Sport Law for Sport Managers

Doyice J. Cotten

T. Jesse Wilde

KENDALL/HUNT PUBLISHING COMPANY
4050 Westmark Drive   Dubuque, Iowa 52002

Cover art (bat and baseball): Images © 1996 PhotoDisc, Inc.

Contents

Foreword

Sport litigation is on the rise in America's litigious society as the sports industry continues to grow. Sport has become a multi-billion dollar industry that involves millions of participants. The American sport environment is filled with troublesome issues which ultimately lead to litigation. There is a trend toward diverse issues that have an impact on the sport industry. As a result of the litigious climate that plagues the sport industry, sport administrators have felt the need for a sport law text that will increase the competency of their sport management students in the various phases of sport law and risk management.

Doyice Cotten and Jesse Wilde accepted the challenge and succeeded. Sport management students and practitioners in sport-related activities are the beneficiaries of their work. Both authors were joined by professionals, acknowledged experts in sport law and risk management. It is a plus for readers of *Sport Law for Sport Managers* who will benefit from the shared expertise and experience of the authors who teach, publish and practice in the field of sport law.

Sport Law for Sport Managers answers two important questions: "What does the law expect from me?" and "What can I do about it?" The book avoids legalese and does not intimidate the reader. The text is a road map for the territory and creates an awareness of problems, issues and strategies sport managers will experience in their everyday operation of sport programs. Legal concepts are presented in addition to practical applications for the sport industry.

Sport Law for Sport Managers is a must for students of sport management and sport-related activities. The book will also be an asset to the practitioner already on the job and should be in every library in the country. Those who master the material will be well on their way to success in dealing with the legal aspects of the sport industry.

I congratulate the authors for producing an appropriate text that is well-conceived and written. It is a valuable addition to sport law and sport management.

Herb Appenzeller, Ed.D
Jefferson-Pilot Professor of
Sport Management Emeritus
Guilford College

Preface

Our aim in creating this book is to provide a non-intimidating, "user friendly" sport law text for use in sport management or sport-related majors and as an informative, practical resource for sport managers. The book strives to assist sport management students and sport managers in developing a basic understanding of principles of law relevant to sport. Recognizing that the law is constantly evolving, each author has utilized recent cases in an effort to insure that the information provided is as current as possible.

We have tried to create a text that is appropriate for an introductory course in sport law, whether at the graduate or undergraduate level. Realizing that different instructors take different approaches and that different courses stress different aspects of sport law, we have made the text as all-inclusive as possible. Included are an Introduction to Sport Law, a large section on Tort Law, four chapters on Contract Law, a comprehensive section on Constitutional Law, and a section presenting various Sport-related Legislation. In most topic areas, there are chapters dealing with the basic concepts of the topic followed by chapters in which these concepts are applied directly to sport management situations.

In an effort to make the text as "user friendly" as possible, we attempted to keep the chapters short and to make each chapter comprehensible for the student taking his or her first sport law course. More chapters are included than can be covered in any one course so that the professor can select those appropriate for the emphasis of his or her course. The chapters are designed to present the fundamentals of the topic. If the student needs or wishes to study more about the topic, references and citations are included.

A consistent format was used in all of the chapters. This format includes a brief introduction to the topic, followed, in most chapters, by a case which will be meaningful to the student. In some chapters the case selected is a landmark case, while in other chapters, the case is merely representative of the type. The Fundamental Concepts section contains the "meat" of the topic, providing the reader with a concise review of essential principles relevant to the topic. In the Recent Trends section, the author summarizes some of the most significant recent developments relating to the topic. The final section is a list of Publications and Cases from which the author researched the chapter.

Who are the authors? We are very fortunate to have authors with tremendous expertise in the field. Each is a member of the Society for the Study of the Legal Aspects of Sport and Physical Activity (SSLASPA), an organization of professionals who are interested in the study and development of sport law. The SSLASPA, formally organized in 1990 with a view to furthering the study and dissemination of information regarding legal aspects of sport and physical activity, is comprised of lawyers and non-lawyers, most of whom teach courses in sport law and/or risk management. Authors were invited to contribute chapters on topics in which they had expertise, as evidenced by presentations and/or publications relating to the topic. In addition, several of our authors have published books on sport law and a number either hold or have held the position of editor of a sport law publication.

As editors of this work, we sincerely thank all who have contributed, and trust that this book will be a valuable resource for students, professors, and sport managers alike.

Doyice J. Cotten
T. Jesse Wilde

Contributors

Editors

DOYICE J. COTTEN

Doyice J. Cotten manages his own risk management and consulting business, Sport Risk Consulting, through which he works with sport-related organizations such as school systems, recreation departments, and health and fitness clubs. He is an emeritus professor of sport management at Georgia Southern University, where he taught graduate and undergraduate courses in sport law and risk management.

Dr. Cotten is very active in professional organizations. Most recently, he has served as President of the Society for the Study of Legal Aspects of Sport and Physical Activity (SSLASPA). He has held several other offices in professional organizations including President of the Georgia Association for Health, Physical Education and Recreation (GAPHERD), as well as Editor of the GAHPERD Journal

Dr. Cotten has spoken on legal issues at such conferences as: the North American Society for Sport Management (NASSM), the American Alliance for Health, Physical Education, Recreation and Dance (AAHPERD), the Athletic Business Conference, The Sports Business Workshop, the International Conference on Sport Business, and the Sport, Physical Education, Recreation, and Law Conference. Dr. Cotten has been the author of over 150 articles, including more than 40 related to sport law. He has published legal articles in such publications as the *Journal of Legal Aspects of Sport*, the *Sports, Parks and Recreation Law Reporter*, the *Exercise Standards and Malpractice Law Reporter*, *The Sports Executive Report*, the *Physical Educator*, *JOPERD*, and *Athletic Business*. Sport-related waivers have been of major interest to Dr. Cotten. He has researched this topic extensively, collecting and analyzing more than 400 relevant cases.

T. JESSE WILDE

Professor Wilde is a Canadian-born attorney, having received his law degree in 1985 from the University of Alberta. After practicing law for three years in Alberta, he returned to graduate school to pursue graduate sport management and sport law studies at the University of Massachusetts at Amherst. Following his graduation in 1990, Professor Wilde joined the faculty at Rice University, Houston, Texas as an assistant professor of sport law and sport management, and director of the university's sport management program. He remained at Rice University from 1990 to July 1996, save for a year's leave of absence during which he taught sport law at the University of Massachusetts. In July 1996, Professor Wilde returned to the private practice of law in his hometown of Lethbridge, Alberta. In addition to his law practice, he operates a sport management/athlete representation firm.

Professor Wilde has published a number of journal articles and trade publications on various topics, including gender equity in college athletics, labor relations in professional sports, sport agent regulation, and trademark infringement. He has also given presentations on a variety of sport law topics at conferences hosted by the North American Society for Sport Management, the International Society for Comparative Physical Education and Sport, the Society for the Study of Legal Aspects of Sports and Physical Activity, and the Sport Lawyers Association. In addition, Professor Wilde has coauthored a comprehensive annotated reference publication with Glenn M. Wong, Esq. entitled *The Sport Attorney's Guide to Legal Periodicals*.

Contributing Authors

JAY M. ABLONDI

Jay M. Ablondi is the Assistant Director of Government Relations for The International Health, Racquet and Sportsclub Association (IHRSA) located in Boston, Massachusetts. IHRSA is the largest trade association for the health club industry representing over 3,000 member clubs worldwide. Since 1990, Mr. Ablondi has monitored and reported on legislation and legal issues affecting the health, fitness and racquet club industry in all fifty states. Mr. Ablondi holds a Bachelor of Arts in political science from the University of New Hampshire and is continuing his studies at the Harvard Extension School in Cambridge, Massachusetts.

RUTH H. ALEXANDER

Ruth H. Alexander is a Distinguished Service Professor at the University of Florida in Gainesville and coordinates the graduate program in Sport Management. She teaches in the area of Issues in Sport Law, Sport Finance and Marketing and Athletic Administration.

ROB AMMON, JR.

Rob Ammon Jr., Ed.D. received his Bachelors degree in Physical Education from the University of Colorado and his Masters in Exercise Physiology from Louisiana State University. After coaching intercollegiate football for seven years he secured his doctorate in Sport Management from the University of Northern Colorado. Dr. Ammon is currently employed at Slippery Rock University where he teaches sport law, event and facility management and management of sport in addition to being the graduate coordinator for the Physical Education department. His research specialties include risk management at sport events and facilities, crowd management, and legal liabilities in sport. Dr. Ammon has authored and coauthored various articles, chapters, and a text pertaining to these areas.

LINDA JEAN CARPENTER

Dr. Carpenter is a Professor in the Department of Physical Education at Brooklyn College, Brooklyn, New York. She is an attorney, having received her law degree from Fordham University in 1981, and is a member of both the New York State Bar and United States Supreme Court Bar. She also holds a Ph.D. degree from the University of Southern California. Dr. Carpenter has published numerous articles and books on sport law topics, including her most recent book, entitled *Legal Concepts in Sport* (1995). In addition, she has made numerous national and regional presentations at sport law conferences on various topics. Dr. Carpenter is perhaps best known for her research on women in sport and related legal and gender equity issues, which has resulted in national recognition from organizations including the Women's Sports Foundation and the National Association for Girls and Women in Sport.

MARGARET E. CICCOLELLA

Margaret E. Ciccolella earned an Ed.D. from BYU in 1978 and a J.D. from Humphreys College in 1993. Dr. Ciccolella is currently a professor in the Department of Sport Sciences at the University of the Pacific in Stockton, California where she teaches undergraduate and graduate course work in sports law, kinesiology, and health education. She consults with a hospital-based fitness program and is a part-time attorney with the San Joaquin County Counsel.

CATHRYN L. CLAUSSEN

Cathryn L. Claussen teaches in the Sport Management Division at Bowling Green State University. She received her J.D. from Georgetown University Law Center in 1992, and her M.A. in sport sociology/philosophy from the University of Iowa in 1986. Her primary teaching and research interests are in sport law, with a special focus on civil and constitutional rights. She has played tennis professionally, and was an assistant tennis coach while at the University of Iowa.

JAMES H. CONN

James H. Conn is a Professor and Chair of the Department of Physical Education at Central Missouri State University. He received his Ph.D. degree from Southern Illinois University in 1986, his M.S. degree from Eastern Washington University in 1972 and his B.A. degree from the University of Northern Colorado in 1969. He has spent 16 years in coaching and teaching, and the last 10 years in higher education.

MARK CONRAD

Mark Conrad is Associate Professor of Legal and Ethical Studies at Fordham University's Graduate and Undergraduate Schools of Business Administration. Professor Conrad earned his B.A. from City College of New York, his J.D. from New York Law School, and his M.S. from Columbia University's Graduate School of Journalism. Professor Conrad teaches a "Sports and the Law" class to both undergraduate and graduate students. He has published in academic journals, as well as such other mainstream publications as the *New York Times* and the

Wall Street Journal. He also writes a monthly sports law column for the *New York Law Journal,* a daily newspaper for lawyers. His recent publications have covered N.C.A.A. rules, advertising restrictions and league governance.

TED CURTIS

Ted Curtis is a sports lawyer and writer in Boca Raton, Florida. He is an attorney with the University of South Florida; General Counsel to Double Eagle Sports Enterprises, a player and event management company; the news editor for The Sports Lawyer, the bimonthly journal of the Sports Lawyers Association; the Associate Director of the Sports Law & Policy Project, a research clearinghouse at the University of Central Florida; and the chair of the Florida Bar's Amateur Sports Committee. He was the editor-in-chief of *The Sports Executive Report* from 1993-96 and has published extensively on issues in sports law, business and finance.

JOHN N. DROWATZKY

John N. Drowatzky, J.D., Ed.D. is Professor Emeritus of Exercise Science at The University of Toledo where he served as Chairman of the Department of Health Promotion and Human Performance. Admitted to practice at the Ohio Bar—he has served as an expert witness for several sport law cases in addition to practicing law. His publications include 10 books and monographs and approximately 60 journal articles, many dealing with sport law issues.

MAUREEN P. FITZGERALD

Maureen P. Fitzgerald is an Assistant Professor at the University of Texas at Austin where she is the Sport Management Coordinator in the Department of Kinesiology and Health Education. She received her B.A. in Government from Saint Mary's College in Notre Dame, Indiana and her M.A. and Ph.D. from The Ohio State University. She was in tennis club management prior to completing her Ph.D. and accepting positions at the University of Missouri-Columbia and the University of Texas, respectively. Her research in sport law has focused on facility owner liability and personnel management issues. Beyond sport law, her research focus has been managerial mobility and retention relative to career development.

ROBERT P. FLEISCHMAN

Robert P. Fleischman, an attorney, is an assistant professor and the graduate program coordinator for sport management at East Stroudsburg University. A graduate of the Hofstra University School of Law, Fleischman is active in the area of sports and education law. He is a former partner in the Manhattan, New York-based law firm of Kirschenbaum, Fleischman and Spiegler. Fleischman previously taught at the University of Massachusetts, where he earned an M.S. Degree in Sport Management.

The author would like to acknowledge the contributions of Rory Fazendeiro, a graduate sport management student at East Stroudsburg University, who assisted with the preparation of his chapters.

GIL B. FRIED

Mr. Fried is an Assistant Professor teaching in the University of Houston's Sports and Fitness Administration Program and at the U of H, Law Center. He teaches sports law, marketing, management and facility administration.

Mr. Fried received a B.S. in Business Administration from California State University, Sacramento and his Master's in Sports Administration and Juris Doctors both from Ohio State University. Mr. Fried went on to be a litigation attorney, the Director of the Sports Law Center and an Adjunct Professor at University of San Francisco. Mr. Fried has served as a lobbyist and board member for several civic and cultural organizations.

LYNNE P. GASKIN

Lynne P. Gaskin is a Professor of Physical Education at the State University of West Georgia. She received her B.S. degree from Wesleyan College, and her M.S. and Ed.D. degrees from the University of North Carolina at Greensboro. Dr. Gaskin has written and spoken extensively at the national and international levels in the area of sport law. She is a member of 15 professional societies, serves as an officer and as a member of the Board of Directors for a number of professional organizations, received the Research Excellence Award from the University of North Carolina at Greensboro, and the Honor Award from the North Carolina Alliance for Health, Physical Education, Recreation and Dance.

GARY R. GRAY

Gary R. Gray is a Professor and Chair of the Department of Health and Physical Education at Montana State University-Billings. He is also Director of Intercollegiate Athletics for the MSU-Billings Yellowjacket athletic program, a member of the NCAA Division II Pacific West Conference. In addition, he serves as Director of the university's employee wellness program. Dr. Gray's research interests are related to identifying risk management behaviors of sport leaders in a variety of environments. He has taught and coached in the United

States and Canada in both public and private schools. Dr. Gray is Past President of the Society of Legal Aspects of Sport and Physical Activity and former Editor of the *Journal of Legal Aspects of Sport.*

JAMES T. GRAY

James T. Gray is a 1986 graduate of Temple University and a 1990 graduate of Marquette University Law School. He serves as assistant director of the National Sports Law Institute and as an adjunct professor at Marquette University Law School. He presently teaches "Regulation of Amateur Athletics" and "Current Issues in Sports Law." He is coauthor of the 700-page book entitled *The Stadium Game* as published by the National Sports Law Institute and a law review article entitled *Citizenship Base Quota Systems in Athletics* for the *Marquette Sports Law Journal*. He has been quoted in many publications in the United States including the *New York Times*, the *National Law Journal* and *U.S. News & World Report*. He sits on the Board of Advisors for the Anglia Sports Law Research Centre based in Chelmsford, England and The Center for the Study of Law, Society and Popular Culture at the University of Westminster in London, England.

RALPH G. HALL

Ralph G. Hall is a professor at Appalachian State University and a practicing Attorney at Law. He holds a Bachelor's and Doctor's Degree from the University of Tennessee, a Master's Degree from the University of Memphis, and a Juris Doctor from Wake Forest University. He teaches courses in public school law, law of higher education, sports law, and educational leadership at Appalachian. Dr. Hall is a regional reporter for National Organization of Legal Problems in Education's *School Law Reporter.*

MARY A. HUMS

Mary A. Hums, Ph.D., an Assistant Professor of Sport Management at the University of Massachusetts-Amherst, earned her Ph.D. in Sport Management from Ohio State University, an M.A. in Athletic Administration and an M.B.A. from the University of Iowa and a B.B.A. from the University of Notre Dame. She is the President-Elect of SSLASPA, and is an active member of NASSM and AAHPERD. Hums formerly was Athletic Director at St. Mary-of-the-Woods College, Terre Haute, IN and previously directed the Sport Management Program at Kennesaw State University, Marietta, GA. She is a 1996 inductee in the Indiana Softball Hall of Fame.

RON KANOY

Ron Kanoy, M.A., ATC (retired), is an assistant professor in the Department of Health, Leisure and Exercise Science at Appalachian State University, Boone, North Carolina. Prior to his current position, he served as Head Athletic Trainer at Appalachian State from 1966 to 1985. He received both his B.S. and M.A. degrees from Appalachian State.

CAROLYN LEHR

Carolyn Lehr is currently an Associate Professor in the Department of Physical Education and Sport Studies at the University of Georgia. She holds a B.A. from Syracuse University, M.Ed. from the State University of New York at Buffalo, and an Ed.D. from the University of New Mexico. Dr. Lehr currently teaches various courses in the graduate program in Sport Management. She has presented papers at state, regional and national conferences, and published numerous articles in the various aspects of sports law.

BERNARD P. MALOY

Bernard P. Maloy earned his B.A. from Wheeling Jesuit College, a J.D. from the University of Notre Dame, and an M.S.A. from Ohio University. He had a law practice for 11 years, and worked in corporate management for three years prior to his appointment at the University of Michigan. Currently, he is an Associate Professor in the Division of Kinesiology where he teaches courses in the legal aspects and management of sport, recreation, and facility management. In 1991, he received a State of Michigan Teaching Excellence Award for his work. In 1995, he was named an Academic Leadership Fellow to the Committee on Institutional Cooperation which is comprised of all the Big Ten universities and the University of Chicago. He is currently researching legal issues in the design and operations of stadiums and arenas. Additionally, he is examining stress disabilities and their relation to management functions and workmen's compensation.

LISA PIKE MASTERALEXIS

Lisa Pike Masteralexis is an Associate Professor of Sport Law in the Sport Management Program at the University of Massachusetts-Amherst where she teaches courses in Amateur and Professional Sport Law, as well as Labor Relations in Professional Sport. She received a B.S. in Sport Management from the University of Massachusetts-Amherst and a J.D. from Suffolk University School of Law. She is a member of the state bar of

Massachusetts, serves the Massachusetts Bar Association as a pro bono attorney for legal issues in sport, and is associated with Sport Ventures International, a professional athlete management firm.

JOHN MERRIMAN

John Merriman, Ed.D., is a professor of sport law and sport ethics in the Department of Health, Physical Education and Athletics at Valdosta State University, Valdosta, Georgia. He is the cofounder of the Sport, Physical Education and Law Conference which was the parent to the Society for the Study of Legal Aspects of Sport and Physical Activity. While an active member of the National Association of Sport and Physical Education, The National Association for Physical Education and Health Education, and the Southern District of the American Alliance for Health, Physical Education, Recreation and Dance, Dr. Merriman is the current president-elect of the Georgia Association for Health, Physical Education, Recreation and Dance.

LORI K. MILLER

Lori K. Miller is currently an Associate Professor and Director of the Sport Administration program (undergraduate and graduate) at Wichita State University. She earned her Ed. D. from East Texas State. She has a Masters of Business Administration from the University and Louisville and a M.Ed. in Physical Education from Texas A&M University. Her undergraduate degree is in Business from Emporia State University. Her research efforts are interdisciplinary in nature and focus on a combination of sport, legal issues, and business topics.

MERRY MOISEICHIK

Merry Moiseichik is an associate professor at the University of Arkansas teaching in the area of recreation management and sport management. She graduated with a Doctor of Recreation from Indiana University. She became interested in legal aspects at Indiana where she did her dissertation on a New York State Law that had been passed for camp safety in 1986. She has been at the University of Arkansas for the last seven years teaching and writing in the area of risk management and legal aspects.

AARON L. MULROONEY

Aaron L. Mulrooney, J.D. holds a Master of Business Administration degree in Finance and is a licensed attorney in the state of Ohio. He coordinates the graduate program in sport administration at Kent State University in the School of Exercise, Leisure and Sport. Prof. Mulrooney has published a variety of articles and given numerous presentations on risk management and liability. Prof. Mulrooney has been involved with the facility management industry for over 15 years and has just recently coauthored a text on facility management. He plans on continuing his research endeavors in facility management and legal research. Prof. Mulrooney is a native Ohioan and a former nationally ranked tennis player who competed in many men's national amateur championships and was invited to the 1984 Olympic trials.

R. GARY NESS

R. Gary Ness, (Ph.D. Stanford University, 1975) currently is an associate professor at the University of New Mexico and graduate coordinator for the Division of Human Performance and Development. During his term as Director (1988-1993), the Department of Athletics finished second in the Western Athletic Conference, operated in the black, reduced long term debt by 60 percent, added two women's sports, and hosted two NCAA Division I national championships. Dr. Ness teaches sports law and finance in the graduate Sports Administration Program.

ANDY PITTMAN

Dr. Andy Pittman, Associate Professor and Coordinator of the Sport Management Program at Baylor University, received a B. S. from Baylor University, an M. Ed. from Ohio University, an M. S. from the University of Baltimore, a Ph.D. from Texas A & M University and has taken post-doctoral work at Baylor University Law School. He has been employed at Baylor since 1981 and prior to that worked for the federal government and the Naval Academy Athletic Association. He has been involved in several national professional organizations to include AAHPERD, NASSM, and SSLASPA and has over 30 refereed presentations and publications primarily in the sport law area.

WILLIAM F. REGAN

William F. Regan is a graduate from the University of Akron School of Law and is receiving his Masters in Sports Administration from Canisius College. Currently working as the Director of Operations/Ski School Director at Cockaigne Ski area, he was a partner in the law firm of LeBlanc, Herrman and Regan, specializing in labor, municipal and school law. He has served as Assistant City Attorney for the City of Lackawanna. He is also a lecturer for undergraduate and graduate Physical Education courses regarding legal aspects of coaches and physical educators. He is currently the assistant men's soccer coach for Canisius College. He is also serving as

Compliance Assistant for the SUNY at Buffalo's Division of Athletics.

GARY M. RUSHING

Gary Rushing, Associate Professor, received his Ed.D. from the University of Northern Colorado. Currently, he is coordinator of Sport Management studies in the Human Performance Department at Mankato State University, Mankato, Minnesota. His research and teaching areas include a variety of Sport Management courses such as Legal Aspects of Sport and Physical Activity. He is published in several law reporters and coaching journals. He has over twenty years of experience in athletics as a coach and athletic administrator.

THOMAS H. SAWYER

Thomas H. Sawyer is professor of Physical Education, Recreation and Sport Management, Coordinator of Sport Management Programs, Indiana State University, Department of Recreation and Sport Management. He received his B.S. from Springfield College, 1968; M.P.E. from Springfield College, 1971; and Ed.D. from Virginia Polytechnic Institute and State University, 1977. Professor Sawyer has written over 70 professional articles and three book chapters, and made over 80 professional presentations at the state, national and international levels. He is the editor of the Indiana *APHERD Journal* and *Newsletter*, and the *Journal for the Legal Aspects of Sport*. He teaches sport law courses on the undergraduate and graduate levels.

LINDA L. SCHOONMAKER

Linda. L. Schoonmaker received her B.S. and M.S. from SUNY at Brockport and her Ph.D. from Ohio State University. She held administrative positions in campus recreational sport for ten years, seven of those years as the Director of Recreational Sports and Facilities at the University of Wisconsin-Whitewater. For the past five years, she has held faculty positions at Tulane University and the University of Missouri-Columbia teaching undergraduate and graduate courses in sport management. Dr. Schoonmaker currently is conducting research in the area of gender equity and interscholastic athletics.

ROBERT E. TRICHKA

Robert E. Trichka received a B.S. degree in Physical Education and an M.A. Degree in Physical Education from The University of Connecticut. He earned his DPE from Springfield College with an emphasis in Administration and Sport Psychology.

Dr. Trichka is currently a Professor of Physical Education and Health Fitness Studies in the Department of Physical Education and Health Fitness at Central Connecticut State University. He has authored articles and has made numerous presentations nationally and statewide in the area of sport law. He has conducted workshops in negligence theory for statewide school districts. During his tenure at Central Connecticut State University, Dr. Trichka has served as a football coach, tennis coach, department chair, and interim Associate Dean of the School of Education and Professional Studies. Currently, he teaches undergraduate and graduate courses in physical education, including sport law and torts in physical activity.

BETTY VAN DER SMISSEN

Dr. Betty van der Smissen is a Professor at Michigan State University where she teaches both graduate and undergraduate courses in legal aspects of sport and leisure services. She is an attorney and a member of the Michigan bar. In addition, she holds a doctorate degree in recreation. Dr. van der Smissen is a well known expert in sport law and risk management, and has given numerous presentations and workshops on topics related to sport law and risk management over the past 15 years. She is perhaps best known for her comprehensive 3-volume sport law reference entitled *Legal Liability and Risk Management*.

JOHN T. WOLOHAN

John T. Wolohan is an attorney and assistant professor in the Health and Human Performance Department at Iowa State University, where he teaches undergraduate and graduate courses in the areas of sports law. Professor Wolohan received his B.A. from the University of Massachusetts, and his J.D. from Western New England College School of Law. Professor Wolohan is a member of the Massachusetts Bar. He has presented and published a number of articles relating to a variety of sport law topics.

1.00 • INTRODUCTION TO SPORT LAW ————————————

The Legal System

Gil B. Fried
University of Houston

If one asked what the term "law" means, one would probably receive a different answer from each person one asked. Law implies a multitude of definitions and concepts. Law is abstract, living, constantly changing and evolving. At the same time, laws provide predictability, accountability, justice, protection, and even compassion. Law consists of the entire conglomeration of rules, values, and principles that govern daily conduct and can be enforced by either the government or individual citizens through courts. Even if there were no written laws, society would establish moral, ethical, and natural laws to protect individual citizens from one another.

Individuals often confuse the law with justice. The law normally provides for one specific interpretation. Justice, however, does not necessarily mean the same thing to all people. Justice varies based on one's education, upbringing, social class, and related factors. Thus, while the law protects one's freedom of speech, many people might not think justice is served by letting a hate group demonstrate on public property. However, our society has determined that laws are often required to protect certain rights or people that the rest of society might not cherish or approve.

■ ■ ■ ■

Representative Case

SAVINO v. ROBERTSON

Appellate Court of Illinois, First District, Second Division
273 Ill. App. 3d 811; 652 N.E.2d 1240; 1995 Ill. App. LEXIS
480; 210 Ill. Dec. 264
June 30, 1995, Decided

OPINION: JUSTICE McCORMICK

Plaintiff John Savino brought a **negligence action** against **defendant** Scott Robertson after plaintiff was struck and injured in the eye by a hockey puck shot by defendant. The **trial court** granted defendant's subsequent motion for summary judgment, but allowed plaintiff to amend the complaint to allege that defendant's conduct was wilful and wanton. Upon another motion by defendant, the trial court granted summary judgment in favor of

defendant on the amended complaint. On appeal from both orders, plaintiff raises the following issues for our consideration: (1) whether a plaintiff must plead and prove wilful and wanton conduct in order to recover for injuries incurred during athletic competition; and (2) whether there was a genuine issue of material fact as to whether defendant's conduct was wilful and wanton in injuring plaintiff. We affirm.

Plaintiff and defendant were teammates in an amateur hockey league sponsored by the Northbrook Park District. Plaintiff and defendant also had met in various "pick-up" games prior to playing in the Northbrook league, but they were neither friends nor enemies. On April 20, 1990, plaintiff and defendant were warming up prior to a game. During warm-up, teams skate around and behind their goal on their half of the ice. Plaintiff was on the ice, "to the right of the face off circle in front of the net." Defendant shot a puck that missed the goal and hit plaintiff near the right eye. Plaintiff lost 80 percent vision in that eye.

On September 11, 1990, plaintiff filed a one-count **complaint** against defendant alleging that defendant was negligent and failed to exercise ordinary care in shooting the puck. Specifically, plaintiff alleged that defendant (a) failed to warn plaintiff that he was going to shoot the puck toward plaintiff; (b) failed to wait until a goalie was present before shooting the puck; (c) failed to warn others that he was shooting the puck; (d) failed to follow the custom and practice of the Northbrook Men's Summer League which required the presence of a goalie at the net before shooting; and (e) failed to keep an adequate lookout.

Defendant filed his **answer to the complaint** and, after **interrogatories** and **discovery depositions** were taken, defendant moved for summary judgment. (735 ILCS 5/2-1005 (West 1992).) Defendant argued that he was entitled to judgment as a matter of law because plaintiff alleged ordinary negligence. To be entitled to relief for injuries incurred during athletic competition, defendant argued, plaintiff had to plead and prove wilful and wanton conduct or conduct done in reckless disregard for the safety of others. The trial court granted defendant's motion for summary judgment and denied plaintiff leave to amend count I of the complaint. Upon reconsideration, the trial court granted plaintiff leave to file an **amended complaint** to allege a count II based on wilful and wanton conduct.

Defendant filed his **answer to plaintiff's subsequent amended complaint** and the parties engaged in discovery as to count II of that complaint. Defendant later filed another **motion for summary judgment**. Defendant argued that, due to plaintiff's admission that his injury was caused by an accident, plaintiff's case presented no genuine issue of material fact with regard to defendant's alleged wilful and wanton conduct. Defendant further argued that plaintiff could not show that defendant's action was anything more than an ordinary practice shot normally taken during warm-up sessions.

Plaintiff, on the other hand, argued in his **response to defendant's motion** that ordinary negligence should be the standard applied to his case rather than wilful and wan-

ton conduct, because, since the hockey game had not officially begun, he was not a participant at the time of his injury. Plaintiff attached the affidavit of Thomas Czarnik, a hockey coach at Deerfield High School, to his response. According to Czarnik, it was the custom of amateur hockey leagues to wait until the goalie was present in the net before any practice shots were taken.

• • •

Czarnik had no knowledge of the rules and usages of the Northbrook Hockey League and had no firsthand knowledge of the incident.

Czarnik also stated that he had seen players in adult hockey leagues take shots at open goals, that is, goals without a goalie present, during the warm-up period and that he had taken shots at open goals. According to Czarnik, the warm-up period was a part of the game of hockey even though the players are not technically playing a game. Czarnik considered plaintiff's injury an accident.

Defendant attached excerpts of Czarnik's deposition in support of his reply to plaintiff's **response to the motion for summary judgment**. Defendant argued that Czarnik's responses demonstrated that plaintiff could not show, as a matter of law, that defendant's conduct was wilful or wanton. Defendant also contended that Czarnik was not a proper **expert** to render an opinion in this case, given his lack of familiarity with adult hockey leagues and lack of knowledge of the rules and usages of the Northbrook Summer Men's Hockey League. The trial court granted defendant's motion for summary judgment. Plaintiff now **appeals** from both orders of the trial court granting summary judgment in favor of defendant.

Our review of the trial court's grant of summary judgment is de novo. (Superior Investment & Development Corp., Inc. v. Devine (1993), 244 Ill. App. 3d 759, 767, 614 N.E.2d 302, 185 Ill. Dec. 168.) The granting of summary judgment is proper when the pleadings, depositions and affidavits show that no genuine issue of material fact exists and the moving party is entitled to judgment as a matter of law. (Estate of Henderson v. W.R. Grace Co. (1989), 185 Ill. App. 3d 523, 527, 541 N.E.2d 805, 133 Ill. Dec. 594.) In determining whether summary judgment is proper, the court must construe the evidence in a light most favorable to the non-movant and strongly against the movant. Schroth v. Norton Co. (1989), 185 Ill. App. 3d 575, 577, 541 N.E.2d 855, 133 Ill. Dec. 644.

Plaintiff first argues that he should not have been required to plead wilful and wanton conduct in this case because he was not actually "playing" the game of hockey at the time his injury occurred, but rather was participating in the warm-up practice.

The seminal case on this issue is Nabozny v. Barnhill (1975), 31 Ill. App. 3d 212, 334 N.E.2d 258. In Nabozny, the plaintiff was the goalkeeper for a teenage soccer league and the defendant was a forward from an opposing team. The game's rules prevented players from making contact with the goalkeeper while he is in possession of the ball in the penalty area. (Nabozny, 31 Ill. App. 3d at 214.) During the game, the ball was passed to the plaintiff while he was in the penalty area. The plaintiff fell onto his knee. The defendant, who had been going for the ball, continued to run towards the plaintiff and kicked the plaintiff in the head, causing severe injuries. (Nabozny, 31 Ill. App. 3d at 214.) The trial court directed a verdict in favor of the defendant, holding that as a matter of law the defendant was free from negligence (owed no duty to the plaintiff) and that the plaintiff was contributorily negligent.

In reversing the trial court, the Nabozny court held that when athletes engage in organized competition, with a set of rules that guides the conduct and safety of the players, then "a player is charged with a legal duty to every other player on the field to refrain from conduct proscribed by a safety rule. (Nabozny, 31 Ill. App. 3d at 215.) The court then announced the following rule:

> "It is our opinion that a player is liable for injury in a tort action if his conduct is such that it is either deliberate, wilful or with a reckless disregard for the safety of the other player so as to cause injury to that player, the same being a question of fact to be decided by a jury." Nabozny, 31 Ill. App. 3d at 215.

Illinois courts have construed Nabozny to hold that a plaintiff-participant injured during a contact sport may recover from another player only if the other's conduct was wilful or wanton. (Novak v. Virene (1991), 224 Ill. App. 3d 317, 586 N.E.2d 578, 166 Ill. Dec. 620; Keller v. Mols (1987), 156 Ill. App. 3d 235, 509 N.E.2d 584, 108 Ill. Dec. 888; Oswald v. Township High School District No. 214 (1980), 84 Ill. App. 3d 723, 406 N.E.2d 157, 40 Ill. Dec. 456.) Plaintiff contends, however, that decisions subsequent to Nabozny have misconstrued the court's holding in that case. According to plaintiff, Nabozny is to be applied only to conduct during a game because Nabozny "involved an injury that occurred during a game and therefore, it implicitly recognizes a distinction with pre-game injuries."

In the case at bar, we believe that plaintiff was no less a participant in a team sport merely because he was engaged in "warm-up" activities at the time of his injury. However, assuming arguendo that we were to view plaintiff's action using an ordinary negligence standard, we must find that plaintiff knowingly and voluntarily assumed the risks inherent in playing the game of hockey. Plaintiff's own testimony bears out this fact. Plaintiff was an experienced hockey player, playing from the time he was eight years old. He had played in organized adult leagues for approximately 10 years prior to his accident. Plaintiff testified that while it was "customary" for players to wait for a goalie to be present prior to taking practice shots, in his experience he had seen players take shots at open nets. There was no written rule against taking shots at open nets. Plaintiff was also aware, at the time he stepped onto the ice, that there was a risk of being hit with a puck during "warm-ups." Indeed, according to plaintiff, that risk "always" existed. Nonetheless, plaintiff chose not to wear a protective face mask, since it was not required, even though in his estimation 65-70 percent of his teammates were wearing protective masks during "warm-up" and despite the inherent risk of being hit with a puck, irrespective of the goalie's presence at the net. Based on plaintiff's testimony, we believe that plaintiff voluntarily consented, understood and accepted the dangers inherent in the sport or due to a co-participant's negligence.

• • •

We find no reason to abandon the well-established **precedent** of this court, and that of a majority of **jurisdictions**, that a participant in a contact sport may recover for injury only where the other's conduct is wilful or wanton or in reckless disregard to safety.

It is undisputed that plaintiff and defendant were teammates in an organized hockey league. There were rules and usages. Reviewing the evidence in a light most favorable to plaintiff, there appears to be no genuine issue of material fact that practice shots were often taken at an open net and such was the custom of the team.

For the foregoing reasons, we **affirm** both orders of the circuit court granting summary judgment in defendant's favor.

Affirmed.

SCARIANO, P.J., and DiVITO, J., concur.

■ ■ ■ ■

Fundamental Concepts

Types of Laws

Two primary areas of law will be discussed in this text: **common law** and **statutory law**. Since laws passed by legislative bodies (statutory laws) can never cover all potential circumstances, conditions, or occasions, common law can be used to provide specific guidance for interpreting the laws. Common law refers to cases that have been resolved by various courts. The decisions of numerous courts over hundreds of years are combined to form our common law system. For example, numerous principles concerning the liability of an individual who fails to live up to a certain standard of conduct have been developed over the past five centuries. These cases comprise common law and provide precedence for future cases involving the same or similar facts. **Precedence** serves to create boundaries by which future cases can be decided. Once a case becomes precedence, all future analysis of the same or similar facts in that jurisdiction will rely upon the prior decision. Subsequent courts cannot ignore or overturn the prior decision unless a legislative body changes the underlying law upon which the decision was based or a higher court overturns the decision. Thus, when the United States Supreme Court concluded that Major League Baseball was exempt from antitrust laws, such a conclusion became precedence. Since there is no higher court than the United States Supreme Court, and the Supreme Court does not want to overturn this decision, the only way baseball can lose its antitrust exemption would be if the United States Congress changed the antitrust laws to specifically cover baseball.

Statutory laws are laws originating from and passed by legislative bodies. Statutory laws are adopted by all forms of government including: national, state, municipal, county and city entities. These laws are only valid for the area governed by that entity and can cover such topics as zoning, advertising, taxes, or building a sports facility. Statutory laws and constitutional laws are analogous in that both types of laws are adopted or changed by a voting system and form the framework of laws which guide our everyday actions. **Constitutional law** refers to laws embodied in the United States Constitution. In addition, each state has its own constitution. An example of constitutional law in sports involves prayer in a locker room. While most athletes are familiar with pre-game prayers, the Constitution prohibits states from endorsing any religion. Thus, if a public high school coach required players to pray before a game, the coach would be violating the constitutionally required separation of church and state.

Administrative laws refer to laws, rules, and regulations that are developed, adopted and enforced by government units responsible for managing specific government agencies. While administrative laws are not as widely applied as statutory or common law, they still affect a variety of sports issues. Large portions of the economy are governed by federal administrative agencies. The regulations adopted by national administrative agencies such as the National Labor Relations Board (NLRB) or the Occupational Safety and Hazard Administration (OSHA) have the force of law. In 1972, Congress passed the law commonly referred to as Title IX. The law requires equal treatment of men and women in programs receiving federal funds. Colleges receiving federal funds are required to provide similar funding to both men's and women's athletic programs. State administrative agencies have jurisdiction over issues such as workmen's compensation, facility rentals, and fair employment practices.

Court System

When a dispute arises involving either the application of a statute or an individual's rights, the dispute is traditionally resolved through an appropriate **court** system. A court is a tribunal established by governments to hear certain cases and administer justice. There are three primary court systems; state, federal, and administrative. Legal authority, procedures, and the types of disputes heard are different in each court system.

A **state court** has jurisdiction (authority) to hear a case if the case involves an event or activity which occurred within the state. In addition, the parties to the lawsuit have to reside or conduct significant business activities in the state. Typical cases brought in state court include breach of contract claims, personal injury suits, and suits involving real estate located in the state.

State court systems traditionally consist of general or superior jurisdiction courts which are referred to by various names in different states. They are commonly called circuit courts, district courts, superior courts, or courts of common pleas. Some states have other special courts such as probate (to handle the estates of deceased persons), juvenile, family law, municipal, tax, city, and small claims courts.

If a party to a suit does not feel the law was properly applied, he or she could appeal the case to an appellate court. An appeal is the process by which a party to a suit can challenge the legal decision rendered by a court. The appeals process is designed to guarantee that the court cannot exercise unchecked or abusive power. If the appellate court's decision is also disputed, the litigant can file another appeal to the state's supreme court. State supreme court decisions are final unless the decision involves an issue regarding the federal Constitution, laws, or treaties. Appellate courts and the state supreme court can only review issues of law. They cannot review the facts or reanalyze evidence.

A majority of cases are brought in state courts. However, if a dispute involves over $10,000, citizens of different states, or a question involving the Constitution or a federal law question, the case would be brought in **federal court**. Federal courts also hear patent, tax, copyright, maritime and bankruptcy matters. If a party determines that the federal court misapplied the law, the party can petition a federal court of appeals. The United States is divided into 12 judicial districts, each with a federal appellate court. The last resort for any party is to request that the United States Supreme Court review a case. The process of applying for review by the Supreme Court involves filing a writ of certiorari. A **writ of certiorari** is sent from the Supreme Court to a lower level court when at least four of the nine Supreme Court Justices vote to hear the case. The writ requires the lower court to turn the case over to the Supreme Court.

Administrative courts or agencies are created by Congress or state legislatures and both create and enforce their own rules. All other courts only enforce or interpret rules made by other courts or legislatures. For example, the NLRB is lawmaker, an executive agency that enforces the law, and a court which interprets and applies the law. If a professional league decided to lock its unionized players out of training camp, the players could file a complaint with the NLRB. The NLRB would investigate and reach a decision concerning the players' complaint. A federal administrator has the power to investigate violations of agency rules and to force individuals to appear before the agency and answer charges against the individuals. Because administrative agencies make, enforce, and judge their own laws, most associations have established separate judicial branches removed from the law-making and enforcing divisions and directed by an administrative law judge. An administrative law judge helps ensure some degree of independence.

A court can only hear a case if it has **jurisdiction** over the people involved or if the issue involved in the case occurred or is located within the court's jurisdiction. Jurisdiction refers to a court's authority to hear and decide a certain case. If a court does not have jurisdiction, then the court cannot hear the case. Jurisdiction can be obtained by a court having jurisdiction over a person or company or the subject matter of the dispute. Thus, federal courts have subject matter jurisdiction over a case if the case involves issues under the Federal Constitution, the amount in controversy is over $10,000 or the disputing parties are located in different states. On the other hand, a state court only has personal jurisdiction if a disputant lives in that state or has significant contacts within the state. Noted track star Butch Reynolds sued the International Amateur Athletic Federation in an Ohio state court. The case centered around IAAF's failure to overturn a competition suspension imposed on Reynolds after an inaccurate drug test. The IAAF did not attend the state court trial which resulted in a $28.3 million verdict against the IAAF. The case was appealed to a federal court which overturned the state court's decision. The federal court's decision was based on the fact that the IAAF was not based in Ohio and did not conduct a significant amount of business in Ohio. Therefore, the Ohio court did not have jurisdiction to hear a case involving a non-Ohio based organization.

Typically courts are distinguished by the types of cases they can hear. **Criminal courts** only resolve criminals matters in which the people, represented by a public prosecutor, bring charges against individual(s) who violate the law through the commission of a misdemeanor or felony. Cases between individuals, corporations, business entities, organizations and government units involving non-criminal matters are resolved primarily in **civil courts**. The O.J. Simpson murder cases provide an excellent distinction between criminal and civil courts. Simpson was first tried by the State of California for allegedly harming state citizens. The criminal case resulted in a not guilty verdict. The double jeopardy rule prohibits Simpson from ever being tried again on the same charges in a criminal case. However, Simpson was subsequently sued by the victims' families in civil court. The criminal court decision has no bearing on the civil court case because a different burden of proof is required by the two courts. In order to convict someone in criminal court, the prosecutors must prove the accused committed the crime beyond a reasonable doubt. On the other hand, a person suing in civil court only has to prove by a preponderance of the evidence that the other side is the guilty party.

Legal Process

Detailed rules specify the how, when, and where questions associated with bringing a lawsuit. These rules differ in each court and are often very complex. An example provides the best method of discussing the structure and processes involved in a lawsuit. The following is a fictitious example of such a case. Sarah Jones was a high school student and interscholastic volleyball star in Houston, Texas. While playing in a sanctioned interscholastic event, Jones attempted to spike a ball, but slipped on a water puddle. Jones tore her knee ligaments. She required over $10,000 in medical bills, missed the remainder of the volleyball season, lost $4,000 from not being able to work, and missed her chance to possibly receive a volleyball scholarship from the University of Houston.

After Jones left the hospital, her father set up an interview with a lawyer to discuss their legal options. The lawyer was Ruth Smith, a young lawyer fresh out of law school. Smith asked numerous questions and discovered from Mr. Jones that he heard one official tell a coach immediately after the accident that the school had failed to sweep the floor prior to the match and the roof had been leaking for over two months. Utilizing her legal prowess, Smith thought she had a great negligence case and accepted the Joneses as clients.

Smith initially performed research and discovered that the likely parties that should be sued included the school, the school district, the volleyball officials, the athletic director, the coach, and the high school athletic association. Jones, who brought the suit to recover her damages, was called the **plaintiff** while all parties being sued were called **defendants**. Jones and all the defendants lived or operated in Texas. Because there was no federal question, or litigants from different states, Smith's only option was to bring the suit in a Texas state court. Based on the medical expenses and potential future damages, Smith had to bring the case in a specific court with proper jurisdiction.

Smith remembered that special rules applied whenever a governmental entity is sued. Thus, after some initial research, Smith filed a **governmental claim** against the school district. Smith filed the claim specifically to avoid a statute of limitations issue. The **statute of limitations** required the suit to be filed within a certain time period, or Jones would have been forever barred from filing suit. *Each state has its own rules concerning filing a claim against the state. These governmental claim rules are designed to provide the state with notice it might be sued. Some states require the filing of a claim while others allow a party just to name the state in a lawsuit.*

Smith prepared a **complaint** which described key facts available to Jones and provided enough information for the opposing side to know why they were being sued. The complaint specifically identified all known defendants, the reason why jurisdiction was proper, and a statement setting forth what remedies Jones demanded. Smith had a specified amount of time within which she had to serve the defendants with a copy of the complaint that she had already filed with the chosen court. Smith was required to personally serve each defendant with the complaint. *Some states allow a party to mail a complaint or to serve the complaint* *through a sheriff. A complaint indicates the title of the case, identifies all the parties, designates in which court the case is being filed, and tells the story of the dispute in a specified legal form.*

Within a specified time after receiving the complaint, the defendants filed an **answer** indicating why they were not liable for Jones' injuries. Along with their answer, the defendants served Jones (through her attorney) with several discovery requests. **Discovery** was used as a means to find out what Jones knew about the incident and her damages. The discovery requests included a request to produce all relevant documents in Jones' possession (e.g., medical bills), a request for admissions (e.g., admitting she did not miss any work or she did not receive lower grades as a result of the injury), interrogatories or specific questions (e.g., her age, her address, if she has a driver's license), and a request to take Jones' deposition. Smith responded by serving similar discovery requests on all the defendants. Jones was required to attend a **deposition** where she had to answer numerous questions, under oath, asked by the defendants' attorneys. Smith had the right to request the same types of discovery from the defendants. *Discovery is the process used to discover information about the opposing parties in a suit. Answers have to be given under oath or the penalty of perjury. Additional discovery tools not specifically addressed above could include: a request to inspect the gym, an independent medical examination of Jones, and possibly an independent psychological evaluation if Jones was claiming severe or extreme emotional distress.*

After several months of discovery, the defendants filed a **motion for summary judgment**. Summary judgment motions are brought when a party concludes that, as a matter of law, the undisputed facts are in their favor and they should win without having to go to trial. These motions are solely based on applicable case law and the facts uncovered through the discovery process. The judge determined that there were still issues of facts that were in dispute and as such, the judge denied defendants' summary judgment motion. The parties tried to settle the case, but when they were unable to reach a mutually acceptable settlement, they started preparing for trial. Each side obtained witnesses on its own behalf. The court chose a trial date which was approximately two years after Jones was first injured. *Summary judgment is one of several possible pretrial motions. Other such motions include a demurrer, motion to sever, motion to strike, motion to remove for lack of subject matter jurisdiction, and other motions which attack the complaint or require the production of requested discovery material. Such motions are brought when, as a matter of law, one party is or should be required to alter its case. For example, an injured high school athlete might have suffered a great injury, but due to governmental immunity bestowed to the high school principal, the principal could bring a summary judgment motion to be dismissed from the case as a matter of law.*

Smith thought the facts favored her client. Her client made a good witness. Thus, Jones demands a trial by **jury**. The plaintiff in a civil case always has the choice of whether or not he or she wants a jury. The twelve member jury was required to decide who was telling the truth and ultimately what were the facts. Each side prepared a trial memorandum explaining its case and provided the memorandum to the judge. After resolving some disputes concerning what evidence would be allowed at trial, the judge allowed the parties to pick a jury. Utilizing a process called **voir dire**, each side interviewed prospective jurors and had the right to dismiss all biased jurors or a limited number of jurors that they just did not want. *The size and role of a jury varies in different states. Some juries only examine facts or certain components of a case while other juries are responsible for analyzing all facts and determining damages.*

Smith provided an eloquent **opening statement** which Perry Mason would have envied. The defendants also had a strong opening statement on their own behalf. The trial proceeded with Smith calling Jones as the first witness. After answering all the questions asked by Smith, Jones was **cross-examined** by defendants' attorneys who were attempting to refute Jones' testimony or highlight any inconsistencies. Jones' father was a **fact witness** because he had specific facts concerning the accident and injuries. Both sides also acquired the services of **expert witnesses** to testify about the standard of care for schools, doctors to testify about Jones' injuries, and several high school volleyball coaches. The trial continued with each side presenting its witnesses and the other side having the opportunity to cross-examine each witness. Documentary evidence was also introduced by each side. Throughout the trial, each side repeatedly made **objections** to certain questions or the introduction of some evidence. The judge was forced to determine, as a matter of law, which side was correct and which questions or evidence were legally allowable. *The plaintiff always presents his or her case first in civil cases.*

Each side concluded its questioning and then made its final **closing statement**. The closing statements provided a summary of the facts and law exposed by each side during the trial. The jury was given specific instructions by the judge concerning the law and how the jury was to apply the facts to the law. Based on the evidence presented, the jury returned a verdict in Jones' favor. The jury awarded Jones $14,000 for **actual damages** (medical expenses and lost wages) and $20,000 for **pain and suffering**. The lost scholarship was too speculative, thus, the jury was barred from awarding damages for that loss.

The defendants were not happy with the jury's conclusion. The defendants' attorneys knew they could not challenge the jury's evidentiary conclusion, but felt the judge gave the jury an incorrect instruction concerning the school's duty to Jones. The judge could have overturned the jury's decision if the judge felt it was not supported by law or the facts. However, the judge affirmed the jury's decision. Defendants filed a **notice of appeal** which is the first step in the appeals process. Each side was required to submit a "brief" that outlined its legal analysis and then argue its case in front of three appellate judges. The appellate court, after carefully reviewing the lower court's actions, determined that the lower court made a **procedural mistake** in using an incorrect jury instruction. Therefore, the appellate court **remanded** (sent back) the case to the lower court to retry the case using the correct instruction. *The number of judges hearing an appeal varies in different courts. An appellate court can remand a case, uphold the lower court's decision, or overturn the lower court's decision.*

Before the new trial began, the sides reached a **settlement** in which the school paid Jones $18,000. By the time Jones finally settled the case, she was in college and three years had elapsed since she brought the suit. The appellate court's reasoning was published in the state's official case registry and became precedence for any future cases dealing with the appropriate jury instruction to give concerning a school's duty to its students. However, from reading the published appellate court's decision, a reader would not know that the case was settled once it was remanded to the lower court. The appellate court report only indicated that it was remanding the case to be retried. Rarely does one discover what happens to cases because lower court decisions are not officially published. Furthermore, most cases are settled and the settlement terms are often confidential. While Jones' fictitious case went to trial, it is estimated that less than five percent of all cases filed ever reach a trial. Most cases are either dismissed prior to trial, settled, or defeated through summary judgment or other defensive maneuvers. *Only state appellate and state Supreme Court cases are officially published. All Federal cases are published. Cases are commonly found in the following reporters: Federal District Court cases can be found in Federal Supplement volumes (cases are cited using the initials "F. Supp."), Federal Appellate cases can be found in the Federal Reporter ("F." or "F.2d" which is the second volume of Federal Reporters), U.S. Supreme Court cases can be found in three different reporters—United States Supreme Court Reports ("U.S."), Supreme Court Reporter ("S. Ct."), and Supreme Court Reports, Lawyer's Edition ("L. Ed."). Nine different reporters exists for various state courts or regional groupings of courts. These cases are found in the following reporters: Atlantic Reporter ("A." or "A. 2d"), Northeastern Reporter ("N.E." or "N.E. 2d."), Northwestern Reporter ("N.W." or "N.W. 2d."), Pacific Reporter ("P." or "P. 2d."), Southeastern Reporter ("S.E." or "S.E. 2d."), Southern Reporter ("So." or "So. 2d."), Southwestern Reporter ("S.W." or "S.W. 2d."), New York Supplement ("N.Y.S."), or California Reporter ("Cal.Rptr.").*

References

Publications

Anderson, R., Fox, I., Twomey, D., (1984). *Business Law*, (12th Ed.) Cincinnati: South-Western Publishing Co.

Coughlin, G. G., (1983). *Your Introduction to Law*, (4th ed.). New York: Barnes & Noble Books.

—— 1.20 ——

Legal Research

William F. Regan
Canisius College

The ability to perform legal research is vital to the sport manager. First, legal research will enable the sport manager to acquire a fundamental understanding of the legal concepts which are germane to one's sport or business. Second, legal research will keep the sport manager up-to-date on the current legal developments affecting the business of sport. To enable the sport manager to perform basic legal research, this chapter will outline and define basic research sources, and explain their use. Remember, this is a basic introduction and should never be considered as a replacement for an attorney's advice on legal issues.

This chapter will divide all resources into one of two areas of authority, primary or secondary. **Primary authorities** represent the actual law, which includes case law and statutory law. **Secondary authorities** are those works which analyze and present an overview on statutes and cases. While not considered legal precedents, secondary authorities do provide generally accurate summaries of relevant law.

A final section, LEXIS/WESTLAW, has been included to give a brief overview of the current computer tools available to the legal researcher.

Secondary Authorities

Secondary authorities are articles, journals, editorials, or other sources that are written to attempt to synthesize and analyze certain topics or areas of the law. The real value of these works, apart from their scholarly contributions, is that they provide the reader with a basic overview and understanding of the law regarding a particular topic.

In addition, the authors often include numerous references to other sources. This permits the researcher to locate cases and statutes, as well as other secondary authority on the research topic.

There are many different sources of secondary authority. For purposes of this chapter the focus will be on those that are most useful in the research of sport-related topics. These sources fall into one of the following categories:

1. Legal Encyclopedias
2. Legal Periodicals
3. Annotations
4. Books/Treatises and Dictionaries

Legal Encyclopedias.   A legal encyclopedia, like a general encyclopedia, contains detailed summaries of numerous points of law. These topics are covered by narrative text which summarizes legal rules of both state and federal courts. The text of a particular topic is supported by references to cases, statutes, and other related resources. Encyclopedias provide a good introduction to the researcher who knows little about the subject (Wren & Wren, 1986). Encyclopedias are a good way to begin your research, but they do have their

11

limitations. They are limited by the fact that they do not provide a detailed explanation of any particular area of law. They also fail to analyze the law.

The two most referenced legal encyclopedias on the national level are *Corpus Juris Secundum* and *American Jurisprudence*. Both are multi-volume sets that arrange topics alphabetically. Each has a topical table of contents at the beginning of each volume as well as an extensive index at the end of the volumes. Each volume is updated with a yearly supplement included at the end of the volume, or by a separate soft-covered supplemental volume.

In addition to national encyclopedias, there are a limited number of state specific encyclopedias. These encyclopedias provide the same type of information and are arranged in a similar fashion to the national encyclopedias. The main difference is that they are specific to the particular state, and should only be referenced when researching a particular state's law.

Legal encyclopedias are arranged by topic, alphabetically. This permits the researcher to go directly to the volume of the encyclopedia which contains the research topic. Prior to reviewing the text, a review of the table of contents will serve two objectives. It will allow the researcher to focus on the pertinent sections of the text, and, it will permit the researcher to confirm that the section of the encyclopedia selected covers the research topic. If the researcher does not know which topic is appropriate for that particular problem, the researcher can use the index to look up a descriptive term or word. The index will then lead the researcher to the appropriate topic and section in the encyclopedia (Wren & Wren, 1986).

Legal Periodicals and Law Reviews.   Legal periodicals and law reviews provide scholarly writings about recent cases and new statutes and critically analyze recent developments in the law. Law reviews are typically published by law schools and are written by students, professors, and practicing attorneys (Elias & Levinkind, 1995). Law review articles provide the reader with critical analysis of current legal developments and recent court decisions, and attempt to predict the future course of the law.

Legal periodicals published by bar associations and other professional organizations are written to provide the reader with a more practical application of recent legal developments. These periodicals are typically published on a monthly or quarterly basis.

The articles found in law reviews and legal periodicals are generally narrow in their focus and often deal with complex legal concepts. These articles do provide great insight into current trends and developments in the law. This, however, also proves to be their biggest limitation. Because of their complexity, one should not use these articles until one has an understanding of the area of law being researched and has reviewed a number of other sources.

The most common approach to accessing periodicals and law reviews is by using the Index to Legal Periodicals and the Current Case Index. Each index is organized by subject, author, and title and contains a table in the front of each volume for the abbreviations of the reviews or journals in which the articles can be located (Elias & Levinkind, 1995). In addition, the Current Case Index includes a table of cases and statutes which are cited and used in the articles. Both the Index to Legal Periodicals and the Current Case Index cover all legal periodicals.

A more suitable tool for the sport manager to research sport-specific topics is *The Sport Lawyer's Guide to Legal Periodicals*, by Wong & Wilde (1994). This index provides references to over 900 sport related articles from 285 Law Journals. This resource indexes articles by subject, journal, title, or author. There are also a number of sport specific journals which are available for the sport manager. Several examples include: *The Marquette Sport Law Journal, Seton Hall Journal of Sport Law, Entertainment & Sports Law Reporter,* and *The Journal of Legal Aspects of Sport*.

Annotations.   Annotations are a series of volumes which represent decisions of federal and state courts which are unique, or establish some precedent. Included with each case is a critical analysis or commentary about the case, and how it may or does affect other cases or the current status of the law. These annotations are published in a series known as the American Law Reports. There are currently five editions in this series, and a federal A.L.R. that deals with federal cases, statutes, and regulations. The volumes in the 3rd, 4th, and 5th series have a pocket part, which must be consulted to determine if there have been any changes to the articles in the series worth noting.

Because the annotations in the A.L.R. are so specific and narrow in focus, if the researcher does not have a case, statute, regulation, or point of law identified, one may not find this resource to be very useful. But, if the researcher has narrowed the focus of the research, the A.L.R.s are beneficial in supplying cases from a number of different jurisdictions.

To use this series, it is best to begin one's research with the most current volume. The newest volumes do not replace previous volumes, but may have superseded the older annotations. The A.L.R. has several tools to locate annotations. The Quick Index volume for each series should be used. This volume contains an index of topics and key words, which are arranged in alphabetical order. The Word Index is for the 1st and 2nd series of the A.L.R.; the researcher would search by using key terms or words as one would in any index (Wren & Wren, 1986). The Digest, a separate volume for the 1st and 2nd series, and a combined volume for the other series, divides the law into legal topics arranged alphabetically, and references A.L.R. annotations. There are also tables of cases and statutes and regulations that contain references to annotations that report a particular case or statute.

Books/Treatises and Dictionaries.   Books and treatises are scholarly works typically written by an expert on a particular aspect of the law. The book or books dedicated to a particular aspect of the law permit an in-depth and, usually, expansive investigation into a particular facet of the law. Due to the comprehensive manner in which topics are covered, the researcher will find defined areas of interest covered in great detail. Also included are annotations or footnotes to cases and statutes. This resource can be accessed through a card catalog in a library or by a computer search.

Law dictionaries will assist the researcher in understanding the unique language of the law. Similar to an ordinary dictionary, the law dictionary will provide the meaning of words and other relevant information.

Primary Authorities

Unlike secondary sources, primary authorities **are** the law. There are two generally accepted sources of primary authority. They are those created by the legislatures in the form of statutes, codes, or regulations and those fashioned by the courts through judicial opinions, rulings, and decisions.

Statutes.   Statutes are the written laws. They are the result of legislative action at both the federal and the state level. The procedure by which statutes are enacted, printed, and published follows a very similar sequence, regardless of whether it is a federal or a state statute. First, the law is adopted by the appropriate legislative measures required of the jurisdiction promulgating the statute. The law is then printed in the form of a slip law. **Slip laws** are often in pamphlet form, published and numbered according to the sequence in which the laws are enacted. The second form in which statutes appear is **session laws**. These are bound, soft covered volumes of slip laws. Typically included with these volumes are tables evidencing which laws have been affected and a subject index. The final form in which statutes are published is in the form of **annotated** and **non-annotated codes**. This is the form in which the researcher will find statutes most accessible.

Annotated and non-annotated codes are the compilation of the adopted statutes organized into common subject categories. Annotated codes are printed with the inclusion of explanatory information about the text of the statute (Elias & Levinkind, 1995). This information consists of a history of the statute, cross references to other related statutes and legal resources, and judicial decisions interpreting that statute. Non-annotated codes will only contain the statute text and do not provide any commentary about the statute nor any court decisions dealing with that particular statute. Most research should utilize annotated statutes because not only is one provided with the text of the statute, but also with numerous other sources and cases that may be germane to a research topic.

It is imperative that, when reviewing statutes, one also examine the yearly supplements that are provided in a pocket part at the back of each volume, or under separate cover. The supplement will provide any revisions, amendments, or deletions to the text of the statue. Without reviewing the annual supplement, one may be relying on outdated and inaccurate law.

Research involving statutes can be performed by several different methods. The method one selects will depend on what knowledge and particular facts one has about the research topic. If one knows the statute and has the correct **citation** (reference to a statute by the volume and section in that volume wherein the statute appears) for that statute, one would merely have to look up the statute in the appropriate volume. If only the popular name of the statute is known, and not its citation, one can still find the statute by using a Popular Names table found in a majority of federal and state codes (Wren & Wren, 1986).

If one does not know the citation or name of a particular statute, but is confident that there is an applicable statute and knows which areas of the code deal with that topic (e.g., Consumer Protection), the researcher can go directly to the appropriate volume or volumes dealing with that topic. The researcher can review the table of contents prior to the first statute or use the index after the last statute of that particular section. Unless familiar with what legal topics are covered by particular sections of the particular code, one will find this method time consuming.

The final method, the one recommended and most often used, is to use key terms and words. This method requires that one use the index volumes of the particular code to look up key terms and words. Most sets of codes have a separate multi-volume set of indexes that arrange terms alphabetically. If successful, the researcher will be referred to a particular section of the code. One must then go to that section to determine whether it is appropriate. If nothing is found, that indicates one of two possibilities: there are no statutes dealing with that particular topic, or, the search terms or words may not coincide with the indices. If the latter is the case, a new key term or word must be used. (Wren & Wren, 1986).

Case Law.   An important source of primary authority is case law, i.e., the decisions and opinions of the courts. The courts' function is to decide questions of law and fact between opposing parties, or to interpret legislative enactments. Reported decisions inform us as to how a court decided a specific legal issue before it. They also serve to provide a basis for predicting how future, similar issues might be decided.

These decisions and opinions are compiled and reprinted in volumes known as Reporters. They are arranged, not by topic, but by the date of the decision. Reports are published at both the State and Federal level. It is important to remember that these decisions do not contain the trial transcript, evidence, or other similar information. What they do contain is a brief history of the case, a statement of the facts, the issues before the court, and the decision and reasoning of the rendering court. Reporters which contain Appellate Court decisions also contain a history of the case in the lower court or courts and, often, a summary of the legal arguments of opposing counsel.

Reporters, as mentioned above, are published for both State and Federal Courts. At the Federal Court level, each court has at least one case reporter for its decisions (Wren & Wren, 1986). Supreme Court decisions are published in several different reports including: United States Reporter, Supreme Court Reporter, and the United States Supreme Court Reporter, Lawyers' Edition.

The decisions of the Federal Court of Appeals are published in the Federal Reporter. Federal District Court decisions can be found in the Federal Reporter for cases decided until 1932, and, since 1932, in the Federal Supplement.

Each State Court also has a separate reporter for the decisions of its highest courts. Some states may also provide reporters for their lower level appellate courts. In addition to individual state reports, which the researcher may not have access to, there are regional reporters. Regional reporters reprint the decisions of the state appellate and supreme courts from specific geographical regions of the county (Wren & Wren,

1986). These regional reporters are as follows: Atlantic, North Eastern, North Western, Pacific, South Eastern, South Western and Southern.

Cases are referred to by citations. All citations are composed of similar elements, viz.; the name of the parties involved in the law suit, the name of the reporter wherein the case is recorded, the volume of the reporter, and the page on which the case begins. For example, *Faer v. Vertical Fitness & Racquet Club* is cited at 462 NYS2d 784 (NY City Cir. Ct. 1983). This case can be located in volume number 462 of the New York Supplement, 2d series on page 784. The parties involved in the lawsuit are Faer and Vertical Fitness & Racquet Club. The parenthetical information in this example lets the researcher know in which lower court this case originated.

Each volume of a reporter contains several tools to aid in locating cases in that particular volume. These tools consist of a table of contents, table of judges (judges who decided the cases), table of statutes, and rules construed. To search for a case this way, unless you are already aware of its citation, would usually be too time consuming. A more practical resource for locating case authority is through use of a digest.

The digest serves as a subject index to reporters. As mentioned earlier, it would be impractical to search for cases about a particular topic by going through each volume of a reporter. The digest provides brief statements of facts and/or court rulings and decisions. These decisions are grouped together based upon their topic. It serves as an annotated subject index for the reported case law of a particular jurisdiction. These brief one- or two-sentence synopses are referred to as headnotes. You will find headnotes in the digests, and similar headnotes at the beginning of the cases reported in the reporters.

The primary publisher of digests is West Publishing Company. West has published digests for state and federal reporters. In addition, West publishes a general digest, referred to as the American Digest System.

All of the digests published by West have similar features that will assist in locating cases. These features are: 1) a descriptive word index volume, 2) Topic Index for each volume, 3) Table of Cases and Defendant-Plaintiff Index, 4) some digests also contain a words and phrases volume.

Like statutes, cases can be located in several ways. The manner in which one searches and the tools used will depend on the information one has when beginning the search. The first method is by the actual citation of the case. If, after reviewing statutes or some secondary source, one locates a case of interest, the researcher would look to see if the citation of the case is given. If a citation can be located, one would then use the citation to look for that case in the appropriate reporter by volume and page number. However, one must remember that there may be many other relevant cases. To locate other cases, review the headnotes at the beginning of the instant case and determine which ones are germane to your topic. Adjacent to each headnote will be a key number. The key number references are a unique feature of the West Digest System. Each topic, or headnote, is given a specific designation, a key number. This key number is readily identified by an image of a key with a number next to it. A key number is assigned to every topic or headnote. One will find that the key number assigned for a particular topic or headnote will be identical in all books published by West, including case reports and encyclopedias. The researcher would then go to the appropriate digest dealing with that topic and which has the same key number. The digest will then provide a number of other relevant cases on that topic. If only the name of the case and not the complete citation is available, the case can be located by the table of cases or the defendant-plaintiff table provided with the digest.

If the researcher does not have a case citation or name to begin the search, and is unsure as to which research topic is appropriate, the word index should be used to begin one's research. If confident of the topic, the researcher can use the corresponding index in the appropriate volume of the digest. Once at the appropriate topic index for the particular topic, use the index as one would any other index. Review the entries to see which are relevant, then examine the cases referenced under these topics.

Shepards.   The final place one must go after having researched a topic is Shepards. Shepardizing is a process whereby one updates research involving cases and statutes. Shepardizing insures that all cases and statutes are still good law.

Shepards follows the history of cases and statutes. The materials reveal what has happened to that case, if it has been followed by other courts, if it has been modified or overturned (reviewed). Without Shepardizing the cases and statutes relevant to the topic, one cannot be sure that the research is current and valid.

Shepardizing is essential, but it can also be intimidating to the beginning researcher. The following summary will guide the researcher on how to Shepardize.

Select the appropriate set of Shepards' Citators covering the reporters or statutes being used. Shepards publishes separate sets of Citators for state reporters, state statutes, West regional reporters, Federal Statutes, Federal Reporter, Federal Supplements, and the U.S. Supreme Court Reports (Wren & Wren, 1986). Each Shepards volume will cover several volumes of Reporters. For example, one volume of Shepards' New York Supplement 2nd series may cover volume 223 through 256 of the New York Supplement 2nd Reporter. Examine the binding of the Shepards Citators to determine which volumes are relevant to your materials.

Each volume of the Citator will cover a particular time period. One must check the most recent paperbound volume of the citator to determine if one has all of the books needed. The front of the paperbound Citator tells what should be in the library (Wren & Wren, 1986). If the case is covered by several volumes, usually the paperbound volumes and one or two hard cover volumes, one must examine all relevant volumes.

Once the correct volumes of the Citator are located, one must examine the tables of citation within those volumes (Wren & Wren, 1986). The volume of the Citator may cover several different series of case reporters. Examine the top of the pages to make sure that the right table is being used. One can also use the table of contents to determine which pages cover the case reporter containing the case (Wren & Wren, 1986).

After determining the correct volumes and tables, one must locate within the appropriate table the volume number of the case reporter that contains the case being Shepardized. The volumes are arranged numerically and are designated by a boldfaced "**Vol.**" This designation may be anywhere on a particular page. Once the correct volume is located, look for the correct page number (Wren & Wren, 1986). This page number will be the beginning page number of the case, and will also be the page number from the citation.

Now one can examine the cases that have dealt with or treated the case or statute. The citation for these cases as well as letters may be seen. These letters designate the history or treatment of the case. To find out what these letters mean, turn to the front of the volume which contains the History of Case and Treatment of Case abbreviations.

This may seem like a cumbersome process, but with practice one will be able to Shepardize quickly. Remember that research is not finished until the relevant cases and statutes have been shepardized.

LEXIS/WESTLAW. The most current sources available to a researcher are LEXIS and WESTLAW. Both are computer data bases that provide easy and quick access to statutes, cases and many secondary sources. The researcher is able to locate a number of resources by using citations or key terms. Although LEXIS and WESTLAW are very useful to the researcher, their availability proves to be their biggest limitation. The researcher can usually only expect to find this resource available through a law school library. But, if one has access the benefit is well worth using.

References

Publications
Elias, S., & Levinkind, S. (1995). *Legal Research: How to Find and Understand the Law*. (4th ed.). (J. Portman, Ed). Berkeley, Calif.: Nolo Press.

Wren, C. G., & Wren, J. L. (1986). *The Legal Research Manual: A Game Plan for Legal Research and Analysis*. (2nd ed.). Madison, Wis.: Adams & Ambrose Publishing.

Ethics and Law

John Merriman
Valdosta State University

Sport managers at all levels are constantly faced with decisions, the outcomes of which usually affect many people. If for no other reason than to avoid offending or upsetting those affected by such decisions, the sport manager should make every effort to see that the decisions are ethical in every respect. **Black's Law Dictionary** defines ethics as:

> Of or relating to moral action, conduct, motive or character; . . . also treating of moral feelings, duties, or conduct; . . . Professionally right or befitting; conforming to professional standards of conduct. (p. 523)

Sport managers are faced with day-to-day decisions and responsibilities in such areas as marketing, planning, budgeting, personnel, facilities, and legal questions. Usually, one is concerned with only the legality of decisions, but concerned and competent managers should also make sure that the actions are ethical. Although training in ethics is not a prerequisite to the making of ethical decisions, certainly training in ethics would be helpful in promoting morally correct actions. As Kretchmar has pointed out, "We are left largely on our own when deciding how to act ethically in our professional roles . . ." (Kretchmar, 1991). Kretchmar is supported by Zeigler, who in lamenting the lack of ethical training stated, "Unfortunately, the child or young person typically learns to make rational ethical decisions poorly and inadequately, a tragic condition because the inclusion of rationality in personality development is so important." (Zeigler, 1992).

This chapter is no substitute for a course in ethics. It is meant to challenge sport managers to think about the subject and to evaluate their actions from an ethical perspective. It is important for a sport manager to act ethically for at least two reasons. One is to promote high morale among those with whom the manager works, and the second is to help avoid actions that might well lead to litigation.

Neither philosophers nor sport managers would agree on a single ethical value system. Among the many value systems, Richard Fox, a professor of philosophy at Cleveland State University (Zeigler, 1992), suggests a three-stage test to determine if an action is ethical. This test begins with Kant's principle of universality, moves to Bentham's and Mill's principle of utility, and ends with Aristotle's principle of intentions. The careful reader will detect inconsistencies and conflicts among the principles of these three philosophers. In addition, there are differences in interpretation of these philosophers by modern ethicists. Further, the reader should be aware that there are many other value systems or principles relating to ethical behavior (e.g., appeal to religion and other varieties of both utilitarian and deontological ethics). One's personal values determine the ethical principles by which one lives, and principles espoused by one philosopher may be in direct conflict with those of a person with different values. One should be careful, however, that one is not using an ethical principle merely as a way to rationalize one's own prejudices.

Simply stated, Kant's **principle of universality** says that all rules or actions must be able to be applied to all people. They cannot be levied against nor favor some while rejecting any others. In other words, Kant believed that for a "rule" to be ethical it must be universally applicable. If exceptions to the rule have to be made, then the rule is either incomplete or unethical. To test any action with this principle, one asks the question: "Is it possible to apply this action or rule to all people on earth?" In other words, one should so act that his or her action could become a universal law of human behavior. Application of this principle is very similar to the application of the Golden Rule and other maxims. One interpretation of Kant's principle of universality has been developed by Hill.[1] He implements the principle through the following rules: 1) you must not coerce others, 2) you must not allow yourself to be coerced, 3) you must treat people as ends and never as means to an end, 4) you must treat all equally unless unequal treatment works for the advantage of all parties and all parties give consent to the unequal treatment, 5) you must not deceive or defraud, 6) you must honor your contracts (keep all vows and promises rightly made), 7) you must support the autonomy of all persons, including oneself. In short, be committed to "self-actualizing" programs and policies.

The **principle of utility** is identified with Jeremy Bentham and John Stuart Mill. Application of this principle is referred to as utilitarianism. Basically this principle, as they apply it, states that action taken which benefits the greatest number of the whole is ethical. Carried to its logical conclusion, utilitarianism becomes "the end justifies the means." It can be argued that any action which benefits the greatest number of the whole is ethical regardless of the means used to accomplish it.

Care must be taken in determining who is included in the whole; the whole is all of those affected by the action. Seldom, if ever, does the whole consist of just the team, sport program, department, or the institution or business. Because sport is so pervasive an influence in our society, one must also consider the effect of one's actions on the community and society itself.

The author's interpretation of Aristotle's **concept of practical virtue** is that, to be virtuous, correct actions must be taken for the right reasons. In other words, if a managerial decision is the ethically correct thing to do but the manager makes that decision for ethically wrong reasons, the manager is not acting ethically.

Read each of the following sport incidents and identify the unethical actions, if any, and determine why each such action is unethical.

> **Incident 1.**   An intercollegiate athletic director is informed that his baseball coach is teaching players the following tactic: With runners on second and third, the batter executes a safety squeeze bunt down the third base line. The home plate official must cover the play at home and the field official must cover the play on the batter at first. With only two umpires, neither is in position to watch the runner at second as he rounds third. The coach teaches the runner coming from second to take advantage of this by making the turn at third well short of the base giving him an advantage in distance and speed in attempting to reach home.

Is the action of the coach unethical? Would a utilitarian consider his act to be ethical since it helped the team to win the game? What group constitutes the whole? Under the principle of universality, would the action be unethical because it involved deceit and taking advantage of the other party?

What action should the athletic director take at this point? What action by the athletic director would be of greatest benefit to the whole? If the athletic director disciplines the coach, under the principle of virtue, what should his motives be?

---

[1]Dr. Jim Hill, professor of psychology at Valdosta State University and an ethicist, must be credited with the development of the rules cited here as interpretation of the principle of universality. Dr. Hill, through many discussions and his class Ethics in Sport, has contributed greatly to the creation of the content of this chapter.

Incident 2.   The swimming team at a school just starting a swimming program has 14 swimmers, only 5 of whom have competitive experience. The new coach is concerned, but after receiving assurance from the head coach of a powerhouse school that his team will "take it easy," he schedules a dual meet at the opponent's school. The inexperienced team is heavily trounced, scoring a total of only 9 points. The opposing team ridicules and embarrasses the young swimmers. In retaliation, the visiting swimmers steal 75 of the host school's towels.

Upon learning of the theft, what action should the visiting coach take? Should all offending athletes be treated equally? Since the athletes had some justification for the theft, should they be punished? Who will benefit if they are punished? What kind of discipline, punishment, or restitution will result in the greatest benefit for the whole? Who constitutes the whole? Under the principle of virtue, why should or should not the coach discipline the players?

Did the coach of the powerhouse school act unethically? Were his assurances intentionally deceptive and in violation of the principle of universality? Was it a violation of the principle of universality for him to promise to "take it easy" on the team? Was it ethical to ask his team to perform less than their best or to substitute weaker swimmers? Did allowing his players to ridicule the other team benefit the greatest number of the whole? Who constitutes the whole? The motives of the coach are unclear, so is it possible to judge whether he has acted ethically?

The Representative Case presented here is meant to illustrate how the application of appropriate ethical principles might help to prevent litigation in sport situations. In reading this case, examine the actions of the coach, the university administrators, and the football players. Determine how the application of the three previously discussed principles would have affected the actions of each of the parties involved.

■ ■ ■ ■

Representative Case

WILLIAMS v. EATON
United States Court Of Appeals For The Tenth Circuit
468 F.2d 1079; 16 Fed. R. Serv. 2d (Callaghan) 1353
October 31, 1972

OPINION: HOLLOWAY, Circuit Judge.

This appeal is a sequel to our earlier consideration of this controversy involving several Black athletes of the University of Wyoming football team. They were dismissed from the team following a dispute over their intentions to wear black armbands during a football game with Brigham Young University. After their dismissal they sought relief by this civil rights action, claiming violation of First Amendment rights.

In the prior appeal we affirmed in part, sustaining the dismissal of claims against the State of Wyoming and all damage claims, but reversed a summary judgment and dismissal of claims for equitable and declaratory relief as to other defendants, and remanded for further proceed-

ings. 443 F.2d 422. After a trial to the court on these remaining claims for declaratory and injunctive relief, the trial court made findings of fact and conclusions of law in favor of the defendants and dismissed again. 333 F. Supp. 107. Essentially the court upheld the defendants' actions in dismissing the athletes from the team on the ground that the Federal and Wyoming Constitutions mandated complete neutrality on religious matters which would have been violated otherwise by the armband display expressing opposition to religious beliefs of the Church of Jesus Christ of Latter-Day Saints on racial matters.

The general circumstances of the controversy have been set out by the trial court and our earlier opinion and need not be repeated. We feel it important to discuss the facts in detail based on the trial record only in respect to two principal issues which will be treated. We believe the controlling issues on this appeal are as follows:

1. whether findings of fact 14 and 15 made by the trial court, dealing with the purpose of the athletes in seeking to wear the armbands and the position they took thereon, are clearly erroneous;
2. whether the determination by the Board of Trustees of the University refusing to permit the athletes to wear the armbands on the field during the game was a reasonable and lawful ruling or regulation under the principles of Tinker v. Des Moines Independent School District, 393 U.S. 503, 89 S. Ct. 733, 21 L. Ed. 2d 731, and similar cases.

We do not treat certain additional propositions forcefully argued for the athletes on this appeal. Arguments are made that the football coaching rule against participation generally by the athletes in demonstrations was invalid. However, we feel that questions concerning the rule need not be decided. The original dismissal of the athletes by Coach Eaton for violation of the rule was not the end of the matter. Later the controversy was considered by the Trustees and President Carlson at a conference with the athletes and the athletic officials. It was found by the trial court that the decision of the Trustees to sustain the dismissal of the athletes was made after this conference during which the athletes insisted on the right to wear the armbands during the game. And it was further found that the Trustees' decision was made on the ground that permitting the wearing of the armbands would be in violation of the constitutional mandate requiring complete neutrality on religion. Therefore our decision focuses on the lawfulness of the Trustees' action.

Findings 14 and 15 and the Purpose of the Athletes in Seeking to Wear the Armbands

The plaintiffs challenge findings 14 and 15 of the trial court, arguing that they are clearly erroneous under the test of United States v. United States Gypsum Co., 333 U.S. 364, 395, 68 S. Ct. 525, 92 L. Ed. 746.

• • •

The plaintiffs first challenge the portion of finding 14 that there is no merit in the contention that one of the purposes of the armband display was protesting against "cheap shots" and name-calling by members of the Brigham Young team. There was testimony by plaintiffs Williams and Hamilton that they were protesting against such conduct by the BYU team; Governor Hathaway and defendants Carlson and Hollon also said the plaintiffs did complain at the meeting with the Trustees about such conduct of the BYU players. However, plaintiffs Williams

and Hamilton also said that at various meetings they were protesting against racial policies, Williams referring to such policies of BYU and Hamilton to those of the Mormon Church. And there was testimony by several defendants that centered on the demand of the athletes to wear the armbands in the game to protest views of the Mormon Church. Viewing the record as a whole we cannot agree with this challenge to the findings.

The plaintiffs also say that there was error in the portion of finding 14 that all of the plaintiffs refused to play against Brigham Young University unless they could wear the armbands. And they argue also that finding 15 was in error in stating that all of the plaintiffs refused to play again for the University if defendant Eaton remained as coach. They say the proof fails to establish these facts as to all of the individual plaintiffs and that there was contrary proof. The evidence was in conflict. There was, however, testimony by Governor Hathaway and President Carlson about the discussions and conduct of the plaintiffs at the meeting which Governor Hathaway and President Carlson had separately with them which supports these findings. Defendant Pence's testimony also supports these findings.

• • •

First Amendment Principles Under Tinker v. Des Moines Independent School District

Both plaintiffs and defendants rely on the principles stated in the Tinker case and similar decisions. The plaintiffs argue that they come within its bounds of freedom of expression recognized therein as applying to students in different places, including the playing field. 393 U.S. at 512, 513, 89 S. Ct. 733, 21 L. Ed. 2d 731. On the other hand the defendants say that their actions were within the exceptions stated in the opinion. We feel the controlling guidelines from the Tinker case are the following:

A student's rights, therefore, do not embrace merely the classroom hours. When he is in the cafeteria, or on the playing field, or on the campus during the authorized hours, he may express his opinion, even on controversial subjects like the conflict in Vietnam, if he does so without "materially and substantially [interfering] with the requirements of appropriate discipline in the operation of the school" and without colliding with the rights of others. . . . But conduct by the student, in class or out of it, which for any reason—whether it stems from time, place, or type of behavior—materially disrupts class work or involves substantial disorder or invasion of the rights of others is, of course, not immunized by the constitutional guarantee of freedom of speech. . . .

•••

... The Constitution says that Congress (and the States) may not abridge the right to free speech. This provision means what it says. We properly read it to permit reasonable regulation of speech-connected activities in carefully restricted circumstances. But we do not confine the permissible exercise of First Amendment rights to a telephone booth or the four corners of a pamphlet, or to supervised and ordained discussion in a school classroom. [citations omitted] 393 U.S. at 512, 513, 89 S. Ct. at 740.

The trial court concluded that had the defendants, as governing officials of the University of Wyoming, permitted display of the armbands, their actions would have been violative of the First Amendment establishment clause and its requirement of neutrality on expressions relating to religion, citing School District of Abington v. Schempp, 374 U.S. 203, 83 S. Ct. 1560, 10 L. Ed. 2d 844, and similar cases. The Court further grounded its conclusions on the provisions of the Wyoming Constitution guaranteeing the free exercise and enjoyment of religion and worship without discrimination or preference.

". . . The government is neutral, and, while protecting all [religious opinions and sects], it prefers none, and it disparages none." Id. at 215, 83 S. Ct. at 1567. Thus stemming from state and federal law there is strong support for a policy restricting hostile expressions against religious beliefs of others by representatives of a state or its agencies. We feel that the Trustees' decision was a proper means of respecting the rights of others in their beliefs, in accordance with this policy of religious neutrality.

The plaintiffs vigorously deny that there would have been state action or a violation of the First Amendment principles on religion by permitting the armband display. Without deciding whether approval of the armband display would have involved state action or a violation of the religion clauses, we are persuaded that the Trustees' decision was lawful within the limitations of the Tinker case itself. Their decision protected against invasion of the rights of others by avoiding a hostile expression to them by some members of the University team. It was in furtherance of the policy of religious neutrality by the State. It denied only the request for the armband display by some members of the team, on the field and during the game. In these limited circumstances we conclude that the Trustees' decision was in conformity with the Tinker case and did not violate the First Amendment right of expression of the plaintiffs. See Sword v. Fox, 446 F.2d 1091, 1097, 1098 (4th Cir.), cert. denied, 404 U.S. 994, 92 S. Ct. 534, 30 L. Ed. 2d 547.

We do not base our holding on the presence of any violence or disruption. There was no showing or finding to that effect and the trial court's conclusions of law state that the denial of the right to wear the armbands during the game ". . . was not predicated upon the likelihood of disruption, although such a demonstration might have tended to create disruption." Instead the trial court referred only to the mandate of complete neutrality in religion and religious matters as the basis for the court's ruling.

We hold that the trial court's findings and this record sustain the Trustees' decision as lawful, made for the reasons found by the trial court, as a reasonable regulation of expression under the limited circumstances involved, in accord with the principles of the Tinker case on free speech.

Affirmed.

■ ■ ■ ■

Suit was filed against officials of University of Wyoming and the football coach by black athletes, who were dismissed from the football team following a dispute over their intention to wear black arm bands during a football game with Brigham Young University. The athletes wanted to wear the arm bands to protest certain religious beliefs alleged to be prejudicial to blacks held at that time by the Church of Jesus Christ of Latter-Day Saints, commonly known as the Mormon Church. The players alleged that actions by the University preventing such a protest constituted a violation of their First Amendment rights. The United States Court of Appeals, in ruling on the District Court dismissal of the case, affirmed the lower court ruling in favor of the defendants. Had the governing officials of the University of Wyoming permitted a display of the armbands, they would have violated the First Amendment requirement of neutrality on expressions relating to religion. Therefore, their refusal to permit black athletes to wear arm bands on field during the football game against Brigham Young University amounted to a reasonable and lawful ruling and did not violate the First Amendment right of expression of the athletes.

Examine the actions of the football players. What was their motive in wanting to wear the arm bands? Was the act virtuous? Was the act of wearing the arm bands supported by the principle of utility—an action to benefit the greatest number of the whole? One aspect of the principle of universality is to honor contracts. By refusing to play without armbands, did they violate this principle?

Examine the actions of the coach. We know now that his decision to disallow the armbands was legal, but was it ethical? In making his decision not to allow armbands, was he applying the principle of universality by not allowing himself to be coerced; by preventing his team from treating the other team as means to an end; and by preventing his black players from treating the other team unequally (infringing upon their right to practice their religion)? Can the morality of his act be determined without knowing his motives? Would the principle of taking the correct action for the right reason support an open discussion and acknowledgment of the players' feelings? Might such discussion have diminished the conflict and made possible a resolution without litigation? Might there be an educational benefit for the greatest number of the whole as they became more aware of the racial issue (principle of utility)?

Examine the actions of the administration. The Federal and Wyoming Constitutions mandated complete neutrality on religious matters, which would have been violated by the armband display expressing opposition to religious beliefs of the Mormon Church. The right of the students to express their opinions was limited by their infringement of the rights of others. Was the administration policy of restricting hostile expressions against the religious beliefs of others an ethical policy? Would it be supported by the principle of universality which says everyone should be treated equally? Would it be supported by the principle of utility—does it benefit the greatest number of the whole? Who constitutes the whole in this situation? Is it supported by the principle of taking correct actions for the right reasons? Would it have been ethical for the administration to try to effect some compromise which would allow the students to protest in some other form?

Another case which exemplifies how the use of ethical principles could have prevented litigation is *Dunham v. Pulsifer* (1970), in which high school tennis players acted to enjoin school authorities from enforcing the school's athletic grooming code. The court ruled that the code—which called for males to have their hair tapered at the sides and in back to have no hair over the collar, and to have neatly trimmed side burns no longer than the ear lobe—was unconstitutional. The plaintiffs showed that the school's justifications for the grooming code (to prevent dissension on the team, to avoid adverse public reaction, and to promote *esprit de corps*) were unfounded since the tennis team had no such problems prior to the implementation of the code. Furthermore, the court cited that there were no corresponding restrictions on the general student population.

Based upon the ethical questions raised earlier in this chapter, suggest alternative courses of action which might have prevented this lawsuit. Could the goals of the school have been accomplished without infringing upon the legal rights of the athletes?

In summary, the sport manager wants to make "good" decisions. Decisions based upon the foregoing ethical principles should avoid preferential treatment and work for the best interests of both the sport-related organization, its employees, and its patrons. That, and a willingness to listen to the concerns of others, should help to resolve conflicts in such a way as to avoid litigation.

References

A. Cases
Dunham v. Pulsifer, 312 F.Supp. 411 (1970).
Williams v. Eaton, 468 F.2d 1079 (1972)

B. Publications

Black, H.C. (1990), *Black's Law Dictionary*. St. Paul, Minn.: West Publishing Co.

Kretchmar, R.S. (1991, Nov/Dec) The Ethics Gap. *Strategies*, 5(3) 15-18.

Kretchmar, R.S. (1994). *Practical Philosophy of Sport*. Champaign, Ill.: Human Kinetics.

Lumpkin, A., Stoll, S.K. & Beller, J.M. (1994). *Sport Ethics: Applications for Fair Play*. St. Louis: Mosby.

Merriman, J. & Hill, J. (1992, Fall). Ethics, Laws and Sport. *Journal of Legal Aspects of Sport*. 56-63.

Watson, J. (1992, June) *Maverick Maneuvers: They'll Get You Nowhere*. *Strategies*, 5(8) 9-11.

Zeigler, E.F. (1992). *Professional Ethics for Sport Managers*. Champaign, Ill.: Stipes Publishing Co.

2.00 • TORT LAW

2.11

Elements of Negligence

Betty van der Smissen
Michigan State University

A tort is a civil wrong. The law suit is brought against the wrongdoer or tortfeasor by a person who was injured in person or property. There are three categories of torts: 1) unintentional acts which harm (negligence), 2) intentional acts that harm (intentional torts), and 3) strict liability (liability without proof of fault). The focus of this chapter is upon negligence.

Negligence is an unintentional tort which injures a person. It may be an act of omission or commission. There are four elements of negligence, *all which must occur for a person to be held liable* for the injury.

1. **Duty.** A special relationship exists between the service provider (defendant) and the injured person (plaintiff), which gives rise to an obligation to protect the individual from unreasonable risk of harm.
2. **The act.** What the service provider did (commission) or did not do (omission) to protect the individual was not in accord with the standard of care a prudent professional should provide.
3. **Proximate cause.** The breach of the standard of care was the reason the injury occurred.
4. **Damage.** The individual received physical or emotional injury.

■ ■ ■ ■

Representative Case

SANDERS v. KUNA JOINT SCHOOL DISTRICT
Court of Appeals of Idaho
125 Idaho 872; 876 P.2d 154; 1994 Ida. App. LEXIS 77
June 16, 1994, Filed

OPINION: PERRY, J.

Josh Sanders appeals from a district court order granting summary judgment in favor of the respondents, Kuna Joint School District and Ron Emry. For the reasons stated below, we affirm the judgment.

Facts and Procedure
The underlying facts of this lawsuit are generally agreed upon by all of the parties. On May 15, 1990, Josh Sanders, a student at Kuna High School, attempted to slide

into first base during a softball game and broke his ankle. Sanders had been enrolled in a specialized physical education class which provided instruction in weight lifting. On the date of the incident, the instructor, respondent Ron Emry, decided to have the class play softball outside instead of weight lifting. The students were not informed of this decision until after they appeared in the school's weight room. According to Sanders, on that particular day he was wearing a pair of "Saucony Shadows," a shoe designed specifically for running. Once on the softball field, Emry did not give instruction in the game of softball and supervised the game from behind a backstop. During one particular sequence of play, Sanders attempted to slide into first base in order to avoid being tagged out. During the slide, Sanders broke his ankle.

Following proper notice as required by I.C. @@ 6-901 et seq., Sanders filed suit against Emry and the school district as Emry's employer. Sanders claimed that Emry had been negligent by requiring the students to play softball, by failing to adequately supervise the students, including inspecting their footwear, and by failing to properly instruct the students on how to play softball.

After initial discovery was completed, the respondents filed a motion for summary judgment on grounds that, accepting the truth of Sanders' evidence, it did not prove a claim of negligence as a matter of fact. The district court granted the respondents' motion. Sanders now appeals to this Court, claiming that the district court improperly granted the summary judgment.

Analysis
• • •

In this case, Sanders would bear the burden of proof at trial to establish the elements of negligence. In Idaho, a cause of action in negligence requires proof of the following: (1) the existence of a duty, recognized by law, requiring the defendant to conform to a certain standard of conduct; (2) a breach of that duty; (3) a causal connection between the defendant's conduct and the resulting injury; and (4) actual loss or damage. Black Canyon Racquetball Club, Inc. v. Idaho First Nat'l Bank, N.A., 119 Idaho 171, 175-76, 804 P.2d 900, 904-05 (1991).

The respondents contended in their summary judgment motion that Sanders had failed to offer sufficient proof of causation. In order to properly analyze the evidence of causation, we must look separately at the negligent instruction and negligent supervision claims.

As to the negligent instruction claim, we agree with the district court that the record reveals a lack of evidence as to causation. Sanders simply claims that Emry failed to instruct the students in the game of softball and that such a failure caused the injury. Sanders does not, however, offer any evidence as to what the instructions should have been, how such instructions would have prevented the injury, or how Sanders improperly slid. We agree with the conclusion of the district court that a rational jury could not find a causal connection between the failure to instruct and the resulting injury on the evidence presented. Therefore, the district court did not err in granting summary judgment as to Emry's alleged negligent instruction.

With respect to the negligent supervision claim, there are two separate issues we must consider—the actual supervision of the game as it was being played and the failure to inspect the footwear of the students. Again, as with the negligent instruction claim, Sanders' allegation of negligent supervision during the actual game must fail for lack of proof of causation. Sanders alleges that Emry failed to supervise the game and that such a failure caused the injury. Sanders does not offer any evidence, however, as to what the supervision of the game should have entailed, how that supervision was related to sliding or how such supervision would have prevented the injury. The only causal connection offered is the naked inference that if Emry had been standing on the field giving instruction to each student as the class played, this injury would not have occurred. Such an implausible inference does not rise to the level of evidence, however. In short, Sanders has failed to offer sufficient evidence of the causal connection between Emry's alleged negligent supervision and the injury. The district court's conclusion that no reasonable jury, on this evidence, could find a causal connection between the two was correct and, therefore, the summary judgment was properly granted as to this issue.

As to the issue of whether Emry was negligent in failing to inspect Sanders' shoes and should have prevented Sanders from playing in them, there is a mere scintilla of evidence presented. Sanders offered his own deposition testimony that he was playing in shoes that were designed for running. In response to the summary judgment motion, Sanders submitted the affidavit of the owner/manager of an athletic shoe store. The witness states that, "from a safety standpoint I would not recommend the use of the Saucony Shadow Shoe for use as a baseball or softball shoe." No evidence was offered, however, beyond the post hoc inference that because this was a running shoe with a wide sole, it must have caused the injury. Further, there was no evidence how a different shoe would have prevented the injury. Offering the mere coincidence that Sanders was injured and that he was wearing running shoes at the time is not sufficient to establish a causal connection. There must be some evidence that the shoe caused the injury. The evidence offered, the testimony of Sanders and the owner/manager of the shoe store, is not a sufficient basis upon which a jury could base a verdict for Sanders.

Jurors may draw inferences of causation where such inferences are within the common experience of the average person. In this case, however, we do not believe that the common experience of the average person includes knowledge of the properties of specialized running shoes versus other types of footware. Nor do we think the average person possesses knowledge in the mechanics of sliding or injuries from sliding. Without sufficient evidence on the differences in design, purpose, and function of the shoes worn by Sanders and other shoes, no reasonable jury could infer causation under the facts as presented in this case. Likewise, with no evidence as to the actual mechanics of this injury, a jury should not be left to speculate as what might have been the cause. Sanders has simply failed to offer any competent evidence as to the cause of this injury. Alleging temporally coincidental events is not a sufficient basis upon which a jury could find or infer causation. Therefore, the district court did not err by granting the summary judgment.

As an alternative basis for its summary judgment argument, the respondents asserted that Sanders had failed to offer sufficient evidence as to the existence of a duty. Having decided that the summary judgment was proper on the issue of causation, we need not consider this issue here.

Conclusion

The respondents in this case properly carried their burden on their motion for summary judgment by showing that Sanders was unable to present sufficient evidence on the causal connection between the alleged negligence and the injury. The burden then shifted to Sanders to show that a genuine issue did exist. Sanders failed to meet this burden and therefore the summary judgment was properly granted.

Costs on this appeal are awarded to respondents; no attorney fees are awarded.

WALTERS, C.J., and LANSING, J., concur.

■ ■ ■ ■

Fundamental Concepts

There are fundamental concepts embodied in each of the four elements of negligence.

Duty

Duty is societal-based, that is, it is the courts and legislatures which determine which members of society owe a duty to another. The larger social consequences of imposing a duty are considered (*Bodaness v. Staten Island Aid, Inc.*, 1991). As society changes, so may a duty; for example, some years ago a college stood *in loco parentis* (in the place of a parent; charged with the parent's rights, duties, and responsibilities) as to its students. Then, the societal attitude changed and, for activities outside of the academic/curricular program or officially sponsored co-curricular activities, including recreation and sport (*Kleinknecht v. Gettysburg College*, 1993), colleges no longer were in an *in loco parentis* relationship. That is, colleges did not owe a duty to protect students or to supervise conduct generally. However, in the late '90s there appears to be a return to *in loco parentis* for certain types of activities and student protection (Snow and Thro, 1994).

Duty, as an element of negligence, arises from a special relationship between the service provider and the user/participant which requires that the provider protect the individual from exposure to unreasonable risks which may cause injury. This duty should be distinguished from duty meaning function. Often it is said that one owes a duty to supervise, to warn, to instruct, to provide protective equipment, et al. These are functions or responsibilities, not relationships (*Woolsey v. Holiday Health Clubs and Fitness Centers, Inc.*, 1991).

Origin of Duty. Duty has three primary origins. They are 1) from a relationship inherent in the situation; 2) from a voluntary assumption of the duty; and 3) from a duty mandated by statute.

There usually is little question that there is a special relationship, for it exists in most provision of services, that is, it is inherent and obvious. The nature of the activity places individuals in a special relationship—the athlete and coach, the director of a sport camp and its participants, the student and instructor, the athlete and athletic trainer, the user of a facility and the maintenance person, the sponsor of a tournament and the entrants (*Dukes v. Bethlehem Cent. Sch. Dist.*, 1995), the rentor of equipment and the user. When a service is provided, usually there also is a concomitant obligation not to expose the participant/user to unreasonable risk of harm.

Duty or the special relationship is established not only by being inherent in the situation but also by voluntary assumption when no duty existed. For example, if a person holding a life guarding certificate is on the beach with a friend, but is not employed as a lifeguard, and a person in the water is struggling, there is no legal obligation to endeavor to rescue the person because there is no special relationship. The holding of a certificate for lifesaving or first aid/CPR does not establish a special relationship with whomever might need the skill and, thus, does not carry a legal obligation to render aid. *There may be a moral obligation, but not a legal one.* However, if the person decides to rescue, then that person establishes voluntarily a special relationship and therefore a duty with an obligation to perform the rescue with the appropriate standard of care. Or, a duty may be established by a person volunteering to be a Little League coach—by such voluntary act a special relationship is established between the coach and young player which requires protection against unreasonable risk to the player (see Chapter 2.22 relating to immunity for volunteers).

A special relationship or duty also may be set forth by statutes, such as those established for employment (see Chapter 2.36 on Employment Torts), supervisory requirements, or rendering of first aid in specified situations. Often violation of such statutes is deemed negligence *per se*, that is, negligence "on the face" where one does not have to prove negligence. However, the violation of a statute is not automatically negligence *per se*, without having to prove negligence. It must still be shown that the violation of the statute was the proximate cause of the injury.

Types of Relationships. There are three categories of relationship frequently set forth—**invitee, licensee**, and **trespasser**. To these should be added a fourth, **recreational user**. However, although these categories are types of relationships, all are related to premises and the status of the entrant onto the premise (facility or area); and, therefore, discussion of these may be found in Chapter 2.34 Safe Environment. The status affects the degree of protection which must be provided to individuals in that type of relationship. The discussion in this chapter focuses only upon the invitee and the requirements to protect against unreasonable risk.

The Act

If the duty is to protect against an unreasonable risk of harm, what is that risk to be protected against and what is "unreasonable"?

Types of Risks. There are two types of risks that relate to negligence—inherent risks and negligent behaviors.

Inherent risks are those integral to the activity. For example, in any of the contact sports, such as football and soccer, it is inherent in the sport that players will collide and may get hurt therefrom. In baseball, the possibility of being hit by a foul ball is an inherent risk taken by spectators. An **inherent risk** is one which, if removed from the game, would essentially alter the sport and thereby the sport would lose its integrity. *There is no liability for injury which occurs due to inherent risks.* A participant, whether player or spectator, assumes such risk and exposure thereto is not "unreasonable" and is not something against which one must protect. These risks are assumed by the participant (see 2.21 Defenses for Negligence—Primary Assumption of Risk).

Negligent behavior is that conduct which is not in accord with the standard of care a prudent professional should give and, hence, the participant is subject to "unreasonable risk" of injury. Behaviors or conduct may be ordinary negligence or gross negligence. Gross negligence is a negligent act done with utter unconcern for the safety of others, or one done with such reckless disregard for the rights of others that a conscious indifference to consequences is implied in law.

A third type of risk, **intentional torts** (see Chapters 2.41, 2.42, and 2.43) really is not a part of the elements of negligence, since negligence is an unintentional tort. Intentional torts, however, do impact the use of waivers, which are valid only for acts of ordinary negligence and void for intentional tort (see Chapter 2.23 on Waivers), and which usually negate any statutory immunity (see Chapter 2.22 on Immunity).

Standard of Care. What is an unreasonable risk? The standard of care required in order not to be "unreasonable" or negligent is that of a prudent professional. By whom is this standard determined? The standard may be set forth by statute, ordinance, or regulation, by organizations or agencies, or by the profession. For example, the National Operating Committee on Standards for Athletic Equipment (NOC-SAE) sets the standard for football helmets; the Red Cross certification programs in first aid and life saving have long been the principal requirement for competence where first aid is required and for life guards; playground equipment standards are set forth by the Consumer Products Safety Commission (CPSC); the American College of Sports Medicine (ACSM) has established competencies for fitness directors and the National Athletic Trainers Association (NATA), for athletic trainers. *It behooves every provider to be aware of published standards and guidelines.* A professional will be held thereto! Where there are no published standards, the practices of the profession are the norm. In court, expert witnesses will attest to the accepted, desirable practices. Hence, it is very desirable for professionals to be knowledgeable and keep up-to-date with the latest and best practices through literature and attendance at conferences, workshops, seminars, et al.

The professional standard of care does not vary based on the qualifications of the person in charge, whether experienced, older, or certified. If one accepts a responsibility for giving leadership to an activity or providing a service, one's performance is measured against the standard of care of a qualified professional for that situation. The participant is entitled to the standard of a prudent professional, not a standard dependent upon the qualifications of whomever happened to be in charge. Thus, *the professional standard of care is situation-determined*—what is the nature of the activity, who are the participants, and what are the environmental conditions?

Nature of the Activity. The provider must be aware of the "requirements" of the activity; if complex, the leader must understand or if simple, then a lesser knowledge about the activity is required. The activity must be understood in order for the inherent risks to be known/identified as well as how one can protect against them, warn against them, et al. If a leader or provider is not familiar with an activity, how can one know the risks and what to do? (See Chapter 2.33 Conduct of Activity.)

Type of Participants. The service provider must not only be aware of the character of the participants, (e.g., experienced or novice, highly skilled or lack motor development, intellectually gifted or mentally retarded, physically disabled or emotionally distressed) but also understand how to work with them in the specific activity, and know which risks a participant may be able to assume and thus better protect them from risks (see Chapter 2.32 Supervision and Chapter 2.33 Conduct of Activity).

Environmental Conditions. What is the physical environment related to the activity—layout or condition of the field or the gymnasium and the weather conditions (e.g., whether a hot and humid day, has there been rain, soggy or muddy field, slippery grass)? What is an "open and obvious" risk, which a participant may assume? (See Chapter 2.21 for secondary assumption of risk or contributory fault and Chapter 2.34 Safe Environment.)

In regard to the foregoing, *there is a duty to be proactive in protecting only when the risk is foreseeable by a prudent professional.* If not foreseeable, how can one protect! Thus, no liability. The test of foreseeability is foresight, not hindsight! For example, a student was foreseen as a healthy, 23-year-old, but in fact, suffered in a one-mile timed run extreme exertional rhabdomyolysis (*Turner v. Rush Medical College*, 1989). On the other hand, a basketball player with an injured nose, which had not yet healed, and with eyes swollen and face bruised, was directed by the coach to participate in scrimmage. It was held predictable or foreseeable that further injury would occur. The injury need only fall into general category of risk reasonably anticipated; the specific or exact injury does not need to be foreseen (*Lamorie v. Warner Pacific College*, 1993). It should be made clear that one can owe a duty to protect, but because there is no foreseeable unreasonable risk, there does not have to be any proactive action. It is not correct to say that there is no duty—the duty is there; there just does not have to be any action.

Proximate Cause

The act which did not meet the standard of a professional must be the cause-in-fact of the injury. Just because the standard is not met does not mean the defendant is liable. For example, there may be inadequate supervision, but lack of supervision may not have been the cause of the injury (*Baker v. Eckelkamp*, 1988), or a written organization standard may not have been complied with, but failure to comply may not be the cause of the injury; or, instruction in the correct manner of using equipment may not have been given, but improper instruction may not have been the cause of the injury (*Burkart v. Health & Tennis Corp. of America*, 1987).

The act does not have to be the sole cause, but may be a "substantial factor." A minor hurt his wrist playing football and then volleyball. A fracture failed to be diagnosed from the x-ray and subsequent surgery was necessary. The court held that there was no evidence of causation between the failure to diagnose the fracture and the subsequent need for surgery; to be proximate cause, negligent conduct must be the substantial factual cause of injury for which damages are sought (*Pascal v. Carter*, 1994). Or, there may be a "superseding cause" by the injured. For example, a swimmer drowned in a city-owned pool. He had entered after hours through a hole in the fence or over a brick wall—a trespasser. Negligence was alleged of the city in failing to keep illegal swimmers out of the pool. The court held that even if the city's negligence was a substantial factor, decedent's conduct of being intoxicated (alcohol level .23 percent) was an unforeseeable superseding cause and the decedent assumed the risk of own conduct (*Garcia v. City of New York*, 1994).

Damage

The fourth element of negligence is that there must be compensable bodily injury or emotional harm. No damage, no liability. Usually damage is not difficult to prove and is not in question because without it a person would not be suing! Generally, compensable injuries fall into four categories: 1) economic loss (medical expenses, present and future, lost occupational earnings, custodial care, costs incurred by required substitute hired to do work while recovering, etc.), 2) physical pain and suffering (usually left to jury to determine value), 3) emotional distress (e.g., fright and shock, anxiety, loss of peace of mind and happiness, loss of consortium, humiliation and embarrassment, inconveniences), and 4) physical impairment (temporary and permanent, partial or total, e.g., eyesight, hearing, use of an extremity). The plaintiff must submit documentation regarding costs and the jury establishes the amount of an award.

The injured/plaintiff also may seek punitive damages. Punitive damages are seldom awarded for ordinary negligence wherein a person is unintentionally injured, inasmuch as punitive damages are beyond compensatory damages and are to "punish" the tortfeasor or wrongdoer for intentional acts which harm. However, intention is implied as related to reckless disregard for the rights or safety of another, the deliberate indifference to an employee's rights, or child abuse (see Chapter 2.41 relating to reckless misconduct and Chapter 2.36 on Employment Torts).

However, damage, the element, and damages, the result of liability, must be distinguished. What often is at issue is not whether there are compensable injuries, but the amount of damages and who should pay. The allocation of damages, including joint and several liability, is addressed in Chapter 2.21 Defenses for Negligence.

Recent Trends

The trends in the late '90s are not so much related to the fundamental concepts of the elements of negligence as to the responsibilities of the injured and defenses. Most of these trends are discussed in other chapters, so only a brief highlighting of some of these trends is stated in this section.

As related to environmental conditions, the participant is expected to be aware of and conduct oneself in a manner to protect oneself against "open and obvious" hazards (see Chapter 2.34 Safe Environment). In order to encourage volunteers to give leadership to an activity or to render aid after injury, and to protect a landowner who permits use of property, there are statutes which provide immunity to volunteers and landowners for ordinary negligence (see Chapter 2.22 Immunity). There are also "shared responsibility" laws, e.g., ski, equine, whitewater responsibility acts or "hazard recreation," which set forth the provider's obligations to protect the participant and the participant's responsibilities for assuming the inherent risks of the sport.

Protection against violence is another area of change for both intentional torts "private violence" of participant against participant and third party crime in society. The liability appears to be ameliorated by lack of "notice," actual or constructive, whereby the danger is not foreseeable. Where there is notice of danger, either in the community or by another participant's behavior, there is a responsibility by the provider to protect the participants from this foreseeable danger (see Chapter 2.41 Assault and Battery and Chapter 5.11 Sport Violence). There also is violence in the workplace, particularly employee abuse of children, older adults, and persons with disabilities. Most states have laws requiring background checks of persons working with children, whether employee or volunteer. This aspect of violence does modify the usual doctrine of *respondeat superior*, making responsible administrative personnel liable individually, as well as the corporate entity, for their "deliberate indifference" to the dangers to which the participant is being exposed by "negligent" hiring, training, supervision, or retention (see Chapter 2.12 Which Parties Are Liable for Negligence?). In terms of damages, the courts (juries) have been generous in interpretation of "emotional distress," including many types of inconveniences to enjoyment of life, including sports and recreation.

References

A. Cases

Baker v. Eckelkamp, 760 S.W.2d 178 (Mo. App. 1988).
Bodaness v. Staten Island Aid, Inc., 567 N.Y.S.2d 63 (App. Div. 1991).
Burkart v. Health & Tennis Corp. of America, 730 S.W.2d 367 (Tex. App. 1987).
Dukes v. Bethlehem Cent. Sch. Dist., 629 N.Y.S.2d 97 (App. Div. 1995).
Garcia v. City of New York, 617 N.Y.S.2d 462 (App. Div. 1994).
Kleinknecht v. Gettysburg College, 989 F.2d 1360 (3rd Cir. 1993).
Lamorie v. Warner Pacific College, 850 P.2d 401 (Or. App. 1993).
Pascal v. Carter, 647 A.2d 231 (Pa. Super. 1994).
Turner v. Rush Medical College, 537 N.E.2d 890 (Ill. App. 1989).
Woolsey v. Holiday Health Clubs and Fitness Centers, Inc., 820 P.2d 1201 (Colo. App. 1991).

B. Publications

Snow, Brian A., and Thro, William. Commentary—Redefining the Contours of University Liability: The Potential Implications of Nero v. Kansas State University, 90 *Ed. Law Rep.* 989 (July 14, 1994).
van der Smissen, B. (1990). *Legal Liability and Risk Management for Public and Private Entities*. Cincinnati: Anderson Publishing Company. (with 1997 supplement). @ chp. 2 Elements of Negligence.

Which Parties Are Liable for Negligence?

Doyice J. Cotten
Sport Risk Consulting

Sport law students often ask "Why did they sue the school system when it was the teacher who was negligent?" or "If I am the supervisor, will I be liable if someone in my charge is negligent?" These questions represent just two of the many issues to be considered in answering the question of which parties may be liable when an injury occurs. Where in the past, the party sued was usually the corporate entity or the "deep pocket," today the trend is to sue everyone associated with the incident leading to the injury. For instance, suppose an aerobics instructor at a health club conducts an aerobics class in a room where speakers have been placed very near the participants. A participant loses his or her balance, falls into the speaker, and suffers injury. The participant might well name as individual defendants not only the aerobics instructor, but the manager of the health club, the program director, the person responsible for room setup and maintenance, the owner of the health club, as well as the health club corporate entity.

The question to be addressed in this chapter is who is liable when a negligent act results in an injury. The reader should remember, however, that since the laws regarding liability in such situations differ somewhat from state to state, the discussion will be general in nature. State law in any one state may differ somewhat from these general concepts.

■ ■ ■ ■

Representative Case

VARGO v. SVITCHAN
Court of Appeals of Michigan
100 Mich. App. 809; 301 N.W.2d 1
May 6, 1980, Submitted
October 22, 1980, Decided

OPINION:

Plaintiffs brought this action against defendants as a result of injuries sustained by Gregory Vargo. On the grounds of governmental immunity, MCL 691.1407; MSA 3.996(107), the trial court granted accelerated judgment to defendants Svitchan, the athletic director, Mayoros, the high school principal, Hagadone, the school district superintendent, and the Riverview Community School District. Leave to appeal was initially denied by this Court. Plaintiffs sought leave to appeal to the Supreme Court which, in lieu of leave to appeal, remanded to this Court to hear the case as on leave granted.

On June 25, 1973, Gregory Roy Vargo, a 15-year-old high school student, reported for the first of a scheduled series of weight lifting training sessions in preparation for high school football team tryouts in the Fall. This session was conducted at the high school in the gymnasium. Allegedly urged on by the coach, Dr. Donald Lessner, to perform to the utmost, Gregory Vargo pushed himself to and beyond his limits, and, while lifting a 250 to 300 pound weight, he fell and received injuries resulting in paraplegia. It is alleged Gregory Vargo's two "spotters," Mark Mayoros and Gary Merker, failed to react quickly enough to seize the barbell before the fall.

Plaintiffs' complaint, twice amended, alleges that appellee Svitchan, the Athletic Director, appellee Ernest Mayoros, the Principal, and appellee Hagadone, the School Superintendent, negligently supervised Coach Lessner and allowed Lessner to abuse students and to threaten and pressure them into attempting athletic feats beyond their capabilities, resulting in Gregory Vargo's injury. The complaint further alleges that the gymnasium facilities were inadequate and defective because lack of sufficient ventilation caused Gregory Vargo to perspire excessively, contributing to his injuries.

MCL 691.1407; MSA 3.996(107), reads:

"Except as in this act otherwise provided, all governmental agencies shall be immune from tort liability in all cases wherein the government agency is engaged in the exercise or discharge of a governmental function."

The question as to whether the protection afforded a governmental unit by the above statute extends to its individual agents or employees is presently unsettled in Michigan. The state of the law in this regard has been accurately assessed by Judge Brennan in his opinion in Cook v Bennett, 94 Mich App 93, 98-100.

• • •

The Court in Cook, supra, 100, then proceeded to evaluate the liability of the defendant principal in terms of the following test:

"The extent to which a school principal is protected by immunity is dependent upon whether the act complained of falls within the principal's discretionary or ministerial powers." Justice Cooley, in Wall v Trumbull, 16 Mich 228, 234 (1867), draws the distinction as follows:

"'A ministerial officer has a line of conduct marked out for him, and has nothing to do but to follow it; and he must be held liable for any failure to do so which results in the injury of another. A judicial officer, on the other hand, has certain powers confided to him to be exercised according to his judgment or discretion; and the law would be oppressive which should compel him in every case to decide correctly at his peril.'

"Discretionary acts are those of a legislative, executive or judicial nature. Sherbutte v Marine City, 374 Mich 48, 54; 130 NW2d 920 (1964). Ministerial acts are those where the public employee has little decision-making power during the course of performance, but rather his conduct is delineated."

Employing these distinctions, the Cook Court concluded that:

"Even though the supervisory powers of the school principal are incident to her public function, she has a duty to reasonably exercise these powers in such a way as to minimize injury to students in her charge. Where the principal negligently performs this duty, government immunity does not operate to insulate her from all liability. Accordingly, the lower court's ruling to the contrary is erroneous." Cook, supra, 101.

In the case at bar, the plaintiffs, in their complaint, have set forth lengthy allegations concerning the purported negligence of Riverview Community High School Principal Ernest Mayoros. The plaintiffs have averred that Principal Mayoros was negligent by "inducing, suggesting, encouraging . . . intimidating and coercing plaintiff Gregory Roy Vargo . . . to attend the weight lifting session and to attempt to lift and lower heavy weights without having inquired as to his experience or capabilities to lift such weights without properly instructing him and other members of the class as to techniques of safety that would avoid injury and without providing proper mechanical and/or human safeguards. . . ." The plaintiffs have further alleged that Principal Mayoros was negligent "by failing to stop the illegally conducting of an organized summer program for varsity football players contrary to Michigan High School Athletic Association rules," and "by failing to promulgate adequate rules, regulations, procedures and safeguards, and by failing to properly instruct and train the coach, assistant coaches, and Athletic Director herein. . . ." The plaintiffs finally claim that Principal Mayoros was negligent because he failed to inspect the activities that were being conducted by Coach Lessner, because he permitted the use of an improperly-equipped room, and because he failed to take action upon receiving a complaint and notice that Coach Lessner was "too rough" on his prospective football players.

According to the analysis set forth in Cook, supra, it appears that the principal in the instant case should not be covered by the cloak of governmental immunity. As in Cook, Principal Mayoros had a duty to reasonably exercise supervisory powers so as to minimize injury to his students. The principal of the school maintains direct control over the use and condition of the facilities. Therefore, if the weight lifting room was, in fact, improperly equipped and designed for that use, the defendant principal would bear direct responsibility. Moreover, if the summer weight lifting program was, in fact, in violation of MHSAA rules and regulations, it would be the principal, Ernest Mayoros, who would be in charge of such a program. Finally, it must be noted that weight lifting is an activity which requires special training and supervision; overexertion and resultant injuries are foreseeable and frequent in the absence of proper supervision. If such a program was to be conducted in the high school, the principal had a duty to minimize injury to the participating students.

Although the liability (or lack thereof) of a school athletic director under the governmental immunity statute has not been previously addressed by this Court, it seems that the above reasoning and outcome should apply with equal vigor to that person who is in direct control of the athletic program under which the plaintiff is injured. In the instant case, athletic director George Svitchan was directly in charge of the football program and Coach Lessner. As athletic director, the summer weight lifting program was not only within his knowledge but was also his direct responsibility. George Svitchan was the person in a position and authority to oversee the practices and stop any unsafe activities. Due to the specialized nature of the position, Mr. Svitchan, more so than the principal, should have promulgated reasonable safety precautions and minimized injury to the students. The athletic director must be presumed to know the nature of the class and the physical requirements and limitations of its participants. One cannot say that all reasonable men would agree that no negligence could be inferred under the circumstances. That question should be left to the jury. Knapp v City of Dearborn, 60 Mich App 18; 230 N.W.2d 293 (1975).

We conclude that the plaintiffs' allegations are of active, personal negligence on the part of the athletic director. The alleged liability is not based upon negligence committed as a public functionary. Since the plaintiff was injured in the course of an athletic activity, a trier of fact could find that defendant Svitchan abused a personal and direct duty to provide a safe weight lifting program. Defendant Svitchan is not entitled to the protection of the governmental immunity statute.

However, the same cannot be said for Superintendent T. E. Hagadone. We are unable to discern in the complaint any allegations of "personal neglect" on the part of the superintendent. The essence of the plaintiffs' allegations is that Mr. Hagadone was negligent in his supervisory responsibilities. The possible negligence of the coach (and other school employees) cannot be imputed to him merely because he was in a supervisory position. But see Bush v. Oscoda Area Schools, 275 N.W.2d 268 (1979).

Plaintiffs also appeal from the trial court's decision that the defendant school district is immune from suit because it is not liable under the defective building exception to the governmental immunity statute, the pertinent part of which follows:

"Governmental agencies have the obligation to repair and maintain public buildings under their control when open for use by members of the public. Governmental agencies are liable for bodily injury and property damage resulting from a dangerous or defective condition of a public building." MCL 691.1406; MSA 3.996(106).

• • •

These cases make it clear that the exception to governmental immunity found in MCL 691.1406; MSA 3.996(106) is no longer to be governed by whether the instrumentality causing the injury was a fixture or structural part of the public building. Of concern now is whether the injury occurred in a "public place" and whether that public place was fit for its assigned and intended use.

In the instant case, the plaintiffs' allegations invoking the public building exception follow the vein of Bush. The plaintiffs do not point to a particular fixture or part of the building as dangerous but aver that the defendant school district was negligent for the following reasons:

". . . providing a school building and room that was defective and inadequate for the activity required or directed to be performed; that there was inadequate ventilation, excessive heat and perspiration which caused or contributed to the injuries sustained, and/or by otherwise failing to use due care in the ownership, maintenance, operation, utilization of such school building and/or by otherwise failing to use due care."

The plaintiffs further allege that, at the time of the accident, the weight lifting room failed to have sufficient numbers of weight lifting safety machines or power racks to be used by the students and that the available floor mats or pads were not being used on the concrete floor to prevent possible slippage and lessen the likelihood of serious injury.

Thus, the plaintiffs in the case at bar, like the plaintiff in Bush, have alleged the existence of a dangerous condition on the basis of "fitness for intended use" and the absence of safety devices.

However, as the defendant school district notes, in the present case, unlike Bush and Lockaby, the complained-of room was being used as expected, as a gymnasium. Plaintiffs' argument that the gymnasium was dangerous because there was inadequate ventilation and consequent excessive perspiration (causing the barbells to slip) would possibly require a distorted interpretation of the statutory exception and the concept of "dangerous or defective." It is a common, and indeed unavoidable, experience that athletes perspire while in action. To allow the plaintiffs' claim in this regard would be to overextend the purpose and meaning of the statute. The plaintiffs' allegations fall more within the tenor of danger caused by the negligence (failure to exercise due care) of individual employees of the school district, rather than danger caused by the building itself. It appears from the facts that the lack of supervision, not a defect in the building, was the cause of the plaintiff's injuries. Justice Ryan's reasoning in his dissent in Bush, supra, 738-739, is applicable to the case at bar:

> "Although I find the majority approach appealing as a substantive rule of law, I am compelled to dissent because such a construction of the 'building' exception does not at all square with the manifest intent of the Legislature as expressed in the governmental immunity statute, MCL 691.1407; MSA 3.996(107).

> "When construing an exception to a general rule, care must be taken not to derogate from the general rule to the extent that its intent and purpose is under-

mined. See Grand Rapids Motor Coach Co v Public Service Commission, 323 Mich 624, 634; 36 NW2d 299 (1949). Today's majority construes and applies the 'building' exception in a way which significantly undermines the intent of the general immunity provision by characterizing as a building defect what is actually the behavior of the school district's employees in utilizing a portion of the school building for a unique and highly specialized and always dangerous purpose, one for which it was not designed, constructed or intended to be used."

In the instant case, the plaintiffs' allegations concerning a defective or dangerous condition stem not from the condition of the building itself but from the activities or operations conducted within the building. To hold otherwise would expand the public building exception far beyond its purpose and intent and do violence to the will of the Legislature.

The order of the trial court granting accelerated judgment to defendants Ernest Mayoros and George Svitchan is reversed, the grant of accelerated judgment to defendants Hagadone and Riverview Community School District is affirmed, and the matter is remanded for trial.

Reversed in part, affirmed in part.

■ ■ ■ ■

Fundamental Concepts

There are three categories of parties that may be liable in any given situation. The first category consists of the **service personnel** involved. This is generally the person who committed the negligent act. This category includes persons who generally have actual contact with the participants e.g., teacher, coach, weight room attendant, referee, scout master. Also included in this category are the maintenance personnel or custodian who are often in direct contact with the participant.

The second category is the **administrative or supervisory personnel**. These are generally individuals who have some sort of administrative or supervisory authority over the service personnel. Examples include the department head, a principal, a head coach, an athletic director, a school superintendent, a manager of a health club, or a general manager of a professional baseball club. It is important to remember, however, that the classification of this individual can vary with the act being performed. For instance, the department head would be categorized as service personnel when teaching a class, but as administrative when performing scheduling duties.

The third category is the **corporate entity**. This category includes the governing body of the organization. Examples include the county school board, the recreation board, the university board of regents, the corporation board of directors, or the local health club corporation.

Who Is Liable?

Service Personnel. The party who performed the negligent act most often falls in the classification of service personnel and is generally legally liable for the injury. In other words, a teacher, a lifeguard, a camp counselor, an assistant coach, an athletic trainer, or a maintenance person who has a duty, breaches that duty by failing to meet the required standard of care, and that breach is the proximate cause of injury to the plaintiff, is negligent and is legally liable.

The aerobics instructor in the foregoing example would fall into the service personnel category. If the instructor breaches a duty to the aerobics class by allowing participation too close to a hazard (the speaker), and that breach is shown to be the proximate cause of the injury, then the instructor is negligent and is legally liable for damages.

Administrative/Supervisory Personnel. Whereas the question regarding liability of service personnel is relatively simple, the question of liability of the administrative or supervisory personnel for the negligence of subordinates is much more complex. The general rule is that administrative/supervisory personnel are not liable for the negligence of subordinates. The administrator is liable, however, if the administrator owes a duty and acts (or omissions) of the administrator enhanced the likelihood of injury (van der Smissen, 1990).

These administrative duties fall into five categories (van der Smissen, 1990). These duties are 1) to employ competent personnel and discharge those unfit; 2) to provide proper supervision and to have a supervisory plan; 3) to direct the services or program in a proper manner; 4) to establish safety rules and regulations and to comply with policy and statutory requirements; and 5) to remedy dangerous conditions and defective equipment or to warn users of dangers involved.

In the example involving the aerobics instructor, the health club manager would fall into the administrative/supervisory personnel category. Normally the manager is not liable for the negligence of the aerobics instructor unless the manager did something that enhanced the likelihood of injury. In this case the manager hired a qualified, certified instructor, supervised the program adequately, and the aerobics program was conducted according to standards suggested by a national association. The manager may have breached an administrative/supervisory duty, however, by failing to establish or enforce safety rules regarding hazards on the floor or minimal clear space requirements or by failing to identify and remedy or warn of dangerous conditions. On the other hand, if the presence of the speaker on the floor was a one-time occurrence and the manager had safety rules regarding hazards and space and regularly enforced them, then the manager would not be liable since the manager breached no duty and did not increase the likelihood of injury.

The Corporate Entity. The next question regards the liability of the corporate entity for the negligence of an employee whether service personnel or administrative/supervisory personnel. The answer to this question is governed by the **doctrine of respondeat superior** which states that *the negligence of an employee is imputed to the corporate entity if the employee was acting within the scope of the employee's responsibility and authority and if the act was not grossly negligent, willful/wanton, and did not involve malfeasance* (van der Smissen, 1990). This doctrine is also referred to as **vicarious liability.** So, according to this doctrine, if an employee commits ordinary negligence while engaged in the furtherance of the employer's enterprise, the employer as well as the employee is liable. Refer to the Recent Trends section for a brief discussion of a broader interpretation of this doctrine.

Acts that are beyond the scope of responsibility and authority of the employee are considered ***ultra vires acts*** and, generally, such an act relieves the corporate entity of liability via respondeat superior. Exceptions to this rule occur when the corporate entity benefited from, had notice of, or condoned the act.

In the foregoing example, the aerobics instructor instructing the class was acting within the scope of responsibility and authority and was engaged in the furtherance of the employer's enterprise. If it is shown that allowing activity too near the speakers was ordinary negligence, then not only is the instructor liable, but liability is also imputed to the health club corporate entity.

Wilful Acts by an Employee. In some cases, the corporate entity can be liable even for **wilful torts** committed by the employee (*Glucksman v. Walters*, 1995; *Rogers v. Fred R. Hiller Company of Ga., Inc.*, 1994; *Pelletier v. Bilbiles,* 1967). Each case involved an instance in which an employee who, while on duty, physically assaulted a patron. Each court stated that a master is liable for the wilful torts of his servant if the tort was committed within the scope of the servant's employment and in furtherance of his master's business. The Glucksman court further stated that the fact that the specific method employed to accomplish the master's orders is not authorized does not relieve the master of liability.

Volunteers, Trainees, and Interns. The question often arises as to whether the acts of a **volunteer**, a **trainee**, or an **intern** fall under the doctrine of respondeat superior. The liability of the corporate entity depends upon whether the organization exerts control over (or has the right to control) the activities of the volunteer, trainee, or intern, and whether the party was acting within the scope of "employment," authority, or responsibility (van der Smissen, 1990; Manley, 1995). It is worth noting that the volunteer, trainee, and intern *are held to the same standard of care as that of an experienced, competent professional.*

University Athlete. An issue that sometimes arises is whether a university is liable under respondeat superior for the negligent acts of a **university varsity athlete** (*Townsend v. The State of California,* 1987; *Hanson v. Kynast,* 1986; *Brown v. Day,* 1990). Courts have ruled the applicability of the doctrine requires an individualized determination of whether a master-servant relationship exists between the tortfeasor and the university (*Townsend v. The State of California, 1987*). The Townsend court concluded that whether on scholarship or not, the athlete is not an employee and the university is not vicariously liable for the athlete's negligent acts.

Limiting Corporate Liability by Contract

Leasing Facilities. The use of sport and recreational facilities by another group or organization is a common practice. The details of these transactions can range from free use by oral agreement to a formal lease with a rental charge. In any case, the question is "What is the liability of the owner of the premises when an injury occurs on the premises while being used by another organization?" To determine liability, one must first determine whether the injury was premise-related (resulting from unsafe premises) or activity-related (resulting from the conduct of the activity) (van der Smissen, 1990). Unless specified in the contract, the owner generally remains liable for premise-related injuries. Second, if the injury is activity-related, one must determine if the owner retained *control* over the activity or the use of the premises. Essentially, the liability for activity-related injury generally lies with the party that had control over the activity. Thus, if a university leases an arena to a promoter of an ice skating event and retains no control over how the activity is conducted, the university would not be liable for activity-related injuries, but might be liable if the injury resulted from an unsafe facility.

It is common practice for facility owners to require that the leasing party indemnify the owner for financial loss resulting from the event. Also, facility owners generally require that the leasing party provide a certificate of insurance showing adequate liability insurance for the event. Many require that the owners be named as a co-insured on the policy.

Independent Contractors. An independent contractor is an individual or a company that contracts to perform a particular task. Examples of persons that are often classified as independent contractors include referees for a contest, an aerobics specialist at a health club, a team physician, or a diving business which teaches SCUBA for a recreation department. Often, whether one is an employee or an independent contractor is at issue. Courts generally rule that one is an employee if one is hired, paid a set wage or salary, and must perform the work as directed by the employer. An independent contractor is one who is generally engaged for a specific project, usually for a set sum, often paid at the end of the project, may do the job in one's own way, often furnishes one's own equipment, is subject to minimal restrictions, and is responsible only for the satisfactory completion of the job (*Jaeger v. Western Rivers Fly Fisher,* 1994).

The general rule is that the corporate entity, in hiring an independent contractor, shifts liability for negligence from the corporation to the independent contractor. Under certain circumstances, however, the employer is held liable. Three such circumstances are 1) when the employer fails to hire a competent contractor or fails to inspect the work upon completion; 2) when the employer fails to keep the premises safe for invitees or to provide employees of the corporate entity a safe place in which to work; and 3) when the activities are inherently dangerous as with fireworks or keeping of vicious animals (van der Smissen, p 93).

Waivers.   The corporate entity may protect itself and its employees from liability by use of waivers of liability or exculpatory agreements in which the participant or service user contractually relieves the business from liability for negligence by the corporate entity or its employees. For more information regarding waivers, see Chapter 2.23.

Corporate Liability in Other Situations

Financial Sponsorship.   Many organizations provide financial sponsorship for recreational activities or teams. This type of sponsorship includes financial support, but the sponsoring organization exercises no control over the activity. An example of this type of sponsorship would be civic clubs or private businesses sponsoring recreation department softball teams. Financial sponsorship of this sort generally carries with it no liability. Whether the organization is liable for injuries that occur due to negligence depends upon several things: 1) was the person in charge an agent of the organization? 2) did the organization have control over the activity? and 3) was a duty owed to the participant? (van der Smissen, 1990).

In *Wilson v. United States of America* (1993), the issue was whether an agency relationship existed between the Boy Scouts of America and adult volunteers of a troop so as to provide for vicarious liability for the negligence of the adult troop leaders. The court stated that liability based upon respondeat superior requires evidence of a master-servant relationship. In this case, there was no liability since the national organization exerts no direct control over the leaders or the activities of individual troops. In an older case, Boy Scouts of America was found liable for the negligence of an adult volunteer at a Scout-o-Rama controlled by the regional council. The key difference was control (*Riker v. Boy Scouts of America*, 1959).

Program Sponsorship and Joint Programming.   Program sponsorship exists when an organization or entity organizes an event or maintains control over an event. Joint programming is when more than one entity is involved in program sponsorship. Examples of such sponsorship or programming include an NCAA championship event, an event sponsored and conducted by the University of Georgia and the Southeastern Conference, and a high school game under the auspices of the state high school athletic association. When leagues or athletic associations exert control over the conduct of the game and the eligibility of the participants, duties are created and liability for negligence emerges.

When two organizations are involved in joint programming or joint sponsorship of an activity, each is fully responsible for negligence under "joint and several" liability. The joint and several doctrine, however, has been modified to some extent in most states (see Chapter 2.21).

Joint Ventures.   A joint venture is "an agreement between two or more persons, ordinarily, but not necessarily limited to a single transaction for the purpose of making a profit." (*Jaeger v. Western Rivers Fly Fisher,* 1994 at p. 1224). Some essential elements for a joint venture include combining of property, money, efforts, skill, labor, knowledge, and a sharing of losses and profits. A group of college students who wanted to go whitewater rafting, put up notices informing other students of the proposed trip, met, planned the trip, shared resources, and went on the trip would form a joint venture. It would not be a joint venture if the campus recreation department conceived the idea of the trip, publicized the proposed trip, helped them plan the trip, and supplied equipment for the trip. In the latter case, the university would be a sponsor of the activity and would be liable in the event of negligence. In a true joint venture, there is no group sponsorship and, hence, no liability for the corporation.

Statutory Immunity for Entities and Individuals. The foregoing discussion is based upon the assumption that no immunity statutes affect the liability of the parties. Many states do have statutes that grant immunity to governmental organizations (e.g., schools, municipalities) and their employees under certain circumstances. Sovereign or governmental immunity, still in effect in some states, generally protects the public corporate entity but not its employees. However, officials of public bodies are generally immune from liability for discretionary acts performed within the scope of authority and a few states do provide the employee with immunity from liability for any act as long as it is in performance of the employee's duties and is not willful and wanton (van der Smissen, 1990). For more information on immunity, see Chapter 2.22.

Many states have passed limited liability statues designed to protect individuals in certain situations. These include recreational user statutes which protect landowners, Good Samaritan statutes protecting some who come to the aid of the injured, and various volunteer statutes. Most states also have passed laws which allow either for the indemnification of a public employee or for liability insurance coverage of the employee. Each of these are examined in detail in Chapters 2.22 and 2.31.

Recent Developments

Broadened Scope of Respondeat Superior Doctrine

Traditionally, under the doctrine of respondeat superior, an employer was liable for injuries to the person or property of third persons resulting from actions by an employee that were within the scope of employment, but the employer carried no liability for unauthorized acts by employees including willful acts to injure another. In recent years, however, many jurisdictions have extended vicarious immunity to include workplace torts (i.e., the wrongdoing of those in positions of authority), sexual assaults, sexual harassment, and abuse by a party in a position of authority over children (Carter, 1995; van der Smissen, 1996; *Williams v. Butler*, 1991). The concept of "acting within the scope of authority" continues to apply, but is more broadly interpreted to mean any activities which carry out the objectives of the employer (van der Smissen, 1996) and those during which the employer was or could have been exercising control of the activities of the employee (*Longin v. Kelly*, 1995).

Apart from the doctrine of respondeat superior, the employer may be held liable for the intentional acts of the employee in cases of employment process negligence (i.e., when the employer in the employment process negligently allows the assignment of an unfit employee or fails to use reasonable care to discover the unfitness of an employee). Liability of the employer can result from negligent hiring, negligent supervision, negligent training, negligent retention, and negligent referral of an employee that is unfit (van der Smissen, 1996; Carter, 1995).

To find a supervisory school official liable for the acts of a subordinate in a case involving physical sexual abuse, the United States Court of Appeals for the Fifth Circuit (*Doe v. Taylor Independent School District*, 1994) established that the supervisor learned of a clear pattern of inappropriate sexual behavior, demonstrated "deliberate indifference" toward the safety of the abused student, and such failure to act resulted in injury to the student. The court in discussing "deliberate indifference," stated that it is sometimes used interchangeably with such terms as "callous disregard," "grossly negligent," and "callous indifference." It explained, however, that "gross negligence" involves a heightened degree of negligence where "deliberate indifference" involves a lesser form of intent. The court held that a supervisory official's liability for the abusive acts of a subordinate arises only when the plaintiff shows that the action or inaction of the official demonstrated "deliberate indifference" to the student's right to personal security and freedom from sexual assault. For more information on these topics, see Chapter 2.36.

References

A. Cases
Brown v. Day and Tippen University, 588 N.E.2d 973 (Ohio, 1990).
Doe v. Taylor Independent School District, 15 F.3d 443 (Texas, 1994).
Glucksman v. Walters, 659 A.2d 1217 (Conn., 1995).
Hanson v. Kynast, 494 N.E.2d 1091 (Ohio, 1986).
Jaeger v. Western Rivers Fly Fisher, 855 F.Supp. 1217 (Utah, 1994).
Longin v. Kelly, 875 F.Supp. 196 (NY, 1995).
Pelletier v. Bilbiles, 227 A.2d 251 (Conn., 1967).
Riker v. Boy Scouts of America, 183 NYS2d 484 (1959).
Rogers v. Fred R. Hiller Company of Georgia, Inc., 448 S.E.2d 46 (Ga., 1994).
Townsend v. The State of California, 237 Cal.Rptr. 146 (Cal., 1987).
Williams v. Butler, 577 So.2d 1113 (La.App. 1 Cir. 1991).
Wilson v. United States of America, 989 F.2d 953 (MO, 1993).

B. Publications
Carter, P. (1995). Employer's Liability for Assault, Theft, or Similar Intentional Wrong Committed by Employee at Home or Business of Customer, 13 A.L.R.5th 217.
Manley, A., (1995). Liability of Charitable Organization Under Respondeat Superior Doctrine for Tort of Unpaid Volunteer, 82 *A.L.R.* 3d 1213.
van der Smissen, B. (1990). *Legal Liability and Risk Management for Public and Private Entities.* Cincinnati: Anderson Publishing Co.
van der Smissen, B. (1996). *Legal liability and Risk Management for Public and Private Entities.* Cincinnati: Anderson Publishing Co. (Pre-publication supplement)

2.21

Defenses
for Negligence

Doyice J. Cotten
Sport Risk Consulting

In today's litigious society, lawsuits are common, however, the fact that a sport enterprise or a sport manager is sued does not necessarily mean that loss of the suit is inevitable. There are many effective defenses which may be used by the defendant. Some of these are presented in this and the subsequent chapters (see Chapters 2.22 and 2.23).

The best defense is that one or more of the elements required for negligence is not present. As discussed in Chapter 2.11, to be liable, one must have a legal duty to the plaintiff, must breach that duty, and the breach of duty must be the proximate cause of an injury to the plaintiff. If one of these elements is missing (duty, breach, proximate cause, or injury), then no other defense is necessary—no negligence, no liability.

■ ■ ■ ■

Representative Case

SHEPPARD v. MIDWAY R-1 SCHOOL DISTRICT

Court of Appeals of Missouri, Western District
904 S.W.2d 257; 1995 Mo. App. LEXIS 1012
May 30, 1995, Filed

OPINION:

On April 15, 1991, Terra Sheppard, a fourteen-year-old girl, participated in a junior high school track meet hosted by Midway R-1 School District and conducted at the Midway High School track. She was entered in the long jump event at the track meet. During one of her jumps, Sheppard was injured as she landed in the long jump pit which had been prepared by Midway employees. She sustained an injury to her knee which required surgical replacement of a ligament in the knee. She has a permanent disability in her right knee which adversely affects the mobility and stability of the knee and which will, for the rest of her life, require her to wear an orthopedic brace when engaging in sports activities.

Sheppard brought suit against Midway in Cass County Circuit Court, pursuant to @ 537.600, n2 alleging that

Midway's long jump pit was in an unreasonably dangerous condition because it was not adequately prepared for long jumping. Midway denied that the long jump pit was inadequately prepared and alternatively alleged assumption of the risk as an affirmative defense. Following a trial, the jury returned its verdict assessing no fault to Midway and the trial court entered judgment in favor of Midway pursuant to the verdict. Sheppard appeals this judgment.

Sheppard raises three points in her appeal. In her first point, she contends the trial court erred in giving its instruction on the issue of assumption of risk because (a) assumption of risk is not applicable as a complete defense in that Midway created the risk of injury by inadequately preparing the long jump pit, a risk not inherent in the long jump event, and (b) the assumption of risk instruction contained no require-ment that the jury find Sheppard knowingly or intelligently assumed a foreseeable risk of the injury she received.

At trial, both sides presented evidence as to the cause of Sheppard's knee injury. Sheppard presented evidence that the long jump pit was wet and muddy, did not have an adequate amount of sand, and was not properly raked between jumps. Her experts testified that this was the cause of her knee injury. Midway, on the other hand, presented evidence that the long jump pit was adequately prepared and that Sheppard's injury was caused by her awkward landing. In the alternative, Midway contended that even if the pit was in fact wet or otherwise inadequately prepared, Sheppard had observed the pit and had jumped into it several times prior to the injury and therefore assumed the risk of jumping into the pit that day.

• • •

In 1983, the Missouri Supreme Court introduced the concept of comparative fault into Missouri negligence law in Gustafson v. Benda, 661 S.W.2d 11 (Mo. banc 1983). The court expressly adopted the Uniform Comparative Fault Act ("UCFA") and declared that "insofar as possible this and future cases shall apply the doctrine of pure comparative fault in accordance with the Uniform Comparative Fault Act." The court attached a copy of the UCFA, with commissioners' comments, to its opinion. The court in Gustafson did not specifically address the role of assumption of risk under comparative fault. However, the UCFA did.

• • •

(b) "Fault" includes acts or omissions that are in any measure negligent or reckless toward the person or property of the actor or others, or that subject a person to strict tort liability. The term also includes breach of warranty, unreasonable assumption of risk not constituting an enforceable express consent, misuse of a product for which the defendant otherwise would be liable, and unreasonable failure to avoid an injury or to mitigate damages. Legal requirements of causal relation apply both to fault as the basis for liability and to contributory fault.

Furthermore, the commissioners' comment states:

"Assumption of risk" is a term with a number of different meanings—only one of which is "fault" within the meaning of this Act. This is the case of unreasonable assumption of risk, which might be likened to deliberate contributory negligence and means that the conduct must have been voluntary and with knowledge of the danger. As used in this Act, the term does not include the meanings (1) of a valid and enforceable consent (which is treated like other contracts), (2) of a lack of violation of duty by the defendant (as in the failure of a land-

owner to warn a licensee of a patent danger on the premises), or (3) of a reasonable assumption of risk (which is not fault and should not have the effect of barring recovery).

While the Missouri Supreme Court has rarely addressed the role of assumption of risk under comparative fault since Gustafson, the issue regarding the role of assumption of risk under comparative negligence has been the subject of discussion by many courts and commentators. Most classify assumption of risk into categories, namely, express, implied primary, and implied secondary (reasonable or unreasonable).

Express assumption of risk occurs when the plaintiff expressly agrees in advance that the defendant owes him no duty. Recovery is completely barred since there is no duty in the first place. In the case at bar, Sheppard did not sign a release or otherwise expressly relieve Midway from liability, so express assumption of risk is not at issue here.

Implied primary assumption of risk, like express assumption of risk, relates to the initial issue of whether the defendant had a duty to protect the plaintiff from the risk of harm. Henkel v. Holm, 411 N.W.2d 1, 4 (Minn. App. 1987). It applies only where the parties have voluntarily entered a relationship in which the plaintiff assumes well-known incidental risks. Id. As to those risks, the defendant has no duty to protect the plaintiff and if the plaintiff's injury arises from an incidental risk, the defendant is not negligent. Id. Implied primary assumption of risk, like express assumption of risk, is based on consent by the plaintiff, but does not possess "the additional ceremonial and evidentiary weight of an express agreement." Kirk v. Washington State Univ., 109 Wash. 2d 448, 746 P.2d 285, 288 (Wash. 1987) (quoting W. Keeton at 496). The plaintiff's consent is implied from the act of electing to participate in the activity. Martin v. Buzan, 857 S.W.2d 366, 369 (Mo. App. 1993). "In such situations, assumption of risk is not actually an absolute defense but a measure of a defendant's duty of care; therefore, it survives the doctrine of comparative fault." Id. See also Springrose v. Willmore, 292 Minn. 23, 192 N.W.2d 826, 827 (Minn. 1971) (Minnesota Supreme Court holding that because there is no duty in the first place, primary assumption of risk is not an affirmative defense.); Arnold v. City of Cedar Rapids, 443 N.W.2d 332, 333 (Iowa 1989); Coker v. Abell-Howe Co, 491 N.W.2d 143 (Iowa 1992).

Implied secondary assumption of risk (reasonable or unreasonable) occurs when the defendant owes a duty of care to the plaintiff but the plaintiff knowingly proceeds to encounter a known risk imposed by the defendant's breach of duty. In this type of case, the question of the reasonableness of the plaintiff's assuming the risk becomes an issue. If the plaintiff's action is **reasonable**, he is not barred from recovery, nor is the defendant entitled to a comparison of fault, because a reasonable assumption of risk "is not fault and should not have the effect of barring recovery." UCFA, @ 1, Commissioners' comment. See also Kirk v. Washington State Univ., 746 P.2d at 291; Knight v. Jewett, 3 Cal. 4th 296, 834 P.2d 696 (Cal. en banc 1992); and Springrose v. Willmore, 292 Minn. 23, 192 N.W.2d 826, 827 (Minn. 1971). On the other hand, if the plaintiff's conduct in voluntarily encountering a known risk is itself unreasonable, it amounts to contributory negligence and is therefore subsumed as an element of fault to be compared by the jury. Regarding the reasonable/unreasonable distinction, one writer said:

> If secondary or implied assumption of risk is to be equated with contributory negligence, the question will be whether the plaintiff acted reasonably or unreasonably in assuming the risk. If his conduct falls in the latter category, he is guilty of contributory negligence and his recovery in a comparative fault jurisdiction will be proportionately diminished. If the plaintiff acted reasonably in assuming the risk, he is not guilty of contributory negligence. The distinction between reasonable and unreasonable assumption of risk is made in many of the cases and some of the statutes. . . . It is made in the Uniform Act where "fault" inter alia is defined as "unreasonable assumption of risk not constituting an enforceable consent."

H. Woods, at 135. See also Kirk at 289 (Implied unreasonable assumption of risk is widely recognized as a form of contributory negligence, and is therefore, subsumed under contributory negligence); Stephens v. Henderson, 741 P.2d 952, 955 (Utah 1987) ("Assumption of risk in its secondary sense . . . is to be treated as contributory negligence."); Swagger v. City of Crystal, 379 N.W.2d 183, 184 (Minn. App. 1985) ("In its 'secondary' sense assumption of risk means simply that the plaintiff was guilty of contributory negligence or fault.").

The Missouri Supreme Court recognized the distinction between primary and secondary assumption of risk in Krause v. U.S. Truck Co., 787 S.W.2d 708, 712 (Mo. banc 1990). And, as stated by Woods, supra, the distinction between reasonable and unreasonable assumption of risk is made in the UCFA where "fault" is defined as "unreasonable assumption of risk not constituting an enforceable consent." Therefore, while express and primary assumption of risk remain a complete bar to recovery, unreasonable implied secondary assumption of risk is to be considered one element of fault to be compared by the jury.

Generally, assumption of risk in the sports context involves primary assumption of risk because the plaintiff has assumed certain risks inherent in the sport or activity. Martin v. Buzan 857 S.W.2d at 369. The nature of the activity creates the risk. For example, the risk of being hit by a baseball is a risk inherent to the game of baseball, and everyone who participates in or attends a baseball game assumes the risk of being hit by a ball. However, "the assumed risks in such activities [that fall within the primary assumption of risk category] are not those created by a defendant's negligence but rather by the nature of the activity itself." Id. See also Kirk, 746 P.2d at 289 ("Assumption of the risk may act to limit recovery but only to the extent the plaintiff's damages resulted from the specific risks known to the plaintiff and voluntarily entered. To the extent a plaintiff's injuries resulted from other risks, created by the defendant, the defendant remains liable for that portion."); Bush v. Parents Without Partners, 17 Cal. App. 4th 322, 21 Cal. Rptr. 2d 178, 181 (Cal. App. 1993) ("In the sports context duty is fashioned 'in the process defining the risks inherent in the sport not only by virtue of the nature of the sport itself, but also by reference to the steps the sponsoring business entity reasonably should be obligated to take in order to minimize the risks without altering the nature of the sport.'") (citing Knight v. Jewett, 3 Cal. 4th 296, 834 P.2d 696 (Cal. 1992)).

Consequently, if, as Sheppard contends, her injury was caused not by a risk inherent in the sport of long jumping but rather by Midway's negligence in preparing the pit, secondary, rather than primary, assumption of risk applies and the question of her negligence in assuming that risk should merely be compared by the jury as an element of comparative negligence rather than being a complete bar to her recovery.

• • •

Therefore, in the sports context, under comparative fault, if the plaintiff's injury is the result of a risk inherent in the sport in which he was participating, the defendant is relieved from liability on the grounds that by participating in the sport, the plaintiff assumed the risk and the defendant never owed the plaintiff a duty to protect him from that risk. If, on the other hand, the plaintiff's injury is the result of negligence on the part of the defendant, the issue regarding the plaintiff's assumption of that risk and whether it was a reasonable assumption of risk, is an element of fault to be compared to the defendant's negligence by the jury.

This brings us to the case at bar. Sheppard contends her knee injury was the result of Midway's negligence in preparing and raking the long jump pit. Substantial evidence was presented at trial to establish that the long jump pit was inadequately prepared and not reasonably safe. This evidence tended to show that Sheppard's injury resulted not from a bad landing, an inherent risk of the sport of long jumping, but rather from the condition of the pit. There can be no question that Sheppard assumed the risks inherent in the sport of long jumping, but she did not assume the risk of Midway's negligent provision of a dangerous facility. Thus, as in Kirk, in a primary sense, she did not assume the risk and relieve Midway of its duty to provide a reasonably safe jumping pit, although based on her observations of the pit and continuing to participate, she may have unreasonably assumed the risk of injury in the secondary sense, i.e., have been contributorily negligent. Thus, Instruction 8, Sheppard's verdict director, and Instruction 10, which submitted contributory negligence (secondary assumption of risk), properly presented the issues for determination by the jury.

By the same token, however, Midway presented substantial evidence to support a finding that Sheppard's injury resulted exclusively from an awkward or bad landing, an inherent risk of participating in the long jump. Thus, contrary to Sheppard's contention, Midway was entitled to an instruction on the affirmative defense of primary assumption of risk. Instruction 9 was given to submit the issue. However, Instruction 9 is fatally flawed. First, it was, as noted previously, overly broad in that it required the jury to find for Midway even if it found Midway negligently prepared the pit, and that the negligent condition of the pit contributed to cause the injury. In effect, it compelled the jury to render a verdict for Midway if it found any assumption of risk, primary or secondary, by Sheppard and, therefore, it negated Instruction 10 entirely.

Instruction 9 also failed to properly instruct the jury that Sheppard must have had knowledge of and appreciated the risk. As our Supreme Court said in Ross v. Clouser, 637 S.W.2d 11 (Mo. banc 1982), while discussing assumption of risk, "based on a voluntary consent, express or implied, to accept the danger of a **known and appreciated risk**, it bars recovery when plaintiff **comprehended the actual danger and intelligently acquiesced in it**." Id. at 14 (emphasis added). The basis of primary assumption of risk is the plaintiff's consent to accept the risk. "This means that he must not only be aware of the facts which create the danger, but must also appreciate the danger itself and the nature, character, and extent which make it unreasonable." Restatement (Second) of Torts @ 496 D(b) (1965). Furthermore, the standard is a subjective one, "what the particular plaintiff in fact sees, knows, understands and appreciates." Id. at @ 496 D(e). Instruction 9 merely directed that if the injury was a reasonably foreseeable risk of participating in the long jump, and that Sheppard assumed the risk by participating, the jury must find for Midway. It did not tell the jury that it must find that Sheppard comprehended the actual danger and intelligently acquiesced in it.

For these reasons, we hold that the trial court erred in submitting instruction 9 to the jury and therefore reverse the judgment and remand for a new trial. Because of our disposition of Sheppard's Point I, we need not address her two other points, which relate to alleged errors in admission and exclusion of evidence, because the manner in which they arose at trial make it unlikely they will recur on retrial.

The judgment is reversed and the case is remanded for a new trial.

JOSEPH M. ELLIS, JUDGE

All Concur.

■ ■ ■ ■

Fundamental Concepts

Contributory Negligence

The Second Restatement of Torts §463 defined contributory negligence as conduct on the part of the plaintiff, contributing as a legal cause to the harm suffered, which falls below the standard to which plaintiff is required to conform for his own protection. Or put more simply, contributory negligence exists when the conduct of the plaintiff in any way helps to cause or aggravate the plaintiff's injury.

Contributory negligence is an affirmative defense and the defendant must show contributory negligence on the part of the plaintiff. Just as with proving negligence, the defendant must show the plaintiff had a duty, breached that duty, and that the breach was the proximate cause of an injury to the plaintiff. If a recreation department requires that a mouthpiece be worn by all players and a player suffers a mouth injury while not wearing a mouthpiece, the department might be found negligent for failure to inspect players for safety equipment or failure to adequately enforce the safety rule. The player, however, might be contributorily negligent for failure to wear the mouthpiece after instructions to do so.

The import of this negligence theory is that *any contributory negligence on the part of the plaintiff, regardless of how slight, serves as a complete bar to recovery on the negligence claim.* Thus, if it can be established that the plaintiff's own negligence was a factor in the plaintiff's injury, the court will not hold the defendant liable. If the defendant is 90 percent to blame for the injury and the plaintiff is 10 percent to blame, the plaintiff cannot win the suit. Obviously this is a harsh law that often leaves the plaintiff with no legal recourse even when the defendant acted in a negligent manner. In the 1960s most states adhered to the contributory negligence doctrine, however that number has decreased to six states and the District of Columbia at present (See Table 1.)

Table 1
Defense Theory Used in Each State[a]

Contributory Negligence	Pure Comparative	49% Rule Comparative	50% Rule Comparative		Slight/Gross Comparative
AL	AK	CT	NH	AR	NE
MD	AZ	DE	NJ	CO	SD
NC	CA	HA	OH	GA	
SC	FL	IL	OK	ID	
VA	KY	IN	OR	KS	
TN	LA	IA	PA	ME	
DC	MS	MA	TX	ND	
	MI	MN	VT	UT	
	MO	MT	WI	WV	
	NM	NV	WY		
	NY				
	RI				
	WA				

a. Table adapted from Mutter, C.A. (1990). Moving to Comparative Negligence in an Era of Tort Reform: Decisions for Tennessee. 57 *Tennessee Law Review* 199 (1990). The information was current as of 1990, but the number of states in each category does change as state law in that state changes. Contributory negligence is presently under attack in several states including Tennessee, South Carolina, and Virginia. (*Langley v. Boyter*, 1984; Mutter, 1990).

It is important to note that this defense acts as a complete bar to recovery only in those few states that are still classified as contributory negligence states. In addition, the defense protects the sport manager or sport business only against negligence claims. The contributory negligence defense does not protect a defendant from the consequences of reckless acts, wilful or wanton conduct, or intentional acts by the defendant.

Age. The question often arises, can a child be contributorily negligent? The general rule has been that children over the age of fourteen are capable of negligence and children under seven are incapable of negligence. Those between seven and fourteen are judged capable of negligence in certain circumstances. These lines of demarcation seem to be weakening in recent years as cases in various jurisdictions have begun to allocate contributory negligence to children six years of age and under (*Grace v. Kumalaa*, 1963; *Lash v. Cutts*, 1991). The contributory negligence of a child is not measured by the standard of care of an adult, but by the "self-care expected of a child of similar age, intelligence and experience under the particular circumstances of the case" (*Robertson v. Travis*, 1980 at 313).

Comparative Negligence

Comparative negligence is not a true defense against liability for negligence. More precisely, it is a method for apportioning blame or the relative degree of responsibility for the injury. Comparative negligence deals with the apportionment of the fault and not the damage done by the fault. In fact, some states use the term "comparative fault" rather than comparative negligence. Comparative negligence is based on the fact that both plaintiff and defendant are negligent. The jury compares the fault of each party and generally allocates the fault by percentage.

Pure Comparative Negligence. This form of comparative negligence has been adopted by 13 states (see Table 1). In this form, the award to the plaintiff is reduced by the percentage of fault assigned to the plaintiff. For example, suppose the award is $100,000 and the fault is apportioned 75 percent to the plaintiff and 25 percent to the defendant. In this case, since the plaintiff is 75 percent to blame, the plaintiff's award would be reduced by 75 percent and the plaintiff would receive $25,000.

Modified Comparative Negligence. Modified comparative negligence operates on the theory that the plaintiff is not entitled to recovery unless the negligence of the defendant is substantial. The modified form falls into three very similar categories: the *49 Percent Rule* type (in which the plaintiff may not recover if plaintiff's fault is equal to or greater than that of the defendant, thus recovery is possible if plaintiff's fault is between one and 49 percent); the *50 Percent Rule* type (in which the plaintiff may not recover if plaintiff's fault is greater than that of the defendant, thus recovery is possible if plaintiff's fault is between one and 50 percent); and the *slight/gross system* (a variation of the 49 percent system in which the plaintiff may recover only if his negligence is slight in comparison with the defendant's [*Chambers v. Dakotah Charter, Inc.*, 1991]). In each case, the qualifying plaintiff's damages are diminished by the percentage of fault attributable to the plaintiff.

Nineteen states have adopted the *50 Percent Rule* of comparative negligence and ten have adopted the *49 Percent Rule* (see Table 1). In most states the one percent difference is not important because the jury can adjust the percentage to fit the law if the jury feels the plaintiff should receive an award. Adjustment is not possible in some states where state law prohibits telling jurors the effects of the allocation. While the two modifications of comparative negligence differ little in most states, there is considerable difference between the pure and modified versions. The *slight/gross system* is an older, disfavored approach and has not been followed in but two jurisdictions. Looking again at the foregoing illustration involving the $100,000 award, the plaintiff received $25,000 under pure comparative negligence, while under modified comparative negligence the plaintiff would receive nothing because plaintiff's fault exceeds the 49 or 50 percent limits. When the fault exceeds these limits, modified comparative negligence has the same effect as contributory negligence—acting as a complete bar to recovery.

Joint Tortfeasors. Laws closely related to comparative negligence are those regarding liability when more than one party is at fault. In the past, most states have followed *joint and several liability* which states that one tortfeasor is not relieved of liability simply because others were also to blame. Under this doctrine, if more than one defendant is found liable, the liability of a defendant is not limited by the proportionate fault of that defendant. In a particularly extreme case, Walt Disney World was held only 1 percent at fault with other defendants 85 percent at fault. Disney had to pay 86 percent of the award. In other words, even if one defendant is found to be 10 percent to blame, that defendant might have to pay as much as 100 percent of the damages. Tort reform in the late 1980s modified this law in many states so that a tortfeasor's liability is limited to its proportionate share of the damages. In fact, at least 35 of the 44 comparative negligence states have legislated changes in the joint and several liability doctrine. Some of these changes have been very minor, but many states have virtually eliminated it (*Mutter*, p. 203).

In addition, in the 1980s most states passed statutes calling for equitable *contribution among joint tortfeasors*. Under these laws, when a tortfeasor has paid more than its share of damages, the tortfeasor can gain contribution from other tortfeasors by suing them in a separate action.

Assumption of Risk

The assumption of risk defense states that one may not recover from an injury to which one consents. In other words, when one voluntarily exposes oneself to known and appreciated risks, that person cannot recover for injuries resulting from those risks. The applicability of the doctrine depends on the nature and scope of the participant's awareness and consent. This defense was one of the most common and effective defenses until the comparative negligence doctrine was adopted by most states. The effectiveness of the defense varies greatly from state to state since in some states the defense was subsumed by comparative negligence while in others its validity has remained unaffected. It is not within the scope of this chapter to examine the assumption of risk doctrine on a state-by-state basis. One should check legislation and case law in one's own state for its law and interpretation. Two types of assumption of risk will be addressed here. They are *primary assumption of risk* and *secondary assumption of risk*.

Primary Assumption of Risk. Primary assumption of risk is a legal theory which involves *consent of the participant* and "relieves the defendant of a duty which he might otherwise owe the plaintiff with respect to participatory risks. ("Effect of Adoption . . . 1995 at p. 5) There are two kinds of primary assumption of risk—*express assumption of risk* and *implied primary assumption of risk*.

Express Assumption of Risk. Express assumption of risk may take the form of documents such as permission forms or agreements to participate in which the participant expressly agrees to accept the inherent risks of the activity. The agreement may be verbal, but is most often written.

More often, the express assumption of risk is in the form of a waiver or release of liability in which the signer expressly agrees that the defendant shall have no duty of ordinary care. The signer assumes the risks of injuries caused by the ordinary *negligence* of the sport business or its employees and relieves them from liability. Through express assumption of risk, the signer may assume risks both known and unknown to the signer. Such contracts are subject to the laws of the state (see Chapter 2.23).

Implied Primary Assumption of Risk. Implied primary assumption of risk is presumed when an individual has voluntarily participated in an activity that involves inherent or well-known risks. Although the individual has signed nothing, one is held to have consented, by virtue of his or her voluntary participation, to those injury-causing events which are known and reasonably foreseeable (*Truett v. Fell*). Implied primary assumption of risk acts as a defense in that it relieves the defendant of a duty which might otherwise be owed to the plaintiff. For example, if a man attends a YMCA, knows and appreciates the risks involved in weight lifting, chooses to lift weights, and injures his back, there is implied primary assumption of risk and the YMCA bears no responsibility absent negligence on its part.

Primary assumption of risk cannot constitute a defense to a strict products liability claim against a manufacturer (*Lamey v. Foley*, 1993). The manufacturer has a nondelegable duty to make a safe product. Invoking assumption of risk of the product user would undermine the policies underlying the doctrine of strict products liability.

Requirements for Implied Primary Assumption of Risk.   To use the implied primary assumption of risk defense, three elements must exist. These are 1) that the risk must be inherent to the activity; 2) that the participant must voluntarily consent to the participation and the subsequent risk exposure; and 3) that the participant must know, understand, and appreciate the risks involved in the activity.

An important point to remember is that even in jurisdictions where the assumption of risk defense is valid, the participant assumes only those risks that are *inherent* to participation in the activity. The participant does not normally assume risks incurred as a result of the negligence of the service provider unless the participant has signed a waiver.

The inherent risks are those that are a normal, integral part of the activity—risks that cannot normally be eliminated without changing the nature of the activity itself. Such injuries as an athlete pulling a hamstring running wind sprints, a softball player breaking an ankle while sliding into a base, or a football player breaking his collarbone while throwing a block may exemplify the inherent risks of the activity. On the other hand, some injuries result from the negligence of the service provider or its employees. The following are some examples where the injury might have been due to negligence: a player injuring a knee when he steps in one of many outfield holes running for a fly ball; a tumbler injured doing a handspring when no spotter is provided; or a player suffering additional injury when the coach fails to secure proper medical treatment for an injury.

One who is playing recreation league softball, a person in a pickup basketball game, or a person on the varsity football team each is participating by choice and meets the second requirement for implied primary assumption of risk—*voluntary consent.* Voluntary consent is sometimes at issue in cases regarding injuries in required physical education classes. If the plaintiff was a student in a required class where gymnastics is a required activity and was injured performing a mandatory back handspring, the voluntary consent requirement would be difficult to meet. On the other hand, if the student elected from among several choices to take weight training to meet the physical education requirement, there might be a degree of voluntary participation.

Thirdly, one cannot assume a risk of which one has no *knowledge, understanding, or appreciation*. Courts have ruled that one must not only know of the facts creating the danger, but also must comprehend and appreciate the nature of the danger to be confronted. Whether one is held to know, understand, and appreciate the risks usually depends upon the age of the plaintiff, experience of the plaintiff, and opportunity of the plaintiff to become aware of the risks. In some jurisdictions, however, knowledge and appreciation are measured by an objective test and can be determined by law when "any person of normal intelligence in [the plaintiff's] position must have understood the danger" (*Leakas v. Columbia Country Club*, 1993).

One way to strengthen the implied primary assumption of risk defense is to ensure that participants know, understand, and appreciate the risks of the activity. One effective way to accomplish this is through the use of an *agreement to participate* (see Chapter 2.24). Use of this document insures that the risks of the activity are explained to the participant in writing (accompanied by verbal explanation). Included in the document is a detailed description of the activity, the types of accidents that might occur in the activity (raft capsizing, falling into icy water, striking a rock), and the possible consequences of such accidents (drowning, broken bones, sprains, paralysis).

Secondary Assumption of Risk. Secondary assumption of risk is a form of contributory negligence which involves the voluntary choice or *conduct of the participant* to encounter a known or obvious risk created by the negligent conduct of the service provider (*Riddle v. Universal Sport Camp*, 1990). This may occur in two types of situations. In the first, the participant voluntarily participates when there is a substantial risk that the defendant will act in a negligent manner (i.e., going up in a plane with someone who has a reputation for wild or careless acts). The second is when the service provider has already been negligent and the participant takes part anyway (i.e., playing softball in an outfield that has obvious rocks and holes scattered about). In each case, the conduct of the participant (electing to participate) falls below the standard to which one is required to conform for one's own protection. If secondary assumption of risk occurs in one of the seven contributory negligence jurisdictions, it serves as a complete bar to recovery. If the incident occurs in a comparative negligence state, secondary assumption of risk will reduce the award by the percentage of fault allocated to the participant, or in some comparative negligence states, will serve as a bar to recovery (see Table 1).

Some jurisdictions break secondary assumption of risk into reasonable and unreasonable assumption of risk (*Riddle v. Universal Sport Camp*, 1990; *Sheppard v. Midway R-1 School Dist.*, 1995). The two are distinguished by weighing the utility of the conduct against the risk involved. Entering a burning building to save a child would be reasonable while entering to retrieve a hat would be unreasonable. If plaintiff's action was reasonable, plaintiff is not barred from recovery and recovery is not reduced under comparative negligence because reasonable assumption of risk is not fault. Unreasonable conduct amounts to contributory negligence and is therefore subsumed as an element of fault to be compared by the jury.

Ultra Vires Act

A defense that can be very helpful to the corporate entity is the defense that the act by the employee was an *ultra vires* act—one that is not within the authority or scope of responsibility of the employee. Normally under the doctrine of respondeat superior, the employer is liable for the negligent acts of the employee (see Chapter 2.12). A major exception to this rule, however, is when the employee had no authority or responsibility to perform the act. In such a case, only the employee is liable for the negligent act. If a coach teaches a skill incorrectly and an injury results from that negligence, the employer would be liable under the doctrine of respondeat superior since the negligence occurred in the process of fulfilling the coach's responsibility. On the other hand, if a coach injured a youngster while administering corporal punishment when the school had a strict rule prohibiting corporal punishment, the act would be outside the authority of the coach and the school system would probably escape liability. The coach would still be liable for the negligent act.

Procedural Noncompliance

Three areas of concern will be addressed in this section. These are jurisdiction of the court, statute of limitations, and notice of claim. Each of these may serve as an effective defense under certain circumstances.

Jurisdiction. Cases must be brought to trial in a court that has jurisdiction over the matter. In other words, the court must have the authority to try the case. One type of jurisdiction is personal jurisdiction which means that the court has power over the defendant's person. This is usually dependent upon geographical area and concerns the residency of the individual. In cases of diversity of citizenship, where the case involves parties from two states, federal court may assume jurisdiction (i.e., if a person goes to another state to ski and is injured due to the alleged negligence of the ski resort).

A second aspect of jurisdiction involves substantive or subject matter jurisdiction. For example, state courts are not the proper forum for cases involving federal laws; some courts require a minimum amount of money to be at issue; and others are designed to hear only cases of a certain type.

Statute of Limitations.   A statute of limitations is a restriction on the length of time an injured party has in which to file suit. The law differs from state to state and also with the nature of claim. In tort claims, states allow one to four years in which to file suit with most allowing two or three years.

A major difference in statute of limitations laws occurs when a minor is the plaintiff. Generally, the statute of limitations does not begin running until the minor has reached the age of majority. So, if a child is injured at age 11 due to the negligence of an employee at a recreation department, the youngster would have one to four years (the length of the statute of limitations in that state) after reaching the age of 18 by which to file suit.

Notice of Claim.   Notice of claim statutes relate usually to tort claim statutes and provide that the plaintiff must provide the defendant agency (public entity) with a notice of intent to file suit. This notice must be filed within a certain number of days following the accident or the right to sue is lost. In essence, the notice of claim is a type of statute of limitations with a similar effect. Not all states have a notice of claim provision in their tort law statutes and the notice of claim requirements apply only when the defendant is a governmental agency.

Other Defenses: Immunity, Waivers, and Agreements to Participate

Effective defenses protecting service providers from liability for negligence are often provided by statutes. Governmental or sovereign immunity as well as other special statutes such as Good Samaritan statutes, recreational user statutes, or volunteer statutes are covered in detail in Chapter 2.22. A waiver, a contract relieving a service provider of liability for negligence, can constitute a defense for the negligence of the service provider. The effectiveness of waivers as a defense is presented in Chapter 2.23. An agreement to participate, a document describing the inherent risks of an activity as well as possible consequences of participation, may be used to strengthen both the contributory negligence and the assumption of risk defenses (see Chapter 2.24).

Recent Trends

Assumption of Risk Regaining Importance

With the adoption of comparative negligence in most states, the assumption of risk defense had diminished in importance. Recent cases seem to indicate that the *implied primary assumption of risk defense* is regaining some of its former importance. The service provider, however, must fulfill more obligations to use the defense than in the past. For example, courts are more likely to require that the service provider warn of the inherent risks or to require that the provider show that the plaintiff knew, understood, and appreciated the inherent risks of the activity.

When determining *secondary assumption of risk*, courts are more likely to consider the *previous experience* of the participant in determining if the plaintiff assumed the risks of the activity (*Lako v. Sports Arena, Inc.*, 1995; *Lamey v. Foley*, 1993; *Riddle v. Universal Sport Camp*, 1990). The courts are also less likely to require that service providers warn of open and obvious dangers. The *open and obvious doctrine* provides that the duty of reasonable care owed by an owner or occupier of land to those lawfully on the premises does not extend to conditions which are known or obvious (*Gunther v. Charlotte Baseball, Inc.*, 1994; *Bucheleres v. Chicago Park District*, 1994; *Higgins v. Pfeiffer*, 1996). In a recent skiing case, the court ruled that the plaintiff assumed the risk because plaintiff had skied the course at least three times prior to the accident and all of the risks involved were perfectly obvious (*Dicruttalo v. Blaise Enterprises, Inc.*, 1995).

Florida's Express Assumption of Risk

Florida has adopted an express assumption of risk doctrine which gives protection to the service provider if the plaintiff recognized the risk involved in a contact sport and proceeded to participate in the face of such danger. The doctrine bars recovery for risks inherent in the sport, but does not protect the provider from liability for injuries caused by the negligence of the provider. Although named "express assumption of risk," this doctrine actually provides for implied primary assumption of risk. Football, horse racing, karate, cheerleading, and softball have been considered contact sports under the doctrine, while diving was not (*City of Miami v. Cisneros*, 1995; *Lenoble v. City of Ft. Lauderdale*, 1995; *Zalkin v. American Learning Systems, Inc.*, 1994; *Mazzeo v. City of Sebastian*, 1989; *Ashcroft v. Calder Race Course, Inc.*, 1986; *Nova University, Inc. v. Katz*, 1993)

References

A. Cases

Ashcroft v. Calder Race Course, Inc., 492 So2d 1309 (Fla., 1986).
Bucheleres v. Chicago Park District, 646 N.E.2d 1326 (Ill., 1994).
Chambers v. Dakotah Charter, Inc., 488 N.W.2d 63 (S.D., 1991)
Chappel v. Franklin Pierce School District No. 402, 426 P.2d 471 (Wash., 1967).
City of Miami v. Cisneros, 662 So.2d 1272 (Fla., 1995).
Dicruttalo v. Blaise Enterprises, Inc., 621 N.Y.S.2d 199 (1995).
Ferrari v. Grand Canyon Dories, 32 Cal.App.4t/h 248 (1995).
Freeman v. Hale, 30 Cal.App.4th 1388 (1994).
Garcia v. City of New York, 617 N.Y.S.2d 462 (1994).
Grace v. Kumalaa, 387 P.2d 872 (Hawaii, 1963).
Gunther v. Charlotte Baseball, Inc., 854 F.Supp. 424 (S.C., 1994).
Higgins v. Pfeiffer, 1996 Mich. App. LEXIS 40.
Lako v. Sports Arena, Inc., 1995 U.S.App. LEXIS 13951 (Ohio).
Lamey v. Foley, 594 N.Y.S.2d 490 (1993).
Langley v. Boyter, 325 SE2d 550 (S.C., 1984).
Lash v. Cutts, 943 F.2d 147 (Me., 1991).
Leakas v. Columbia Country Club, 831 F.Supp. 1231 (Md., 1993).
Lenoble v. City of Fort Lauderdale Umpires, Inc., 663 So.2d 1351 (Fla., 1995).
Mazzeo v. City of Sebastian, 550 So.2d 1113 (Fla., 1989).
Melerine v. State of Louisiana, 505 So.2d 79 (La., 1987).
Nova University, Inc. v. Katz, 636 So.2d 729 (Fla., 1993).
Riddle v. Universal Sport Camp, 786 P.2d 641 (Kan., 1990).
Robertson v. Travis, 393 So.2d 304 (La., 1980).
Sheppard v. Midway R-1 School District, 904 S.W.2d 257 (Mo.App. W.D. 1995).
Springrose v. Wilmore, 192 N.W.2d 826 (Minn., 1971).
Truett v. Fell, 68 N.Y.2d 432.
Zalkin v. American Learning Systems, Inc., 639 So.2d 1020 (Fla. 3d DCA 1994).

B. Publications

Effect of Adoption of Comparative Negligence Rules on Assumption of Risk, 16 A.L.R.4th 700.

Kaiser, Ronald A. *Liability and Law in Recreation, Parks, and Sports*. Englewood Cliffs, N.J.: Prentice-Hall 1986.

van der Smissen, B. (1990). *Legal Liability and Risk Management for Public and Private Entities*. Cincinnati: Anderson Publishing Co

Mutter, C.A. (1990). Moving to Comparative Negligence in an Era of Tort Reform: Decisions for Tennessee. 57 Tenn. L. Rev. 199.

2.22

Immunity

Bernard P. Maloy
University of Michigan

An important defense for negligent conduct is immunity—the freedom or exemption from penalty or liability for negligence. Thus one who has the protection of immunity is not held liable for one's negligent conduct. Immunity, however, does not protect one from liability for behavior which is reckless, wanton and willful, or intentional. This chapter will examine the types of immunity applicable to sport, recreation, and physical activity. It will concentrate on sovereign or governmental immunity, review statutory immunity, and briefly examine some other concepts related to immunity.

■ ■ ■ ■

Representative Case

OIEN v. THE CITY OF SIOUX FALLS
Supreme Court of South Dakota
393 N.W.2d 286
September 10, 1986

OPINION:

This appeal arises from a personal injury action initiated by plaintiff Kay Oien (Oien), as Guardian Ad Litem for her four-year-old child, Casie Oien (Casie), against the defendant City of Sioux Falls (City). City filed a motion for summary judgment on grounds that SDCL 9-38-55 and SDCL 9-38-105 immunized it from liability under the facts of this case. The trial court found that SDCL 9-38-55 and SDCL 9-38-105 afforded City municipal immunity and granted City's motion for summary judgment. Oien appeals and we reverse and remand.

• • •

City employees chemically treated the water in a municipal swimming pool and left a quantity of the water treatment chemicals on the pool's edge. Casie came into contact with the chemical solution when she sat down at the pool's edge. The solution caused severe chemical burns on the child's buttocks. Immediate medical treatment was required. The child suffered pain and faces permanent scarring and potential infection. Oien alleged that City's employees negligently left some of the chemical solution on the edge of the pool during swimming hours and thereby violated City's duty of care to protect pool users from contact with such chemicals.

City asserts that SDCL 9-38-55 and 9-38-105 (park immunity statutes) shield it from negligence actions arising from its operation of parks and public recreation facilities. City relies on our holding in Grosz v. City of Sioux Falls, 346 N.W.2d 446 (S.D. 1984), wherein we stated we believe that the plain import of SDCL 9-38-55 and 9-38-105 is to immunize municipalities from tort liability arising out of the construction and maintenance of public parks, recreation areas and playgrounds.

Oien alleges that the park immunity statutes are unconstitutional under the provisions of South Dakota Constitution art. VI, @ 20, the so-called "open courts" provision which provides:

All courts shall be open, and every man for an injury done him in his property, person or reputation, shall have remedy by due course of law, and right and justice, administered without denial or delay.

The issue thus presented to us is: Is the legislative attempt to extend sovereign immunity to municipal operation of parks, playgrounds and pools unconstitutional? We hold that it is.

In High-Grade Oil Co., Inc. v. Sommer, 295 N.W.2d 736 (S.D. 1980), we discussed sovereign immunity in relation to article VI, @ 2O, as pertains to state government. In that regard, we said:

To say that sovereign immunity is a constitutional violation is on its face an incongruity. In our republican form of government the people are the sovereign. The rights granted under the constitution are such rights as the sovereign grants. The sovereign can retain rights or qualify the grant. As we have noted . . . the doctrine of sovereign immunity predates our constitution. . . . While . . . the doctrine [of sovereign immunity] is "judge made law," we are reminded that it is a doctrine of long standing; so long in fact, that it antecedes the federal and state constitutions.

• • •

We then noted that our state constitution took cognizance of the doctrine of sovereign immunity when it provided in article III, @ 27, that "the legislature shall direct by law in what manner and in what courts suits may be brought against the state."

• • •

And further:

There is not, legally speaking, any distinction in the capacity in which the government of the state acts, or in the essential nature of its operation as a matter of law, in the performance of any one function intrusted to it by the people as compared with the performance of other functions so intrusted. We therefore hold that there cannot be successfully maintained, as a matter of law, in this state, under the circumstances here involved, a distinction between what has been frequently denominated as a [governmental] and [proprietary] capacity of the state.

• • •

In discussing the doctrine of sovereign immunity on a municipal level as it relates to article VI, @ 20, and in the light of the provisions of article III, @ 27, we are first reminded that "[a] court, in construing a constitutional provision, must give regard to the whole instrument, must seek to harmonize the various provisions, and must, if possible, give effect to all the provisions."

South Dakota Auto. Club, Inc. v. Volk, 305 N.W.2d 693, 696 (S.D. 1981). In addition, we are of course mindful that Oien bears the burden of proving beyond a reasonable doubt that the statutes violate the state constitutional provisions. There is a strong presumption that the laws enacted by the legislature are constitutional and that presumption is rebutted only when it clearly, palpably and plainly appears that the statute violates a provision of the constitution. . . . Constitutional review of legislative enactments must be handled without regard for the legislative wisdom behind the enacted law, we must focus on its constitutionality. . . . Finally, this court must adopt any reasonable and legitimate construction of the statutes which will permit us to uphold the legislature's enactments.

• • •

In Grosz, supra, we acknowledged that shortly after the decision in Norberg v. Hagna, 46 S.D. 568, 195 N.W. 438 (1923), the South Dakota Legislature enacted what is now known as SDCL 9-38-55 and in 1949 enacted what is now SDCL 9-38-105. The Grosz decision reiterated the Conway statement that "the power to define tort liability of a municipality rests with the legislature subject to constitutional limitations." 346 N.W.2d at 447. We further held: (1) the construction and maintenance of bicycle paths falls within the purview of the statute; (2) under the statute it is immaterial whether the city was engaged in proprietary or governmental functions; and (3) the plain import of the park immunity statutes is to immunize municipalities from tort liability from activities within their purview. It is important to note that the constitutionality of the parks immunity statutes was not questioned in the briefs nor mentioned in the opinion. Oien is the first case in which anyone has sought to test the enactment of those statutes under the provisions of article VI, @ 20.

• • •

In In re Heartland Consumers Power District, 85 S.D. 205, 208-9, 180 N.W.2d 398, 400 (1970), we reiterated that holding, stating: "The Constitution of South Dakota is not a grant but a limitation upon the lawmaking powers of the state legislature and it may enact any law not expressly or inferentially prohibited by the state or federal constitutions." And further, "in order to determine that an act is unconstitutional we must find some provision that prohibits the enactment of a statute rather than for grants of such power." In High-Grade Oil, supra, we characterized article III, @ 27, as recognition of the doctrine of sovereign immunity; authority for a qualified grant of a right of action against the sovereign. Thus, we do not perceive article III, @ 27, as any grant of authority to enact the parks immunity statutes. Instead, we must examine article VI, @ 20, to determine whether it is indeed a prohibition against the enactment of the parks immunity statutes.

In Simons v. Kidd, 73 S.D. 41, 46, 38 N.W.2d 883, 886 (1949) (quoting Mattson v. Astoria, 39 Or. 577, 65 P. 1066, 1067 (1901)), we characterized article VI, @ 20, the "open courts" provision, as "a guarantee that 'for such wrongs as are recognized by the law of the land the courts shall be open and afford a remedy.'" That is to say, where a cause of action is implied or exists at common law without statutory abrogation, a plaintiff has a right to litigate and the courts will fashion a remedy. Did Oien have a remedy under the common law? We think she did.

Under the common law sovereign immunity only extended to the state and its agencies and subdivisions. Municipal corporations are not considered in all respects to be agencies or subdivisions of the state. In South Dakota, sovereign immunity extends to municipalities only to the extent that they are acting as agents for the state, i.e., in a governmental capacity.

As early as 1893, this court recognized in O'Rourke v. Sioux Falls, 4 S.D. 47, 51, 54 N.W. 1044, 1045-46, that there are two kinds of duties imposed upon a municipal corporation, in respect to which there is a clear distinction—one is imposed for governmental purposes, and is discharged in the interest of the public, and the other arises from the grant of some special power, in the exercise of which the municipality acts as a legal individual. In the latter case the power is not held or exercised by the municipality as or because it is one of the political subdivisions of the state, and for public governmental purposes, but as and because it is, as an individual might be, the grantee of such power for private purposes. In such case the municipality is on the same footing with a private grantee of the same power, and is, like him, liable for an injury caused by the improper use of such power. But where the power is conferred upon the municipality as one of the political divisions of the state, and conferred, not for any benefit to result therefrom to such municipality, but as a means in the exercise of the sovereign power for the benefit of the public, the corporation is not answerable for nonfeasance or misfeasance by its public agents.

See also Jensen v. Juul, 66 S.D. I, 5, 278 N.W. 6, 8 (1938) wherein we held:

Although a corporation may be public, and not private, because established and controlled by the state for public purposes, it does not follow that such corporation is in effect the state and that the same immunity from liability attaches. Generally, in reference to liability for torts a municipal corporation has a dual character. It is vested with powers of a governmental character for the administration of general laws of the state and no liability for tort ordinarily attaches for damages caused by negligence while in the exercise of such powers. In so far, however, as municipal corporations exercise powers not of this character. there is no immunity from liability.

In Board of County Commissioners, 53 S.D. at 630, 222 N.W. at 592, we further held:

Municipal corporations enjoy their immunity from liability for torts only in so far as they partake of the state's immunity, and only in the exercise of those governmental powers and duties imposed upon them as representing the state. In the exercise of those administrative powers conferred upon, or permitted to, them solely for their own benefit in their corporate capacity, whether performed for gain or not, and whether of the nature of a business enterprise or not, they are neither sovereign nor immune. They are only sovereign and only immune in so far as they represent the state. They have no sovereignty of their own, they are in no sense sovereign per se.

In Norberg, supra, we held the City of Watertown liable for negligence in the maintenance of its swimming area and in Jensen, supra, we held the Town of Irene liable for negligence in the maintenance of a baseball field. In both cases we determined that such activities did not constitute the exercise of a governmental function.

Since construction, maintenance, and operation of parks, playgrounds and pools have traditionally been held to be a proprietary function, the park immunity statutes which attempt to expand sovereign immunity to municipalities acting in a proprietary capacity and to thereby defeat a cause of action for negligent acts committed in that capacity clearly violates the constitutional limitations of article VI. @ 20 of the South Dakota Constitution.

We reverse the judgment of the trial court and remand for further proceedings.

■ ■ ■ ■

Fundamental Concepts

Sovereign or Governmental Immunity

Sovereign immunity is recognized as a defense for state governments and their agencies, boards, departments, and institutions; similarly, governmental immunity is recognized as a defense for city and other local governmental entities and schools. Two limitations to sovereign or governmental immunity are 1) that they apply only to governmental entities—not private bodies, and 2) that *they primarily apply only to the governmental entity and not to the officers, agents, or employees of the entity* (van der Smissen, 1990), although some statutes do give some protection to employees, especially by indemnification when acting in the scope of responsibility or authority. The concept of discretionary function (see later discussion) also protects employees and officials of a public agency or institution. While there is a legal distinction between sovereign immunity and governmental immunity, that distinction has meaning only to those litigating immunity cases. In this chapter, the terms will be used synonymously.

The essence of governmental immunity is that public agencies can be sued only if they give their consent. Historically, immunity has afforded governmental bodies very broad protection from liability for negligence. The purpose of broad governmental immunity protection was two-fold: first, to protect the public treasury from claims; and, second, to permit unfettered decision-making by public officials. The general protection it offered public agencies and their employees included virtually all job-related conduct, except wanton and willful or reckless behavior. Governmental immunity remained fairly broad in its coverage until the post-World War II years. In the 1950s, important changes began to occur in the application of immunity protection. Van der Smissen (1990) provides an excellent historical perspective on the changes affecting governmental immunity. She states that immunity has undergone five eras of change in the last 40 years. Each era has restricted or limited the "broad-brush" approach to governmental immunity in its own way. The common theme in all of the eras has been that immunity protection for the negligent acts of public agencies is unfair to the injured.

In response, legislatures began to permit public agencies to purchase liability insurance; they passed tort claims acts which allowed negligence suits against public agencies for certain types of claims; and, they began to classify which type of governmental conduct would be protected, and which would not. Over the last 40 years, governmental immunity has been greatly limited or restricted in a number of different ways. The most important limitations, or restrictions, are the governmental-proprietary function distinction, the discretionary acts-ministerial acts distinction, and the real property exception.

The Representative Case (*Oien v. Sioux Falls*, 1986) is of interest for three reasons. It pinpoints the "fairness" aspect of immunity protection showing that getting relief from the courts is a limited constitutional right. The concept of immunity should be understood in the context of limiting the ability of a citizen to pursue legal remedies. Secondly, it helps to understand the distinction set forth by the court between governmental function and proprietary function. Finally, the case highlights the subtle distinctions between sovereign immunity and governmental immunity as far as the functions of the state are distinguished from the functions of cities and local governmental agencies.

Governmental-Proprietary Function.   Prior to the early 1970s most states had adopted an immunity classification termed the governmental function-proprietary function test. Basically, what this legal test did was classify the *functions* of public agencies. Some public functions were deemed necessary public duties and were protected by immunity. These public functions under the broad umbrella of public welfare included public health, public education, and emergency services. This meant the police and fire departments, hospitals, and schools were protected under governmental immunity for the functions they performed. Other functions of public agencies which were, by nature, based on leisure activities which could be as easily provided by private entities, competitive enterprise, or the benefit of particular segments of the public were called proprietary functions and were not protected by immunity.

The major problem with the governmental-proprietary function distinction is that public agencies which charge fees for services, or which derive revenues from their activities, may be seen as performing pecuniary or for-profit services. The governmental-proprietary function test presented another dilemma for courts in looking at the application of governmental immunity. Since it was clear that certain functions such as public welfare, health, or education were protected, public schools and universities, as state agencies, were protected for their educational functions. What was not clear was whether an intercollegiate athletic program could be considered an educational function (*University of Texas-Pan American v. Valdez,* 1993).

Discretionary Acts-Ministerial Acts. By the early 1980s, only a few states still adhered to this distinction, with most having abandoned the function test in favor of the discretionary acts-ministerial acts test. Discretionary acts may be defined as "those which require personal deliberation, decision, and judgement" (van der Smissen, 1990, p. 165). Discretionary acts generally include the planning, deliberation, and decision-making activities of a public body. Under this test, *the public body and those with the authority to make decisions of this nature are protected by immunity.* Ministerial acts may be defined as "those which constitute merely an obedience to orders or a performance of a duty in which the individual has little or no choice . . . the distinction between 'discretionary' and 'ministerial' acts is that the latter involves the execution of a decision-making" (van der Smissen, 1990, p. 165). Activities which are operational in nature, for example, teaching, supervision, and facility maintenance, are ministerial acts and are not protected by immunity. The purpose of protecting the deliberative or discretionary functions is to free elected and public officials, charged with making decisions in the public welfare, from suits which might inhibit them from discharging their duties.

Under the discretionary acts-ministerial acts test, it is the **nature** of the employee act that determines the liability of the governmental body. If the employee is engaged in a discretionary act within the scope of responsibility and authority and not acting with malice or wilful misconduct, neither the employee nor the public body is liable. In contrast, if the employee is performing a ministerial act, the negligence of the employee is imputed to the public body and neither the public body nor its employee is protected by immunity (van der Smissen, 1990).

It should be noted that the determination of whether a particular act is discretionary or ministerial may vary greatly among states. Some states define a discretionary act as almost any act taken by an administrator in the scope of the administrator's authority and responsibility (*Hennessy v. Webb,* 1980). In such states, immunity is a very strong defense.

Real Property Exception. During the era when legislatures were enacting tort claims acts which specified the parameters within which a public agency could be sued or permitted agencies to purchase liability insurance, a notable exception to governmental immunity, the real property exception, emerged. Under the real property exception, public agencies are charged with the duty of maintaining public premises in a reasonably safe condition. In those states which have the real property exception, the exception to immunity applies regardless of whether the state follows the governmental-proprietary distinction or the discretionary acts-ministerial acts distinction. Owners and operators of public parks, public physical education and athletic facilities, and public recreation areas need to be aware of the law in their states because the real property exception, if applicable, eliminates the protection that would otherwise be afforded public agencies by immunity (Keaton, et al., 1988).

Some have attempted to apply this exception to all types of injuries occurring at public facilities. The exception, however, applies only to those directly relating to the care and maintenance of the facility itself. In a Pennsylvania case, a youngster was injured at a city swimming pool by a group of rowdies. His parents alleged the city failed to properly supervise the pool. The city had no immunity under the real property exception because the injury was not caused by a defective condition of the pool area (*Kasavage v. City of Philadelphia*, 1987).

Statutory Immunity

There are several types of statutory immunity: 1) recreational user acts related to land use, 2) legislation relating to volunteers, and 3) statutes related to rendering of emergency care.

Recreational Use Immunity. Recreational use immunity is instituted in most states to encourage landowners to open their lands to the general public for recreational use at no cost. The purpose of recreational use statutes is to supplement the current park and recreation system by providing opportunities for the general public to enjoy recreational activities on private lands. It fulfills this purpose by granting immunity to landowners who make their land available for recreational purposes. The immunity, like governmental immunity, only applies to negligent conduct. It will not protect a landowner from liability for conduct or behavior which is found to be wanton and willful, or reckless misconduct (Miller).

Recreational use laws have four characteristics: 1) The immunity protection is primarily for private landowners though a number of states do extend recreational use immunity to public agencies as well. 2) The protection extends to land which is largely undeveloped, and rural in nature. Recreational use immunity generally does not extend to urban areas although there are some exceptions. The recreational uses for which the immunity is named usually refer to outdoor activities like swimming, hunting, boating, and hiking. 3) The landowner's only obligation under recreational use immunity is to provide a warning for any concealed danger which would not be apparent to the recreational user. This does not require warnings for naturally occurring conditions. 4) The landowner cannot charge a fee or payment for his permission to use the premises for recreational activities.

Recreational use immunity protects both private landowners and, in some states, public agencies which control and operate public lands. There are a number of underlying theories for extending recreational use immunity protection to public agencies. The most prevalent seems to be that tort claims acts have severely restricted governmental immunity protection for public agencies making them susceptible to lawsuits just like private citizens. Recreational use immunity was extended, therefore, to afford the public agencies the same rights and protections as a private citizen (Miller). In practice, the application of this immunity protection for public agencies has not been the same as that for private citizens. The effect of the unequal treatment has been to provide public agencies with greater recreational immunity protection than that afforded private landowners in two circumstances.

As stated, the purpose of recreational use immunity has been to protect landowners who make their unimproved, rural lands available for recreational purposes. **Unimproved lands** means real estate for which there has not been a labor cost or capital improvement intended to enhance its value for another purpose. In a Pennsylvania case, a student was injured when she stepped into a hole while practicing on a lacrosse field. The court stated that the school was not protected by recreational use immunity since it applied to unimproved lands (*Seiferth v. Downington Area School Dist., 1992*). In another Pennsylvania case, an urban basketball court operated by a public recreational agency was not unimproved land and recreational use immunity did not apply (*Walsh v. City of Philadelphia.* 1990).

In many jurisdictions, however, recreational use immunity has been extended to protect previously unprotected activities on public lands. For example, in Ohio, recreational use immunity was extended to include municipal property when spectators were injured near a softball field. The court, by ruling the spectators were recreational users, changed the nature of the lands which were protected under recreational use law (*Licause v. City of Canton*, 1989).

The inequality is that a private landowner of urban improved real estate is not provided the same protection as a public agency. It is generally held that homeowners are not protected by recreational use immunity for injuries which occur to social guests in their home even if the injury was from a recreational use.

A basic concept of recreational use immunity provides that a landowner cannot charge a **fee** or payment for permission to use the land. However, in a number of cases, public agencies have been permitted to charge nominal fees for admission to the land without forfeiting their immunity. Private landowners have not been permitted to charge such fees.

In a Georgia case, a camper was injured while on the way to a laser light show in Stone Mountain Park. The court stated that the payment of an admission fee, a camping fee, and concession charges did not constitute fees within the meaning of the state recreational use law since she was injured in an activity for which no fee was charged (*Hogue v. Stone Mountain Memorial Association*, 1987). The same result was reached in a Michigan case where the plaintiff was injured while unloading a boat at a dock in a state park. The court ruled that a nominal admission fee did not constitute the "valuable consideration" barred by the state recreational use law (*Schiller v. Muskegon State Park*, 1986).

However, recreational use immunity does not protect a public agency if a fee is charged for the particular activity in which the injury occurs. In an Arizona case, the court noted that the injured plaintiff's participation in a softball league was conditioned on payment of the $250 team participation fee. Recreational use immunity did not apply (*Prince v. City of Apache Junction*, 1996).

Volunteer Immunity. Absent legislation to the contrary, volunteers, like employees, are liable for their own negligent acts. This exposure to liability coupled with the difficulty of obtaining liability insurance prompted more than 20 state legislatures to pass immunity statutes relieving volunteers of liability for ordinary negligence. Volunteer immunity seeks to encourage people to donate their time and effort working for nonprofit organizations dedicated to the public welfare by protecting them from liability. Volunteer immunity, like the other kinds of immunity that have been discussed, will not protect volunteers for injuries caused by gross negligence, reckless misconduct, or wanton and willful behavior.

Volunteer immunity, however, should not be viewed as protecting the unsafe practices of untrained volunteers. In a New Jersey case, a coach in a youth baseball program permitted a youngster to warm up a pitcher without a wearing a catcher's mask. The youngster was hit in the eye with a ball and severely injured. The New Jersey law states that a coach, manager, or official must meet the requirement of a safety training program in order to enjoy immunity protection. In spite of the fact that the league had not established a safety program, the court clearly stated that volunteer immunity protection is contingent upon the completion of such a program (*Byrne v. Fords-Clara Boys Baseball League, Inc.*, 1989). The *Byrne* case set forth as public policy that volunteers in youth sports should not be protected by volunteer immunity without some minimal training in the skills and rules of the activity.

Good Samaritan Statutes. Good Samaritan statutes have been enacted to provide immunity from liability for those who voluntarily come to the aid of injured persons. These laws seek to protect those individuals who do not owe any legal responsibility to render aid, but act when they come upon an accident or situation wherein a victim needs emergency care or rescue. Van der Smissen (1990) emphasizes that "Persons owing a duty because of professional relationships should not presume they can use the Good Samaritan laws for limited liability or immunity" (p. 103). By this token, authorities in a sport setting have no immunity under these laws since they owe a duty of emergency care to their patrons.

Concepts That Function Like Immunity

Workmen's Compensation is a type of insurance required by the state to provide benefits to employees who are injured on the job. The employer bears the cost of this insurance in return for limited immunity from lawsuits by employees for negligent behavior of the employer (see Chapter 5.70).

In loco parentis is a relationship where a person or agency stands in the place of a parent in providing for a child and is charged with a parent's rights, duties, and responsibilities. In the past, this relationship conferred the tort immunity of a parent to teachers, coaches, and athletic administrators. Note that only Illinois continues to confer on teachers the status of *in loco parentis* in non-disciplinary as well as disciplinary matters.

Another concept relating to immunity is that which has been granted to **participants** in organized contact sports. When a participant's actions result in an injury to another participant in organized contact sports, the offending participant has not been held liable for ordinary negligence. Reckless conduct has been recognized as the standard of behavior required for liability (Narol, 1991; Berry and Wong, 1993). For further discussion of this topic, see Chapter 2.41.

Recent Developments

Sport managers should note that there is a growing trend to recognize an equipment exception to immunity. Like the real property exception, the recognition of a safe equipment exception would further limit the protection afforded to those who teach, manage, and administer sports, recreation, and physical education programs. There is a legal obligation on the part of coaches, teachers, administrators, and premises operators to provide reasonably safe sports and athletic equipment. In fact, in Illinois the obligation to provide safe equipment is considered an exception to *in loco parentis* immunity which still protects teachers and coaches in that state (*Poelker v. Macon Community Unit School Dist. 5,* 1990).

References

A. Cases

Byrne v. Fords-Clara Boys Baseball League, Inc., 236 N.J.Super. 185, 564 A.2d 1222 (1989).
Hennessy v. Webb, 264 S.E.2d 878 (GA 1980).
Hogue v. Stone Mountain Memorial Association, 358 S.E.2d 852 (Ga. App. 1987).
Kasavage v. City of Philadelphia, 524 A.2d 1089 (Pa. Commw. 1987).
Licause v. City of Canton, 42 Ohio St.3d 109, 537 N.E.2d 1298 (1989).
Oien v. City of Sioux Falls, 393 N.W.2d 286 (S.D. 1986).
Poelker v. Macon Community Unit School Dist. 5, 571 N.E.2d 479 (Ill. App. 1990).
Prince v. City of Apache Junction, 912 P.2d 47 (Ariz. App. 1996).
Seiferth v. Downington Area School Dist., 604 A.2d 757 (Pa. Commw. 1992).
Schiller v. Muskegon State Park, 395 N.W.2d 75 (Mich. App. 1986).
University of Texas-Pan American v. Valdez, 869 S.W.2d 446 (Tex. App. 1993).
Walsh v. City of Philadelphia, 585 A.2d 445 (Pa. 1990).

B. Publications

Berry, R.C. & Wong, G.M. (Vol. II, 2d ed., 1993). *Law and Business of the Sports Industries: Common Issues in Amateur and Professional Sports,* Westport, Conn.: Praeger Publishers.
Miller, R.C., Annotation. Effect of Statute Limiting Landowner's Liability for Personal Injury to Recreational User, 47 A.L.R.4th 262.

Narol, M. (1991). Sports Participation with Limited Litigation: The Emerging Reckless Standard, 1 *Seton Hall Journal of Sport Law* 29.

Keeton, W.P., et al. (5th ed., 1988). *Prosser and Keeton on the Law of Torts*. St. Paul, Minn.: West Publishing Co.

van der Smissen, B. (Vol. 1, 1990). *Legal Liability and Risk Management for Public and Private Entities*. Cincinnati: Anderson Publishing Co.

2.23

Exculpatory Agreements or Waivers

Doyice J. Cotten
Sport Risk Consulting

An **exculpatory agreement** or **waiver** of liability in the sport setting is a contract in which the participant or user of a service agrees to relinquish the right to pursue legal action against the service provider in the event that negligence of the provider results in an injury to the participant. While injuries result from one of three causes, 1) inherent risks of the activity (common accidents), 2) negligence by the service provider or its employees, and 3) more extreme acts by the service provider or its employees (gross negligence, reckless conduct, wilful/wanton conduct, or intentional acts), it is important to understand that **the waiver is meant to protect the service provider from liability for the *ordinary negligence* of the service provider or its employees**.

Although waivers are used by many sport-related businesses, many people feel that waivers are worthless and offer no protection to the service provider. The validity of a waiver, however, is determined by the law in each state and subsequently, the validity of waivers will vary depending upon the state. Cotten has placed states into four categories depending upon the degree of rigor required by the state for a valid waiver. The first category consists of three states in which waivers will not protect the service provider from liability for negligence. The second category includes 19 states that allow waivers, but maintain very rigorous requirements for a waiver to be upheld. The third category includes 19 states in which waivers are allowed and the requirements for validity are moderate in nature. The final category includes seven states that not only allow waivers, but have very lenient requirements for their validity. No sport-related waiver cases were found in New Mexico or Rhode Island. Thus, well-written waivers, signed by adults, can be used to protect the sport business from liability for negligence by the business or its employees in at least 45 states.

Table 1
Categorization of States Based on
the Rigor Required for a Valid Waiver

Not Enforceable			Rigorous			Moderate			Lenient		
LA	MT	VA	AK	AR	AK	CO	HA	IA	AL	GA	ID
			CA	CT	DE	IL	IN	KS	MD	MI	SC
			FL	KY	ME	MA	MN	MS	TN		
			MO	NH	NJ	NC	ND	NE			
			NV	NY	OR	OH	OK	PA			
			TX	UT	VT	SD	WA	WV			
			WI			WY					

■ ■ ■ ■

Representative Case

GROVES v. FIREBIRD RACEWAY, INC.
United States Court of Appeals for the Ninth Circuit
1995 U.S. App. LEXIS 28191
September 14, 1995, Argued and Submitted, Seattle, Washington
September 28, 1995, Filed

OPINION: MEMORANDUM

Gary Groves ("Mr. Groves") and Kathy Groves ("Mrs. Groves") appeal from the grant of summary judgment in favor of Firebird Raceway, Inc. ("Firebird") and the National Hot Rod Association ("NHRA"). Mr. Groves contends that the district court erred in concluding that the release of tort liability signed by Mr. Groves is unambiguous and does not violate public policy. Mrs. Groves maintains that the district court erred in concluding that the agreement signed by her husband releasing Firebird of tort liability for the physical injuries sustained by Mr. Groves also precludes her separate claim for loss of consortium.

We affirm the grant of summary judgment regarding the validity of the release signed by Mr. Groves because it is not ambiguous and does not violate public policy. We reverse the judgment dismissing Mrs. Groves' claim for loss of consortium because we conclude that the Idaho Supreme Court would hold that the agreement signed by Mr. Groves releasing Firebird of any tort liability sustained by Mr. Groves does not bar her separate claim for loss of consortium.

I
• • •

On August 14, 1992, Mr. Groves paid the entry fee and signed a document entitled, "Release and Waiver of Liability and Indemnity Agreement," in order to participate in the Pepsi Nightfire National Races at Firebird Raceway. In the past, Mr. Groves had signed similar agreements before participating in other racing events.

• • •

During a race, Mr. Groves' vehicle crashed and burst into flames. Firebird's employees responded to the accident and extinguished the fire. Mr. Groves suffered serious burns and incurred substantial medical costs.

On August 12, 1993, the Groves filed a complaint in the district court against Firebird in this diversity action containing claims for negligence and loss of consortium. On April 26, 1994, the district court granted summary

judgment in favor of Firebird and entered a final judgment dismissing this action.

II
• • •

Mr. Groves alleges that the district court erred in granting Firebird's motion for summary judgment based on its conclusion that the release barred recovery of his claim of negligent firefighting.

A

Mr. Groves contends that the release does not bar claims for negligent firefighting. Specifically, Mr. Groves asserts that the terms " EVENT(S)" and "NEGLIGENT RESCUE" are undefined, thereby rendering the release ambiguous and unenforceable.

A federal court, in exercising its diversity jurisdiction, must apply state law. Erie R.R. Co. v. Tompkins, 304 U.S. 64, 78, 82 L. Ed. 1188, 58 S. Ct. 817 (1938). Accordingly, Idaho law applies to the matter sub judice. The Idaho Supreme Court has recognized that "a party may contract to absolve [itself] from certain duties and liabilities[.]" Anderson & Nafziger v. G.T. Newcomb, Inc., 100 Idaho 175, 595 P.2d 709, 712 (Idaho 1979). Such contracts must "speak clearly and directly to the conduct of the defendant which caused the harm at issue." Id. Where the clear purpose of the release is to preclude all liability, however, the parties need not have contemplated the precise occurrence which resulted in harm. Rawlings v. Layne & Bowler Pump Co., 93 Idaho 496, 465 P.2d 107, 110 (Idaho 1970).

Although the agreement does not specifically preclude negligent firefighting claims, read in its entirety, its effect is to bar such claims. The release provides that, "[Mr. Groves] . . . COVENANTS NOT TO SUE [Firebird and the NHRA] . . . FOR ANY AND ALL LOSS . . . ON ACCOUNT OF INJURY TO THE PERSON . . . CAUSED BY THE NEGLIGENCE OF [Firebird and the NHRA] . . . INCLUDING NEGLIGENT RESCUE OPERATIONS[.]" (emphasis added). In addition, the release contains provisions under which Mr. Groves expressly acknowledges that he recognized that the "ACTIVITIES OF THE EVENT(S) ARE VERY DANGEROUS", and assumes "FULL RESPONSIBILITY FOR ANY RISK OF BODILY INJURY[.]" In fact, Mr. Groves acknowledges that "INJURIES RECEIVED MAY BE COMPOUNDED OR INCREASED BY NEGLIGENT RESCUE OPERATIONS." Nevertheless, he agreed to absolve Firebird and the NHRA from all liability. The release is drafted in clear and unambiguous terms.

• • •

B

Mr. Groves contends that the release is unenforceable because it violates public policy. Under Idaho law, contracts that violate public policy are void. Salinas v. Vierstra, 107 Idaho 984, 695 P.2d 369, 375 (Idaho 1985). Express agreements which exempt one party from liability for negligence may violate public policy if: "(1) one party is at an obvious disadvantage in bargaining power; [or] (2) a public duty is involved." Rawlings, 465 P.2d at 111.

Mr. Groves failed to present any evidence to the district court to support the contention that he raises before this court that he was at an obvious disadvantage in bargaining power. The district court's order granting Firebird's motion for summary judgment notes that " the plaintiffs do not contend that Gary Groves, being a person who makes his living building and racing cars, was at an obvious disadvantage in bargaining power when he signed the release." The Supreme Court has instructed that to avoid an adverse ruling on a motion for summary judgment, the nonmovant must "designate 'specific facts showing that there is a genuine issue for trial.'" Celotex Corp. v. Catrett, 477 U.S. 317, 324, 91 L. Ed. 2d 265, 106 S. Ct. 2548 (1986) (quoting Fed. R. Civ. P. 56(e)). Mr. Groves has failed to demonstrate that there is a genuine issue of material fact concerning whether he was at an obvious disadvantage in bargaining power.

Further, the Idaho legislature has not imposed a public duty on persons involved in conducting automobile races. The Rawlings court cited public utilities and common carriers as examples of entities engaged in a "public duty." Rawlings, 465 P.2d at 111. As interpreted by the Idaho Supreme Court, the legislature can create a "public duty." Lee v. Sun Valley Co., 107 Idaho 976, 695 P.2d 361, 363 (Idaho 1984). Under Idaho law, a public duty is created, when:

the legislature has addressed the rights and duties pertaining to personal injuries arising out of the relationship between two groups, i.e., employers/employees, outfitters and guides/participants, and has

granted limited liability to one group in exchange for adherence to specific duties, then such duties become a "public duty" within the exception to the general rule validating exculpatory contracts.

• • •

In summary, Firebird's activities are not similar to the public duties performed by a public utility or a common carrier. Further, the Idaho legislature has not enacted legislation governing the automobile racing industry. Accordingly, the release does not violate Idaho public policy.

III

Mrs. Groves contends that the district court erred in granting Firebird's motion for summary judgment based on its conclusion that the release signed by Mr. Groves precludes her claim for loss of consortium. The district court rejected Mrs. Groves' contentions that a claim for loss of consortium is a separate and independent cause of action. It was also unmoved by her argument that she cannot be bound by a release agreement she did not sign.

• • •

There are no Idaho appellate decisions that address the question whether a release signed by a person subsequently injured by an alleged tortfeasor's negligent conduct also precludes his or her spouse from recovering for loss of consortium. Thus, "in the absence of such express guidance, we must interpret and apply the law as we predict the state's highest court would interpret and apply it." S & R Metals, Inc. v. C. Itoh & Co. (Am.), Inc., 859 F.2d 814, 816 (9th Cir. 1988).

A

• • •

Courts in other states have recognized that although a claim for loss of consortium is "viewed as derivative, and not cognizable unless the defendant is liable to the injured spouse, a loss of consortium cause of action constitutes a separate and distinct cause of action personal to the deprived spouse . . ."

• • •

C

The basis of Mrs. Groves' loss of consortium claim is that Firebird's allegedly tortious conduct caused her harm. The fact that Mr. Groves signed a release does not support a logical inference that Firebird did not commit a tortious act. See Quick v. Crane, 111 Idaho 759, 727 P.2d 1187, 1211 (Idaho 1986) (citations omitted) (the question of liability of a defendant who is a party to a release "is wholly immaterial."). Instead, the release signed by Mr. Groves is a "complete abandonment of [his tort] cause of action." Holve v. Draper, 95 Idaho 193, 505 P.2d 1265, 1267

(Idaho 1973). The Idaho Supreme Court stated in Quick that "[a] release . . . discharges [a] defendant from any possible liability for any tort of which such defendant possibly might have been guilty." Quick, 727 P.2d at 1211-12 (citations omitted). The court noted that "whether [an alleged tortfeasor] was, in fact guilty of tort is immaterial where such defendant does not desire to try out the question and is willing to pay consideration and in good faith secure such release and covenant not to sue." Id. at 1212.

Further, the fact that we have upheld the validity of the release as to Mr. Groves does not resolve the question whether Firebird is responsible to Mrs. Groves for loss of consortium. The release signed by Mr. Groves did not mention Mrs. Groves, nor did it refer in any way to her loss of consortium claim. Because she was not a party to the release and did not receive any consideration for abandoning her own claim, Mrs. Groves is not bound by the release. See Lomas & Nettleton Co. v. Tiger Enters., Inc., 99 Idaho 539, 585 P.2d 949, 952 (Idaho 1978) (a release is a type of contract); Vance v. Connell, 96 Idaho 417, 529 P.2d 1289, 1291 (Idaho 1974) (some consideration is a necessary element to all contracts); see also Karnes v. Quality Pork Processors, 532 N.W.2d 560, 562 (Minn. 1995) ("as with any other contract, a release requires consideration. . . ."); Brown v. Kentucky Lottery Corp., 891 S.W.2d 90, 92 (Ky. Ct. App. 1995) ("it is well established that a release must be supported by valuable consideration.").

• • •

IV

We are persuaded that the Idaho Supreme Court would follow the reasoning of the overwhelming majority of state courts that have addressed this issue and hold that a release executed by a spouse does not bar the other spouse's loss of consortium claim. As noted above, the Idaho Supreme Court has recognized that a spouse has a separate cause of action for loss of consortium. Rindlisbaker, 519 P.2d at 424. We have not found any Idaho Supreme Court decision that would support the conclusion that a spouse's separate cause of action for loss of consortium is within the control of the spouse who was directly injured by a tortfeasor. Such a conclusion would appear to be inconsistent with Idaho cases which recognize that loss of consortium is a separate cause of action.

Further, in Runcorn, 107 Idaho 389, 690 P.2d 324, the Idaho Supreme Court looked to New York law in deciding that the non-physically injured spouse's loss of consortium claim would be reduced by the percent of negligence attributable to the directly injured spouse. 690 P.2d at 329. Accordingly, we believe that the Idaho Supreme Court would likewise look to Champagne, 185 A.D.2d 835, 586 N.Y.S.2d 813, in deciding that a release signed by the directly injured spouse does not bar the other spouse's loss of consortium claim.

The release agreement executed by Mr. Groves bars him from recovering damages in a tort action for the injuries he sustained as the result of Firebird's alleged negligence. Mrs. Groves was not a party to the release agreement. Therefore, the release does not preclude her from pursuing her separate claim against the alleged tortfeasor for loss of consortium.

The summary judgment in favor of Firebird concerning Mr. Groves' negligence action is AFFIRMED. The summary judgment in favor of Firebird dismissing Mrs. Groves' action for loss of consortium is REVERSED and REMANDED.

■ ■ ■ ■

Fundamental Concepts

Requirements for a Valid Waiver

Public Policy. A contract or waiver is not valid if it is against public policy—that is, not in the best interest of the public or opposed to the duty one has to one's fellowman. A waiver is generally against public policy if 1) it pertains to a service important to the public, 2) if the parties are not of equal bargaining power, 3) if there is an employer-employee relationship, or 4) it attempts to preclude liability for extreme forms of conduct such as gross negligence, reckless misconduct, wilful and wanton conduct, or intentional acts. The general rule is that sport-related waivers are not against public policy. A possible exception is when a public school attempts to require students to sign waivers to relieve the school of liability for its negligence.

Clarity of Language. Courts agree that for a waiver to be enforceable, the intent of the document must be clear. The language needs to be clear, explicit, and comprehensible to such a degree that it clearly notifies the signer that the signer is relinquishing the right to pursue legal action against the service provider in the event the signer is injured as a result of the negligence of the service provider.

The following are drawn from court rulings in determining if the agreement was clear. 1) The agreement should state clearly that the agreement releases the service provider from liability for negligence. Use of the word "negligence" is required in only a few states (AK, FL, NJ, NY, TX), however, specific reference to the "negligence" of the service provider is strongly urged in several other states (AR, AZ, CA, DE, NH, ME, MO, WI). Good practice would suggest its use in waivers in all states because its use helps to clarify the question of intent. 2) The format should emphasize the intent of the agreement, i.e., the title should say **waiver** or **release of liability** (not **sign up sheet** or **roster**), the agreement and the exculpatory language should be in easy-to-read type, and the exculpatory language should be conspicuous (bold, caps, underlined, colored). 3) The signer should be given an opportunity to read the document and provided a reader if the person is unable to read. In general, however, the agreement is binding even if the signer fails to read it. Note, however, that failure to provide opportunity to read has caused a waiver to be overturned (*Eder v. Lake Geneva Raceway, Inc.*, 1994). 4) The waiver should be worded carefully to include the activities, circumstances, or situations for which protection is needed.

Consideration.   A valid contract requires that something of value be exchanged between parties. The courts have held that the opportunity to participate constitutes consideration on the part of the service provider. Waivers usually include language such as "In consideration for . . ."

Parties to the Contract.   Three important points relate to the parties involved in an exculpatory agreement. They are capacity to contract (generally relating to age), parties barred from redress, and parties protected by the contract.

The general rule is that a **minor** may disaffirm a contract made by the minor or by a parent on the minor's behalf. However, courts in three states (California, Georgia, and Indiana) have indicated that under some circumstances exculpatory agreements signed by the parent or by the parent and the minor may not be disaffirmed (*Hohe v. San Diego Unified Sch. Dist.*, 1990; *Dekalb County School System v. White*, 1979; *Smoky v. McCray*, 1990; *Huffman v. Monroe County Community School*, 1991). A more effective procedure, when dealing with minors, would be to use an agreement to participate (see Chapter 2.24).

When signing a waiver, the signer is obviously relinquishing the rights of the signer to hold the service provider liable in the event of injury. However, the **spouse or heirs** often file suit against the service provider when the signer is seriously injured or killed. While the law varies by state, the majority of states provide that the loss of consortium or wrongful death claim of the spouse or heirs is derivative upon whether the signer has or would have had a valid claim. A phrase in which the signer relinquishes, on behalf of self, spouse, heirs, estate, and assigns, the right to recover for injury or death is usually included in the waiver and is enforceable in most states.

Finally, the waiver generally specifies the **parties protected** by the agreement. Parties such as the corporation, management, employees, sponsors, and any others meant to be protected should be listed followed by an inclusive phrase such as ". . . and all others who are involved."

Form of the Waiver

Waivers are generally found in one of two forms. They appear as a stand-alone document such as the one in the *Groves v. Firebird Raceway, Inc.* case. They also appear as a part of another document such as a membership agreement, an entry form, a rental agreement, or a team roster. Both forms, the stand-alone waiver and the waiver that is part of another document, can protect the service provider if they are well-written and used with care.

Waivers on Tickets. Waivers or, more accurately, disclaimers of liability are often found on the back on tickets; however, no cases have been found in which the waiver provided the service provider with protection. In many cases, the patron is not even aware of the language on the ticket. In addition, the patron signs no agreement, therefore intent to release the provider from liability is not evident. There is no harm in including such disclaimers on the back of a ticket, but the service provider should operate on the assumption that the statement will not effectively protect the business.

Recent Developments

Negligent Rescue Operations. In a 1982 Wisconsin case (*Arnold v. Shawano*), the Wisconsin Supreme Court ruled that the waiver signed by an injured driver did not protect the track from liability since the injury was caused by negligent rescue operations rather than by risks contemplated by the parties to the waiver. In two recent cases involving auto racing, the wording in the waivers has been broadened to include negligent rescue operations. In *Groves v. Firebird Raceway, Inc.* (1994), the plaintiff alleged inadequate firefighting equipment and a slow response contributed to severe burns. Cadek (*Cadek v. Great Lakes Dragaway, Inc.*, 1994) made similar allegations regarding firefighting equipment charging that the negligence resulted in extensive damage to his vehicle. The courts in each case ruled that the exculpatory language in each document referred specifically to negligent rescue operations and protected the racetracks from liability.

Violation of Equal Protection Claim. A trial court decision in favor of the defendant was overturned by the Supreme Court of Appeals of West Virginia because the court found that the waiver violated the equal protection provisions of the West Virginia Constitution (*Kyriazis v. University of West Virginia*, 1994). The university required students playing rugby to sign a waiver but did not require waivers of students participating in intramural sports or in other club sports. The court ruled that by doing so, the university was treating rugby players differently from players of other sports. This is the first case found in which equal protection violation was the basis for rejecting the waiver.

Enumeration of Risks in the Waiver. An inexperienced rider was injured when she fell from a spooked horse after renting the horse and signing a waiver (*Swierkosz v. Starved Rock Stables*, 1993). She alleged she was inexperienced and unaware of the actions of a horse and the risks of falling. The court supported the waiver saying that plaintiff's inexperience was less of a factor because the risks of riding were specifically listed in the waiver. Waiver language had referred to the unpredictability of the behavior of a horse and to the impact of falls This case serves as evidence of the desirability of enumerating risks in the waiver. In another case, *Maurer v. Cerkvenik-Anderson Travel, Inc.* (1994), the court did not uphold a waiver because the agency failed to disclose material dangers known to the agent. The court stated that the agency had a duty to alert the patron to the specific risks that patron is asked to waive. In *Coughlin v. T.M.H. International Attractions, Inc.* (1995), an inexperienced spelunker died due to the negligence of the tour leader. The court did not uphold the waiver because the waiver failed to adequately warn the novice of the dangers of spelunking.

Need for a Severability Clause. A severability clause is a statement within the waiver which says that if any part of the waiver is held void, this will have no effect upon the validity of the remainder of the waiver. In a 1995 case (*Farina v. Mt. Bachelor, Inc.*), a court ruled that an Oregon waiver was invalid because the court interpreted protection from negligence to include gross negligence and other extreme forms of conduct. Since seeking protection from liability for gross negligence is against public policy in that state and since there was no severability clause in the waiver, the court ruled that the entire waiver was invalid.

Use of the Word "Negligence."   As mentioned earlier, most states do not require the specific reference in the waiver to the "negligence" of the defendant. More states, however, seem to be gravitating toward either requiring the use of the word or toward such strict scrutiny that the word is almost required for validity of the waiver. Texas has broadened its "express negligence doctrine" to include waivers. The doctrine states that the intent of the parties must be expressed in specific terms within the four corners of the contract and expressly list negligence as a claim being relinquished by the buyer (*Rickey v. Houston Health Club, Inc.*, 1993). In New Hampshire, the *Wright v. Loon Mountain Recreation Corp.* (1995) court did not say that the word "negligence" must be used, but emphasized that "the contract must clearly state that the defendant is not responsible for the consequences of his negligence." (p. 5) In addition, in Missouri a court (*Hornbeck v. All American Indoor Sports, Inc.*, 1995) ruled that a waiver must clearly and unambiguously exonerate the defendant from liability for negligence and that general language would not suffice. Another Missouri court (*Alack v. Vic Tanny International of Missouri, Inc.*, 1995) clarified that while the word "negligence" is mandated in indemnity agreements, the same is not true for waivers. However, the court did say that best practice would be to include an explicit reference to the "negligence" of the exculpated party in the agreement.

References

A. Cases

Alack v. Vic Tanny International of Missouri, Inc., 1995 Mo. App. LEXIS 1473.

Arnold v. Shawano, 330 N.W. 2nd 773 (Wis., 1982).

Cadek v. Great Lakes Dragaway, Inc., 843 F. Supp. 420 (Ill., 1994).

Coughlin v. T.M.H. International Attractions, Inc., 1995 U.S. Dist. LEXIS 12499 (Ky).

Dekalb County School System v. White, 260 S.E.2d 853 (Ga., 1979).

Eder v. Lake Geneva Raceway, Inc., 523 N.W.2d 429 (Wis., 1994).

Farina v. Mt. Bachelor, Inc., 66 F.3d 233; U.S. App. LEXIS 26136 (Cal., 1995).

Groves v. Firebird Raceway, Inc., 849 F. Supp. 1385 (Id, 1994).

Hohe v. San Diego Unified Sch. Dist., 274 Cal.Rptr. 647 (1990).

Hornbeck v. All American Indoor Sports, Inc., 898 S.W.2d 717 (Mo.App., 1995); 1995 Mo. App. LEXIS 1001.

Huffman v. Monroe County Community School, 564 N.E.2d 961 (Ind., 1991).

Kyriazis v. University of West Virginia, 450 S.E. 2d 649 (W.V., 1994).

Maurer v. Cerkvenik-Anderson Travel, Inc., 165 Ariz. Adv. Rep. 51 (1994).

Rickey v. Houston Health Club, Inc., 1993 Tex. App. LEXIS 2401.

Smoky, Inc. v. McCray, 396 S.E.2d 794 (Ga., 1990).

Swierkosz v. Starved Rock Stables, 607 N.E. 2d 280 (Ill., 1993).

Wright v. Loon Mountain Recreation Corp., 663 A.2d 1340; 1995 N.H. LEXIS 119 (1995).

B. Publications

Cotten, D. J. Ambiguity as a Factor in the Validity of Exculpatory Agreements, *Journal of Legal Aspects of Sport*, 4 (2) 1994, 7-20.

Cotten, D. J. Effect of Exculpatory Agreement on Minors and Non-Signing Spouses or Heirs, *Journal of Legal Aspects of Sport*, 4 (1) 1994, 66-77.

Cotten, D. J. Effectiveness of Ticket Disclaimers as Exculpatory Instruments, *The Sports, Parks, and Recreation Law Reporter*, Vol 7 (2) Sept., 1993, 17-21.

Cotten, D. J. Analysis of State Laws Governing the Validity of Sport-Related Exculpatory Agreements, *Journal of Legal Aspects of Sport*, 3 (2), 1993, 50-63.

van der Smissen, B. (1990). *Legal Liability and Risk Management for Public and Private Entities*. Cincinnati: Anderson Publishing Co.

2.24

Agreements to Participate

Doyice J. Cotten
Sport Risk Consulting

In today's litigious climate, sport managers should be concerned with limiting liability in the event of an accident. One way of limiting liability is through the use of a document called an *agreement to participate*. The agreement to participate is a document which helps to inform participants of 1) the nature of the activity, 2) the risks to be encountered through participation in the activity, and 3) the behaviors expected of the participant. In the agreement to participate, the participant verifies the assumption of the inherent risks of the activity (van der Smissen, 1990).

The agreement to participate has two major purposes. First, it helps to establish the assumption of risk defense. It is well established that the assumption of risk defense is valid only if 1) the risk was inherent to the activity, 2) the participation was voluntary, and 3) the participant knew, understood, and appreciated the risk (*Riddle v. Universal Sport Camp*, 1990; *Leakas v. Columbia Country Club*, 1993). The agreement to participate provides evidence that the participant was aware of the risks of the activity and that participation was voluntary. The second purpose is to help to establish the contributory negligence defense by showing that the participant knew the expected participant behaviors and agreed to adhere to them.

■ ■ ■ ■

Representative Case

FERARRI v. GRAND CANYON DORIES

Court of Appeal of California, Third Appellate District
32 Cal. App. 4th 248; 1995 Cal. App. LEXIS 116; 38 Cal.
Rptr. 2d 65; 95 Cal. Daily Op. Service 1095; 95 Daily Journal DAR 1927
February 10, 1995, Decided

OPINION:

Plaintiff appeals from a judgment of dismissal following an order granting defendants' motion for summary judgment. Plaintiff's complaint seeks damages for injuries suffered when her head struck the metal frame of a raft during a commercial rafting trip sponsored and conducted by defendants. The trial court concluded plaintiff's negligence claim is barred by the doctrine of primary assumption of risk and her product liability claim fails because defendants supplied a service, not a product. We shall affirm.

I

Plaintiff participated in a five-day commercial raft trip on the Colorado River sponsored and conducted by defendant Grand Canyon Dories, also known as GCD Raft Trips (hereafter GCD). Rubber rafts used on the trip were equipped with metal frames laid across the top of the gunnels and secured by straps. These frames are constructed of metal tubing joined together in the shape of a rectangle which is covered by fabric to form a flat surface on which supplies and equipment may be secured. The frame is positioned in the center of the raft and extends across its entire width and over approximately half its length, leaving room at the front and rear of the raft for passengers. Oar locks are attached to each side of the frame and in the center is a place for a "guide" to sit and row or steer.

Prior to embarking on the trip, plaintiff signed a "release" absolving GCD of responsibility for injuries she might sustain during the trip. Plaintiff was also **given safety instructions. For example, she was told where to sit, that it was necessary to hold onto the raft while navigating rapids and where to hold on, and how to react if thrown out of the raft into the water** [emphasis added].

During the trip, as the raft was approaching a rapids, plaintiff was kneeling in the rear taking photographs. She asked the guide if she could remain in that location and continue taking pictures. He advised she could but admonished her to hold on. Plaintiff held onto the raft with one hand and held the camera with the other. While traversing the rapids, the raft made a "violent movement," causing plaintiff to strike her head on the metal frame several times, resulting in the injuries complained of in this action.

Plaintiff initiated this action against GCD and one of its partners, George Wendt. Also named as defendants are Outdoors Unlimited River Trips and Oars, Inc. Professional River Outfitters, the manufacturer of the metal frame, was added as a Doe defendant but entered into a good faith settlement and was dismissed.

The complaint alleges negligence and product liability. Defendants moved for summary judgment relying on express and implied assumption of risk and the fact they provided a service, not a product. The court granted summary adjudication as to the product liability claim only. Defendants renewed their motion on the negligence claim and the court granted the motion on the basis of implied assumption of risk.

II
• • •

In their motion for summary judgment, defendants argued the type of injury suffered by plaintiff is a risk inherent in white water rafting and hence plaintiff's claim is barred by the doctrine of primary assumption of risk.

In Knight v. Jewett (1992) 3 Cal.4th 296 [11 Cal.Rptr.2d 2, 834 P.2d 696] (Knight) and Ford v. Gouin (1992) 3 Cal.4th 339 [11 Cal.Rptr.2d 30, 834 P.2d 724] (Ford), the court explained primary assumption of risk occurs when a party voluntarily participates in a sporting event or activity involving inherent risks. Such risks include, for example, an errantly thrown ball in baseball or a carelessly extended elbow in basketball. (3 Cal.4th at p. 316.) Primary assumption of risk is merely another way of

saying no duty of care is owed for risks inherent in a given sport or activity. It is a complete bar to recovery. (3 Cal.4th at pp. 314-315.)

The overriding consideration in the application of primary assumption of risk is to avoid imposing a duty which might chill vigorous participation in the implicated activity and thereby alter its fundamental nature. (Knight, supra, 3 Cal.4th at pp. 318-319.) For example, in Ford, the court held the driver of a boat owed no duty to a skier who was injured when his head struck a limb extending over the water. In rejecting the plaintiff's argument that primary assumption of risk should not apply to a cooperative activity such as water-skiing, the court explained: "Even when a water-skier is not involved in a 'competitive' event, the skier has undertaken vigorous athletic activity, and the ski boat driver operates the boat in a manner that is consistent with, and enhances, the excitement and challenge of the active conduct of the sport. Imposition of legal liability on a ski boat driver for ordinary negligence in making too sharp a turn, for example, or in pulling the skier too rapidly or too slowly, likely would have the same kind of undesirable chilling effect on the driver's conduct that the courts in other cases feared would inhibit ordinary conduct in various sports." (Ford, supra, 3 Cal.4th at p. 345.)

In Knight and Ford, the court held negligent conduct of a participant in an active sport is an inherent part of the game. Certain sports have inherent risks which do not involve the want of ordinary care by other participants. Skydiving is an obvious example. In snow skiing, the risk of falling on steep slopes or uneven terrain is an inherent part of the sport. "'Each person who participates in the sport of skiing accepts the dangers that inhere in that sport insofar as the dangers are obvious and necessary. Those dangers include, but are not limited to, injuries which can result from variations in terrain; surface or subsurface snow or ice conditions; bare spots; rocks, trees and other forms of natural growth or debris; collisions with ski lift towers and their components, with other skiers, or with properly marked or plainly visible snow-making or snow-grooming equipment.'" (Danieley v. Goldmine Ski Associates, Inc. (1990) 218 Cal.App.3d 111, 123 [266 Cal.Rptr. 749], quoting from Mich. Stat. Ann., @ 18.483 (22)(2).)

Plaintiff acknowledges that white water rafting has certain inherent risks. For example, violent movement of the raft while traversing rapids can cause the raft to overturn or the occupants to be thrown into the water where they risk striking rocks or even drowning. The risk of being thrown involuntarily about inside the raft and colliding with objects or people therein is also an inherent part of the activity. Rafting trips are generally rated according to the difficulty of the rapids encountered in order that those embarking on a trip may know what to expect.

"[T]he scope of the legal duty owed by a defendant frequently will depend on the defendant's role in, or relationship to, the sport." (Knight, supra, 3 Cal.4th at p. 317.) It is generally recognized commercial operators of recreational activities "have a duty to use due care not to increase the risks to a participant over and above those inherent in the sport. Thus, although a ski resort has no duty to remove moguls from a ski run, it clearly does have a duty to use due care to maintain its towropes in a safe, working condition so as not to expose skiers to an increased risk of harm. The cases establish that the latter type of risk, posed by a ski resort's negligence, clearly is not a risk (inherent in the sport) that is assumed by a participant." (Knight, supra, 3 Cal.4th at pp. 315-316.)

• • •

As the commercial sponsors and operators of the rafting trip, defendants owed plaintiff a duty not to increase the risks inherent in the activity. Plaintiff contends defendants breached this duty in two ways: 1) by permitting her to sit in the back of the raft and take pictures while traversing the rapids; and 2) by using a raft configured with a metal frame superstructure.

Permitting plaintiff to sit in the back of the raft did not increase the risk inherent in the activity. According to the undisputed testimony, passengers normally sit in either the front or rear of the raft. **Plaintiff was instructed before the trip to hold onto the raft while in rapids and was reminded again to hold on** when she was given permission to remain in the back of the raft just before the injury occurred [emphasis added]. To quarrel with the fact plaintiff was not then reminded to hold on with both hands is mere hairsplitting, as plaintiff was already aware holding on with two hands rather than one reduced the risk of injury.

• • •

The judgment is affirmed.

■ ■ ■ ■

Fundamental Concepts and Principles

Participatory Forms

Sport managers often confuse the three commonly used participatory form—waivers, parental permissions, and agreements to participate. Each is important in reducing risk to the corporate entity, but their roles differ greatly. It is important that the sport manager know how the agreement to participate differs from the other forms.

Comparison with a Waiver. The agreement to participate and the waiver are often confused. A waiver is an agreement by which the signer relinquishes his or her right to redress or compensation for injury caused by the negligence of the sport business or its employees. In other words, the signer releases the sport business from liability for its own negligence. However, a waiver is a contract and is subject to the laws of contracts—one of which is that one must be of majority age to be bound by the contract. Thus, waivers, being contracts, are not binding on minors in most states and may be voided at the will of the minor. This is usually true even if the parent signs the waiver (Cotten, 1994). For this reason, the agreement to participate is the agreement of choice when the sport business is attempting to control its exposure to liability when dealing with minor participants.

The agreement to participate, on the other hand, is not a contract. It is simply an agreement by which the participant affirms his or her assumption of the inherent risks of participation in the activity. In establishing that the participant, minor or adult, was aware of the inherent risks of the activity, the assumption of risk defense is strengthened. It should be noted, however, that *an agreement to participate has no effect on liability for injury caused by the negligence of the sport business or its employees.*

The agreement to participate also serves to inform the participant of the conduct to which he or she is expected to adhere. By establishing that the participant was aware of the conduct expected, the contributory negligence defense is strengthened because some of the responsibility for the safety of the participant is transferred to the participant. Whether the state is governed by contributory negligence or comparative negligence, the participant has a duty to protect himself or herself from unreasonable risk of foreseeable harm. If the participant acted negligently by departing from the expected behaviors, any award the participant might be due is subject to either be reduced or barred completely.

Comparison with a Parental Consent Form. The agreement to participate must not be confused with a parental consent or parental permission form. The consent or permission form merely means that the parent agrees to allow the minor to participate in the activity. By having the parent sign the permission form, neither the assumption of risk nor the contributory negligence defense is being strengthened. Furthermore, as with the agreement to participate, neither the parent nor the minor is relinquishing any rights to redress by signing the permission form. While this document might have some public relations value in informing the parent of the activity in which the child will be participating, it has no legal value and provides no protection to the sport business. It can be used, however, to gain permission for emergency medical treatment and to assign financial responsibility for such treatment.

Contents of the Agreement to Participate

There are no "magic phrases" that are either legally required or even universally useful in the construction of agreements to participate. There also is no ironclad format that is required. However, certain information should be in any agreement to participate and the following would serve as a logical order for inclusion.

Section I: Nature of the Activity. It is important that the activity be described in some detail. The description should be specific to the activity and not generic in nature. It should include a description of what the activity is like remembering that the less familiar the participant is with the activity, the more detail required in the description. Include negative or unpleasurable aspects that the participant should expect, how much physical stress is involved, and the intensity level of the activity. A general introductory statement pointing out that "Every sport has certain inherent risks and regardless of the precautions taken, it is impossible to ensure the safety of the participant" might serve as an effective way to begin the section.

Section II: Possible Consequences of Injury. Two areas should be covered in this section. First, the participant should be made aware of the types of accidents that may occur in the specific sport involved. Here one should list some insignificant accidents that are common to the sport (being struck by the ball in racquetball), as well as some serious accidents that occur occasionally (falling and striking one's head on the floor in racquetball). Second, include some of the injuries that can occur in the sport. List some minor injuries that are common to the sport (i.e., bruises, strains, sprains in racquetball), some more serious injuries (i.e., loss of vision, broken bones, concussions), as well as catastrophic injuries (i.e., paralysis and death). Use phrases such as "some of the. . . ," "injuries such as. . . ," and "including, but not limited to . . ." in listing both accidents and injuries. It is critical that the accidents and injuries be specific to the sport for which the agreement applies, thus generic agreements to participate would not be effective.

Section III: Behavioral Expectations of the Participant. The major purpose of this section is to transfer some of the responsibility for the participant's safety from the sport business to the participant. One might list on the agreement to participate several very important rules to which the participant is expected to adhere. An example in racquetball might be that participants are required to wear eye protection at all times. If there are few rules, they might be listed on the front of the agreement. If there are numerous rules, the participant might be referred to the back of the sheet where they are listed. In either case, giving the participant a copy of these rules would be desirable. Once again, the list should not be made all-inclusive. "Some of the rules which the participant agrees to follow" is one example of phraseology that could be used.

Figure 1

Agreement to Participate in *Racquetball*

(Substitute Information Appropriate to other Sports for Italicized Sections)

Participation in all sports and physical activities involves certain inherent risks and regardless of the care taken, it is impossible to ensure the safety of the participant. *Racquetball* is an activity requiring *considerable coordination, agility, and a high level of cardiovascular fitness.* It involves *vigorous activity for as long as an hour or more, many quick bursts of speed, and being alert to fast moving objects in a confined space.* While it is a reasonably safe sport as long as safety guidelines are followed, some elements of risks cannot be eliminated from the activity.

A variety of injuries may occur to a *racquetball* participant. Some examples of those injuries are:
1. Minor injuries such as *scrapes, bruises, strains, and sprains*;
2. More serious injuries such as *broken bones, cuts, concussions, and eye injuries (including loss of vision)*;
3. Catastrophic injuries such as *heart attacks, paralysis, and death.*

These, and other injuries, sometime occur in racquetball as a result of hazards or accidents such as *slips, being struck by a ball, being struck by a racket, colliding with another player, colliding with the wall, falling to the floor, or excessive stress placed on the cardiovascular system.*

To help reduce the likelihood of injury to yourself and to other participants, participants are expected to follow the following rules:
1. *All participants are expected to wear proper footwear.*
2. *All participants are expected to keep the racquet strap around the wrist during play.*
3. *All participants are expected to wear protective eyewear during play.*
4. *All participants are expected to avoid swinging when it might endanger another player.*
5. *All participants are expected to follow all posted safety rules as well as those associated with the rules of racquetball.*

I agree to follow the preceding safety rules, all posted safety rules, and all rules common to the sport of *racquetball.* Further, I agree to report any unsafe practices, conditions, or equipment to the management.

I certify that 1) I possess a sufficient degree of physical fitness to safely participate in *racquetball*, 2) I understand that I am to discontinue activity at any time I feel undue discomfort or stress, and 3) I will indicate below any health-related conditions that might affect my ability to play *racquetball* and I will verbally inform activity management immediately.

Circle: Diabetes   Heart Problems   Seizures   Asthma   Other _____

I have read the preceding information and it has been explained to me. I know, understand, and appreciate the risks associated with participation in *racquetball* and I am voluntarily participating in the activity. In doing so, I am assuming all of the inherent risks of the sport. I further understand that in the event of a medical emergency, *management will call EMS to render assistance and that I will be financially responsible for any expenses involved.*

Signature of Participant	Date	Signature of Parent	Date

WAIVER OF LIABILITY: In consideration of being permitted to play *racquetball,* on behalf of myself, my family, my heirs, and my assigns, I hereby release the *sport business* from liability for injury, loss, or death to myself, while *using the facility or in any way associated with participating in the activity of racquetball* now or in the future, resulting from the ordinary negligence of the *sport business*, its agents, or employees.

Signature of Participant	Date

Section IV: Condition of the Participant. The participant should affirm that he or she possesses the physical condition and required competencies to participate in the activity safely. The required level, which will vary with the activity, should be described in Section I of the agreement. The participant will also affirm that the participant has no physical conditions that would preclude participation in the activity and will identify any conditions of which the sport business should be aware (i.e., heart problems, seizures, asthma). Particularly for vigorous activities, a statement that the participant can discontinue the activity if undue discomfort or stress occur should be included. Participant affirmation of condition is generally adequate for activities such as 5K runs, health club memberships, and between-inning promotions at baseball games. Other situations might require more confirmation of condition. For example, residential camps usually require health histories and schools generally demand pre-participatory physical exams prior to varsity competition.

Section V: Concluding Statement. This concluding section should contain several items. A statement by which the participant affirms knowledge, understanding, and appreciation of the inherent risks of the activity should be included. The participant should also affirm that participation is voluntary, if that is the case. A third item that may be included is an assumption of risk statement. A fourth area that can be covered in the concluding paragraph is notice of the procedures to be followed in the event of an emergency and the financial responsibility of the participant for emergency actions. Insurance requirements can also be specified here. Finally, a space for the signature of the participant and the parent (if the participant is a minor) should be at the bottom of the agreement. The critical signature is that of the minor, however the parent's signature is important for public relations purposes.

Section VI: Exculpatory Clause. This is an optional section which may be used with agreements to participate that are meant for adults. If an exculpatory clause is included, it should be carefully worded to release the sport business from liability for injury caused by the negligence of the sport business or its employees (see Chapter 2.23 Waivers). This section should follow the signature section of the agreement to participate and provide space for a second signature by the participant relating specifically to the exculpatory clause.

While noted earlier that there is no particular format or wording dictated by law, a sample format including the critical information is given in Figure 1. All information in italics is specific to racquetball. The agreement preparer can substitute information specific to other activities when using this format as a guide.

Using the Agreement to Participate

Some guidelines regarding the use of the agreement to participate can help to insure the effectiveness of the agreement in strengthening the assumption of risk and the contributory negligence defenses. First, presentation of the agreement should be accompanied by a verbal explanation of the risks participants will encounter through participation and of their responsibility for their own safety. Second, it is important to provide an opportunity for the signer to ask questions and gain clarification. Third, stress the participant's duty to inform you of any dangerous practices, hazardous conditions, or faulty equipment of which they may become aware while participating. This, however, in no way reduces or relieves the sport business of its duty to inspect the facility, examine the equipment, or supervise the activity. In addition, the language used in both the agreement and the verbal explanation should be appropriate to the age and maturity of the participant.

Finally, keep in mind that the agreement to participate can serve as important evidence in the event of a lawsuit. These records should be safely stored so that they may be retrieved when needed. The time during a which a person may file a timely suit varies from one to four years after the injury, depending upon the state. However, keep in mind that a minor who is injured can generally file a suit until one to four years after reaching the age of majority. So in the event of an injury, it would be helpful to make and carefully store a file on that individual which would include the agreement to participate along with all other pertinent documentation (i.e., accident report, written statements by witnesses, parental permission slips).

Recent Developments

The major recent development in this area is that the courts are increasingly calling upon the service provider to warn the participant of the inherent risks of the activity. In recent cases involving such activities as spelunking, travel tours, skiing, and horseback riding, the courts have stressed the need to warn participants of the inherent risks of the activity (*Coughlin v. T.M.H. International Attractions, Inc.*, 1995; *Maurer v. Cerkvenik-Anderson Travel, Inc.*, 1994; *McBride v. Minstar, Inc.*, 1994; *McGuire v. Sunday River Skiway Corp.*, 1994; *Swierkosz v. Starved Rock Stables*, 1993). The use of an agreement to participate or the inclusion of the same information within a waiver will help service providers effectively meet this requirement.

References

A. Cases

Coughlin v. T.M.H. International Attractions, Inc., 1995 U.S. Dist. LEXIS 12499 (Ky).

Leakas v. Columbia Country Club, 831 F. Supp. 1231 (Md., 1993).

Maurer v. Cerkvenik-Anderson Travel, Inc., 890 F.2d 69; 1994 Ariz. App. LEXIS 105; 165 Ariz Adv. Rep. 51.

McBride v. Minstar, Inc., 283 N.J.Super. 471 (1994).

McGuire v. Sunday River Skiway Corp., 1994 U.S. Dist. LEXIS 13061.

Riddle v. Universal Sport Camp, 785 P.2d 641 (Kan., 1990).

Swierkosz v. Starved Rock Stables, 607 N.E.2d 280 (Ill., 1993).

B. Publications

Cotten, D. J. (1992). 'What am I Getting Myself Into?' Agreements to Participate, *Strategies* 5: (4) p. 13-16.

Cotten, D.J. (1994). Effect of Exculpatory Agreements on Minors and Non-signing Spouses or Heirs, *Journal of Legal Aspects of Sport*, 4(1), pp. 66-77.

van der Smissen, B. (1990). *Legal Liability and Risk Management for Public and Private Entities*. Cincinnati: Anderson Publishing.

2.31

Emergency Care

Ralph Hall • Ron Kanoy
Appalachian State University

The term "emergency care" encompasses a broad span of situations where health care is provided to an injured person. This chapter will focus on the rendering of emergency medical care to persons injured while participating in organized sport programs. It is essential that managers who oversee these programs develop a plan for rendering emergency care. The degree to which sport managers plan for occurrences which require emergency care may well determine whether or not they and the organization for which they work will ultimately be found liable for negligence in providing such care.

In planning for emergency care the sport manager must understand the extent of the duty to provide emergency care and to whom the duty extends. It is in the planning stage that attention must be given to the who, what, when and how questions of emergency care and to consider the appropriate answers. Who should give emergency care? What should be done? When should it be given? How should it be done? Once a plan is developed to provide emergency services, then it is essential that all personnel understand the plan and their role in its implementation. Finally it is critical that the sport manager ensure that the steps in the plan are rehearsed and enforced.

■ ■ ■ ■

Representative Case

WELCH v. DUNSMUIR JOINT UNION HIGH SCHOOL DISTRICT

District Court of Appeal, Third District, California
326 P.2d 633
June 9, 1958

OPINION:

Anthony L. Welch, a minor, brought this action through his guardian ad litem against the defendant Dunsmuir Joint Union High School District to recover damages for personal injuries received while participating in a high school football scrimmage between the Dunsmuir High School team and the Enterprise High School team on September 10, 1955. The jury returned a verdict in favor of the plaintiff in the sum of $325,000, and judgment was entered thereon with interest at the rate of seven percent per annum.

• • •

A few days prior to September 10, the respective coaches of the schools arranged for an inter-school scrimmage between the two teams on that date at Tiger Field in Redding. Prior to the opening of school on August 29, plaintiff was given a physical examination by a Doctor

Reynolds and found to be physically fit. The coaches were on the field directing or supervising the play and there were no "game officials" there. The teams alternated in carrying the ball, and after each sequence of plays the coaches stopped the activity and instructed the players. No downs were called and no score was kept. Plaintiff was a T-formation quarterback and directed the play of his team while they were on offense. Plaintiff took the ball on a "quarterback sneak" and was tackled shortly after he went through the line. As he was falling forward another player was coming in to make the tackle and fell on top of him. After this play plaintiff was lying on his back on the field and unable to get to his feet. Coach Reginato of the Dunsmuir school suspected that plaintiff might have a neck injury and had him take hold of his hands to see if there was any grip in them. Plaintiff was able to move his hands at that time.

The evidence was conflicting as to whether or not Doctor Saylor, who was admittedly present at the scrimmage, examined plaintiff before he was moved to the sidelines. Franklin Barr, a member of the Dunsmuir team, testified on plaintiff's behalf that Doctor Saylor was from 20 to 25 yards away when plaintiff was injured but did not go over to see him until after he had been removed from the place of injury. Thereupon Johnson, another member of the team, testified on plaintiff's behalf that he did not see the doctor on the field. Barr testified further that he assisted in carrying plaintiff from the field; that he was moved by eight boys, four on each side; and that no one directed the moving. Other witnesses testified that Doctor Saylor came out to the boy immediately after the accident. It was not claimed that the doctor was an agent or employee of the defendant.

The undisputed and only medical testimony was that the plaintiff is a permanent quadriplegic caused by damage to the spinal cord at the level of the fifth cervical vertebra; that there was a fracture of this vertebra without significant displacement; that the fracture was the result of severe trauma; that the removal of the plaintiff from the field without the use of a stretcher was an improper medical practice in view of the symptoms. In answer to the question: "Doctor, in determining just exactly what did damage to the spinal cord, is movement of the fingers, hands and feet the most significant thing?" he testified, "Actually far more important than any kind of examination that one can make of the local injury. This follows from what I have previously said about the fact that the level of injury precludes, if it is complete, the movement of the hands and feet in any effective fashion. If the injury has already been sustained and if the individual can, following the injury, move the hands and feet, he should continue to be able to move the hands and feet." It appears that

after the plaintiff was moved off the field to the sidelines he was unable to move his hands, fingers and feet. With these circumstances in mind the doctor testified it was his opinion that the plaintiff must have sustained additional damage to the spinal cord after being tackled. The doctor's testimony stands undisputed in the record.

• • •

Defendant contends that the court erred in giving certain instructions at plaintiff's request and in failing to give certain instructions proposed by defendant.

• • •

Defendant contends next that the court erred prejudicially in giving an instruction in the language of BAJI 102-D as follows: "Because of the great danger involved in moving an injured human being a person of ordinary prudence will exercise extreme caution when engaged in such an activity. Hence it is the duty of anyone managing or participating in such an activity to exercise extreme caution." Defendant claims that the giving of this instruction was prejudicial for the reason that it set up a false standard of conduct and placed upon the defendant a burden that is not consistent with the existing law. We do not agree with defendant. In this case it appears that the challenged instruction, read with the other instructions, correctly informed the jury that the standard of care required of the defendant was that of ordinary care under the circumstances. Tucker v. Lombardo, 47 Cal.2d 457, 303 P.2d 1041; Jensen v. Minard, 44 Cal.2d 325, 282 P.2d 7, Immediately preceding this instruction the court gave the following instruction:

> Inasmuch as the amount of caution used by the ordinarily prudent person varies in direct proportion to the danger known to be involved in his undertaking, it follows that in the exercise of ordinary care, the amount of caution required will vary in accordance with the nature of the act and the surrounding circumstances.

> To put the matter in another way, the amount of caution involved in the exercise of ordinary care, and hence required by law, increases or decreases as does the danger that reasonably should be apprehended. (BAJI 102-A.)

The standard was still one of ordinary care, that is, of a person of ordinary prudence, where the factual situation shows that great danger was involved in the activity. There was evidence in the case that the moving of a person with suspected grave injuries is inherently a hazardous activity.

We find no merit in the defendant's contention that the court erred in failing to give the following two proposed instructions:

1. If you find that Dr. Saylor attended the plaintiff after the accident and before the plaintiff was moved from the place where he was injured: then, in that event, I instruct you that the responsibility of the coach to render first aid ended when the doctor's responsibility began.
2. I instruct you that the evidence in this case did not establish that Dr. Saylor was an agent, servant or employee of the Dunsmuir Joint Union High School District and if you find that the doctor was negligent, such negligence is not chargeable to the defendant.

The first of the above refused instructions is taken substantially from the Red Cross textbook which says: "The responsibilities of the first aider stop when the physician's begin. First aid tells what to do until the doctor comes." It is claimed that the instruction would have given the jury a measuring stick by which they could have determined when the responsibility of the coach would have ended and the responsibility of the doctor would have commenced. The second instruction was proposed on the theory that the doctor alone was negligent. In lieu thereof the court gave the following instruction which the defendant claims was prejudicial:

When the negligent acts or omissions of two or more persons, whether committed independently or in the course of jointly directed conduct, contribute concurrently and as proximate causes to the injury of another, each of such persons is liable. This is true regardless of the relative degree of the contribution. It is no defense for one of such persons that some other person, not joined as a defendant in the action, participated in causing the injury even if it should appear to you that the negligence of that other person was greater in either its wrongful nature or its effect. (BAJI 104-B)

Under the evidence in this case the jury could reasonably have inferred that both the doctor and the coach were negligent in the removal of the plaintiff from the field to the sidelines; the coach in failing to wait for the doctor and allowing plaintiff to be moved, and the doctor in failing to act promptly after plaintiff's injury. Therefore, the court properly gave the above instruction and properly refused defendant's proposed instruction. See Palmer v. Brown, 127 Cal.App.2d 44, 62, 273 P.2d 306. Further there was no pleading and no evidence introduced on the issue of Doctor Saylor's agency. An instruction should be given only where it is applicable to the issues raised by the pleadings or is pertinent to some issue or theory developed by the evidence. Leo V. Dunham.

• • •

The purported appeal from the order denying defendant's motion for a new trial is dismissed. The judgment is affirmed.

■ ■ ■ ■

Fundamental Concepts

Duty and Liability Related to Emergency Care

As was discussed under negligence theory (see Chapter 2.11), to be liable, a sport manager must owe a duty to the injured party, the duty to provide care must be breached, and the breach must be the proximate cause of the damage. Whether the law will impose a duty to provide emergency care depends on factors inherent in the situation, such as the risk of conducting the activity, the foreseeability of the injury, the social utility of the activity versus the likelihood of injury, and the magnitude of the burden on the sport manager to provide the emergency care.

In addition, there may be statutory regulations which require that emergency care be provided and which define the extent of that duty. Sharp has stated that administrators have two primary responsibilities when providing for emergency care of injuries: 1) they must be sure all personnel who have teaching or coaching assignments are competent in the administering of emergency first aid and CPR procedures, and 2) they must be concerned with the development of emergency procedures for timely medical assistance and adherence to those procedures. (Sharp, 1990). Who will be providing the emergency care? Must the organization have a certified athletic trainer? Must the coaches be certified in CPR and first aid?

The sport manager should consult the statutes in the state of employment and the requirements or recommendations of state governmental agencies and professional associations for help in answering these questions. States vary greatly in their regulations requiring personnel to hold certificates in first-aid and CPR, requiring sport facilities to have certain equipment such as stretchers and oxygen tanks, requiring medical personnel to be present at athletic practices and games (van der Smissen, part C, 1990). Two other sources of requirements or standards for the sport manager are state governmental agencies and professional associations. Finally, the duty of the sport manager will depend on the relationship between the parties, whether it be coach to player, manager of a sports arena to the spectators and participants, recreation park director to the participants in the park's programs or other relationships.

A 1994 case addressing the duty of facility owners to provide emergency medical care at a concert was remanded for a new trial. In the trial, an expert witness testified that sports or entertainment facilities could expect to experience one medical emergency per hour for every 10,000-20,000 patrons in attendance (*Leane v. The Joseph Entertainment Group*, 1994).

One who has a duty must recognize the signs and symptoms of emergencies and react to them. One must understand what action is required and the importance of immediate action. In *Barth by Barth v. Board of Education* (1986), the court found willful and wanton misconduct on the part of a school staff in failing to obtain prompt medical treatment for a student injured in a physical education class. In this case, the injured student was taken for treatment approximately one and one-half hours after the injury occurred even though the student was experiencing headaches, nausea, vomiting, weakness, blurred vision, and a hospital and ambulance service were located directly across the street from the school. Testimony by doctors revealed that the delay in treatment allowed a hematoma to grow from the size of a walnut to the size of an orange, resulting in impaired intellectual function, headaches, and weakness in the left side of the body. Another relevant case is the *Jarreau* case discussed in Recent Developments at the end of this chapter.

It is important to understand that the duty to provide emergency care encompasses not only the rendering of care once the injury has occurred but also the preparation for emergency care prior to the conducting of the activity in which the accident occurs. A sport manager may do everything humanly possible under the circumstances of the moment to provide care to an injured participant in a sporting event but unless there has been adequate planning for the emergency situation and the appropriate training of personnel to carry out the plan, the standard of care required may not have been met. That is, the ultimate finding of liability may be the result of inadequate planning, administration, and supervision of the emergency care program.

Planning for Emergency Care

It is critical that a sport manager plan for appropriate care in the event of injury. While some jurisdictions find that there is no duty to prepare beforehand for medical emergencies (*Applebaum v. Nemon,* 1984), most jurisdictions support a duty to prepare for emergency care before emergencies occur (van der Smissen, 1990). The injured party to whom a duty is owed may be a participant in the activity, a spectator, or member of the staff. An emergency plan must be tailored to the kind of organization being managed. A plan need not be complex but must be carefully prepared to ensure that all critical elements are included. It should be reviewed regularly and updated as needed. An effective plan should include: assessment, personnel, emergency plan review, and consent.

Assessment. Planning starts with an assessment of the risk of the activity, the potential dangers, and the type of injuries to which an emergency response must be made. Although it may not be possible to anticipate (foresee) all types of accidents which result in injury requiring a response, it is important for the sport manager to be as thorough as possible at the initial stage of the planning process in identifying the risks of the activity. Assessment serves as a foundation for a comprehensively planned program of emergency care. It is also at this stage that the sport manager must make risk management decisions as to the extent and degree the organization can or cannot afford to shoulder the financial burden of a comprehensive emergency care program.

Personnel.   All sport-related programs, whether health club, professional team, ski resort, or school athletic program, need personnel who are trained and qualified to administer emergency care. Facility operators and those sponsoring mass gatherings have a duty to provide reasonable response to life-threatening situations. Further, this duty exists regardless of the training of personnel, thus prudent administrators will insure that their personnel are adequately trained for emergency care (van der Smissen, 1990).

A successful school sports program should have well-trained individuals filling every needed position. The team approach in providing emergency care to both participants and spectators consists of physicians, certified athletic trainers, coaches, student trainers, health services staff (colleges and universities), and Emergency Medical Technicians (EMTs) provided by the local emergency medical services system.

Whether the team physician is community based or an employee, such as with a university, all medical decisions should rest with that physician. Beginning with the pre-season physical examination of the athlete, the physician should also be involved with on-site medical attention to the injured athlete, medical treatment subsequent to injury, and return-to-play decisions (Gallup, 1995).

The best approach for the health and welfare of the athletes is for the school to provide a team physician who attends as many practices as possible and who is present on the sidelines for events. In the absence of a physician, emergency care decisions must be made by trainers, coaches, or EMTs. Because of special skills and training, doctors, trainers and physical therapists are held to a higher standard of care in the treatment of the sick and injured (Schubert, 1986).

The National Athletic Trainers Association (NATA), through its certification process, prepares trainers to meet the needs of athletes ranging from the public schools through the professional ranks. Through their preparation and experience, athletic trainers can provide the highest quality professional care to athletes. States providing licensure for athletic trainers are Alabama, Arkansas, Delaware, Florida, Georgia, Illinois, Iowa, Maine, Massachusetts, Mississippi, Nebraska, New Mexico, North Dakota, Ohio, Oklahoma, Rhode Island, South Dakota, Texas (McMullan, 1996).

College athletic training staffs usually consist of the head trainer, possibly one or more assistants, and several student trainers who plan to make athletic training their chosen profession. Since all sports practices and events need emergency care coverage of some type, the student trainer often performs in the absence of a full-time trainer. However, serious liability problems arise when uncertified students act without proper supervision. In practice, many schools fail to have a trainer present at every practice or game, in which case the duty of the trainer falls upon the coach. Coaches have a duty to supervise their athletes and should be required to be certified in CPR and first aid so that they will be better able to perform emergency care procedures in the absence of a trainer. Situations in which coaches handle the athletic training also present significant liability concerns. Although not trained to the level of a trainer, the coach has a duty to use reasonable care in providing care to the injured athlete. This duty includes arranging for medical treatment whenever necessary.

All sport-related businesses and organizations will reduce their exposure to legal liability by having well-trained and qualified personnel to provide emergency care. Some sport businesses such as ski slope providers have certifications specific to their area (e.g., National Ski Patrol System) and should employ only those with appropriate certification. Other businesses, such as spas and health clubs, may have no certifications specific to that particular business, but should employ those with EMT credentials, NATA certification, American Heart Association CPR, American Red Cross CPR or from similar respected certification programs. The sport manager must consult with state statutes in order to make astute professional judgments in determining the credentials and expertise needed by the personnel in the organization.

Emergency Plan Review.   To insure that the emergency care plan is functioning effectively, it should be reviewed by all personnel on a regular basis. This review should include an analysis of any incidents and suggestions for improvement in procedures.

Consent for Emergency Care. Consent for emergency care should be obtained prior to any athletic participation. If the participant is a minor, parental consent should be obtained. The sport manager should check the state statutes regarding regulations governing parental consent. A system is needed to maintain records of written consent forms which allows for regular review and immediate retrieval when needed. Coaches or trainers should take copies of athletes' consent forms on road trips.

Record Keeping

It is important that sport businesses collect and keep records relating to emergency care of injuries. This is important regardless of the type of sport business involved. Schools probably use more types of records relating to injury than most organizations. Some of these include:

1. medical history
2. pre-participation physical examination form
3. consent for treatment
4. injury/accident report
5. physician referral
6. diagnosis and prescribed treatment from physician
7. daily treatment log maintained by trainer
8. daily notification to coaches by trainer

In the event of an accident, care should be taken to store these records until the statute of limitations expires—one to four years depending upon the state. When the injured party is a minor, the statute of limitations begins when the minor reaches the age of majority.

Good Samaritan Laws

All 50 states and the District of Columbia have enacted "Good Samaritan" statutes. Some states apply the statute to all citizens who otherwise owe no duty to act. Other states limit the applicability of the statute to certain classes of persons (e.g., health care personnel) and to certain circumstances. It should be noted that "persons owing a duty because of a professional relationship should not presume they can use the Good Samaritan laws for limited liability or immunity" (van der Smissen, part C, p. 103.)

Recent Developments

Duty of Emergency Care

In a 1993 Pennsylvania case (*Kleinknecht v. Gettysburg*), a lacrosse player collapsed and died of cardiac arrest during a practice session under the supervision of the lacrosse coach. The United States Court of Appeals, Third Circuit, ruled that a college owed a student lacrosse player a duty of reasonable care based on the theory a special relationship existed between the college and the lacrosse player by virtue of his status as a member of an intercollegiate athletic team. In this case, the Court limited its finding of a **duty based on the special relationship** to intercollegiate athletes as a class of persons to whom a duty is owed. The court also found a **duty based on the theory of foreseeability**. The court distinguished the foreseeability that determines a duty of care as opposed to proximate cause stating that foreseeability in the former means the likelihood of the occurrence of a general type of risk where in the latter it means the likelihood of occurrence of the precise chain of events leading to the injury. The court recognized, as a matter of law, that under the facts of this case, a supervised practice, the college owed a duty to the lacrosse players to provide prompt treatment in the event they suffered a life-threatening injury.

In Pennsylvania, the **Good Samaritan law** provides immunity to persons rendering emergency care if they are holders of certificates showing that they have completed training in first-aid and basic life support. The court found that "persons "in the law applied only to natural persons, thus did not provide immunity to the college.

Failure to Obtain Prompt Medical Attention

In *Jarreau v. Orleans Parish School Board* (1992), the court found a school board vicariously liable for a high school coach's and team trainer's negligence in failing to immediately refer an injured player for medical treatment. In this case the football player fractured his wrist during a game and the coach continued to play the student even though the player continued to experience swelling and pain. Only at the end of the season did the trainer refer the player for treatment by a physician. The court stated that coaches are not expected to diagnose the extent of the injury, but "should recognize their limitations in this regard and seek expert medical advice for their players in the face of continuing complaints involving pain and swelling" (p. 1393). Plaintiffs also alleged, and the trial court found, that the school board was negligent for failing to train the coaches to diagnose injuries and for failure to have a physician present. Since, the appellate court had already found the school board vicariously liable for the acts of its employees, it did not address these issues.

References

A. Cases
Applebaum v. Nemon, 678 S.W.2d 533 (Texas, 1984).
Barth by Barth v. Board of Education, 490 N.E.2d 77 (Ill.App.1Dist. 1986).
Jarreau v. Orleans Parish School Board, 600 So.2d 1389 (La. 1992).
Leane v. The Joseph Entertainment Group, 642 N.E.2d 852 (Ill., 1994).
Kleinknecht v. Gettysburg College, 786 F.Supp 449 (M.D.Pa. 1992), rev'd, 989 F.2d 1360 (3rd Cir. 1993).
Mogabgab v. Orleans Parish School Board, 239 So.2d 456 (La.App. 1970).
Stineman v. Fontbonne College, 664 F.2d 1082 (8th Cir. 1981).
Welch v. Dunsmuir, 326 P.2d 633 (Cal.App. 1958).

B. Publications
Gallup, E. (1995). *Law and the Team Physician*. Champaign, Ill.: Human Kinetics.
McMullan, D. (1996). New Law Targets Respect for Athletic Trainers and Restraints on Imitators. *NATA News*, February, p.4.
Schubert, G., Smith, R. & Trentadue, J. (1986). *Sports Law*. St. Paul, Minn.: West Publishing Co.
Sharp, L. (1990). Sport Law. NOLPE.
van der Smissen, B. (1990). *Legal Liability and Risk Management for Public and Private Entities*. Cincinnati: Anderson Publishing Co.
Wong, G. (1994). *Essentials of Amateur Sports Law*. Westport, Conn.: Praeger.

Supervision

Lynne P. Gaskin
State University of West Georgia

Supervision is a broad term denoting responsibility for an area and for the programs that take place in that area (Kaiser, 1986). When individuals are injured while participating in sporting activities and negligence is alleged, most such suits involve questions about supervision. In fact, van der Smissen (1990) estimated that approximately 80 percent of all negligence suits involve allegations of lack of supervision or improper supervision.

Even though most case law involving allegations of improper supervision comes from the school setting, the legal concepts and principles presented in this chapter also apply to the broad area of sport management. Program sponsors (schools, colleges and universities, municipalities, public and private agencies, and sport-related businesses) are expected to exercise due care to prevent unreasonable risk of harm to participants, spectators, or others on the premises.

■ ■ ■ ■

Representative Case

BRAHATCEK v. MILLARD SCHOOL DISTRICT, SCHOOL DISTRICT #17

Supreme Court of Nebraska
202 Neb. 86; 273 N.W.2d 680
January 10, 1979, Filed

OPINION:

This is a wrongful death action brought by Darlene Brahatcek as administratrix of the estate of her son, David Wayne Brahatcek, hereinafter called David, against Millard School District No. 17. David died as a result of being accidentally struck in the left occipital region of his skull by a golf club during a physical education class. Trial was had to the court. The District Judge entered judgment in favor of the plaintiff in the amount of $3,570.06 special damages, $50,000 general damages, and costs. Defendant appeals.

Defendant essentially alleges four assignments of error: (1) The insufficiency of the evidence; (2) the failure

to find decedent contributorily negligent; (3) the failure to hold the negligence of the classmate who struck decedent was an intervening cause of death; and (4) the award of general damages was excessive. We affirm.

David, who was a ninth grade student 14 years of age, was injured on April 3, 1974, during a physical education class conducted in the gymnasium of Millard Central Junior High School. He was struck by a golf club swung by a fellow student, Mark Kreie. He was rendered unconscious and died 2 days later without regaining consciousness.

Mandatory golf instruction during physical education classes at the school began on Monday, April 1, 1974. Because decedent was absent from school on that day, his first exposure to the program was when his class next met on Wednesday, the day of the accident. Classes on both dates were conducted in the school gymnasium because of inclement weather. Instruction was coeducational. Decedent's class of 34 boys combined with a girls' physical education class having an enrollment of 23. Two teachers, one male and one female, were responsible for providing supervision and instruction. The faculty members present on Monday were Max Kurtz and Vickie Beveridge, at that time Vickie Lindgren.

On Monday, after attendance was taken, the students were gathered around in a semicircle and received instruction on the golf grip, stance, swing, etiquette, and safety. Mr. Kurtz then explained to them the procedure that would be followed in the gym.

• • •

Approximately 12 mats were placed across the width of the gym, in two rows of six each. One row of mats was located in the south half of the gym about even with the free throw line on the basketball court. The other row was placed along the free throw line in the north half of the gym. . . . A golf club and three or four plastic "wiffle" balls were placed by each mat.

The students were divided into groups of four or five students and each group was assigned to the use of one of the mats. The boys used the mats on the south side of the gym and hit in a southerly direction. The girls used the mats on the north, and hit the golf balls in a northerly direction. At the start of the class all of the students were to sit along the center line of the basketball court between the two rows of mats. On the signal of one of the instructors one student from each group would go up to the assigned mat, tee up a ball, and wait for the signal to begin. After the student had hit all of the balls on the mat he was to lay the club down and return to the center of the gym. When all of the students were back at the center line, the next student in each group was directed to retrieve the balls and the procedure was repeated.

Mr. Kurtz was not present for class on Wednesday, the day of the accident, because his wife had just given birth to a baby. His place was taken by a student teacher, Tim Haley, who had been at the school for approximately 5 weeks and had assisted with four to six golf classes on Monday and Tuesday. At the beginning of the class on Wednesday, Mrs. Beveridge repeated the instructions which had been given by Mr. Kurtz on Monday. The groups were again divided. One student went up to each mat and Mrs. Beveridge testified she gave the signal for the first balls to be hit.

Plaintiff's decedent, who prior to the date of his death had never had a golf club in his hands, was either the second or third student to go up to the easternmost mat on the boys' side of the gym. He had difficulty and asked his group if anyone could help him. Mark Kreie, who had been the last to use the club, came forward and showed decedent how to grip the club and told him that he (Kreie) would take two practice swings then hit the ball. Decedent moved to the east and stood against the folded up bleachers about 10 feet to the rear of Kreie. Kreie looked over his shoulder to observe decedent before taking two practice swings. He then stepped up to the ball and took a full swing at it. Unaware that decedent had moved closer, he hit decedent with the club on the follow-through. During all of this time, Mr. Haley was helping another boy a few mats away. Mark did not know whether Mr. Haley saw decedent and him standing together at the mat. Mrs. Beveridge was positioned along the west end of the girls' line.

• • •

Mrs. Beveridge testified she was in charge of the entire class on Wednesday but after telling the students when they could hit the ball, she concentrated on the girls. At the time of the accident she was standing on the west side of the gym, between the center line and the row of girls' mats. She testified that had she seen Mr. Haley devoting all of his attention to one boy she would have watched the entire class. She did not instruct Mr. Haley prior to class that he should not spend too much time with one student. Neither did she see the decedent get hit.

Mr. Haley, who was a second semester senior at Wayne State Teachers College, had been student teaching at Millard Central Junior High School for approximately 5 weeks. He testified he told the boys when to start and Mrs. Beveridge told the girls. He testified during the class he walked up and down between the boys standing at the mats and those seated at the center of the gym. A short time after the first student went up to the mats a few boys in decedent's group stood up, although not close to the mats. He told them to sit down and they complied. At the time of the accident Mr. Haley was giving individualized instructions to a boy near the middle of the gym. He did not see decedent get hit.

• • •

Mark Kreie stated he was simply doing what Mrs. Beveridge instructed, namely to assist a student in need. During his instruction of David he did not receive any warning or admonition from either teacher. During the class various students from each group were intermingling around the court, visiting with each other. Mrs. Beveridge did not hear what instructions, if any, student teacher Haley gave his charges and did not see the incident which led up to the fatal injury of David.

Ike F. Pane, principal of Millard Central Junior High School, testified golf was a mandatory course of instruction. . . . Pane identified exhibit 9 as his school's written rules of instruction which stated the objectives to be achieved in teaching golf to the ninth grade class, and specifically setting forth in what manner or procedure the instruction was to be undertaken and achieved. . . . On page 2 of exhibit 9, the following appears: "Safety should be stressed at all times, especially when you are rained out. If in the gym, one can set up stations on the floor along one side of the bleachers, divide all students into that many stations and have them sit on the outstretched bleachers on the opposite side. Have the first person hit four or five balls, (sic) to the second person across the gym. When the first is done hitting, he will go to the end of his group and the second person hits and the third retrieves the ball and so on."

On the next page of exhibit 9, the following appears under "Safety Hints": "1. Never hit a shot until you are sure those in front of you are out of your range. If you hit another player, you may be liable for damages. 2. Never swing a club, especially on the tees, unless you are sure no one is standing close to you."

Pane testified he approved of exhibit 9 and the procedure set forth therein, and that it was his understanding the instruction was undertaken in conformity with exhibit 9. However, after David's fatal injury he discovered that the physical arrangements for instruction were quite different than that specified.

Pane acknowledged that if the instructions had been followed it would have been difficult to have two people on a mat at the same time. It was not until after the accident that he realized the arrangement was different from what was recommended. He recognized that in any of the areas where there might be danger there is a potential for harm if the students were not properly supervised. If the procedure recommended had been followed, it would have made it more difficult for another student from the group to walk across the width of the gymnasium. It was Mr. Kurtz and Mrs. Beveridge who decided to vary the placement of the mats from that recommended in exhibit 9.

Mr. Kurtz testified that on Monday when he was giving the instruction, one from each group would go up all at the same time to the respective mats. Both he and Mrs. Beveridge would see that only one individual was at each mat when the students were to commence their swings. While the students were shooting their two or three balls, he would walk up and down in the back of them, more or less patrolling to make sure everything was okay. They walked the students through the hitting of the first ball. The second ball the students would hit on their own. In the

instruction, he followed the curriculum guide, which is exhibit 9.

After each person had hit his three balls, he was supposed to lay his club down on the carpet and go back to his group and sit down. After all the stations had been cleared and no one else was standing, the next golfer would be told to go out and gather the wiffle balls, bring them back, and set them on the carpet, standing there by the proper mat. Then when that group had gathered all the balls and the designated students were standing at their respective mats, they would go through the same procedure again.

It is evident the instruction procedure used Monday was not followed on Wednesday. If it had been, the instructor would have observed the dilemma of the deceased and given him the instruction he had missed. Also, the students would not have been assisting one another.

Mr. Haley testified he had received no instruction from any of the regular teachers or faculty prior to the commencement of the class, nor did he have a lesson plan because Mrs. Beveridge was going to handle that. He further stated he gave no oral instruction to any of the students as a whole. He recognized he was teaching unskilled young people in a game dealing with potentially dangerous instruments. At the time David was injured, Haley was at the fifth mat, giving some individual instruction. Haley testified that if he had seen another student approach the mat, he would have directed him to sit down. At the time in question his attention was diverted from those students who were supposed to be observing rather than using the clubs. When he was giving specialized instruction the only persons he was seeing were the individuals who were using that particular mat he was working with. Haley was asked the following question: "'Who told you after ——— instructed you, if anybody, that once the instructions started on the mat that you were to lead the group from center court and go down and pass in review, more or less, in front of the mats, and if the students needed help to give them help. A. Who told me personally to do that? Q. Yes. A. No one.'"

• • •

Mr. Kurtz and Mrs. Beveridge testified they did not use the procedure outlined in exhibit 9 because they did not want the wiffle balls hit toward other students. They also felt there was a danger of a golf club flying loose. Mrs. Beveridge also envisioned a problem with wiffle balls going underneath the bleachers if they were hit across the width of the gym.

Recovery in this case is sought on the ground of lack of supervision. Where lack of supervision by an instructor is relied on to impose liability, such lack must appear as the proximate cause of the injury, with the result that the liability would not lie if the injury would have occurred notwithstanding the presence of the instructor.

In the instant case, we are dealing with a ninth grader who had never before swung a golf club. The instruction was conducted indoors, in close quarters. There was some testimony, which the trial court could have accepted, that the physical arrangement, which was contrary to defendant's suggestion, as indicated by exhibit 9, would have prevented the opportunity for injury if followed. There is a question as to whether there was adequate safety instruction regarding the use of a golf club prior to the commencement of the class at which the fatal injury occurred. There is evidence, which the court could have accepted, that on the day the accident occurred the teaching procedure outlined by the regular instructor was not followed by the student teacher. The record would also indicate the student teacher may not have been properly informed as to the procedure to be followed. There is no question the trial judge could have found that, at the very best, there was ineffective observation and attention on the part of the student teacher when ordinary care or supervision would have prevented the occurrence which resulted in the death of David. In Scarborough v. Aeroservice, Inc., 155 Neb. 749, 53 N. W. 2d 902 (1952), we held: "Inattention to the duty to exercise care in a situation which reasonably may be regarded as hazardous is negligence, notwithstanding the act or omission involved would not in all cases, or even ordinarily, be productive of injurious consequences.

> "The risk reasonably to be perceived defines the duty to be obeyed; it is the risk reasonably within the range of apprehension, of injury to another person, that is taken into account in determining the existence of the duty to exercise care."

In this instance, working with ninth graders, who were not familiar with the rules of golf, and in the case of the deceased, who had never before been exposed to the game, includes a duty to anticipate danger that is reasonably foreseeable.

We have no difficulty in finding that the lack of supervision was a proximate cause of the death of David. "Proximate cause" as used in the law of negligence is that cause which in the natural and continuous sequence, unbroken by an efficient intervening cause, produces the injury and without which the injury would not have occurred. Daniels v. Andersen, 195 Neb. 95, 237 N. W. 2d 397 (1975).

The judgment of the trial court is affirmed.

Affirmed.

■ ■ ■ ■

Fundamental Concepts and Principles

There is an inherent duty to supervise when participants are taking part in sponsored activities in most public and private educational institutions, park and recreation agencies, or other profit and nonprofit sport organizations. Supervision includes inspecting and preparing the facility; providing adequate and proper equipment; instructing properly; warning of dangers inherent in the activity; communicating and enforcing rules and regulations; monitoring the conduct of the activity, the use of the facility or area, and the behavior of those on the premises; and rendering first-aid and providing access to medical treatment. Supervision, which may be general, specific, or transitional, should be predicated on the age, experience, judgment, and physical condition of participants and the activity involved. It must be related to foreseeable consequences and causation.

General, Specific, and Transitional Supervision

General supervision is overseeing individuals or groups involved in activity and does not require constant, unremitting scrutiny of the activity or facility. General supervision usually is expected for observing participants and activities on the playground, in the gymnasium, in the weight room, or in the swimming pool when the supervisor is not expected to have every individual under supervision (*Fagan v. Summers*, 1972; *Stevens v. Chesteen*, 1990).

Specific supervision is constant and continuous, the type of supervision that is more appropriate for individuals or small groups receiving instruction, involved in high risk activities, or using areas that have the potential for serious injury. For example, participants who are learning an activity or skill need specific, direct supervision. Similarly, participants who are not able to perform a skill adequately need specific supervision. Specific supervision also is mandated when participants are behaving or are likely to behave in ways which may injure themselves or others.

According to van der Smissen (1990), supervision cannot be categorized simply as general **or** specific but frequently is transitional in nature—i.e., changing from specific, to general, to specific, depending on such factors as the participants' need for instruction, their ability to perform certain activities, their use of equipment, their involvement with others, and their use of the facility. As the potential for harm increases, the degree of supervision should increase proportionally, and specific supervision is appropriate when the supervisor perceives a situation as dangerous. Whether involved in general or specific supervision, or moving from one to the other, supervisors are expected to identify dangerous activities and intervene either to stop the activity or facilitate its continuing safely.

Appropriateness of Supervision for the Age and Experience of Participants

Although program sponsors cannot insure the safety of participants, they are expected to exercise reasonable supervision over participants. The responsibility to supervise varies with the age and experience of participants, their mental condition, and the nature of the activity in which they are engaged.

Supervisors observing young children have a high duty of care (*Ferguson v. DeSoto Parish School Bd.*, 1985).

> Ordinarily it is necessary to exercise greater caution for the protection and safety of a young child than for an adult person who possesses normal physical and mental faculties. One dealing with children must anticipate the ordinary behavior of children. The fact that they usually cannot and do not exercise the same degree of prudence for their own safety as adults, that they often are thoughtless and impulsive, imposes a duty to exercise a proportional vigilance and caution on those dealing with children, and from whose conduct injury to a child might result. (*Calandri v. Ione Unified School Dist.*, 1963)

> Children have a known proclivity to act impulsively without thought of the possibilities of danger. It is precisely this lack of mature judgment which makes supervision so vital. The mere presence of the hand of authority and discipline normally is effective to curb this youthful exuberance and to protect the children against their own folly. (*Ohman v. Board of Educ.*, 1949)

Adults generally require less supervision than children. When adults are novices, however, and unfamiliar with the activity and the inherent risks involved, they require closer supervision. Supervisors also must be alert to adults who may be involved in horseplay and be prepared to intervene if necessary.

The reasonableness of supervision also is related to the abilities of participants. Moreover, greater caution is required for participants with disabling conditions—e.g., mentally handicapped children on a Special Olympics team walking three blocks away from campus to a gymnasium to practice basketball (*Foster v. Houston General Insurance Co.*, 1982) and mentally retarded children with poor eye-hand coordination running on the playground with other children (*Rodriguez v. Board of Educ.*, 1984).

A higher degree of supervision also is necessary for certain activities that are considered to be more dangerous than others. Wrestling, for example, requires continuous and constant supervision (*Carabba v. Anacortes School District No. 103*, 1967). In *Carabba*, a high school wrestler was severely injured when the referee looked away while the opponent applied an illegal hold on the plaintiff. The court found negligent supervision since the referee's failure to break the illegal hold was the proximate cause of the injury.

Quality of Supervision. Supervisors must be competent to adequately supervise the participants involved, activities conducted, and facilities utilized. Whenever possible, supervisors should be regular, full-time employees who have appropriate qualifications.

It is foreseeable that participants who are unacquainted with an activity (or novices) may be injured primarily because they are unfamiliar with, and inexperienced in, the activity. The court found negligent supervision in the *Brahatcek* case where one student swung a golf club and hit another student due to inattention on the part of a student teacher (*Brahatcek v. Millard School Dist.*, 1979). Negligent supervision was also found in the case of two student assistants who failed to detect a novice swimmer who sank to the bottom of the swimming pool and drowned (*Morehouse College v. Russell*, 1964).

All supervisors should be properly trained and undergo regular staff development to improve their skill and knowledge. Furthermore, if an activity is dangerous or has the potential to be dangerous, supervisors should provide participants with instructions, familiarize them with basic rules and procedures essential in executing skills, and warn them of reasonably foreseeable dangers before they attempt the skill (*Green v. Orleans Parish School Board*, 1978).

Not only must supervisors warn of dangers, they also must see that the warnings are heeded. A teacher warned students to slow down a merry-go-round because it was going too fast. She was liable for negligent supervision when she resolved a dispute over a basketball between other students rather than making sure that the students slowed the merry-go-round (*Rollins v. Concordia Parish School Board*, 1985).

The courts have provided direction in defining non-negligent supervision. In *Toller v. Plainfield School District 202* (1991), for example, the court determined that a teacher used reasonable care by teaching the rules of wrestling; demonstrating wrestling maneuvers; matching students according to height, weight, and size; and closely supervising them.

Number of Supervisors. The number of persons required to provide reasonable supervision depends on the participants and the nature of the activity. Moreover, when plaintiffs allege negligence due to an insufficient number of supervisors, they must prove that inadequate supervision was the proximate cause of the injury and that additional supervisors would have prevented the injury (*Kaczmarcsyk v. City & County of Honolulu*, 1982). Except for swimming pool and school playground cases, however, the courts generally have not imposed liability when there has been at least one supervisor present (*Fosselman v. Waterloo Community School Dist.*, 1975; *Banks v. Terrebonne Parish School Board*, 1976). More than one life guard may be required to supervise swimmers depending on the size of the swimming pool and the number of swimmers (*YMCA v. Bailey*, 1963).

When considering the number of supervisors required for children on a school playground, the courts have held that one supervisor for approximately 50 children on a playground was reasonable (*District of Columbia v. Cassidy*, 1983; *Ferguson v. DeSoto Parish School Bd.*, 1985), that six to eight adult supervisors for more than 250 children was reasonable (*Capers v. Orleans Parish School Bd.*, 1978), and that three supervisors for 170 students was reasonable (*Hampton v. Orleans Parish School Bd.*, 1982). In one situation, however, two teachers and a principal provided insufficient supervision for 200 students when the principal failed to prevent a child from misusing a volleyball stand after he had warned the students previously not to play with the stands (*Santee v. Orleans Parish School Bd.*, 1983). In a recent case involving children at a park playground, the court held that three teachers and 11 parents provided adequate supervision for 78 kindergarten students (*Clanker v. Rapids Parish School Board*, 1993).

Foreseeability and Causation Factors

When injured plaintiffs allege improper supervision, they must demonstrate that the injury was reasonably foreseeable and that inadequate supervision was the proximate cause of the injury. Supervisors are expected to be on site in reasonable proximity to the activity they are supervising. Even if the supervisor is not present at the time an injury occurs, however, there will be no liability if the injury would have occurred notwithstanding the supervisor's absence.

An injured plaintiff prevailed in a case in which he alleged negligent supervision since it was reasonably foreseeable that a catcher chasing a foul ball would trip over spectators who were allowed to congregate close to the base line. The supervisors had stopped the game twice prior to the injury to move the spectators back away from the third base line and against the fence. The court found the teachers negligent for failing to control the crowd and found that the plaintiff was not guilty of contributory negligence (*Domino v. Mercurio,* 1963).

Non-negligent supervision entails supervisors taking action to prevent reasonably foreseeable injuries to participants. When supervisors leave participants alone, they may be liable for negligent supervision. For example, it was reasonably foreseeable that, when left unattended, boys would throw rocks at girls with the likelihood of serious injury—in this case one of the girls was blinded (*Sheehan v. St. Peter's Catholic School,* 1971). Similarly, in *Dailey v. Los Angeles Unified School District* (1970), a boy died as a result of a head injury incurred during a slap-boxing incident. The person on duty at the time was in his office eating lunch. Since the injury to the boy was foreseeable and proper supervision would have prevented the injury, the court found that the person on duty was liable for negligent supervision.

When the plaintiff alleges that the supervisor's absence was the proximate cause of the injury, the plaintiff must prove that the supervisor's presence would have prevented the injury. There are a number of cases, however, which demonstrate that there are situations in which no amount of supervision would have prevented an injury—e.g., a player running head first and colliding with a catcher blocking home plate; basketball players bumping heads while jumping for the ball; roller skater being struck by another skater (*Passantino v. Board of Educ.,* 1977; *Kaufman v. City of New York,* 1961; *Blashka v South Shore Skating, Inc.,* 1993).

In summary, if the potential for injury is foreseeable and the presence of the supervisor would have prevented the injury, the probability of liability is strong. If, however, the injury would have occurred even if the supervisor had been there, there can be no liability.

Recent Developments

Currently, there are two principal developments pertaining to supervision: 1) the change in the status of individuals on the premises and 2) the use of a supervisory plan to delineate specific procedures for supervising areas and facilities, and the conduct of individuals on the premises.

Visitor Status

In the past, the status of adult individuals on the premises (invitees, licensees, trespassers) has been used in determining the duty owed, with invitees requiring the greatest protection, licensees moderate protection, and trespassers minimum protection. There has been a trend away from using such classifications. Some states (led by California, Hawaii, and New York) have abandoned this approach and have applied the "reasonable care under the circumstances" standard. Such a decision provides impetus for basing the amount and kind of supervision on what is reasonable for a specific situation.

Supervisory Plan

A second consideration is the need to develop, implement, and evaluate a supervisory plan for facilities and individuals on the premises. Regardless of the situation, a systematic procedure should be developed to document specifically each component to be addressed in supervision: **who, what, when, where,** and **how**. There should be both a master plan including all the facilities, when they will be used, by whom, for what, and who will be supervising and a detailed supervisory plan for each area and activity.

Several cases in school settings have indicated the necessity of adequate supervisory plans. In *Dailey v. Los Angeles Unified School Dist.* (1970), negligent supervision was at issue when the supervisory plan did not provide for a formal supervisory schedule and allowed too much discretion on the part of subordinates. In a Florida case (*Broward County School Board v. Ruiz* [1986]), the supervisory plan failed to provide for supervision in an after-school waiting area. Due to inadequate supervisory plans, negligence was found in each of these cases. In *Butler v. D.C.* (1969), no negligence was found was found since the school was utilizing a supervisory plan. In another Florida case (*Comuntzis v. Pinellas County School Board,* [1987]), a child was beaten. No supervisory plan was in use and negligent supervision was found.

An effective supervisory plan requires detailed planning, development, implementation, evaluation, and revision. Supervisors should be involved in developing supervisory plans, evaluating them, and revising them with primary emphasis on maintaining the safety of participants in a safe environment. Although the framework for a supervisory plan may vary, the plan should be in writing, be specific, and be evaluated regularly and periodically to assess its effectiveness.

The supervisory plan in Figure 1 is an example of a supervisory plan for step aerobics at a health club. The activity, time, place, date, number of participants, assigned supervisor with acceptable certification(s), and location of participants and the supervisor are designated in the sample plan. Specific details of the actions of the supervisor are specified for managing behavior, rendering first aid, communicating and enforcing rules and regulations, and being alert to dangerous conditions. A similar plan should be designed, implemented, and evaluated for any activity or facility to demonstrate a systematic approach to supervision.

Figure 1. Supervisory Plan

SUPERVISORY PLAN		
	FOR:	*Step Aerobics*
	BY:	*Lynne P. Gaskin*
	DATE:	*January 6, 1997*

SITUATION:

Step aerobics exercise session from 5:00 - 6:00 pm; 50-75 participants in the gymnasium (all adults)

NUMBER OF SUPERVISORS:

One, leading the exercise—on duty at all times

QUALIFICATIONS OF SUPERVISORS:

Aerobics and Fitness Association of America (AFAA), American Council of Exercise (ACE), National Dance-Exercise Instructor's Training Association (NDEITA) certification

LOCATION OF SUPERVISORS:

(Diagram facility to be supervised and show the placement of the supervisors.)
Instructor:

Elevated, in front of group with view of all participants

$$\boxed{X}$$

```
X  X  X  X  X  X  X  X  X  X
X  X  X  X  X  X  X  X  X  X
X  X  X  X  X  X  X  X  X  X
X  X  X  X  X  X  X  X  X  X
X  X  X  X  X  X  X  X  X  X
```

FUNCTIONS OF SUPERVISORS:

Managing Behavior

Be alert to any problem behavior.

Observe, anticipate, respond to address safety concerns

Rendering Emergency First Aid

Sprains/strains—provide ice and refer to personal physician or activate EMS system[a] if necessary.

Respiratory/Cardiac Difficulty—cease activity, monitor vital signs, activate EMS system if necessary.

Respiratory/Cardiac Emergencies—administer rescue breathing/CPR and activate EMS system.

Neck or Spinal Injury—check vitals, stabilize individual, and activate EMS system.

Bleeding—administer appropriate first aid and activate EMS system if necessary.

Other—e.g., epilepsy, diabetes, stroke—administer proper first aid and activate EMS system if necessary.

Communicating and Enforcing Rules and Regulations (only one person per set of steps)

Participants must
- wear proper attire.
- provide evidence of physical examination prior to participating.
- situate steps 6′ from persons on either side or from walls.
- use progression in adding steps.
- adjust to activity according to individual ability/needs.

Being Alert to Dangers Conditions

1 Dangerous Activities: stop participants from jumping on steps rather than stepping.

2 Defective Equipment and Hazards: be observant of broken steps and report them (remove from use)

a. "An emergency medical services (EMS) system is a network of community resources and medical personnel that provides emergency care to victims of injury or sudden illness" (American Red Cross, 1996, p. 4).

References

A. Cases

Banks v. Terrebonne Parish School Board, 339 So.2d 1295 (La.Ct.App. 1976).

Blashka v. South Shore Skating, Inc,. 598 N.Y.S.2d 74 (App.Div., 2d Dept.1993).

Brahatcek v. Millard School Dist., 202 Neb. 86, 273 N.W.2d 680 (Neb.1979).

Broward County School Board v. Ruiz, 493 So.2d 474 (Fla. App. 1986).

Butler v. D.C., 417 F.2d 1150 (1969).

Calandri v. Ione Unified School Dist., 219 Cal. App.2d 542, 33 Cal. Rptr. 333, 1963.

Capers v. Orleans Parish School Bd., 365 So.2d 23, (La.Ct.App.1978).

Carabba v. Anacortes School District No. 103, 72 Wash.2d 939, 435 P.2d 936 (Wash.1967).

Clanker v. Rapids Parish School Board, 610 So.2d 1020 (La.Ct.App.1993).

Comuntzis v. Pinellas County School Board, 508 So.2d 750 (Fla.App. 1987).

Dailey v. Los Angeles Unified School District, 470 P.2d 360 (Cal., 1970).

Daniel v. S-Co Corp., 255 Iowa 869, 124 N.W. 2d 522 (1963).

District of Columbia v. Cassidy, 465 A.2d 395, (DC 1983).

Domino v. Mercurio, 17 A.D.2d 342, 234 N.Y.S.2d 1011 (1962), aff'd, 13 N.Y.S.2d 922, 193 N.E.2d 893, 244 N.Y.S.2d 69 (1963).

Ely v. Northumberland Gen. Ins. Co., 378 So.2d 1024 (La.1979).

Fagan v. Summers, 498 P.2d 1227 (Wyo.1972).

Ferguson v. DeSoto Parish School Bd., 467 So.2d 1257 (La.Ct. App.), cert denied, 469 So.2d 978 (La.1985)

Fosselman v. Waterloo Community School Dist., 229 N.W.2d 280 (Iowa 1975).

Foster v. Houston General Insurance Co., 407 So.2d 759 (La.Ct. App.1982).

Green v. Orleans Parish School Board, 365 S.2d 834 (1978).

Hampton v. Orleans Parish School Bd., 422 So.2d 202 (La.Ct.App.1982).

Kaczmarcsyk v. City & County of Honolulu, 63 Hawaii 612, 656 P.2d 89 (Hawaii 1982).

Kaufman v. City of New York, 30 Misc.2d 285, 214 N.Y.S.2d 767 (1961).

Kungle v. Austin, 380 S.W. 2d 354 (Mo 1964).

Morehouse College v. Russell, 109 Ga.App. 301, 136 S.E.2d 179 (1964).

Ohman v. Board of Educ., 300 N.Y. 306, 90 N.E.2d 474 (1949).

Passantino v. Board of Educ., 41 N.Y.S.2d 1022, 363 N.E.2d 1373, 395 N.Y.S.2d 628 (1977), revg 52 A.D.2d 935, 383 N.Y.S.2d 639 (1976).

Rodriguez v. Board of Educ., 104 A.D.2d 978, 480 N.Y.S.2d 901 (1984).

Rollins v. Concordia Parish School Board, 465 So.2d 213 (La.Ct.App.1985).

Santee v. Orleans Parish School Bd., 430 So.2d 254 (La.Ct.App.1983).

Sheehan v. St. Peter's Catholic School, 29 Minn. 1, 188 N.W.2d 868 (1971).

Stevens v. Chesteen, 561 So.2d 1100 (Ala.1990).

Toller v. Plainfield School District 202, 582 N.E.2d 237 (Ill.App.1991).

YMCA v. Bailey, 107 Ga.App, 417, 130 S.E.2d 242 (1963).

B. Publications

American Red Cross. (1996). *American Red Cross First Aid—Responding to Emergencies* (2d ed.). St. Louis, Mo.: Mosby Lifeline.

Champion, W. T., Jr. (1993). *Sports Law in a Nutshell*. St. Paul, Minn.: West.

Kaiser, R. A. *(1986). Liability and Law in Recreation, Parks, and Sports.* Englewood Cliffs, N.J.: Prentice-Hall.

van der Smissen, B. *(1990). Legal Liability and Risk Management for Public and Private Entities.* Cincinnati, Ohio: Anderson, 1990.

Conduct of the Activity

Robert E. Trichka
Central Connecticut State University

How physical activity is conducted has long been a concern for sport-related service providers in both the public and private sectors. The service provider must possess a thorough understanding of all activities in which participants engage. Actions must conform to recognized standards of the professional field in which the practitioner is engaged. Under normal circumstances, this standard is that of a reasonably prudent person qualified to undertake the conduct of physical activity. Teachers, activity leaders, coaches, and exercise specialists are expected to select or allow only those activities which are reasonable for the ability levels of the participants in the activity. Adequate instruction must be planned and carried out; participants must be warned of danger; proper safety rules and regulations must be taught and adhered to; and, in the area of physical education, a prescribed curriculum of activities must be followed and not modified. In addition, care must be taken to see that the facilities are properly maintained. The prudent service provider, therefore, must carefully examine all elements of the program and take reasonable steps to remove or control identifiable risks.

■ ■ ■ ■

Representative Case

FANTINI v. ALEXANDER
Superior Court of New Jersey, Appellate Division
172 N.J. Super. 105; 410 A.2d 1190
January 16, 1980, Argued
January 25, 1980, Decided

OPINION:

Plaintiff, a college student, instituted suit to recover damages for personal injuries he received while participating in the activities of a karate club of which defendant was the instructor in charge. The injury was received when plaintiff, who had about 20 hours of instruction, was kicked in the head by a more advanced student with whom plaintiff was engaging in a "free fight" which was being staged only for demonstration purposes. He appeals from a judgment of dismissal granted at the close of plaintiff's case.

The allegation of negligence was:

Defendant failed to properly instruct and supervise the karate class and in particular the plaintiff. Defendant was negligent in instructing the plaintiff who was a complete novice to participate in a karate fight when he should have known that plaintiff did not have sufficient experience to so participate.

The applicable rule for measuring defendant's conduct is set forth in Restatement, Torts 2d, @ 299A at 73 (1965):

Unless he represents that he has greater or less skill or knowledge, one who undertakes to render services in the practice of a profession or trade is required to exercise the skill and knowledge normally possessed by members of that profession or trade in good standing in similar communities.

• • •

Plaintiff called Ronald J. Gaeta, who owned and taught in a karate school, as an expert witness. It is admitted that Gaeta was well qualified and accomplished in the field of karate. After an examination out of the presence of the jury, the trial judge examined a report Gaeta had submitted to plaintiff's attorney and then ruled that Gaeta had not established any generally accepted standard in this type of situation. He based his ruling on Fernandez v. Baruch, 52 N.J. 127 (1968), and Sesselman v. Muhlenberg Hospital, 124 N.J. Super. 285 (App.Div.1973).

The determination of an expert's competency to testify and of the sufficiency, as distinguished from the weight of the testimony, is primarily for the discretion of the trial judge. An appellate court, however, will interfere where there has been a clear abuse of discretion. Sanzari v. Rosenfeld, supra, 34 N.J at 136; Henningsen v. Bloomfield Motors, Inc., 32 N.J. 358, 411 (1960). We find that there was a clear abuse of discretion in the holding of the trial judge, induced probably by the judge's consideration of the report submitted by Gaeta to plaintiff's attorney. Gaeta's testimony makes clear that in his opinion there was a generally recognized standard in the profession of karate instruction of when a student should be permitted to "free fight." He was asked a hypothetical question by the judge:

. . . [w]as there any standard that would govern whether or not that man should be sent in to free fight with an Orange Belt with instructions to the Orange Belt, to both of them, to take it easy, and that was supposed to be—supposed to be a no contact situation, would that violate a standard in your opinion?

THE WITNESS: Definitely.

THE COURT: What standard would it violate?

THE WITNESS: Not enough time. Not enough time and training. Fourteen hours is ridiculous amount of time.

THE COURT: Twenty hours.

THE WITNESS: Twenty hours is not enough time. Not—not with sporadic training once a week. I would never have a student spar after that.

THE COURT: Do you know of any people who do it, other than instructors who do it?

THE WITNESS: Not in my organization, no. I do know of other acquaintances.

Shortly after that testimony Gaeta testified on redirect examination:

Q. My question is, is it a recognized principle of good practice among karate instructors not to permit that type of situation?

A. I have to say, yes, from my experience.

Q. Notwithstanding that, it may be violated by other instructors from time to time, is that correct?

A. Yes, it's always violated. When I started karate it was violated.

Q. So that there is a minimum standard or practice?

A. Well—

Q. Or principle which can be violated, is that correct?

A. Yes, sir.

A standard does not mean a principle which every practitioner in the applicable profession will follow. It is a generally recognized standard. There are always going to be persons in every profession who do not follow what the vast majority of practitioners recognize as proper conduct. Although it may be that Gaeta's testimony was weak, it was sufficient to constitute a question of fact. Cf. Skupienski v. Maly, 27 N.J. 240, 246 (1958).

It is apparent from reading the transcript of Gaeta's testimony that he had some difficulty in distinguishing between the way in which he operated his school and the generally recognized standard. What he himself did would not be establishing the generally recognized standard and should not be offered to the jury. In re Hyett, 61 N.J. 518, 531 (1972). Upon the retrial, that problem can be adequately controlled by the trial judge.

The weight to be given to Gaeta's testimony is not for the trial judge but rather for the jury. Polyard v. Terry, 160 N.J. Super. 497, 511 390 A.2d 653 (App.Div.1978), aff'd o.b. 79 N.J. 547 401 A.2d 532 (1979); Sanzari v. Rosenfeld, supra, 34 N.J. at 138, 167 A.2d 625.

Under the allegation of negligence asserted above, cases such as Jackson v. Hankinson, 51 N.J. 230, 238 A.2d 685 (1968), and Titus V. Lindberg, 49 N.J. 66, 228 A.2d 65 (1967), are not applicable. It is apparent, however, from the argument on the motion to dismiss, which was granted because plaintiff had failed to adduce testimony from an expert witness establishing a generally recognized standard of care from which defendant departed, that plaintiff wished to contend that there were other bases to support negigence which did not involve the conduct of defendant as a professional. Since plaintiff should have a proper opportunity to prepare his case, on remand a pretrial conference will be held well in advance of the retrial.

The judgment of dismissal is reversed. The matter is remanded to be proceeded with in accordance with this opinion. We do not retain jurisdiction.

■ ■ ■ ■

Fundamental Concepts

It is a generally recognized tenet that professionals are held accountable for the quality of services rendered. The professional is held to a standard of care which is commensurate with the activities being conducted. This point is emphasized by the "reasonable person standard" which is utilized by the courts to determine proper conduct in negligence cases. Not meeting, or not living up to this standard can be considered as malpractice. Malpractice, as defined by Black's Law Dictionary (1990) is:

> The failure of one rendering professional services to exercise that degree of skill and learning commonly applied under all circumstances in the community by the average, prudent, reputable member of the profession with the result of injury, loss or damage to the recipient of those services or to those entitled to rely upon them. (p. 959)

Although in its usual application, malpractice is more often referred to as undesirable conduct within the medical or legal professions, the term can be applied to professions in which faulty teaching or inadequate instruction may result in injury to the participant. In the sport and physical activity area, the failure to conduct the activity properly is negligence. Van der Smissen (1990) stated:

> The application of educational malpractice to negligent conduct of activity is an unusual application. However, . . . in the broader context, [educational malpractice] can be applied to any individual who has instructional responsibility . . . whether in the school, community recreation, commercial enterprises, or private-not-for-profit organization settings. (p. 210)

Standards of Conduct

If professionals are expected to meet standards, the question then arises, "What are the standards against which professional conduct is assessed?" The court in *Fantini v. Alexander* (1988) held that a standard is a generally recognized principle, set or approved by a professional organization, even though not every member of the profession will follow the principle. The standard does not imply perfect conduct, nor does it imply superiority, but is that of a reasonably prudent and careful individual possessing and exercising the knowledge and the skill of a member of the profession. For example, standards for developmentally appropriate activity have been set by the Council on Physical Education for Children (COPEC). The fitness industry has adopted standards set forth by the American College of Sports Medicine (ACSM) and the National Strength and Conditioning Association (NSCA). The National Recreation and Parks Association (NRPA) has developed standards for practitioners in the recreation profession.

Participants

The prudent service provider will be informed of the participants' physical and emotional condition, as well as their size, maturation, and skill level. These factors should be considered in the conduct of the activity.

The activity leader has been held liable when the leader required participation by a participant who had a known physical or mental condition which precluded safe participation. When a participant possesses neither the physical skill nor the mental attitude critical to safe participation, the activity leader should not allow the participation to continue. Physical and emotional condition were at issue in *Bellman v. San Francisco High School District* (1938) and obesity was an issue in *Landers v. School District No. 203* (1978). In *Morris v. Union High School District* (1931), football coaches and the school district were found liable for allowing participation of an unfit football player.

Mismatching. Common sense would indicate that service providers should use care in matching or pairing opponents in activities which involve physical contact. The careful matching of opponents must not ignore such attributes as physical size, experience, and skill level. However, court decisions have not been consistent in ruling that matching is required. The sport of wrestling punctuates the need for determining differences among participants. The weight difference between wrestling opponents was at issue with the plaintiff prevailing in *Stehn v. Bernarr MacFadden Foundation, Inc.,*(1970). However, in *Edelson v. Uniondale Free School District* (1995), the court ruled in favor of the defendant, stating there was no duty to match opponents. The plaintiff had prevailed in cases involving the sport of football in *City of Miami v. Cisneros* (1995) and *Tepper v. City of New Rochelle* (1988). No mismatch was found in *Vendrell v. School District No. 26C, Malheur County* (1962) and *Benitez v. City of New York Board of Education* (1969) as the courts stated that the participants had assumed the inherent risk of injury in the activity.

Instruction

When instruction is offered, the service provider has a duty to insure that such instruction is adequate. It cannot be disputed that activity leaders have a duty to teach the correct techniques. Appropriate instruction was defined by the court in *Green v. Orleans Parish School Board* (1978) to include an explanation of the basic rules and procedures; suggestions for proper performance including feedback; and an identification of the safety rules and regulations. An improper classification of the ability level of a non-swimmer was at issue in *Morehouse College v. Russell* (1964). Knowledge of potential risks involved in any activity, the type of injuries which might occur, how such injuries might occur, and how they can be prevented are also aspects of adequate instruction.

One aspect of instruction is the selection and organization of appropriate physical activities, made in relation to the maturity level, age, and size of the participant. A higher standard of care is required when activity is conducted for young children, and when the possibility of injury is greater due to the nature of the activity.

Proper instruction has been held to be essential in contact sports such as football (*Vendrell v. School District 26C*, 1962) and soccer (*Darrow v. Genessee Central School District*, 1973). In the non-contact sports of gymnastics (*Gardner v. State, 1939*), golf (*Larson v. Independent School District*, 1973) and baseball *(Passantino v. Board of Education of New York City*, 1977), proper instruction was a critical issue. Allegations related to improper instruction in weight training were at issue in *Vargo v. Svitchen* (1981).

Proper orientation to the use of fitness equipment is another aspect of adequate instruction. Too often fitness equipment is simply supplied to individuals without appropriate instruction for its use. As a result, many individuals are injured because they do not understand how a machine works or how to use it properly, (*Ostrosky v. Universal Gym Equipment Co.*, 1990 and *Woolsey v. Holiday Health Clubs and Fitness Centers, Inc.*, 1991).

The courts have identified six other areas of concern which fall under the broad heading of instruction. These are addressed in the subsequent paragraphs.

Warnings.   Activity leaders have a duty to warn participants of the dangers inherent in the activity. In addition, there may be need to warn of risks regarding equipment, dress, skill level, physical conditioning, and danger of third party attacks. Landowners are required to warn participants of environmental conditions and non-apparent hazards. Courts emphasize that risks must be known, understood, and appreciated by the participant; thus it is important that clear and regular warnings are given to remind participants about safety practices and procedures.

Where the risk is elevated such as in the activities of football and gymnastics, clear warnings of the specific risks involved in the activity are necessary (*Brown v. Quaker Valley School District*, 1984). In *Pell v. Victor J. Andrews High School and AMF, Inc.* (1984), the warning labels on a mini-trampoline were facing in the wrong direction when the teacher assembled the bed of the trampoline.

Coercion.   Litigation against activity leaders who motivate through coercion is common. Coercion is the application of undue pressure on participants to perform or to perform beyond their capabilities. In *Morris v. Union High School District* (1931), a football player was coerced into playing without the consent of the parent. In another case, a junior high school student was instructed to squat press weights totaling 360 pounds in his physical education class despite his protest (*Koch v. Gillings School District No. 2*, 1992). A common, but dangerous, practice in both physical education and recreational activities is that of allowing or coercing participants to engage in the activity either barefoot or in stocking feet because they do not have the appropriate footwear. Coercing participants to engage in an activity without the proper footwear has been at issue in *Passaferro v. Board of Education of the City of New York* (1974) and *Brod v. Central School District No. 1* (1976).

Dangerous Activities and Conditions.   When a dangerous activity is included in the program, strict supervision is essential. For the activities of dodgeball and bombardment, courts have questioned the appropriateness of the game and the dangers which exist through improper supervision of the activity. Zakrajsek (1988) stated, "Where else in the school curriculum do we condone throwing objects at each other?" (p. 51). Williams (1992) called dodgeball ". . . a litigation action waiting to happen" (p. 57). Cases in which the allegation of dangerousness was at issue include *Rivera v. Board of Education* (1975), *Fosselman v. Waterloo Community School District* (1975), and *Acosta v. Los Angeles Unified School District* (1995).

The control of the activity and/or the activity area is basic to properly conducting any activity. Overcrowding and/or overlapping activity areas has been an issue. Excessive numbers of participants in a limited area and activities which overlap boundaries or utilize the same boundaries can cause a dangerous condition to arise. With the rise in popularity of fitness establishments, activity leaders must be cognizant of space problems which may exist at the facility. Attempting to put too many participants in too little space can give rise to litigation. Overcrowding was alleged in *Mannone v. Holiday Health Club and Fitness Center, Inc.* (1992). The courts have held the defendants negligent in the cases of *Bauer v. Board of Education* (1995), *Keesee v. Board of Education* (1962), *Sutphen v. Benthian and the Vernon Township Board of Education* (1979), *Driscol v. Delphi Community School Corp.* (1972), and *Zawadzki v. Taylor* (1976).

Violations of Game Rules.   One aspect of proper instruction is enforcement of the rules of the game. If a rule has been adopted for safety reasons, lack of enforcement or a permitted violation of such rule will be difficult to defend when injury occurs. If the activity leader modifies a safety rule, the modification of the rule should be in the direction of making the activity more safe and not less safe. Litigation in the sports of football, baseball, and recreational softball dominate this area (*Peterson v. Multnomah County School District No. 1*, 1983; *Albo v. School Board of Broward County*, 1994; *Darrah v. Legnon and Liberty Mutual Ins.*

Co., 1992; *Ross v. Clouser,* 1982; and *Ceplina v. So. Milwaukee School Board,* 1976). Most courts have ruled that a participant in a game involving a contact sport, or the possibility of contact, is liable for injuries only if the conduct is such that it is willful or constitutes a reckless disregard for the safety of other participants. In *Nabozny v. Barnhill* (1975), the court held that the defendant was reckless and negligent when, during a soccer game, the defendant kicked the goalie in the head while the goalie was in the penalty area. See Chapter 2.41 for more information regarding injuries caused by other participants.

Safety Equipment.   It is necessary to realize that a legal duty exists to inform participants of needed protective or safety equipment as well as to furnish such equipment. The activity leader also must exercise reasonable care in supplying equipment that is suitable for the purpose for which it is being provided. Failure to supply safety equipment to participants is central to court action in a number of cases. When inadequate or defective safety equipment is the cause of injury, usually the defendants in the case are the activity leader, the public or private entity, and/or the manufacturer of the equipment. The failure to issue protective equipment in physical education class, varsity sports, or recreational activities was an issue in *Brackman v. Adrian* (1971), *Sutphen v. Benthian* (1979), *Berman v. Philadelphia Board of Education* (1983), *Locilento v. John Coleman Catholic High School* (1987), *Ausmus v. Board of Education, City of Chicago* (1987), *Parisi v. Harpursville Central School District* (1990), *Meese v. Brigham Young University* (1981), and *Leahy v. School Board of Hernando County* (1984).

In the past few years, litigation with complaints of poor equipment maintenance have plagued the fitness industry. Fitness machines and apparatus must be properly maintained at periodic intervals, with a log recording when and what was done in terms of the maintenance. Recent cases include *Kantor v. Health and Tennis Corp. of Amer. and Bally's* (1993), *Johnson v. Midtown Athletic Club and Stairmaster Inc.* (1992), *Savage v. Eagle Performance Systems, Inc.* (1986), *Lomas v. Family Fitness Center and Nautilus Industries* (1991), and *Ostrosky v. Universal Gym Equipment* (1989). In a suit adjoining the *Ostrosky* case, the equipment manufacturer claimed poor maintenance on the part of the fitness center (*Universal Gym Equipment v. Vic Tanny,* 1990).

Facilities.   Activity leaders owe a duty to participants to provide a safe learning and play environment. Not only must equipment be properly maintained, but facilities and grounds should be inspected regularly for unreasonable risks with such risks clearly marked or if possible, eliminated. Previous rulings have indicated the need for inspection of grounds for exposure to unreasonable risks (*Short v. Griffitts,* 1979, *Sears v. City of Springfield,* 1974, and *Scaduto v. State,* 1982); regularly checking the gymnasium area (*Wilkinson v. Hartford Accident and Indemnity Co.,* 1982); and proper maintenance of swimming pools (*Burgert v. Tietjens,* 1974 and *Pleasant v. Blue Mound Swim Club,* 1970). Maintenance of facility was at issue in the following recreational softball cases: *Paterek v. 6600 Limited* (1990), *Scrapchansky v. Town of Plainfield* (1986), *Bailey v. City of North Platte* (1984), *Edwards v. City of Birmingham* (1984), *Perretti v. City of New York* (1987), and *Chase v. Shasta Lake Union School District* (1988). The courts, in hearing cases involving poor maintenance of facilities, require that the condition was the proximate cause of the injury and that the disrepair was known to, or should have been known to the entities responsible for upkeep (*Gauthier v. Town of Fairfield,* 1990; *Krasenics v. City of West Haven,* 1990).

Recent Developments

Proper Instruction

In an attempt to slide into first base, the plaintiff broke his ankle and sued the school district for negligence in requiring the students to play softball, failing to adequately supervise, and failing to properly instruct the students on how to play softball. The Appellate Court upheld summary judgment on the part of the school district due to the failure of the plaintiff to present sufficient information on the causal connection between the alleged negligence and the injury. The proper use of lesson plans and adherence to the curriculum should be a central concern for activity leaders (*Sanders v. Kuna Joint School District,* 1994).

Mismatch

Action was brought against a wrestling referee and other school officials for negligent and reckless supervision and instruction after the athlete was injured while practicing a wrestling move with the referee. The trial court granted summary judgment for the referee and the plaintiff appealed. The Supreme Court held that ordinary negligence is a proper cause of action when negligent supervision or negligent instruction is involved in a sporting activity (*Hearon v. May,* (1995).

Elementary school football coaches, the school district, and the professional liability insurer were sued for alleged negligence. The plaintiff, an eighth grader was injured when tackled by a 270-pound player in a scrimmage football game. The trial court granted summary judgment for the defendants and on appeal, the Court held that elementary school football coaches owed no duty to players to protect against risk of injury from playing football against players of different weights (*Laiche v. Kohen,* 1993).

Warnings

Plaintiff sustained injury when diving head first into a lake in an area controlled by the park district. The Appellate Court held that a material question of fact as to the adequacy of signs prohibiting diving or warning of dangers of diving precluded summary judgment for the defendant. This case points to the need to have adequate signage so that knowledge, understanding, and comprehension or risks is not a question. It would be prudent to ensure that specific risks are understood by the participant by warning of the possible extent of any injury and the nature of these injuries (*Bucheleres v. Chicago Park District,* 1995).

Safety Equipment

A father brought action against the school district and Board of Education on behalf of his daughter who was injured during practice for the high school field hockey team. The Supreme Court, Appellate Division held that material issues of fact existed as to the coach's conduct in allowing athletes to participate without a mouthpiece (*Baker v. Briarcliff School District,* 1994).

References

A. Cases

Acosta v. Los Angeles Unified School District, 37 Cal. Rptr. 2d 171 (1955).
Albo v. School Board of Broward County, Circuit 91-28771, (FL 1994).
Ausmus v. Board of Education, 508 N.E. 2d 298 (Ill. 1987).
Bailey v. City of North Platte, 216 Neb. 810; 319 N.W. 2d 776 (1984).
Baker v. Briarcliff School District, 613 N.Y.S. 2d 660 (S.C. App. Div. 2d, 1994).
Bauer v. Board of Education, 285 App. Div. 1148; 140 N.Y.S. 2d 167 (1955).
*Bellman v. San Francisco High School District,*73 P.2d 596 (1937).
Benitez v. New York City Board of Education, 543 N.Y.S. 2d 29 (Ct. App. 1969)
Berman v. Philadelphia Board of Education, 456 A. 2d 545 (1983).
Brackman v. Adrian, 472 S.W. 2d 735 (TN 1971).
Brod v. Central School District, 386 N.Y.S. 2d 1255 (1976).
Brown v. Quaker Valley School District, 486 A. 2d 526 (PA 1984).
Bucheleres v. Chicago Park District, 646 N.E. 2d 1326 (IL App. 1 Dist. 1995).

Burgert v. Tietjens, 499 F. 2d 1, 4 (10th Cir. 1974, KS).

Ceplina v. South Milwaukee School Board, 73 Wis. 2d 338, 243 N.W. 2d 183 (1976).

Chase v. Shasta Lake Union School District, 66 Cal. Rptr. 517 (1988).

City of Miami v. Cisneros, 662 So. 2d 1272 (FL 1995).

Darrah v. Legnon & Liberty Mutual Ins. Co., District Ct 399-4 (LA August 1992).

Darrow v. Genessee Central School District, 41 A.D. 2d 897, 342 N.Y.S. 2d 611 (1973).

Driscol v. Delphi Community School Corp., 155 Ind. App. 56, 290 N.E. 2d 769 (1972).

Edelson v. Uniondale Free School District, 631 N.Y.S. 2d 391 (A.D. 2 Dept. 1995).

Edwards v. City of Birmingham, 477 So. 2d 704 (AL 1984).

Fantini v. Alexander, 172 NJ Super. 105, 410 A. 2d 1190 (1988).

Fosselman v. Waterloo Community School District, 229 N.W. 2d 280 (1975).

Fuller v. Board of Education, 614 N.Y.S. 2d 557, 206 A.D. 2d 452 (1994).

Gardner v. State, 22 N.E. 2d 344 (1939).

Gauthier v. Town of Fairfield, 16 Conn. Law Trib. 24 (CT 1990).

Green v. Orleans Parish School Board, 365 So. 2d 183 (LA 1979).

Hearon v. May, 540 N.W. 2d 124 (NE 1995).

Johnson v. Midtown Athletic Club & Stairmaster, CV 92-4022 (IA 1992).

Kantor v. Health & Tennis Corp. of Amer. & Bally's, CV 93-01-0294 (OH 1993).

Keesee v. Board of Education, 37 Misc. 2d 414, 235 N.Y.S. 2d 300 (1962).

Koch v. Gillings School District No. 2, 833 P.2d 181 (1992).

Krasenics v. City of West Haven, CV 89-0292185 (CT 1990).

Laiche v. Kohen, 621 So. 2d 1162 (LA 1993).

Landers v. School District No. 203, 383 N.W. 2d 645 (1978).

Larson v. Independent School District, 289 N.W. 2d 112 (MN 1980).

Leahy v. School Board of Hernando County, 450 So. 2d 833 (1964).

Locilento v. John A. Coleman Catholic High School, 523 N.Y.S. 2d 198 (1987).

Lomas v. Family Fitness Center & Nautilus Industries, CV 100-3810 (CA 1991).

Mannone v. Holiday Health Clubs and Fitness Centers, 92 CV 0707 (CO 1992).

Meese v. Brigham Young University, 639 P.2d 720 (UT 1981).

Morehouse College v. Russell, 109 Ga. App.301, 136 S.E. 2d 179 (1964).

Morris v. Union High School District, 160 Wash. 121, 294 P. 998 (1938).

Nabozny v. Barnhill, 31 IL App. 3rd 212, 334 N.E. 2d 255 (1975).

Ostrosky v. Universal Gym Equipment Co., CV 90-386148 (MI 1990).

Parisi v. Harpursville Central School District, 553 N.Y.S. 2d 566 (1990).

Passaferro v. Board of Education, 43 A.D. 2d 918, 353 N.Y.S. 2d 125 (1976).

Passantino v. Board of Education, 395 N.Y.S. 2d 628 (1977).

Paterek v. 6600 Limited, 465 N.W. 2d 342 (MI App. 1990).

Pell v. Victor J. Andrews High School & AMF, Inc., 462 N.E. 2d 858 (IL 1984).

Perretti v. City of New York, 132 A.2d 537, 517 N.Y.S. 2d 272 (1987).

Peterson v. Multnomah County School District, 668 P.2d 385 (1983).

Pleasant v. Blue Mound Swim Club, 128 IL App.2d 277, 262 N.E. 2d 107, 112 (1970).

Rivera v. Board of Education, 11 A.D. 2d 7, 201 N.Y.S. 2d 372 (1960).

Ross v. Clouser, 637 S.W. 2d 11 (MO 1982).

Sanders v. Kuna Joint School District, 876 P.2d 154 (ID App. 1994).

Savage v. Eagle Performance Systems, Inc., CDV 85-919 (MT 1986).

Scaduto v. State, 86 A.D. 2d 682, 446 N.Y.S. 2d 21 (1982).

Scrapchansky v. Town of Plainfield, 226 CT 629, 522 A. 2d 795 (1987).

Short v. Griffitts, 255 S.E. 2d 479 (1979).

Stehn v. Bernarr MacFadden Foundation, Inc., 434 F. 2d 811 (1970).

Sutphen v. Benthian, 165 N.J. Super. 79, 397 A. 2d 709 (1979).

Tepper v. City of New Rochelle School District, 53 N.Y.S. 2d 367 (A.D. 2 Dept. 1988).

Universal Gym v. Vic Tanny, 91-414310-22 (MI 1990).

Vargo v. Svitchan, 301 N.W. 2d 1 (1981).

Vendrell v. School District No. 26C, Malheur County, 233 OR 1, 376 P. 2d 406 (1962).

Wilkinson v. Hartford Accident & Indemnity Co., 411 So. 2d 479 (1992).

Woolsey v. Holiday Health Clubs and Fitness Centers, 820 P. 2d 1201 (CO 1991).

Zawadzki v. Taylor, 70 MI App. 545, 246 N.W. 2d 161 (1976).

B. References

Black, H.C. (1990). *Black's Law Dictionary*, St. Paul, Minn.: West Publishing Co.

Hart, J & R. Ritson (1993). *Liability and Safety in Physical Education and Sport*. Reston, Va.: AAHPERD Publications.

Shubert, G., R. Smith & J. Trentadue (1986). *Sports Law.* St. Paul, Minn.: West Publishing Co.

van der Smissen, B. (1990). *Legal Liability and Risk Management for Public and Private Entities*. Cincinnati, Ohio: Anderson Publishing Co.

Williams, N. (1990). The Physical Education Hall of Shame. *JOHPERD*, 63(6), pp. 57-60.

Zakrajsek, D. (1986). Premeditated Murder: Let's Bump Off Killer Ball. *JOHPERD*, 7(7), pp. 49-51.

Wong, G. (1994). *Essentials of Amateur Sports Law.* Westport, Conn.: Praeger Press.

Safe Environment

Bernard P. Maloy
University of Michigan

This chapter examines tort liability issues that relate to a safe environment for sport, recreation, and physical activity. Such a discussion might logically start with the obligations relating to the design and construction of the premises for sport, recreation, and physical activity. Most liability problems dealing with safe environment, however, stem from maintenance and operation of the premises, not their design and construction. In fact, a large majority of the personal injury lawsuits involving park facilities allege poor maintenance so that processes like cleaning, inspection, and repair become critical areas of concern.

Sport environments include such locations as an indoor gymnasium, an outdoor track, a parking lot at a health club, or a concession area in an arena. Because physical activity can take place anywhere, it is difficult to limit environment to a building, a field, or a park. Much physical activity and exercise takes place in natural outdoor settings like lakes, trails, and woods. The safe environment concept, therefore, has few limitations regarding the type of facility for activity; thus premises will refer to any area in which sport, physical activity, or exercise is performed.

■ ■ ■ ■

Representative Case

JACOBS v. COMMONWEALTH HIGHLAND THEATRES, INC.
Court of Appeals of Colorado, Division Three
738 P.2d 6
October 30, 1986, Decided

OPINION:

Defendant, Commonwealth Highland Theatres, Inc., appeals the judgment entered against it on a jury verdict awarding plaintiff, Betty Jacobs, $100,000 compensatory and $150,000 exemplary damages. We affirm in part and reverse in part.

In 1982, plaintiff was walking down the center aisle of defendant's theater when she stumbled on a step and fell, breaking her hip. The theater was dark, and the step was not lighted. Although two signs warned of the step, neither

was close to the step, and one was below eye level. Ushers often forgot to warn patrons about the step. Moreover, the dark pattern of the carpet in the aisle obscured the step, giving it the appearance of a continuous ramp. Patrons entering the theater from the brightly lit lobby tended to be distracted by the screen and the choice of seating.

Plaintiff underwent surgery for a fractured femur, which was replaced with a metal prosthesis. Because of the injury, she was permanently disabled. Her injury also necessitated additional medical treatment and surgery.

There was evidence that the same step had been the cause of similar falls on ten prior occasions between 1978 and 1982, some resulting in injury to patrons. Although defendant's district manager was aware of each incident, no corrective measures were taken, other than to install additional lighting in the general area between 1978 and 1979. The manager knew that ushers and doormen routinely failed to warn patrons of the step and that doormen were often called from their stations to work at the concession stand. The problem was regularly reported to defendant's home office, but was not corrected until after plaintiff was injured.

I

Defendant first asserts that evidence of prior similar incidents involving slips and falls on the same step at the theater was inadmissible to establish defendant's negligence. Thus, defendant contends that the trial court erred in failing to dismiss the complaint because plaintiff did not establish a prima facie case of negligence. We disagree.

Evidence of prior similar incidents cannot alone establish a prima facie case of negligence. Griffith v. City & County of Denver, 55 Colo. 37, 132 P. 57 (1913). However, such evidence may be admissible when offered for a valid purpose, when relevant to a material issue, and when its probative value outweighs any prejudice resulting from its admission. See Griffith v. City & County of Denver, supra; College v. Scanlan, 695 P.2d 314 (Colo. App. 1985) CRE 404(b).

Here, evidence of similar incidents was admitted not to prove defendant's negligence, but to show the existence of a hazardous condition, see Cameron v. Small, 182 S.W.2d 565 (Mo. 1944); cf. Griffith v. City & County of Denver, supra, and to show that defendant had notice of this condition. See City & County of Denver v. Brubaker, 97 Colo. 501, 51 P.2d 352 (1935); CRE 404(b).

Existence of a hazardous condition and the fact that defendant had notice of it are elements of a claim for premises liability. Griffith v. City & County of Denver, supra; City & County of Denver v. Brubaker, supra. Moreover, evidence of prior similar occurrences was also relevant to establish plaintiff's entitlement to exemplary damages in that it tended to show defendant's continued failure to correct a dangerous condition known to it. See Bodah v. Montgomery Ward & Co., 724 P.2d 102 (Colo. App. 1986); cf. Palmer v. A. H. Robins Co., 684 P.2d 187 (Colo. 1984). Consequently, we conclude that the trial court did not abuse its discretion in admitting this evidence. See Uptain v. Huntington Lab, Inc., 723 P.2d 1322 (Colo. 1986).

Plaintiff presented sufficient other evidence, independent of prior accidents, that the step was unsafe, that defendant's agents knew of the danger, and that no steps had been taken to correct it. Such evidence established a prima facie case of negligence on defendant's part, and thus, the court did not err in refusing to dismiss the complaint. See Kenney v. Grice, 171 Colo. 185, 465 P.2d 401 (1970).

Defendant's argument that expert testimony was required to establish the hazardous nature of the step is without merit. See Blackburn v. Tombling, 148 Colo. 161, 365 P.2d 243 (1961).

II

Defendant also asserts that plaintiff failed to establish prima facie her claim for exemplary damages. Again, we disagree.

For exemplary damages to be awarded, @ 13-21-102, C.R.S., requires the injury complained of to be attended by "a wanton and reckless disregard of the injured party's rights and feelings." Here, the issue is whether defendant's failure to remedy the hazardous condition of the step after repeated notice constitutes such "wanton and reckless disregard" as to support a claim for exemplary damages.

While mere negligence cannot support an award of exemplary damages, Tri-Aspen Construction Co. v. Johnson, 714 P.2d 484 (Colo. 1986), repeated failure to correct a known dangerous condition may convert mere negligence into wanton and reckless disregard. See Palmer v. A. H. Robins Co., supra. This is so if the failure to act creates a substantial risk of harm to another and purposefully occurs with awareness of the risk in disregard of consequences, see Coale v. Dow Chemical Co., 701 P.2d 885 (Colo. App. 1985), or if the defendant, while conscious of its conduct and cognizant of existing conditions, knew or should have known that injury would probably result from its omissions. See Pizza v. Wolf Creek Ski Development Corp., 711 P.2d 671 (Colo. 1985).

On the basis of evidence presented concerning defendant's awareness of the hazard and its repeated failure to remedy it, we conclude that plaintiff presented a prima facie case of wanton and reckless disregard which would support an award of exemplary damages. Because the jury could reasonably infer from the lack of corrective measures taken with regard to the step that defendant's failure to act was purposeful, with knowledge of the risk involved to patrons, the trial court did not err in refusing to dismiss plaintiff's claim for exemplary damages. See Bodah v. Montgomery Ward & Co., supra.

• • •

VII

Defendant next argues that the trial court improperly refused its tendered instruction on corporate liability for exemplary damages. We disagree.

Defendant's tendered instruction would have instructed the jury that a negligent act or omission of an employee attended by circumstances of a wanton and reckless disregard of plaintiff's rights and feelings is attributable to the corporation only if the corporation authorized or ratified the act or omission. Defendant's instruction is an incorrect statement of Colorado law as applied to the facts of this case. See Fitzgerald v. Edelen, 623 P.2d 418 (Colo. App. 1980).

Both Holland Furnace Co. v. Robson, 157 Colo. 347, 402 P.2d 628 (1965) and Frick v. Abell, 198 Colo. 508, 602 P.2d 852 (1979), relied upon by defendant, concerned liability of the principal for the torts of nonmanagerial agents. The correct rule for assessing exemplary damages against a corporation for the actions of an agent employed in a managerial capacity is stated in Fitzgerald v. Edelen, supra:

> Punitive damages can properly be awarded against a master or other principal because of an act by an agent if, but only if . . . the agent was employed in a managerial capacity and was acting in the scope of employment. See Restatement (Second) of Agency @ 217C (1958).

Here, it is undisputed that the acts or omissions upon which the exemplary damages were predicated were attributable to defendant's district manager, and fell within the scope of his employment. Thus, the rule in Fitzgerald applies in this case, and since defendant's tendered instruction was not a correct statement of Colorado law, it was properly refused. See I.M.A., Inc. v. Rocky Mountain Airways, Inc., 713 P.2d 882 (Colo. 1986).

• • •

That part of the judgment awarding prejudgment interest on the exemplary damages is reversed, and the cause is remanded with directions to modify the judgment by deleting that part of the award. The judgment is affirmed in all other respects.

JUDGE SMITH and JUDGE METZGER, concur.

■ ■ ■ ■

Fundamental Concepts

Premises Operators

The legal responsibility for providing safe premises is placed upon the possessor or occupier of the area. The legal theory holding the possessor or occupier liable for injury to patrons is simple. The possessor of the premises is in the best position to discover and control any risks or hazards. Unfortunately, the possessor is often the party who is responsible for creating risks and hazards as well. Obviously, ownership of the land or building vests one with the right of possession or occupation of the premises. However, those who lease or contract with ownership to use the premises can also be deemed possessors or occupiers.

The responsibility for operating a safe environment for sport, fitness, and physical activity is not limited to the owner. The legal responsibilities of the premises operator are shared by the coaches or program supervisors and by employees. Coaches and supervisors have a responsibility to provide reasonably safe premises for those involved in their organized programs or activities. They could be referred to as premises operators for the limited role they play in the supervision of their programs. Employees are charged with reasonably performing the functions of customer contact, premises maintenance, and general operational duties (*Daniels v. Thistledown Racing Club, Inc.*, 1995). They, too, can be referred to as premises operators in the limited role of their job. The legal policy for imposing liability on possessors and their agents was recently stated by the Supreme Court of Vermont in a case dealing with the liability of a ski operator:

> [Possessors] . . . have the expertise and opportunity to foresee and control hazards, and to guard against the negligence of their agents and employees. They alone can properly maintain and inspect their premises, and train their employees in risk management. They alone can insure against risks . . . (*Dalury v. S-K-I Ltd.*, 1995, p. 799).

For reference and convenience, the premises operator will include the possessor, as well as coaches, supervisors, and employees in their limited roles as premises operators.

Premises Users

Three practical terms to describe visitors or patrons using the premises are users, participants, and spectators. The user is a person who is using the premises for some personal benefit or plan (e.g., family members using a public park for a picnic, a person working out in a fitness center). The participant, or player, is a person utilizing the facility as part of an organized athletic or fitness activity (e.g., a recreational league softball player, a participant in a supervised aerobics class). Finally, there is the spectator who is on the premises strictly for the purpose of observing an event or activity.

There is little legal distinction between participant and user except for some legal subtleties regarding the degree of shared responsibility by the premises operator, coaches, and activity supervisors. The legal distinction between a participant or user and spectator, on the other hand, is dramatic for two reasons. First, a spectator is not expected to have the same degree of knowledge about the risks of the event or activity that he has come to view as the participant or user. Second, the spectator has limited access to the premises compared to the participant or user. In legal terms, this refers to the "area of invitation" discussed in the following section on invitees.

The nature of the duty owed to those on the premises depends upon the relationship between the visitor and the premises operator. Traditionally, these relationships have been defined in terms of the status of the visitor—invitee, licensee, and trespasser. State statutes have now created a fourth category—the recreational user (van der Smissen, 1990). Each category will be discussed below.

Invitees. Generally, users, participants, and spectators of sports premises are legally termed invitees. **Invitee** is the legal designation for an individual who has paid for use of the premises (a business invitee), or who has been solicited or "invited" as a member of the public to use the premises (a public invitee). An operator owes an invitee the obligation to exercise reasonable care to keep the invitee safe. The obligation requires the operator to protect patrons from unreasonable risk, and to avoid acts that can create risks. That means the operator owes the invitee all the duties of care listed in the section concerning the legal obligations for providing safe premises.

The business invitee is the patron whose presence will produce direct or indirect economic gain for the premises operator. Examples are a spectator who pays admission to watch an event, a user who has paid a membership fee to join a health club, or a potential customer who is browsing the sporting goods store. The payment, or expected economic benefit for the operator, is the key to this legal designation. The public invitee is on the premises because his presence was encouraged by the operator. The key to this designation is the encouragement (or invitation) given to the general public to use the premises (*City of Bloomington v. Kuruzovich*, 1987). An example would be citizens freely using public park facilities built specifically for public use. In fact, the public invitation has also been recognized in such diverse activities as public lectures, church meetings, and even for spectators who are located on a public sidewalk watching a chamber of commerce parade (*Straley v. Urbana Chamber of Commerce*, 1992).

Generally, a student is deemed an invitee of his or her school; a player is deemed an invitee performing at the stadium, field, or arena; and, an employee is an invitee in the workplace. In a relevant case, a professional jockey was injured when he fell from his horse and was impaled on a metal anchor called a "goose neck" on the inside rail. He was an invitee so the track operator had a duty to reasonably protect the jockey from an unsafe inside rail (*Thompson v. Ruidoso-Sunland, Inc.*, 1987).

It should be noted that invitee status is limited to a specific area for the purpose designated by the operator. This concept, called "area of invitation," means that an operator owes invitees the obligations of reasonable care within the designated area. A safe entrance and safe exit to the facility are always part of the area of invitation. The rest of the designated area depends on the purpose for which the invitee is on the premises. In a Washington case, it was ruled that the "area of invitation" for a skier was the general area served by the chair lifts. The obligation of the ski operator was to discover hazards within that area, and repair them, or at least warn of their danger (*Codd v. Stevens Pass, Inc.*, 1986). Conversely, when a couple left the clubhouse of a country club which was hosting a dance, they left the area of invitation. When the male fell into an open basement in an unlit area, he was no longer an invitee who was owed a duty of care because he had left the area of invitation (van der Smissen, 1990).

Licensee. A **licensee** is a person who uses the premises with the bare consent of the operator. Bare consent means permission has been given to the person to use the premises but the operator has no real or expected benefit from the licensee's use. A licensee enters upon the premises for his own purpose. An example would be a hunter who is hunting on land with the owner's permission, or a swimmer using a lake or swimming hole with the owner's permission. The only obligation an operator owes to a licensee is to warn of hazards or dangers which the licensee may not be able to discover. The theory is that the licensee has the same right as the operator to know of premises risks. The operator, however, does not have to inspect or discover dangers, nor give any warnings to the licensee for conditions which are obvious. In an Ohio case, a women and her young daughter were in a women's locker room of a university recreational facility after a free fitness class. The daughter was injured when a set of lockers fell on her as she apparently tried to climb on them. It was determined that the woman and her daughter were licensees at the time of the accident. The university's only legal obligation was to warn them of dangers of which they might be unaware (*Light v. Ohio University*, 1986).

Trespasser. A **trespasser** is a person who enters the premises without the permission of the operator. Generally, since no consent has been given to use the premises the only obligation owed by the operator is to refrain from any intentional conduct which would cause injury to the trespasser.

Recreational User. A **recreational user** must be on the land specifically for recreational purposes, must not have paid a fee for the recreational use of the land, and must be directly involved in the activity. The duty owed a recreational user is comparable to that owed a trespasser. The premises operator owes no duty to keep the premises safe for recreational use nor to give warning of dangerous conditions. Further, no invitee or licensee status is conferred even if the premises operator directly or indirectly invited the visitor to the premises (van der Smissen, 1990).

The Legal Obligations for Providing Safe Premises

The legal obligations owed by a premises operator to patrons are based on the proposition that the premises operator is in the best position to discover hazards and risks. The obligation is that a premises operator will protect patrons from those risks of which the operator is aware or should be aware. In the *Jacobs* case, the step was a risk that the operator should have known about, and additionally became a risk of which the operator had actual knowledge after a fall by a previous patron. The operator had a duty to properly fix or respond to the condition. The obligation to provide a safe theater was the duty of all three positions, the corporate office, the theater management, and the ushers. Although a patron is supposed to be careful and protect himself or herself, the change of lighting and the screen created distractions causing the patron to focus on things other than the step. The role of proper warnings and lighting becomes increasingly important to overcome the distractions that affect patrons.

As noted earlier, many activities may be conducted in natural settings. There are three general rules regarding liability for injuries caused by natural conditions. First, the traditional rule of English and American courts is that an operator is not obligated to remedy or correct any natural conditions on the land. Second, the operator can be held liable for any changes or alterations he makes to natural conditions on the land. Finally, the law regarding natural conditions is generally applicable only to rural and unimproved areas. It is not suited or applicable to urban areas (van der Smissen, 1990).

An operator must take ordinary care to keep the premises in a reasonably safe condition for its users, participants, and spectators. That obligation for ordinary care includes the duties to: 1) inspect regularly for hazards or dangers; 2) maintain the premises and correct defects; 3) warn users, participants, and spectators about hazards or dangers that are not readily apparent; 4) warn users, participants, and spectators about participatory risks of the sport or activity; and 5) keep users and spectators safe during their use of the premises by having a plan for reasonable supervision and security; using reasonable employee recruiting, selection, hiring, and training practices; and having an emergency medical plan.

The Legal Obligation of Inspection.   Operators have a duty to reasonably protect invitees from known risks of injury. This means that operators must inspect the premises for risks or hazards that threaten invitees. Inspection is a duty which is shared by premises operators, coaches, and employees.

> Those in charge of sports facilities will be liable for any harm caused by the dangers they should have discovered. Moreover, if their employees are aware of the danger, this awareness is imputed to the owner or operator who become liable if they fail to take reasonable steps to remedy the problem or to warn participants. (Yasser, 1985, p. 238)

In *Lindgren v. Voge* (1961), the court stated that the obligation to inspect required the track operators to inspect the premises, including the rest rooms, in a more timely and thorough manner. Although the track operator did not have knowledge of the hazard, the court ruled that the operator failed to exercise reasonable care by not inspecting the rest rooms during the race. Sport and recreation facilities have the legal obligation to repair dangers which are discovered as a result of inspection; or, minimally, to warn patrons of the dangers if remedial steps cannot be taken immediately.

Inspections may be classified according to type or frequency. They may be informal or they can involve comprehensive checklists. The inspection may be a general inspection of the total facility or focus on a designated location. Inspections may be conducted daily, weekly, monthly, seasonally, or annually. The critical feature of any inspection plan is to meet the facility's obligation to discover hazards (Vivian and Maloy, 1992).

An effective inspection program can help to protect the facility from liability as it did in the case of *Byrd v. State* (1994). The court stated that the state had fulfilled its duty to maintain the park in a safe condition by conducting daily inspections and correcting defects as soon as possible. In contrast, in *Gray v. Louisiana Downs* (1991) the track operator was aware that accumulated debris was a hazard, but failed to have track employees inspect or remove trash from the area. The court felt it would not be unreasonable to have the stands inspected during race events or to provide trash receptacles for the spectators.

The Legal Obligation of Maintenance and Repair.   The premises operator has a duty to keep the facility in safe repair. A premises maintenance plan is a vital ingredient in fulfilling this legal obligation. Such a plan should include the correction of defects found through inspections as well as regularly scheduled maintenance of all areas of the facility. Such a plan helps to insure follow-up of inspections and will minimize risks which might not be revealed by inspection. For example, in situations involving bleacher defects, collapse of bleachers, or the fracture of wooden seats, backboards, or steps, reasonable inspection may reveal the hazard or danger. In situations where a hazard is not visible, a plan for maintenance of bleachers may call for replacement of defects before they become visible through inspection and will thereby minimize the possibility of accidents.

Bleacher cases are a problem when the premises have been leased, and the lease agreement is not clear regarding the maintenance responsibilities of the lessor or lessee. The general rule is, absent agreement otherwise, the owner or lessor is responsible for the maintenance of the bleachers on the premises (Berry and Wong, 1993).

The role of maintenance is especially important in insuring the safety of users and participants because they usually have greater access to the facility than spectators. For example, activity areas, locker rooms, showers, and private entrances and exits may be available to users and participants, but not to spectators. In a recent Illinois case, a high school tennis player sued the Board of Education for failure to maintain a tennis court. The player stepped into a hole on the court and injured his ankle. The issues were whether the Board was aware of the danger, had disregarded the defective condition of the court, failed to respond to previous complaints, and failed to inspect (*Carter v. New Trier East High School*, 1995).

The Legal Obligation to Warn of Concealed Dangers. The premises operator has a duty to warn users, participants, and spectators of concealed dangers that are not usually visible or apparent. The duty of the operator, therefore, is to warn the user or spectator about the risk. The warning must be reasonably sufficient to bring the plaintiff's attention to the danger. The operator may be required to provide a barrier near the hazard or to prevent access to the hazard if the warning is not sufficient to make the risk of danger apparent to the patrons. In one case, a student was injured when a junior high physical education class walked across a mopped floor after having been warned not to at the beginning of the class. It was determined that the type of warning given was not adequate to make junior high school age students aware of the danger (*Jolivette v. Iberia Parish School Bd.*, 1992).

In a Louisiana case, a plaintiff was injured while attending a baseball game at the Louisiana State University baseball stadium. As the plaintiff was proceeding down the steps of the temporary bleachers, he slipped and fell on what was termed an "awkward" step. It was disclosed that the temporary bleachers did not fit together properly. The university argued that it had no duty to warn of the non-uniform step since the step was obvious to all the patrons, and there had been no injuries when the temporary bleachers were used previously. The court disagreed (*Rispone v. Louisiana State University,* 1994).

Some premises risks and hazards are obvious to the patron. There is no legal duty to warn of such dangers. For example, in an Illinois case, a teenage spectator was injured while watching a tennis match from within the court. The court ruled that he was aware of the risks of tennis and, in encountering an obvious risk, assumed the risk of injury. The school did not owe him a warning of the obvious risk (*Chareas v. Township High School Dist.,* 1990).

The concept of open and obvious danger can apply in situations where the facility may have breached an obligation. For example, a plaintiff attended a performance at a dinner theater and was descending a stairway when she fell. The height of the handrail along the stairs did not conform to state code. The plaintiff, however, had been a frequent visitor to the theater over the course of four years and was familiar with the area. The court stated that premises liability is imposed when the operator is aware of the dangers but the injured party is not *(Wicichowski v. Gladieux Enterprises*, 1988).

The Legal Obligation of Advising of Participatory Risks. The premise operator has a duty to warn of participatory risks, those risks that are incidental to the game or activity. The user, participant, or spectator will usually assume risks and hazards that are inherent to the activity itself.

Participatory risks are treated much like open and obvious risks. There are, however, certain preconditions which have to be met before a user, spectator, or player assumes a participatory risk. The first, and foremost, precondition is that the user, spectator, or player has to know, understand, and appreciate the risk. The obligation here is called advising of participatory risks. It is a shared obligation of the operator, coaches, and premises supervisors who will be dealing directly with patrons.

There is also a distinction regarding the extent of the warning to be given for participatory risks. An operator may rely to an extent on a user's or participant's past experience for recognizing an activity hazard or risk. If the user or participant is just learning the activity, or is a minor child, then the operator has an affirmative obligation to advise of the risks of the activity. Coaches, supervisors, or instructors all have the obligation to warn the participants of participatory risks. An operator can be liable under the vicarious liability theory because the coaches or employees did not advise participants of the participatory risks of the activity. In *Maddox v. City of New York* (1985), an outfielder was injured when he slipped on wet grass. The court stated that there was no duty on the part of the stadium to warn the player of the risk since he was an experienced professional baseball player, was aware of the wet grass, and had examined the field before he chose to play. In contrast, in a Wisconsin case, an amateur baseball pitcher was struck in the eye by a batted ball. While normally being hit by a batted ball is a participatory risk, in this case, since the city acknowledged that the lighting was poor, the risk was created by the facility and was not a participatory risk (*Kloes v. Eau Claire Cavalier Baseball Assoc.*, 1992).

There is a difference when dealing with a spectator who is viewing the activity. Unlike the user or participant who may be familiar with the nature of the activity, an operator should not assume that a spectator is knowledgeable about participatory risks. The operator's obligation in this regard is to affirmatively advise spectators of the participatory risks. It is not unusual to see signs on the premises warning fans of baseball foul balls or flying hockey pucks. Often, the written warning is accompanied by a public address announcement warning of the participatory risks. Again, the operator is wise to assume spectators are not aware of the participatory risks of the activity they are watching. There are two other components of this obligation. First, in addition to providing warnings, an operator has to provide a reasonable number of seats protected by screens or barriers from participatory risks for those spectators who ask for them. Second, as noted under the obligation to maintain and repair, an operator is responsible to maintain and repair protective screens and barriers (van der Smissen, 1990).

The Legal Obligation to Keep Safe.   Three aspects of this personnel-related duty of the premises operator will be discussed. These are the duty to hire competent personnel, the duty to provide supervision, and the duty to provide for emergency care. These duties are illustrated in *Fish v. Los Angeles Dodgers Baseball Club* (1976) where a young spectator was knocked unconscious and temporarily exhibited incoherent speech after being struck by a foul ball. His examination by the contracted physician was incomplete and he was permitted to return to the game. Before leaving the stadium he began exhibiting renewed symptoms of serious injury. It was later determined that he had suffered a fractured skull the complications of which, if properly attended, would not have been fatal. The child's parents alleged *failure to hire competent personnel, failure to provide adequate supervision,* and *failure to provide emergency medical services* in their lawsuit against the Dodgers, as operators of the stadium, and the physician as their agent.

Failure to Hire Competent Personnel.   In most instances, the primary issues in the obligation to hire competent personnel are the employee recruiting, selection, and hiring process; and, the training process utilized by the operator for new employees. See Chapter 2.36 for more information relating to this topic.

Failure to Provide Supervision.   Three issues should be considered in determining if there was proper supervision in an injury situation. The first issue is whether the supervisors who were present were competent. The second issue is whether the supervisors were properly located. The final issue is whether there were sufficient supervisors for the event. See Chapter 2.32 for further information on supervision.

An illustration of inadequate planning and supervision is the 1993 football game between the University of Michigan and the University of Wisconsin at Madison, Wisconsin. Although the university anticipated potential crowd control problems and added more security for the game. their efforts were ineffective. About 12,000 fans surged onto the field crushing and injuring spectators. Many thought crowd control demanded more security staff than had been added.

Reacting to Emergency Medical Situations.   The third aspect of the keep safe obligation refers to the operator's ability to reasonably and properly react to medical emergencies. As noted in the *Fish v. Los Angeles Dodgers* case, it was maintained the physician failed to reasonably react to the youngster's head injury. By the same token, the response of other facility personnel to fan or participant injury is just as important. In the *Dodgers* case, part of the medical response involved the ushers and security who responded to the injured youngster in his seat. In the Wisconsin situation, it took more than one half hour for many of the injured to receive emergency medical treatment. The size of the crowd, the location of the injured parties, and the inability to clear the area of other fans all contributed to the delay in emergency medical help.

Finally, one of the most asked questions is whether there is an obligation for the operator to hire personnel who are also certified medical personnel. Generally, the obligation is that the operator must use reasonable efforts to obtain quick and capable medical assistance. Additionally, the operator should refrain from taking any actions that could aggravate the injury. This means that the operator has to be able to recognize when serious injury has occurred (as in the *Dodgers* case). There are a number of states where an operator has to provide certified medical personnel at certain events. For example, a physician or person trained in emergency medical care has to be in attendance at interscholastic football games in some states (Berry and Wong, 1993). Additionally, there are a number of states that require schools to have at least one person on school grounds during normal school hours who is certified to administer first aid (van der Smissen, 1990). There is no general common law obligation, however, to provide personnel who are trained in emergency medical care. An operator should know whether there is a state statute which would require employees to have those qualifications. For more information regarding emergency medical care, see Chapter 2.31.

Recent Trends

Dram Shop.   Traditionally, dram shop laws have focused on operators who *sold* alcoholic beverages to visibly intoxicated persons on the premises. The operator was then liable to third parties who were later injured by the intoxicated person. An operator should check the state law, however, to see if potential liability has been extended to include *providing* alcoholic beverages, as well as selling them.

ADA.   The 1990 Americans with Disabilities Act has significant impact for operators. Implicitly, this act recognizes that the disabled have been effectively barred from many physical activities simply due to the design and construction of facilities. The act obligates the operator to provide the disabled with access to facilities and programs in sport, recreation, and physical activity. Operators should be aware of this obligation and should realize that future construction, or the renovation of existing facilities, requires compliance with this law.

References

B. Cases
Byrd v. State, 614 N.Y.S.2d 446, 447 (N.Y.A.D. 1994).
Carter v. New Trier East High School, 272 Ill.App.3d 551, 208 Ill.Dec. 963, 650 N.E.2d 657 (1995).
Chareas v. Township High School Dist., 553 N.E.2d 23 (Ill. App. 1990).
City of Bloomington v. Kuruzovich, 517 N.E.2d 409 (Ind.App. 1987).
Codd v. Stevens Pass, Inc., 725 P.2d 1008 (Wash. App. 1986).
Daniels v. Thistledown Racing Club, Inc., 103 Ohio App.3d 281, 659 N.E.2d 346 (1995).
Dalury v. S-K-I Ltd., 670 A.2d 795, 799 (Vt. 1995).
Fish v. Los Angeles Dodgers Baseball Club, 128 Cal. Rptr. 807, 56 Cal. App. 3d 620 (1976).
Gray v. Louisiana Downs, 585 So.2d 1238 (La. App. 1991).
Jacobs v. Commonwealth Highland Theatres, Inc., 738 P.2d 6 (Colo. App. 1986); cert.den. June 8, 1987.
Jolivette v. Iberia Parish School Bd., 601 So.2d 812 (La. App. 1992).
Kloes v. Eau Claire Cavalier Baseball Assoc., 487 N.W.2d 77, 81 (Wis. App. 1992).
Light v. Ohio University, 502 N.E.2d 611 (Ohio 1986).
Lindgren v. Voge, 260 Minn. 262, 109 N.W.2d 754 (1961).

Maddox v. City of New York, 455 N.Y.S.2d 102 (N.Y. App. Div. 1982), 467 N.Y.S.2d 972, 121 Misc. 2d 358 (N.Y. App. Div. 1983), *rev'd,* 487 N.Y.S.2d 354 (N.Y. App. Div. 1985).

Straley v. Urbanna Chamber of Commerce, 413 S.E.2d 47 (Va. 1992).

Thompson v. Ruidoso-Sunland, Inc., 734 P.2d 267 (N.M. App. 1987).

Wicichowski v. Gladieux Enterprises, 561 N.E.2d 1012 (Ohio. App. 1988).

A. Publications

Berg, R. Stem the Stampede: The University of Wisconsin Hopes It Has Its Crowds Under Control. *Athletic Business,* November, 1994.

Berry, R.C. and Wong, G.M. (1993). *Law and Business of the Sports Industries: Common Issues in Amateur and Professional Sports,* Westport, Conn.: Praeger Publishers.

Flynn, R.B., Ed. (1993). *Facility Planning for Physical Education, Recreation, and Athletics.* Reston, Va.: American Alliance for Health, Physical Education, Recreation and Dance.

Keeton, W.P., et al. (1988). *Prosser and Keeton on the Law of Torts.* St. Paul, Minn.: West Publishing Co.

Maloy, B.P. (1988). *Law in Sport: Liability Cases in Management and Administration.* Indianapolis,: Benchmark Press, Inc.

Schubert, G.W., Smith, R.K., and Trentadue, J.C. (1986). *Sports Law.* St. Paul, Minn.: West Publishing Co.

van der Smissen, B. (1990). *Legal Liability and Risk Management for Public and Private Entities* (Vol. 1 & 2). Cincinnati, Ohio: Anderson Publishing Co.

Vivian, J. and Maloy, P. Developing a Risk-Management Partnership. *American Hockey Magazine,* Vol. 14, No. 2, February, 1992; Vol. 14, No. 3, March, 1992; and, Vol. 14, No. 3, April, 1992.

Yasser, R.L. (1985). *Torts and Sports.* Westport, Conn.: Quorum Books.

Transportation

Andy Pittman
Baylor University

Those organizations involved in transporting athletes must be concerned about their safety and welfare. The potential for liability extends not only to transporting them to and from events, but also to the use of vehicles in completing special tasks associated with the event (such as transporting injured persons to a hospital) and to supervisory concerns before, during, and after transport.

Private agencies, public agencies, and individuals must be aware of the duty of care required by law when transportation is provided. The potential for liability of public colleges and universities, public secondary schools, school boards and districts or other public agencies such as recreation departments, however, must be considered in light of applicable legislation. Most states have enacted State Tort Claims Acts which limit the liability of these institutions with respect to negligence in the operation of motor vehicles. In most states, in instances where no motor vehicle is involved (e.g., the existence of a duty to provide a safe bus stop or the placement of a bus stop), liability will attach only if the action at issue is ministerial in nature as opposed to discretionary. How these terms are defined varies by jurisdiction. Generally speaking, a **ministerial act** is one in which a particular course of action is required and violation of the act creates a presumption of negligence. In contrast, a **discretionary act** is one in which several courses of action are available and the course of action chosen is generally immune from liability.

■ ■ ■ ■

Representative Case

MURRAY v. ZARGER

Commonwealth Court of Pennsylvania
164 Pa. Commw. 157; 642 A.2d 575; 1994 Pa. Commw. LEXIS 229
March 1, 1994, Argued
May 18, 1994, Filed

OPINION: OPINION BY JUDGE MCGINLEY

Richard J. Zarger (Zarger) appeals from an order of the Erie County Court of Common Pleas (common pleas court) that denied his motion for post-trial relief. We reverse.

This action originally involved a negligence claim brought by Margaret Murray (Murray) as administratrix of the Estate of Cherise R. Silvis, a/k/a Cherise R. Murray (Decedent). Decedent was a high school freshman and member of the diving team at Corry Area High School when she sustained fatal injuries in an automobile accident on January 18, 1985. At the time of the accident Decedent and three other students were traveling to a swim meet in a car driven by Zarger and owned by Corry Area High School swim coach Jack McIntyre (McIntyre).

On May 23, 1988, Corry Area School District (School District) filed a motion for summary judgment alleging that the motor vehicle was not in the possession or control of the School District at the time of the accident, and that Zarger was not an employee of the School District at the time of the accident. The common pleas court denied the motion without prejudice. On July 25, 1988, the common pleas court approved Zarger's and McIntyre's requests to plead governmental immunity. The School District subsequently assumed McIntyre's defense, but not Zarger's. Zarger filed a motion for partial summary judgment seeking a determination that he was for all relevant purposes an employee of the School District and entitled to indemnification.

A jury trial began on October 11, 1988, and ended in a mistrial the same day. Zarger filed a praecipe with the common pleas court to place the motion for partial summary judgment on the argument list. The motion was granted by a January 5, 1989, order of the common pleas court. On November 21, 1989, this Court reversed the partial grant of summary judgment on the basis that such an order is not appropriate without an underlying judicial determination that the alleged employee caused the injury.

Before trial a settlement was executed among all the parties. As a part of the settlement the School District and Zarger agreed to preserve the issues of Zarger's employment and right to indemnification for subsequent determination and on June 11, 1990, a non-jury trial was held before the common pleas court. On June 11, 1992, the common pleas court issued an opinion and order. The common pleas court determined that Zarger was a volunteer diving coach who was provided remuneration by McIntyre, the swim coach, to assist him in coaching the diving squad and swim team and to drive students to meets. The common pleas court determined that Zarger was not an employee of the School District at the time of the accident, nor did he possess a good faith belief that he was acting within the scope of his alleged employment with the School District.

Zarger presents two issues on appeal: (1) did the common pleas court err in determining that Zarger was not an employee of the School District at the time of the accident; and (2) did the common pleas court err in determining that Zarger did not have a good faith belief that he was acting within the scope of his employment at the time of the accident?

Section 8501 of the Judicial Code (Code), 42 Pa. C.S. @ 8501, defines an "employee" for the purposes of indemnification, providing in relevant part: "Employee" Any person who is acting or who has acted on behalf of a government unit, whether on a permanent or temporary basis, whether compensated or not and whether within or without the territorial boundaries of the government unit, including any volunteer firemen or any elected or appointed officer, member of a governing body or other person designated to act for the government unit. Independent contractors under contract to the government unit and their employees and agents and persons performing tasks over which the government unit has no legal right of control are not employees of the government unit.

In Zarger I, we noted that the School District contended that Zarger was not an employee on the following grounds: that the School District had no control over the manner in which Zarger performed; that Zarger was not responsible for the swim team's performance; that there was no agreement between Zarger and the School District; that Zarger was used by McIntyre for his special diving skills only; and that Zarger was employed in a distinct occupation at the Corry YMCA and as an industrial engineer at McInnis Steel. Zarger I, 129 Pa. Commonwealth Ct. at 616, n.2, 566 A.2d at 648, n.2. These allegations on the part of the School District would, if proven, tend to establish that Zarger was an independent contractor and thus exempt from the definition of an employee set forth in the Code. Consequently, in our decision to remand, we observed that in Schuylkill County v. Maurer, 113 Pa. Commonwealth Ct. 54, 536 A.2d 479 (1988), a governmental immunity case, this Court held that when determining whether a person is an independent contractor or an employee, the proper guide to be utilized is that stated in Hammermill Paper Co. v. Rust Engineering Co., 430 Pa. 365, 243 A.2d 389 (1968). See Zarger I, 129 Pa. Commonwealth Ct. at 616, 566 A.2d at 648. In Hammermill, the Supreme Court stated:

> While no hard and fast rule exists to determine whether a particular relationship is that of employer-employee or owner-independent contractor, certain guidelines have been established and certain factors are required to be taken into consideration: 'Control of manner work is to be done; responsibility for result only; terms of agreement between the parties; the nature of the work or occupation; skill required for performance; whether one is engaged in a distinct occupation or business; which party supplies the tools; whether payment is by the time or by the job; whether work is part of the regular business of the employer, and also the right to terminate the employment at any time.' (citations

omitted). Hammermill, 430 Pa. at 370, 243 A.2d at 392.

•••

As Zarger contends, the definition of employee in the Act is broad. Zarger is not exempted from indemnification under the statute because he was a volunteer: Section 8501 specifically states that an "employee" may be a person acting on behalf of a government unit whether compensated or not.

At the trial, Zarger testified that after the former swim coach retired and McIntyre was approached by the School District about becoming head swimming coach, McIntyre asked him about working with him coaching the Corry High School divers in exchange for a portion of McIntyre's salary. Notes of Testimony, June 11, 1990, (N.T.) at 18. Zarger stated that McIntyre subsequently became head swimming coach and Zarger assisted him by coaching and transporting the divers to practice in Union City, a town twelve miles away. N.T. at 19. Zarger testified that McIntyre's predecessor, Bill Cochran, had started the practice of taking divers to the Union City Pool for practice. N.T. at 33. Zarger stated that, with regard to swim meets, he would go to the meets on the bus with the students, warm them up, prepare diving sheets and work with them throughout the event. Id. These were his duties throughout the 1985 season. Id. Also, he was given a one-time payment of approximately $300 by McIntyre for the 1985 season. N.T. at 45. It was Zarger's belief that the School Board was aware of his activities because the School Board president's daughter was on the diving team. N.T. at 49. Zarger also testified that he transported a diver to a meet in State College, Pennsylvania, and transported three divers to a district meet prior to the accident, and was reimbursed for mileage by the School District. N.T. at 125.

Zarger also called McIntyre as a witness. McIntyre stated that before he was hired he had a conversation with William Nichols (Nichols), supervisor of secondary education, and that he recollected that he was told whoever he wished to assist and however he wanted to split his salary was up to him. N.T. at 57-58. He stated that subsequent to that conversation he made arrangements with Zarger to assist him in return for approximately $200 and then to split his salary with David Cochran (Cochran). N.T. at 59. McIntyre stated that Zarger's duties were primarily to coach the divers, and that he occasionally transported them to meets. N.T. at 60, 65. He stated that he did not inform the school administration that he paid Zarger and Cochran. N.T. at 80.

McIntyre stated that on the day of the accident Zarger borrowed his car to transport the divers to an invitational swim meet at Iroquois High School with McIntyre's approval. N.T. at 66. McIntyre stated that he had submitted a written request to Gerard Rushin (Rushin), the Corry High School athletic director, requesting use of the school van for January 18, 1985, to transport the divers, but was told to use a car and that he would be reimbursed. N.T. at 68.

Rushin also testified at the trial and stated that he was aware prior to the date of the accident that Zarger was assisting McIntyre in some manner in his coaching duties. N.T. at 93. Rushin stated that he saw Zarger at swim meets with McIntyre and assumed he was helping out. N.T. at 112. Rushin stated that he had no objection to Zarger volunteering. N.T. at 123. Rushin stated that he did not know that the divers were practicing at Union City. N.T. at 117. Rushin confirmed that he approved the use of McIntyre's car to transport the divers to the meet on January 18, 1985. N.T. at 98. Rushin stated that he did not know that Zarger was the driver of McIntyre's car until he contacted Cochran after receiving a phone call from the Iroquois athletic director asking him why his divers had not arrived at the meet. N.T. at 107.

Nichols also testified and stated that he told McIntyre that he could use volunteers and pay them out of his salary if he wanted. N.T. at 131. Nichols stated that Cochran was specifically mentioned as someone whom McIntyre might use, and that although Zarger was not specifically discussed, Nichols would have had "no hesitation with recommending him also." Id. Nichols testified that he would have had to approve Zarger's transportation of students to meets prior to the date of the accident, and that he was surprised when Zarger testified to this, but he did not question Zarger's testimony. N.T at 152.

Despite the argument of Appellees McIntyre and the School District that this testimony does not establish that there was a position of "diving coach" or "assistant swim coach," that the school provided other alternatives for students riding to meets than being driven by Zarger, and that on the day of the accident, Rushin believed that McIntyre was to drive the students to the meet, the evidence is clear that Zarger acted on behalf of the School District in assisting with interscholastic athletics, a part of the regular business of the School District, and that he was authorized to drive students to meets prior to the accident.

The School District argues that Zarger is not an employee under 42 Pa. C.S. @ 8501, as he was a person over whom the School District had no legal right of control, and that if Zarger had refused to take the students to the meet on the day of the accident, there would have been no recourse against him. As we have stated, the definition of "employee" in Section 8501 of the Act does not require that an employee be compensated or possess a formal employment contract with the government unit, as long as he is acting in its interests. In Wilson v. Miladin, 123 Pa. Commonwealth Ct. 405, 553 A.2d 535 (1989), this Court held that a varsity football player was an "employee" under the Political Subdivisions Tort Claim Act when he knocked down a spectator while leading his team out of the locker room at a game, because he was acting on behalf of his school district by wearing a school uniform and participating in the game. This case presents an even clearer example of an individual servicing the school district. We do not believe that the issues the School District has raised concerning the informality of Zarger's relationship are persuasive when contrasted with Zarger's history of School District service, including the transport of swim team members to a diving meet.

Zarger also takes issue with the finding of the common pleas court that he did not possess a good faith reasonable belief that he was an employee of the School District at the time of the accident. The Act does not require an employee to have a "good faith reasonable belief" that he is an employee, although 42 Pa. C.S. 8548 states that indemnity will only issue under the act if the employee in good faith reasonably believes the action was within the scope of his duties. There is no evidence to establish that Zarger did not possess a good faith reasonable belief that transportation of the diving team to a diving meet was one of his duties as an assistant diving coach.

The order of the common pleas court is reversed.

BERNARD L. MCGINLEY, Judge

■ ■ ■ ■

Fundamental Concepts

Duty to Provide Transportation

Generally, when sport-related activities are sponsored by an organization, there may be a corresponding duty to provide transportation, and such transportation must be provided in a safe manner regardless of the mode of travel, who is doing the driving, or the point of departure. The duty to provide transportation usually begins at the point of departure and continues until those using the transportation have been returned to the original departure point. Liability exists regardless of whether the participants meet at the organization and are then assigned a particular vehicle or they are picked up by the driver at their homes or elsewhere.

It may be possible to avoid liability by establishing a policy that no transportation will be provided for anyone for a particular event. In that case, athletes are instructed to convene at the site of the event. However, this policy may not be practical if large numbers of people are involved, the distance to travel is far, or participants do not have access to an alternative form of transportation. The organization also needs to establish a policy governing the conditions under which a participant can leave an event by other transportation than that provided by the organization. For minors, parental permission should be required.

Duty of Care

When an organization provides transportation, it owes a duty of care with respect to such transportation. Generally, reasonable and ordinary care under the circumstances is the appropriate standard of care. However, there is authority which indicates that the operators of school buses are in the same general position as common carriers and that the highest degree of care consistent with the practical operation of the bus is required. The standard of care required of the drivers will be based on the particular circumstances. Some factors that may be considered in determining the standard of care include the age, knowledge, judgment, and experience of the passengers.

In a situation where a driver or organization has violated a specific statute enacted for the protection of the passengers and such violation is the proximate cause of an injury, the standard of care is deemed irrelevant. In that instance, the organization would be held absolutely liable.

Jurisdictions differ as to the duty required in regard to supervision. In some jurisdictions the duty of care includes a duty to provide a location where participants can wait for the transportation with reasonable safety and a duty to select a discharge point that does not needlessly expose them to any serious safety hazards. The duty to provide a reasonably safe location also may impose a duty upon the organization to provide proper supervision. In contrast, courts in other jurisdictions have ruled that the duty of an organization toward participants under its control applies only during the period they are transported to and from the event, commencing when the participant enters the vehicle and continuing until they have been safely discharged. Likewise, absent the existence of a special duty, this duty may not extend to situations where the participant is no longer under the organization's authority or is no longer under its physical custody.

Transportation Options

The transportation of participants to and from sport events and activities can be accomplished in one of four ways: a) independent contractor, b) use of organization-owned vehicles, c) use of employee vehicles, and d) use of non-employee vehicles. The potential for liability varies from situation to situation with the least potential for liability existing where independent contractors are used and the greatest potential where private vehicles are used. The risk of liability is not as high when one independently contracts because most of the risk is transferred. The risk of liability is greatest when non-employee vehicles are used because the organization has the least control. The keys to the determination of liability are the ownership of the vehicle and the relationship of the driver to the corporate entity responsible for the participants.

Independent Contractor. If an organization can afford it, using an independent contractor for transportation would be the best legal option, since the contract for service shifts liability to the contractor. The independent contractor may be of two types: common or private carrier. A common carrier is one who is in the business of transporting goods or persons for hire. A private carrier, on the other hand, only hires out to deliver goods or persons in particular cases. A common carrier may be held to a higher standard of care regarding the qualifications of the driver and the condition of the vehicle than a private carrier or a non-commercial driver.

There is authority which holds that an organization may delegate its duty of safe transportation to third party independent contractors. However, whether a person is an independent contractor is determined by who has the right to control the manner in which the work is done, the method of payment, the right to discharge, the skill required, and who furnishes the tools, equipment, or materials needed to accomplish the work. With respect to transportation, if factors such as the use of specific vehicles, the driver, the route, the enroute stops, and the manner of driving are all within the control of the transportation company and its employees, then it is likely the relationship is that of an independent contractor.

However, an organization may not be able to avoid liability if the organization is negligent in its selection of an independent contractor. Thus, it is always good administrative practice to investigate independent contractors carefully prior to entering into a contract with them. Several questions and concerns should be addressed in selecting an independent contractor. First, the independent contractor should be required to verify that it has sufficient liability insurance by providing a copy of its certificate of insurance regardless of whether it is a common or private carrier. Other items to consider when hiring a transportation company include requiring proof of insurance for each vehicle, evidence of an International Commerce Commission license number, age of equipment, company safety record, and availability of information demonstrating preventive maintenance.

Organization-owned Vehicles. For some agencies, the use of an independent contractor is not a viable option because of cost. Organization-owned vehicles are the most common means of transporting participants and provide the next best transportation option. Since the organization owns the vehicles, it has the legal responsibility for the safe transportation of the participants. The organization has a duty to see that the vehicles are in safe operating condition and to see that the drivers are properly qualified.

With all organization-owned vehicles, the organization is responsible for maintenance, and failure to do so leaves the organization liable. Any vehicle with defects such as broken mirrors, defective lights, broken windshield wipers, emergency doors which cannot be opened, or worn tires should not be used until the condition is corrected. At a minimum, each vehicle should be supplied with necessary emergency equipment including flares, markers, first aid kit, spare tire, tire jack, and approved traction devices (e.g., chains, snow tires) for use during inclement weather.

The organization is responsible for insuring that all persons assigned to drive vehicles are well qualified, well trained, and have the appropriate licenses. If the employee driver commits an *ultra vires* act, an act beyond the power authorized by law, the negligence of the employee is not imputed to the corporate entity. Examples of *ultra vires* acts include exceeding the speed limit, running a red light or stop sign, and deviating from the designated route.

In all states, the right to use a vehicle owned by a school to transport students to activities other than classes is controlled by state law. Some states have no restrictions while others restrict the use of school buses to providing transportation to and from classes. Other states restrict use depending upon the source of operating funds, which may be a critical factor in the application of governmental immunity. Until the 1970s, cities or schools were often not held liable for injuries resulting from negligence of employees due to immunity laws. Since that time, the doctrine of governmental immunity has been changed in many states by the passage of State Tort Claims Acts.

Employee and Non-Employee Vehicles. In some cases, organizations may find it necessary to use privately owned vehicles for transportation. Such vehicles may be owned by employees or by non-employees (e.g., parents, volunteers, participants). In either case, liability for negligence is generally retained by the organization.

Before the use of private vehicles is permitted, risk management policies should be established to be certain that both vehicles and drivers conform to acceptable safety standards. Such policies might relate to a physical inspection of the vehicle, maintenance records of the vehicle, vehicle insurance, and vehicle registration. Policies should also ensure that the driver is properly licensed, has a good driving reputation, has a violation-free driving record, and has no impairments which would preclude driving.

Employee Vehicles. When an employee, as a part of his or her employment, uses a personal vehicle for transporting students or patrons, a principal-agent relationship is established. An organization is vicariously liable for employee negligence committed within the course and scope of employment. Use of privately-owned vehicles does increase the risks to the organization; therefore, the establishment and enforcement of risk management policies regarding the driver and the vehicle is essential.

If the employee uses his or her privately-owned vehicle as a service to the organization and in accordance with organization policy, most jurisdictions require that the driver exercise reasonable and ordinary care. The employee will be personally liable for negligent operation of the vehicle, notwithstanding the vicarious liability of the organization.

Non-Employee Vehicles. When an organization has a duty to provide transportation and uses a private vehicle provided by someone who is not an employee, a principal-agent relationship is created. The organization is liable for the negligence of the driver. Because an organization has the least control when non-employee vehicles are used, this category creates the greatest risk of liability to the organization. It is imperative that the organization institute and enforce the risk management policies suggested at the beginning of this section.

Recent Developments

Independent Contractor. In *Chainani v. Board of Education of the City of New York* (1995), two children were struck, one by a school bus after she had departed it and the other by a car while she was trying to cross a highway to catch her bus at an undesignated stop. The court, in a consolidation of two cases, held for the school districts in both instances because transportation services had been contracted out to independent contractors. Ordinarily, the corporate entity is not liable for the acts of independent contractors in that, unlike the master-servant relationship, the corporate entity cannot control the manner in which the independent contractor's work is performed.

Negligence in Maintaining Vehicle and Selecting Driver. In 1986, a single-vehicle accident caused by the blowout of the right rear tire on a van carrying members of the Delgado Community College baseball team resulted in injuries to several of the team members. A student-coach, who was not qualified to drive the van because of the lack of a proper license, was driving the van at the time of the accident. Evidence indicated that the tire which blew out had been underinflated for much of its life and was underinflated by 30 pounds per square inch at the time of the accident. The court held that the college was negligent in maintaining the van and in selecting and training the driver and returned damages in excess of $3 million against the college (*Clement v. Griffin*, 1994).

Respondeat Superior. Plaintiff Christopher Foster, a senior high school basketball recruit, was visiting Butler County Community College and was injured in a motor vehicle accident. The driver, George Johnson, a student at the college and not an employee, had picked Foster up at the request of the head basketball coach. Johnson did not have liability insurance, his vehicle was unregistered, and he did not have a valid driver's license. The court stated that several facts were relevant in determining the scope of an employment situation: 1) the purpose of the employee's act rather than the method of performance; 2) whether the employee had express or implied authority to do the acts in question; and 3) whether the employee's acts were reasonably foreseeable by the employer. The fact that the act of driving was gratuitous was not fatal to the existence of an employer/employee relationship. The court upheld a judgment in excess of $2 million for the plaintiff (*Foster v. Board of Trustees*, 1991).

No Constitutional Duty to Supervise. Jack Reeves, a freshman high school football player, was injured as a result of a hazing incident on the return bus ride after a football game. The bus was driven by the football coach, who did nothing to stop the incident. Rather than file a tort claim (negligence or failure to supervise), Reeves sued the school and football coach on Constitutional grounds, alleging a violation of his civil rights. The defendants filed a summary judgment to dismiss the case. In upholding the summary judgment, the court found that the plaintiff was not deprived of any right, privilege, or immunity guaranteed by the Constitution. The court, in ruling that the coach did not violate Reeves' due process rights by failing to prevent hazing on the team bus, stated

> If the court were to accept the Plaintiff's argument here that the Constitution somehow imposes a duty on school officials to provide for the safety of students with respect to extracurricular activities, even though their participation in those activities is wholly voluntary, then there would no longer be any practical distinction between ordinary state-law negligence claims and federal constitutional violations, so long as the negligent party was acting under the color of state law. (*Reeves by Jones v. Besonen*, 1991, p.1140)

The court further stated that, even if this duty existed, the doctrine of qualified immunity shielded the coach from liability. School officials are not **constitutionally** required to protect students from assaults by fellow students during extracurricular activities, even if school officials are aware that some students are prone to "rough up" other students in connection with athletic events.

References

A. Cases

Anderson v. Shaughnessy, 526 N.W.2d 625 (MN. 1995).

Bishop v. State, Department of Corrections, 837 P.2d 1207 (Ariz. App. Div. 1 1992).

Bowers by Bowers v. City of Chattanooga, 855 S.W.2d 583 (Tenn. 1993).

Chainani v. Board of Education, 1995 WL 641390 (N.Y.).

Clement v. Griffin, 634 So.2d 412 (La. App. 4 Cir. 1994).

Cooper v. Millwood ISD #37, 887 P.2d 1370 (Okla. App. 1994).

Cunningham v. Niagara Falls, 272 N.Y.S. 720 (1934).

Dixon v. Whitfield, 654 So.2d 1230 (Fla. App. 1 Dist. 1995).

Durham Transportation v. Valero, 897 S.W.2d 404 (Tex. App.-Corpus Christi 1995).

Foster v. Board of Trustees of Butler County Community College, 771 F.Supp. 1122 (D. Kan 1991).

Gardner v. Biggart, 417 S.E.2d 858 (S.C. 1992).

Gorton v. Doty, 69 P.2d 136 (1937).

Goston v. Hutchison, 853 S.W.2d 729 (Tex. App.-Houston[1st Dist.] no writ 1993).

Gutierrez v. Dade County School Board, 604 So.2d 852 (Fla. App.3 Dist. 1992).

Hewett v. Miller, 898 S.W.2d 213 (Tenn. App. 1994).

Hoover v. Charlotte-Mecklenburg Board of Education, 361 S.E.2d 93 (N.C.App. 1987).

Kirby v. Spate, 448 S.E.2d 7 (Ga. App. 1994).

LeLeaux v. Hamshire-Fannett School District, 835 S.W.2d 49 (Tex. 1992).

Lofy v. Joint School District #2, City of Cumberland, 166 N.W.2d 809 (1969).

Luna v. Harlingen Consolidated School District, 821 S.W.2d 442 (Tex. App.-Corpus Christi 1991, writ denied).

Malmquist v. Hellenic Community of Minneapolis, Inc., 203 N.W.2d 420 (1925).

Merchants Parcel Delivery v. Pennsylvania Public Utility Commission, 28 A.2d 340 (1942).

Murray v. Zarger, 642 A.2d 575 (Pa. Cmwlth. 1994).

O'Campo v. School Board of Dade County, 589 So. 2d 323 (Fla. App. 3 Dist. 1991).

Plummer v. Dace, 818 S.W.2d 317 (Mo. App. 1991).

Reeves by Jones v. Besonen, 754 F. Supp. 1135 (E.D. Mich. 1991).

Robertson v. Travis, 393 So. 2d 304 (La. App. 1st Cir. 1980), cert den (La) 397 So. 2d 805 and cert den (La) 397 So. 2d 806 (1981).

Sparks v. L. D. Folsom Company, 31 Cal. Rptr. 640 (1963).

Stokes v. Tulsa Public School, 875 P.2d 445 (Okl. App. 1994).

Swearinger v. Fall River Joint Unified School District, 212 Cal. Rptr. 400 (Cal. App. 3 Dist. 1985).

Tryer v. Ojai Valley School, 12 Cal. Rptr. 2d 114 (Cal. App. 2 Dist. 1992).

Wenger v. Goodell, 632 N.Y.S.2d 865 (A.D.3 Dept. 1995).

Yurkovich v. Rose, 847 P.2d. 925 (Wash. App. Div. 1 1993).

B. Publications

Barron, T., A Fleet for the Street, *College Athletic Management*, 3 (3), 1991, 19-21.

Beth, B., Smooth Traveling, *College Athletic Management,* 2 (6), 1990, 47-49.

78A C.J.S., *Schools and School Districts* §474-477, 1995.

Gregory, S. L., Chartering the Route, *College Athletic Management*, 2 (4), 1990, 14, 16-17.

Hart, J. E. and Ritson, R.E., (1993) *Liability and Safety in Physical Education and Sport*, Reston, VA: AAHPERD.

Korpela, A.E., Annotation, Tort Liability of Public Schools and Institutions of Higher Learning for Accidents Associated With the Transportation of Students, 34 *A.L.R.*3d, 1970, 1212-1245.

Lyke, R., Smooth Driving, *College Athletic Management*, 1 (3), 1989, 79-80 and Voyaging with Vans, *College Athletic Management,* 1 (5), 1989, 58.

Nygaard, G. and Boone, T.H., (1989) *Law for Physical Educators and Coaches,* Columbus, Ohio: Publishing Horizons, Inc.

Speiser, S.M., et al., 2 The American Law of Torts 1985, §6.27, 128-134.

van der Smissen, B. (1990). *Legal Liability and Risk Management for Public and Private Entities*. Cincinnati: Anderson Publishing Co.

— 2.36 —

Employment Torts

Betty van der Smissen
Michigan State University

Whereas torts have been thought of primarily in terms of negligence (unintentional torts) and participant/spectator injuries (see Chapters 2.31 through 2.35), in the decade of the '90s, torts in employment, that is, employee-related torts, have become a major concern. Both intentional torts and negligence are involved, federal and state legislation has been passed, and negligence theory (see Chapters 2.12 and 2.21) has been modified.

Two primary areas of employment torts are addressed in this chapter—1) participant abuse and the employment process, and 2) the working environment and gender discrimination. Perhaps employment torts are a product of the '90s society with its seemingly paradoxical behaviors of violence and human rights. And, sport, as a microcosm of society, has experienced these behaviors, as illustrative cases evidence.

■ ■ ■ ■

Representative Case

DOE v. TAYLOR INDEPENDENT SCHOOL DISTRICT
United States Court of Appeals for the Fifth Circuit
15 F.3d 443; 1994 U.S. App. LEXIS 3846
March 3, 1994, Decided

OPINION: E. GRADY JOLLY and W. EUGENE DAVIS

Jane Doe was sexually molested by her high school teacher in Taylor, Texas. Defendant Eddy Lankford, principal of Taylor High, and defendant Mike Caplinger, superintendent of the Taylor Independent School District, were sued in their supervisory capacity by Jane Doe for permitting violations of her substantive due process right to bodily integrity. The district court denied their claim of qualified immunity, and they have filed this interlocutory appeal on that issue. We hold, first, that schoolchildren do have a liberty interest in their bodily integrity that is protected by the Due Process Clause of the Fourteenth Amendment and that physical sexual abuse by a school employee violates that right. Second, we hold that school officials can be held liable for supervisory failures that result in the molestation of a schoolchild if those failures manifest a deliberate indifference to the constitutional rights of that child. Next, we conclude that each of these legal principles was clearly established in 1987, when the violations took place. Finally, in analyzing whether Caplinger and Lankford fulfilled the duty that they owed to Jane Doe, we reverse the district court's denial of immunity to defendant Caplinger, but we affirm its denial of immunity to Lankford.

I

Facts

• • •

Defendant Jesse Lynn Stroud, a twenty-year veteran of Texas's public education system, was employed by the Taylor Independent School District as a biology teacher and assistant coach from 1981 until 1987. It was no secret within the school community that Coach Stroud behaved inappropriately toward a number of young female students over the course of his employment at Taylor High. He made little effort to conceal his fancy for these female students: he wrote notes to them, he let them drive his truck, he exhibited explicit favoritism toward them in class, and often touched them in an overly familiar, inappropriate way.

Defendant Eddy Lankford became the principal of Taylor High in August 1983. By the fall semester of 1985, complaints about Stroud's behavior had reached his office through various channels. During the previous 1984-1985 school year, Stroud had "befriended" one of his female freshman students. Their friendship far transgressed the boundaries of a normal, appropriate teacher-student relationship.

• • •

By the fall of 1985, approximately one year after their "relationship" had begun, rumors about Stroud and the freshman student (by then a sophomore) were circulating not only among students and faculty but also among the town residents of Taylor. Stroud's favoritism in the classroom was also well-known within the school community. In addition, Stroud had also befriended a new female freshman student, and began a similar inappropriate relationship (note-writing, gift-giving, walking to class, etc.) with her. Principal Lankford approached Stroud outside the fieldhouse during the 1985 football season and spoke to him about being "too friendly" with the sophomore student.

Also during the fall of 1985, the school librarian, Mary Jean Livingood, . . . reported the inappropriate behavior she had witnessed to Principal Lank-ford and also informed him of the two telephone calls she had received from parents.

• • •

In May of 1986, Livingood reported to Lankford that she had witnessed an episode of "child molestation" involving Stroud and two freshman female students. . . .

• • •

Lankford downplayed the incident. . . . Lankford did not warn or discipline Stroud—even mildly—for any incident or conduct. Indeed, Lankford failed to document any of the complaints he received about Stroud.

All of this behavior occurred before defendant Mike Caplinger ever moved to Taylor or worked for the Taylor Independent School District. Caplinger became the superintendent of the Taylor ISD in July 1986; Lankford did not inform Caplinger of any problems—real or potential—with Stroud or with his pattern of conduct.

Plaintiff Jane Doe entered Taylor High as a freshman in August 1986; she was a student in Stroud's biology class. Stroud began his seduction of Doe by writing personal—often suggestive—comments on her homework and test papers.

• • •

By late fall, Stroud was touching and kissing Jane Doe. It began with a kiss on her cheek as she was leaving the school fieldhouse one day. Eventually, he began taking her into the laboratory room adjacent to his classroom and to the fieldhouse to engage in kissing and petting. Their physical relationship escalated to heavy petting and undressing in January 1987, when Stroud took Doe and some of her friends, including his own daughter, to a rock concert. There, he bought her alcoholic beverages, took her back to the fieldhouse, and began caressing her in the most intimate of ways. He suggested intercourse, but she refused.

Rumors about Doe and Stroud were rampant among the students and faculty by this time. The two were constantly together—walking to class, riding in the car, going out to lunch. Doe often went to Stroud's classroom during other class periods. Coaches and students frequently teased Stroud about his relationship with Doe, often mentioning the two freshman girls he had befriended during the two previous years. Sometime in January 1987, Lankford heard that Stroud had taken Doe and other students to the rock concert; that month he also received complaints from four female students in Stroud's biology class about Stroud's favoritism toward certain students. Lankford spoke with Stroud about this complaint, and, for the first time, notified Caplinger about possible problems with Coach Stroud.

In early February 1987, Mickey Miller, the assistant principal of Taylor's middle school, reported to Caplinger that at a basketball game he had witnessed Stroud behaving inappropriately with several freshman girls, including Jane Doe. . . . Caplinger instructed Lankford to speak with Stroud about this incident, which he did; the athletic director, Eddy Spiller, also spoke with Stroud about the report.

• • •

On Valentine's Day, Stroud gave Jane Doe a valentine that read: "To my most favorite, prettiest, sweetest, nicest sweetheart in the world! Please don't change cause I need you. I'm in love with you. Forever—for real—I love you." A friend and classmate of Jane Doe's, Brittani B., found the valentine in Doe's purse

• • •

Brittani took the note to Lankford the next day; . . . Lankford did not keep a copy of the note and did not investigate the matter further; he did not tell Superintendent Caplinger about the incident, nor did he speak with Stroud or Doe. His only action was to transfer Brittani out of Stroud's biology class.

• • •

In late March or early April 1987, Stroud and Doe had intercourse for the first time. She was fifteen years old. Stroud was her first sexual partner.

Over the next several months, Stroud and Doe had repeated sexual contact. Sex occurred at different locations, both on and off the school grounds. Their romantic relationship—although perhaps not the extent of it—was common knowledge within the Taylor High community, not only among students, but also among the faculty and the parents of many students. Lankford asked a friend whose daughter was a student at the high school to "keep his ears open" for information about Doe and Stroud. On Stroud's performance evaluation by Lankford for the 1986-1987 academic year, however, there was nothing to indicate that Stroud's performance was anything less than fully satisfactory. Indeed, Lankford still had not even informally documented any incident or pattern of conduct relating to Stroud.

In June 1987, Stroud took Doe and some other girls, along with his family, to a local fair, the Corn Festival, . . . Two concerned parents, both prominent members of the community, reported to Caplinger that Stroud was behaving inappropriately with Jane Doe at this festival, that Mrs. Stroud had left the festival because of his behavior, and that there was a possibility that he and Doe had left the festival together. One of the parents also showed Caplinger notes that Stroud had written to his daughter.

In response to the report, Caplinger contacted the parents of the girl who, according to the story, was intoxicated and misbehaving at the festival in the company of Doe and Stroud. When the girl's mother assured him that her daughter had not even been at the festival, that she had been sick and at home, Caplinger dismissed the report as unfounded without investigating further or contacting Jane Doe's parents to discuss the report with them.

• • •

In July 1987, Doe's parents discovered photographs of Stroud among Doe's possessions with such handwritten inscriptions by Stroud as: "Please don't ever change and don't ever leave me. I want to be this close always—I love you—Coach Lynn Stroud." Doe's parents immediately

scheduled a meeting with Caplinger. . . . He promised to convene a meeting of all the parties involved. After speaking with Doe's parents, Caplinger spoke with Jane Doe privately in his office. He showed her the photographs her parents had just presented to him and inquired about the nature of her relationship with Stroud. Doe suggested that the notes on the photos were just "friendly gestures." She explicitly denied any sexual relations with Stroud.

Caplinger called Lankford after the meeting with the Does, who in turn called Stroud. . . . There, the three men discussed the situation. Caplinger and Lankford warned Stroud to keep his distance from Jane Doe, and that he would be fired "if something was going on." No further action was taken, however; the meeting that Caplinger had promised to schedule never took place, and Stroud did not hear from either Lankford or Caplinger again until October 6, the day he was suspended from employment.

Although Jane Doe was able to stay away from Stroud for the remainder of the summer vacation, when classes resumed in the late summer of 1987, Stroud's sexual advances towards her resumed as well, and soon thereafter they began having intercourse again. Lankford admits that he watched Stroud no more closely than he previously had. The sexual contact continued into the fall of Jane Doe's sophomore year, until October 5, when Doe's mother found more love letters from Stroud among Jane's possessions. The Does then consulted their family lawyer, who agreed to discuss the matter with Jane. Upon meeting with Jane, the attorney learned the truth about her sexual involvement with Stroud. Doe explained that she had kept the matter a secret because she feared the repercussions of disclosure.

The attorney reported the information to Caplinger at once. . . . Caplinger ordered Stroud immediately suspended from employment. Stroud later resigned his position and pled guilty to criminal charges stemming from his molestation of Jane Doe.

II

Procedural History

Jane Doe brought this @ 1983 civil rights lawsuit against Stroud, the school district, Superintendent Caplinger, and Principal Lankford. She charged inter alia that these defendants, while acting under color of state law, deprived her of her constitutional rights guaranteed by the Fourteenth Amendment's Due Process and Equal Protection Clauses, in violation of 42 U.S.C. @ 1983. Following the denial of their motions for summary judgment on qualified immunity grounds, Caplinger and Lankford filed this appeal. Both contend that they are entitled to qualified immunity because: (1) Jane Doe was not deprived of any constitutional right when she was sexually molested by Coach Stroud; (2) even if Doe was deprived of a constitutional right, they owed her no duty in connection with this constitutional violation; (3) even if Doe was deprived of a constitutional right and they owed her a duty with respect to that right, these issues of law were not "clearly established" in 1987 when the violations took place; and (4) in any event, their response to the situation satisfied any duty that they owed to Doe.

III

Due Process

A

The first step in deciding whether Caplinger and Lankford are entitled to claim qualified immunity from this lawsuit is to determine whether the Constitution, through the Fourteenth Amendment's substantive due process component, protects school-age children attending public schools from sexual abuse inflicted by a school employee. "Section 1983 imposes liability for violations of rights protected by the Constitution, not for violations of duties of care arising out of tort law." . . . To state a cause of action under @ 1983 for violation of the Due Process Clause, plaintiffs "must show that they have asserted a recognized 'liberty or property' interest within the purview of the Fourteenth Amendment, and that they were intentionally or recklessly deprived of that interest, even temporarily, under color of state law." . . . "The Supreme Court has expanded the definition of 'liberty' beyond the core textual meaning of that term to include [not only] the . . . privileges [expressly] enumerated by the Bill of Rights, [but also] the 'fundamental rights implicit in the concept of ordered liberty' and 'deeply rooted in this Nation's history and tradition' under the Due Process Clause."

• • •

Jane Doe's substantive due process claim is grounded upon the premise that schoolchildren have a liberty interest in their bodily integrity that is protected by the Due Process Clause of the Fourteenth Amendment and upon the premise that physical sexual abuse by a school employee violates that right. This circuit held as early as 1981 that "the right to be free of state-occasioned damage to a person's bodily integrity is protected by the fourteenth amendment guarantee of due process."

• • •

If the Constitution protects a schoolchild against being tied to a chair or against arbitrary paddlings, then surely the Constitution protects a schoolchild from physical sexual abuse—here, sexually fondling a 15-year-old school girl and statutory rape—by a public schoolteacher. Stroud's sexual abuse of Jane Doe, earlier detailed in this opinion, is not contested by the defendants. Thus, Jane

Doe clearly was deprived of a liberty interest recognized under the substantive due process component of the Fourteenth Amendment. It is incontrovertible that bodily integrity is necessarily violated when a state actor sexually abuses a schoolchild and that such misconduct deprives the child of rights vouchsafed by the Fourteenth Amendment.

• • •

B

Having concluded that Stroud's physical sexual abuse of Jane Doe violated her constitutional right to substantive due process, we next must decide whether school officials, like the appellants in this case, owe any duty to a schoolchild when a subordinate violates that child's constitutional rights.

• • •

This circuit has held that supervisors can be liable for "gross negligence" or "deliberate indifference" to violations of their subordinates.

• • •

In Lopez, we applied these same principles when we adopted a narrow duty on the part of school officials: a duty not to "callously disregard" a student's constitutional rights. Id. 817 F.2d at 355. The Lopez panel, throughout its opinion, interchangeably used the terms "callous disregard," "deliberately indifferent," "grossly negligent," and "callous indifference."

• • •

In Canton, the Supreme Court held that a municipality is responsible in certain circumstances under @ 1983 for a failure to train its employees that results in the violation of a plaintiff's right to receive necessary medical attention while in police custody. Id. The Court explained, however, that such liability, predicated on a violation of the plaintiff's right under the Due Process Clause of the Fourteenth Amendment, depends on a showing of (1) a "deliberately indifferent" policy of training that (2) was the "closely related" cause of the violation of the plaintiff's federally protected rights.

• • •

The most important difference between City of Canton and this case is that the former dealt with a municipality's liability whereas the latter deals with an individual supervisor's liability. The legal elements of an individual's supervisory liability and a political subdivision's liability, however, are similar enough that the same standards of fault and causation should govern. A municipality, with its broad obligation to supervise all of its employees, is liable under @ 1983 if it supervises its employees in a manner that manifests deliberate indifference to the constitutional rights of citizens. We see no principled reason why an individual to whom the municipality has delegated responsibility to directly supervise the employee should not be held liable under the same standard. Other circuits have reached substantially the same result.

• • •

The similarities between the cases, however, are more important than the differences: Both cases involve alleged failures of supervisors to prevent substantive due process violations occasioned by their subordinates. Thus, in Gonzalez v. Ysleta Independent School District, 996 F.2d 745, 753-60 (5th Cir.1993), we applied City of Canton to an elementary school student's @ 1983 claim against a school district for supervisory failures that led to a teacher's violation of her substantive due process right to bodily security. We concluded that the school district could be held liable for supervisory failures resulting in the molestation of the student only if those failures "manifested a deliberate indifference to the welfare of the school children." Id. 996 F.2d at 760. We therefore hold that a school official's liability arises only at the point when the student shows that the official, by action or inaction, demonstrates a deliberate indifference to his or her constitutional rights.

• • •

Using this standard, we adopt the following test, which determines the personal liability of school officials in physical sexual abuse cases. A supervisory school official can be held personally liable for a subordinate's violation of an elementary or secondary school student's constitutional right to bodily integrity in physical sexual abuse cases if the plaintiff establishes that:

1. the defendant learned of facts or a pattern of inappropriate sexual behavior by a subordinate pointing plainly toward the conclusion that the subordinate was sexually abusing the student; and

2. the defendant demonstrated deliberate indifference toward the constitutional rights of the student by failing to take action that was obviously necessary to prevent or stop the abuse; and

3. such failure caused a constitutional injury to the student.

C

We must next consider these legal principles in the context of qualified immunity. Under the shield of qualified immunity, Caplinger and Lankford cannot be held liable under @ 1983 unless (1) Jane Doe's liberty interest under the substantive due process component of the Fourteenth Amendment, and (2) Caplinger's and Lankford's duty with respect to Jane Doe's constitutional right were "clearly established" at the time these events took place. See Stem v. Ahearn, 908 F.2d 1, 5 (5th Cir.1990), cert.

denied, 498 U.S. 1069, 111 S. Ct. 788, 112 L. Ed. 2d 850 (1991). For a constitutional right to be clearly established, "the contours of the right must be sufficiently clear that a reasonable official would understand that what he is doing violates that right."

• • •

The "contours" of a student's substantive due process right to be free from sexual abuse and violations of her bodily integrity were clearly established in 1987. In 1987 this court held that it was clearly established in 1985 that the Due Process Clause protects a schoolchild from being lashed to a chair for the better part of two days for "instructional purposes." . . . Indeed, this much seems crystal clear: No reasonable public school official in 1987 would have assumed that he could, with constitutional immunity, sexually molest a minor student.

Not only was the underlying violation clearly established in 1987, but Lankford's and Caplinger's duty with respect to that violation was also clearly established at that time. . . . In Bowen v. Watkins, 669 F.2d 979, 988 (5th Cir.1982), we observed generally that:

> Although supervisory officials cannot be held liable solely on the basis of their employer-employee relationship with a tortfeasor, they may be liable when their own action or inaction, including a failure to supervise that amounts to gross negligence or deliberate indifference, is a proximate cause of the constitutional violation.

In the face of this precedent, Lankford and Caplinger point to no authority from this circuit involving school officials which would enable them to reasonably believe, in 1987, that they could be deliberately indifferent to their subordinate's violation of a student's constitutional rights and escape supervisory liability under @ 1983. In fact, Lopez and our earlier cases arguably announced a broader duty on the part of school officials than we adopt today. See Lopez, 817 F.2d at 355. By narrowing the duty that @ 1983 imposes on supervisors, the courts have not affected its status as "clearly established."

D

Having established that Jane Doe's constitutional right to bodily integrity and the appellants' duty with respect to that right were clearly established in 1987 when these events occurred, we must determine whether, on the record before us, Lankford and Caplinger have established that they satisfied their duty to Doe, and are thus entitled to summary judgment as a matter of law. The plaintiff in this case has adduced clear summary judgment evidence of deliberate indifference by defendant Lankford toward her constitutional rights. By 1987, Lankford had certainly received notice of a pattern of inappropriate behavior that had been committed by Stroud that suggested misconduct of a sexual nature. He had spoken with Stroud two years earlier, in 1985, about being "too friendly" with a particular female student. He had received complaints from parents about Stroud's favoritism toward certain girls in the classroom. The school librarian reported Stroud's inappropriate behavior with female students to Lankford on two occasions, and at one point described the incident she witnessed as "child molestation." More importantly, Lankford received knowledge that Stroud was directing his inappropriate sexual behavior specifically toward Doe. He had heard about Mickey Miller's report of Stroud's misconduct with freshman girls, including Jane Doe, at a school basketball game. A jury could find that Lankford then received a clear signal that Stroud and Doe were engaged in a sexual relationship when Brittani B. gave him the valentine in February 1987. Later that year, Lankford received reports about Stroud's inappropriate behavior with Doe at the Corn Festival and learned that Doe's parents had discovered Stroud's autographed photographs in Doe's possession. Thus, under the facts construed in the light most favorable to Jane Doe and considering all the information Lankford received about Stroud's relationship with Doe, she has satisfied the first prong of the test with respect to defendant Lankford—knowledge of facts or a pattern of inappropriate sexual behavior by Stroud pointing plainly toward the conclusion that he was sexually abusing Doe.

Doe has also illustrated, in a manner sufficient to survive a summary judgment motion, that Lankford demonstrated deliberate indifference to the offensive acts by failing to take action that was obviously necessary to prevent or stop Stroud's abuse. When certain parents complained about Stroud's favoritism, Lankford suggested that their children were "jealous" of the favorite students. Lankford similarly dismissed the librarian's report of "child molestation." In perhaps the most striking example of his apathy, he responded to Brittani B.'s presentation of the valentine—which he admitted appeared to bear Stroud's handwriting—by transferring Brittani (not Jane Doe) out of Stroud's class. He never bothered to discuss the valentine incident with Caplinger, Stroud, Doe, or Doe's parents. He did not record any of these complaints of inappropriate conduct in Stroud's personnel file. He did not take the obvious steps of removing Doe from Stroud's class and directing Stroud to stay away from Doe. Both Stroud and Doe stated that they did not begin having sexual intercourse until late March or early April 1987. A jury could reasonably conclude that had Lankford taken actions that were obviously necessary in response to the valentine—indeed, if he had responded at all—the relationship might have been derailed at that point and the vio-

lation of Jane Doe's rights would not have been as severe or prolonged. Thus, Jane Doe has, in a manner sufficient to withstand a motion for summary judgment, stated a claim under @ 1983 that defendant Lankford was deliberately indifferent to his subordinate's violation of her constitutional right to bodily integrity.

With respect to whether defendant Caplinger is immune from this lawsuit, however, the evidence presented tells a different story. The first time Caplinger heard of any potential misconduct by Stroud was when he received the report from Mickey Miller in February 1987. He promptly notified Lankford and instructed him to speak with Stroud about the incident. There is no evidence that Lankford informed Caplinger at that time about Stroud's past behavior, and it is undisputed that Lankford never documented any of the reports he had received about Stroud.

Caplinger did not receive any other reports about Stroud until June 1987, when two parents reported the Corn Festival incident to him. Again, Caplinger promptly responded by contacting the parents of one of the allegedly misbehaving students reportedly at the festival. He was assured that the accused student was not even at the event. We cannot say that Caplinger's decision not to pursue the investigation further, after the parents assured him that their child had not even attended the Corn Festival, exhibited deliberate indifference.

When Doe's parents met with Caplinger concerning the photographs of Stroud in July 1987, Caplinger again responded appropriately, if ineffectively, to the situation.

• • •

Although after the July photograph incident Caplinger had received notice of a pattern of inappropriate sexual behavior sufficient to satisfy the first prong of the test, he certainly did not respond to the misconduct with deliberate indifference. He instructed Lankford to speak with Stroud about the incident at the basketball game; he personally investigated the report concerning the Corn Festival report; and he met with Stroud immediately after learning of the photographs, reprimanded him for his conduct, and unequivocally warned him of the consequences if any further misconduct was reported. His actions were ineffective, but not deliberately indifferent. Summary judgment should have been granted to defendant Caplinger on the grounds of qualified immunity.

• • •

V

The sole question before us is the propriety of the district court's denial of qualified immunity to the appellant school officials. The school officials' main argument that the liability of a school official for ignoring a subordinate's sexual abuse of a 15-year-old student was not clearly established in 1987.

Appellants, however, agree that by 1987 the Constitution clearly protected the most hardened criminal inmate from abuse by his guard and imposed liability on the guard's supervisor who was consciously indifferent to such abuse. Similarly, appellants cannot seriously contest that the @ 1983 liability of a police chief was not clearly established in 1987 when the chief was consciously indifferent to his officer's physical abuse of a citizen. In short, supervisory liability for deliberate indifference to constitutional violations committed by subordinates was clearly established when the events in this case occurred. Consequently, the school officials' argument that with constitutional immunity they could ignore the teacher/coach's

physical sexual abuse of an impressionable 15-year-old student is, as a practical matter perverse, and, as a legal matter, not supported by the case law. Such an argument neither legally nor logically makes any sense.

For the reasons stated above, we affirm the district court's order denying qualified immunity to defendant Lankford and reverse the district court's order denying qualified immunity to defendant Caplinger. We also remand this case to the district court for further proceedings consistent with this opinion.

AFFIRMED in part, REVERSED in part and REMANDED.

■ ■ ■ ■

Fundamental Concepts

Participant Abuse and the Employment Process

Increasingly there has been concern regarding the physical and sexual abuse of participants, particularly children, but also persons with disabilities and the elderly,[1] by employees and volunteers who provide services, including sport and recreation, to these individuals, whether it be in the public sector of schools and municipalities, the nonprofit sector, or commercial enterprise (see Chapter 2.41 Assault and Battery).

Statutes. Both the federal government and more than three-fourths of the state governments have responded by passing legislation.[2] There are three approaches used in legislation—1) making child abuse a crime[3] and maintaining a registry of child abusers, 2) requiring those working with children to report suspected child abuse to a federal or state agency[4] and giving protection to them for reporting, and 3) requiring criminal background checks for all persons working with children. It is the third approach that applies particularly to employment process negligence.

---

[1]Illustrations relate only to children as that is where the preponderance of cases is and the greatest concern to sport.

[2]e.g., National Child Protection Act of 1993, P.L. 103-209, criminal justice agency of each state must report child abuse crime information to National Criminal History Background Check System; Victims of Child Abuse Act of 1990, Subtitle E of Crime Control Act of 1990 - Title II, P.L. 101-647, child care worker employee background checks. See your agency or institution personnel office for legislation and regulations specific to your state.

Action on abuses also may be brought under Title IX, e.g., *Leija v. Canutillo Indep. Sch. Dist.* (1995) second grade student allegedly sexually abused by physical education teacher/coach, in "teacher-student sexual abuse cases" under Title IX acts of teachers are imputed to school district under strict liability principles, $1.4 M awarded.

Action also may be brought on deprivation of liberty interest under 14th amendment's substantive due process, e.g., *Doe v. Taylor Indep. Sch. Dist.* (1994) assistant coach/biology teacher sexually molested student, "deliberate indifference" on part of school officials held deprived student of Constitutional right (see the Representative Case).

[3]e.g., *State v. Laird*, (1989) teacher/coach convicted of molesting a 14-year-old student, 8 year sentence at hard labor with 5 years suspended, not an excessive sentence; *People v. Arnold* (1992) 2 female high school students brought action under sexual battery statute against wrestling coach, convicted of 5 felony counts and 6 misdemeanor counts; *People v. Peters* (1992) 13-year-old student sued gym teacher/swim coach under sexual abuse crime statute.

[4]e.g., *C.B. v. Bobo* (1995) physical education teacher allegedly sexually abused student, private right of action did not exist under Child Abuse Reporting Act; *Doe v. Rains Indep. Sch. Dist.* (1995) teacher/coach had sexual relationship with minor student who had been baby-sitting for him, held violation of state statute to report abuse within 48 hours not "state action" required to sustain sec. 1983 suit.

Modifications in the Doctrine of *Respondeat Superior.* There have been two major modifications in the doctrine of *respondeat superior* (see Chapter 2.12). First, under the doctrine, the corporate entity has not been liable for the intentional torts or criminal acts of its employees, since such acts are considered outside the scope of authority and responsibility and not for the benefit of the employer. Secondly, the doctrine has deemed that administrative/supervisory personnel are not responsible as individuals for such acts of employees working under them. However, as related to employment torts, both the corporate entity and the administrative/supervisory personnel, as individuals, are liable. They are liable for the injury caused by the intentional tort because they were negligent as related to the employment process which enhanced the likelihood of such intentional tort or crime occurring. This misfeasance most often is an act of omission and referred to as *deliberate indifference.* Deliberate indifference occurs when one is aware of the situation or potential problem, but is indifferent to it by inaction. To be deliberately indifferent implies intent.

Concept of Negligence. The employment process encompasses not only the hiring process, but also retention, supervision, training, and referral. The term negligent is placed in front of each of these processes, e.g., negligent hire, negligent supervision, et al. However, there is modification in meaning of the term. Negligence usually means failure to conduct an activity or provide a service in accord with appropriate professional standards. In this sense, employment process negligence would mean employing an incompetent person to conduct the activity or provide the service; however, when reference is made to negligent hire, et al, the term means that an employee is hired or a volunteer is assigned who is *unfit, i.e., has a propensity for physically violent or sexually abusive behavior.* The individual may very well be highly competent as related to the activity or service. Further, this "qualification" for a position, consideration of "fitness," also impinges upon discrimination in hiring, wherein it is normally stated that only qualifications to do the job or task are pertinent (see Section 5.80). But in this situation, "unfitness" is a legal disqualification.

Negligent hire is the most common of the employment processes involved in child abuse and is the subject of the statutes and regulations. The majority of states recognize negligent hiring as an actionable tort. A key element in the appropriate standard of care is foreseeability (see Chapter 2.11 Elements of Negligence), and for negligent hire *foreseeability is characterized by appropriate and adequate background checks.* Was the employer diligent in checking background records so as to eliminate those potential employees who had backgrounds which evidenced foreseeability of possible violent or sexual abuse behaviors? Did the school, agency, or institution do all that was "reasonable" in conducting the background check? If so, then neither the corporate entity nor the administrator is held liable. However, if not, then both are held on "negligent hire."[1] This background checking must be done for volunteers as well as employees, and there are many volunteers in sport, especially youth sport coaches; **all must have their backgrounds checked!**

Not only must there be initial checking of backgrounds for those working with children and youth, but if a person's position is changed from not having contact with children to having contact, then that person must then also have background checked. For example, a person had been hired for a janitorial position and then was promoted to a supervisory position at the city recreation center. The background was not checked when the change in assignment occurred; but, in fact, there was a felony conviction. Action was brought against the city, the city recreation and parks commission, and the gym supervisor for employee's alleged sexual molestation of several young girls and a young boy. The city also had not complied with its own policies regarding background checking. The personnel department, which usually examined applicants carefully, did not do so in this situation because they were aware that the area supervisor had some knowledge of the applicant-employee (*Williams v. Butler*, 1991). Beware—one may not know acquaintances or even "friends"

---

[1] e.g., *Doe v. Village of St. Joseph* (1992) action against school for alleged sexual molestation by recreational supervisor of 13-year-old, records check had been conducted prior to hiring and no information suggested any criminal record or propensity; *Doe v. Coffee County Board of Education* (1992) 4 students allegedly sexually abused by basketball coach, background check had been made upon employment. See also *Camacho*, 1993.

as well as one might expect. There may be "hidden" backgrounds!! Every one, even long-standing friends, should be subjected to the same checks. *It is essential that an organization, agency, or institution establish well-defined policies and procedures for checking applicant backgrounds AND HAVE THEM CARRIED OUT METICULOUSLY.*

Negligent supervision, as negligent hire, is not the supervision of how an activity is conducted, but rather an assessment of the behaviors of the individual as related to "fitness," that is, a propensity towards violence or sexual molestation. When such conduct is evidenced, whether observed directly (actual notice) or would have been if proper supervision had been given (constructive notice) or reported by someone else (e.g., participant, parent, other leader), the supervisor/administrator in charge must take immediate action to protect the participants. A principal was found to be *deliberately indifferent* when he received numerous reports about a teacher/coach molesting a 15-year-old student. He regularly dismissed the reports and students' complaints, did not record incidents, and declined to talk with involved students, parents, or the accused teacher/coach. The court distinguished gross negligence and deliberate indifference in that the former is a heightened degree of negligence, while the latter is a lesser form of intent. Further, it was stated that the deliberate indifference standard is to be applied in determining an individual supervisor's liability under federal civil rights statute.[1]

A third employment tort is **negligent referral**. A critical element in checking backgrounds are references and evaluations of past performances; yet, with the litigious society, individuals may sue for defamation if a "bad" reference is given, particularly as related to "unfit" characterizations. The protection of society (participants) from danger by persons with a propensity for violence or sexual abuse must be balanced with the desire to protect the confidentiality of the individual and an individual's right to a "second chance." It is a very difficult situation for those who are asked to give referrals, and some refuse saying "no comment" or merely providing factual data of dates employed and position description. The courts have tried to help the situation by providing "qualified privilege" to employers giving referrals. Legal action also may be taken against the employer for failure to provide an appropriate referral which included warnings of behaviors which had been evidenced.

After one has observed behaviors of "unfitness" or has obtained information evidencing the propensity for violence or sexual abuse, but does not discharge or remove the person from the position which gives contact with participants (children and youth), action can be brought for **negligent retention** of an employee or volunteer. A 55-year-old park employee worked at the neighborhood playground both in general maintenance and checking out basketballs, games, ropes, et al. On this day, he told a 9-year-old child to return the jump rope to him at the maintenance shed at 5 p.m., where he then for two hours repeatedly raped, assaulted, and sexually abused her, as well as threatened to kill her. He had begun work 7 months earlier as part of a work program and had put on his application he had no arrest or conviction record. Subsequent to employment, a fingerprint check was made and the personnel department received his record of substantial criminal activity, but took no action. He was considered a utility worker, not involved in working with children. Because this was in a mandated welfare work program, there was no action for negligent hire; however, knowing of the background, this was considered negligent retention. The court held that the doctrine of governmental immunity from tort liability (see Chapter 2.22 Immunity) for discretionary function was inapplicable and that the strong public policy favoring rehabilitation of ex-convicts did not excuse the city from

---

[1] *Doe v. Taylor Indep. Sch. Dist.* (1994). See also *Hagan v. Houston Indep. Sch. Dist.* (1995) 3 former students brought civil rights action against principal for failing to prevent coach's alleged sexual abuse, principal had taken action on complaints so not deliberately indifferent; *D.T. by M.T. v. Indep. Sch. Dist. No. 16* (1990) alleged acts of sexual molestation against 3 boys' basketball team members engaged in fund-raising activities for summer basketball camp by elementary school teacher/coach, held that school's established procedure in investigating, hiring, and supervising teacher/coach did not amount to deliberate indifference or reckless disregard for civil rights of students.

compliance with its own procedures requiring informed discretion in the placement of persons with criminal records. $2.5M were awarded in damages (*Haddock v. City of New York*, 1990).

The Working Environment and Gender Discrimination

Gender discrimination in employment under Title IX (see Chapter 4.25) and Title VII (see Chapter 5.81) usually is thought of as relating to equal opportunity in employment; however, there are two forms of gender discrimination. The other is that which is sexually motivated, referenced as sexual harassment, which gives rise to a hostile workplace. It was almost 10 years after Title VII was enacted that the first case was brought on sexual harassment, but the court found no basis under the statute. However, several years later the court overturned this decision and several cases holding similarly, and established the two forms of discrimination, making sexual harassment actionable under Title VII.

Sexual Harassment. The Equal Employment Opportunity Commission (EEOC) issued guidelines in 1980 defining *sexual harassment as unwelcome sexual advances, requests for sexual favors, and other verbal or physical conduct of a sexual nature . . . when submission to such conduct is made either explicitly or implicitly a term or condition of an individual's employment, the basis for employment decisions affecting such individual or has the purpose or effect of unreasonably interfering with an individual's work performance or creating an intimidating, hostile or offensive working environment.*

Submission to sexual favors which are either a term or condition of an individual's employment or as a basis for employment decisions affecting that individual is known as *quid pro quo sexual harassment*. Power by the one seeking the sexual favors serves as its basis, in that the employee is afraid not to accommodate the sexual favor requested because of the "power" which the person holds over the person's position, e.g., salary, work assignment, promotion, dismissal, et al. The other type of sexual harassment relates to interference with work performance creating a hostile workplace.

Hostile Work Environment. A hostile work environment is created when there is unreasonable interference with an individual's work performance or creation of an intimidating, hostile or offensive working environment. The concept of a hostile work environment is difficult to define, but five elements appear essential: 1) that the employee belongs to the protected category, 2) that the employee is subject to unwelcome sexual harassment, 3) that the harassment was based on sex, 4) that the harassment complained of affected the term, condition or privilege of employment, and 5) that the employer knew or should have known of the harassment and failed to take prompt, effective remedial action.[1] The last element is critical. What did the employer know and what was done? **Every school, institution, agency, and organization must have established policies and procedures for dealing with sexual harassment.** To whom does an employee make a complaint? A concern in making a complaint to a superior about a supervisor is that of retaliation, an actionable claim as exemplified in a case of coaches harassing female gymnasts (*Koop v. Indep. Sch. Dist.*, 1993). The *Giordano* case (*Giordano v. William Paterson College*, 1991; see also, *Bell v. Chesapeake & Ohio Ry. Co.*, 1991) set forth several factors to determine whether an employer's response was sufficiently prompt and adequate to avoid *respondeat superior* liability: 1) whether the employer investigated alleged acts of harassment, 2) type of investigation conducted, 3) post-investigation remedial steps taken, 4) was a grievance procedure and policy against discrimination in place, and 5) was harassment ended after remedial measures were taken. If the harassment continues, under the *doctrine of continuing violation*, the statute of limitations does not run.

---

[1] See landmark decision, *Meritor Savings Bank, FSB v. Vinson* (1986); Weddle, (1995); *Faragher v. City of Boca Raton* (1994) former city lifeguards sued city and two supervisors for sexual harassment based on inappropriate touching and lewd remarks, i.e., "hostile environment" claim under Title VII, city had constructive knowledge of supervisors' sexual harassment proving *respondeat superior*, judgment for lifeguards.

What is harassment? One is familiar with the "reasonable man" concept, but at the turn of the decade the *reasonable woman standard* became important in hostile work environment cases. However, in 1993 (*Harris v. Forklift Systems, Inc.* [1991]; Childers, [1993]; Adler and Pevice, [1993]; Schimmel, [1994]), the Supreme Court did not refer to the "reasonable woman," but rather referred to the gender-neutral "reasonable person." There are two dimensions required for the work environment: 1) that the behavior be severe or pervasive enough to create an objectively hostile or abusive work environment, an environment that a "reasonable person" would find hostile or abusive; and 2) the employee must subjectively perceive that the environment is abusive. Thus, it must be noted that what constitutes a hostile environment is very much subjective to the person involved and, therefore, there is no objective standard or specific criteria against which to measure an environment for hostility.

Other Types of Harassment.   While the focus in the mid to late '90s is on gender harassment, a hostile workplace also may occur when there is racial, ethnic, age, disability, or religious harassment.

Recent Developments

Essentially this entire area of employment torts has developed in this decade. For this reason, no recent developments were selected for this section.

References

A. Cases

Bell v. Chesapeake & Ohio Ry. Co., 929 F.2d 220 (6th Cir. 1991).
C.B. v. Bobo, 659 So.2d 98 (Ala. 1995).
Doe v. Coffee County Board of Education, 852 S.W.2d 899 (Tenn. Ct. App. 1992).
Doe v. Rains Indep. Sch. Dist., 66 F.3d 1401 (5th Cir. 1995).
Doe v. Taylor Indep. Sch. Dist., 15 F.3d 443 (5th Cir. 1994).
Doe v. Village of St. Joseph, 415 S.E.2d 56 (1992).
D.T. by M.T. v. Indep. Sch. Dist. No. 16, 894 F.2d 1176 (10th Cir. 1990).
Faragher v. City of Boca Raton, 864 F.Supp. 1552 (S.D. Fla. 1994).
Giordano v. William Paterson College, 804 F.Supp. 637 (D.N.J. 1992).
Haddock v. City of New York, 553 N.E.2d 987 (N.Y. 1990).
Hagan v. Houston Indep. Sch. Dist., 51 F.3d 48 (5th Cir. 1995).
Harris v. Forklift Systems, Inc., 929 F.2d 220 (6th Cir. 1991).
Koop v. Indep. Sch. Dist., 505 N.W.2d 93 (Minn. Ct. App. 1993).
Leija v. Canutillo Indep. Sch. Dist., 887 F.Supp. 947 (W.D. Tex. 1995).
Meritor Savings Bank, FSB v. Vinson, 477 U.S. 57 (1986).
People v. Arnold, 7 Cal.Rptr. 2d 833(1992).
People v. Peters, 590 N.Y.S.2d 916 (1992).
State v. Laird, 547 So.2d 1 (La.Ct.App. 1989).
Williams v. Butler, 577 So.2d 1113 (La.Ct.App. 1991).

B. Publications

Adler, Robert S., and Ellen R. Pevice. The Legal, Ethical, and Social Implications of the "Reasonable Woman" Standard in Sexual Harassment Cases, 61 *Fordham Law Review* 773-827 (1993).
Camacho, Rodolfo. How to Avoid Negligent Hiring Litigation, 14 *Whittier Law Review* 787-807 (1993).

Childers, Jolynn. Notes—Is There a Place for a Reasonable Woman in the Law? A Discussion of Recent Developments in Hostile Environment Sexual Harassment, 42 *Duke Law Journal* 854-904 (1993).

Schimmel, David. Commentary—Sexual Harassment in the Workplace: When Are Hostile Comments Actionable? 89 *Ed. Law Rep.* 337 (May 5, 1994).

van der Smissen, Betty. (1990) *Legal Liability and Risk Management for Public and Private Entities.* Cincinnati: Anderson Publishing Company. 1997 supplement @ 1.7.

Weddle, Justin S. Title VII Sexual Harassment: Recognizing an Employer's Non-delegable Duty to Prevent a Hostile Workplace, 95:3 *Columbia Law Review* 724-748 (April 1995).

2.37

Products Liability

Lori K. Miller
Wichita State University*

Products liability significantly influences sport and sport businesses. Social policy and business ethics mandate the prudent manufacture and distribution of sporting goods products. This chapter traces the fundamental concepts and principles associated with products liability including the following: a) evolution of products liability, b) elaboration on the three causes of actions available to an injured plaintiff, c) the distributor and resultant liability, d) defenses, e) the current tort reform movement, f) concluding comments.

■ ■ ■ ■

Representative Case

Everett v. Warren

Supreme Judicial Court of Massachusetts
376 Mass. 280; 380 N.E.2d 653
February 17, 1978, Argued
September 5, 1978, Decided

OPINION:

In this case the plaintiff seeks damages from the suppliers of a protective helmet he was wearing when, while playing in a hockey game, he was struck in the head by a puck and was seriously injured. The question before us is whether, on the various counts brought under both negligence and strict liability theories, the evidence was sufficient to support the verdicts for the plaintiff.

• • •

The controversies in this case revolve around the design of the protective helmet worn by the plaintiff when he was injured. It is described as a three-piece helmet because its protective components are three sections of high-impact plastic lined on the inside with shock foam.

One piece covers the back of the head, extending from the nape up about six inches, and running horizontally between positions slightly behind each ear; the second piece, approximately two inches wide, rings the front of the head from the same positions, thus covering the forehead; and the third piece joins the tops of these two sections and covers the top of the head. This top piece is loosely connected to the other two sections by six strips of leather, each 1½ to 1¾ inches in width and 1½ to 2 inches in length. The side pieces are linked by a ¾-inch wide elastic strap, whose length is adjustable. The result of this three-piece design and loose method of linking the sections is that there are gaps within the helmet where no

*Dr. Lawrence W. Fielding, Indiana University, made significant contributions to this chapter. The author wishes to recognize these contributions and express a genuine gratitude to Dr. Fielding.

plastic piece covers. The gap between the top piece and the two side pieces ranges from ½ to ¾ of an inch. The gaps between the two side pieces vary with the size of the wearer's head and the tension with which the elastic straps are adjusted, and range from zero to ¾ of an inch. This three-piece design, characterized by the internal gaps, was somewhat unique, and there were available at the time of the plaintiff's injury and for some time prior thereto helmets that were designed as one-piece units and were therefore without such gaps.

When the injury occurred the plaintiff, who was approximately nineteen years old, was a post-graduate student and a member of the hockey team at the defendant New Preparatory School (New Prep) in Cambridge, Massachusetts. On January 10, 1970, the New Prep team went to Providence, Rhode Island, to play the Brown University freshman team. During the game the plaintiff, a defenseman, attempted to block the shot of a Brown player by throwing himself into a horizontal position on the ice, about ten to fifteen feet in front of the shooting player and perpendicular to the intended line of flight of the puck. The puck struck the plaintiff above and slightly back from his right ear, and penetrated into the gap of the helmet formed where the three helmet sections came together. As a result of this penetration the puck hit his head and caused a fracture of the skull. This serious injury subsequently required that a plate be inserted in the plaintiff's skull, and caused the plaintiff to have headaches that will continue indefinitely.

The helmet was being worn by the plaintiff on the night of his injury as a result of its being supplied to him through the following process. The helmet was manufactured by J. E. Pender (Pender), a proprietorship engaged in the manufacture of sporting goods and represented in this action by the defendant George Whittie, executor of the will of James E. Pender. In 1967 through 1969 Pender sold at least fourteen helmets of the type worn by the plaintiff to the defendant Bucky Warren, Inc. (Bucky Warren), a retailer in sporting goods, which in turn sold them to New Prep. The helmets had been specially ordered by Owen Hughes, the coach of the New Prep team, who was the person authorized by the school to make such purchases. They were painted in the colors of the school to match the team uniforms. Each player on the plaintiff's team was supplied with one of these helmets for practice and games use, although Hughes's testimony indicated that, had a player so wished, he could have worn a different helmet of his own choosing. Rather than purchasing his own helmet, the plaintiff chose to wear the one supplied to him by the school authorities.

The plaintiff brought this action claiming that, because of the gaps, the Pender helmet was defectively designed,

and that therefore all three defendants, Pender, Bucky Warren, and New Prep, were liable to him in negligence for supplying him the helmet, and that the defendants Pender and Bucky Warren were also liable to him in tort on a strict liability theory. At trial, motions for directed verdicts were denied, and fourteen special questions were submitted to the jury. The jury found that all three defendants were negligent, that the helmet was not in a reasonably safe condition when sold by Pender and Bucky Warren, that the plaintiff's injury was caused by the condition of the helmet and the negligence of the defendants, and that the plaintiff himself neither assumed the risk of the injury nor was contributorily negligent. The plaintiff was awarded $85,000 in damages. After proper motions the judge, notwithstanding the jury verdicts, entered judgments in favor of all defendants on the negligence counts, holding that, as matter of law, the plaintiff assumed the risk of his injury. He entered judgment for the plaintiff for $85,000 on the strict liability counts, however, on the ground that assumption of the risk was not a defense to this cause of action. Appeals and cross-appeals were claimed, and we granted an application for direct appellate review. G. L. c. 211A, @ 10 (A).

The issues raised here are whether there was sufficient evidence for the jury to find that: (a) the defendants Pender and New Prep were negligent, (b) the plaintiff was not negligent and did not assume the risk of his injury, and (c) the helmet was defective and unreasonably dangerous as sold by Pender and Bucky Warren. Additionally, we address certain evidentiary and procedural matters raised by the defendants.

• • •

1. Negligence. "A manufacturer is under a duty to use reasonable care to design a product that is reasonably safe for its intended use." W. Prosser, Torts @ 96, at 645 (4th ed. 1971). The Pender helmet was designed by James E. Pender, who possessed no engineering background. It was intended to protect the vital areas of the head, the temples and cranium. It was designed in three pieces, however, not for safety reasons, but to facilitate adjustment. Pender indicated in his deposition—he was deceased at the time of trial—that the helmet was consciously designed so that there would be gaps between its sections when it was properly adjusted; the larger the head of the wearer, the larger would be the gaps. The jury could reasonably have concluded from the examination of the helmet that Pender knew, or should have known, that a puck could penetrate between the sections and cause serious injury to the wearer. Pender was aware that other manufacturers were producing helmets of a one-piece design, but he nevertheless failed to make any tests of his own helmet to determine its safety. We hold that this evidence was

sufficient to support the answer of the jury that Pender was negligent in the design of the helmet.

We reach a similar conclusion with regard to the defendant New Prep. As stated in its brief, the issue with regard to New Prep is whether "it was bad practice for a hockey coach to supply the plaintiff with the helmet in question and the supplying of said helmet to the plaintiff was causally related to his injuries." As to the claim of lack of causation we see no serious question; the jury could clearly have concluded that the presence of the gaps in the helmet was the cause of his injury. The more substantial issue here is whether the jury were warranted in finding that New Prep, through its agent, Coach Owen Hughes, was negligent in supplying the helmet to the plaintiff. As a supplier New Prep was required to exercise reasonable care not to provide a chattel which it knew or had reason to know was dangerous for its intended use. See Restatement (Second) of Torts @ 388 (1965). Hughes, as a person with substantial experience in the game of hockey, may be held to a higher standard of care and knowledge than would an average person. Restatement (Second) of Torts @ 289(b), Comment m (1965). Since many of the teams that New Prep played prior to 1970 wore one-piece helmets, the jury could have found that Hughes knew, or should have known, of their availability. He conceded in his testimony that the one-piece helmets were safer than the Pender model since the gaps in the latter would allow for the penetration of a puck. There was sufficient evidence to permit the jury to decide whether, in these circumstances, the supplying of the helmet to the plaintiff was negligent conduct.

Having determined that the jury were warranted in finding negligence on the parts of the defendants, we turn now to a consideration of the defenses of assumption of the risk and contributory negligence. Unlike contributory negligence, assumption of the risk involves a subjective standard, keyed not to the knowledge or understanding of the hypothetical reasonable man, but to "what the particular plaintiff in fact sees, knows, understands and appreciates." D'Andrea v. Sears, Roebuck & Co., 109 R.I. 479, 487 (1972), quoting from Restatement (Second) of Torts @ 496D, Comment c (1965). Kennedy v. Providence Hockey Club, Inc., R.I., a (1977). In order to rule that a plaintiff assumed the risk of his injury as matter of law, the facts must be so plain that reasonable men could draw only one inference. Kennedy, supra at b. The facts here are not so plain. The plaintiff testified that he did not know of any dangers that he was exposed to by wearing the helmet. He believed, he said, that it would protect his head from injury. The helmet had been supplied to him by a person with great knowledge and experience in hockey, a person whose judgment the plaintiff had reason to trust, and it was

given to him for the purpose implied, if not expressed, of protecting him. On the other hand, the obviousness of the gaps in the helmet would support an inference that he was actually aware of the risks he ran. It was on this basis that on the negligence counts the judge entered judgments for the defendants notwithstanding the verdicts for the plaintiff. But we do not think that these gaps were so large or so obvious as to require the conclusion, as matter of law, that the plaintiff possessed the awareness necessary to support an assumption of the risk defense. Rather it was the function of the jury to balance the obviousness of the helmet design against the plaintiff's testimony and the circumstances in which he received the helmet in order to arrive at a conclusion as to what the plaintiff knew at the time of the injury. That he knew that the game of hockey carries with it certain other risks, such as being hit in his unprotected face, is not relevant to this issue; the question is whether the plaintiff appreciated the risk of the injury that befell him.

• • •

We note simply that the question of contributory negligence is rarely to be taken from the jury and decided as matter of law, Mirick v. Galligan, 372 Mass. 146, 151 (1977); Halley v. Hugh Nawn, Inc., 356 Mass. 28, 30 (1969); Robitaille v. Brousseau, 115 R.I. 27, 32 (1975), and we find no exceptional circumstances in this case that would justify such as an action.

2.   Strict liability in tort. In Ritter v. Narragansett Elec. Co., 109 R.I. 176, 188 (1971), the Supreme Court of Rhode Island adopted the law of strict liability in tort as it is defined in the Restatement (Second) of Torts @ 402A (1965). The plaintiff claims that the three-piece design of the Pender helmet, with the gaps in it, was defective and unreasonably dangerous as defined in the Restatement, and therefore that the manufacturer and retailer are liable to him. We hold that there was sufficient evidence to reach the jury on this theory. For a product to be in a defective condition it does not have to be the result of errors made during the manufacturing process; it is defective as well "when it is properly made according to an unreasonably dangerous design" and does not meet a consumer's reasonable expectation as to its safety. W. Prosser, Torts @ 99, at 659 (4th ed. 1971). The focus is on the design itself, not on the manufacturer's conduct. Factors that should be weighed in determining whether a particular product is reasonably safe include "the gravity of the danger posed by the challenged design, the likelihood that such danger would occur, the mechanical feasibility of a safer alternative design, the . . . cost of an improved design, and the adverse consequences to the product and to the consumer that would result from an alternative design." Back, supra at 642, quoting from Barker v. Lull Eng'r Co., 20 Cal. 3d

413, 431 (1978). In this case the gravity of the danger posed by the three-piece design was demonstrated by the injuries to the plaintiff. There was substantial evidence that tended to show that helmets of the one-piece design were safer than the Pender model, that these one-piece helmets were in manufacture prior to the plaintiff's injury, and that, while more expensive than the Pender helmets, they were not economically unfeasible. This evidence provided a sufficient basis for the jury's findings that the helmet was "unreasonably dangerous."

The defendants also argue that the plaintiff is barred from recovery on the strict liability counts because he assumed the risk of injury. In view of our holding earlier in this opinion that the jury were warranted in finding that the plaintiff had not assumed the risk, we need not decide whether assumption of the risk would be a defense to a strict liability claim under Rhode Island law. See Kennedy v. Providence Hockey Club, Inc., R.I., (1977); c Restatement (Second) of Torts @ 402A, Comment n (1965).

3. Miscellaneous issues.

• • •

(b) The defendant New Prep contends that it was error for the judge to admit in evidence certain testimony of Hughes, the plaintiff's coach at New Prep, who is now also the owner of a business dealing in hockey equipment. Specifically New Prep objects to the admission of Hughes's testimony (1) that he could have acquired one-piece helmets for New Prep prior to the plaintiff's injury, and (2) that it was his present opinion that the one-piece

helmets were safer than the Pender helmet. This evidence, it is claimed, was irrelevant because it dealt with Hughes's current knowledge and opinions rather than those he held at the time of the injury. The testimony, however, was clearly relevant to the issue of reasonable safety of the Pender helmet under the strict liability counts, since on this issue the jury are entitled to compare the challenged product with alternative, feasible designs. Back v. Wickes Corp., 375 Mass. 633, 642 (1978). For the same reasons evidence of the relative costs of the two helmet types was properly admitted. Since this evidence was admissible for one purpose, and no limiting instruction was requested, there was no error.

• • •

(c) New Prep also argues that a model of a one-piece helmet was wrongly admitted against it because there was a lack of evidence showing that it was aware of that helmet before the plaintiff's injury. We hold, however, that there was sufficient evidence of the helmet's availability during this period to justify an inference that the school officials were aware, or should have been aware, of this helmet. Therefore there was no error.

4. The judgments on the strict liability counts are affirmed. The judgments on the negligence counts are reversed with instructions that judgments be entered on the verdicts.

So ordered.

■ ■ ■ ■

Fundamental Concepts and Principles

The Privity of Contract Requirement

Privity of contract is a time-honored concept adopted by the United States courts from England's judicial system (*Winterbottom v. Wright*, 1842). The privity of contract requirement provided recourse to an injured plaintiff when a manufacturer breached a contractual warranty. However, recourse was contingent upon a direct relationship between the product manufacturer and the end user. The end user's ability to recover for product injuries was not problematic during the agrarian or pre-industrial era when consumers typically entered into direct consumer transactions, or exchanges, with a local manufacturer. However, development of the distributive trade (e.g., wholesalers and retailers) precluded recourse opportunities available to the end user (Jeanblanc, 1937; Kessler, 1943; Traynor, 1965). As explained by Jeanblanc (1937):

> With the intervention of middlemen the consumer was no longer in privity of contract with the maker of the goods, and the system of warranties, which theretofore had afforded him adequate protection, was rendered ineffective. (p. 134)

The problem, as argued by consumer advocates like Ralph Nader (1972), is that manufacturers induced purchases via mass marketing. Consumers, persuaded by businesses' marketing tactics, would then purchase desired products. Unfortunately, the end user sustaining product-related injuries was left powerless and unable to seek legal recourse against the manufacturer. The use of the independent distributors forced consumers to accept demanded products on a *caveat emptor* basis.

Courts, regardless of the alleged inequities, upheld precedent and sanctified the privity of contract requirement as legal and binding (Kessler, 1943; *Printing and Numerical Registering Co. v. Sampson*, 1875). The English court and subsequent American courts feared a flood of cases should the privity of contract be abandoned.

Strict Liability

Strict liability is a concept of "liability regardless of fault." As explained by Bruns, "The doctrine of strict liability is being interpreted to mean a manufacturer's product no longer needs to be at fault to be guilty, but simply needs to be involved in an accident" (Products Liability Insurance, 1977, p. 413). By 1964, the concept of enterprise liability (i.e., strict liability) dominated judicial outcomes. Compensation of the injured meant that someone had to pay. Social justice ideology conspired with court opinion to target the manufacturer.

Despite concerns regarding a massive increase in litigation, the judiciary gradually evolved to become the champion of consumer rights. The justice pendulum swung away from the manufacturer and became fastened on the side of the consumer. Landmark decisions between 1960 and 1964 brought an end to the privity of contract requirement and solidified the pro-plaintiff movement in products liability litigation. *Henningsen v. Bloomfield Motors, Inc.* (1960) was the beginning of this revolution in products liability (Priest, 1985; Prosser, 1966). The *Henningsen* case (1960) echoed the socially just concept of risk distribution inbred within workmen's compensation statutes. Risk distribution advocates argue that it is better to spread losses among society than to invoke a substantial loss on one individual who is unable to pay. As expounded by this theory, businesses are in an ideal position to distribute resultant loss via higher prices or insurance. Legal scholars and consumer advocates further argue that a business's cognizance of possible loss makes it more safety-oriented and willing to upgrade quality control practices (Garrett, 1972; Nader, 1972; Plant, 1957). Prosser, responsible for Section 402A of the Second Restatement of Torts, solidified the concept of strict liability in 1964 (Cantu, 1993, p. 328). As stated by Prosser in Section 402A, a seller (i.e., manufacturer) is liable if an "unreasonably" dangerous or defective product causes injury. The definition of "unreasonably" dangerous was given wide latitude by the courts. Section 402A(2) was even more problematic as it imposed liability on a seller even though the seller "exercised all possible care in the preparation and sale of his product." This made the defendant manufacturer strictly liable. As stated by Cantu (1993, p. 345), "Any argument that the defendant acted as a reasonable, prudent person is totally irrelevant." Section 402(A)(2)(b) further nullified the privity of contract requirement by stating that the seller was liable in the above situation regardless of an existing contractual relationship between the consumer and seller.

The New Jersey Supreme Court's decision in *O'Brien v. Muskin Corporation* (1983) illustrates the hardships strict liability imposes on sporting goods manufacturers. In the *O'Brien* case, a 23-year-old plaintiff was seriously injured when he dove into an outdoor, above ground swimming pool with an embossed vinyl liner. The plaintiff alleged that the manufacturer was strictly liable for failure to warn and for using the vinyl liner. There was a warning on the pool which stated, "DO NOT DIVE" in 1.5" letters. The plaintiff's expert witness testified that he knew of no other type of lining, other than vinyl, used in above-ground swimming pools. The New Jersey Supreme Court remanded the question of whether the use of the vinyl lining constituted a design defect. As stated by the *O'Brien* court (1983), "Even if there are no alternative methods of making bottoms for above-ground pools, the jury might have found that the risk posed by the pool outweighed its utility" (p. 306). The precedent set by this case is dangerous. As reflected in the *O'Brien* case, strict liability eliminated the manufacturer's use of traditional products liability defenses (e.g., product misuse, alteration) and absolved the consumer of any responsibility for injuries. Rather, manufacturers became a provider of social insurance.

Although not common, repair service providers have also been held strictly liable. Courts reasoned that customers rely on their expertise, they are able to spread the cost of accidents, and imposing strict liability would induce them to invest in safety (*Gentile v. MacGregor Mfg. Co.*, 1985). The sporting goods service sector repair industry continues to grow as manufacturers downsize, sporting goods product lines expand, new sporting goods are introduced, and entrepreneurs look for profitable ventures. Consequently, it is important that these sport managers be cognizant of the court precedent regarding liability.

Negligence

Manufacturers and sellers liable under negligence theory have breached the standard of reasonable care owed to the consumer. The Court of Appeals decision in the 1916 case, *MacPherson v. Buick Motor Co.*, is a landmark decision as it was the first to hold the manufacturer liable for negligent product design, construction, and/or failure to warn. Negligence, in comparison to strict liability or breach of warranty, requires that the plaintiff prove fault. There are three common causes of action under the negligence doctrine: a) improper design, b) improper construction, and c) failure to warn.

Improper Design. The Supreme Court of Arizona (*Byrns v. Riddell, Incorporated*, 1976) and the Supreme Judicial Court of Massachusetts (*Everett v. Bucky Warren, Inc.*, 1978) itemized factors used for analysis regarding whether a product is designed in a "reasonably" safe manner. The following seven factors include: 1) the gravity of danger; 2) the likelihood of injury; 3) the obviousness of the danger; 4) the feasibility of an alternate design; 5) common knowledge and normal expectation of danger; 6) the ability to avoid injury by use of instructions or warnings; 7) the ability to eliminate the danger without impairing the usefulness of the product or making it unduly expensive.

As decided in the *Everett* case, the manufacturer of a three-piece hockey helmet marketed an "unreasonably dangerous" product. The seriousness and obviousness of the danger was foreseeable (i.e., obvious) as the three-piece helmet had gaps ranging between ½ to ¾ of an inch between each section. The court concluded that it was likely that a puck could hit the head in the "gap area" and cause critical damage to the skull. The feasibility of adopting an alternative design was obvious as other manufacturers were already producing one piece helmets and the cost was not prohibitive in light of the safety benefits. The plaintiff-player expected the helmet to provide protection as it was furnished to him for the purpose of protecting him.

Improper Construction. Improper product construction alleges that there is nothing faulty with the design of the product. Rather, the plaintiff is alleging that the product's improper construction, defective at the time it left the manufacturer, was the direct cause of injury. *Curtiss v. YMCA* (1972) is a good illustration of improper product construction resulting in injury. In the *Curtiss* case, a 17-year-old plaintiff performed a gymnastic maneuver on the parallel bars. The plaintiff fell between five and seven feet when the top bar became detached from the metal saddles at each end of the bar due to a manufacturing defect.

A common tenet in the analysis of whether a manufacturer improperly constructed a product focuses on whether that manufacturer engaged in reasonable testing or inspection (van der Smissen, 1990; Wittenberg, 1992). In *McCormick v. Lowe & Campbell Athletic Goods Co.* (1940), the plaintiff was injured when using a vaulting pole manufactured by the defendant company. The court explained that a manufacturer of a product is under duty to exercise ordinary care to test the product for defects.

The elaborate testing employed by the defendant manufacturing company was of critical importance in refuting a strict liability claim alleging that a catcher's mask was defective (*Roseboro v. Rawlings Manufacturing Company*, 1969). In comparison, the irregularities of the testing process used by defendant manufacturer Bike Athletic Co. was harmful to the defendant's case in *Austria v. Bike Athletic Co.* (1991).

The degree and amount of testing should be commensurate with the probability of danger (van der Smissen, 1990). In other words, more elaborate testing is required of a football helmet than of a wiffle ball.

Failure to Warn. The issue of warnings is critical to the analysis of liability. The purpose of a warning is to "apprise uninformed users of potential danger so they can take appropriate measures to protect themselves" (Eaton and Woltjen, 1988, p. 13). Courts view the warning as an inexpensive responsibility that generates a great deal of utility (*Crispin v. Volkswagenwerk A.*, 1991; *Michalko v. Cooke Color & Chem. Corp.*, 1982). The Court of Civil Appeals of Texas, in a 1.5 million dollar decision against the defendant (*Rawlings Sporting Goods Co., Inc. v. Daniels*, 1981), stated that the manufacturer, who has superior knowledge of the limitations of the product has a duty to warn the consumer, who will rely on the protective ability of the product.

In negligent failure to warn cases, the plaintiff is alleging that another reasonably prudent manufacturer would have warned in a like or similar circumstance. In other words, the manufacturer had actual or constructive notice of the latent danger of a product yet failed to communicate this danger to the user. For example, the United States Court of Appeals (Seventh Cir.) held that defendant manufacturer had constructive notice of consumer risk when approximately 100 sunglasses were returned daily for lens replacement. Common practice within the industry and prior injuries resulting from similar situations, although not dispositive, are factors indicating that warnings should have been used (*Back v. Wickes Corp.*, 1978; *Matz v. Mile Hi Concrete, Inc.*, 1991).

Manufacturers also have a responsibility to warn of defects discovered after a product has been marketed. Again, referring to the 1995 *Arnold v. Riddell, Inc.* case, the United States District Court (D. Kansas), in deciding for the plaintiffs, recognized the defendant's failure to warn players and coaches although it "knew its helmets did not perform as well as others on crown impacts."

Warnings must include dangers inherent in normal use of the product as well as dangers resulting from foreseeable misuses (van der Smissen, 1990; *Whitacre v. Optical Products, Inc.*, 1987). However, courts continue to recognize that manufacturers have no duty to warn about open and obvious dangers.

There is an interesting *caveat* regarding the use of warnings. A manufacturer, in an attempt to comply with its responsibility to warn, may provide too many warnings, "creating a kind of sensory overload which will lessen rather than promote the impact of proper warnings" (Eaton and Woltjen, 1988, p. 13).

Breach of Warranty

A breach of warranty is an allegation based on contract law. Recovery based upon a breach of warranty surfaced in the late nineteenth and early twentieth centuries (Clark and Smith, 1984). The Uniform Sales Act approved by the National Conference of Commissioners on Uniform State Laws in 1906 further solidified the concept of express and implied warranties. Acceptance of the Uniform Commercial Code by all states except Louisiana in the 1950s provided the plaintiff with a widely recognized cause of action based upon breach of warranty. As explained by van der Smissen (1990, p. 340),

> An express warranty arises through advertising, sales literature, product labeling, and oral statements and is an assertion of fact or promise by the seller relating to the quality of goods that induces the buyer to purchase the goods.

For example, in *Hauter v. Zogarts* (1975), a golf training device was packaged with the following language, "COMPLETELY SAFE BALL WILL NOT HIT PLAYER." The language on the package encouraged the player to "drive the ball with full power." The plaintiff was seriously injured when the cord attached to the ball wrapped around his club and hit him in the head. The court found for the plaintiff on the breach of express warranty. According to the court, this statement was "a misrepresentation of material fact upon which plaintiffs justifiably relied" (p. 381). Sport managers responsible for advertising campaigns or other product or service packaging should use caution when using descriptive terms such as "safe" and "foolproof." First, very few sport-related products will ever be 100 percent "safe" as sport in itself invites injury. Second, as explained by the Supreme Court of California in the *Hauter* (1975) decision, "Courts have come to construe unqualified statements . . . liberally in favor of injured consumers."

Implied warranties include both the implied warranty of fitness and the implied warranty of merchantability. Black (1990, p. 1587) defines the terms as follows:

Implied Warranty of Fitness

When the retailer, distributor, or manufacturer has reason to know any particular purpose for which the consumer goods are required, and further, that the buyer is relying on the skill and judgment of the seller to select and furnish suitable goods, then there is an implied warranty that the goods shall be fit for such purpose and that when there is a sale of an assistive device sold at retail in the state, then there is an implied warranty by the retailer that the device is specifically fit for the particular needs of the buyer.

Implied Warranty of Merchantability

The consumer goods meet each of the following: 1) Pass without objection in the trade under the contract description; 2) Are fit for the ordinary purposes for which such goods are used; 3) Are adequately contained, packaged, and labeled; 4) Conform to the promises or affirmations of fact made on the container or label.

Filler v. Rayex Corporation (1970) is a case commonly used to illustrate the implied warranty of fitness concept. In the *Filler* case, a high school baseball coach purchased sunglasses from the defendant based upon the advertisement guaranteeing "instant eye protection." Unlike other sunglasses, advertisements and product packaging specifically identified baseball as a sport where players would be protected by the "scientific lenses." The plaintiff-athlete lost his right eye when a ball hit the lens and it shattered. As explained by the court of appeals "Since they lacked the safety features of plastic or shatterproof glass, the sunglasses were in truth not fit for baseball playing, the particular purpose for which they were sold" (*Filler v. Rayex Corporation,* 1970, p. 338). The implied warranty of fitness extends to the intended product uses as well as foreseeable misuses. There is no liability for the "unforeseeable misuse of a product" (*Back v. Wickes Corp.,* 1978, p. 969).

The implied warranty of merchantability assures one, for example, that a football helmet serves and protects as any ordinary football helmet on the market. Similarly, a baseball bat meets the implied warranty of merchantability if it performs as an ordinary baseball bat. Referring again to the *Hauter* case (1975), the court found that the defendant also breached the implied warranty of merchantability. The golf training device, intended for use by novices, did not serve as an ordinary training device as it was foreseeable that the device would injure users.

The Liability of the Distributor

Although only five percent of product sellers are actually held liable in product liability cases, they are frequently required to expend monies preparing a defense. This translates into an unnecessary expense that is ultimately passed on to the consumer. More alarming is the fact that 34 states currently treat product sellers as if they were an actual manufacturer. In other words, "they are absolutely liable for a manufacturer's mistakes" (Schwartz, 1993). The logic of holding product sellers liable as manufacturers is two-fold. First, this argument assumes that the product sellers can exert buyer power on the manufacturer by demanding top quality products and refusing to sell products of substandard quality. However, the demand associated with sporting goods equipment neutralizes this argument as buyers (i.e., retailers) are often forced to take what they can get in order to fill orders. Second, this logic assumes that all product sellers will have the monies and resources needed to seek indemnification from manufacturers. The fallacy of this argument is obvious as transaction costs, expended time of personnel, public relations problems, and diminished goodwill often devastate the net income generated by retailers. Even a school may be viewed as a "distributor" within the realm of products liability litigation. In *Everett v. Bucky Warren, Inc.* (1978) the court concluded that a jury could find the school negligent when the coach, acting as an agent of the school, negligently selected hockey helmets.

Defenses

Defenses available to defendants involved in products liability litigation often focus on plaintiff actions. For example, the following plaintiff actions illustrate viable defenses: a) improper equipment installation or maintenance, b) modification of equipment without involvement of the manufacturer, c) use of the product for unforeseeable purposes, and d) failure to use product in accordance with instructions. The above defenses magnify the importance of proper warnings and instruction. Further, the defendant may allege that the product was not the proximate cause of injury. Knowledge of the consumer and the facts involving the injury are imperative to a defendant.

Tort Reform

The current products liability system is complex and inefficient. Attempts at reform have been advanced since the early 1970s when Congress first became alerted to the many problems both consumers and manufacturers faced in navigating the system. Six products liability reform bills have been presented to Congress since 1981. Philip K. Howard's recent best seller, *The Death of Common Sense* (1994), points out severe problems in product safety law as does the more highly publicized *Contract with America* (Gillespie and Schellhas, 1994). These recent works are merely additions to a call for reform voiced by American manufacturers since the late 1960s.

Proponents of reform argue that uniform legislation is necessary to bring about a more efficient and predictable products liability system (Product Liability Fairness Act, 1993). At the present time products liability law varies among the 50 states (Schloerb, Blatt, Hammesfahr, and Nugent, 1988). Products liability reform advocates believe that a uniform products liability law would resolve many of the inefficiencies and deficiencies within the current products liability system. As explained by Schwartz (1993, p. 270), "Products are uniform, and standards of and for safety should have uniformity." Schwartz believes that state-by-state products liability laws are inefficient since only 30 percent of all products manufactured are sold in the state in which a particular manufacturing company resides (Schwartz, 1993). Individual state legislation, therefore, only provides manufacturers with operating parameters and guidelines for 30 percent of its manufactured goods. Manufacturers, product sellers, insurers, and consumer-plaintiffs are all disadvantaged by this unpredictability in how liability will impact company operations and expenses. Manufacturing companies are further hindered by the courts' willingness to redistribute wealth from out-of-state manufacturers to in-state plaintiff(s). As Justice Richard Neely, West Virginia Supreme Court of Appeals, testifies (Product Liability Fairness Act, 1993), an in-state plaintiff, in-state (elected) judge, in-state jury, in-state witnesses, and in-state spectators frequently are biased against the out-of-state manufacturer. Manufacturers, on the other hand, are unable to contour product prices on a state-by-state basis to conform to individual state liability laws. Higher prices result for all as the pro-plaintiff products liability laws force manufacturers to price products in a way that protects against potential liability loss (Hay, 1992).

Advocates of products liability reform argue that the expense associated with the current system hinders the ability of American companies to compete both domestically and globally. Transaction costs, insurance costs, punitive damages, delayed or eliminated research and development, and the expenses associated with unpredictability are all factors placing the U.S. companies at a competitive disadvantage. Many products are not brought to market due to the lack of demand associated with a premium price, the inability to get insured, or because of a foreign competitor's low cost production (Product Liability Reform Act, 1990). The manufacturers' inability to compete on price curtails the manufacturing of goods which directly impacts job development, employment rates, and the generation of needed tax monies.

Recent Developments

Case Updates.   United States District Court (D. Kan.) denied manufacturer's request for judgment notwithstanding verdict. District court jury found in favor of plaintiff, awarding damages in excess of $12 million (Arnold v. Riddell, Inc., 1995).

A plaintiff was awarded $2 million, five hundred times the $4000 in compensatory damages, when BMW failed to tell him his new car had been "touched up" with paint to cover minor imperfections. In a 5-4 decision the Supreme Court described the Alabama jury award as "grossly excessive" (*BMW v. Gore*, 1996). Three factors used to determine the reasonableness of such awards include: a) "the degree of reprehensibility of the defendant's conduct," b) "the ratio between the punitive award and the actual harm to the plaintiff," and c) "the difference between the award and penalties provided in 'comparable cases'" (Felsenthal and Schmitt, 1996, p. B7).

Tort Reform.   Individual states pass tort reform legislation as a way to curb products liability woes. For example, in March, 1995, Illinois passed a reform bill limiting awards for pain and suffering to $500,000 and capping punitive damages at 3 times economic damages. Since the mid-1980s, 30 states have passed some type of tort reform legislation (Johnson and Eldridge, 1996; Schmitt, 1995). However, the defeat of California's tort reform legislation in March, 1996, raises doubts about the likelihood of nationwide tort reform (Zachary, 1996). Pro-business advocates spent an estimated $12.5 million on the California initiative. Opponents of the legislation attribute the victory to a growing anti-business sentiment.

Products Liability Legislation.   A products liability bill limiting punitive damages to two times the amount of compensatory damages or $250,000, whichever was greater, passed the House with a vote of 259-158 and the Senate with a vote of 59-40. The bill was later vetoed by President Clinton who argued the bill imposed on the rights of the states and harmed consumers (Schmitt, 1996; The Lawyers' Veto, 1996).

References

A. Cases
Arnold v. Riddell, Inc., 882 F. Supp. 979 (D. Kan. 1995).
Austria v. Bike Athletic Co., 810 P.2d 1312 (Or. App. 1991).
Back v. Wickes Corp., 378 N.E.2d 964 (Mass. 1978).
BMW v. Gore, 116 S. Ct. 1589 (1996).
Byrns v. Riddell, Inc., 113 Ariz. 264, 550 P.2d 1065 (1976).
Crispin v. Volkswagenwerk Ag., 591 A.2d 966 (N.J. Super. A.D. 1991).
Curtiss v. YMCA, Wash., 511 P. 2d 991 (1973).
Everett v. Bucky Warren, Inc., 376 Mass. 280, 380 N.E. 2d 653 (1978).
Filler v. Rayex Corporation, 435 F.2d 336 (1970).
Gentile v. MacGregor Mfg. Co., 493 A.2d 647 (N.J. Super.L. 1985).
Hauter v. Zogarts, 120 Cal. Rptr. 681, 534 P.2d 377 (1975).
Henningsen v. Bloomfield Motors, Inc., 32 N.J. 358, 161 A.2d 69 (1960).
MacPherson v. Buick Motor Co., 111 N.E. 1050 (1916).

Matz v. Mile Hi Concrete, Inc., 819 P.2d 530 (Colo.App. 1991).

McCormick v. Lowe & Campbell Athletic Goods Co., 144 S.W. 2d 866 (1940).

Michalko v. Cooke Color & Chem. Corp., 91 N.J. 386, 451 A.2d 179 (1982).

O'Brien v. Muskin Corporation, 463 A.2d 298 (N.J. 1983).

Printing and Numerical Registering Co. v. Sampson, L.R. 19 Eq. 462 (1975).

Rawlings Sporting Goods Co., Inc. v. Daniels, 619 S.W.2d 435 (Tex. Civ. App. 1981).

Roseboro v. Rawlings Manufacturing Company, 79 Cal. Rptr. 567 (1969).

Whitacre v. Halo Optical Products, Inc., 501 So.2d 994 (La. App. 2 Cir. 1987).

Winterbottom v. Wright, 10 M.&W. 112.

B. Publications

Black, H.C. (1990). *Black's Law Dictionary* (6th ed.). St. Paul, Minn: West Publishing Co.

Burke, R. (1969). AGMA Warned of Ambulance Chasers. *Sporting Goods Dealer,* 140(2), 17.

Cantu, C. E. (1993). Twenty-five Years of Strict Product Liability Law: The Transformation and Present Meaning of Section 402A. *St. Mary's Law Journal*, 25(1), 327-353.

Clark, Barkley and Smith, Christopher (1984). *The Law of Product Warranties.* New York: Warren, Gorham & Lamont, Inc.

Eaton, J. Timothy and Woltjen, Maria (Summer, 1988). *Product Warnings in the Marketplace.* The Brief, pp. 12-15, 29-33.

Felsenthal, E. and Schmitt, R. B. (1996, May 22). BMW Ruling Seen Affecting Many Cases. *The Wall Street Journal*, p. B7.

Garrett, M. C. (1972). Allowance of Punitive Damages in Products Liability Claims. *Georgia Law Review,* 6(3), 613-630.

Gillespie, E. G. and Schellhas, B. (Eds.) (1994). *Contract with America.* New York: Times Books.

Hay, B. L. (1992). Conflicts of Law and State Competition in the PRODUCT LIABILITY SYSTEM. *The Georgetown Law Journal*, 80(3), 617-652.

Howard, P. K. (1994). *The Death of Common Sense.* New York: Random House, Inc.

Jeanblanc, L. R. (1937). Manufacturers' Liability to Persons Other Than Their Immediate Vendees. *Virginia Law Review*, 24(2), 629-642.

Johnson, K. and Eldridge, E. (1996, May 21). Ruling in BMW Case Divides Legal Arena. *The USA Today*, pp. 1-2B.

Kessler, F. (1943). Contracts of Adhesion: Some Thoughts about Freedom of Contract. *Columbia Law Review,* 43(5), 629-642.

Nader, R. (1972). *Unsafe at Any Speed: The Designed-in Dangers of the American Automobile.* New York: Grossman.

Plant, M. L. (1957). Strict Liability of Manufacturers for Injuries Caused by Defects in Products: An Opposing View. *Tennessee Law Review*, 24(7), 938-951.

Priest, G. L. (1985). The Invention of Enterprise Liability: A Critical History of the Intellectual Foundations of Modern Tort Law. *The Journal of Legal Studies*, 14(3), 461-527.

Product Liability Fairness Act, 1993. Hearings on S. 687 Before the Subcomm. on Consumer of the Committee on Commerce, Science, and Transportation, 103rd Cong., 1st Sess. (1993). (Statement of Judge Richard Neeley).

Product Liability Insurance, 1977: Hearings Before the Subcommittee for Consumers of the Senate Committee on Commerce, Science, and Transportation, 95th Cong., 1st Sess. (1977). (Statement of William Bruns, President, SGMA).

Product Liability Reform Act, 1990: Hearings on S. 1400 Before the Subcommittee on the Consumer of the Committee on Commerce, Science, and Transportation, 101st Cong., 2nd Sess. (1990).

Prosser, W. L. (1966). The Fall of the Citadel (Strict Liability to the Consumer). *Minnesota Law Review,* 70(4), 791-848.

Restatement (Second) of Torts 402A (1965).

Schloerb, R. G., Blatt, R. N., Hammesfahr, R. W. & Nugent, L. S. (1988). *Punitive Damages: A Guide to the Insurability of Punitive Damages in the U.S. and its Territories.* Chicago: Peterson, Ross, Schloerb & Seidel.

Schmitt, R. B. (March 18, 1996). Planned Veto of Liability Bill Is Business's Loss. *The Wall Street Journal,* pp. A2, A8.

Schmitt, R. B. (June 16, 1995). While Congress Debates, States Limit Civil Lawsuits. *The Wall Street Journal,* pp. B1, B4.

Schwartz, V. E. (1993). Product Liability Fairness Act, S. 687. *Journal of Products & Toxics Liability,* 15(4), 267-277.

Traynor, R. J. (1965). The Ways and Means of Defective Products and Strict Liability. *Tennessee Law Review,* 32(3), 363-377.

van der Smissen, B. (1990). *Legal Liability and Risk Management for Public and Private Entities,* Cincinnati, Ohio: Anderson Publishing Company.

Wittenberg, J. D. (1992). *Products Liability: Recreation and Sports Equipment.* New York: Law Journal Seminars-Press.

Zachary, G. Pascal (1996, March 28). California's Defeat of Legal, Insurance Overhaul Raises Questions About Tort Reform Nationwide. *The Wall Street Journal,* p. A16.

2.41

Assault and Battery

Mary A. Hums
University of Massachusetts-Amherst

Sport managers need to be aware of different contexts in which assault and battery may occur in the sport setting. Examples of such incidents are players striking officials, players attacking fans, fans attacking other fans, ushers roughly attempting to physically move unruly patrons, third persons attacking patrons, and coaches physically handling athletes. Controlling for situations in which assault and battery may occur should be a part of any sport organization's risk management plan.

The "Ice Ball" incident at Giants Stadium, where fans pelted players, workers, and other fans with ice balls, illustrates what can happen when crowds get out of control. Only one offender was apprehended in this incident. The well-documented attacks on Nancy Kerrigan and Monica Seles should make sport managers aware of security issues surrounding highly visible athletes. The NBA experienced two serious physical confrontations between players and officials during the 1995-96 season. The NBA responded by levying stiff fines and imposing strong suspensions against the players involved. Recent episodes have occurred involving players retaliating against fans' verbal abuse. One example of this is Albert Belle of the Cleveland Indians throwing a ball into the stands at a heckler. These highly visible incidents occurred in professional sports; however, the sport manager needs to realize that assault and battery may also occur in a health club, on the recreation field, at the little league game, on a rafting trip, or in any other sports setting.

■ ■ ■ ■

Representative Case

BAUGH v. REDMOND

Court of Appeal of Louisiana, Second Circuit
565 So. 2d 953; 1990 La. App. LEXIS 1604
June 20, 1990, Rendered

OPINION:

In this action for damages as the result of a battery, defendant, Maurice Redmond, appealed the judgment of the trial court in favor of plaintiff, Jimmie Baugh, and defendant's insurer, Aetna Casualty and Surety Company. Finding the trial court did not err in holding defendant lia- ble for plaintiff's damages and in its apportionment of fault between the parties but erred in holding the insurer was not liable for the intentional tort under the policy provisions, we affirm in part and reverse in part.

Issues Presented

On appeal, defendant presents the following assignments of error:

1. The trial court erred in finding plaintiff had proven by a preponderance of the evidence that defendant intended to commit a battery;
2. The trial court erred in failing to mitigate the general damage award as plaintiff's actions precipitated and provoked the incident;
3. The trial court erred in failing to acknowledge the applicability of comparative fault in an intentional tort case; and,
4. The trial court erred in finding the insurer was not liable based upon a provision excluding liability for bodily injury which was expected or intended from the standpoint of the insured.

Factual Context

On May 20, 1987 plaintiff was umpiring an adult softball game between teams from the Ouachita Parish Sheriff's Department and Ouachita Electric Service, Inc., a Redmond corporation which sponsored the team. During the game plaintiff called a Ouachita Electric Service player out for leaving a base early on a fly ball and defendant became enraged by plaintiff's call. Throughout the remainder of the game, defendant verbally harassed plaintiff and defendant's team eventually lost the game. Following the game, plaintiff and defendant had a confrontation upon exiting the field in which heated words were exchanged and eventually resulted in defendant striking plaintiff in the face. As a result of the blow, plaintiff's eyeglasses were knocked off his face and he incurred a bloody mouth with extensive damage to his teeth.

On August 21, 1987 plaintiff instituted this action for damages naming as defendants Maurice Redmond and Ouachita Electric Service, Inc. Ouachita Electric Service, Inc. was later dismissed from the litigation. In his petition, plaintiff alleged defendant had punched him in the face without provocation, knocking him to the ground, breaking his eyeglasses and causing extensive damage to plaintiff's teeth and bones in his mouth necessitating extensive dental treatment and oral surgery.

Defendant filed a third-party demand naming as third-party defendant his insurer, Aetna Casualty and Surety Company. Defendant alleged the altercation was covered by the liability provisions of the homeowner's policy issued to him by the insurer. Further the insurer was obligated to provide legal representation on the behalf of defendant. However, despite demand, third-party defendant had failed to provide such representation. In its answer, the insurer alleged the incident was not covered by the liability provisions of the policy due to a provision which excluded coverage for any acts which were expected or intended by the insured.

Defendant filed an amending and supplemental answer in which he alleged plaintiff was guilty of contributory negligence which partially contributed to the incident and therefore his recoverable damages should be reduced in proportion to the degree or percentage of fault attributed to him. In the event the court deemed contributory negligence inapplicable, defendant alleged that any damages awarded should be mitigated due to the conduct of plaintiff in escalating the confrontation.

At the trial on the merits the testimony as to the actual battery was conflicting. Plaintiff testified he had served as an umpire for the West Monroe Adult Softball League for approximately ten years. He said defendant began to verbally abuse him after a call, requiring him to warn the team that if defendant did not quiet down he would forfeit the game. Plaintiff allowed the team to play the remaining inning during which defendant continually verbally abused him. After the game ended and he was exiting the Ouachita Electric Service dugout, plaintiff was confronted and threatened by defendant. Plaintiff stated he told defendant he would report the incident to the recreation department and defendant would not be allowed back at the ballpark. Plaintiff turned to walk toward the concession stand with the defendant walking slightly behind him and was struck once unexpectedly by defendant. Plaintiff stated he did not make any threatening gestures and he had placed his face mask underneath his arm. As the result of the blow, plaintiff said he was knocked up against a fence, his glasses were broken and he was bleeding from the mouth. He stated that several officers from the Sheriff's Department had to restrain defendant after the initial blow. Plaintiff was treated at a local hospital and was eventually required to undergo extensive dental treatment and oral surgery, including four root canals and crowns.

Ray Zeigler, another umpire at the game, testified that defendant had harassed plaintiff after the adverse call. Zeigler stated plaintiff stopped the game and warned the Ouachita Electric Service team that if harassment did not cease by their spectators he would have to call the game. He stated defendant was quieter but could still be heard in the background talking about the call. Zeigler stated that upon finishing a game the umpires usually go directly to the concession stand. When he and plaintiff exited the dugout, defendant was just outside. Zeigler stated plaintiff did not push, bump or make any threatening moves toward defendant. Plaintiff began to walk away from defendant and after going one step was struck in the mouth. The force of the blow popped the lens out of his eyeglasses and after the initial blow, defendant was restrained. Zeigler stated that throughout the incident he had a clear view and indicated plaintiff had his mask underneath his arm when he was talking to defendant.

Theresa Van Carter Redmond, defendant's daughter-in-law, testified she had attended the softball game. Mrs. Redmond stated that the spectators believed there had been bad calls by the umpire and some comments were made. She testified that plaintiff warned the spectators he would call the game and then told defendant "You shut up" or he would have him thrown out of the park. Mrs. Redmond testified that after the game defendant went into the dugout and she could hear plaintiff and defendant "hollering" as they came out. The parties were talking as they were walking and plaintiff was a step or two ahead of defendant. Mrs. Redmond stated plaintiff told defendant that he could have defendant thrown out of the park and then quite suddenly turned back toward the defendant with his mask in his right hand. At that time defendant punched plaintiff with a quick sharp punch. Mrs. Redmond was approximately two feet away from the parties when the blow occurred. She stated plaintiff's glasses fell to the ground and plaintiff stepped on them. Mrs. Redmond said that the force of the blow did not knock the plaintiff down but rather caused him to stumble backwards.

Defendant testified that during the course of the game plaintiff came over to the fence and became angry at him. He was told plaintiff would eject him from the park. After the game ended defendant proceeded to the dugout. When plaintiff walked through the dugout, defendant stated plaintiff's shoulder hit him in the chest and defendant went into the dugout after him. Defendant said they talked as they proceeded through the dugout and plaintiff "hollered" he bet defendant $100 he would be ejected from the ballpark. Plaintiff then turned around with his mask in his hand. Defendant testified he thought at that moment that plaintiff would strike him and he struck plaintiff in the face. He stated he did not intend to hit plaintiff but rather intended to keep plaintiff from striking him. Defendant testified he did not intend that plaintiff be injured or incur damage to his teeth. Defendant stated the testimony of the witnesses as to plaintiff's bleeding surprised him as he did not think he had struck plaintiff that hard.

After the trial on the merits, the trial court found in favor of plaintiff and third-party defendant. In its written opinion, the trial court reviewed the testimony of the parties and witnesses as to the confrontation and found that the evidence established that defendant had allowed himself to become outraged at plaintiff over the call made against his team. His anger rekindled at losing the game and he confronted plaintiff inside the playing area where he had no reason to be and there, without any legal justification or provocation, committed a battery upon plaintiff

by striking him in the mouth, causing the injuries and damages sustained by him. The court found plaintiff had proven the battery by a preponderance of the evidence. The court noted the medical testimony established that the blow to plaintiff's mouth was consistent with and caused significant trauma to six upper teeth requiring four root canals as well as other oral surgery. The court observed that plaintiff's injuries were quite painful and plaintiff had missed work and lost wages due to his dental treatments which began immediately after the battery and continued until January, 1988. As general damages for plaintiff's pain and suffering, the court found the sum of $20,000 was fair and adequate under the circumstances. The court further awarded plaintiff special damages in the amount of $4812.80 for past medical expenses and lost wages incurred as a result of the battery. The trial court found that as this matter was an intentional tort, contributory and/or comparative negligence was not applicable. The court further stated it had considered all the evidence in light of defendant's request for mitigation of damages and declined to grant the same. The court found that defendant's conduct after the game was unnecessary and his actions toward plaintiff were deliberate and intentional. In examining defendant's third-party demand, the trial court held the policy exclusion as to bodily injury which was expected and intended by the insured was applicable and, accordingly, the trial court denied defendant's claim.

On defendant's motion for a new trial, the trial court agreed it should have applied the principles of comparative fault to this matter. However, upon reviewing all of the testimony and the factors to be considered in apportioning fault, the trial court found the testimony did not establish by a preponderance of the evidence that plaintiff was at fault in causing or contributing to his injuries. Rather, the evidence established there was unprovoked battery committed by defendant when plaintiff was only trying to exit the playing field. The court further found there was nothing in the record to reverse its previous decision that the insurer's policy of insurance did not provide coverage to defendant for this incident.

Liability for Battery

It is well-settled that a Court of Appeal may not set aside a trial court's finding of fact in the absence of "manifest error" or unless it is "clearly wrong" and, where there is conflict in the testimony, reasonable evaluations of credibility and reasonable inferences of fact should not be disturbed upon review, even though the appellate court may feel its own evaluations and inferences are as reasonable. The trial judge is in a better position to evaluate the credibility of the witnesses and the weight of the evidence than an appellate court who does not see or hear the witnesses. For this reason, a reviewing court should adopt the trial court's findings as its own in the absence of clear error, even if other conclusions from the same evidence are equally reasonable.

• • •

A battery is any intentional and unpermitted contact with the plaintiff's person or anything attached to it or practically identified with it. In order to recover for a battery, plaintiff must prove by a preponderance of the evidence that his damages resulted from an unprovoked attack by defendant. The intention of the defendant need not be malicious nor need it be an intention to inflict actual damage. It is sufficient if the actor intends to inflict either a harmful or physical contact without the other's consent. Liability for a battery depends upon the facts and circumstances of each case. Where the defendant relies upon provocation as justification for a battery, he must prove some conduct or action by the plaintiff sufficient to provoke and arouse defendant to the point of physical retaliation. Louisiana's aggressor doctrine precludes tort recovery by plaintiff if the evidence establishes he was at fault in provoking the difficulty in which he was injured, unless the person retaliating has used excessive force to repel the aggression.

• • •

On appeal, defendant argues the trial court erred in finding plaintiff had proven by a preponderance of the evidence that defendant intended to commit a battery upon the plaintiff. We disagree.

The record shows that defendant had become angry with plaintiff during the game and verbally harassed plaintiff periodically throughout the remainder of the game. After the game concluded defendant proceeded to his team's dugout and confronted plaintiff as he was proceeding through the dugout area, which was his normal practice at the end of each game. Defendant verbally harassed plaintiff about his authority to eject defendant from the park if disruptive during a game. The evidence established that plaintiff continued to walk through the dugout toward the concession stand and was followed closely behind by defendant who was apparently intent upon provoking a confrontation with plaintiff through verbal harassment. There was no evidence that plaintiff pushed or made any threatening moves toward defendant in any manner so as to cause defendant to believe it was necessary to defend himself. Rather, it is clear that the blow to plaintiff was completely unexpected and unprovoked.

Considering all the circumstances surrounding this incident, it appears clear that defendant did intend to strike plaintiff and the trial court was not manifestly erroneous in this determination.

Comparative Negligence

Contributory negligence is conduct on the part of plaintiff which falls below the standard to which he should conform for his own safety and protection, that standard being that of a reasonable man under like circumstances. Harris v. Pineset, supra. La. C.C. Art. 2323 provides that a plaintiff whose negligence contributes to his own injuries for which he seeks damages shall have his claim reduced in proportion to his degree of fault. The determination and apportionment of fault are factual matters and the trial court's findings in this regard should not be disturbed by a reviewing court unless they are erroneous.

• • •

In assessing comparative fault the trial court must consider the nature of each party's conduct and the extent of the causal relationship between the conduct and the damages claimed. Relevant factors concerning the nature of each party's conduct include: (1) whether the conduct resulted from inadvertence or involved an awareness of the danger, (2) how great a risk was created by the conduct, (3) the significance of what was sought by the conduct, (4) the capacities of the actor, whether superior or inferior, and (5) any extenuating circumstances which might require the actor to proceed in haste, without proper thought.

• • •

It is well-settled that it is within the trial court's discretion to mitigate a general damage award when plaintiff's conduct helps create the circumstances giving rise to the injury. Mere words, even though designed to excite or irritate, cannot excuse a battery. However, words which are calculated to provoke and arouse to the point of physical retaliation may mitigate damages in a civil action. How and when damages are mitigated are determinations which are within the discretion of the trial court.

• • •

Defendant argues the trial court erred in failing to mitigate the general damage award as plaintiff's actions precipitated and provoked the incident and further the trial court erred in failing to acknowledge the applicability of comparative fault in an intentional tort case. This argument is without merit. It is clear from the opinion of the trial court in its denial of defendant's motion for a new trial that the trial court found it should have applied the principles of comparative fault to this matter. However, the court concluded upon a review of the testimony and the factors to be considered in apportioning fault that the testimony did not establish by a preponderance of the evidence that plaintiff was at fault in causing or contributing to his injuries so as to require a reduction of his damages. We agree.

The record shows that when defendant began his attempts to confront plaintiff following the conclusion of the game, plaintiff attempted to avoid such a confrontation by walking ahead of defendant and toward the concession stand. Defendant continued to walk behind plaintiff and to verbally harass him as to his authority to eject defendant from the park. There was no evidence that plaintiff acted verbally or physically to escalate the situation but rather was attempting to avoid any type of confrontation when struck unexpectedly by defendant. Under these circumstances we find plaintiff was not guilty of any comparative fault so as to reduce his recovery for injuries sustained by him.

Insurance Coverage
• • •

In defendant's homeowner's insurance policy which was issued by third-party defendant, Aetna Casualty & Surety Company, the policy provides that personal liability coverage and medical payments to others do not apply to bodily injury or property damage which is expected or intended by the insured.

• • •

A review of the record in light of the above jurisprudence establishes that the trial court erred in holding that the insurer's policy of insurance did not provide coverage to defendant for this incident.

• • •

The circumstances surrounding the conduct of defendant demonstrates his actions were not premeditated and not intended to inflict the serious injury plaintiff sustained. Defendant testified he did not think he had struck plaintiff with enough force to inflict a bloody mouth and he did not intend for plaintiff to be injured. Defendant characterized his blow as a "sharp, quick punch" more in the nature of a provocative gesture rather than a forceful blow intended to inflict serious injury. It is significant to note this incident occurred at a sporting event in which defendant was interested as a sponsor of the team, which circumstance would support the conclusion that the blow was more a gesture of anger and frustration rather than a deliberate effort on the part of the defendant to inflict bodily harm upon plaintiff. As we find the evidence demonstrates defendant did not intend or expect such a serious injury to result from his conduct, we find that coverage under defendant's homeowner policy is not excluded.

• • •
Decree
For these reasons, the judgment of the trial court in favor of plaintiff and against defendant is AFFIRMED. The judgment dismissing the third-party demand is REVERSED, and there is judgment in favor of the third-party plaintiff, Maurice Redmond, and against the third-party defendant, Aetna Casualty and Surety Company, for the amount of the judgment on the main demand against defendant, and for attorney fees in the sum of $3000.

■ ■ ■ ■

Fundamental Concepts

When the terms assault and battery come to mind, they are most often thought of in terms of criminal law; however, the sport manager is more often concerned with civil assault and battery. A distinction must be made between criminal assault and battery, which is a crime, and civil assault and battery, which is an intentional tort. The same act can be either or both a crime and an intentional tort. For instance, suppose an irate parent punches an umpire at a little league baseball game. The umpire has the option of filing a civil suit against the parent. If his suit is successful, he may be awarded monetary damages. He also has the option of filing criminal charges against the parent. If the parent is convicted, he may serve jail time, be fined, or be punished in some other way by the state. If both civil and criminal remedies are pursued, the outcome of one is independent of the outcome of the other. This chapter focuses on civil assault and battery.

A final point to keep in mind when discussing assault and battery is that while these two terms are often used together, they are, in fact, separate concepts. These intentional torts may occur together, or may be independent of each other. In basic terms, assault is the threat (non-contact) to use force while battery is the actual use (contact) of force.

Assault

Assault may be defined as the intentional creation of a reasonable apprehension of an imminent and offensive contact without the person's consent. No actual physical contact need occur for an assault to be committed. If a football coach draws back his hand, threatening to strike a youngster, he has committed assault. If he shouts at the boy or threatens to make him run laps, no assault has occurred. In order to understand the definition of assault, it is helpful to break it down into several parts. Specifically, we should define what is meant by *reasonable, apprehension* and *imminent*.

First, what is meant by *reasonable*? The court will look in hindsight at what occurred and ask the question, "Would a reasonable person have believed the contact to be imminent?" If the answer to this question is yes, then an assault has occurred. The courts, however, cannot see into the mind of the person committing the assault. It does not matter if the person committing the assault pointed an unloaded gun, for example. There was no way the person being assaulted could have known whether or not the gun was loaded, or could have known if the person intended to carry out the assault. The fact is, if someone points a gun at another person, it is reasonable for that person to assume he or she is about to be shot.

Next, one must understood what is meant by *apprehension*. Normally, apprehension is associated with fear or being scared. However, when looking at an assault situation, apprehension is more accurately defined as awareness rather than fear. Here the courts will ask whether the person was aware that some sort of contact was about to occur. If the answer is no, no assault occurred. Because of this, technically one could not assault a person who is asleep or unconscious. A sleeping or unconscious individual is incapable of being aware of imminent contact. Once again the reasonable person standard is applied in determining apprehension on the part of the person who was assaulted.

Finally, *imminent* implies that something is going to happen immediately. The person being threatened believes something is going to happen immediately, not at some unknown time in the future.

Elements of Assault. In order to establish an assault has occurred, the following three elements must be present:

1. the defendant intended to cause harm (or apprehension)
2. the plaintiff felt reasonable apprehension of immediate harm
3. there was lack of consent by the plaintiff.

Defenses for Assault. A successful defense to assault can be brought by the defendant if he or she can prove that any one of the three elements is missing.

Battery

Battery is defined as the intentional, unpermitted, unprivileged, and offensive touching of the person of one individual by another. In battery, touching means any physical contact. The contact does not have to result in an injury to anyone, the mere contact is enough. The lifeguard who seizes an unruly swimmer by the arm and escorts the swimmer from the pool area may be charged with battery.

The "person" of someone is not confined to their physical body, but includes items they are carrying. Snatching a purse or stealing a backpack off one's shoulder could be considered battery. As opposed to assault, awareness is not required. It is possible for battery to occur if the person touched is asleep, unconscious, or even if he or she just had his or her back turned to the assailant.

Elements of Battery. Three elements are required for battery. The plaintiff must prove:

1. the defendant intended to touch the plaintiff
2. actual touching occurred
3. there was lack of consent by the plaintiff.

Defenses for Battery. There are two fundamental defenses for battery. The first is that the touching was not intentional. The second is that the plaintiff consented to the touching.

Damages

If a defendant is found to have committed civil assault and battery, actual damages may be awarded to the plaintiff. These damages are monetary and can include lost wages, lost earning capacity, medical expenses, and pain and suffering.

Privilege

Some situations in which threatening force or touching without consent occur are not assault and battery because of certain special circumstances. A person may be considered to have what is known as **privilege**, which allows him or her to act in ways normally considered assault and battery. The two most common examples of privilege are acting in self-defense and acting in defense of a third party.

Laws regarding self-defense vary from state to state. In general if a person harms another person and claims self-defense, the circumstances must be examined. First, did the person use reasonable force to get away from the situation? The courts attempt to look into the mind of the person being attacked to determine the answer to this question. Reasonable force can mean different things to different people. If two individuals of the same size are involved in an altercation, striking back with a fist may seem reasonable. If a smaller individual is attacked by a much larger individual, the smaller person may think it reasonable to pick up an implement and strike back, as opposed to just fighting back with fists. Secondly, did the person who was attacked retreat from the situation when there was opportunity? The duty to retreat once an escape option is available must be considered.

Laws regarding defense of a third party also differ on a state-by-state basis. One issue is the definition of a *third party*. Often this privilege is extended only to people who are defending a family member. The definition of *family member* may differ from state to state.

Standard of Care Owed Other Participants

While an ordinary citizen is legally responsible for assaulting or battering another individual, the expectations are different for the participant in a sporting event. Society accepts a certain amount of violence in sport as being part of the game which would not be considered acceptable outside of competition. Throwing a 95-mph fastball at a batter's head is sometimes considered strategy in baseball, but throwing a 95-mph fastball at a heckling fan is assault and/or battery.

Traditionally a distinction has been made between the standard of care one participant owes another in contact and non-contact sports. In non-contact sports, participants have generally been held liable for negligent acts that injure fellow participants. For example, if a golfer hits toward the green while another foursome is on the green and strikes another participant, that golfer could be considered negligent and liable for any injury incurred.

In contact sports, reckless misconduct was established as the standard of care in the *Nabozny v. Barnhill* case in 1975. A soccer player recklessly kicked Nabozny in the face and was found liable. The court said that a player was liable for injury if his action was made with a reckless disregard for the safety of the other player.

The tort of **reckless misconduct** falls in between negligence, an unintentional tort, and assault and battery, which are intentional torts. "Reckless misconduct occurs when the actor has intentionally performed an act in total disregard of a known risk, when the risk is so great as to make the harm highly probable" (Berry and Wong, 1993, p. 417). In other words, a person intends to commit a certain act, but does not intend for another person to be harmed. This type of action is often called reckless, or willful and wanton, and is accompanied by a knowing disregard of the circumstances. For example, a javelin thrower is practicing on a windy day while his teammates are running on the track. The thrower decides he wants to scare his friends by throwing the javelin so it lands next to the track. He misjudges the distance and the wind and strikes a runner in the leg with the javelin. The thrower intended to throw the javelin near the runners, but did not intend to hit any of them. The javelin thrower knew there was a possibility that if he threw the javelin near people, especially on a windy day, someone could be hit. He disregarded the potential harm and threw the javelin anyway.

The courts have recently been giving mixed signals regarding the standard of care that one participant owes to another in contact sports. In *Crawn v. Campo* (1993), softball catcher Crawn brought action against a runner who violently slid into him at home plate. The trial court used the standard of negligence, but the appellate court remanded the case with a directive to use reckless conduct as the standard of care. Both the *Martin v. Buzan* (1993) and *Pfister v. Schusta* (1995) courts continued to uphold the position that participants owed each other the duty to refrain from reckless, wilful and wanton, or intentional misconduct, but were not liable for injuries caused by ordinary negligence. In *Martin*, the plaintiff catcher was injured in a collision at home plate. The court stated that reasonable minds would have concluded the plaintiff assumed the risk of the defendant colliding with her at home plate; and the plaintiff, by her participation, consented to an injury which was a reasonably foreseeable consequence of participating in the competition. In *Pfister*, the plaintiff injured his hand and arm when pushed during a spontaneous "kick the can" game in a residence hall. Under the exception to the standard of ordinary care for contact sports created by the appellate court, voluntary participants in contact sports are not liable for injuries caused by simple negligent conduct.

In contrast, in *Lestina v. West Bend Mutual Insurance Company* (1993), a soccer player was injured when the defendant slide-tackled him during a recreational league game in which slide-tackling was against the rules. The court held that negligence, rather than recklessness, was the appropriate standard to govern cases involving injuries during recreational team contact sports.

Recent Developments

One issue sport managers, especially facility managers, need to be aware of is that of third party assaults which may occur on their premises. Facility managers need to know they may be found negligent if such incidents do occur and if the incidents were foreseeable. According to Walker, Sawyer and Sharp (1996), the courts have considered three approaches in determining if third party assaults were foreseeable—1) the no duty rule, 2) the prior similar acts (or incidents) rule, and 3) the totality of circumstances rule. Traditionally, the courts have relied on the prior similar acts rule, where landowners were not expected to anticipate a third party attack if one had not previously occurred on the premises. In a key case *(Small v. McKennan Hospital,* [1989]), the lower court used the prior similar acts rule. However, on appeal the court favored the totality of circumstances rule and reversed the decision. Under totality of circumstances, a landowner may be held liable for criminal attacks, depending on the surrounding facts and circumstances (Walker, Sawyer, and Sharp, 1996). According to Eiesland (1990), when using the totality of circumstances test, the plaintiff's lawyer should examine: a) any prior similar acts, b) the nature of the premises, c) the nature of the area where the attack occurred, and d) the nature of the operation being carried on by the defendant.

In order to help protect their patrons from attack and themselves from liability, facility managers need to monitor such things as prior violent activity, nonviolent crime activity, lighting, security personnel, warning signs, access control, location, physical layout, maintenance, and any patron complaints or suggestions

(Eiesland, 1990). Facility operators need to use reasonable care in seeing that patrons can safely enter and exit a facility (Walker, Sawyer, and Sharp, 1996).

References

A. Cases

Baugh v. Redmond, 565 So.2d 953 (La.App. 2 Cir. 1990).

Crawn v. Campo, 630 A.2d. 368 (N.J. Super. A.D. 1993).

Lestina v. West Bend Mutual Insurance Company, 501 N.W.2d 28 (Wis. 1993).

Martin v. Buzan, 857 S.W. 2d 366 (Mo.App. E.D. 1993).

Nabozny v. Barnhill, 334 N.E.2d 258 (Ill. 1975).

Pfister v. Shusta, 657 N.E. 2d. 1013 (Ill. 1995).

Small v. McKennan Hospital, 403 NW 2d. 410 (S.D. 1987); 437 N.W.2d 194 (S.D. 1989).

B. Publications and Presentations

Berry, R.C., & Wong, G.M. (1993). *Law and the Business of the Sport Industry.* (Vol. II). (2nd. Ed.). Westport, Conn.: Praeger.

Eiesland, G. (1990). Attacks in Parking Lots. *Trial*, Sept., p. 108-113.

Walker, M., Sawyer, L. & Sharp, L. (1996). An Update of Recent Litigation Affecting Sport Facilities. *North American Society for Sport Management Annual Conference*, Fredericton, New Brunswick, Canada.

Defamation

Lori K. Miller
Wichita State University*

The tort of defamation, dating back to early 16th century common law, provides recourse for false, insidious, or irresponsible statements which damage individual reputations. As defined by **Black's Law Dictionary** (1990),

> Defamation is that which tends to injure reputation; to diminish the esteem, respect, goodwill or confidence in which the plaintiff is held, or to excite adverse, derogatory or unpleasant feelings or opinions against him. (p. 417)

The tort of defamation includes both slander and libel. Defamatory comments made orally, such as those heard on television, exemplify **slander**. A comment is slanderous *per se* if it falls into one of the following categories: 1) accuses the plaintiff of criminal conduct, 2) accuses the plaintiff of having a loathsome disease, 3) accuses the female plaintiff of being unchaste, 4) accuses the plaintiff of misconduct in public office, or 5) injures the plaintiff's profession, business, or trade. For example, false comments accusing someone of murder, having AIDS, having sex with an entire basketball team, or illegal recruiting practices could be construed as slanderous *per se* (Carpenter, 1995).

Libel is a broader category of communication. Written comments, photographs, and cartoons, such as those appearing in newspapers and in other written documents, are examples of libel. Some states classify statements as libel *per se* if they fall into one of the above five categories characterizing slander *per se*.

Slander and libel were originally recognized as two distinct types of defamation. Libel was thought to be more damaging as the material containing the libelous statement had greater longevity. For example, newspapers and magazines could be retained for weeks while statements made on television vanished within seconds. Technology now secures media statements in a tangible form and most jurisdictions refer to the two terms (i.e., slander and libel) interchangeably (Pember, 1990).

As explained by the **Restatement (Second) of Torts**, the following four elements must exist to constitute any claim of defamation: a) a false statement, b) publication to a third party, c) fault or negligence of the publisher, and d) damage. The plaintiff retains the burden of proof in a defamation action (**Restatement (Second) of Torts**). Plaintiffs alleging slander (or libel) *per se* have an advantage as they are not required to prove damages, often "the most difficult element of defamation to prove" (Carpenter, 1995, p. 53).

Elaborating on the importance of defamation law to an individual, Justice Stewart said, "The right of a man to the protection of his own reputation from unjustified invasion and wrongful hurt reflects no more than our basic concept of the essential dignity and worth of every human being . . ." (*Rosenblatt v. Baer*

*Dr. Lawrence W. Fielding, Indiana University, made significant contributions to this chapter. The author wishes to recognize these contributions and express a genuine gratitude to Dr. Fielding.

p. 92). Critics say defamation law stifles individual commentary which contributes to the marketplace of ideas. The judicial system attempts to balance the right to preserve one's reputation with individual constitutional rights. To promote balance between plaintiff and defendant, Supreme Court decisions have categorized individuals into three groups: public officials, public figures, and private figures. The burden of proof differs among the categories and hence, varies the "accuracy" required of defendants.

■ ■ ■ ■

Representative Case

GOMEZ v. MURDOCH

Superior Court of New Jersey, Appellate Division
193 N.J. Super. 595; 475 A.2d 622; 54 A.L.R.4th 861
January 10, 1984, Argued
February 6, 1984, Decided

OPINION:

This appeal involves a libel action. Plaintiff, a professional jockey, filed a complaint based upon an article by defendant Kerrison in a daily newspaper, the New York Post. The complaint alleges that "defendant Murdoch is the publisher of . . . the New York Post, which is published by defendant, News Group Publications, Inc. . . ." Defendants made a motion for summary judgment which was granted. This is plaintiff's appeal from the order granting summary judgment. We affirm.

Defendants' application for summary judgment was based upon the contention that plaintiff was a public figure and, therefore, was required to prove "actual malice" within the meaning of New York Times v. Sullivan, 376 U.S. 254, 84 S.Ct. 710, 11 L.Ed.2d 686 (1964). In that case, the Court defined a statement made with actual malice as one made ". . . with knowledge that it was false or with reckless disregard of whether it was false or not." Id. at 279-280, 84 S.Ct. at 725-726. Although New York Times v. Sullivan dealt with a public official, the same test of actual malice was ultimately applied to a public figure. Gertz v. Welch, 418 U.S. 323, 94 S.Ct. 2997, 41 L.Ed.2d 789 (1974); Lawrence v. Bauer Pub. & Print., Ltd., 89 N.J. 451, 466 (1982).

There are two questions for us to resolve on this appeal. First, was plaintiff a public figure at the time of the publication of the article about which he complains? Second, if plaintiff was a public figure, was there a disputed question of fact as to actual malice so as to preclude summary judgment? We answer the first question "yes," and the second question "no."

In determining plaintiff's status as a public figure, the trial judge stated that plaintiff had been "a flat track jockey" since 1975 or 1976 and on September 25, 1981, had a mount at the Meadowlands racetrack. It was defendant Kerrison's derogatory article in the New York Post about plaintiff's handling of his horse in a race on that date which formed the basis of plaintiff's libel action. It is not necessary for us here to repeat that article in full. Suffice it to say that the article charged in forceful and caustic terms that plaintiff deliberately tried to keep his horse from making its best effort. The article ended with a declaration that plaintiff "robbed" those persons who bet on the horse "as if he had plucked the money out of their wallets."

In his colloquy with plaintiff's counsel at the time of argument on the motion for summary judgment, the trial judge said that "there is no way in the world that a man could decide to become a jockey, put the silks on and ride before hundreds of thousands of people as he has and not call himself a public figure." The judge also stated that "any people on television see him run," and further mentioned "the public interest in horseracing." Finally, the judge declared that plaintiff "voluntarily made himself publicly seen, publicly known, publicly printed." It is undisputed that it is the function of the trial judge, rather than the jury, to decide the question of whether a plaintiff in a libel action is a public figure. See Lawrence v. Bauer Pub. & Print., Ltd., supra, 89 N.J. at 462. We agree with the trial judge's view that plaintiff here was a public figure.

The trial court relied in large part on Gertz v. Welch, supra. That case distinguished between an individual of "pervasive fame or notoriety" who is a public figure in all contexts and an individual who "becomes a public figure for a limited range of issues." 418 U.S. at 351, 94 S.Ct. at 2997. In the matter now before us, the trial court stated that plaintiff was not a public figure "as far as private life is concerned," but "when he gets on the back of a horse, and he becomes a jockey, he certainly takes on all aspects of being a public figure." Thus, although the judge did not specifically so articulate it, he obviously found plaintiff to be a public figure for a limited range of issues within the Gertz dichotomy. Accordingly, adverse newspaper comment about plaintiff's performance in his professional capacity as a jockey must be considered under the law of defamation relating to public figures. We are not here dealing with comments about plaintiff's activities outside of his professional life, which comments would not be privileged except in the case of a person of pervasive fame or notoriety.

In Time, Inc. v. Johnston, 448 F.2d 378 (4 Cir.1971), the court held that a retired professional basketball player was a public figure. There, the court quoted Cepeda v. Cowles Magazine & Broadcasting Co., 392 F.2d 417 (9 Cir.1968), cert. den. 393 U.S. 840, 89 S.Ct. 117, 21 L.Ed.2d 110 (1968), a case involving a professional baseball player, in which the court stated that public figures are those persons involved in issues in which the public has a justified and important interest, and include athletes. Consistent with this definition, a college athletic director, Curtis Publishing Co. v. Butts, 388 U.S. 130, 87 S.Ct. 1975, 18 L.Ed.2d 1094) (1967), a basketball coach, Grayson v. Curtis Publishing Co., 72 Wash.2d 999, 436 P.2d 756 (1968), and a professional boxer, Cohen v. Marx, 94 Cal.App.2d 704, 211 P.2d 320 (1950), have all been held to be public figures. We likewise find to be a public figure a professional jockey who chooses to perform publicly in a sport which commands widespread public interest, and regarding which the communications media regularly report. "Professional athletes, at least as to their playing careers, generally assume a position of public prominence." Chuy v. Philadelphia Eagles Football Club, 595 F.2d 1265, 1280 (3 Cir.1979). We note the emphasis in plaintiff's reply brief on the question of plaintiff's access to the media to respond to allegations against him. While it is true that this is a factor to be considered, see Gertz v. Welch, supra, an affidavit submitted by defendant Kerrison in support of the motion for summary judgment reveals that there was a "press box" at Meadowlands racetrack. There is no indication that plaintiff could not visit that facility in order to give his side of the story.

We move now to the subject of whether the trial judge should have abstained from granting summary judgment because a jury question remained as to whether defendants acted with actual malice. After determining that plaintiff was a public figure, the judge said: "Having made that conclusion, all the other dominoes can click, click, click and fall in place." This statement failed to fulfill the requirement of R. 4:46-2 that on a motion for summary judgment, the trial court "shall find the facts and state its conclusions." Ordinarily, this lack of compliance with the rule by the trial judge would make a remand necessary. However, we are satisfied that under the circumstances of this case a remand would serve no useful purpose and could not change the result. Our conclusion in this respect is based on three factors: (1) affidavits submitted by defendants in support of their motion for summary judgment; (2) the absence of any opposing affidavit or certification on the part of plaintiff and (3) plaintiff's answers to interrogatories.

Defendants submitted affidavits from defendant Kerrison and a racetrack steward, Sam Boulmetis. In his affidavit, defendant Kerrison, who is the author of the newspaper article in question, stated that while in the press box at Meadowlands racetrack, he noticed a press release which announced that plaintiff had been suspended for "failing to persevere with his mount" in the fourth race on September 25, 1981. Kerrison declared that upon consulting the "chart," he found that it stated that the horse ridden by plaintiff "made a good late run, while remaining under restraining through the drive." Several days later, according to the Kerrison affidavit, Kerrison spoke with three state stewards and viewed a videotape of the suspect race approximately six times. Kerrison further stated that one of the stewards, Sam Boulmetis, called to his attention that the videotape revealed that plaintiff was not "pushing" his horse toward the end of the race, while all the other jockeys were pushing theirs. The Kerrison affidavit also quoted Boulmetis as saying that plaintiff's explanation that his saddle had slipped was "ridiculous" as plaintiff "had his feet on the dashboard." The affidavit of Boulmetis confirmed Kerrison's affidavit.

Despite the damning nature of Kerrison's affidavit, plaintiff offered no countervailing affidavit to indicate that the critical article was written with actual malice, i.e., that it was made with knowledge that it was false or with reckless disregard of whether or not it was false. See R. 4:46-5(a). Moreover, with regard to plaintiff's answers to interrogatories, when plaintiff was asked the basis of his claim of actual malice he responded: "See prior answers; article has no basis in fact." All the questions and answers have not been supplied to us, but plaintiff has made no claim to us that they tend to prove actual malice. Certainly, an assertion that an offending article has "no basis in fact" is insufficient to establish actual malice.

• • •

However, in a libel action where a qualified privilege exists, the plaintiff has the burden of proving actual malice. . . . Plaintiff here has failed to raise any question of fact as to actual malice. At the least, the evidence must permit the conclusion that defendants entertained serious

doubt as to the truth of the publication. . . . In conclusion, we note the statement in Kotlikoff v. The Community News, 89 N.J. 62 (1982) that in libel cases trial courts are encouraged "to give particularly careful consideration to identifying appropriate causes for summary judgment disposition." Id. at 67-68.

Affirmed.

■ ■ ■ ■

Fundamental Concepts and Principles

The Public Official

The 1964 Supreme Court decision in *New York Times v. Sullivan* revolutionized the way the judiciary interpreted and applied defamation law. As stated by Pember (1990, p. 129), "This is one of the most important First Amendment cases ever decided . . ." In the *NY Times* case, the Supreme Court prohibited *public officials* from recovering damages for defamatory comments relating to official conduct unless the plaintiff could prove that the statement was made with *actual malice*. The Supreme Court believed that the public had a right to know, and to evaluate for themselves, how leaders governed. Further, open debate, although at times caustic and unpleasant, assured the exchange of ideas necessary to bring about political and social change desired by the people.

Pember succinctly defines a **public official** as "someone who works for a government and draws a salary from the public payroll" (1990, p.133). The Supreme Court also attempted to define the public official. In *Rosenblatt v. Baer* (1966) the Court questioned whether all individuals employed by the state are public officials or just those employed in "high powered" positions. As stated by Justice Douglas in a concurring opinion, "anyone on the public payroll" qualifies as a public official (1966, p. 89).

It would appear from the above decisions that subsequent court decisions would classify all teachers, coaches, and recreation supervisors as public officials. However, a contrary decision was issued by the Supreme Court of Kentucky in *Warford v. Lexington Herald* in 1990. As decided by this court, an assistant basketball recruiting coach at the University of Pittsburgh was not classified as either a public official or a public or limited purpose public figure (see the section below dealing with the public figure and limited purpose public figure).

Communication made with actual malice was defined by the *NY Times* court (1964, p. 380) as communication made, "with knowledge that it was false or with reckless disregard of whether it was false or not." Proof of actual malice is a significant departure from early defamation law. Subsequent Supreme Court cases provide evidence of the difficulty associated with proving actual malice (*Garrison v. Louisiana,* 1964; *St. Amant v. Thompson,* 1968).

The Public Figure

In a subsequent landmark case, *Curtis Publishing Co. v. Butts* (1967), the Supreme Court extended the constitutional protection given to statements about public officials in the *New York Times* case to public figures as well. Similar to the standard of proof established in the *New York Times* case, the *Curtis* court stated that individuals falling into the status of a public figure must prove actual malice to recover for damages. As explained by the Supreme Court in *Curtis Publishing Co. v. Butts,* a public figure is an individual who has, because of his or her activities, "commanded sufficient continuing public interest" (1967, p. 155). The Supreme Court recognized the appellee in this case, the Athletic Director of the University of Georgia (Wally Butts), as a public figure. District courts adopted and extended the Supreme Court ruling. As explained in a footnote concerning public figures by the *Waldbaum* court (*Waldbaum v. Fairchild Publications, Inc.*, 637 F.2d 1287 [1980, p. 1294])

> Many well-known athletes, entertainers, and other personages endorse commercial products, . . . This phenomenon, regardless of whether it is justified, indicates that famous persons may be able to transfer their recognition and influence from one field to another. (p. 1294)

Athletes, like politicians, can sway individual thinking. Consequently, their individual actions are open to public debate and scrutiny.

The *Curtis* court provided two reasons for its extension of the actual malice standard as defined in the *NY Times* case to public figures. First, the plaintiff-public figure voluntarily "thrusts" himself or herself into the "vortex" of "important public controversies" (*Curtis*, 1966). As explained by the United States Court of Appeals (Third Circuit) in *Chuy v. Philadelphia Eagles Football Club* (1979),

> If society chooses to direct massive public attention to a particular sphere of activity, those who enter that sphere inviting such attention must overcome the *Times* standard. (p. 267)

Second, the 1966 *Curtis* court rationalized that, like public officials, public figures had "sufficient access to the means of counter argument" via the media.

The Limited Purpose Public Person. The 1974 Supreme Court decision in *Gertz v. Robert Welch, Inc.* introduced the limited purpose public person as ". . . an individual [who] voluntarily injects himself or is drawn into a particular public controversy and thereby becomes a public figure for a limited range of issues" (p. 351). Persons with instant national recognition and constant national media exposure such as Johnny Carson, Mohammed Ali, Wayne Newton, and William F. Buckley are considered all-purpose public figures (Barron and Dienes, 1979). The limited purpose public figure has instant local recognition and constant media coverage on a local level. The courts further assert that total community recognition need not be present to qualify as a limited purpose public figure. Rather, it is sufficient if the particular subculture in which the individual is involved is exposed to the defamatory publication (*Rosenblatt v. Baer*, 1966; *Scott v. News-Herald*, 1987; *Washington v. Smith*, 1995). Most sport-related figures (e.g., coaches, athletes, sport broadcasters) tend to be classified as limited purpose public figures. Persons in both public figure classifications (all-purpose and limited-purpose) are required to prove actual malice in order to recover for the tort of defamation.

The Private Figure

The "private figure" classification refers to individual citizens who are not involved in public issues or employed as a public official. Distinguishing between a public versus private figure is a critical issue for a plaintiff. Classification as a private person is important as private figures need only prove that an alleged defamatory statement was negligently made. Negligence is the failure to exercise "reasonable care." This is a much lower standard of proof than that required for public officials, public figures, or limited purpose public figures.

The difficulty comes in ascertaining who qualifies as a "private figure." Defendants allege that private citizens involved in matters of interest to the public constitute limited purpose public figures, at minimum, and are subject to the grueling standard of proof required by the *NY Times* case. According to the Supreme Court's plurality decision in *Rosenbloom v. Metromedia, Inc.* (1971), all publication regarding matters of general interest or public concern should be protected by requiring plaintiffs to prove actual malice.

Subsequent courts, concerned about the improper balance between competing interests, repudiated the "public interest" or "subject matter" standard established in the 1971 *Rosenbloom* case.

Two dominant reasons explain why the Court preserved the private person status granting individuals a lower standard of proof. First, it is assumed that private individuals do not have the same ability to access the media as public officials and public figures. Access to the media provides public officials and public figures with an opportunity to refute defamatory statements. The value of media access is illustrated by the Iowa Libel Research Project. According to this research project, almost 75 percent of defamed plaintiffs indicated they would have found adequate recourse if "the news medium would have published or broadcast a correction, retraction or apology" (Pember, 1990). Second, it is said that public figures and public officials relinquish rights when they voluntarily become entangled in an issue of public concern. Private individuals, in comparison, are not attempting to influence society and are not desirous of media attention.

Although private figures are not required to show actual malice in order to recover for defamation, they must prove actual injury. As defined by the Supreme Court in *Gertz* (1974, p. 350), actual injury includes "Impairment of reputation and standing in the community, personal humiliation, and mental anguish and suffering." Injury is difficult to prove and the likelihood of winning a monetary award is slight.

A more common strategy is to attempt to recover presumed or punitive damages. In order to recover presumed or punitive damages, a private figure must show actual malice. There are two benefits to this strategy. First, proving actual malice eliminates the need to prove actual injury. Second, defamation cases historically last over a decade. Without punitive damages, it is often not financially feasible for the plaintiff to pursue the case as the recovered damages are not enough to offset litigation expenses. Litigation time and expense, when combined with the need to prove actual malice, place plaintiffs at a distinct disadvantage (Anderson, 1991).

Fact v. Opinion

Early common law protected statements of opinion from defamatory allegations. The Supreme Court affirmed this sentiment in the *Gertz* case in 1974. As stated by the Supreme Court, "Under the First Amendment there is no such thing as a false idea" (*Gertz*, 1974, p. 339). However, statements based upon false facts, or undisclosed facts, are actionable. In other words, if an opinion is stated, then all the facts which were used in deriving the opinion should be disclosed. This enables an individual to read the facts and then draw his or her own conclusion (i.e., opinion) which may differ from that of the writer or publisher. The decision as to whether a statement constitutes fact or opinion is a question of law for the court to decide.

The Supreme Court in *Milkovich v. Lorain* (1990) further narrowed the protection given to statements of opinion. As explained by the Court, merely prefacing a statement with "In my opinion, . . ." does not insulate an individual from defamation liability. More specifically, the Court stated,

> Even if the speaker states the facts upon which he bases his opinion, if those facts are either incorrect or incomplete, or if his assessment of them is erroneous, the statement may still imply a false assertion of fact. Simply couching such statements in terms of opinion does not dispel these implications. . . . (p. 2706)

The U.S. Court of Appeals, in *Ollman v. Evans* (1984), established four factors to delineate between fact and opinion. The four factors, although none singularly dispositive, include: 1) the specific language used; 2) whether the statement is verifiable; 3) the general context of the statement; and 4) the broader context in which the statement appeared. Unfortunately, for the sport-related plaintiff, this four-factor analysis of whether a comment is fact or opinion is of little help. For example, in *Stepien v. Franklin* (1988) the Court of Appeals of Ohio held an assortment of disparaging adjectives to be constitutionally protected opinion. The adjectives included the following:

"Stupid," "dumb," "buffoon," "nincompoop," "scum," "a cancer," "an obscenity," "gutless liar," "unmitigated liar," "pathological liar," "egomaniac," "nuts," "crazy," "irrational," "suicidal," "lunatic." (p. 1327)

As illustrated above, the specific language used by the defendant is overtly injurious. However, the syllabus by the court, justifying its action, stated, "The area of sports is a traditional haven for cajoling, invective, and hyperbole; . . ." (p. 1326).

Factor two, whether the statement is verifiable, is also problematic. In *Gertz,* the Supreme Court recognized that the First Amendment requires that we "protect some falsehood in order to protect speech that matters" (1974, p. 341). As explained by the Supreme Court in *Philadelphia Newspapers, Inc. v. Hepps* (1986),

> There will always be instances when the fact finding process will be unable to resolve conclusively whether the speech is true or false; . . . there will be some cases in which plaintiffs cannot meet their burden despite the fact that the speech is in fact false . . . where the scales are in such an uncertain balance, we believe that the Constitution requires us to tip them in favor of protecting true speech.

Factors three and four, referring to the context in which the statement appeared, are also difficult to apply. Society commonly accepts rowdy behavior as "part of the game." Even during the 1960s, the era of individual rights, the heckling involved in sport was viewed as common-place. As explained by the Supreme Court of North Carolina in *Toone v. Adams* (1964, p. 136),

> For present day fans, a goodly part of the sport in a baseball game is goading and denouncing the umpire when they do not concur in his decisions, and most feel that, without one or more rhubarbs, they have not received their money.

The Supreme Court of Ohio (*Scott v. News-Herald,* 1986) concluded that most information conveyed in the sports section of a newspaper is "constitutionally protected." The *Scott* court's decision, although of limited precedential value, is precarious because it suggests that comments about a sport-related figure, regardless of their veracity or the publisher's degree of fault, are constitutionally protected.

Defenses

Truth is an absolute defense to all claims of defamation. However, defendants are no longer required by courts to prove the accuracy of these claims as the plaintiffs must prove falsity.

Privilege, a second defense, refers to "a particular and peculiar benefit or advantage enjoyed by a person, company, or class, beyond the common advantages of other citizens" (Black, 1990, p. 1197). Privileged statements made without malice are immune from defamation liability (*Iacco v. Bohannon*, 1976; *Institute of Athletic Motivation v. Univ. of Ill.*, 1982). Two common types of privilege include absolute privilege and qualified privilege. **Absolute privilege** is enjoyed by those in: a) a legislative forum (e.g., congressmen, congresswomen, senators, city council members), b) the judicial forum (e.g., judges, lawyers, plaintiffs, defendants), and c) administrative and executive branches of government (e.g., Presidents, mayors, department heads). Other individuals may enjoy a **qualified privilege**. As explained by Carpenter (1995), qualified statements are those statements made: a) without knowledge of falsity, b) by a person with reason to communicate the statement, and c) communicated only to a person with a "justifiable interest in knowing." Media defendants commonly use the fair comment doctrine as a defense. As explained by Black (1990, p. 596), **fair comment** is:

A form of qualified privilege applied to news media publications relating to discussion of matters which are of legitimate concern to the community as a whole because they materially affect the interests of all the community.

The fair comment defense is only appropriate when comments are made without malice and statements are based on true facts (Black, 1990; *Cohen v. Cowles Publishing Co.*, 1954; *Conkwright v. Globe News Publishing Company,* 1965).

Failure to comply with the **statute of limitations** is a third defense available to defendants. Although states vary, the majority of statutes stipulate a one or two year statute of limitations (Carpenter, 1995; Pember, 1990) which begins to run at the point when the plaintiff discovers the defamatory comment.

Neutral reportage is another defense available to media defendants in certain circuits (Kaufman, 1989). Based upon the U.S. Court of Appeals landmark decision in *Edwards v. National Audubon Society, et al.* (1977), media defendants can publish statements made by responsible or prominent organizations even though the publisher doubts the veracity of the statements. As explained by the Court of Appeals (1977, p. 120),

> When a responsible prominent organization ... makes serious charges against a public figure, the First Amendment protects the accurate and disinterested reporting of those charges, regardless of the reporter's private views regarding their validity. What is newsworthy about such accusations is that they were made ...

The protection afforded by constitutional rights is another common defense. As discussed above, defendants have constitutional protection via the First Amendment and Fourteenth Amendment when commenting about public officials, public figures, or limited purpose public figures so long as the statements are not made maliciously.

Recent Developments

In *Washington v. Smith* (1995), the women's basketball coach at the University of Kansas sued publishers of preseason preview publications for defamation. Defendants' comments included a statement that the coach "usually finds a way to screw things up." The interesting *caveat* regarding this case is the decision by the U.S. District court (Dist. of Columbia) to overlook whether plaintiff should be classified as either a public official, public figure, limited purpose public figure, or private figure. Rather, the court adopted the "public concern" test applied in the vacated Supreme Court decision of *Rosenblatt v. Baer* (1966).

Liability protection for intentional torts is becoming more common. Employment practices liability insurance, or EPL insurance, covers areas including defamation, invasion of privacy, and sexual harassment. Coverage for these types of claims had originally been viewed as against public policy. EPL insurance is expensive and industry experts worry that employees with knowledge of an employer's EPL coverage will be more likely to sue. As stated by Jonathan Segal, a labor lawyer, "One question you have to ask yourself is, 'Is (the money) better spent on preventing the problem or on buying insurance to cover it?'" (Schwartz, 1996, p. K18).

References

A. Cases

Brooks v. Paige, 773 P.2d 1098 (Colo. App. 1988).

Cepeda v. Cowles Magazines and Broadcasting, Inc., 392 F.2d 417 (9th Cir. 1968).

Chuy v. Philadelphia Eagles Football Club, 595 F.2d 1265 (3rd Cir. 1979).

Curtis Publishing Co. v. Butts, 388 U.S. 130 (1967).

Edwards v. National Audubon Soc., 556 F.2d 113 (2nd Cir.), cert. denied, 434 U.S. 1002 (1977).

Garrison v. Louisiana, 379 U.S. 64 (1964).

Gertz v. Robert Welch, Inc., 418 U.S. 323 (1974).

Gomez v. Murdoch, 475 A.2d 622 (N.J. Super. A.D. 1984).

Hotchner v. Castillo-Puche, 551 F.2d 910 (2nd Cir. 1977).

Iacco v. Bohannon, 245 N.W.2d 791 (Mich. 1976).

Institute of Athletic Motivation v. Univ. of Ill., 170 Cal.Rptr.411 (Cal. App., 1981).

Milkovich v. Lorain Journal Co., 497 U.S. 1 (1990).

New York Times Co. v. Sullivan, 376 U.S. 254 (1964).

Ollman v. Evans, 750 F.2d 970 (D.C. Cir.) cert. denied, 471 U.S. 1127 (1985).

Philadelphia Newspapers, Inc. et al. v. Hepps et al., 475 U.S. 767 (1986).

Rosenblatt v. Baer, 383 U.S. 75 (1966).

Rosenbloom v. Metromedia, Inc., 403 U.S. 29 (1971).

St. Amant v. Thompson, 390 U.S. 727 (1968).

Scott v. News-Herald, 496 N.E.2d 699 (Ohio 1986).

Stepien v. Franklin, 528 N.E.2d 1324 (Ohio App. 1988).

Toone v. Adams, 137 S.E.2d 132 (1964).

Waldbaum v. Fairchild Publications, Inc., 637 F.2d 1287 (D.C. Cir.) cert.denied, 449 U.S. 898 (1980).

Washington v. Smith, 893 F.Supp. 60 (D.D.C. 1995).

Wolston v. Reader's Digest Ass'n, 443 U.S. 157 (1979).

B. Publications

Anderson, D. (1984). Reputation, Compensation, and Proof. *William & Mary Law Review*, 25(5), 747.

Anderson, D. A. (1991). Is Libel Law Worth Reforming? *University of Pennsylvania Law Review, 140*(2), 487-554.

Barron, J. and Dienes, C.T. (1979). *Handbook of Free Speech and Free Press*. Boston: Little, Brown.

Black, H.C. (1990). *Black's Law Dictionary* (6th ed.). St. Paul, Minn.: West Publishing Co.

Carpenter, L. J. (1995). *Legal Concepts in Sport: A Primer*. Reston, Va.: AAHPERD.

Mayer, M.F. (1987). *The Libel Revolution: A New Look at Defamation and Privacy*. Chelsea, Mich.: BookCrafters.

Pember, D.R. (1990). *Mass Media Law* (5th ed.). Dubuque, Iowa: Wm. C. Brown Publishers.

Ransom, E. (1995). The Ex-Public Figure: A Libel Plaintiff Without a Class. *Seton Hall Journal of Sport Law*, 5(2), 389-417.

Schwartz, K. (1996, February 18). Liability Insurance for Employment Practices is Increasingly Common. *The Courier Journal*, p. K18.

Smolla, R.A. (1983). Let the Author Beware: The Rejuvenation of the American Law of Libel. *University of Pennsylvania Law Review*, 132(1), 1-94.

Other Intentional Torts

*Invasion of Privacy, Breach of Fiduciary Duty,
and Tortious Interference with Contract*

Gary Rushing
Mankato State University

Intentional torts are deliberate wrongs done to others that cause harm. This type of tort differs from negligence torts in that lack of due care or engaging in abnormally dangerous activity is immaterial. Liability for intentional torts is predicated upon the tortfeasor purposely causing harm to another person or engaging in an activity that is substantially certain to harm another (Restatement of Torts, Second, Torts 8A, 1965). Sport-related intentional torts can occur on or off the playing field. This chapter will discuss three common "off-field" intentional torts. They are invasion of privacy, breach of fiduciary duty, and tortious interference with contract.

■ ■ ■ ■

Representative Case

THE DETROIT LIONS, INC. v. ARGOVITZ

United States District Court for the Eastern District of
Michigan, Southern Division
580 F. Supp. 542
February 10, 1984

OPINION: MEMORANDUM OPINION

The plot for this Saturday afternoon serial began when Billy Sims, having signed a contract with the Houston Gamblers on July 1, 1983, signed a second contract with the Detroit Lions on December 16, 1983. On December 18, 1983, the Detroit Lions, Inc. (Lions) and Billy R. Sims filed a complaint in the Oakland County Circuit Court seeking a judicial determination that the July 1, 1983, contract between Sims and the Houston Gamblers, Inc. (Gamblers) is invalid because the defendant Jerry Argovitz (Argovitz) breached his fiduciary duty when negotiating the Gamblers' contract and because the contract was otherwise tainted by fraud and misrepresentation. Defendants promptly removed the action to this court based on our diversity of citizenship jurisdiction.

For the reasons that follow, we have concluded that Argovitz's breach of his fiduciary duty during negotiations for the Gamblers' contract was so pronounced, so egregious, that to deny recision would be unconscionable.

• • •

Sometime in February or March 1983, Argovitz told Sims that he had applied for a Houston franchise in the newly formed United States Football League (USFL). In May 1983, Sims attended a press conference in Houston at which Argovitz announced that his application for a franchise had been approved. The evidence persuades us that Sims did not know the extent of Argovitz's interest in the Gamblers. He did not know the amount of Argovitz's original investment, or that Argovitz was obligated for 29 percent of a $1.5 million letter of credit, or that Argovitz was the president of the Gamblers' Corporation at an annual salary of $275,000 and 5 percent the yearly cash flow. The defendants could not justifiably expect Sims to comprehend the ramifications of Argovitz's interest in the Gamblers or the manner in which that interest would create an untenable conflict of interest, a conflict that would inevitably breach Argovitz's fiduciary duty to Sims. Argovitz knew, or should have known, that he could not act as Sims' agent under any circumstances when dealing with the Gamblers. Even the USFL Constitution itself prohibits a holder of any interest in a member club from acting "as the contracting agent or representative for any player."

Pending the approval of his application for a USFL franchise in Houston, Argovitz continued his negotiations with the Lions on behalf of Sims. On April 5, 1983, Argovitz offered Sims' services to the Lions for $6 million over a four-year period. The offer included a demand for a $1 million interest-free loan to be repaid over 10 years, and for skill and injury guarantees for three years. The Lions quickly responded with a counter offer on April 7, 1983, in the face amount of $1.5 million over a five-year period with additional incentives not relevant here. The negotiating process was working. The Lions were trying to determine what Argovitz really believed the market value for Sims really was. . . . On June 1, 1983, Argovitz and the Lions were only $500,000 apart. We find that the negotiations between the Lions and Argovitz were progressing normally, not laterally as Argovitz represented to Sims. The Lions were not "dragging their feet." Throughout the entire month of June 1983, Mr. Frederick Nash, the Lions' skilled negotiator and a fastidious lawyer, was involved in investigating the possibility of providing an attractive annuity for Sims and at the same time doing his best to avoid the granting of either skill or injury guarantees. The evidence establishes that on June 22, 1983, the Lions and Argovitz were very close to reaching an agreement on the value of Sims' services.

Apparently, in the midst of his negotiations with the Lions and with his Gamblers franchise in hand, Argovitz decided that he would seek an offer from the Gamblers. Mr. Bernard Lerner, one of Argovitz's partners in the Gamblers agreed to negotiate a contract with Sims. Since Lerner admitted that he had no knowledge whatsoever about football, we must infer that Argovitz at the very least told Lerner the amount of money required to sign Sims and further pressed upon Lerner the Gamblers' absolute need to obtain Sims' services. In the Gamblers' organization, only Argovitz knew the value of Sims' services and how critical it was for the Gamblers to obtain Sims. In Argovitz's words, Sims would make the Gamblers' franchise.

On June 29, 1983, at Lerner's behest, Sims and his wife went to Houston to negotiate with a team that was partially owned by his own agent. When Sims arrived in Houston, he believed that the Lions organization was not negotiating in good faith; that it was not really interested in his services. His ego was bruised and his emotional outlook toward the Lions was visible to Burrough and Argovitz. Clearly, virtually all the information that Sims had up to that date came from Argovitz. . . . Lerner offered Sims a $3.5 million five-year contract, which included three years of skill and injury guarantees. The offer included a $500,000 loan at an interest rate of 1 percent over prime. It was from this loan that Argovitz planned to receive the $100,000 balance of his fee for acting as an agent in negotiating a contract with his own team. Burrough testified that Sims would have accepted that offer on the spot because he was finally receiving the guarantee that he had been requesting from the Lions, guarantees that Argovitz dropped without too much quarrel. Argovitz and Burrough took Sims and his wife into another room to discuss the offer. Argovitz did tell Sims that he thought the Lions would match the Gamblers financial package and asked Sims whether he (Argovitz) should telephone the Lions. But, it is clear from the evidence that neither Sims nor Burrough believed that the Lions would match the offer. We find that Sims told Argovitz not to call the Lions for purely emotional reasons. As we have noted, Sims believed that the Lions' organization was not that interested in him and his pride was wounded. Burrough clearly admitted that he was aware of the emotional basis for Sims' decision not to have Argovitz phone the Lions, and we must conclude from the extremely close relationship between Argovitz and Sims that Argovitz knew it as well. When Sims went back to Lerner's office, he agreed to become a Gambler on the terms offered. At that moment, Argovitz irreparably breached his fiduciary duty. As agent for Sims he had the duty to telephone the Lions, receive its final offer, and present the terms of both offers to Sims. Then and only then could it be said that Sims made an intelligent and knowing decision to accept the Gamblers' offer.

During these negotiations at the Gamblers' office, Mr. Nash of the Lions telephoned Argovitz, but even though Argovitz was at his office, he declined to accept the telephone call. . . . When he declined to accept Mr. Nash's call, Argovitz's breach of his fiduciary duty became even more pronounced. Following Nash's example, Argovitz left for his weekend trip, leaving his principal to sign the contracts with the Gamblers the next day, July 1, 1983. The defendants, in their supplemental trial brief, assert that neither Argovitz nor Burrough can be held responsible for following Sims' instruction not to contact the Lions on June 30, 1983. Although it is generally true that an agent is not liable for losses occurring as a result of following his principal's instructions, the rule of law is not applicable when the agent has placed himself in a position adverse to that of his principal.

• • •

On July 1, 1983, it was Lerner who gave lip service to Argovitz's conspicuous conflict of interest. It was Lerner, not Argovitz, who advised Sims that Argovitz's position with the Gamblers presented a conflict of interest and that Sims could, if he wished, obtain an attorney or another agent. Argovitz, upon whom Sims had relied for the past four years, was not even there. Burrough, conscious of Sims' emotional responses, never advised Sims to wait until he had talked with the Lions before making a final decision. Argovitz's conflict of interest and self dealing put him in the position where he would not even use the wedge he now had to negotiate with the Lions, a wedge that is the dream of every agent. Two expert witnesses testified that an agent should telephone a team that he has been negotiating with once he has an offer in hand. Mr. Woolf, plaintiff's expert, testified that an offer from another team is probably the most important factor in negotiations. Mr. Lustig, defendant's expert, believed that it was prudent for him to telephone the Buffalo Bills and inform that organization of the Gamblers' offer to Jim Kelly, despite the fact that he believed the Bills had already made its best offer to his principal. The evidence here convinces us that Argovitz's negotiations with the Lions were ongoing and it had not made its final offer. Argovitz did not follow the common practice described by both expert witnesses. He did not do this because he knew that the Lions would not leave Sims without a contract and he further knew that if he made that type of call Sims would be lost to the Gamblers, a team he owned.

On November 12, 1983, when Sims was in Houston for the Lions game with the Houston Oilers, Argovitz asked Sims to come to his home and sign certain papers. He represented to Sims that certain papers of his contract had been mistakenly overlooked and now needed to be signed. Included among those papers he asked Sims to sign was a waiver of any claim that Sims might have against Argovitz for his blatant breach of his fiduciary duty brought on by his glaring conflict of interest. Sims did not receive independent advice with regard to the wisdom of signing such a waiver. Despite having sold his agency business in September, Argovitz did not even tell Sims' new agent of his intention to have Sims sign a waiver. Nevertheless, Sims, an unsophisticated young man, signed the waiver. This is another example of the questionable conduct on the part of Argovitz who still had business management obligations to Sims. In spite of his fiduciary relationship he had Sims sign a waiver without advising him to obtain independent counseling.

Argovitz's negotiations with Lustig, Jim Kelly's agent, illustrates the difficulties that develop when an agent negotiates a contract where his personal interests conflict with those of his principal. Lustig, an independent agent, ignored Argovitz's admonishment not to "shop" the Gamblers' offer to Kelly. Lustig called the NFL team that he had been negotiating with because it was the "prudent" thing to do. The Gamblers agreed to pay Kelly, an untested rookie quarterback $3.2 million for five years. His compensation was $60,000 less than Sims', a former Heisman Trophy winner and a proven star in the NFL. Lustig also obtained a number of favorable clauses from Argovitz; the most impressive one being that Kelly was assured of being one of the three top paid quarterbacks in the USFL if he performed as well as expected. If Argovitz had been free from conflicting interests he would have demanded similar benefits for Sims. Argovitz claimed that the nondisclosure clause in Kelly's contract prevented him from mentioning the Kelly contract to Sims. We view this contention as frivolous. Requesting these benefits for Sims did not require disclosure of Kelly's contract. Moreover, Argovitz's failure to obtain personal guarantees for Sims without adequately warning Sims about the risks and uncertainties of a new league constituted a clear breach of his fiduciary duty.

The parties submitted a great deal of evidence and argued a number of peripheral issues. Although most of the issues were not determinative factors in our decision, they do demonstrate that Argovitz had a history of fulfilling his fiduciary duties in an irresponsible manner. One cannot help but wonder whether Argovitz took his fiduciary duty seriously. For example, after investing approximately $76,000 of Sims' money, Argovitz, with or without the prior knowledge of his principal, received a finder's fee. Despite the fact that Sims paid Argovitz a 2 percent fee, Argovitz accepted $3800 from a person with whom he invested Sims' money. In March 1983, Argovitz had all of his veteran players, including Sims, sign a new agency contract with less favorable payment terms for the players even though they already had an ongoing agency agreement with him. He did this after he sold his entire agency business to Career Sports. Finally, Argovitz was prepared to take the remainder of his 5 percent agency fee for negotiating Sims' contract with the Gamblers from monies the Gamblers loaned to Sims at an interest rate of 1 percent over prime. It mattered little to Argovitz that Sims would have to pay interest on the $100,000 that Argovitz was ready to accept. While these practices by Argovitz are troublesome, we do not find them decisive in examining Argovitz's conduct while negotiating the Gamblers' contract on June 30 and July 1, 1983. We find this circumstantial evidence useful only insofar as it has aided the court in understanding the manner in which these parties conducted business.

We are mindful that Sims was less than forthright when testifying before the court. However, we agree with plaintiff's counsel that the facts as presented through the testimony of other witnesses are so unappealing that we can disregard Sims' testimony entirely. We remain persuaded that on balance, Argovitz's breach of his fiduciary duty was so egregious that a court of equity cannot permit him to benefit by his own wrongful breach. We conclude that Argovitz's conduct in negotiating Sims' contract with the Gamblers rendered it invalid.

Conclusions of Law
• • •

3. The relationship between a principal and agent is fiduciary in nature, and as such imposes a duty of loyalty, good faith, and fair and honest dealing on the agent. Anderson v. Griffith, 501 S.W. 2d 695, 700 (Tex. Civ. App. 1973).

4. A fiduciary relationship arises not only from a formal principal-agent relationship, but also from informal relationships of trust and confidence. Thigpen v. Locke, 363 S.W. 2d 247, 253 (Tex. 1962); Adickes v. Andreoli, 600 S.W. 2d 939, 945-46 (Tex. Civ. App. 1980).

5. In light of the express agency agreement, and the relationship between Sims and Argovitz, Argovitz clearly owed Sims the fiduciary duties of an agent at all times relevant to this lawsuit.

6. An agent's duty of loyalty requires that he not have a personal stake that conflicts with the principal's interest in a transaction in which he represents his principal. As stated in Burleson v. Earnest, 153 S.W. 2d 869 (Tex. Civ. App. 1941):

(The) principal is entitled to the best efforts and unbiased judgment of his agent . . . (The) law denies the right of an agent to assume any relationship that is antagonistic to his duty to his principal, and it has many times been held that the agent cannot be both buyer and seller at the same time nor connect his own interests with property involved in his dealings as an agent for another. Id. at 874.

7. A fiduciary violates the prohibition against self-dealing not only by dealing with himself on his principal's behalf, but also by dealing on his principal's behalf with a third party in which he has an interest, such as a partnership in which he is a member. In Daniel v. Henderson, 183 S.W. 2d 242 (Tex. Civ. App. 1944), aff'd sub nom., Southern Trust & Mortgage Co. v. Daniel, 143 Tex. 321, 184 S.W. 2d 465 (1944), the court held:

The trustee violates his duty to the beneficiary not only where he purchases the trust property for himself individually, but also where he has a personal interest in the purchase of such a substantial nature that it might affect his judgment in making the sale. Thus, a trustee violates his duty if he sells trust property to a firm of which he is a member or to a corporation in which he has a controlling or substantial interest. 183 S.W. 2d at 245 (quoting Restatement of Trusts Section 170(c) (1935)).

8. Where an agent has an interest adverse to that of his principal in a transaction in which he purports to act on behalf of his principal, the transaction is voidable by the principal unless the agent disclosed all material facts within the agent's knowledge that might affect the principal's judgment. Burleson v. Earnest, 153 S.W. 2d at 874-75.

9. The mere fact that the contract is fair to the principal does not deny the principal the right to rescind the contract when it was negotiated by an agent in violation of the prohibition against self-dealing. As stated in Burleson:

The question, therefore, does not relate to the mala fides of the agent nor to whether or not a greater sum might have been procured for the property, nor even to whether or not the vendor received full value therefor. The self-interest of the agent is considered a vice which renders the transaction voidable at the election of the principal without looking into the matter further than to ascertain that the interest of the agent exists.

10. Once it has been shown that an agent had an interest in a transaction involving his principal antagonistic to the principal's interest, fraud on the part of the agent is presumed. The burden of proof then rests upon the agent to show that his principal had full knowledge, not only of the fact that the agent was interested, but also of every material fact known to the agent which might affect the principal and that having such

knowledge, the principal freely consented to the transaction.

11. It is not sufficient for the agent merely to inform the principal that he has an interest that conflicts with the principal's interest. Rather, he must inform the principal "of all facts that come to his knowledge that are or may be material or which might affect his principal's rights or interests or influence the action he takes." Anderson v. Griffith, 501 S.W. 2d 695, 700 (Tex. Civ. App. 1973).

12. Argovitz clearly had a personal interest in signing Sims with the Gamblers that was adverse to Sims' interest—he had an ownership interest in the Gamblers and thus would profit if the Gamblers were profitable, and would incur substantial personal liabilities should the Gamblers not be financially successful. Since this showing has been made, fraud on Argovitz's part is presumed, and the Gamblers' contract must be rescinded unless Argovitz has shown by a preponderance of the evidence that he informed Sims of every material fact that might have influenced Sims' decision whether or not to sign the Gamblers' contract.

13. We conclude that Argovitz has failed to show by a preponderance of the evidence either: 1) that he informed Sims of the following facts, or 2) that these facts would not have influenced Sims' decision whether to sign the Gamblers' contract:

    c. Argovitz's 29 percent ownership in the Gamblers; Argovitz's $275,000 annual salary with the Gamblers; Argovitz's five per-

cent interest in the cash flow of the Gamblers.

    d. That both Argovitz and Burrough failed to even attempt to obtain for Sims valuable contract clauses which they had given to Kelly on behalf of the Gamblers.

    e. That Sims had great leverage, and Argovitz was not encouraging a bidding war that could have advantageous results for Sims.

14. Under Texas law, a nonbinding prior act cannot be ratified, and the right to seek recision cannot be waived, unless the party against whom these defenses are asserted had full knowledge of all material facts at the time the acts of ratification or waiver are alleged to have occurred.

15. At no time prior to December 1, 1983, was Sims aware of the material nondisclosures outlined above; accordingly, the defenses of ratification and waiver must be rejected.

16. Defendants asserted defenses of estoppel and latches are also without merit.

17. As a court sitting in equity, we conclude that recision is the appropriate remedy. We are dismayed by Argovitz's egregious conduct. The careless fashion in which Argovitz went about ascertaining the highest price for Sims' service convinces us of the wisdom of the maxim: no man can faithfully serve two masters whose interests are in conflict.

Judgment will be entered for the plaintiffs rescinding the Gamblers' contract with Sims.

IT IS SO ORDERED.

■ ■ ■ ■

Fundamental Concepts—Invasion of Privacy

Privacy, as defined by the courts, is "the right to be left alone; to live one's life as one chooses free from assault, intrusion or invasion except as they can be justified by the clear needs of the community under a government of law" (*Rosenbloom v. Metromedia, Inc.*, 1971). The legal principles that serve as the bases for privacy protection are found primarily in three sources of the law—the Fourteenth Amendment, the Constitution, and tort law. The Fourteenth Amendment and the Constitution are concerned with the rights claims against any of the various governmental entities. Tort law is devoted to rights claims against a person or persons (Samar, 1991). Further, most states recognize the right of privacy either by means of common-law case decisions or by applicable statutes (Carper, 1995).

Right of privacy, as found in tort law, involves four distinct theories or ways in which one's privacy can be invaded. Keeton, et al. (1984) explains that these ways are not one tort, but a complex of four kinds of invasion. They have little in common except that each represents an interference with the right "to be let alone" which is at the center of all wrongful invasion suits. The four types of invasion are: 1) unreasonable intrusion on the seclusion of another; 2) appropriation of the another's name or likeness 3) unreasonable disclosure of private facts; and 4) publicity that unreasonably places the other in a false light before the public.

Unreasonable Intrusion on Seclusion

This form of privacy invasion is straightforward and concerns the invasion of one's home or illegally searching one's personal belongings. Courts have extended this tort to include eavesdropping by wiretap, unauthorized examination of a bank account, compulsory blood testing, and window peeping (Cross & Miller, 1995). The information acquired in these or similar ways is invasion of privacy even if the information is the truth and it serves the public's right to know (Schubert, 1986). The intrusion must be offensive or objectionable to a reasonable person. (Keeton, et al., 1984)

Appropriation

This invasion of privacy tort involves the unauthorized use of a person's name or likeness for commercial purposes such as advertising or trade. The protection provided by this law is especially important to sport figures because it gives them some control over the extent to which their name and likeness can be commercially exploited. Without this control athletes would lose a significant source of income from commercial endorsements, trading cards, and other enterprises.

Sport figures do not have complete control over the use of their names or likenesses. Courts have upheld unauthorized uses for editorial purposes and when reused by publishers and broadcasters for campaigns to increase circulation or to increase broadcasting audiences. A use in this manner is considered to be protected incidental use. (Dill, 1986)

In a case which illustrates the salient issues in this area, Joe Namath sued *Sports Illustrated* (*Namath v. Sports Illustrated,* [1967]) for the unauthorized use of his photo to promote subscription sales. He contended that this use was commercial and violated his right to privacy. Further, because he was in the business of endorsing products and selling the use of his name and likeness, it interfered with his right to profit from such sale. The photo had originally been used without objection from Namath in conjunction with a 1969 Super Bowl article. However, when it was reprinted to promote subscription sales, he felt he should be compensated for its use. In ruling for *Sports Illustrated*, the court noted that the use of the photo was merely "incidental" advertising since it was used to illustrate the quality and content of the periodical in which it originally appeared.

In another case, *Palmer v. Schonhorn Enterprises, Inc.* (1967), a toy manufacturing company appropriated the names and career profiles of golfers, Arnold Palmer, Gary Player, Doug Sanders, and Jack Nicklaus, for use in a game. In this situation, the court sided with the plaintiffs because the commercial use of their names and profiles was done without their permission and without compensation.

Public Disclosure of Private Facts

Action for invasion of privacy in this area involves public disclosure of private facts about an individual that an ordinary person would find objectionable. Public disclosure suits are sometimes referred to as embarrassment suits because they arise from objections to publicity of embarrassing private information. (Dill, 1986) At issue in this type of suit is the balance between the public's right to know and the extent of the intrusion into one's private life.

Although there are secondary issues that must be satisfied to prevail in an embarrassment suit (see Keeton, et al., 1984 pp. 856-857), where public figures are concerned, there are two major issues that the courts will address: 1) whether the disclosed information was truly private and 2) whether the disclosed information was highly offensive to an ordinary person.

Private v. Public Facts.   For a plaintiff to succeed in a public disclosure suit, it must be shown that the publicity disclosed was in an area where there was a legitimate expectation of privacy. In other words, the disclosure must involved truly private matters. Average citizens can expect a higher degree of privacy protection than sports personalities, who have little privacy protection due to their public figure status. A public figure is someone who by "his [or her] accomplishments, fame, or mode of living, or by adopting a profession or calling which gives the public a legitimate interest in his doings, his affairs, and his character, has become a 'public personage'" (Keeton, et al., 1984, p.859). The Constitution, which provides the media with the privilege of reporting matters of public interest, deprives public figures of some of their right to privacy. Hence, sport figures cannot expect privacy in public matters such as their game performance, sport associations, or character (Schubert, 1986). Furthermore, most reported information that has already been made accessible to the public through public records or other documentation, or that is newsworthy, is not considered to be purely private in nature and therefore is discloseable (Berry & Wong, 1993).

Highly Offensive Material.   Even though some facts may be newsworthy, they may not be published if they can be viewed as highly offensive to the average person. Since community norms vary from jurisdiction to jurisdiction, courts may have mixed decisions regarding what is permissible disclosure. However, where public figures are concerned, even conservative courts will allow most private truthful facts, although embarrassing, to be disclosed unless they are "unredeemably offensive and not even remotely in the public interest" (Dill, 1986, p.137).

False Light Intrusion

Under this theory, an invasion of privacy occurs when publicity places the plaintiff in a "false light" in the public eye. For example, in a sport setting, this could occurs if someone in the media uses a photograph or makes a statement about a sport figure that gives a false impression to the public. This false impression could emanate from "made-up" details, omitted facts, or misleading context (Dill, 1986).

However, for sport figures to prevail in a false light suit, they must not only show that the published information was false, but also that the disclosure was done by one knowing it was false or who had reckless disregard for the truth. This standard was established in *Time, Inc. v. Hill* (1967), which held that the First Amendment protects reports of newsworthy matters.

False light action is different from libel in that the publicity does not have to be defamatory. The depiction in question could be either complimentary or defamatory. Although most false light cases involve unflattering portrayals, the central issue is "being let alone" from the effects of a false reputation or false publicity (Samar, 1991). Both false light and libel complaints are permitted in some states; however, other states do not recognize false light claims and permit only libel suits.

An example of false light invasion occurred in the case of *Spahn v. Messner* (1967). This case centered on an unauthorized biography written about Warren Spahn, a celebrated pitcher for the Milwaukee Braves. The author used "invented dialogue, and imaginary incidents" which he knew to be false and knew to present an untruthful depiction of Spahn. Spahn objected to this portrayal even though parts of the story were complimentary. The court awarded Spahn $10,000 in damages and enjoined further publication of the book.

Fundamental Concepts—Breach of Fiduciary Duty

Another intentional tort is breach of fiduciary duty or responsibility. Black's Law Dictionary (1979), defines a fiduciary as "[a] person having duty, created by his undertaking, to act primarily for another's benefit in matters connected with this undertaking." As an adjective, it means ". . . relating to or founded upon a trust or confidence" (p. 563). Carper (1995) clarifies this by adding that a fiduciary relationship is one involving a person in a position of trust who undertakes to act for the benefit of another. Examples of fiduciary relationships include lawyer-client, parent-child, and coach-athlete.

In the sport setting, the fiduciary relationship that is most troublesome is the association between a professional athlete and his or her agent (Powers, 1994; Ehrhart & Rodgers, 1988). An agent can be responsible for managing many of the athlete's financial concerns. These may include "negotiating the athlete's employment agreement; securing, bartering and reviewing commercial opportunities; providing financial advice and income management; and counseling on legal and tax matters" (Sobel, 1987, p.705). Because many of these dealings are legally binding to the represented athlete, the law imposes a high obligation of trustworthiness upon the agent. If an agent violates this trust and the athlete is harmed as a result, the agent is guilty of tortious conduct and may have to make restitution. (Restatement (Second) of Torts #874 p. 300)

A fiduciary duty requires that the sports agent act with complete honesty in all dealings with athlete-clients. In addition, the agent must avoid any personal **conflicts of interest**. In other words, the interests of the athlete must come before those of the agent. Also, an agent must not represent two adverse parties in the same transaction. For example, representing two or more players vying for the same endorsement contracts or representing a player and the company he is negotiating with for a contract. Finally, an agent must not receive hidden compensation or profits from third parties for transacting the player's business or take advantage of any business opportunity that rightfully belongs to the athlete (Schubert, et al., 1986). An agent can avoid liability in this area by fully disclosing any possible conflict of interest or other potentially improper conduct and obtaining the athlete's prior consent to the action.

Detroit Lions, Inc. v. Jerry Argovitz (1984) offers an instructional example of breach of fiduciary duty. In this case, Billy Sims' agent, Jerry Argovitz, engaged in a series of unethical practices with the intent of inducing Sims to sign a contract with the Houston Gamblers of United States Football League. After the Gamblers made an offer to Sims, Argovitz failed to give the Detroit Lions an opportunity to match the bid. Sims signed with the Gamblers believing theirs to be the best offer. After it was revealed Argovitz was a substantial owner in the Gamblers' franchise and that he had withheld information which might have swayed Sims' decision, the court allowed Sims to rescind his contract and sign with the Detroit Lions. Sims was unaware of the extent of Argovitz's association with the Gamblers.

Fundamental Concepts—Tortious Interference With Contract

This tort involves the intentional inducement of another to breach his or her contractual obligations (Schubert, 1986). Because contracts play a vital role in sport, this is a significant area of concern. Inducement to break contracts has been alleged in situations such as teams competing for talented players (*Cincinnati Bengals v. Bergey et al.*, 1974), boxing promoters arguing over promotion rights (*Don King Productions v. James "Buster" Douglas, & others*), and agents interfering with a college player's eligibility (Woods & Mills, 1988).

There are three elements necessary to prove the existence of a wrongful interference tort:

1. A valid, enforceable contract must exist between two parties.
2. The defendant must have known of the contract's existence.
3. The defendant must have, without justification, knowingly induced either of the two parties from full performance of the contract. This interference must have been done for the purpose of advancing the economic interest of the inducer and it does not matter if the action was done in bad faith or with malice (the intention to harm another), even though in most cases bad faith or malice is usually a factor. (Cross & Miller, 1995)

Plaintiff has the burden to prove that the defendant knew of the contract's existence and knowingly induced the breach of the contractual relationship. The defendant can refute the charge if it can be shown that the interference was justified or permissible. For example, aggressive marketing and advertising strategies may entice customers to break contracts with competitors but are not unlawful.

In a significant case involving a tortious interference complaint, the Cincinnati Bengals sued Bill Bergey, their premier linebacker, the Virginia Ambassadors, and the other 11 teams of the newly formed World Football League (WFL). At the heart of this complaint, was the claim that the WFL defendants were inducing a breach of contract by Bergey and, unless enjoined, would do the same with other key players on the Bengals. While under contract with the Bengals, Bergey had negotiated and signed a contract with the Virginia team for his future services. His new contract was to begin when his existing Bengals contract expired. The Bengals felt that his signing of a contract with a different team while under contract with the Bengals would cause him not to perform his current contractual duties with them. The court denied an injunction, primarily because the Bengals failed to show how the negotiations and the subsequent contract signing interfered with the performance of his existing contract.

Recent Developments

In a recent invasion of privacy case (*Montana v. San Jose Mercury News, Inc.*, 1995), Joe Montana brought action against the San Jose Mercury News for misappropriation of his name, photograph, and likeness. At issue was the reproduction of Montana's photograph which originally appeared in conjunction with a 1990 Super Bowl victory for the San Francisco 49ers. His photo had been reproduced in poster form, some of which were sold for five dollars each and the rest were donated to charitable organizations.

The court reached a decision similar to that of the Namath case and found in favor of the newspaper for two reasons. First, the original newspaper account and the subsequent photograph constituted matters in the public interest, and second, the posters were sold to advertise the quality and content of its newspaper. They contained no information that was not originally included in the newspaper and did not convey Montana's endorsement.

References

A. Cases

Cincinnati Bengals v. William Bergey, et al., 453 F. Supp. 129 (1974).

Detroit Lions, Inc. v. Argovitz, 580 F.Supp. 542 (1984).

Don King Productions v. James "Buster" Douglas, et al,. 735 F.Supp. 522 (1990).

Montana v. San Jose Mercury News, Inc., 34 Cal. App. 4th 790. (1995).

Namath v. Sports Illustrated, 48 A.D.2d 487; 371 N.Y.S.2d 10. (1975).

*Palmer v. Schonhorn Enterprises, Inc.,*323 A.2d 458 (1967).

Rosenbloom v. Metromedia, Inc., 403 U.S. 29; 29 L.Ed.2d 296 (1971).

Spahn v. Messner, Inc., 18 N.Y.2d 324; 274 N.Y.S.2d 877; 221 N.E.2d 543; vacated 387 U.S. 239;18 L.Ed.2d 744 (1966).

Time, Inc. v. Hill, 385 U.S. 374 (1967).

B. Publications

Carper, D.L., et al. (1995) *Understanding the Law*. St. Paul, Minn.: West Publishing Co.

Black, H.C., (1979). *Black's Law Dictionary*, 5th ed. St. Paul, Minn.: West Publishing Co.

Berry, R.C. and Wong G.M. (1993). *Law and Business of the Sports Industries* (Vol.II). 2nd ed. Westport, Conn.: Praeger Publishers.

Cross, F.B. & Miller, R.L (1995). *West's Legal Environment of Business*. St. Paul, Minn.: West Publishing Co.

Dill, B. (1986). *The Journalist's Handbook on Libel and Privacy*. New York: The Free Press.

Ehrhardt, C.W. & Rodgers, J.M. (1988). Tightening the Defense Against Offensive Sports Agents. 16 *Florida State University Law Review* 634-74.

Keeton, W.P., et al., (1984). *Prosser and Keeton on Torts*. St. Paul, Minn.: West Publishing Co.

Powers, A. (1994). The Need to Regulate Sports Agents. 4 *Seton Hall Journal of Sport Law* 253-274.

Restatement (Second) of Torts #874

Samar, V.J. (1991). *The Right to Privacy*. Philadelphia: Temple University Press.

Schubert, G., et al.(1986). *Sport Law*. St. Paul, Minn.: West Publishing Co.

Sobel, S. (1987). The Regulation of Sports Agents: An Analytical Primer, 39 *Baylor Law Review* at 705-09.

Woods, R.P. & Mills, M.R. (1988). Tortious Interference With An Athletic Scholarship: A University Remedy For The Unscrupulous Sports Agent. 40 *Alabama Law Review* at 141-180.

2.51

Risk Management Process

Rob Ammon Jr.
Slippery Rock University

Risk management is the formal process of assessing exposure to risk and taking whatever action is necessary to minimize its impact (National Association of Independent Schools, 1988). While risk management is a relative newcomer to sport management literature, risk management has been found in business periodicals for many years. The literature from corporate risk management, however, has traditionally been limited primarily to financial risks controlled through the purchase of insurance (van der Smissen, 1990). In contrast, when discussing the specific risk management needs of the sports industry, a broader approach is evident. While economic problems concern all companies, individuals associated with sports and athletics have identified as their number one priority the safety and welfare of participants and spectators (Sharp, 1990).

In sport, the risk management approach has been to combine the traditional corporate interest of limiting financial risk with the interest of the sport industry—providing for increased safety. By the reduction of injury, the business is at the same time reducing financial exposure. Increasing the safety and security of individuals to the fullest extent is a difficult task that is possible only through the development and utilization of a comprehensive **risk management plan** for controlling risks. Miller (1989) observes that when a good risk management plan is implemented, the potential for litigation diminishes. Sport managers have a moral, ethical, and legal duty to provide an environment as free of dangers as possible to their members, clients, and patrons. Unrecognized and untreated, these risks may result in injury and provide the basis for negligence claims. Thus, by combining business interest with that of the sport industry, risk management may be viewed as the control of financial and personal injury losses from sudden, unforeseen, unusual accidents and intentional torts (Ammon, 1993).

Of the thousands of sport-related cases litigated in recent years, many could have been prevented by the implementation of effective risk management plans. Just a few examples of causes of sport-related litigation that might have been avoided by appropriate risk management procedures include: water present on locker room floors, missing bolts on gymnasium track railings, non-shatterproof glass in gymnasium windows and doors, concrete in a base path, poorly maintained sports equipment, missing handles on pommel horses, and failure to warn about the inherent dangers in sports and physical activity (Ross, 1985).

Sport managers have been exposed to a new society during the past 20 years—a society that has become enchanted with litigation, and to which many professionals in the sports environment have fallen victim. Society will not tolerate inappropriate behavior, and sport managers, especially those managing sport facilities, must develop an awareness of the hazards for which they will be held accountable. An effective risk management plan will help to diminish the risks that confront today's sport managers.

Fundamental Concepts

The D. I. M. Process: Establishing a Risk Management Program

The "D. I. M. Process" is a tool that can be used to construct a practical and effective risk management plan. This process involves three basic steps: 1) developing the risk management plan; 2) implementing the risk management plan; and 3) managing the risk management plan. Risk management strategies in sport-related organizations contain similar goals regardless of whether they are associated with corporations, university athletic departments, or municipally owned stadiums (M. Wagner, personal communication, June 30, 1992). By adopting anticipatory techniques such as the D. I. M. Process, rather than reacting to situations, an organization will be able to diminish the chances for litigation.

Developing the Risk Management Plan

Developing a risk management plan consists of three separate stages: 1) the identification of risks, 2) the classification of risks, and 3) the selection of methods of treatment for the risks.

Identification of Risks. Van der Smissen states that risks normally fall into one of four different classifications. 1) **Property loss or damage** usually pertains to facilities or equipment. This includes owned or leased properties and equipment and potential risks include natural elements such as fire and flood as well as theft and vandalism. 2) **Non-negligent public liability** includes discrimination, product liability, contractual liability, and employee actions such as violation of dramshop laws and social host liability, defamation of character, invasion of privacy, and assault and battery. 3) **Negligent public liability** includes risk of bodily injury, whether minor or major, resulting from negligence of the sport-related organization or its employees in supervised services or in unsupervised areas. Failure to supervise, instruct, or properly train employees are examples of causes of action that could have been avoided by appropriate risk management. 4) **Business operations** refers to potential financial losses that may occur in the various aspects of business due to personnel-related and non-personnel related risks (van der Smissen, 1990).

Each sport-related organization, whether university, professional team, or private business, has unique risks. The risk manager may identify risks by conducting inspections, examining operational policies and procedures, studying accident records, observing operations, talking with employees and patrons, and talking with other sport managers in similar sport-related organizations. The following table lists some of the areas where risks lie. While certainly not all-inclusive, the list presented in Table 1 can serve as a starting point for the sport manager in the identification of risks in a sport-related organization.

Classification of Risks. Once the risks have been identified, they must be classified to enable the sport manager to select the proper treatment for the risk. There are two aspects to classification. The first involves determining the severity of the risk or the potential impact of the risk upon the sport-related organization. Some risks are minor such as scratches, sprains, wind damage to a sign, or marking on a wall in the building. These have little impact upon the financial stability of the organization. Others such as paralysis or death, destruction of the building by fire, or embezzlement of a large sum of money are more severe. These are of more importance to the organization and must be prepared for because they demand different treatments.

Table 1
Selected Sources of Risk in Sport-Related Organizations

Administrative Areas	Facilities	Equipment
Accident Reports	Contracts	Distribution
Activity Selection	Design Factors	Proper Fit
Civil Rights of Athletes	Emergency Care System	Inspection
Contracts	Maintenance Schedule	Maintenance Schedule
Documentation System	Safety Audits	Purchase Records
Emergency Plans	Signage	Reconditioning
Employees	Spectators	Warranties
Player Physicals	Supervision	
Safety Audits	Training of Personnel	
Travel and Transportation		

The second aspect of classification relates to the frequency or likelihood of occurrence of the risk. In a recreation center basketball program, sprains would be a likely occurrence while a fire in the building would be less likely to occur. The two would require different approaches to treatment. The classification of each risk is determined by the risk manager based upon such factors as accident records, the manager's previous experience, and the recommendations of experts.

Method of Treatment.   The final step in the development of a risk management plan concerns the selection of treatments for the identified and classified risks. Four distinct choices of treatment are available.

One method of treatment is to **eliminate the risk**. This may involve the recognition of a significant risk before instituting an activity and avoiding it completely by not adding the activity. In addition, it may involve the recognition of a significant risk in the current program and the elimination of the activity posing the risk. This treatment is most often chosen with high severity types of risks, particularly those with high frequency or likelihood. To illustrate, suppose a recreation program includes the use of a trampoline. After identifying and classifying the potential risks or injuries that program members may incur on the trampoline and the risk posed to the recreation program, management may decide to get rid of the equipment before injury occurs. Sport managers may not feel that elimination is a desirable choice since they are in the activity business, but elimination is an appropriate choice when the organization is unable to provide the standard of care required for the safe conduct of the activity (van der Smissen, 1990).

A second approach is to **transfer the risk** from the sport-related organization to another organization or individual. This is a popular method for risks classified as moderate and high severity. Insurance is one popular method of transferring the risk. In this situation, the sport-related organization pays an insurance company a premium to cover selected physical or financial damages that may occur (See Chapter 2.53 for more detail on insurance). Risk is also transferred by contract. Independent contractors such as doctors, referees and aerobic instructors are examples of transfer by contract. As independent contractors, these individuals are personally liable for their negligent acts and the sport-related organization is not generally liable under respondeat superior. Another contractual transfer of risk involves an indemnification agreement, also termed a "hold harmless agreement," by which one organization or individual agrees to repay another organization for expenses incurred and thereby transfers the risk to another. One final way in which the sport-related organization transfers risk is by use of an exculpatory agreement or waiver by which the risk is transferred to the participant.

Retention of the risk is a third approach that the sport-related organization can take. The sport-related organization, whether a university, sport facility, or small sport business, that chooses retention becomes financially responsible for any injuries or financial risks that may occur. This expense must be planned for in advance and the budget must provide funds to pay for expenses that may be incurred by the organization. Normally this treatment is used for minor injury pay-outs, first aid treatment, ambulance service, and other low severity types of risks.

Another form of retention involves the use of insurance deductibles because the deductible amount is the amount of risk retained by the organization. The sport manager needs to realize that while all risks may be transferred by having no deductible, this is an expensive approach. Insurance premiums decrease measurably as the size of the deductible increases.

The final approach to risk treatment is the **reduction of risks** which is the heart of the risk management program. This treatment involves taking a proactive approach to reducing all forms of risk, thereby decreasing the likelihood of injury, and subsequently, reducing the chances of being sued. Requiring employees to undertake in-service training, extensive inspections coupled with preventative maintenance, and compiling and utilizing extensive records (e.g., accident reports) are three examples of prevention techniques. **A concerted risk reduction approach should be used in conjunction with each of the other three approaches to treatment.**

A hypothetical situation can help to clarify each of the steps in the D. I. M. Process. *Clint Davis, a recent sport management graduate, is hired as the director of his hometown recreation program. The program has been besieged by several negligence suits in the last two years and one of his responsibilities is to implement a risk management plan for the recreation program. Clint's first priority is to develop the plan. After several weeks of reading reports and records, observing various activities, analyzing operational policies and procedures, talking to participants, and questioning other recreation directors, Clint begins to make a list of the risks he has observed and identified. The city recreation program includes a men's basketball league which Clint decides poses some potential physical hazards that need to be addressed. There have been many injuries reported, mostly involving twisted ankles, jammed fingers, skin abrasions, and occasionally small lacerations. After identifying these risks Clint classifies them as low-medium frequency and low severity.*

When selecting a treatment for the risks, Clint must decide among four options. First, he could eliminate the basketball league to insure that the risks didn't occur, but this would not be sensible. The decision would be unpopular with the basketball participants and could potentially cause a great deal of negative publicity. Second, Clint could amend the insurance policy to cover this type of injury. That would transfer the risk to an outside agency, but would increase the cost of the insurance policy considerably. He could also transfer the risk by having each participant sign a waiver and assumption of risk statement. Since this is an adult league, such documents could provide considerable protection. Third, he could retain the risk and pay for any of the identified minor injuries from the recreation program operating budget. If the potential injuries were classified correctly retention would be a possible choice. Finally, Clint could attempt to avert the risks through preventative measures. Educating the participants about proper stretching techniques, training the league referees to keep better control of the games, and instituting certain safety rules could significantly reduce the injuries. Here, Clint's best options might be to select two of the approaches—transfer (by requiring that participants sign a waiver and assumption of risk statement) and risk reduction (by instituting the measures to reduce risk). In Clint's situation transfer and risk reduction offer realistic, yet achievable, solutions to his identified risk. Clint would proceed to develop his plan by identifying, classifying, and selecting methods of treatment for his other risks.

Implementing the Risk Management Plan

The "I" of the D. I. M. process consists of implementing the risk management plan. In order for the plan to be implemented successfully it must be communicated to everyone involved. Risk management should be practiced by every employee in the organization because it is a shared responsibility. If administrators, supervisors, and employees collaborate, risk management becomes a successful enterprise (Nygaard & Boone, 1989). The use of printed guidelines outlining risk reduction is one method of communicating a plan and can be inserted in the employee handbook at orientation. Examples of the items covered in the guidelines include: the facility, layout, and operation; personnel and organizational management; rules and regulations of the business; responsibilities of various employees; correct methods of documenting records and reports; and emergency procedures.

An additional method used to communicate risk management policies should be through in-service training. These instructional periods help to review policies and procedures and to identify specific employee training needs that have arisen since the initial employee orientation meetings.

In our scenario, Clint implements his plan by providing a condensed risk management manual to each employee including contracted personnel such as referees. The books explain appropriate policies, rules and regulations, and emphasize emergency care procedures. In addition, he conducts training sessions for the league referees to make certain they understand and enforce the local safety rules instituted by the program. Clint also implements an emergency medical plan for which his supervisory personnel are well trained.

Manage the Risk Management Plan

The final step of the D. I. M. process is to manage the plan. Management of the plan is initiated through the hiring or selection of a risk manager and the establishment of an employee risk management committee. The authority and responsibilities of both the risk manager and the employee risk management committee should be described in the policy statement of the organization and in the risk management manual. It is important that the risk manager and the employee risk management committee be given the authority to act effectively. Support of the organization's governing board is important if the risk manager is to function effectively.

Organizations that do not have a risk manager should at least establish an employee risk management committee (Miller, 1989; Sharp, 1990). Employees should have input into a risk management plan and be made to feel an "ownership" in the plan. The safety committee should monitor the risk management plan, implement changes, assist in fostering a genuine safety attitude amongst other employees, conduct inspections, review accidents, and supervise in-service training (van der Smissen, 1990). In addition to employees, travel and facility personnel, insurance experts, administrators, and anyone else whose expertise may improve the quality of the risk plan should be included on the committee (Miller, 1989). The size of the committee depends on the overall goals and extent of the organization.

Clint was hired with the understanding that his duties as director of the recreation program would include the duties of a risk manager. He is fortunate that the organization policy statements provide him with the essential authority to carry out these various responsibilities and to manage the plan effectively. He establishes an employee risk management committee to assist him in the management of the risk management plan. Once the risk management plan has been developed, Clint gets needed help, advice, information, and support from the employee risk management committee. From this input, Clint manages the plan and makes regular modification in the plan.

With the litigious nature of today's society, risk management is now a sports management necessity. There is no such thing as a perfectly safe program and it is unreasonable for a sport manager to expect to eliminate all injuries and financial losses. Even though many risks can be identified, classified, and treated, hazards will still exist in all sport-related organizations—private businesses, university athletic departments, fitness centers, sport facilities, and recreation programs—and accidents will occur. The ability to recognize and reduce the likelihood of these mishaps is the essence of a successful risk management program.

Recent Developments

Settlements

In order to reduce expenses, insurance companies often find that it is less expensive to settle lawsuits than litigate the claims. Settlements are often made in cases where the insurance company would have won in court. Such decisions to cut potential expenses may have short term economic benefits, but send the wrong message to potential litigants (Kozlowski, 1988). This strategy may actually backfire by increasing the number of lawsuits since plaintiffs feel that even with a weak case, they can settle for a substantial sum. As insurance companies gain the reputation of paying off claims, the number of suits will continue to grow.

An additional problem which occurs because of settling lawsuits, involves individual employees defended by the organization. If the facility pays off the claim, the employee has no opportunity to prove his or her innocence. This stigma can be quite traumatic and remain with the employee for a long time. An alternative to paying off claims involves the use of "alternative dispute resolutions" (ADR). When a dispute occurs, the parties use an ADR method such as arbitration, fact finding, or conciliation. This option may be written into contracts and agreements as a cost saving measure (van der Smissen, 1990).

Assumption of Risk

A Florida case demonstrates the need for effective risk management programs and insurance coverage to counter the risks of negligence claims. An appeals court ruled that while a high school football player assumed the risks inherent to the sport of football, he did not assume the risk of negligent supervision (*Zalkin v. American Learning Systems, Inc.*, 1994). The player had been injured a week prior to a play-off game, but the high school football coach allowed the plaintiff to participate in the play-off game where he further irritated his injury. An effective risk management plan could have instituted policies related to participation or return-to-participation by injured athletes.

References

A. Cases
Ashcroft v. Calder Race Course, Inc., 492 So.2d 1309 (Fla. 1986).
Zalkin v. American Learning Systems, Inc., 630 So.2d 1020 (Fla. App. 3 Dist. 1994).

B. Publications
Ammon, Jr., R. (1993). Risk and Game Management Practices In Selected Municipal Football Facilities (Doctoral dissertation, University of Northern Colorado, 1993). Dissertation Abstracts International, 54, 3366A.
Barringer, F. (1992, August 19). Fullback Sues School Over Her Injury. *The New York Times*, p. D20.
Kozlowski, J. C. (1988, September). A Common Sense View of Liability. *Parks & Recreation*, 56-59.
Miller, A. W. (1989). Risk Management. In G. Nygaard & T. Boone (Eds.), *Law for Physical Educators and Coaches* (pp. 419-437). Columbus, Ohio: Publishing Horizons.
National Association of Independent Schools. (1988). *Risk Management for Schools*. Boston: Author.
Nygaard, G., & Boone, T. (1989). *Law for Physical Educators and Coaches* (2nd Ed.). Columbus, Ohio: Publishing Horizons.
Ross, C. T. (1985, June). Managing Risk. *Athletic Business*, 22, 24, 26-27, 29.

Sharp, L. A. (1990). Sport Law. National Organization on Legal Problems of Education (Whole No. 40).

van der Smissen, B. (1990). *Legal liability and Risk Management for Public and Private Entities*. Cincinnati: Anderson Publishing Co.

Wolohan, J. T. (1995, July/August). The Assumption Of Risk Defense Takes a Beating in Florida. *The Sports Lawyer*, 13, 4, 12.

2.52

Risk Identification and Reduction

Gary R. Gray
Montana State University-Billings

Assessing the risks involved in specific sports activities has become an important topic in the professional literature (Clement, 1988; Koehler, 1988; Sharp, 1990; van der Smissen, 1990). Although various types of processes are possible, the risk management planning process involves: 1) identifying the risks related to participating in a specific sport or activity; 2) evaluating the risks to determine their probability and severity; 3) selecting the appropriate means of dealing with each risk, including a) transfer (e.g., waivers and insurance), b) avoidance (i.e., eliminating the activity or components of it), c) reduction (i.e., devising appropriate safety strategies), and d) retention (e.g., budgeting for certain losses); and 4) implementing the appropriate administrative procedures to put the risk management plan into action.

Sport administrators must be diligent in planning and implementing comprehensive administrative practices to reduce the likelihood of unreasonable injuries in their programs. Important program-related areas that deserve special attention include: 1) selecting and training program personnel; 2) supervising personnel and the program; 3) conducting the program in a reasonable manner; 4) developing a documentation system; and (5) maintaining the facility where the program will be conducted.

■ ■ ■ ■

Representative Case

BERMAN v. PHILADELPHIA BOARD OF EDUCATION

Superior Court of Pennsylvania
310 Pa. Super. 153; 456 A.2d 545
June 2, 1982, Argued
February 4, 1983, Filed

OPINION:

In April, 1976, Brad Berman was an eleven-year-old, fifth-grade student, attending Sharswood Elementary School in Philadelphia. In response to a flyer distributed to each classroom announcing an after-school floor hockey league, Brad enrolled in the program and was assigned to play for the Capitals, one of the eight league teams. All games were played in the school's gymnasium.

Daniel Caputo, a physical education instructor at Sharswood, began the program during the 1974-75 school year. He instructed the student players, at the beginning of each season, that slapshots, raising hockey sticks above the waist, checking and foul language were prohibited. During the 1975-76 school year, which included the date of April 21, 1976 at issue here, the students were equipped with hockey sticks composed of wooden shafts and plastic blades; however, no helmets, face masks, mouth guards, shin guards or gloves were provided.

On April 21, 1976, Brad Berman was facing an opposing player moving toward goal. The opposing player made a backhanded shot and his follow-through motion caused the stick blade to strike Brad's mouth. Three maxillary and two mandibular teeth were severed resulting in severe pain and extensive dental treatment.

As a result of the injuries, Brad Berman, a minor, by his parents and natural guardians, Leonard and Sheila Berman, and Leonard and Sheila Berman in their own individual capacities, filed a Complaint in Trespass against appellant, the Philadelphia Board of Education, in the Court of Common Pleas of Philadelphia County. A non-jury trial was conducted on December 12, 1980; however, a verdict was not then returned because the lower court reopened the case for the purpose of admitting life expectancy tables on Brad's life. On April 14, 1981, a verdict was finally entered for Brad Berman in the amount of $83,190.00 and for Leonard and Sheila Berman in the amount of $1,810.00. The appellant's exceptions and amended exceptions to the order of April 14, 1981 were denied, and an Order for Judgment in favor of the appellees in the amounts stated above was entered on August 4, 1981. This appeal followed.

It is the appellant's first contention that there was insufficient evidence to support a finding of negligence. The expert testimony of Cosmo R. Castaldi, a pediatric dentist, and member of the Safety and Protective Equipment Committee of the Amateur Hockey Association of the United States, testified on cross examination that no regulation existed in April, 1976, requiring any kind of mouth guards for participants of amateur ice or floor hockey; consequently, the appellant reasons, no standard of care was established upon which a finding of negligence could stand. Without a regulation to the contrary, Daniel Caputo, as the appellant's agent, was not required to furnish mouth guards. His general instructions, officiating games and calling penalties were sufficient actions to satisfy any applicable standard of care. We disagree with this reasoning and hold that the record supports a finding of negligence.

• • •

. . . we find enough evidence supporting a determination of negligence. Daniel Caputo was familiar with the safety and protective equipment available for ice or floor hockey. He was also aware that mouth injuries were recurring consequences of playing the sport. In fact, he appreciated the inherent risks enough to request on two or three separate occasions during the program's first year (1975-76) that the appellant purchase safety equipment for the students. The Philadelphia Board of Education, however, turned a deaf ear to these continual requests; no helmets, shin guards, gloves, face masks or mouth guards were provided for the students until 1977.

The standard of care was not diminished by Dr. Castaldi's admission that no rules or regulations for the adornment of mouth guards were imposed on floor hockey in 1976. The absence of a mouth guard mandate does not necessarily excuse the appellant's failure to impose similar rules itself. A duty of care is imposed upon a board of education for the safety and welfare of students under conditions such as those before us. Ayala v. Philadelphia Board of Public Education, 453 Pa. 584, 305 A.2d 877 (1973). Having found sufficient evidence to support a breach of that duty of care, we must defer to the lower court's judgment.

• • •

Judgment affirmed.

■ ■ ■ ■

Fundamental Concepts and Principles

A Risk Identification and Reduction Instrument

Although there is no single "right" method to identify and reduce the risks associated with any particular sport or physical activity, the critical factor is to approach the risk identification and reduction process in a systematic manner. That is to say, rather than arguing which system might be preferred, a sport manager should at the very least use or design a system that is feasible for his or her own specific situation. The instrument and process described in this chapter have been used in planning 27 sport competitions in the Iowa Games, Iowa's annual amateur sports festival involving over 14,000 athletes. In addition, this system has been adopted by the National Congress of State Games and recommended to all 44 member states that offer annual State Games competition. Sport managers can use this instrument and process to increase the awareness of safety and risk management planning among their employees as well as make their programs safer as a result of implementing the safety strategies identified by their staff members.

The instrument consists of two parts: (1) the **Sport Risk Assessment Form** and (2) the **Strategies to Reduce Identified Risks Form**. Completing the Sport Risk Assessment Form causes sport managers to bring their employees together to discuss the physical risks intrinsic to the sports and physical activities offered in a program. These are the naturally inherent risks that sport managers and their employees need to minimize and to communicate to their participants. Everyone participating in the sport risk assessment process will contribute to and benefit from the discussion of safety concerns related to the specific sport analyzed. This open exchange of information and opinions can help sport managers make their programs safer. The Strategies to Reduce Identified Risks Form, also to be completed by sport managers and their staffs in a group setting, facilitates discussion of proposed strategies or methods to deal with each identified risk so that the various sports offered can be made as safe as possible.

Following are instructions for completing the Sport Risk Assessment Form and the Strategies to Reduce Identified Risks Form. To complete the forms, follow these steps:

1. Complete the introductory information at the top of the Sport Risk Assessment Form so that the appropriate individuals can be contacted if questions arise or if additional information is needed.

2. Identify, within reason and to the best of your ability, the typical, inherent risks related to participation in the sport. Be specific but concise as you identify the particular risks that might lead to injury in the sport. If you are familiar with the specific facilities in which the sport will take place, you may identify facility-related possibilities of injury. Otherwise, keep facility concerns general in nature (i.e., facility characteristics that might be related to injury regardless of where the sport is played). Do not feel that you must complete each of the 20 lines. However, if more space is needed, continue the list of identified risks on another sheet.

3. On a scale of 1 through 9, estimate the probability (P) or likelihood that each identified risk could cause injury to one of the participants. Assume that "1" indicates a risk that is "extremely unlikely/almost impossible" and that "9" indicates a risk that is "extremely likely/almost certain." The center of the scale ("5") represents an "average" probability or likelihood. Place the number in the column marked "P" on the same line as each identified risk. Attempt to arrive at group consensus or take the average of the numbers proposed by group members.

4. On a scale of one through nine, estimate the severity (S) of injury that would likely occur if each identified risk resulted in an actual injury to a participant. Assume that "1" indicates an injury that is "extremely minor/almost inconsequential" and "9" indicates an injury that is "extremely serious/catastrophic." The center of the scale ("5") represents an injury of average severity. Place the number in the column marked "S" on the same line as the identified risk. Again, attempt to arrive at group consensus or take the average of the numbers proposed by group members. In discussing the appropriate numbers to place in the "P" and the "S" columns, group members might disagree since assigning numbers is dependent upon each individual's perception of risk based upon experience with the sport and the types of injuries observed. The numbers assigned are likely to vary depending upon such factors as age, experience, and level of expertise of the participants in any given situation. One must remember that the numbers assigned are relative rather than absolute.

5. For each identified risk, multiply the number in the "P" column by the number in the "S" column to determine the "PS Quotient" for each identified risk.

6. Add the numbers in the "PS Quotient" column to determine the "Total PS Quotient" for the sport.

7. On the Strategies to Reduce Identified Risks Form, identify at least one strategy that could be implemented to decrease either the probability or severity of injury (or both) for each identified

risk related to the sport. Write the strategy on the same numbered line as the identified risk from the previous form. If the group can develop safety and injury prevention strategies for the sport that are related to many of the identified risks or to the entire sport in general, place those strategies in the section labeled "Other" at the bottom of the page.

Table 1
Sport Risk Assessment Form

Name of Sport: Floor Hockey   **Date**: April 11, 1996
Assessment form completed by:
   J. Smith, R. Jones, A. Murphy, D. Andrews

Risk Identification	P		S		PS Quotient
1. Getting hit in eye with puck	3	x	7	=	21
2. Getting hit in eye with stick	3	x	8	=	24
3. Getting hit in mouth with puck	3	x	5	=	15
4. Getting hit in mouth with stick	3	x	7	=	21
5. Getting hit on hands by opponent's stick	8	x	3	=	24
6. Getting hit on shins by opponent's stick	9	x	3	=	27
7. Getting hit on feet/ankles by opponent's stick	9	x	3	=	27
8. Inadvertent collisions between opponents	7	x	4	=	28
9. Body checking/bumping opponent to obtain puck	5	x	4	=	20
10. Goalie getting hit with stick around goal	6	x	3	=	18
11. Goalie getting hit in face with puck	8	x	7	=	56
12. Goalie getting hit in torso with puck	9	x	3	=	27
13. Running into protruding stage at side of gym	3	x	6	=	18
14. Slipping on floor due to chronic dust problem	6	x	3	=	18
15. Plastic head of stick coming off wooden handle	2	x	4	=	8
16. _____	—	x	—	=	—
17. _____	—	x	—	=	—
18. _____	—	x	—	=	—
19. _____	—	x	—	=	—
20. _____	—	x	—	=	—
	TOTAL			=	352

Table 2
Strategies to Reduce Identified Risks Form

1. Provide and require the wearing of eye guards/goggles
2. Provide and require the wearing of eye guards/goggles
3. Provide and require the wearing of mouth guards
4. Provide and require the wearing of mouth guards
5. Provide and require the wearing of heavy, work-type gloves
6. Provide and require the wearing of field hockey shin guards
7. Teach how to execute short, low follow-through; do not chop at puck
8. Teach students to stick handle puck (dribble) with head up
9. Enforce no body checking rule (two-minute penalty); then expulsion
10. Enlarge goal crease to offer goalie more protection/space
11. Provide and require goalie to wear full face mask
12. Provide and require goalie to wear baseball-type chest protector
13. Warn students of stage and pad with gym mats
14. Sweep floor before each class session
15. Require students to inspect sticks prior to each class session
16. _____
17. _____
18. _____
19. _____
20. _____

Other _____

_____

_____

_____

_____

Once both forms have been completed, it is absolutely critical to implement the identified strategies to decrease the probability and/or severity of injury to program participants. At a later date, the group can evaluate to what degree the probability and severity of injury were actually reduced as a result of implementing the identified strategies by going through the risk identification and evaluation process again. Injury report forms completed after these strategies have been implemented can be studied to determine whether the number and the extent of various injuries have decreased. The group can continue to plan new strategies, if appropriate, to make the sport even safer. This cycle continues as risks related to the activity are periodically assessed, as "new and better" safety strategies are implemented, and as evaluation takes place concerning the degree to which the safety strategies reduced the probability and severity of injuries related to the identified risks.

Risk Identification and Reduction

The heart of any risk management program involves the identification of risks and the subsequent reduction of those risks. The following four areas should help to guide the sport manager in identifying and reducing the risks in his or her sport program.

Selecting and Training Program Personnel. Sport administrators should develop a systematic process for selecting staff members, including paid and volunteer positions. Interview each candidate thoroughly and check letters of recommendation, certifications, and other credentials carefully. Talk to people who know the candidates well, such as former colleagues and employers, even if no letters of recommendation are included in the candidates' application materials. Make the interview process more than just a social chat or a personality evaluation. Assess the candidate's skills, knowledge, and philosophies. Pose specific "what would you do if . . ." questions to the candidate to assess how he or she will react to certain situations. Enlist the expertise and advice of several staff members in the selection process to benefit from many opinions and judgments. Remember, the program will benefit if the best candidate is selected in an objective way from the largest pool possible.

Train all employees well. Give them the information that will allow them to perform their jobs successfully, such as department manuals or handbooks. Identify clear expectations of each person; it is hard for a person to do a good job if the person never knows exactly what the job is. Provide a written job description and then give the employees the help they need to succeed. Plan on-going in-service workshops, such as safety clinics in which first aid updates and CPR refreshers can be provided, as part of regular staff meetings. Make sure that employees know their legal responsibilities and how to fulfill these responsibilities in a reasonable manner. Require coaches and other employees to attend clinics, conferences, and workshops to stay current in their fields. Provide financial assistance so that employees can remain professionally active.

Supervising Personnel and the Program. Provide continuing feedback to employees through frequent, informal supervision by observing them at work. In sports situations, attend practices and games in order to observe employees in action. Offer helpful feedback whenever appropriate. In terms of risk management, look specifically for unsafe activities and intervene if necessary. Even if one is not an expert in a specific sport or activity, one's knowledge of sport in general will help in assessing the manner in which activities are being conducted. Knowledge of acceptable professional behaviors, such as coaching techniques, should allow one to do this well.

Evaluate staff members on measurable criteria annually. Provide written assessments as a result of those evaluations. Reinforce employees' strengths and plan strategies with them to improve weaknesses. Set dates to re-evaluate employees' performance after they have had an opportunity to show growth.

Make sure that employees are with the program participants when they are supposed to be (e.g., coaches in attendance at athletic practices and other training sessions, such as weight lifting sessions) and that they are actively supervising and interacting with the participants. Require written program plans, such as athletic practice plans, and help employees plan for safety within each of their activities.

In addition, make use of supervisory plans for all activities. For more information on supervisory plans, see Chapter 2.32.

Mentor new employees, particularly if they are relatively inexperienced in their field. Schedule regular meetings with them, communicate effectively with them, and provide the structure that they need to help them be successful. Generally, inexperienced employees need closer supervision than more experienced employees. Know the details of the program's insurance coverage, including excess medical coverage and liability coverage. Explain these details to all employees so that they will understand what is covered and what is not covered.

Conducting the Program in a Reasonable Manner. Sport managers should make a diligent effort to determine that activities conducted as part of their programs are done in accordance with professional expectations within the industry. In addition to ensuring that programs are conducted in a professionally acceptable manner, sport managers should also scrutinize each program to determine that each program is conducted in a reasonable manner. That is to say, programs must be conducted within the parameters of reasonable foresight being exercised by staff members. Normally, doing what is professionally acceptable is reasonable; however, there might be some activities that are routinely done within an industry that, if evaluated in court, would not meet the standard of reasonableness. In any event, always be sure to evaluate programs and activities with the "yardstick" of reasonableness.

Sport managers should insure that their employees do not induce, encourage, intimidate, or coerce participants to perform physical activities without examining the participants' abilities and experience related to those activities. Do not require program participants to perform specific physical activities without providing adequate instruction related to the correct manner in which the activities should be performed.

One should be concerned with rules established by the governing entity, operational rules of the organization, and rules of games or activities. Appropriate rules should be established, communicated, and enforced. Establish all necessary rules, but eliminate rules that are not considered important enough to enforce. Be certain that all rules are communicated both to appropriate personnel and to participants. Be certain all clearly understand the rules. And finally, enforce all rules. Enforcement must be effective and consistent. Do not conduct programs that are in violation of pertinent regulatory agencies' rules or policies, and be sure that program personnel are aware of those rules and policies.

Regularly inspect physical activity facilities to determine whether they are properly equipped and maintained for safe use by program participants. Develop, communicate, and consistently implement reasonable safety precautions, including safety equipment and supervision, to minimize the risk of injury to program participants. Know the physical nature, requirements, and limitations of program participants and supervise them in a reasonable manner.

Finally, be prepared for emergency situations. This would involve the implementation of an emergency plan (see Chapter 2.31) and having personnel that are qualified and trained to react appropriately in emergency situations.

Developing a Documentation System. Wise sport managers develop a carefully planned documentation system. Perhaps the first area that should be committed to writing is a policy and procedures manual. Carefully worded policies and detailed procedures for virtually every area within a sport program should be developed, communicated, implemented, evaluated, and revised whenever necessary. For the purpose of this chapter, it should be stressed that safety and risk management policies and procedures must be created. These policies and procedures include but are not necessarily limited to the following conceptual areas: appropriate use of independent contractors; appropriate use of warnings and waivers; first aid and medical emergencies; injury/incident report forms; facility inspection and evacuation; equipment inspection; transportation of participants; severe weather contingencies; program postponement and cancellation; and security emergencies. Some of these will be discussed in more detail in the following paragraphs.

Written Warnings/Agreements to Participate. Sport managers should warn the participants in writing of the inherent risks related to participation in each sport activity. In addition, participants should sign and date these written warnings. Written warnings, or agreements to participate as they are often known, can be much more effective than verbal warnings alone. Putting a warning in writing makes it easier to communicate to participants in an effective manner. It is something they can read, think about, ask questions about, and refer to at any time. A verbal warning is not so long-lasting. Certainly, a combination of written warnings followed by verbal reminders of the inherent risks is best. See Chapter 2.24 for more information on agreements to participate.

The other advantage of a written warning over a verbal warning is the fact that the written warning is documentation in itself of how the participants were warned. Since a verbal warning is not documented, it is often more difficult to determine the exact nature of how the participants were warned. The exact words and examples used in a verbal warning might not be very clear in the minds of participants two or three years later, when a lawsuit might be filed. A written warning, on the other hand, exists as long as it is saved in a file to provide exact documentation of how participants were warned of the inherent risks related to participation in a specific activity or program.

First Aid and Medical Emergencies. Sharp (1990) identified two obligations of sport leaders toward those who are injured in sport programs: 1) to render emergency first aid assistance until medical personnel arrive, and 2) to exercise reasonable care in procuring medical treatment for the injured party (i.e., develop emergency procedures for timely medical assistance and adhere to those procedures). Offer appropriate first aid to injured participants or see that it is offered promptly and correctly. Develop a system for accurately reporting in writing the important information related to injuries, such as the injured participant's name, address, and phone number; the specific body part injured; the type of injury; when and where the injury occurred; a description of the circumstances surrounding the injury as reported to the person in charge of the event; and the names, addresses, and phone numbers of witnesses.

Know the health and physical condition of program participants. This can be accomplished by requiring participants to complete written health history forms so that program leaders can become aware of relevant health and physical condition factors that relate to safe participation in a particular program. For some programs, such as interscholastic and intercollegiate athletics, it is appropriate, and even required, to have participants complete a physical examination by a medical doctor.

Obtain appropriate written permission, commonly referred to as consent-to-treat, from a parent or legal guardian to obtain necessary medical treatment for minor participants when the parent or guardian is unavailable to grant such permission in an emergency situation. This signed document could be instrumental in securing timely medical treatment from a physician when a minor is in need of such treatment and the parent cannot be reached. Remember to take these signed forms on trips such as athletic contests. This consent-to-treat authorization can easily be combined with a "permission slip," a document in which parents indicate that it is acceptable for their child to participate in a specific program. Permission slips are excellent communication and public relations tools by which program leaders can communicate very important, specific information to parents in a caring manner.

Maintaining the Program's Facility. Sports participants practice and compete using both indoor and outdoor sports facilities. In some situations, a problem with the design or condition of the facility might contribute to an injury sustained by a participant or spectator. Sport managers should focus their attention on designing a preventive and corrective maintenance program to minimize the likelihood of injury to program participants. A regular inspection process, one which is documented for later follow-up purposes, should identify any potential problems that might exist with a facility. This systematic process should involve making at least the following decisions: 1) which facilities, parts of facilities, or areas should be inspected; 2) who should perform the facility safety inspections for each area identified; 3) what criteria will be used to determine whether each facility is reasonably safe for its intended use; and 4) what process will be used to document each inspection and to correct any problems identified. Certainly, it is important not to use a portion of a facility while it is being repaired or while corrective maintenance is being conducted.

Recent Developments

Adams (1985) reported that an unpublished court decision in February, 1982 (*Thompson v. Seattle Public School District*), opened a new era in sport litigation with far-reaching implications for sport at all levels. In that case, a young man was awarded $6.3 million in a lawsuit against the Seattle school district and a coach for a football injury that left him a quadriplegic. The young player was a 15-year-old sophomore at the time of the injury. He was injured when he was running with the football and lowered his head to ward off tacklers. He was hit on the top of his helmet, causing an injury to his spinal cord. The player sued his coach for failure to warn of the dangers inherent in football and for improper instruction in coaching. The Seattle School District appealed the trial court's decision, but settled the case for $3.84 million prior to the appellate court's decision. This ruling placed new emphasis on the duty to warn of risks inherent in an activity.

References

A. Cases
Berman v. Philadelphia Board of Education, 310 Pa. Super. 153, 456 A. 2d 545 (1983).

B. Publications
Adams, S. (1985). Implications of the Seattle Decision. In H. Appenzeller (Ed.), *Sports and Law: Contemporary Issues* (pp. 17-22).

Clement, A. (1988). *Law in Sport and Physical Activity*. Indianapolis, Ind.: Benchmark Press.

Koehler, R. W. (1987). *Law, Sport Activity, and Risk Management*. Champaign, Ill.: Stipes Publishing Co.

Sharp, L. A. (1990). Sport law. NOLPE.

van der Smissen, B. (1990). *Legal Liability and Risk Management for Public and Private Entities*. Cincinnati, Ohio: Anderson Publishing Co.

2.53
Managing Risk Through Insurance

Doyice J. Cotten
Sport Risk Consulting*

Insurance is a method by which an individual or business pays a defined expenditure (premium) to protect against the possibility of a large, undetermined future loss or expense. Insurance spreads the financial risks and costs of an individual or business among a large group of persons or businesses so that the losses of those few who experience them are shared with the many who do not. In so doing, insurance provides protection against financial catastrophe and is an indispensable risk management technique.

Many persons look at insurance and risk management as one and the same. This, however, is not true. Risk management involves the identification of risks, determination of the extent of the risks, and the implementation of one or more control approaches. Control approaches include: 1) elimination of the activity, 2) reduction of risks through operational control, 3) retention (through such techniques as self-insurance, current expensing, and deductibles), 4) transfer by contract (through indemnity agreements, exculpatory clauses, and by requiring insurance by the other party), and 5) by purchasing insurance from an insurance company.

Obviously, insurance is but one of many techniques available to help manage risks in a sport-business. The sport manager should purchase insurance to protect against all risks that could have a significant impact upon the financial integrity of the sport-business, but should not try to insure against every possible risk and potential loss. It is usually less expensive to simply pay for minor losses when they occur. It is obviously important that the sport manager be knowledgeable enough to determine which risks are of such a magnitude as to allow retention by the sport-business, which can be transferred by contract, and which require protection through insurance coverage. The purpose of this chapter is to help the sport manager become more informed about this aspect of risk management and, subsequently, be able to better protect the sport-business from financial risks.

Fundamental Concepts

Understanding the Policy

One of the first steps in becoming more knowledgeable about insurance and being able to better protect your sport-business from financial risks is learning to read and understand an insurance policy. Most can be long and confusing, particularly if one does not know exactly what to look for. The major sections found in most policies are summarized below.

*Special thanks to Mr. Bryan Burke, partner in Blount, Burke, Wimberly & Hendricks Insurors, and Mr. John Lee, partner in Lee, Hill & Johnson Insurors, Statesboro, Georgia, for their efforts in reading this chapter and making suggestions for its improvement.

Declarations.   This is the section that includes the facts and figures regarding your particular policy. This section includes such items as the name of the insured, address, policy period, coverages, amounts of insurance, the applicable deductibles, and the cost of the policy. If parties other than the corporate entity are covered (i.e., employees, directors), they should be named in the declarations section. Careful study of this section can help one to better understand the coverage of the policy.

Contractual Agreement.   This is the actual contractual agreement between the insurance company and the sport-business. The statement of agreement may be quite short. The section simply states that the insurance company agrees to insure the sport-business to the extent indicated in the declarations in exchange for the agreed-upon premium.

This agreement is generally followed by a list of definitions. Many key words or phrases used in the document are carefully defined. Examine these carefully because many terms have specific meanings in insurance that may differ from the sport manager's concept of the term. For instance, one might assume that "personal injury" refers to physical injuries of an individual. However, personal injury refers to injuries caused by such things as slander, libel, false arrest, false imprisonment, humiliation, and invasion of privacy.

Coverages.   The coverages section includes a listing of what is being insured in the policy. Following each coverage is a detailed explanation of what is included in the coverage. For example, the building might be listed including any attached structures. The section might state that rental structures away from the main building are not included. This section will also include the perils which the insurance covers (e.g., fire, theft). Additional Benefits Coverage includes coverage of newly acquired property.

Exclusions.   This section of the policy describes what is not covered by the policy. Items that are often excluded from a standard commercial policy include landscaping, buildings under construction, and cash. Some perils that are usually excluded from the standard policy are earthquake, volcanic eruption, water damage from floods, sewers, or surface ground water, power interruption, war, and nuclear hazard. When a coverage is needed by the sport-business that is not listed in the inclusions and is excluded by the exclusions, riders or endorsements adding the coverage to the policy may be purchased.

Conditions.   This section sets forth the various things the sport-business must do to meet the obligations of the insured. Some of these conditions might include reporting obligations following a loss, giving sworn affirmation of loss, providing an inventory, or provision of receipts.

This section also includes the responsibilities of the insurance company in the event of a claim. Specified here are such things as when cash replacement is mandated, when replacement items may be utilized, procedures to be followed if the insurer and insured fail to agree on the loss, and whether repair is the option of the insurance company.

Endorsements.   Endorsements are detailed listings of inclusions added to your policy. The final section of the policy is an identification of the specific endorsements included with your policy. Endorsements may be added when the policy is purchased or at a later date as the needs of the sport-business change. Examples of endorsements might include adding insured persons, coverage of fine art, and peak season coverage (which increases inventory coverage by 25 percent during the peak season when inventory is higher than usual). A separate Difference in Conditions policy or endorsement might be purchased to protect against earthquake and flood.

It is important that the sport manager develop an understanding of insurance and select an insurance agent who has a basic understanding of sport-related businesses. The better the agent understands the sport-business, the more helpful the agent can be in recommending important coverages that might be critical to the sport-business and in eliminating, or reducing, unnecessary coverages.

Determining Necessary Coverage for a Sport-business

In reviewing a current insurance policy or when considering the initial purchase of insurance coverage, the sport-business must take four steps to make a wise insurance purchase. First, examine the risks and potential losses which the organization might encounter. Then, establish an effective risk reduction program to reduce the likelihood of the risks occurring. Third, identify the remaining risks and determine which are of a magnitude that can be safely retained by the sport-business and which might be handled by transfer by contract. Finally, the remaining risks which can significantly impact the sport-business should then be covered by an insurance policy which will protect the sport-business from financial loss.

Table 1 provides a list of financial risks faced by sport businesses. Of course, the risks faced vary from one type of sport-business to another, so many of the risks listed in the table will not apply to a particular sport-business and some sport-businesses may encounter risks that are not listed. Nevertheless, the table can serve as a guide or checklist in helping the sport manager make certain the sport-business is properly covered.

Types of Insurance Coverage

There are several types of insurance coverage. Each is designed to offer protection from loss for certain risks. The two types that are most indispensable for a sport-business are property insurance and general liability insurance. Other types of insurance include umbrella liability, liability protection for employees, motor vehicle, workmen's compensation, and participant liability and accident insurance. Each type will be explained below.

Property Insurance. Property insurance is the primary means of protecting the sport-business from loss from damage or destruction of its facility, the facility contents, and accompanying properties. There are three levels of property coverage offered: basic, broad (or extended coverage), and special form (sometimes referred to as all-risks). The basic coverage includes protection against a limited number of hazards (fire, malicious mischief, lightning, and vandalism) whereas extended coverage includes protection against more exposures (hail, riot, explosion, windstorm, aircraft, vehicle damage, and smoke). Special form includes all risks not excluded on the policy (e.g., collapse, burglary, and theft). Even with special form coverage, some property risks are not covered and if the sport manager feels coverage is needed, additional endorsements must be purchased. Some property that might not be included and might require additional endorsements include theft by employees, vehicles such as golf carts, and boilers. Property insurance also does not include normal wear and tear, cracking, settling, vermin, earthquakes, or floods.

Two endorsements of special importance to many sport-businesses are *extra expense insurance* and *business income insurance*. Extra expense protects the sport-business against certain indirect losses that may occur. For instance, if a health spa is destroyed by fire, some expenses that may be encountered are rental of another building during rebuilding, leasing equipment, and advertising expense. Business income coverage includes loss of income due to the insured peril and continuing expenses such as the salaries of key personnel while the sport-business is closed.

Table 1
Typical Financial Risks Faced by Sport-Businesses

Property Exposures
Fire
Smoke
Natural Elements
Wind & Tornado Damage
Flood
Lightning
Rain
Hail
Earthquake
Debris Removal
Vandalism & Malicious Mischief
Riot
Explosion
Boiler & Machinery
Damage to Signs
Glass Coverage
Damage to Parking Lots & Fences
Damage by Aircraft
Valuable Papers
Electronic Data Processing
Computer Systems
Money & Property
Theft, Burglary, Disappearance
Embezzlement & Employee Dishonesty
Off Premises Coverage
Counterfeit Losses

Moveable Equipment (golf carts, mowers, etc.)
Golf Green Coverage
Damage to Property of Others (on your premises)

Company Vehicles
Damage to Vehicle (collision)
Damage to Vehicle (non-collision: theft, vandalism, tree limb)
Damage to Vehicle (uninsured motorist)
Damage to other Vehicles or Property

Public Liability (Excluding Negligence)
Malpractice by Personnel
Products Liability
Contractual Liability (Including Indemnification)
Advertisers Liability
Dram Shop/Host Liquor Liability

Intentional Torts (Personal Injury)
Defamation
False Arrest or Imprisonment
Malicious Prosecution
Invasion of Privacy
Wrongful Entry or Eviction
Assault and Battery

Employment Practices
Sexual Discrimination
Racial Discrimination
Handicap Discrimination
Age Discrimination
Sexual Harassment
Civil Liberty Violations

Business Operations
Business Interruption
Loss of Income
Extra Expenses
Sickness/Accidents/Disability of Employees
Health of Key Personnel
Workmen's Compensation

Public Liability (Negligence)
Death
Paralysis
Brain Damage
Loss of Limbs
Loss of Senses
Internal Organ Injuries
Infliction of Emotional Stress
Broken Bones
Damaged Ligaments & Tendons
Sprains and Strains
Cuts, Punctures, Abrasions, & Bruises

Vehicles:
Injury to Other Persons
Damage to Property of Others
Damage to non-owned or Leased Vehicles

Directors & Officers Liability
Professional Liability
Independent Contractors Liability
Adventure & Tripping Liability
Sponsor Liability
Trip Liability
Event Liability

Watercraft
Injury to Other Persons
Damage to Property of Others

Injury to Participant
Catastrophic Injury to Participant
Pollution Liability
Suits by Employees (For Wrongful Termination, Breach of Employment Contract)

Adapted from van der Smissen, B. (1990). *Legal Liability and Risk Management for Public and Private Entities*. Cincinnati: Anderson Publishing Company.

The sport manager has other choices when purchasing property insurance. One is whether to purchase *cash value* or *replacement cost* insurance. Replacement cost is usually preferred because it pays the entire cost to replace the property rather than an estimate of the actual current value of the property (which might fall far short of what is needed to replace the item). Most policies have a *coinsurance* clause which requires the sport-business to insure the property to at least 80 percent of the replacement cost or actual cash value, depending upon the form chosen. Failure to coinsure for the amount specified in the policy will result in a significant decrease in benefits in the event of a loss. The amount of the *deductible* is another decision that must be made. The sport-business pays the deductible when a claim is made. For instance, if a storm does $3,000 damage to the building and the sport-business carries a $500 deductible, the sport-business pays the first $500 and the insurance covers the remaining $2500. The higher the deductible, the lower the cost of the insurance, so a sport-business can save money by carrying a high deductible and retaining that degree of risk.

The sport manager should determine what exposures are covered by the property insurance, determine from Table 1 and a knowledge of the risks of the particular sport-business what property exposures are uncovered, and with the help of the insurance agent, determine the best way to provide the protection needed. Most companies offer packages combining several endorsements at a cost less than purchasing the endorsements individually.

General Liability Insurance.   The purchase of this coverage protects the sport-business from financial loss in the event a person suffers injury or property loss as a result of the negligence of the sport-business or its employees. The policy is called Commercial General Liability (CGL). If the sport-business is sued, CGL will cover the legal costs and any award for damages up to the limit of the policy. The insurance company also has the option of paying a settlement to the plaintiff in order to avoid court expenses and risk of a larger award.

Sport-businesses should and usually do carry general liability insurance with coverage of one million dollars or more. Like property insurance, endorsements may be added to supplement the basic coverage. Some of the common endorsements by sport-businesses include the following. *Contractual liability* would protect the sport-business in the event it rented a facility and signed an indemnity agreement with the owner. Contractual liability passes that liability to the insurance company. *Errors and omissions* (professional liability or malpractice liability) can protect the sport-business from liability for errors by medical personnel, or, in sport settings, by trainers, therapists, or exercise physiologists. *Cross liability* coverage broadens the policy to protect the sport-business from suits from within the organization. For example, CGL would not protect if an injured volunteer worker sued an employee or if an injured employee sued a director. Cross liability would expand the coverage to include suits other than third party suits. *Products liability* protects against claims resulting from products manufactured or sold by the sport-business. Products include not only items such as those sold in a pro shop, but also food and concessions. *Liquor liability* coverage protects the sport-business for liability incurred through dispersal of alcohol. The sport-business is protected in the event one to whom the sport-business either sold or gave alcohol then causes injury or damage by a negligent act. The liability of the sport-business varies tremendously among states because of the differences in the laws (Dram Shop and Host Liquor) in those states. *Personal Injury liability* protects against liability for acts such as defamation (libel and slander), invasion of privacy, false arrest, or false imprisonment. *Advertising liability* protects the sport-business if advertising claims inadvertently result in a claim charging libel, slander, unfair competition or infringement on a copyright, title, or slogan. Many companies offer a package of several of the above coverages at less than buying the endorsements separately.

There are numerous other exclusions from a CGL policy for which endorsements are available. Some of these are damage to the property of others which is stored on your property (saddle animals, watercraft, golf clubs, etc.), fire damage to adjacent property, advertising, adventure and tripping programs, wrongful dismissal, pollution or contamination of the environment, owned saddle animals, owned watercraft, and human rights violations such as sexual harassment.

Umbrella Liability. Umbrella liability is a policy which greatly increases the liability protection at a reasonable cost. The policy might increase liability coverage from one million to five million or more and would come into effect only after the limit of the CGL has been surpassed. This extension of coverage generally applies to the CGL policy, the vehicle coverage, and the workmen's compensation insurance.

Liability Protecting Employees. Some sport-businesses not only purchase liability insurance to protect the sport-business, but also purchase insurance to protect employees in the event of legal action. The most common of these is *directors and officers liability* which generally provides general liability protection and liability for their "wrongful acts" of $1 million or more. Wrongful acts include error, misstatement, misleading statement, act, omission, and neglect of duty in the person's insured capacity. Coverage generally excludes: actions not within the scope of their duties; breach of contract; fines and penalties; dishonesty, infidelity, or criminal activities; human rights or sexual harassment violations; and failure to maintain adequate insurance.

Some sport-businesses provide *professional* or *malpractice insurance* for some or all employees. The professional insurance is designed to protect the employee from liability for negligence in acts related to giving professional advice or counsel. Suits often name the employee personally because the practice today is to sue all who may be potentially at fault, because the act may be an ultra vires act leaving only the employee as vulnerable, and because with governmental entities, the entity may be immune leaving only the employee. Malpractice insurance applies primarily to persons in legal or health-related areas. Malpractice insurance protects both the individual and the sport-business.

Professional and malpractice insurance can also be purchased by the individual employee. Policies are often available through a professional organization at very reasonable rates. They may also be purchased though one's insurance company, but the charge will be significantly higher. One should be aware that many exclusions exist on the policies.

Automobile Insurance. The sport manager must be certain that all sport-business vehicles are adequately covered. Maintain coverage for damage to the sport-business vehicles (collision, comprehensive, and uninsured motorist), damage to other vehicles, property, or persons (liability), and medical coverage for injured parties. Sport-business vehicles should be covered with a commercial automobile policy. One's personal automobile policy generally is inadequate for use with business vehicles.

In automobile insurance, as in property insurance, the amount of the deductible must be decided for both collision (damages to your automobile from the collision with another object) and comprehensive (damage to your automobile other than from collisions, e.g., vandalism to your auto, tree limb falling on your auto). Once again, the higher the deductible, the smaller the premium.

In some sport-businesses, employees occasionally must drive personal automobiles for business purposes. A *Non-owned Automobile* endorsement may be purchased to insure the sport-business in such cases. Coverage may also be extended to include volunteers who use their own vehicles. If the organization cannot insure the sport-business use of personal vehicles for employees or volunteers, procedures should be instituted to insure that the owners of all such vehicles have adequate coverage.

Many sport-businesses have occasion to rent or lease vehicles for varying periods of time. The sport-business may purchase a stand-alone policy or an endorsement on the firm's automobile policy that covers *Hired Vehicles*. This policy can provide both liability protection and coverage for the rental vehicle. Be aware, however, that neither the stand-alone policy nor the endorsement (or for that matter, insurance purchased from the rental company) will cover the loss or theft of personal property or equipment stored in the vehicle.

Another desirable endorsement is *Uninsured/Underinsured Motorist Coverage*. This coverage applies in the event that the other party has no insurance or the limits of that party's insurance have been reached. Typically this policy carries a $250 property damage deductible.

Workmen's Compensation. Workmen's compensation is insurance protection which provides for compensation to employees who suffer injury in the course of their employment. The worker receives compensation for lost income, both temporary and long term, and medical expenses incurred. The amount of the income is limited by the law in each state. All sport-businesses with three or more full-time employees are required to carry workmen's compensation insurance coverage. The cost of this insurance varies with the amount of risk involved in that type of sport-business and with the claims record of each individual sport-business. The premium is based on a certain number of dollars per hundred of payroll for the sport-business. Representative costs per $100 dollars of payroll might range from $15 for a riding club, $6 for a country club, $2 for a health spa, to less than one dollar for a sport-business involving all clerical or desk work.

Injured workers simply file a claim in order to receive compensation for work-related injuries. They neither have to file suit against the employer nor prove negligence or fault on the part of the employer. The employee, however, generally cannot receive compensation for pain and suffering through workmen's compensation. The employee's option to file suit against the employer varies from state to state, but when legal action is instituted, the employee generally forfeits rights to benefits from workmen's compensation.

Event Insurance. Many sport-businesses sponsor or conduct events either on an occasional or a regular basis. For any event, the sport-business should purchase additional liability insurance if the event is not included in the CGL policy of the sport-business. Additional insurance coverage depends upon the event and how much investment in involved and/or whether the sport-business is dependent upon a profit from the event. Also, many parties (i.e., venue, merchandisers, media, sponsors, concessionaires, and competing teams) may need to be named as additional insureds on your policy.

A common event liability policy would include bodily injury, personal injury, and property damage; an incident policy which would cover payment for medical expense for minor injuries (injured files a claim; no suit necessary); and settlement for uncontested claims in exchange for a release.

An important coverage in many events is that for *non-appearance/cancellation of event.* Bases for cancellation are specified and the policy generally includes costs, anticipated revenues, and anticipated profits. For some events, *life or accident coverage of participants* is purchased. Other typical endorsements include *automobiles, crime, prize indemnity, fire* (for damages that may not fall under the CGL), and *media coverage* (i.e., loss of signal, failure of transmission, breach of contract by media).

Recent Trends

There are two significant new trends in insurance coverage that may be particularly relevant to the sport manager.

Employee-Related Liability Insurance. This type of insurance protects the sport-business against lawsuits by employees. Protection may be provided for such claims as 1) wrongful termination, 2) sexual harassment, 3) equal pay violations, and 4) discrimination (racial, sex, age, and disability). Some policies cover any violation of certain state and federal statutes, including anti-discrimination laws, ADA, ADEA, and the Equal Pay Act.

By way of example, one such company, Evanston, writes $500,000/$1,000,000 per claim with a $1,000,000 aggregate coverage. The minimum premium is $3500 and increases with the size of the company.

Pollution Liability. A second coverage now purchased by some sport-businesses (e.g., golf courses) is pollution liability. This coverage protects the sport-business if acts by the sport-business result in pollution and damage to neighboring property. For instance, a chemical spill in a stream on a golf course could result in damage to the property of others and subsequent legal action against the sport-business.

References

Brooks, D. (1985). Property Insurance. *Risk Management Today.* Washington: ICMA.

Castle, G., Cushman, R., and Kensicki, P. (1981). *The Business Insurance Handbook.* Homewood, Ill.: Dow Jones-Irwin.

Corbett, R. (1995). *Insurance in Sport and Recreation.* Edmonton, Alberta: Centre for Sport and Law.

Mattman, J. Tips to Keep Insurance Premiums Down. *Facility Manager.* Spring, 1991.

Mehr, R., Cammack, E., and Rose, T. (1985). *Principles of Insurance.* Homewood, Ill,: Richard D. Irwin, Inc.

Sundheim, F. (1983). *How to Insure a Business.* Santa Barbara, Calif: Venture Publications.

Ten Tips for Buying Insurance. *Community Risk Management & Insurance.* 4 (1), Jan., 1995.

van der Smissen, B. (1990). *Legal Liability and Risk Management for Public and Private Entities.* Cincinnati: Anderson Publishing Co.

Wilkinson, D.G., Editor, (1988). *The Event Planning Process.* Levine, M.A., Kirke, G., Zitterman, D.B., and Kert, E. Insurance. Willowdale, Ontario, Can.: The Event Management & Marketing Institute.

3.00 • CONTRACT LAW

——— 3.10 ———

Contract Essentials

T. Jesse Wilde
Huckvale & Company Law Offices

Negotiated contracts are a focal point of the day-to-day operations of any business, including sport organizations. It, therefore, becomes fundamental that the sport manager be well versed in contract law principles when, for example, negotiating a player or coaching contract, hammering out a television or sponsorship deal, scheduling a contest, making an equipment purchase, leasing a facility, negotiating a licensing agreement, or limiting liability through insurance coverage.

Encouraging a sport manager's familiarity with contract law principles is not to displace the need for competent legal counsel. Often the negotiation of sport-related contracts is done by or in concert with legal counsel. Sport managers are encouraged to seek legal assistance, particularly from an attorney with a familiarity with sports-related issues. For the sport manager, hopefully this chapter, and the other related chapters that follow, will be instructive of principles and issues relevant to sport-related contracts, and thereby prevent difficulties before they arise. While an exhaustive discussion of contract law principles is well beyond the scope of this brief chapter, the following review will outline contract law concepts particularly relevant to the administration of sport organizations. The chapter will also serve as an introduction to ensuing chapters in which specific sport-related contract law topics are discussed in greater detail.

Fundamental Concepts

Except for a few American jurisdictions where contract law has been codified, the law of contracts is based in common law, embodied in court decisions. As such, contract law has evolved through time as courts have considered the essentials of an offer, or the nature of acceptance, or when agreements might be unenforceable, void or voidable, or what remedies might be available to the victim of a contractual breach.

For guidance and clarity, the American Law Institute published a code-like document in 1932 called the *Restatement of Contracts*. Although not having the force of law, the *Restatement*, as revised in the 1979 *Second Restatement*, is a highly persuasive summary of this country's common law of contract.

Even though basic contract law is governed by common law principles, many legislative enactments impact requirements for certain types of contracts, such as insurance policies, employment contracts, labor agreements, and commercial contracts. For example, the Uniform Commercial Code (UCC), enacted by all states except Louisiana, governs commercial transactions. Most of the provisions of the UCC do not affect basic contract law. Those that do are primarily contained in Article 2, which deals with the sale of goods, and, for a sport manager, would affect such contracts as the sale of sporting equipment or game tickets (Wong, 1994).

Formation of a Contract

All contracts begin with a promise, but not all promises become contracts. Although there may be a moral obligation to keep all promises seriously made (see Chapter 1.30), it does not follow that there will be any legal obligation. Contract law is concerned with legally binding promises. The most quoted definition of a "contract" is that found in section 1 of both the first and second *Restatement of Contracts*: "a promise, or set of promises, for breach of which the law gives a remedy, or the performance of which the law in some way recognizes as a duty." When does a promise become legally binding? Fundamentally, not until an offer to exchange consideration has been made by one party and accepted by the other party to whom the offer was made, where it appears that the parties intend to be bound by their bargain.

The Offer. An offer is a conditional promise made by one party, the offeror, to another party, the offeree. It is essentially a promise to do or refrain from doing some specified thing in the future (Calamari, 1987). Most offers contain a pair of promises, a conditional promise made by one party that is premised on the second party's promise in return. This exchange of promises is characterized as a **bilateral contract**, a contract consisting of the two promises and both parties are bound to perform (Wong, 1994). A characteristic of bilateral contracts is that each party will be both a promisor and a promisee, since each has an obligation to perform for the other and each has a right to performance by the other. For example, A promises to pay B $50,000 if B promises to coach A's basketball team for the upcoming year; or A promises to pay B $100,000 if B promises to provide A with exclusive title sponsorship rights to an upcoming event.

Some offers do not involve an exchange of promises, rather they involve a promise by the offeror in exchange for an act by the offeree. These offers which require acceptance by performance of an act are called **unilateral contracts**. Once the offeree has performed the act, he is not obligated to do anything more. All obligation under the contract then rests with the offeror to perform his half of the bargain. For example, A promises a $1000 reward to any fan returning a homerun baseball. Fan B returns the ball, then A is bound to pay. Or, A promises to pay $100,000 to a lucky fan if he makes a half court shot. The lucky fan sinks the half court shot, then A is bound to pay.

An offer may no longer be accepted by the offeree in circumstances where the offer has either lapsed or has been revoked by the offeror. An offer may lapse where the offeree fails to accept within a time specified in the offer, fails to accepts within a reasonable time if the offer has not specified any time limit, or when either of the parties dies or loses mental capacity prior to acceptance. An offeror may revoke or withdraw his offer at any time before acceptance, unless he by a separate contract has agreed to keep the offer open for acceptance for a specified period of time. Such an agreement to keep an offer open exclusively for another party for a specified period of time is called an option contract (Corbin, 1964).

Acceptance. Acceptance must be made in some positive form, whether in words or by conduct, and can only be made by the party to whom the offer was made. Under common law, acceptance must mirror the offer as to the offer's essential terms, which normally include the subject matter, the time and place for performance, and the price to be paid. In normal business negotiations parties make a number of offers and counter-offers, but until a specific offer by one side is accepted without qualification by the other, under common law there will be no contract and the parties will have no legal obligation to one another. When an offer is put forward and the offeree, though interested, chooses to vary some of its features, he has not accepted, rather he has rejected the offer and made a counter-offer of his own. The making of a counter-offer amounts to a rejection of the original offer and brings it to an end. Further, the original offer does not revive if the counter-offer is in turn also rejected. The offeree can only accept the original offer if the offeror agrees to renew it. In sale of goods contracts, however, the UCC has created an exception such that an acceptance differing from the offer will be enforceable as long as the acceptance is not expressly conditioned on the offeror's accepting the new terms (Wong, 1994).

Consideration. Fundamental to contract law is the concept of a bargain, that one party must pay a price, that is make some contribution, or suffer legal detriment, for the promise he obtains from the other party. In a unilateral contract, the price paid for the promise of the offeror is the act done by the acceptor. In a bilateral contract, the price paid by each of the parties for the promise of the other is his own promise. This price is called consideration.

To create an enforceable contract, there must be a mutual exchange of consideration by the parties, such that one party agrees to give up or do something in return for the other's doing the same. Agreements which do not contain a mutual exchange of value are void for lack of consideration. For example, a promise to make a gift or a promise to perform service without remuneration are nothing but gratuitous promises, for which the promisee, in general terms, has, in most circumstances, no legal recourse if the gift remains ungiven or the services unperformed. Exceptions to this rule—including where a gratuitous promise is made under seal, or where a gratuitous promise is relied upon by the promisee—may be enforced under the doctrine of **promissory estoppel**. Under this doctrine a promisee may enforce a promise, even though without consideration, if it was reasonably intended that the promise should be relied upon and in fact was relied upon to the promisee's detriment, and if a failure to enforce the promise would amount to sanctioning the perpetration of a fraud or result in injustice to the promisee (Farnsworth, 1990). For example, during the course of recruiting high school prospect A, coach B offers A an athletic scholarship for the upcoming academic year, and orally reassures A that an athletic scholarship with B's institution is a four year commitment. Relying on this promise or inducement of a four year commitment, A accepts B's scholarship offer. Even though the scholarship contract offered to A is, by its terms, a one year contract, A may be successful in binding B's institution to the four year scholarship promise, under the doctrine of promissory estoppel.

Intention to Create Legal Relations. Even when an apparently valid offer has been accepted and consideration is present, there may be no contract in law. An intention on the part of both sides to create a legally enforceable agreement must also be present. Of course, parties do not often direct their minds to the legal effects of their bargains. It is well settled that parties need not manifest an intent to be bound or consciously consider the legal consequences that might arise upon a breach; however, if, from the statements or conduct of the parties or the surrounding circumstances, it appears that the parties do not intend to be bound or do not intend legal consequences, then there is no contract (Calamari, 1987). The law presumes that the necessary intention is present in almost all instances where an agreement is seriously made. This presumption is especially strong in dealings between strangers, and in commerce generally. On the other hand, it is easier to rebut this presumption in arrangements between friends or members of a family, where it is often obvious that there was no intention to create legal relations.

Void, Voidable and Unenforceable Contracts

A contract is void (a contradiction in terms really), when it produces no legal obligation upon the part of a promisor. For example, as noted above, agreements which do not contain a mutual exchange of value are void for lack of consideration. It would be more exact to say that no contract has been created (Calamari, 1987).

A contract is voidable if one or more of the parties has the power to elect to avoid the legal relations created by the contract or by ratification to extinguish the power of avoidance (Calamari, 1987). As will be examined below, this power to avoid or ratify is sometimes given to an infant contracting party and to persons who have been induced to enter contracts by fraud, mistake, or duress.

Unenforceable contracts are those which have some legal consequences but which may not be enforced in an action in the face of certain defenses such as the Statute of Frauds, discussed below, and the statute of limitations (Calamari, 1987). Contracts which are tainted by illegality but are neither wholly void nor voidable may also be classified as unenforceable (Restatement, Second, Contracts 8).

Capacity.   Under common law, certain classes of individuals lack the ability, competence, or capacity in certain respects to enter into contracts which will be binding upon them. Individuals who have reached the age of majority (the age of 18 in most states) and are mentally competent have the capacity to enter into a contract. Conversely, a contract entered into by a minor (one who has not reached the age of majority) or by someone who is mentally incompetent, is generally considered voidable (Wong, 1994). For minors, the general rule is that the contract of a minor is unenforceable against him, but enforceable by him against the other side. As a result, a minor may often disregard his promises with impunity, as, for example, when a minor signs a waiver agreeing to relinquish the right to pursue legal action against the provider of the waiver in the event that negligence of the provider results in his injury. In most circumstances, the waiver will be ineffective to shield the provider from suit by the minor. One recognized exception to this general rule is when the subject matter of the contract involves necessaries of life, which have been held by courts to include food, clothing, lodging, medical attention, legal advice, and transportation.

The law also protects individuals who lack the capacity to contract by virtue of some mental defect, or who lose capacity through the consumption of alcohol or drugs, in the same way as a minor. The law makes such contracts, except for necessaries, voidable at the individual's option but enforceable by him or her against the other contracting party.

Unlike natural persons, business organizations, such as corporations and labor unions, have no physical existence, and derive their capacity to contract through the statutes creating or empowering them. Since these organizations are not natural persons, they must enter into contracts through authorized agents. An athletic director, for example, may be the authorized agent to enter into scheduling contracts, television contracts, lease agreements, and so forth, on behalf of his institution. Or the general manager of a professional sports franchise may be the authorized agent to negotiate player contracts with athletes.

Misrepresentation, Undue Influence, and Duress.   Misrepresentation is a false assertion of fact which induces another party to enter into a contract. If the assertion was made with knowledge of its falsity, or without an honest belief in its truth, the misrepresentation is fraudulent or intentional. If, on the other hand, the assertion was made in the belief that it was true, the misrepresentation is innocent or unintentional (Farnsworth, 1990). In general terms, if the misrepresentation is innocent, the contract is considered voidable, and the party who relied on the misrepresentation, upon learning the true facts, may repudiate or rescind the contract and free himself from his obligations under it, so long as he renounces the agreement promptly upon learning of the true facts. If he allows an unreasonable length of time to elapse without repudiating, or takes further benefits under the contract, he will lose his right to repudiate. He may also be entitled to recover money or property in the hands of the other party. If the misrepresentation is fraudulent, the contract is also considered voidable at the option of the victim, and the injured party has an additional tort action for fraud, upon the tort known as deceit. Money damages for deceit may often be a valuable supplement to simply rescinding or repudiating the contract (Farnsworth, 1990).

Undue influence is a concept originated as a ground for setting aside transactions that have been imposed by a dominant party upon a subservient party, where the domination of one party over the mind of the other party is such as to unfairly persuade or cause that party to enter into a contractual relationship that he would not otherwise have entered into absent the domination (Calamari, 1987).). A contract formed as the result of undue influence is voidable at the option of the victim. This claim normally arises where the parties to the contract stand in a special relationship to each other, such as where one party is in a dominant position in relation to the other, or where one party has a special skill or knowledge causing the other to place his confidence and trust in him. Examples of such a relationship might include a lawyer and client, a team doctor and an athlete, or possibly a coach and an athlete.

Duress is any wrongful act or threat which coerces a party to enter into a contract. The effect of duress is similar to that of undue influence in that the contract is voidable at the option of the victim (Farnsworth, 1990). This principle was originally available to provide relief in circumstances of fear of loss of life or limb, but now includes economic pressure where such overcomes the free will of a party and causes him to enter into a contract that he would not have absent the pressure. For example, an athlete agreeing to an unconstitutional drug test as a prerequisite to receiving scholarship assistance may be able to set aside such an agreement on the basis that the economic pressure of being unable to attend college without the scholarship robbed him of his free will and motivated his decision to submit to the drug test.

Mistake. Perhaps the most difficult task in the law of contract is to state clearly the circumstances in which the courts will afford a remedy for mistake. Historically, while relief was available for certain kinds of mutual mistake, it was unavailable for unilateral mistake unless the other party knew or had reason to know the mistake. This summary is no longer entirely accurate, causing many to argue that the distinction between mutual and unilateral mistake should be dropped, yet the distinction in law remains (Calamari, 1987).

A **mutual mistake** arises when both parties share a common, mistaken assumption about a vital existing fact upon which they based their bargain. In such circumstances, the transaction may be avoided if, because of the mistake, a quite different exchange of values occurs from the exchanges of values originally contemplated (Farnsworth, 1990). The same rule holds true if the parties are operating under differing mistakes about the same vital fact. If, for example, unbeknownst to the parties, the subject matter of the contract no longer exists, then the contract is void, or never existed. If the mistake goes to the quality of the subject matter, the contract is not void, but may be voidable. The court may set aside the contract in whole or in part as a means of reaching a fair and equitable result.

A **unilateral mistake** arises when only one party is mistaken about a fact vital to the bargain. Until recently, the commonly stated rule has been that avoidance is not available for unilateral mistake except where the other party knows or has reason to know of the mistake. More recently avoidance is allowed if two conditions concur: 1) enforcement of the contract against the mistaken party would be oppressive, or, at least, result in an unconscionably unequal exchange of values, and 2) rescission would impose no substantial hardship on the other (Calamari, 1987).

Illegality. As a general rule, if the formation or contemplated performance of a contract is criminal, tortious, or otherwise opposed to public policy, the contract will be unenforceable (Restatement, Contracts 512; Restatement, Second, Contracts 178). Two basic policies underlie this principle. First, a refusal to enforce illegal bargains will deter the making of such contracts in the future. Second, while it may not discourage the making of such contracts, it keeps the courts respectable (Calamari, 1987). Examples of contracts that may be declared illegal include: gambling and bribery, agreements contemplating the violation of statutory laws such as criminal, antitrust, or tax laws, or contracts contemplating the commission of torts such as battery, defamation, fraud or incitement to break an existing contract.

Statute of Frauds. Under common law, certain types of contracts are unenforceable unless they are in writing. The rule dates to the passage of the Statute of Frauds in 1677 by the English parliament, designed to promote certainty with specific types of contracts. The rules created by the application of the Statute of Frauds have often been criticized as promoting more frauds than they prevent, since parties to otherwise valid oral contracts have often been able to avoid their obligations solely because these contracts have been held to come within the scope of the Statute. The Statute identifies an extensive list of contracts which must be in writing to be enforceable. Those most relevant to sport managers include: contracts involving the sale, mortgage, or lease of an interest in land (e.g., facility lease agreements, land purchases) and contracts that will not be performed within one year from the date of their making (e.g., scheduling contracts for contests to be performed beyond one year, long term coaching contracts) (Wong, 1994). Under section 2-201 of the Uniform Commercial Code, a contract for the sale of goods for the price of $500 or more is also unenforceable if not in writing (e.g., equipment purchases, game tickets) (see U.C.C. 2-201).

To satisfy the writing requirement under the Statute of Frauds, the note or memorandum of the contract must contain all the essential terms of the contract and be signed by the party to be charged, or, in other words, the defendant in a suit brought upon the contract. It should be emphasized here, as a matter of good business practice, all contracts, and not simply those within the Statute of Frauds, should be reduced to writing. The effective administrator will anticipate future problems with contractual agreements. The substance of negotiations and the final agreement should all be documented to provide for both evidence and clarity should contractual disputes arise. The prudent administrator will also ensure that the final signed agreement is in fact an accurate reflection of the negotiated deal. Under common law, the final agreement made by the parties supersedes tentative terms discussed in earlier negotiations. When the parties reduce their agreement to writing, as they always should, the written agreement will stand as the final embodiment of their bargain and may not, as a general rule, be contradicted by other evidence. This principle, known as the **parol evidence rule**, provides that a term, previously agreed upon between the parties but not included in the final written contract, cannot later be added to the contract, unless the contract is ambiguous, in which case evidence of preliminary agreements, writings and oral understandings may be used to explain the ambiguity (Corbin, 1964).

Remedies for Contractual Breach

When a contract is broken, depending on the type of breach committed and the subject matter of the contract, the aggrieved party may have several remedies including an action for damages and the equitable remedy of specific performance.

Damages. The purpose of an award of damages is to place the aggrieved party in the same economic position as if the contract had been performed. Damages must be a reasonably foreseeable consequence of the breach, and generally will not be awarded to compensate an aggrieved party for some unusual or unexpected consequence. In determining the economic harm as a consequence of a breach, and thus the damages to be awarded to an aggrieved party, courts consider three legally protected economic interests: an expectation interest, a reliance interest, and a restitution interest. An expectation interest is the benefit that was bargained, and the remedy is to put the aggrieved party in a position equal to his or her economic position had the contract been performed. A reliance interest is the loss suffered by relying on the contract and taking actions consistent with the expectation that other party will abide by it. The remedy is reimbursement that restores the aggrieved party to his or her economic position before the contract was made. A restitution interest is that which restores to the aggrieved party any benefit he or she conferred on the other party (Wong, 1994).

An aggrieved party's ability to recover damages as a consequence of a breach is limited by his **duty to mitigate**. A party who has been wronged by a breach of contract may not unreasonably sit idly by and allow damages to accumulate. The damages such a party will be able to recover at law will not include what loss he might reasonably have avoided (Calamari, 1987).

In some circumstances, the damages associated with a breach may be specifically contemplated in the contract. While penalty clauses designed to deter a party from breaching his contract have been held unenforceable, liquidated damage clauses are permitted under certain conditions to determine in advance what damages will be assessed in the event of a breach. Distinguishing between these clauses can be difficult; however, courts have listed three criteria by which a valid liquidated damages clause may be distinguished from a penalty: first, the parties must intend to provide for damages rather than for a penalty; second, the injury caused by the breach must be uncertain or difficult to quantify; and third, the sum stipulated must be a reasonable pre-estimate of the probable loss (Farnsworth, 1990). Such liquidated damage clauses, for example, have been used effectively in coaching contracts to assist in quantifying the damages occasioned to a university as a result of a coach failing to perform the full term of his contract.

Specific Performance.   Specific performance is a discretionary, equitable remedy, developed to provide relief when an action for damages is inadequate. Such a remedy takes the form of a decree ordering a party to carry out his contractual duties. Circumstances in which a claim for specific performance may be granted include the breach of a contract to convey an interest in land or a contract for the sale of goods where the goods are unique or in limited supply (e.g., rare trading cards or other memorabilia). By contrast, courts will not generally require a contract for personal services to be specifically performed (e.g., a player holding out and refusing to perform his contract). The granting of such relief would be tantamount to enforcing involuntary servitude (Wong, 1994). Similarly, requiring the specific performance of an agreement by a person to refrain from exercising his trade or calling, standing alone, is viewed as being illegal and contrary to public policy, since it is contrary to the interests of a free market society. However, if a covenant not to compete forms part of a legitimate transaction, such as a coach agreeing not to coach elsewhere for the duration of his current contract, then courts have specifically enforced such clauses. In *New England Patriots Football Club, Inc. v. University of Colorado*, (1st Cir. 1979), for example, the Patriots successfully enforced a clause in their head coach's contract requiring him to refrain from contracting elsewhere for his coaching services during the term of his employment with the Patriots. The First Circuit upheld an injunction enjoining the University of Colorado from employing the Patriot's head coach while he was under contract with the NFL club.

Recent Developments

This *Contract Essentials* chapter is followed by a series of chapters devoted to examining sport-specific applications of contract law principles outlined above. While these ensuing chapters will also highlight recent sport-related contract law litigation, a few issues or developments are summarized below which may not directly relate to any of the sport-specific contract law chapter topics in this text.

Failure to Provide Promised Educational Opportunity.   In *Ross v. Creighton University*, (7th Cir. 1992), the court considered claims brought by Kevin Ross, a student-athlete, in tort and breach of contract against the university. The claims had been dismissed on summary judgment by the U.S. District Court for the Northern District of Illinois. Ross claimed that the university had breached an alleged duty owed to him to provide him a meaningful educational opportunity, and had breached an alleged contract to provide him with an opportunity to obtain a meaningful college education and degree. The Seventh Circuit affirmed the dismissal of the tort claims for various public policy reasons; however, did allow Ross to proceed on the contract claim, concluding that the breach of contract claims were sufficiently specific to allow a court to determine on remand whether Creighton had provided any real access to its academic curriculum to enable Ross to participate in the academic life of the university in a meaningful way. For further discussion, see Rafferty, Daniel P., Technical Foul! Ross v. Creighton University Allows Courts to Penalize Universities Which do not Perform Specific Promises Made to Student-Athletes, 38 *South Dakota Law Review* 173-188 (1993).

Enforcement of Covenant Not to Compete.   In *Prince William Professional Baseball Club v. Boulton*, (D.Del. 1995), the purchaser of an interest in a baseball team brought action against the seller, alleging the breach of a noncompetition clause in the sale agreement. On the purchaser's motion for partial summary judgment, the court held that the seller's retention of the team's general manager in a consulting capacity to the seller's new team within the one-year period proscribed by the noncompetition clause, constituted a breach and precluded the seller's recovery of the remaining portion of the purchase price.

Agent Sues Player for Breach of Contract.   In *Total Economic Athletic Management of America, Inc. v. Pickens*, (Mo. App. W.D. 1995) a sports agent firm brought a successful suit for anticipatory breach of contract against a professional football player following the player's retention of another agent. The agent brought an appeal on a quantum of damages issue, contending that the damage award of $20,000 did not provide adequate compensation for the agent's loss occasioned by the player's breach. The Missouri Court of Appeals dismissed the appeal, finding that the award was within the range of the evidence, and that the damage claim based on amounts the player would earn as a professional football player after trial were too speculative and could not be established with reasonable certainty.

Student Athletes Fail in Attempt to Reinstate Wrestling Program. In *Cooper v. Peterson*, (N.Y. Sup. Ct. 1995) members of the varsity wrestling team at St. Lawrence University sought a temporary injunction prohibiting the university from eliminating their sport prior to the graduation of their class. The plaintiffs contended that by recruiting them to attend St. Lawrence, the university entered into a four year contract to support a wrestling program. The court held that the plaintiff's contract claim was barred by the Statute of Frauds, since the alleged unwritten contract could not be performed within one year. Further, the Plaintiff's promissory estoppel claim, that they had been promised a four year program and came to St. Lawrence in reliance on that promise, was unsupported by the evidence.

References

A. Cases

Cooper v. Peterson, 626 N.Y.S.2d 432 (Sup. Ct. 1995).

New England Patriots Football Club, Inc. v. University of Colorado, 592 F.2d 1196 (1st Cir. 1979).

Prince William Professional Baseball Club v. Boulton, 882 F. Supp. 1446 (D.Del. 1995).

Ross v. Creighton University, 957 F.2d 410 (7th Cir. 1992).

Total Economic Athletic Management of America, Inc. v. Pickens, 898 S.W.2d 98 (Mo. App. W.D. 1995).

B. Publications

Calamari, John D. and Perillo, Joseph M. (1987). *The Law of Contracts*, (3d ed.).

Corbin, A.L. (1964). *Corbin on Contracts*.

Farnsworth, E. Allan. (1990). *Farnsworth on Contracts*.

Rafferty, Daniel P., Technical Foul! Ross v. Creighton University Allows Courts to Penalize Universities Which do not Perform Specific Promises Made to Student-Athletes, 38 *South Dakota Law Review* 173-188 (1993).

Ross v. Creighton University Allows Courts to Penalize Universities Which do not Perform Specific Promises Made to Student-Athletes. 38 *South Dakota Law Review* 173-188.

Wong, Glenn M. (1994). *Essentials of Amateur Sports Law*, (2d ed.).

C. Other

Uniform Commercial Code (1987).

Restatement of Contracts (1932).

Restatement (Second) of Contracts (1981).

3.21

Coaching Contracts

Robert P. Fleischman
East Stroudsburg University

A coaching contract, on its most basic level, is an agreement between an individual coach and either a professional organization, a university, or a high school in which the coach agrees to coach a particular team for a specified duration in return for compensation. However, in today's complex and multi-faceted sport marketplace, coaching contracts must be intricately drafted to include each party's rights and obligations. Coaching contracts, like other personal service contracts, can be based on written agreements, verbal agreements, letter agreements, or other written memoranda. The past practices of the parties can also be used in determining the terms and conditions of these contracts when the contracts fail to adequately identify certain conditions. Relative to other forms of coaching contracts, the written agreement is the most effective means used to define the rights and obligations of the parties. A written agreement better enables the parties to eliminate ambiguities within the agreement and provides each party with a clear understanding of its respective responsibilities. This becomes particularly important in determining whether, in fact, a breach has occurred and what restitution may be available.

Although coaching contracts are entered into every day on all levels of sport, many observers feel that these contracts are often broken as quickly as they are made, by one party or the other, for many different reasons (Graves, 1986). Therefore, sport managers must pay particular attention to the terms when drafting these contracts. This is especially true in situations involving major college and professional team coaches' contracts. The terms of these agreements are often determined by state law, thus the drafters of coaching contracts must be well versed in the particular law of the state in which they are operating. This is particularly true with respect to contract clauses involving restrictive covenants, workmen's compensation laws, termination rights and obligations, and arbitration proceedings. A well-written coaching contract uses clear and unambiguous language which adequately serves to define the rights and obligations of the parties and to protect all parties—that is, team, institution, and coach—from liability in the event a claim is made for breach of contract.

■ ■ ■ ■

Representative Case

RODGERS v. GEORGIA TECH ATHLETIC ASSOCIATION
Court of Appeals of Georgia
166 Ga. App. 156; 303 S.E.2d 467
March 16, 1983, Decided

OPINION:

Franklin C. "Pepper" Rodgers brought this breach of contract action against the Georgia Tech Athletic Association to recover the value of certain perquisites which had been made available to him as the head coach of football at the Georgia Institute of Technology. Both parties moved for summary judgment, Rodgers' motion encompassing only the issue of liability under his contract of employment with the Association. The trial court granted the Association's motion and denied Rodgers' motion. The issue presented for resolution by this appeal is whether Rodgers is entitled to recover the value of certain perquisites or "fringe benefits" of his position as head coach of football under the terms of his contract of employment with the Association.

Rodgers was removed from his coaching position by vote of the Association's Board of Trustees on December 18, 1979, notwithstanding a written contract of employment through December 31, 1981. In addition to an annual salary, the contract provided that Rodgers, as an employee of the Association, would be entitled "to various insurance and pension benefits and perquisites" as he became eligible therefor. Rodgers makes no claim for base salary, health insurance and pension plan benefits, all of which were provided voluntarily by the Association through December 31, 1981, the expiration date of the contract. Rather, his claim is solely for the value of the aforesaid "perquisites," to which he claims entitlement under this employment contract.

Rodgers lists some 29 separate items as such perquisites. In support of his motion for summary judgment, Rodgers categorized these items into two groups: A. Items provided directly to him by the Association but discontinued when Rodgers was relieved of his duties, and B. Items provided by sources other than the Association by virtue of his position as head coach of football. These items are listed in the Appendix to this opinion.

The subject contract was in the form of a letter from the Association dated April 20, 1977 offering Rodgers the position of head coach of football for three years at an annual salary plus certain benefits and perquisites. This contract provided that Rodgers could be terminated for illness or other incapacity continuing for three months, death, or "any conduct or activity involving moral turpitude or which in the opinion of [the Board of Trustees] would constitute an embarrassment to the school." Rodgers accepted this contract on April 25, 1977. This contract was extended until January 1, 1982 by a subsequent letter agreement between the parties. At its December 18, 1979 meeting, the Association's Board of Trustees determined that a change should be made in the position of head coach of football.

• • •

2. Rodgers contends that he was terminated or fired from his employment by the Association. However, the evidence of record supports the Association's view that Rodgers was merely relieved of his duties as the head coach of football yet remained an employee of the Association, albeit without any function or duties, for the duration of his contract. In either event, this disassociation of Rodgers from his position and duties was not "for cause" pursuant to the terms of the contract. Therefore, the Association was obligated to pay Rodgers that part of the amount set forth in the contract "which he himself was entitled to receive as compensation for his services." Southern Cotton Oil Co. v. Yarborough, 26 Ga. App. 766, 770 (107 SE 366) (1921); see also Dinnan v. Totis, 159 Ga. App. 352 (1) (283 SE2d 321) (1981).

In addition to a salary, health insurance and pension benefits, the contract provided that Rodgers, as an employee of the Association, was entitled to "perquisites" as he became eligible therefor. The term "perquisites" is defined as "moluments or incidental profits attaching to an office or official position, beyond the salary or regular fees." Black's Law Dictionary 1299 (4th ed. 1968). The term is also defined as "a privilege, gain, or profit incidental to an employment in addition to regular salary or wages; esp: one expected or promised [e.g.,] the [perquisites] of the college president include a home and car. . . ." Webster's Third New International Dictionary 1685 (1981). Thus, Rodgers was entitled to the perquisites (or their value) for which he was eligible during the duration of his contract. The problem presented here for resolution is to determine whether any of the items listed in the Appendix were indeed perquisites to which Rodgers was entitled pursuant to his contract.

First, we must determine the intention of the parties as to the scope of the perquisites to which Rodgers was entitled under the contract. See Code Ann. @ 20-702 (now OCGA @ 13-2-3). The pertinent language of the contract provides: "You, as Head Coach of Football, will devote your time, attention, skill, and efforts to the performance of your duties as Head Coach under the policies established by the Athletic Board and the Athletic Director, and you will receive compensation at annual rate of $35,175.00 payable in equal monthly installments. In addition, as an employee of the Association, you will be entitled to various . . . perquisites as you become eligible therefor." The Association contends that the language "as an employee of the Association" limited Rodgers' eligibility for perquisites to those items common to all Association employees. Rodgers argues that he was not only entitled to those perquisites common to all Association employees, but that he was also entitled to additional perquisites for which he became eligible as the head coach of football. Since the contract is susceptible to either construction, it is ambiguous. This ambiguity may be resolved by applying the appropriate rules of construction.

"If a contract is so framed as to be susceptible of two constructions, that interpretation which is least favorable to the author . . . should generally be accepted. [Cits.] 'When it is possible to do so without contravening any rule of law, the courts will construe a contract as binding on both the parties, where, from the language of the contract, the conduct of the parties, and all the attendant circumstances, it appears that the intention of the parties was that both should be bound, and substantial justice requires that the contract be given effect. [Cits.]'" Bridges v. Home Guano Co., 33 Ga. App. 305, 309 (125 SE 872) (1924); see Clear-Vu Cable v. Town of Trion, 244 Ga. 790 (1) (262 SE2d 73) (1979); see also Asa G. Candler, Inc. v. Ga. Theatre Co., 148 Ga. 188 (5) (96 SE 226) (1918). The subject contract was drafted by the Association. Moreover, the record discloses that Rodgers, during his tenure as head coach of football, did receive perquisites in addition to those received by other Association employees. Accordingly, we conclude that the parties intended that Rodgers would receive perquisites, as he became eligible therefor, based upon his position as head coach of football and not merely as an employee of the Association.

We must next determine the nature of the items for which Rodgers seeks damages, i.e., whether the items listed in the Appendix are perquisites vel non.

• • •

(a) The Association asserts that Rodgers was not entitled to any of the items listed in Section A because they were expense account items—"tools" to enable him to more effectively execute his duties as head coach of football. Rodgers counters that those items were an integral part of the total compensation package that he received as head coach of football and constituted consideration for his contract of employment. . . . The fact that these items were not reported as taxable income by Rodgers is not conclusive as to their nature (see Mullinax v. Mullinax, 234 Ga. 553, 555 (216 SE2d 802) (1975)), nor is the fact that Rodgers reimbursed the Association for occasional "personal" expenses which it had paid. Thus, with three exceptions, we cannot say as a matter of law either that Rodgers was entitled to the items listed in Section A as perquisites of his employment, or that he was not.

The three exceptions to this finding are the services of a secretary, the services of an administrative assistant, and the cost of trips to football conventions, clinics, etc. The undisputed purpose of the services of the secretary and administrative assistant was to assist Rodgers in fulfilling his duties under the contract. Since Rodgers had been relieved of his duties as head coach of football, and, thus, had no responsibilities under the contract, he had no need for these support services.

• • •

(b) We turn our attention finally to those items in . . . the Appendix—items which Rodgers asserts were perquisites he received from sources other than the Association by virtue of his position as head coach of football at Georgia Tech. The Association argues that Rodgers' claim for recovery of these items was in the nature of a tort claim for humiliation and injury to feelings. Rodgers counters that these items were perquisites within the contemplation of the parties which constituted part of the consideration for the contract even though they were provided by sources other than the Association.

We do not construe Rodgers' claim for recovery of the items in [the Appendix] to be in the nature of a personal injury tort. "All pleadings shall be so construed as to do substantial justice." Code Ann. @ 81A-108(f) (now OCGA @ 9-11-8(f)). Also, pleadings will be construed to serve the best interests of the pleader. Riviera Equip. v. Omega Equip. Corp., 147 Ga. App. 412, 416 (249 SE2d 133) (1978). The several and ancient cases from other jurisdictions cited by the Association in support of its contention all involve situations wherein the party wrongfully removed from his employment by his employer's breach of the employment contract brought suit to recover damages for personal injury such as loss of reputation, humiliation, etc. In the case at bar Rodgers claims that the items in [the Appendix] were part of the consideration of his contract. No claim for personal injury appears. Furthermore, the State Court of Fulton County, where this case was brought, has no jurisdiction over personal injury claims. Construing Rodgers' complaint to serve his best interests, we hold that the Association's argument here is without merit. Nevertheless, we must now determine whether Rodgers may recover the items in [the Appendix] under his breach of contract theory.

"[T]he consideration of a contract need not flow directly from the promis[or] [here, the Association], but may be the promise or undertaking of one or more third persons." Bing v. Bank of Kingston, 5 Ga. App. 578, 580 (63 SE 652) (1908). "Damages growing out of a breach of contract, in order to form the basis of a recovery, must be such as can be traced solely to the breach, must be capable of exact computation, must have arisen naturally and according to the usual course of things from such breach, and must be such as the parties contemplated as a probable result of the breach." Sanford-Brown Co. v. Patent Scaffolding Co., 199 Ga. 41 (33 SE2d 422) (1945). "As a general rule, a party is entitled to recover profits that would have resulted from a breach of a contract into which he has entered, where the breach is the result of the other party's fault. And while a breach of the original contract will not ordinarily entitle a plaintiff to recover as damages the profits of collateral enterprises or subcontracts, yet where the knowledge of the subcontract [or collateral enterprise] is within the contemplation of the parties when the original contract is made, and is known to have been made with reference thereto, anticipated profits shown to be certain, fixed in amount, and the direct fruit of the contract, are recoverable. Profits are excluded only when there are no criteria, definite and certain, upon which an adjudication can be based. They then become speculative and imaginary." Carolina Portland Cement Co. v. Columbia Improvement Co., 3 Ga. App. 483 (2) (60 SE 279) (1908).

We will apply the foregoing legal principles to the facts of record. Can Rodgers' loss of the items in [the Appendix] be traced solely to the Association's breach of the contract? Rodgers testified that he received these perquisites as a result of his being head coach of football at Georgia Tech. The record discloses, however, that the items relating to housing and the cost of premiums on a life insurance policy were discontinued several years prior to the Association's breach of contract and were, in fact, not related to the breach. Thus, these items were properly excluded by the trial court. The remaining items were discontinued as the direct result of Rodgers being relieved of his duties as head coach of football.

Are the remaining items in [the Appendix] capable of exact computation? A "gift" is defined as "voluntary transfer of personal property without consideration." Black's Law Dictionary 817 (4th ed. 1968). A gift, then, being a voluntary transaction and without consideration, can not form an enforceable part of the consideration of a contract. Although Rodgers may have received gifts of money and personalty during his tenure as head coach of football, such voluntary contributions to his financial well-being are totally incapable of exact computation, for a gift made in one year is no assurance of a similar gift in the next. In fact, Rodgers concedes that he did not receive these gifts each year. Thus, the item which listed various financial gifts was properly excluded from recovery. The items now remaining are sufficiently capable of computation. See generally Hoffman v. Louis L. Battey Post etc. Am. Legion, 74 Ga. App. 403, 410-1 (39 SE2d 889) (1946).

Did these remaining items arise naturally and according to the usual course of things, and were they such as the parties contemplated as a probable result of a breach? There is no evidence of record showing that the Association had any knowledge of Rodgers' free lodging at certain Holiday Inns or of his membership in Terminus International Tennis Club. Thus, the loss of these items could not be such as was contemplated as a probable result of a breach of the contract. The evidence was in dispute as to the remaining items—profits from his television and radio shows and from his summer football camp plus the loss of use of a new automobile and tickets to professional sporting events—i.e., whether such items were contemplated by the parties at the time the contract was executed as perquisites or fringe benefits to which Rodgers would be entitled as the result of his position as head coach of football at Georgia Tech. These items are of the type commonly provided to head coaches at major colleges and universities. There was some evidence that the Association knew that Rodgers would receive (and, in fact, did receive) these benefits as the result of his head coaching position and that his removal from that position would result in the loss of these benefits. In fact, some members of the Association assisted Rodgers in obtaining many of these items. Also, there was at least some evidence by which the amount of these items could be fixed. Therefore, summary judgment in favor of the Association as to these items was inappropriate. See Glennville Hatchery, Inc. v. Thompson, 164 Ga. App. 819 (3) (298 SE2d 512) (1982). For these same reasons, summary judgment in favor of Rodgers was properly denied.

In summary, a question of fact remains as to whether Rodgers is entitled to recover those items listed in . . . the Appendix not excluded in this opinion . . . any recovery being subject to proof of the amount of his damages as set forth in this opinion. All items which have been excluded are denoted by asterisks in the Appendix.

Judgment affirmed in part; reversed in part.

Appendix

A. Benefits and Perquisites Received by Rodgers Directly from the Georgia Tech Athletic Association.

1. gas, oil, maintenance, repairs, other automobile expenses;
2. automobile liability and collision insurance;
3. general expense money;
4. meals available at the Georgia Tech training table;
5. eight season tickets to Georgia Tech home football games during fall of 1980 and 1981;
6. two reserved booths, consisting of approximately 40 seats at Georgia Tech home football games during fall of 1980 and 1981;
7. six season tickets to Georgia Tech home basketball games for 1980 and 1981;
8. four season tickets to Atlanta Falcon home football games for 1980 and 1981;
9. four game tickets to each out-of-town Georgia Tech football game during fall of 1980 and 1981;
10. pocket money at each home football game during fall of 1980 and 1981;
11. pocket money at each out-of-town Georgia Tech football game during fall of 1980 and 1981;
12. parking privileges at all Georgia Tech home sporting events;
*13. the services of a secretary;
*14. the services of an administrative assistant;
15. the cost of admission to Georgia Tech home baseball games during spring of 1980 and 1981;
*16. the cost of trips to football coaches' conventions, clinics, and meetings and to observe football practice sessions of professional and college football teams;
17. initiation fee, dues, monthly bills, and cost of membership at the Capital City Club;
18. initiation fee, dues, monthly bills, and cost of membership at the Cherokee Country Club;
19. initiation fee and dues at the East Lake Country Club.

B. Benefits and Perquisites Received by Rodgers from Sources Other Than the Georgia Tech Athletic Association by Virtue of Being Head Coach of Football.

1. profits from Rodgers' television football show, "The Pepper Rodgers Show," on Station WSB-TV in Atlanta for the fall of 1980 and 1981;
2. profits from Rodgers' radio football show on Station WGST in Atlanta for the fall of 1980 and 1981;
3. use of a new Cadillac automobile during 1980 and 1981;
4. profits from Rodgers' summer football camp, known as the "Pepper Rodgers Football School," for June 1980 and June 1981;
*5. financial gifts from alumni and supporters of Georgia Tech for 1980 and 1981;
*6. lodging at any of the Holiday Inns owned by Topeka Inn Management, Inc. of Topeka, Kansas, for the time period from December 18, 1979 through December 31, 1981.
*7. the cost of membership in Terminus International Tennis Club in Atlanta for 1980 and 1981;
8. individual game tickets to Hawks basketball and Braves baseball games during 1980 and 1981 seasons;
*9. housing for Rodgers and his family in Atlanta for the period from December 18, 1979 through December 31, 1981;
*10. the cost of premiums of a $400,000.00 policy on the life of Rodgers for the time period from December 18, 1979 through December 31, 1981.

■ ■ ■ ■

Fundamental Concepts

Form of Coaching Contracts

Written Contracts.   In the typical employment relationship, the primary purpose of a written agreement is to clearly specify the nature and duration of the employment, the compensation to be paid the employee, and any other relevant terms and conditions of the employment arrangement (Graves, 1986). Like other employment agreements, coaching contracts contain many of the usual clauses dealing with salary, benefits, and other matters of state law (Selvaggi, 1993). The employment relationship between a coach and team or institution, however, significantly differs from the typical working relationship that an employer has with its employees. Today's coaches are under amazing pressures to win—to win now and win often. As already noted herein, due to the uncertain nature of the coaching profession, these contracts are often terminated prematurely.

With regard to major college and professional coaching contracts, the compensation package usually extends beyond the coach's base salary to include various fringe benefits. These benefits often include pension and retirement plans, revenues from television and radio shows, and athletic summer camp opportunities. Other incidental benefits include guarantees of product endorsements or similar personal appearance opportunities and the use of free cars, free housing, life insurance, lodging, complimentary club memberships, trust funds, and complimentary athletic tickets (Graves, 1986).

The courts have held these benefits to be recoverable as damages for breach of contract where knowledge of these terms is found to be within the contemplation of the parties when the original contract is made (*Rodgers v. Georgia Tech Athletic Association*, 1983). In order to recover such damages there must be evidence of the following: 1) That the items were contemplated by the parties as fringe benefits of the coaching position at the time the contract was executed; 2) That these damages are capable of exact computation; and 3) That these damages have arisen naturally and according to the usual course of things from such breach (*Rodgers v. Georgia Tech Athletic Association*, 1979). Therefore, when drafting these contracts, sport managers must carefully distinguish between the benefits a coach receives for being in the position—and those which will be discontinued upon termination as coach.

Letter Agreements.   Due to several high profile incidents of litigation over coaching contracts beginning with the Pepper Rodgers (*Rodgers v. Georgia Tech Athletic Association*, 1983) and Chuck Fairbanks (*New England Patriots Football Club, Inc. v. University of Colorado*, 1979) cases, professional team front office personnel and university counsel have paid closer attention to how these contracts are drafted. However, many teams and institutions still appoint coaches by short-form letter agreements similar to the type that caused trouble for the Georgia Tech Athletic Association when it decided to terminate Rodgers (Stoner and Nogay, 1989). The problem with these short-form agreements is that they are often incomplete when standing alone, and therefore tend to incorporate by reference the terms and conditions of other documents—such as collective bargaining agreements, administrative rules, and state and federal regulations (*Monson v. Oregon,* 1995). These agreements, although enforceable, lack the necessary clarity in defining each party's rights.

As suggested by Stoner and Nogay (1989), when drafting coaching contracts, there is no substitute for a comprehensive, carefully drafted written agreement. The following should be included: 1) The compensation a coach receives relating to the coaching position; 2) The explicit items the parties intend to be paid as compensation; 3) A statement indicating that no terms other than those included in the contract are to be provided as compensation; and 4) The exact terms of the contract and the repercussions, including reassignment terms and restrictions on subsequent employment in the event either side prematurely terminates the contract. In addition, the sport manager must also be aware of any athletic association or league policies which may affect the contract.

Oral Contracts.   In contrast to written contracts, the courts are reluctant to enforce an oral promise to employ a coach for an indefinite period of time. Therefore, coaches without written contracts have generally been considered *at-will* employees by the courts. *At-will* employment relationships are generally terminable at any time, by either party, and with or without cause. Under these circumstances, breach of contract claims resulting from the wrongful termination of a coach are difficult to sustain. The claim of the coach was successful where the coach has made some sacrifice (e.g., relinquishing a job and spending money on relocation) that probably would not have been made absent a guarantee of employment (*Smith & Gremer v. Board of Education of Urbana School District*, 1982). Courts have also supported claims where promises made by the employer (in recruiting the employee or set forth in an employee handbook) cause the employee to rely on an employment relationship (Wong, 1994). In general, however, the existence of an oral coaching agreement is difficult to prove at trial and the courts have found these promises to be unenforceable.

Any discussion of oral coaching contracts would not be complete, however, without mentioning the role of the Statute of Frauds as a bar to recovery under a breach of contract claim. According to this doctrine, certain contracts must be in writing in order to be enforceable. In the area of personal service contracts, to satisfy the statute's requirements, contracts not capable of being completely performed within one year of contract, are unenforceable unless they are in writing. Therefore coaching contracts lasting a year or more, must be in some form of writing (e.g., written contract, letter agreement or other memoranda) to be considered valid (Wong, 1994). In summary, the most effective means by which to employ coaches is to utilize a well-written document which is clear, comprehensive, and unambiguous.

Important Elements of Coaching Contracts

Clarity of Language.   A contract utilizing clear and precise language is critical in defining each party's responsibilities under the agreement and in protecting against any unintended court interpretations of the contractual language. Because of the lack of job security in coaching, and the amount of money paid to coaches for their services, meticulously drafted employment contracts have become a necessity for both the coach and the team or institution who employs the coach (Greenburg, 1991). This is because the courts rely upon the terms of these agreements in deciding cases involving termination of coaches.

The following are drawn from coaching termination cases where the court's ruling was determined by the language in the contract:

1. A contract term is ambiguous when it is reasonably capable of being understood in more than one sense because the language or expression is not definite or due to the term having a double or multiple meaning. The courts are more likely to grant summary judgment in cases involving contract language which is clear, unambiguous, and not subject to different interpretations.
2. When a contract is ambiguous, parol evidence may be introduced to aid in its interpretation (*Lewis v. Board of Education of North Clay Community School District,* 1989).
3. If a contract is so framed as to be susceptible of two constructions, that interpretation which is least favorable to the author will generally be accepted (*Rodgers v. Georgia Tech Association*, 1983).
4. When the language of a contract is plain and unambiguous then construction of the agreement is a matter of law for the court to decide (*Whirlpool v. Dailey Constitution, Inc.*, 1993; *Babb v. Harnett County Board of Education*, 1995).

In summary, when drafting these contracts, sport managers and their legal counsel should be certain the language is clear, comprehensive, unambiguous, and concise language to avoid a situation where the agreement is capable of several interpretations.

Consideration. Consideration has been defined as a bargained-for legal detriment involving an exchange of value wherein one party agrees to give up or do something in exchange for another party doing the same (Wong, 1994). In addition to the mutual assent of the parties, it is essential to the formation of a contract that there be some form of consideration. Otherwise, the agreement could be rendered unenforceable.

Applied to coaching contracts, if a coach agrees to work for one institution or team for a set period of time and, in fact, receives compensation for his or her services, there is sufficient consideration to support the formation of a valid contract (i.e., the exchange of coaching services in return for compensation). As noted earlier, courts have held that certain perquisites or fringe benefits received by a head coach in consideration of his or her position, may be compensable as damages in the event of a breach. Therefore, when drafting coaching contracts, it is important to draft terms clearly identifying the consideration underlying the agreement. This will assist the court in computing the damages related to a breach of contract.

Termination. In addition to the damage issues associated with termination, an institution or team may also encounter procedural problems in attempting to rid itself of its coach prior to the expiration of his or her contract (Wong, 1994). In *Yukica v. Leland* (1985), when Dartmouth College attempted to fire a football coach with one year remaining on his contract, the coach challenged the decision by seeking a court order restraining the college from making the move. The broad legal question raised, but not answered, in the case was whether an employee in a personal services contract can force an employer to fulfill the terms of the contract, or whether the employee is entitled only to a financial settlement (Asher, 1986). The New Hampshire Superior Court, however, in directing Dartmouth to honor the terms of the contract, ruled that the college had violated the terms of the coach's contract by failing to comply with the termination procedures which were required.

High School Coaching Contracts

High school coaches, unlike college coaches, are generally hired for two separate jobs in the school system—that is, to teach and to coach. As a result, most enter into a separate, divisible contract for each job. As a teacher, the high school coach is eligible for tenure and other benefits which are generally provided for under collective bargaining agreements or state policies. Most states, however, do not grant tenure for coaching positions (Wong, 1994). Therefore, problems arise when a coach is dismissed or resigns from his coaching position, but continues to teach because his teaching contract is protected under the tenure provisions of the school system.

In these cases, the courts have generally held that coaching jobs are classified as "non-academic" positions which are not offered the same protection given to teaching positions under the state tenure system. Accordingly, most state courts give local school boards broad discretion to hire or terminate any coach based on the determination of whether the particular coach is the most qualified person to coach the team (*Smith and Gremer v. Board of Education of Urbana School District*, 1983). This determination generally has no effect on a coach's teaching position. The courts, however, have found exceptions to the general rule that high school coaches are hired to teach and coach under separate divisible contracts. These exceptions have been found in cases where the contracts to coach and teach were not clearly separate and divisible (Wong, 1994). When drafting these agreements, it is important to define the rights and duties of the high school coach in his respective capacities as teacher and as coach. If it is the intention of the parties to distinguish between these two jobs, then the contracts must be drawn to clearly reflect this intention. Thus, in the event a coach is either terminated or resigns from his coaching position, the issue regarding tenure and job security in the teaching position should be made clear by reading the contract.

Recent Developments

Due Process Protection Rights

In a 1988 case, the United States Supreme Court held that when the University of Nevada at Las Vegas imposed disciplinary sanctions against its basketball coach, Jerry Tarkanian, under orders from the NCAA, the action did not constitute state action prohibited by the Fourteenth Amendment of the United States Constitution (*NCAA v. Tarkanian*, 1988). While the Fourteenth Amendment guarantees that no person can be deprived of liberty or property interest without due process of law, most claims brought by coaches under the Fourteenth Amendment fail because coaches generally are not entitled to the same due process protection as teachers under State Teacher Tenure Acts (Wong, 1994). The courts, however, in several states including West Virginia and Ohio, have held that coaches are entitled to procedural due process protection with respect to their coaching positions.

Most recently, the North Carolina Court of Appeals held that a disputed sentence in the addendum to a coaching contract did not apply, and therefore the former basketball and football coach had no property interest in coaching pursuant to contract (*Babb v. Harnett County Board of Education*, 1995). The North Carolina Court ruled that the language of the coaching contract allowed the principal to unilaterally choose not to assign the plaintiff any coaching duties. Hence, the coach had no property interest in the position.

Fringe Benefits

In a 1994 breach of contract case against the Charlotte Hornets, former coach Dick Harter claimed that his contract was breached by the Hornets and he, therefore, was entitled to damages for all the perquisites he enjoyed in his position. These included the use of an automobile, free game tickets, a radio show, endorsement agreements and a summer basketball camp (*Harter v. Charlotte Hornets*, 1994). The court, however, ruled in favor of the defendant team in denying Harter's claim for damages. In contrast to the Pepper Rodgers case, the Harter court effectively ruled that since Harter was no longer coaching the Hornets, he was precluded from making a claim for the benefits he enjoyed in the position. Notwithstanding their respective outcomes, both the Harter and Rodgers cases involved situations in which the contracts were not clear on the compensation to be paid to the coach in the event of termination. Therefore, in order to avoid any unintended interpretations, contracts must be specific in defining the benefits which will continue to be paid to a coach in the event of termination.

Non-Renewal

In a recent Arkansas case involving the non-renewal of a high school coach, the Arkansas Supreme Court held that the non-renewal notice given to a coach failed to comply with Arkansas' Teacher Fair Dismissal Act (*Hamilton v. Pulaski Co. Sp. School District*, 1995). Athletic administrators and sport managers need to be aware of state laws and rules which might supersede the terms of the contract.

Breach of Contract

In a 1995 case brought by Baylor University against its former basketball coach Darrel Johnson (*Baylor University v. Johnson*, 1995), Baylor claimed that the coach had violated his contract by breaking various NCAA and university rules. In essence, Baylor asserted that Johnson had helped athletes to cheat to meet certain academic requirements. While the lawsuit was subsequently dropped, it establishes the possibility that colleges and universities may be willing to bring suit to enforce the obligations owed by coaches under contract.

Miscellaneous

Many professional and college coaching contracts contain clauses which grant bonuses for winning percentages, conference and league championships, and playoff success. In recent years, several universities have provided contract bonuses to coaches based on team graduation rates and other academic successes. Specific coaching contract clauses, however, are not limited to the relative success of the team. In fact, one professional coach has a provision in his contract where he will be terminated in the event he is found to have consumed any alcoholic beverages during the course of the season.

References

A. Cases
Babb v. Harnett County Board of Education, 454 S.E.2d 833 (N.C. App. 1995).

Baylor University v. Johnson, Case no. W-95-CA-365 (W.D. TX., 1995).

Hamilton v. Pulaski Co. Sp. School Dist., 900 S.W. 2d 205 (Arkansas, 1995).

Harter v. Charlotte Hornets, Inc., et al., Case no. C-C-91-418-MU (W.D.N.C., 1994).

Lewis v. Board of Education of North Clay Community School District, 181 Ill. App. 3d 694; 537 N.E. 2d 440 (1989).

Monson v. Oregon, 136 Ore. App. 225; 901 P. 2d 904 (1995).

National Collegiate Athletic Association v. Tarkanian, 109 S. Ct. 454 (1988).

New England Patriots Football Club, Inc. v. University of Colorado, 592 F. 2d 1196 (1st Cir., 1979).

Rodgers v. Georgia Tech Athletic Association, 303 S.E. 2d 467 (Ga. Ct. App., 1983).

Smith and Gremer v. Board of Education of Urbana School District, No. 116 of Champaign County, 708 F. 2d 258 (7th Cir., 1982).

Yukica v. Leland, Case No. 85-1E-191 (N.H. Superior Court, 1985).

Whirlpool v. Dailey Constitution, Inc., 110 N.C. App. 468; 429 S.E. 2d 748 (1993).

B. Publications
Asher, M., Contracts Getting Closer Looks, *Miami Herald,* February 7, 1986, p. 2E.

Graves, J., Coaches in the Courtroom: Recovery In Actions for Breach of Employment Contracts, 12 *Journal of College and University Law* 545-58, (1985-86).

Greenburg, M., College Coaching Contracts: A Practical Perspective, *Marquette Sports Law Journal,* pp. 207-82 (Spring 1991).

Selvaggi, M., The College v. The Coach, 3 *Seton Hall Journal of Sports Law,* 221-235, (1993).

Stoner, E. and Arlie Nogay, The Model University Coaching Contract ("MCC"): A Better Starting Point for Your Next Negotiation, 16 *Journal of College and University Law*, 43-92 (Summer 1989).

Wong, G., (1994). *Essentials of Amateur Sports Law* (2nd Ed.). Westport, Conn.: Praeger Publishing Co.

3.22
Letters of Intent and Scholarships

Mark A. Conrad
Fordham University

A letter of intent is a document, signed by a high school athlete and the parent or guardian, which serves as a notification of the student's intention to attend a particular undergraduate institution. The institution promises to award the student a scholarship in exchange for this commitment. The letter of intent (formally known as a National Letter of Intent or NLI) binds the student to an irrevocable commitment to that college for at least one year and penalizes the student if he or she reneges on that commitment.

The NLI also binds the institution to awarding a scholarship to the student, whereby the student's tuition, room and board, and books will cost the student nothing (or in some cases, these costs will be reduced). The failure of the student to perform his or her responsibilities—not attending practices, failing to show up for games and, not insignificantly, failing to maintain academic eligibility—will result in the forfeiture of the scholarship. However, if the student forfeits a scholarship, he or she still must remain in school as the NLI is binding for the academic year.

The NLI has been a mainstay of college athletics since the 1960s. It was developed by the College Commissioners' Association (CCA) to ease recruiting for schools, preventing the situation where one school could recruit and sign an athlete and subsequently "lose" the athlete to another institution without any legal recourse. Today, it is the CCA, not the NCAA, that enforces the NLI. Nearly every four-year undergraduate institution in the United States utilizes them, despite the fact that the NCAA has never formally required them. The NLI binds a high school senior to the promise of attending the chosen school thus preventing a student from impetuously "jumping ship" from one institution to another. It gives college administrators an accurate way to determine the number of students with athletic scholarships entering the freshman class and fosters a sense of responsibility on the prospective students and their families that their obligation to enter the institution is just that, an obligation. Penalties for forfeiture of the NLI accrue if the student breaches the letter of intent.

Although on the surface the length and terms of the NLI and the resulting scholarship obligations seem straightforward, the scope and enforceability of both the NLI and the athletic scholarship have been grounds for considerable discussion and debate. The basic question involves whether the letter of intent and the resulting scholarship constitute a "contractual" relationship under the general rules of contract law and, if so, what rights and responsibilities exist for the student and the institution. Some have argued that the Letter of Intent and the resulting scholarship are contracts and should be treated as such—in other words, binding and irrevocable commitments. Others claim that they are documents that, at best, constitute a "gentleman's agreement" with little enforcement powers. A third contention is that since the student is frequently under the age of majority when he or she signs the document, the student should have the right to avoid the agreement due to a lack of competency.

With so much at stake for the college and the student, the rules and contractual validity of NLI and the resulting scholarships will be discussed in some detail.

218

■ ■ ■ ■

Representative Case

COOPER v. PETERSON

Supreme Court of New York, St. Lawrence County
164 Misc. 2d 878; 626 N.Y.S.2d 432; 1995 N.Y. Misc. LEXIS 179
April 12, 1995, Decided

OPINION: David Demarest, J.

Plaintiffs, by order to show cause, move for a temporary injunction prohibiting St. Lawrence University (SLU) from eliminating the varsity sport of wrestling prior to the graduation of the 1994 freshman class. Defendants, by notice of cross motion returnable January 13, 1995, move for an order pursuant to CPLR 3211 (a) (7) and 3016 (b) dismissing plaintiffs' complaint on the grounds that it fails to state a valid claim upon which relief can be granted.

In mid-October 1994 the SLU administration announced its decision to eliminate the intercollegiate wrestling program after the 1994-1995 season. Shortly thereafter plaintiffs commenced this action alleging five causes of action: breach of contract; misrepresentation; fraud; estoppel; and sexual discrimination. Upon presentment of their order to show cause, plaintiffs sought a temporary restraining order, which was denied. Plaintiffs' motion seeks issuance of a preliminary injunction prohibiting elimination of the sport until the May 1998 graduation of the current freshman class.

Since the summer of 1991, David S. Hudson, as SLU head wrestling coach, recruited the freshman, sophomore, and junior class wrestlers. Plaintiffs present Hudson's sworn affidavits wherein he unequivocally states he made representations to the plaintiffs as prospective student wrestlers, which included statements that the wrestling program was "a strong program"; "it would be around for four years"; "you will be part of a long standing traditional support at St. Lawrence University which is greatly supported by the university and athletic department"; "you will get an excellent education and be able to wrestle for four years while getting the education." Mr. Hudson concedes he does not know the exact dates, times or places the representations were made, but that he made the representations believing he was authorized to do so in his capacity as head wrestling coach. Further, Mr. Hudson states he "had absolutely no idea during coaching at St. Lawrence University that the wrestling program was even being considered for termination."

• • •

It is defendants' position that the decision to terminate the sport followed the budgeting process for the 1995-1996 academic year. The process was begun during the summer of 1994, and in mid-September 1994 the senior officers in the university's administration made their recommendations. Dean Bambrey recommended elimination of the wrestling program and, after conclusion of the board of trustees' September 1994 meeting and further consultation with senior staff, it was decided in mid-October 1994 to eliminate the wrestling program. Defendants allege that elimination of the program was the result of its efforts to meet its budget constraints and was, therefore, in SLU's best interest.

Defendants' Cross Motion: Dismissal of Plaintiffs' Complaint

Plaintiffs' Breach of Contract Cause of Action:

It is defendants' position that the plaintiffs' first cause of action, breach of contract, is barred since the unwritten contract could not be performed within one year and is, therefore, void under the Statute of Frauds. (General Obligations Law @ 5-701 [a].)

• • •

Importantly, SLU, as in Gonyo v Drake Univ. (837 F Supp 989 [SD Iowa 1993]), continues to offer its financial assistance despite termination of the wrestling program. Unlike Gonyo, the plaintiffs are not recipients of any athletic scholarships, having been awarded financial aid on the same criteria as all other SLU students. Further, plaintiffs' financial aid packages have already been awarded and/or are available. As in Hysaw v Washburn Univ. (690 F Supp 940 [D Kan 1987]), plaintiffs received financial aid allocations promised them. Moreover, plaintiffs set forth nothing more than "understandings" and "expectations" that they were even promised a position on the SLU wrestling team. (Supra, at 947.) Based on these facts, it cannot be said that the acts performed by plaintiffs are "unequivocally referable" to the purported wrestling agreement; and, in fact, their actions in attending SLU and wrestling on the team are equally consistent with their status as SLU students. Plaintiffs' assertions of part performance do not remove the contract from the Statute of Frauds.

In any event, other courts faced with this same type of case, albeit dealing only with the issue of temporary relief, have been reluctant to dictate to education institutions, "[i]n areas of policy, administrative decisions, and the every day routine of running the institution" (Soderbloom v Yale Univ., 1992 WL 24448, 2 [Conn Super Ct 1992]).

• • •

Additionally, Soderbloom (supra, at 4) held that "even if varsity wrestling were considered part of a contract between the plaintiffs and Yale, and even if Yale had not specifically reserved the right to make changes, courts have recognized that universities must have the flexibility to make changes in furtherance of their educational responsibilities." "'Certainly in the period of time between a student's matriculation and graduation, an educational institution, which is a living, changing thing, may not reasonably be expected to remain static; and, conversely, change may reasonably be expected. Hence, each statement in a publication of what now is true does not necessarily become a term in the contract between the school and the student.'" (Supra, at 4, quoting Peretti v State of Montana, 464 F Supp 784, 786 [D Mont 1979], revd on other grounds 661 F2d 756 [9th Cir 1981].) The court then went on to hold that it did not find a valid binding contract to provide the sport of varsity wrestling during the plaintiffs' academic careers and that as a result they failed to show a protectable interest was at stake nor that they would prevail on the merits, to a reasonable degree of certainty; plaintiffs' application for a temporary injunction was denied.

In light of the foregoing, not only does plaintiffs' cause of action for breach of contract fail to sustain its entitlement to a preliminary injunction, the court also finds it fails to state a cause of action as it is barred by the Statute of Frauds and should be dismissed.

Plaintiffs' Misrepresentation, Fraud, and Estoppel Causes of Action:

• • •

Although, as it has been set forth above, the affidavit of Mr. Hudson specifies the actual statements made to all potential SLU recruits who expressed an interest in the wrestling program, and therefore sufficiently supplements the complaint in this respect, there has been no attempt to identify when the statements were made and whether if any of the actual plaintiffs heard, and relied upon, any of these particular statements.

Also lacking in plaintiffs' pleadings is the element of scienter on the part of the defendants. There are no allegations that anyone knew the program was doomed when representations were made. Defendants, in support of their cross motion, set forth uncontroverted allegations that it was only after the plaintiffs had been accepted and agreed to attend SLU that any discussions concerning the academic budget ensued, making the existence of scienter factually impossible.

Constructive fraud, existing where the parties have a special confidential or fiduciary relationship, vitiates the necessity of scienter, but plaintiffs have failed to plead any such relationship. (See, Matter of Gordon v Bialystoker Ctr. & Biakur Cholim, 45 NY2d 692 [1978]; Manheim Dairy Co. v Little Falls Natl. Bank, 54 NYS2d 345 [Sup Ct, Herkimer County 1945]; see also, Costello v Costello, 209 NY 252 [1913].)

The court, upon review of the second, third, and fourth causes of action, is of the opinion that they, too, fail to state a cause of action.

• • •

It is, therefore, the decision of this court, and it is hereby ordered, that the cross motion of the defendants be, in all respects, granted, dismissing the complaint, in its entirety, for failure to state a valid claim upon which relief can be granted. Plaintiffs' application for a preliminary injunction is thereby rendered moot.

■ ■ ■ ■

Fundamental Concepts

In the following pages, a sample letter of intent will be reproduced. The accompanying text will analyze the salient provisions of the NLI, discuss the parties, contractual enforceability, performance, and defenses to the NLI and the accompanying scholarship.

1996 NATIONAL LETTER OF INTENT (NLI)

Administered by the Collegiate Commissioners Association (CCA)

Do not sign prior to 7:00 am (local time) on the following dates or after the final signing date listed for each sport.

	SPORT	INITIAL SIGNING DATE	FINAL SIGNING DATE
_____	Basketball (Early Period)	November 8, 1995	November 15, 1995
_____	Basketball (Late Period)	April 10, 1996	May 15, 1996
_____	Football (Midyear JC Transfer)	December 20, 1995	January 15, 1996
_____	Football (Regular Period)	February 7, 1996	April 1, 1996
_____	Women's Volleyball, Field Hockey, Soccer, Water Polo	February 7, 1996	August 1, 1996
_____	All Other Sports (Early Period)	November 8, 1995	November 15, 1995
_____	All Other Sports (Late Period)	April 10, 1996	August 1, 1996

(Place an "X" on the proper line)

IMPORTANT - READ CAREFULLY

It is important to read this entire document before signing it in triplicate One copy is to be retained by you and two copies are to be returned to the institution, one of which will be filed with the appropriate conference commissioner.

---

1. **Initial Enrollment in Four-Year Institution.** This NLI is applicable only to prospective student-athletes who will be entering four-year institutions for the first time as full-time students, except for 4-2-4 transfers who are graduating from junior college as outlined in paragraph 8-b.

2. **Financial Aid Requirement.** I must receive in writing an award for athletics financial aid for the entire 1996-97 academic year from the institution named in this document at the time of my signing A mid-year junior college transfer must receive athletics financial aid for the remainder of the 1995-96 academic year The award letter shall list the terms and conditions of the award, including the amount and duration of the financial aid If such conditions are not met, this NLI shall be invalid.

    a. **Professional Sports Contract.** If I sign a professional sports contract, I will remain bound by the provisions of this NLI even if the institution named in this document is prohibited from making athletically-related financial aid available to me under NCAA rules.

3. **Provisions of Letter Satisfied.**

    a. **One-year Attendance Requirement Met.** The terms of this NLI shall be satisfied if I attend the institution named in this document for at least one academic year.

    b. **Junior College Graduation.** The terms of this NLI shall be satisfied if I graduate from junior college after signing a NLI while in high school or during my first year in junior college.

4 . **Basic Penalty. I understand that if I do not attend the institution named within this document for one full academic year, and I enroll in another institution participating in the NLI program, I may not represent the latter institution in intercollegiate athletics competition until I have completed two full academic years of residence at the latter institution. Further, I understand that I shall be charged with the loss of two seasons of intercollegiate athletics competition in all sports, except as otherwise provided in this NLI. This is in addition to any eligibility expended at the institution at which I initially enrolled.**

    a. **Early Signing Period Penalties. A prospective student-athlete who signs a NLI during the early signing period (November 8-15, 1995) will be ineligible for practice and competition in football for a two-year period and also shall be charged with two seasons of competition in the sport of football.**

5. **Mutual Release Agreement.** A formal release procedure shall be provided in the event the institution and I mutually agree to release each other from any obligations to the NLI. I understand that if I receive this formal release, I shall not be eligible for competition at a second NLI institution during my first academic year of residence there, and I shall lose one season of competition. This mutual release form must be signed by me, my parent or legal guardian, and the Director of Athletics of the institution named in this document, and I must file a copy of the mutual release form with the conference which processes this NLI. (NOTE: This mutual release form may be obtained from the institution named in this document.)

   a. **Authority to Release.** A coach is not authorized to void, cancel or give a release to this NLI.

   b. **Extent of Mutual Release.** A mutual release from this NLI shall apply to all participating institutions and shall not be conditional or selective by institution.

6. **Appeal Process.** I understand that the NLI Steering Committee has been authorized to issue interpretations, settle disputes and consider petition for a full release from the provisions of this NLI where there are extenuating circumstances. I further understand its decision may be appealed to the NLI Appeals Committee, whose decision shall be final and binding.

7. **Letter Becomes Null and Void.** This NLI shall be declared null and void if any of the following occurs:

   a. **Admissions Requirement.** This NLI shall be declared null and void if the institution with which I signed notifies me in writing that I have been denied admission.

      (1) It is presumed that I am eligible for admission and financial aid until information is submitted to the contrary Thus, it is mandatory for me, upon request, to provide a transcript of my previous academic record and an application for admission to the institution named in this document.

      (2) If I am eligible for admission, but the institution named in this document defers admission to a subsequent term, this NLI shall be rendered null and void However, if I defer my admission, the NLI remains binding.

   b. **Eligibility Requirements.** This NLI shall be declared null and void if, by the institution's opening day of classes in the fall of 1996, I have not met (a) the institution's requirements for admission, (b) its academic requirements for financial aid to athletes, AND (c) the NCAA requirement for freshman financial aid (NCAA Bylaw 14.3) or the NCAA junior college transfer rule.

      (1) If I become a nonqualifier (per NCAA Bylaw 14.3), this NLI shall be rendered null and void.

      (2) If I am a midyear junior college football transfer signee, the NLI remains binding for the following fall term if I was eligible for admission and financial aid and met the junior college transfer requirements for competition for the winter or spring term, but chose to delay my admission.

   c. **One-Year Absence.** This NLI shall be null and void if I have not attended any institution (or attended an institution, including a junior college, that does not participate in the NLI Program) for at least one academic year after signing this NLI, provided my request for athletics financial aid for a subsequent fall term is not approved by the institution with which I signed. To receive this waiver, I must file with the appropriate conference commissioner a statement from the Director of Athletics at the institution named in this document that such financial aid will not be available to me for the requested fall term.

   d. **Service in the U.S. Armed Forces. Church Mission.** This NLI shall be null and void if I serve on active duty with the armed forces of the United States or an official church mission for at least eighteen (18) months.

   e. **Discontinued Sport.** This NLI shall be null and void if my sport is discontinued by the institution named in the document.

   f. **Recruiting Rules Violation.** If the institution (or a representative of its athletics interests) named in this document violated NCAA or conference rules while recruiting me, as found through the NCAA or conference enforcement process or acknowledged by the institution, this NLI shall be declared null and void. Such declaration shall not take place until all appeals to the NCAA or conference for restoration of eligibility have been concluded.

8. **Only One Valid NLI Permitted**. I understand that I may sign only one valid NLI, except as listed below.

   a. **Subsequent Signing Year.** If this NLI is rendered null and void under Item 6, I remain free to enroll in any institution of my choice where I am admissible and shall be permitted to sign another NLI in a subsequent signing year.

   b. **Junior College Exception.** If I signed a NLI while in high school or during my first year in junior college, I may sign another NLI in the signing year in which I am scheduled to graduate from junior college. If I graduate, the second NLI shall be binding on me; otherwise, the original NLI I signed shall remain valid.

9. **Recruiting Ban After Signing**. I understand that all participating conferences and institutions are obligated to respect my signing and shall cease to recruit me upon my signing this NLI. I shall notify any recruiter who contacts me that I have signed.

10. **Institutional Signatures Required Prior to Submission.** This NLI must be signed and dated by the Director of Athletics or his/her authorized representative before submission to me and my parents (or legal guardian for our signatures. This NLI may be mailed prior to the initial signing date. When a NLI is issued prior to the initial signing date, the "date of issuance" shall be considered to be the initial signing date and not the date that the NLI was signed or mailed by the institution.

11. **Parent/Guardian Signature Required.** My parent or legal guardian is required to sign this NLI regardless of my age or marital status. If I do not have a living parent or a legal guardian, this NLI may be signed by the person who is acting in the capacity of a guardian. An explanation of the circumstances shall accompany this NLI.

12. **Falsification of NLI**. If I falsify any part of this NLI, or if I have knowledge that my parent or guardian falsified any part of this NLI, I understand that I shall forfeit the first two years of my eligibility at any NLI participating institution as outlined in Item 4.

13. **14-Day Signing Deadline.** If my parent or legal guardian and I fail to sign this NLI within 14 days of issuance to me, it will be invalid. In that event, another NLI may be issued within the appropriate signing period. (NOTE: This does not apply to the early signing period).

14. **Institutional Filing Deadline.** This NLI must be filed with the appropriate conference by the institution named in this document within 21 days after the date of final signature or it will be invalid. In that event, another NLI may be issued.

15. **No Additions or Deletions Allowed to NLI.** No additions or deletions may be made to this NLI or the Mutual Release Agreement.

16. **Official Time for Validity.** This NLI shall be considered to be officially signed on the final date of signature by myself or my Parent (or guardian). If no time of day is listed, then 11:59 p.m. is presumed.

17. **Statute Of Limitations.** This NLI shall carry a four-year statute of limitations.

18. **Nullification of Other Agreements.** My signature on this NLI nullifies any agreements, oral or otherwise, which would release me from the conditions stated within this NLI.

19. **If Coach Leaves**. I understand that I have signed this NLI with the institution and not for a particular sport or individual. For example, if the coach leaves the institution or the sports program, I remain bound by the provisions of this NLI.

20. **Coaching Contact Prohibited at Time of Signing.** A coach or an institutional representative may not hand-deliver this NLI or be present at the time I sign it. This NLI may be delivered by express mail, courier service, regular mail or facsimile machine.

NATIONAL LETTER OF INTENT PROGRAM

1996 NATIONAL LETTER OF INTENT (NLI)

Name of Prospect _____

| Last | First | Middle |

Type Proper Name, Including Middle Name or Initial)

Permanent Address _____

| Street | City | State | Zip Code |

Submission of thus NLI has been authorized by:

SIGNED _____   _____

Director of Athletics   Date Issued to Prospect

_____   _____

Sport (Men's)   Sport (Women's)

❑ Check here if signee is a junior college transfer student.

This is to certify my decision to enroll at _____

Name of Institution

I certify that I have read all terms and conditions included in the four pages of this document, I have discussed them with the coach and/or other staff representatives of the institution named above, and I fully understand, accept and agree to be bound by them. (All three copies of this NLI must be signed individually)

SIGNED _____ _____ _____

Prospect's Signature   Date (Mth/Day/Yr)   Time (A.M./P.M.)

_____

Prospect's Social Security Number

SIGNED _____ _____ _____

Parent or Legal Guardian Signature (circle one)   Date (Mth/Day/Yr)   Time (A.M./P.M.)

_____   _____

Print Name of Parent/Legal Guardian   Telephone Number (including area code)

Standard Provisions

As one can see from the sample, some of the key clauses in the National Letter of Intent include:

- A student **commitment to matriculate for at least one year** in return for a commitment to an athletic scholarship. This binds the student to a one-year obligation. After that time, the student's obligations cease and he or she could transfer to another institution with no violation of the NLI. The NCAA's transfer rules would apply requiring the transferring student-athlete to sit out one year after enrollment in a school of the same division.

- The **failure to attend** the institution for one year and the subsequent attendance of that student in another institution results in a two-year ban on representing the new institution in intercollegiate sports.

- If the school and the student **agree to release each other** from the obligations of the NLI, there shall be no penalty on the student, except that he or she will not be eligible to represent the new institution in intercollegiate athletics for one year.

- Only **one NLI may be signed,** unless the student elected to go to a Junior College. In that case, the student may sign another Letter of Intent during his or her second (graduation) year at the Junior College. That second NLI will be binding; the first will be rescinded.

- Once the agreement is signed, the commissioner notifies all other conference commissioners that the student is committed. This is a **central reason** why the NLI is signed.

- The **student-athlete and at least one parent or guardian must sign** the Letter of Intent within a specified calendar period, depending on the given sport.

- The NLI must be signed by the student and a parent or guardian within **14 days of issuance** (if that period is within the stated signing period). The failure to sign renders the document null and void, although another NLI may be issued within the appropriate signing period.

- The NLI **must be signed and dated by the college's athletic director** or authorized representative before it is sent to the student-athlete.

- Any **prior oral or written promises** made by the student are nullified by the signature on the NLI. This is a variation of the "parol evidence" rule, a traditional contract law doctrine which prohibits prior oral statements which contradict the terms of the contract from being introduced into evidence at a trial. This section is a reminder that it is the writing that is paramount and any oral promises or representations made before the document is consummated are worthless.

- **No additions or deletions** are allowed in the agreement.

- The NLI **must be filed** with the appropriate athletic conference within 21 days after signature.

- **If the coach of the institution leaves,** the student remains bound by the contract.

Parties

There are always three parties who sign the Letter of Intent: a representative of the institution, the student, and an adult co-signer (usually a parent or a legal guardian). The signature of the adult co-signer is an attempt to ensure that the agreement will be enforceable. Generally, an adult party who co-signs an agreement is liable for damages if the minor breaches the obligation. However, as a practical matter, it is difficult to bring an action against the adult co-signer for remedies under this arrangement if the student breaches his or her obligations. The adult is not the one receiving the scholarship and it is difficult to employ the traditional standard of "monetary damages" for the breach.

A representative of the undergraduate institution also is required to sign the Letter of Intent. If the document conforms to contractual standards, that person (usually the athletic director or coach) binds the college to the terms of the agreement. Under agency law, a representative of the contracting party has the authority to bind the institution. It would be difficult for the institution to back out of the agreement, even if the President or Dean was not aware of the agreement.

Contractual in Nature

The Letter of Intent, coupled with the offer of scholarship aid, has been deemed a binding contract by a number of courts (*Begley v. Corporation of Mercer University*, 1973; *Taylor v. Wake Forest University*, 1972; *Barile v. University of Va.*, 1981). At first glance, all the elements of a contract—offer and acceptance, consideration, capacity, and legality—are contained. There is an offer and acceptance. The college is making an offer to the student which stipulates that the institution will confer a scholarship if the student accepts by giving an irrevocable commitment to attend the school for at least one year. If the student accepts, a bilateral contract occurs. Assuming contractual assent, the requirement of consideration (the exchange of exclusive commitment for scholarship money) is met. The student is presumed to have the capacity to make this contract, even if the student is a minor (under the age of 18 in most states) because the student's parent or guardian signs the contract as a guarantor.

It is important to note that not every court or commentator considers that the NLI and the resulting scholarship is a contract. Weistart & Lowell have questioned the application of contract law, arguing that the scholarship should be categorized as an educational grant. Cloaked in "academic" rather than "contractual" garb, they claim that the athletic scholarship is akin to a music student who has been provided financial aid with the understanding that he or she will "engage in public performances as part of the educational program" (Weistart & Lowell, 1979). Certain courts have agreed with this argument *(Ewing v. State, 1972)*. But the prevalent thinking points towards the conclusion that the NLI and scholarship create a contract.

Assuming that contract law applies, important interpretational questions come up. Is the contract a binding one year obligation? Or are there circumstances where the student's scholarship can be terminated during that one-year period? Section 15.3.4 of the NCAA's rules says that a school can drop the scholarship during the contract year in four instances: where the student 1) becomes ineligible for intercollegiate competition; 2) fraudulently misrepresents any information on an application, letter of intent, or financial aid agreement; 3) engages in serious misconduct warranting substantial disciplinary penalties; or 4) voluntarily withdraws from a sport for personal reasons. If there is any reduction or cancellation of aid, the student does have a right to a hearing. (NCAA rules sec. 15.4.1.3).

A second contractual issue involves continuation of scholarship benefits after the one-year period. Generally, a school has no obligation to renew a scholarship, but if the institution decides not to renew or reduces financial aid for the next academic year, the institution is required to inform the student that he or she may request a hearing before the institutional agency making the award. (NCAA rules sec. 15.3.5.1.1). The institution is required to establish "reasonable procedures" for conducting the hearing.

Another contractual issue involves conditions, requirements that must be adhered to before a contract is effective. The sample NLI states a number of apparent conditions that must be completed as a prerequisite to enforceability. For example, the NLI *must* be filed with the appropriate athletic conference within 21 days after the "final signature." What happens if that does not occur? Is the scholarship withdrawn? Is the entire agreement negated? Is the institution in breach? Can the student go somewhere else? The NLI only states that another Letter of Intent may be issued within the appropriate signing period.

In contrast, the NLI directly addresses two important conditions: entry requirements to the institution and falsification of information. It specifically states that the student must meet the institution's requirements for admission under the NCAA's minimum requirements by the opening day of classes. If not, the NLI is null and void. Also, if the athlete falsified any information in the NLI, the first two years of eligibility are forfeited.

Scholarship as Contract.   It has been earlier noted that the scholarship offer is a part of the contract created when the student signs the NLI. It lasts for one-year and renewal is at the discretion of the institution. It is the consideration that binds the student to the agreement with the institution. The rules and regulations of the institution and the academic requirements of the NCAA must be fulfilled, as will be noted in the "performance" section of the chapter.

Good Faith Standards.   General contract law mandates that the parties negotiating a contract do so in good faith *(U.C.C. sec. 1-203; Restatement (2d) of Contracts, sec. 205)*. However, the NLI specifically states that the terms of this agreement cannot be modified or changed. In other words, it is a "take it or leave it" contract. Does that violate the "good faith" standard? There is no clear answer, although in certain circumstances, the issue could be one which a court could grapple. General contract law states that a "contract of adhesion" will be looked upon with greater disfavor by the courts, especially if there is an inequality of bargaining power by one of the parties *(Oxford Companion to Law, 1980)*. It would be difficult to apply the contract of adhesion concept to a case where a student is being recruited by a number of schools. That student still retains considerable power of choice in the selection of an institution, despite the "finality" of the NLI standardized form. If students could make individual "deals" and bargain for "bonuses" in their NLI's the basic goals would be adversely affected and the athletic scholarship would become more than financial aid for tuition, books, and room and board. It would be like an athlete negotiating with a professional team.

Performance.   Contract law generally mandates that the parties perform their obligations as required under a contract to avoid a breach. Once a NLI is signed by the student and the scholarship is received, the student is generally required to perform his or her obligations in good faith. That has been interpreted to mean complying with NCAA academic standing and amateurism requirements, conference rules, and the academic rules of the institution. The relationship between the student and the institution is akin to a personal services obligation (despite the NCAA's requirement of "amateurism") where a performer is obligated to perform a service and the institution must "compensate" the performer for it.

Factors such as the amount of playing time, starting positions, and practice rules are not disputable. These are in the purview of the coach of the team and the student will not have a right to "walk" out of his obligations if the coach's decisions do not agree with the student's ideas. On the other hand, a student cannot guarantee a "good game." If his or her performance during a match or during an entire season is disappointing or not commensurate with the athlete's abilities, it will not give the institution the right to unilaterally terminate the scholarship. However, the failure to maintain a minimally acceptable academic average, the acceptance of other types of compensation besides the scholarship benefits, or the signing of a contract with an agent will result in the loss of "eligibility" and deprive the athlete of scholarship benefits.

An interesting case noted that a junior college's requirements prohibiting facial hair and imposing hair length and "proper" dress requirements as conditions for being on the baseball team were not violations of a student's constitutional rights, since the student voluntarily accepted these restrictions as part of his choice to participate. These restrictions were not a part of the scholarship agreement, but rather were *unwritten* rules and regulations made by the college's athletic department. (*Lesser v. Neosho City College, 1990*).

Contract Defenses.   The contractual nature of the NLI recognizes various contract defenses. If one of the parties can show that the contract was made by duress, undue influence, fraud, misrepresentation, mutual mistake, or a lack of capacity, a court could rescind the agreement, freeing the party who successfully pleads that his or her assent was defective or faulty.

As practical matter, it is difficult for a student to rescind a co-signed contract for lack of capacity, but not impossible. For a student under the age of 18 when he or she signed the NLI and committed to a scholarship, a number of jurisdictions hold that the fact that the contract had been co-signed by an adult does not alter the right of a minor to disaffirm a contract. (*Campbell v. Fender, 1951*). Also, some courts could interpret the NLI as a contract for a "necessary" matter, something indispensable for maintaining an existence. Education, along with food, clothing, and shelter are deemed "necessaries." If the NLI fits into this category, the student would be precluded from dis-affirming the agreement once it has been performed or "executed" by the student. So when the student enrolls in the institution, he or she has "executed" the contract and the student's right to disaffirm ends.

As to other contract defenses, if it can be shown that a student was fraudulently induced to sign a NLI or acted under duress, contract law permits the aggrieved party to rescind the contract. In one case, a court ruled that a prime facie case for fraudulent misrepresentation was presented when a coach made claims that a student would receive "maximum exposure to major college and professional scouts" while attending and the coach would not "turn the athletes loose." The athlete sued after he was cut from the team. (*Lesser v. Neosho City College, 1990*).

Release

The NLI permits the student to terminate before entry to school if the student engages in military service for eighteen months or works as a religious missionary for the same period of time. It also permits release if the student's sport is discontinued by the institution, or he or she is subsequently denied an athletic scholarship by the institution after the Letter of Intent is signed. These events will release the student without any penalty.

Recent Developments

A recent case shows what can happen if a student signs a NLI after developing a relationship with the college coach, who is subsequently fired. Katie Coleman was recruited by Purdue University, as well as Northwestern and Illinois. After participating in Dunn's summer basketball camp for two years, she knew Dunn well and knew what to expect from her. In October, 1995, Katie and her parents signed the NLI. Shortly afterward, Dunn was fired from Purdue. This action came despite a prior statement to Katie's father who was "assured" by the university's Athletic Director that Dunn would be rehired. Coleman's request for a release of her obligation was denied. Complicating the matter is the fact that Purdue has released five current players of the team. Purdue officials insisted that if they gave recruits the releases, there could be a "mass exodus" before a new coach could be hired. Coleman may appeal the denial. But given the language in the NLI, it is unlikely she will win.

A year earlier, quarterback Chris Redman won an appeal from the Collegiate Commissioners Association committee after he signed with Illinois. Redman sought to leave when the team's offensive coordinator, who recruited Redman, was fired shortly after Redman committed to Illinois. The committee released Redman from his Letter and restored his eligibility immediately because Illinois supported the claim. He transferred to the University of Louisville.

References

A. Cases

Barile v. University of Va., 441 N.E. 2d 608 (Ohio App. 1981).
Begley v. Corporation of Mercer University, 367 F. Supp. 908 (E.D. Tenn. 1973).
Campbell v. Fender, 235 S.W.2d 957 (1951).
Ewing v. State, 331 N.Y.S.2d 287 (Court of Claims, N.Y. 1972).
Lesser v. Neosho City College, 741 F. Supp. 854 (D. Ks. 1990).
Taylor v. Wake Forest University, 191 S.E.2d 379, cert. den. 192 S.E.2d 196 (N.C. 1972).

B. Publications

Farnsworth, E.A., (1990). *Farnsworth on Contracts*, 2d, secs. 4.4-4.5.
Weistart, J.C. and Lowell, C.H., (1979). *The Law of Sports*. New York: Bobbs-Merrill Company, Inc.
Oxford Companion to Law, p. 24 (1980).
Cozzillo, Michael J., The Athletic Scholarship and the College National Letter of Intent: A Contract by Any Other Name, 35 *Wayne Law Review* 1275-1380 (1989).

C. Legislation

U.C.C. sec. 1-203; Restatement (2d) of Contracts, sec. 205.
NCAA Rules, secs. 15.3.4, 15.4.1.3, 15.3.5.1.1.

3.23
Game and Event-Related Contracts

Robert P. Fleischman
East Stroudsburg University

Game and event-related contracts in the sport setting are similar to other performance contracts—that is, they identify the parties, specify the dates, times, and places of performance, and define the consideration bargained for between the parties. Traditionally, contracts involving games and events have been relatively free of litigation; however, in recent years the sport marketplace has become increasingly complex. (Berry and Wong, 1993). The sport marketplace has blossomed into a thriving industry which generates immense sums of money. As a result, it is important that sport managers recognize that these changes have increased the potential for litigation arising from sport-related activities. Therefore, when drafting game and event-related contracts, sport managers must be clear and unambiguous in defining the obligations and rights of the parties.

Although contracts are used in many sport-related games and events—ranging in sophistication from simple high school game contracts to the multiple comprehensive agreements associated with major events such as the Super Bowl or Olympics—many novice sport managers fail to recognize the astoundingly important role these contracts play in staging games and events (Ernst & Young, 1992). Some game contracts, for example, include such areas as television and radio rights, hotel and travel accommodations, practice sites, eligibility and competition rules, licensing rights, luxury boxes, locker room details, security, media areas, darkroom provisions, concessions, complimentary tickets, parking, handicapped access, wheelchair seating, insurance liability, special events, promotions, and marketing rights.

■ ■ ■ ■

Representative Case

SULT v. GILBERT
Supreme Court of Florida, En Banc
148 Fla. 31; 3 So. 2d 729
August 1, 1941; Rehearing Denied September 15, 1941

OPINION: TERRELL, J.

Florida High School Athletic Association is a voluntary organization of all high schools recognized as such by the State Department of Education. Membership in the association is exercised by the supervising principal of each high school and its affairs are regulated by a Constitution, the officers required being a president, two vice presidents, a legislative council, executive committee, and executive secretary.

•••

In June, 1939, Palmetto High School entered into an agreement with Sarasota High School to play a game of football in November, 1939. In April, 1940, Sarasota High School severed athletic relations with Palmetto High School and a controversy arose as to whether a football game would be played between them in November, 1940. On the reverse side of the 1939 contract, the following was inserted:

It is hereby understood that Sarasota High School will give Palmetto High School, for the year 1940, one of the following contracts:

A. The same contract as this year;

B. A $200.00 guarantee;

C. A fifty-fifty split on the gate.

(Palmetto to have the choice of accepting one of the above.)

Article IX, Constitution of the Association, provides:

. . . A contract shall not be cancelled except by the mutual consent of the parties to the contract. In case of failure of the parties to reach agreement concerning cancellation the matter shall be referred to the executive secretary for adjudication. His decree, or the decree of the executive committee in case of appeal, shall be final, and the provisions of the decree shall be carried out by the parties to the contract. Failure to comply with the decision of the executive secretary or executive committee on the part of either member school signing the contract, within thirty days, shall result in the suspension of the school so failing from the Association for a period of one year.

The two high schools could not reconcile their differences so the controversy as to the 1940 game was submitted by the principal of Palmetto High School to the executive secretary of the Association as provided in Article IX of the Constitution above quoted. After due consideration, the executive secretary held that the contract between the two high schools provided for but one game of football which had been played in 1939 as per agreement, that the terms written on the reverse side of the contract were doubtless intended to provide for an additional game in 1940 but not having been covered in the contract as originally executed or by subsequent provision, it could not be enforced. Palmetto High School accepted the finding of the executive secretary and did not appeal to the executive committee.

In October, 1940, Palmetto High School filed its bill of complaint in the circuit court praying that Sarasota High School be required to play football with it in November, 1940. The chancellor ruled that the contract between them could not be enforced as to the 1940 game by specific performance.

Immediately after filing this suit, the executive secretary cited Palmetto High School to show cause why it should not be suspended from the Association; after a full hearing the executive secretary held that refusal of Palmetto High School to accept his decision as to the 1940 game with Sarasota and the institution of court proceedings to compel the game was a violation of the rules of the Association for which he would be bound to suspend it for a period of one year. On appeal and full hearing by both sides, the executive committee affirmed the decision of the executive secretary.

Palmetto High School then filed its bill of complaint in which it named the Florida High School Athletic Association, Sarasota High School, Winter Haven High School, and Bradenton High School as defendants. The bill prayed that said high schools be required to play football games with complainant in 1940 as per schedule or contract with them and that complainant be not suspended from membership in the Florida High School Athletic Association.

The court entered a temporary restraining order enjoining the suspension of Palmetto High School from the Association and requiring Winter Haven and Bradenton High Schools to perform their agreements to play football with complainant. The latter part of the order was promptly obeyed and thereafter a motion to dissolve the injunction and dismiss the bill of complaint was granted. The court further found that the suspension order was regular and in compliance with the Constitution of the Association and should not be disturbed. This appeal is from the order of dismissal.

The question presented is whether or not the order of the executive secretary as affirmed by the executive committee suspending Palmetto High School from the Florida Athletic Association for a period of one year is valid and enforceable.

•••

The Constitution of the Florida High School Athletic Association shows that it is a voluntary nonprofit organization. When Palmetto High School was a member of the Association, it had a right to make contracts with member schools for athletic meets. The loss of this right was all that was lost by the suspension and that being the case, we find no showing of a contractual or property right that would authorize the courts to interfere. It was purely an internal affair of the Association and there is no showing of mistake, fraud, collusion, or arbitrariness in the proceedings.

We do not overlook the contention of appellant that it should not be penalized for going into court to assert what it considered to be a material property or contract right. In fact, at the oral argument, it was virtually agreed that the question presented was whether or not the act of going into court constituted a disregard of the decision of the Florida Athletic Association.

If we were answering this question in response to impulse or predilection, we would have to say no, but the Constitution of the Association provides the answer in that it makes the decision of the executive committee final and requires it to be acquiesced in good faith by all members schools. The appellant subscribed to and agreed to abide by the Constitution. We think that under all the circumstances the penalty in this case was too harsh but was not more than was authorized.

We have examined the cases relied on by appellant but we do not think they rule the case at bar. They arise from constitutional or factual conditions different from those presented in this case. The Constitution in this case was substantially complied with so the judgment is affirmed.

Affirmed.

■ ■ ■ ■

Fundamental Concepts

Distinguishing Between Game and Event-Related Contracts

Similar to one another in several ways, game and event-related contracts often differ in respect to their form and scope. For instance, a game contract, in its simplest form, generally addresses of a single contest or competition. The game contract may run from one page to many pages depending upon the type of game.

Event-related contracts are generally found in one of several forms. They appear as a separate document such as the promoter's contract used in most boxing events (*Mara v. Tunney*, 1932). These contracts may also appear as part of other documents such as license agreements, arena or stadium leases, insurance agreements, endorsement agreements, television and radio broadcast agreements, sponsorship agreements, or independent contractor agreements. A tournament or event agreement may require that several separate contracts be drawn to provide for a variety of competitions, teams, athletes, sponsors, vendors, licensees, spectators, and the media. For the 1984 Olympic Games, 4,400 such contracts were signed (Ernst & Young, 1992).

All contracts, whether used alone or together can serve to clarify the role and responsibilities of the various parties and to protect each party against unforeseen circumstances which may occur during the staging of an event. For the purposes of the following discussion, game and event-related contracts will be considered together.

Factors to Include in Game and Event Contracts

Terms. In its simplest form, a game contract is used by athletic organizations and programs on all levels of sport, from high school through professional, to schedule contests between teams. Most often, the game contract consists of a single form document covering the following terms: 1) The parties, location, date, and time of the contest; 2) the provision for and payment of officials; 3) the corresponding association or conference rules governing eligibility and competition for the contest; 4) the radio and television rights pertaining to the contest; 5) the financial guarantees and complimentary tickets for the contest; 6) the termination provisions under the agreement; 7) renewal provisions; and 8) remedies available in the event of a breach by one party of the contract (Sharp, 1990).

In contrast to game contracts, event-related contracts are often more complex in nature and comprehensive in scope. They frequently include numerous contracts to which the promoter/manager of the event may be a party. For example, some contracts may be with the venue, while others may deal with matters such as the split of parking revenues, ticket sales, and merchandise revenues.

It is important to remember that situations sometimes occur between the initial signing and the completion of the contract which may change the original contract or cause unforeseen or opposing interpretations

(Ernst & Young, Id.). Therefore, when drafting these agreements, sport managers must be careful to include language which is clear, explicit, and comprehensible so that it provides for the various contingencies which might occur prior to the final outcome of the event. A carefully drawn contract serves to notify the parties of their rights and obligations and to protect their interests in the event that claims are made for breach of contract or negligence by one of the parties or its employees.

Jurisdiction. The law governing game and event-related contracts is determined by state law and, consequently, a contract's effect may vary depending on the laws of the state having jurisdiction. To determine jurisdiction in matters involving game and event-related contracts, the courts generally consider the following: 1) the residence or place of business of the parties; 2) the location where the contract is to be performed; or 3) the law of the state designated in the contract.

Therefore, in order to avoid any uncertainty regarding the interpretation of a game or event-related contract, sport managers should specify, within the contract, the appropriate state law to be applied to the contract. In fact, several experts have recommended that an arbitration clause be included in a game or event contract to avoid the excessive delays involved in civil litigation (Graham, Goldblatt & Delpy, 1995).

Liquidated Damages. While teams may generally cancel a contract by mutual consent, the issue of breach by either party must be addressed (Sharp, 1990). Accordingly, the game contract should define the conditions under which the parties will be considered to be in breach. It should also provide for damages in the event a breach is found to have occurred. This may be accomplished by drafting a *liquidated damages* clause into the agreement. Liquidated damages is "the sum which party to contract agrees to pay if he breaks some promise and, which having been arrived at by good faith effort to estimate actual damage that will probably ensue from breach, is recoverable as agreed damages if breach occurs" (Black, 1990, p. 391). In drafting these clauses, sport managers must be careful to determine an amount which bears a *"reasonable"* relationship to the actual damage or loss incurred by the non-breaching party. The following matters must be considered: 1) what benefit(s) does the innocent party expect to receive when the contract is fully executed? 2) what money will be spent in reliance on the contract? and 3) what is the value of any benefit which will be conferred on the breaching party? The courts have refused to enforce liquidated damage clauses where they have been found to be excessive, thereby imposing a penalty on the party breaching the contract. Therefore, these clauses must be carefully drafted to reflect a reasonable relationship to the actual damages a party expects to suffer in the event a breach occurs.

Integration Clause. When drafting game contracts it is important to incorporate all the terms and conditions of the agreement into the written document. The contract should also contain an *"integration clause,"* or a statement representing it to be the *"entire understanding between the parties"* and a statement that any changes or other modifications can only be made in a writing executed by both parties. Integration clauses are useful in the event litigation arises regarding the contract, as they invoke the parol evidence rule. The parol evidence rule precludes the use of extrinsic evidence to contradict, vary, defeat, or modify a complete and unambiguous written instrument, or to change, add to, or subtract from it (*J.M. Montgomery Roofing Co. v. Howland*, 1957). Thus parties are unable to offer testimony to change or modify the contract through prior conversations, documents, or agreements (Wong, G., 1994).

Consideration. In order for a contract to be legally enforceable, it must be supported by consideration. Consideration is present when a promisee, in return for a promise, does anything which he or she is not legally bound to do, or refrains from doing anything which he or she has a right to do (*Dorman v. Publix-Saenger-Sparks Theatres, Inc.*, 1938). Consideration may include both monetary sums and benefits running from one party to the other. In other words, a valid contract requires that something of value be exchanged between the parties. The courts have held that the agreement to engage in an athletic contest, without more, is sufficient consideration to support the contract. Notwithstanding this fact, it is common practice to compensate teams in exchange for their agreeing to play or compete. Accordingly, game contracts often include language such as, "In consideration for . . ." or "in compensation for . . ." Regardless of form, a game contract should specifically refer to the consideration agreed upon between the parties.

Recent Developments

State High School Associations

In a 1995 Pennsylvania case (*East Stroudsburg Area School District v. Pennsylvania Interscholastic Athletic Association*), the Court of Common Pleas of Pennsylvania ruled that the Pennsylvania Interscholastic Athletic Association (PIAA) was precluded from interfering with a scheduled contest between two high school football teams. The PIAA had invoked a rule which limited the number of contests a team could play, claiming that both teams had reached the maximum permissible number. In granting an injunction which allowed the teams to play despite the PIAA ruling, the Court held that the action taken by the PIAA was contrary to its rules and outside the scope of the association's authority.

Damages for Cancellation

In a recent situation involving a scheduled men's basketball game between the University of Arizona and Saint Joseph's University in Philadelphia, Arizona cancelled the game because it decided not to travel due to reports of bad weather. Arizona officials claimed the decision not to travel was based on safety concerns. Saint Joseph's has sent a bill to the University of Arizona asking for money damages for lost ticket sales and other revenue. Arizona is attempting to make a cash settlement (Blum, D., 1996).

Concert Tour Promotions

In a recent action involving a concert tour promotions contract, several consumers brought a claim against a ticket distribution operation and concert promoter. The plaintiffs alleged that defendants entered into contracts in restraint of trade and engaged in monopolistic practices that illegally shut out competition and created unreasonably high service charges. The Court held that a violation had not occurred because the defendant had previously disclosed its fees and did not engage in any collusive practices (*Sands v. Ticketmaster-New York*, 1994). This further emphasizes the care and precision which must accompany the drafting of complex event-related contracts.

References

A. Cases

Dorman v. Publix-Saenger-Sparks Theatres, Inc., 184 So 886 (Fla 1938).

East Stroudsburg Area School District and Stroudsburg Area School District v. Pennsylvania Interscholastic Athletic Association, Inc., Civ. Case No. 3195 (Ct. Com. Pleas, 1995).

J.M. Montgomery Roofing Co. v. Fred Howland, Inc., 98 So2d 484 (Fla 1957).

Mara v. Tunney, 236 N.Y. App. Div. 82 (1st Dept. 1932).

Sands v. Ticketmaster-New York, 616 N.Y.S.2d 362; 207 A.D. 2d 687 (N.Y.A.D. 1 Dept., 1994).

Sult v. Gilbert, 3 So. 2d 729 (S Ct. Fla 1941).

B. Publications

Berry, R. and Wong, G.M., (1993). *Law and Business of the Sports Industries*, Vol. 2 (2d ed.), Westport, Conn.: Praeger.

Black, H.C. (1990). *Black's Law Dictionary* (6th ed.). St. Paul, Minn.: West Publishing Co.

Blum, D., Saint Joseph's University Sends University of Arizona Bill for Cancelled Game, *Chronicle of Higher Education*, February 25, 1996, p. A43.

Cutherwood, D. and van Kirk, R. (1992). *The Complete Guide to Special Event Management.* Toronto: John Wiley and Sons.

Graham, S., Goldblatt, J. and Delpy, L. (1995). *The Ultimate Guide to Sport Event Management and Marketing.* Chicago: Richard D. Irwin, Inc.

Sharp, L., *Sport Law* (NOLPE No. 40, NOLPE Monograph Series), (1990). USA: Pace Setter Graphics, Inc.

4.00 • CONSTITUTIONAL LAW

4.11
Judicial Review, Standing, and Injunctions

Lisa Pike Masteralexis
University of Massachusetts-Amherst

Sport managers make decisions regarding athletic rules and regulations daily. When making decisions sport managers must realize that they do not possess complete control over rules and regulations, as their decisions may be reviewed by courts. Although courts generally take a "hands-off" approach to reviewing decisions of private athletic organizations, in a limited number of situations courts will review the actions of private athletic organizations. A court may grant a review of an athletic organization's action provided the plaintiff has standing, which is a right to bring an action in court. A plaintiff seeking judicial review of an athletic organization's decision will be asking the court to grant an order to bar the athletic organization from going forward with its decision. The granting of court orders is also called providing injunctive relief.

■ ■ ■ ■

Representative Case

CHRIST THE KING REGIONAL HIGH SCHOOL
v.
CATHOLIC HIGH SCHOOLS ATHLETIC ASSOCIATION, DIOCESE OF BROOKLYN
Supreme Court of New York, Queens County
624 N.Y.S.2d 755 (1995)

OPINION:

In this action seeking, inter alia, a permanent injunction, plaintiff Christ the King Regional High School moves herein for a preliminary injunction restraining the defendant, the Catholic High Schools Athletic Association, Diocese of Brooklyn, from implementing and enforcing a directive of the Principals' Committee of said association, which suspends plaintiff's girls' varsity basketball team from playing in postseason league and tournament play for the 1994/1995 season.

The issue confronting the court on this day, March 10, 1995, is whether movant should be allowed to play tomorrow, Saturday, March 11, 1995 in the Diocese championships and for any games remaining in this season.

Granting or denying the preliminary injunction herein amounts to a determination of the entire action. For that reason the court notified the attorneys on March 8, 1995, that it was prepared to consider the motion as one for summary judgment, and directed them to provide a stipulation of agreed facts and any other documents and affidavits they chose to produce.

The plaintiff is a member of the defendant athletic association and is governed by the association's constitution and bylaws. Its members are subject to the discipline of its Eligibility and Infractions Committee, whose recommendations for sanctions are, in turn, subject to ratification by the Principals' Committee. Pursuant to the bylaws, teams of the member schools are restricted to one trip outside the metropolitan area during any competitive season. It is undisputed that the plaintiff's girls' basketball team travelled to western Pennsylvania in early December and to Ohio at the end of that month. It further appears that the Eligibility and Infractions Committee of the girls league conducted hearings regarding plaintiff's violation of the travel rule on January 12, 1995, and on January 18, 1995 made a recommendation to the Principals' Committee that suspension was not required, and that a sufficient sanction would be to restrict plaintiff's tournament play for the 1995/1996 season to the confines of the metropolitan area. The Principals' Committee convened on February 9, 1995 and rejected the Eligibility and Infractions Committee's determination. In a letter to plaintiff dated February 16, 1995, the president of the Principals' Committee informed plaintiff that its girls' varsity basketball team will be suspended from league play for the remainder of this season and for at least one additional season, effective February 22, 1995.

It is well settled that the law of associations accords judicial relief to an association member suspended without adherence to its rules, and the courts of this State have consistently recognized the right to such relief. Whether by analogy to the law of associations, on the basis of a "supposed contract," or simply as a matter of essential fairness to its members and their students, it has been held that when an association has adopted a rule or guideline establishing the procedure to be followed in relation to suspension, that procedure must be substantially observed. This court recognizes that private educational organizations may to a large extent order their own affairs; but, at the very least, their conduct may not be arbitrary or capricious or violative of the applicable constitutions, bylaws, rules or regulations.

Section G6 of the girls league bylaws entitled "Procedures for Review of Infractions" is specifically applicable to this case, and provides as follows:

a. A proceeding under this article shall be commenced by the filing of a notice of infraction by the principal of a member school with the Eligibility and Infractions Committee.

b. The Committee shall commence an investigation within 14 days of receipt of the notice and shall make a decision regarding penalties or sanctions it deems appropriate within 60 days after the commencement of the investigation.

c. No decision or enforcement procedure requesting penalties or sanctions shall be implemented without review and ratification by the Principals' Committee.

Article V, subdivision (2) (e) of the constitution specifically limits the authority of the Principals' Committee as follows: "The Principals' Committee will review and authorize any sanctions recommended by the Eligibility and Infractions Committees of the boys and girls leagues."

In the opinion of this court, the Eligibility and Infractions Committee is given the exclusive right to investigate alleged infractions and to decide upon penalties or sanctions. The Principals' Committee is limited to the review and ratification of the Eligibility and Infractions Committee's recommendations, and is not empowered by the constitution or bylaws to supersede and independently assume the fact-finding and penalty-imposing authority of the Eligibility and Infractions Committee.

In light of the foregoing, the court finds that the sanction of suspension imposed by defendant's Principals' Committee against plaintiff's girls' varsity basketball team was ultra vires, and was arbitrary and capricious because it was meted out without proper authority in violation of defendant's own constitution and bylaws.

Accordingly, plaintiff's motion, deemed one for summary judgment, is granted, and defendant's cross motion to dismiss is denied for lack of merit. The defendant is hereby restrained and prohibited from barring and interfering with participation of plaintiff's girls' varsity basketball team in postseason tournaments for the 1994/1995 scheduled season.

■ ■ ■ ■

Fundamental Concepts

Judicial Review

Scope of review. As a general rule, courts decline to intervene in the internal affairs of the private, voluntary organizations which govern professional and amateur sports. The reasoning behind this policy is that membership in the organizations are voluntary and the organizations are self regulating. The court will, however, review the decisions where one of the following conditions is met:

1. The rule or regulation challenged by the plaintiff exceeds the scope of the athletic association's authority.
2. The rule or regulation challenged by the plaintiff violates an individual's constitutional rights.
3. The rule or regulation challenged by the plaintiff is applied in an arbitrary and/or capricious manner.
4. The rule or regulation challenged by the plaintiff violates public policy because it is considered fraudulent or unreasonable.
5. The athletic association breaks one of its own rules.

The harshness of a rule is not by itself grounds for judicial review. Relief is granted only where the plaintiff can prove to the court that one of the above conditions has been met. Even where a rule is subject to review, the court's role is limited. A court will not review the merits of the rule, but simply decide whether the application of the rule is invalid on the basis of meeting one of the five conditions listed above.

Application. Despite the standards listed above, often the decisions in cases involving athletic associations may vary. Among the reasons why cases vary is that there may be due to variations in precedent across jurisdictions or due to variation in regional standards, such as when a community is given the right to determine standards. An example would be in the distinction between free speech and obscenity. The Supreme Court has deferred to communities to define obscenity, such that what may be considered obscene in Lincoln, Nebraska may not be obscene in New York City. One area where there has been some variation is where an amateur athletic association has imposed rules barring married students from participation in high school athletics. In one case, *Estay v. La Fourche Parish School Board* (La. Ct. App. 1969), a married high school student challenged his exclusion from all extracurricular activities. The Louisiana Court of Appeals held that the school board had the authority to adopt the regulation. The regulation survived equal protection scrutiny because the court found there was a rational relationship between the rule and its stated objective of promoting completion of high school before marriage. Finally, the court held that the rule was not arbitrary and capricious for it was applied uniformly and impartially against all who sought to participate in extracurricular activities, not simply athletics. Eight years later and in another jurisdiction, *Beeson v. Kiowa County School District* (Colo. Ct. App. 1977) the Colorado Court of Appeals ruled for the student-athlete, stating that he possessed a fundamental right to marry and the reasons proffered by the school board did not establish a compelling state interest to justify the violation of the plaintiff's equal protection rights.

Similarly, jurisdictions vary when enforcing rules which prohibit the use of alcohol and drugs, often called good conduct rules. If the rules address a legitimate sports-related purpose courts will often find that they are within the scope of the association's authority. But where the rule is intrusive and broadly attempts to regulate the conduct of a student athlete during the off-season or conduct unrelated to athletic participation, a court will likely strike it down. In *Braesch v. De Pasquale*, 265 N.W. 2d 842 (Neb. Sup. Ct. 1978), the Supreme court of Nebraska ruled that a rule prohibiting drinking served a legitimate rational interest by directly affecting the discipline of a student athlete. The court also ruled that the rule was not arbitrary nor an unreasonable means to attain the legitimate end of deterring alcohol use among student-athletes. On the other hand, in *Bunger v. Iowa High School Athletic Association* (Sup. Ct. 1972) another court struck down a good conduct rule prohibiting the use of alcoholic beverages. During the summer, the plaintiff was riding in a car containing a case of beer. The car was pulled over by the police and the four minors in the car were issued citations. The plaintiff reported the incident to his athletic program and was suspended in accordance with the state athletic association rule. The Iowa Supreme Court held the rule was invalid on the grounds that it exceeded the scope of the athletic association's authority. The Court based its decision on the fact that the incident was outside of the football season, beyond the school year, and did not involve the illegal use of alcohol.

Finally, cases examining athletic association rules which infringe upon the constitutional right to freedom of expression have exhibited variation. In *Williams v. Eaton* (10th Cir., 1972), a group of fourteen African-American football players for the University of Wyoming sought permission from their coach to wear black armbands in their game against Brigham Young University to protest the beliefs of the Mormon Church. The coach dismissed them from the team for violating team rules prohibiting protests. In a court action challenging the rule the court held that the First Amendment rights of the players to freedom of speech could not be paramount to the rights of others to practice their religion free from a state-supported (University of Wyoming) protest. On the other hand *Tinker v. Des Moines Independent School District* (1969) held that student-athletes wearing politically motivated black armbands protesting the Vietnam War in a public high school were found to have a constitutionally protected right to freedom of expression.

Standing

Standing concerns a plaintiff's right to bring a complaint in court. In order to establish standing the plaintiff must meet three criteria:

1. The plaintiff bringing the action must have sustained an injury in fact.
2. The interest which the plaintiff seeks to be protected is one for which the court possesses the power to grant a remedy.
3. The plaintiff must have an interest in the outcome of the case.

The question of standing is generally one raised by the defense seeking to dismiss a case and not one which the court will raise on its own. In other words, as an initial matter, the plaintiff does not possess a burden of proof with regard to standing, but may be forced to show standing when the issue is raised by the defendant in a case.

Injunctive Relief

Scope. When a plaintiff seeks judicial review of an athletic association decision, the plaintiff will also request some form of injunctive relief to bar the rule from being applied. Injunctive relief is designed to prevent future wrongs, rather than to punish past actions. It is only used to prevent an irreparable injury which is suffered when monetary damages will not provide adequate compensation to the injured party. An injury is considered irreparable when it involves the risk of physical harm or death, the loss of a special opportunity, or the deprivation of unique, irreplaceable property. For example a high school senior student-athlete may be granted an injunction to compete in a championship game because he/she may never have that opportunity again.

Types of Injunctive Relief. There are four types of injunctive relief available to courts review: the temporary restraining order, the preliminary injunction, the permanent injunction, and specific performance. The **temporary restraining order** is generally issued to a plaintiff in an emergency situation, without notice (appearance at hearing) to the defendant, and is usually effective for a maximum of 10 days. Before a court will grant the temporary restraining order a plaintiff must prove that he/she will face irreparable harm and that money damages would be an inadequate remedy. The **preliminary injunction** is granted to a plaintiff prior to a full trial on the merits of a legal action and lasts throughout the trial process of the case. The defendant is given notice to appear at the hearing for the injunction and may argue against the granting of the preliminary injunction. To be awarded a preliminary injunction, the plaintiff must prove:

1. The plaintiff will face irreparable harm without the preliminary injunction.
2. Money damages are an inadequate remedy.
3. The plaintiff can prove that the balance of the hardships favor the plaintiff.
4. The plaintiff possesses a likelihood of success on the merits of the pending case.

A **permanent injunction** requires the plaintiff to prove the same four elements, but is awarded as a remedy following a full hearing on the merits of the case.

Finally, **specific performance** is a court order which may be available to the victim of a breach of contract. Specific performance requires that a defendant comply with (honor) the contract. Since money is generally an adequate remedy for a contract breach, specific performance is rarely used. The court will grant this remedy in situations where the subject matter is extremely rare. An example in sport where a court may be willing to grant specific performance is with a breach of a contract for the sale of sports memorabilia. For example, there may be only one Honus Wagner baseball card in the world and money may not be an adequate remedy to replace the card if the seller were to break the contract. In such a case the non-breaching party might seek an injunction for specific performance because the card is priceless and rare. One area where specific performance will not be granted is to enforce a contract of a professional athlete. While there may be only one Michael Jordan, if he were to break his contract with the Chicago Bulls, the court will not grant the Bulls a specific performance injunction to force Jordan to honor his contract with the Bulls. The reason is that by granting such an injunction the court would be forcing Jordan to work and would find its order in conflict with the U.S. Constitutional prohibition against slavery. In these cases, however, there is a remedy for professional teams. Courts are willing to grant negative injunctions against athletes who breach their contracts. A negative injunction is actually a preliminary or permanent injunction (depending on the time it is sought by the team—prior to trial or as part of a breach of contract award at the end of trial). The effect of the negative injunction is to prohibit the player from playing his or her sport for any other team or event than the plaintiff. In this way the court is not ordering the athlete to work, but simply prohibiting him/her from playing his/her sport anywhere but for the team possessing the valid and enforceable contract.

References

A. Cases

Beeson v. Kiowa County School District, 567 P. 2d 801 (Colo. Ct. App. 1977)

Braesch v. De Pasquale, 265 N.W. 2d 842 (Neb. Sup. Ct. 1978)

Bunger v. Iowa High School Athletic Association, 197 N.W. 2d 555 (Sup. Ct. 1972)

Christ the King Regional High School v. Catholic High Schools Athletic Association, 624 N.Y.S. 2d 755 (Sup. 1995)

Estay v. La Fourche Parish School Board, 230 So. 2d 443 (La. Ct. App. 1969)

Tinker v. Des Moines Independent School District, 383 F. 2d 988, rev'd 393 U.S. 503 (1969)

Williams v. Eaton, 468 F. 2d 1079 (10th Cir. 1972)

B. Publications

Wong, Glenn M. (1994). *Essentials of Amateur Athletics*, Second Edition. 135-61, 310-320.

Wong, Glenn M. and Masteralexis, Lisa Pike. (1996). "Sports Law," in Bridges, Francis J. and Roquemore, Libby L., *Management for Athletic/Sport Administration: Theory and Practice*.

4.12

State Action

T. Jesse Wilde
Huckvale & Company Law Offices

Save for the Thirteenth Amendment's prohibition on slavery, the United States Constitution does not seek to govern or regulate the affairs of individuals and private entities. The Constitution governs American governments, not Americans (Strickland, 1991). The individual rights and liberties guaranteed by the Constitution are, for the most part, freedoms from governmental action. The first eight Amendments apply, either expressly or impliedly, only to actions of the federal government. Similarly, the Due Process and Equal Protection Clauses of the Fourteenth Amendment expressly apply only to state governments. Only the Thirteen Amendment's prohibition of slavery directly restricts the actions of private citizens. With that exception, the important constitutional liberties apply to and restrict only governmental actions (Strickland, 1991). Thus, athletes, coaches and administrators seeking redress from allegedly unconstitutional conduct must, as a threshold issue, demonstrate state action; that is, that the conduct complained of "may be said to be that of the state" (*Shelley v. Kraemer*, 1948). Where the alleged wrongdoer is an extension of the government, such as a public high school or state-sponsored university, state action is a given. Where, however, the wrongdoer is an otherwise private organization, such as a college conference or professional sports league, the relevant state action inquiry is whether there is a sufficient connection between the wrongdoer and the government to justify a constitutional claim (Schwartz, 1989).

■ ■ ■ ■

Representative Case

NATIONAL COLLEGIATE ATHLETIC ASSOCIATION v. TARKANIAN
Supreme Court of the United States
488 U.S. 179 (1988)

OPINION: JUSTICE STEVENS delivered the opinion of the Court.

When he became head basketball coach at the University of Nevada, Las Vegas (UNLV), in 1973, Jerry Tarkanian inherited a team with a mediocre 14-14 record. App. 188, 205. Four years later the team won 29 out of 32 games and placed third in the championship tournament sponsored by the National Athletic Association (NCAA), to which UNLV belongs.

Yet in September 1977 UNLV informed Tarkanian that it was going to suspend him. No dissatisfaction with Tarkanian, once described as "the 'winningest' active basketball coach," motivated his suspension. Rather, the impetus was a report by the NCAA detailing 38 violations of NCAA rules by UNLV personnel, including 10 involving Tarkanian. The NCAA had placed the university's basketball team on probation for two years and ordered UNLV to show cause why the NCAA should not impose further penalties unless UNLV severed all ties during the probation between its intercollegiate athletic program and Tarkanian.

Facing demotion and a drastic cut in pay, Tarkanian brought suit in Nevada state court, alleging that he had been deprived of his Fourteenth Amendment due process rights in violation of 42 U. S. C. @ 1983. Ultimately Tarkanian obtained injunctive relief and an award of attorney's fees against both UNLV and the NCAA. 103 Nev. 331, 741 P. 2d 1345 (1987) (per curiam). NCAA's liability may be upheld only if its participation in the events that led to Tarkanian's suspension constituted "state action" prohibited by the Fourteenth Amendment and was performed "under color of" state law within the meaning of @ 1983. We granted certiorari to review the Nevada Supreme Court's holding that the NCAA engaged in state action when it conducted its investigation and recommended that Tarkanian be disciplined. 484 U.S. 1058 (1988). We now reverse.

• • •

Embedded in our Fourteenth Amendment jurisprudence is a dichotomy between state action, which is subject to scrutiny under the Amendment's Due Process Clause, and private conduct, against which the Amendment affords no shield, no matter how unfair that conduct may be. Shelley v. Kraemer, 334 U.S. 1, 13 (1948); see Jackson v. Metropolitan Edison Co., 419 U.S. 345, 349 (1974). As a general matter the protections of the Fourteenth Amendment do not extend to "private conduct abridging individual rights." Burton v. Wilmington Parking Authority, 365 U.S. 715, 722 (1961).

"Careful adherence to the 'state action' requirement preserves an area of individual freedom by limiting the reach of federal law" and avoids the imposition of responsibility on a State for conduct it could not control. Lugar, 457 U.S., at 936-937. When Congress enacted @ 1983 as the statutory remedy for violations of the Constitution, it specified that the conduct at issue must have occurred "under color of" state law; thus, liability attaches only to those wrongdoers "who carry a badge of authority of a State and represent it in some capacity, whether they act in accordance with their authority or misuse it." Monroe v. Pape, 365 U.S. 167, 172 (1961). As we stated in United States v. Classic, 313 U.S. 299, 326 (1941):

> Misuse of power, possessed by virtue of state law and made possible only because the wrongdoer is clothed with the authority of state law, is action taken "under color of" state law.

In this case Tarkanian argues that the NCAA was a state actor because it misused power that it possessed by virtue of state law. He claims specifically that UNLV delegated its own functions to the NCAA, clothing the Association with authority both to adopt rules governing UNLV's athletic programs and to enforce those rules on behalf of UNLV. Similarly, the Nevada Supreme Court held that UNLV had delegated its authority over personnel decisions to the NCAA. Therefore, the court reasoned, the two entities acted jointly to deprive Tarkanian of liberty and property interests, making the NCAA as well as UNLV a state actor.

These contentions fundamentally misconstrue the facts of this case. In the typical case raising a state-action issue, a private party has taken the decisive step that caused the harm to the plaintiff, and the question is whether the State was sufficiently involved to treat that decisive conduct as state action. This may occur if the State creates the legal framework governing the conduct, e. g., North Georgia Finishing, Inc. v. Di-Chem, Inc., 419 U.S. 601 (1975); if it delegates its authority to the private actor, e. g., West v. Atkins, 487 U.S. 42 (1988); or sometimes if it knowingly accepts the benefits derived from unconstitutional behavior, e. g., Burton v. Wilmington Parking Authority, supra. Thus, in the usual case we ask whether the State provided a mantle of authority that enhanced the power of the harm-causing individual actor.

This case uniquely mirrors the traditional state-action case. Here the final act challenged by Tarkanian—his suspension—was committed by UNLV. A state university without question is a state actor. When it decides to impose a serious disciplinary sanction upon one of its tenured employees, it must comply with the terms of the Due Process Clause of the Fourteenth Amendment to the Federal Constitution. Accord, Cleveland Board of Education v. Loudermill, 470 U.S. 532 (1985); Board of Regents of State Colleges v. Roth, 408 U.S. 564 (1972). Thus when UNLV notified Tarkanian that he was being separated from all relations with the university's basketball program, it acted under color of state law within the meaning of 42 U. S. C. @ 1983.

The mirror image presented in this case requires us to step through an analytical looking glass to resolve the case. Clearly UNLV's conduct was influenced by the rules and recommendations of the NCAA, the private party. But it was UNLV, the state entity, that actually suspended Tarkanian. Thus the question is not whether UNLV participated to a critical extent in the NCAA's activities, but whether UNLV's actions in compliance with the NCAA rules and recommendations turned the NCAA's conduct into state action.

We examine first the relationship between UNLV and the NCAA regarding the NCAA's rulemaking. UNLV is among the NCAA's members and participated in promulgating the Association's rules; it must be assumed, therefore, that Nevada had some impact on the NCAA's policy determinations. Yet the NCAA's several hundred other public and private member institutions each similarly affected those policies. Those institutions, the vast majority of which were located in States other than Nevada, did not act under color of Nevada law. It necessarily follows that the source of the legislation adopted by the NCAA is not Nevada but the collective membership, speaking through an organization that is independent of any particular State. Allied Tube & Conduit Corp. v. Indian Head, Inc., 486 U.S. 492, 501 (1988) ("Whatever de facto authority the [private standard-setting] Association enjoys, no official authority has been conferred on it by any government . . .").

State action nonetheless might lie if UNLV, by embracing the NCAA's rules, transformed them into state rules and the NCAA into a state actor. See Lugar, 457 U.S., at 937. UNLV engaged in state action when it adopted the NCAA's rules to govern its own behavior, but that would be true even if UNLV had taken no part in the promulgation of those rules. In Bates v. State Bar of Arizona, 433 U.S. 350 (1977), we established that the State Supreme Court's enforcement of disciplinary rules transgressed by members of its own bar was state action. Those rules had been adopted *in toto* from the American Bar Association Code of Professional Responsibility. It does not follow, however, that the ABA's formulation of those disciplinary rules was state action. The State Supreme Court retained plenary power to reexamine those standards and, if necessary, to reject them and promulgate its own. So here, UNLV retained the authority to withdraw from the NCAA and establish its own standards. The university alternatively could have stayed in the Association and worked through the Association's legislative process to amend rules or standards it deemed harsh, unfair, or unwieldy. Neither UNLV's decision to adopt the NCAA's standards nor its minor role in their formulation is a sufficient reason for concluding that the NCAA was acting under color of Nevada law when it promulgated standards governing athlete recruitment, eligibility, and academic performance.

Tarkanian further asserts that the NCAA's investigation, enforcement proceedings, and consequent recommendations constituted state action because they resulted from a delegation of power by UNLV. UNLV, as an NCAA member, subscribed to the statement in the Association's bylaws that NCAA "enforcement procedures are an essential part of the intercollegiate athletic program of each member institution." It is, of course, true that a State may delegate authority to a private party and thereby make that party a state actor. Thus, we recently held that a private physician who had contracted with a state prison to attend to the inmates' medical needs was a state actor. West v. Atkins, 487 U.S. 42 (1988). But UNLV delegated no power to the NCAA to take specific action against any university employee. The commitment by UNLV to adhere to NCAA enforcement procedures was enforceable only by sanctions that the NCAA might impose on UNLV itself.

Indeed, the notion that UNLV's promise to cooperate in the NCAA enforcement proceedings was tantamount to a partnership agreement or the transfer of certain university powers to the NCAA is belied by the history of this case. It is quite obvious that UNLV used its best efforts to retain its winning coach—a goal diametrically opposed to the NCAA's interest in ascertaining the truth of its investigators' reports. During the several years that the NCAA investigated the alleged violations, the NCAA and UNLV acted much more like adversaries than like partners engaged in a dispassionate search for the truth. The NCAA cannot be regarded as an agent of UNLV for purposes of that proceeding. It is more correctly characterized as an agent of its remaining members which, as competitors of UNLV, had an interest in the effective and evenhanded enforcement of the NCAA's recruitment standards. Just as a state-compensated public defender acts in a private capacity when he or she represents a private client in a conflict against the State, Polk County v. Dodson, 454 U.S. 312, 320 (1981), the NCAA is properly viewed as a private actor at odds with the State when it represents the interests of its entire membership in an investigation of one public university.

The NCAA enjoyed no governmental powers to facilitate its investigation. It had no power to subpoena witnesses, to impose contempt sanctions, or to assert sovereign authority over any individual. Its greatest authority was to threaten sanctions against UNLV, with the ultimate sanction being expulsion of the university from membership. Contrary to the premise of the Nevada Supreme Court's opinion, the NCAA did not—indeed, could not—directly discipline Tarkanian or any other state university employee. The express terms of the Confidential Report did not demand the suspension unconditionally; rather, it requested "the University . . . to show cause" why the NCAA should not impose additional penalties if UNLV declines to suspend Tarkanian. Even the university's vice president acknowledged that the Report gave the university options other than suspension: UNLV could have retained Tarkanian and risked additional sanctions, perhaps even expulsion from the NCAA, or it could have withdrawn voluntarily from the Association.

Finally, Tarkanian argues that the power of the NCAA is so great that the UNLV had no practical alternative to compliance with its demands. We are not at all sure this is true, but even if we assume that a private monopolist can impose its will on a state agency by a threatened refusal to deal with it, it does not follow that such a private party is therefore acting under color of state law. Jackson, 419 U.S., at 351-352 (State's conferral of monopoly status does not convert private party into state actor).

In final analysis the question is whether "the conduct allegedly causing the deprivation of a federal right [can] be fairly attributable to the State." Lugar, 457 U.S., at 937. It would be ironic indeed to conclude that the NCAA's imposition of sanctions against UNLV—sanctions that UNLV and its counsel, including the Attorney General of Nevada, steadfastly opposed during protracted adversary proceedings—is fairly attributable to the State of Nevada. It would be more appropriate to conclude that UNLV has conducted its athletic program under color of the policies adopted by the NCAA, rather than that those policies were developed and enforced under color of Nevada law.

The judgment of the Nevada Supreme Court is reversed, and the case is remanded to that court for further proceedings not inconsistent with this opinion.

It is so ordered.

DISSENT: JUSTICE WHITE, with whom JUSTICE BRENNAN, JUSTICE MARSHALL, and JUSTICE O'CONNOR join, dissenting.

All agree that UNLV, a public university, is a state actor, and that the suspension of Jerry Tarkanian, a public employee, was state action. The question here is whether the NCAA acted jointly with UNLV in suspending Tarkanian and thereby also became a state actor. I would hold that it did.

I agree with the majority that this case is different on its facts from many of our prior state-action cases. As the majority notes, in our "typical case raising a state-action issue, a private party has taken the decisive step that caused the harm to the plaintiff." In this case, however, which in the majority's view "uniquely mirrors the traditional state-action case," the final act that caused the harm to Tarkanian was committed, not by a private party, but by a party conceded to be a state actor. Because of this difference, the majority finds it necessary to "step through an analytical looking glass" to evaluate whether the NCAA was a state actor.

But the situation presented by this case is not unknown to us and certainly is not unique. In both Adickes v. S. H. Kress & Co., 398 U.S. 144 (1970), and Dennis v. Sparks, 449 U.S. 24 (1980), we faced the question whether private parties could be held to be state actors in cases in which the final or decisive act was carried out by a state official. In both cases we held that the private parties could be found to be state actors, if they were "jointly engaged with state officials in the challenged action."

• • •

On the facts of the present case, the NCAA acted jointly with UNLV in suspending Tarkanian. First, Tarkanian was suspended for violations of NCAA rules, which UNLV embraced in its agreement with the NCAA. As the Nevada Supreme Court found in its first opinion in this case, University of Nevada v. Tarkanian, 95 Nev. 389, 391, 594 P. 2d 1159, 1160 (1979), "[a]s a member of the NCAA, UNLV contractually agrees to administer its athletic program in accordance with NCAA legislation." Indeed, NCAA rules provide that NCAA "enforcement procedures are an essential part of the intercollegiate athletic program of each member institution."

Second, the NCAA and UNLV also agreed that the NCAA would conduct the hearings concerning violations of its rules. Although UNLV conducted its own investigation into the recruiting violations alleged by the NCAA, the NCAA procedures provide that it is the NCAA Committee on Infractions that "determine[s] facts related to alleged violations," subject to an appeal to the NCAA Council. As a result of this agreement, the NCAA conducted the very hearings the Nevada Supreme Court held to have violated Tarkanian's right to procedural due process.

Third, the NCAA and UNLV agreed that the findings of fact made by the NCAA at the hearings it conducted would be binding on UNLV. By becoming a member of the NCAA, UNLV did more than merely "promise to cooperate in the NCAA enforcement proceedings." It agreed, as the university hearing officer appointed to rule on Tarkanian's suspension expressly found, to accept the NCAA's "findings of fact as in some way superior to [its] own." App. 74. By the terms of UNLV's membership in the NCAA, the NCAA's findings were final and not subject to further review by any other body, and it was for that reason that UNLV suspended Tarkanian, despite concluding that many of those findings were wrong.

In short, it was the NCAA's findings that Tarkanian had violated NCAA rules, made at NCAA-conducted hearings, all of which were agreed to by UNLV in its membership agreement with the NCAA, that resulted in Tarkanian's suspension by UNLV. On these facts, the

NCAA was "jointly engaged with [UNLV] officials in the challenged action," and therefore was a state actor.

• • •

The majority states in conclusion that "[i]t would be ironic indeed to conclude that the NCAA's imposition of sanctions against UNLV—sanctions that UNLV and its counsel, including the Attorney General of Nevada, steadfastly opposed during protracted adversary proceedings—is fairly attributable to the State of Nevada." I agree. Had UNLV refused to suspend Tarkanian, and the NCAA responded by imposing sanctions against UNLV, it would be hard indeed to find any state action that harmed Tarkanian. But that is not this case. Here, UNLV did suspend Tarkanian, and it did so because it embraced the NCAA rules governing conduct of its athletic program and adopted the results of the hearings conducted by the NCAA concerning Tarkanian, as it had agreed that it would. Under these facts, I would find that the NCAA acted jointly with UNLV and therefore is a state actor.

I respectfully dissent.

■ ■ ■ ■

Fundamental Concepts

State Action Analysis

Determining when private conduct is state action and thus subject to constitutional claims has long been one of the most troublesome issues in constitutional law (Strickland, 1991). Nearly every article about the state action doctrine published in the last twenty years quotes and concurs with Professor Charles Black's characterization of the doctrine as "a conceptual disaster area" (Black, 1967).

The first significant set of decisions of the United States Supreme Court regarding the state action doctrine were *The Civil Rights Cases*, (1883), wherein the Court held that conduct which is exclusively private is not governed by the Fourteenth Amendment, and that the guarantees of equal protection and due process apply only to state action. An act by a state government is clearly state action. However, less clear are those cases where a private entity acts in concert with a state government (Westover, 1989). Two basic theories have evolved to find state action when the challenged act of a private entity is attributable to the state: when either the state is sufficiently "involved" or "entangled" with the private action, or when the private action constitutes the performance of a "public function" (Graglia, 1989).

Nexus or Entanglement Theory. The nexus or entanglement theory examines whether the state's involvement or entanglement with a private actor's conduct is sufficient to transform the private conduct into state action, and thus subject the conduct to constitutional review. In *Jackson v. Metropolitan Edison Co.* (1974), Justice Rehnquist, addressing the nexus or entanglement approach, stated:

> While the principle that private action is immune from the restrictions of the Fourteenth Amendment is well established and easily stated, the question whether particular conduct is "private," on the one hand, or "state action," on the other, frequently admits of no easy answer. . . . It may well be that acts of a heavily regulated activity with at least something of a governmentally protected monopoly will more readily be found to be "state" acts than will the acts of an entity lacking these characteristics. But the inquiry must be whether there is a *sufficiently close nexus* between the State and the challenged action of the regulated entity so that the action of the latter may be fairly treated as that of the State itself. (349-351)

The scope of this state action theory was curtailed by three 1982 Supreme Court decisions in *Blum v. Yaretsky*, *Rendell-Baker v. Kohn*, and *Lugar v. Edmondson Oil Co.* In *Blum*, the Court held that privately owned nursing homes reimbursed by the state were not state actors for purposes of Fourteenth Amendment claims. The mere receipt of state funds did not transform otherwise private acts into state action, unless the state exercises coercive power or provides significant encouragement, either overt or covert, such that the private acts are deemed to be that of the State. In *Rendell-Baker*, the Court held that a private school funded primarily from public funds and regulated by public authorities was not a state actor since the school's decision to discharge employees was not compelled or influenced by state funding or state regulation. In *Lugar*, the Court found the state action requirement to be met when a private party jointly participated with state officials in the seizure of disputed property, and depriving a citizen of his due process rights. The net result of this Supreme Court trilogy restricts the nexus or entanglement theory, such that neither state funding nor state regulation, without more, is enough to command a state actor determination, and that significant joint participation between the state and the private party is essential for the state actor label to attach (Westover, 1989).

Public Function Theory. In a line of decisions beginning with *Marsh v. Alabama*, (1946), the Supreme Court recognized a public function theory of state action that departed from earlier notions of state action through entanglement or joint participation. Under this theory a court can find state action in the activities of a private party if that party undertakes functions or assumes powers that the government ordinarily performs or exercises (Strickland, 1991). In *Marsh*, the Court held that a company-owned town which took on all of the functions and characteristics of a regular public municipality was subject to the requirements of the Constitution, and that its attempt to curtail the distribution of Jehovah's Witness literature on its streets violated both the First and Fourteenth Amendments.

Subsequent to *Marsh*, the Court has used this public function theory to apply constitutional restrictions in several other contexts, including: elections held by private political associations (*Terry v. Adams*, 1953); the operation of a public park (*Evans v. Newton*, 1966); and the maintenance of common areas of a shopping center (*Amalgamated Food Employees v. Logan Valley Plaza*, 1968). No Supreme Court decision since *Logan Valley* has used the public function theory to apply the Fourteenth Amendment to private conduct. In fact, in *Hudgens v. NLRB*, (1976) the Court overruled *Logan Valley*, holding that a shopping center's refusal to permit the distribution of literature on its premises is not state action subject to the Fourteenth Amendment (Strickland, 1991). In two additional cases, *Jackson v. Metropolitan Edison Co.*, (1974) and *Flagg Bros. v. Brooks*, (1978), the Court further clarified and restricted the public function theory, such that private activities will only constitute state action under this theory if: 1) the activities involve a function that traditionally has been performed only by government; and, 2) the private entity's assumption of the function substantially replaces the government's traditional performance of the function (Strickland, 1991).

Application to Athletic Organizations

Courts have consistently held that the activities of public schools and state-funded universities constitute state action. A more difficult analysis involves whether state action exists in the conduct and administration of private voluntary athletic associations, including high school athletic associations, college conferences, national organizations governing college athletics, Olympic organizations, and professional sport leagues. In such an analysis, there are, for the most part, no hard and fast rules. Instead, as the Court stated in *Lugar*, the recognition of state action depends upon an ad hoc analysis of the facts of each case.

High School Athletic Associations. Historically, the overwhelming majority of cases have found state high school athletic associations to be state actors and therefore subject to the requirements of the Constitution. Many such cases find state action under a nexus or entanglement theory based on the fact that the majority of schools within an association are tax supported institutions, that the association is the beneficiary of tax funds or tax concessions from the state, and that the association uses public facilities, athletic stadiums and gymnasiums, which have been constructed and maintained with tax funds, for its events. (See, for example, *Louisiana High School Athletic Association v. St. Augustine High School*, 1968; *Wright v. Arkansas Activities Association*, 1974; *Yellow Springs Exempted School District v. Ohio High School Athletic*

Association, 1978). In *Barnhorst v. Missouri State High School Athletic Association*, (W.D. Mo. 1980), the court relied on the public function test in finding the association a state actor, based on the similarities between the functions served by the association and the state as regulators of school age children.

A contrary view is expressed in *Anderson by Anderson v. Indiana H.S. Athletic Association*, (S.D. Ind. 1988), where the court concluded that the imposition of a suspension based upon an association transfer rule was not state action. Based upon the Supreme Court's 1982 trilogy of state action cases, the court undertook a more rigorous examination of the constitution and activities of the association, concluding that the association was not a state actor since it is not an official arm of the State, nor subject to coercive state regulation, nor performing a public function that can fairly be said to be traditionally performed only by government.

College Conferences. The determination of whether a college conference is a state actor involves an analysis similar to that involving high school athletic associations. Courts concluding that conferences are state actors have focused on the conference's membership, that the majority of its schools are tax-supported institutions, that the conference is the direct or indirect beneficiary of tax funds or tax concessions from the state, and that the conference uses public facilities, athletic stadiums and gymnasiums, which have been constructed and maintained with tax funds, for its events. For example, in *Stanley v. Big Eight Conference*, (W.D. Mo. 1978) the court held that because the Big Eight is composed solely of state-supported public universities which have delegated supervisory functions to the conference, the actions of the Big Eight conference amounted to state action (McKenna, 1992).

National Organizations Governing College Athletics. National organizations governing college athletics, such as the National Collegiate Athletic Association (NCAA), the National Association of Intercollegiate Athletics (NAIA), and the National Junior College Athletic Association (NJCAA), are private voluntary associations composed of both public and private institutions. The determination of whether the activities of such national organizations constitute state action is best reflected in a series of cases involving the NCAA.

The NCAA is a privately funded, unincorporated association of approximately 1000 member schools. State-funded colleges and universities comprise roughly half the association's membership. Despite the NCAA's status as a private association, federal courts throughout the 1970s found state action in the association's enforcement of its rules and regulations. In *Buckton v. NCAA*, (D.Mass. 1973) the court concluded that the NCAA was a state actor, when it denied intercollegiate hockey eligibility to Canadian student-athletes because they had participated in junior hockey in Canada, based on the fact that more than half of the NCAA members schools received state funding and the NCAA's nationwide sovereign-like role in supervising and policing intercollegiate athletics. In *Howard University v. NCAA*, (D.C. Cir. 1975) the D.C. Circuit found state action in the NCAA's enforcement of its five year competition rule, its 1.6 GPA rule, and its foreign student rule, based on the significant role of state-supported institutions in the association's governance and control. In *Parish v. NCAA*, (5th Cir. 1975) the Fifth Circuit also found state action in the NCAA's enforcement of its 1.6 GPA rule, based on the fact that state-supported institutions play a substantial role in the administration of the NCAA, and that the association, by engaging in the regulation of education through organized athletics, fulfills a role that is beyond the reach of one state and thus performs a traditional governmental function.

The trend toward finding state action in NCAA cases reversed in the 1980s, following the Supreme Court's 1982 trilogy of state action cases, which restricted the nexus or entanglement theory, such that neither state funding nor state regulation, without more, is enough to command a state actor determination, and that significant joint participation between the state and the private party is essential for the state actor label to attach (Westover, 1989). In *Arlosoroff v. NCAA*, (4th Cir. 1984), relying on these Supreme Court rulings, the Fourth Circuit held that mere indirect involvement of state governments could no longer suffice to convert the acts of a private entity into state action (Thompson, 1994). The court concluded that the NCAA was not a state actor since there was no indication that the state-funded schools within the association caused or procured the adoption of the NCAA bylaws governing student-athlete eligibility, and thus the state did not order or cause the action. Further, the regulation of intercollegiate athletics was not a function traditionally reserved exclusively to the state (Thompson, 1994). Results similar to *Arlosoroff* followed in *Barbay v. NCAA*, (E.D. La. 1987) and *Hawkins v. NCAA*, (C.D. Ill. 1987). In *Barbay*, the court held that the NCAA's adoption, enforcement and implementation of its drug testing program did not constitute state action. The plaintiff had failed to demonstrate that the state-funded members of the association had caused or procured the implementation of the testing program. In *Hawkins*, the court held that the NCAA's imposition of sanctions against Bradley University did not constitute state action under reasoning similar to *Arlosoroff* and *Barbay*.

In 1988, the United States Supreme Court was presented with the issue of whether the NCAA was a state actor in *NCAA v. Tarkanian*, (1988). The edited text of the Court's decision is included above. In summary, by a five to four majority, the Court held that the NCAA's conduct, ultimately resulting in the suspension of Coach Tarkanian for two years by the University of Nevada, Las Vegas (UNLV), was not state action. The Court found that neither UNLV's decision to adopt the NCAA's standards nor its minor role in their formulation is a sufficient reason for concluding that the NCAA's conduct amounted to state action when it promulgated standards governing athlete recruitment, eligibility and academic performance. The Court also rejected Tarkanian's contention that the NCAA became a state actor in these circumstances where it acted jointly with UNLV, a state-funded institution, to allegedly deny Coach Tarkanian his due process rights under the Fourteenth Amendment. The Court reasoned that the NCAA could not mandate UNLV to take any action against Tarkanian, and it could do nothing directly to suspend the coach. UNLV retained full authority to act as it deemed appropriate toward its coach. The institution retained authority not only to reject NCAA rules, but also to avoid the suspension of Tarkanian, and simply chose to abide by the NCAA sanction rather than risk further penalties (Strickland, 1991). The four dissenting Justices found this joint participation theory compelling, and would have held the NCAA to be a state actor because it acted jointly with UNLV in suspending Tarkanian.

Olympic Organizations.   Even though it is a creature of statute, is federally regulated, and is the recipient of federal financial support, courts have held that activities of the United States Olympic Committee (USOC) do not constitute state action. In *DeFrantz v. USOC*, (D.D.C. 1980), aff'd, (D.C. Cir. 1980), the court held that the USOC's decision not to send an American team to participate in the 1980 Moscow Olympics could not be considered state action, since the government did not exert its control or influence on the USOC so as to become a joint participant with the USOC in the boycott. Similarly, in *San Francisco Arts & Athletics, Inc. v. USOC*, (1987) the U.S. Supreme Court, in a five to four decision, held that the USOC's refusal to grant SFAA permission to use the word "Olympics" was not state action and thus could not violate the Fifth Amendment. The USOC's federal charter, its federal funding, and its federal grant of exclusivity to the word "Olympic" did not constitute sufficient federal involvement with the USOC to entangle it with the state. In addition, because the USOC's activities traditionally were performed by private entities rather than the government, the Court held that the USOC was not a state actor under the public function doctrine (Strickland, 1991).

Professional Sport Leagues.   Described as joint ventures of independent clubs or as a single entity comprised of separately managed divisions, sports leagues are a cooperative effort of largely private business owners to produce sporting exhibitions for a profit (Weiler, 1991). Under most circumstances, acts of these private business entities, will not constitute state action since their business activities are typically not entangled with the state sufficient to transform otherwise private conduct into state action, nor do professional teams and leagues perform a function that has traditionally been performed exclusively by the state.

That is not to say, however, that professional teams and leagues have never been considered state actors. In *Ludtke v. Kuhn*, (S.D.N.Y. 1978) the court found state action in the New York Yankees' enforcement of the baseball commissioner's policy to deny female reporters access to Major League Baseball clubhouses. The fact that the Yankees leased the stadium from the city, that they had obtained significant rent concessions from the city, that public funds had been used to improve the stadium in order to enhance the Yankee's drawing power and profitability, and that the city provided the Yankees with additional police presence on game days created the appearance of government authorization of and participation in the unconstitutional policies and practices of the Yankees and Major League Baseball (Gregus, 1993).

In a day when more and more professional franchises are seeking significant concessions from their home states and local municipalities, in terms of stadium construction and revenue, tax concessions and the like, it may be argued that professional teams and leagues are sufficiently entangled with the state to warrant constitutional scrutiny of their activities (Gregus, 1993).

Recent Developments

Enforcement of NFL Drug Testing Not State Action.   In *Long v. NFL*, (N.D.Pa. 1994) the U.S. District Court for the Northern District of Pennsylvania dismissed the complaint of Terry Long, a former member of the Pittsburgh Steelers, who was suspended for testing positive for steroid use. The complaint alleged that the NFL testing policies violated Long's federal and state guarantees against unreasonable search and seizure. The NFL contended that its drug testing policies and procedures were not the product of state action and therefore not subject to a constitutionally-based claim. The court examined the business relationship between the City of Pittsburgh, the Steelers and the NFL, including the City's involvement in the construction of Three Rivers Stadium, and the City's collection of an amusement tax on the sale of Steeler game tickets, and concluded that the business association between the NFL and the City was insufficient to establish state action necessary to support the constitutional violations claimed (Cruz, 1995).

High School Athletic Associations as State Actors.   In a number of recent decisions, the activities of high school athletic associations in enforcing rules and regulations have been considered state action. In *Mississippi High School Activities Association, Inc. v. Coleman* (1994), the Mississippi Supreme Court found state action in the association's enforcement of its anti-recruiting rule. In *Jordan v. Indiana High School Athletic Association* (1994), the U.S. District Court for the Northern District of Indiana found state action in the association's enforcement of its eligibility rules. The Seventh Circuit dismissed the IHSAA appeal as moot since the player had graduated, this notwithstanding the association's arguments that its rules authorized it to take certain actions against the player's school and the player despite his graduation. And, in *Beck v. Missouri State High School Activities Association* (1994), the U.S. District Court for the Eastern District of Missouri found state action in the association's enforcement of its one-year transfer rule, but struck down an exemption to the rule for transfers from nonpublic to public schools as violative of the Equal Protection Clause. The Eighth Circuit dismissed the association appeal as moot since more than a year had passed since Beck had brought the action, and he was now eligible to play varsity basketball under the transfer rule.

References

A. Cases
Amalgamated Food Employees v. Logan Valley Plaza, 391 U.S. 308 (1968).
Anderson by Anderson v. Indiana H.S. Athletic Association, 699 F.Supp. 719 (S.D. Ind. 1988).
Arlosoroff v. NCAA, 746 F.2d 1019 (4th Cir. 1984).

Barbay v. NCAA, 1987 WL 5619 (E.D. La. 1987).

Barnhorst v. Missouri State High School Athletic Association, 504 F.Supp. 449 (W.D. Mo. 1980).

Beck v. Missouri State High School Activities Association, 837 F.Supp. 998 (E.D. Mo. 1993), dismissed as moot, 18 F.3d 604 (8th Cir. 1994).

Blum v. Yaretsky, 457 U.S. 991 (1982).

Buckton v. NCAA, 366 F.Supp. 1152 (D.Mass. 1973).

The Civil Rights Cases, 109 U.S. 3 (1883).

DeFrantz v. USOC, 492 F.Supp. 1181 (D.D.C. 1980), aff'd, 701 F.2d 221 (D.C. Cir. 1980).

Evans v. Newton, 382 U.S. 296 (1966).

Flagg Bros. v. Brooks, 436 U.S. 149 (1978).

Hawkins v. NCAA, 652 F.Supp. 602 (C.D. Ill. 1987).

Howard University v. NCAA, 510 F.2d 213 (D.C. Cir. 1975).

Hudgens v. NLRB, 424 U.S. 507 (1976).

Jackson v. Metropolitan Edison Co., 419 U.S. 345 (1974).

Jordan v. Indiana High School Athletic Association, 813 F. Supp 1372 (N.D. Ind. 1993), dismissed as moot, 16 F.3d 785 (7th Cir. 1994).

Long v. NFL, 870 F.Supp. 101 (N.D.Pa. 1994).

Louisiana High School Athletic Association v. St. Augustine High School, 396 F.2d 224 (5th Cir. 1968).

Ludtke v. Kuhn, 461 F.Supp. 86 (S.D.N.Y. 1978).

Lugar v. Edmondson Oil Co., 457 U.S. 922 (1982).

Marsh v. Alabama, 326 U.S. 501 (1946).

Mississippi High School Activities Association, Inc. v. Coleman, 631 So.2d 768 (1994)

NCAA v. Tarkanian, 488 U.S. 179 (1988).

Parish v. NCAA, 506 F.2d 1028 (5th Cir. 1975).

Rendell-Baker v. Kohn, 457 U.S. 830 (1982).

San Francisco Arts & Athletics, Inc. v. USOC, 483 U.S. 522 (1987).

Shelley v. Kraemer, 334 U.S. 1 (1948).

Stanley v. Big Eight Conference, 463 F.Supp. 920 (W.D. Mo. 1978).

Terry v. Adams, 345 U.S. 461 (1953).

Wright v. Arkansas Activities Association, 501 F.2d 25 (8th Cir. 1974).

Yellow Springs Exempted School District v. Ohio High School Athletic Association, 443 F.Supp. 753 (S.D. Ohio 1978) reversed on other grounds, 647 F.2d 651 (6th Cir. 1981)).

B. Publications

Black, Charles. (1967). The Supreme Court, 1966 Term—Forward: "State Action," Equal Protection, and California's Proposition 14. 81 *Harvard Law Review* 69-95.

Cruz, Anthony, Jr. (May 1995). NFL Drug Testing Survives a Former Player's Suit. 2 *Sports Law Monthly* 9-10.

Graglia, Lino A. (1989). State Action: Constitutional Phoenix. 67 *Washington University law Quarterly* 777-798.

Gregus, Daniel R. (Winter 1993). The NFL's Drug-Testing Policies: Are They Constitutional? 10 *The Entertainment and Sports Lawyer* 1-4, 25-28.

McKenna, Kevin M. (1992). Courts Leave Legislatures to Decide the Fate of the NCAA in Providing Due Process. 2 *Seton Hall Journal of Sport Law* 77-128.

Schwartz, J.M. (1989). NCAA v. Tarkanian: State Action in Collegiate Athletics. 63 *Tulane Law Review* 1703-1710.

Strickland, Henry C. (1991). The State Action Doctrine and the Rehnquist Court. 18 *Hastings Constitutional Law Quarterly* 587-666.

Thompson, Ronald J. (1994). Due Process and the National Collegiate Athletic Association: Are There Any Constitutional Standards? 41 *UCLA Law Review* 1651-1684.

Weiler, Paul C. and Roberts, Gary R. (1993). *Sports and the Law; Cases: Materials and Problems*.

Westover, Susan. (1989). National Collegiate Athletic Association v. Tarkanian: If NCAA Action Is Not State Action, Can Its Members Meaningfully Air Their Dissatisfaction? 26 *San Diego Law Review* 953-976.

Due Process

Linda L. Schoonmaker

Although the framers of the United States Constitution and its Amendments did not have sport, athletes, coaches or athletic and sport governing bodies in mind when they drafted those documents, it is fair to say that the guarantees and rights granted to citizens that are contained in those documents have had, and in all likelihood will continue to have, an impact upon the sport industry. As result, sport managers must have an understanding of our constitutionally protected rights and how sport is impacted by those protected rights.

One of the rights contained in the U.S. Constitution is that of due process. This constitutional guarantee is found in both the Fifth and Fourteenth Amendments to the U.S. Constitution. Enacted in 1791, the Fifth Amendment applies to acts of the federal government. It states "No person shall . . . be deprived of life, liberty, or property without due process of law." The Fourteenth Amendment was enacted in 1868 and extends the applicability of the due process guarantee to the states. The Amendment reads:

> . . . nor shall any state deprive any person of life, liberty, or property without due process of law.

Many state constitutions also prohibit the denial of due process. The due process guarantee applies to governmental action and not to those of private entities.

■ ■ ■ ■

Representative Case

HALL v. UNIVERSITY OF MINNESOTA
United States District Court, District of Minnesota
530 F. Supp. 104 (1982)

OPINION:

Findings of Fact Conclusions of Law and Order

This Court is presented with a serious and troubling question concerning the academic standing and athletic eligibility of a University of Minnesota varsity basketball player. The plaintiff in this action is a 21-year-old black senior at the defendant University of Minnesota. He is also a formidable basketball player who, up to this season, played for the defendant University of Minnesota men's intercollegiate varsity basketball team. He is before the Court seeking an injunction ordering the University to admit him to a degree program, a prerequisite to the athletic eligibility he lost.

• • •

The plaintiff does meet the Big Ten eligibility standards with respect to grade point average and credit accumulation, but unless he is enrolled as a "candidate for a degree," he is ineligible to practice or play on the defendant University's basketball team. According to the coach of the University basketball team, the plaintiff is the only player he has known who has met the grade and credit criteria of the Big Ten but has been refused admission into a degree program.

• • •

According to the evidence, if the plaintiff is accorded the opportunity to represent the University of Minnesota in intercollegiate varsity basketball competition during winter quarter of 1982, his senior year, he will have a significant opportunity to be a second round choice in the National Basketball Association draft this year, thereby acquiring a probable guarantee of his first year's compensation as a player in the National Basketball Association. If the plaintiff is denied the opportunity to participate in intercollegiate basketball competition on behalf of the University of Minnesota during winter quarter 1982, his chances for a professional career in basketball will be impaired; and it will be extremely unlikely that his compensation as a first year player in the National Basketball Association will be guaranteed. The evidence indicates that without an opportunity to play during the winter quarter of 1982, the plaintiff would likely be a sixth round choice in the National Basketball Association draft.

This Court has no hesitation in stating that the underlying reason for the plaintiff's desire to be enrolled in a degree program at the defendant University is the enhancement of his chances of becoming a professional basketball player. The plaintiff will probably never attain a degree should he be admitted to a degree program since the National Basketball Association draft occurs in April of 1982, well before the plaintiff could accumulate sufficient credits for a degree. The plaintiff was a highly recruited basketball player out of high school who was recruited to come to the University of Minnesota to be a basketball player and not a scholar. His academic record reflects that he has lived up to those expectations, as do the academic records of many of the athletes presented to this Court.

The plaintiff applied for admission to the UWW twice, once in August of 1981 and once in October of 1981. In each case, the UWW admissions committee determined, based on the plaintiff's application, that he should be admitted to the UWW introductory program. In each case, the directors of the program (further up in the hierarchy of the UWW) intervened in the admissions process and effectively directed the admissions committee to reject plaintiff's application. This interference by the directors never occurred in any other case as to any other student.

• • •

It seems apparent that the plaintiff was not judged solely on the basis of his applications and the information therein. Each time the admissions committee reviewed the plaintiff's application, they recommended that he be admitted. After the intervention of the directors and the communication of the information outlined in the above-mentioned memorandum, the plaintiff was denied admission. However, in both of the rejection letters sent to the plaintiff, none of the allegations noted in the memorandum were listed as reasons for the plaintiff's failure to gain admission to the UWW.

The plaintiff asserts that he has been denied his right to due process of law arising under the Fourteenth Amendment. Due process protects life, liberty and property. Protected property interests are usually created and defined by sources such as state laws. Board of Regents v. Roth, 408 U.S. 564, 92 S. Ct. 2701, 33 L. Ed. 2d 548 (1972). A student's interest in attending a university is a property right protected by due process. Abbariao v. Hamline University School of Law, 258 N.W.2d 108, 112 (Minn.1977); citing Dixon v. Alabama State Bd. of Education, 294 F.2d 150 (5th Cir. 1961), cert. denied 368 U.S. 930, 82 S. Ct. 368, 7 L. Ed. 2d 193 (1961); Gaspar v. Bruton, 513 F.2d 843, 850 (10th Cir. 1975). The defendant asserts that while in cases of expulsion, public education may be a property right, in cases of nonadmission, public education is but a mere privilege, citing Davis v. Southeastern Community College, 424 F. Supp. 1341 (E.D.N.C.1976), aff'd in part, vacated in part and remanded, 574 F.2d 1158, reversed on other grounds, 442 U.S. 397, 99 S. Ct. 2361, 60 L. Ed. 2d 980 (1979). However, the right versus privilege distinction has long been abandoned in the area of due process. See Goldberg v. Kelly, 397 U.S. 254, 262, 90 S. Ct. 1011, 1017, 25 L. Ed. 2d 287 (1970). And in any event, even though the plaintiff was denied admission, the circumstances of this case make it more like an expulsion case than a non-admission case. The plaintiff lost existing scholarship rights; he cannot enroll in another college without sitting out one year of competition under athletic rules; and although he has attended the defendant University for several years, he may no longer register for day classes at the defendant University.

But to say that due process applies in the area of a student's interest in attending a university does not finish the analysis. One must answer the question of what process is due. "Due process is flexible and calls for such procedural protection as the particular situation demands." Morrissey v. Brewer, 408 U.S. 471, 481, 92 S. Ct. 2593, 2600, 33 L.

Ed. 2d 484 (1972). Factors balanced to determine what process is due are: (1) the private interest affected by the action; (2) the risk of an erroneous deprivation of such interest through the procedures used and the value of additional procedural safeguards; and (3) the government's interest involved, including fiscal and administrative burdens. Mathews v. Eldridge, 424 U.S. 319, 96 S. Ct. 893, 47 L. Ed. 2d 18 (1976).

The private interest at stake here, although ostensibly academic, is the plaintiff's ability to obtain a "no cut" contract with the National Basketball Association. The bachelor of arts, while a mark of achievement and distinction, does not in and of itself assure the applicant a means of earning a living. This applicant seems to recognize this and has opted to use his college career as a means of entry into professional sports as do many college athletes. His basketball career will be little affected by the absence or presence of a bachelor of arts degree. This plaintiff has put all of his "eggs" into the "basket" of professional basketball. The plaintiff would suffer a substantial loss if his career objectives were impaired.

The government's interest, i.e., the defendant University's interest, is the administrative burden of requiring a hearing or other due process safeguards for every rejection of every student who applies to the University. This burden would be tremendous and this Court would not require the defendant University to shoulder it.

The key factor in this case which weighs heavily in the plaintiff's favor is the risk of an erroneous deprivation given the nature of the proceedings used in processing the plaintiff's application. This Court is aware that in the area of academic decisions, judicial interference must be minimal. See Board of Curators of the University of Missouri v. Horowitz, 435 U.S. 78, 98 S. Ct. 948, 55 L. Ed. 2d 124 (1978). However, an academic decision is based upon established academic criteria. See Horowitz, supra at 89-90, 98 S. Ct. at 954-55. In this case, the plaintiff's applications to the UWW were treated very differently than all other applications. The directors intervened in the process and provided the admissions committee with allegations concerning the plaintiff's conduct, a facet of the proceedings that taints this "academic" process and turns it into something much like a disciplinary proceeding. Given this aspect of the proceedings, it would appear that the plaintiff should have at least been notified that allegations had been made regarding his conduct so that he could have presented evidence in his own behalf. Without this safeguard, there exists a chance that the plaintiff may have been wrongfully accused of actions which then form the basis for his rejection.

This is not to say that all applicants who are rejected by the defendant University must be given an opportunity to rebut evidence used in evaluating a college application; however, if the defendant University intends to interject evidence concerning allegations of improper conduct of the applicant into the admissions process, it must provide the applicant an opportunity to give his or her side of the story.

Finally, one must consider all that has occurred in light of the standards utilized by the Courts in this Circuit in evaluating the propriety of issuing a preliminary injunction. Four factors determine whether a preliminary injunction should issue. They are: (1) the threat of irreparable harm to the moving party, (2) the state of balance between that harm and the injury that granting the injunction will inflict on other parties, (3) the public interest, and (4) the probability that the movant will succeed on the merits of the claim. Dataphase Systems, Inc. v. C.L. Systems, Inc., 640 F.2d 109, 113 (8th Cir. 1981); Medtronic Inc. v. Catalyst Research Corp., 518 F. Supp. 946, 950 (D.Minn.1981); Brotherhood, etc. v. Burlington Northern, Inc., 513 F. Supp. 1023, 1027 (D.Minn.1981).

With respect to the first factor, if the plaintiff is not eligible to play basketball by January 4, 1982, he will not play his senior year. This poses a substantial threat to his chances for a "no cut" contract in the National Basketball Association, according to his coach, and his overall aspirations regarding a career as a professional basketball player. It would be difficult indeed to measure the loss to the plaintiff in terms of dollars and cents. The injury is substantial and not really capable of an accurate monetary prediction. Thus, it would be irreparable. See Danielson v. Local 275, Laborers Intern. Union of North America, AFL-CIO, 479 F.2d 1033 (2d Cir. 1973); see also, Phillips v. Crown Central Petroleum Corp., 602 F.2d 616 (4th Cir. 1979), cert. denied, 444 U.S. 1074, 100 S. Ct. 1021, 62 L. Ed. 2d 756.

The harm to the other parties, i.e., the defendant University, is difficult to assess. On the one hand, this Court doubts that the University men's intercollegiate varsity basketball team and coaching staff would characterize the reinstatement of the plaintiff to the team in terms of "harm." But the defendant University academic wing argues that if this Court orders the plaintiff into a degree program, its academic standards and integrity would be undermined. The plaintiff and his fellow athletes were never recruited on the basis of scholarship and it was never envisioned they would be on the Dean's List. Consequently we must view with some skepticism the defendant University's claim, regarding academic integrity. This Court is not saying that athletes are incapable of scholarship; however they are given little incentive to be scholars and few persons care how the student athlete performs academically, including many of the athletes themselves.

The exceptionally talented student athlete is led to perceive the basketball, football, and other athletic programs as farm teams and proving grounds for professional sports leagues. It well may be true that a good academic program for the athlete is made virtually impossible by the demands of their sport at the college level. If this situation causes harm to the University, it is because they have fostered it and the institution rather than the individual should suffer the consequence.

• • •

This Court is of the opinion that the plaintiff has shown a substantial probability of success on at least his claim regarding the UWW. It is conceivable that the UWW may have had reason to deny the plaintiff admission to its degree program. However, the manner in which the UWW processed the plaintiff's application strongly suggests that he has been treated disparately and in a manner violative of due process. The plaintiff was given no notice nor any opportunity to answer the allegations leveled against him by the Dean of the General College. It is equally conceivable that the plaintiff would have had a "good answer" to these charges had he been given an opportunity to respond. Balancing all of the above factors, this Court concludes that an injunction should issue requiring the defendant University to admit the plaintiff into a degree program on January 4, 1982 and to declare him eligible to compete in intercollegiate varsity basketball competition.

■ ■ ■ ■

Fundamental Concepts

A definition of due process appears in a 1877 U.S. Supreme Court decision, *Pennoyer v. Neff*, (1877). In this case, the Court defined due process as ". . . a course of legal proceedings according to those rules and principles which have been established by our jurisprudence for the protection and enforcement of private rights" (p.715).

The plaintiff must clear two hurdles before he/she can proceed with a deprivation of due process claim. First, is the state action requirement. Second, the deprivation must infringe upon a life, liberty, or property interest.

State Action. As discussed earlier, to maintain a due process claim, the plaintiff must demonstrate that the deprivation is the result of action taken by a federal or state government or a representative of the government.

Life, Liberty, or Property Interest. Rarely is a deprivation of a life interest raised in the sport industry, as a result, deprivation of a liberty and/or property interest usually is the issue.

Liberty Interest. The U.S. Supreme Court has defined liberty as follows: "Without doubt, it denotes not merely freedom from bodily restraint but also . . . generally to enjoy those privileges long recognized . . . as essential to the orderly pursuit of happiness by free men" (*Meyer v. Nebraska*, 1923). As regards due process and deprivation of a liberty interest, the Court in a 1971 case stated "where a person's good name, reputation, honor, or integrity is at stake because of what the government is doing to him, notice and an opportunity to be heard are essential" (*Wisconsin v. Constantineau*, 1971). In a later case, the Court extended the requirements that are necessary to invoke a liberty interest. In that case, the Court concluded that: ". . . this line of cases does not establish the proposition that reputation alone, apart from some more tangible interests such as employment, is either "liberty" or "property" by itself sufficient to invoke the . . . protections of the Due Process Clause" (*Paul v. Davis*, 1976). This "more tangible interests" requirement has become known as the "stigma plus" test.

An example of the application of this "stigma plus" test in the sport industry is found in *Stanley v. Big Eight Conference* (1978). In this case, Stanley was relieved as head football coach at Oklahoma State University because of an NCAA investigation which implicated him in NCAA rules violations. Stanley brought a due process suit claiming that the action taken would have a stigmatizing effect upon his ability to pursue his livelihood as a coach. The ruling of the court states that: ". . . the 'more tangible interest' is Stanley's employment with OSU which has recently been terminated due at least in part to the allegations contained in the report, and his professional reputation which will determine his future employment opportunities" (*Stanley v. Big Eight Conference,* 1978).

Property Interest. The U.S. Supreme Court has defined a "property" interest as follows: "To have a property interest in a benefit, a person clearly must have more than an abstract need or desire for it. He must have more than a unilateral expectation of it. He must, instead, have a legitimate claim of entitlement" (*Board of Regents v. Roth,* 1972).

In the collegiate setting, plaintiffs have asserted that they either have a property right in an athletic scholarship or in a future professional career. In *Hall v. University of Minnesota* (1982), the court ruled that Hall did have a protected property right based upon his future opportunity to play professional basketball. In another example, *Gulf South Conference v. Boyd* (1979), the court found that there was a property right of present economic value in a college athletic scholarship.

Although the athlete who possesses a scholarship and/or a legitimate professional career opportunity may have a protected property interest, the same can not be said for an athlete who has neither, for the courts generally have not recognized a right to participate in intercollegiate athletics (*Colorado Seminary v. NCAA,* 1976/1978).

In the interscholastic setting, the "entitlement" must often asserted in the sport setting is that of the right to participate in athletics. This right to participate arises from the threshold issue of whether there is a right to an education. The Supreme Court has specifically stated that education is not among the rights afforded explicit or implicit protection in the Constitution (*San Antonio Independent School District v. Rodriguez,* 1972). Even though the right to an education is not grounded in the U.S. Constitution, a state may grant a right to an education either explicitly and implicitly by requiring school attendance (*Goss v. Lopez,* 1974). After determining that the plaintiff has a right to an education based upon mandatory attendance, the determination must be made of whether or not that right includes the right to participate in interscholastic athletics.

Usually the courts do not find a right to participate in interscholastic athletics, but rather find that participation is a privilege. Over time, the courts, both at the federal and state levels, have generally been consistent in this view (See *Morrison et al. v. Roberts,* 1938; *State of Indiana v. Lawrence Circuit Court,* 1959; *Scott v. Kilpatrick,* 1970; *Taylor v. Alabama High School Athletic Ass'n,* 1972; *Kentucky High School Athletic Association v. Hopkins County Board of Education,* 1977; *Pegram v. Nelson,* 1979; *Pennsylvania Interscholastic Athletic Association, Inc. v. Greater Johnstown School District,* 1983; *Niles v. University Interscholastic League,* 1983; and *Spring Branch Independent School District v. Stamos,* 1985).

Although the overwhelming majority of courts have not found a right to participate in interscholastic athletics, interestingly at least two courts have found otherwise (*Moran v. School District #7, Yellowstone County,* 1972; *Duffley v. New Hampshire Interscholastic Athletic Association,* 1982). And, at least one court has ruled that although there is no right to participate in interscholastic athletics, a student's interest in participating is not entirely unprotected (*Stone v. Kansas State High School Activities Association,* 1988). The court's rationale for this opinion is that participation is part of the total educational experience provided by schools.

Due Process Analysis

After a plaintiff has cleared the above discussed hurdles, he/she can then proceed with demonstrating to the court how their due process rights have been violated.

Due process of law is composed of two areas of inquiry. The first is **substantive due process**, which requires the regulation or rule to be fair and reasonable in content as well as application. The essence of substantive due process is protection from arbitrary and capricious actions. The inquiry in substantive due process poses two questions: 1) Does the regulation or rule have a proper purpose? and, 2) does the regulation or rule clearly relate to the accomplishment of that purpose?

Over time, courts have adopted general principles that serve to guide them in their decisions regarding rules and regulations of voluntary associations. As a general rule, courts will not interfere with the internal affairs of voluntary associations. In the absence of mistake, fraud, collusion or arbitrariness, the decisions of the governing body of an association will be accepted as conclusive. Voluntary associations may adopt reasonable bylaws and rules which will be deemed valid and binding upon the members of the association unless the bylaw or rule violates some law or public policy. It is not the responsibility of the courts to inquire into the expediency, practicability or wisdom of the bylaws and regulations of voluntary associations. These general principles are equally applicable to cases involving athletic governing bodies (*Kentucky High School Athletic Association v. Hopkins County Board of Education,* 1977). Examples of courts upholding the rules and regulations of athletic governing bodies include: *Spring Branch I.S.D. et al. v. Stamos,* 1985; *Berschback v. Grosse Pointe Public School District,* 1986; *Ternan v. Michigan High School Athletic Association, Inc.,* 1986; and, *Palmer v. Merluzzi,* 1989. In each of these cases, the court deemed the rule or regulation at issue to be rationally related to its stated purpose. In the following cases, courts found that the actions of the athletic governing body was unreasonable, capricious and arbitrary: *Tiffany v. Arizona Interscholastic Association, Inc.,* 1986; *Manico v. South Colonie Central School District,* 1992; and, *Diaz v. Board of Education of the City of New York,* 1994.

The second area of due process inquiry involves **procedural due process,** which addresses the methods used to enforce the regulation or rule. Procedural due process examines the decision-making process that is followed to determine whether the regulation or rule has been violated and what sanction, if any, will be imposed. The goal of procedural due process is to assure fair treatment.

After it has been determined that procedural due process is due to the plaintiff, the question becomes what procedures should be followed to insure fair treatment? Over time, the U.S. Supreme Court has provided guidance to us in answering that question. "Due process is flexible and calls for such procedural protections as the particular situation demands" (*Morrissey v. Brewer,* 1972). "Parties whose rights are to be affected are entitled to be heard; and in order that they may enjoy that right they must be notified" (*Baldwin v. Hale*). The greater the deprivation, the greater procedural due process owed to the plaintiff (*Goldberg v. Kelly,* 1970). Finally, the Court developed a balancing test to be used to determine the extent to procedural due process (*Mathews v. Eldridge,* 1976). In that case the Court stated, "First, the private interest that will be affected by the official action; second, the risk of an erroneous deprivation of such interest through the procedures used, and the probable value, if any, of additional or substitute procedural safeguards; and finally, the Government's interest, including the function involved and the fiscal and administrative burdens that the additional or substitute procedural requirement would entail" (*Mathews v. Eldridge,* 1976).

As these procedural due process requirements apply to an educational setting, we look to the opinion of the U.S. Supreme Court in *Goss v. Lopez* (1975). In *Goss,* a number of students in schools in the Columbus, Ohio school district were suspended from school for 10 days for disruptive behavior. The students brought suit claiming their due process rights had been violated. The Court ruled that for suspensions of 10 days or less the students "must be *some* kind of notice and afforded *some* kind of hearing." The Court further outlined the procedures that needed to be followed to meet the standard they had established. Specifically, the student must be given oral and written notice of the charges against him and, if he denies them, an explanation of the evidence the authorities have and an opportunity to present his side of the story. And that there be no delay between the time of the notice and the time of the hearing (*Goss v. Lopez,* 1975).

We can see the application of the standards established in *Goss* in two sport cases, *Pegram v. Nelson* (1979) and *Palmer v. Merluzzi* (1989). In both the cases, student-athletes were suspended from school for 10 days and from athletics for four months and sixty days, respectively. In both cases, the student-athletes were given notice and a hearing which afforded them the opportunity to refute the allegations against them. The courts in both cases ruled that the procedures that were followed afforded the student-athletes all the procedural due process they were owed (*Pegram v. Nelson,* 1979 and *Palmer v. Merluzzi,* 1989).

Three sport cases can provide the sport manager with further guidance in the development of due process procedures. In the first case, *Kelley v. Metropolitan County Board of Education of Nashville* (1968), the plaintiff high school student-athlete was suspended from athletic competition by the Board of Education without being formally charged with a rule violation. The court held that due process requires published standards, formal charges, notice, and a hearing and granted an injunction that prevented the enforcement of the suspension.

In the second case, *Behagen v. Intercollegiate Conference of Faculty Representatives* (1972), two student-athletes were suspended for fighting with their opponents during a collegiate basketball game. They brought suit claiming they were denied due process. The court held that their due process rights had been violated. In its opinion, the court outlined the procedures that needed to be followed to meet rudimentary requirements of due process. The procedures are as follows: 1) written notice of the time and place of the hearing at least two days in advance, 2) notice of the specific charges, 3) a hearing in which the athletic director hears both sides of the story; it should include the presentation of direct testimony in the form of statements by each of those directly involved in relating their versions of the incident, 4) a list of witnesses to the plaintiff prior to the hearing, 5) a written report of the findings of fact and the basis for punishment, 6) tape recordings of the proceedings, and 7) an appeals procedure (*Behagen v. Intercollegiate Conference of Faculty Representatives,* 1972).

The third case is *Stanley,* discussed earlier. Stanley was relieved as head football coach at Oklahoma State University following an NCAA investigation which implicated him in NCAA rules violations. Stanley filed suit claiming his due process rights had been violated. In its opinion, the court provided guidance as to steps that could be followed to meet the demands of due process, including: 1) notice the infractions with which plaintiff is charged, 2) a list of witnesses the defendants will utilize to support each charge could be provided to the plaintiff, 3) plaintiff could report in writing each charge he specifically denies, 4) a list of witnesses the plaintiff wishes to have produced for confrontation and cross-examination could be provided to the defendant, and 5) the plaintiff could furnish the names of the witnesses he will rely upon in his defense of each charge (*Stanley v. Big Eight Conference,* 1978).

Recent Developments

The NCAA and Due Process. After the U.S. Supreme Court decision in *NCAA v. Tarkanian* (1988), wherein the Court held that the NCAA was not a state actor, four state legislatures, Nevada, Illinois, Florida, and Nebraska, passed state laws that imposed upon intercollegiate athletic governing bodies the need to provide certain due process procedures to an athlete before the athlete could be declared ineligible. The NCAA brought suit challenging the Nevada statute, claiming that the statute violated the Commerce Clause and the Contract Clause of the U.S. Constitution. The District Court, in June 1992, declared the statute unconstitutional, on the basis that the statute would require the NCAA to adopt the Nevada standards across the country if it wished to have uniform enforcement procedures (*NCAA v. Miller,* 1992). On appeal, the Ninth Circuit upheld the decision of the lower court (*NCAA v. Miller,* 1993). The NCAA also challenged the Florida statute on the same grounds it had asserted in the Nevada case, with the same result (NCAA News, August 31, 1994). The statute was declared unconstitutional for the same reasons that the courts had articulated in both *Miller* decisions. (NCAA News, Nov. 21, 1994).

Due Process and the Olympics. The Constitution and by-laws of the International Olympic Committee (IOC), its member National Olympic Committees (NOC), International Sport Federations (IFs), and National Sport Federations (NFs) all contain policies and procedures that are to be followed to ensure due process is afforded to all who are involved in competitions governed by these entities. Over time it became apparent that an international arbitration panel was needed that would serve as the final authority in dispute resolution. As a result, in 1983, the IOC established the Court of Sport Arbitration (CAS). (Netzle, 1992). The CAS operated as an arm of the IOC until 1994 when it was restructured as an independent agency and renamed the International Court for the Arbitration of Sport (ICAS). The restructuring was deemed necessary following criticism that the CAS was too closely tied to the IOC. Beginning with the 1996 Summer Olympics in Atlanta, the IOC and its member NOCs, IFs, and NFs have all agreed to submit disputes to mandatory and binding arbitration conducted by the ICAS. In addition, there is a mandatory and binding arbitration clause in the Olympic entry form that all athletes, coaches, and officials must sign as a condition of their Olympic participation. (Reuben, 1996).

References

A. Cases

Baldwin v. Hale, 1 Wall. 223.

Behagen v. Intercollegiate Conference of Faculty Representatives, 346 F. Supp. 602 (D. Minn. 1972).

Berschback v. Grosse Pointe Public School District, 397 N.W.2d 234 (Mich. App. 1986).

Board of Regents v. Roth, 408 U.S. 564, 92 S.Ct. 2701, 33 L.Ed.2d 548 (1972).

Colorado Seminary v. NCAA, 417 F. Supp. 885 (D. Colo. 1976), aff'd, 570 F.2d 320 (10th Cir. 1978).

Diaz v. Board of Education of the City of New York, 618 N.Y.S.2d 984 (Sup. 1994).

Duffley v. New Hampshire Interscholastic Athletic Association, 446 A.2d 462 (Sup. Ct. N. H. 1982).

Goldberg v. Kelly, 397 U.S. 266, 90 S.Ct. 1028, 252 L.Ed.2d 307 (1970).

Goss v. Lopez, 419 U.S. 565, 94 S.Ct. 1405, 39 L.Ed.2d 465 (1974).

Gulf South Conference v. Boyd, 369 So. 553 (Sup. Ct. Ala. 1979).

Hall v. University of Minnesota, 530 F. Supp. 104 (D. Minn. 1982).

Kelley v. Metropolitan County Board of Education of Nashville, 293 F. Supp. 485 (M.D. Tenn. 1968).

Kentucky High School Athletic Association v. Hopkins County Board of Education, 552 S.W.2d 685 (Ky. App. 1977).

Manico v. South Colonie Central School District, 584 N.Y.S.2d 519 (Sup. Ct. 1992).

Mathews v. Eldridge, 424 U.S. 319, 96 S.Ct. 893, 47 L.Ed.2d 18 (1976).

Meyer v. Nebraska, 262 U.S. 390, 43 S.Ct. 625, 67 L.Ed. 1042 (1923).

Moran v. School District #7, Yellowstone County, 350 F. Supp. 1180 (D. Mont. 1972).

Morrison et al. v. Roberts, 183 Okl. 359, 82 P.2d 1023 (Sup. Ct. Okl. 1938).

Morrissey v. Brewer, 408 U.S. 471, 92 S.Ct. 2593, 33 L.Ed.2d 484 (1972).

NCAA v. Miller, 795 F. Supp. 1476 (D. Nev. 1992), aff'd 10 F.3d 633 (9th Cir. 1993).

NCAA v. Tarkanian, 488 U.S. 179, 109 S.Ct. 454, 102 L.Ed.2d 469 (1988).

Niles v. University Interscholastic League, 715 F.2d 1027 (5th Cir. 1983).

Palmer v. Merluzzi, 868 F.2d 90 (3rd Cir. 1989).

Paul v. Davis, 424 U.S. 693, 96 S.Ct. 1155, 47 L.Ed.2d 405 (1976).

Pegram v. Nelson, 469 F. Supp. 1134 (M.D. N.C. 1979).

Pennoyer v. Neff, 95 U.S. 714 (1877).

Pennsylvania Interscholastic Athletic Association, Inc. v. Greater Johnstown School District, 463 A.2d 1198 (Pa. Cmwlth. 1983).

San Antonio Independent School District v. Rodriguez, 411 U.S. 1, 93 S. Ct. 1278, 36 L.Ed.2d 16 (1972).

Scott v. Kilpatrick, 286 Ala. 129, 237 So.2d 652 (Sup. Ct. Ala. 1970).

Spring Branch Independent School District v. Stamos, 695 S.W.2d 556 (Tex. 1985).

Stanley v. Big Eight Conference, 463 F. Supp. 920 (W.D. Mo. 1978).

State of Indiana v. Lawrence Circuit Court, 162 N.E.2d 250 (Sup. Ct. Ind. 1959).

Stone v. Kansas State High School Activities Association, 761 P.2d 1255 (Kan. App. 1988).
Taylor v. Alabama High School Athletic Ass'n, 336 F. Supp. 54 (M.D. Ala. 1972).
Tiffany v. Arizona Interscholastic Association, Inc., 726 P.2d 231 (Ariz. App. 1986)
Wisconsin v. Constantineau, 400 U.S. 433, 91 S.Ct. 507, 27 L.Ed.2d 515 (1971).

B. Publications

Berry, Robert and Wong, Glenn M. (1993). *Law and Business of the Sport Industries,* Vol. 2, (2d ed.). Westport, Conn.: Praeger Publishers.

Clement, Annie (1988). *Law in Sport and Physical Education.* Indianapolis: Benchmark Press, Inc.

Due-process Law in Florida Struck Down. (1994, November 21). *NCAA News,* p.1, p.20.

NCAA Sues, Challenges Florida Law. (1994, August 31). *NCAA News,* p.1, p. 13.

Nerzle, Stephen (1992). The Court of Arbitration for Sport: An Alternative For Dispute Resolution in U.S. sports. *The Entertainment and Sports Lawyer,* 10, 1-4, 25-28.

Polvino, Anthony, T. (1994). Arbitration as Preventive Medicine for Olympics Ailments: The International Olympic Committee's Court of Arbitration for Sport and the Future for the Settlement of International Sporting Disputes. *Emory International Law Review, 8,* 347-381.

Rapp, James A. (1986). *Education Law.* New York: Matthew Bender and Co., Inc.

Reuben, Richard (1996). And the Winner Is . . . Arbitrators to Resolve Disputes as They Arise at Olympics. *ABA Journal,* 20.

Sharp, Linda A. (1990). *Sport Law.* NOLPE.

Equal Protection

Cathryn L. Claussen
Bowling Green State University

"No state shall . . . deny to any person within its jurisdiction the equal protection of the laws." With this language, the Equal Protection Clause of the Fourteenth Amendment to the United States Constitution provides a guarantee that laws, rules, and regulations will be applied in a fair and non-discriminatory fashion. While this clause is aimed at the several states, its content is considered applicable to the federal government as well under the Due Process Clause of the Fifth Amendment. Therefore, the Equal Protection Clause serves to place a limit on the government at all levels. The essence of equal protection is that, absent a constitutionally permissible reason for different treatment, similarly situated people should receive similar treatment by the law. Thus, the Equal Protection Clause provides individuals with a means of challenging the constitutionality of a rule or law which has singled them out for different treatment based on their membership in a prescribed category of people.

Originally, the Fourteenth Amendment, along with the Thirteenth and Fifteenth Amendments, was aimed at eliminating the vestiges of African American slavery in the aftermath of the Civil War. Over the intervening years, numerous court decisions have applied the Equal Protection Clause to laws which have classified people based on characteristics other than race. In the context of sport, this means that public institutions may not, without good reason, discriminate in the provision of services, participation opportunities, or employment.

■ ■ ■ ■

Representative Case

INDIANA HIGH SCHOOL ATHLETIC ASSOCIATION v. RAIKE
Court of Appeals of Indiana
329 N.E.2d 66 (1975)

OPINION:

Facts

The essential facts most favorable to the trial court's judgment are:

On November 27, 1971, Raike was a senior in good standing enrolled in the Rushville High School in Rushville, Indiana. On that date, Raike, being seventeen years of age, married a sixteen-year-old Rush County female and approximately two weeks later, a child was born to Mrs. Raike. The trial court specifically found that this marriage "conformed exactly to the statutory mandate of Burns Ind. Stat. Ann. @ 44-101 (IC 1971, 31-1-1-1)" [now 31-1-1-1, et seq.]

Prior to this marital union Raike actively participated in Rushville's athletic program, including football, wrestling and baseball.

Being aware of certain rules adopted by IHSAA and Rushville prohibiting married students from participating in athletics, Raike sought unsuccessfully prior to his marriage to avoid operation of these rules.

He then filed, on December 16, 1971, a complaint against Rushville and IHSAA seeking a Declaratory Judgment and a Temporary Restraining Order (with Affidavits). The Temporary Restraining Order was granted the same day (ex parte) and on September 21, 1972, the Superior Court of Marion County, Room No. 6, made findings of fact and conclusions of law and entered a Declaratory Judgment and Permanent Injunction against IHSAA and Rushville enjoining them from enforcing their restrictive rules prohibiting married high school students from engaging in athletic competition and extra-curricular activities. In granting injunctive relief the trial court specifically found that the rules in question violated equal protection of the laws guaranteed Raike under the Fourteenth Amendment to the Constitution of the United States and that the same rules were also violative of due process of law as guaranteed Raike by the Fourteenth Amendment of the Constitution of the United States.

The parties have stipulated that enforcement of the rules in question constitutes State action.

• • •

Issue

Do the Rules of Rushville and IHSAA prohibiting married high school students from participating in athletics and extra-curricular activities deny Raike equal protection of the laws as guaranteed by the Fourteenth Amendment of the U. S. Constitution?

Additional Facts

Raike attacks these rules as being discriminatory:

The Rushville Rule:

Married students, or those who have been married, are in school chiefly to meet academic needs and they will be disqualified from participating in extra-curricular activities and Senior activities except Commencement and Baccalaureate.

The IHSAA Rule:

Students who are or have been at any time married are not eligible for participating in intraschool athletic competition. (Rule 14 of its By-laws) (Collectively referred to as the Rules)

The trial court found that Rushville was subject to the rules and regulations of IHSAA and evidence was introduced showing IHSAA's avowed purpose to be:

The purpose of this Association shall be to encourage and direct wholesome amateur athletics in the schools of Indiana. In keeping with this purpose the Association shall regulate, supervise, and administer interscholastic athletic activities among its member schools. All such activities shall remain an integral factor in the total secondary educational program. (As emphasized in Haas v. South Bend Community School Corp., infra. Article Two of the Constitution of IHSAA)

Also, there was evidence that IHSAA was originally organized in 1903 in an attempt to establish and maintain uniformity of rules and regulations in athletic events.

High school principals, teachers, coaches and consultants testified to the reasons justifying the existence of the Rules. Their testimony may be summarized as follows:

1. Married students need time to discharge economic and family responsibilities, and participating in athletics and extra-curricular activities would interfere with these responsibilities.
2. Teenage marriages should be discouraged so as to reduce the high percentage of divorce and school dropout rates among married students.
3. Athletes serve as models or heroes to other students and teenage marriages are usually the result of pregnancy so that immorality is encouraged if married students participate without sanction in athletics.
4. If married students participate in athletics, a double standard must be applied, thereby causing discipline, training and administrative problems.
5. Unwholesome interaction between married and nonmarried students is prevented by avoidance of undesirable "locker room talk."

After Raike was permitted to participate in athletics as a married person, his athletic and academic career showed marked improvement. He won the sectional wrestling championship and was elected captain of the wrestling team. Similarly, in baseball Raike's batting average improved by almost 100 points from the prior year and the baseball team's record improved from the prior year.

Raike was able to maintain a B average, hold down a part-time job, engage in athletics and at the same time discharge his family responsibilities.

Conclusion

It is our opinion that the Rules prohibiting a married high school student from participating in athletics and extra-curricular activities do not bear a fair and substantial relation to the objective sought, and therefore deny Raike equal protection of the laws contrary to the Fourteenth Amendment of the U. S. Constitution.

• • •

In reviewing a classification for equal protection impurity, classic constitutional methodology requires us to determine the appropriate standard of review to be used. That choice determines how closely the justification for the classification will be scrutinized.

A. Standards of Review

A two-tier approach has been developed by the United States Supreme Court in evaluating and reviewing equal protection cases. . . . The "low" tier or low scrutiny test presumes constitutionality of the classification and will not disturb the state action unless the classification bears no "rational relationship" to a legitimate governmental interest . . . a minimal test. If it bears some rational relationship to a legitimate government purpose, the classification can withstand equal protection scrutiny, even though there be significant deviation from an ideal classification.

At the other end of the scale of judicial review of challenged classifications is the second tier approach or high scrutiny test. If the classifying criteria are grounded upon certain "suspect traits," such as race, alienage or national origin, or if that classification impinges upon rights deemed "fundamental," e.g., the right to vote, interstate travel, the right to appeal a criminal conviction, freedom of association, then "strict" judicial scrutiny will be brought to bear on the classification and it will not stand unless justified by a compelling governmental interest.

The rigidity of the two-tier test inevitably led to a blurring of this somewhat artificial dualism. In recent years various courts and commentators have sensed modification of the two-tier approach. They point to a "new" or hybrid approach to equal protection which is more flexible. By its terms, the classification must be justified by something more than any "reasonably conceivable" set of facts. Rather it:

> must rest upon ground of difference having a fair and substantial relation to the object of the legislation, so that all persons similarly circumstanced shall be treated alike. (Village of Belle Terre v. Boraas (1974), 416 U.S. 1)

• • •

In summary, then, under the traditional two-tier approach of the United States Supreme Court, the classification was initially examined to determine if it was "suspect" or if a "fundamental right" was violated by the statutory or regulatory scheme; if not, the low scrutiny, rational basis test for review was used. Judicial review of classifications will be more flexible if the "new" or intermediate approach is followed by the reviewing court. The general principle seems to be that the more important and closer the individual's interest comes to a specific constitutional guarantee, the greater the degree of judicial scrutiny. The importance of the standard of review adopted is that the result reached is in large part a product of that initial decision.

• • •

With this background as to the standards of judicial review available for examination of classifications questioned as violative of the equal protection clause, it is meet that we now inspect the classification before us.

• • •

B. Intermediate or Sliding Scale Scrutiny

While it is true high school students do not have a fundamental or absolute right to participate in interscholastic athletics, it is, nevertheless, a right that "should be encouraged as it provides students the opportunity to cultivate good habits and to develop their mental and physical abilities." Haas v. South Bend Community School Corp., supra, 259 Ind. at 524, 289 N.E.2d at 499-500.

High school students, with some limitations, also enjoy "the vital personal right(s)" of marriage (Loving), which is considered by some to rise to the level of a fundamental right.

A classification which prohibits participation in athletic competition solely because of the marital status of the high school student shackles two important rights, and thereby prompts us to adopt as a standard of review the intermediate scrutiny test. Our specific authority for this constitutional methodology is Haas, a case holding IHSAA's rule prohibiting females from engaging in interscholastic golf competition to be violative of the equal protection clause. Justice Hunter, speaking for the majority, cited and relied on Reed v. Reed, supra. To withstand constitutional challenge, then, the classification:

> must be reasonable . . . and must rest upon some ground of difference having a fair and substantial relation to the object of the legislation, so that all persons similarly circumstanced shall be treated alike. (Reed v. Reed, (1971), 404 U.S. 71, 76, 92

S.Ct. 251, 254, 30 L.Ed.2d 225, 229; Royster Guano Co. v. Virginia (1920), 253 U.S. 412, 415, 40 S.Ct. 560, 64 L.Ed. 989." Haas, 259 Ind. at 522, 289 N.E.2d at 498)

So our next task is to ascertain the objective of the Rules. If the classification created bears a fair and substantial relation to the objective treating all persons similarly situated alike, then the classification is not violative of equal protection.

Article Two of the Constitution of IHSAA declares that:

> The purpose of this Association shall be to encourage and direct wholesome amateur athletics in the schools of Indiana. In keeping with this purpose the Association shall regulate, supervise and administer interscholastic athletic activities among its member schools.

So the avowed purpose of IHSAA in promulgating its rules and regulations, including those in question, is to regulate and supervise interscholastic high school athletics so as to create a wholesome atmosphere . . . an atmosphere free of corrupting influences. To this stated purpose must be added the testimony of IHSAA's experts and various high school officials. Throughout their testimony runs the same thread . . . the elimination of immoral or corrupting influences, and married students inject an immoral and corrupting influence into an otherwise wholesome atmosphere.

Other reasons are given in justification of the Rules, such as the desirability of eliminating premarital sex and teenage marriages with or without resulting pregnancies, and the reduction of high dropout rates and high divorce rates among married high school students. But such justification appears to be more an effect of the Rules than their ultimate objective.

Thus we arrive at the conclusion that the objective of the Rules is to preserve the integrity and wholesome atmosphere of amateur high school athletics by prohibiting married students from participating therein because they are bad examples and their participation interjects an unwholesome influence. The unwholesome influence is said to result from discussion of marital intimacies and other corrupting "locker room talk," and further, from hero worship of married students (who may or may not have engaged in premarital sex with resultant pregnancy and forced marriage).

It is obvious that the classification used to attain the desired objective is one prohibiting all married high school students from participating in athletics solely on the basis of their present or previous married status; i.e.,

dissimilar treatment is afforded married and unmarried students . . . all in the name of preventing married students from exerting an unwholesome effect on high school athletics.

While the Rules as drawn may reasonably contribute in some measure to the realization of that goal, they are unreasonable in that the classification is not narrowly drawn—it is both over- and under-inclusive.

The classification is over-inclusive in that it includes some married students of good moral character who would not corrupt the morality of their fellow students or contribute to an unwholesome atmosphere.

It is under-inclusive in that it includes neither unmarried high school students who participate in athletics as team members, student managers or trainers, and yet may engage in premarital sex nor unmarried high school students who may be of a depraved nature, all of whom are as likely to be a corrupting influence as married high school students.

The classification simultaneously catches too many fish in the same net and allows others to escape.

In effect, those similarly situated are not similarly treated, and therefore there is no fair and substantial relation between the classification and the objective sought.

In the succinct words of Reed, "all persons similarly circumstanced shall be treated alike" . . . and they were not.

Insofar as the classification discourages teenage marriages resulting from pregnancies, it is also defective in that it contravenes established public policy allowing teenage high school students of Raike's age to legitimate offspring resulting from premarital sex.

• • •

C. "Low" Tier (Low Scrutiny)

It is possible to apply the low scrutiny test to the Rules and conclude that there is no rational basis whatsoever to support such a classification. Judge Eschbach, in Wellsand v. Valparaiso Community School Corp., supra, No. 71 H 122(N.D. Ind. 1971)(2) (Unpublished opinion), after examining each of IHSAA's six reasons justifying the same "marriage rule" now before us, concluded that it was constitutionally defective as a violation of equal protection because there was no "rational basis for the classification of students into different groups and a different treatment accorded each group."

• • •

We prefer to rest our decision on the reasoning of Haas, Sturrup, and Reed, recognizing that such reliance does not necessarily eliminate the possibility that there may be some rational basis or rational connection between a classification and the object sought to be obtained.

■ ■ ■ ■

Fundamental Concepts

State Action

To find a violation of the Equal Protection Clause requires a finding of state action. The concept of state action is discussed in more detail in Chapter 4.12. It is enough to reiterate here that the government must have been sufficiently involved with the deprivation of an individual's rights to warrant invoking the protection of the Constitution. Public schools and universities, as well as state or local departments of recreation, are considered branches of the government; hence, they are state actors for purposes of equal protection analysis. Courts have also, upon occasion, declared that private entities sufficiently intertwined with publicly-owned facilities have engaged in state action.

Purposeful Discrimination

Equal Protection Clause analysis requires a finding that the government engaged in purposeful, rather than unintentional, discrimination. By itself, an unintended discriminatory effect is insufficient grounds for an equal protection violation.

Standards of Review

Deprivation of Fundamental Right—Strict Scrutiny. There are two possible bases on which to challenge a law on equal protection grounds. The first is to allege selective deprivation of a right that is considered to be fundamental in our society, such as the right to vote or the right to travel freely among the different states. A law that deprived people of such a fundamental right would receive heightened scrutiny by the courts because of the serious nature of the deprivation. Since sport participation has commonly been ruled to be a privilege rather than a right, this basis for a lawsuit has limited relevance in the sport management context.

Classification into Group to Receive Different Treatment. The second basis for an equal protection challenge is to claim that the particular law unfairly discriminates by classifying people into a group singled out for different treatment. The Supreme Court has, over the years, established a three-tiered standard of review for this type of equal protection claim. The Court has ruled that certain classifications are more suspicious than others and therefore trigger different levels of judicial review. Thus, this hierarchically arranged set of tests is based on the type of classification found in the law at issue. Laws containing suspect classifications (race, ethnicity, national origin, alienage) will be subjected to strict scrutiny, the highest level of review. Classifications based on gender or legitimacy of birth are considered quasi-suspect classifications, and laws containing these will receive intermediate level scrutiny. The lowest level of scrutiny, called rational basis review, is used to judge all group classifications other than those established by the Court as suspect or quasi-suspect.

A. Strict Scrutiny. Laws that include classifications based on race, ethnicity, national origin, or alienage are considered suspect classifications because there is virtually never any constitutionally permissible justification for segregating people on such bases. Suspect classifications are considered unjustifiable for three primary reasons. The first is that people have historically been subjected to discrimination on the basis of race or national origin, so to continue to classify people on such bases would tend to make one suspect the perpetuation of prejudice. The second reason is that groups defined by race or national origin have suffered from political powerlessness because they are discrete and insular minority groups. In other words, they have not traditionally been part of the mainstream culture, have tended to remain to themselves, and so have not been able to fend for themselves politically and effect change for their benefit. Finally, the third reason race and national origin are considered suspect classifications is that they are based on immutable characteristics, that is, traits which are unchangeable. It is deemed fundamentally unfair to discriminate against individuals based on these characteristics that cannot be altered.

The courts will be suspicious of any law that makes such a suspect classification and will give it strict, or highest level, scrutiny. The test for a law under strict scrutiny is whether that law is **necessary** to achieve a **compelling** governmental interest. In other words, the government must have an essential objective in mind, and the law it passed must be the only way to accomplish that objective. If there is a less discriminatory means to achieve a worthy end, it must be used instead of the challenged law. Almost every law containing a suspect classification fails the test of strict scrutiny and is ruled unconstitutional.

In *Louisiana High School Athletic Association v. St. Augustine High School* (E.D. La. 1967), the state high school athletic association had a membership admission rule which allowed the existing members to vote to deny membership to an all-black high school which otherwise met all the conditions for membership. The court was suspicious of this voting requirement because it had been first instituted at the annual meeting in which for the first time in the history of the association an all-black school was to be considered for membership. The court believed that the purpose of this voting provision was to enable the association to deny membership without having to justify its action. Based on this conclusion, the court found sufficient evidence that membership was denied on the basis of race, and concluded that since there was no compelling reason to distinguish between white and black schools, the rule violated the Equal Protection Clause.

B. Intermediate Scrutiny. In *Craig v. Boren* (U.S. 1976), decided one year after *Raike*, the Supreme Court refined the middle tier of equal protection review and has since applied it to the quasi-suspect classifications of gender and legitimacy of birth. These are considered somewhat suspect because of their similarity to suspect classifications like race in that they are based on immutable characteristics that have often in the past been used as reasons for discrimination. Yet, they are only suspect because, in the estimation of the Court, it is justifiable to differentiate on the basis of sex more frequently than on the basis of race, for example. In other words, sex differences may make a difference in ability to perform certain tasks, whereas racial differences rarely make a legitimate difference.

Nevertheless, such instances are increasingly uncommon, and the courts will be fairly suspicious of laws that include quasi-suspect classifications, and will subject them to intermediate scrutiny. The test under intermediate scrutiny is whether the challenged law is **substantially related** to an **important** governmental interest. Although this language appears synonymous with the strict scrutiny test, it is meant to be a slightly less rigorous examination of the law at issue. Still, most laws containing quasi-suspect classifications are also struck down as unconstitutional violations of equal protection.

In *Ludtke v. Kuhn* (S.D.N.Y. 1978), a female sports reporter was denied access to the locker room of the New York Yankees solely because of her sex. State action existed because the stadium was owned by the city and supported by public funds, and the profitability of the city's lease depended in part on publicity about the team. The defendants argued that there were three important interests at stake in excluding female reporters: 1) protecting the privacy of the players; 2) preserving baseball's status as a family sport; and 3) adhering to traditional standards of decency and propriety. The court found only the first to be an important interest meriting consideration under intermediate scrutiny. However, totally excluding female reporters from the locker room was not substantially related to achieving that important interest, because the court was able to identify less discriminatory means to accomplishing the goal of protecting player privacy (such as the use of backdrops or the wearing of towels). Therefore, the court held that the exclusion policy violated the Equal Protection Clause.

In *Haffer v. Temple University* (E.D. Pa. 1987), Temple was spending far less money in support of its women's athletics programs than its men's programs. The university argued that it was justified in spending more on men's sports because of their greater potential for garnering publicity and generating revenue. The court agreed that the university had important interests in using intercollegiate athletics to secure favorable publicity and revenue, but questioned whether the disparity in expenditures was substantially related to accomplishing those goals. The plaintiffs had produced evidence that certain women's teams might generate interest and revenue if they received greater expenditures for marketing and promotion, so spending less on the women's programs was not a well-tailored attempt to accomplish the university's goals.

C. Rational Basis Review. The lowest level of equal protection scrutiny is applied to all group classifications other than those established by the Supreme Court as suspect or quasi-suspect. These are classifications that have not historically been sufficiently associated with invidious discrimination so as to raise the suspicion of the Court. The test for a law under rational basis review is whether that law is **reasonably related** to a **legitimate** governmental interest. As long as the government can articulate an arguably legitimate goal and appears to have a rational basis for enacting the law at issue in an attempt to realize that goal, the law will be upheld. Nearly all classifications receiving rational basis review are found to be constitutional under the Equal Protection Clause. In *Schaill by Kross v. Tippecanoe County School Corp.* (N.D. Ind. 1988), the school district had a rule which singled out student-athletes from the rest of the student body for drugtesting. Since the category of student-athletes is not a suspect or quasi-suspect classification, the drug-testing policy received rational basis review. In the view of the court, the school district had a legitimate interest in maintaining a drug-free environment for athletics based on concern for the health and safety of student-athletes. The court concluded that the drug-testing program was a reasonable means of attaining that goal, given the heightened health and safety concerns associated with the physical and mental intensity of athletics participation compared to other school activities. Thus, the court held that the drug-testing rule did not violate equal protection.

Under- and Over-inclusiveness

Sometimes courts will invalidate a law because, in its application, it is either under-inclusive or over-inclusive, or both at the same time. If the law is not well-tailored to accomplishing its purpose, it may sweep with too wide a net and affect too broad a spectrum of people, with the result that it is over-inclusive. Or, it may not sweep wide enough to accomplish its purpose and affect the lives of too narrow a range of people, with the result that it is under-inclusive. Or, finally, it may do both at the same time. Affecting too many people unnecessarily or affecting too few exclusively are both unfair applications of a law which result in unequal protection. This is because either similarly situated people are being treated dissimilarly, or dissimilarly situated people are being treated alike.

In *Indiana High School Athletic Association v. Raike* (Ind. App. 1975), the state association had a rule prohibiting married high school students from participating in interscholastic athletics. Prior to the mid-1970s, the usual reason that high school age students got married was because they had engaged in premarital sex and the girl had become pregnant. The association's purpose for having the rule was to encourage students to avoid such problems by depriving them of the opportunity to participate if they did have to get married. The rule was held to violate equal protection because it was both over-inclusive and under-inclusive. The court, using intermediate scrutiny because the rule burdened the near-fundamental right of marriage, found that the rule was not narrowly tailored to achieve the association's important purpose of preserving a wholesome atmosphere in athletics. It was over-inclusive because it excluded all married students, even those who might have been of high moral character. It was simultaneously under-inclusive because it only excluded married students, and overlooked those unmarried students who might have engaged in premarital sex. Over- or under-inclusiveness, and especially both together, were evidence of the lack of precision required for the rule to be substantially related to the government's important purpose of preserving wholesomeness. Hence, the court decided that the rule violated equal protection.

Recent Developments

Reverse Discrimination

At issue in *Kelley v. Board of Trustees, University of Illinois* (7th Cir. 1994) was whether the university's decision to eliminate the men's swimming program as part of its effort to better comply with Title IX constituted reverse discrimination on the basis of sex. The plaintiffs, who had been members of the men's swimming team, sued under Title IX and the Equal Protection Clause, claiming that the university's decision discriminated against them because they were males. The court held that neither law was violated by targeting a men's sport for elimination because the university's action was an attempt to comply with federal law. Furthermore, the court concluded that Title IX itself does not violate the Equal Protection clause because Congress had articulated an important goal of prohibiting sex discrimination in educational institutions; moreover, the statute is substantially related to achieving that goal because as a remedial measure it directly protects the disproportionately burdened sex.

Learning Disabilities

Recently, the NCAA's academic eligibility standards were challenged on the basis that they unfairly discriminated against student-athletes with learning disabilities. In response to an investigation of this issue by the United States Justice Department, the NCAA Council has sponsored legislation to change some of their eligibility requirements. If they had failed to act, learning disabled students might have been able to bring a lawsuit against the NCAA under the Americans With Disabilities Act for denying access to individuals with disabilities. The athletes would, however, have no grounds for an equal protection claim because, since the mid-1980s, the NCAA has been held to be a private and voluntary association and hence the application of NCAA rules involves no state action.

State action would be present, though, in the case of academic eligibility rules implemented by public schools or state high school athletics associations. Such organizations would do well to revisit their academic eligibility policies to ensure that they include procedures for providing reasonable accommodations to enable student-athletes with learning disabilities to have access to athletics participation.

In *Hoot by Hoot v. Milan Area Schools* (E.D. Mich. 1994), a student-athlete brought suit against the state high school athletics association for discrimination based on his learning disability. The athlete had requested a waiver of the association's academic eligibility rule requiring completion of a minimum number of credit hours during the semester prior to competition. He asserted that his learning disability (Attention Deficit Hyperactivity Disorder) had prevented him from being able to satisfy this requirement. The plaintiff claimed violations of the: 1) Equal Protection Clause, because he had been singled out for different treatment on the basis of disability; 2) Michigan Handicappers' Civil Rights Act; 3) Americans with Disabilities Act; and 4) Rehabilitation Act. The state athletics association moved for summary judgment on all four claims, but the court denied the motion. In discussing the equal protection claim, the judge concluded that the student had established legitimate issues of fact as to whether the application of the academic eligibility requirements violated his equal protection rights, and whether the state athletics association contributed further to the discrimination by failing to grant his requested waiver of the requirements. The judge cited the Supreme Court decision in *City of Cleburne v. Cleburne Living Center, Inc.* (U.S. 1985) which applied rational basis review to distinctions based on mental retardation, implying that in a trial on the merits this would be the appropriate test for the issue of discrimination on the basis of learning disabilities.

References

A. Cases

City of Cleburne v. Cleburne Living Center, Inc., 473 U.S. 432 (1985).

Craig v. Boren, 429 U.S. 190 (1976).

Haffer v. Temple University, 678 F. Supp. 517 (E.D. Pa. 1987).

Hoot by Hoot v. Milan Area Schools, 853 F. Supp. 243 (E.D. Mich. 1994).

Indiana High School Athletic Association v. Raike, 329 N.E.2d 66 (Ind. App. 1975).

Kelley v. Board of Trustees, University of Illinois, 35 F.3d 265 (7th Cir. 1994).

Ludtke v. Kuhn, 461 F. Supp. 86 (S.D.N.Y. 1978).

Schaill by Kross v. Tippecanoe County School Corp., 679 F. Supp. 833 (N.D. Ind. 1988).

St. Augustine High School v. Louisiana High School Athletic Association, 270 F. Supp. 767 (E.D. La. 1967), *aff'd,* 396 F.2d 224 (5th Cir. 1968).

B. Publications

————. (April 29, 1996). Council to Sponsor Learning Disability Legislation. *NCAA News*, v. 33, no. 17, pp. 1, 24.

Stone, Geoffrey R., Seidman, Louis M., Sunstein, Cass R., and Tushnet, Mark V. (1986). *Constitutional Law*, Boston: Little, Brown and Company.

C. Constitution

U.S. Constitution, Amend. XIV.

4.15

Search and Seizure/Right to Privacy

Margaret E. Ciccolella
University of the Pacific

The right of privacy is fundamental to American heritage and to rights guaranteed by the United States Constitution. It should be noted that the word "privacy" is not found in the United States Constitution. However, privacy interests are found in the "penumbra" of rights guaranteed throughout the Constitution, e.g., the First, Fourth, Fifth, and Fourteenth Amendments safeguard privacy interests relevant to freedom of expression, substantive due process, equal protection, and search and seizure of one's person and/or personal effects.

The heart of search and seizure privacy protections is found in the Fourth Amendment of the United States Constitution. It is the primary purpose of this chapter to focus upon privacy interests of student athletes as they relate specifically to the Fourth Amendment of the United States Constitution. Perhaps no issue illustrates this better than case law on urinalysis-drug-testing of high school and intercollegiate athletes. The significant case for this chapter, *University of Colorado v. Derdeyn* (1993), considered random, suspicionless drug testing of college athletes by using a Fourth Amendment analysis. It may be helpful for the reader to refer to Chapter 4.26, for a review of its significant case, *Vernonia v. Acton* (1995). These two cases came to different conclusions regarding the constitutionality of drug testing of athletes and offer an opportunity for legal and factual comparisons.

■ ■ ■ ■

Representative Case

UNIVERSITY OF COLORADO v. DERDEYN
Supreme Court of Colorado
863 P.2d 929 (1993)

OPINION:

We granted certiorari in order to determine whether random, suspicionless urinalysis-drug-testing of intercollegiate student athletes by the University of Colorado, Boulder (CU), violates the Fourth Amendment to the United States Constitution or Article II, Section 7, of the Colorado Constitution. Following a bench trial conducted in August of 1989 in which a class of current and prospective CU athletes challenged the constitutionality of CU's

drug-testing program, the Boulder County District Court permanently enjoined CU from continuing its program. The trial court found that CU had not obtained voluntary consent from its athletes for such testing, and it declared such testing unconstitutional under both the federal and state constitutions. The Colorado Court of Appeals generally affirmed. See Derdeyn v. University of Colorado, 832 P.2d 1031 (Colo. App. 1991). We agree with the court of appeals, that in the absence of voluntary consents, CU's random, suspicionless urinalysis-drug-testing of student athletes violates the Fourth Amendment to the United States Constitution and Article II, Section 7, of the Colorado Constitution. We further agree, that the record supports the finding of the trial court that CU failed to show that consents to such testing given by CU's athletes are voluntary for the purposes of those same constitutional provisions. Accordingly, we affirm the judgment of the court of appeals.

I

CU began a drug-testing program in the fall of 1984 for its intercollegiate student athletes. CU has since amended its program in various ways, but throughout the existence of the program participation was mandatory in the sense that if an athlete did not sign a form consenting to random testing pursuant to the program, the student was prohibited from participating in intercollegiate athletics at CU.

• • •

CU's third amended program, which became effective August 14, 1988, contained numerous changes. First, it added alcohol, "over-the-counter drugs," and "performance-enhancing substances such as anabolic steroids" to the list of drugs for which students could be tested. Second, the term "athlete" was defined to include "all student participants in recognized intercollegiate sports, including but not limited to student athletes, cheerleaders, student trainers and student managers." Third, random "rapid eye examination (REE)" testing was substituted for random urinalysis, and a urinalysis was performed only after a "finding of reasonable suspicion that an athlete has used drugs," and at the athlete's annual physical examination. Failure to perform adequately on an REE was considered "prima facie reasonable suspicion of drug use [except with regard to steroids]," and the student was required to provide a urine specimen for testing purposes if the student did not perform adequately on the REE. In addition, if a student exhibited "physical or behavioral characteristics indicating drug use including, but not limited to: tardiness, absenteeism, poor heath [sic] habits, emotional swings, unexplained performance changes, and/or excessive aggressiveness," this was also considered reasonable suspicion of drug use, and the student was required to take a urine test. Fourth, urine samples were to be collected "within the Athletic Department facilities," and athletes were "directed to provide a urine specimen in a private and enclosed area" while a monitor remained outside. The monitor would then receive "the sample from the athlete and check the sample for appropriate color, temperature, specific gravity and other properties to determine that no substitution or tampering has occurred." Fifth, the athletes

were required to give their consent to releasing test results to the Head Athletic Trainer at [CU]; my parent(s) or legal guardian(s), if I am under the age of 21; the head coach of any intercollegiate sport in which I am a team member; the Athletic Director of [CU]; my work supervisor (if applicable) and the Drug Counseling Program at the Wardenburg Student Health Center.

• • •

Following a bench trial conducted in August of 1989, the trial court entered its written findings of fact, conclusions of law, and order and judgment. The trial court found that "obtaining a monitored urine sample is a substantial invasion of privacy." It found that the REE does not function, in any sense, as "reasonable suspicion" of drug use. Because of its disastrous ability to predict drug use, it functions more as an avenue to inject arbitrary judgments into an otherwise random selection of students for testing. Similarly, it found that "like the REE, the [other] reasonable suspicion criteria [as set forth by CU] are incapable of indicating drug use to any degree" (emphasis in original). The trial court also found that while the University labels the program as a "Drug Education Program", there is little education. . . . There is no ongoing educational component of the program. Testing is clearly its major focus. Finally, the trial court found that there is no evidence that the University instituted its program in response to any actual drug abuse problem among its student athletes. There is no evidence that any person has ever been injured in any way because of the use of drugs by a student athlete while practicing or playing a sport.

• • •

The fact that CU's athletes signed forms consenting to random drug testing did not alter the trial court's conclusion. Rather, the trial court found that CU failed to demonstrate that the consents given by the athletes were voluntary, and also held that "no consent can be voluntary where the failure to consent results in a denial of the governmental benefit."

On these bases, the trial court declared that CU's drug-testing program was unconstitutional. It permanently enjoined CU from "requiring any urine samples from student athletes for the purposes of drug testing, whether those tests occur on a random basis or as a result of the 'reasonable suspicion' criteria stated," and it permanently enjoined CU from "requiring student athletes participation in the Rapid Eye Exam procedure." In addition, the trial court held that "reasonable suspicion" is not the appropriate standard to warrant urinalysis-drug-testing of athletes by CU, and that such testing is impermissible absent probable cause under either the Fourth Amendment or Article II, Section 7, of the Colorado Constitution.

The Colorado Court of Appeals generally affirmed.

• • •

We granted CU's petition for writ of certiorari on the following issues:

In the context of the University's drug-testing program, is suspicionless drug testing constitutionally reasonable?

Can student athletes give valid consent to the University's drug-testing program if their consent is a condition of participation in intercollegiate athletics at the University?

• • •

II

The Fourth Amendment to the United States Constitution protects individuals from unreasonable searches conducted by the government, Von Raab, 489 U.S. at 665, even when the government acts as the administrator of an athletic program in a state school or university. See Schaill ex rel. Kross v. Tippecanoe County Sch. Corp., 864 F.2d 1309 (7th Cir. 1989); Brooks v. East Chambers Consol. Indep. Sch. Dist., 730 F. Supp. 759 (S.D. Tex. 1989); cf. New Jersey v. T.L.O., 469 U.S. 325, 333-37, 83 L. Ed. 2d 720, 105 S. Ct. 733 (1985) (holding that the Fourth Amendment prohibits unreasonable searches and seizures conducted by public school officials acting as civil authorities). Furthermore, because it is clear that the collection and testing of urine intrudes upon expectations of privacy that society has long recognized as reasonable, . . . these intrusions must be deemed searches under the Fourth Amendment Skinner, 489 U.S. at 617. It follows that CU's urinalysis-drug-testing program must meet the reasonableness requirement of the Fourth Amendment.

A search must usually be supported by a warrant issued upon probable cause. Von Raab, 489 U.S. at 665. However, neither a warrant, nor probable cause, nor any measure of individualized suspicion is an indispensable component of reasonableness in every circumstance. Id.; Skinner, 489 U.S. at 618-24. Rather, where a Fourth Amendment intrusion serves special governmental needs, beyond the normal need for law enforcement, it is necessary to balance the individual's privacy expectations against the Government's interests to determine whether it is impractical to require a warrant or some level of individualized suspicion in the particular context.

• • •

CU advances alternative theories to support its claim that its drug-testing program is reasonable under the Fourth Amendment. First, CU argues that its drug-testing program is reasonable under the Fourth Amendment because of the student athletes' diminished expectations of privacy and the compelling governmental interests

served by the program. Second, CU argues that even if its drug-testing program is not otherwise constitutionally reasonable, there is no constitutional violation because its student athletes voluntarily consent to testing. We address these arguments in turn.

A

CU argues that its drug-testing program is reasonable under the Fourth Amendment because of the student athletes' diminished expectations of privacy and the compelling governmental interests served by the program. We therefore consider in turn (1) the degree to which CU's drug-testing program intrudes on the reasonable expectations of privacy of student athletes and (2) the magnitude of the governmental interests served by the program. We then balance these factors in order to determine whether CU's drug-testing program is reasonable under the Fourth Amendment.

1

[W]e now consider CU's arguments that the magnitude of the intrusion of its drug-testing program on the reasonable expectations of privacy of its student athletes was minimal.

(a) CU argues that collection of the urine sample in a closed stall with aural monitoring minimizes any intrusion. We agree that aural monitoring is less intrusive than visual monitoring, but as we have already noted, the trial court found that CU and the other defendants have refused to agree that they will not return to the policy which was initially challenged in this class action [i.e., the policy according to which students were visually monitored while providing a urine sample]. In fact, defendants have indicated that there are circumstances under which they would return to that policy.

• • •

(b) CU argues that student athletes' expectations of privacy with regard to urinalysis are diminished because they routinely give urine samples as part of an annual, general medical examination, and because they regularly undergo close physical contact with trainers. In this regard, it is true that the United States Supreme Court has recognized that urine tests are less intrusive when the "sample is . . . collected in a medical environment, by personnel unrelated to the [employee's] employer, and is thus not unlike similar procedures encountered often in the context of a regular physical examination." Skinner, 489 U.S. at 626-27. Similarly, the Seventh Circuit Court of Appeals has stated that if an individual is required by his job to undergo frequent medical examinations, then that individual will perceive random urinalysis for drug-testing purposes as being less intrusive. Dimeo, 943 F.2d at 682. In this case, however, the trial court heard testimony that samples for random urinalysis-drug-testing were not collected in a medical environment by persons unrelated to the athletic program.

• • •

(c) CU argues that student athletes' expectations of privacy with regard to urinalysis are diminished because they submit to extensive regulation of their on- and off-campus behavior, including maintenance of required levels of academic performance, monitoring of course selection, training rules, mandatory practice sessions, diet restrictions, attendance at study halls, curfews, and prohibitions on alcohol and drug use.

• • •

Although it is obviously not amenable to precise calculation, it is at least doubtful that the testimony relied upon by CU fully supports CU's assertion that its student athletes are "extensively regulated in their on and off-campus behavior," especially with regard to all of the particulars that CU asserts. More importantly, none of the types of regulation relied on by CU entails an intrusion on privacy interests of the nature or extent involved in monitored collection of urine samples.

(d) argues that student athletes' expectations of privacy with regard to urinalysis are diminished because they must submit to the NCAA's random urinalysis-drug-testing program as a condition of participating in NCAA competition. In this regard, CU's athletic director testified that at NCAA championship events, the NCAA conducts random drug testing of athletes as well as testing of the top three finishers and certain starting players, and evidence in the record suggests that NCAA athletes are required to sign consent forms to such testing.

• • •

Despite the fact that students might dislike the NCAA drug-testing program, it seems that they must consent to it in order to be NCAA athletes, and submission to one such program could reduce the intrusiveness of having to submit to another. On the other hand, the trial court heard testimony suggesting that part of what is intrusive about the CU program is that it transformed what might otherwise be friendly, trusting, and caring relations between trainers and athletes into untrusting and confrontational relations.

(e) CU argues that student athletes' expectations of privacy with regard to urinalysis are diminished because the consequences of refusing to provide a urine sample are not severe. We appreciate that in comparison to losing one's job, as would be the consequence in some government employee/drug-testing cases, e.g., Bostic, 650 F.Supp. at 249, not being able to participate in intercollegiate athletics can be regarded as less of a burden. It is, to be sure, only a very small percentage of college athletes whose college "careers" are essential as stepping stones to lucrative con-

tracts—or to any contract—as professional athletes. On the other hand, however, we must also recognize that many intercollegiate athletes who otherwise could not afford a college education receive athletic scholarships that enable them to obtain a college degree and thereby increase their earning potential.

• • •

(f) Finally, CU argues that student athletes expectations of privacy with regard to urinalysis are diminished because positive test results are confidential and are not used for the purposes of criminal law enforcement. It is true that an intrusion by the government outside the context of criminal law enforcement is generally less of an intrusion than one for the purposes of law enforcement. However, as a matter of law, we already take this fact into account when we analyze this case according to the standards of cases like Skinner and Von Raab, rather than according to the standards of typical cases in the area of criminal procedure where there are very few and well defined exceptions to the requirement of a warrant based on probable cause. In other words, were we to attribute less weight to the students' privacy interests because this is not a criminal case, and also start with the premise that Skinner and Von Raab control, we would be, in effect, giving double weight in our analysis to the fact that we are not dealing with an issue in criminal procedure.

• • •

(g) Having reviewed the record in light of each of CU's assertions, it is clear that in some places CU seems to overstate its case, while in others, it has a valid point. On balance, however, we are in full agreement with the conclusion of the trial court that CU's random, suspicionless urinalysis-drug-testing of athletes is an "intrusion [that] is clearly significant."

2

CU asserts several interests in maintaining its drug-testing program. These interests are preparing its athletes for drug testing in NCAA championship events, promoting the integrity of its athletic program, preventing drug use by other students who look to athletes as role models, ensuring fair competition, and protecting the health and safety of intercollegiate athletes.

We begin our consideration of these interests by observing that suspicionless urinalysis-drug-testing by the government has been upheld in numerous cases, and in many of those cases, courts have characterized the relevant government interests as "compelling." Skinner, 489 U.S. at 628 (government has "compelling" interest in testing railroad employees whose "duties [are] fraught with such risks of injury to others that even a momentary lapse of attention can have disastrous consequences"); Von

Raab, 489 U.S. at 670 (government has "compelling interest in ensuring that front-line [drug] interdiction personnel [in the United States Customs Service] are physically fit, and have unimpeachable integrity and judgment"); id. at 677 (government has a compelling interest in protecting truly sensitive information from those who might compromise such information); id. at 679 (government has "compelling interests in preventing the promotion of drug users to positions where they might endanger the integrity of our Nation's borders or the life of the citizenry"); Cheney, 884 F.2d at 610 (government has a "compelling safety interest in ensuring that the approximately 2,800 civilians who fly and service its airplanes and helicopters are not impaired by drugs"). However, the Supreme Court has not held that only a "compelling" interest will suffice, see Skinner, 489 U.S. at 624; cf. Von Raab, 489 U.S. at 666, and some courts have upheld suspicionless urinalysis-drug-testing by the government without finding a compelling interest. Dimeo, 943 F.2d at 681, 683, 685 (explaining that decreasing levels of intrusiveness require decreasing levels of government justification, declining to characterize as compelling the government's interest in protecting professional jockeys, starters, and outriders from injuring one another at the race track, characterizing the state's financial interest as "substantial," and holding that these two interests outweigh "the very limited privacy interest[s]" of professional jockeys, starters, and outriders); International Bhd. of Elec. Workers, Local 1245 v. Skinner, 913 F.2d 1454, 1462, 1463, 1464 (9th Cir. 1990) (finding that the government has a "great" interest in the safety of the natural gas and hazardous liquid pipeline industry, and holding that this "strong" interest is sufficient to justify random urinalysis testing of pipeline workers). Hence, rather than trying to characterize CU's interests as "compelling," "strong," "substantial," or of some lesser degree of importance, we think it is more instructive simply to compare them with other types of commonly asserted interests that have been held sufficient or insufficient to justify similar intrusions.

• • •

CU asserts no significant public safety or national security interests. This is not by itself dispositive, but absent a showing by CU that its athletes have a greatly diminished expectation of privacy or that its program is not significantly intrusive, the great majority of cases following Skinner and Von Raab clearly militate against the conclusion that CU's program is a reasonable exercise of state power under the Fourth Amendment. This is so despite the fact that CU's interest in protecting the health and safety of its intercollegiate athletes, like its interest in protecting all of its students, is unquestionably significant.

We have not been persuaded that CU's athletes have a greatly diminished expectation of privacy, nor are we persuaded that CU's program is not significantly intrusive. In addition, we question whether some of the interests asserted by CU are even significant for Fourth Amendment purposes. For example, although the integrity of its athletic program is, like all the other interests asserted by CU, a valid and commendable one, it does not seem to be very significant for Fourth Amendment purposes. See Local 1245 v. NRC, 966 F.2d at 525 (In evaluating a program for random drug testing of employees absent individualized suspicion, the court said, "The NRC wisely decided to refrain from pursuing its integrity of the workforce rationale on appeal. This rationale has almost uniformly been rejected by the courts as insufficient to justify drug testing of employees."); O'Grady, 888 F.2d at 1196. Similarly, although the promotion of fair competition builds character in athletes and enhances the entertainment value of athletic events, CU does not explain why the promotion of fair competition is itself an important governmental interest, just as it does not explain why preventing the disqualification of its athletes at sporting events is an important governmental interest.

We therefore hold, based on a balancing of the privacy interests of the student athletes and the governmental interests of CU, that CU's drug-testing program is unconstitutional under the Fourth Amendment. More specifically, we hold that random, suspicionless urinalysis-drug-testing by CU of student athletes is unconstitutional under the Fourth Amendment if that testing is conducted according to the procedures utilized in any of CU's drug-testing programs to the date of trial, or if that testing is conducted in a manner substantially similar to any of the procedures utilized in any of CU's drug-testing programs to the date of trial. Furthermore, because the Colorado Constitution provides at least as much protection from unreasonable searches and seizures as does the Fourth Amendment, CU's drug-testing program is also unconstitutional under Article II, Section 7, of the Colorado Constitution.

B

CU asserts, however, that even if its drug-testing program is not otherwise constitutionally reasonable, there is no constitutional violation because its student athletes voluntarily consent to testing. We next address that argument.

A warrantless search of an individual is generally reasonable under the Fourth Amendment if the individual has voluntarily consented to it. Schneckloth v. Bustamonte, 412 U.S. 218, 219, 222, 36 L. Ed. 2d 854, 93 S. Ct. 2041 (1973). A voluntary consent to a search is "a consent intelligently and freely given, without any duress, coercion or subtle promises or threats calculated to flaw the free and unconstrained nature of the decision." People v. Carlson, 677 P.2d 310, 318 (Colo. 1984) (citing Bustamonte, 412 U.S. 218, 36 L. Ed. 2d 854, 93 S. Ct. 2041, and People v. Helm, 633 P.2d 1071 (Colo. 1981)). Whether consent to a search was voluntary "is a question of fact to be determined from all the circumstances. . . ." Bustamonte, 412 U.S. at 248-49.

• • •

The trial court heard specific direct testimony from several intercollegiate student athletes who described how and when they were presented with consent forms to sign, and why they signed them. CU had the opportunity to cross-examine these students, and to present direct testimony of its own. The intercollegiate student athlete who testified on behalf of CU was not asked about how or when she was told of the drug-testing program, how or when she was presented with a consent form to sign, or why she signed the form. The Athletic Director for CU and CU's Head Athletic Trainer testified in general about how and when intercollegiate student athletes are notified about the drug-testing program, although neither testified about how and when the students are actually presented with consent forms to sign.

• • •

The evidence produced during this trial failed to establish that the consents given by the University's student-athletes are voluntary. It is quite clear that they are "coerced" for constitutional purposes by the fact that there can be no participation in athletics without a signed consent.

• • •

The trial court permanently enjoined CU "from requiring any urine samples from student athletes for the purposes of drug testing. . . ." In view of our conclusion that it was unnecessary to address the unconstitutional conditions issue, we recognize the possibility that in the future CU might be able to devise a program involving truly voluntary consents to drug testing. In such event, CU is free to apply for modification or dissolution of the injunction.

III

For the foregoing reasons, we affirm the judgment of the court of appeals.

■ ■ ■ ■

Fundamental Concepts

The Fourth Amendment

The Fourth Amendment to the United States Constitution states:

> The right of the people to be secure in their persons, houses, papers, and effects against unreasonable searches and seizures, shall not be violated, and no Warrant shall issue, but upon probable cause, supported by Oath or affirmation, and particularly describing the place to be searched, and the persons or things to be seized. (*United States Constitution, Amendment IV*)

The Fourth Amendment, made applicable to the states by virtue of the Fourteenth Amendment, guarantees that individuals are protected against "arbitrary invasions by governmental officials." (*O'Connor v. Ortega*, 1987) Note that only unreasonable searches and seizures are prohibited. Also, in the context of conduct by law enforcement, warrants based upon probable cause are required.

Once a search or seizure is characterized as "unreasonable," it is unconstitutional and therefore is prohibited. In the context of athletics, searches of lockers, personal items, or a person become potentially serious invasions of privacy by the language of the Fourth Amendment. Valid warrants based upon probable cause are rarely the situation in athletics because school searches are not typically under the authority of law enforcement. More commonly, in the context of public school aged and college aged athletes, searches and seizures occur under the authority of school officials.

It is important to distinguish constitutionally permissible from constitutionally prohibited conduct as determined by the Fourth Amendment. Fourth Amendment analysis of search and seizure privacy interests must consider three basic issues. First, does the conduct represent state (governmental) action? Second, is the conduct a search? Third, is the search reasonable?

1. Is There State Action? The Fourth Amendment protects individuals from invasions of privacy by the government. It does not protect against the conduct of private individuals or organizations. The NCAA is not subject to Fourth Amendment scrutiny because the regulatory functions of the NCAA are considered to represent private and not state action. (*Arlosoroff v. NCAA*, 1984) Action or conduct by state, local, or federal officials is state or governmental action for purposes of the Fourth Amendment. For example, public but not private schools are subject to Fourth Amendment standards of review.

2. Is the Conduct a Search? Under Fourth Amendment analysis, a search occurs when an expectation of privacy which society is prepared to consider is infringed. (*Schaill v. Tippecanoe County School Corp.*, 1989) The United States Supreme Court has held that the collection and testing of urine constitute a search under the Fourth Amendment. (*Skinner v. Railway Labor Executives' Assn.*, 1989) This is especially relevant to athletes subject to mandatory urine testing. In *Skinner*, the Court stated:

> It is not disputed, however, that chemical analysis of urine, like that of blood, can reveal a host of private medical facts about an employee, including whether he or she is epileptic, pregnant, or diabetic. Nor can it be disputed that the process of collecting the sample to be tested, which may in some cases involve visual or aural monitoring of the act of urination, itself implicates privacy interests. (p. 1413-14)

There remains a legitimate expectation of privacy for both the college and public school student that a student athlete's urine is not subject to public scrutiny. The courts continue to hold that the mandatory urine testing of student athletes constitutes a search and seizure. (*Derdeyn*, 1993; *O'Halloran v. University of Washington*, 1988; *Vernonia*, 1995)

This does not mean that mandatory urine testing of athletes will result in a violation of the Fourth Amendment. In *O'Halloran* (1988), the constitutionality of drug testing college athletes was upheld even though it was concluded that, "the NCAA's urine testing program is a search for Fourth Amendment analysis." In 1995, the Supreme Court held that mandatory, random urinalysis testing of public school athletes represented a reasonable search under a Fourth Amendment analysis. (*Vernonia*, 1995)

It is clear that urine testing of student athletes represents a search. The more crucial question is whether the search is reasonable. Reasonableness, by considering all of the events or the "totality of the circumstances" surrounding a search, will ultimately determine whether a Fourth Amendment violation has occurred.

3. Is the Conduct a Reasonable Search? Only unreasonable searches are prohibited by the Fourth Amendment. However, the test of reasonableness under the Fourth Amendment is not capable of precise definition or mechanical application. The Supreme Court consistently asserts what is "reasonable" depends on the context within which a search takes place. (*O'Connor*, 1987; *Skinner*, 1989; *National Treasury Employees Union v. Von Raab*, 1989) In *New Jersey v. T.L.O.* (1985), the proper standard for assessing the legality of a school search by school officials was determined. In this case, school officials searched a student's purse for drugs. The Supreme Court held that reasonableness of a search involved a two-fold inquiry. First, was the search justified at its inception e.g., was there reasonable suspicion for the search. Second, was the search reasonable in it scope, e.g., were the measures adopted reasonably related to the objectives of the search and not excessively intrusive in light of the age and sex of the student and the nature of the infraction?

In light of the *T.L.O.* (1985) holding and in the context of warrantless school searches, it is common for a court to determine reasonableness by a) considering the existence of reasonable suspicion for the search and b) balancing the degree of intrusion on individual privacy interests against governmental interests in conducting the search.

a.   Reasonable suspicion.   Reasonable suspicion has been defined as "the existence of reasonable circumstances, reports, information, or reasonable direct observation" leading to the belief that illegal drugs have been used. (*Horsemen's Benevolent & Protective Assn. v. State Racing Commission*, 1989) The University of Colorado (CU) amended its suspicionless urine testing program by including a rapid eye examination (REE). REE became the basis for a subsequent mandatory urinalysis on the basis that a positive REE test provided reasonable suspicion of drug use. Other physical and behavioral characteristics were also used as a basis for reasonable suspicion including excessive aggressiveness and poor health habits. (*Derdeyn*, 1993)

Vernonia (1995), which held that random, suspicionless urinalysis testing of public school athletes met the requirements of the Fourth Amendment, had dissents from Justices O'Connor, Stevens, and Souter who spoke strongly to the historical requirement of suspicion in safeguarding Fourth Amendment privacy interests:

> For most of our constitutional history, mass, suspicionless searches have been generally considered *per se* unreasonable within the meaning of the Fourth Amendment. p. 2398.

> [W]hat the Framers of the Fourth Amendment most strongly opposed, with limited exceptions wholly inapplicable here, were general searches—that is, searches by general warrant, by writ of assistance, by broad statute, or by any other similar authority. p. 2398.

> Protection of privacy, not evenhandedness, was then and is now the touchstone of the Fourth Amendment. p. 2399.

> [T]here is a substantial basis for concluding that a vigorous regime of suspicion-based testing . . . would have gone a long way toward solving Vernonia's school drug problem while preserving the Fourth Amendment rights of James Acton. p. 2403-2404.

T.L.O. (1985) required individualized suspicion, but because of the facts of that case, the Court was not required to consider whether circumstances could ever exist that could negate the need for individualized suspicion. *Vernonia* (1995) may well have provided the circumstances missing in *T.L.O.* It is interesting to consider the possible role of sport as a factual circumstance leading to this diversion from *T.L.O.* Given the dissent noted above, it will be equally interesting to consider factual distinctions made by the Supreme Court in the future and the role of sport in providing those distinctions.

b.   Balancing Test.   In addition to considering the existence of reasonable suspicion, the courts typically balance the degree of the intrusion on an individual's privacy interests against the government's interests in testing.

Privacy Interests of the Student Athlete

Privacy interests of athletes have included the following arguments (*Hill v. NCAA*, 1994, citations omitted):

1. There are few activities in our society more personal or private than the passing of urine. Therefore, the visual or aural monitoring of urination implicates privacy interests.
2. Monitored urine collection is embarrassing and degrading thereby violating privacy and dignitary interests protected by the Fourth Amendment.
3. Chemical analysis of urine violates medical confidentiality because it can reveal a host of private medical facts, e.g., epilepsy, pregnancy, diabetes.

4. Urinalysis testing interferes with privacy rights associated with the right to control one's own medical treatment, including the right to choose among legal medications.
5. Urinalysis testing attempts to regulate "off-the-field" personal conduct thereby violating the right to engage in constitutional protections for enormously diverse personal action and belief.

Alternatively, it has been argued that athletes subject to drug testing have diminished expectations of privacy rendering a Fourth Amendment analysis an insufficient basis on which to declare a Constitutional violation. For example, "communal undress" inherent in athletic participation suggests a reduced expectation of privacy. Also, health examinations are fairly routine to participants in vigorous activities. In the context of such examinations, viewing and touching is tolerated among relative strangers that would be firmly rejected in other contexts. (*O'Halloran*, 1988) More recently the Supreme Court of the United States in *Vernonia* (1995) has stated:

> Legitimate privacy expectations are even less with regard to student athletes. School sports are not for the bashful. They require "suiting up" before each practice or event, and showering and changing afterwards. Public school locker rooms, the usual sites for these activities, are not notable for the privacy they afford. (pp. 2392-2393).

Governmental Interests Served by Urine Testing

The other side of the balancing test considers the governmental interests served by urine testing. In the context of urine testing of student athletes, the government must show a special need because the testing exceeds the normal need for law enforcement and occurs in the absence of a warrant or probable cause. A search unsupported by probable cause can be constitutional, we have said, "when special needs, beyond the normal need for law enforcement, make the warrant and probable-cause requirement impracticable." *Vernonia*, (1995) p. 2391.

Examples of special needs which have been successfully asserted to justify warrantless, mandatory urine testing of the intercollegiate athlete include: 1) providing fair and equitable competition, 2) guarding the health and safety of student-athletes, and 3) deterring drug use by testing. (*Hill*, 1994; *O'Halloran*, 1988) With regard to public school athletes, these needs as well as the role of the school standing *in loco parentis* to the children entrusted to it has recently and successfully been argued to support mandatory, random urinalysis testing of public school athletes. (*Vernonia*, 1995) The doctrine of *in loco parentis* has no role in higher education. The role of guardian may help distinguish disparate holdings of cases dealing with random, suspicionless drug testing of college as opposed to public school athletes:

> [A] proper educational environment requires close supervision of schoolchildren, as well as the enforcement of rules against conduct that would be perfectly permissible if undertaken by an adult. *T.L.O.* (1985) p. 741.

> Fourth Amendment rights ... are different in public schools than elsewhere; the "reasonableness" inquiry cannot disregard the schools' custodial and tutelary responsibility for children ... So also when the government acts as guardian and tutor the relevant question is whether the search is one that a reasonable guardian and tutor might undertake. *Vernonia* (1995) p. 2392, 2397.

> We therefore find of only marginal relevance holdings by other courts that high school student athletes have a diminished expectation of privacy under the Fourth Amendment. *Derdeyn* (1993) p. 939. [in reference to drug testing of college athletes by the University of Colorado]

Comparison of Derdeyn to Vernonia

In *Vernonia* (1995), the Supreme Court of the United States held that random urinalysis drug testing of students who participate in public school athletics did not violate students' federal or state constitutional rights to be free from unreasonable searches. As in *Derdeyn* (1993), the Fourth Amendment to the United States Constitution was the heart of the analysis. In contrast to *Derdeyn*, the *Vernonia* court held that the governmental interests in drug testing outweighed a student athlete's Fourth Amendment privacy interests.

In reconciling these two cases, it may be helpful to consider that *Vernonia* involved public school aged athletes. The circumstance of children entrusted to the schools via "loco parentis" was likely the most crucial factor distinguishing the holdings of the two cases. Additionally, in *Derdeyn*, visual and aural monitoring of urine for both males and females was at issue while in *Vernonia*, visual monitoring of males was limited and only aural monitoring occurred with females. Finally, in *Derdeyn*, the intent of the program included safeguarding health, safety, integrity, and fairness in the athletic program and deterring drug use by other students who see athletes as role models. In *Vernonia*, these arguments were also used. However, a emphatic argument included the disciplinary problems faced by schools faced with a sharp increase in drug use by students.

Other Privacy Issues

Privacy protections are seen beyond Fourth Amendment protections. As with the Fourth Amendment, interpretation of the nature and extent of privacy protections has been contested within the context of athletics. First Amendment protections dealing with personal conduct and expression have been challenged by considering the authority of the schools to regulate hair length (*Menora v. Illinois High School Assn.*, 1982; *Tinker v. Des Moines Indep. Comm. School District*, 1969), dress (*Dunham v. Pulsifer*, 1970; *Zeller v. Donegal School District*, 1975), on- and off- court/field behavior (*Bunger v. Iowa H.S. Athletic Assn.*, 1972) and marriage/parenthood of student athletes (*Indiana High School Athletic Assn. v. Raike*, 1975; *Estay v. LaFourche Parish School Board*, 1969; *Davis v. Meek*, 1972; *Perry v. Granada Municipal School District*, 1969). Confidentiality of educational records protected by the *Family Educational Rights and Privacy Act*, also known as the "Buckley Amendment" has been challenged. (*Marmo v. NYC Board of Education*, 1968) The Freedom of Information Act, often used as a basis on which to challenge confidentiality has been challenged itself. (*Arkansas Gazette Co. v. Southern State College*, 1981) Clearly, privacy exceeds Fourth Amendment protections and is addressed throughout the constitution and in federal statutory law.

Concluding Remarks

Our continued legal determination of fundamental educational questions will ultimately dictate the policies which shape the future of privacy interests of student athletes in this country. More importantly, our decisions regarding constitutional protections may have repercussions on our most basic rights. As the *Derdeyn* trial court emphasized:

> We must remember that, after all, it is only athletic games we are concerned with here ... The integrity of athletic contests cannot be purchased at the costs of privacy interests protected by the Fourth Amendment ... A government that invades the privacy of its citizens without compelling reason, no longer abides by the constitutional provisions essential to a free society.

Do we sacrifice Constitutional principles in order to dictate either conduct of or information about athletes? Perhaps, we should be mindful of the Supreme Court's admonition that students "do not shed their constitutional rights ... at the schoolhouse gate." (*Tinker*, 1969, p. 736) Perhaps there is no real disagreement that all students have constitutional rights, "in" or "out" of the schoolhouse gate. It may well be that what we must continue to resolve is the nature of those rights based upon such factors as age and circumstance.

References

A. Cases

Arlosoroff v. NCAA, 746 F.2d 1019, 1021 (1984).
Arkansas Gazette Co. v. Southern State College, 620 S.W.2d 258 (1981).
Bunger v. Iowa H.S. Athletic Assn., 197 N.W.2d 555 (1972).
University of Colorado v. Derdeyn, 863 P.2d (1993).
Davis v. Meek, 344 F.Supp. 298 (1972).
Dunham v. Pulsifer, 312 F.Supp. 41 (1970).
Estay v. LaFourche Parish School Board, 230 So.2d 443 (1969).
Hill v. NCAA, 7 Cal.4th 1 (1994).
Horsemen's Benevolent & Protective Assn. v. State Racing Commission, 532 N.E.2d 644 (1989).
Indiana High School Athletic Assn. v. Raike, 329 N.E.2d 66 (1975).
Marmo v. NYC Board of Education, 289 N.Y.S.2d 51 (1968).
Menora v. Illinois High School Assn., 683 F.2d 1030 (1982).
National Treasury Employees Union v. Von Raab, 109 S.Ct. 1384 (1989).
New Jersey v. T.L.O., 105 S.Ct. 733 (1985).
O'Halloran v. University of Washington, 679 F.Supp. 997 (1988).
O'Connor v. Ortega, 107 S.Ct. 1492 (1987).
Perry v. Granada Municipal School District, 300 F.Supp. 748 (1969).
Schaill v. Tippecanoe County School Corporation, 864 F.2d. 1309 (1989).
Skinner v. Railway Labor Executives' Assn., 109 S.Ct. 1402 (1989).
Tinker v. Des Moines Indep. Comm. School District, 89 S.St. 733 (1969).
Vernonia v. Acton, 115 S.Ct. 2386 (1995).
Zeller v. Donegal School District, 517 F.2d 600 (1975).

B. Federal and State Constitutional Law

California Constitution, Article 1.
United States Constitution, First, Fourth and Fourteenth Amendments.

4.21
Voluntary Athletic Associations

James Conn
Central Missouri State University

For more than a century amateur athletes and sport teams have joined organizations that govern their participation. The legal reporters customarily refer to these amateur sports regulatory organizations as voluntary associations (*Meyer v. Arkansas Activities Association*, 1991). Individuals and groups voluntarily join and agree to abide by the rules and regulations of the association. (Dougherty, 1994). Voluntary associations based their regulatory authority in federal, state, and local laws, and league and organizational rules. The major governing voluntary associations for amateur athletics in the United States include the National Federation of State High School Associations, National Collegiate Athletic Association, National Association of Intercollegiate Athletics, Amateur Athletic Union, and the United States Olympic Committee.

Provided that voluntary associations adopt reasonable by-laws, rules and regulations, such will generally withstand legal challenge unless the rules and regulations violate law or public policy. Courts generally avoid interfering with the administration of voluntary associations, or inquiring into the expediency, practicality or wisdom of their rules and regulations. Finally, courts avoid eliminating imprudent and inappropriate rules so long as the association interprets them fairly and reasonable.

The voluntary associations receiving focus in this chapter are high school athletic associations. The regulation of high school athletics rests with the high school athletic association of each state. The membership of these voluntary associations includes both public and private high schools that wish to participate in the association's sponsored events. The members agree to abide by the rules of the association. The rules and regulations empower the state associations to judge on the infringements. Some of the rules and regulations may include, but not limited to athletic eligibility (*Indiana High School Athletic Association v. Schafer*, 1992), age (*University Interscholastic League v. Buchanan*, 1993), years of participation (*Maroney v. University Interscholastic League*, 1985), academic standards, transfers (*Beck v. Missouri State High School Activities Association*, 1993), boys playing on girls' teams (*Kleczek v. Rhode Island Interscholastic League*, 1992), girls playing on boys' teams (*Israel v. West Virginia Secondary Schools Activities Commission*, 1989), red-shirting, recruitment (*Simkins by Simkins v. South Dakota High School Activities Association*, 1989), number of semesters in school (*California Interscholastic Federation v. Jones*, 1988), and out of season (*Zuments v. Colorado High School Activities Association*, 1987). In sum, the state high school athletic associations oversee and regulate amateur interscholastic athletic relationships among the membership to ensure a spirit of fair play, friendly rivalry, and good sportsmanship (Trichka, 1995).

■ ■ ■ ■

Representative Case

STONE v.
KANSAS STATE HIGH SCHOOL ACTIVITIES ASSOCIATION, INC.
Court of Appeals of Kansas
761 P.2d 1255 (1988)

OPINION:

The Kansas State High School Activities Association (KSHSAA) appeals from a preliminary injunction enjoining the enforcement of its eligibility rules. Following the spring 1987 semester, Lance Stone, a student at Tonganoxie High School, had been certified academically ineligible to play football during the fall 1987 semester. Although he later made up his academic deficiency, a KSHSAA rule prevented him from regaining his eligibility. Stone challenged the "no make-up" rule on due process and equal protection grounds and sought a preliminary injunction enjoining its enforcement. The district court granted the injunction, holding that the no make-up rule was unreasonable and denied Stone the due process and equal protection guaranteed by the United States Constitution. KSHSAA contends that the district court abused its discretion in granting the injunction. We agree with KSHSAA for reasons explained later in this opinion. Accordingly, we reverse.

The Kansas State High School Activities Association, Inc., (KSHSAA) is a voluntary association of Kansas high schools that oversees interscholastic activities between member schools. Its existence is authorized by K.S.A. 72-130 et seq. To carry out its responsibilities, KSHSAA has enacted a comprehensive set of fifty-one rules and regulations. These rules and regulations are binding on member schools and on students of member schools participating in interscholastic activities.

KSHSAA Rule 12 requires member schools to certify that each student participating in an activity is eligible. Rule 13 requires a student to pass at least five subjects of unit weight in the current semester in order to be eligible in the next semester. Rule 14 prevents a student from making up work after the end of the semester for the purpose of regaining eligibility.

During the 1986-87 school year, Lance Stone was a junior at Tonganoxie High School, a member school of KSHSAA. In the spring 1987 semester, he enrolled in six classes. He withdrew from one class, passed four classes,

and failed English. On June 8, 1987, Lee Smith, the principal of Tonganoxie High School, certified to KSHSAA that Stone was ineligible for the fall 1987 semester.

While Smith was on vacation in July, Stone's parents made arrangements with Stephen McClure, the superintendent for the district, for Stone to receive 45 hours of tutoring from his English teacher so that Stone could raise his failing grade. Tutoring was necessary because Tonganoxie does not offer summer school classes. McClure did not realize when he approved the arrangement that Rule 14 prevented students from regaining eligibility by making up failing grades after the semester was over.

When Smith returned from vacation, McClure learned from him that Rule 14 would prevent Stone from regaining his eligibility and that, under standards set by the Kansas Board of Education, 60 hours of tutoring rather than 45 would be required for one unit of credit.

Stone completed the remaining 15 hours during the fall semester through a combination of tutoring and attending a night school English class. The school then noted on his transcript: "English III by arrangement-completed 10/7/87."

On September 22, 1987, Stone, his parents, and their attorney appeared before the KSHSAA executive board and requested that Stone's eligibility be restored. The executive board denied this request. The next day, Stone, his parents, their attorney, and Superintendent McClure appeared before the KSHSAA board of directors. The superintendent asked the board to amend Rule 14 so that students could regain eligibility through summer school, night school, and tutoring. The board declined to act on this request.

On October 8, 1987, Stone and his parents filed the present action seeking a declaratory judgment that Rule 14 as applied to Stone violated Stone's constitutional rights and a permanent injunction enjoining KSHSAA from declaring Stone ineligible for the fall 1987 semester. The next day, Stone sought and obtained a temporary restraining order prohibiting KSHSAA and the school district from "preventing, in any way, Lance Stone from participating in any interscholastic or interschool activity during the Fall Semester of 1987."

At a hearing on October 23, 1987, on Stone's application for a temporary injunction, the trial court acknowledged that the rule denying eligibility to a student who did not pass five courses was desirable, but stated:

> However, it seems to the Court that, basically, that if they go ahead and cure that defect, the defect being of flunking the course, that they should be eligible for sports the next semester.

> So the rule that they cannot make it up, I think, is unreasonable and arbitrary and doesn't provide the student really the right that he should have as far as participating.

Stone also alleged in his petition that a student at Eudora High School had been declared eligible even though that student had apparently made up some failed courses in summer school before transferring to Kansas from Iowa. Unlike Kansas, Iowa permits make-up work, and this student would have been eligible had he remained in Iowa. He became eligible in Kansas under a rule providing that a transfer student may be considered eligible if he would have been eligible under similar rules in the state from which he transferred. The trial court concluded:

> I do believe that that is unequal treatment if you would allow a student from another jurisdiction who has flunked courses and is not all right academically to come into your jurisdiction and then participate in sports. I don't think that would be right.

> I think that's arbitrary and unreasonable in view of what you have in your rules for the Kansas students.

> I just don't think that that would be reasonable.

The court filed a written opinion and issued a preliminary injunction on October 23, 1987.

• • •

The first question we must address is whether Stone may even challenge KSHSAA rules on due process and equal protection grounds since KSHSAA is not a government body and these guarantees protect against only government actions. We hold that he may. KSHSAA exercises substantial control over the public schools of this state and it does so as a result of its exclusive recognition by the legislature. See K.S.A. 72-130 et seq. When KSHSAA acts, it acts, in effect, as a government body. Accordingly, we hold that KSHSAA's rules are subject to the same constitutional scrutiny that we would apply had these rules been adopted directly by either the legislature or the school districts of this state.

• • •

Due Process

At the outset, we note that participation in extracurricular school activities is not a fundamental right. Since the right to an education is not a fundamental right, San Antonio School District v. Rodriguez, 411 U.S. 1, 36 L. Ed. 2d 16, 93 S. Ct. 1278 (1973), it follows that the right to participate in school-related activities is also not a fundamental right. It does not, however, follow that a student's interest in participating in such activities is entirely unprotected. See Goss v. Lopez, 419 U.S. 565, 572-75, 42 L. Ed. 2d 725, 95 S. Ct. 729 (1975) (a student may not be deprived of his statutory right to an education without due process of law). Accordingly, we respectfully differ from those courts which hold that a student's interest in participating in extracurricular activities is "not of constitutional magnitude," Hardy v. University Interscholastic League, 759 F.2d 1233, 1235 (5th Cir. 1985), is not constitutionally protected, Colorado Seminary (U of Denver) v. N.C.A.A., 570 F.2d 320, 321 (10th Cir. 1978), or falls "outside the protection of due process," Walsh v. Louisiana High Sch. Athletic Ass'n, 616 F.2d 152, 159-60 (5th Cir. 1980), cert. denied, 449 U.S. 1124 (1981). We are unwilling to hold that an athletic association may enact and enforce, free of judicial review, rules that are arbitrary and capricious.

Since a fundamental right is not involved, the test for due process is whether the legislative means selected have a real and substantial relation to the object sought, or, whether regulation is reasonable in relation to its subject and is adopted in the interest of the community. State ex rel. Schneider v. Liggett, 223 Kan. 610, 614, 576 P.2d 221 (1978).

KSHSAA has supplied several justifications for its no make-up rule. First, in KSHSAA's judgment, the rule encourages a student to study so that he or she can pass classes when first taken. Second, the rule treats students throughout the state fairly. Many schools do not offer summer school, and not every parent can arrange or afford tutoring. In the judgment of KSHSAA, a different rule would be unfair to those students who would not have the opportunity to make up their work. A different rule would also be unfair to students who participate in extracurricular activities in the spring. Because there is only a short break between fall and spring semesters, these students, unlike the students who participate in fall extracurricular activities, would have no real opportunity to make up their work. KSHSAA also believes that the no make-up rule is not overly harsh since a student at most Kansas high schools may enroll in up to six or seven classes per semester and is required to pass only five of these classes to be eligible the next semester.

When the trial court stated that the no make-up rule was unreasonable because it did not allow a student to rectify his or her mistake, it also acknowledged that a different judge might reach a different conclusion:

> And to be perfectly frank with you, Mr. Forbes, I can see how a judge might think differently, might come to a logical conclusion the other way, but my personal feeling on logic is that . . . I agree totally with Dr. McClure's reasoning. . . .

Although the trial court disagreed with the reasoning behind the no make-up rule, it is not the role of the trial court to substitute its own judgment for that of the KSH-SAA. "Courts can no longer sit as a 'super legislature' and throw out laws they feel may be unwise, improvident or inappropriate." Liggett, 223 Kan. at 614. If reasonable people can differ on the theory underlying the no make-up rule, a court may not hold that the rule is invalid under a rational basis standard. As the court observed in Art Gaines Baseball Camp, Inc. v. Houston, 500 S.W.2d 735 (Mo. App. 1973):

> Undoubtedly this [eligibility] rule will engender strong and diverse feelings. However, this does not constitute unreasonableness or arbitrariness. The volume and competence of the testimony as to the need for and desirability of this rule show that a rational basis for the rule does exist and that its enactment by the members was justified. We cannot say that this rule is unreasonable and therefore we should not substitute our judgment for that of the Association. (500 S.W.2d at 741)

We conclude that the no make-up rule has a rational basis and its application to Stone therefore did not violate his due process rights. We note that the many federal and state courts that have considered this question have reached the same result. See Bailey v. Truby, W.Va., 321 S.E.2d 302, 314-15 (1984) (citing numerous cases holding that similar eligibility rules do not violate a student's due process rights).

Equal Protection

The trial court also held that enforcement of the no make-up rule denied Stone the equal protection of the laws because the Iowa transfer student had been declared eligible under the out-of-state transfer rule even though he had also made up some failed courses. We hold that this did not violate Stone's equal protection rights.

Different classes of people may be treated differently under the equal protection clause of the United States Constitution. When the classification is on the basis of a suspect category, such as race or religion, equal protection requires the government to show that a compelling state interest requires the classification. However, when the classification is on any other basis, equal protection requires only that the classification have a reasonable or rational basis. Liggett, 223 Kan. at 616-18. Such classification need not be exact; "it is sufficient if a classification is practical and not palpably arbitrary." Manzanares v. Bell, 214 Kan. 589, 612, 522 P.2d 1291 (1974).

The record before us demonstrates that there is a rational basis for distinguishing between students transferring to Kansas from other states and nontransfer students. Different states have different eligibility rules. Students in other states plan their coursework in reliance upon their state's rules. These students have no knowledge of KSH-SAA's rules, and often they will not learn that their families are moving until after they have finished the semester. Accordingly, KSHSAA has determined that it would be unfair to deny eligibility to students who move to Kansas when they would have been eligible had they remained in their former states.

Because the distinction between Kansas students and students moving into Kansas has a rational basis and is not based upon any suspect category, we hold that its application does not deny Stone the equal protection of the laws under the United States Constitution.

A district court is vested with a large measure of discretion in granting a temporary injunction. Augusta Medical Complex, Inc. v. Blue Cross, 227 Kan. 469, 473, 608 P.2d 890 (1980). However, it is an abuse of discretion for a district court to grant a temporary injunction to which the plaintiff, as a matter of law, is not entitled.

• • •

Reversed.

■ ■ ■ ■

Fundamental Concepts

Courts infrequently overrule the rules, regulations and restrictions of voluntary associations. Generally, courts refrain from interfering with the internal affairs of voluntary associations, and support the rule-making and decision-making authority associations unless there is evidence of mistake, fraud, collusion or arbitrariness (Champion, 1993). Berry and Wong (1993) claim that judicial review of the decision of a voluntary athletic association will only be successful if it is demonstrated that: 1) the association exceeded the scope of its authority; 2) the association violated its own rules; 3) the association unreasonably or arbitrarily applied its own rules; or 4) the association's rules violated constitutional rights.

Exceeding Authority

The decisions of voluntary athletic associations may sometimes transcend the scope of their authority. For example, in *Indiana High School Athletic Association v. Schafer* (1992), the plaintiff requested that a prior year of athletics participation be disregarded when determining remaining eligibility. The Indiana High School Athletic Association denied the request, yet the Indiana Court of Appeals found the association's application of the eligibility rule to be indefensible. By contrast, in *Mississippi High School Activities Association, Inc. v. Coleman* (1994), the Supreme Court of Mississippi denied a student's contention that the association's application of its anti-recruiting rule was overbroad, on grounds that it provided no transfer exceptions for students for legitimate reasons which had nothing to do with overzealous recruiting practices.

Violating Own Rules

Even though courts generally refrain from interfering with the decisions of voluntary associations, when decisions violate association bylaws, rules or regulations, such decisions are subject to judicial review. In *California State University, Hayward v. National Collegiate Athletic Association* (1975), the university sought an injunction to prevent the NCAA from declaring its intercollegiate athletic program ineligible for postseason play. The court ruled that a voluntary association remains subject to judicial review when it clearly breaches one of its own rules. In *Christ the King Regional High School v. Catholic High Schools Athletics Association, Diocese of Brooklyn*, a private high school sought a preliminary injunction to restrain the high school athletic association from barring its girls high school basketball team from playing in postseason competition. In finding for the school, the court held that the association had not followed its own procedures in barring the team's participation.

Arbitrariness and Constitutional Violations

Courts may also interfere with the rulings of a voluntary association if they deprive a person of a protected constitutional right, or its actions deemed arbitrary or capricious. In *University Interscholastic League v. Buchanan* (1993), the court granted a permanent injunction to the plaintiffs based on its finding that the voluntary organization failed to reasonably accommodate disabled athletes. The high school athletes in question suffered from a learning disability, whereby one repeated the first and seventh grades and the other repeated the fourth and seventh grades. Each sought a waiver of the association's age limitation rule.

Recent Developments

Challenges to the authority of state associations have reached a new twist. Recent issues have involved the constitutionality of state athletic associations and compliance with the Americans with Disabilities Act.

Constitutionality of State Associations. In *Robinson v. Kansas State High School Athletic Association* (1995), the constitutionality of the state high school athletic association was challenged. The KSHSAA was founded in 1910 and functioned without legislative approval until 1954. Without ruling on the merits of the case, which involved out-of-state competition rules, the trial judge found that a Kansas statute, passed in 1954, delegating rule-making authority to the KSHSAA was unconstitutional. Consequently, all rules and regulations of the KSHSAA were without legal foundation. The trial court ruling has been stayed pending appeal to the Kansas Supreme Court.

Americans with Disabilities Act. Since its passage, the Americans with Disabilities Act has proved an effective cause of action in challenging the decisions of voluntary athletic associations. The Act's application has proved particularly relevant to issues involving age limitation rules (*Reaves v. Mills*; *Johnson v. Florida High School Activities Assn., Inc.*, 1995; *University Interscholastic League v. Buchanan*, 1993; *Pottgen v. Missouri State High School Athletic Association*, 1994; and, *Sandison v. Michigan High School Athletic Association*, 1994), transfer *rules (Crocker v. Tennessee Secondary School Athletic Association*, 1992), and academic eligibility rules. The Americans with Disabilities Act and Section 504 of the Rehabilitation Act prohibit discrimination against individuals with disabilities. According to the requirements of these statutes, schools and colleges may not discriminate against an otherwise qualified individual because of that individual's disability. In terms of sports participation, this means that an athlete who otherwise meets all criteria for participation must be allowed to play. In these situations courts have been called on to determine if the eligibility criteria in question is necessary and if either a waiver or modification or the criteria would be reasonable (Osborne, 1996).

References

A. Cases

Beck v. Missouri State High School Activities Association, 837 F.Supp. 998 (E.D. Mo. 1993).

California Interscholastic Federation v. Jones, 243 Cal. Rptr. 271 (Ct. App. 1988).

*California State University, Hayward v. National Collegiate Athletic Asso*ciation 121 Cal. Rptr. 85 (Ct. App. 1975).

Christ the King Regional High School v. Catholic High Schools Athletics Association, Diocese of Brooklyn, 624 N.Y.S.2d 755.

Crocker v. Tennessee Secondary School Athletic Association, 980 F.2d 382 (6th Cir 1992).

Indiana High School Athletic Association, Inc. v. Schafer, 598 N.E.2d 540 (Ind. Ct. App. 1992).

Israel v. West Virginia Secondary Schools Activities Commission, 388 S.E.2d 480 (W.V. Sup. Ct. 1989).

Johnson v. Florida High School Activities Assn., Inc., 899 F.Supp. 579 (M.D. Fla. 1995).

Kleczek v. Rhode Island Interscholastic Leagues, Inc., 612 A.2d 734 (R.I. Sup. Ct. 1992).

Maroney v. University Interscholastic League, 764 F.2d 403 (5th Cir. 1985).

Meyer v. Arkansas Activities Association, 805 S.W. 2d 58 (Ark. Sup. Ct. 1991).

Mississippi High School Activities Association, Inc. v. Coleman, 631 So.2d 768 (Miss. 1994)

Pottgen v. Missouri State High School Athletic Association, 40 F.3d 926 (8th Cir. 1994).

Reaves v. Mills, 904 F. Supp. 120 (W.D. N.Y.).

Robinson v. Kansas State High School Athletic Association, #95 C 1064, 18th Judicial District, Civil Department, Sedgwick County, Kansas. (1995).

Sandison v. Michigan High School Athletic Association, 863 F.Supp. 483 (E.D. Mich. 1994).

Simkins by Simkins v. South Dakota High School Activities Association, 434 N.W.2d 367 (S.D. 1989).

Stone v. Kan. State High School Activities Assn., 761 P.2d 1255 (Kan. App. 1988).

Sturrup v. Mahan, 305 N. E. 2d 877.

University Interscholastic League v. Buchanan, 848 S.W.2d 298 (Tex. Ct. App. 1993).

Zuments v. Colorado High School Activities Association, 737 P. 2d 1113 (Col. Ct. App. 1987).

B. Publications

Berry, R. C. and Wong, G. M. (1993). *Law and Business of the Sport Industries*, Vol. 2, (2d ed.).

Carpenter, L. J. (1995). *Legal Concepts in Sport: A Primer*. Reston, Va.: The American Alliance for Health, Physical Education, Recreation and Dance:

Champion, W. T. (1993). *Sports Law*. St. Paul, Minn.: West Publishing Company.

Dougherty, N. J. Auxter, D., Goldberger, A. S. & Heinzmann, G. S. (1994). *Sport, Physical Activity, and the Law*. Champaign, Ill.: Human Kinetic Publishers.

Osborne, A. G. and Battaglino, L. (1996, February 8). Eligibility of students with disabilities for sports: Implications for policy. *Education Law Reporter*, 105(2), 379-388.

Trichka, R. E. (1995). State high school athletic association's rules and regulations pertaining to transfers and recruiting. A paper presented to the Society for the Study of Legal Aspects of Sport and Physical Activity. Jekyll Island, Ga.

Eligibility Issues

R. Gary Ness
University of New Mexico

An individual's eligibility to participate in an organized sport setting is determined by one or more qualifications agreed upon by those who organize, manage, and supervise the competition. Even the earliest local youth sports organizations require that participants meet specific age and residence qualifications and pay the necessary fees. These qualifications for eligibility reflect the goals of the organization, e.g., to provide baseball competition for registered kids ages 8-12 from the northeast quadrant of the city, and extend the privileges of participation to those who meet those qualifications.

The rules and policies for participation by individuals representing schools and colleges, moreover, reflect an explicit and primary educational mission. Yet, because athletic prowess on the part of individuals and institutions may generate notoriety and wealth for athletes and enormous revenues for institutions, the race for such rewards may serve to compromise the educational mission. Consequently, eligibility rules were enacted by high school or college athletics organizations to protect the welfare of student-athletes, to preserve the integrity of educational institutions, and to promote amateur athletics. The eligibility requirements thus enacted for inter-scholastic and intercollegiate athletic competition and their legal challenges are the focus of this chapter.

■ ■ ■ ■

Representative Case

BECK v.
MISSOURI STATE HIGH SCHOOL ACTIVITIES ASSOCIATION
United States District Court, Eastern District of Missouri
837 F. Supp. 998 (1993)

OPINION:

On July 12, 1993, plaintiff instituted this action for injunctive and declaratory relief pursuant to the First and Fourteenth Amendments of the United States Constitution and 28 U.S.C. @ 2201. Plaintiff asks the Court to consider the constitutionality of @ 238.3 of the Bylaws of the Missouri State High School Activities Association ("MSH-SAA" or "Association"). That particular bylaw restricts a student's eligibility to participate in interscholastic ath-

letic activities for a period of 365 days following the student's transfer from one school to another This provision contains nine (9) exceptions, one of which is the basis of this suit. Specifically, plaintiff challenges the exception contained in @ 238.3(a)(2) which affords students transferring from a non-public to a public school eligibility for interscholastic competition within five (5) days of transfer, as opposed to the 365 day waiting period imposed on students such as plaintiff who transfer from a public school to non-public school.]

Plaintiff alleges that because of the inclusion of this particular provision, the entire transfer restriction bylaw violates his Equal Protection and Due Process rights under the Fourteenth Amendment, as well as his First Amendment rights of Freedom of Religion and Association, by depriving him of eligibility to participate in interscholastic basketball competition as a consequence of his transfer from a public school to a parochial school.

I. Findings of Fact

1. Plaintiff Sean Beck is a minor, sixteen years of age, who resides with his parents in St. Charles, Missouri and currently attends Lutheran High School ("Lutheran") in St. Peters, Missouri.
2. Plaintiff transferred to Lutheran, a private parochial school, from Francis Howell North High School ("Francis Howell"), a public school, on January 25, 1993.
3. Defendant MSHSAA is a voluntary, non-incorporated association of private and public junior and senior high schools.
4. Both Francis Howell and Lutheran are members of MSHSAA, and both field teams in various sports that compete with teams of other member schools.
5. MSHSAA is an activities association established by junior and senior high schools for the purpose of adopting uniform standards to regulate interscholastic activities and contests among member schools. Activities encompassed by MSHSAA include athletics, speech and debate, music, and cheerleading.

• • •

8. The eight individuals on the Board represent eight geographical districts within the State of Missouri and are selected by schools within each of the districts; each of the individuals is either a principal or a superintendent of a public school in his or her respective district. Local school boards have input into the formulation and enforcement of MSHSAA policies and rules through their district representatives.
9. Section 238.3(a)(2) of the MSHSAA bylaws specifically provides:

Transfer from Nonpublic to Public—If a student transfers from a nonpublic school to a public school located in the district where the student's parents reside, he/she may be eligible as soon as certified in accordance with By-law 234 provided the student is transferring to the

public school for the first time and the principals of both the public and nonpublic schools involved concur that undue influence is not involved in the transfer.

However, the bylaws lack a similar provision covering transfers from a public school to a non-public school.

10. Bylaw 238.3(a)(9) contains a waiver which confers limited eligibility upon a student who transfers schools under circumstances which would otherwise make him ineligible to participate in interscholastic athletics at his or her new school for 365 days. The student is eligible under the following terms: "A student whose name has been included on a school eligibility roster at any level for a given sport during the twelve (12) calendar months preceding the date of such transfer can be eligible only for sub-varsity competition in that sport. A student may have unrestricted eligibility in all other sports. . . ."
11. Any transferring student is permitted to practice with teams at any level, in any sport, regardless of his involvement with that sport at his or her prior school.
12. During the 1992-93 school year, while in the tenth grade, plaintiff transferred from Francis Howell to Lutheran. While at Francis Howell, plaintiff participated on the junior-varsity basketball team.
13. Participation in interscholastic athletics was not an impetus to plaintiff's decision to transfer, nor did it play any part in the decision. Neither plaintiff nor his parents were ever "recruited," solicited, or influenced by any official, teacher, or other person affiliated with Lutheran in connection with the decision to transfer.]
14. Plaintiff's decision to transfer from Francis Howell to Lutheran was made after consultation with his parents, and was based on their belief that Lutheran offered plaintiff smaller classes, a better educational experience, and improved prospects of attending an outstanding university.
15. At the time the transfer decision was made, plaintiff and his parents were aware that Lutheran was a member of MSHSAA and that one of MSHSAA's rules generally prohibited a transfer student from participating in interscholastic athletic competition for a period of 365 days from the time of transfer.

16. Subsequent to plaintiff's enrollment at Lutheran, he inquired about participation in the school's varsity basketball program. The school advised plaintiff that he would not be eligible to compete in interscholastic competitions between member schools until approximately January 25, 1994.

• • •

20. MSHSAA relies on the transfer rule to combat the evils associated with "school-hopping" and improper recruiting. However, defendants failed to demonstrate the existence, much less the prevalence, of either such evil.

21. There are no allegations of recruiting, "school-hopping" or undue influence in this case, and it is unlikely that plaintiff's participation on Lutheran's basketball team, if permitted, would afford that team any significant advantage over other teams, as plaintiff labels himself an "average player."

• • •

II. Conclusions of Law
• • •

2. The Transfer of Enrollment Standards Contained in @ 238.3 of MSHSAA's Bylaws Do Not Violate Plaintiff's Freedom of Religion or Freedom of Association Rights.

Plaintiff argues that he is "penalized" by the transfer restriction, which denies him eligibility to participate in interscholastic athletic competition for 365 days because he transferred from a public to a religious school. This "penalty" allegedly impairs his right to freely exercise his religious beliefs and to freely associate with those holding similar religious beliefs, both in violation of his First Amendment rights to Free Exercise of Religion and the right of his parents to direct the education of their child. For the reasons set forth below, the Court rejects both arguments.

The Free Exercise Clause prohibits government from punishing an individual on the basis of his or her religious beliefs. However, it does not prohibit the regulation of conduct engaged in for religious reasons, when the regulation is necessitated by reasons independent of the religious nature of the conduct. See, e.g., Church of the Lukumi Babalu Aye v. City of Hialeah, 124 L. Ed. 2d 472, 113 S. Ct. 2217, 2226 (1993) (acknowledging that a law might be upheld despite the incidental effect of burdening a particular religious practice); Braunfeld v. Brown, 366 U.S. 599, 607, 6 L. Ed. 2d 563, 81 S. Ct. 1144 (1961). The rule at issue makes no reference to religion and thus does not facially interfere with plaintiff's exercise of his religious beliefs.

• • •

Plaintiff also alleges that his freedom of association rights are restricted. The freedom of association is not explicitly provided in the Constitution but rather is implied from other, explicitly provided, constitutional rights. In this case, plaintiff argues that his parents have a right to select the school he attends, and any burden on his parents' right impairs his implied right to freely associate with those sharing similar religious beliefs. Plaintiff's reliance on Pierce v. Society of Sisters, 268 U.S. 510, 69 L. Ed. 1070, 45 S. Ct. 571 (1925), as supporting his position is misplaced. In Pierce, the Supreme Court held that states could not prevent students from attending non-public schools. However, because the bylaw at issue does not impose such a restriction, Pierce is inapplicable. There is no evidence that temporarily restricting plaintiff's eligibility to compete in a basketball game restricts his ability to choose a particular school or to associate with whomever he chooses. The bylaw does not unduly interfere with the religious beliefs of plaintiff or his parents, or their ability to freely choose a school. Therefore, the Court finds no constitutional violation. See, e.g., In re U.S. ex rel Missouri State High School Activities Ass'n, 682 F.2d 147 (8th Cir. 1982) [hereinafter In re MSHSAA]; Griffin High School v. Illinois High School Ass'n, 822 F.2d 671 (7th Cir. 1987).

3. By-Law 238.3 Is Not Over-Inclusive, Arbitrary or Capricious.

Relying on ABC League v. Missouri State High School Activities Ass'n, 530 F. Supp. 1033, 1048 (E.D. Mo. 1981) [hereinafter ABC League], plaintiff argues that the Transfer of Enrollment Standards provided in @ 238.3 are over-inclusive because they impact many transfers which do not involve the harms that @ 238.3 was adopted to prevent. The Eighth Circuit expressly rejected that argument in In re MSHSAA, 682 F.2d at 152, and accordingly, plaintiff's argument cannot succeed.

Plaintiff also attacks the "hardship exception," contained in @ 238.3(a)(8), as being arbitrary and capricious. Again relying on ABC League, plaintiff alleges that the hardship exception is "vague and amorphous" because it lacks specific standards as to what constitutes a "hardship." The Eighth Circuit found that the prior version of the rule contained at least one definite standard that was sufficient to narrow the scope of the bylaw. "The exception can only be invoked in cases involving no choice by the student or his parents. . . . The [Board] has a very narrow ambit of discretion which is constitutionally acceptable."

In re MSHSAA, 682 F.2d at 153. The current version of the transfer rule contains a similar limitation, because it can be invoked only if the transfer was for non-athletic reasons and there was no undue influence. Additionally, the current version of the rule replaces the "no choice" language of the prior version with a specific description of the circumstances which might give rise to a hardship exception. The Count finds that the range of discretion afforded the Board is not contrary to constitutional strictures.

4. The Exception to MSHSAA's Transfer Rule Contained in @ 238.3(a)(2) Violates the Equal Protection Clause

Finally, plaintiff attacks the constitutional validity of the entire Transfer of Enrollment Standards provision because of the inclusion of subsection (a)(2), which allegedly causes students transferring from public schools to non-public schools to be treated differently than students transferring from non-public schools to public schools. The Constitution requires heightened judicial scrutiny when a law classifies individuals so as to create a "suspect class," or when a constitutionally protected fundamental right is infringed. Plaintiff does not contend that the classification created by the rule—students transferring from public to non-public schools—is based upon "suspect" criteria. Thus, consistent with the Court's findings above, there is no unconstitutional deprivation in this case, and plaintiff is correct to frame his argument in terms of a rational basis analysis.

Under the transfer policy in effect before this dispute arose, students who transferred to or from MSHSAA member schools were subsequently ineligible for participation in interscholastic competition among member schools for a period of 365 days, unless their parents had actually changed residences from one school district to another. The alleged purpose of this policy was to prevent the recruitment of student athletes, and based on that purpose, the Eighth Circuit upheld that prior version of the transfer rule against constitutional challenges similar to those raised here. See In re MSHSAA, supra. However, that case contained a version of the transfer rule which "attaches a restriction to all transfers whether to private or public schools. . . ." Id. at 153. Because the current version of @ 238.3 is similar to the Transfer of Enrollment Standards upheld by the Eighth Circuit, with the primary difference being the addition of @ 238.3(a)(2), the Court declines plaintiff's invitation to invalidate @ 238.3 in its entirety. Rather the Court will extrapolate from the Eighth Circuit's opinion in evaluating only the addition to the Transfer Standards, @ 238,3(a)(2).

In support of upholding the entire bylaw, defendant relies on Griffin High School v. Illinois High School Ass'n, alleging that the transfer restriction at issue in that case was identical to the rule at issue here. In Griffin, the Seventh Circuit upheld the transfer rule, which distinguished between transfers to public and private schools, against similar First Amendment, Due Process and Equal Protection challenges. However, in Griffin the Seventh Circuit relied, at least in part, on the findings of an ad hoc committee which concluded that in Illinois "private schools . . . enjoy an unfair advantage." 822 F.2d at 673. The appellate court determined that adjusting for this "perceived inequity" was a legitimate purpose and that the transfer rule was rationally related to achieving that purpose.

The Court finds Griffin distinguishable and inapplicable because the case at bar lacks comparable evidence as to the existence of a "private school advantage." MSHSAA did convene an ad hoc committee to consider the alleged advantages enjoyed by private schools, as in Griffin, but at trial, the parties presented little evidence as to the findings of the ad hoc committee. In fact, the specific portion of the transfer rule at issue was drafted and enacted completely independent of the ad hoc committee.

In this case, Mr. Miles, a former MSHSAA Executive Director, provided the majority of the evidence as to the alleged private school advantage. He testified that public schools were disadvantaged because private schools could select students from an unlimited geographical area, whereas a public school may only enroll students from the school district in which a student's parents reside. Mr. Miles also cited the "financial incentives" that private schools were able to offer to attract student athletes. Mr. Miles' testimony was similar to the evidence the Seventh Circuit considered in Griffin, where that court found that, "differences between public and private schools . . . [in the view of the ad hoc committee], rendered competition between the two groups of schools inequitable, despite the facial neutrality of the [Illinois High School Association] transfer policy." 822 F.2d at 673.

In this case, however, it is not evident to this Court how these "differences" provide non-public schools an advantage over public schools. Public schools are free to all who reside within the district area, so a scholarship or even partial financial assistance afforded non-public school students merely places the non-public schools on an equal plain as the public school. Defendants argue that public schools are limited to accepting students who live within their district, while non-public schools can enroll students from theoretically anywhere. Also, it would seem that the public schools have larger student populations from which to select their athletes. Regardless of the reality of these "differences," the Association and its ad hoc committee acknowledged at least their potential existence and in response, agreed to impose attendance areas on non-public schools. Neither party has claimed that this solution is inadequate or that the "problem" remains an issue.

Additionally, in contrast to Griffin, this Court concludes that the bylaw raises a potential equal protection problem. In Griffin, the Seventh Circuit concluded that the rule was facially neutral because it did not classify students based on their religion. 822 F.2d at 674. However, in this action, @ 238(a)(2), on its face, causes similarly situated individuals to be treated differently. Nevertheless, this constitutional infirmity might not be fatal to the bylaw, if defendant can show that the regulation addresses a legitimate state purpose and is rationally related to serving that legitimate purpose.

As indicated above, the parties in this action have failed to present the Court with evidence that a problem of "school-hopping" or recruiting actually occurs in the school system. Rather, Mr. Miles admitted knowledge of only a few incidents of "school-hopping," upon which he did not elaborate. There was also testimony that recruiting is not a problem. This Court has searched in vain for an explanation of the "advantage" that nonpublic schools are afforded over public schools which might justify such an exception to the transfer restriction. While the Court acknowledges the existence of cases from other jurisdictions reaching different conclusions, based on the record created by the parties in this case, and the materials submitted in support of their respective positions, it is unclear that this bylaw protects a legitimate state interest being protected by this bylaw. That is not to say that it may not exist; however, based on the evidence adduced at trial, this Court finds an insufficient basis upon which to uphold the challenged provision.

• • •

Accordingly, for the foregoing reasons, [it is hereby ordered] . . . that Section 238.3(a)(2) of the Missouri State High School Activities Association By-Laws is invalidated.

■ ■ ■ ■

Fundamental Concepts

High School Privilege

High School eligibility rules are essentially the products of state high school activities/athletics associations. Such associations are usually privately chartered and may or may not have direct advisory functions to a state board of education. Typically, local school districts' representatives to the association decide in parliamentary fashion the rules for conducting the athletic events throughout the state. Such agreement is necessary to ensure that fairness reigns in athletics competition across the state. Because each state association is unique, rule variance exists between states. However, despite their distinctions, consistency is readily apparent.

These associations are created to deal with the management of *extracurricular activities* which, by definition, are all those activities for students that are sponsored or sanctioned by an educational institution that supplement or complement, but are not a part of, the institution's required academic program or regular curriculum. Participation is voluntary and, more important, a **privilege** in the reasoning of courts, which may be extended at the discretion of the school board. The board, therefore, may decide, usually through its participation in the state high school athletics association, the terms under which students may exercise the privilege. When eligibility standards are challenged in the courts, they must, in most circumstances withstand only rational basis scrutiny. (See Chapter 4.14.) This means that if the requirements are rationally related to the purpose of activity and not arbitrary, capricious, or unjustly discriminatory, they will be upheld by the courts (Wong, 1994).

Academic Standards. Alternative means of demonstrating academic eligibility for athletic participation in high schools include grade point average (GPA), courses passed in previous and/or current semesters, courses passed in previous year, percent daily attendance, enrollment in minimum number of classes, enrollment in minimum full-credit courses, GPA or passing grades in current or previous grading periods, and maintaining a grade of 70 in each class during six-week grading period to stay eligible for the next six-week grading period (Texas). Thus, a variety of standards are used by different states to demonstrate academic qualification for athletic participation in high schools.

The Texas standard (above) is a notorious statute ("no pass, no play rule" passed by the legislature in 1985, and challenged all the way to the U.S. Supreme Court in 1986. The Supreme Court refused to hear the Texas law citing the lack of federal question. In so doing, it allowed a Texas court decision affirming the law to stand. In 1995 the Texas legislature modified the law to make it more permissive. For instance, failing students could rejoin the team if they are passing after three weeks; plus, failing students can practice or rehearse during the suspension period.

Transfer Rules. High School associations create transfer rules to preclude student-athletes from "jumping" (enrolling in different school) for reasons pertaining to athletics. There are many legitimate reasons for transfers involving such things as family relocations, employment, divorce, etc., and as such, constitute a basis for exceptions within the rules. Oregon has passed a statute preventing implementation of the transfer rule if the student moved with his or her parent as opposed to moving in with friends just to play for another school.

Transfer rules appear to be popular targets for legal challenges based upon claims of violations of equal protection, freedom of religion, right to travel and due process. (See *Beck v. Missouri State High School Activities Association*, above.) Yet, courts have generally upheld transfer rules under rational judicial scrutiny. Considering that no fundamental right is violated, nor any suspect class established, the transfer rule need only be rationally related to the purpose stated above to be upheld by the court. If, however, the student-athlete plaintiff can establish fraud, collusion, or arbitrariness the possibility exists for a successful challenge. (Notice the judge's order to invalidate a section of the bylaw which violates the equal protection clause.)

Redshirting. The practice of delaying or postponing an athlete's competition in order to extend the athlete's career is known as "redshirting." For purposes of maximizing athletic success, redshirting is an effective strategy to take advantage of an extra year's growth and maturity and, of course, skill development. Moreover, parents of team sport athletes have demonstrated a willingness to "hold back" students a year in school so as to create an aggregate of student-athletes more likely to win championships. High school athletics association rules do not permit the practice of redshirting because it is antithetical to the educational mission. Furthermore, redshirting creates unfair competition advantages, possible dangerous mismatches, and unwarranted exclusion of peer student-athletes.

On the other hand, high school athletics associations recognize illness and/or injury and purely academic determinations of grade level as legitimate reasons for exceptions to rules precluding redshirting and make appropriate allowances. To handle the problem of redshirting, however, rules of **longevity** must be invoked. Longevity rules determine the limits for participation in terms of a) semesters/years allowed to complete competition and b) a maximum age beyond which interscholastic competition may not continue. For example, most high school association rules limit a student athlete to eight consecutive semesters in which to complete interscholastic competition. Similarly, most associations do not permit competition among student/athletes who have reached their nineteenth birthday before beginning his/her senior year.

In general, courts have agreed with the rational argument that longevity and redshirting regulations preserve the privilege of interscholastic sports competition, consistent with their educational mission.

Intercollegiate Regulations

Individual eligibility rules for intercollegiate competition begin at the specific institution where the student in enrolled. Depending upon the institution's characteristics and mission, specific eligibility standards for representing that institution in intercollegiate athletic competition may be imposed. Such standards must reflect at a minimum the requirements of the conference in which it competes and, further, the association of conferences and institutions in which it holds membership. The largest such association of four-year institutions is the National Collegiate Athletics Association (NCAA). This discussion will focus on the eligibility rules and bylaws of the NCAA and various legal challenges of those rules.

Article 1.3.1 of the *NCAA Manual* declares its basic purpose:

> The competitive athletics programs of member institutions are designed to be a vital part of the educational system. A basic purpose of this Association is to maintain intercollegiate athletics as an integral part of the educational program and the athlete as an integral part of the student body and, by so doing, retain a clear line of demarcation between intercollegiate athletics and professional sports.

Thus, the NCAA is a private, voluntary association of four-year institutions which share a common interest in preserving amateur intercollegiate athletics as part of the educational mission.

Academic Regulations. To maintain the educational mission, the NCAA has legislated at the annual conventions of its members explicit rules for qualifying individuals academically for competition on two dimensions: initial and continuing. To meet *initial* qualifications, i.e., to be academically eligible to compete upon matriculation, the student-athlete must currently demonstrate the following (Bylaw 14.02.9.1):

a. Graduation from high school;
b. Successful completion of a required core curriculum of a minimum number of courses in specified subjects;
c. Specified minimum GPA in the core curriculum, and
d. Specified minimum SAT or ACT score.

Determination of initial eligibility is currently made at a centralized clearinghouse by a consulting service under direction of the NCAA staff. If the student satisfactorily meets the standards, the student is deemed a "qualifier" and academically eligible to participate and receive athletically-related financial aid. If the standards are not met, the applicant is restricted from competing (but may practice), may not receive athletically-related financial aid, and surrenders one of his/her four years of competition eligibility.

To satisfy *continuing eligibility* requirements, the student- athlete must demonstrate a consistent record of progress toward a degree. To register "satisfactory progress" the student-athlete's academic record at the beginning of the fall semester or quarter of each year in residence must indicate completion of a requisite percent of course requirements in the student-athlete's particular academic program at a requisite percent of the GPA required for graduation at the particular institution.

In addition, the student-athlete must be enrolled full-time (minimum 12 semester credit hours) in order to maintain current athletic eligibility. Dropping below full-time enrollment immediately disqualifies the student for athletic competition.

Transfer Rules. NCAA rules governing eligibility following transfer from one institution to another are rather complex because of the great mobility of the age group. The purposes of transfer rules is to preclude recruitment of athletes from one institution to another, and to discourage interruptions of academic progress due to transfers because of reasons pertaining to athletics. The general principle stated in Bylaw 14.5.1 requires a student who transfers to a member institution from any other collegiate institution to complete one full academic year of residence at the certifying institution before being eligible to compete. There are multiple exceptions to this requirement most notable being those involving transfers from two-year colleges.

Longevity. The NCAA, too, is concerned with the problems presented by interminable eligibility and older than expected participants. With regard to the former, the NCAA decided four years of intercollegiate competition is the maximum allowable, regardless of where or at how many institutions the competition takes place. Further, the individual student-athlete is permitted five consecutive calendar years from original matriculation to complete four years of eligibility. Thus, an accommodation is possible following a transfer, or even a redshirt year for maturation or injury, etc.

With regard to age, the membership became alarmed at the infusion of older athletes, particularly foreign athletes with the advantage of seasoning and experience, supplanting the scholarships of younger athletes. So, in 1980 the membership passed "the age rule," Bylaw 14.2.4.5 which credits any organized sports competition in a particular sport in each 12-month period following the athlete's twentieth birthday as a year of NCAA competition eligibility.

Challenges/Defenses

The annual edition of *The NCAA Manual* is voluminous and complex. Despite efforts to simplify the manual, the rules, and their complexity the quantity and complexity continues to grow. Challenges of specific bylaws first appears in discussions on the floor of the convention. The debate seldom quells the dissatisfaction so that once controversial proposals are passed and implemented affected parties seek relief in the courts.

The constitutionality of specific bylaws is the most frequent complaint. For example, there are many who feel that the inclusion of standardized test scores as a factor in determining initial eligibility favors wealthier, better prepared students and discriminates against economically disadvantaged students. Thus, many feel that "Proposition 48," the informal name for the initial proposal passed in the 1986 NCAA convention, violates the Fourteenth Amendment guaranteeing equal protection under the law. (See Chapter 4.14) However, the Fourteenth Amendment protects only against actions taken by *state actors*; and does not protect against the actions or conduct of a private organization. (See Chapter 4.12 for an explanation of state action.) A successful challenge of Proposition 48, therefore, must be based on a finding that the NCAA is a state actor.

Although court decisions rendered in the 1970's found the NCAA a state actor, particularly involving the NCAA's enforcement activities, more recent cases have contradicted that view. Two notable challenges, *Parish v. NCAA* and *Howard University v. NCAA,* failed in their arguments that the 1.600 Rule, precursor to Proposition 48, violated constitutional rights even though federal courts deemed the NCAA a state actor in both cases. In *Parish*, the Fifth Circuit Court of Appeals held that the rule did not violate constitutional rights because participating in athletics fell outside the protection of the law. In *Howard University*, the 1.600 Rule was upheld as being narrowly and reasonably related to the private goals of the NCAA and not an infringement on constitutional rights.

In the only test of the NCAA as a state actor to reach the United States Supreme Court, *NCAA v. Tarkanian*, in a 1988 decision the court agreed with the NCAA, holding that the NCAA in no way acted with state authority. Tarkanian had argued that the NCAA's Infractions Committee, which had found his involvement in thirty-eight recruiting violations, forced UNLV, his employer, to suspend him. Tarkanian's argument that the threaten of NCAA sanctions forced his suspension was countered by the court's judgment that UNLV could, at any time, withdraw its NCAA membership. Furthermore, the court confirmed the NCAA is a private organization with no actual ties to the state or state authority so that any actions taken by the NCAA were private and not within the umbrella of protection of the Fourteenth Amendment.

In light of the *Tarkanian* decision and others it appears that student-athlete challenges of NCAA bylaws, be they eligibility rules or others, will be severely limited on constitutional grounds.

Recent Developments

Eligibility Rights of the Disabled.   Federal statutes protecting the educational rights of students with disabilities, i.e., the Individuals with Disabilities Education Act (IDEA), the Federal Rehabilitation Act (section 504), and the Americans with Disabilities Act (ADA), safeguard students' participation in school athletics in two general ways. First, section 504 and the ADA bars schools from administering school sports in a manner that discriminates against students with disabilities. Second, under IDEA, athletics participation is a component of the "free, appropriate, public education" to which every student with disabilities is entitled. Indeed, under IDEA, athletic activities may be included in a child's personal individualized education program ("IEP"). The antidiscrimination protection of section 504 and the ADA apply, however, even when sport participation is not considered necessary to assure an appropriate education for an individual.

Section 504 mandates that "no otherwise qualified individual with a disability . . . shall, solely by reason of her or his disability, be excluded from the participation in, be denied the benefits of, or be subjected to discrimination under any program or activity receiving Federal financial assistance." The Supreme Court has defined an **otherwise qualified individual** as one who is able to meet all of a program's requirement in spite of his handicap." Furthermore, the Court has held that if a person with disabilities requires **reasonable accommodations** to meet those requirements, he or she may still be an otherwise qualified individual. However, individuals are not deemed otherwise qualified if a) the accommodations necessary would substantially lower standards, b) if they would require fundamental alteration of the nature of the program, or c) if they create undue financial and administrative burdens.

The more recently enacted ADA provides similar mandates but, in addition, defines **qualified individual with a disability** as "an individual with a disability, who, with or without reasonable modifications to rules, policies, or practices . . . meets the essential eligibility requirements for . . . participation in programs or activities provided by a public entity."

Equivocal Litigation.   Results of litigation over claims of discrimination brought by disabled students denied participation in athletics has been mixed and somewhat confusing. When schools bar students from participation directly because of their disabilities, courts have consistently overturned those exclusions. Courts consistently reject paternal arguments that participation may be unsafe to the disabled student. Where courts struggle, however, is with discrimination claims in which the student's disability is not directly related to his failure to meet eligibility requirements. For example, an early learning disability is responsible for a student's exceeding the high school association's age limit by the time the student reaches his senior class. This identical problems was treated differently in two federal courts.

In *Sandison v. Michigan High School Athletic Association, Inc.*, the federal district court for the Eastern District of Michigan granted a preliminary injunction barring enforcement of the age limit against two students who wanted to join their track and cross country teams. The court employed a four-factor test: 1) whether plaintiffs had a disability under the statutes; 2) whether they were otherwise qualified to participate on the teams; 3) whether they were being excluded from the athletic program "solely by reason of their disabilities"; and 4) whether the interscholastic sports program run by the athletic association received federal funds.

The court acknowledged that the disability satisfied the definition found under ADA. Secondly, the court reasoned that abolishing the requirement for the plaintiffs was a "reasonable accommodation," thus making them "otherwise qualified" to participate. The court also acknowledged that although the MHSAA rule was necessary, protection of high school students from older, more physically developed athletes was not advanced by its application to non-contact track competition. Further, in repelling the defendants' argument that they would suffer an undue burden by an increase in eligibility challenges, the court commented, "The conclusion I reach today is not universal." Finally, the court found that the state athletic association was an indirect recipient of federal financial assistance and subject to ADA.

Just two months later, the Eighth Circuit Court of Appeals reviewed the grant of an injunction under almost identical circumstances in *Pottgen v. Missouri State High School Activities Association*, but reached the opposite conclusion. The court found that the award of preliminary relief was an abuse of the district court's discretion. The circuit court rejected complete waiver of the age rule in *Pottgen* as a "fundamental alteration" and, thus, concluded that since the plaintiff can never meet the essential eligibility requirement, he is not an "otherwise qualified individual." Furthermore, the court reasoned that the individualized inquiry through evidentiary hearings would, indeed, present an undue administrative burden. With no likelihood of success on the merits, the court reversed the district court's grant of a preliminary injunction barring enforcement of the eligibility rule against Pottgen.

Subsequently, an appeal of the *Sandison* decision to the Sixth Circuit Court ultimately returned a decision more akin to that in the *Pottgen* appeal. Specifically, the Court of Appeals held that: 1) appeal from portion of injunction requiring that students be permitted to participate in track meets was mooted by the end of track season and the students' graduation from high school; 2) appeal from portion of the injunction prohibiting the MHSAA from penalizing high schools for allowing students to participate in sports was not moot; 3) the age requirement did not violate the Rehabilitation Act or Department of Education regulations; and 4) the age requirement did not violate the Americans with Disabilities Act.

Inadequacy of Injunctions. The granting of injunctions against enforcing eligibility rules so that plaintiffs may compete for a three month competitive season leads to a persistent interpretive conflict demonstrated by the *Sandison* and *Pottgen* cases. There is a predictable process of litigation: a preliminary injunction is granted or denied quickly to resolve the immediate issue of the student's participation, but the case becomes moot when the season ends. The essential legal claims of the plaintiff, however, are evaluated only against the flexible standard of whether there is some likelihood of success on the merits. Alas, no final, appealable decision as to how section 504 and the ADA apply to general athletic eligibility which may exclude a student with disabilities is rendered.

Conflict Continues. Looking to other courts for clarification of the issue of discrimination against disabled students by interscholastic eligibility rules finds waters no less muddy. State and federal courts in Tennessee and Texas have interpreted the federal antidiscrimination statutes to prohibit the enforcement of general athletic eligibility standards against students with disabilities, while other courts in New York, Indiana, and Texas have permitted schools and state athletic associations to apply such eligibility restrictions to students with disabilities.

Even the federal Office of Civil Rights (OCR), the agency which conducts investigations of discrimination complaints where federal statutes are at issue has rendered inconsistent opinions. The OCR for the Ohio region has ruled that section 504 was not violated when a student with disabilities was removed from his high school golf team because he failed to meet minimum academic requirements. The office was persuaded by the argument that (academic) eligibility rules, on their face and as applied, were not discriminatory on the basis of handicap."

In contrast, another OCR regional office for New Mexico ordered the state athletic association to declare a disabled student older than the 19 year age ceiling eligible because inappropriate early education led to his late graduation.

NCAA Eligibility for Disabled Students. Complaints from students with learning disabilities unable to meet NCAA qualifications for initial eligibility have prompted the U.S. Department of Justice to examine the issue. Most recently, the Justice Department issued a letter to the NCAA with suggestions of how to apply rules less strictly to accommodate athletes with special needs. The NCAA's Academic Requirements Committee is meeting to consider the suggestions.

Home Schooled Student Eligibility.   Should students schooled at home be permitted to participate for local school athletic teams? In *McNatt v. Frazier School District, 1995 WL 568380 (W.D. Pa.)*, a student, schooled at home, sued the local school board for denying him eligibility to play for the district's junior high basketball team, thereby denying his rights under the Equal Protection Clause of the Fourteenth Amendment and the Civil Rights Act. The District Court upheld the decision of the school board. As "home schooling" becomes more prevalent and more acceptable, expect state legislatures to consider statutes providing accommodations for such students.

References

A. Cases

Beck v. Missouri State High School Activities Association, 837 F. Supp. 998 (E.D. Mo. 1993)

Howard University v. National Collegiate Athletic Association, 510 F.2d 213 (D.C. Cir. 1975)

McNatt v. Frazier School District, 1995 WL 568380 (W.D. Pa.)

National Collegiate Athletic Association v. Tarkanian, 488 U.S. 179 (1988)

Parish v. National Collegiate Athletic Association, 506 F.2d 1028(5th Cir. 1975)

Pottgen v. Missouri State High School Activities Association, 40 F.3d 926 (8th Cir. 1994)

Sandison v. Michigan High School Athletic Association, Inc., 863 F. Supp. 483 (E.D. Mich. 1994)

B. Publications

Foster, Linda. (1995). Activities' Bylaws Restricting Students Participation May Violate Equal Protection Clause. 5 *Seton Hall Journal of Sports Law* 669-673.

Goedert, J.C. (1995). Schools, Sports and Students with Disabilities: The Impact of Federal Laws Protecting the Rights of Students with Disabilities on Interscholastic Sports. 24 *Journal of Law and Education* 403-421.

Hendrix, S.D. (1995). Challenges to Proposition 48: Do Athletes Have a Constitutional Right to Compete? 24 *Journal of Law and Education* 133-139.

Wong, Glenn M. (1994). *Essentials of Amateur Sports Law*, (2d ed.).

C. Opinions

Northern (OH) School District, OCR Opinion, 17 EHLR 541 (1990)

New Mexico State Dept. of Education, OCR Opinion, 18 IDLR 219 (1991)

D. Legislation

Americans with Disabilities Act, 42 U.S.C. §§ 12101-12213 (West. Supp. 1993)

Federal Rehabilitation Act (§ 504), 29 U.S.C. § 79 (West Supp. 1973)

Individuals with Disabilities Education Act, 20 U.S.C. §§ 1400 et. seq. (West Supp. 1992)

Conduct Issues

Cathryn L. Claussen
Bowling Green State University

Grooming and dress codes, rules against the use of alcohol and drugs, prohibitions against high school marriages, rules against unsportsmanlike conduct, and rules requiring generally worthy conduct are all examples of good conduct rules used in amateur athletics. The source of such rules may be an athletics association, school, or coach. While marriage of high school athletes is no longer a real issue, the other types of conduct rules remain viable and continue to affect student eligibility to participate in athletics.

■ ■ ■ ■

Representative Case

PALMER v. MERLUZZI
United States District Court for the District of New Jersey
689 F. Supp. 400 (1988)

OPINION:

This litigation involves, inter alia, plaintiff Daniel Palmer's (Palmer) claim that defendants, Peter L. Merluzzi (Merluzzi) and the Hunterdon Central Board of Education (The Board of Education) violated plaintiff's Fourteenth Amendment right to due process when they suspended him from participating in extracurricular events for sixty days. In the instant motion, defendants have moved for summary judgment. Plaintiff opposes this motion and has cross-moved to compel defendants to provide certain discovery. These motions were referred to me by the Honorable Clarkson S. Fisher, U.S. District Judge.

Background
At all relevant times, Palmer was a senior at Hunterdon Central High School (the High School) located in Raritan Township. Merluzzi was the Superintendent of Schools for the Hunterdon Central Regional School District. The Board of Education is the duly elected governing body for the Hunterdon Central Regional School District.

Daniel Palmer was a starting wide receiver on the high school football team. He also was enrolled in a high school course known as "Careers in Broadcasting." On the evening of September 28, 1986, in conjunction with this course, Palmer and three other students had been assigned to the high school radio station. The next morning, school administrators questioned the students, including Palmer, about the discovery of beer stains and a marijuana pipe at the radio station. At this meeting, Palmer admitted to Dr. Paul Grimm, the school disciplinarian, that he had smoked marijuana and drank beer the previous night at the radio station.

Palmer was then suspended by Dr. Grimm for ten days pursuant to Policy 5380 of the High School and the Student Handbook. This suspension applied to both curricular and extracurricular activities of the school. Dr. Grimm telephoned Palmer's father, James Palmer, later that morning to inform him about the incident and the resulting suspension. Written confirmation of the ten day suspension dated September 30, 1986 was mailed to Palmer's parents and received on or about October 2, 1986. In that letter, Dr. Grimm specified the dates of suspension as being September 30 through October 13, 1986. This letter made no mention that any additional penalties were being considered.

On or about October 3, 1986, Dr. Grimm, Merluzzi, and several other administrators met to consider whether additional punishment should be imposed upon Palmer and the other students. Specifically, the possibility of suspending the students from extracurricular activities was discussed. Apparently, the majority of the administrators present agreed that suspension from extracurricular activities was warranted. However, a definitive decision to impose an additional penalty was not made at this juncture.

Thereafter, Merluzzi contacted two local drug and alcohol rehabilitation centers for a recommendation as to how to handle the situation. Specifically, Merluzzi sought information concerning "what would [be] . . . a reasonable period of time to accomplish some change in attitude amongst those individuals." Merluzzi did not inform the representatives he questioned that he was considering suspending the students from extracurricular activities. Merluzzi was told that sixty days was a reasonable period of time "to undergo some change." Id. Besides the incident in question, there was no evidence before Merluzzi that Palmer was a drug/alcohol abuser or that he had even previously used drugs or alcohol; Merluzzi did not even review Palmer's file before contacting the rehabilitation centers.

On or about October 9, 1986, Palmer's father heard rumors that additional penalties might be imposed on his son. Mr. Palmer telephoned Dr. George Collier, President of the Board of Education, to discuss his concerns. During that conversation, Mr. Palmer was advised by Dr. Collier to address the matter in writing to the Superintendent of Schools, and further, that the matter might be discussed in more detail at a Board of Education meeting scheduled for October 13, 1986. Neither Mr. Palmer or his son ever received formal notice that further disciplinary action against Dan Palmer was being considered or that they should attend the upcoming Board meeting.

Sometime before the October 13th Board of Education meeting, Merluzzi decided to recommend to the Board that Palmer and the other students be suspended from extracurricular activities for sixty days. In reaching this decision, Merluzzi primarily relied on Policy 138 which states in pertinent part:

No student may participate in a scheduled event if he was not in attendance on the day of the athletic event, or the day preceding a weekend event. No student may participate who has not demonstrated good citizenship and responsibility. No student who has not returned all equipment may participate in a succeeding season.

• • •

After the imposition of the extracurricular suspension, plaintiff made application before the New Jersey State Commissioner of Education for review of the actions of the Board of Education and Merluzzi. Specifically, Palmer sought injunctive relief 1) to set aside the ten day school suspension, 2) to set aside the sixty day suspension from extracurricular activities, and 3) to order the reinstatement of Palmer and the expungement of the incident from his records.

On October 20, 1986, a hearing was conducted before the Honorable Bruce R. Campbell, A.L.J. Judge Campbell, in a written opinion, found that the "ten-day out-of-school suspension was procedurally faultless and consistent with announced policy." D.K.P. By His Guardian Ad Litem J.P. and J.P. and B.P. v. Board of Education of Hunterdon Central Regional School District and Peter L. Merluzzi, Superintendent, OAL Dkt. No. EDU 7004-86 at 3 (October 21, 1986). Therefore, the request to set aside and expunge the ten-day suspension was denied.

Concerning the extracurricular suspension, Judge Campbell found that the defendant's conduct denied Palmer due process and thus he remanded this issue to the Board for proceedings consistent with the decision.

• • •

The Commissioner of Education affirmed the finding of the Administrative Law Judge regarding the suspension for ten days. However, the Commissioner set aside the stay of the sixty day extracurricular suspension previously imposed. . . . The Commissioner directed the Board of Education to grant Palmer and his parents an immediate opportunity to informally present their reasons for mitigation or the setting aside of the suspension.

Plaintiff appealed the Commissioner's ruling to the Appellate Division of the Superior Court of New Jersey seeking to stay the ban from all extracurricular activities. The Appellate Division denied this application. Plaintiff then appealed the decision of the Appellate Division to the New Jersey Supreme Court. The New Jersey Supreme Court declined to hear the matter.

On October 27, 1986, Palmer's attorney presented oral argument to the Board. The next day, plaintiff was notified in writing of the Board's decision affirming the penalty imposed by Merluzzi.

On November 25, 1986 plaintiff filed a complaint in this court. On March 25, 1987, on petition by plaintiff, the

Commissioner dismissed the matter without prejudice. The only pending action is the one before this Court.

Discussion

1. Property Interest—Due Process

Palmer alleges in Count I of his complaint that the defendants violated his right to due process under the Fourteenth Amendment when they suspended him from participating in extracurricular activities for sixty days without notice and a hearing. Palmer claims that participation by students in extracurricular activities rises to the level of a property interest and, therefore, he had the right to procedural due process before defendants imposed the suspension on him. Defendants have moved for summary judgment on the ground that New Jersey and the majority of jurisdictions do not recognize a student's property interest in extracurricular activities, and, there being no property interest, Palmer was not entitled to due process protection before the suspension was imposed.

The purpose of the summary judgment rule is the avoidance of the delay and expense of an unnecessary trial where the circumstances of the case, the applicable law and the facts, are ripe for such procedure. Goodman v. Mead Johnson Co., 534 F.2d 566, 573 (3d Cir. 1976), cert. denied 429 U.S. 1038, 50 L. Ed. 2d 748, 97 S. Ct. 732 (1977). Celotex v. Catrett, 477 U.S. 317, 106 S. Ct. 2548, 91 L. Ed. 2d 265 (1986). Fed. R. Civ. P. 56 provides for the granting of summary judgment if "the pleadings, depositions, answers to interrogatories, and admissions on file, together with the affidavits, if any, show that there is no genuine issue as to any material fact and that the moving party is entitled to a judgment as a matter of law." As the moving party bears the burden of demonstrating that there is clearly no genuine issue of material fact, all doubts will be resolved against the moving party. Adickes v. S.H. Kress and Co., 398 U.S. 144, 157, 90 S. Ct. 1598, 1611, 26 L. Ed. 2d 142, 155, 26 L. Ed. 2d 142 (1970); Anderson v. Liberty Lobby, 477 U.S. 242, 106 S. Ct. 2505, 2519, 91 L. Ed. 2d 202, 216 (1986).

• • •

The Fourteenth Amendment to the United States Constitution prohibits state action which deprives "any person of life, liberty or property without due process of law." The threshold question in this case is whether Daniel Palmer's interest in participating in extracurricular activities rises to the level of a property interest protected by procedural due process. If Palmer has a property interest in participating in extracurricular activities then the inquiry shifts to what process he is due before his "right" to participate is denied. Morrissey v. Brewer, 408 U.S. 471, 92 S. Ct. 2593, 33 L. Ed. 2d 484 (1974). If Palmer has no protectible liberty or property interest then the constitutional guarantee of due process is not applicable to defendants' interference with his participation in extracurricular activities.

First, I will consider Palmer's claimed property interest. Property interests are not created by the constitution but rather "are created and their dimensions defined by existing rules or understandings that stem from an independent source such as state law." Board of Regents v. Roth, 408 U.S. 564, 92 S. Ct. 2701, 33 L. Ed. 2d 548, 561 (1972); Bishop v. Wood, 426 U.S. 341, 344, 96 S. Ct. 2074, 48 L. Ed. 2d 684, 690 (1976). Property interests must reflect a person's "legitimate claim of entitlement to a specific government benefit" and not an "abstract need or desire" or a "unilateral expectation." Board of Regents v. Roth, supra.

On the basis of state law, Palmer undeniably had a legitimate claim of entitlement to a public education. Goss v. Lopez, 419 U.S. 565, 95 S. Ct. 729, 42 L. Ed. 2d 725 L. Ed. 2d (1975). New Jersey law requires that local authorities are to provide a free education to all residents over five and under twenty years of age, N.J.S.A. 18A:38-1, and compulsory attendance in schools is required of all students between the ages of six and sixteen, N.J.S.A. 18A:38-25. While no New Jersey statute or law specifically creates an obligation on schools to provide extracurricular activities, New Jersey does, however, require public schools to offer "[a] breadth of program offerings designed to develop the individual talents and abilities of pupils." N.J.S.A. 18A:7A-5(d). And "extracurricular activities, including interscholastic athletics, play an integral part in satisfying the breadth of programs requirement . . ." Burnside v. N.J.S.J.A., Docket Number A-625-84T7, November 15, 1984 (unpublished opinion). See also, Smith v. Paramus Bd. of Ed., 1968 S.L.D. 62, citing, Evaluative Criteria (1960 ed) of National Study of Secondary School Evaluation ("The School provides for two general kinds of educational experience, the regular classroom activities, and those called extracurricular or cocurricular. Together they form an integral whole aimed toward a common objective.").

New Jersey case law on whether a student has a property interest in extracurricular activities is scant to say the least. However, this is where the court must turn to determine whether Palmer has such a protectible interest. In Burnside v. N.J.S.A., supra, high school students and parents challenged a rule promulgated by the New Jersey State Interscholastic Athletic Association (N.J.S.I.A.A.) which required that students pass 23 academic credits per year in order to be eligible to compete in interscholastic athletic competition. The students claimed that they had a constitutional right to participate on their high school's interscholastic athletic teams.

The Appellate Division disagreed. While the court found that extracurricular activities, including interscholastic athletics, "are important factors toward a sound and comprehensive academic education," Id. at 5, it emphasized that "each pupil does not have a right to participate in interscholastic athletics. . . . [but] each pupil has a right to the opportunity to participate in interscholastic athletics and other extracurricular activities. That opportunity may not be hampered by discrimination in the participants selection."

• • •

New Jersey is not alone in recognizing that students do not have a federally protected property interest in extracurricular activities. The great majority of state and federal courts which have considered this issue have reached a similar conclusion.

• • •

A minority of decisions, however, have held that students have a property interest in extracurricular activities. These cases rest on the premise that extracurricular activities, specifically interscholastic athletics, serve as a springboard to college scholarships and professional opportunities. For example, in Duffley v. N.H. Interscholastic Athletic Assoc., 122 N.H. 484, 446 A.2d 462 (N.H. 1982), the New Hampshire Supreme Court, finding a due process right under the State Constitution, held that:

It is apparent that interscholastic athletics are considered an integral and important element of the educational process in New Hampshire. It follows that the right to participate in them at least rises above that of a mere privilege. Recognizing this, and the stark fact that a student's ability to attend college and further his education may, in many instances, hinge upon his athletic ability and athletic scholarships we hold that the right of a student to participate in interscholastic athletics is one that is entitled to the protections of procedural due process under Part I, Article 15 of our State Constitution. See also, Boyd v. Board of Education of McGehee School District No. 17, 612 F. Supp. 86, 93 (D.Ark. 1985) (a student's participation in interscholastic athletics is important to a student's education and economic development. Thus, the "privilege of participating in interscholastic athletics must be deemed a property interest protected by the due process of the Fourteenth Amendment.") Behagen v. Intercollegiate Conference of Faculty Representatives, 346 F. Supp. 602, 604 (D.Minn. 1972) (participation in athletics has "the potential to bring students great economic rewards").

Another view advanced by one court is to analyze the degree of exclusion from extracurricular activities in determining whether procedural due process is implicated. Pegram v. Nelson, 469 F. Supp. 1134, 1140 (M.D.N.C. 1979). For example, in Pegram the court found that the denial of a student's opportunity to participate in one or several extracurricular activities would not give rise to a right to due process. Id. "However, total exclusion from participation in that part of the educational process designated as extracurricular activities for a lengthy period of time could, depending upon the particular circumstances, be a sufficient deprivation to implicate due process." Id. (emphasis in original). In Pegram, a four month extracurricular suspension did not constitute a lengthy amount of time. See also, Dallam v. Cumberland Valley School District, 391 F. Supp. 358, 361 (M.D. Pa. 1975):

The property interest in education created by the State is participation in the entire process. The myriad activities which combine to form that education process cannot be dissected to create hundreds of separate property rights, each cognizable under the Constitution. Otherwise, removal from a particular class, dismissal from an athletic team, a club or any extracurricular activity would each require ultimate satisfaction of procedural due process. Id. at 361.

Notwithstanding these few cases which hold that a property interest exists because of the potential for future education or professional opportunities or which implicate the due process clause because of the nature and length of the extracurricular suspension, it is clear that this Court must look to New Jersey law in determining whether Daniel Palmer had a property interest in participating in extracurricular activities. Board of Regents v. Roth, supra.

Here, New Jersey case law, consistent with the majority of state and federal courts, specifically rejects the notion that participation in extracurricular activities is anything but a privilege. Dennis v. Holmdel Board of Education, supra. Therefore, Palmer has no property interest in playing varsity football and his suspension from that activity as well as other extracurricular activities, did not have to comport with due process. Thus, it is recommended that summary judgment be entered in favor of defendants on these claims.

Equal Protection

Palmer claims that his suspension from extracurricular activities violated his right to equal protection.

Essentially, Palmer argues that no other student has ever received a penalty of this magnitude and the penalty is not rationally related to a legitimate governmental objective.

The Fourteenth Amendment to the United States Constitution provides in pertinent part:

No state shall . . . deny to any person within its jurisdiction the equal protection of the laws.

In analyzing an equal protection claim a court must first determine what standard of review to employ. The first standard, strict scrutiny, should be used in cases involving 1) a government act classifying people in terms of their ability to exercise a fundamental right or 2) a governmental classification that distinguishes between persons in terms of any right, upon some suspect basis. Hawkins v. National Collegiate Athletic Assoc., 652 F. Supp. 602, 613 (C.D. Ill. 1987) citing U.S. v. Carolene Products Company, 304 U.S. 144, 152 n.4, 58 S. Ct. 778, 783 n.4, 82 L. Ed. 1234 (1938). The second standard, the rational relationship test, mandates that "classifications that neither regulate suspect classes nor burden fundamental rights be sustained if they are rationally related to a legitimate governmental interest." In re Asbestos Litigation, 829 F.2d 1233, 1238 (3d Cir. 1987).

It is well settled law that a right to a public education is not a fundamental right under the federal constitution. . . . Because neither a fundamental right nor a suspect class is involved here the defendants' conduct must be analyzed under the rational relationship test.

Under this test, I must determine whether the extracurricular suspension of Daniel Palmer was "rationally related to a legitimate governmental interest." In re Asbestos Litigation, supra. The defendants' articulated interest

in suspending Palmer was to ensure that only students who display "good citizenship and responsibility" may participate in interscholastic sports and to see "a change in attitude from an individual involved with drugs or alcohol."

• • •

Keeping in mind the Supreme Court's reluctance to have federal courts "second guess" policy decisions, I find that Palmer's suspension was rationally related to enforcing the legitimate goal of ensuring compliance with school drug policy. Superintendent Merluzzi consulted with faculty members, drug rehabilitation programs and school policies regarding drug/alcohol abuse before imposing the suspension. While the penalty was severe, it reflected an approach to deal with a complex social program that I cannot find irrational. See New Jersey v. T.L.O., supra ("maintaining security and order in the schools requires a certain degree of flexibility in school disciplinary procedures. . . .").

Palmer's argument that defendant's conduct was arbitrary and capricious because his punishment was more severe than other students violating school policy is similarly without merit. . . . All students involved in the incident at the radio station, including Palmer, received the same punishment. To go back and view the penalties meted out to others for similar offenses would constitute an unnecessary foray into second guessing the judgment of the Board in many different situations. That is simply unwarranted.

In conclusion, because Palmer has not demonstrated an equal protection violation, nor could he do so even with further discovery, I recommend that his equal protection claim be dismissed with prejudice.

■ ■ ■ ■

Fundamental Concepts

Authority to Regulate Conduct

In most states, the state legislature has the authority to regulate education. Typically, the legislature delegates that authority, including the authority to make rules governing extracurricular activities like athletics, to school boards or similar supervisory bodies. Often, a state statute will grant further authorization for school boards to join athletics associations or conferences, which are the bodies responsible for most of the rule-making concerning athletics participation. Where such statutory authorization to join athletics associations has not been granted by the state legislature, an issue may arise concerning whether in joining such an association the school board has improperly delegated its discretionary power. Generally, delegated authority may not be redelegated if it is a discretionary, decision-making type of authority. However, an agency may redelegate authority to carry out routine, ministerial functions. In *Bunger v. Iowa High School Athletic Association* (Iowa 1972), the court examined the delegation of authority issue, and concluded that in the absence of any statutory authorization enabling the school board to delegate rule-making authority to the athletics association, the rules of that association were invalid and could not be enforced.

Standards for Valid Conduct Rules

Non-Constitutional Standard. The school districts, individual schools, and coaches as agents of the schools, are vested with broad discretionary authority to promulgate and enforce rules that are reasonably related to carrying out the functions of the institution. There are two criteria for determining the validity of a rule under an administrative law standard, used when no constitutional challenge is brought against the relevant rule. These criteria are: 1) the rule must govern conduct which directly affects the effective operation of the school; 2) the rule must not be arbitrary or unreasonable. In *Bunger*, the leading case illustrating the application of this non-constitutional standard, the conduct rule in question prohibited "possession, consumption or transportation of alcoholic beverages or dangerous drugs." In addition, a student would lose eligibility if caught "in a vehicle stopped by a law officer and alcoholic beverages and/or dangerous drugs are found in the vehicle," and it was determined that the athlete had knowledge that such beverages or drugs were in the vehicle. The Iowa Supreme Court acknowledged that ineligibility could be enforced if a student consumes, "possesses, acquires, delivers, or transports beer," whether during an athletics season or during any part of the school year. The court even indicated its probable support of a rule making an athlete ineligible for violating a beer law during summer vacation. These situations were thought to have a direct bearing on the operation of the school. However, the student in Bunger was simply riding in a car, outside of the school year, with knowledge of the presence of beer but having committed no improper or illegal use of the substance. In this instance, the court felt that the part of the beer rule prohibiting such conduct did not directly affect the effective operation of the school. Further, while asserting that rules applying to extracurricular activities may reasonably be broader in scope than other school rules because athletes represent the school and are role models, the court concluded that the beer rule at issue went beyond the bounds of reasonableness. In the words of the court:

> School authorities may make reasonable beer rules, but we think this rule is too extreme. Some closer relationship between the student and the beer is required than mere knowledge that the beer is there. The rule as written would even prohibit a student from accepting a ride home in a car by an adult neighbor who had a visible package of beer among his purchases. (*Bunger* at 565)

Constitutional Standard. There are three primary grounds for a constitutional challenge to good conduct rules: the Equal Protection Clause of the Fourteenth Amendment, the Due Process Clause of the Fourteenth Amendment, and the First Amendment Freedom of Speech and Religion Provisions.

A. Due Process Clause. In *Palmer v. Merluzzi* (D.N.J. 1988), a high school student who had smoked marijuana and drunk beer on campus was suspended from the football team for sixty days in addition to the usual ten-day suspension from school. At issue was whether the penalty of suspension from football violated the Due Process Clause by depriving the student-athlete of a property interest in athletic participation. The court reviewed decisions in New Jersey as well as several other jurisdictions, the vast majority of which had concluded that the state had created no legitimate claim of entitlement to participate. In contrast to the entitlement to a public education, participation in athletics is considered a privilege rather than a right. It should be noted that a small minority of jurisdictions have found a protectible property interest in participation in school athletics programs based on the idea that such participation may serve as a training ground for later opportunities to receive college athletics scholarships or professional sport contracts. The majority position, however, is that the potential for such future opportunities is too speculative in any given case to be considered an existing, and hence protectible, property interest.

    B.   Equal Protection Clause.   In *Dunham v. Pulsifer* (D. Vermont 1970), a high school tennis player challenged a grooming code specifying acceptable hair length, a rule which did not apply to any group of students except athletes. The court ruled that choice of hair style was a fundamental right that could not be regulated unless the rule passed the test of strict scrutiny. The school board's justifications for the grooming rule were reviewed in order to determine whether it was necessary to accomplish a compelling governmental interest. The school board asserted four interests it claimed were compelling: 1) maximizing performance by eliminating the potential detrimental effects of long hair; 2) preventing dissension on the team; 3) maintaining team discipline; 4)enforcing conformity to social norms and providing uniformity in hair length rules between the various sports teams. The court found that: 1)long hair did not hinder performing well in tennis; 2) there was no evidence of dissension on the team; 3) discipline may be a compelling interest, but demanding obedience to a rule unrelated to the objectives of participation was unreasonable; 4) requiring conformity and uniformity for their own sakes and unrelated to any performance objective was unreasonable. In light of these findings, the court held that the grooming code violated the Equal Protection Clause. (It should be noted that federal courts across the country are divided on the issue of whether dress and grooming codes are constitutional.)

    In *Palmer v. Merluzzi* (D.N.J. 1988), the student's suspension from football for drug and alcohol use was issued under a school policy prohibiting athletics participation by students who had "not demonstrated good citizenship and responsibility." The court, finding that there is no fundamental right to participate in athletics and finding no suspect classification to be involved, applied rational basis review to the rule singling out athletes to be held to a good citizenship standard. The school's use of suspension from an extracurricular activity to accomplish its objective of enforcing compliance with its drug policy was held to be a reasonable means of achieving a legitimate end, and the court dismissed the equal protection claim.

    C.   Freedom of Speech and Religion.   Conduct issues can include expressive conduct (for example, student protest activities) and conduct involved in the practice of one's religious beliefs. Rules governing these types of conduct may be challenged on First Amendment grounds.

        1. **Freedom of Speech**. In the public school context, expressive conduct that would elsewhere be protected by the First Amendment Freedom of Speech is protected unless it constitutes a substantial disruption of the educational environment. In *Tinker v. Des Moines Independent School District* (U.S. 1969), students wearing black armbands and planning a demonstration to protest United States involvement in Vietnam were suspended for violating their school's policy against such protests. They claimed their freedom of speech was violated, and the Supreme Court agreed, ruling that the school's policy was unconstitutional because there was no evidence that the protest activity had substantially interfered with the learning environment.

        2. **Freedom of Religion**. Grooming and dress codes can sometimes conflict with traditional religious practices. In *Menora v. Illinois High School Association* (7th Cir. 1982), a Jewish athlete wished to wear his yarmulke during basketball competition in order to practice his religious belief that males must keep their heads covered at all times. The defendant league argued in support of their "no headgear rule," claiming that loose head coverings could create dangerous playing conditions. The court ruled against the student, reasoning that the safety concerns were a valid basis for the rule, and thus the rule did not impermissibly infringe on his right to freely exercise his religion. The court did, however, state that the schools should consider adopting a rule that permitted *secure* forms of head coverings for such athletes, since this would constitute a means of accomplishing their safety objective that would be less restrictive to individuals than the total ban on headgear.

In a similar case, but one in which there were no safety considerations, the decision went in favor of the students. In *Moody v. Cronin* (C.D. Ill. 1980), two students refused to attend required physical education classes because they would have had to wear shorts and shirts in a coeducational setting, which would have violated their religion's views on propriety and modesty. Despite the school's arguments that physical education classes were a required part of the curriculum and that Title IX had been interpreted to require such classes to be offered in a coeducational setting, the court found for the plaintiffs. It ruled that the school could not force the students to violate their religious beliefs by requiring their participation in such a setting.

Recent Developments

Recently, Attention Deficit Hyperactivity Disorder has been identified as a disability which can cause disruptive behavior. In *Hoot by Hoot v. Milan Area Schools* (E.D. Mich. 1994), a student was denied the opportunity to participate in interscholastic football because his disruptive behavior had resulted in a one-semester expulsion from school. This expulsion prevented him from meeting the Michigan High School Athletic Association's rule requiring that a certain amount of coursework be completed in the semester prior to competition. The athlete alleged that his misconduct stemmed from his ADHD condition, and therefore denying him the opportunity to play football violated his rights under several laws, including the Equal Protection Clause (for subjecting him to different treatment on the basis of his disability), the Rehabilitation Act, and the Americans with Disabilities Act. Following a hearing on the defendant high school's motion for summary judgment, the court concluded that material issues of fact existed for all claims, and therefore declined to decide the case in favor of the defendant without a full trial on the merits.

References

A. Cases
Bunger v. Iowa High School Athletic Association, 197 N.W.2d 555 (Iowa 1972).
Dunham v. Pulsifer, 312 F. Supp. 411 (D. Vermont 1970).
Hoot by Hoot v. Milan Area Schools, 853 F. Supp. 243 (E.D. Mich. 1994).
Menora v. Illinois High School Association, 683 F.2d 1030 (7th Cir. 1982).
Moody v. Cronin, 484 F. Supp. 270 (C.D. Ill. 1980).
Palmer v. Merluzzi, 689 F. Supp. 400 (D.N.J. 1988).
Tinker v. Des Moines Independent School District, 393 U.S. 503 (1969).

C. Publications
Fischer, Louis, Schimmel, David, & Kelly, Cynthia. (1995). *Teachers and the Law*, 4th ed., White Plains, N.Y.: Longman Publishers, pp. 418-20.
Weistart, John C. & Lowell, Cym H. (1979). *The Law of Sports*, Charlottesville, Va.: The Michie Company, pp. 45-46.

B. Constitution
U.S. Constitution, Amend. I.
U.S. Constitution, Amend. XIV.

4.24

Gender Equity
Opportunities to Participate

Linda Jean Carpenter
Brooklyn College

Sport is the laboratory experience through which students gain skills such as decision making, risk evaluation, teamwork, leadership, self appraisal and personal esteem. These skills are the same skills which allow graduates to successfully use their other academic skills in their adult lives and employment circumstances.

Sport's place on campus in the form of intramurals, athletics, and physical education is defensible, not because of any possible revenue generation, or because of fan support, but because of the valuable skills it provides which are not easily obtained elsewhere in the educational setting.

The skills obtainable through sport have value to both female and male participants. The legal imperatives for equity found in the 14th Amendment of the United States Constitution and Title IX of the Education Amendments of 1972 (and a variety of similarly worded state legislation) are the two most frequently used tools to judicially increase gender equity in sport.

■ ■ ■ ■

Representative Case

ROBERTS v. COLORADO STATE UNIVERSITY

998 Federal Reporter, 2d Series
United States Court of Appeals,
Tenth Circuit.
July 7, 1993.

Plaintiffs, CSU students and former members of the fast pitch softball team, brought suit in their individual capacities against SBA and CSU in June 1992 after CSU announced that it was discontinuing the varsity fast pitch softball program. In February of this year the district court found that SBA and CSU had violated Title IX, and issued a permanent injunction reinstating the softball program. Approximately three weeks later, the district court held a status conference and, in the face of apparent foot-dragging by defendant, amplified its earlier orders to require defendant to hire a coach promptly, recruit new members

for the team, and organize a fall season. This court denied a motion for a stay but expedited the appeal.

• • •

A

This controversy concerns one subpart of the regulations implementing Title IX. 34 C.F.R. § 106.41(c) provides:

A recipient which operated or sponsors interscholastic, intercollegiate, club or intramural athletics shall provide equal athletic opportunity for members of both sexes. In determining whether equal opportunities are available the Director [of the Office for Civil Rights] will consider, among other factors:

(1) Whether the selection of sports and levels of competition effectively accommodate the interests and abilities of members of both sexes[.]

Although § 106.41(c) goes on to list nine other factors that enter into a determination of equal opportunity in athletics, an institution may violate Title IX simply by failing to accommodate effectively the interests and abilities of student athletes of both sexes.

• • •

In 1979, the Department of Health, Education, and Welfare issued a policy interpretation explaining the ways in which institutions may effectively accommodate the interests and abilities of their student athletes.

The Policy Interpretation delineates three general areas in which the OCR will assess compliance with the effective accommodation section of the regulation, as follows:

a. The determination of athletic interests and abilities of students;
b. The selection of sports offered; and
c. The levels of competition available including the opportunity for team competition.

The OCR assesses effective accommodation with respect to opportunities for intercollegiate competition by determining:

(1) Whether intercollegiate level participation opportunities for male and female students are provided in numbers substantially proportionate to their respective enrollments; or

(2) Where the members of one sex have been and are underrepresented among intercollegiate athletes, whether the institution can show a history and continuing practice of program expansion which is demonstrably responsive to the developing interest and abilities of the members of that sex; or

(3) Where the members of one sex are underrepresented among intercollegiate athletes, and the institution cannot show a continuing practice of program expansion such as that cited above, whether it can be demonstrated that the interests and abilities of the members of that sex have been fully and effectively accommodated by the present program.

In effect, "substantial proportionality" between athletic participation and undergraduate enrollment provides a safe harbor for recipients under Title IX. In the absence of such gender balance, the institution must show that it has expanded and is continuing to expand opportunities for athletic participation by the underrepresented gender, or else it must fully and effectively accommodate the interests and abilities among members of the underrepresented gender.

In addition to assessing whether individuals of both sexes have the opportunity to compete in intercollegiate athletics, the OCR also examines whether the quality of competition provided to male and female athletes equally reflects their abilities. This will depend on whether, program wide, the competitive schedules of men's and women's teams "afford proportionally similar numbers of male and female athletes equivalently advanced competitive opportunities," id., or "[w]hether the institution can demonstrate a history and continuing practice of upgrading the competitive opportunities available to the historically disadvantaged sex as warranted by developing abilities among the athletes of that sex." However, "[i]nstitutions are not required to upgrade teams to intercollegiate status or otherwise develop intercollegiate sports absent a reasonable expectation that intercollegiate competition in that sport will be available within the institution's normal competitive regions."

B

The district court found that plaintiffs met their burden of showing that defendant could not take shelter in the safe harbor of substantial proportionality. The district court reviewed a substantial quantity of statistical data, and made the undisputed finding that following the termination of the varsity softball program, the disparity between enrollment and athletic participation for women at CSU is 10.5 percent. Defendant maintains that, as a matter of law, a 10.5 percent disparity is substantially proportionate.

The OCR has instructed its Title IX compliance investigators that "[t]here is no set ratio that constitutes 'substantially proportionate' or that, when not met, results in a disparity or a violation." Investigator's Manual at 24. However, in the example immediately preceding this statement, the Manual suggests that substantial proportionality entails a fairly close relationship between athletic participation and undergraduate enrollment. Furthermore, in a Title IX compliance review completed in 1983, the OCR found that CSU's athletic participation opportunities for men and women were not substantially proportionate to their respective enrollments. During the three years that were the subject of that review, the differences between women enrolled and women athletes were 7.5 percent, 12.5 percent, and 12.7 percent. The district court relied on these sources, as well as expert testimony that a 10.5 percent disparity is statistically significant, in concluding that CSU could not meet this first benchmark. *See also Cohen v. Brown Univ.,* 809 F.Supp. 978, 991 (D.R.I.1992) (11.6 percent disparity not substantially proportionate) *aff'd,* 991 F.2d 888 (1st Cir.1993). Without demarcating further the line between substantial proportionality and disproportionality, we agree with the district court that a 10.5 percent disparity between female athletic participation and female undergraduate enrollment is not substantially proportionate. The fact that many or even most other educational institutions have a greater imbalance than CSU does not require a different holding.

C

The district court also found that defendant could not prove a history and continuing practice of expansion in women's athletics at CSU. Defendant argues that the district court should have given greater weight to its dramatic expansion of women's athletic opportunities during the 1970s. In essence, defendant suggests reading the words "continuing practice" out of this prong of the test. In support of this position, defendant offers anecdotal evidence of enforcement at other institutions, and the OCR's 1983 finding of compliance for CSU, which was contingent upon CSU's fulfilling the provisions of a plan that CSU never met.

Although CSU created a women's sports program out of nothing in the 1970's, adding eleven sports for women during that decade, the district court found that women's participation opportunities declined steadily during the 1980s. Furthermore, although budget cuts in the last twelve years have affected both men and women athletes at CSU, the district court found that women's participation opportunities declined by 34 percent, whereas men's opportunities declined by only 20 percent. The facts as found by the district court (and largely undisputed by defendant) can logically support no other conclusion than that, since adding women's golf in 1977, CSU has not maintained a practice of program expansion in women's athletics, and indeed has since dropped three women's sports.

We recognize that in times of economic hardship, few schools will be able to satisfy Title IX's effective accommodation requirement by continuing to expand their women's athletics programs. Nonetheless, the ordinary meaning of the word "expansion" may not be twisted to find compliance under their prong when schools have increased the relative percentages of women participating in athletics by making cuts in both men's and women's sports programs. Financially strapped institutions may still comply with Title IX by cutting athletic programs such that men's and women's athletic participation rates become substantially proportionate to their representation in the undergraduate population.

• • •

The heart of the controversy is the meaning of the phrase "full and effective accommodation of interests and abilities." Defendant maintains that even if there is interest and ability on the part of women athletes at CSU, the university is obliged to accommodate them only to the extent it accommodates men. Thus, the argument goes, plaintiffs cannot be heard to complain because both women's softball and men's baseball were eliminated in the last round of cuts and there are more disappointed male than female athletes at CSU. The First Circuit rejected this position in *Cohen,* and so do we. "[T]his benchmark sets a high standard: it demands not merely some accommodation, but full and effective accommodation. If there is sufficient interest and ability among members of the statistically underrepresented gender, not slaked by existing programs, an institution necessarily fails this prong of the test." Id. at 898.

Based on the district court's subsidiary findings of fact, we conclude that plaintiffs met the burden of showing that CSU has not accommodated their interest and abilities fully and effectively. Questions of fact under this third prong will be less vexing when plaintiffs seek the reinstatement of an established team rather than the creation of a new one. Here, plaintiffs were members of a successful varsity softball team that played a competitive schedule as recently as the spring of 1992. Although apparently four plaintiffs have transferred and one has been dismissed, seven or eight plaintiffs remain at CSU for at least part of the 1993-94 school year and would be eligible to play on a reinstated team. We agree with the district court that CSU fails the third prong of effective accommodation test.

■ ■ ■ ■

Fundamental Concepts

Constitutional Issues

The Equal Protection Clause of the 14th Amendment is the generic protector of equal rights. It guarantees that no *state actor* such as a federal, state or local governmental agency or, for example, public school and recreation programs, can gratuitously classify people and treat them differently based on those classifications without having a defensible reason.

Level of Scrutiny

Strict/High (Strict Scrutiny). The defensible reason required to constitutionally treat people differently varies depending on the classification scheme employed. If, for example, a public school (*state actor*) classified its students by race and then treated its African American students differently, the reason used to defend the constitutionality of such an action would have to withstand the Court's highest level of scrutiny. The school would need to show that its racially based discrimination was: ***necessary to accomplish a compelling state interest.*** It is difficult to imagine a reason for racial discrimination which would meet such a test.

Mild/Low (Rational Basis). As an alternative example, consider the scenario where a public school's (*state actor*) physical education program classified its students by skill level and, as a result, only allowed its beginning level students in a beginning level course while allowing the more highly skilled students to have access to a variety of advanced electives. The Court would use a lower level of scrutiny to determine if discrimination based on skill level was constitutional. The school would only have to show that its discrimination was: ***rationally related to a legitimate state interest.*** Protecting beginners from the injuries likely to occur if they participated with highly skilled athletes or performed advanced movements for which they were either untrained or unconditioned would appear to be rationally related to the legitimate state interest of protecting the health and safety of the community's school children.

An Evolving Middle Ground (Intermediate Standard). Most classification schemes are reviewed by the courts using either the strict/high or mild/low levels of scrutiny. Typically only those classifications based on race, alienage or nationality face strict/high scrutiny. Almost all other classification schemes face only the mild/low level.

Because the level of scrutiny to be applied is not statutorily determined, it is only prior case law which gives us a degree of confidence in predicting the level of scrutiny the courts will apply in future cases. In the last few decades, we have seen the judicial review of classification schemes based on age, gender and disability elevated from the low level of scrutiny to a reasonably amorphous mid-level of scrutiny.

In its June, 1996 decision involving coeducation at Virginia Military Institute, the Supreme Court elevated the scrutiny applied to *gender* discrimination even higher within this middle ground to a level requiring an exceedingly persuasive justification. Thus if a state actor discriminates on the basis of gender, it will need to show that doing so was considerably more than rationally related to a legitimate state interest, but it will not need to show that it was necessary to accomplish a compelling state interest.

Why is discrimination based on age, disability, and particularly gender becoming more difficult to justify constitutionally? The change probably reflects the changing attitudes of society to this type of discrimination wherein society, as reflected in various civil rights legislation such as Title VI, VII and IX has acknowledged its awareness that such classification schemes are often insidiously and significantly unfair and are extremely unlikely to have a justifiable basis.

Cases involving gender discrimination in sport have used the 14th Amendment but the more prevalently used tool is Title IX. For this reason, and because of the presence of a fuller discussion of constitutional issues elsewhere in this text, the remaining portion of this chapter will focus on Title IX.

Title IX

A Brief History.   Title IX was enacted by Congress on June 23, 1972 to prohibit gender discrimination in the nation's education programs. There are three basic elements which must all exist in order for Title IX's jurisdiction to be triggered. The elements are:

- *Gender discrimination.* Title IX does not protect against discrimination based on race or age or discrimination; it protects solely against gender discrimination.

- *Federal funding.* The receipt of Federal funding is required so that the enforcement of Title IX has administrative teeth. If an institution is found to be violating Title IX, its Federal funding may be terminated.

- *Education program.* The definition of this element brought early controversy to the implementation of Title IX. The U.S. Supreme Court's 1984 *Grove City* decision resulted in the word 'program' being defined as a 'subunit' of an institution. As a result of *Grove City*, any subunit which did not receive Federal funding would not be obligated to refrain from gender discrimination. Thus college level athletics and physical education programs, which typically receive no Federal funding, were no longer obligated by Title IX to refrain from gender discrimination. However in 1988 Congress passed the Civil Rights Restoration Act of 1987 over presidential veto saying, in effect, that the Court had misunderstood Congress' intent to have Title IX apply on an institution wide basis. So, as of 1988 Title IX once again applies to college level athletics and physical education programs, as well as to all education programs in institutions which receive Federal funding.

Title IX Enforcement.   There are three main pathways to enforce Title IX. The complainant or plaintiff may select any of the three and need not exhaust in house remedies first.

Each institution under the jurisdiction of Title IX must have a designated Title IX officer. The Title IX officer's job is to educate the faculty, staff and students about the rights and responsibilities imposed by Title IX and to deal with any Title IX complaints filed in-house.

The second method of enforcement is through the Office for Civil Rights of the U.S. Department of Education. Once an administrative complaint is filed with the OCR (legal standing is NOT required in order to file), the OCR investigates, and, if violations are found negotiates a 'letter of resolution' with the institution in which the institution agrees to a time frame and list of changes to be made.

The third method involves the filing of a federal lawsuit by someone with legal standing. This method has found increased favor among plaintiffs since the Supreme Court's 1992 Franklin decision which made it clear that compensatory and even punitive damages are available to victims of intentional gender discrimination under Title IX.

Title IX Requirements.   When Title IX was enacted in 1972, there was only the one sentence law saying:

> No person in the United States shall, on the basis of sex, be excluded from participation in, be denied the benefits of, or be subjected to discrimination under any education program or activity receiving Federal financial assistance.

In addition to the one sentence law, formal Regulations were promulgated and ultimately gained the force of law.

Even though most Title IX cases and controversies have related to its application to sport, Title IX applies to all of education. However, because of continuing controversy about the details of Title IX's implementation in the area of sport, Policy Interpretations were adopted in 1979. Although it does not have the force of law, the 1990 OCR Investigator's Manual is another source of guidance concerning the application of Title IX to athletics situations.

Athletics Application. There are many specific requirements of Title IX relating to coaching, facilities, equipment, travel and so on. However, if a female is not provided an opportunity to participate, it matters very little if she would have had equal access to coaching, facilities, equipment, travel and so on. Therefore let's focus on participation opportunities.

Title IX's Regulations require that "the selection of sports and levels of competition effectively accommodate the interests and abilities of members of both sexes." According to the Policy Interpretations, an institution has effectively accommodated the interests of its students if it satisfies any one of the following three benchmarks:

1. Participation opportunities for male and female students are provided in numbers substantially proportionate to their respective enrollments; or
2. The institution can show a history and continuing practice of program expansion demonstrably responsive to the developing interest and abilities of the members of the under represented sex; or
3. The institution can show that it is fully and effectively meeting the interests and abilities of the under represented sex.

Institutions which effectively responded to Title IX's 1978 mandatory compliance and which have maintained their commitment to the legal requirements of gender equity over the years have had no difficulty in meeting either benchmark 2 or 3 and thus don't even need to address the issue of proportionality found in benchmark 1.

However, institutions which have ignored the requirements of Title IX or which have failed to implement plans to provide equitable athletic participation opportunities for their female students, 23 years after the passage of Title IX, are now facing a quandary. They have not satisfied benchmark 2. If a group of female athletes demonstrate interest and ability sufficient to support the creation of a team in a particular sport in which it would be reasonable to find suitable competition in the school's traditional competitive region, the institution cannot claim that it has satisfied benchmark 3. That leaves benchmark 1: proportionality. For many reasons, including past discrimination and societal influences, very few schools meet benchmark 1. Typically, the courts have found such institutions to be violating Title IX's requirement to effectively accommodate the interests and abilities of students athletes of both sexes. Such institutions are therefore at risk of losing their Federal funding in addition to being liable for possible compensatory and punitive damages.

Recent Developments

Does Title IX Protect Members of Discontinued Men's Teams? No. Title IX protects the participation rights of the historically under represented sex. In the athletics programs of most schools' the historically under represented sex would be female. In a 1994 Illinois case (*Kelley v. University of Illinois*) the men's swimming team was cut but the women's team was not. The U.S. Court of Appeals, Seventh Circuit held that even after the cut, men's participation in athletics was more than substantially proportionate to their enrollment and indeed, if the women's team had been cut the university would have increased the lack of proportionality sufficiently to be vulnerable to a Title IX claim by the women.

Is the Lack of Money a Defense to Title IX?   No. Budgetary constraints which either force teams to be cut or prohibit their addition are not a defense to the requirements of Title IX. Cases demonstrating this principle include: *Cook v. Colgate University* (1992) and *Favia v. Indiana University of Pennsylvania* (1993).

Should Either Satisfaction or Failure of Benchmark 1 (Proportionality) Create an Irrebuttable Presumption of Either Compliance with or Violation of Title IX's Accommodation/Opportunity Requirement?   According to the discussion found in a 1996 Louisiana case *(Pederson v. Louisiana State University)* benchmark 1 should not be used as the solitary indicia of compliance or failure concerning participation opportunities. In the absence of information concerning the interests and abilities of female athletes, reliance solely on benchmark 1 is inappropriate, according to the U.S. District Court for the Middle District of Louisiana.

Discussion concerning benchmark 1's role in determining if sufficient participation opportunities exist has been heated in the past few years. Some voices have accused the OCR of focusing solely on benchmark 1 as the determinative indicia. OCR has, in turn, restated the commitment to the Policy Interpretation's three part test. In effect, the *LSU* decision supports OCR's restatement that where benchmark 1 is not satisfied, proceeding to determine if either benchmark 2 or 3 is met is appropriate. The First Circuit's decision in *Cohen v. Brown University* (currently on appeal) supports this view. The district court in *LSU* goes one step further, however, by saying that where an institution meets benchmark 1 (not the case at LSU), additional information should be sought concerning the interests and abilities of the female athletes (benchmark 3) before finding an institution in compliance.

References

A. Cases
Cohen v. Brown University, 991 F. 2d 888 (1st Cir. 1993), 8879 F. Supp. 185 (D.R.I. 1995), currently under appeal.
Grove City v. Bell, 465 U.S. 555 (1984)
Favia v. Indiana University of Pennsylvania, 7 F. 3d 332 (3rd Cir. 1993).
Franklin v. Gwinnett County Public Schools, 112 S. Ct. 1028 (1992).
Kelley v. University of Illinois, 35 F.3d 265 (7th Cir. 1994).
Pederson v. Louisiana State University, Civil No. CV 94-247-A-MI (M.D. La. 1995).
Roberts v. Colorado State University, 814 F. Supp. 1507 (D. Colo.) aff'd in relevant part sub nom. Roberts v. Colorado *State Bd. of Agric.*, 998 F. 2d 824 (10th Cir.), cert. denied, 114 S. Ct. 580 (1993).

B. Legislation and Regulation
Education Amendments of 1972, §§ 901-909 as amended, 20 U.S.C.A. §§ 11681-1688.
40 Fed. Reg. 24, 128 (1975) currently appearing at 34 C.F.R. §§ 106 (1992)
U.S. Department of Education Athletic Guidelines; Title IX of the Education Amendments of 1972; A Policy Interpretation; Title IX and Intercollegiate Athletics, 44 Fed. Reg. 71,413, 71,423 (1979).

Gender Equity
Coaching and Administration

Maureen P. Fitzgerald
University of Texas at Austin

When people in scholastic and intercollegiate athletics hear the term "gender equity," most think of what it means relative to participation opportunities for student-athletes. Certainly, the accommodation of students' interests and abilities in participating in athletics is a key gender equity issue, however, the term also encompasses other important legal concerns such as the equitable selection and/or treatment of the coaches and athletics administrators.

Decisions regarding the selection, hiring, and compensation of coaches or administrators should not be based on gender. Yet, at a time when the participation opportunities for female athletes have been increasing there has been a dramatic decline in the number of females coaching and administering female teams (Acosta & Carpenter, 1992).

The recent success of plaintiffs and the increased attention focused on gender equity issues and concerns suggest that efforts are being made to ensure equitable apportionment of participation opportunities for females in collegiate athletics (Wilde, 1994). However, until recently two groups were consistently and conspicuously left out of any discussion regarding equity in athletics: female coaches and administrators.

A heightened sense of urgency and pressure to provide equitable opportunities was placed upon academic institutions when the Supreme Court, in *Franklin v. Gwinnett* (1992), ruled that compensatory damages were available for plaintiffs under a Title IX a cause of action. Since *Franklin*, there have been several plaintiffs who have filed employment discrimination claims using Title IX, the Equal Pay Act, and Title VII. Even though no such case has made it to the Supreme Court, the lower court decisions are instructive of pay equity issues in coaching and administration, and can assist in shaping the selection, hiring, and compensation decisions of managers in sport.

Three recent cases, *Tyler v. Howard University* (1993), *Pitts v. Oklahoma* (1994), and *Stanley v. University of Southern California* (1994) examined issues associated with pay equity in college coaching. Of the three, *Stanley*, a Ninth Circuit review of a federal district court denial of injunctive relief, provides valuable insight into relevant legislation, causes of action, and defenses associated with gender equity in athletic employment.

■ ■ ■ ■

Representative Case

STANLEY v. UNIVERSITY OF SOUTHERN CALIFORNIA
United States Court of Appeals for the Ninth Circuit
13 F.3d 1313 (1994)

OPINION:

Marianne Stanley, former head coach of the women's basketball team at the University of Southern California (USC), appeals from an order denying her motion for a preliminary injunction against USC and Michael Garrett, the athletic director for USC (collectively USC).

Coach Stanley contends that the district court abused its discretion in denying a preliminary injunction on the ground that she failed to present sufficient evidence of sex discrimination or retaliation to carry her burden of establishing a clear likelihood of success on the merits. Coach Stanley also claims that the court misapprehended the nature of the preliminary injunction relief she sought. In addition, she argues that the district court clearly erred in finding that USC would suffer significant hardship if the preliminary injunction issued. Coach Stanley further asserts that she was denied a full and fair opportunity to present testimonial evidence at the preliminary injunction hearing and to demonstrate that USC's purported justification for paying a higher salary to George Raveling, head coach of the men's basketball team at USC, was a pretext for sex discrimination and retaliation. We affirm because we conclude that the district court did not abuse its discretion in denying the motion for a preliminary injunction. We also hold that the district court did not deny Coach Stanley a full and fair opportunity to present evidence of sex discrimination, retaliation, and pretext.

I. Pertinent Facts

Coach Stanley signed a four-year contract with USC on July 30, 1989, to serve as the head coach of the women's basketball team. The expiration date of Coach Stanley's employment contract was June 30, 1993. Coach Stanley's employment contract provided for an annual base salary of $60,000 with a $6,000 housing allowance.

Sometime in April of 1993, Coach Stanley and Michael Garrett began negotiations on a new contract. The evidence is in dispute as to the statements made by the parties. Coach Stanley alleges in her declarations that she told Garrett that she "was entitled to be paid equally with the Head Men's Basketball Coach, George Raveling[,] and that [she] was seeking a contract equal to the one that USC

had paid the Head Men's Basketball Coach" based on her outstanding record and the success of the women's basketball program at USC. She also requested a higher salary for the assistant coaches of the women's basketball team. According to Coach Stanley, Garrett verbally agreed that she should be paid what Coach Raveling was earning, but he asserted that USC did not have the money at that time. He indicated that "he would get back [to her] with an offer of a multi-year contract . . . that would be satisfactory." Garrett alleges in his affidavit, filed in opposition to the issuance of the preliminary injunction, that Coach Stanley told him that "she wanted a contract that was identical to that between USC and Coach Raveling."

On April 27, 1993, Garrett sent a memorandum which set forth an offer of a three-year contract with the following terms:

1993-94 Raising your salary to $80,000 with a $6,000 housing allowance.

1994-95 Salary of $90,000 with a $6,000 housing allowance.

1995-96 Salary of $100,000 with a $6,000 housing allowance.

Presently, Barbara Thaxton's base salary is $37,000 which I intend to increase to $50,000. It is not my policy to pay associate or assistant coaches housing allowances. Therefore that consideration is not addressed in this offer.

The memorandum concluded with the following words: "I believe this offer is fair, and I need you to respond within the next couple of days so we can conclude this matter. Thank you." According to Garrett, Coach Stanley said the offer was "an insult."

Coach Stanley alleged that, after receiving this offer, she informed Garrett that she "wanted a multi-year contract but his salary figures were too low." Coach Stanley also alleged that she told Garrett she "was to make the same salary as was paid to the Head Men's Basketball Coach at USC." Garrett asserted that Coach Stanley demanded a "three-year contract which would pay her a total compensation at the annual rate of $96,000 for the first 18 months and then increase her total compensation to the same level as Raveling for the last 18 months." He rejected her counter offer.

Coach Stanley alleged that Garrett stated to her that he thought his proposal was fair and he would "not spend a lot of time negotiating a contract." According to Coach Stanley, Garrett's attitude toward her changed and he became "hostile." Garrett told her that she would not be paid the same as Coach Raveling and that she should be satisfied with being the second highest paid women's basketball coach in the PAC-10 Conference.

After this discussion, Coach Stanley retained attorney Timothy Stoner to negotiate the terms of the new contract. Coach Stanley alleged that Garrett rejected her offer "to negotiate a contract that would allow me to gradually work my way to the contract salary and benefits level that USC had provided to George Raveling." He withdrew the multi-year contract offer he previously made to her. Coach Stanley also alleged that Garrett told her attorney that he would offer a one-year contract at a $90,000 salary, plus a $6,000 housing allowance.

• • •

Garrett alleged that Coach Stanley did not accept the offer. The following day, Coach Stanley sent a memorandum requesting additional time to consider the offer because she was too distressed to make a decision. Garrett sent a memorandum to Coach Stanley on July 15, 1993, in which he stated, inter alia:

My job as athletic director is to look out for the best interests of our women's basketball program as a whole, and that is what I have been trying to do all along. The best interests of the program are not served by indefinitely extending the discussions between you and the University, which have already dragged on for weeks. That is why I told you on Tuesday that I needed a final answer that day.

Since I did not hear from you, as it now stands the University has no offers on the table. If you want to make any proposals, I am willing to listen. Meanwhile, for the protection of the program, I must, and am, actively looking at other candidates. I am sorry that you feel distressed by this situation. As I have said, I have to do what is best for our women's basketball program.

Finally, I was not aware that you were in Phoenix on official University business. Your contract with the University expired at the end of June, and I must ask you not to perform any services for the Univer-

sity unless and until we enter into a new contract. I will arrange for you to be compensated on a daily basis for the time you have expended thus far in July on University business.

• • •

Coach Stanley did not reply to Garrett's July 15, 1993 memorandum. Instead, on August 3, 1993, her present attorney, Robert L. Bell, sent a letter via facsimile to USC's Acting General Counsel in which he indicated that he had been retained to represent Coach Stanley. Bell stated he desired "to discuss an amicable resolution of the legal dispute between [his] client and the University of Southern California." Bell stated that if he did not receive a reply by August 4, 1993, he would "seek recourse in court." On August 4, 1993, USC's Acting General Counsel sent a letter to Bell via facsimile in which he stated that "we are not adverse to considering carefully a proposal from you for an 'informal resolution.'"

II. Procedural Background

On August 5, 1993, Coach Stanley filed this action in the Superior Court for the County of Los Angeles. She also applied ex parte for a temporary restraining order (TRO) to require USC to install her as head coach of the women's basketball team.

The complaint sets forth various federal and state sex discrimination claims, including violations of the Equal Pay Act (EPA), 29 U.S.C. 206(d)(1) (1988), Title IX, 20 U.S.C. § 1681(a) (1988), the California Fair Employment and Housing Act (FEHA), Cal. Gov't Code @ 12921 (West Supp. 1993), and the California Constitution, Cal. Const. art. 1, @ 8 (West 1983). The complaint also alleges common law causes of action including wrongful discharge in violation of California's public policy, breach of an implied-in-fact employment contract, intentional infliction of emotional distress, and conspiracy. As relief for this alleged conduct, Coach Stanley seeks a declaratory judgment that USC's conduct constituted sex discrimination, a permanent injunction restraining the defendants from discrimination and retaliation, an order "requiring immediate installation of plaintiff to the position of Head Coach of Women's Basketball at the USC," three million dollars in compensatory damages, and five million dollars in punitive damages.

On August 6, 1993, the Los Angeles Superior Court issued an oral order granting Coach Stanley's ex parte application for a TRO, pending a hearing on her motion for a preliminary injunction. . . . On the same day that the TRO was issued, USC removed the action to the District Court for the Central District of California. On August 11, 1993, the district court ordered that the hearing on Coach

Stanley's motion for a preliminary injunction be held on August 26, 1993, and that the TRO issued by the state court be extended and remain in effect until that date.

• • •

Pursuant to Coach Stanley's request, the district court reviewed Coach Raveling's employment contract in camera. Later that day, the district court denied the motion for a preliminary injunction.

III. Discussion

The gravamen of Coach Stanley's multiple claims against USC is her contention that she is entitled to pay equal to that provided to Coach Raveling for his services as head coach of the men's basketball team because the position of head coach of the women's team "requires equal skill, effort, and responsibility, and [is performed] under similar working conditions." She asserts that USC discriminated against her because of her sex by rejecting her request. She also maintains that USC retaliated against her because of her request for equal pay for herself and her assistant coaches. According to Coach Stanley, USC retaliated by withdrawing the offer of a three-year contract and instead presenting her with a new offer of a one-year contract at less pay than that received by Coach Raveling.

We begin our analysis mindful of the fact that we are reviewing the denial of a preliminary injunction. There has been no trial in this matter. Because the hearing on the preliminary injunction occurred 21 days after the action was filed in state court, discovery had not been completed. Our prediction of the probability of success on the merits is based on the limited offer of proof that was possible under the circumstances. We obviously cannot now evaluate the persuasive impact of the evidence that the parties may bring forth at trial.

A. Standard of Review.

We review the denial of a motion for preliminary injunction for abuse of discretion. . . . An order is reversible for legal error if the court did not apply the correct preliminary injunction standard, or if the court misapprehended the law with respect to the underlying issues in litigation. An abuse of discretion may also occur if the district court rests its conclusions on clearly erroneous findings of fact.

• • •

Coach Stanley argues that she did not seek a mandatory preliminary injunction. She asserts that she was "not seeking to be instated by USC, she was seeking to continue her employment with USC." Appellant's Opening Brief at 28. Coach Stanley maintains that she requested a prohibitory preliminary injunction and that the district court erred in applying the test for a mandatory preliminary injunction.

A prohibitory injunction preserves the status quo. Johnson v. Kay, 860 F.2d 529, 541 (2n Cir. 1988). A mandatory injunction "'goes well beyond simply maintaining the status quo *pendente lite* [and] is particularly disfavored.'" Anderson v. United States, 621 F.2d 1112, 1114 (9th Cir. 1979) quoting Martinez v. Mathews, 544 F.2d 1233, 1243 (5th Cir. 1976). When a mandatory preliminary injunction is requested, the district court should deny such relief "'unless the facts and law clearly favor the moving party.'" Id. Our first task is to determine whether Coach Stanley requested a prohibitory injunction or a mandatory injunction.

Coach Stanley's four-year contract terminated on June 30, 1993. She was informed by Garrett on July 15, 1993, that her employment contract had expired and that she should not perform any services for the university until both parties entered into a new contract. On August 6, 1993, the date this action was filed in state court, Coach Stanley was no longer a USC employee.

Accordingly an injunction compelling USC to install Coach Stanley as the head coach of the women's basketball team and to pay her $28,000 a year more than she received when her employment contract expired would not have maintained the status quo. Instead, it would have forced USC to hire a person at a substantially higher rate of pay than she had received prior to the expiration of her employment contract on June 30, 1993. The district court did not err in concluding that Coach Stanley was seeking a mandatory injunction, and that her request was subject to a higher degree of scrutiny because such relief is particularly disfavored under the law of this circuit. Anderson, 612 F.2d at 1114.

B. There Has Been No Clear Showing of a Probability of Success on the Merits of Coach Stanley's Claim for Injunctive Relief.

In light of our determination that Coach Stanley requested a mandatory preliminary injunction, we must consider whether the law and the facts clearly favor granting such relief. To obtain a preliminary injunction, Coach Stanley was required to demonstrate that her remedy at law was inadequate. Beacon Theatres, Inc. v. Westover, 359 U.S. 500, 506-07 & n.8, 3 L. Ed. 2d 988, 79 S. Ct. 948 (1959) ("The basis of injunctive relief in the federal courts has always been irreparable harm and inadequacy of legal remedies.") (footnote omitted).

• • •

To the extent that Coach Stanley is seeking money damages and back pay for the loss of her job, her remedy at law is adequate. Cf. Anderson v. United States, 612 F.2d at 1115 (mandatory injunction is inappropriate where retroactive promotion and back pay are available if the employee succeeds on the merits). The district court, however, construed the motion for a preliminary injunction as including a request that future discrimination or retaliation based on the fact that she is a woman be enjoined. We do so as well for purposes of resolving the present appeal.

1. Merits of Coach Stanley's Claim of Denial of Equal Pay for Equal Work.

The district court concluded that Coach Stanley had failed to demonstrate that there is a likelihood that she would prevail on the merits of her claim of a denial of equal pay for equal work because she failed to present facts clearly showing that USC was guilty of sex discrimination in its negotiations for a new employment contract. The thrust of Coach Stanley's argument in this appeal is that she is entitled, as a matter of law, "to make the same salary as was paid to the Head Men's Basketball Coach at USC." Appellant's Opening Brief at 9. None of the authorities she has cited supports this theory.

In her reply brief, Coach Stanley asserts that she has "never said or argued in any of her submissions that the compensation of the men's and women's basketball coaches at USC or elsewhere must be identical." Appellant's Reply Brief at 2. Coach Stanley accuses USC of mischaracterizing her position. This argument ignores her insistence to Garrett that she was entitled to the "same salary" received by Coach Raveling. The denotation of the word "same" is "identical." Webster's Third New International Dictionary 2007.

In her reply brief, Coach Stanley asserts that she merely seeks equal pay for equal work. In Hein v. Oregon College of Education, 718 F.2d 910 (9th Cir. 1983), we stated that to recover under the Equal Pay Act of 1963, 29 U.S.C. @ 206(d)(1) (1988), "a plaintiff must prove that an employer is paying different wages to employees of the opposite sex for equal work." Hein, 718 F.2d at 913. We concluded that the jobs need not be identical, but they must be "substantially equal." Id. (internal quotation and citation omitted).

The EPA prohibits discrimination in wages "between employees on the basis of sex . . . for equal work, on jobs the performance of which requires equal skill, effort, and responsibility, and which are performed under similar working conditions." 29 U.S.C. @ 206(d)(1) (1988). Each of these components must be substantially equal to state a claim. Forsberg v. Pacific Northwest Bell Tel., 840 F.2d 1409, 1414 (9th Cir. 1988).

Coach Stanley has not offered proof to contradict the evidence proffered by USC that demonstrates the differences in the responsibilities of the persons who serve as head coaches of the women's and men's basketball teams. Coach Raveling's responsibilities as head coach of the men's basketball team require substantial public relations

and promotional activities to generate revenue for USC. These efforts resulted in revenue that is 90 times greater than the revenue generated by the women's basketball team. Coach Raveling was required to conduct twelve outside speaking engagements per year, to be accessible to the media for interviews, and to participate in certain activities designed to produce donations and endorsements for the USC Athletic Department in general. Coach Stanley's position as head coach did not require her to engage in the same intense level of promotional and revenue-raising activities. This quantitative dissimilarity in responsibilities justifies a different level of pay for the head coach of the women's basketball team. See Horner v. Mary Inst., 613 F.2d 706, 713-14 (8th Cir. 1980) (evidence that male physical education teacher had a different job from a female physical education teacher because he was responsible for curriculum precluded finding that jobs were substantially similar; court may consider whether job requires more experience, training, and ability to determine whether jobs require substantially equal skill under EPA).

The evidence presented by USC also showed that Coach Raveling had substantially different qualifications and experience related to his public relations and revenue-generation skills than Coach Stanley. Coach Raveling received educational training in marketing, and worked in that field for nine years. Coach Raveling has been employed by USC three years longer than Coach Stanley. He has been a college basketball coach for 31 years, while Coach Stanley has had 17 years experience as a basketball coach. Coach Raveling had served as a member of the NCAA Subcommittee on Recruiting. Coach Raveling also is the respected author of two bestselling novels. He has performed as an actor in a feature movie, and has appeared on national television to discuss recruiting of student athletes. Coach Stanley does not have the same degree of experience in these varied activities. Employers may reward professional experience and education without violating the EPA. Soto v. Adams Elevator Equip. Co., 941 F.2d 543, 548 & n.7 (7th Cir. 1991).

Coach Raveling's national television appearances and motion picture presence, as well as his reputation as an author, make him a desirable public relations representative for USC. An employer may consider the marketplace value of the skills of a particular individual when determining his or her salary. Horner, 613 F.2d at 714. Unequal wages that reflect market conditions of supply and demand are not prohibited by the EPA. EEOC v. Madison Community Unit Sch. Dist. No. 12, 818 F.2d 577, 580 (7th Cir. 1987).

The record also demonstrates that the USC men's basketball team generated greater attendance, more media interest, larger donations, and produced substantially more revenue than the women's basketball team. As a result, USC placed greater pressure on Coach Raveling to promote his team and to win. The responsibility to produce a large amount of revenue is evidence of a substantial difference in responsibility. See Jacobs v. College of William and Mary, 517 F. Supp. 791, 797 (E.D. Va. 1980) (duty to produce revenue demonstrates that coaching jobs are not substantially equal), aff'd without opinion, 661 F.2d 922 (4th Cir.), cert. denied, 454 U.S. 1033 (1981).

Coach Stanley did not offer evidence to rebut USC's justification for paying Coach Raveling a higher salary. Instead, she alleged that the women's team generates revenue, and that she is under a great deal of pressure to win. Coach Stanley argues that Jacobs is distinguishable because, in that matter, the head basketball coach of the women's team was not required to produce any revenue. Jacobs, 517 F. Supp. at 798. Coach Stanley appears to suggest that a difference in the amount of revenue generated by the men's and women's teams should be ignored by the court in comparing the respective coaching positions. We disagree.

• • •

At this preliminary stage of these proceedings, the record does not support a finding that gender was the reason that USC paid a higher salary to Coach Raveling as head coach of the men's basketball team than it offered Coach Stanley as head coach of the women's basketball team. Garrett's affidavit supports the district court's conclusion that the head coach position of the men's team was not substantially equal to the head coach position of the women's team. The record shows that there were significant differences between Coach Stanley's and Coach Raveling's public relations skills, credentials, experience, and qualifications; there also were substantial differences between their responsibilities and working conditions. The district court's finding that the head coach positions were not substantially equal is not a "clear error of judgment." Martin v. International Olympic Comm., 740 F.2d 670, 679 (9th Cir. 1984).

2. Merits of Coach Stanley's Claim of Retaliation

The district court also rejected Coach Stanley's claim that USC terminated her contract or failed to renew her contract in retaliation for her involvement in protected activities. Rather, the court found that her contract had expired and she refused to accept any of the renewal options that USC offered. This finding is not clearly erroneous. Although Coach Stanley contends that she accepted the multi-year contract and continued only to negotiate the terms of the compensation, the district court found this assertion to be "contrary to the weight of the evidence which clearly suggests that Ms. Stanley failed to accept USC's three-year contract because she was dissatisfied with the proposed compensation." The record supports this finding. Coach Stanley rejected the three-year contract offered by USC. She made a counter offer which USC did not accept. The disagreement on the amount of pay precipitated an impasse in the negotiations.

• • •

IV. Conclusion

The district court did not abuse its discretion in denying a mandatory preliminary injunction. Coach Stanley did not meet her burden of demonstrating the irreducible minimum for obtaining a preliminary injunction: "that there is a fair chance of success on the merits." Martin v. International Olympic Comm., 740 F.2d at 675. Because mandatory preliminary injunctions are disfavored in this circuit, we are compelled to review the record to determine whether the facts and the law clearly favor Coach Stanley. Anderson, 612 F.2d at 1114. The evidence offered at the hearing on the motion for a preliminary injunction demonstrated that Coach Stanley sought pay from USC equal to Coach Raveling's income from that university, notwithstanding significant differences in job pressure, the level of responsibility, and in marketing and revenue-producing qualifications and performance. A difference in pay that takes such factors into consideration does not prove gender bias or violate the Equal Pay Act. The unfortunate impasse that occurred during the negotiations for the renewal of the employment contract of an outstanding basketball coach followed the offer of a very substantial increase in salary—not sex discrimination or retaliation. Because Coach Stanley failed to demonstrate that the law and the facts clearly favor her position, the judgment is AFFIRMED.

■ ■ ■ ■

Fundamental Concepts

The causes of action most relevant to employment discrimination in athletics include actions under the Equal Pay Act of 1964, Title VII of the Civil Right Act of 1963, Title IX, and the Equal Protection Clause of the Fourteenth Amendment (using Section 183 of Civil Rights Act of 1871) of United States Constitution.

The Equal Pay Act of 1963. The Equal Pay Act (EPA) of 1963 (29 U.S.C. § 206 (d) (l) 1982) prohibits an employer from discriminating between employees on the basis of sex,

> ... by paying wages to employees in such establishment at a rate less than the rate at which he pays wages to employees of the opposite sex in such establishment for equal work on jobs the performance of which requires equal skill, effort and responsibility, and which are performed under similar working conditions, except where such payment is made pursuant to (i) a seniority system; (ii) a merit system; (iii) a system which measures earnings by quantity or quality of production; or (iv) a differential based on any other factor other than sex ...

The plaintiff must prove that the employer paid different wages to an employee of the opposite sex for equal or "substantially equal" work (*Laffey v. Northwest Airlines, Inc.*, 1976). Employers are prohibited from paying unequal wages to employees of the opposite sex for substantially equal work. The EPA established and courts have affirmed (*Schultz v. Wheaton Glass Co.*, 1970; *Corning Glass Works v. Brennan*, 1974) that job content is measured as equal based on four statutory factors: skill, effort, responsibility, and the working conditions required to perform the job. A defendant can utilize one of four affirmative defenses: seniority system, merit system, system which measure earnings by quantity or quality of production, or pay differential which is based on any factor other than the sex of the employee (29 U.S.C. § 206 (d) (l) (1982). In sex-based pay discrimination cases, the fourth affirmative defenses (i.e., any factor other than sex) has been a "catch-all defense" which has been utilized by and provided the most success for defendant employers (Luna, 1990).

The courts have established that the equality of work does not have to be identical but must be "substantially equal" (*Schultz v. Wheaton Glass Company*, 1970). The Department of Labor regulations, require job content, not job title, be the basis for establishing equality (29 C.F. R. § 800.121 (1980)). As per the Department of Labor regulations, equal skill is "based upon the experience, training, education and ability required in performing the job; effort is defined as the amount or degree of physical or mental exertion required to perform the job successfully; and responsibility is judged on the degree of accountability required with emphasis on the importance of the job obligation" (Luna, 1990).

In order to prevail in an EPA claim, a plaintiff must establish that the defendant is paying different wages to individuals of the opposite sex for work that is equal (*Hein v. Oregon College of Education*, 1983). The *Stanley v. USC* decision, recognizing the differences in the areas of responsibilities, skills, efforts, and working conditions (for coaches of men's and women's teams) potentially hinders the EPA from being a truly effective cause of action. In *Stanley*, the Ninth Circuit was of the opinion that the areas of public relations, promotional activities, and years spent as a coach illustrated how different wages for the coaches of two similar teams was justified. "Employers may reward professional experience and education without violating the EPA . . ." (*Soto v. Adams Elevator Equipment Company*, 1991). In addition, the *Stanley* court concluded that the market place value of skills (e.g., coaches of men's team receive higher salaries than coaches of women's teams—nationally) and the duty to generate revenue are important factors in justifying greater pay for coaches of male teams.

The willingness of the *Stanley* court to accept the arguments of the defendants suggests that perhaps the EPA is not the most effective cause of action. However, since wage discrimination cases in higher education and athletic administration are relatively scarce in comparison to private industry, the outcome of *Stanley*, when tried on the merits should serve to clarify the potency of the EPA in these types of cases. At this time there is no clear precedent.

Title VII of Civil Rights Act of 1964. Another cause of action which can be utilized in sex-based wage discrimination cases/suits is Title VII of the Civil Rights Act of 1964. In its current form, Title VII (42 U.S.C. § 2000 - 2 (a) (1) (2) (1982)) provides:

It shall be an unlawful employment practice for an employer:

1. to fail or refuse to hire or to discharge any individual, or otherwise to discriminate against any individual with respect to his compensation, terms, conditions, or privileges of employment, because of such individual's race, color, religion, sex, or national origin; or

2. to limit, segregate, or classify his employees or applicants for employment in any way which would deprive or tend to deprive any individual of employment opportunities or otherwise adversely affect his status as an employee, because of such individual's race, color, religion, sex, or national origin.

Title VII was originally directed at prohibiting racial discrimination in employment. In an effort to cause the defeat of the bill, gender-based discrimination was included under the coverage of Title VII via an amendment that added the word "sex" (110 Congressional Record 2577, 1964). In an effort to clarify the interpretative relationship between the EPA and Title VII, Senator Bennett "inserted a memorandum in the 1965 Congressional Record" (Luna, 1990). What has come to be called the Bennett Amendment, was offered by the Senator in an effort to assure that the EPA was not nullified (Greenlaw & Kohl, 1994). "Virtually every federal court through 1979 which ruled on the relationship between the Bennett Amendment and the EPA held that sex-based wage discrimination claims must first meet the EPA criteria" (Luna, 1990).

In *County of Washington v. Gunther* (1981), the Supreme Court "rejected such a far-reaching interpretation of the Bennett Amendment, ruling that the Bennett Amendment does not bar a claim of sex-based wage discrimination merely because the employees failed to establish the equal work requirement of the Equal Pay Act. The Court construed the Bennett Amendment to incorporate into Title VII only the affirmative defenses of the Equal Pay Act" (Perry, 1991, p. 159). In other words, in *Washington*, the Supreme Court clarified that Title VII cases do not have to satisfy the narrow prima facie case requirements of the Equal Pay Act. Such a narrow interpretation (EPA prima facie requirement for Title VII cases) "would have precluded all pay equity suits except those alleging unequal pay for equal work" (Perry, 1991, p. 159).

To establish a prima facie Title VII case of discrimination a plaintiff must establish: a) the defendant was subject to the provisions the statute; b) the plaintiff is entitled to protection of the statute; and c) the plaintiff has not been provided the benefits of the statute. If the plaintiff is able to establish these three conditions, the burden then shifts to the defendant who must advance evidence of legitimate nondiscriminatory reasons for its conduct. In this context, it is important to note that *County of Washington v. Gunther* (1981) established that Title VII incorporated only the four affirmative defenses against wage discrimination claims (e.g., seniority system, merit system, system that measure quantity or quality of work or differential is based on "factor other than sex") and not the "equal work standard."

The two legal theories for establishing sex discrimination under Title VII are disparate treatment and disparate impact. Disparate treatment in pay equity, and other employment discrimination, cases would require the plaintiff to establish that the employer consciously intended to discriminate. *County of Washington v. Gunther* (1981) was one of the rare cases where the employee was able to establish such intent. Pamela L. Perry (1991) addressed the difficulties that the plaintiff faces when she wrote:

. . . the employers can defend against disparate discrimination by explaining that it set pay according to a facially neutral criterion, rather than (the) sex of the employees . . . by explaining that they set pay by the market, rather than by the sex of the incumbents in similarly situated jobs. Unless the employees can demonstrate the facially innocent explanation to be a pretext for a discriminatory purpose, employees will lose despite the evidence of sex discriminatory pay. (p. 134)

Utilizing the disparate impact theory of Title VII, ". . . the plaintiff may establish a prima facie case of wage discrimination by showing that an employer engaged in a facially neutral practice which nevertheless disadvantaged female employees" (Luna, 1990). The cases where the plaintiff has successfully utilized this theory have been rare. It has been said that the, ". . . disparate impact doctrine requires the courts to examine the business justification for these policies. The courts, however, have strongly resisted this view. Only one court, the district court in *AFSCME v. Washington* (1985) applied the disparate impact analysis to challenge sex-based wage discrimination between jobs of different content (Perry, 1991). Obviously, Title VII has a history of being an ineffective cause of action in pay discrimination cases.

Title IX of Education Amendments Act of 1972. The third key cause of action for plaintiffs in sex-based wage discrimination cases in athletics is Title IX of the Education Amendments of 1972. It is beyond the scope of this chapter to address the multiple events, cases, and pieces of legislation that helped to shape how Title IX is interpreted and enforced today. However, relative to Title IX's effectiveness in gender discrimination in athletic employment cases, it is appropriate to provide cursory analysis of the legal ramifications of those three key cases and the impact the Civil Rights Amendment of 1987 can have on employment discrimination cases.

Prior to the *Grove City College v. Bell* (1984) decision, the courts had been split over how to interpret/apply Title IX. Some courts had ruled that only those programs or activities which directly received federal financial assistance were required to comply with Title IX—'program-specific' approach. At the same time, other courts were ruling that if any program or activity within an institution received federal monies then every program/activity must abide by Title IX—'institution-wide' approach. In *Grove City College v. Bell* (1984), the Supreme Court ruled in favor of the 'program-specific' approach which severely limited the applicability of the statute relative to athletic departments/programs. The Civil Rights Restoration Act of 1987 ". . . clarified that entire institutions and agencies are covered by Title IX . . . if any program or activity within the organization receives federal aid" (Pub L. No. 100-259, 102. 28 (1988)).

The reestablishment of the institution-wide interpretation of Title IX, in conjunction with the Supreme Court's decision in *North Haven Board of Education v. Bell* (1982), set the stage for the filing of employment discrimination cases in athletic employment. *North Haven v. Bell*, (1982) established that Title IX is a viable cause of action for employees in education while in 1979, the Supreme Court ruled in *Cannon v. University of Chicago* that Title IX provided a private right of action. The combination of these two cases and the institution-wide interpretation afforded by the Civil Rights Restoration Act of 1987 means that Title IX provides another viable cause of action for employment discrimination cases in educational institutions.

In addition, of the multiple Title IX regulations, Subparts D and E address employment discrimination in educational institutions. It has been suggested that Subpart E, in particular, was intended to provide equity for all employees (including those in athletics) at federally funded institutions. Therefore, these specific Title IX regulations might provide ". . . a basis on which coaches can sue for sex-based employment discrimination without regard to the effect discrimination has on their athletes, and without having to prove program noncompliance with Title IX" (Claussen, 1996).

Perhaps the greatest potential for successfully litigating a pay discrimination case in athletics lies in the utilization of Title IX as a cause of action. The acceptance, by the Ninth Circuit, of USC's argument that factors other than sex (e.g., skills, responsibilities, etc.) and market forces are the basis for the different wages paid to coaches of males and female teams suggests that both the EPA and Title VII may not be the most effective causes of action. However, as noted by the Ninth Circuit Court, the *Stanley* case has yet to be heard on its merits.

It is important to note that the Ninth Circuit's analysis in *Stanley v. USC* (1994) decision was limited to a review of a denial of a preliminary injunction. In fact, the Ninth Circuit stated that it could not ". . . evaluate the persuasive impact of the evidence that the parties may bring forth at trial" (p. 1024). By contrast, *Tyler v. Howard University*, a similar suit brought by the women's basketball coach contending the university had violated the Equal Pay Act, Title IX and the District of Columbia Human Rights Act by paying her less than the men's basketball and football coaches, was decided by a jury trial based on the evidence after the full discovery phase of the trial. In *Tyler*, the jury awarded (after the judge merged remedies that factually and legally overlapped) $1,060,000 to the plaintiff.

In *Pitts v. Oklahoma*, the head women's golf coach successfully utilized Title VII and Title IX to win a decision against Oklahoma State University. Ann Pitts, the women's coach, was paid $28,000 less than the men's coach. In the end, the university was found to have violated Title VII and Title IX but not the Equal Pay Act. Similarly, Pam Bowers sued Baylor University for back pay and benefits (compensatory damages of $1 million, and punitive damages in excess of $3 million) utilizing only Title IX as a cause of action. She claimed that as the head women's basketball coach at Baylor she was not paid equitably relative to the men's coach and further that the University had retaliated against her for reporting discriminatory practices. An out-of-court settlement was reached between Bowers and Baylor University prior to the scheduled trial date of September 5, 1995.

Section 1983 of the Civil Rights Act of 1871.   In addition to the aforedescribed causes of action, it has been suggested that a constitutional challenge using the equal protection clause of the fourteenth amendment might be the most effective legal theory to utilize in an effort to provide pay equity for male and female coaches of same-sport teams (Dessem, 1980). Section 1983 of the Civil Rights Act of 1871 ". . . provides a vehicle for obtaining a remedy for violations of other federally protected rights. Section 1983 is most frequently used to enforce rights governed under the Equal Protection Clause of the Fourteenth Amendment to the United States Constitution which prohibits discrimination based on gender. Thus sex discrimination involving state action violates the Equal Protection Clause and Section 1983 provides a remedy for such violations. Under the Equal Protection Clause, discriminatory state action based on gender is allowed only if it is necessary to achieve "important governmental objectives" and the discriminatory action is substantially related to the achievement of those objectives (Henson, 1992).

Recent Developments

There is clearly a lack of case law on pay equity in intercollegiate athletics. Court decisions in each new case further defines this area of law and, in turn, necessarily impacts how administrators must approach gender equity and discrimination in employment. If courts in the future share the same view as the Ninth Circuit in *Stanley*, it is likely that the existence and the content of job descriptions and performance appraisals will become more important. These management tools could aid a plaintiff or a defendant in their respective efforts to clearly establish the responsibilities and duties required of a particular position. If the head men's and women's coaching positions are indeed not substantially the same then these differences should be quite evident and easily discernible within the job descriptions and performance appraisals.

Of the four key cases in the area of pay equity for collegiate coaches, only *Stanley* has not yet been heard on the merits or resulted in an out of court settlement. Both *Tyler v. Howard University* and *Pitts v. Oklahoma* resulted in the court finding for the plaintiff. The finding in *Tyler* was based on the Equal Pay Act, Title IX, and the District of Columbia Human Rights Act. In *Pitts*, Title VII and Title IX were the effective causes of action. In *Bowers v. Baylor University*, Coach Bowers' claim was based on Title IX as the cause of action. As noted above, the case was settled prior to trial.

Until other pay equity cases in intercollegiate athletics are litigated, and/or *Pitts v. Oklahoma, Stanley v. USC*, or *Tyler v. Howard* are heard by the Supreme Court, no clear precedent exists. Thus, it will be up to individual administrators and their institutions to eliminate pay discrimination and work toward gender equity in employment. Athletics administrators must examine the salaries of employees relative to their duties and responsibilities, and the opportunities provided to the individual in that position (e.g., only offering alumni speaking engagements to coaches of male teams) rather than basing salary decisions on the sex of the individual or the students which they teach/coach. If administrators and institutions begin to do this it will provide an important step toward achieving gender equity for female coaches and administrators.

References

A. Cases

AFSCME v. Washington, 770 F.2d 1401 (9th Cir. 1985), aff'd, 813 F.2d 1034 (9th Cir. 1987)

Bowers v. Baylor University, 862 F. Supp. 142 (W.D. Tex. 1994)

Cannon v. University of Chicago, 441 U.S. 677 (1979)

Cohen v. Brown, 991 F.2d 888 (1st Cir. 1993)

Cook v. Colgate, 802 F.Supp. 737 (N.D. N.Y. 1992), vacated, 992 F.2d 17 (2d Cir. 1993)

Corning Glass Works v. Brennan, 417 U.S. 188 (1974)

County of Washington v. Gunther, 452 U.S. 161 (1981)

EEOC v. Madison Community School District No. 12, 818 F.2d 577 (7th Cir. 1987)

Favia v. Indiana University of Pennsylvania, 812 F. Supp. 578 (W.D. Pa. 1993)

Franklin v. Gwinnett County Public Schools, 503 U.S. 60 (1992)

Grove City v. Bell, 464 U.S. 555 (1984)

Hein v. Oregon College of Education, 718 F.2d 940 (9th Cir. 1983)

Horner v. Mary Institute, 613 F.2d 706 (8th Cir. 1980)

Kouba et v. Allstate Insurance Company, 691 F.2d 873 (9th Cir, 1982)

Laffey v. Northwest Airlines, Inc., 567 F.2d 429 (D.C. Cir. 1976), cert. denied, 434 U.S. 1906 (1978)

North Haven v. Bell, 456 U.S. 512 (1982)

Pitts v. Oklahoma, No. CIV-93-1341-A, (W.D. Okla. 1994)

Schultz v. Wheaton Glass Company, 421 F. 2d at 259 (3rd Cir.), cert. denied, 398 U.S. 905 (1970)

Soto v. Adams Elevator Equipment Company, 914 F.2d 543 (7th Cir. 1991)

Stanley v. University of Southern California, 13 F.3d 1313 (9th Cir. 1994)

B. Publications

Claussen, C.L. (1996). Title IX and Employment Discrimination in Coaching Intercollegiate athletics, *Entertainment & Sports Law Review*, 1, 1-20.

Dessem, R.L. (1980). Sex Discrimination in Coaching. *Harvard Women's Law Journal*, 3, 97-117.

Greenlaw, P.S. & Kohl, J.P. (1994). Thirty Years of Civil Rights: The EPA/Title VII Sex-based Wages Discrimination Controversy. *Labor Law Journal*, (April), 240-247.

Henson, D. (1992). "Gender Equity in Sport: What Is She Entitled To?" Presented at The University of Texas Gender Equity in Sport Conference, Austin, Texas, March 8, 1992.

Luna, G. (1990). Understanding Gender-base Wage Discrimination: Legal Interpretation and Trends of Pay Equity in Higher Education. *Journal of Law and Education*, 3, 371-384.

Perry, P.L. (1991). Let Them Become Professionals: An Analysis of the Failure to Enforce Title VII's Pay Equity Mandate. *Harvard Women's Law Journal*, (Spring), 127-184.

Wilde, J. (1994). Gender Equity in Athletics: Coming of Age in the 90s. *Marquette Sports Laws Journal*, 4, 217-258.

C. Legislation
Civil Rights Act of 1987 (Pub. L. No. 100-259, 102 Stat. 28)
Civil Rights Act of 1871, 16 Stat. 433
District of Columbia Human Rights Law, D.C. Code §1-2501 et seq.
Equal Pay Act of 1964 (29 U.S.C. § 206 (d) (1) (1982))
Fair Labor Standards Act of 1938, 52 Stat. 1060
Title VII of Civil Rights Act of 1964 (42 U.S.C. §2000 2(a) (1) (2) 1982)
Title IX of the Educational Amendments of 1972, 86. Stat. 235 (codified at 20 U.S.C. §1681-1688 (1990))

—— 4.26 ——

Drug Testing

Ted Curtis
Attorney, University of South Florida

Few areas of sports law are as controversial as drug testing. For every athlete, parent, school administrator, or league official who vehemently supports athlete drug testing, someone rises to strenuously protest it. So it was no surprise that when the U.S. Supreme Court upheld the random drug testing of high school student-athletes in June, 1995, the story became front-page news across the country.

Athlete drug testing programs already are in place throughout amateur and professional sports. Many high schools and colleges test their student-athletes for illegal narcotics. The National Collegiate Athletic Association has conducted a drug testing program at its national championship tournaments since 1986. And most professional leagues and many national sports governing bodies also require athletes to submit to drug tests either on a random or regular basis.

However, many of these recent programs have come under fire from opponents to athlete drug testing. These legal challenges have included claims that drug testing violates Constitutional rights such as the right to due process and the right to be free from unreasonable searches and seizures. Other athletes have challenged the validity of drug testing on state grounds, including litigation based on state privacy laws.

Understanding this struggle between the supporters and detractors of drug testing at the scholastic, intercollegiate, Olympic, and professional athletics levels now has become an integral part of sports law and athletics administration. It will continue to be so for many years to come.

■ ■ ■ ■

Representative Case

VERNONIA SCHOOL DISTRICT 47J v. ACTON
Supreme Court of the United States
115 S. Ct. 2386 (1995)

OPINION: JUSTICE SCALIA delivered the opinion of the Court.

The Student Athlete Drug Policy adopted by School District 47J in the town of Vernonia, Oregon, authorizes random urinalysis drug testing of students who participate in the District's school athletics programs. We granted certiorari to decide whether this violates the Fourth and Fourteenth Amendments to the United States Constitution.

I

A

Petitioner Vernonia School District 47J (District) operates one high school and three grade schools in the logging community of Vernonia, Oregon. As elsewhere in small-

328

town America, school sports play a prominent role in the town's life, and student athletes are admired in their schools and in the community.

Drugs had not been a major problem in Vernonia schools. In the mid-to-late 1980's, however, teachers and administrators observed a sharp increase in drug use. Students began to speak out about their attraction to the drug culture, and to boast that there was nothing the school could do about it. Along with more drugs came more disciplinary problems. Between 1988 and 1989 the number of disciplinary referrals in Vernonia schools rose to more than twice the number reported in the early 1980's, and several students were suspended. Students became increasingly rude during class; outbursts of profane language became common.

Not only were student athletes included among the drug users but, as the District Court found, athletes were the leaders of the drug culture. 796 F. Supp. 1354, 1357 (D. Ore. 1992). This caused the District's administrators particular concern, since drug use increases the risk of sports-related injury. Expert testimony at the trial confirmed the deleterious effects of drugs on motivation, memory, judgment, reaction, coordination, and performance. The high school football and wrestling coach witnessed a severe sternum injury suffered by a wrestler, and various omissions of safety procedures and misexecutions by football players, all attributable in his belief to the effects of drug use.

Initially, the District responded to the drug problem by offering special classes, speakers, and presentations designed to deter drug use. It even brought in a specially trained dog to detect drugs, but the drug problem persisted. According to the District Court:

> The administration was at its wit's end and . . . a large segment of the student body, particularly those involved in interscholastic athletics, was in a state of rebellion. Disciplinary problems had reached 'epidemic proportions.' The coincidence of an almost three-fold increase in classroom disruptions and disciplinary reports along with the staff's direct observations of students using drugs or glamorizing drug and alcohol use led the administration to the inescapable conclusion that the rebellion was being fueled by alcohol and drug abuse as well as the student's misperceptions about the drug culture. (Ibid.)

At that point, District officials began considering a drug-testing program. They held a parent "input night" to discuss the proposed Student Athlete Drug Policy (Policy), and the parents in attendance gave their unanimous approval. The school board approved the Policy for implementation in the fall of 1989. Its expressed purpose is to prevent student athletes from using drugs, to protect their health and safety, and to provide drug users with assistance programs.

B

The Policy applies to all students participating in interscholastic athletics. Students wishing to play sports must sign a form consenting to the testing and must obtain the written consent of their parents. Athletes are tested at the beginning of the season for their sport. In addition, once each week of the season the names of the athletes are placed in a "pool" from which a student, with the supervision of two adults, blindly draws the names of 10 percent of the athletes for random testing. Those selected are notified and tested that same day, if possible.

The student to be tested completes a specimen control form which bears an assigned number. Prescription medications that the student is taking must be identified by providing a copy of the prescription or a doctor's authorization. The student then enters an empty locker room accompanied by an adult monitor of the same sex. Each boy selected produces a sample at a urinal, remaining fully clothed with his back to the monitor, who stands approximately 12 to 15 feet behind the student. Monitors may (though do not always) watch the student while he produces the sample, and they listen for normal sounds of urination. Girls produce samples in an enclosed bathroom stall, so that they can be heard but not observed. After the sample is produced, it is given to the monitor, who checks it for temperature and tampering and then transfers it to a vial.

The samples are sent to an independent laboratory, which routinely tests them for amphetamines, cocaine, and marijuana. Other drugs, such as LSD, may be screened at the request of the District, but the identity of a particular student does not determine which drugs will be tested. The laboratory's procedures are 99.94 percent accurate. The District follows strict procedures regarding the chain of custody and access to test results. The laboratory does not know the identity of the students whose samples it tests. It is authorized to mail written test reports only to the superintendent and to provide test results to District personnel by telephone only after the requesting official recites a code confirming his authority. Only the superintendent, principals, vice-principals, and athletic directors have access to test results, and the results are not kept for more than one year.

If a sample tests positive, a second test is administered as soon as possible to confirm the result. If the second test is negative, no further action is taken. If the second test is positive, the athlete's parents are notified, and the school principal convenes a meeting with the student and his parents, at which the student is given the option of (1) participating for six weeks in an assistance program that includes weekly urinalysis, or (2) suffering suspension from athletics for the remainder of the current season and the next athletic season. The student is then retested prior to the start of the next athletic season for which he or she is eligible. The Policy states that a second offense results in automatic imposition of option (2); a third offense in suspension for the remainder of the current season and the next two athletic seasons.

C

In the fall of 1991, respondent James Acton, then a seventh-grader, signed up to play football at one of the District's grade schools. He was denied participation, however, because he and his parents refused to sign the testing consent forms. The Actons filed suit, seeking declaratory and injunctive relief from enforcement of the Policy on the grounds that it violated the Fourth and Fourteenth Amendments to the United States Constitution and Article I, @ 9, of the Oregon Constitution. After a bench trial, the District Court entered an order denying the claims on the merits and dismissing the action. 796 F. Supp. at 1355. The United States Court of Appeals for the Ninth Circuit reversed, holding that the Policy violated both the Fourth and Fourteenth Amendments and Article I, @ 9, of the Oregon Constitution. 23 F.3d 1514 (1994). We granted certiorari. 513 U.S. _____ (1994).

II

The Fourth Amendment to the United States Constitution provides that the Federal Government shall not violate "the right of the people to be secure in their persons, houses, papers, and effects, against unreasonable searches and seizures, . . ." We have held that the Fourteenth Amendment extends this constitutional guarantee to searches and seizures by state officers, Elkins v. United States, 364 U.S. 206, 213, 4 L. Ed. 2d 1669, 80 S. Ct. 1437 (1960), including public school officials, New Jersey v. T. L. O., 469 U.S. 325, 336-337, 83 L. Ed. 2d 720, 105 S. Ct. 733 (1985). In Skinner v. Railway Labor Executives' Assn., 489 U.S. 602, 617, 103 L. Ed. 2d 639, 109 S. Ct. 1402 (1989), we held that state-compelled collection and testing of urine, such as that required by the Student Athlete Drug Policy, constitutes a "search" subject to the demands of the Fourth Amendment. See also Treasury Employees v. Von Raab, 489 U.S. 656, 665, 103 L. Ed. 2d 685, 109 S. Ct. 1384 (1989).

As the text of the Fourth Amendment indicates, the ultimate measure of the constitutionality of a governmental search is "reasonableness." At least in a case such as this, where there was no clear practice, either approving or disapproving the type of search at issue, at the time the constitutional provision was enacted, whether a particular search meets the reasonableness standard "'is judged by balancing its intrusion on the individual's Fourth Amendment interests against its promotion of legitimate governmental interests.'" Skinner, supra, at 619 (quoting Delaware v. Prouse, 440 U.S. 648, 654, 59 L. Ed. 2d 660, 99 S. Ct. 1391 (1979)). Where a search is undertaken by law enforcement officials to discover evidence of criminal wrongdoing, this Court has said that reasonableness generally requires the obtaining of a judicial warrant, Skinner, supra, at 619. Warrants cannot be issued, of course, without the showing of probable cause required by the Warrant Clause. But a warrant is not required to establish the reasonableness of all government searches; and when a warrant is not required (and the Warrant Clause therefore not applicable), probable cause is not invariably required either. A search unsupported by probable cause can be constitutional, we have said, "when special needs, beyond the normal need for law enforcement, make the warrant and probable-cause requirement impracticable." Griffin v. Wisconsin, 483 U.S. 868, 873, 97 L. Ed. 2d 709, 107 S. Ct. 3164 (1987) (internal quotation marks omitted).

We have found such "special needs" to exist in the public-school context. There, the warrant requirement "would unduly interfere with the maintenance of the swift and informal disciplinary procedures [that are] needed," and "strict adherence to the requirement that searches be based upon probable cause" would undercut "the substantial need of teachers and administrators for freedom to maintain order in the schools." T. L. O., supra, at 340, 341. The school search we approved in T. L. O., while not based on probable cause, was based on individualized suspicion of wrongdoing. As we explicitly acknowledged, however, "'the Fourth Amendment imposes no irreducible requirement of such suspicion,'" id., at 342, n. 8 (quoting United States v. Martinez-Fuerte, 428 U.S. 543, 560-561, 49 L. Ed. 2d 1116, 96 S. Ct. 3074 (1976)). We have upheld suspicionless searches and seizures to conduct drug testing of railroad personnel involved in train accidents, see Skinner, supra; to conduct random drug testing of federal customs officers who carry arms or are involved in drug interdiction, see Von Raab, supra; and to maintain automobile checkpoints looking for illegal immigrants and contraband, Martinez-Fuerte, supra, and drunk drivers, Michigan Dept. of State Police v. Sitz, 496 U.S. 444, 110 L. Ed. 2d 412, 110 S. Ct. 2481 (1990).

III

The first factor to be considered is the nature of the privacy interest upon which the search here at issue intrudes. The Fourth Amendment does not protect all subjective expectations of privacy, but only those that society recognizes as "legitimate." T. L. O., 469 U.S. at 338. What expectations are legitimate varies, of course, with context, id., at 337, depending, for example, upon whether the individual asserting the privacy interest is at home, at work, in a car, or in a public park. In addition, the legitimacy of certain privacy expectations vis-a-vis the State may depend upon the individual's legal relationship with the State. For example, in Griffin, supra, we held that, although a "probationer's home, like anyone else's, is protected by the Fourth Amendment," the supervisory relationship between probationer and State justifies "a degree of impingement upon [a probationer's] privacy that would not be constitutional if applied to the public at large." 483 U.S. at 873, 875. Central, in our view, to the present case is the fact that the subjects of the Policy are (1) children, who (2) have been committed to the temporary custody of the State as schoolmaster.

Traditionally at common law, and still today, unemancipated minors lack some of the most fundamental rights of self-determination—including even the right of liberty in its narrow sense, i.e., the right to come and go at will. They are subject, even as to their physical freedom, to the control of their parents or guardians.

• • •

Fourth Amendment rights, no less than First and Fourteenth Amendment rights, are different in public schools than elsewhere; the "reasonableness" inquiry cannot disregard the schools' custodial and tutelary responsibility for children. For their own good and that of their classmates, public school children are routinely required to submit to various physical examinations, and to be vaccinated against various diseases. According to the American Academy of Pediatrics, most public schools "provide vision and hearing screening and dental and dermatological checks. . . . Others also mandate scoliosis screening at appropriate grade levels." Committee on School Health, American Academy of Pediatrics, School Health: A Guide for Health Professionals 2 (1987). In the 1991-1992 school year, all 50 States required public-school students to be vaccinated against diphtheria, measles, rubella, and polio. U.S. Dept. of Health & Human Services, Public Health Service, Centers for Disease Control, State Immunization Requirements 1991-1992, p. 1. Particularly with regard to medical examinations and procedures, therefore, "students within the school environment have a lesser expectation of privacy than members of the population generally." T. L. O., 469 U.S. at 348 (Powell, J., concurring).

Legitimate privacy expectations are even less with regard to student athletes. School sports are not for the bashful. They require "suiting up" before each practice or event, and showering and changing afterwards. Public school locker rooms, the usual sites for these activities, are not notable for the privacy they afford. The locker rooms in Vernonia are typical: no individual dressing rooms are provided; shower heads are lined up along a wall, unseparated by any sort of partition or curtain; not even all the toilet stalls have doors. As the United States Court of Appeals for the Seventh Circuit has noted, there is "an element of 'communal undress' inherent in athletic participation," Schaill by Kross v. Tippecanoe County School Corp., 864 F.2d 1309, 1318 (1988).

There is an additional respect in which school athletes have a reduced expectation of privacy. By choosing to "go out for the team," they voluntarily subject themselves to a degree of regulation even higher than that imposed on students generally. In Vernonia's public schools, they must submit to a preseason physical exam (James testified that his included the giving of a urine sample, App. 17), they must acquire adequate insurance coverage or sign an insurance waiver, maintain a minimum grade point average, and comply with any "rules of conduct, dress, training hours and related matters as may be established for each sport by the head coach and athletic director with the principal's approval." Record, Exh. 2, p. 30, P8. Somewhat like adults who choose to participate in a "closely regulated industry," students who voluntarily participate in school athletics have reason to expect intrusions upon normal rights and privileges, including privacy. See Skinner, 489 U.S. at 627; United States v. Biswell, 406 U.S. 311, 316, 32 L. Ed. 2d 87, 92 S. Ct. 1593 (1972).

IV

Having considered the scope of the legitimate expectation of privacy at issue here, we turn next to the character of the intrusion that is complained of. We recognized in Skinner that collecting the samples for urinalysis intrudes upon "an excretory function traditionally shielded by great privacy." Skinner, 489 U.S. at 626. We noted, however, that the degree of intrusion depends upon the manner in which production of the urine sample is monitored. Ibid. Under the District's Policy, male students produce samples at a urinal along a wall. They remain fully clothed and are only observed from behind, if at all. Female students produce samples in an enclosed stall, with a female monitor standing outside listening only for sounds of tampering. These conditions are nearly identical to those typically encountered in public restrooms, which men, women, and especially school children use daily. Under such conditions, the privacy interests compromised by the process of obtaining the urine sample are in our view negligible. The other privacy-invasive aspect of urinalysis is, of course, the information it discloses concerning the state of the subject's body, and the materials he has ingested. In this regard it is significant that the tests at issue here look only for drugs, and not for whether the student is, for example, epileptic, pregnant, or diabetic. See Skinner, supra, at 617. Moreover, the drugs for which the samples are screened are standard, and do not vary according to the identity of the student. And finally, the results of the tests are disclosed only to a limited class of school personnel who have a need to know; and they are not turned over to law enforcement authorities or used for any internal disciplinary function. 796 F. Supp. at 1364; see also 23 F.3d at 1521.

Respondents argue, however, that the District's Policy is in fact more intrusive than this suggests, because it requires the students, if they are to avoid sanctions for a falsely positive test, to identify in advance prescription medications they are taking. We agree that this raises some cause for concern. In Von Raab, we flagged as one of the salutary features of the Customs Service drug-testing program the fact that employees were not required to disclose medical information unless they tested positive, and, even then, the information was supplied to a licensed physician rather than to the Government employer. See Von Raab, 489 U.S., at 672-673, n. 2. On the other hand, we have never indicated that requiring advance disclosure of medications is per se unreasonable. Indeed, in Skinner we held that it was not "a significant invasion of privacy." Skinner, 489 U.S. at 626, n. 7. It can be argued that, in Skinner, the disclosure went only to the medical personnel taking the sample, and the Government personnel analyzing it, see id., at 609, but see id., at 610 (railroad personnel responsible for forwarding the sample, and presumably accompanying information, to the Government's testing lab); and that disclosure to teachers and coaches—to persons who personally know the student—is a greater invasion of privacy. Assuming for the sake of argument that both those propositions are true, we do not believe they establish a difference that respondents are entitled to rely on here.

The General Authorization Form that respondents refused to sign, which refusal was the basis for James's exclusion from the sports program, said only (in relevant part): "I . . . authorize the Vernonia School District to conduct a test on a urine specimen which I provide to test for drugs and/or alcohol use. I also authorize the release of information concerning the results of such a test to the Vernonia School District and to the parents and/or guardians of the student." App. 10-11. While the practice of the District seems to have been to have a school official take medication information from the student at the time of the test, see App. 29, 42, that practice is not set forth in, or required by, the Policy, which says simply: "Student athletes who . . . are or have been taking prescription medication must provide verification (either by a copy of the prescription or by doctor's authorization) prior to being tested." App. 8. It may well be that, if and when James was

selected for random testing at a time that he was taking medication, the School District would have permitted him to provide the requested information in a confidential manner—for example, in a sealed envelope delivered to the testing lab. Nothing in the Policy contradicts that, and when respondents choose, in effect, to challenge the Policy on its face, we will not assume the worst. Accordingly, we reach the same conclusion as in Skinner: that the invasion of privacy was not significant.

V

Finally, we turn to consider the nature and immediacy of the governmental concern at issue here, and the efficacy of this means for meeting it. In both Skinner and Von Raab, we characterized the government interest motivating the search as "compelling." Skinner, supra, at 628 (interest in preventing railway accidents); Von Raab, supra, at 670 (interest in insuring fitness of customs officials to interdict drugs and handle firearms). Relying on these cases, the District Court held that because the District's program also called for drug testing in the absence of individualized suspicion, the District "must demonstrate a 'compelling need' for the program." 796 F. Supp. at 1363. The Court of Appeals appears to have agreed with this view. See 23 F.3d at 1526. It is a mistake, however, to think that the phrase "compelling state interest," in the Fourth Amendment context, describes a fixed, minimum quantum of governmental concern, so that one can dispose of a case by answering in isolation the question: Is there a compelling state interest here? Rather, the phrase describes an interest which appears important enough to justify the particular search at hand, in light of other factors which show the search to be relatively intrusive upon a genuine expectation of privacy. Whether that relatively high degree of government concern is necessary in this case or not, we think it is met.

That the nature of the concern is important—indeed, perhaps compelling—can hardly be doubted. Deterring drug use by our Nation's schoolchildren is at least as important as enhancing efficient enforcement of the Nation's laws against the importation of drugs, which was the governmental concern in Von Raab, supra, at 668, or deterring drug use by engineers and trainmen, which was the governmental concern in Skinner, supra, at 628. School years are the time when the physical, psychological, and addictive effects of drugs are most severe. . . . And of course the effects of a drug-infested school are visited not just upon the users, but upon the entire student body and faculty, as the educational process is disrupted. In the present case, moreover, the necessity for the State to act is magnified by the fact that this evil is being visited not just upon individuals at large, but upon children for whom it has undertaken a special responsibility of care and direction. Finally, it must not be lost sight of that this program is directed more narrowly to drug use by school athletes, where the risk of immediate physical harm to the drug user or those with whom he is playing his sport is particularly high. Apart from psychological effects, which include impairment of judgment, slow reaction time, and a lessening of the perception of pain, the particular drugs screened by the District's Policy have been demonstrated to pose substantial physical risks to athletes.

• • •

VI

Taking into account all the factors we have considered above—the decreased expectation of privacy, the relative unobtrusiveness of the search, and the severity of the need met by the search—we conclude Vernonia's Policy is reasonable and hence constitutional.

We caution against the assumption that suspicionless drug testing will readily pass constitutional muster in other contexts. The most significant element in this case is the first we discussed: that the Policy was undertaken in furtherance of the government's responsibilities, under a public school system, as guardian and tutor of children entrusted to its care. Just as when the government conducts a search in its capacity as employer (a warrantless search of an absent employee's desk to obtain an urgently needed file, for example), the relevant question is whether that intrusion upon privacy is one that a reasonable employer might engage in, see O'Connor v. Ortega, 480 U.S. 709, 94 L. Ed. 2d 714, 107 S. Ct. 1492 (1987); so also when the government acts as guardian and tutor the relevant question is whether the search is one that a reasonable guardian and tutor might undertake. Given the findings of need made by the District Court, we conclude that in the present case it is.

• • •

The Ninth Circuit held that Vernonia's Policy not only violated the Fourth Amendment, but also, by reason of that violation, contravened Article I, P9 of the Oregon Constitution. Our conclusion that the former holding was in error means that the latter holding rested on a flawed premise. We therefore vacate the judgment, and remand the case to the Court of Appeals for further proceedings consistent with this opinion.

It is so ordered.

■ ■ ■ ■

Fundamental Concepts

I. Search and Seizure

The Fourth Amendment to the U.S. Constitution affords individuals the right "to be secure in their persons, houses, papers and effects, against unreasonable searches and seizures." The Fourteenth Amendment to the U.S. Constitution applies that amendment—in addition to the remainder of the original ten Amendments—to states, government-run organizations, and any other "state actors." A state actor is an entity that conducts activities that have such a close connection to the state that the entity may be considered to be an extension of the state itself. Public school athletic departments or state-sponsored athletic associations are examples of state actors, and, therefore, generally are subject to the search and seizure restrictions of the Fourth Amendment. However, Constitutional requirements and restrictions are not necessarily applicable to private non-state actors, such as private sports leagues and the NCAA.

Drug Testing as a Search. In 1989, the U.S. Supreme Court recognized that a drug test constitutes a search and seizure subject to Fourth Amendment restrictions, *Skinner v. Railway Labor Executives' Assn.*, 489 U.S. 602 (1989).

Three-Part Test. In order to determine whether a particular drug test violates the Fourth Amendment as an unreasonable search and seizure, courts generally examine the following three factors as part of a balancing test weighing the interests of the athlete against the interests of the entity conducting the drug test:

1. *Legitimate Expectation of Privacy.* The first consideration is whether the athlete subject to the test had a "legitimate expectation of privacy," that is, whether the athlete legitimately expected that he would not be required to be subjected to a drug test. That expectation depends upon a number of factors.

At the scholastic level, the age and grade of the student-athlete is a significant factor. In upholding the drug test in *Vernonia School District 47J v. Acton* (above), the U.S. Supreme Court emphasized that a high school student-athlete's expectation of privacy is lesser than that of an adult athlete due to the nature of the high school setting, where teachers and coaches take on quasi-parental roles and subject students to high degrees of supervision in every aspect of school life.

At every level of competition, the degree to which an athlete's privacy *already* has been limited also must be considered. An athlete may *explicitly* agree to limitations on his privacy by signing injury waivers, eligibility statements, or standard player contracts. An athlete may *implicitly* consent to limitations on his privacy by playing under a coach or athletic program that requires regulation of the athlete's diet, sleep, or other daily regimens. An athlete also may implicitly consent to limitations on his privacy by participating in the usual locker room setting with its open showers and communal undress. As the Supreme Court offered in *Acton*, "school sports are not for the bashful."

2. *The Character of the Intrusion.* The second factor generally examined in a Fourth Amendment analysis is the nature and extent of a drug test's physical and informational intrusion into an athlete's life.

In analyzing the degree of the *physical intrusiveness* of a drug test, courts examine how the test actually is given and who physically monitors the athlete's production of a test sample. Not surprisingly, courts differ as to what level of physical intrusion is overly excessive: In *Acton*, the U.S. Supreme Court allowed a program requiring a monitor to stand behind a student-athlete and listen for sounds indicating that a sample was being given. However, in *Hill v. NCAA*, 865 P.2d 633 (Cal. 1994), even though the California Supreme Court upheld the NCAA's drug testing program on state privacy grounds utilizing an analysis similar to a Fourth Amendment inquiry, the court called the NCAA's procedure requiring a monitor's direct observation of an athlete "particularly intrusive."

Examining the degree to which a drug test intrudes upon an athlete's *informational privacy* requires a consideration of the extent to which the test permits the release of information that an athlete otherwise would not readily disseminate. For example, in addition to drug use, certain urine sample tests also could provide information on pregnancy, AIDS, or other information that the athlete might not otherwise wish to be released. As with physical privacy, the greater the intrusion on informational privacy, the greater the chance that a drug test will be held to be unconstitutional.

3. *Nature and Immediacy of the Governmental Interest.* The final factor to be considered in a Fourth Amendment analysis of a drug test is the importance and immediacy of the test administrator's interest in conducting the search, usually defined as the "governmental interest" in the search. Since courts have disagreed as to whether this interest must be defined as "compelling," "significant," or "important," it may be most accurate instead to state, as the U.S. Supreme Court did in *Acton*, that the government's interest in conducting the athlete drug test "must be *important enough* to justify the particular search at hand." In other words, an examination of the nature of the government interest must not be considered alone—it is here where a consideration of the first two factors also must be brought into play. By balancing the intrusiveness of the drug test and the athlete's legitimate expectation of privacy against the nature of the governmental interest in conducting the test, a court may reach a conclusion as to the Constitutionality of the test under the Fourth Amendment.

In *Acton*, the U.S. Supreme Court held that the protection of the health and safety of student-athletes was enough to justify a drug test where the students were minor children with lessened expectations of privacy, and where submission to the monitored drug test was no different than circumstances similar to "those typically encountered in a public restroom." However, an opposite conclusion was reached in *University of Colorado v. Derdeyn*, 863 P.2d 929 (Colo. 1993), where the Supreme Court of Colorado held that the same governmental interest involved in *Acton* was *not* enough to justify the intrusive testing of college-aged student-athletes under state and federal search and seizure laws. The *Derdeyn* court recognized that while the university may have an interest in protecting the welfare of its student-athletes, and that while a student-athlete may consent to other limitations on his private life by participation in intercollegiate athletics, nothing entails "an intrusion on privacy interests of the nature and extent involved in monitored collection of urine samples."

Similarly, in *Shoemaker v. Handel*, 795 F.2d 1136 (3rd Cir. 1986), the U.S. Court of Appeals for the Third Circuit held that a state horse racing commission's interest in preserving racing integrity was sufficient to uphold drug testing of jockeys. However, that decision has been criticized by a number of state and federal courts, i.e., *Horsemen's Benevolent and Protective Assn. v. State Racing Commission*, 532 N.E.2d 644 (Mass. 1989); *Penny v. Kennedy*, 846 F.2d 1563 (6th Cir. 1988).

II. Due Process

The Fourteenth Amendment to the U.S. Constitution provides that no state may deprive any individual "of life, liberty, or property, without due process of law." Under the legal concept of "procedural due process," no individual may be deprived of any right without prior notice and an opportunity to participate in a hearing at which time the individual may contest the deprivation of the benefit. Therefore, attempts to strike down drug testing programs on a procedural due process basis traditionally involves an athlete's claim that a testing program fails to afford the athlete either notice of the test and its consequences or a chance for the athlete to defend himself in the face of disciplinary actions following a failed drug test.

1. **Educational Setting.** Students have had mixed results challenging drug tests on due process grounds. This may be demonstrated best by the 1985 federal court ruling in *Anabele v. Ford*, 653 F.Supp. 22 (W.D.Ark. 1985), in which one court announced two different decisions in two separate cases involving the same school district. In the first case, the federal court held that an Arkansas school violated a student's procedural due process guarantees when it required the student, who was suspected of using marijuana, to submit to a drug test. According to the court, the due process violation was "brought about by the [school's] failure to inform [the student] of all of the evidence against her prior to utilization of the [drug] test" and by the school's request that the student voluntarily withdraw from school without being afforded a hearing on the issue. On the other hand, in the case of an alcohol-related suspension of a second student, the *Anabele* court held that the same Arkansas school's alcohol use policy, breathalyzer test requirement, and subsequent expulsion procedures did not violate due process. The court found that the student understood these policies, and that the school's procedures specifically gave the student the opportunity to challenge any disciplinary action as a result of a failed alcohol test, the opportunity to present a case in the student's defense, and the opportunity to cross-examine all witnesses.

2. **Professional Setting.** It is rare for a drug test to be successfully challenged on a procedural due process claim at the professional athletics level. In most, if not all, instances, the drug testing policy of a professional sports league is contained in a written document, agreed upon by both management and the players (thus satisfying the notice requirement) and specifies an athlete's opportunity to present a defense to any disciplinary action taken for a failed drug test (therefore satisfying procedural due process' hearing requirement).

III. Equal Protection

In addition to guaranteeing due process, the 14th Amendment to the U.S. Constitution guarantees that no state actor may "deny to any person within its jurisdiction the equal protection of the laws"—that is, that no rule may be made that adversely affects one group while leaving another group untouched.

Under equal protection claims, courts uniformly have held that where a rule affects a "suspect" class of people, such as those definable by race or national origin, the rule only may be upheld upon a showing that the restriction is narrowly tailored to advance a *compelling* state interest, such as national security. Where a rule affects a "non-suspect" class of people, the rule will be upheld upon a showing that the rule supports an *important* or *legitimate* state interest.

As student-athletes may be defined as a "non-suspect" class of people, a drug testing program that affects student-athletes, but *not* non-student-athletes, may be upheld upon a showing that the testing satisfies a legitimate state interest. However, a drug testing program which, for example, requires the testing only of all student-athletes of one national origin may fall within the former test and would require a compelling state interest in order to be upheld under equal protection scrutiny.

IV. Self Incrimination

The Fifth Amendment to the U.S. Constitution provides that "no person shall be compelled in any criminal case to be a witness against himself." However, an argument that a drug test violates this Constitutionally guaranteed right against self incrimination invariably may fail as courts have consistently and uniformly held that urine and blood testing do not constitute the "testimonial" evidence protected by the Fifth Amendment. Courts also have held that the fact that the results of a drug test may be utilized in future criminal proceedings against the athlete is too remote of a possibility to warrant a finding that a drug test is illegal under the Fifth Amendment.

V. Contract Claims

An athlete also may attempt to advance a claim challenging a drug test based in contract claims, contending that the sports league responsible for administering the test could not subsequently impose sanctions against the athlete since the league failed to follow its own testing procedures. Such arguments have been particularly successful in intercollegiate and Olympic athletics when a misapplication of the sports organization's testing procedures *actually* had been demonstrated.

VI. Invasion of Privacy Under State Law

Technically, the U.S. Constitution does not recognize an individual's "right to privacy." However, a number of states, including New York, Massachusetts, and California, have codified a right of privacy into state law. Often, drug testing litigation involving such state privacy claims require an analysis similar to the test for a search and seizure case. For example, in *Hill v. NCAA*, where two Stanford University student-athletes challenged the NCAA's drug testing program at NCAA national championship tournaments, California's high court utilized the familiar three-part Fourth Amendment test outlined above to reach the conclusion that the NCAA's drug testing program did not violate California's Constitutionally guaranteed right to privacy. Similarly, in *Bally v. Northeastern*, 532 N.E.2d 49 (Mass. 1989), the Massachusetts Supreme Judicial Court held that Massachusetts' right of privacy law was not implicated by Northeastern University's student-athlete drug testing program since the student's informational privacy was not violated as required for a violation of the state law.

VII. Consenting to a Drug Test

A sports organization's primary defense against an athlete's legal challenge of a drug testing program is that a test must stand because the athlete expressly consented to the test. However, even where consent is given by an athlete, determining whether this consent is valid is not always an easy matter.

A consent is valid if it is given voluntarily, intelligently and freely, "without any duress, coercion or subtle promises or threats calculated to flaw the free and unconstrained nature of the decision," *Schneckloth v.*

Bustamonte, 412 U.S. 218 (1973). A league or athletic association need not necessarily expressly announce those threats to an athlete in order to invalidate an athlete's consent to a drug test. For example, in striking down the University of Colorado's student-athlete drug testing program, the Supreme Court of Colorado ruled in *Derdeyn* that the student-athletes' signed consents to the test were invalid since they were required to be given as a prerequisite to intercollegiate athletic participation at the school. According to the court, the price for failing to sign the consents—potentially automatic ineligibility from athletic participation—was simply too high for the court to consider the consents to have been given freely.

Recent Developments

NFL Drug Testing Upheld.   Ruling that the National Football League's drug testing program did *not* involve state action, a federal district court in Pennsylvania refused to strike down the league's suspension of former Pittsburgh Steelers player Terry Long, after the player allegedly tested positive for performance enhancing steroids, *Long v. NFL,* 870 F.Supp. 101 (N.D.Pa. 1994). Long claimed that the drug test violated state and federal guarantees against unreasonable searches and seizures. However, in its November 22, 1994 ruling, the U.S. District Court for the Western District of Pennsylvania held that the NFL's relationship with the City of Pittsburgh failed to pass both the "symbiotic relationship" and the "close nexus" tests for determining state action. In ruling that no "symbiotic relationship" existed between the Steelers and Pittsburgh, the court found that while the city may profit from the activities of its NFL franchise, this business association was too tenuous to justify a finding that the league should be considered a state actor and therefore should be subject to federal Constitutional claims. Second, in finding that Long's complaint failed to sufficiently allege a "close nexus" between the NFL and the state, the court disagreed with the player's contention that a legally sufficient relationship between the NFL and Pittsburgh was evident by the city's acquiescence and implied support of the NFL's drug testing program. "Acquiescence or indirect involvement," the court concluded, "is not enough to show the requisite state action."

NCAA Toughens Standards.   At its annual convention in January, 1996, NCAA member colleges and universities overwhelmingly approved an amendment to Association bylaws that calls for the permanent ineligibility of a student-athlete who fails two drug tests. The measure, adopted as 1996 Proposal 68, becomes effective on August 1, 1996. Prior NCAA bylaws provided that a student-athlete who fails two drug tests would become permanently ineligible only if that second failed drug test came *after* the student-athlete's eligibility had been restored following the temporary loss of eligibility after a first failed test.

References

A. Cases
Anabele v. Ford, 653 F.Supp. 22 (W.D.Ark. 1985)
Bally v. Northeastern, 532 N.E.2d 49 (Mass. 1989)
Hill v. NCAA, 865 P.2d 633 (Cal. 1994)
Horsemen's Benevolent and Protective Assn. v. State Racing Commission, 532 N.E.2d 644 (Mass. 1989)
Long v. NFL, 870 F.Supp. 101 (N.D.Pa. 1994)
O'Halloran v. University of Washington, 679 F.Supp. 997 (W.D. Wash. 1988)
Penny v. Kennedy, 846 F.2d 1563 (6th Cir. 1988)
Schneckloth v. Bustamonte, 412 U.S. 218 (1973)
Schaill v. Tippecanoe County School Corp., 864 F.2d 1309 (7th Cir. 1988)
Shoemaker v. Handel, 795 F.2d 1136 (3rd Cir. 1986)

Skinner v. Railway Labor Executives' Assn., 489 U.S. 602 (1989)

University of Colorado v. Derdeyn, 863 P.2d 929 (Colo. 1993)

Vernonia School District 47J v. Acton, 115 S.Ct. 2386 (1995)

B. Publications

———. (August 1994). Butch Reynolds Runs Into a Stumbling Block. *Sports Law Monthly*, 3.

1995-96 NCAA Manual. National Collegiate Athletic Association: Overland Park, KS.

Official Notice, 1996 NCAA Convention, at 146-47. National Collegiate Athletic Association: Overland Park, KS.

4.27

Disabled Athletes

John T. Wolohan
Iowa State University

In athletics, the line between lawful refusal to extend eligibility requirements and illegal discrimination against handicapped persons is getting cloudier all the time. This is especially true since 1990, when the Americans with Disabilities Act [hereinafter cited as ADA] was signed into law. Yet, even with the enactment of the ADA, handicapped athletes still face a number of obstacles in their struggle to participate in athletics. There are two primary areas of concern involving handicapped athletes. The first area of concern is with those athletes who have either lost the use of a limb or vital organ (Wong, 1994). In an attempt to protect or shield themselves from liability, as well as to protect the athlete, a number of athletic organizations have developed policies prohibiting athletes with certain medical conditions or disabilities from participating in athletics or other extra curriculum activities. The rationale behind prohibiting athletes with disabilities from participating in athletics often has been based on the American Medical Association's (AMA) Recommendations for Participation in Competitive Sports (American Medical Association, 1976). The AMA guidelines recommend barring athletes with particular disabilities from certain sports (Wong, 1994). The guidelines which were intended to assist physicians in making participation decisions concerning athletes with certain medical conditions or disabilities, were last revised in 1976, and are no longer distributed by the AMA (Mitten, 1992).

The second area of dispute involves students who due to their disability were withheld in school and now wish to participate in high school athletics after reaching the state athletic association's age requirement (Wolohan, 1996). Every State high school athletic association has a cut off date after which a student is denied the opportunity to participate in interscholastic athletics. These age limit rules, which are designed to equalize competition between individuals and teams, have been defended on the grounds that: 1) it prevents older and more mature students from endangering the health and safety of younger students; 2) 19-year-old students are not the average high school student; and 3) it eliminated the possibility of athletes red-shirting in order to gain a competitive advantage (Wolohan, 1996). However, since it may often take a student with a disability extra time to finish high school, a state athletic associations' age requirement often prevents disabled students from participating in extracurricular activities, such as athletics.

■ ■ ■ ■

Representative Case

POOLE v. SOUTH PLAINFIELD BOARD OF EDUCATION
United States District Court, District of New Jersey
490 F. Supp. 948 (1980)

OPINION:

Richard Poole, a young man who was born with one kidney, was denied the right to participate in South Plainfield High School's interscholastic wrestling program due to his handicap. As a result, he has brought this suit against the South Plainfield Board of Education seeking compensatory damages. His complaint alleges a cause of action under 42 U.S.C. § 1983 for a violation of his Fourteenth Amendment rights and under 29 U.S.C. § 794, also known as § 504 of the Rehabilitation Act of 1973, "which prohibits discrimination against an 'otherwise qualified handicapped individual' in federally funded programs 'solely by reason of his handicap.'" Southeastern Community College v. Davis, 442 U.S. 397, 400, 99 S. Ct. 2361, 2364, 60 L. Ed. 2d 980 (1979) quoting 29 U.S.C. § 794.

• • •

The Board has urged several grounds for rejection of the plaintiff's § 504 claim. As an initial matter, they assert that § 504 does not create a private cause of action. Although the question of whether this section creates a private cause of action is a matter in dispute nationally. See Southeastern Community College v. Davis, 442 U.S. 397, 404 fn. 5, 99 S. Ct. 2361, 2366, 60 L. Ed. 2d 980 (1979), it has been resolved in favor of a private party's standing in the Third Circuit. Doe v. Colautti, 592 F.2d 704, 708 fn. 8 (1979). The Board has also argued that even if § 504 creates a private cause of action, it only creates an action for injunctive relief and not one for damages. It is true that in Doe v. Colautti the plaintiff was only seeking injunctive relief, but in Leary v. Crapsey, 566 F.2d 863 (2d Cir. 1977), the first case cited by the Third Circuit in support of the proposition that a private cause of action exists, the plaintiff was seeking monetary as well as injunctive relief. The decision in Leary is a sound one.

There are many plaintiffs for whom injunctive relief can only come too late. Mr. Poole is one of these, since he has already graduated from the South Plainfield High School and cannot, therefore, participate in its wrestling program. If he can prove that he was a victim of illegal discrimination, he should be entitled to some form of relief.

Monetary damages are the most usual form of relief given to successful plaintiffs, and I conclude that they are appropriately sought here.

• • •

The Board's second objection is that its interscholastic wrestling program does not come within the purview of § 504 since it "was not the recipient of federal funds for its interscholastic athletic program during the period of plaintiff's enrollment in the school system." Defendant's brief at page 7.

It is, of course, clear from the statutory language that § 504 is only applicable to a "program or activity receiving Federal financial assistance." What is not clear is the definition of "program or activity."

The Board admits in the affidavit of William Foley that it receives federal assistance for a number of its projects and activities. It argues, however, that unless the federal aid is received for the specific program that a handicapped individual is denied access to, in this case interscholastic athletics, that § 504 does not apply. The Board has cited no authority other than the statutory language itself in support of this proposition.

The Board's restrictive definition does not seem to be in keeping with the broad remedial purpose of the Rehabilitation Act of 1973. See 29 U.S.C. § 701 (Congressional declaration of purpose). Moreover, it is a definition that the Department of Health, Education and Welfare has rejected in its regulations interpreting § 504.

According to 45 CFR § 84.2 the regulations are applicable to each "recipient" of Federal Assistance from HEW. A "recipient" is defined as:

(A)ny state or its political subdivision, any instrumentality of a state or its political subdivision, any public or private agency, institution, organization, or other entity, or any person to which Federal financial assistance is extended directly or through another recipient, including any successor, assignee, or transferee of a recipient, but excluding the ultimate beneficiary of the assistance.

45 CFR § 84.3(f).

The South Plainfield Board of Education certainly meets this definition of a "recipient." What, then, are the duties of "recipients" like the defendants here, who operate schools? As the plaintiff's brief has pointed out, the regulations at 45 CFR § 84.37 state:

Nonacademic services:

(a) General.

(1) A recipient to which this subpart applies shall provide nonacademic and extracurricular services and activities in such manner as is necessary to afford handicapped students an equal opportunity for participation in such services and activities.

(2) Nonacademic and extracurricular services and activities may include counseling services, physical recreational athletics, transportation, health services, recreational activities, special interest groups or clubs sponsored by the recipients, referrals to agencies which provide assistance to handicapped persons, and employment of students, including both employment by the recipient and assistance in making available outside employment.

• • •

(c) Physical education and athletics.

(1) In providing physical education courses and athletics and similar programs and activities to any of its students, a recipient to which this subpart applies may not discriminate on the basis of handicap. A recipient that offers physical education courses or that operates or sponsors interscholastic, club, or intramural athletics shall provide to qualified handicapped students an equal opportunity for participation in these activities.

(2) A recipient may offer to handicapped students physical education and athletic activities that are separate or different from those offered to nonhandicapped students only if separation or differentiation is consistent with the requirements of § 84.34 and only if no qualified handicapped student is denied the opportunity to compete for teams or to participate in courses that are not separate or different."

Section 84.34, which is referred to in the regulation that I have just read, states in relevant part:

In providing or arranging for the provision of nonacademic and extracurricular services and activities, including meals, recess periods, and the services and activities set forth in § 84.37(a)(2), a recipient shall ensure that handicapped persons participate with nonhandicapped persons in such activities and services to the maximum extent appropriate to the needs of the handicapped person in question.

45 CFR § 84.34(b). It is clear from 45 CFR § 84.31 that these regulations are applicable to a recipient, even though the funds received are not for the specific program involved in the handicapped person's claims. According to § 84.31,

(these regulations apply) to preschool, elementary, secondary, and adult education facilities that receive or benefit from Federal financial assistance and to recipients that operate . . . such programs or activities.

I am convinced that in promulgating these regulations, the Secretary of HEW manifested his belief that § 504 of the Rehabilitation Act of 1973 was applicable to entities like the South Plainfield Board of Education in all of its interscholastic athletic activities if it received federal moneys for any of its programs, athletic or otherwise.

• • •

I agree with the agency's interpretation, however, insofar as it finds § 504 applicable to all of the activities engaged in by a school system receiving federal funds. It seems absurd to ban discrimination in a discrete area of a school system that receives federal funds while permitting it throughout the rest of the system. I do not believe that Congress intended to ban discrimination during school hours while permitting it in officially sponsored extracurricular activities. This belief is supported by the fact that federal aid to any program in a school system releases local money for other uses, thereby benefiting those programs that are not direct beneficiaries of the federal aid. . . . I hold, therefore, that § 504 is applicable to the interscholastic athletic activities of a school system receiving federal funding even if none of the federal funds are specifically spent on interscholastic athletics.

Having dispensed with the defendant's objections to the plaintiff's standing and its assertion that § 504 is inapplicable to its athletic program, it is necessary to deal with the defense's substantive claim that the allegations made by Richard Poole do not make out a violation of § 504.

• • •

Richard Poole, at the time in question, was a vigorous, athletically inclined high school student in good health. His only physical problem was the absence of one kidney from birth. His single kidney was, however, a healthy one. Mr. Poole, the son of a former state champion wrestler, participated in the school wrestling program in his eighth, ninth and tenth grades. He was denied the right to participate during his eleventh and twelfth grade years, however, when the Medical Director of the South Plainfield Board of Education, Dr. John F. Scalera, advised the Board that it should not allow Mr. Poole to participate in its wrestling program because of his physical condition. Both Richard and his parents wanted Richard to participate in the high school wrestling program, even after they were made aware of the school system's concern over possible injury to his kidney. Despite protests and an offer to sign a waiver by Richard and his parents, the Board decided to heed Dr. Scalera's advice. The Pooles' subsequent appeal to the New Jersey Commissioner of Education proved unsuccessful and by the time Richard graduated from South Plainfield High School in June 1978, he had been denied participation in the wrestling program for two school years.

Although some doctors, and especially the school system's medical director, Dr. Scalera, believe that it is inadvisable for a student with one kidney to participate in wrestling, there is also medical opinion, represented by the opinions of Drs. Fred Lathrop and Joseph S. Torg, that Richard could safely participate in the sport of wrestling. Giving the plaintiff the benefit of all doubts, it could be concluded that the better view was that participation in wrestling was safe for Richard.

The Board, however, decided to prohibit Richard's participation, after seeking a legal opinion from their counsel as well as the medical opinion of Dr. Lathrop. It seems that their decision was based on a serious concern over the possibility of injury to Richard's kidney and their moral and legal responsibility in the event of such an eventuality. This view is reflected in the opinions of both their physician and their lawyer. Dr. Scalera wrote to the Board that:

> It is in the best interest of the students to bar them from contact sports despite the wrath from both students and parents. How can you justify and explain to the student who has one kidney and the other destroyed that his death or lifelong attachment to a kidney machine was worth the "glory."

Affidavit of Leonard A. Tobias, filed March 31, 1980, Exhibit B. In a similar vein, the Board's attorney, Robert J. Cirafesi, included the following conclusion in his opinion letter to the Board:

> Although, at first blush, a complete release and waiver would appear to resolve the problem at hand, such an approach side-steps the basic question of responsibility. In other words, in my opinion, the Board of Education cannot abrogate its responsibility towards the pupils in question by

placing the entire burden of responsibility upon the pupils and parents. In this type of situation, the school board stands in loco parentis, which means literally "in place of the parents." As such, it is for the Board of Education to exercise its collective judgment in this matter and a waiver or release from the parents based upon their own judgments that their sons should be allowed to participate cannot, in my opinion, abrogate the Board's ultimate responsibility.

Brief of Defendant, Exhibit A.

From these letters, together with the medical evidence discussed above, it could be inferred that the Board of Education decided that it was part of its function to protect its students against rational judgments reached by themselves and their parents. In effect, the Board's decision stands the doctrine of in loco parentis on its head. Traditionally, this doctrine has meant that a school system must act "in place of the parents" when the parents are absent. See Brinkerhoff v. Merselis' Executors, 24 N.J.L. 680, 683 (Sup.Ct.1855); A.S. v. B.S., 139 N.J.Super. 366, 369, 354 A.2d 100 (Ch.1976). Here, the South Plainfield Board has acted in a manner contrary to the express wishes of parents, who, together with their son, have reached a rational decision concerning the risk involved in wrestling.

As the Supreme Court recently recognized in Parham v. J.R., 442 U.S. 584, 99 S. Ct. 2493, 61 L. Ed. 2d 101 (1979), a state may sometimes disregard wishes of parents "when (a child's) physical . . . health is jeopardized." Id. at 603, 99 S. Ct. at 2504, but the same decision also makes it clear that such instances are rare and usually premised upon child neglect or abuse rather than upon a mere difference of rational opinion.Id. at 602-603, 99 S. Ct. at 2504-2505.

• • •

It can be concluded, therefore, that the South Plainfield Board's perception of its role in the face of disagreeing parents armed with respectable medical authority was an unusual one. To find it unusual, however, is not to say that it is prohibited. Many unusual things may be done so long as they violate neither statutory, common, nor constitutional law. The question of whether the Board's actions violated § 504 of the Rehabilitation Act of 1973 is, of course, the nub of this lawsuit.

I will now address that question on the basis of the facts that I have just outlined, with all inferences drawn in favor of the plaintiff.

In Southeastern Community College v. Davis, cited supra, the Supreme Court decided that a woman with a serious hearing impairment, requiring her to read lips, could be rejected from a training program for Registered Nurses on the basis of her handicap without violating

§ 504. In that case the Court's primary focus was on the question of whether the plaintiff was "qualified" for the nursing program. The court found that:

> It is not open to dispute that, as Southeastern's Associate Degree Nursing program currently is constituted, the ability to understand speech without reliance on lipreading is necessary for patient safety during the clinical phase of the program . . . this ability also is indispensable for many of the functions that a registered nurse performs.

Id., 442 U.S. at 407, 99 S. Ct. at 2367. Since the Court held that § 504 did not require the college to change its program to accommodate handicapped students, Id. at 411-12, 99 S. Ct. at 2369-2370, the college's hearing requirement was sustained. The Court's holding, as it affects this case, can be summarized by quoting its definition of the language of § 504: "An otherwise qualified person is one who is able to meet all of a program's requirements in spite of his handicap." Id. at 406, 99 S. Ct. at 2367.

The question to be decided in this case, then, is whether Richard Poole Jr., was able to meet all of South Plainfield's interscholastic wrestling program's requirements in spite of the fact that he was born with one kidney. The Board's position is that Richard is unqualified because he failed to pass the physical that he was required to take in order to participate. It is clear, however, that the only reason he failed the exam was the absence of a paired organ, i. e., one kidney, and the doctor's legitimate fear of injury to the other. The Board has nowhere suggested that Richard was incapable of pinning his adversary to the mat or meeting the training requirements of a team sport. The board seems to have premised its decision on fear of injury to Richard's only kidney. It is undoubtedly true that injury to Richard's kidney would have grave consequences, but so might other injuries that might befall him or any other member of the wrestling team. Hardly a year goes by that there is not at least one instance of the tragic death of a healthy youth as a result of competitive sports activity. Life has risks. The purpose of § 504, however, is to permit handicapped individuals to live life as fully as they are able, without paternalistic authorities deciding that certain activities are too risky for them.

Much of the school's brief is devoted to the proposition that Richard, as a minor, could not execute a legally binding waiver or consent form relieving the Board of responsibility. I believe that this argument misconceives the Board's role. This is not a contract. This is a young man who, with his parents' support and approval, wishes to live an active life despite a congenital defect. The Board's responsibility is to see that he does not pursue this course in a foolish manner. They therefore have a duty to alert Richard and his parents to the dangers involved and to require them to deal with the matter rationally.

In the present case, the Pooles not only consulted their family physician, Dr. Lathrop, but Dr. Torg of the Temple University Center for Sports Medicine and Science as well. Both of these doctors felt that Richard could participate. The Pooles also consulted with Gerald C. Leeman, a wrestling coach at Lehigh University, as to the types and frequencies of injuries encountered by wrestlers. The Board knew of these consultations but insisted nonetheless in imposing its own rational decision over the rational decision of the Pooles. I hold that it had neither the duty nor the right under § 504 to do so. This conclusion is shared by HEW, as reflected in a policy interpretation of § 504 published at 43 Fed.Reg. 36034, 35 (August 14, 1978).

Whatever duty the Board may have had towards Richard was satisfied once it became clear that the Pooles knew of the dangers involved and rationally reached a decision to encourage their son's participation in interscholastic wrestling. I believe that if the plaintiff can prove the facts as I have inferred them to exist in this opinion, then he will be entitled to a judgment that the Board violated § 504.

I have not addressed any of the constitutional issues raised because I have been able to resolve the questions presented on a statutory basis.

• • •

The defendant's motion must, therefore, be denied.

■ ■ ■ ■

Fundamental Concepts

As recently as 1970, children with learning disabilities were denied access into a number of state public school systems because it was thought that their presence would interfere with the learning environment of non handicapped students (Clement, 1988). In the early 1970's, Congress began enacting federal legislation designed to increase the opportunities available to handicapped individuals (Clement, 1988). The first law passed by Congress to impact athletes and their fight to participate in athletics was **The Rehabilitation Act of 1973**. Section 504 of the Rehabilitation Act states that:

> No otherwise qualified handicapped individual in the United States, . . . shall solely by reason of his handicap, be excluded from participation in, be denied the benefits of, or be subjected to discrimination under any program or activity receiving Federal financial assistance . . . (29 U.S.C. 794 (Supp. V 1993))

One of the stated intents of the Rehabilitation Act was to provide handicapped individuals with the opportunity to participate in physical education and athletic programs or activities without being discriminated against due to their handicap.

In order for an individual to successfully pursue a claim under §504, he or she must establish four elements: 1) that he or she is a **handicapped individual;** 2) that he or she is **otherwise qualified** for the athletic activity; 3) that he or she is being excluded from athletic participation **solely by reason of** their disabilities; and 4) that the **school, or institution is receiving federal financial assistance** (29 U.S.C. 794. (Supp. V 1993)).

Since most challenges under § 504 hinge on the determination of the **otherwise qualified** element or the **solely by reason of** element, an examination of the meaning of those two elements is important. The United States Supreme Court in *Southeastern Community College v. Davis*, interpreted the phrase otherwise qualified person to mean someone who is able to meet all of a program's requirements in spite of his handicap (422 U.S. 397, at 406 (1979)). Davis, who suffered from a serious hearing disability, sought entry into Southeastern Community College's school of nursing. The Supreme Court, in upholding the school's rejection of Davis' application, stated that § 504 of the Rehabilitation Act does not compel an institution to disregard the disabilities of handicapped individuals or to make substantial modifications in their programs to allow disabled person to participate. In finding that Davis' hearing disability made it impossible for her to safely complete the nursing program, the Supreme Court held that neither the language nor the purpose of § 504 required recipients of federal funds to make substantial modifications to accommodate the handicapped.

In *Alexander v. Choate*, the Supreme Court addressed what types of modifications would be required under § 504 when it held that while a grantee need not be required to make fundamental or substantial modifications to accommodate the handicapped, **it may be required to make reasonable ones**. Reasonable accommodation may include: 1) Making facilities used by employees readily accessible to and usable by handicapped persons; and 2) job restructuring, part-time or modified work schedules, acquisition or modification of equipment or devices, the provision of readers or interpreters, and similar actions (34 C.F.R. § 104.12. (b)).

The excluded **solely by reason of** the disability requirement is met if the handicapped individual is being excluded due to their handicap or disability. For example in Poole, the plaintiff was being excluded from participation in athletics "solely by reason of" the fact he had one kidney. The issue of whether someone is being excluded "solely by reason of" their disability is more difficult when an individual due to an illness or learning disability is over the athletic association's maximum age requirement by the time he or she reaches their senior year in high school. *University Interscholastic League (UIL) and Bailey Marshall v. Buchanan* is a perfect illustration the problem presented in these cases. In *UIL v. Buchanan* two 19-year-old students, who were diagnosed with learning disabilities, sought a permanent injunction against the enforcement of UIL's rule requiring all athletes to be under 19 years old. In support of the age requirement, the UIL argued that the age requirement was necessary to ensure the safety of the participating student athletes and to ensure the equality of competitors. The UIL also argued that the age rule did not discriminate against the plaintiffs because of their handicaps, but was applied equally against both handicapped and non-handicapped students. Therefore, the plaintiffs were ineligible due to their ages, not their handicaps. The Court of Appeals, in affirming the trial court's injunction, enjoining UIL from enforcing the age rule against the plaintiffs, held that except for their handicaps the students would have turned nineteen after September 1 of their senior year and would have been age-eligible to participate in interscholastic athletics (at 302). In determining whether

UIL had made reasonable accommodations for the plaintiffs' disabilities, the Court of Appeals examined the waiver mechanism UIL had in place for other eligibility rules. The waiver of the age rule, the Court of Appeals found would be a reasonable accommodation by UIL to ensure that handicapped athletes achieve meaningful access. The UIL's no exception policy to the age requirement, therefore, had to yield to the reasonable accommodation requirement of § 504 of the Rehabilitation Act.

On the heels of the Rehabilitation Act of 1973, Congress enacted the Education for all Handicapped Children Act of 1975. The purpose of the Education for all Handicapped Children Act was to increase the educational opportunity available to handicapped children by providing all handicapped children a free appropriate public education that emphasizes special education and related services designed to meet their unique needs (20 U.S.C. 1400 (c)). In 1990, the Education for all Handicapped Children Act was amended and renamed the Individuals with Disabilities Education Act (IDEA).

In order to satisfy the goal of the IDEA, local educational agencies, together with the handicapped student's teacher and parents are required to develop a written statement or individualized education program (IEP) outlining achievable educational objectives for the student. Although less specific with regard to athletics than those pursuant to § 504 of the Rehabilitation Act, the regulations adopted under the IDEA do require each public agency to ensure that a variety of educational programs and services, including physical education, available to non disabled children are available to those covered under the Act. Besides providing educational programs and services, each public agency is also required to provide nonacademic and extra-curricular activities and services in such manner as is necessary to afford children with disabilities an equal opportunity for participation in those services and activities (34 C.F.R. § 300.306(a)). For example, in *Lambert v. West Virginia State Board of Education*, a high school basketball player, who has been deaf since birth, won the right to require her school to provide her with a sign language interpreter so that she could compete on the girl's basketball team. The student was provided with a signer for her basic courses, but the State Board of Education refused to provide a signer for her vocational classes or her extracurricular activities. In holding that the Board of Education was required to provide a signer for the plaintiff, the court found that the assistance of a signer was a reasonable accommodation that provided the plaintiff with equal access to extracurricular activities.

Another example of a student-athletes successfully using the IDEA to gain participation rights is *Crocker v. Tennessee Secondary School Athletic Association (TSSAA)*. In *Crocker* the plaintiff transferred from a private school into his local public high school so that he could receive the special education he needed, which was not available in the private school. When the plaintiff attempted to participate in interscholastic athletics at his new school, the TSSAA ruled that he was ineligible. According to TSSAA rules, any student who transfers from one TSSAA member school to another is ineligible to participate in interscholastic sports for 12 months. The plaintiff argued that the TSSAA, by enforcing its transfer rule, was depriving him of his rights guaranteed under the IDEA. In ruling for Crocker, the court held that since the plaintiff's transfer was motivated by his handicap, TSSAA's refusal to waive its transfer rule violated the IDEA.

The court in *Crocker*, however, failed to address the issue of whether the plaintiff's participation in interscholastic athletics was a related service that should have been incorporated into his "Individual Education Program" (IEP). The importance of including participation in interscholastic athletics in a student's IEP can be seen in *T.H. v. Montana High School Association (MHSA)*. In *T.H. v. MHSA*, the plaintiff, after being diagnosed as having a learning disability, was provided with an IEP in accordance with the IDEA. One component of T.H.'s IEP was that he participates in interscholastic athletics as a motivational tool. Before his senior year, the Montana High School Association ruled T.H. ineligible to compete in interscholastic athletics due to his age. In finding for the plaintiff, the court held that while students have no constitutional right to participate in interscholastic sports; it is a privilege that may be withdrawn by the school or a voluntary association, when participation in interscholastic sports is included as a component of the IEP as a related service, the privilege of competing in interscholastic sports is transformed into a federally protected right (at 10).

Another piece of legislation effecting the rights of handicapped athletes is the Amateur Sports Act. The Amateur Sports Act names the United States Olympic Committee (USOC) as the coordinator of amateur athletics in the United States (Wong, 1996). As the coordinator of amateur athletics, one of the goals of the USOC is to "encourage and provide assistance to amateur athletic programs and competition for handicapped individuals, including, where feasible, the expansion of opportunities for meaningful participation by handicapped individuals in programs of athletic competition for able-bodied individuals" (36 U.S.C. § 374 (13)). In order to accomplish its goal the USOC established the Committee on Sports for the Disabled. The Committee helps disabled athletes by breaking down unnecessary barriers to competition and supporting organizations that provide sports experiences for disabled individuals. (Wong, 1996).

Recent Developments

The Americans with Disabilities Act (ADA). Perhaps the most powerful weapon handicapped athletes have in their fight to participate in interscholastic athletics is the ADA. Signed into law July 26, 1990, the purpose of the ADA is "to provide a clear and comprehensive national mandate for the elimination of discrimination against individuals with disabilities." The ADA focuses on eradicating barriers, by requiring public entities to consider whether reasonable accommodations could be made to remove any barrier created by a person's disability (Wolohan, 1996). The ADA defines a "qualified individual with a disability" as any handicapped or physically or mentally disabled individual "who, with or without reasonable modifications to rules, policies, or practices, the removal of architectural, communication . . . barriers, or the provision or auxiliary aids and services, meets the essential eligibility requirements for the receipt of services or the participation in programs or activities provided by a public entity" (42 U.S.C. 12115). The ADA is divided into five sections covering the rights of the disabled in the area of employment, public services, transportation and telecommunications. The three sections athletic administrators should be aware of are Title I which covers Employment, Title II which covers Public Services and Title III which covers Public Accommodations and Services operated by Private Entities.

Title I—Employment. Title I provides that: "no covered entity shall discriminate against a qualified individual with a disability because of the disability of such individual in regard to job application procedures, the hiring, advancement, or discharge of employees, employee compensation, job training, and other terms, conditions, and privileges of employment" (42 U.S.C. § 12112). Although the ADA has not provided for any preferential treatment or established any quotas in employment matters, athletic administrators should be aware that they may be required to make reasonable modifications to rules, policies, practices, including the removal of architectural barriers, or provide auxiliary aids and services in order for disabled or handicapped individuals to meet the essential eligibility requirements of the job. However, just because an employer is required to make reasonable modifications, disabled individuals must still be able to perform the essential functions of the job.

Title II—Public Services. The section that covers the activities of high school athletic associations is Title II—Public Services. Title II, which is based on § 504 of the Rehabilitation Act, provides that: "no qualified individual with a disability shall, by reason of such disability, be excluded from participation in or be denied the benefits of the services, programs, or activities of a public entity, or be subjected to discrimination by any such entity" (42 U.S.C. § 12132).

In interpreting the meaning of Title II, the courts use the case history of § 504 of the Rehabilitation Act. Therefore to establish a violation of Title II of the ADA an individual must establish the following elements: 1) that he or she is a "qualified individual with a disability"; 2) that he or she is "otherwise qualified" for the activity; 3) that he or she is being excluded from athletic participation "solely by reason of" their disabilities; and (4) that he or she is being discriminated against by a public entity.

Once again the more prevalent issues under Title II are those dealing with overaged students who wish to participate in interscholastic athletics. Two jurisdictions, the Eighth Circuit in *Pottgen v. Missouri State High School Activities Association*, and the Sixth Circuit in *Sandison v. Michigan High School Athletic Association*, have held that waiving a state high school athletic association's age requirement was not required under the ADA since it would constitute a fundamental alteration in the nature of the state's interscholastic programs and would impose an undue hardship on the organization. In other jurisdictions, the courts are evenly divided on whether or not students have the right to participate after reaching the age requirement.

Title III—Public Accommodations and Services Operated by Private Entities. The provisions of Title III provide that: "no individual shall be discriminated against on the basis of disability in the full and equal enjoyment of the goods, services, facilities, privileges, advantages, or accommodations of any place of public accommodation by any person who owns, leases, or operates a place of public accommodation" (42 U.S.C. § 12182).

In *Anderson v. Little League Baseball, Inc.*, a youth baseball coach, who is confined to a wheelchair and had coached Little League Baseball for the previous three years as an on-field coach, sued the League after it adopted a policy prohibiting coaches in wheel chairs from on-field coaching. In support of the policy, the League pointed out that the ADA specifically "does not require a public accommodation to permit an individual to participate . . . when that individual poses a direct threat to the health or safety of others" (28 C.F.R. § 36.208). The stated intent of the policy was to protect the players from collisions with the wheel chair during the game. In ruling for the coach, the court rejected the League's argument and held that the League's policy fell markedly short of the requirements of the ADA. The found no evidence indicating that the plaintiff posed a direct threat to the health or safety of others.

Athletes with AIDS. A growing area of concern for athletic administrators is whether individuals testing HIV positive or with the AIDS virus should be allowed to participate in athletic competitions. The United States Supreme Court in *School Board of Nassau County v. Arline* held that individuals with contagious diseases could be defined as handicapped persons under the meaning of § 504 of the Rehabilitation Act (480 U.S. at 287).

While the plaintiff in *Arline* had tuberculosis, not HIV or AIDS, and the Supreme Court refused to address whether § 504 would cover individuals with HIV or AIDS, the issue was addressed in *Doe v. Dolton Elementary School District*. In Doe v. Dolton Elementary School District, a twelve-year-old student who was infected with AIDS was excluded from attending school. In ruling for the student, the court relying on *School Board of Nassau County v. Arline* held that an individual with AIDS was likely to qualify as a handicapped individual under § 504. Although the court did allow Doe to attend classes, it also placed certain limits on the activities the plaintiff could engage in, one of the limits being contact sports (Hums, 1991).

With increased public awareness about the transmission of HIV and the AIDS virus, however, administrators should expect to address questions involving the participation by individuals testing HIV positive or with the AIDS virus (Hums, 1991). For example, should athletes who test HIV positive be excluded from participation in contact sports, such as football? The issue has yet to been tested in the courts, yet as illustrated by Magic Johnson and Tommy Morrison, administrators should be prepared to address the issue.

References

A. Cases

Alexander v. Choate, 469 U.S. 287 (1985).
Booth v. El Paso Independent School District, Civil No. A-90-CA-764 (Tex. Dist. Ct. 1990).
Crocker v. Tennessee Secondary School Athletic Association, 980 F.2d 382 (6th Cir. 1992).

Doe v. Dolton Elementary School District, 694 F.Supp. 440 (1988).

Interscholastic League and Bailey Marshall v. Buchanan, 848 S.W. 2d. 298 (1993).

T.H. v. Montana High School Association, CV 92-150-BLG-JFB (1992).

Johnson v. Florida High School Activities Association, 899 F.Supp. 579 (M.D.Fla. 1995).

Lambert v. West Virginia Secondary School Activities Comm'n, 447 S.E.2d 901 (W.Va. 1994).

Poole v. South Plainfield Board of Education, 490 F.Supp. 948 (D.N.J. 1980).

Pottgen v. Missouri State High School Activities Association, 40 F.3d 926 (8th Cir. 1994).

Sandison v. Michigan High School Athletic Association, 863 F.Supp. 483 (E.D.Mich. 1994).

School Board of Nassau County v. Arline, 480 U.S. 273 (1987).

Southeastern Community College v. Davis, 422 U.S. 397 (1979).

B. Publications

Medical Evaluation of the Athlete: A Guide, rev'd. (1976). Chicago, American Medical Association.

Clement, Annie. (1988). *Law in Sport and Physical Activity*.

Hums, Mary A. (1991). AIDS and Sports Participants: Legal and Ethical Considerations for School Sports Programs. 1 *Journal of Legal Aspects of Sport* 22-35.

Mitten, Matthew J. (1992). Amateur Athletes with Handicaps or Physical Abnormalities: Who Makes the Participation Decision? 71 *Nebraska Law Review* 987.

Wong, Glenn M. (1994). *Essentials of Amateur Sports Law*, (2d ed.).

C. Legislation

The Rehabilitation Act of 1973, 29 U.S.C. § 701 *et seq.*

The Individuals with Disabilities Education Act, 20 U.S.C. § 1400 *et seq.*

The Americans with Disabilities Act, 42 U.S.C. § 12101 *et seq.*

The Amateur Sports Act, 36 U.S.C. § 371-396.

D. Selected Readings

Jones, Cathy J. (1992). College Athletes: Illness or Injury and the Decision to Return to Play, 40 *Buffalo Law Review* 113.

Hums, Mary A. (1994). AIDS in the Sports Arena: After Magic Johnson, Where Do We Go from Here. 4 *Journal of Legal Aspects of Sport* 59-65.

Shepard, Robert E. (1991). Why Can't Johnny Read or Play? The Participation Rights of Handicapped Student-Athletes. 1 *Seton Hall J. Sport Law* 163.

Religious Issues

Thomas H. Sawyer
Indiana State University

Do invocations delivered before high school games or invocations and benedictions before and after high school graduation ceremonies violate the Establishment Clause and the three-part *Lemon* test? In 1993 the answer is yes, even though the United States Supreme Court is narrowly divided on the issue evidenced by the 1992, 5-4 decision rendered in *Lee v. Weisman* (1992).

The United States District Court for the Northern District of Georgia found that invocations given only by Protestant Christian clergy before football games are unconstitutional; however, the court held open the door for invocations provided that a system be employed to randomly select students, parents, or staff from the school district to deliver messages before the games (*Jager v. Douglas County School District and School Board*, 1987). But, the court did find that the practice of delivering invocations violated the Establishment Clause of the First Amendment.

■ ■ ■ ■

Representative Case

JAGER v. DOUGLAS COUNTY SCHOOL DISTRICT
United States Court of Appeals for the Eleventh Circuit
862 F.2d 824 (1989)

OPINION: JOHNSON, Circuit Judge:

This case involves invocations which are delivered prior to public high school football games in Douglas County, Georgia. These football games are school-sponsored activities which are played at a stadium owned by the school system. The schools furnish the equipment used by the participants, and the coaches who supervise these activities are employed by the school system. Taxpayer funds are used to pay the operating costs for the stadium lights and public address system. We hold that the practice of beginning these games with an invocation violates the Establishment Clause of the First Amendment.

I. Facts

In the fall of 1985, Doug Jager, then a member of the Douglas County High School marching band, objected to his school principal about the practice of having pre-game invocations delivered at home football games. The invocations often opened with the words "let us bow our heads" or "let us pray" and frequently invoked reference to Jesus Christ or closed with the words "in Jesus' name we pray." These invocations conflict with the Jagers' sincerely held religious beliefs. The Douglas County High School principal informed the band director of Doug

Jager's objections to the prayers. The band director proceeded to lecture Doug on Christianity.

On June 2, 1986, Douglas County School Superintendent Kathryn Shehane, the school system attorney, the Jagers and their counsel, and Reverends Jamie E. Jenkins and Donald Mountain of the Douglas County Ministerial Association ("DCMA") met and discussed two alternative proposals for modifying the invocation practices: an inspirational wholly secular speech and an "equal access" plan that would retain some religious content. The Jagers rejected the equal access approach, and notified the school system attorney that the secular inspirational speech was the only feasible alternative to the invocation practice. Upon the Jagers' rejection of the equal access plan, Reverends Jenkins and Mountain drafted a compromise proposal. The stated purpose of the alternative draft was to "perpetuate and regulate the traditional invocation as part of the opening ceremonies of school athletic events." R1-24-16. In August 1986, the plaintiffs agreed to reconsider the Jenkins/Mountain version of the equal access plan if prayers voluntarily ceased at football games in the interim.

In September 1986, Superintendent Shehane met with the principals of Douglas County high schools. The group decided to proceed with pregame invocations pursuant to the equal access plan. On September 15, 1986, the high school principals informed their schools that the equal access plan, which the district court found to be coextensive with the Jenkins/Mountain plan, would govern future games, including those scheduled for September 26, 1986.

Under the terms of the equal access plan, all school clubs and organizations can designate club members to give invocations, and any student, parent or school staff member can seek to deliver an invocation. The plan specifies that the student government will randomly select the invocation speaker, and no ministers will be involved in selecting invocation speakers or in delivering invocations. In addition, the schools will not monitor the content of the invocations.

On September 19, 1986, the Jagers filed a complaint in the United States District Court for the Northern District of Georgia. The district court issued a temporary restraining order enjoining the Douglas County School District ("the School District") from conducting or permitting religious invocations prior to any athletic event at the school stadium.

The case was tried in the district court in November 1986. On February 3, 1987, the district court (1) declared the pregame invocations unconstitutional, (2) denied the Jagers' request for a permanent injunction, (3) rejected the Jagers' claim based on the Free Exercise of Religion Clause of the First Amendment, and (4) rejected the Jag-

ers' claim that the School District violated the Georgia Constitution.

After the School District filed a Motion for Clarification, the district court entered an additional order in which it held that the equal access plan was constitutional on its face and did not violate the Establishment Clause. The court expressly declined to determine whether the equal access plan was unconstitutional as applied. The district court denied the Jagers' request for declaratory and injunctive relief relating to the equal access plan.

On June 2, 1987, the district court determined that the Jagers were "prevailing parties" under 42 U.S.C.A. § 1988 and thus were entitled to attorneys' fees. On August 31, 1987, the district court awarded attorneys' fees, after decreasing the amount sought by the Jagers by 25 percent. The appeals and cross-appeals from the district court's orders on the merits and on the question of attorneys' fees were then consolidated.

II. Discussion

A. Equal Access Plan's Facial Validity

The district court held that the equal access plan, which involves the random selection of an invocation speaker, was constitutional on its face. The Jagers challenge this holding on appeal.

The Establishment Clause of the First Amendment forbids the enactment of any law or practice "respecting an establishment of religion." U.S. Const. Amend. I. The religion clauses of the First Amendment require that states "pursue a course of complete neutrality toward religion." Wallace v. Jaffree, 472 U.S. 38, 60, 105 S. Ct. 2479, 2491, 86 L. Ed. 2d 29 (1985) ("Jaffree II"). To determine whether state action embodies the neutrality that comports with the Establishment Clause, this Court must apply a three-pronged analysis. See Lemon v. Kurtzman, 403 U.S. 602, 612-13, 91 S. Ct. 2105, 2111, 29 L. Ed. 2d 745 (1971). We must ask whether (1) the Douglas County School Superintendent and the school principals had a secular purpose for adopting the equal access plan, (2) the plan's primary effect is one that neither advances nor inhibits religion, and (3) the plan does not result in an excessive entanglement of government with religion. Id. at 612-13, 91 S. Ct. at 2111. State action violates the Establishment Clause if it fails to meet any of these three criteria. Edwards v. Aguillard, 482 U.S. 578, 107 S. Ct. 2573, 2577, 96 L. Ed. 2d 510 (1987).

The School District argues that the Lemon test does not apply here. Instead, the School District contends that Marsh v. Chambers, 463 U.S. 783, 103 S. Ct. 3330, 77 L. Ed. 2d 1019 (1983), provides the standard for determining whether the equal access plan violates the Establishment Clause. In Marsh, the Supreme Court upheld Nebraska's practice of commencing state legislative sessions with a prayer delivered by a chaplain employed by the state. In refusing to declare Nebraska's legislative invocation unconstitutional, the Court relied on the "unique history" associated with the practice of opening legislative sessions with a prayer. Id. at 791, 103 S. Ct. at 3335-3336. The practice existed at the time of the adoption of the First Amendment and had continued in many states to the present. See id. at 792, 103 S. Ct. at 3336 ("In light of the unambiguous and unbroken history of more than 200 years, there can be no doubt that the practice of opening legislative sessions with prayer has become part of the fabric of our society.") Since the Continental Congress and the First Congress opened their sessions with prayers, the Marsh Court concluded that the drafters of the Establishment Clause undoubtedly perceived no threat from legislative prayer and did not intend to prohibit legislative invocations. Id. at 791, 103 S. Ct. at 3335-3336.

Because Marsh was based on more than 200 years of the "unique history" of legislative invocations, it has no application to the case at bar. The instant case involves the "special context of the public elementary and secondary school system," Edwards, 107 S. Ct. at 2577, in which the Supreme Court "has been particularly vigilant in monitoring compliance with the Establishment Clause." Id. As the Supreme Court recently explained:

> The Lemon test has been applied in all cases since its adoption in 1971, except in Marsh v. Chambers, where the Court held that the Nebraska legislature's practice of opening a session with a prayer by a chaplain paid by the State did not violate the Establishment Clause. The Court based its conclusion in that case on the historical acceptance of the practice. Such a historical approach is not useful in determining the proper roles of church and state in public schools, since free public education was virtually nonexistent at the time the Constitution was adopted.

Edwards, 107 S. Ct. at 2577 n. 4 (citations omitted). Similarly, the present case does not lend itself to Marsh's historical approach because invocations at school-sponsored football games were nonexistent when the Constitution was adopted. Therefore, the Lemon test guides this Court's analysis in the case at bar.

1. Secular Purpose

The first prong of the Lemon test asks whether the challenged practice had a secular purpose. "In applying the purpose test, it is appropriate to ask 'whether government's actual purpose is to endorse or disapprove of religion.'" Jaffree II, 472 U.S. at 56, 105 S. Ct. at 2489 (quoting Lynch v. Donnelly, 465 U.S. 668, 690, 104 S. Ct.

1355, 1368, 79 L. Ed. 2d 604 (1984) (O'Connor, J., concurring)). Clearly, the equal access plan in the case at bar was adopted with the actual purpose of endorsing and perpetuating religion.

The district court found that pregame invocations serve four purposes: (1) to continue a long-standing custom and tradition, (2) to add a solemn and dignified tone to the proceedings, (3) to remind the spectators and players of the importance of sportsmanship and fair play, and (4) "to satisfy the genuine, good faith wishes on the part of a majority of the citizens of Douglas County to publicly express support for Protestant Christianity." R1-24-19. The School District could serve all of its cited secular purposes by requiring wholly secular inspirational speeches about sportsmanship, fair play, safety, and the values of teamwork and competition. Indeed, the Jagers offered to accept a pre-game invocation consisting of a secular inspirational speech. Since the School District rejected this compromise even though it would have fulfilled the three secular purposes of pregame invocations, it is clear that the School District was most interested in the fourth purpose served by the invocations. That is, the School District wanted to have invocations that publicly express support for Protestant Christianity.

"The unmistakable message of the Supreme Court's teachings is that the state cannot employ a religious means to serve otherwise legitimate secular interests." Karen B. v. Treen, 653 F.2d 897, 901 (5th Cir. Unit A 1981), aff'd mem., 455 U.S. 913, 102 S. Ct. 1267, 71 L. Ed. 2d 455 (1982). In choosing the equal access plan, the School District opted for an alternative that permits religious invocations, which by definition serve religious purposes, just like all public prayers. See Jaffree v. Wallace, 705 F.2d 1526, 1534 (11th Cir. 1983) ("Recognizing that prayer is the quintessential religious practice implies that no secular purpose can be satisfied. . . ."), aff'd, 472 U.S. 38, 105 S. Ct. 2479, 86 L. Ed. 2d 29 (1985) ("Jaffree I"). The School District's rejection of the alternative of wholly secular invocations makes it very clear that the School District's actual purpose in having pre-game invocations was religious. Consequently, the equal access plan fails to survive the Lemon test.

The conclusion that an intrinsically religious practice cannot meet the secular purpose prong of the Lemon test finds support in other cases. In Stone v. Graham, 449 U.S. 39, 101 S. Ct. 192, 66 L. Ed. 2d 199 (1980), the Supreme Court held that Kentucky's statute requiring the posting of a copy of the Ten Commandments in all public classrooms had no secular purpose. The Kentucky legislature required the following notation in small print at the bottom of each copy of the Ten Commandments: "The secular application of the Ten Commandments is clearly seen in its adoption as the fundamental legal code of Western Civilization and the Common Law of the United States." Id. at 41, 101 S. Ct. at 193 (quoting Ky.Rev.Stat. § 158.178 (1980)). Nonetheless, the Supreme Court held that "the pre-eminent purpose for posting the Ten Commandments on schoolroom walls is plainly religious in nature. The Ten Commandments are undeniably a sacred text in the Jewish and Christian faiths, and no legislative recitation of a supposed secular purpose can blind us to that fact." Id. at 41, 101 S. Ct. at 194 (footnote omitted). Likewise, the facts in the present case demonstrate that, although the School District emphasized at trial the secular purposes behind the pregame invocations, the pre-eminent purpose behind having invocations was to endorse Protestant Christianity. This is prohibited by the Establishment Clause. See Abington School Dist. v. Schempp, 374 U.S. 203, 223, 83 S. Ct. 1560, 1572, 10 L. Ed. 2d 844 (1963) (daily reading of Bible verses and Lord's Prayer in the public schools held unconstitutional, despite school district's assertion of such secular purposes as "the promotion of moral values, the contradiction to the materialistic trends of our times, the perpetuation of our institutions and the teaching of literature"); Graham v. Central Community School District, 608 F. Supp. 531, 535 (S.D.Iowa 1985) (striking down commencement invocation and benediction for lack of secular purpose). In light of the controlling case law and the nature of the challenged practice, we hold that, because the equal access plan fails to satisfy the first prong of the Lemon test, the plan violates the Establishment Clause of the First Amendment.

2. The Primary Effect

Even assuming, arguendo, that the equal access plan survives the first prong of the Lemon test, we would still find that the plan is facially unconstitutional because it fails the primary effect prong of the Lemon test. "The effect prong asks whether, irrespective of government's actual purpose, the practice under review in fact conveys a message of endorsement or disapproval [of religion]." Jaffree II, 472 U.S. at 56 n. 42, 105 S. Ct. at 2489 n. 42 (quoting Lynch, 465 U.S. at 690, 104 S. Ct. at 1368 (O'Connor, J., concurring)).

In the present case, as noted above, the School District could satisfy its secular objectives by prescribing a strictly secular invocation. The equal access plan, however, permits religious invocations. When a religious invocation is given via a sound system controlled by school principals and the religious invocation occurs at a school-sponsored event at a school-owned facility, the conclusion is inescapable that the religious invocation conveys a message that the school endorses the religious invocation. See Jaffree I, 705 F.2d at 1534-35 ("The primary effect of prayer is the advancement of ones religious beliefs.") This mes-

sage becomes even clearer when the context of these pregame prayers is understood. In the past, pregame invocation speakers at the Douglas County High School, with very few exceptions, have been Protestant Christian ministers. In addition, Protestant Christianity is the majority religious preference in Douglas County. Therefore, the likely result of the equal access plan will be the continuation of Protestant Christian invocations, which have been delivered since 1947. Moreover, the equal access plan places those attending football games in the position of participating in a group prayer. Consequently, the plan violates the primary effect prong of the Lemon test. Accord Graham, 608 F. Supp. at 536 ("invocation and benediction portions of defendant's commencement exercises have as their primary effect the advancement of the Christian religion").

3. Entanglement

On the face of the equal access plan, the School District is not entangled with religion at all. The School District does not monitor the content of the invocations, and the DCMA will no longer choose the invocation speakers or deliver the pregame prayers. Nonetheless, the lack of entanglement cannot save the equal access plan because the plan violates the first two prongs of the Lemon test.

4. The School District's Arguments

The School District sets forth several arguments for distinguishing school prayer cases, claiming that these distinctions permit a finding that religious invocations at high school football games are constitutional. The School District first argues that the school prayer cases are not implicated here because pregame invocations occur outside the instructional environment of the classroom. This argument is meritless. Even though not occurring in the classroom, the invocations take place at a school-owned stadium during a school-sponsored event. In Doe v. Aldine Ind. School Dist., 563 F. Supp. 883 (S.D.Tex.1982), the United States District Court for the Southern District of Texas rejected the argument that the School District asserts here. In Doe, a public high school sponsored extracurricular activities at which a prayer was sung. The defendants argued that the prayer did not violate the Establishment Clause because it occurred outside the classroom. The Doe court rejected this argument:

Pep rallies, football games, and graduation ceremonies are considered to be an integral part of the school's extracurricular program and as such provide a powerful incentive for students to attend. . . . "It is the Texas compulsory education machinery that draws the students to the school event and provides any audience at all for the religious activities. . . ." Since these extracurricular activities were school sponsored and so closely identified with the school program, the fact that the religious activity took place in a nonreligious setting might create in a student's mind the impression that the state's attitude toward religion lacks neutrality.

Id. at 887 (citation omitted). The Doe court's reasoning applies equally well in the present case.

The School District next contends that football invocations do not invoke the teacher-student relationship, and are directed to a far less impressionable audience of adults and sixteen- to eighteen-year-olds. However, the equal access plan does permit teachers to deliver religious invocations, thereby impacting on the teacher-student relationship. Furthermore, to persons of any age who do not believe in prayer, religious invocations permitted by the equal access plan convey the message that the state endorses religions believing in prayer and denigrates those religions that do not. If these prayers are delivered by authority figures, such as teachers, as is possible under the equal access plan, the message endorsing prayer becomes even stronger.

The School District argues further that the invocations are constitutional because they are given at public events at which attendance is entirely voluntary. Courts upholding invocations at graduation ceremonies have stressed that attendance is voluntary. See, e.g., Wood v. Mt. Lebanon Township School District, 342 F. Supp. 1293, 1294 (W.D.Pa.1972). However, the Supreme Court and this Court have not held that public prayer becomes constitutional when student participation is purely voluntary. See Engel v. Vitale, 370 U.S. 421, 430, 82 S. Ct. 1261, 1266-1267, 8 L. Ed. 2d 601 (1962) ("Neither the fact that the prayer may be denominationally neutral nor the fact that its observance on the part of the students is voluntary can serve to free it from the limitations of the Establishment Clause"); see also Karen B. v. Treen, 653 F.2d at 902. The School District attempts to distinguish these cases on the

ground that they involved students who were compelled by law to be in attendance in the classrooms where prayer took place. The School District suggests that, because attendance at football games is voluntary, a constitutional violation is avoided. This argument lacks merit because whether the complaining individual's presence was voluntary is not relevant to the Establishment Clause analysis. Bell v. Little Axe Ind. School Dist. No. 70, 766 F.2d 1391, 1405 (10th Cir. 1985). The Establishment Clause focuses on the constitutionality of the state action, not on the choices made by the complaining individual.

• • •

None of the arguments offered by the School District are persuasive in the present case. Each alleged distinction overlooks the single fact that a state or its subdivision cannot endorse or advance religion. Nor can a state use religious means to achieve secular purposes where, as here, secular means exist to achieve those purposes.

In short, the equal access plan is unconstitutional because it has a religious purpose and a primary effect of advancing religion. By using a purely secular invocation, the School District could avoid any problems of entanglement, fulfill its secular purposes, and not advance religion, thereby complying with the requirements of Lemon and its progeny. Because the School District rejected the alternative of a purely secular pregame speech, and instead adopted a plan which fails to satisfy the Lemon test, we hold that the equal access plan is unconstitutional on its face.

• • •

III. Conclusion

In sum, we REVERSE the district court's order declaring the equal access plan constitutional on its face, and we AFFIRM the lower court's order declaring that the pregame invocations were unconstitutional. Because we award relief to the plaintiffs on both of their Establishment Clause claims, we REMAND to the district court to determine the amount of attorneys' fees to be awarded.

■ ■ ■ ■

Fundamental Concepts

The Jager Case and Its Impact on High School Athletics. The Jagers argued that the practice of delivering invocations before football games violated all three prongs of the *Lemon* test. They alleged first that no secular purpose existed for the practice of delivering the invocations. Citing *Doe v. Aldine* (1982), in which a federal court found unconstitutional the practice of delivering prayers before high school graduation exercises, the plaintiffs said that "as a matter of law . . . prayer recitation lacked a secular purpose" (*Doe v. Aldine*, 1982). Further, if government purpose can be achieved through nonreligious means, the state may not employ religious ones" (*Doe v. Aldine*, 1982, p.886).

With respect to the second prong, primary effect, the Jagers stated that . . . "whether the defendants intended to or not, they created the impression that the Douglas County public school sanctioned the tradition of a school-sponsored forum for religious invocations by Protestant clergymen. Therefore, the primary effect of the practice was to maintain a school-sponsored forum for the expression of the religious views held by the majority in Douglas County and to inhibit and divide those with nonconforming beliefs on religious matters" *(Doe v. Aldine*, 1982).

Finally, the defendants failed the entanglement test because the school district could not supervise the equal access plan without becoming closely involved in determining what messages would be presented at the games. If the school district did not "encourage a more diverse presentation of views, the invocations were likely to sound much like the previous prayers, and if the school took action to promote diverse views, the district would become entangled in a costly, divisive program to identify and favor religious and nonreligious minorities" (Schimmel, 1992).

The court held that the custom and practice of invocations before Douglas County High School football games violated the Establishment Clause of the First Amendment to the United States Constitution. The court found that the pregame prayers violated the first prong of the *Lemon* test and thus that it was unnecessary to consider whether the second and third parts of the test had been violated.

Pre-game Team Prayers and Invocations: Are They Constitutional or Unconstitutional? In 1987 Doug Jager, a junior at Douglas County High School, and his father, William Jager sued the Douglas County School District and Board of Education to stop the practice of offering invocations before Douglas County High School football games (*Jager v. Douglas County School District and School Board*, 1989). The practice of offering invocations before games in Douglas County was initiated about 1947 (*Jager*, 1989). The federal district court found that invocations before football games are unconstitutional. Two years later, in 1989, the Eleventh Circuit Court of Appeals ruled the pre-game invocations violate the First Amendment. In May 1989, the Supreme Court refused to review the *Jager* decision.

Since 1989 numerous school districts have probably complied with the *Jager* decision. However, a few notably have not, namely: 1) the Suwanee County, Florida, school board voted to continue pre-game invocations . . . "we just felt like we didn't need to change it unless somebody complained" (Education Week, 1989); 2) during the 1989 football season *USA Today* reported that "dozens of school systems are disregarding . . ." the *Jager* decision and that "defiance is getting enthusiastic support" (Mayfield and Rota, 1989); 3) *Time* reported that a variety of strategies to evade the decision have been used, such as ministers using bullhorns led the crowd in a prayer at the beginning of the annual football jamboree in Escambia County, Florida, or ministers in Sylacauga, Alabama, who sat at various locations in the stands, and cued the fans who chanted the Lord's prayer, and fans in Chatsworth, Georgia, who were encouraged to take radios to the game and turn up the volume when a local radio station broadcasted a prayer (Trippett, 1989).

On November 7, 1989, voters in Palatka, Florida voted to disapprove (seventy-eight percent) of the *Jager* decision (*USA Today*, 1989). Despite large public support, efforts to evade the *Jager* decision are unlikely to be successful in view of the line of court decisions on organized, devotional prayer in public school settings over the past quarter of a Century (Bjorlun, 1990).

The *Jager* decision, which bans pre-game invocations, may increase the use of team prayers conducted by a team member, coach, or another school official in a locker room before or after the game. Team prayers are much less visible than an invocation given over the public address system at the site of the athletic contest. They may be less visible but they are not constitutional. They like invocations are in violation of the First Amendment in most cases (Bjorlun, 1990).

The Limitations of the First Amendment. The First Amendment guarantees basic freedoms of speech, religion, press, and assembly, and the right to petition the government for redress of grievances. The various freedoms and rights are protected by the First Amendment have been held applicable to the states through the due process clause of the Fourteenth Amendment. Further, it encompasses two distinct guarantees: 1) the government shall make no law respecting an establishment of religion or 2) prohibiting the free exercise thereof. Both have the common purpose of securing religious liberty. Through vigorous enforcement of both clauses by the courts, religious liberty and tolerance is promoted for all. Further, the conditions which secure the best hope of attainment of that end are nurtured (*Lee v. Weisman*, 1992).

"The First Amendment rests upon the premise that both religion and government can best work to achieve their lofty aims if each is left free from the other within its respective sphere" (*McCollum v. Board of Education*, 1948). The First Amendment protects speech and religion by quite different mechanisms. Speech is protected by insuring its full expression even when the government participates, for the very object of some of our most important speech is to persuade the government to adopt an idea as its own (*Abood v. Detroit Board of Education*, 1977; *Meese v. Keene*, 1987; and *Keller v. State Bar of California*, 1990). The method for protecting freedom of belief and freedom of conscience in religious matters is quite the reverse. In religious debate or expression the government is not a prime participant, for the Framers deemed religious establishment contrary to the freedom of all. The Free Exercise Clause embraces a freedom of belief and conscience that has close parallels in the speech provisions of the First Amendment, but the Establishment Clause is a specific prohibition on forms of state intervention in religious affairs with no precise counterpart in the speech provisions. The explanation lies in the lesson of history that was and is the inspiration for the Establishment Clause, the lesson that in the hands of government what might begin as a tolerant expression of religious views may end in a policy to indoctrinate and coerce. A state-created orthodoxy puts at grave risk that freedom of belief and conscience are the sole assurance that religious faith is real, not imposed (*Buckley v. Valeo*, 1976).

The lessons of the First Amendment are as urgent in the modern world as in the 18th Century when it was written. One timeless lesson is that if citizens are subjected to state-sponsored religious exercises, the State disavows its own duty to guard and respect that sphere of inviolable belief and conscience which is the mark of a free people (*Buckley*, 1976).

In *Engel v. Vitale* the Supreme Court held that organized, devotional prayers (invocations and/or benedictions) in public schools are unconstitutional even if participation is voluntary. The court said," . . . it is no part of the business of government to compose official prayers for any group of American people to recite . . ." (*Engel*, 1962).

In 1963, a year later, the court extended this principle by holding the student recitation of a non-government composed prayer, Lord's Prayer, violated the Establishment Clause (*School District of Abington Township v. Schempp* and *Murray v. Curlett* (1963). Further, the court ruled that governmental bodies cannot advance secular goals through religious means even if those secular goals are commendable. Therefore, while achieving team unity might be a commendable secular goal, it cannot be promoted by prayer, which is a religious activity. Finally, the court rejected the voluntary nature of participation as valid justification for devotional prayers when it stated voluntary participation in religious activities "furnishes no defense to a claim of unconstitutionality under the Establishment Clause" (Bjorlun, 1990, p.10).

Bjorlun (1990) found that devotional team prayers led by a team member, a coach, or another school or non-school person are in violation of the Establishment Clause. Further he stated this would also apply to periods of silence held before and/or after games if they are designated by the coach for meditation or prayer. In *Wallace v. Jaffree* (1985), the Supreme Court ruled that an Alabama statute that authorized schools to begin the day with a moment of silence for meditation or voluntary prayer violated the Establishment Clause because it gave students a clear signal that prayer was a favored way of using the period of silence (*May v. Cooperman*, 1985).

However, the court also indicated in *Wallace* (1985) that a moment of silence statute could be adopted to meet a genuine secular purpose, and if it was worded so as not to favor prayer, it would be constitutional. "Thus, a coach could set aside a 'quiet' time before and/or after the game for reflection by the players. They could then choose to pray or think about any other matter they wished. Such a practice would probably not violate the Establishment Clause" (Bjorlun, 1990, p.10).

Free Exercise (of Religious Belief or Conscience) Clause. The First Amendment provides that "Congress shall make no law respecting an establishment of religion, or prohibiting the free exercise thereof" (Black, 1990, p.635). Further, free exercise provides for freedom to individually believe and to practice or exercise one's belief (*Re Elwell*, 1967). This First Amendment protection embraces the concept of freedom to believe and freedom to act, the first of which is absolute, but the second of which remains subject to regulation for protection of society (*Oney v. Oklahoma City, C.C.A. Okl.*, 1941). Such freedom means not only that civil authorities may not intervene in affairs of church; it also prevents church from exercising its authority through state (*Eastern Conference of Original Free Will Baptists of N.C. v. Piner*, 1966).

The *Lee* (1992) majority declared vigorously that "if citizens are subjected to state-sponsored (e.g., invocation prior to an athletic event or invocation before and a benediction after a graduation ceremony) religious exercises, the State disavows its own duty to guard and respect that sphere of inviolable belief and conscience which is the mark of a free people" (*Lee v. Weisman*, 1992). If this equation expressed by the Court is followed, the affirmative intensity of judicial protection of an individual's beliefs and conscience should be in direct proportion to the negative intensity of judicial exclusion of religious activities from the public sector. However, the evidence is to the contrary; while the Court may vigorously assert the protection of the conscience of dissenters under the establishment clause where religion and the public sector are concerned, it has not demonstrated the same vigorous intensity in protecting individual beliefs and conscience under the Free Exercise Clause (Mawdsley and Russo, 1992).

Judge Souter's concurring opinion in *Lee* (1992) underscores the dilemma regarding the disparity between the two religion clauses—1) Establishment, and 2) Free Exercise. Souter disavows that the state has a legitimate function in promoting a diversity of religious views. Such a function, he observed, "would necessarily compel the government and, inevitably, the courts to make wholly inappropriate judgments about the number of religions the State should sponsor and the relative frequency with which it should sponsor each" (*Lee v. Weisman*, 1992). However sound such reasoning regarding diversity of views may seem under the aegis of the Establishment Clause, the application of such reasoning to the Free Exercise Clause is catastrophic (Bjorlun, 1990)

Establishment Clause. During the eighties the United States Supreme Court has been called on in a number of cases to resolve questions involving religion and government on a variety of issues. The overwhelming majority of Supreme Court decisions addressing religion clauses of the First Amendment have dealt with issues regarding Establishment rather than Free Exercise (Mawdsley, 1992).

The Establishment Clause prohibits public school students from being exposed to religion in form of "nonsectarian" prayer given by school-selected clergymen at athletic events or graduation ceremonies, even though students were subjected to a variety of ideas in courses, with freedom of communication being protected by the First Amendment (U.S.C.A. Const. Amends. 1, 14). Further, under the free speech portion of the First Amendment it was contemplated that government would be a participant in expression of ideas, while under the Establishment Clause it was provided that government would remain separate from religious affairs.

The United States Supreme Court first reviewed a challenge to state law under the Establishment Clause in *Everson v. Board of Education* (1947). Relying on the history of the clause, and the Court's prior analysis, Justice Black outlined the considerations that have become the touchstone of Establishment Clause jurisprudence: "Neither a state nor the Federal Government can pass laws which aid one religion, aid all religions, or prefer one religion over another. Neither a State nor the Federal Government, openly or secretly, can participate in the affairs of any religious organization and vice versa" (*Lee v. Weisman*, 1992, p.2662). "In the words of Jefferson, the clause against establishment of religion by law was intended to erect 'a wall of separation between church and state'" (*Reynolds v. United States*, 1879).

In Engel (1962) the Court considered for the first time the constitutionality of prayer in a public school setting. Students said aloud a short prayer selected by the State Board of Regents: "Almighty God, we acknowledge our dependence upon Thee, and we beg Thy blessings upon us, our parents, our teachers, and our Country" (*Engel v. Vitale*, 1962). Justice Black, writing for the Court, again made clear that the First Amendment forbids the use of power or prestige of the government to control, support, or influence the religious beliefs and practices of the American people. Even though the prayer was "denominationally neutral" and "its observance on the part of the students [was] voluntary," (*Engel*, 1962) the court found that it violated this essential precept of the Establishment Clause. In 1963, a year later, the Court again invalidated government-sponsored prayer in public schools in *Schempp* (1963).

Because the schools' opening exercises were government-sponsored religious ceremonies (e.g., reading from the Bible, and recitation of the Lord's prayer), the Court found that the primary effect was the advancement of religion and held, therefore, that the activity violated the Establishment Clause. In 1968, five years later, the Court reiterated the principle that government "may not aid, foster, or promote one religion or religious theory against another or even against the militant opposite" (*Epperson v. Arkansas*, 1968).

Justice Scalia, in 1989, joined an opinion recognizing that the Establishment Clause must be construed in light of the "government policies of accommodation, acknowledgment, and support for religion [that] are an accepted part of our political and cultural heritage" (*Allegheny County v. Greater Pittsburgh ACLU*, 1989). That opinion affirmed that "the meaning of the Clause is to be determined by reference to historical practices and understandings" (*Allegheny County*, 1989). Finally, Scalia concludes: ". . . to deprive our society of that important unifying mechanism (religion), in order to spare the nonbeliever what seems to me the minimal inconvenience of standing or even sitting in respectful nonparticipation, is as senseless in policy as it is unsupported in law" (*Lee v. Weisman*, 1992, p.2686).

In *Lee* (1992) Justice Scalia, the Chief Justice, and Justices White and Thomas dissented. Justice Scalia did not join in the opinion because the majority opinion was conspicuously bereft of any reference to history. Thus in holding that the Establishment Clause prohibits invocations and benedictions at public-school graduation ceremonies, the court lays waste a tradition that is as old as public-school graduation ceremonies themselves, and that is a component of an even more long-standing American tradition of nonsectarian prayer to God at public celebrations generally.

The *Lemon* test (The "Effects" Test). In 1971 the United States Supreme Court enunciated the *Lemon* test (*Lemon v. Kurtzman*, 1971), yet the Court has yet to interpret the test in a clear and consistent manner. In the wake of *Lemon*, no fewer than twenty-eight Supreme Court cases, generating more than one-hundred opinions, have addressed the establishment of religion both in education and noneducation settings (Underwood, 1989). The *Lemon* test is a three-part test. To avoid violating the Establishment Clause, a governmental act must: 1) have a secular purpose; 2) be (its principal and primary effect) one that neither advances or inhibits religion; and 3) not foster excessive government entanglement with religion (*Lee v. Weisman*, 1992). Should the governmental action violate any one of the three parts of the test, then the action must be struck down as unconstitutional.

Justice Souter and Thomas are key components in the future definition and application of the *Lemon* test. It is not clear what their views are at the present time. Although Justice Souter's exact sentiments concerning *Lemon* are yet to be expressed in a judicial opinion. During his confirmation hearings Souter expressed an awareness of "the difficulty of applying the three-part *Lemon v. Kurtzman* test. . . . The concerns that have been raised about [the *Lemon* test] naturally provoke a search, not only perhaps for a different test of the standard which we think we are applying today, but a deeper reexamination about the very concept behind the Establishment Clause. However, Justice Souter, in *Lee* concludes: "When public officials . . . convey an endorsement of religion to their students, they strike near the core of the Establishment Clause. However 'ceremonial' their message may be, they are flatly unconstitutional" (*Lee v. Weisman*, 1992, p.923). According to Souter the Establishment Clause forbids government aid to religion, it prohibits all state-sponsored prayers in public schools. Since the invocation of God's blessing is a religious activity supervised by school officials, it violates the Establishment Clause even if there is no coercion. Finally, he argues that the principle of neutrality, which prohibits government favoritism or endorsement of some religions or all, is the core of the Establishment Clause.

Lee neither overrules the *Lemon* test nor endorses it. The consideration of the *Lemon* test has merely been postponed. Since a majority of the Justices have criticized *Lemon*, it remains a critically weak precedent that is likely to be replaced or substantially revised in the next few years.

Coercion Test.   The implication for pre-game invocations are obvious. The student-athlete must attend the game, stand for the invocation, and remain silent during the invocation. All three are expressions of participation in the prayer. The student-athlete is faced with public pressure, peer pressure, and social pressure during the pre-game invocation. Is this "peer-pressure" or "psychological" coercion?

Justice Scalia, in this case, attacked the notion that graduation prayers are different from prayers at other public ceremonies on the ground that they involve "psychological coercion" (Schimmel, 1992, p. 919). Scalia wrote: "Since the Court does not dispute that students exposed to prayer at graduation ceremonies retain (despite 'subtle coercive pressures') the free will to sit, there is absolutely no basis for the Court's decision." He further argues that "peer-pressure" or "psychological" coercion is not the kind of coercion the Establishment Clause was intended to prohibit. Rather, it is "coercion of religious orthodoxy and of financial support by force of law and threat of penalty. However, Scalia concedes that constitutional tradition also prohibits government endorsement of "sectarian" religion "in the sense of specifying details" upon which believers differ. But the nondenominational prayers of a rabbi, "with no one legally coerced to recite them," are not violations.

Endorsement Test.   Over the years, the Supreme Court has declared the invalidity of many noncoercive state laws and practices conveying a message of religious endorsement. In *Allegheny County*, the Court ". . . forbade the prominent display of a nativity scene on public property; without contesting the dissent's observation that the crèche coerced no one into accepting or supporting whatever message it proclaimed, five Members of the Court found its display unconstitutional as a state endorsement of Christianity" (*Allegheny County v. Greater Pittsburgh ACLU*, 1989). Likewise, in *Wallace* (1985), the Court struck down a state law requiring a moment of silence in public classrooms not because the statute coerced students to participate in prayer (for it did not), but because the manner of its enactment . . . "conveyed a message of state approval of prayer activities in the public schools" (*Wallace v. Jaffree*, 1985). Further, Justice O'Connor, in *Lynch*, declared that the government can run afoul of the Establishment Clause in two ways: 1) excessive entanglement with religious institutions, and 2) government endorsement or approval of religion (the latter being a more direct infringement). Moreover this "endorsement" concept has both an objective component (the message intended by the government based on the words themselves) and a subjective component (the message actually communicated to the audience or some portion of the audience) (*Lee v. Weisman*, 1992).

Civic Religion.   The Court in *Lee* explained why the government cannot be involved with prayers. Justice Kennedy writes ". . . in the Religion Clauses (Establishment and Free Expression) which mean that religious beliefs and religious expression are too precious to be either proscribed or prescribed by the State" (*Lee v. Weisman*, 1992, p. 2672). Therefore, the Constitution is designed to guarantee that the "transmission of religious beliefs and worship is a responsibility and a choice committed to the private sphere." However, the Religion Clauses are not just designed to protect the nonbeliever but equally important "to protect religion from government interference." These concerns, writes Kennedy, "have particular application in the case of school officials, whose effort to monitor prayer will be perceived by the students as inducing a participation they might otherwise reject."

> The Court rejects the argument that nonsectarian prayers at public ceremonies should be recognized as part of this country's "civic religion" and should be tolerated when sectarian prayers are not. This proposal, writes Kennedy, conflicts with the "central meaning of the Religion Clauses . . . which is that all creeds must be tolerated and none favored." The idea that government may establish a civic religion "as a means of avoiding the establishment of a religion" is an unacceptable contradiction. (Schimmel, 1992)

Implications.   The Court, in *Everson*, articulated six examples of paradigmatic practices that the Establishment Clause prohibits ". . . 1) neither a state nor the Federal Government can set up church; 2) neither can pass laws which aid one religion, aid all religions, or prefer one religion over another; 3) neither can force or influence a person to go to or to remain away from church against his will or force him to profess a belief or disbelief in any religion; 4) no person can be punished for entertaining or professing religious beliefs or disbeliefs, for church attendance or non-attendance; 5) no tax in any amount, large or small, can be levied to support any religious activities or institutions, whatever they may be called, or whatever form they may adopt to teach or practice religion; and 6) neither a state not the Federal Government can openly or secretly, participate in the affairs of any religious organizations or groups" (*Everson v. Board of Education*, 1947). These articulated examples are still used in Establishment Clause jurisprudence. The second example has the greatest effect on public schools relating to pre-game invocations, and invocations and benedictions delivered at graduation ceremonies, even today 45 years later as evidenced in the *Lee* case.

Today public schools are faced with considerable support for pre-game prayers, and prayers at graduation ceremonies even though they violate the First Amendment's Establishment Clause and their use can lead to liability problems for coaches, principals, superintendents, and school boards. Coaches who lead team prayers or moments of silence or permit others to lead them could be liable for damages for violation of the Constitution. If coaches are liable, so are principals, superintendents, and school board members if they know or knew about the team prayers and took no action to stop them. Further the school district could be liable for such actions by its personnel. The school board need not have a policy permitting or condoning team prayers in order to be liable for their occurrence. An unwritten policy or custom that encourages or condones such prayers at pre-game or graduation ceremonies can be the basis for an award of damages against the district.

Bjorklun suggests that "voluntary cessation of an unconstitutional practice," such as pre-game prayers or prayers at graduation ceremonies, "does not moot the issue unless it can be shown that the practice is not likely to be resumed" (Bjorlun, 1990, p.14). The burden of proving that resumption will not occur is on the school board and it is a high standard to meet. Parents are regarded as having an interest their children's religious education which includes an interest in having their children educated in public schools that do not permit or impose religious practices. "Thus, as long as any parents, party to the suit, have children in the schools, the issue cannot be moot" (Bjorlun, 1990, p.14).

Finally, if the Court adopts a modification of *Lemon* similar to those suggested by Justice O'Connor (the Endorsement test), the Court, in the future, is likely to permit prayer at Douglas County football games and Rhode Island public school graduation ceremonies since participation was voluntary and no attempt was made to proselytize or coerce members of the audience. The test that emerges from *Lee* ". . . may well revise and revive the interaction between religion and the government for the next several decades" (Mawdsley, 1992, p.202).

Educators and attorneys need to be able to explain the historic and contemporary reasons for government neutrality concerning religion and how separation of church and state in the public schools can protect religious as well as nonreligious students (*Wisconsin v. Yoder*, 1972, p.929).

Recent Developments

University of Wisconsin at Madison Football Team Changes Ties with Priest. Staff lawyers at the University of Wisconsin—Madison decided that the Badger football team's ties to a local Catholic priest may violate the constitutional principle of separation of church and state. University officials issued new guidelines that will, among other things, require Father Burke to make his own travel arrangements for away games and cover his own expenses. But the changes still did not satisfy the Freedom from Religion Foundation that brought the charges.

In the past, coaches and other officials participated in and invited players to join in team prayers before and after games. This involvement by coaching staff in these prayers could raise questions about the state promoting a religious activity. Under the new guidelines, players will be told at the beginning of the season that they can decide for themselves—without due influence or guidance from coaches—whether to put prayers on their schedule. If the players choose to supplement the established routine, and invite the participation of a Catholic priest or other clergy, that will be their prerogative.

Student Prayer Fails Court Test in Mississippi. On November 26, 1993, Bishop Knox, who was fired as Wingfield High School Principal on November 24, 1993, said he does not regret allowing a broadcast of a prayer because students voted 490-96 in favor of it. His firing was later reduced to a suspension. That same year the Mississippi legislature enacted a state statute legalizing student-led prayer. However a federal judge halted enforcement of the law from the beginning, but many schools in the state proceeded or continued allowing student prayer.

Almost three years later, on Wednesday, January 10, 1996, the Mississippi law that allowed student-led prayer in public schools was struck down by a Federal Appeals court. The panel said the law "tells students that the state wants them to pray," thereby violating the constitutional ban on state-established religion.

The ruling is a blow to efforts by the religious right to reintroduce prayer in public schools by arguing that students have a free speech right to initiate prayers. This ruling reaffirms that student-led prayer can be just as coercive and involuntary as teacher-led prayer. The Supreme Court banned teacher-led prayer in public schools in 1962.

The ruling leaves in place an earlier decision by the same appeals court that allows student prayer at graduation in the judicial district that includes Louisiana, Mississippi, and Texas.

References

A. Cases

Abood v. Detroit Board of Education, 431 U.S. 209 (1977).
Allegheny County v. Greater Pittsburgh ACLU, 492 U.S. 573 (1989).
Board of Education of Westside Community Schools v. Mergens, 496 U.S. 226 (1990).
Buckley v. Valeo, 424 U.S. 1 (1976).
Committee for Public Education v. Nyquist, 413 U.S. 756 (1973).
Doe v. Aldine, 563 F. Supp. 883 (S.D. Tex. 1989).
Douglas County School District v. Doug Jager, 109 S.Ct. 2431 (1989).
Engel v. Vitale, 370 U.S. 421 (1962).
Employment Division v. Smith, 494 U.S. 872 (1990).
Epperson v. Arkansas, 393 U.S. 97 (1968).
Everson v. Board of Education, 330 U.S. 1 (1947).
Grand Rapids School District v. Ball, 473 U.S. 373 (1985).

Jager and Jager v. Douglas County School District and Douglas County School Board, No. 86-2037A (D.Ga. Feb. 27, 1987).

Jager v. Douglas County School District, 862 F.2d 824 (11th Cir. 1989).

Keller v. State Bar of California, 496 U.S. 1 (1990).

Lee v. Weisman, 112 S.Ct. 2649, (1992).

Lemon v. Kurtzman, 403 U.S. 602 (1971).

May v. Cooperman, 780 F.2d 240 (3rd Cir. 1985).

McCollum v. Board of Education, 333 U.S. 203 (1948).

Meese v. Keene, 481 U.S. 465 (1987).

Mueller v. Allen, 463 U.S. 388 (1983).

Oney v. Oklahoma City, C.C.A. Okl., 120 F.2d 861 (3rd Cir. 1941).

Reynolds v. United States, 98 U.S. 145 (1879).

School District of Abington Township v. Schempp, cited in Murray v. Curlett, 374 U.S. 203 (1963).

Wallace v. Jaffree, 472 U.S. 38 (1985).

Wisconsin v. Yoder, 406 U.S. 205 (1972).

B. Publications

Black, Henry Campbell. (6th Ed) (1990). *Black's Law Dictionary*. Charlottesville, VA: Michie.

Eastern Conference of Original Free Will Baptists of N.C. v. Piner, 267 N.C. 74, 147 S.E.2d 581 (1966).

Education Week, VIII (May 10, 1989), p. 3.

Gordon, Bill. (1981). "Team Prayer: Does It Infringe on a Player's Constitutional Rights?" *St. Petersburg Times* (July 1), pp. 1c and 11c.

Hall, Mimi (1993). School Doesn't Have a Prayer—or Principal. *USA Today*, 2A (Friday, November 26).

Mawdsley, Ralph D. and Charles J. Russo. (1992). "Lee v. Weisman: The Supreme Court Pronounces the Benediction on Public School Graduation Prayers," 77 *Ed. Law Rep.* 1071 (Dec. 17).

Mauro, Tony (1996). Student Prayer Fails Court Test. *USA Today*, 5A (Thursday, January 11).

Mayfield, Mark and Kelly Rota. (1989). "Hands Together for Prayer, Applause in South," *USA Today* (Oct. 10), p. 34.

Schimmel, David. (1992). "Graduation Prayers Flunk Coercion Test: An Analysis of *Lee v. Weisman*." 76 *Ed. Law Rep.* 913 (Nov. 5).

———. (1989). "Election Results from Across the USA," *USA Today* (November 8).

Walden, John C. (1987). "Are Prayers at High School Football Games Unconstitutional?" 39 *Ed. Law Rep.* 493 (Aug. 6).

4.29

Private Clubs

Discriminatory Issues

Thomas H. Sawyer
Indiana State University

The purpose of this chapter is to: 1) describe the nature of "truly private" clubs, 2) define the meaning of public accommodation (§2000a) and outline the impact on private clubs, 3) discuss the issues that surround the freedom of association and the right to discriminate, and 4) provide the reader with some strategies to open the doors to so-called private clubs.

Professional women, who like men, need to join golf and other clubs to expand their business network are learning that swinging a club can be easier than joining one. Women golfers suffer from discrimination, similar to the Jews and blacks, when it comes to joining private golf clubs. Not long ago, Vice President Quayle canceled a second round at Monterey's all-white Cypress Point because he felt it might look bad to play there; but, had no problem playing at all-male Burning Tree, where he holds an honorary membership (Maclean, 1991).

Many private golf clubs all over America discriminate against women in subtle ways. Other clubs bar women altogether and go to extremes to protect their policy to do so. However, outright exclusion of women from courses is rare among the nation's 5,276 private clubs (PGA, 1991). Nevertheless this is a form of deliberate sex discrimination and it should be pursued as vigorously as racial discrimination.

■ ■ ■ ■

Representative Case

U.S. v. LANSDOWNE SWIM CLUB

United States District Court, Eastern District of Pennsylvania
713 F. Supp. 785 (1989)

OPINION:

The United States brought this action against the Lansdowne Swim Club ("The Club," "LSC"), alleging that it is a place of public accommodation that discriminates in its membership policies and practices against blacks on the basis of their race or color in violation of Title II of the Civil Rights Act of 1964, 42 U.S.C. § 2000a-2000a-6. The Attorney General is authorized to bring this action on behalf of the United States. 42 U.S.C. § 2000a-5(a). I have

jurisdiction under 42 U.S.C. § 2000a-6(a) and 28 U.S.C. § 1345.

LSC denies that it is a place of public accommodation, claims that it is a private club exempt from the coverage of Title II, and denies that it has discriminated. This Memorandum sets forth my findings of fact and conclusions of law as to these issues, as required by Fed. R. Civ. P. 52(a).

For the reasons that follow, I conclude that LSC is a place of public accommodation, is not a private club, and has engaged in a pattern or practice of discrimination against blacks in its membership policies.

I. Background

Lansdowne Swim Club is a Pennsylvania nonprofit corporation which owns and maintains facilities at the corner of Burmont Road and Baltimore Pike in Lansdowne, PA. Stipulation of Facts ("Stip.") 1, 3; Defendant's Exhibit ("DX") 1. It is the only swimming facility in Lansdowne, except for pools located on personal property. Stip. 6. LSC opened its facilities in 1958 (Stip. 2) and has been open every summer since then.

LSC's recreational facilities include a swimming pool with diving and sliding boards, a wading pool, lounging and sunbathing areas, shower and dressing facilities, ping pong tables, horseshoes, lounge chairs, umbrellas, picnic tables, and basketball and volleyball facilities. Stip. 21-31, 33-39. There is an entrance gate into the Club property off Burmont Road that leads to the parking area, where the basketball and volleyball equipment is located. Kressley Testimony, Tr. 6/17/88, at 18; Stip. 91. From the parking area, a ramp leads to an enclosed area where the pool is located. Kressley, at 18. The pool is accessible through a gate, which is staffed by LSC employees who admit members, associates and guests during normal pool hours. See Cunningham Testimony, Tr. 6/16/88, at 4-5; Kressley, at 18-19. LSC leases a portion of its facilities to a concessionaire as a snack bar. Stip. 52.

The Club is managed by a twelve-person Board of Directors, including a President, Vice-President, Secretary and Treasurer. DX 3a (Art. II, Secs. 1, 2(a)). The shareholder members of the LSC are referred to in the Club's Bylaws as "active" members. Stip. 106; DX 2 (Art. IV, Sec. 1). Membership is evidenced by a capital share, or "bond," which has a par value of $250. Stip. 108; DX 1 (Art. 9). The Club limits its shareholder members to 500. Stip. 142. LSC also permits persons and families, known as "associates", to use its facilities for one season only. Stip. 107. The Club's general policy is that before being elected to membership an applicant must use the facilities of LSC for one swimming season as an associate. Stip. 110.

Prior to 1979, all applicants for shareholder membership or associate privileges were required to be approved by the Membership Committee and elected to membership by the Board of Directors. Stip. 113-114; DX 2 (Art. IV, Sec. 2). Since 1979, all applicants must be approved by ninety percent of the shareholders present and voting at the annual meeting. Stip. 115-117. At this meeting, voting members cast ballots anonymously: an affirmative vote is cast by not listing the applicant's name on the ballot, and

a negative vote is cast by listing the applicant's name. Stip. 118-119. Since 1985, the attendance of one of the applicant's sponsors at the annual meeting has also been required. Stip. 173-175.

II. Public Accommodation

Title II of the Civil Rights Act prohibits discrimination in places of public accommodation. An establishment is a place of public accommodation within the meaning of Title II if its operations affect commerce and it is one of four categories of establishments which serve the public. 42 U.S.C. § 2000a(b). The categories relevant to this case are:

> any restaurant, cafeteria, lunchroom, lunch counter, soda fountain, or other facility principally engaged in selling food for consumption on the premises. Id. § 2000a(b)(2).

> any motion picture house, theater, concert hall, sports arena, stadium or other place of exhibition or entertainment. Id. § 2000a(b)(3).

> any establishment (A)(i) which is physically located within the premises of any establishment otherwise covered by this subsection, or (ii) within the premises of which is physically located any such covered establishment, and (B) which holds itself out as serving patrons of such covered establishment. Id. § 2000a(b)(4).

The operations of an establishment covered by section 2000a(b)(2) affect commerce if the establishment "serves or offers to serve interstate travelers or a substantial portion of the food which it serves . . . has moved in commerce." Id. § 2000a(c)(2). The operations of an establishment covered by section 2000a(b)(3) affect commerce if the establishment "customarily presents films, performances, athletic teams, exhibitions, or other sources of entertainment which move in commerce." Id. § 2000a(c)(3). The operations of an establishment covered by section 2000a(b)(4) affect commerce if the establishment "is physically located within the premises of, or there is physically located within its premises, an establishment the operations of which affect commerce within the meaning of this subsection." Id. § 2000a(c)(4).

A. Place of Entertainment

The Lansdowne Swim Club is a place of entertainment pursuant to section 2000a(b)(3). At its facilities, members, associates and guests (and members of the public in some instances), are amused and entertained by swimming, diving, sunbathing and "people-watching." They also consume snack food and beverages; talk to and associate with each other; play basketball, volleyball, ping pong and horseshoes; participate in and observe swimming and diving meets; and attend pool parties which sometimes include musical entertainment. See Stip. 20-47.

It is well-established that a place of entertainment includes an establishment where entertainment takes the form of direct participation in an activity or sport. See Daniel v. Paul, 395 U.S. 298, 306-08, 23 L. Ed. 2d 318, 89 S. Ct. 1697 (1969); see also, e.g., Evans v. Seaman, 452 F.2d 749, 751 (5th Cir.) (roller skating rink), cert. denied, 408 U.S. 924, 33 L. Ed. 2d 335, 92 S. Ct. 2493 (1972); Miller v. Amusement Enters., Inc., 394 F.2d 342, 350-51 (5th Cir. 1968) (en banc) (amusement park); Brown v. Loudoun Golf & Country Club, 573 F. Supp. 399, 402 (E.D. Va. 1983) (golf club); United States v. Slidell Youth Football Ass'n, 387 F. Supp. 474, 482 (E.D. La. 1974) (youth football league). This interpretation of the term entertainment comports with its generally accepted meaning and the overriding purpose of Title II, "to remove the daily affront and humiliation involved in discriminatory denials of access to facilities ostensibly open to the general public." Daniel, 395 U.S. at 307-08. In accordance with the holding and rationale of Daniel, the Court of Appeals for the Second Circuit concluded that a swim club is a place of entertainment. Olzman v. Lake Hills Swim Club, Inc., 495 F.2d 1333, 1340 (2d Cir. 1974).

Although LSC concedes that its swimming and other recreational areas constitute a place of entertainment, it contends that this designation is limited to its "recreational areas." Defendant's Brief in Support of its Proposed Findings of Fact and Conclusions of Law [hereinafter Defendant's Brief], at 4. Thus, LSC appears to be dividing its facilities into entertainment and nonentertainment areas. This bifurcation has no support in the plain language of the Act or the case law interpreting it. Once an establishment is determined to be a place of entertainment, the entire facility is identified as such. See Daniel, 395 U.S. 298, 23 L. Ed. 2d 318, 89 S. Ct. 1697 (recreational facility including swimming, boating, sunbathing and picnicking areas, miniature golf, dancing facilities, and a snack bar); Olzman, 495 F.2d 1333 (swim club including swimming pool, wading pool, parking area and snack bar); Miller, 394 F.2d 342 (amusement park including mechanical rides, ice skating rink during winter, and small concession stand); United States v. Johnson Lake Inc., 312 F. Supp. 1376 (S.D. Ala. 1970) (recreational complex including swimming, picnicking and dancing areas, snack bar, pool tables, jukebox and gum machine); Evans v. Laurel Links, 261 F. Supp. 474 (E.D. Va. 1966) (golf course with lunch counter); cf. Martin v. United Way, 829 F.2d 445, 449-50 (3d Cir. 1987) (noting that the Supreme Court in Daniels "held that the entire

facility was a place of entertainment 'affecting commerce' . . .").

As a place of entertainment, the operations of LSC affect commerce because LSC customarily presents sources of entertainment which move in interstate commerce. A "source of entertainment" is "the utilization of a device or an implement to engage in an entertaining activity." Slidell Youth Football Ass'n, 387 F. Supp. at 483. The sliding board at LSC, which the Club bought in 1968, was manufactured in Texas. Stip. 444(c), (d); Government's Exhibit ("GX") 108. 0 The sliding board is a source of entertainment because patrons use the slide to entertain themselves in the pool.

Participants in activities are also considered sources of entertainment for purposes of Title II. See Scott v. Young, 421 F.2d 143, 144 (4th Cir.), cert. denied, 398 U.S. 929, 26 L. Ed. 2d 91, 90 S. Ct. 1820 (1970); Brown, 573 F. Supp. at 402; Johnson Lake, 312 F. Supp. at 1380; Laurel Links, 261 F. Supp. at 477. Some of the persons who have used the Club's facilities are out-of-state residents. Stip. 51. For example, in 1986, the Club's guest receipts show that there were 117 visits by out-of-state guests; in 1987 there were 165 visits. See GX 106, 107. 1 Therefore, the sources of entertainment in this case are the sliding board and the Club's out-of-state visitors.

• • •

B. Snack Bar as Covered Establishment

LSC is an establishment within the premises of which is physically located a covered establishment, a facility engaged in selling food for consumption on the premises, and which holds itself out as serving patrons of that covered establishment, the snack bar.

The snack bar at LSC is leased to a concessionaire who operates it. Stip. 52. Food and drink purchased from the bar cannot be taken from the snack bar and ticket booth areas. See GX 56 (1962 Rules and Regulations); GX 57 (1964 Pool Regulations); GX 58 (1978 Pool Regulations); GX 59 (1979 Pool Regulations); GX 60 (1986 Pool Regulations). The bar sells hamburgers, hot dogs, french fries, coffee, pizza, candy, tea, soda and hot chocolate to the members, guests and employees of the Club. Stip. 53-62.

When John and Carolyn Doucas operated the snack bar, the carbonated "Coca-Cola" soft drinks sold at the snack bar were purchased from the Coca-Cola Bottling Co. of Philadelphia. Stip. 444(a). These beverages were manufactured using syrup concentrate produced in Baltimore, Maryland. Stip. 444(b). The coffee sold at the snack bar comes from beans grown outside the continental United States. GX 120.

Nonresidents of Pennsylvania have been served by the operators of the snack bar. Stip. 64, 66.

It is undisputed that the snack bar sells food for consumption on the premises. Stip. 53. Thus, the snack bar at the Club is a "facility principally engaged in selling food for consumption on the premises" pursuant to 42 U.S.C. § 2000a(b)(2). Accord Daniel, 395 U.S. at 303-04 (snack bar in recreational area); Fazzio Real Estate v. Adams, 396 F.2d 146, 150 (5th Cir. 1968) (snack bar in bowling alley); United States v. Beach Assocs., Inc., 286 F. Supp. 801, 806 (D. Md. 1968) (restaurant adjoining beach club); Johnson Lake, 312 F. Supp. at 1378-81 (snack bar in recreational area).

The Club holds itself out as serving patrons of the snack bar: the bar serves the members, associates, guests and employees of LSC, Stip. 63-66; conversely, LSC provides entertainment to those who patronize the bar. Cf. Adams v. Fazzio Real Estate, 268 F. Supp. 630, 638-39 (E.D. La. 1967), aff'd, 396 F.2d 146 (5th Cir. 1968)(to satisfy "holding out" requirement, not necessary to show that primary function of bowling alley is to serve patrons of refreshment counter). Defendant disputes that the snack bar satisfies this requirement because the bar is not independent of the other facilities and, as such, "there are no 'patrons' of the snack bar who are not already 'patrons' of LSC." Defendant's Brief, at 6. The Supreme Court's decision in Daniel refutes defendant's argument, however. In Daniel, the snack bar encompassed only a small portion of a larger recreational area, the Lake Nixon Club, to which blacks were denied admission. See Daniel, 395 U.S. at 301. Thus, it appears there were no patrons of the snack bar who were not already patrons of the recreational facility. The Supreme Court did not discuss whether the Lake Nixon Club held itself out as serving patrons of the Club's snack bar. See id. at 302-08. Moreover, the Court did not distinguish the decision in Adams, 396 F.2d 146, on which it relied to reach its conclusion that the snack bar brought the entire facility within the coverage of the Title II. Daniel, 395 U.S. at 305. Any distinction between the cases apparently was not material to the Court's conclusion.

The operations of LSC's snack bar affect commerce because it serves and offers to serve interstate travelers. This standard is "satisfied by minimal evidence." Adams, 268 F. Supp. at 639 n.19. It is undisputed that nonresidents have used the Club's facilities and have been served at the snack bar. The statute does not designate how many nonresidents must be served within a certain period of time in order to "affect commerce." I have already concluded that the number of out-of-state guests who have patronized LSC is significant. See supra p. slip op. at 12. This requirement need not be fulfilled by showing solicitation of out-of-state residents. Cf. Daniel, 395 U.S. at 304; Newman v. Piggie Park Enters., 256 F. Supp. 941, 951 (D. S.C. 1966), rev'd on other grounds, 377 F.2d 433 (4th Cir. 1967) (both

cases showing that out-of-state residents were patrons of facility because it advertised). As I have previously stated, evidence of solicitation is simply a substitute for direct evidence of attendance by out-of-state residents, see supra p. slip op. at 13; in this case the government need not show that LSC advertised for nonresident patrons because it has been stipulated that the snack bar has in fact served them.

I also find that the snack bar offers to serve interstate travelers because LSC offers to serve all persons who use the Club's facilities, including out-of-state guests. See Daniel, 395 U.S. at 304; Gregory v. Meyer, 376 F.2d 509, 510 (5th Cir. 1967); United States v. All Star Triangle Bowl, Inc., 283 F. Supp. 300, 302 (D. S.C. 1968); Laurel Links, 261 F. Supp. at 476.

Finally, the operations of the snack bar affect commerce because a "substantial" portion of the food served at the bar has moved in interstate commerce in accordance with 42 U.S.C. § 2000a(c)(2). Substantial has been defined as "anything more than a minimal or insignificant amount." Gregory, 376 F.2d at 511 n.1, cited with approval in Daniel, 395 U.S. at 305; accord Newman, 256 F. Supp. at 950-51 (Substantial is "something of real worth and importance; of considerable value; valuable; something worthwhile as distinguished from something without value or merely nominal.") (footnote omitted).

Ingredients in the soda and coffee sold at the snack bar originated outside Pennsylvania. I take judicial notice of the fact that many of the purchases at a swimming pool's snack bar, open during the hot summer months, include a cold drink. The primary cold drinks sold at the snack bar are "Coca-Cola" soft drinks, which contain an essential ingredient that has moved in commerce.

• • •

The operations of LSC affect commerce because the snack bar is physically located within its premises. "The snack bar's status as a covered establishment automatically brings the entire . . . facility within the ambit of Title II." Daniel, 395 U.S. at 305.

For all of the above reasons, I find that the Club is a place of public accommodation within the meaning of 42 U.S.C. § 2000a(b)(4), as well as under § 2000a(b)(3).

III. Private Club Exemption

LSC claims that it is exempt from the coverage of Title II because it is a private club pursuant to 42 U.S.C. § 2000a(e). 2 That section provides, in pertinent part: "The provisions of [Title II] shall not apply to a private club or other establishment not in fact open to the public. . . ." "The test of whether a private club, or an establishment not open to the public, is exempt from title II, relates to whether it is, in fact, a private club, or whether it is, in fact, an establishment not open to the public." 110 Cong. Rec. 13,697 (1964) (remarks of Sen. Long).

LSC bears the burden of demonstrating that it is a private club. . . . The statute itself does not define a private club: "the statute sets forth a factual test of sorts—'not in fact open to the public,' but it does not define 'private club'." Cork Club, 315 F. Supp. at 1150 (footnote omitted). The limited legislative history of section 2000a(e) provides me with only broad guiding principles. The private club exemption "must be examined in the light of the Act's clear purpose of protecting only 'the genuine privacy of private clubs . . . whose membership is genuinely selective . . .'" Nesmith, 397 F.2d at 101-02 (citing remarks of Sen. Humphrey, 110 Cong. Rec. 13,697 (1964)). This exemption must also be examined in light of the remedial purpose of the Act, to eliminate racial discrimination in places open to the public. See Cork Club, 315 F. Supp. at 1150; see also supra p. 795 & n. 21 (discussing general remedial purpose of Title II).

The few decisions of the Supreme Court addressing the scope of section 2000a(e) are of limited value in developing a comprehensive definition of a private club, perhaps because they clearly involved shams. . . . Other Courts interpreting section 2000a(e) have not relied on a single test to determine if an establishment is a private club. Instead, they have weighed a variety of relevant factors. "Each factor is considered and either tips the balance for or against private club status." Cork Club, 315 F. Supp. at 1150; see also Nesmith, 397 F.2d at 101-02. I agree that a factor analysis is appropriate. The following factors are relevant to this determination and will be considered:

1. The genuine selectivity of the group in the admission of its members.
2. The membership's control over the operations of the establishment.
3. The history of the organization.
4. The use of the facilities by nonmembers.
5. The purpose of the club's existence.
6. Whether the club advertises for members.
7. Whether the club is profit or nonprofit.
8. The formalities observed by the club, e.g., by-laws, meetings, membership cards.

Upon consideration of the factors listed above, I conclude that LSC has not established that it is a private club.

• • •

In sum, I find that, upon consideration of all of the evidence and the applicable law, the government has sustained its burden of proving that the Lansdowne Swim Club has engaged in a widespread pattern or practice of discrimination against blacks from its inception to the present. When the Club was organized, it did not solicit blacks from the Lansdowne community and, when blacks inquired about membership, they were referred to the nearby "black" swim club. When black and part-black families requested or inquired about membership, the Club regularly failed to respond; the Club also had a reputation for discrimination, which deterred black and part-black families from applying. When black and part-black families satisfied the qualifications of Club membership, all but one were denied membership because of their race. "As [discriminatory] behavior has become more unfashionable, evidence of intent has become harder to find. But this does not mean that racial discrimination has disappeared." Lofts Realty, 610 F.2d at 1043 (citation omitted). The evidence in this case convinces me that such discrimination has existed in LSC.

V. Conclusions of Law

1. The Lansdowne Swim Club is a place of public accommodation within the meaning of 42 U.S.C. § 2000a (b)(3), (b)(4).
2. The operations of the Club affect commerce within the meaning of 42 U.S.C. § 2000a (c)(3), (c)(4).
3. The Club is not a private club or other establishment not in fact open to the public within the meaning of 42 U.S.C. § 2000a (e).
4. The United States has sustained its burden of demonstrating that the Club has engaged in a pattern or practice of resistance to the full and equal enjoyment by black persons of the rights secured by 42 U.S.C. §§ 2000a -2000a-6, and that the pattern or practice is of such a nature and is intended to deny the full exercise of these rights.

■ ■ ■ ■

Fundamental Concepts

What Is a "Truly Private" Club? According to Black's Law Dictionary (1990) **private** is defined as, "affecting or belonging to private individuals as distinct from the public in general" (*People v. Powell*, 1937). **Club** is defined as, "a voluntary, incorporated or unincorporated association of persons for common purposes of a social, literary, investment, political nature, or the like. Association of persons for promotion of some common object, such as literature, science, politics, good fellowship, etc., especially one jointly supported and meeting periodically, and membership is usually conferred by ballot and carries privilege of exclusive use of club quarters, and word also applies to a building, apartment or room occupied by a club." Therefore a **private club** might very well be a group of private individuals, regardless of race, religion or gender, banned together exclusively to participate in the activity of golf. And a **private golf club** would have periodic meetings, membership conferred by ballot, membership carries privilege of exclusive use of the club quarters, and could exclude (discriminate) individuals (i.e., race, religion, and gender) who do not share the views and values that the club's members wish to promote.

In *Wright v. Salisbury Club, Ltd.* (1979, 1980), *U.S. v. Eagles* (1979), *Perkins v. New Orleans Athletic Club* (1976), *Cornelius v. Benevolent Protective Order of Elks* (1974), *Solomon v. Miami Women's Club* (1973), *Moose Lodge No. 107 v. Irvis* (1972), *Sims v. Order of United Commercial Travelers of America* (1972), *Tillman v. Wheaton-Haven Recreation Association, Inc.* (1971, 1973), *Daniel v. Paul* (1969), *Sullivan v. Little Hunting Club, Inc.* (1969) and *Nesmith v. Young Men's Christian Association of Raleigh, N.C. Inc.* (1968) the courts have begun to define the characteristics of a "truly private" club. The term "truly private" was established by the Supreme Court in *Tillman v. Wheaton-Haven Recreation Association* (1973) to distinguish between "private" in the sense of non-government and "private" in the association sense. The courts have adopted criteria to be considered for determining whether or not an organization is a "truly private" club within public accommodations provision, including, but not limited to:

genuine selectiveness of group in admission of its members,

existence of formal membership procedures,

degree of membership control over internal governance, particularly with regard to new members,

history of organization,

use of club facilities by nonmembers,

substantiality of dues,

whether organization advertises,

whether club is profit or nonprofit,

purpose of club's existence, and

formalities observed by club (Civil Rights Act of 1964).

In *Wright v. Salisbury Club, Ltd.* (1980, 1979) the court found that whether a particular club is "truly private" is a determination to be made in the light of the facts of each case. Further, the test for private club status is whether, without regard to race, the club's membership policies and practices manifest a plan or purpose of exclusiveness. The principal consideration in determining whether a club is "truly private" is whether the club is genuinely selective and exclusive (*Olzman v. Lake Hills Swim Club* (1974) and *Clover Hill Swimming Club, Inc. v. Goldsboro* (1966)).

The Salisbury Club (*Wright v. Salisbury Club, Ltd.*, 1980, 1979) membership policy indicated that membership was not tied to a limited geographic area and the procedures consisted of the following steps: 1) one must file an application, 2) receive the endorsement of two members, 3) be recommended by the membership committee, 4) be approved by seventy-five percent of the board of directors present at the meeting in which the vote is taken, and 5) payment of a substantial initiation fee and membership dues are required.

Interestingly enough the Salisbury Club was found to be genuinely selective and exclusive as determined by the membership procedures. However, the Salisbury Club engaged in extensive advertisement and membership solicitation and had become the crown jewel of the developer's marketing effort which the court found to be inconsistent with the genuinely selective and exclusive nature of a "truly private" club. The court determined that exclusive means that a club does not advertise extensively for new members, does not link itself with other entities, like subdivisions, does not become part of a developer's marketing effort, and does deny membership to prospective members.

In *Solomon v. Miami Women's Club* (1973) the court indicated that selectivity has often been said to be the essence of a private club and selection by recommendation serves to draw a line of demarcation between admitting the general public and only a select few. Other courts have noted that the requirement of member recommendations may be a significant indication of exclusivity (*Durham v. Red Lake Fishing and Hunting Club, Inc.*, 1987; *Lloyd Lions Club of Portland v. International Association of Lions Clubs*, 1986; *U.S. Power Squadrons v. State Human Rights Appeal Board*, 1983, 1981; *Golden v. Biscayne Bay Yacht Club, City of Miami*, 1973; *Smith v. Young Men's Christian Association of Montgomery, Inc.*, 1972; *Wright v. Cork Club*, 1970; *U.S. v. Johnson Lake, Inc.*, 1970; *U.S. v. Jack Sabin's Private Club*, 1967; and *Nesmith v. Young Men's Christian Association of Raleigh, N.C., Inc.*, 1967).

In *Sullivan v. Little Hunting Park, Inc.* (1969) and later in *Tillman v. Wheaton-Haven Recreation Association* (1973) the court determined if a club is "truly private," there cannot be any connection between club membership and property necessary to implicate civil rights statutes dealing with the right of all persons to acquire property. In *Tillman* the Supreme Court found that when an organization links membership benefits to residency in a narrow geographical area, that decision infuses those benefits into the bundle of rights for which an individual pays when buying or leasing within that area.

Further, in *Cornelius v. Benevolent Protective Order of Elks* (1974) the court found that Elks and Moose Lodges did discriminate racially with respect to membership. Since they do, they stand to forfeit state aid, direct or indirect, which amounts to "encouragement." Moreover, only genuinely selective and exclusive "truly private" clubs are exempted from the 1866 and 1964 civil rights statutes. Those who believe that racial exclusion fosters fraternity are free to act out their belief, but they may not promote prejudice for profit. If a lodge were to diverge from their ways and become an establishment where economic opportunity was the attraction, it would cease to be exempt: To have their privacy protected, clubs must function as extensions of the member's home and not as extensions of their businesses.

Finally, other decisions have looked to the extent to which the membership exercised rights of control over the alleged clubs. Courts denying the private club exemption have considered as relevant evidence that A) members did not own club facilities (*Daniels v. Paul*, 1969); B) profits from the use of the club facilities were retained by the operator (*U.S. v. Richberg*, 1968); and C) members had no control over the operations of the establishment (*Wright v. Cork Club*, 1970).

What Is a Public Accommodation?   A primary force behind the passage of the 1964 Civil Rights Act was the need for antidiscrimination legislation covering "**public accommodations**." The public accommodations title exempted from its coverage "private club[s and] other establishment[s] not in fact open to the public (42 U.S.C.A. 2000 a(e))." The exemption reflects the simple fact that the harm to which the legislation was primarily addressed was discrimination in public accommodations rather than in private groups.

According to the United States Code Annotated (1992) any place or organization defined as a public accommodation will be without discrimination or segregation on the grounds of race, color, religion, sex, or national origin. Further all persons shall be entitled to the full and equal enjoyment of the goods, services, facilities, advantages, and accommodations of any place of public accommodation (*Delaney v. Central Valley Golf Club*, 1941).

A public accommodation is defined as:

> any establishments affecting interstate commerce or supported in their activities by State action as places of public accommodation;

> lodgings, such as inns, hotels, motels, and any other establishment which provide lodging to transient guests;

> facilities principally engaged in selling food for consumption on the premises, such as restaurants, cafeterias, lunchrooms, lunch counters and soda fountains;

> gasoline stations;

> places of exhibition, amusement, or entertainment, such as motion picture houses, theaters, concert halls, sports arenas or stadiums, or race tracks;

> any establishment which is physically located within the premises of a public accommodation; and

> any establishment which holds itself out as serving patrons of a public accommodation

> (42 U.S.C.A. 2000 §a(e), 1992).

The courts have developed a number of factors which could be examined to determine whether, under the public accommodations title, alleged clubs were "truly private" or in fact "sham clubs" actually open to the (white male) public, including, but not limited to A) the absence of formal membership selection procedures (*Stout v. YMCA*, 1968); B) failure to reject a significant number of white applicants (*Nesmith v. Young Men's Christian Association of Raleigh, N.C., Inc.*, 1967); C) extending club facilities to nonmembers in disregard of club bylaws (*U.S. v. Jack Sabin's Private Club*, 1967); D) the absence or insubstantiality of dues and exceedingly large membership lists (*Bradshaw v. Whigham*, 1966); and E) several courts have cited advertising as evidence of a lack of selectivity (*U.S. v. Jordan*, 1969).

In *Evans v. Laurel Links, Inc.* (1966) it was decided that a lunch counter at a golf course was an "establishment affecting commerce" within the public accommodations provisions of the Civil Rights Act of 1964. The lunch counter did serve and offered to serve the general public, including interstate travelers. And because the lunch counter was located within the golf course facilities it brought the entire golf course within public accommodation provisions.

Annually at Laurel Links, a Virginia golf course, a golf team from the District of Columbia played in a tournament. The court determined that tournaments and/or team matches which are played on the defendant's facilities (Laurel Links) make it a place of exhibition and entertainment within the public accommodation provisions. The court further decided the operation of such an establishment affects commerce if it customarily presents athletic teams which move in commerce (across state lines). "Custom" is defined (Black, 1990) as habitual practice or course of action that characteristically is repeated in like circumstances (*Jones v. City of Chicago*, 1986). The golf team from Washington, D.C., played on the course on a regular annual basis and the court determined that greater frequency is not required to establish that it is "customarily presented" (*Fuller Brush Co. v. Industrial Commission of Utah*, 1940).

Some courts have looked at the intent of the organizers of the club, denying an exemption where the club was formed to evade public accommodations provisions, including when A) a country club owned and operated for profit-making corporation was not a "private club" (*Bell v. Kenwood Golf & Country Club, Inc.*, 1970); B) a recreational facility which was a business operation for profit with none of the attributes of self-government and member-ownership traditionally associated with private clubs (*Daniel v. Paul*, 1969); C) a beach club which sells season and individual tickets, refreshments and other accommodations is not a 'private club' (*U.S. v. Johnson Lake, Inc.*, 1970); D) a health and exercise club which did not exercise selectivity and which was a business operated for profit and not controlled by club membership was not exempt from Equal Accommodations Act (*Vidrich v. Vic Tanny Intern, Inc.*, 1980; *Gardner v. Vic Tanny Compton, Inc.*, 1960); E) an organization which admits members based upon objective, and not subjective, criteria may not be considered a "private club" (*U.S. Power Squadron v. State Humans Right Appeal Board*, 1981, 1983; *People of State of N.Y. by Abrams v. Ocean Club, Inc.*, 1984); and F) a golf club, whose formal admission procedures did not operate in practice to make club's membership selective, was a place of public accommodation (*Brown v. Loudoun Golf and Country Club, Inc.*, 1983).

Freedom of Association and the Right to Discriminate. A 1975 article in the *Yale Law Journal,* dealing with the rights of private groups to discriminate, made the following interesting points relating to private clubs and discrimination, and affirm points already discussed.

Jones v. Alfred H. Mayer Co. (1968) revitalized the Civil Rights Act of 1866 as an instrument with which to attack racial discrimination by private clubs and private schools. *Jones* consequently reawakened the conflict between **freedom of association**, which many have believed gives private groups a right to discriminate, and **freedom from racial discrimination**, guaranteed by the **principles of equality** undergirding the Thirteenth and Fourteenth Amendments.

Freedom of Association (*NAACP v. Alabama*, 1958; *Shelton v. Tucker*, 1960; *NAACP v. Button*, 1963; *Gibson v. Florida Legislative Investigating Commission*, 1963; and *U.S. v. Robel*, 1967) evolved to protect the ability of an individual to join with others for the expression or promotion of political ideas. This freedom of association has little to do with a right to exclude others on the basis of race. Indeed, the right to exclude arguably impairs the freedom to associate of the person who wants to join. Most social and golf clubs are apolitical and would find it difficult to prove that they require a right to discriminate for the purpose of political expression (*Yale Law Journal*, 1975).

Because the freedom of association cases did not deal with the exclusive question, some commentators have suggested that the question of a right to discriminate could be better conceptualized as deriving from the right of privacy. Supreme Court cases (*Griswold v. Connecticut*, 1965; *Stanley v. Georgia*, 1969; *Eisenstadt v. Baird*, 1972; and *Roe v. Wade*, 1973) have established this right to freedom from government intrusion in specific situations involving the family, procreation, and the home, but in several cases (*Roe v. Wade*, 1973; *Paris Adult Theater I v. Slaton*, 1973; *U.S. v. 12 200-ft Reels of Super 8 mm Film*, 1973; and *Village of Belle Terre v. Boraas*, 1974) the court has specifically refused to extend the right beyond these limited contexts. Therefore, while the concept of a zone of privacy might be the best foundation upon which a constitutional right to discriminate could be based, no decision has yet established that right as a matter of law (*Yale Law Journal*, 1975).

At What Cost Do We Protect Private Discrimination? The greatest cost of protecting private discrimination is denial of equal opportunity. White- and white male-only private social and golf clubs have denied access to non-white and females for generations (country clubs, city clubs, athletic clubs, fraternal clubs). These private clubs have been a part of American society and more than likely will remain as a tradition. Membership in some clubs can be an important source for business opportunities and networking. Country clubs and downtown clubs are often the setting for new business contacts and business entertaining. There is evidence that executive job promotion is often dependent on the club membership. In some areas clubs may hold a local monopoly on a particular type of recreational facility or dining establishment. The continuance of blanket racial, religious, and gender exclusion would deny these advantages to blacks, Jews, and women, regardless of how well they might meet other nonracial, or gender admissions' criteria.

In resolving the conflict between private groups and individual quality, the courts should recognize the existence of several alternative solutions for reconciling the opposing interests. The courts can maintain a meaningful freedom for private groups to choose social intimates without granting a blanket and absolute right to practice racial, religious, and/or gender discrimination.

Recent Developments

While discrimination (whether it be equal access to admission into a club, equal tee times, or equality in governance) is unacceptable in any forum, the right to form and belong to private clubs is also a basic American right (freedom of association and right to privacy) no matter how distasteful it is. These issues create polarities that need to be managed.

Recently a great deal of attention has been given to discrimination issues in golf. The LPGA and the PGA tours have taken strong positions against discrimination. While some clubs have refused to change their policies, many clubs are considering the minority and women's issues very seriously.

Kerry Graham, (Graham, 1991) president of the LPGA's teaching division and a teaching professional at McCormick Ranch Golf Club (Scottsdale, Arizona), indicates that separate tee times have historical reasons for existing. For many years, when most women did not work, women golfers were pleased to play their primary golf on weekdays, leaving weekends golf times for the men. Golf mirrors our cultural transitions, so as women play a bigger role in business, government, and corporate America, women want greater accessibility and control of their leisure time.

When the difficult economic conditions are added to the cultural transitions more and more clubs (new ones in particular) are trying to attract minorities and women as members and customers. Further current trends of continued cultural change are evidenced clearly by litigation and legislation across the country in the past ten years. Bellwether states like Minnesota, Michigan, and California (Graham, 1991) have taken action by passing laws against discrimination in private clubs. As a result, many clubs are searching for ways to reduce restrictions, such as restricted tee times.

Graham suggests the following creative solutions to reduce restrictions such as 'priority membership' systems, 'special fees' for priority times, and priority tee times by 'handicap.'

She further indicates that we are in a period of increasing women's involvement and leadership. The pressures to continue toward more equal tee times access, etc. will continue. While it cannot happen overnight, private clubs will need to be creative in finding ways to serve women.

Is There Any Reason for a Private Golf/tennis Club Not to Have Gender-neutral Rules Regarding Membership and Use of Its Facilities? In Minnesota (Mackenzie, 1991) a recently passed state law denies a lower property tax rate for private golf courses that discriminated on the basis of gender. Tee-time restrictions based on sex disappeared.

The broader issue behind the tee-time controversy is the clash between the traditional right of the private clubs and associations to make their own rules about membership and privileges versus the obligation of government to act to prevent discriminatory conduct.

Changing societal values have caused state legislatures and courts to reevaluate this issue. They have decided that government-regulated privileges, such as property tax benefits, liquor licenses, and environmental permits, may be withheld from private clubs that discriminate. They have decided that some clubs that receive revenue from nonmembers or where the club is used for furtherance of business opportunities are places of public, not private, accommodation. Therefore they are subject to the same rules that apply in the workplace and school.

Tee-Time Barrier Broken

A settlement regarding the prohibition of women from prime-time tee times at Cheval Country Club in Tampa, Florida, is being touted as an example of private clubs' reversing their policies about tee-time barriers. On April 11, 1994 the Florida attorney general's office notified the club it is violating the law by not allowing women to tee off on Saturday mornings or eat in the men's grill. The state said Cheval must comply with the law or face a lawsuit.

Cheval's prompt action was taken after Molly O'Dea, a Xerox executive and Cheval member, filed a complaint with the Florida attorney general's office in October 1993. O'Dea's complaint was the first under a 1993 Florida law against discrimination. The law states thar private clubs with more than 400 members that provide regular meal service must not publish any statements denying certain privileges of the club because of race, religion, color, gender or national origin.

A similar complaint to O'Dea's was filed earlier this month [time] by Ruth Hanno and Mary Stiegler against Carrollwood Village Golf and Country Club in Tampa. In response to the complaint, Carrollwood removed gender-based language from the club's bylaws and implemented new rules restricting play from 7:30 AM to 1:00 PM on Saturdays to the member and their guest, be it a man or woman.

In Florida the number of clubs, mostly private, that restrict tee-times or food and beverage service is on the decline. The clubs are changing as a reflection of what society is doing.

Sex Discrimination—Martial Dissolution: What Are Your Rights?

In 1995, Welch and other women members of the Wildwood Golf Club brought action under §§ 1983 and 1985(3) against club and owners of land on which club was located, seeking to be free from sexual discrimination, to travel freely, and to conduct business, and one plaintiff alleged in pendent state claim that the club violated her right to effect marital dissolution and distribution of marital property. The district held that: 1) club did not violate women's rights to interstate travel; 2) club was not conducting conspiracy aimed at thwarting capacity of law enforcement authority to provide equal protection of laws; and 3) golf club did not act under color of state law (*Welch v. Bd. Directors of Wildwood Golf Club*, 877 F.Supp. 955 (W.D. Pa. 1995)).

New Jersey Attacking Sex Discrimination at Golf Clubs

In 1996, legislation was introduced to the New Jersey Assembly addressing the issue of sex discrimination in private golf clubs by amending Public Law 1945, c.169 (NJ Law Against Discrimination). This bill has been introduced to amend a loophole that has allowed private clubs to discriminate against women who wish to hold full club membership. It should add teeth to existing antidiscrimination laws. If the bill becomes law, private clubs will have to comply with equal gender treatment regulations. Club membership categories limited solely on the basis of gender should cease.

References

A. Cases
Augusta Golf Association, Inc. v. United States, 338 F.Supp. 272 (S.D.Ga. 1971).
Bell v. Kenwood Golf & Country Club, Inc., 312 F.Supp. 753 (D.C.Md. 1970).
Baker v. Mid Maine Medical Center, et al., 499 A.2d 464 (Me. 1985).
Booth v. City of Minneapolis, 203 N.W. 625 (Minn. 1925).
Bradshaw v. Whigham, 11 Race Rel. L. Rep. 934 (S.D. Fla. 1966)
Brown v. Loudoun Golf and Country Club, Inc., 573 F.Supp. 399 (D.C. Va. 1983).
Clover Hill Swimming Club, Inc. v. Goldsboro, 219 A.2d 161, 47 N.J. 25 (N.J. 1966).

Cornelius v. Benevolent Protective Order of Elks, 382 F.Supp. 1182 (D.C.Conn. 1974).

Daniel v. Paul, 395 U.S. 298, 89 S.Ct. 1697, 23 L.Ed. 318 (1969).

Delaney v. Central Valley Golf Club, 28 N.Y.S.2d. 932, aff'd 31 N.Y.S.2d 834, 263 App.Div. 710, appeal denied 32 N.Y.S.2d 1016, 263 App.Div. 870, aff'd 43 N.E.2d 716, 289 N.Y. 577 (N.Y.Sup. 1941).

Durham v. Red Lake Fishing and Hunting Club, Inc., 666 F.Supp. 954 (W.D.Texas 1987).

Eisenstadt v. Baird, 405 U.S. 438 (1972).

Evans v. Laurel Links, Inc., 261 F.Supp. 474 (E.D.Va. 1966).

Fuller Brush Co. v. Industrial Commission of Utah, 104 P.2d 201, 203 (Utah 1940).

Gardner v. Vic Tanny Compton, Inc., 6 Cal.Rptr. 490, 182 C.A.2d 506, 87 A.L.R.2d 113 (Cal.App. 1960).

Gibson v. Florida Legislative Investigating Committee, 372 U.S. 539 (1963).

Golden v. Biscayne Bay Yacht Club, City of Miami, 370 F. Supp. 1038 (S.D. Fla. 1973).

Griswold v. Connecticut, 381 U.S. 479 (1965).

Jones v. City of Chicago, 787 F.2d 200, 204 (7th Cir. 1986)

Jones v. Alfred H. Mayer Co., 392 U.S. 409 (1968).

Lloyd Lions Club of Portland v. International Association of Lions Clubs, 724 P.2d 887, 81 Or.App. 151 (Or. App. 1986).

Moose Lodge No. 107 v. Irvis, 407 U.S. 163, 92 S.Ct. 1965, 32 L.Ed. 627 (1972).

NAACP v. Alabama, 357 U.S. 449 (1958).

NAACP v. Button, 371 U.S. 415 (1963).

Nesmith v. Young Men's Christian Association of Raleigh, N.C., Inc., 397 F.2d 96 (1968)

Olzman v. Lake Hills Swim Club, 495 F.2d 1333 (1974).

Paris Adult Theater I v. Slaton, 413 U.S. 49 (1973).

People v. Powell, 274 N.W. 372, 373 (Mich. 1937).

People of State of N.Y. by Abrams v. Ocean Club, Inc., 602 F.Supp. 489 (D.C.N.Y. 1984).

Perkins v. New Orleans Athletic Club, 429 F.Supp. 661 (E.D.La. 1976).

Roe v. Wade, 410 U.S. 113 (1973).

Shelton v. Tucker, 364 U.S. 479 (1960).

Sims v. Order of United Commercial Travelers of America, 343 F.Supp. 112 (1972).

Smith v. Young Men's Christian Association of Montgomery, Inc., 316 F. Supp. 899, modified 462 F.2d 634 (D.C.Ala 1972).

Solomon v. Miami Women's Club, 359 F.Supp. 41 (D.C. Fla 1973).

Stanley v. Georgia, 394 U.S. 557 (1969).

Stout v. YMCA, 404 F.2d 687 (5th Cir. 1968).

Sullivan v. Little Hunting Club, Inc. 396 U.S. 229, 90 S.Ct. 400, 24 L.Ed. 2d 386 (1969).

Tillman v. Wheaton-Haven Recreation Association, Inc., aff'd, and certiorari granted, 451 F.2d 1211 (4th Cir. 1971), denied rehearing, 451 F.2d 1225 (4th Cir. 1971), rev'd and remanded, 410 U.S. 431, 93 S.Ct. 1090, 35 L.Ed.2d 403 (1973).

U.S. v. Eagles, 472 F.Supp. 1174 (E.D.Wis. 1979).

U.S. v. Lansdowne Swim Club, 713 F.Supp. 785 (E.D.Pa. 1989), rehearing denied, 894 F.2d 83 (3rd Cir. 1990).

U.S. v. Jack Sabin's Private Club, 265 F.Supp. 90 (La. Ct. App. 1967).

U.S. v. Johnson Lake, Inc., 312 F.Supp. 1376 (D.C.Ala 1970).

U.S. v. Jordan, 302 F.Supp. 370 (E.D.La. 1969).

U.S. Power Squadrons v. State Human Rights Appeal Board, 445 N.Y.S.2d 565, 84 A.D.2d 318 (N.Y.A.D. 1981); aff'd, 465 N.Y.S.2d 871, 59 N.Y.2d 401, 452 N.E.2d 1199, reargument dismissed 468 N.Y.S.2d 107, 60 N.Y.2d 682, 455 N.E.2d 666 (N.Y.A.D. 1983).

U.S. v. Richberg, 398 F.2d. 523 (5th Cir. 1968).

U.S. v. Robel, 389 U.S. 258 (1967).

U.S. v. 12 200-ft Reels of Super 8 mm Film, 413 U.S. 123 (1973).

Vidrich v. Vic Tanny Intern, Inc., 301 N.W.2d 482, 102 Mich.App. 230 (Mich. App. 1980).

Village of Belle Terre v. Boraas, 416 U.S. 1 (1974).

Welch v. Bd. Directors of Wildwood Golf Club, 877 F.Supp. 955 (W.D. Pa. 1995)

Wright v. Cork Club, 315 F.Supp. 1143 (D.C. Tex 1970).

Wright v. Salisbury Club, Ltd., 479 F.Supp. 378 (D.C.Va. 1979). rev'd on other grounds, 632 F.2d 309 (C.A.Va. 1980).

B. Publications

Bardshaw v Yorba Linda Country Club and American Golf Corporation Settled Out-of-Court (1989) reported in Maclean, P.A. (1991). Tee'd Off. *Women's Sports & Fitness*, 64, 41-48.

Maclean, P.A. (1991). Tee'd Off. *Women's Sports & Fitness*, 64,41-48.

Notes (1975). Section 1981 and Private Groups: The Right to Discriminate Versus Freedom from Discrimination. *Yale Law Journal*, 84:1441-1476.

PGA (1991). Annual Membership Report.

Pike, Steve (1994). Female Pioneer Breaks Through Tee-Time Barrier. *Golfweek*, 3-4.

Sawyer, T.H. (1990). Unpublished Study Completed by Students in an Undergraduate Sports Law Class.

C. Legislation

Civil Rights Act of 1966, 42 U.S.C.A. § 1981 (1970).

Civil Rights Act of 1964, 42 U.S.C.A. § 2000a (1970).

42 U.S.C.A. § 2000 a(a)(b)(c)(d)(e) (1970)

42 U.S.C.A. § 1981 (1970)

5.00 • SPORT AND LEGISLATION

Aaron L. Mulrooney
Kent State University

Violence in sport is not a new topic of discussion. As long as competition between athletes is present, the propensity for violence will exist in many sports. Sport by its very nature, especially in today's society, is a battle ground for the survival of the fittest. Looking simply at the popularity of the Ultimate Fighting Championships, where martial artists fight with virtually no rules until one combatant submits or is no longer able to physically continue, one could discern that violence not only exists in sport, but is a sport as well, that fans both condone and applaud.

The question though, is when does violence in sport turn into to criminal behavior. The crimes of assault and battery are present in jurisdictions throughout the country and are defined by both statute and case law. The commission of a crime requires that an individual meet certain elements dealing with the act and mental state of the defendant. In this respect, criminal law is much the same as tort law. Like tort law, criminal law affords defenses to excuse what might otherwise be described as criminal conduct. With respect to violence in sport, the two most prominent defenses are self-defense and consent. This section will explore these concepts and will explain them relative to sport.

Most sport law texts examine *Regina v. Maki* (1970) or *Regina v. Green* (1970) when discussing criminal conduct in sport. In the following case, the principles outlined in *Maki* and *Green* are applied to a situation involving amateur athletics. While reading this case try to determine if the facts of the cases are truly different or could different standards apply to amateurs versus professionals?

■ ■ ■ ■

Representative Case

PEOPLE v. FREER
District Court of New York, First District, Suffolk County
381 N.Y.S.2d 976 (1976)

OPINION:

Defendant was charged with the crime of assault in the third degree in violation of section 120.00 of the Penal Law. The case was tried by the court without a jury since the defendant is an apparently eligible youth.

The complainant and the defendant were playing as participants on opposite teams in a football game. The defendant was carrying the ball when the complainant tackled him. In the course of the tackle the complainant punched the defendant in the throat. Both fell to the ground and there was a pileup. After all of the players got off of the defendant he punched the complainant in the eye with intent to cause physical injury, causing the damage including a laceration requiring plastic surgery, as shown in the hospital report received in evidence.

The area of law involving the above facts, "violence in organized sports," is an extremely current, controversial and a "grey" area in the law. Many questions remain unanswered.

There are generally two defenses presented to assaultive attacks by participants in sporting events. Generally, these are: (1) that the act was consented to as being part of the game, referred to as the "consent defense." Secondly, (2) that the act was justified as an act of "self defense."

1. The Consent Defense:

In 1969 an altercation during the course of a professional hockey game resulted in the prosecution of two participants, Edward "Ted" Green and Wayne Maki, for assault. The incident began during the game when Green struck Maki in the face with a gloved hand. While the testimony was conflicting, it appeared that Maki retaliated by striking Green in the lower abdomen with his hockey stick. A stickfight ensued in which Green first struck Maki near the shoulder and Maki countered with a blow which fractured Green's skull. Maki was charged with "Assault causing bodily harm." Green was charged with simple assault. Both individuals were acquitted.

The first of these cases to be tried, Regina v Maki, in 1970 in Ontario Provincial Court (10 CRNS 268; 13 Amer Crim L Rev, p 235), discussed the consent defense in dicta. The court in that case concluded (p 241) that the defense could not apply on the facts of the particular case saying "no athlete should be presumed to accept malicious, unprovoked, or overly violent attack." The theory of the consent defense is simply that in all sports participants "consent" by the very nature of the sport to certain acts of violence. In Regina v Green, tried in 1970 in Ontario Provincial Court (16 DLR3d 137; 13 Amer Crim L Rev, p 235), the Judge determined that the victim had consented to being struck in the face by a gloved hand, because the victim knew this was a common practice in hockey games and was not likely to be seriously injured.

The courts in the above cases drew two conclusions. (1) There is a limit to the magnitude and dangerousness of a blow to which another is deemed to consent. (2) In all sports players consent to many risks, hazards and blows.

In these particular instances the court felt that a blow to the face by a gloved hand was consented to by the participant.

2. The Defense of Justification. "Self Defense":

"Section 35.00 et seq. of the Penal Law governs the defense of justification. Section 35.10 provides that the use of physical force is justifiable and not criminal when (under subd. 6) a person is defending himself or another, defending property, making an arrest or preventing escape. Section 35.15 provides that a person is justified in using physical force on another in order to defend himself or a third party from what he reasonably believes to be the use or imminent use of unlawful physical force, to such a degree as the actor reasonably believes is necessary. However, a person is not justified if he provoked the use of such unlawful physical force, or he was the initial aggressor (with an exception for situations where the actor has withdrawn from the encounter and communicated such withdrawal); or the force involved was the result of agreed upon combat not authorized by law." (People v Gibaldi, 75 Misc 2d 811, 812.)

In the case at bar one player tackles another and in doing so allegedly throws a punch; after an intervening pileup the player receiving it punches back, causing injury to the eye of the alleged initial aggressor.

Initially it may be assumed that the very first punch thrown by the complainant in the course of the tackle was consented to by defendant. The act of tackling an opponent in the course of a football game may often involve "contact" that could easily be interpreted to be a "punch." Defendant's response after the pileup to complainant's initial act of "aggression" cannot be mistaken. Clearly, defendant intended to punch complainant. This was not a consented to act.

Hypothetically speaking, if defendant, after receiving the alleged initial punch, believed he was vulnerable to further attack, and was lying on the ground in a pileup, his actions may very well be justified, especially if complainant ended up on top of defendant. If, however, defendant rolled free and was not vulnerable to further attack his actions could not be deemed reasonable.

The statute, subdivision 1 of section 35.15 of the Penal Law, uses the language, "what he reasonably believes." Since it is impossible to determine what defendant believed, we can only infer his feelings by witnesses' observations concerning whether or not it appeared that defendant could have been vulnerable to further attack.

Initially it should be noted that justification for an assault should not be presumed. Although the burden of proof rests with the People, the defendant must go forward in the first instance to show the justifiableness of an assaultive act. (See People v Gibaldi, 75 Misc 2d 811, 813 supra.) In the Gibaldi case, the court dealt with the question of whether or not it was reasonable for the defendant to believe that complainant would attack him. In the case at bar, a similar question must be answered, to wit, whether or not defendant believed he was under attack and whether he had a right to this belief.

The court in the Gibaldi case, notes that the test of whether the defense of justification may be asserted, is dependent upon whether there was reasonable ground for the belief. "Any person who commits violence in his personal defense must not only believe he is in danger but he must in fact have reasonable ground for that belief." (People v Gibaldi, supra, p 812, citing People v Governale, 193 NY 581.) Further, "the question is not merely what did the defendant believe, but what did he have a right to believe." (People v Gibaldi, supra, p 812, citing People v Rodawald, 177 NY 408.)

In the case before the court the testimony made it abundantly clear that any attack which the defendant may have believed was being made upon him was terminated by the pileup which ensued after the initial contact between the complainant and the defendant at the time of the tackle. After the other players got up and off of the defendant he got up on one knee while the complainant was lying supine and forcibly struck the complainant with his fist. The court has no alternative other than to find that the time and acts intervening between the two occurrences deprived the defendant of any reasonable basis to believe that he was in danger.

The court finds that the People have proved beyond a reasonable doubt that the defendant is guilty of the crime of assault in the third degree in violation of section 120.00 of the Penal Law of the State of New York. This matter is set down for determination of defendant's eligibility for youthful offender treatment and sentencing on May 21, 1976. A probation report shall be ordered and the defendant is requested to communicate with the Probation Department to assist them in commencing their investigation.

■ ■ ■ ■

Fundamental Concepts

Assault and battery are crimes that are generally coupled when spoken of in day to day conversation. But, these crimes each have separate elements. Both of these crimes will be discussed, but it should be noted that today, some jurisdictions have encompassed the crime of battery in their definition of assault. (See Model Penal Code sec. 211.1) Before discussing the specific crimes of assault and battery, we will first examine the two essential elements of many crimes, the Actus Reus and Mens Rea.

Actus Reus

For most crimes, including assault and battery, it is necessary to show that the defendant performed some type of voluntary act or failed to act when a legal duty was imposed to do so. The act in question must be not only voluntary but conscious as well. This infers that acts, that are pure reflex acts, will not meet the requirements for actus reus. This element of assault and battery is not usually an issue in sport since the competitors are quite aware and able to control their actions in most instances.

Mens Rea

Mens rea refers to the mental state of the defendant at the time the alleged crime took place (see State v. Forbes, 1975). When mens rea is combined with actus reus, the basis for criminal liability has been established. The three main mental states in criminal law are general intent, specific intent and criminal negligence.

General intent refers to the state of mind that is required to commit the actus reus. This means that the defendant would need to know or have an awareness that the act is probably going to occur. Throwing a punch or other blow would easily meet general intent as a presumption may be drawn that intent is present by simply committing the act.

Specific intent is a higher level of mental state. It requires that the defendant go beyond simply doing an act. The defendant must also intend to cause some additional act or consequence. An example would be if the defendant threw a punch intending to injure a person in a particular way, such as knocking out some teeth.

Criminal negligence is similar to negligence in tort law but a greater degree of culpability is required for criminal negligence. This means that the defendant would have to either have some sort of subjective awareness of the risk at hand or there must be a rather large deviation from the reasonable care standard found in an ordinary negligence case.

Assault

The two basic types of assault include: assault for attempted battery and assault for intentionally placing someone in apprehension of physical harm or injury.

Assault for attempted battery occurs when the defendant wishes to not only complete the physical act (actus reus) but also is intending on causing some type of injury. The mental state of the defendant requires specific intent. In other words the defendant intends to make physical contact but for some reason is unable to do so.

Assault for intentionally placing someone in apprehension of physical danger or injury occurs when the defendant threatens an individual in some manner. It is important to understand that simple verbal threats are insufficient to meet the actus reus in this case. The apprehension of injury must be reasonable and immediate. Therefore words must be accompanied by some threatening action at a minimum. The mental state again is specific intent. The defendant must have intentionally place the victim in apprehension of harm.

Battery

Battery occurs when the defendant inflicts illegal force upon another. In most jurisdictions, the force need not cause an injury to the victim but simple offensive touching will suffice. The mens rea involved in battery usually is that of general intent and sometimes criminal negligence. This means that under general intent, the simple doing or completion of the act will suffice in proving liability.

Assault and Battery in Sports

Using a strict reading of the crimes defined above, one could make the argument that assault and battery occurs in every single athletic contest. This may be true if there were no defenses that can be used to justify conduct that may otherwise be deemed as assault and battery. However, as discussed in *The People of the State of New York v. John Freer,* presented earlier, the defenses of consent and self-defense exist in order to justify what may otherwise be viewed as criminal conduct.

Consent

Consent is usually a defense to minor assault and batteries when there is not a threat that the victim will suffer serious bodily harm. For consent to operate as a defense, the defendant must show that the consent was voluntarily given, no fraud was used in obtaining the consent and the victim had capacity to give his or her consent. Implicitly in sport, all participants consent to the ordinary/normal instances of "violence" that are peculiar to their sport. It is when these bounds are exceeded the defense of consent no longer will work for the defendant (see *Regina v. Maloney,* 1976).

Self-Defense

Self-defense permits an individual to use such force as is reasonably necessary to protect himself or herself from the imminent use of illegal force against them. In most jurisdictions there is no duty to retreat placed upon the victim. The key facts involved in self-defense are the amount of force used and the timing of the "self-defense." As a general rule, someone who is asserting self-defense may not escalate the violence that is already occurring. If this occurs, the person who escalates the violence may become the aggressor and will no longer be able to claim self-defense. Timing is important in much the same way. If the aggressor who initiates the altercation retreats and shows no signs of further aggression then an attack by the victim will not be viewed as self-defense (see *Regina v. Leyte*, 1973).

Legislative Attempts to Control Sport Violence

In the 1980's legislative attempts were made to stem the violence in professional hockey. One of these attempts occurred at the state legislature level in Massachusetts. Two other pieces of legislation were introduced at the federal level in the U.S. House of Representatives.

After a fight that occurred during a Boston Bruins hockey game the president of the Boston City Council proposed an ordinance that required the police officers to arrest players who interrupted play by fighting. The proposed ordinance (proposed by Councilor Bolling, Dec. 19, 1986; filed without further action, Feb. 27, 1987) provided in part:

> Section 2. Any professional athlete engaged in competition within the City of Boston, shall be subject to immediate arrest by any member or members of the Boston Police Department upon the commission of any violent act during said competition.

In 1980, Congressmen Mottl introduced the following *Sports Violence Act* which, if passed, would have made violence in sport a federal criminal offense (H.R. 7903, 96th Congress, 2d Session (1980)). The bill provided in part:

> (a) Whoever, as a player in a professional sports event, knowingly uses excessive physical force and thereby causes a risk of significant bodily injury to another person involved in that event shall be fined not more than $5,000 or imprisoned not more than one year, or both.
>
> (b) As used in this section, the term—
>
> > (1) "excessive physical force" means physical force that—
> >
> > > (A) has no reasonable relationship to the competitive goals of the sport;
> > >
> > > (B) is unreasonably violent; and
> > >
> > > (C) could not be reasonably foreseen, or was not consented to, by the injured person, as a normal hazard of such person's involvement in such sports event; and
> >
> > (2) "professional sports event" means a paid-admission contest, in or affecting interstate or foreign commerce, of players paid for their participation.

In 1983, Congressman Daschle introduced the *Sports Violence Arbitration Act* in an attempt to pick up where Congressman Mottl left off. (H.R. 4495, 98th Congress, 1st Session (1983)). Excerpts from the bill are outlined below.

A BILL

To provide for the establishment of an arbitration system to reduce the number and costs of injuries resulting from the use of excessively violent conduct during professional sports events.

Be it enacted by the Senate and House of Representatives of the United States of America in Congress assembled,

SHORT TITLE (in part)

Section 1. This Act may be cited as the "Sports Violence Arbitration Act of 1983."

STATEMENT OF PURPOSE

Section 2. It is the purpose of this Act to reduce the number and costs of injuries resulting from the use of excessively violent conduct during professional sports events by establishing an arbitration system empowered to settle grievances resulting from such conduct.

DEFINITIONS

Section 3. As used in this Act, the term—

(2) "excessively violent conduct" means physical force or contact employed during a professional sports event which creates a risk of injury and which

(A) is unnecessary for effective participation in the sport consistent with the competitive goals of that sport;

(B) is intended to injure; or

(C) is intended to create a threat of injury;

ESTABLISHMENT OF ARBITRATION SYSTEMS

Section 4.
(a) Each professional sports league shall establish an arbitration system in accordance with this Act for the arbitration of grievances resulting from the use of excessively violent conduct.

ARBITRATION OF GRIEVANCES

Section 5.
(a) Any player or professional sports club which sustains injury as the result of excessively violent conduct, or is the object of excessively violent conduct, may bring a grievance before the arbitration board against the player who allegedly engaged in such excessively violent conduct and the professional sports club which employed such player.

(b) Any person who acted as a league game official at a professional sports event may bring a grievance before the arbitration board against any player who allegedly engaged in excessively violent conduct during such professional sports event and against the professional sports club which employed such player.

(c) Upon the bringing of any grievance the arbitration board shall conduct an investigation and hold proceedings in accordance with the policies, rules, and procedures established by the Federal Mediation and Conciliation Service pursuant to section 8 of this Act. Upon the completion of such proceedings, the arbitration board shall issue a written decision and order. Such decision and order may include the following:

   (1) An award of compensation to any party which sustained injury as a result of the excessively violent conduct which is the subject of the grievance. The award of compensation shall be paid by the professional sports club which employed the player who engaged in such excessively violent conduct.

   (2) The imposition of disciplinary sanctions against the player who engaged in such excessively violent conduct, against the professional sports club which employed such player, or against both such player and such professional sports club. The disciplinary sanctions which may be imposed include fines, suspension from play without pay, and loss of a draft choice.

(d) The factors which the arbitration board shall take into account in fixing the amount of compensation awarded under subsection (c)(1) of this section shall include—

   (1) the extent of any injuries sustained by any player injured as a result of such excessively violent conduct;

   (2) the duration of any period during which such injured player was unable to participate in professional sports events as a result of such injuries;

   (3) the amount of salary paid to such injured player by the professional sports club which employs such player during that period which such player was unable to participate in professional sports events as a result of such injuries;

   (4) the amount of any medical or other expenses incurred by such injured player or the professional sports club which employs such player as a result of such injuries; and

   (5) any other factors which the arbitration board may deem relevant.

(e) The factors which the arbitration board shall take into account in imposing disciplinary sanctions under subjection (c)(2) of this section shall include—

   (1) the extent of any injuries sustained by any player injured as a result of conduct;

   (2) the duration of any period during which such player was unable to participate in professional sports events as a result of such injuries;

(3) the risk of serious injury which was created by the use of such excessively violent conduct, whether or not such conduct actually resulted in injuries;

(4) any prior history of excessively violent conduct on the part of the player who engaged in such excessively violent conduct;

(5) the apparent intent on the part of the player who engaged in such excessively violent conduct to cause injury; and

(6) any other factors which the arbitration board may deem relevant.

ADDITIONAL REMEDIES

Section 7.
Any player or professional sports club bringing an action before an arbitration board under section 5(a) of this Act shall not, by reason of such action, be barred from instituting a civil action in any court of competent jurisdiction based upon the occurrence which is the subject of the action brought before the arbitration board, except that any compensation awarded by the arbitration board under section 5(c)(1) of this Act shall be reduced by an amount equal to the amount for any monetary settlement or award in any such civil action.

Recent Developments

Violence in sport remains a current problem throughout professional sport. But, nowhere is the violence problem better exhibited than in professional hockey. As mentioned previously, Canadian courts have wrestled with the issue of criminal sanctions against players who engage in violent conduct during the course of the game. Yet, due to the status of professional athletes and the public acceptance of violence in hockey, convictions for assault and battery have been difficult.

However, in 1988, in *Regina v. Ciccarelli* (1988), Dino Ciccarelli of the then Minnesota North Stars, was convicted of assault for hitting Luke Richardson of the Toronto Maple Leafs twice over the head with his stick and punching him once in the mouth. Ciccarelli was ejected from the game and suspended for 10 games by the NHL and he served a one-day jail sentence and was ordered to pay a fine of $1000. Although many may applaud the efforts of the court in this case, a one day jail sentence and a $1000 fine is less than a slap on the hand given the length of jail term and amount of fines an ordinary person would be subjected to if they committed these same acts.

Professional sport leagues have also attempted to reduce violence through instituting new rules that are both punitive and preventative in nature. For example, in the NHL, rules have been introduced that create penalties for instigating fights and for a player entering a fight involving a teammate (see *Official NHL Playing Rules*, 1996). In the NBA, the length of suspensions and the maximum amounts of fines for fighting have been increased and rules have been instituted that penalize trash talking and flagrant fouls (see *NBA Official Rules*, 1996). Although the rules are a step in the right direction, the problem with these rules is that they still do not have a high enough level of monetary punishment. The $25,000 maximum fine in the NBA is a game's salary for many player's in the league. If leagues truly wish to reduce violence in their respective sports they should dramatically increase the amounts of fines to a point where these athletes will think twice before committing acts of violence.

References

A. Cases

The People of the State of New York v. John Freer, 86 Misc. 2d 280; 381 N.Y.S.2d 976 (1976).
Regina v. Ciccarelli, (Ontario Prov. Ct. 1988).
Regina v. Green, 16 DLR 3d 137 (Ont. Prov. Ct. 1970).
Regina v. Leyte, 13 C.C.C. 2d 458 (Ont. Prov. Ct. 1973).
Regina v. Maloney, (1976) 28 C.C.C. 2d 323 (Ont. Prov. Ct. 1970).
Regina v. Maki, 14 DLR 3d 164 (Ont. Prov. Ct. 1970).
State v. Forbes, No. 63280 (Minn. Dist. Ct. 1975).

B. Publications

Berry, Robert and Wong, Glenn M. (1986). *Law and Business of the Sports Industries*. Vol. 2. Dover, Mass.: Auburn House.
Loewy, A. (1987). *Criminal Law in a Nutshell*. St. Paul, Minn.: West Publishing.
Official NHL Playing Rules. (1996). National Hockey League, New York.
NBA Official Rules. (1996). National Basketball Association, New York.
Schubert, G., Smith, R., and Trentadue, J. (1986). *Sports Law*. St. Paul, Minn.: West Publishing.
Weistart, J. and Lowell, C. (1979). *The Law of Sports*. Charlottesville, Va.: The Michie Company.
Weiler, P. and Roberts, G. (1993). *Sports and the Law*. St. Paul, Minn.: West Publishing.
White, D. (1986). Sports Violence as Criminal Assault: Development of the Doctrine by Canadian Courts. *1986 Duke Law Journal* 1030.

C. Legislation

Model Penal Code § 211.1.
Sports Violence Act, H.R. 7903, 96th Congress, 2d Session (1980).
Sports Violence Arbitration Act, H.R. 4495, 98th Congress, 1st Session (1983).

Criminal Law

Gambling, Ticket Scalping, Wire and Mail Fraud

Andy Pittman
Baylor University

Intro

Gambling and ticket scalping have been problems in the sports industry for many years. Indeed, long before the Black Sox scandal of 1919 professional baseball players routinely accepted bribes to throw games. Sports gambling has grown to the point now that the Federal Bureau of Investigation (FBI) estimates that sports betting accounts for 50 percent of the $28 billion bet annually in the United States. Like gambling, ticket scalping has long been a problem in the entertainment and sport industries. In an early case in California (*Ex parte Quarg*, 1906), scalpers challenged anti-scalping legislation, alleging that it violated their right of free enterprise. At major college and professional sporting events today, it is not unusual to find scalpers fanning their tickets at would-be buyers, selling them for whatever price the market may bear. Unlike gambling and ticket scalping, wire and mail fraud is relatively new to sports. The seminal case in this area is *U. S. v. Walters* (1989) in which two sports agents were accused of using the mail to defraud higher education institutions. Due to improved technology and subsequent expanded use of electronic mail, wire and mail fraud violations in sport may become more frequent in the twenty-first century.

■ ■ ■ ■

Representative Case

NATIONAL FOOTBALL LEAGUE v. GOVERNOR OF THE STATE OF DELAWARE
United States District Court for the District of Delaware
435 F. Supp. 1372 (1977)

OPINION: STAPLETON, District Judge:

In August 1976, the Office of the Delaware State Lottery announced a plan to institute a lottery game based on games of the National Football League ("NFL"). Immediately thereafter, the NFL and its twenty-eight member clubs filed suit in this Court against the Governor and the Director of the State Lottery seeking preliminary and permanent injunctive relief barring such a lottery scheme. The State of Delaware intervened, and the complaint was amended to add a request that the Court create a construc-

tive trust on behalf of the NFL clubs of all revenues derived from such a lottery. Finding no threat of immediate irreparable injury to the NFL, the Court denied the prayer for a temporary restraining order.

During the week of September 12, 1976, the football lottery games commenced. Upon defendants' motion, the Court dismissed plaintiffs' claims that the games violated the Equal Protection Clause of the Fourteenth Amendment and the Commerce Clause of the Constitution. With respect to twelve other counts, defendants' motion to dismiss or for summary judgment was denied. The lottery games continued through the season.

In late Fall, a six day trial on the merits was held. That was followed by extended briefing. The matter is now ripe for disposition. This Opinion constitutes the Court's findings of fact and conclusions of law on the questions presented.

Factual Background

The Delaware football lottery is known as "Scoreboard" and it involves three different games, "Football Bonus," "Touchdown" and "Touchdown II." All are weekly games based on regularly scheduled NFL games. In Football Bonus, the fourteen games scheduled for a given weekend are divided into two pools of seven games each. A player must mark the lottery ticket with his or her projections of the winners of the seven games in one or both of the two pools and place a bet of $1, $2, $3, $5 or $10. To win Football Bonus, the player must correctly select the winner of each of the games in a pool. If the player correctly selects the winners of all games in both pools, he or she wins an "All Game Bonus." The amounts of the prizes awarded are determined on a pari-mutuel basis, that is, as a function of the total amount of money bet by all players.

In Touchdown, the lottery card lists the fourteen games for a given week along with three ranges of possible point spreads. The player must select both the winning team and the winning margin in each of three, four or five games. The scale of possible bets is the same as in Bonus and prizes are likewise distributed on a pari-mutuel basis to those who make correct selections for each game on which they bet.

Touchdown II, the third Scoreboard game, was introduced in mid-season and replaced Touchdown for the remainder of the season. In Touchdown II, a "line" or predicted point spread on each of twelve games is published on the Wednesday prior to the games. The player considers the published point spread and selects a team to "beat the line", that is, to do better in the game than the stated point spread. To win, the player must choose correctly with respect to each of from four to twelve games. Depending upon the number of games bet on, there is a fixed payoff of from $10 to $1,200. There is also a consolation prize for those who beat the line on nine out ten, ten out of eleven or eleven out of twelve games.

Scoreboard tickets are available from duly authorized agents of the Delaware State Lottery, usually merchants located throughout the State. The tickets list the teams by city names, e.g., Tampa or Cincinnati, rather than by nicknames such as Buccaneers or Bengals. Revenues are said to be distributed pursuant to a fixed apportionment

schedule among the players of Scoreboard, the State, the sales agents and the Lottery Office for its administrative expenses.

The Parties' Claims

The core of plaintiffs' objections to Scoreboard is what they term a "forced association with gambling." They complain that the football lottery constitutes an unlawful interference with their property rights and they oppose its operation on a host of federal, state and common law grounds. Briefly stated, their complaint includes counts based on federal and state trademark laws, the common law doctrine of misappropriation, the federal anti-gambling laws, the Civil Rights Act of 1871 (42 U.S.C. § 1983), the Delaware Constitution and the Delaware lottery statute.

The defendants deny that the state-run revenue raising scheme violates any federal, state or common law doctrine. Further, they have filed a counterclaim for treble damages under the Sherman and Clayton Acts for federal antitrust law violations charging, inter alia, that the plaintiffs have brought this litigation for purposes of harassment and that they have conspired to monopolize property which is in the public domain.

For the reasons which follow, I have determined that the plaintiffs are entitled to limited injunctive relief, in the nature of a disclaimer on all Scoreboard materials disseminated to the public. The Touchdown II game will also be invalidated. In all other respects, their claims for relief are denied. The defendants' claim for treble damages is likewise denied.

• • •

IV. Delaware Lottery Law

The plaintiffs assert that the State Lottery Office is acting ultra vires in conducting the Scoreboard games. The NFL points to Article II, Section 17 of the Delaware Constitution which prohibits all forms of gambling in the State except lotteries under state control, pari-mutuel wagering on State licensed races, and Bingo. The heart of their contention based on Section 17 is that Scoreboard is not a lottery. The NFL further contends that, even if Scoreboard is a lottery within the meaning of the Constitution, the Lottery Office is operating it in a manner inconsistent with the requirements for state lotteries established by the General Assembly. The State's first line of defense is that the NFL lacks standing to raise these ultra vires arguments.

A. Standing

The question of standing with respect to claims based on the State Constitution and a State statute is governed by Delaware law. In the past, the Delaware Supreme Court has looked to and followed the rules of standing established in the federal courts on the law of standing as well as to its own precedents. I have done likewise here.

In Mills v. Trans-Caribbean Airways, Inc., 272 A.2d 702, 703 (Del. 1971), the court held that standing to attack the constitutionality of a statute or any action taken thereunder depends on a showing that "a right of the complainant is affected thereby." Association of Data Processing Service Organizations, Inc. v. Camp, 397 U.S. 150, 25 L. Ed. 2d 184, 90 S. Ct. 827 (1970), sets forth a three-part analysis by which to determine whether such a litigable right exists. Camp held that a party must allege injury in fact; he must show that he is "arguably within the zone of interests to be protected or regulated by the statute or constitutional guarantee in question"; and finally, the complainant must establish that judicial review has not been precluded. 397 U.S. at 152-156. Later cases have emphasized that the interest the plaintiff alleges must not be one which is held in common by all members of the public. Plaintiff must be suffering or threatened with a concrete, particularized injury. Schlesinger v. Reservists to Stop the War, 418 U.S. 208, 220, 41 L. Ed. 2d 706, 94 S. Ct. 2925 (1974).

The original version of Section 17 contained a general prohibition of all forms of gambling in the State. It is fair to assume that it was based on some generalized belief that gambling was a corrupting, dangerous influence in society from which the people of the State should be protected.

Over the years, the constitutional provision has been amended in stages. Each amendment was designed to exempt from the general prohibition some particular form of gambling. Undoubtedly the amendments reflect a changing perception about the evils of gambling. Nevertheless, Section 17 continues to reflect a concern about the potentially deleterious influence of gambling on society.

A police power regulation of this kind is for the benefit of the society at large. As a component of that society, the NFL is within the zone of interests to be protected. In addition, the NFL has alleged a concrete injury in fact to itself. The NFL charges that the likelihood that games will be fixed or, more likely, that the public will imagine that the games have been fixed to produce a large payoff will hurt its reputation. In addition, it asserts that the same ill will toward gambling that prompted the legislature to enact the constitutional provisions will drive away those NFL fans who believe that the NFL has consented to or approved gambling on its games. This is a sufficient stake in the outcome to ensure that the matter has been presented in a true adversary context. Finally, the State does not contend that review has been precluded. Accordingly, the NFL has standing to make its constitutional claim.

The standing analysis with respect to NFL's contention that Scoreboard violates the lottery statute, 29 Del. C. §

4801, et seq., is much the same. The lottery statute embodies the same underlying mistrust for gambling, qualified by the idea that State control will obviate the undesirable aspects of gambling while providing the State with a source of income. The zone of interests protected is the same and the same allegations of injury are sufficient.

• • •

V. The Federal Anti-gambling Law Claims

Plaintiffs maintain that defendants are operating the Delaware Lottery in a manner which violates a number of sections of the federal anti-gambling laws, e.g., 18 U.S.C. §§ 1301, 1302, 1304 and 1084. I assume, without deciding, that this is true. Nevertheless, the relief sought cannot be granted on this ground.

A. Plaintiffs Have No Civil Claim Based Directly Upon the Federal Anti-Gambling Statutes

The Supreme Court recently observed in Piper v. Chris-Craft Industries, Inc., 430 U.S. 1, 97 S. Ct. 926, 51 L. Ed. 2d 124, 45 U.S.L.W. 4182 (February 23, 1977), that "the reasoning of . . . [the cases which have implied a private cause of action where none has been expressly provided by Congress] is that, where congressional purposes are likely to be undermined absent private enforcement, private remedies may be implied in favor of the particular class intended to be protected by the statute." 430 U.S. at 25, 97 S. Ct. at 941. The opinion in Piper also reaffirmed the court's position in Cort v. Ash, 422 U.S. 66, 45 L. Ed. 2d 26, 95 S. Ct. 2080 (1975) that four factors are "'relevant' in determining whether a private remedy is implicit in a statute not expressly providing one." 422 U.S. at 78. They are: (1) whether plaintiff is one of the class for whose especial benefit the statute was enacted; (2) whether there is any indication of legislative intent, explicit or implicit, either to create such a remedy or deny one; (3) whether it is consistent under the underlying purposes of the legislative scheme to imply such a remedy for the plaintiff; and (4) whether the cause of action is one traditionally relegated to state law.

The anti-gambling laws upon which plaintiffs rely restrict the utilization of interstate commerce in aid of gambling enterprise. They were enacted at the turn of the century "to protect the citizen from the demoralizing or corrupting influence" of solicitations to gamble. United States v. Horner, 44 F. 677 (S.D.N.Y. 1891), aff'd, 143 U.S. 207, 36 L. Ed. 126, 12 S. Ct. 407 (1892). I believe the suggestion that they were enacted for the "especial" benefit of sports entrepreneurs to be simply far fetched.

It is true that Congress in 1974 enacted 18 U.S.C. § 1307 for the purpose of exempting state sponsored lotteries from certain of the prohibitions of Sections 1301-1304 and defined "lottery" for this purpose as not including "the placing or accepting of bets or wagers on sporting events or contests." While this clearly exhibits an intent to exclude state sponsored sports betting from the exclusion, it does not alter the basic purpose of the statute or those who comprise its direct beneficiaries. Moreover, Section 1307 cannot be read to justify implication of a private right of action in favor of sports entrepreneurs without inferring a congressional intent to create a cause of action against state governments and the Supreme Court has cautioned that such an intent should not be inferred absent clear evidence in the legislative history.Employees of the Department of Public Health and Welfare of Missouri v. Department of Public Health and Welfare of Missouri, 411 U.S. 279, 285, 36 L. Ed. 2d 251, 93 S. Ct. 1614 (1973).

No legislative history has been cited to the Court which indicates any congressional intent to create a private cause of action of any kind, much less a private cause of action by a commercial enterprise against a State. Nor is there any indication that private enforcement is necessary to effectuate the restrictions on interstate commerce which Congress sought to impose. For these reasons, I hold that plaintiffs have no private cause of action under the federal anti-gambling statutes.

B. Plaintiffs Have No Unfair Competition Claim Under Which Defendants' Duty Is Measured by the Federal Anti-Gambling Statutes

Plaintiffs have cited a number of cases which hold that a commercial enterprise has an unfair competition claim against a competitor who achieves a competitive advantage by conducting his business in an illegal manner. In Featherstone v. Independent Service Station Association,

10 S.W.2d 124 (Tex. Civ. App. 1928), for example, the owner of a filling station was granted injunctive relief against a chain of competing stations which was promoting its own services and products by means of a lottery illegal under state law.

I do not question the reasoning of these cases. An entrepreneur who is willing to obey the law should not be put at a disadvantage by a competitor who is less scrupulous. This reasoning cannot be stretched to cover a situation like the one before this Court, however, without emasculating the settled principles discussed above which circumscribe judicial creation of private causes of action.

Moreover, the only potential injury to the NFL which this Court is able to perceive arises not from the aspects of defendants' activities which are alleged to violate the federal gambling statutes, but rather from those aspects of the Delaware Lottery which have produced confusion as to sponsorship. Stated another way, if such confusion is eliminated, this record does not support the view that the existence of the Delaware Lottery, whether legal in all respects or not, will cause injury to the NFL plaintiffs.

• • •

Conclusion

For all of the reasons discussed in the foregoing Opinion, the Court will enter an Order (1) enjoining the defendants to include in publicly disseminated Scoreboard materials a clear and conspicuous statement that Scoreboard is not associated with or authorized by the National Football League and (2) declaring Touchdown II in violation of 29 Del. C. §§ 4805(a)(11) and 4815. All other requests for relief are denied.

■ ■ ■ ■

Fundamental Concepts

Gambling

Since the Black Sox scandal of 1919, professional sports figures have been implicated in gambling, point shaving, and game fixing. Pete Rose has been jailed and suspended from baseball, Len Dykstra was placed on probation, Denny McLain was suspended, Paul Hornung, Alex Karras, and Art Schlicter were suspended from the NFL. Michael Jordan has allegedly accumulated massive gambling debts.

There have also been problems in college sports—Boston College, Kentucky, New York City College, Rhode Island, Seton Hall, and Tulane University basketball teams have been implicated in point shaving scandals. UNLV basketball players have been charged with associating with known gamblers.

Gambling in some form is now legal in 48 of the 50 states. Three states currently allow legalized sports gambling: Delaware, Nevada, and Oregon. Largely due to the relative failure of the gambling statutes in Delaware and Oregon, other states have not attempted to legalize sports gambling.

The debate over federal sports gambling legislation has focused primarily on two issues: 1) the appropriateness of broadening and applying the Lanham Act specifically for the protection of the trademarks and goodwill of sports leagues and teams, and 2) the intrusion of the proposed legislation upon states rights, including state governments' ability to raise revenues in any lawful manner it so chooses.

The Lanham Act, a federal act enacted in 1946, protects service marks and trademarks. Many who have criticized the use of the Lanham Act to protect sports teams state that it amounts to nothing more than special interest legislation favoring the professional sports leagues over other trademark holders. However, professional sports leagues have been successful in arguing the application of the Lanham Act to protect the reputation and good will of the leagues.

Commentators have argued that the federal preemption issues are deceptive on several counts. Most of the states that are considering legalizing sports betting would only allow betting on out-of-state teams. Therefore the concern of the states of the impact of gambling on the citizens of that state and teams in that state should be minimal. Also, most states have never had the right to legalize sports gambling. In 1979, the United States Congress made it a crime to bribe or attempt to bribe an individual in order to influence the outcome of a sporting contest (18 U. S. C. § 224). Lastly, those who have advocated the right of states to legalize sports gambling have ignored the fact that many amateur and professional sport organizations have attempted to police and protect their administrators, officials, owners, and players from the gambling element.

Gambling Legislation

Prohibition of Illegal Gambling Businesses (1994). Whoever conducts, finances, manages, supervises, directs or owns all or part of an illegal gambling business shall be fined under this title or imprisoned not more than five years or both. **Illegal gambling business** means a gambling business which is a violation of the law of a state or political subdivision in which it is conducted; involves five or more persons who conduct, finance, manage, supervise, direct, or own all or part of such business and has been or remains in substantially continuous operation for a period in excess of thirty days or has a gross revenue of $2,000 in any single day. **Gambling** includes but is not limited to pool-selling, bookmaking, maintaining slot machines, roulette wheels or dice tables, and conducting lotteries, policy, bolita or numbers games, or selling chances therein. This section of the law does not apply to any bingo game, lottery, or similar game of chance conducted by an organization exempt from tax under paragraph (3) of subsection (c) of section 501 of the Internal Revenue Code of 1986, as amended, if no part of the gross receipts derived from such activity inures to the benefits of any private shareholder, member, or employee of such organization except as compensation for actual expenses incurred by him in the conduct of such activity.

The Professional and Amateur Sports Protection Act (1994). This makes it unlawful for a governmental entity or a person to sponsor, operate, advertise, promote, license, or authorize by law or compact a lottery, sweepstakes, or other betting gambling or wagering scheme on one or more competitive games in which amateur or professional athletes participate. Section 3703 allows a civil action to enjoin a violation to be commenced in an appropriate district court of the United States by the Attorney General of the United States or by a professional or amateur sports organization whose competitive game is alleged to be the basis of such violation.

Exceptions to this law are: 1) lotteries, sweepstakes, or other betting or gambling schemes in operation in a state or other governmental entity in effect beginning January 1, 1976 and ending August 31, 1990; 2) a scheme authorized by statute as in effect on October 2, 1991; 3) a betting, gambling, or wagering scheme other than a lottery, conducted exclusively in casinos located in a municipality, and 4) pari-mutuel animal racing or jai-alai games.

Ticket Scalping

Ticket scalping is commonly defined as the reselling of tickets at a price higher than the established value. Ticket scalping is a large economic enterprise plagued by several problems. Recognizing the problems as they have existed in the sports and entertainment industries, several state legislatures have recently enacted anti-scalping legislation in an attempt to curb the nuisances associated with ticket scalping. Currently 45 states have some form of regulation.

Today, despite the enactment of anti-scalping legislation, ticket scalping continues as an inherent and integral part of the sports and entertainment industries. Ticket scalping is now so pervasive in our society that it is impossible to accurately depict the full scope of the industry. Ticket scalping currently permeates through every aspect of the sports and entertainment industries and is practiced by a wide variety of people, both amateur and professional.

Ticket scalping restrictions vary among the states. In Kentucky, for example, a person will be found guilty of ticket scalping by the mere act of selling a ticket in excess of the price printed on that ticket. California only prohibits the act of reselling tickets on the grounds of, or in the stadium, arena, or other venues where an event is being held. Conversely, Georgia, Connecticut, and Illinois restrict the selling of the tickets at a price greater than the price fixed for admission but allow an increase in price for taxes and service charges. New Jersey forbids a person to engage in the business of reselling tickets unless that person obtains a license to resell or engage in the business of reselling tickets. Alabama and New York require a person wishing to engage in the act of reselling tickets to procure a license and pay a fee for that license. Ohio permits municipal corporations to regulate, by license or otherwise, the act of selling tickets to theatrical and amusement events. Illinois permits a ticket broker meeting certain licensing requirements to sell a ticket for more than the price printed on that ticket. Pennsylvania holds a person, not possessed of authority, guilty of ticket scalping for selling, bartering, of transferring a ticket to an event for any consideration.

Legitimate Interest in Protecting the Welfare of the Public. Generally the courts have recognized that a state has a legitimate interest in protecting the welfare of the public. In *People v. Johnson*, a New York court noted that the purpose and thrust of anti-scalping legislation, the preservation of public welfare and advancement of the arts and theater, is to be given effect in order to accomplish the legislature's intention.

Legitimate Interest in Ensuring Public Access to Entertainment and Sports Events. In *People v. Shepherd*, the California District Court of Appeals held that the unregulated use of the Los Angeles Memorial Coliseum by peddlers of tickets or other property would add congestion, annoyance and inconvenience in areas where crowds must move rapidly and safely.

Legitimate Exercise of a State's Police Power. If not enacted in a discriminatory or otherwise unconstitutional manner, antiscalping legislation will most likely be upheld as a legitimate exercise of a state's police power. This standard was set forth in *Nebbia v. New York*, where the Supreme Court held that a state, in an effort to promote public welfare and in the absence of other constitutional restrictions, is free to adopt whatever economic policy it deems necessary and enforce that policy by way of legislation adapted to its purpose.

Statute Merely Must be Rationally Related to Stated Legitimate Goals. When pursuing this legislative action, a state is not required to solve the entire problem or provide the best remedy. In *State v. Major* the Court held that the statute merely has to be rationally related to stated legitimate goals. The three defendants were accused of selling at an illegal price admission tickets to a football game between the Atlanta Falcons and the Minnesota Vikings at the Atlanta-Fulton County Stadium. The tickets were allegedly sold at five to eleven dollars above the printed price on the ticket. The defendants challenged the constitutionality of Georgia Code § 96-602, which stated that only authorized ticket agents at established business locations may charge a fee not to exceed $1 in excess of the printed price. The Court reasoned that prohibiting the scalping of tickets is a proper legislative objective and does not violate any due process or property rights that an individual ticket holder may possess.

Wire and Mail Fraud

Federal legislation regarding wire and mail fraud has been criticized by many. Most of the policy concerns with wire and mail fraud legislation are raised in association with overcriminalization. The overcriminalization debate concerns the proper limit at which point the law can legitimately punish behavior without crossing the point where society feels it is not the law's business. These concerns are focused on two points: discriminatory enforcement and waste of judicial resources. One of the dangers of an expansive interpretation of the mail fraud statute is that it will not be enforced uniformly, but based on prejudices and passions of the day. Also, many believe that wire and mail fraud legislation is too blunt an instrument to address the myriad problems in college sports. An additional concern raised concerning NCAA enforcement of wire and mail fraud is that some people feel that giving athletes money is not normatively wrong. It is wrong only because the NCAA says that it is wrong.

According to Title 18 U.S.C. §§ 1341-1346 (1994), it is illegal to use the mails for the purpose of executing a scheme to defraud. There are two basic elements to the crime of mail fraud: 1) a scheme to defraud; and 2) use of the mails to execute the scheme.

Scheme to Defraud. A scheme to defraud is behavior calculated to deceive persons of ordinary prudence and comprehension. This element has two components: fraudulent intent and contemplation to harm or injury. To prove **fraudulent intent,** the government must show a scheme to defraud by proving that the defendant actually devised or intended to devise such a scheme. The focus is not upon conduct but on the state of mind or scheme. A **contemplation of harm or injury** may be inferred when a scheme has an injurious effect as a necessary result of its execution.

Causing the Use of Mails. This has been interpreted to mean that the person acts with the knowledge that use of the mails will follow in the ordinary course of business, or where use of the mails can reasonably be foreseen even though not actually intended. There are limitations on the mailing element of the statute: letters mailed before the scheme is conceived or after it is completed are not subject to the mail fraud statute because mailing either before a scheme is conceived or after it has reached fruition does not further the scheme and cannot support a mail fraud conviction. In *U.S. v. Walters*, the Court of Appeals for the Seventh Circuit held that the defendant, Norby Walters, did not cause the universities to use the mails and that the mailing of the forms was not sufficiently integral to his scheme to support a mail fraud conviction. Deceit was an ingredient of his plan, but no evidence existed that he conceived a scheme in which mailings played a role. There was no evidence to indicate that he actually knew that the colleges would mail the athletes' forms.

Recent Developments

Gambling   Case Results

Specific Intent Crime v. General Intent Crime. In *United States v. Blair*, defendant pleaded guilty to knowingly using wire communication facility for transmission of bets or wagers and knowingly and willfully conspiring to commit offense of illegal gambling against the United States. He appealed and the Court of Appeals upheld his conviction.

Blair's arguments were premised on the contention his crimes were specific intent crimes and that a specific intent crime requires a showing the defendant was cognizant of the illegality of his actions. A **specific intent crime** is one in which an act was committed voluntarily and purposely with the specific intent to do something the law forbids. In contrast, a **general intent crime** is one in which an act was done voluntarily and intentionally, and not because of mistake or accident. In short, a specific intent crime is one in which the defendant acts not only with knowledge of what he is doing, but does so with the objective of completing some unlawful act. Specific intent crimes do not, as a rule, necessitate a showing the defendant intentionally violated a known legal duty. While it is true that such a requirement has been imposed in the context of income tax crimes and violations of the Bank Secrecy Act, such a requirement has been imposed only in those circumstances where there was a clear directive from Congress. Absent such intent, the general rule, deeply rooted in the American legal system is that ignorance of the law or a mistake of law is no defense to criminal prosecution and is one that has been applied by the United States Supreme Court in numerous cases construing criminal statutes.

Ticket Scalping

Legitimate Government Interest. In *People v. The Concert Connection, Ltd.* (A.D. 2 Dept. 1995), the Attorney General brought action against a Connecticut corporation and its president, seeking to enjoin defendants from continuing illegal ticket scalping. The Supreme Court, Appellate Division, held that the ticket scalping statute did not violate due process, equal protection or the commerce clause. The regulation of ticket sales to protect the public against fraud, extortion, exorbitant rates and similar abuses is a legitimate government interest and does not offend any notions of due process. Specifically, the statute treats all ticket brokers alike while exempting certain other classes of people from the application of the "maximum premium price." The statute permits operators and their agents to impose a service charge that reflects "special services" provided to consumers in making tickets available. Also exempted are corporations that purchase tickets for their own use or for use by their agents or employees. Not-for-profit corporations are also exempt so long as the profit realized from ticket reselling is wholly dedicated to the purposes of such not-for-profit organization.

Wire and Mail Fraud

Under Color of Law. In *Thomas v. Pearl*, a basketball player brought suit against a former assistant basketball coach at a competing state university alleging that the coach violated federal and state wiretapping laws by recording a telephone conversation while the coach was attempting to recruit him. The Court of Appeals held that the coach did not act under color of law for purposes of exception to liability in federal wiretapping statute. There are two exceptions to violations of the federal wiretapping statute, 18 U.S.C. §§ 2510-2520. One of the exceptions is a person acting under color of law. The phrase "under color of law" initially was interpreted to refer to state officials who exercised power possessed by virtue of state law and made possible only because the wrongdoer is clothed with the authority of state law. The Supreme Court extended that definition in *Monroe v. Pape* to include not just fully authorized acts by state officials but acts committed by officials exceeding their authority. However, Congress has not said whether color of law means the same thing under the federal wiretapping statutes as it does under the civil rights statutes. Prior case law has been careful to restrict definitions of color of law to the civil rights arena.

References

A. Cases
Ex parte Quarg, 84 P. 766 (Cal. 1906).
Monroe v. Pape, 365 U.S. 167 (1961).
National Football League v. Governor of the State of Delaware, 435 F. Supp. 1372 (D. Del. 1977).
Nebbia v. New York, 291 U.S. 502 (1934).
People v. Johnson, 278 N.Y.S.2d 80 (1967).
People v. Shepherd, 141 Cal. Rptr. 379 (1977), cert. denied 436 U.S. 917 (1978).

People v. The Concert Connection, Ltd., 629 N.Y.S.2d 254 (A.D. 2 Dept. 1995).
State v. Major, 253 S.E.2d 724 (Ga. 1979).
Thomas v. Pearl, 998 F.2d 447 (7th Cir. 1993).
U.S. v. Blair, 54 F.3d 639 (10th Cir. 1995).
U.S. v. Walters, 711 F. Supp. 1435 (N.D. Ill. 1989), rev'd on other grounds, 913 F.2d 388 (7th Cir. 1990), 775 F. Supp. 1173 (N.D. Ill. 1991), and 997 F.2d 1219 (7th Cir. 1993).

B. Legislation
Delaware Code Annotated, Title 29 State Government, Chapter 48 Lotteries, § 4801 (as amended 1994).
Federal Trademark Act of 1946, Lanham Act § 45, 15 U.S.C. §§ 1051-1127 (1946).
Nevada Revised Statutes Annotated (Michie), Title 41: Gaming; Horse Racing; Sporting Events (1993).
Oregon Revised Statutes, § 461.213 (1990).
Professional and Amateur Sports Protection, 28 U.S.C. §§ 3701-3704 (1994).
Prohibition of Illegal Gambling Businesses, 18 U.S.C. § 1955 (1994).
Sentencing Reform Act of 1984, Public Law 98-473, Title II, Chapter II, §§ 211-39, 98 Stat. 1987 (1984) (codified at 18 U.S.C. §§3551-3586 (1994)).
Title 18, Crimes and Criminal Procedure, Chapter 63 Mail Fraud, U.S.C. §§1341-1346 (1994).
Title 18, Crimes and Criminal Procedure, Chapter 119 Wire and Electronic Communications Interception and Interception of Oral Communications, U.S.C. §§ 2510-2522 (1994).

Antitrust and Labor Law

Professional Sport Applications

Lisa Pike Masteralexis
University of Massachusetts-Amherst

The application of antitrust and labor law to the professional sport industry is unique for a number of reasons. First, the professional sport of baseball possesses a judicially granted exemption from the antitrust laws. Second, professional sports leagues have adopted many restrictive policies unmatched in other industries for the efficient operation of their leagues. These policies restrict players, owners, prospective owners, competitor leagues, cities possessing and seeking franchises, broadcasters, among others. No other industry employs such rules as restraints on employee movement as drafts, trades, and salary caps, or such stringent restrictions on franchise ownership and relocation, and thus, the professional sport industry may be more likely to face antitrust challenges. Third, players associations are different than unions in other industries. For instance, unlike other unions, members of players associations possess a wide range and variety of skills, and thus there is a disparity in the interests and demands of union members from the superstars to the practice players. On the other hand though, very few individuals possess the bargaining power and leverage of professional athletes and thus, few industries pay employees wages comparable to those earned by athletes. As a result, when restraints in the professional sports industry are successfully challenged by players, treble damage awards may amount to millions of dollars and severely debilitate the industry. Fourth, players associations have a high turnover rate due to their members' short careers. This translates to a lack of true job security. All of these factors impact the labor-management relationship in professional sport.

■ ■ ■ ■

Representative Case

MACKEY v. NATIONAL FOOTBALL LEAGUE

United States Court of Appeals for the Eighth Circuit
543 F.2d 606 (1976)

OPINION: LAY, Circuit Judge.

This is an appeal by the National Football League (NFL), twenty-six of its member clubs, and its Commissioner, Alvin Ray "Pete" Rozelle, from a district court judgment holding the "Rozelle Rule" to be violative of § 1 of the Sherman Act, and enjoining its enforcement. (The Rozelle Rule essentially provides that when a player's contractual obligation to a team expires and he signs with a different club, the signing club must provide compensation to the player's former team. If the two clubs are unable to conclude mutually satisfactory arrangements, the Commissioner may award compensation in the form of one or more players and/or draft choices as he deems fair and equitable.)

This action was initiated by a group of present and former NFL players, appellees herein, pursuant to §§ 4 and 16 of the Clayton Act, 15 U.S.C. §§ 15 and 26, and § 1 of the Sherman Act, 15 U.S.C. § 1. Their complaint alleged that the defendants' enforcement of the Rozelle Rule constituted an illegal combination and conspiracy in restraint of trade denying professional football players the right to freely contract for their services. Plaintiffs sought injunctive relief and treble damages.

The district court, the Honorable Earl R. Larson presiding, conducted a plenary trial which consumed 55 days and produced a transcript in excess of 11,000 pages. At the conclusion of trial, the court entered extensive findings of fact and conclusions of law. The court granted the injunctive relief sought by the players and entered judgment in their favor on the issue of liability. This appeal followed.

The district court held that the defendants' enforcement of the Rozelle Rule constituted a concerted refusal to deal and a group boycott, and was therefore a per se violation of the Sherman Act. Alternatively, finding that the evidence offered in support of the clubs' contention that the Rozelle Rule is necessary to the successful operation of the NFL insufficient to justify the restrictive effects of the Rule, the court concluded that the Rozelle Rule was invalid under the Rule of Reason standard. Finally, the court rejected the clubs' argument that the Rozelle Rule was immune from attack under the Sherman Act because it had been the subject of a collective bargaining agreement between the club owners and the National Football League Players Association (NFLPA).

The defendants raise two basic issues on this appeal: (1) whether the so-called labor exemption to the antitrust laws immunizes the NFL's enforcement of the Rozelle Rule from antitrust liability; and (2) if not, whether the Rozelle Rule and the manner in which it has been enforced violate the antitrust laws. Ancillary to these contentions, appellants attack a number of the district court's findings of fact and raise several subsidiary issues.

History

We first turn to a brief examination of the pertinent history and operating principles of the National Football League.

The NFL, which began operating in 1920, is an unincorporated association comprised of member clubs which own and operate professional football teams. It presently enjoys a monopoly over major league professional football in the United States. The League performs various administrative functions, including organizing and scheduling games, and promulgating rules. A constitution and bylaws govern its activities and those of its members. Pete Rozelle, Commissioner of the NFL since 1960, is an employee of the League and its chief executive officer. His powers and duties are defined by the NFL Constitution and Bylaws.

Throughout most of its history, the NFL's operations have been unilaterally controlled by the club owners. In 1968, however, the NLRB recognized the NFLPA as a labor organization, within the meaning of 29 U.S.C. § 152(5), and as the exclusive bargaining representative of all NFL players, within the meaning of 29 U.S.C. § 159(a). Since that time, the NFLPA and the clubs have engaged in collective bargaining over various terms and conditions of employment. Two formal agreements have resulted. The first, concluded in 1968, was in effect from July 15, 1968 to February 1, 1970. The second, entered into on June 17, 1971, was made retroactive to February 1, 1970, and expired on January 30, 1974. Since 1974, the parties have been negotiating; however, they have not concluded a new agreement.

For a number of years, the NFL has operated under a reserve system whereby every player who signs a contract with an NFL club is bound to play for that club, and no other, for the term of the contract plus one additional year at the option of the club. The cornerstones of this system are § 15.1 of the NFL Constitution and Bylaws, which requires that all club-player contracts be as prescribed in the Standard Player Contract adopted by the League, and the option clause embodied in the Standard Player Contract. Once a player signs a Standard Player Contract, he is bound to his team for at least two years. He may, however, become a free agent at the end of the option year by playing that season under a renewed contract rather than signing a new one. A player "playing out his option" is subject to a 10 percent salary cut during the option year.

Prior to 1963, a team which signed a free agent who had previously been under contract to another club was not obligated to compensate the player's former club. In 1963, after R. C. Owens played out his option with the San Francisco 49ers and signed a contract with the Baltimore Colts, the member clubs of the NFL unilaterally adopted the following provision, now known as the Rozelle Rule, as an amendment to the League's Constitution and Bylaws:

Any player, whose contract with a League club has expired, shall thereupon become a free agent and shall no longer be considered a member of the team of that club following the expiration date of such contract. Whenever a player, becoming a free agent in such manner, thereafter signed a contract with a different club in the League, then, unless mutually satisfactory arrangements have been concluded between the two League clubs, the Commissioner may name and then award to the former club one or more players, from the Active, Reserve, or Selection List (including future selection choices) of the

acquiring club as the Commissioner in his sole discretion deems fair and equitable; any such decision
by the Commissioner shall be final and conclusive.

This provision, unchanged in form, is currently
embodied in § 12.1(H) of the NFL Constitution. The
ostensible purposes of the rule are to maintain competitive
balance among the NFL teams and protect the clubs'
investment in scouting, selecting and developing players.

During the period from 1963 through 1974, 176 players played out their options. Of that number, 34 signed
with other teams. In three of those cases, the former club
waived compensation. In 27 cases, the clubs involved
mutually agreed upon compensation. Commissioner
Rozelle awarded compensation in the four remaining
cases.

We turn now to the contentions of the parties.

The Labor Exemption Issue

We review first the claim that the labor exemption
immunizes the Commissioner and the clubs from liability
under the antitrust laws. Analysis of this contention
requires a basic understanding of the legal principles surrounding the labor exemption and consideration of the
factual record developed at trial.

History

The concept of a labor exemption from the antitrust
laws finds its basic source in §§ 6 and 20 of the Clayton
Act, 15 U.S.C. § 17 and 29 U.S.C. § 52, and the Norris-
LaGuardia Act, 29 U.S.C. §§ 104, 105 and 113. Those
provisions declare that labor unions are not combinations
or conspiracies in restraint of trade, and specifically
exempt certain union activities such as secondary picket-
ing and group boycotts from the coverage of the antitrust
laws. . . . The statutory exemption was created to insulate
legitimate collective activity by employees, which is
inherently anticompetitive but is favored by federal labor
policy, from the proscriptions of the antitrust laws.

The statutory exemption extends to legitimate labor
activities unilaterally undertaken by a union in furtherance
of its own interests. . . . It does not extend to concerted
action or agreements between unions and non-labor
groups. The Supreme Court has held, however, that in
order to properly accommodate the congressional policy
favoring free competition in business markets with the
congressional policy favoring collective bargaining under
the National Labor Relations Act, 29 U.S.C. § 151 et seq.,
certain union-employer agreements must be accorded a
limited nonstatutory exemption from antitrust sanctions.

The players assert that only employee groups are entitled to the labor exemption and that it cannot be asserted
by the defendants, an employer group. We must disagree.
Since the basis of the nonstatutory exemption is the

national policy favoring collective bargaining, and since
the exemption extends to agreements, the benefits of the
exemption logically extend to both parties to the agreement.

• • •

The clubs and the Commissioner claim the benefit of
the nonstatutory labor exemption here, arguing that the
Rozelle Rule was the subject of an agreement with the
players union and that the proper accommodation of federal labor and antitrust policies requires that the agreement
be deemed immune from antitrust liability. The plaintiffs
assert that the Rozelle Rule was the product of unilateral
action by the clubs and that the defendants cannot assert a
colorable claim of exemption.

To determine the applicability of the nonstatutory
exemption we must first decide whether there has been
any agreement between the parties concerning the Rozelle
Rule.

The Collective Bargaining Agreements

The 1968 Agreement

At the outset of the negotiations preceding the 1968
agreement, the players did not seek elimination of the
Rozelle Rule but felt that it should be modified. During the
course of the negotiations, however, the players apparently presented no concrete proposals in that regard and
there was little discussion concerning the Rozelle Rule. At
trial, Daniel Shulman, a bargaining representative of the
players, attributed their failure to pursue any modifications to the fact that the negotiations had bogged down on
other issues and the union was not strong enough to per-
sist.

The 1968 agreement incorporated by reference the
NFL Constitution and Bylaws, of which the Rozelle Rule
is a part. Furthermore, it expressly provided that free agent
rules shall not be amended during the life of the agreement.

The 1970 Agreement

At the start of the negotiations leading up to the 1970
agreement, it appears that the players again decided not to
make an issue of the Rozelle Rule. The only reference to
the Rule in the union's formal proposals presented at the
outset of the negotiations was the following:

> The NFLPA is disturbed over reports from players
> who, after playing out their options, are unable to
> deal with other clubs because of the Rozelle Rule.
> A method should be found whereby a free agent is
> assured the opportunity to discuss contract with all
> NFL teams.

There was little discussion of the Rozelle Rule during
the 1970 negotiations.

Although the 1970 agreement failed to make any express reference to the Rozelle Rule, it did contain a "zipper clause":

> This Agreement represents a complete and final understanding on all bargainable subjects of negotiation among the parties during the term of this Agreement. . . .

While the agreement did not expressly incorporate by reference the terms of the NFL Constitution and Bylaws, it did require all players to sign the Standard Player Contract, and provided that the Standard Contract shall govern the relationship between the clubs and the players. The Standard Player Contract, in turn, provided that the player agreed at all times to comply with and be bound by the NFL Constitution and Bylaws. At trial, Tex Schramm, a bargaining representative of the club owners, and Alan Miller, a bargaining representative of the players, testified that it was their understanding that the Rozelle Rule would remain in effect during the term of the 1970 agreement.

Since the beginning of the 1974 negotiations, the players have consistently sought the elimination of the Rozelle Rule. The NFLPA and the clubs have engaged in substantial bargaining over that issue but have not reached an accord. Nor have they concluded a collective bargaining agreement to replace the 1970 agreement which expired in 1974.

Based on the fact that the 1968 agreement incorporated by reference the Rozelle Rule and provided that free agent rules would not be changed, we conclude that the 1968 agreement required that the Rozelle Rule govern when a player played out his option and signed with another team. Assuming, without deciding, that the 1970 agreement embodied a similar understanding, we proceed to a consideration of whether the agreements fall within the scope of the nonstatutory labor exemption.

Governing Principles

Although the cases giving rise to the nonstatutory exemption are factually dissimilar from the present case, certain principles can be deduced from those decisions governing the proper accommodation of the competing labor and antitrust interests involved here.

We find the proper accommodation to be: First, the labor policy favoring collective bargaining may potentially be given pre-eminence over the antitrust laws where the restraint on trade primarily affects only the parties to the collective bargaining relationship. . . . Second, federal labor policy is implicated sufficiently to prevail only where the agreement sought to be exempted concerns a mandatory subject of collective bargaining. . . . Finally, the policy favoring collective bargaining is furthered to the degree necessary to override the antitrust laws only where

the agreement sought to be exempted is the product of bona fide arm's-length bargaining.

Application

Applying these principles to the facts presented here, we think it clear that the alleged restraint on trade effected by the Rozelle Rule affects only the parties to the agreements sought to be exempted. Accordingly, we must inquire as to the other two principles: whether the Rozelle Rule is a mandatory subject of collective bargaining, and whether the agreements thereon were the product of bona fide arm's-length negotiation.

Mandatory Subject of Bargaining

Under § 8(d) of the National Labor Relations Act, 29 U.S.C. § 158(d), mandatory subjects of bargaining pertain to "wages, hours, and other terms and conditions of employment. . . ."

Whether an agreement concerns a mandatory subject depends not on its form but on its practical effect.

In this case the district court held that, in view of the illegality of the Rozelle Rule under the Sherman Act, it was "a nonmandatory, illegal subject of bargaining." We disagree. The labor exemption presupposes a violation of the antitrust laws. To hold that a subject relating to wages, hours and working conditions becomes nonmandatory by virtue of its illegality under the antitrust laws obviates the labor exemption. We conclude that whether the agreements here in question relate to a mandatory subject of collective bargaining should be determined solely under federal labor law. Cf. Meat Cutters v. Jewel Tea, supra.

On its face, the Rozelle Rule does not deal with "wages, hours and other terms or conditions of employment" but with inter-team compensation when a player's contractual obligation to one team expires and he is signed by another. Viewed as such, it would not constitute a mandatory subject of collective bargaining. The district court found, however, that the Rule operates to restrict a player's ability to move from one team to another and depresses player salaries. There is substantial evidence in the record to support these findings. Accordingly, we hold that the Rozelle Rule constitutes a mandatory bargaining subject within the meaning of the National Labor Relations Act.

Bona Fide Bargaining

The district court found that the parties' collective bargaining history reflected nothing which could be legitimately characterized as bargaining over the Rozelle Rule; that, in part due to its recent formation and inadequate finances, the NFLPA, at least prior to 1974, stood in a relatively weak bargaining position vis-a-vis the clubs; and that "the Rozelle Rule was unilaterally imposed by the NFL and member club defendants upon the players in

1963 and has been imposed on the players from 1963 through the present date."

On the basis of our independent review of the record, including the parties' bargaining history as set forth above, we find substantial evidence to support the finding that there was no bona fide arm's-length bargaining over the Rozelle Rule preceding the execution of the 1968 and 1970 agreements. The Rule imposes significant restrictions on players, and its form has remained unchanged since it was unilaterally promulgated by the clubs in 1963. The provisions of the collective bargaining agreements which operated to continue the Rozelle Rule do not in and of themselves inure to the benefit of the players or their union. Defendants contend that the players derive indirect benefit from the Rozelle Rule, claiming that the union's agreement to the Rozelle Rule was a quid pro quo for increased pension benefits and the right of players to individually negotiate their salaries. The district court found, however, that there was no such quid pro quo, and we cannot say, on the basis of our review of the record, that this finding is clearly erroneous.

In view of the foregoing, we hold that the agreements between the clubs and the players embodying the Rozelle Rule do not qualify for the labor exemption. The union's acceptance of the status quo by the continuance of the Rozelle Rule in the initial collective bargaining agreements under the circumstances of this case cannot serve to immunize the Rozelle Rule from the scrutiny of the Sherman Act.

Antitrust Issues

We turn, then, to the question of whether the Rozelle Rule, as implemented, violates § 1 of the Sherman Act, which declares illegal "every contract, combination . . . or conspiracy, in restraint of trade or commerce among the several States." 15 U.S.C. § 1. The district court found the Rozelle Rule to be a per se violation of the Act. Alternatively, the court held the Rule to be violative of the Rule of Reason standard.

Players' Services as a Product Market

The clubs and the Commissioner first urge that the only product market arguably affected by the Rozelle Rule is the market for players' services, and that the restriction of competition for players' services is not a type of restraint proscribed by the Sherman Act.

• • •

In other cases concerning professional sports, courts have not hesitated to apply the Sherman Act to club owner imposed restraints on competition for players' services. See Kapp v. National Football League, 390 F. Supp. 73 (N.D. Cal. 1974); Robertson v. National Basketball Ass'n., 389 F. Supp. 867 (S.D. N.Y. 1975). See also

Radovich v. National Football League, supra; Smith v. Pro-Football, supra; Boston Professional Hockey Ass'n., Inc. v. Cheevers, supra; Denver Rockets v. All-Pro Management, Inc., 325 F. Supp. 1049 (C.D. Cal. 1971), stay vacated, 401 U.S. 1204, 91 S. Ct. 672, 28 L. Ed. 2d 206 (1971) (Justice Douglas, Opinion in Chambers).

• • •

We hold that restraints on competition within the market for players' services fall within the ambit of the Sherman Act.

Per Se Violation

We review next the district court's holding that the Rozelle Rule is per se violative of the Sherman Act.

The express language of the Sherman Act is broad enough to render illegal nearly every type of agreement between businessmen. The Supreme Court has held, however, that only those agreements which "unreasonably" restrain trade come within the proscription of the Act. The "Rule of Reason" emerged from these cases.

As the courts gained experience with antitrust problems arising under the Sherman Act, they identified certain types of agreements as being so consistently unreasonable that they may be deemed to be illegal per se, without inquiry into their purported justifications.

• • •

Among the practices which have been deemed to be so pernicious as to be illegal per se are group boycotts and concerted refusals to deal. . . . The term "concerted refusal to deal" has been defined as "an agreement by two or more persons not to do business with other individuals, or to do business with them only on specified terms." . . . The term "group boycott" generally connotes "a refusal to deal or an inducement of others not to deal or to have business relations with tradesmen."

• • •

The district court found that the Rozelle Rule operates to significantly deter clubs from negotiating with and signing free agents. By virtue of the Rozelle Rule, a club will sign a free agent only where it is able to reach an agreement with the player's former team as to compensation, or where it is willing to risk the awarding of unknown compensation by the Commissioner. The court concluded that the Rozelle Rule, as enforced, thus constituted a group boycott and a concerted refusal to deal, and was a per se violation of the Sherman Act.

There is substantial evidence in the record to support the district court's findings as to the effects of the Rozelle Rule. We think, however, that this case presents unusual circumstances rendering it inappropriate to declare the Rozelle Rule illegal per se without undertaking an inquiry into the purported justifications for the Rule.

First, the line of cases which has given rise to per se illegality for the type of agreements involved here generally concerned agreements between business competitors in the traditional sense. See generally Worthen Bank & Trust Co. v. National BankAmericard Inc., supra. Here, however, as the owners and Commissioner urge, the NFL assumes some of the characteristics of a joint venture in that each member club has a stake in the success of the other teams. No one club is interested in driving another team out of business, since if the League fails, no one team can survive. See United States v. National Football League, 116 F. Supp. 319, 323 (E.D. Pa. 1953). Although businessmen cannot wholly evade the antitrust laws by characterizing their operation as a joint venture, we conclude that the unique nature of the business of professional football renders it inappropriate to mechanically apply per se illegality rules here, fashioned in a different context. This is particularly true where, as here, the alleged restraint does not completely eliminate competition for players' services. Compare Kapp v. National Football League, supra with Smith v. Pro-Football, supra.

• • •

Second, one of the underpinnings of the per se analysis is the avoidance of lengthy and burdensome inquiries into the operation of the particular industry in question. Here, the district court has already undertaken an exhaustive inquiry into the operation of the NFL and the effects of and justifications for the Rozelle Rule. Accordingly, the instant case lacks much of the basis for application of the per se doctrine.

In view of the foregoing, we think it more appropriate to test the validity of the Rozelle Rule under the Rule of Reason.

Rule of Reason

The focus of an inquiry under the Rule of Reason is whether the restraint imposed is justified by legitimate business purposes, and is no more restrictive than necessary.

• • •

In defining the restraint on competition for players' services, the district court found that the Rozelle Rule significantly deters clubs from negotiating with and signing free agents; that it acts as a substantial deterrent to players playing out their options and becoming free agents; that it significantly decreases players' bargaining power in contract negotiations; that players are thus denied the right to sell their services in a free and open market; that as a result, the salaries paid by each club are lower than if competitive bidding were allowed to prevail; and that absent the Rozelle Rule, there would be increased movement in interstate commerce of players from one club to another.

We find substantial evidence in the record to support these findings. Witnesses for both sides testified that there would be increased player movement absent the Rozelle Rule.

• • •

In support of their contention that the restraints effected by the Rozelle Rule are not unreasonable, the defendants asserted a number of justifications. First, they argued that without the Rozelle Rule, star players would flock to cities having natural advantages such as larger economic bases, winning teams, warmer climates, and greater media opportunities; that competitive balance throughout the League would thus be destroyed; and that the destruction of competitive balance would ultimately lead to diminished spectator interest, franchise failures, and perhaps the demise of the NFL, at least as it operates today. Second, the defendants contended that the Rozelle Rule is necessary to protect the clubs' investment in scouting expenses and player developments costs. Third, they asserted that players must work together for a substantial period of time in order to function effectively as a team; that elimination of the Rozelle Rule would lead to increased player movement and a concomitant reduction in player continuity; and that the quality of play in the NFL would thus suffer, leading to reduced spectator interest, and financial detriment both to the clubs and the players. Conflicting evidence was adduced at trial by both sides with respect to the validity of these asserted justifications.

The district court held the defendants' asserted justifications unavailing. As to the clubs' investment in player development costs, Judge Larson found that these expenses are similar to those incurred by other businesses, and that there is no right to compensation for this type of investment. With respect to player continuity, the court found that elimination of the Rozelle Rule would affect all teams equally in that regard; that it would not lead to a reduction in the quality of play; and that even assuming that it would, that fact would not justify the Rozelle Rule's anticompetitive effects. As to competitive balance and the consequences which would flow from abolition of the Rozelle Rule, Judge Larson found that the existence of the Rozelle Rule has had no material effect on competitive balance in the NFL. Even assuming that the Rule did foster competitive balance, the court found that there were other legal means available to achieve that end—e.g., the competition committee, multiple year contracts, and special incentives. The court further concluded that elimination of the Rozelle Rule would have no significant disruptive effects, either immediate or long term, on professional football. In conclusion the court held that the Rozelle Rule was unreasonable in that it was overly broad, unlimited in duration, unaccompanied by procedural safeguards, and employed in conjunction with other anticompetitive practices such as the draft, Standard Player Contract, option clause, and the no-tampering rules.

We agree that the asserted need to recoup player development costs cannot justify the restraints of the Rozelle Rule. That expense is an ordinary cost of doing business and is not peculiar to professional football. Moreover, because of its unlimited duration, the Rozelle Rule is far more restrictive than necessary to fulfill that need.

We agree, in view of the evidence adduced at trial with respect to existing players turnover by way of trades, retirements and new players entering the League, that the club owners' arguments respecting player continuity cannot justify the Rozelle Rule. We concur in the district court's conclusion that the possibility of resulting decline in the quality of play would not justify the Rozelle Rule. We do recognize, as did the district court, that the NFL has a strong and unique interest in maintaining competitive balance among its teams. The key issue is thus whether the Rozelle Rule is essential to the maintenance of competitive balance, and is no more restrictive than necessary. The district court answered both of these questions in the negative.

We need not decide whether a system of inter-team compensation for free agents moving to other teams is essential to the maintenance of competitive balance in the NFL. Even if it is, we agree with the district court's conclusion that the Rozelle Rule is significantly more restrictive than necessary to serve any legitimate purposes it might have in this regard. First, little concern was manifested at trial over the free movement of average or below average players. Only the movement of the better players was urged as being detrimental to football. Yet the Rozelle Rule applies to every NFL player regardless of his status

or ability. Second, the Rozelle Rule is unlimited in duration. It operates as a perpetual restriction on a player's ability to sell his services in an open market throughout his career. Third, the enforcement of the Rozelle Rule is unaccompanied by procedural safeguards. A player has no input into the process by which fair compensation is determined. Moreover, the player may be unaware of the precise compensation demanded by his former team, and that other teams might be interested in him but for the degree of compensation sought.

• • •

Conclusion

In conclusion, although we find that non-labor parties may potentially avail themselves of the nonstatutory labor exemption where they are parties to collective bargaining agreements pertaining to mandatory subjects of bargaining, the exemption cannot be invoked where, as here, the agreement was not the product of bona fide arm's-length negotiations. Thus, the defendants' enforcement of the Rozelle Rule is not exempt from the coverage of the antitrust laws. Although we disagree with the district court's determination that the Rozelle Rule is a per se violation of the antitrust laws, we do find that the Rule, as implemented, contravenes the Rule of Reason and thus constitutes an unreasonable restraint of trade in violation of § 1 of the Sherman Act.

• • •

With the exception of the district court's finding that implementation of the Rozelle Rule constitutes a per se violation of § 1 of the Sherman Act and except as it is otherwise modified herein, the judgment of the district court is AFFIRMED. The cause is remanded to the district court for further proceedings consistent with this opinion.

■ ■ ■ ■

Fundamental Concepts

Antitrust Law

In 1890 Congress passed the Sherman Antitrust Act to break up business trusts and monopolies. Section one of the act prohibits "every contract, combination, . . . or conspiracy in restraint of trade or commerce among the several states [interstate commerce]" (15 U.S.C. §1) and section two makes illegal, "to monopolize, attempt to monopolize, or combine or conspire . . . to monopolize" (15 U.S.C. §2). Violators of the Sherman Act must pay treble damages.

The Sherman Act has been dependent upon judicial interpretation as its vague language lends itself to different opinions as to the intent and meaning of crucial terms (Roberts, 1990). As a result the Supreme Court has adopted three approaches to Section one of the Sherman Act. First, the **"rule of reason"** is founded on the notion that some restraints are necessary business practices. In other words, where the defendant can prove the conduct which restrains trade is a legitimate business practice and is the least restrictive means for the defendant to achieve that business practice/objective, the rule of reason is a defense. Thus, the plaintiff must convince the court that the defendant's conduct is an unreasonable restraint. This defense requires the court to inquire as to the necessary business practices of the industry. This theory has been advanced in sport on many occasions due to the numerous and arguably necessary anti-competitive rules and restrictions.

The second approach is where the anti-competitive conduct is deemed **illegal per se**. Illegal per se activities are conclusively presumed to have no benefit to competition in the industry. Use of the illegal per se approach is limited and is applied in two situations: where the Court is examining agreements between traditional business competitions and where the Court is seeking to avoid a lengthy inquiry into an industry's business operations. (Greenberg, 1993).

Finally, a third approach in which the Court focuses solely on the effect a challenged practice has on **consumer welfare** has emerged (Roberts, 1990). This approach, however, has yet to be applied in cases based in the professional sport industry. Roberts (1990) has argued that this consumer welfare standard will be very important for sport-related antitrust cases and if applied, would likely limit a plaintiff's success for the plaintiff would be forced to demonstrate that the league conduct injures consumer welfare.

Antitrust Law Applied to Baseball. Baseball possesses a unique status in professional sport, as well as American business, by virtue of its exemption from the antitrust laws. The exemption results from the 1922 Supreme Court decision, Federal Baseball Club of Baltimore, Inc. v. National League of Professional Baseball Clubs, et al. (1922), in which the Court concluded that baseball was neither interstate nor commerce; two elements which must be present for the Sherman Act to apply. The Supreme Court viewed baseball as a business presenting local exhibitions deemed purely state affairs. It found that the travel of players across state lines was purely incidental and not an essential element of the business of baseball. Finally, the Court focused on the players and found that the business was related to personal effort, rather than production of goods, and thus, was not a subject of commerce. Over time the exemption has faced attack, but the *Federal Baseball* decision is still viewed as controlling.

In *Toolson v. New York Yankees* (1953) and in *Flood v. Kuhn* (1972), baseball players contended that the player reserve system was violative of antitrust law. Major League Baseball's reserve system was made up of two parts. First, every uniform player's contract contained a clause in which they agreed to play for the team the following year at the club's option. Second, each team possessed a reserve list in which the team could protect its players. There was a gentlemen's agreement among the clubs and no team would sign a player on another team's reserve list. Under this system, if a team wanted to retain a player's services that player was perpetually bound to the team. In both decisions the Supreme Court reaffirmed baseball's exemption by stating that the exemption could only be challenged by Congress. Congress has time and again revisited the question of whether baseball should continue to remain exempt from antitrust, but has yet to wage any serious threat to the league's protected status. In *Flood,* the Court encouraged baseball players to use labor relations rather than antitrust law to resolve their disputes over the reserve clause. The *Flood* Court stated that the antitrust exemption only extended to baseball, as the court reiterated that all other team and individual sports were subject to antitrust laws.

The Major League Baseball Players Association did successfully challenge the player reserve system under labor law in *In Re Twelve Clubs Comprising the National League and Twelve Clubs Comprising the American League and Major League Baseball Players Association* (also known as the Messersmith-McNally arbitration decision, 1976). Arbitrator Peter Seitz found that the reserve clause was limited to a one year renewal favoring the club and that placing a player's name on a club's reserve list did not perpetually bind a player to that team. The current free agency clause in the baseball collective bargaining agreement resulted from labor-management negotiations following this decision.

Antitrust Law Applied to Other Sports. Antitrust laws have been applied to the other professional sports by players, owners, prospective owners, and others involved in the business of professional sports. *United States v. International Boxing Club* (1955) was the first case in which antitrust laws were applied to a professional sport (boxing). Soon after, the Supreme Court applied the antitrust laws to football in *Radovich v. National Football League* (1957). In *Radovich* a football player challenged a rule which restricted his signing a contract with a team other than the one which held his rights and which blacklisted him from signing as a player-coach with a team affiliated with the NFL. Radovich contended that the blacklist was a group boycott in restraint of trade. The trial and appellate courts dismissed Radovich's claims on the ground that football, like baseball was exempt from antitrust due to the *Federal Baseball* precedent. The Supreme Court reversed and held that by broadcasting its games nationally on radio and television football was engaged in interstate commerce. In addition, the Court made clear that the judgment granting the antitrust exemption in *Federal Baseball* was specifically limited to the sport of baseball.

Antitrust Exemption for Sport Broadcasting Contracts. In 1961 Congress passed a law exempting sports leagues national television deals from antitrust liability (15 U.S.C. §§ 1291-1294). This statute granted teams in professional leagues the right to pool their television rights together in order to increase their bargaining power when negotiating league wide television packages without the threat of antitrust challenges.

Antitrust Challenges by Competitor Leagues. There have been three cases brought under Section two of the Sherman Act where new competitor leagues have challenged the practices of established leagues as monopolistic. Only one of these cases, *Philadelphia World Hockey, Inc. v. Philadelphia Hockey Club, Inc.* (1972), was substantially successful for the plaintiff. In this case, the World Hockey League successfully argued that the NHL monopolized the labor pool of talented players with the National Hockey League's reserve system. The NHL's reserve system, like that in baseball, perpetually bound players to a team. The World Hockey Association successfully argued that the system restrained their ability to acquire marquee players from the NHL.

The other two cases brought by upstart competitors were not as successful. First, in *American Football League v. National Football League* (4th Cir. 1963), the plaintiff was unable to prove that the NFL, by expanding into Dallas and Minneapolis, two cities the AFL was considering for expansion, was monopolizing the market for professional football in those sites. Second, in *United States Football League v. National Football League* (S.D.N.Y. 1986), a jury found that the NFL had monopolized the market for football in the United States, but the jury awarded nominal damages ($1.00 trebled to $3.00).

Antitrust Challenges by Prospective Team Owners and Team Owners. Individual franchise owners have challenged league rules on the theory that the rules diminish their abilities to compete in the market. Many league rules restrict the opportunities of the individual in favor of the good of the joint venture, the league. Prospective team owners have brought antitrust cases challenging league ownership restrictions which have kept them from becoming owners. The courts in *Levin v. National Basketball Association* (S.D.N.Y. 1974) and *Mid-South Grizzlies v. National Football League* (3d Cir. 1983) upheld rules requiring three-fourths approval of league owners for transfer of ownership (*Levin*) and admission to the league (*Mid-South Grizzlies*). The most recent of these prospective owner challenges, *Piazza v. Major League Baseball* (E.D.Pa. 1993) involved potential owners who attempted to purchase and relocate the San Francisco Giants baseball franchise, as well as a challenge to baseball's antitrust exemption. The case settled out of court just after the *Piazza* court entered a declaratory judgment that the claim should not be dismissed on the authority of baseball's antitrust exemption. In other words, the Federal District Court in Eastern Pennsylvania expressed a willingness to reconsider baseball's exemption.

Until recently, the most celebrated case involving an owner challenging a restriction involved Al Davis in *Los Angeles Memorial Coliseum and the Los Angeles Raiders v. National Football League*, (9th Cir. 1984). This case involved the Raiders' successful antitrust challenge to league restraints on franchise relocation. The Raiders convinced the court that the three-fourths vote needed for relocation into the Los Angeles market was unreasonable. A new breed of owners who have made large investments to purchase and operate teams have been more willing to challenge league rules or policies on antitrust grounds. The increase can be traced to the different vantage point where the new owners sit. Many recent owners view team ownership as an investment opportunity and believe they should be able to control the profits of their teams. In addition, recent owners such as Jerry Jones of the Dallas Cowboys do not believe they should share their profits with established owners who paid far less for their teams, have already earned their return on their investment and who may not (in Jones' opinion) be contributing their fair share of the marketing and licensing revenues to the league. This represents a major shift from the "league think" philosophy championed by National Football League Commissioner Pete Rozelle. The challenges vary from rules restricting the number of games telecast nationally on a superstation [*Chicago Bulls and WGN v. National Basketball Association*, (7th Cir. 1992)]; ownership policies, such as restrictions against public ownership [*Sullivan v. National Football League* (D. Mass 1995)(pending) and *Kiam v. National Football League* (D. Mass 1995)(pending)]; and marketing and revenue sharing [*Dallas Cowboys v. NFL Trust* (N.D. Cal 1995) (pending)].

Antitrust Challenges by Individual Athletes.   One additional area in which the antitrust laws have been used is where a disciplined player challenges the league. For example, in *Molinas v. National Basketball Association*, (S.D.N.Y. 1961), the plaintiff NBA player had been suspended for wagering on games in which he was participating. Molinas application for reinstatement with the league was rejected and Molinas argued that the expulsion from the league restrained trade because he had no economic alternative to playing basketball in the NBA. The court upheld the suspension, finding that the restraint was a reasonable one as the NBA had a legitimate interest in banning gambling and in restoring the public confidence by keeping admitted gamblers out of the NBA.

Convergence of Labor and Antitrust Law

In the three to four decades following its enactment employers used the broad language of the Sherman Act against labor movements, claiming the acts of workers who organized boycotts and carried out work slowdowns or stoppages were combinations or conspiracies in restraint of trade. Employers sought injunctions to thwart labor activities and the threat of treble damages to chill the labor movement.

In 1914 Congress responded to the use of the Sherman Act against labor movements by enacting the Clayton Act. The Clayton Act declared that the labor of a human being [was] not a commodity or article of commerce and thus, labor's actions were not subject to the Sherman Act. The Clayton Act, thus, granted an antitrust exemption to organized labor, provided the workers were acting in their own self-interest. However, as organized labor soon discovered, the federal courts willingly continued to grant injunctions against boycotts. As a result in 1932, Congress passed the Norris-LaGuardia Act, often called the anti-injunction act because it restricted the federal judiciary's power to grant injunctions against labor unions in cases arising out of labor disputes. Finally, in 1935 Congress enacted the Wagner Act, also called the National Labor Relations Act, to grant numerous rights to employees and unions. In addition, through the National Labor Relations Act Congress created the National Labor Relations Board to enforce labor laws throughout the nation.

During the Term of the Collective Bargaining Agreement.   The combination of the Clayton and Norris-LaGuardia Acts created an antitrust exemption for unions acting in their own self-interest, but did not protect union-management actions, such as entering into collective bargaining agreements. Collective bargaining agreements are contracts which contain restrictive provisions and as such, could be deemed "contracts, combinations or conspiracies in restraint of trade." The U.S. Supreme Court addressed this issue in three non-sports cases involving multi-employer bargaining units, *Allen Bradley Co. v. Local Union No. 3, International Brotherhood of Electrical Workers* (1945), *Local Union No. 189, Amalgamated Meat Cutters, and Butcher Workmen of North America, AFL-CIO v. Jewel Tea* (1965), and *United Mineworkers of America v. Pennington* (1965) when it established the labor exemption to antitrust law. In these cases the Supreme Court balanced the interests of antitrust law against the federal labor policy. The goal of the federal labor policy is to bring labor and management together to negotiate an arrangement which best suits their needs. The Court found that Congress did not intend for antitrust laws to subvert the goal of achieving labor peace through labor management relations. The objective of the labor exemption is to protect those mandatory subjects agreed to through good faith bargaining from antitrust scrutiny by a party to the collective agreement. For it would not be fair to agree to a restrictive practice, receive concessions in exchange for the agreement and then turn around and sue a counterpart for antitrust violations caused by that restrictive practice. As a result it has been well established that during the term of a collective bargaining agreement, terms negotiated between labor and management in their collective agreement, which outside a collective agreement would be deemed subject to antitrust law, are in fact exempt from antitrust scrutiny.

Three Part Test for Application of the Labor Exemption.   To raise the labor exemption as a defense to an antitrust challenge, the defendant must satisfy the following three-part test: 1) The injured party (the plaintiff) must be a party to the collective bargaining agreement; 2) The subject being contested on antitrust grounds must be a mandatory subject for bargaining (a mandatory subject is one which deals with hours, wages, and other terms and conditions of employment); 3) The collective bargaining agreement must have been achieved through bona fide arms length bargaining.

Scope of the Labor Exemption.   A number of cases have addressed the scope of the labor exemption in the professional sport industry. First, injured parties under part one of the labor exemption test may include past, present, and future players. For instance, in *Wood v. National Basketball Association* (2d Cir. 1987), a college senior challenged the salary cap, draft, and restricted free agency (right of first refusal) clauses in the collective bargaining agreements under antitrust laws. The player argued that he was not in the league when the agreement was negotiated and thus, did not agree to these restrictive practices. The court found that at the time these provisions would limit his earning capacity, Wood would be an NBA player and thus, he must take the burdens of collective bargaining in order to receive the benefits. In *Reynolds v. National Football League* (8th Cir. 1978) sixteen past and current players challenged a settlement agreement negotiated between the NFL and the NFLPA as a result of the players' successful verdict in *Mackey v. National Football League* (8th Cir. 1976). The court found that once a union is in existence, it is the exclusive bargaining representative and that once a collective bargaining agreement is negotiated to the satisfaction of a majority of players, it is not the court's role to review the merits of the agreement.

In terms of the second criteria for the labor exemption, courts have examined restrictive practices such as restrictions on free agency, the draft, and salary caps as mandatory subjects. So long as the restriction effects hours, wages, or terms and conditions of employment, courts have found the provisions to be mandatory subjects. For instance, in *Mackey v. National Football League* (8th Cir. 1976) the court found that while the Rozelle Rule did not directly deal with hours, wages, terms and conditions of employment, its effect was to depress player salaries (wages) and thus it was deemed a mandatory subject.

Finally, two cases, *Mackey v. National Football League* (8th Cir. 1976) and *McCourt v. California Sports, Inc.* (6th Cir. 1978) are useful in examining the concept of arms length bargaining. In *Mackey*, above, a number of former and current football players challenged the Rozelle Rule, a restriction on free agency which required teams signing free agents to pay compensation to the athlete's former team. The owners argued that the labor exemption provided them with a defense to the antitrust claim as the Rozelle Rule was in the collective bargaining agreement. The court found there was no bona fide arms length bargaining because the Rozelle Rule remained unchanged from the time it was unilaterally implemented in 1963 and there was no evidence that the players agreed to the Rozelle Rule as a quid pro quo for better pension benefits and the right to individually negotiate their salaries (as was argued by the NFL in its defense). In fact the *Mackey* court found that there was no direct bargaining on the Rozelle Rule. Contrast *Mackey* with *McCourt* where the NHL's By-Law 9A, a similar free agent compensation structure, was subject to antitrust attack by Dale McCourt, a player named as compensation. The court found that the labor exemption protected the NHL. The difference was that in *McCourt* the court found evidence that the players association had bargained vigorously against By-Law 9A. The court stated that benefits were bargained for in connection with the reserve system. In sum, the court stated that the inclusion of this free agent compensation was not the result of collusion, but rather good faith bargaining. It was not a failure to negotiate, but rather a failure to succeed in eliminating By-Law 9A.

Duration of the Labor Exemption. A number of recent cases have raised the issue of whether the labor exemption to antitrust continues to protect parties from antitrust scrutiny after a collective bargaining agreement has expired. Under labor law, the subjects of a collective bargaining agreement will survive its expiration as under labor law the parties have a duty to maintain the status quo and continue bargaining for a new agreement until reaching impasse. Impasse occurs when there is a total breakdown in negotiations between union and management. Impasse often leads to a strike (by the union) or a lockout (by management). However, a strike or lockout is not necessarily evidence of impasse as the National Labor Relations Board may find that either may be a negotiating tactic and not necessarily evidence of impasse being reached.

Like the subjects of the collective bargaining agreement, the labor exemption survives the agreement's expiration provided the parties maintain the status quo. If this were not the case the players may have no incentive to bargain, instead opting to drag its feet in negotiations until the expiration of the agreement and then seeking treble damages through an antitrust court action in an effort to increase its leverage in negotiations. The NFLPA has used this tactic successfully after the *Mackey* and *McNeil* verdicts, both of which resulted in settlements which included new collective bargaining agreements. On the other hand, if management favors the collective bargaining agreement, it may have no incentive to bargain, instead opting to maintain the status quo after expiration and drag its feet in negotiations leaving the union with few options short of striking.

The duty to maintain the status quo only extends to impasse and once an employer has bargained in good faith to impasse, the employer may unilaterally impose changes provided those changes are consistent with the latest proposals made to the union prior to impasse. In other words, the employer must have a good faith belief that the unilateral changes it is implementing will be in the next agreement.

Recent Developments

Major League Baseball's Antitrust Exemption Has Been Challenged in Congress and in the Judiciary. In recent years many committees and subcommittees in Congress and the Senate have held hearings questioning whether baseball's antitrust exemption should continue, particularly in light of the maneuvering for limited city resources achieved by many teams who threaten their home cities with a move to a viable market. Baseball has been accused of limiting expansion and holding cities seeking franchises "hostage" for use by teams to gain leverage when negotiating with their home cities. An example is the saga of the Tampa-St. Petersburg region of Florida. It has recently been selected as an expansion site. The decision was likely in response to political pressure from the state of Florida as a result of the games played with that region by many teams who were in the midst of negotiations with their home cities.

In addition, some courts have shown a willingness to narrow baseball's exemption. In *Henderson Broadcasting Corp. v. Houston Sports* (S.D. Tex. 1982) a radio broadcaster brought an antitrust claim against the owner of a baseball team and another broadcaster for conspiracy to impose restraints on the area's radio market. The court held that broadcasting was not central enough to baseball to be encompassed within the exemption as the suit involved a business enterprise which was related to, but separate and distinct from baseball. As mentioned above, in *Piazza v. Major League Baseball* (E.D. Pa. 1993) the court granted a declaratory judgment on the question of whether baseball's exemption continued to protect it from antitrust scrutiny. *Piazza* concluded that baseball's antitrust exemption was limited to the reserve system and was not applicable to the business of baseball. The case settled before a full trial on the merits of the antitrust claims, so *Piazza* has no precedential value. However, another case arising from the same dispute, *Butterworth v. Major League Baseball* (Fla. S. Ct. 1994) held that major league baseball was subject to Florida's state antitrust statute. Prior to *Butterworth* the only other case to deal with the issue of the application of state antitrust laws to baseball was *State v. Milwaukee Braves* (Wisc. S.Ct. 1966). In that decision the Supreme Court of Wisconsin held the application of the Wisconsin state antitrust laws would conflict with the national policy granting baseball its antitrust exemption.

The Duration of the Labor Exemption Is Not Well-Settled. In *Brown v. Pro-Football, Inc.* (1995), the plaintiff, a developmental squad player, alleged that a salary cap of $1,000 per week imposed unilaterally by the NFL was illegal as a violation of the antitrust laws. The District Court found in favor of the plaintiff and held that the labor exemption did not extend past the expiration of the collective bargaining agreement. The appellate court in *Brown* (DC Cir. 1995) reversed, holding that the nonstatutory labor exemption shielded antitrust challenges imposed through collective bargaining provided that the challenged actions are lawful under labor law. Since the parties had reached impasse, the court found that the NFL's unilateral change was a legitimate economic weapon available to the owners under labor law. In arriving at this decision the appellate court followed *Powell v. National Football League* (8th Cir. 1989), *National Basketball Association v. Williams* (2d Cir. 1995) and *Caldwell v. American Basketball Association* (2d Cir. 1995) which have extended the exemption past expiration and impasse provided that a collective bargaining relationship exists for the players and management. The case is currently on appeal to the U.S. Supreme Court.

The effect of Brown and other similar decisions leaves decertification of their bargaining unit, and the resulting elimination of their bargaining relationship with management, as the only means to mount a successful antitrust challenge. NFL players found success using this tactic. In *McNeil v. National Football League*, 790 F.Supp. 871 (D.Minn. 1992), several players challenged the "Plan B" free agency system unilaterally imposed by the owners after the players and owners had reached an impasse in their negotiations (as represented by the players' 1987 strike) and after the decertification of the NFL Players Association as the exclusive bargaining representative of the players. The players prevailed as the Plan B system did not qualify for the labor exemption to antitrust since a bargaining relationship no longer existed between NFL owners and their players.

A similar tactic was recently attempted by a number of NBA players as a means to abolish the salary cap in the NBA. The players had been unsuccessful at the bargaining table and so superstars Michael Jordan, Patrick Ewing, and Alonzo Mourning led an effort to decertify the NBPA in order to open the door for an antitrust suit to challenge the cap. It is the belief of many players that the salary cap, imposed at a time when the NBA was in dire financial need, is no longer necessary for the league's financial success. The decertification election was defeated, perhaps as evidence of the disparity in player interests and demands between superstars and the average players.

References

A. Cases

Allen Bradley Co. v. Local Union No. 3, International Brotherhood of Electrical Workers, 325 U.S. 797 (1945)

Bridgeman v. National Basketball Association, 675 F. Supp. 960 (D.N.J. 1987)

Brown v. Pro-Football, Inc., 782 F. Supp. 125 (D.D.C. 1991), rev'd 50 F. 3d 1041 (D.C. Cir. 1995), *cert. granted* 64 U.S. L.W. 3410 (1995)

Butterworth v. National League of Professional Baseball Clubs, 644 So. 2d 1021 (Fla. 1994)

Chicago Bulls and WGN v. National Basketball Association, 961 F.2d 667 (7th Cir. 1992)

Dallas Cowboys v. NFL Trust, 94-C-9426 (N.D. Cal 1995)

Federal Baseball Club of Baltimore, Inc. v. National League of Professional Baseball Clubs, et al., 259 U.S. 200 (1922).

Flood v. Kuhn, 407 U.S. 258 (1972)

Henderson Broadcasting Corp. v. Houston Sports, 541 F.Supp. 263 (S.D. Tex. 1982)

Local Union No. 189, Amalgamated Meat Cutters, and Butcher Workmen of North America, AFL-CIO v. Jewel Tea, 381 U.S. 676 (1965)

Los Angeles Memorial Coliseum and the Los Angeles Raiders v. National Football League, 726 F.2d 1381 (9th Cir. 1984)

Mackey v. National Football League, 543 F.2d 606 (8th Cir. 1976)

McNeil v. National Football League, 790 F.Supp. 871 (D.Minn. 1992)

Mid-South Grizzlies v. National Football League, 550 F.Supp. 558 (E.D.Pa. 1982), aff'd 720 F.2d 772 (3d Cir. 1983), *cert. denied*, 467 U.S. 1215 (1984)

Molinas v. National Basketball Association, 190 F. Supp. 241 (S.D.N.Y. 1961)

National Basketball Association v. Williams, 43 F.3d 684 (2d Cir. 1995)

Philadelphia World Hockey, Inc. v. Philadelphia Hockey Club, Inc., 351 F. Supp. 462 (E.D.Pa. 1972)

Piazza v. Major League Baseball, 831 F. Supp 420 (E.D. Pa. 1993)

Powell v. National Football League, 930 F.2d 1293 (8th Cir. 1989)

Radovich v. National Football League, 352 U.S. 445 (1957)

Sullivan v. National Football League, 92-10592 (D. Mass. 1995)

State v. Milwaukee, 144 N.W.2d 1 (Wisc. S.Ct. 1966)

Toolson v. New York Yankees, 346 U.S. 356 (1953)

United Mineworkers of America v. Pennington, 381 U.S. 657 (1965)

United States v. International Boxing Club, 348 U.S. 236 (1955)

Wood v. National Basketball Association, 809 F.2d 954 (2nd Cir. 1987)

B. Publications

Gold, Michael E. (1989). *An Introduction to Labor Law*.

Greenberg, Martin J. (1993). *Sports Law Practice* 3-78.

Roberts, Gary. (1990). *Antitrust Issues in Professional Sports*, in Uberstine, Gary (Ed.), *Law of Professional and Amateur Sports*.

Antitrust Law
and Amateur Sports

John N. Drowatzky
The University of Toledo

Following the initial development and rapid growth of the industrial revolution, the economic and market climate produced larger and larger businesses. This trend finally resulted in the development of large monopolies that controlled both the development of competitors and the prices of goods and services. Concerned about this evolution in the market place, Congress passed a series of laws to assure a competitive economy and fair conduct and fair practices on the part of businesses.

The first of these laws, the Sherman Antitrust Act, 15 U.S.C.A. § 1 et seq., was passed in 1890 to stop monopolies and protect fair competition. It made every combination of activities that restrain interstate commerce illegal by casting them into the form of a conspiracy. Under this Act, every person who monopolizes or combines to monopolize is guilty of a felony. In addition, the Sherman Antitrust Act prohibits unreasonable restraints upon interstate and foreign commerce. Sport received little consideration in this area when the acts were passed and professional baseball even received an exemption from antitrust legislation with a Supreme Court decision. In the late 1950s, the Supreme Court made it clear that other sports would not receive the same treatment under the antitrust laws and by early 1970s, the other sports had been covered by the antitrust legislation. The changes occurring in professional sports since that time have been well documented in the sports pages.

Other significant federal antitrust and trade regulatory statutes are the Federal Trade Commission Act of 1914, the Clayton Act of 1914 and the Robinson-Patman Act of 1935. The Clayton Act prohibits certain kinds of price and other discriminations such as exclusive dealing and total requirements dealing that tend to substantially lessen competition. The Robinson-Patman Act prohibits certain discrimination in prices and practices in connection with the sale of commodities in interstate or foreign commerce. Of the three acts, the Sherman Antitrust Act has been used in professional and amateur sport during the past few years.

■ ■ ■ ■

Representative Case

NATIONAL COLLEGIATE ATHLETIC ASSOCIATION
v.
BOARD OF REGENTS OF THE UNIVERSITY OF OKLAHOMA
& UNIVERSITY OF GEORGIA ATHLETIC ASSN.
Supreme Court of the United States
468 U.S. 85 (1984)

OPINION: JUSTICE STEVENS delivered the opinion of the Court.

The University of Oklahoma and the University of Georgia contend that the National Collegiate Athletic Association has unreasonably restrained trade in the televising of college football games. After an extended trial, the District Court found that the NCAA had violated § 1 of the Sherman Act and granted injunctive relief. 546 F.Supp. 1276 (WD Okla. 1982). The Court of Appeals agreed that the statute had been violated but modified the remedy in some respects. 707 F.2d 1147 (CA10 1983). We granted certiorari, 464 U.S. 913 (1983), and now affirm.

I

The NCAA

• • •

The NCAA has approximately 850 voting members. The regular members are classified into separate divisions to reflect differences in size and scope of their athletic programs. Division I includes 276 colleges with major athletic programs; in this group only 187 play intercollegiate football. Divisions II and III include approximately 500 colleges with less extensive athletic programs. Division I has been subdivided into Divisions I-A and I-AA for football.

Some years ago, five major conferences together with major football-playing independent institutions organized the College Football Association (CFA). The original purpose of the CFA was to promote the interests of major football-playing schools within the NCAA structure. The Universities of Oklahoma and Georgia, respondents in this Court, are members of the CFA.

History of the NCAA Television Plan

In 1938, the University of Pennsylvania televised one of its home games. From 1940 through the 1950 season all of Pennsylvania's home games were televised. App. 303. That was the beginning of the relationship between television and college football.

On January 11, 1951, a three-person "Television Committee," appointed during the preceding year, delivered a report to the NCAA's annual convention in Dallas. Based on preliminary surveys, the committee had concluded that "television does have an adverse effect on college football attendance and unless brought under some control threatens to seriously harm the nation's overall athletic and physical system." Id., at 265. The report emphasized that "the television problem is truly a national one and requires collective action by the colleges." Id., at 270. As a result, the NCAA decided to retain the National Opinion Research Center (NORC) to study the impact of television on live attendance, and to declare a moratorium on the televising of football games. A television committee was appointed to implement the decision and to develop an NCAA television plan for 1951. Id., at 277-278.

The committee's 1951 plan provided that only one game a week could be telecast in each area, with a total blackout on 3 of the 10 Saturdays during the season. A team could appear on television only twice during a season. The plan also provided that the NORC would conduct a systematic study of the effects of the program on attendance. Id., at 279. The plan received the virtually unanimous support of the NCAA membership; only the University of Pennsylvania challenged it. Pennsylvania announced that it would televise all its home games. The council of the NCAA thereafter declared Pennsylvania a member in bad standing and the four institutions scheduled to play at Pennsylvania in 1951 refused to do so. Pennsylvania then reconsidered its decision and abided by the NCAA plan. Id., at 280-281.

During each of the succeeding five seasons, studies were made which tended to indicate that television had an adverse effect on attendance at college football games. During those years the NCAA continued to exercise complete control over the number of games that could be televised. Id., at 325-359.

From 1952 through 1977 the NCAA television committee followed essentially the same procedure for developing its television plans. It would first circulate a questionnaire to the membership and then use the responses as a basis for formulating a plan for the ensuing season. The plan was then submitted to a vote by means of a mail referendum. Once approved, the plan formed the basis for NCAA's negotiations with the networks. Throughout this period the plans retained the essential purposes of the original plan. See 546 F.Supp., at 1283. Until 1977 the contracts were all for either 1- or 2-year terms. In 1977 the NCAA adopted "principles of negotiation" for the future and discontinued the practice of submitting each plan for membership approval. Then the NCAA also entered into its first 4-year contract granting exclusive rights to the American Broadcasting Cos. (ABC) for the 1978-1981 seasons. ABC had held the exclusive rights to network telecasts of NCAA football games since 1965.Id., at 1283-1284.

The Current Plan

The plan adopted in 1981 for the 1982-1985 seasons is at issue in this case. This plan, like each of its predecessors, recites that it is intended to reduce, insofar as possible, the adverse effects of live television upon football game attendance.

• • •

In separate agreements with each of the carrying networks, ABC and the Columbia Broadcasting System (CBS), the NCAA granted each the right to telecast the 14 live "exposures" described in the plan, in accordance with the "ground rules" set forth therein. Each of the networks agreed to pay a specified "minimum aggregate compensation to the participating NCAA member institutions" during the 4-year period in an amount that totaled $131,750,000.

• • •

The plan also contains "appearance requirements" and "appearance limitations" which pertain to each of the 2-year periods that the plan is in effect. The basic requirement imposed on each of the two networks is that it must schedule appearances for at least 82 different member institutions during each 2-year period. Under the appearance limitations no member institution is eligible to appear on television more than a total of six times and more than four times nationally, with the appearances to be divided equally between the two carrying networks. See id., at 1293. The number of exposures specified in the contracts also sets an absolute maximum on the number of games that can be broadcast.

Thus, although the current plan is more elaborate than any of its predecessors, it retains the essential features of each of them. It limits the total amount of televised intercollegiate football and the number of games that any one team may televise. No member is permitted to make any sale of television rights except in accordance with the basic plan.

Background of This Controversy

Beginning in 1979 CFA members began to advocate that colleges with major football programs should have a greater voice in the formulation of football television policy than they had in the NCAA. CFA therefore investigated the possibility of negotiating a television agreement of its own, developed an independent plan, and obtained a contract offer from the National Broadcasting Co. (NBC). This contract, which it signed in August 1981, would have allowed a more liberal number of appearances for each institution, and would have increased the overall revenues realized by CFA members.

In response the NCAA publicly announced that it would take disciplinary action against any CFA member that complied with the CFA-NBC contract. The NCAA made it clear that sanctions would not be limited to the football programs of CFA members, but would apply to other sports as well. On September 8, 1981, respondents commenced this action in the United States District Court for the Western District of Oklahoma and obtained a preliminary injunction preventing the NCAA from initiating disciplinary proceedings or otherwise interfering with CFA's efforts to perform its agreement with NBC. Notwithstanding the entry of the injunction, most CFA members were unwilling to commit themselves to the new contractual arrangement with NBC in the face of the threatened sanctions and therefore the agreement was never consummated.

• • •

II

There can be no doubt that the challenged practices of the NCAA constitute a "restraint of trade" in the sense that they limit members' freedom to negotiate and enter into their own television contracts. In that sense, however, every contract is a restraint of trade, and as we have repeatedly recognized, the Sherman Act was intended to prohibit only unreasonable restraints of trade.

It is also undeniable that these practices share characteristics of restraints we have previously held unreasonable. The NCAA is an association of schools which compete against each other to attract television revenues, not to mention fans and athletes. As the District Court found, the policies of the NCAA with respect to television rights are ultimately controlled by the vote of member institutions. By participating in an association which prevents member institutions from competing against each other on the basis of price or kind of television rights that can be offered to broadcasters, the NCAA member institutions have created a horizontal restraint—an agreement among competitors on the way in which they will compete with one another. restraint of this type has often been held to be unreasonable as a matter of law. Because it places a ceiling on the number of games member institutions may televise, the horizontal agreement places an artificial limit on the quantity of televised football that is available to broadcasters and consumers. By restraining the quantity of television rights available for sale, the challenged practices create a limitation on output; our cases have held that such limitations are unreasonable restraints of trade. Moreover, the District Court found that the minimum aggregate price in fact operates to preclude any price negotiation between broadcasters and institutions, thereby constituting horizontal price fixing, perhaps the paradigm of an unreasonable restraint of trade.

Horizontal price fixing and output limitation are ordinarily condemned as a matter of law under an "illegal per se" approach because the probability that these practices are anticompetitive is so high; a per se rule is applied when "the practice facially appears to be one that would always or almost always tend to restrict competition and decrease output." Broadcast Music, Inc. v. Columbia Broadcasting System, Inc., 441 U.S. 1, 19-20 (1979). In such circumstances a restraint is presumed unreasonable without inquiry into the particular market context in which it is found. Nevertheless, we have decided that it would be inappropriate to apply a per se rule to this case. This decision is not based on a lack of judicial experience with this type of arrangement, on the fact that the NCAA is organized as a nonprofit entity, or on our respect for the NCAA's historic role in the preservation and encouragement of intercollegiate amateur athletics. Rather, what is critical is that this case involves an industry in which horizontal restraints on competition are essential if the product is to be available at all.

As Judge Bork has noted: "[Some] activities can only be carried out jointly. Perhaps the leading example is league sports. When a league of professional lacrosse teams is formed, it would be pointless to declare their cooperation illegal on the ground that there are no other professional lacrosse teams." R. Bork, The Antitrust Paradox 278 (1978). What the NCAA and its member institutions market in this case is competition itself—contests between competing institutions. Of course, this would be completely ineffective if there were no rules on which the competitors agreed to create and define the competition to be marketed. A myriad of rules affecting such matters as the size of the field, the number of players on a team, and the extent to which physical violence is to be encouraged or proscribed, all must be agreed upon, and all restrain the manner in which institutions compete. Moreover, the NCAA seeks to market a particular brand of football—college football. The identification of this "product" with an academic tradition differentiates college football from and makes it more popular than professional sports to which it might otherwise be comparable, such as, for example, minor league baseball. In order to preserve the character and quality of the "product," athletes must not be paid, must be required to attend class, and the like. And the integrity of the "product" cannot be preserved except by mutual agreement; if an institution adopted such restrictions unilaterally, its effectiveness as a competitor on the playing field might soon be destroyed. Thus, the NCAA plays a vital role in enabling college football to preserve its character, and as a result enables a product to be marketed which might otherwise be unavailable. In performing this role, its actions widen consumer choice— not only the choices available to sports fans but also those available to athletes—and hence can be viewed as pro-competitive.

• • •

Respondents concede that the great majority of the NCAA's regulations enhance competition among member institutions. Thus, despite the fact that this case involves restraints on the ability of member institutions to compete in terms of price and output, a fair evaluation of their competitive character requires consideration of the NCAA's justifications for the restraints.

Our analysis of this case under the Rule of Reason, of course, does not change the ultimate focus of our inquiry. . . . Under the Sherman Act the criterion to be used in judging the validity of a restraint on trade is its impact on competition.

III

Because it restrains price and output, the NCAA's television plan has a significant potential for anticompetitive effects. The findings of the District Court indicate that this potential has been realized. The District Court found that if member institutions were free to sell television rights, many more games would be shown on television, and that the NCAA's output restriction has the effect of raising the price the networks pay for television rights. Moreover, the court found that by fixing a price for television rights to all games, the NCAA creates a price structure that is unresponsive to viewer demand and unrelated to the prices that would prevail in a competitive market. And, of course, since as a practical matter all member institutions need NCAA approval, members have no real choice but to adhere to the NCAA's television controls.

The anticompetitive consequences of this arrangement are apparent. Individual competitors lose their freedom to compete. Price is higher and output lower than they would otherwise be, and both are unresponsive to consumer preference. This latter point is perhaps the most significant, since "Congress designed the Sherman Act as a 'consumer welfare prescription.'" Reiter v. Sonotone Corp., 442 U.S. 330, 343 (1979). A restraint that has the effect of reducing the importance of consumer preference in setting price and output is not consistent with this fundamental goal of anti-trust law. Restrictions on price and output are the paradigmatic examples of restraints of trade that the Sherman Act was intended to prohibit. See Standard Oil Co. v. United States, 221 U.S. 1, 52-60 (1911). 5 At the same time, the television plan eliminates competitors from the market, since only those broadcasters able to bid on television rights covering the entire NCAA can compete. Thus, as the District Court found, many telecasts that would occur in a competitive market are foreclosed by the NCAA's plan.

Petitioner argues, however, that its television plan can have no significant anticompetitive effect since the record indicates that it has no market power—no ability to alter the interaction of supply and demand in the market. We must reject this argument for two reasons, one legal, one factual.

As a matter of law, the absence of proof of market power does not justify a naked restriction on price or output. To the contrary, when there is an agreement not to compete in terms of price or output, "no elaborate industry analysis is required to demonstrate the anticompetitive character of such an agreement." Petitioner does not quarrel with the District Court's finding that price and output are not responsive to demand. Thus the plan is inconsistent with the Sherman Act's command that price and supply be responsive to consumer preference. We have never required proof of market power in such a case. This naked restraint on price and output requires some competitive justification even in the absence of a detailed market analysis.

As a factual matter, it is evident that petitioner does possess market power. The District Court employed the correct test for determining whether college football broadcasts constitute a separate market—whether there are other products that are reasonably substitutable for televised NCAA football games. Petitioner's argument that it cannot obtain supracompetitive prices from broadcasters since advertisers, and hence broadcasters, can switch from college football to other types of programming simply ignores the findings of the District Court. It found that intercollegiate football telecasts generate an audience uniquely attractive to advertisers and that com-petitors are unable to offer programming that can attract a similar audience. These findings amply support its conclusion that the NCAA possesses market power. Indeed, the District Court's subsidiary finding that advertisers will pay a premium price per viewer to reach audiences watching college football because of their demographic characteristics is vivid evidence of the uniqueness of this product. Moreover, the District Court's market analysis is firmly supported by our decision in International Boxing Club of New York, Inc. v. United States, 358 U.S. 242 (1959), that championship boxing events are uniquely attractive to fans and hence constitute a market separate from that for nonchampionship events. See id., at 249-252. 9 Thus, respondents have demonstrated that there is a separate market for telecasts of college football which "[rests] on generic qualities differentiating" viewers. Times-Picayune Publishing Co. v. United States, 345 U.S. 594, 613 (1953). It inexorably follows that if college football broadcasts be defined as a separate market—and we are convinced they are—then the NCAA's complete control over those broadcasts provides a solid basis for the District Court's conclusion that the NCAA possesses market power with respect to those broadcasts. "When a product is controlled by one interest, without substitutes available in the market, there is monopoly power."

Thus, the NCAA television plan on its face constitutes a restraint upon the operation of a free market, and the findings of the District Court establish that it has operated to raise prices and reduce output. Under the Rule of Reason, these hallmarks of anticompetitive behavior place upon petitioner a heavy burden of establishing an affirmative defense which competitively justifies this apparent deviation from the operations of a free market.

IV

Relying on Broadcast Music, petitioner argues that its television plan constitutes a cooperative "joint venture" which assists in the marketing of broadcast rights and hence is procompetitive.

• • •

The District Court did not find that the NCAA's television plan produced any procompetitive efficiencies which enhanced the competitiveness of college football television rights; to the contrary it concluded that NCAA football could be marketed just as effectively without the television plan. There is therefore no predicate in the findings for petitioner's efficiency justification. Indeed, petitioner's argument is refuted by the District Court's finding concerning price and output. If the NCAA's television plan produced procompetitive efficiencies, the plan would increase output and reduce the price of televised games. The District Court's contrary findings accordingly undermine petitioner's position. In light of these findings, it cannot be said that "the agreement on price is necessary to market the product at all." Broadcast Music, 441 U.S., at 23.3 In Broadcast Music, the availability of a package product that no individual could offer enhanced the total volume of music that was sold. Unlike this case, there was no limit of any kind placed on the volume that might be sold in the entire market and each individual remained free to sell his own music without restraint. Here production has been limited, not enhanced. No individual school is free to televise its own games without restraint. The NCAA's efficiency justification is not supported by the record.

Neither is the NCAA's television plan necessary to enable the NCAA to penetrate the market through an attractive package sale. Since broadcasting rights to college football constitute a unique product for which there is no ready substitute, there is no need for collective action in order to enable the product to compete against its non-existent competitors. This is borne out by the District Court's finding that the NCAA's television plan reduces the volume of television rights sold.

V

Throughout the history of its regulation of intercollegiate football telecasts, the NCAA has indicated its concern with protecting live attendance. This concern, it should be noted, is not with protecting live attendance at games which are shown on television; that type of interest is not at issue in this case. Rather, the concern is that fan interest in a televised game may adversely affect ticket sales for games that will not appear on television.

Although the NORC studies in the 1950's provided some support for the thesis that live attendance would suffer if unlimited television were permitted, the District Court found that there was no evidence to support that theory in today's market.

• • •

There is, however, a more fundamental reason for rejecting this defense. The NCAA's argument that its television plan is necessary to protect live attendance is not based on a desire to maintain the integrity of college football as a distinct and attractive product, but rather on a fear that the product will not prove sufficiently attractive to draw live attendance when faced with competition from televised games. At bottom the NCAA's position is that ticket sales for most college games are unable to compete in a free market. The television plan protects ticket sales by limiting output—just as any monopolist increases revenues by reducing output. By seeking to insulate live ticket sales from the full spectrum of competition because of its assumption that the product itself is insufficiently attractive to consumers, petitioner forwards a justification that is inconsistent with the basic policy of the Sherman Act.

"[The] Rule of Reason does not support a defense based on the assumption that competition itself is unreasonable."

VI

Petitioner argues that the interest in maintaining a competitive balance among amateur athletic teams is legitimate and important and that it justifies the regulations challenged in this case. We agree with the first part of the argument but not the second.

Our decision not to apply a per se rule to this case rests in large part on our recognition that a certain degree of cooperation is necessary if the type of competition that petitioner and its member institutions seek to market is to be preserved. It is reasonable to assume that most of the regulatory controls of the NCAA are justifiable means of fostering competition among amateur athletic teams and therefore procompetitive because they enhance public interest in intercollegiate athletics. The specific restraints on football telecasts that are challenged in this case do not, however, fit into the same mold as do rules defining the conditions of the contest, the eligibility of participants, or the manner in which members of a joint enterprise shall share the responsibilities and the benefits of the total venture.

The NCAA does not claim that its television plan has equalized or is intended to equalize competition within any one league. The plan is nationwide in scope and there is no single league or tournament in which all college football teams compete. There is no evidence of any intent to equalize the strength of teams in Division I-A with those in Division II or Division III, and not even a colorable basis for giving colleges that have no football program at all a voice in the management of the revenues generated by the football programs at other schools. The interest in maintaining a competitive balance that is asserted by the NCAA as a justification for regulating all television of intercollegiate football is not related to any neutral standard or to any readily identifiable group of competitors.

The television plan is not even arguably tailored to serve such an interest. It does not regulate the amount of money that any college may spend on its football program, nor the way in which the colleges may use the revenues that are generated by their football programs, whether derived from the sale of television rights, the sale of tickets, or the sale of concessions or program advertising. The plan simply imposes a restriction on one source of revenue that is more important to some colleges than to others. There is no evidence that this restriction produces any greater measure of equality throughout the NCAA than would a restriction on alumni donations, tuition rates, or any other revenue-producing activity. At the same time, as the District Court found, the NCAA imposes a variety of other restrictions designed to preserve amateurism which are much better tailored to the goal of competitive balance than is the television plan, and which are "clearly sufficient" to preserve competitive balance to the extent it is within the NCAA's power to do so. And much more than speculation supported the District Court's findings on this score. No other NCAA sport employs a similar plan, and in particular the court found that in the most closely analogous sport, college basketball, competitive balance has been maintained without resort to a restrictive television plan.

Perhaps the most important reason for rejecting the argument that the interest in competitive balance is served by the television plan is the District Court's unambiguous and well-supported finding that many more games would be televised in a free market than under the NCAA plan. The hypothesis that legitimates the maintenance of competitive balance as a procompetitive justification under the Rule of Reason is that equal competition will maximize consumer demand for the product. The finding that consumption will materially increase if the controls are removed is a compelling demonstration that they do not in fact serve any such legitimate purpose.

VII

The NCAA plays a critical role in the maintenance of a revered tradition of amateurism in college sports. There can be no question but that it needs ample latitude to play that role, or that the preservation of the student-athlete in higher education adds richness and diversity to intercollegiate athletics and is entirely consistent with the goals of the Sherman Act. But consistent with the Sherman Act, the role of the NCAA must be to preserve a tradition that might otherwise die; rules that restrict output are hardly consistent with this role. Today we hold only that the record supports the District Court's conclusion that by curtailing output and blunting the ability of member institutions to respond to consumer preference, the NCAA has restricted rather than enhanced the place of intercollegiate athletics in the Nation's life. Accordingly, the judgment of the Court of Appeals is

Affirmed.

■ ■ ■ ■

Fundamental Concepts

Antitrust Analysis

Over the years, two ways to interpret an antitrust controversy have evolved; either looking at the issue as falling under the Rule of Reason approach or as a per se violation. After much experience, courts have developed the rather mechanical *per se* review when the problems before them include certain types of agreements that are so consistently unreasonable that the court deems them as illegal without any further inquiry into the rationale given for their existence. However, the per se concept was developed to preserve economic competition between traditional business entities and has not been applied to the amateur athletics.

When this level of unreasonableness is not reached, then the courts will use the Rule of Reason approach. Using the Rule of Reason analysis, the courts focus their inquiry on the issue of whether the restraint as imposed is justified by legitimate purposes and whether it is no more restrictive than necessary. For reasons mentioned above, the Rule of Reason, rather than the per se analysis has been used in amateur sports. Thus, the Rule of Reason analysis poses the question of whether the restraint in question is reasonable under all the circumstances involved. In carrying out this analysis, the issue is evaluated using the following questions:

1. Is the rule in keeping with the purposes of the group or is it intended to protect the association from competition by outsiders?
2. Is the rule a reasonable means of achieving an otherwise proper goal?
3. Are the procedural aspects of the group's enforcement activities reasonable and appropriate?

When using this analysis, there is no presumption that the defendant's act is unreasonable and the burden is on the plaintiff to show that the practice is improper. Specifically, the plaintiff must show that the rule in question restrains trade and that the restraint is unreasonable when viewed in the light of the justification which the defendants have established.

Antitrust and Amateur Sport

As mentioned earlier, sport, especially amateur sport, received little consideration as to whether antitrust legislation should apply. In contrast to the professional sports which are commercial ventures with profit being the sole purpose, amateur sports have a different nature. While the National Collegiate Athletic Association (NCAA) and the member institutions do have concerns about profitability, other noncommercial goals have a central role in their programs. One of the major purposes of the NCAA is to keep the opportunities provided through participation in sport allied with the basic educational functions of member institutions. The courts have, and continue to, view this purpose as an important aspect of NCAA regulatory activities.

Trade Court Cases. Thus, for many years, while antitrust charges were being brought against many businesses, no such charges were considered against amateur sport. Four early cases concerning Sherman Antitrust Act violations involved athletic associations or conferences and the Trade Court. In the early 1970's the Sherman Act was used in *Marjorie Webster College v. Middle States Association* (1970) when the association denied membership to the College because it was operated for a profit. The court found the rule in question was an incidental restraint of trade and did not warrant application of the Sherman Act. Shortly after this case, the dispute between the NCAA and the Amateur Athletic Union (AAU) over participation by track athletes in "certified" meets reached the courts. In *Smara v. NCAA* (1973) two track athletes who attended institutions that were members of the NCAA were invited to participate in the Russian-American Track and Field Meet which was conducted by the AAU. This meet was not certified by the NCAA so participation by the athletes would violate NCAA regulations and result in loss of eligibility. The athletes analogized their situation to a "group boycott" and brought a complaint in the Trade Court charging the NCAA with a violation of the Sherman Antitrust Act. The Trade Court supported the NCAA position and dismissed the action.

Another visit to the Trade Court was made in 1975. The College Athletic Placement Service, Inc. was started to locate athletic scholarships offered by colleges and universities to high school student athletes in return for the payment of a contractual fee by the student's parents. This service was targeted primarily toward student athletes participating in less popular college sports for which there was little publicity or recruitment. *College Athletic Placement Service, Inc. v. NCAA* (1975) litigated a charge that the NCAA violated the Sherman Act by adopting a rule that precluded students who used this athlete's placement service from being eligible for collegiate competition. The Court held that there was no anticompetitive intent as there was no competition; hence, the Sherman Act did not apply. In *Kupec v. Atlantic Coast Conference* (1975), allegations were made that the Atlantic Coast Conference (ACC) controlled the compensation paid to a student athlete enrolled in member institutions and this practice was in violation of the Sherman Antitrust Act. This claim was also denied by the courts. Following these initial challenges to NCAA and other athletic association regulations, creative use of the Sherman Antitrust Act was employed to challenge a variety of NCAA policies.

Over the course of time, the NCAA has become larger and more important in the regulation of intercollegiate sport. Between 1950 and 1970, its membership more than doubled and today the NCAA conducts college championships in a large number of sports in which participation is limited to eligible students attending member institutions. Without doubt, it is the predominant intercollegiate sports organization. By 1970, the NCAA had regulations that possessed many interstate aspects which, according to the purposes of the Sherman Antitrust Act, would be classified as interstate commerce activities. Such activities as the nationwide recruitment of athletes, teams involved in contests that occur in more than one state and the regulation of radio and television broadcasting of NCAA contests and sales of advertising at NCAA tournaments all support the finding that the NCAA and its member institutions are engaged in activities that affect interstate commerce.

Consequently, it was a given that the NCAA would be faced with antitrust litigation focusing on the application of the Sherman Antitrust Act to its activities. It wasn't until the later 1970's that the NCAA became involved in the Federal Court System with cases initially involving constitutional issues related to its regulatory activities. Since that time, the four issues in which the NCAA was faced with antitrust litigation were economic issues, limits on coaches, eligibility issues and implementation of a governance plan for women athletes.

Economical Issues (TV and Radio).   The money issue arose with the development of "big time" television of collegiate football. The NCAA developed a television plan which restricted the number of football games that could be televised and the number of appearances a team could make during the season. The NCAA set the fees that would be received for the telecasts and indirectly the amount of money a team would receive for its appearance. Further, this money was distributed to many member institutions through limitations on the number of appearances a given institution could make on television. Recognizing the potential for increased revenue to support their own programs, the College Football Association (CFA) schools sought control over the marketing of their own games through a legal challenge brought by the Universities of Oklahoma and Georgia. A total of seven visits to the federal court system was related to this issue.

The text of the landmark decision, *NCAA v. Board of Regents* (1984) is printed above. In summary, the University of Oklahoma (OU) and the University of Georgia (UG) charged that the NCAA has unreasonably restrained trade in televising college football games under the Sherman Antitrust Act § 1. The NCAA television plan provided that only one game per week could be televised in each area of the country with a total blackout on 3 of the 10 Saturdays during the season. Further, teams were limited to two appearances during a season. The plan was modified in 1977 when the American Broadcasting System (ABC) was granted exclusive rights for the 1978-1981 seasons. A new plan was adopted in 1981 for the 1982-1985 seasons and is the subject of this action. This plan, as with the others, had the intention to reduce adverse effects upon attendance at live football games and provided that all forms of televised football by NCAA members came under the plan. The NCAA Television Committee awarded the rights to televise the 14 live games allowed by the plan to ABC and the Columbia Broadcasting System (CBS). Following the plan, each of the recommended fees were set for the different types of telecasts and the amount a team received did not vary with the size of the viewing audience. Under this plan, the total number of college football games televised was limited as was the number of games that any one team may televise. Any sales of football games by NCAA members must be made under the provisions of the basic plan. The CFA composed of the major football playing universities was formed and believing that it should have more control over the sales of its football games, investigated the possibility of negotiating a television agreement. It obtained a contract offer from the National Broadcasting Company (NBC) which allowed more liberal appearances and resulted in increased revenue for CFA members. The NCAA announced that it would take disciplinary action against any CFA university that complied with the CFA-NBC contract. Subsequently, OU and UG brought an action to prevent the NCAA enforcement of its policy.

The District Court found that the NCAA plan restrained competition in the relevant market and the Court of Appeals held that the NCAA television plan constituted illegal *per se* price fixing. These decisions were appealed to the Supreme Court which granted Certiorari. Using the Rule of Reason, the Supreme Court determined, there was no doubt but what the television plan of the NCAA constituted a "restraint of trade" when it limited the members' freedom to enter into contracts of their own to televise their football games. Since the Sherman Act prohibited "unreasonable" restraints of trade, the question is whether the NCAA plan constituted an unreasonable restraint of trade. A fair evaluation of the CFA members' competitive character required consideration of the NCAA's justification for the restraints imposed by the plan.

Because the NCAA television plan on its face constituted a restraint on a free market and operated to raise prices while reducing output, the Rule of Reason required the NCAA meet a heavy burden of establishing an affirmative defense to justify its plan. The NCAA position was that the television plan was necessary to protect live football game attendance, which the court felt was based on a fear that the product was not sufficiently attractive to out draw the televised games. The NCAA argued that the interest in maintaining a competitive balance between amateur athletic teams was an important, legitimate goal and justified the restrictions imposed by the plan. The court believed that the television plan was not designed to serve this interest and that many more games would be televised in a free market than under the NCAA plan and the increased consumption in such a market was a compelling demonstration that the television plan controls do not serve any legitimate purpose. The court affirmed the judgment of the Court of Appeals holding, ". . . that by curtailing output and blunting the ability of member institutions to respond to consumer preference, the NCAA has restricted rather than enhanced the place of intercollegiate athletics in the Nation's life." (at 82 L.Ed.2d 96)

A careful reading of this case indicates that while the restrictions on televised football games were not appropriate on a national basis, other commercial issues were not decided. The court indicated that the NCAA had great diversity among its members and the individual members, television networks and consumers had significant financial interests that dictated the outcome of this case. The question remains as to what would be the court's decision if a conference regulated television activities of its members to promote equity within the conference? Further, what if the NCAA or a conference decided to address the court's concern about the lack of controls that promote equity and achieve equity through regulations on salary of coaches and other related aspects of collegiate sport, would such restrictions pass Sherman Act concerns? Given the current atmosphere in collegiate sports, it's not likely that these issues will arise in the near future, but the decision did not answer all questions that might arise.

Limits on Coaches.   Another economic issue that brought the NCAA into court was the issue of restrictions on the number of coaches and the economic impact suffered by loss of jobs because of NCAA regulations. The first antitrust issue arose in *NCAA v. Owens* (1976) which challenged an NCAA By-Law (12-1) that was adopted to limit the number of coaches permitted by a university. The University of Oklahoma (OU) had more assistant football coaches than permitted by this By-Law. OU obtained a temporary injunction staying enforcement of the By-Law until its validity could be determined. The Oklahoma Supreme Court evaluated the trial court's determination that the bylaw operated to restrain trade and was a per se violation of 79 O.S.1871 § 1 (the state's equivalent law to the Sherman Antitrust Law). Finding that the NCAA was a virtual monopoly, the court proceeded to determine whether the bylaw was an unreasonable restraint under the antitrust laws. The court held that the bylaw provision was neither contrary to the public policy of the State of Oklahoma nor did it unreasonably restrain trade in violation of 15 O.S. 1971 § 217.

The *Owens* case was an Oklahoma jurisdiction issue, but a second case litigating the same issue in the Federal Courts soon followed. *Hennessey v. NCAA* (1977) resulted after the NCAA special convention in August 1975 voted to limit the number of assistant football and basketball coaches that could be employed in Division I schools. The By-Law 12-1 scheduled to take effect on August 1, 1976 caused the plaintiffs to be reduced from full-time assistant coach status to part-time coaches. This action requested the court to declare the By-Law invalid or inapplicable which would permit their employment as full-time coaches again. The court noted that the University of Alabama (UA) had one-year contracts and that when the head coach left or was terminated, any employment commitment to the assistant coaches also disappeared. Thus, UA was able to comply with the provisions of By-Law 12-1. The court dismissed the plaintiff's claims that the NCAA engaged in a tortious interference with their contract rights as no ill will or malice was present and the NCAA did not seek anything from them, rather it acted as a matter of direct interest between itself and its member institutions. A person's interest in continuation of his occupation is not a "fundamental right" and the action did not trigger the strict scrutiny test required by the Equal Protection clause. Likewise, the requirements for procedural due process under the Fourteenth Amendment were not met. Sherman Anti-Trust § 1 claims are limited to "unreasonable restraints upon interstate commerce. While the plaintiffs had standing and the NCAA was not totally exempt from antitrust actions, the court held that this action by the NCAA was not an unreasonable restraint and the plaintiffs did not prevail.

Eligibility Issues.   The plaintiffs in *McCormack v. NCAA* (1988) were a group of Southern Methodist University (SMU) alumni, football players and cheerleaders who, after SMU was forced to suspend their football program for violations, charged that the NCAA violated the antitrust and civil rights laws by promulgating and enforcing rules restricting the benefits that may be awarded student athletes. The plaintiffs tried to analogize themselves as shareholders bringing a derivative suit, but unlike shareholders, they own no interest in SMU. The court reasoned that because only a person injured may seek damages for a violation of antitrust laws, the plaintiffs had no standing. The football player plaintiffs could not show a property right that was injured by the NCAA actions. Finally, the Sherman Antitrust Act does not forbid every restraint of trade, only those that are unreasonable. The court held that the NCAA's eligibility rules are reasonable and the plaintiffs failed to allege any thing to the contrary; these rules did not violate antitrust laws.

Weiss v. Eastern College Athletic Conference and NCAA (1983) was a case involving the transfer rule. Weiss was a varsity tennis player during his freshman year at Arizona State University (ASU) who transferred to the University of Pennsylvania (Penn). The NCAA transfer rule required that Weiss be in residence for one academic year and one calendar year before he was eligible to play tennis for Penn. Desiring to play tennis professionally, Weiss brought this action for injunctive relief prohibiting application of the transfer rule against him as he felt that college competitive experience was critical for a professional career. The plaintiff alleged that the transfer rule violated the federal antitrust laws as well as the equal protection and due process clauses. The court held that Weiss did not show evidence that established he would suffer irreparable harm if relief was not granted. All that was shown was that the plaintiff would be considered ineligible for NCAA post-season competition and a potential trip to England at Penn's expense. The record was too sparse to decide other legal questions and injunctive relief was denied.

The plaintiffs in *Justice v. NCAA* (1983) were University of Arizona (UA) football players who were provided compensation or extra benefits such as free airline transportation, free lodging, and cash and bank loans that exceeded NCAA rules. At no time did the plaintiffs or UA deny their guilt. They brought this action with claims under both 42 U.S.C. § 1983 and Sherman Antitrust Act § 1. Specifically they alleged that the NCAA's imposition of sanctions deprived them of their right: a) to be free of punishment in the absence of guilt; b) to participate in intercollegiate football and receive exposure critical to obtaining a professional football contract; and c) to pursue the vocation of their choice and exercise freedom of expression without prior restraints. The court in this case operated under the belief that action by the NCAA constituted state action (later Supreme Court decisions held the NCAA was not a state actor) and was therefore subject to constitutional scrutiny. Consequently the first test was to determine if the plaintiffs held a property interest that was protected under the Fourteenth Amendment. The court reiterated the proposition that receipt of an athletic scholarship did not create a property interest in participation in college athletics. Any oral representations on the part of the coaching staff were expectations rather than an entitlement. Furthermore, Arizona state law did not recognize or create a protectable property right of participation in intercollegiate competition. Likewise the plaintiffs had no constitutionally protected right to play in post-season competition or on television nor do they have a protected interest in receiving television exposure to assist in obtaining a professional football contract. The fact that the plaintiffs were innocent of the wrong doing does not elevate the interest at stake to a level which is protected by the Due Process Clause of the Fourteenth Amendment. The NCAA did not impose arbitrary or irrational sanctions; the fostering of amateur intercollegiate athletics is a legitimate objective of the NCAA. Denial of participation in television and post season games by the NCAA does not constitute prior restraint of First Amendment rights. No Sherman Antitrust cause of action was found because, according to the court, the plaintiffs were not able demonstrate an injury nor did they show the proximate cause between the alleged antitrust violation and the threatened injury. The NCAA "is now engaged in two distinct kinds of rule making activity . . . the protection of amateurism . . . and discernible economic purpose. Because the sanctions evince no anticompetitive purpose, are reasonably related to the association's central objectives, and are not over broad, the NCAA's action does not constitute an unreasonable restraint under the Sherman Act." (at 383)

Women's Sport Issues. Changes in the management and administration of women's athletic events produced *Association for Intercollegiate Athletics for Women (AIAW) v. NCAA* (1983). During the January 1981 Convention, the NCAA adopted the concept of NCAA sponsoring championships for women collegiate athletes and legislation was proposed by the Governance Committee to implement an overall governance plan for women's athletes. AIAW members opposed to the concept of NCAA championships for women vigorously lobbied against this proposal. Many of the AIAW Division I schools chose to participate in the NCAA Division I women's championships rather than the AIAW's tournaments for the same sport. Thus, the AIAW sponsored championships no longer received any television coverage, sponsors of AIAW major awards terminated their agreements and the AIAW encountered numerous other problems. The AIAW ceased doing business as an organization on June 30, 1982.

Subsequently, the AIAW initiated its action against the NCAA charging Sherman Act violations, specifically Section 1 and Section 2 claims. The Section 1 claim of conspiracy named the NCAA as the sole defendant and alleged that the NCAA conspired with various of its own officials to anticompetitive ends. The district court dismissed this allegation stating "that an entity cannot conspire with itself, and subordinates of an enterprise are generally not regarded as separate entities to establish the concerted action necessary to a Section 1 claim." (at 498) Section 2 prohibits competition to the excess and the AIAW alleged that the NCAA engaged in excessively aggressive competitive conduct intended to drive the AIAW from the market altogether. According to the AIAW, the NCAA engaged in unreasonable restraint of trade through its contract between it and CBS for the purchase of television rights to televise the NCAA's Division I men's basketball championship. The AIAW contended that the NCAA "tied" this television right to its new women's basketball championship. According to the court, the main thrust of this action is that the NCAA is a unitary monopolist that is able to dominate, without connivance, the women's market and stifle competition there by projecting its dominant position in the men's intercollegiate market. The court further held that the AIAW action against the NCAA must be treated as an attempted monopoly.

The district court concluded that the AIAW proved the probability of the NCAA's success as a monopolist but failed to prove the alleged predatory acts of injurious conduct through predatory pricing, the development of chaos in women's intercollegiate athletics, intentional conflict with championship dates or interference with commercial relationships. Finally, the push to include women's athletics in the NCAA framework came from the membership rather than the NCAA's "conspiratorial leadership." This plan took shape in the public view for more than a year and the "process through which it was adopted was the antithesis of conspiratorial plotting from a would-be monopolist to acquire surreptitious control of a market to control prices or destroy competition." (at 506)

The AIAW appealed this ruling (1983) which was affirmed by the U.S. Court of Appeals with one exception; namely, the district court's position that intent is a separate and essential prerequisite to civil antitrust liability of organizations such as the NCAA. Supreme Court precedent dealing with regulatory or nonprofit organizations emphasized competitive effect rather than intent. However, the court also held that this was a harmless error and did not affect the outcome, affirming the finding of the District Court.

Recent Developments

NCAA Eligibility and the NFL Draft. Braxton Banks (1992, 1993), a University of Notre Dame scholarship football player, decided to exercise his option to participate in the National Football League (NFL) draft upon completion of his junior year of eligibility. He had been recovering from a knee injury for the past two years and decided to try out rather than risk further injury through participation in collegiate sports. To participate in the draft, he had to sign releases regarding two NCAA rules.

> Rule 12.2.4.2 (the no-draft rule) . . . (a)n individual loses amateur status in a particular sport when the individual asks to be placed on the draft list or supplemental draft list of a professional league in that sport . . .

> Rule 12.3.1 (the no-agent rule) . . . An individual shall be ineligible for participation in a intercollegiate sport if he or she ever has agreed (orally or in writing) to be represented by an agent for the purpose of marketing his or her athletics ability or reputation in that sport.

Banks was not drafted or signed as a free agent and believed that his previous knee injury made him suspect, rather than a lack of playing skills. Consequently, he wanted to participate in Notre Dame football for his senior year of eligibility to enhance his promise as a professional. Since either of these two rules would prohibit his play, he brought suit against the NCAA for: 1) a class action with him acting as a class representative; 2) a Sherman Antitrust § 1 claim asserting an anticompetitive impact on a relevant market (*Banks v. NCAA*, 1993). The court denied both aspects of the suit.

Banks did not file to obtain a ruling on class certification until 8 days before his claim for injunctive relief became moot and therefore lacked standing for the purpose of obtaining class certification before his own claim became moot. If he had filed for a ruling on a motion for class certification immediately after his failure to be selected for the draft or as a free agent, Banks would have had 70 days to obtain a ruling. The court held that his lack of timely filing made his claim for injunctive relief transitory and his action moot. His antitrust claim was also dismissed because he failed to allege that the NCAA rules had an anticompetitive impact on any identifiable market. It is important to note that the circuit court reviewed the complaint ". . . because the NCAA for some reason failed to raise the defense of waiver." (at 1087)

This claim failed because of Banks did not explain how the no-draft restrains trade in the college football market and the rule has no more impact on college players than other rules such as grades, requiring a high school diploma or enrollment in a certain number of hours. Consequently, the court held that Banks was without standing to pursue the merits of the claim on behalf of a class and that he failed to state a claim upon which relief can be granted for any anticompetitive impact upon a discernible market. According to the court, Banks, at best, attempted to frame his complaint in antitrust language. The U.S. Supreme Court reviewed and Certiorari was denied.

Like Banks, Gaines (1990) decided to enter the NFL draft although he had one more year of eligibility remaining at Vanderbilt University. He signed the petition acknowledging that he was giving up his remaining year of intercollegiate eligibility and worked with an agent, thus violating the "no agent" rule of the NCAA. Gaines argued that the NCAA, by preventing football players like himself from returning if they are not successful in the NFL draft violates 15 U.S.C. § 2 by engaging in an unlawful exercise of monopoly power. Gaines filed suit against the NCAA under 15 U.S.C. § 26 which provides that any party threatened by a violation of antitrust laws may seek injunctive relief. The court accepted the distinction between commercial activities subject to antitrust regulation (televising football games, for example) and those NCAA activities not subject to antitrust activities (regulations to promote amateurism). The court held the NCAA had a very narrow exemption for an antitrust analysis when the overriding purpose of the eligibility rule was to prevent commercializing influences from destroying the unique "product" of NCAA college football; these rules had the opposite effect from that prohibited by antitrust regulation. Finally, the court held that "the NCAA has demonstrated strong business justifications for enforcing the current eligibility rules, leading to the conclusion that the Rules cannot be deemed unreasonably anticompetitive or exclusionary." (at 748) Mr. Gaines' application for a Preliminary Injunction was denied (*Gaines v. NCAA*, 1990).

Restricted Earnings Coaches. In 1991 the NCAA adopted a bylaw creating a restricted earnings basketball coach position for Division I basketball programs. This was developed by the NCAA's Cost Reduction Committee charged with recommending ways to reduce costs without compromising student athlete access to higher education or disturbing the competitive balance of NCAA members. The Committee identified personnel as the largest expense in intercollegiate athletics and focused its attention on staff curtailment, proposing the restricted earnings coach. In *Law v. NCAA* (1995), restricted earnings coaches commenced a class action suit against the NCAA, contending that the NCAA rule violates federal antitrust law. The district court applied a rule of reason analysis in evaluating the NCAA's proffered competitive justifications for the restraint on trade governed by the Sherman Antitrust Act. The court found that this restricted earnings rule stabilized and in some cases depressed the market prices for coaching services. According to the court, the NCAA did not demonstrate any link between the stated objectives of the bylaw and its results. No evidence was offered to support the belief that requiring all institutions to pay their fourth coach the same low salary promoted competitive equity, especially when there was no limit on how much the three more senior coaches could be paid. Likewise, there was no evidence that the restricted earnings rule achieved an overall reduction in costs. Therefore, the court found that the NCAA failed to meet the burden of proof and the rule was found violative of the antitrust laws. The decision is currently under appeal. If not overturned, *Law* demonstrates that the NCAA must be able to establish a suitable nexus between its rules and their purposes when faced with antitrust challenges.

References

A. Cases

Association for Intercollegiate Athletics for Women v. National Collegiate Athletic Association, 558 F. Supp. 487 (D.C. D.C. 1983), *aff'd,* 735 F.2d 577 (D.D.C. 1984)

Banks v. NCAA, 977 F.2d 1081 (7th Cir. 1992), *cert. denied*, 113 S.Ct. 2336, 124 L. Ed.2d 247, 61 U.S.L.W. 3771 (1993)

College Athletic Placement Service, Inc. v. National Collegiate Athletic Association, (1975) Trade Cases ¶ 60,117

Gaines v. NCAA, 746 F. Supp. 738 (M.D. Tenn 1990)

Hennessey v. NCAA, 564 F.2d, 1136 (5th Cir., 1987)

Justice v. National Collegiate Athletic Association, 577 F. Supp. 356 (D. Ariz. 1983)

Kupec v. Atlantic Coast Conference, 399 F. Supp 1377 (M.D.N.C. 1975)

Law v. National Collegiate Athletic Association, 902 F. Supp. 1394 (D.Kan. 1995)

Marjorie Webster College v. Middle States Association, 432 F 2d 650 (D.C.Cir. 1970)

McCormack v. NCAA, 845 F.2d 1338 (5th Cir. 1988)

NCAA v. Owens, 555 P.2d 879 (Okl., 1976)

NCAA v. University of Oklahoma and University of Georgia, 463 U.S. 1311, 77 L.Ed.2d 1294, 104 S. Ct. 1 (1983)

NCAA v. University of Oklahoma and University of Georgia, 464 U.S. 913, 78 L.Ed.2d 253, 104 S. Ct. 272 (1983)

NCAA v. University of Oklahoma and University of Georgia, 468 U.S. 85, 82 L.Ed.2d 70, 104 S. Ct. 2948 (1984)

Smara v. NCAA, (1973) Trade Cases ¶ 74,536

University of Oklahoma v. NCAA, 561 P.2d 499 (Okla, 1977)

University of Oklahoma and University of Georgia v. NCAA, 546 F. Supp. 1276 (W.D.Okla., 1982)
University of Oklahoma and University of Georgia v. NCAA, 707 F.2d 1147 (10th Cir. 1983)
University of Oklahoma and University of Georgia v. NCAA, 601 F. Supp. 307 (W.D.Okla. 1984)
Weiss v. Eastern College Athletic Conference and the NCAA, 563 F. Supp. 192 (E.D.Penn. 1983)

B. Publications

Henn, H. C. (1970). *Law of Corporations*. 2nd ed.
Weistart, J. C. and Lowell, C. H. (1979). *The Law of Sports*.

C. Legislation

The Clayton Act of 1914. 15 U.S.C.A. §§ 12-27
Federal Trade Commission Act of 1914. 15 U.S.C.A. §§ 41-58
The Robinson-Patman Act of 1935. 15 U.S.C.A. §§ 15-21a
Oklahoma Statutes 79 O.S.1871 § 1
Oklahoma Statutes 15 O.S.1971 § 217
Sherman Antitrust Act, 1980. 15 U.S.C.A. § 1-7

5.31

Trademark Law
General Principles

T. Jesse Wilde
Huckvale & Company Law Offices

What's in a team nickname? Or logo? The appetite of the sports-crazed fan for merchandise linked with an athletic team or sporting event has fueled what is now a multi-billion dollar industry. Sports fans proclaim their affiliation with their favorite team by wearing T-shirts, jerseys, hats or coats emblazoned with their favorite team's name or emblem. They commemorate attendance at sporting events with merchandise decorated with the name of the competition. And, they are eager to pay significantly more for a product bearing the insignia or name of a team or sporting event than for the same goods without such decorations.

Trademark law affords protection to the owner of a name or emblem and precludes another from palming off goods or business as the goods or business of the original source. A trademark performs a variety of functions, including: designating the source or origin of a particular product or service, even though the source is unknown to the consumer; denoting a particular standard of quality which is embodied in the product or service; identifying a product or service and distinguishing it from the products or services of others; symbolizing the goodwill of its owner and motivating consumers to purchase the trademarked product or service; representing a substantial advertising investment; protecting the public from confusion and deception, ensuring that consumers are able to purchase the products and services they want; and, enabling courts to fashion a standard of acceptable business conduct.

■ ■ ■ ■

Representative Case

BOSTON ATHLETIC ASSOCIATION v. MARK SULLIVAN
United States Court of Appeals for the First Circuit
867 F.2d 22 (1989)

OPINION: **BOWNES, Circuit Judge.**

In this service mark infringement case, Boston Athletic Association (BAA) and Image Impact, Inc. (Image) appeal the denial of their motion for summary judgment and the concurrent granting of the defendants', Mark Sullivan d/b/a Good Life (Sullivan) and Beau Tease, Inc. (Beau Tease), motion for summary judgment. This case arises out of the sale by the defendants of T-shirts (hereinafter called shirts) and other wearing apparel with designs alleged to infringe on BAA's service marks "Boston Marathon," "BAA Marathon" and its unicorn logo. We agree with the district court that there are no genuine issues of material fact, but disagree with the district court's determination of which side was entitled to summary judgment. We, therefore, reverse.

I. The Starting Line

The standard for granting summary judgment in a trademark infringement case is as follows:

Summary judgment is proper only "if the pleadings, depositions, answers to interrogatories, and admissions on file, together with the affidavits, if any, show that there is no genuine issue as to any material fact and that the moving party is entitled to a judgment as a matter of law."

• • •

II. The Start in State Court

We have taken the facts mainly from the district court opinions. BAA is a charitable organization whose principal activity has been conducting the Boston Marathon since it was first run in 1897. The race is run annually from Hopkinton to Boston on Patriots' Day, the third Monday in April. In recent years, a day or two prior to the race an exposition has been put on by Conventures, Inc. under BAA's sponsorship. At the exposition, various businesses set up booths and sell shirts, running apparel, and sports items. The registered runners also pick up their numbers and official materials from the BAA booth.

Defendant Sullivan, a resident of Hopkinton, Massachusetts, retails wearing apparel under the name "Good Life" at a store in Hopkinton. Defendant Beau Tease, Inc. is a Massachusetts corporation doing business in Cambridge. It imprints and distributes merchandise, including shirts, to the trade.

In an effort to defray the costs of the race, BAA began an active campaign to market its name via licensing agreements. It registered the names "Boston Marathon" and "BAA Marathon" and its unicorn logo in Massachusetts in 1983 and "Boston Marathon" in the United States Patent and Trademark Office in 1985.

As early as 1978, the defendants were imprinting and selling shirts with the name "Boston Marathon" and various other terms including the year on them. In 1984, defendant Sullivan negotiated an agreement under which Beau Tease sold to BAA a large quantity of shirts which BAA gave away to the athletes and volunteers during the 1985 race. In 1986, Image, through its President, Mickey Lawrence, entered into an exclusive license with BAA for the use of BAA's service marks on wearing apparel including shirts. Starting in 1986, Image and BAA gave notice to imprinters, wholesalers, and retailers that Image was the exclusive licensee of the BAA and that any unauthorized use on merchandise of the name "Boston Marathon," or a similar name or a colorable imitation thereof, would violate the exclusive rights of BAA and its licensee.

By March of 1986, Beau Tease was imprinting and Sullivan was selling in the Boston area shirts imprinted as follows:

1986 Marathon
[picture of runners]
Hopkinton-Boston

BAA brought suit in Massachusetts Superior Court against the current defendants, and others, alleging that the above design infringed upon its marks. The superior court denied its request for a preliminary injunction, Boston Athletic Association v. Graphtex, Inc., Suffolk Superior Court No. 82365, slip op. (April 11, 1986); the denial was affirmed by a single justice of the Massachusetts Court of Appeals, No. A.C.-86-0169-CV (April 18, 1986) (Fine, J.). The action was discontinued without prejudice; the parties reserved their right to assert their positions in any future action.

In late 1986 and early 1987, Beau Tease began to imprint and Sullivan began to retail shirts and other apparel imprinted as follows:

1987 Marathon
[picture of runners]
Hopkinton-Boston

The 1987 shirts and the 1986 shirts were of poorer quality than plaintiffs' both as to manufacture and materials. The defendants were planning to sell their shirts and other items at the exposition.

III. The Contestants Reach Federal Court

In 1987, the exposition was held on Saturday April 18 and the race on Monday April 20. On April 1, 1987, BAA and Image filed suit in the United States District Court for the District of Massachusetts alleging that defendants' 1986 and 1987 shirts, with the logos described above, infringed BAA's marks. The complaint alleged confusion in violation of the Lanham Act, 15 U.S.C. § 1114, and a similar provision in Massachusetts law, Mass. Gen. Laws Ann. ch. 110B, § 11. The complaint also included additional state law counts for dilution, Mass. Gen. Laws Ann. ch. 110B, § 12, sale of counterfeits and imitations, Mass. Gen. Laws Ann. ch. 110B, § 13, and unauthorized use of a name, Mass. Gen. Laws Ann. ch. 214, § 3A. Along with the complaint, plaintiffs filed a motion for a preliminary injunction, seeking to stop the manufacture and sale of any article bearing the name "Boston Marathon" or any similar name.

On April 8, 1987, the district court held a hearing at which it consolidated the preliminary injunction hearing with a trial on the merits; the defendants were deemed to have made a general denial. Prior to the trial, the parties agreed to certain facts including BAA's registration of its marks in 1983 and 1985. Also prior to trial, several affidavits were filed with the court.

Three days of trial were held on April 13, 14, and 15. During the trial, the plaintiffs presented most of their case. Lawrence, president of plaintiff Image, testified to instances in which people bought defendants' shirts at the 1986 exposition thinking they were plaintiffs'. This testimony was admitted over objection. On April 16, because the exposition was only two days away and the parties were concerned about whether the defendants could sell their shirts at the exposition, the district court received offers of proof as to the remaining witnesses and heard oral argument on the motion for a preliminary injunction.

In a bench opinion the court found that plaintiffs would probably succeed in showing that: 1. BAA's mark was valid and effective at all relevant times; 2. the name "Boston Marathon" when used on products would cause the average person to infer sponsorship by somebody, even if the average person did not realize that BAA was the sponsor; 3. defendants' designs referred to the Boston Marathon; 4. plaintiffs' shirts were of a higher quality than defendants'; and 5. people who attend the exposition, given their interest in running, would infer sponsorship by BAA of Beau Tease's shirts sold at the exposition. The court also found that sale of the same shirts in any other milieu, such as along the race course, would not cause an average person to infer sponsorship by BAA. Based on these findings, the court did not enjoin Sullivan in any way, but did preliminarily enjoin Beau Tease from selling shirts directly at the exposition or marketing to anyone who it knew would sell Beau Tease's 1987 shirts at the exposition.

On April 17, BAA appealed and moved for an injunction in this court. That same day, we denied the injunction because of a lack of irreparable harm. We noted that trademark infringement ordinarily causes intangible injuries which make injunctive relief appropriate. We felt, however, that such relief was not suitable in this case because of the annual and discrete nature of the harm, the availability of a damages remedy and the late date at which plaintiffs' instituted suit in federal court. On April 28, the appeal was dismissed on motion by the plaintiffs.

When the case returned to district court, the parties submitted cross-motions for summary judgment. The motions were bolstered by affidavits—some had been filed pretrial and some filed with the motions—and by references to the trial materials. Plaintiff Image's affidavit, executed by Lawrence, included instances of people buying defendants' 1987 shirts believing them to be plaintiffs'. Lawrence Newman, press liaison for BAA, submitted along with a second affidavit a series of newspaper articles and summaries of the articles, referring to the Boston Marathon and BAA for every tenth year from 1897 to 1967 and for every year from 1972 to 1983 and for 1986 and 1987. On July 24, plaintiffs moved to amend their complaint to include a declaratory judgment claim with respect to their rights in the name "Boston Marathon." The motion also asked that their claim be broadened to include an injunction against defendants' design, already described, with any year on it. The district court allowed this motion on August 17, 1987.

On February 4, 1988, plaintiffs moved to amend their complaint further by including defendants' 1988 shirts and a design:

Boston
[picture of runner/s]
19xx

Plaintiffs also sought a preliminary injunction. On March 7, the district court rendered its decision. On March 11, the district court found the preliminary injunction request moot in light of its March 7 decision. It stated that it had considered the plaintiffs' motion relative to the 1988 shirts and that the March 7 opinion applied to those shirts as well.

The district court's March 7 decision found that BAA's marks were its most valuable asset and were at all relevant times valid and enforceable. It found that an average person would infer sponsorship by someone of a product carrying the logo "Boston Marathon," and that defendants' logos referred to the marathon. The court stated that there was a dispute whether the public would associate BAA with the Boston Marathon but that this dispute was not material. It held that the public would not infer that the defendants' logos were sponsored by BAA. The court explicitly disregarded Lawrence's affidavit evidence of confusion because it was hearsay and the court found no other evidence that any "disinterested" person was confused as to the source of defendants' shirts. The court also held that BAA's rights did not extend beyond the use of its exact service marks. The court ruled as a matter of law that there was no confusion between the defendants' and plaintiffs' shirts. The court concluded its opinion: "More precisely, this Court rules that the specific T-shirt logo challenged in this action does not, as a matter of law, give rise to any colorable confusion with products authorized by the BAA as part of its sponsorship of the particular road race in question." Judgment for the defendants was entered and the preliminary injunction was dissolved. This appeal followed.

IV. BAA'S Right to Run

Defendants argue that they should prevail because BAA's marks are entitled to no protection for two reasons: 1. "Boston Marathon" has become a generic term inasmuch as it now refers to both the race and the services rendered by BAA; and 2. defendants' use of "Boston Marathon" on shirts from 1978 constitutes a prior usage.

• • •

The burden of proof is on the party seeking to have a registered mark declared a generic to show that it has become so under the above test. 3 R. Callman, The Law of Unfair Competition, Trademarks, and Monopolies § 18.25 at 231 (L. Altman 4th ed. 1983) Here, the defendants have introduced no evidence on the issue of "primary significance" and thus, have failed to meet the burden of proof.

With respect to prior usage, it is axiomatic that "registration does not create the underlying right in a trademark. That right, which accrues from the use of a particular name or symbol, is essentially a common law property right. . . ." Keebler Co. v. Rovira Biscuit Corp., 624 F.2d 366, 372 (1st Cir. 1980); see also Volkswagenwerk, 814 F.2d at 815-816 (quoting Keebler). Therefore, BAA's failure to register its marks until the mid-1980s is not dispositive. . . . We agree with the district court that BAA has had valid and enforceable marks for the entire relevant time frame.

V. The Longest Stretch: Likelihood of Confusion

Having held that BAA has enforceable rights in its marks, we turn to the central issue in this and most infringement cases: the likelihood of confusion. Claims for infringement of a registered trademark are governed by § 32(1) of the Lanham Act, 15 U.S.C. § 1114(1), which provides, in pertinent part:

Any person who shall, without the consent of the registrant—(a) use in commerce any reproduction, counterfeit, copy, or colorable imitation of a registered mark in connection with the sale, offering for sale, distribution, or advertising of any goods or services on or in connection with which such use is likely to cause confusion or to cause mistake, or to deceive; . . . shall be liable in a civil action by the registrant for the remedies hereinafter provided.

In order to determine whether defendants' shirts are "likely to cause confusion. . . ," we must first ask, "confusion as to what?" In the "typical" trademark infringement case, the "likelihood of confusion" inquiry centers on whether members of the purchasing public are likely to mistake defendants' products or services for plaintiffs' protected products or services within the same category. See e.g., Pignons S.A. de Mecanique de Precision v. Polaroid Corp., 657 F.2d 482 (1st Cir. 1981) (cameras); Keebler Co. v. Rovira Biscuit Corp., 624 F.2d 366 (1st Cir. 1980) (crackers); President and Trustees of Colby College v. Colby College-New Hampshire, 508 F.2d 804 (1st Cir. 1975) (colleges). One question before us is whether members of the purchasing public are likely to mistake defendants' T-shirts for those of plaintiffs. This was the main issue that was addressed and decided below.

There is, however, a distinct but inseparably related issue, not adverted to directly below, that is involved in this case. Defendants are using the Boston Marathon sponsored and operated by the BAA to promote the sale of goods which are adorned so as to capitalize on the race. This implicates what is called a "promotional goods" issue. . . . Under this issue, the "likelihood of confusion" inquiry focuses upon whether the purchasing public is likely to believe that the sponsor of the Boston Marathon produces, licenses, or otherwise endorses defendants' shirts.

We start with the matter decided below, "confusion of goods." Many of our findings and rulings also bear on the related issue of "promotional goods."

A. Confusion of Goods

The First Circuit has identified eight factors to be weighed in assessing likelihood of confusion.

(1) the similarity of the marks; (2) the similarity of the goods; (3) the relationship between the parties' channels of trade; (4) the relationship between the parties' advertising; (5) the classes of prospective purchasers; (6) evidence of actual confusion; (7) the defendant's intent in adopting its mark; and (8) the strength of the plaintiff's mark. Astra, 718 F.2d at 1205; Pignons, 657 F.2d at 487. Examining the evidence favorable as it applies to [defendants], we must determine on the whole whether there is any genuine issue as to likelihood of confusion. No one factor is necessarily determinative, but each must be considered. Astra, 718 F.2d at 1205; Pignons, 657 F.2d at 487-92.

1. Similarity of the Marks

"'Similarity is determined on the basis of the total effect of the designation, rather than a comparison of the individual features.'" Pignons, 657 F.2d at 487 (omitting citations). Volkswagenwerk, 814 F.2d at 817. Meaning alone, without reference to appearance and sound, may be sufficiently close to constitute similarity. See 3A Callman § 20.18.

It is evident that defendants' logos refer specifically to the "Boston Marathon." There is but one Boston marathon race; defendants' logos use the term "Marathon" and depicts runners. It is run annually; defendants' logos refer to a specific year implying an annual event. The race begins at Hopkinton and ends in Boston; defendants' logos include these cities. Despite this, defendants have introduced no evidence showing that they have taken steps to turn their similarly marked products into dissimilar ones by clearly distinguishing their products, and their lack of BAA sponsorship, from those sold by plaintiffs. When one uses a mark similar to one already in use, there is generally an affirmative duty to avoid the likelihood of confusion.

• • •

Here, the meaning of the two marks is more than similar, it is identical. This overcomes any difference in appearance between them.

2. Similarity of the Goods

The parties offer virtually the same goods: shirts and other wearing apparel. Thus, "under this factor, there is a strong likelihood of confusion." Volkswagenwerk, 814 F.2d at 818; compare id. (both parties were in the business of automobile sales and service) with Astra, 718 F.2d at 1205-1206 (plaintiff sold a local anesthetic while defendant sold a blood analyzer) and Pignons, 657 F.2d at 487-488 (plaintiff sold an expensive, high quality camera while defendant sold a relatively inexpensive instant camera).

3. Relationship Between the Parties' Channel of Trade

4. Relationship Between the Parties' Advertising

5. Classes of Prospective Purchasers

As in some of our previous cases, we treat these three factors simultaneously. See Volkswagenwerk, 814 F.2d at 818.

The parties sell their shirts predominantly in Boston-area retail shops, at the exposition, and along the race date. Sales are largely seasonal, centering on the race date. The parties use the same general method of advertising: displays in store windows, in booths at the exposition, and along the race course. Prospective purchasers are drawn from the public at large. The shirts involved here retailed for about $7-10 and were sometimes sold under hectic conditions. Inexpensive items, bought by the casual purchaser, are not likely to be bought with great care.

"Courts have found less likelihood of confusion where goods are expensive and purchased after careful consideration." Pignons, 657 F.2d at 489; see also 3A Callman § 20.10 at 60.

The virtual identity between the parties' sales outlets and advertising methods, as well as the purchasing public's lack of opportunity to exercise discrimination in making such purchases, all point toward a likelihood of confusion.

• • •

6. Evidence of Actual Confusion

Mickey Lawrence, president of Image Impact, reported in her affidavit that she had encountered a shopper at the Filene's department store who expressed surprise when Lawrence told her that defendants' shirt, which the shopper was wearing, was not an "official" Boston Marathon shirt. The district court refused to consider this account, holding that it was inadmissible hearsay. We think that the account was not hearsay, however, because it was not "offered in evidence to prove the truth of the matter asserted." Fed. R. Evid. 801(c). The statement was made not to prove that the defendants' shirts were in fact officially authorized, but rather to show that the declarant, a member of the public, believed that they were officially authorized.

Lawrence described two other instances where members of the public had bought defendants' shirts believing them to be officially sponsored shirts; one incident involved a 1986 shirt bought at the exposition, the other a 1987 shirt bought at the race. . . . While not as accurate as a survey might have been, this evidence shows that some people were actually confused as to who sponsored defendants' shirts. This factor, then, weighs in favor of a likelihood of confusion.

7. Defendants' Intent in Adopting Their Marks

The facts can only be interpreted to mean that defendants sought to profit from BAA's sponsorship of the Boston Marathon. The defendants chose designs that obviously referred to the Marathon, put those designs on the same types of clothing sold by the plaintiffs, sold those shirts at the same time and in the same manner as the plaintiffs to the same general purchasing public. Defendants' actions clearly show their intent to trade on BAA's sponsorship and management of the Boston Marathon.

8. Strength of BAA's Mark

"The distinctiveness and reknown [sic] of a trademark determine its relative strength or weakness, which, in turn, defines the scope of protection to be accorded the mark against others which are confusingly similar." 3A Callman § 20.43 at 345 (footnote omitted). We have found the following factors useful in determining a trademark's relative strength: the length of time a mark has been used and the plaintiff's relative renown in its field, Pignons, 657 F.2d at 491; the strength of the mark in plaintiff's field of business, especially by looking at the number of similar registered marks, Astra, 718 F.2d at 1209; and the plaintiff's actions in promoting its mark, Volkswagenwerk, 814 at 819.

Here, although BAA has only relatively recently registered its marks, it used them for a long period of time before registration. The Boston Marathon is one of the oldest and most prestigious marathons in this country. BAA, as a charitable organization, does not have the same impetus to advertise that a for-profit company would have. Nonetheless, its broad media exposure serves a similar purpose; it makes known to the public the BAA's sponsorship of the Boston Marathon. Finally, no evidence was introduced that others have obtained, or have not been able to obtain, registration of similar marks in the United States Patent and Trademark Office or its Massachusetts counterpart. Compare Astra, 718 F.2d at 1209 (plaintiff or its parent company held all five federal trademarks using "ASTRA" in the health products field, and thus, had "a certain degree of strength").

The "strength" factors militate in favor of a finding that the mark held by BAA in "Boston Marathon" is a strong one. Therefore, broad protection of the mark is warranted.

Based on the undisputed facts and the pertinent law, plaintiffs have proved that the purchasing public are likely to confuse defendants' shirts with those of plaintiffs.

B. The Promotional Goods Issue

The question here is whether the purchasing public is likely to believe that the sponsor of the Boston Marathon, produces, licenses or endorses defendants' shirts. Whether or not purchasers happen to know that the sponsor of the Boston Marathon is an organization called the "Boston Athletic Association" is irrelevant to this "likelihood of confusion" analysis. See 15 U.S.C. § 1127, as amended (defining "service mark" as a mark "indicat[ing] the source of the services, even if that source is unknown"). Cf. 1 J.T. McCarthy, Trademarks and Unfair Competition § 15:2, at 663-64 (2d ed. 1984). In order to establish infringement in a promotional goods case, it has traditionally been the plaintiff's burden to show that prospective purchasers are in fact likely to be confused or misled into thinking that the defendant's product was produced, licensed, or otherwise sponsored by the plaintiff.

• • •

In the present case, the facts clearly show that defendants intentionally referred to the Boston Marathon on

their shirt in order to create an identification with the event and, thus, to sell their shirts. This evidence is itself sufficient to raise the inference of a likelihood of confusion. Given this presumption in favor of plaintiffs and the fact that defendants offered no evidence that would rebut the presumption, there is no genuine issue of material fact about the "likelihood of confusion."

We acknowledge that a trademark, unlike a copyright or patent, is not a "right in gross" that enables a holder to enjoin all reproductions. See University of Notre Dame du Lac v. J.C. Gourmet Food Imports Co., 703 F.2d 1372, 1374 (Fed. Cir. 1983). In Justice Holmes's words, "When the mark is used in such a way that does not deceive the public we see no such sanctity in the word as to prevent it being used to tell the truth. It is not taboo." Prestonettes, Inc. v. Coty, 264 U.S. 359, 68 L. Ed. 731, 44 S. Ct. 350 (1924). But when a manufacturer intentionally uses another's mark as a means of establishing a link in consumers' minds with the other's enterprise, and directly profits from that link, there is an unmistakable aura of deception. Such a use is, by its very nature, "likely to cause confusion, or to cause mistake, or to deceive." 15 U.S.C. § 1114(1). Unless the defendant can show that there is in fact no likelihood of such confusion or deception about the product's connection to the trademark holder, such a use can be enjoined.

VI. The Finish

Applying the pertinent law to the facts as considered in the light most favorable to defendants, we hold as follows:

1. There is no genuine issue of fact with respect to the likelihood of confusion of goods. Nor is there any genuine issue of fact that the purchasing public will likely believe that the sponsor of the Boston Marathon produces, licenses or otherwise endorses defendants' shirts and other goods with logos referring to the Boston Marathon. These two findings stem from the same set of facts.

2. The plaintiff, BAA, owns the name "Boston Marathon" and the defendants' shirts imprinted with logos suggesting that event constitute an infringement of BAA's mark. This includes the design "Boston; [runner/s]; 19xx," which was the subject of plaintiffs' amended complaint submitted on February 4, 1988.

3. The judgment of the district court is reversed. Judgment shall issue for the plaintiffs, which shall include the following permanent injunction:

The defendants, Mark Sullivan d/b/a/ Good Life and Beau Tease, Inc., and all persons and entities acting in concert or in participation with them, are hereby enjoined from manufacturing or selling goods displaying the name "Boston Marathon" or any other design which is confusingly similar to or a colorable imitation of "Boston Marathon," including goods which are imprinted with "19xx Marathon; [runners]; Hopkinton—Boston," or with "Boston; [runner/s]; 1988."

Costs awarded to appellants.

■ ■ ■ ■

Fundamental Concepts

Suits to enjoin trademark infringement are governed by the Trademark Act of 1946 (the Lanham Act) and the common law tort of unfair competition. Frequently, infringement claims under both the Lanham Act and the common law doctrine of unfair competition are pursued simultaneously.

The Lanham Act

Trademarks and Service Marks. The Lanham Act provides protection for both trademarks and service marks. Under the Act, a trademark is defined as including "any word, name, symbol, or device or any combination thereof adopted and used by a manufacturer or merchant to identify and distinguish goods . . . from those manufactured or sold by others." By contrast, a service mark is described as "a mark used in the sale or advertising of services to identify and distinguish the services of one person, including a unique service, from the services of others and to indicate the source of the services, even if that source is unknown." While a trademark serves to identify and distinguish the source and quality of a tangible product, a service mark functions to identify and distinguish the source and quality of an intangible service. Professional sports franchise marks, for example, are registered as service marks, identifying and representing entertainment services in the form of professional sporting events and exhibitions. These same marks, a team name, logo and color scheme, however, may also simultaneously serve as a trademark, and indicate the source of goods or products produced by that organization.

Trademark Infringement. Under the Lanham Act, determining the outcome of a trademark or service mark dispute involves, in general terms, a two-pronged analysis, namely: does the plaintiff have a protectable property right in the name or mark it seeks to defend; and second, is the defendant's use of a similar mark likely to cause confusion, mistake or deception in the market as to the source, origin, or sponsorship of the products on which the marks are used.

Protectable Property Interest. Under the statute, the registration of a mark with the U.S. Patent and Trademark Office (USPTO) constitutes prima facie evidence that the registrant owns the mark and has the exclusive right to use the mark, and that the registration itself is valid. Section 32(1) of the Act provides a cause of action for trademark infringement in favor of the owner of a registered mark, placing the onus on the one challenging the mark to rebut the statutory presumption of validity. While registration of a mark confers procedural advantages, it does not enlarge the registrant's proprietary interest in the mark, for ownership of a mark rests on adoption and use, not on registration. In fact, the statute affords owners of unregistered marks a cause of action for false designation of origin, under section 43(a) of the Act, against an infringer where the plaintiff can establish that the public recognizes its mark as identifying its goods or services and distinguishes them from those of others. This distinguishing feature of a mark, or the extent to which the mark identifies and distinguishes the goods and services of a mark owner from those of others, is referred to as the "strength" of the mark.

Trademark Strength. Under the Act, trademark or service mark strength is divided into three broad groups in descending order of strength: those marks which 1) are **inherently distinctive**, 2) have acquired **secondary meaning**, or 3) are **generic**. Marks that are **inherently distinctive** include "arbitrary or fanciful" and "suggestive" marks. Arbitrary or fanciful marks are the strongest marks, and include coined words, or words which are not typically associated with the product. Such marks are strong since they serve as an indicator of the source of the goods, rather than describing the product. Examples include "Nike" for sports apparel, "Spalding" for sports equipment, "Ping" for golf clubs, and so forth. Even team nicknames have been described by courts as being fanciful, and, therefore, inherently distinctive. Suggestive marks are also strong marks, although not quite as strong as arbitrary or fanciful marks. Suggestive marks are those which suggest a quality or attribute of the product for which the mark is used.

A mark that is not inherently distinctive cannot be given federal trademark protection unless it has acquired **secondary meaning**, through widespread use and public recognition, such that the mark has become primarily indicative of the source of goods or services, rather than the goods or services themselves. Secondary meaning converts a word, originally incapable of serving as a mark into a protectable trademark or service mark. It tests the connection in the consumer's mind between the product bearing the mark and its source, where the consumer, through public use and recognition, associates symbols, words, colors, and designs with goods of a single source. Professional and collegiate team logos and color schemes, for example, not in and of themselves inherently distinctive, become associated through use in the market place with their respective teams or institutions. The city names or regional designations associated with professional sports franchises are nondistinctive, yet when used with a fanciful nickname, gain secondary meaning. Even some surnames may be entitled to trademark protection if the user can establish secondary meaning, that is, if the name is regarded as identifying the source of the product, rather than the name of the individual, such as "Air Jordan" basketball shoes produced by Nike.

The third category of marks identified above, **generic marks**, receive no trademark protection. A mark becomes generic when it primarily denotes a product, and not the product's producer. When a mark becomes so common or so descriptive that it is not indicative of the source or sponsorship of the good or service, all are be free to use the generic term.

Consumer Confusion. Whether the action is one of trademark infringement or false designation of origin, the key issue in determining the outcome of most infringement cases is whether or not an alleged infringement creates a likelihood of market confusion. Absent a showing of likelihood of confusion, there is no actionable wrong. In determining whether a likelihood of confusion exists, courts have enumerated several factors for consideration. In *Boston Athletic Association v. Sullivan* (1st Cir. 1989), for example, the United State Court of Appeals for the First Circuit, identified eight factors to be weighed in assessing likelihood of confusion, namely: 1) the similarity of the marks; 2) the similarity of the goods; 3) the relationship between the parties' channels of trade; 4) the relationship between the parties' advertising; 5) the classes of prospective purchasers; 6) evidence of actual confusion; 7) the defendant's intent in adopting its mark; and 8) the strength of the plaintiff's mark. While all courts have relied on the same basic factors in their likelihood of confusion analysis, each has placed different weight upon the various factors, while at the same time creating a few of their own. With any of these multi-factored tests, each factor must be considered to globally determine whether or not an alleged infringement creates a likelihood of market confusion.

Defenses/Bars to Recovery

Beyond establishing that the plaintiff has no proprietary interest in the challenged mark or that its use by the defendant is not likely to cause consumer confusion, other defenses may also bar a plaintiff's infringement claim.

Abandonment.   The defendant may allege that the plaintiff has abandoned its mark. Unlike other forms of intellectual property law, trademark law rests on the principle that the owner must "use it or lose it." Whereas a patent lasts for 17 years, and a copyright gives protection for the life of the author plus 50 years, a trademark lasts indefinitely, as long as it is used. However, the corollary is that if it is not used, it is lost. Abandonment is a question of fact. Under the Lanham Act, however, a mark is deemed abandoned when any of the following occurs:

> (1) When its use has been discontinued with intent not to resume such use. Intent not to resume may be inferred from circumstances. Non-use for two consecutive years shall be prima facie evidence of abandonment. "Use" of a mark means the bona fide use of that mark made in the ordinary course of trade, and not made merely to reserve a right in a mark.

> (2) When any course of conduct of the owner, including acts of omission as well as commission, causes the mark to become the generic name for the goods or services on or in connection with which it is used or otherwise to lose its significance as a mark. Purchaser motivation shall not be a test for determining abandonment . . . 15 U.S.C. § 1127.

An abandoned mark may be claimed and used by the public at large. As with any affirmative defense, the burden of proof of abandonment rests on the defendant, the alleged infringer.

Laches.   In circumstances where the plaintiff mark holder has neglected to make a timely assertion of its trademark right, this lapse of time may bar a right to relief, where to grant such would cause prejudice to an adverse party. Under the equitable doctrine of laches, a plaintiff mark holder may be denied equitable relief, such as an injunction for example, where the plaintiff has been guilty of unconscionable delay in seeking that relief, resulting in prejudice to the defendant. This defense underscores the importance of preserving trademark interests through the active assertion of trademark rights and timely prosecution of known infringers.

Functionality.   Features of a product which are purely functional cannot receive protection under the Lanham Act. According to the Supreme Court, a product feature is functional if it is essential to the use or purpose of the article or if it affects the cost or quality of the article. The mere fact that a product characteristic serves a functional purpose, does not, however, preclude the product from receiving trademark protection. If the design of an item is nonfunctional and has acquired secondary meaning, the design may become the subject matter of a trademark even if the item itself is functional. In *Dallas Cowboys Cheerleaders, Inc. v. Pussycat Cinema, Ltd.* (2nd Cir. 1979), for example, the defendants argued that the cheerleading uniform in question was a purely functional item necessary for the performance of cheerleading routines and that it was incapable of becoming a trademark. The court, however, concluded that the combination of the white boots, white shorts, blue blouse, and white star-studded vest was an arbitrary design which made the otherwise functional cheerleading uniform trademarkable.

Disclaimers.   Though criticized by a number of commentators, another possible defense to an infringement claim may be the prior use of a disclaimer. Under this claim, the defendant will argue that a conspicuously placed disclaimer will alert the consuming public that the product or service does not contain certain attributes or features, such as source sponsorship, which the consumer might otherwise logically be inclined to impute to that product or service. The use of disclaimers in the sports arena was upheld in *NFL v. Governor of Delaware* (D.Del. 1977), wherein the NFL unsuccessfully sought to enjoin the State of Delaware from conducting a weekly sport lottery tied to the outcome of NFL games. The court concluded that a disclaimer on the lottery tickets and advertising materials informing consumers that the NFL was not associated with the lottery, dispelled any likelihood of consumer confusion that the NFL was sponsoring the lottery. *National Hockey League v. Pepsi-Cola Canada, Ltd.* (B.C.S.C. 1992), although a Canadian case, provides another example of the use of a disclaimer to bar recovery for alleged trademark infringement.

Tort of Unfair Competition

Unfair competition is a broader area of the law than statutory trademark infringement. Unfair competition is almost universally regarded as a question of whether the defendant is passing off his goods or services as those of the plaintiff by virtue of substantial similarity between the two, leading to confusion on the part of potential customers. Such activity thus allows the defendant to cash in or misappropriate the plaintiff's goodwill by creating the false impression that its product or business is in some way approved, authorized or endorsed by the plaintiff, or that there is some business connection between the defendant and the plaintiff.

Recent Developments

Abandonment of Trademark.   In *Major League Baseball Properties Inc. v. Sed Non Olet Denarius, Ltd.* (S.D.N.Y. 1993), the Los Angeles Dodgers and MLB Properties were unsuccessful in their trademark infringement action against three individual defendants and their corresponding corporations that had opened a restaurant in Brooklyn, New York called "The Brooklyn Dodger Sports Bar and Restaurant." Following a trademark search in October 1987, the defendants registered the name "The Brooklyn Dodger" as a service mark with the New York Secretary of State and the USPTO. The restaurant also registered a logo resembling the L.A. Dodger mark, sharing similar style, script and color. The defendants displayed the registered logo on both the front of the restaurant and on promotional items sold therein. The establishment made further use of the logo by dividing the terms "Dodger" and "Brooklyn" and using them separately on merchandise and food products. Inside the restaurant the defendants also exhibited memorabilia collected from the Brooklyn Dodgers professional baseball team. After considering all relevant factors, the court held that the defendants' use of the Brooklyn Dodger name did not raise a likelihood of confusion and that the Los Angeles Dodgers had abandoned the Brooklyn Dodgers name, thereby preventing them from having any superior rights to the mark.

Likelihood of confusion. In *Indianapolis Colts, Inc. v. Metropolitan Baltimore Football Club Limited Partnership* (7th Cir. 1994), the Indianapolis Colts and the NFL brought suit for trademark infringement against the Canadian Football League's Baltimore franchise for using the nickname "Baltimore CFL Colts," which the NFL plaintiffs contended was confusingly similar to the NFL's mark "Indianapolis Colts." In affirming the decision of the district court to enjoin the Baltimore football club's use of the name "Colts" or "CFL Colts," the Court of Appeals held that the Baltimore team's use of the "Colts" nickname was likely to confuse substantial numbers of consumers, warranting the issuance of a preliminary injunction. (For further discussion see, Curtis, Ted and Stempler, Joel H., "So What Do We Name the Team? Trademark Infringement, the Lanham Act and Sports Franchises," 19 *Columbia/VLA Journal of Law and the Arts*, 23-44 (1994-95)).

Use of Disclaimer.   In the spring of 1990, Pepsi-Cola Canada conducted a consumer contest called the "Pepsi $4,000,000 Pro Hockey Playoff Pool," whereby fans matching information under bottle caps with actual NHL playoff results became eligible for prizes. The promotion was advertised through television commercials and hangtags on Pepsi bottle-necks. On commercial spots and on all promotional materials there was a boldly printed disclaimer disassociating Pepsi-Cola Canada and its promotion from the NHL. The NHL commenced an action (*National Hockey League v. Pepsi-Cola Canada Ltd.* (B.C.S.C. 1992)), alleging that Pepsi-Cola Canada had infringed on NHL trademarks and engaged in unfair competition, by using marks confusingly similar to those owned by the NHL. In finding for Pepsi-Cola Canada, the British

Columbia Supreme Court found that the contest was not likely to mislead the public into believing that it was in any way approved, authorized or endorsed by the NHL, and, in any case, the disclaimer was adequate to dispel any such misconceptions.

Ambush Marketing. In September 1995, NFL Properties, the league's merchandising and marketing arm, commenced an action against Texas Stadium Corp., the Dallas Cowboys and owner Jerry Jones, alleging that the sponsorship deals consummated between Texas Stadium and both Nike and Pepsi violate Dallas Cowboys agreements with NFL Properties regarding the licensing of club marks and logos. The NFL characterizes Jones' agreements with Nike and Pepsi-Cola as ambush marketing deals that undermine existing NFL Properties' sponsorship contracts, specifically with NFL official apparel sponsor Reebok and soft drink sponsor Coca-Cola. The $300 million suit seeks recovery of damages suffered as a result of the Nike and Pepsi deals, and an injunction to prevent the Cowboys from signing any additional outside sponsorship deals. Jones contends in defense that the Nike and Pepsi deals with Texas Stadium, an entity separate from the Cowboys, do not violate trademark licensing agreements between the Cowboys and NFL Properties. Jones' sponsorship deals with Nike and Pepsi-Cola are seen by the NFL as a clear challenge to the league's current merchandising agreement, wherein each franchise shares an equivalent portion of licensing revenues regardless of team's popularity for merchandise in the market place. Such a system of revenue sharing is an NFL tradition that allows small market teams such as Green Bay and Cincinnati to survive. Jones has vocally criticized this system and maintains that individual franchises should be rewarded for their popularity. In 1994, his Cowboys were responsible for 24 percent of NFL Properties' merchandise sales, yet received an equal share with all other NFL clubs.

References

A. Cases

Bd. of Gov's of the Univ. of North Carolina, et al. v. Helpingstine, 714 F. Supp. 167 (M.D.N.C. 1989).
Boston Athletic Association v. Sullivan, 867 F.2d 22 (1st Cir. 1989).
Boston Professional Hockey Association, Inc. v. Dallas Cap & Emblem Mfg., Inc., 510 F.2d 1004 (5th Cir. 1975), cert. denied, 423 U.S. 868.
Dallas Cowboys Cheerleaders, Inc. v. Pussycat Cinema, Ltd., 604 F.2d 200 (2nd Cir. 1979).
Georgia Athletic Association v. Laite, 756 F.2d 1535 (11th Cir. 1986).
Indianapolis Colts, Inc. v. Metropolitan Baltimore Football Club Limited Partnership, 34 F. 3d 410 (7th Cir. 1994).
Major League Baseball Properties Inc. v. Sed Non Olet Denarius, Ltd., 817 F. Supp. 1103 (S.D.N.Y. 1993).
NFL v. Governor of Delaware, 435 F. Supp. 1372 (D.Del. 1977).
National Football League Properties, Inc. v. New Jersey Giants, Inc., 637 F. Supp. 507 (D.N.J. 1986).
National Football League Properties, Inc. v. Wichita Falls Sportswear, Inc., 532 F. Supp. 651 (W.D. Wash. 1982).
National Hockey League v. Pepsi-Cola Canada, Ltd., 92 D.L.R. 4th 349 (B.C.S.C. 1992).
University of Pittsburgh v. Champion Products Inc., 686 F.2d 1040 (3rd. Cir., 1982).

B. Publications

Berry, Robert and Wong, Glenn M. (1993). *Law and Business of the Sports Industries*, Vol. 2, (2d ed.).
Brill, Howard W. (1994). The Name of the Departed Team: Who Can Use It? 15 *Whittier Law Review* 1003-1016.
Curtis, Ted and Stempler, Joel H. (1994-95). So What Do We Name the Team? Trademark Infringement, the Lanham Act and Sports Franchises. 19 *Columbia/VLA Journal of Law and the Arts* 23-44.

Cyrlin, Alan I. (1990). Trademark Protection of Public Spectacles: Boston Athletic Changes the Rules. 10 *Loyola Entertainment Law Journal* 335-351.

Hay, Steven B. (1986). Guarding the Olympic Gold: Protecting the Marketability of Olympic Trademarks Through Section 110 of the Amateur Sports Act of 1978. 16 *Sw. Univ. Law Review* 461.

Kelly, David M. (1983). Trademarks: Protection of Merchandising Properties in Professional Sports. 21 *Duquesne Law Review* 927-964.

McCarthy, J. Thomas. (1984). *Trademarks and Unfair Competition* (2d ed.).

McKelvey, Stephen M. (1994). Atlanta '96: Olympic Countdown to Ambush Armageddon. 4 *Seton Hall J. of Sport Law* 397-445.

McKelvey, Stephen M. (Fall 1992). *NHL v. Pepsi-Cola Canada*, Uh-Huh! Legal Parameters of Sports Ambush Marketing. 10 *Entertainment and Sports Law Journal* 5-17.

Robinson, Mark A. (1994). Injunctive Relief for Trademark Infringement Is Not Available When Likelihood of Confusion Does Not Exist as to the Source of the Goods or Services or When an Entity Abandons a Trademark. 4 *Seton Hall J. of Sport Law* 205-228.

C. Legislation

The Lanham Act of 1946, ch. 540, 60 Stat. 427 (1946) (codified as amended by 15 U.S.C. §§ 1051-1127 (1982 & Supp. V. 1987)).

Sport Management Applications

Ruth H. Alexander
University of Florida

The preceding chapter reviewed concepts relating to the acquisition of trademark rights and the remedies available for trademark infringement. Ownership of a mark, be it a name or symbol grants the owner the exclusive right to use the name or symbol in commerce, and forbids the reproduction, counterfeiting, copying, or imitation thereof by an unauthorized user. In practical terms for sport managers, the ownership of names, logos or symbols, and the ability to dictate who will put their name, logo, or symbol on a cap, shirt, pennant or other souvenir, has translated into a significant revenue source for sport organizations, through the sale of logoed merchandise. Sport organization's have capitalized on a fan's desire to identify with his team or a participant's interest in commemorating his athletic experience (Wong, 1994). Professional sport leagues, for example, have developed licensing programs, authorizing manufacturers to produce and sell products bearing NFL names and logos, to capitalize on the multi-billion dollar public demand for the NFL. Olympic organizations and college athletic departments have done likewise.

■ ■ ■ ■

Representative Case

NATIONAL FOOTBALL LEAGUE PROPERTIES, INC. v. WICHITA FALLS SPORTSWEAR, INC.

United States District Court, Western District of Washington
532 F. Supp. 651 (1982)

OPINION:

The Parties

Plaintiff National Football League Properties, Inc. (hereinafter referred to as "NFLP") is a California corporation jointly owned by the twenty-eight member clubs of the National Football League (hereinafter referred to as "member clubs"). NFLP is the exclusive licensing agent for the registered and common law marks of the member clubs. Plaintiff Seattle Professional Football Club is a general partnership organized and existing under the laws of the State of Washington. The Seattle Club operates a pro-

fessional football team known as the "Seattle Seahawks." Defendant Wichita Falls Sportswear, Inc. (hereinafter referred to as "Wichita") is a Texas corporation in the business of manufacturing and selling garments.

The controversy between the parties concerns Wichita's manufacture of "NFL football jersey replicas." An NFL football jersey replica is a football style shirt bearing large numerals, colors corresponding to an NFL team, sleeve design, and either the full team name (i.e., "Seattle Seahawks"), the team nickname (i.e., "Seahawks"), the "home" city name or regional designation of the respective NFL team (i.e., "Seattle") or the name of a team player (i.e., "Jim Zorn").

Jurisdiction

Plaintiffs seek to enjoin Wichita from manufacturing or selling NFL football jersey replicas. They allege that such activity constitutes: (1) infringement of the federally registered service marks of the member clubs in violation of § 32(1) of the Lanham Act, 15 U.S.C. § 1114(1); (2) infringement of the common law trademarks of the member clubs; (3) false designation of the origin and sponsorship of Wichita's goods, in violation of § 43(a) of the Lanham Act, 15 U.S.C. § 1125(a); (4) unfair competition and misappropriation of the commercial properties of the member clubs, in violation of the common law; (5) infringement of the registered trademarks of the Seattle Club, in violation of RCW § 19.77.140; (6) deceptive business practices, in violation of RCW § 19.86.020; (7) misappropriation of the rights of publicity of the member clubs, in violation of the common law right of publicity; and (8) tortious interference with the business relationships of NFLP, its licensees and the consuming public, in violation of the common law.

Facts

NFLP was created by the member clubs of the NFL in 1963. Each member club grants an exclusive license, either directly or through a trust, to NFLP to act as licensing representative for the trademarks and other commercial identifications of the member clubs. NFLP then authorizes manufacturers to produce merchandise bearing the NFL member club's marks. An NFLP licensee is required to pay to NFLP a royalty fee of 6.5 percent of all net sales of licensed products. Royalties paid by licensees are the sole source of funding for a charitable foundation known as NFL Charities. Since 1971, NFLP has donated almost five million dollars to NFL Charities, including the United Way and the National Negro College Fund.

NFLP conducts a nationwide comprehensive program of trademark protection on behalf of the member clubs. It has investigators in each city with a franchise club to investigate claims of trademark infringement. Complaints are received from a variety of sources, including retailers, licensees and consumers. In every instance, appropriate action to protect the trademarks is taken. The vast majority of these matters are settled amicably. NFLP has, however, gone to court to defend its trademark rights.

• • •

NFLP also maintains a quality control program to monitor the quality and appearance of its licensees' merchandise. This program is in addition to whatever quality control the individual licensees maintain.

Wichita was founded by its president Leo Cooke in 1976. It began as a manufacturer of softball uniforms for local area teams. Defendant began the manufacture of NFL football jersey replicas in 1977.

NFLP became aware of defendant's activities in 1978. In accordance with its standard procedures, NFLP sent defendant a "cease and desist" letter. The matter seemed to have been resolved amicably in 1979. In the spring of 1980, however, NFLP again received evidence of defendant's allegedly infringing activity. After Wichita declined to cease and desist, plaintiffs commenced the present action.

A preliminary injunction was granted by Judge Rothstein on October 3, 1980. Defendant was enjoined from producing shirts bearing "large numerals and the team colors, stripe configuration, and the team name and/or the "home' city name or regional designation of the respective Member Clubs." After the decision in International Order of Job's Daughters v. Lindeburg & Co., 633 F.2d 912 (9th Cir. 1980), cert. denied, 452 U.S. 941, 101 S. Ct. 3086, 69 L. Ed. 2d 956 (1981) (hereinafter referred to as "Job's Daughters"), the preliminary injunction was modified on March 13, 1981. In lieu of a full injunction, defendant was ordered to place a disclaimer label on each of its NFL football jersey replicas which read "Not authorized or sponsored by the NFL." Although less restrictive in impact, the order was expanded in scope to include jerseys bearing the name of any player of a member club.

A contempt hearing was held before Judge Rothstein on November 21, 1981. Wichita was found in contempt for selling jerseys with team nicknames before the injunction was modified. Evidence was also introduced of defendant having sold shirts without the proper phrasing of the disclaimer and other potential violations of the order, but were not found contemptuous. Damages and attorneys' fees resulting from defendant's contemptuous activity were left for this Court to determine.

Plaintiffs seek reinstatement of the original injunction with an inclusion of player names. Defendant responds that it is legally competing in the NFL football jersey replica market and cannot be restrained.

Trademark Infringement-Common Law and § 43(a)

An NFL football jersey replica consists of four separate elements: First, the shirt must bear official team colors of an NFL member club. Second, it must bear a large numeral. Third, an NFL football jersey replica usually has some sleeve design. Finally, it must have a descriptive term which relates the shirt to an NFL team. This term can be an NFL full team name, a team nickname, a city or regional designation or the name of a team player. It is this fourth element, the descriptive term, that the actual controversy is about. Absent this fourth element, the NFLP has disclaimed any interest in the shirts of other manufacturers. The issue then is whether plaintiffs have trademark rights in these descriptive terms when presented with the other three elements or a colorable imitation thereof.

Plaintiffs' federal cause of action is premised on § 43(a) of the Lanham Act, 15 U.S.C. § 1125(a). The statute provides in part:

> Any person who shall affix, apply, or annex, or use in connection with any goods or services, or any container or containers for goods, a false designation of origin, or any false description or representation, . . . and shall cause such goods or services to enter into commerce, . . . shall be liable to a civil action . . . by any person who believes that he is or is likely to be damaged by the use of any such false description or representation.

In order to sue under the statute, it is not necessary for a mark or trademark to be registered. New West Corp. v. NYM Co. of California, Inc., 595 F.2d 1194, 1198 (9th Cir. 1979). Whether the theory is § 43(a) of the Lanham Act or state unfair competition law, the ultimate test is whether the public is likely to be deceived or confused by the similarity of the marks. Id. at 1201. The burden on plaintiffs is twofold: First, plaintiffs must establish secondary meaning in their use of the descriptive terms in the football context. Second, defendant's activities must be shown to have created a likelihood of confusion.

To meet their burden, plaintiffs prepared a nationwide probability survey. Since it would be impossible to bring every potentially confused consumer into court and have him or her testify, a survey can be highly probative on the issues of secondary meaning and likelihood of confusion. See McCarthy, § 32:46 at 498-500. The survey must, however, have been fairly prepared and its results directed to the relevant issues.

• • •

The first step in designing a survey is to determine the relevant "universe." "The universe is that segment of the population whose characteristics are relevant to the mental associations at issue." McCarthy, § 32:47 at 500. A survey of the wrong universe is of little probative value. The universe selected by plaintiffs was the entire population of the continental United States between the ages of thirteen and sixty-five.

Defendant argues that the only relevant universe is likely purchasers of NFL football jersey replicas. Plaintiffs respond, with some authority, that the relevant universe is the entire population. The last word by the Ninth Circuit would indicate the relevant universe is potential purchasers. "In assessing the likelihood of confusion to the public, the standard used by the courts is the typical

buyer exercising ordinary care." AMF Inc. v. Sleekcraft Boats, 599 F.2d 341, 353 (9th Cir. 1979). The Court does not reach the issue, however, because plaintiffs' survey is separately projectable for the universe defendant claims is legally relevant. Separate data is available for prior purchasers of NFL football jersey replicas, "fans" and "fans plus" of NFL member clubs. Even defendant's own expert conceded that these groupings were likely potential purchasers of the NFL football jersey replicas. Moreover, even assuming the relevant universe is potential purchasers, the response of the entire population is of some relevance absent a showing that potential purchasers would have a significantly different response to the survey.

In general, the Court is impressed with the steps plaintiffs took to insure the reliability of the survey. It was well-designed, meticulously executed and involved some of the best experts available. The Court was not persuaded by defendant's efforts to challenge plaintiffs' survey. In view of the fact that defendant offered no survey data of its own, plaintiffs' survey results were essentially uncontroverted.

Secondary Meaning

Secondary meaning has been defined as association, nothing more. Carter-Wallace, Inc. v. Procter & Gamble Co., 434 F.2d 794, 802 (9th Cir. 1970). The basic element of secondary meaning is a mental recognition in buyers' and potential buyers' minds that products connected with the symbol or device emanate from or are associated with the same source. Levi Strauss & Co. v. Blue Bell, Inc., 632 F.2d 817, 208 U.S.P.Q. 713, 716 (9th Cir. 1980). The public does not have to know the specific corporate identity of the single source as long as the public associates the product bearing the mark with a single, though anonymous source.

In order to establish secondary meaning, plaintiffs' survey was directed toward answering this question: When presented with football replica jerseys do people associate such jerseys with the National Football League or its franchised team? The data indicates a significantly high association in the public's mind between the jerseys and the NFL or member clubs. The association level varied from 55-80 percent depending upon the descriptive term employed (nickname, city name or player name).

Defendant argues, however, that the relevant inquiry for secondary meaning in this context is not whether the public associates the products bearing the marks in question with the NFL or a member club but whether the mark primarily denotes to the consumer that the jersey replica was produced, sponsored or endorsed by the NFL member club. That is, because plaintiffs do not manufacture the products in question (but, instead, license the right to manufacture the jerseys with the marks to a number of producers), there is no single though anonymous source of the product.

Trademark law does not just protect the producers of products. The creation of confusion as to sponsorship of products is also actionable. See HMH Publishing Co., Inc. v. Brincat, 504 F.2d 713, 716 (9th Cir. 1974); Dallas Cowboys Cheerleaders, Inc. v. Pussycat Cinema, Ltd., 604 F.2d 200, 204-05 (2nd Cir. 1979). The standard, however, applied by the courts in determining whether a showing of secondary meaning has been made in a sponsorship context is not well-defined. See, e.g., HMH Publishing, 504 F.2d at 718 (secondary meaning is demonstrated by a showing that the purchasing public generally believes that a product which bears that mark is "in some fashion connected" with the products of the registrant); Wyatt Earp Enterprises, Inc. v. Sackman, Inc., 157 F. Supp. 621, 625 (S.D.N.Y.1958) (collapsing the analysis of likelihood of confusion and secondary meaning).

The correct standard should be reachable deductively. There is a symmetry between the concepts of secondary meaning and likelihood of confusion. Secondary meaning requires an examination of the non-infringing party's mark and product, and tests the connection in the buyers' mind between the product bearing the mark and its source. Likelihood of confusion in a sponsorship context focuses on the product bearing the allegedly infringing marks and asks whether the public believes the product bearing the marks originates with or is somehow endorsed or authorized by the plaintiff.

• • •

After considering the survey results, the testimony of the witnesses and the other evidence presented, the Court is satisfied that plaintiffs have made a sufficient showing of secondary meaning in their marks.

Likelihood of Confusion

Likelihood of confusion is the keystone to any trademark infringement action. Despite the levels of secondary meaning established, absent a showing of likelihood of confusion there is no actionable wrong. The stronger the evidence of secondary meaning, however, the stronger the mark and the more likely is confusion.

Likelihood of confusion as interpreted by the Ninth Circuit is a conclusion reached after applying a multi-factor analysis.

In order to determine whether there is a likelihood of confusion in a trademark infringement case, the Court must consider numerous factors, including inter alia the strength or weakness of the marks, similarity in appearance, sound, and meaning, the class of goods in question, the marketing channels, evidence of actual confusion, and evidence of the intention of defendant in selecting and using the alleged infringing (mark).

A strong mark is inherently distinctive and will be afforded the widest ambit of protection from infringing uses. AMF Inc. v. Sleekcraft Boats, 599 F.2d 341, 349 (9th Cir. 1979). The more arbitrary and fanciful the mark, the more distinctive. Focusing on the descriptive terms in a football context, the team nicknames seem extremely fanciful. Why one team is a bear and another a lion is anyone's guess. As for the city name/regional designations, these marks are inherently nondistinctive as they describe the geographic location of the team. By establishing secondary meaning in the city names/regional designations in a football context, plaintiffs nonetheless may be entitled to trademark protection. See Norm Thompson Outfitters, Inc. v. General Motors Corp., 448 F.2d 1293, 1296 (9th Cir. 1971). A similar showing of secondary meaning was made for player names. Moreover, even if plaintiffs' marks are "weak," they still would be entitled to limited protection. Plaintiffs do not seek a monopoly over the word "Seattle," for example, but only use of the term as it relates to NFL football jersey replicas.

The Court is struck with the physical similarity between the "official" NFL football jersey replicas and Wichita's product. There is some variation in design and striping and color, but the differences are not significant. Indeed, Wichita's product, when considered with the testimony of defendant's witnesses, is a calculated effort to create distinctions in the products which will have no real meaning in the minds of consumers. Moreover, the strong correlation in survey data between those responding to questions after having seen the "official" jerseys and those answering after having seen the defendant's product, supports the conclusion of similarity.

The next factor in the likelihood of confusion analysis is evidence of actual confusion. Actual confusion is not a necessary finding in order to establish likelihood of confusion. See Fleischmann Distilling Corp. v. Maier Brewing Co., 314 F.2d 149, 159 (9th Cir. 1963). Evidence that defendant's use has already led to confusion is a persuasive factor, however, that future confusion is likely.

The evidence of actual confusion concerns the testimony of a retail purchaser of defendant's products and the survey itself. The purchaser assumed defendant's product (shirts bearing the word "Chargers" on them) were licensed. In the survey, interviewees confronted with identical copies of defendant's jersey were asked if they felt authorization was required in order to manufacture the jersey. Depending on the descriptive term employed on the jersey, 41.8 percent of the general public who saw shirts with the city name/regional designation, 53.6 percent of the interviewees who were shown jerseys with a player's name on the front and 47.8 percent of those shown shirts with the team nickname felt that authorization from the

NFL or the member club was required. The results were higher for people in the potential purchaser category.

The final factor is the intent of the defendant. Although a plaintiff need not prove that defendant intended to exploit the good will and reputation associated with a mark, where such intent is shown, the inference of likelihood of confusion is readily drawn. HMH Publishing Co. v. Brincat, 504 F.2d 713, 720 (9th Cir. 1974). There is some authority that a showing of intent shifts the burden to the defendant to prove that his efforts have been unsuccessful.

• • •

Plaintiffs have demonstrated that a substantial number of the public at large and of the consuming public for NFL football jersey replicas are likely to be confused by defendant's product. 3 Defendant's activities infringe on plaintiffs' rights as trademark owners to "prevent consumer confusion as to who produced the goods and to facilitate differentiation of the trademark owner's goods." Job's Daughters, 633 F.2d 912, 919 (9th Cir. 1980).

Bars to Recovery

Defendant asserts three "defenses" to the charge of trademark infringement. First, Wichita argues that the marks are functional and therefore not subject to trademark status. Second, granting plaintiffs trademark rights is said to constitute a product monopoly in violation of the doctrine of Sears, Roebuck & Co. v. Stiffel Co., 376 U.S. 225, 84 S. Ct. 784, 11 L. Ed. 2d 661 (1964), and Compco Corp. v. Day-Brite Lighting, Inc., 376 U.S. 234, 84 S. Ct. 779, 11 L. Ed. 2d 669 (1964) (hereinafter referred to as "Sears-Compco"). Finally, the marks are claimed to be generic.

Trademark law does not prevent a person from copying the functional features of a product. Job's Daughters, 633 F.2d 912, 917 (9th Cir. 1980). Functional features constitute the actual benefit that the consumer wishes to purchase, as distinguished from an assurance that a particular entity made, sponsored or endorsed a product. Id. Functionality is not, however, limited to tangible items which "work" (such as a chair or a doorknob) but includes features which are aesthetically pleasing.

• • •

Wichita asserts that the descriptive terms in the context of an NFL football jersey replica are crucial ingredients in the commercial success of plaintiff's licensing program. In other words, no consumer who wishes to purchase an NFL football jersey replica would buy a jersey unless it has the descriptive term which relates the jersey to a member club. An attractive feature is not per se functional. See Keene Corp. v. Paraflex Industries, Inc., 653 F.2d 822, 825 (3rd Cir. 1981) (finding it anomalous that the more attractive the mark, the less protection and thus creating a dis-

incentive for development of imaginative and attractive design). The feature must be "that aspect of (the) product which satisfies (the) consumers' tastes for beauty." Vuitton Et Fils S.A. v. J. Young Enterprises, Inc., 644 F.2d 769, 774 (9th Cir. 1981) (refusing to find functionality as a matter of law simply because a feature is attractive).

Even assuming the marks are functional does not, however, preclude trademark protection. A functional feature may additionally serve as a trademark and be protected as such. As the Court stated in Job's Daughters:

> Our holding does not mean that a name or emblem could not serve simultaneously as a functional component of a product and a trademark. That is, even if the Job's Daughters' name and emblem, when inscribed on Lindeburg's jewelry, served primarily a functional purpose, it is possible that they could serve secondarily as trademarks if the typical customer not only purchased the jewelry for its intrinsic functional use and aesthetic appeal but also inferred from the insignia that the jewelry was produced, sponsored or endorsed by Job's Daughters.

633 F.2d at 919. It is exactly this showing of trademark significance that plaintiffs made in their demonstration of secondary meaning and likelihood of confusion.

Defendant's next argument is that trademark protection would constitute an impermissible product monopoly under the doctrine of Sears-Compco. Assuming the applicability of Sears-Compco to plaintiffs' cause of action, Wichita's argument misses the point. Sears-Compco concerned the prohibition of copying a product not protected by a federal patent or copyright. Plaintiffs do not seek to prohibit the manufacture of jerseys, only jerseys which bear their marks. The jerseys are the product and not the marks. "(It) is clear that Sears-Compco did not redefine the permissible scope of the law of trademarks insofar as it applies to origin and sponsorship."

Trademarks always grant "product monopolies" in that they allow exclusive use of features which connote origin or sponsorship. Adopting Wichita's definition of "product" would subsume all trademark law.

Defendant's final defense is the genericness doctrine. In other words, defendant contends that the marks are generic for NFL football jersey replicas. "The genericness doctrine in trademark law is designed to prevent . . . anticompetitive misuse of trademarks. At its simplest, the doctrine states that when a trademark primarily denotes a product, not the product's producer, the trademark is lost." Anti-Monopoly, Inc. v. General Mills Fun Group, 611 F.2d 296, 301 (9th Cir. 1979). A generic mark no longer serves a trademark function. Considering plaintiffs' establishment of secondary meaning and likelihood of confusion, the Court finds that the primary significance of the marks is source identification. Defendant is a trademark infringer of plaintiffs' marks and has violated § 43(a) of the Lanham Act.

The Court finds it unnecessary to reach plaintiffs' other causes of action.

• • •

Pursuant to the above stated reasons, defendant's use of the marks is found to create a likelihood of confusion and to violate § 43(a) of the Lanham Act. Plaintiffs are entitled to full injunctive relief. The injunction, as well as findings of fact and conclusions of law, accompany this memorandum opinion. Should this opinion contain findings of fact or conclusions of law not separately set forth in the appropriate section, they shall be treated as so set forth and are to be incorporated therein.

■ ■ ■ ■

Fundamental Concepts

Economic Impact

The economic benefits to owners of trademarks were realized in the early 1980s after key legal battles involving professional and collegiate sport properties. Since the early 80s, the licensed sale of sports products has generated billions of dollars. For example, Major League Baseball retail merchandise sales since 1988 alone increased from $650 million to $2.4 billion in 1992. This represented almost a 30 percent increase in four years. In 1992, the top merchandise selling franchises included the Chicago White Sox, the Atlanta Braves and the New York Yankees (*Team Licensing Business*, 1993, p. 15). In 1993, Major League Baseball merchandise sales continued to climb to $2.5 billion, but dropped to $2.1 billion in 1994 following the strike. Sales bounced back in 1995, however, to an all time high of $2.8 billion. The top selling franchises in 1995 included the Colorado Rockies, Atlanta Braves, Chicago White Sox and Florida Marlins (*Team Licensing Business*, 1994, 16).

The National Basketball Association feared its sales in logo merchandise would fall with the retirement of Larry Bird and Magic Johnson, however, Michael Jordan and Charles Barkley smoothly moved into the spotlight and the NBA's sales continued to grow. Newcomer, Shaquille O'Neal, is doing his share to keep the American public positioned in this retail business, especially since "I like Mike" exited, but has since returned. Bill Marshall, general manager for licensing in the NBA Properties indicated that children's licensing products had grown more than 170 percent in a single season—from 8 percent to 15 percent—at the end of the calendar year on December 31, 1992. Top merchandise selling franchise in 1992 was the Chicago Bulls, followed by the Charlotte Hornets and the Los Angeles Lakers. Interestingly, the Orlando Magic was sixth in sales in 1993 even though the Magic finished tenth in league standings (*Team Licensing Business*, 1993, p. 16). In 1993-1994, sales climbed to $2.1 billion, and to $2.5 billion in 1994-1995. Projected sales for the 1995-96 season were $2.65 billion. Approaching the 1995-96 season, the Charlotte Hornets had taken over the lead in merchandise sales, with the Chicago Bulls and Orlando Magic second and third respectively (*Team Licensing Business*, 1995, p. 16).

The National Football League's retail sales went from $1.1 billion in 1988-1989 to $3 billion in 1993-1994. During 1993-94, Los Angeles Raiders merchandise was the NFL's most popular seller, followed closely by the Dallas Cowboys. Raiders merchandise accounted for 17.3 percent of total sales, Cowboys for 14.5 percent, with the Redskins a distant third at 8.9 percent of total sales (*Team Licensing Business*, 1993, p. 17). The 1994-1995 total sales marked an increase $3.8 billion, with the Cowboys assuming the lead in single team sales, followed by the San Francisco '49ers, Kansas City Chiefs and the Miami Dolphins. (*Team Licensing Business*, 1995, p. 18) Some new and innovated twists to the NFL marketing efforts are its expanding retail programs such as the "Spirit for Women"—a domestic home furnishing thrust; "Fitness with Jake" from "Bodies by Jake"; "Cross Training" and the "Country Western" line. NFL Rock and

Country videos are also in demand along with its footwear line called "Apex One" (*Team Licensing Business*, 1993, p. 18).

The National Hockey League has the lowest retail sales in comparison to the other professional sport leagues, but, even so, the growth has been tremendous in recent years, from $100 million in 1988 to $800 million in the 1993 season. Merchandise sales in 1994 reached $1 billion.

On the collegiate scene, the Collegiate Licensing Company from Atlanta handles much of the domestic college licensing and Crossland Enterprises Inc. focuses on American Collegiate licensed products overseas. Retail sales have grown from $221 million in 1987-1988 to $700 million in $1991-1992 to $2.4 billion in 1993-1994. The University of Michigan, Georgetown University, Florida State University and Duke University are the top selling schools in the Collegiate Licensing Company fold. Some big-time institutions find it more lucrative to independently market their own retail logo products and include Notre Dame University, University of Miami, UCLA, Ohio State University, University of Florida and University of South Carolina to name a few. One of these independent schools, the University of Miami, for example, realized an increase in merchandise sales from $18,000 in 1982-1983 to $3.5 million in 1992-1993. On an annual basis, collegiate logo merchandise sales for all institutions have reached close to a $4 billion industry as institutions realize from several thousand to several million dollars annually.

Trademark Enforcement

For a sport manager seeking to maximize profit from merchandise sales, enforcement of trademark rights becomes a key issue as many manufacturers will attempt to use the mark without permission, to benefit from the consumer demand for such products. An organization must aggressively police the unauthorized use of its mark, or join with a licensing group that provides this service as part of the contractual arrangement. In fact, enforcement alone may be the compelling reason for many organizations to contract with a licensing agent who has the resources to police and enforce infringement (Wong, 1994). Each of the major professional sports leagues has a "Properties" division which, in addition to entering into agreements with manufacturers for the authorized production and sale of logoed merchandise, investigates and prosecutes the unauthorized reproduction of its marks. A number of licensing agents handle licensing programs for collegiate athletic departments and perform this same function.

Advantages and Disadvantages of a Licensing Company

An organization may not have the time, money or expertise to undertake all that is involved in developing a licensing program for the production and sale of its merchandise. In such circumstances, many athletic organizations have entered into agreements with licensing companies with expertise in registering of trademarks, negotiating agreements with manufacturers, marketing products on a local, state or national scale, policing the market for trademark infringers, and litigating when necessary (Wong, 1994). One sport organization, such as a college athletic department, may simply not have the resources to operate an effective licensing program, but a number of athletic departments linked together, through a single licensing agent, can reap the benefits of all that such a company can provide.

While the use of a licensing company may appear to be advantageous, an organization operating its own licensing program maintains flexibility in agreements and control of fees and other factors. A university that contracts with a licensing agent pays 40 percent to 50 percent of the royalty revenues generated which means the net royalty revenues for the university may be reduced from 6 percent to 10 percent, to 3 percent to 4 percent. In addition, when an organization contracts with a licensing company it loses a measure of control in the selection of manufacturers and the quality of products (Wong, 1994). As outlined above, some college athletic departments have certainly profited handsomely by operating their own independent licensing program.

Recent Developments

The *Jaguars* Dispute.   When the NFL's Jacksonville expansion franchise chose "Jaguars" as its nickname, Jaguar Cars filed a trademark infringement suit in the federal district court for the Southern District of New York (*Jaguar Cars, Ltd. v. NFL, NFL Properties, Inc. and Jacksonville Jaguars, Ltd.*, 1994). The complaint alleged that the Jacksonville Jaguars' team name and logo was similar to that of the car company, caused a likelihood of consumer confusion, and thus violated the Lanham Act. In response, the NFL Jaguars filed suit in federal district court in Jacksonville, seeking declarations that the team's name and logo did not violate federal trademark or unfair competition laws (*Jacksonville Jaguars, Ltd. v. Jaguar Cars, Ltd.*, 1994). The NFL also filed a motion with the district court for the Southern District of New York, seeking a change in venue of the New York based action from New York to Jacksonville. In January 1995, the NFL's change of venue motion was denied. That same month, the NFL Jaguars announced a redesigning of its logo. The leaping jaguar was replaced with a prowling version, while a snarling jaguar head for the sides of its helmets and a clawing jaguar for other merchandise were introduced by the team. The redesigned logo apparently led to a settlement between the parties, which included the announcement that Ford Car Company, the parent of Jaguar Cars, had become the team's official automobile partner (Curtis, 1994-1995).

University of Wisconsin Obtains Trademark Registration for Name and Logo.   In June 1994 the U.S. Patent and Trademark office ruled that the University of Wisconsin had exclusive rights to the term "Wisconsin Badgers" and its athletic team logo, a drawing of "Bucky Badger" (*The University Book Store v. Board of Regents of the University of Wisconsin System*, 1994). After applying for trademark protection for its team name and logo, the university encountered opposition from three interested parties who contended that the university should not be entitled to the marks, and that the parties should be permitted to continue to produce and sell merchandise with the "Wisconsin Badgers" and "Bucky Badger" marks. In ruling for the University of Wisconsin, the Administrative Trademark Judge held that the University of Wisconsin had not abandoned the marks by permitting uncontrolled used of the marks by book stores and clothes manufacturers. Rather than abandoning its marks, such permitted use by the university was described as a royalty free, non-exclusive, implied license to use the marks. Further, contrary to claims that the marks were geographically descriptive or aesthetically functional, and therefore incapable of trademark protection, the Judge held that the marks had acquired secondary meaning through use in the market, in that a significant portion of the purchasing public associated the marks with University of Wisconsin (Curtis, November 1994).

References

A. Cases

Jaguars Cars, Ltd. and the Jaguar Collection Ltd. v. National Football League, National Football League Properties, Inc. and Jacksonville Jaguars, Ltd., 866 F.Supp. 335 (S.D.N.Y. 1995).

Jacksonville Jaguars, Ltd. v. Jaguar Cars, Ltd., No. 94-537-Civ-J-10 (M.D. Fla., filed June 2, 1994).

National Football League v. Wichita Falls Sportswear, Inc., 532 F.Supp. 651 (W.D.Wash. 1982).

The University Book Store v. Board of Regents of the University of Wisconsin System, Pat. & T.M. opposition nos.: 84,223; 84,224; 84,288; 84,289; 84,290; 84,789 (1994).

B. Publications

1993 Annual Industry Report. (May 1993). *Team Licensing Business*, 15-20.

1995 Annual Industry Report. (June 1995). *Team Licensing Business*, 14-19.

Curtis, Ted. (November 1994). Bucky Wins One for the University of Wisconsin. *Sports Law Monthly*, 3.

Curtis, Ted and Stempler, Joel H. (1994-95). So What Do We Name the Team? Trademark Infringement, the Lanham Act and Sports Franchises. 19 *Columbia/VLA Journal of Law and the Arts* 23-44.

Rotunda, Ronald D. (1989). *Modern Constitutional Law, Cases and Notes*, (3d ed.).

Wong, Glenn M. (1994). *Essentials of Amateur Sports Law*, (2d ed.).

C. Legislation

The Lanham Act of 1946, ch. 540, 60 Stat. 427 (1946).

5.40

Copyright Law

Merry Moiseichik
University of Arkansas

Copyright affects sport and recreation daily. When we use writings of another individual, play music in our fitness centers, or have university bands provide entertainment, is the copyright being violated? Can we remove an artist's mural from walls and floors and how does protection of copyright affect the use of videos or games or recordings?

Congress enacted the United States Copyright Act of 1909 to protect the work of authors and other creative persons from the unauthorized use of their copyrighted materials and to provide a financial incentive for artists to produce, thereby increasing the number of creative works available in society. This legislation was completely revised in 1976 to take into account the changing technology, and to become more inclusive of the types of medium technology has produced and would produce in the future. In 1989 the United States became a member of the Berne Convention where an international copyright treaty was created. This brought about the new revision of the Copyright Act in 1990. The act was revised still again in 1994 because of the United States' entrance into the North American Free Trade Agreement and the passing of the Visual Rights Act of 1990. This is a complicated law and, although many know of its existence, most are not aware of its specific contents.

■ ■ ■ ■

Representative Case

NATIONAL FOOTBALL LEAGUE v. McBEE & BRUNO'S, INC.
United States Court of Appeals for the Eighth Circuit
792 F.2d 726 (1986)

OPINION: ARNOLD, Circuit Judge.

This lawsuit, brought by the National Football League (NFL) and the St. Louis Football Cardinals (Cardinals), alleges that defendants, the owners of several St. Louis restaurants, violated federal copyright and communications law by showing Cardinals' home games which had been "blacked out" in the St. Louis area. According to plaintiffs, defendants picked up the signals for such games by means of satellite dish antennae. The District Court, which had already issued a temporary restraining order

and a preliminary injunction, entered a permanent injunction against defendants after a trial on the merits. NFL v. McBee & Bruno's, 621 F. Supp. 880 (D. Mo. 1985). The decision was based on the Copyright Act of 1976, 17 U.S.C. § 101 et seq., and the Federal Communications Act, 47 U.S.C. § 705 (formerly 47 U.S.C. § 605). In the main, we affirm.

444

I

The Cardinals, a professional football team, is one of 28 teams composing the NFL, an unincorporated non-profit association through which the member clubs schedule games and manage their affairs as a group, including contracts with the three major television networks. One provision of those television contracts is that games which are not sold out within 72 hours of game time are to be "blacked out," that is, not broadcast within a 75-mile radius of the home team's playing field. Officials of the league and club testified at trial that such a rule boosts team revenue directly by increasing ticket sales and indirectly because a full stadium contributes to a more exciting television program and therefore makes the right to broadcast games more valuable.

Witnesses also described the process by which a live football game is telecast by the networks, in this case CBS. As television cameras capture the visual portion of the game, announcers describe and discuss the action from a sound booth of some kind. Those simultaneous audio and video signals are combined at an earth station outside the stadium. This signal—called an uplink—is transmitted up to a satellite, which then sends the signal back—called a downlink—to a network control point on Long Island. Because that signal contains no images other than those from the stadium, this stage is referred to as a "clean feed." The signal is then sent by cable to CBS studios in New York; commercials and other interruptions, such as station breaks, are inserted, and it is now described as a "dirty feed." There is another uplink to the satellite, and then a downlink to local affiliates, who insert local material and finally put the live broadcast on the air. The process apparently takes far longer to describe than to occur; at argument, counsel for the NFL called the procedure "simultaneous, instantaneous," and said that the delay between the action on the field and the broadcast by local affiliates was considerably less than two seconds.

The defendants are owners, corporate or individual, of St. Louis bar-restaurants within 75 miles of Busch Stadium, the Cardinals' home field. All defendants have satellite dish antennae that enable them to receive transmissions in the so-called C-band frequency, approximately 3200-4200 megahertz, in which the satellite sends and receives transmissions. There is no question that prior to November 19, 1984, all defendants but two picked up the clean feed (from the satellite to CBS) and thereby showed blacked-out home games of the Cardinals. On that date, plaintiffs requested and the District Court entered a temporary restraining order, preventing defendants from intercepting and showing the home game scheduled for the following Sunday; after a hearing, the Court issued a preliminary injunction in basically the same terms, dealing with the last home game of the season. Trial on the merits was held on May 7, 1985. The District Court found that the telecasts were copyrightable under Section 102 of the Copyright Act, that the plaintiffs were owners of those copyrights, and that display of the clean feed transmissions of those telecasts violated plaintiffs' exclusive right of display and performance under Section 106 of the Act, as well as Section 705 of the Communications Act. A permanent injunction issued on September 13, 1985, prohibiting the defendants from intercepting and showing plaintiffs' programming, whether in the form of the clean or dirty feed transmissions.

II

The owners of the defendant restaurants challenge the District Court's Copyright Act decision on a variety of grounds: that the evidence presented by plaintiffs to show irreparable injury was too speculative to support the issuance of a permanent injunction; that defendants' display of blacked-out home games falls under statutory limitations on exclusive rights of a copyright owner, 17 U.S.C. § 110(5); that defendants did not infringe on plaintiffs' copyright because they intercepted the clean feed rather than the dirty feed, which was the transmission actually "fixed" under the Copyright Act and registered with the Copyright Office; and that under 17 U.S.C. § 411, no permanent injunction can issue concerning works which are not already in existence. Although some of these arguments have more substance than others, we consider all to be ultimately without merit.

A

Defendants first allege that plaintiffs have not shown that either the League or the local team will suffer the sort of irreparable injury necessary to justify a permanent injunction. Instead, say the restaurant owners, the plaintiffs' evidence is mere "bluster," Appellants' Supplemental Brief at 5, insufficient to make out a claim of copyright infringement under Sony Corp. of America v. Universal City Studios, Inc., 464 U.S. 417, 78 L. Ed. 2d 574, 104 S. Ct. 774 (1984), which they say requires factual evidence of harm.

Defendants have read Sony too broadly. Copyright law has long held that irreparable injury is presumed when the exclusive rights of the holder are infringed. . . . Although the District Court recognized this presumption of irreparable harm, id. at 888, it also stated "that more persons attend the games if a televised showing is not available than if it is," id.; noting that a full stadium translates into greater ticket sales and a more exciting—and therefore more marketable—television entertainment program. This finding is not clearly erroneous, nor is it contradicted by Malrite TV of New York v. Federal Communications

Comm'n., 652 F.2d 1140 (2d Cir. 1981), cert. denied, 454 U.S. 1143, 102 S. Ct. 1002, 71 L. Ed. 2d 295 (1982), cited by defendants for the proposition that the NFL and its member clubs have never been able to support their claim that the black-out rule protects their interests. That decision upheld changes by the FCC in the rules governing transmission of cable television signals and is inapplicable here for a variety of reasons: the standard of review was that used for agency rulemaking; the continuation of the home black-out rule was explicitly assumed; and no question of copyright infringement, with its presumption of injury, was raised.

B

Defendants' second and most considerable argument is that their display of plaintiffs' blacked-out games falls into the category of non-infringing acts under Section 110(5) of the Copyright Act. Under that provision, no copyright liability can be imposed for "communication of a transmission embodying a performance . . . by the public reception of the transmission on a single receiving apparatus of a kind commonly used in private homes. . . ." The District Court rejected this argument, finding that satellite dish antennae, which in the United States are outnumbered by television sets by more than 100-to-one, were outside the statutory exemption. 621 F. Supp. at 887.

• • •

The home-use exemption was included in the 1976 Copyright Act specifically in response to the Supreme Court's decision in Twentieth Century Music Corp. v. Aiken, 422 U.S. 151, 45 L. Ed. 2d 84, 95 S. Ct. 2040 (1975). Aiken held that the owner of a small fried-chicken restaurant was not "performing" copyright works when he played a conventional radio through four in-the-ceiling speakers for the benefit of customers and employees. According to the legislative history of the 1976 Act, an act such as Aiken's would be considered a performance; to decide whether an infringement had occurred, the critical question instead would be the type of equipment used by the putative infringer. Calling "the use of a home receiver with four ordinary loudspeakers . . . the outer limit of the exemption," the drafters then said:

> the clause would exempt small commercial establishments whose proprietors merely bring onto their premises standard radio or television equipment and turn it on for their customers' enjoyment, but it would impose liability where the proprietor has a commercial 'sound system' installed or converts a standard home receiving apparatus . . . into the equivalent of a commercial sound system.

Common sense alone says that it does not matter how well speakers amplify a performance if a receiver cannot pick up the signal in the first place. Moreover, both the legislative history and the plain language of the statute—which speaks of a "receiving set"—contemplate that how the signal is captured will be as much at issue under the exemption as how good the captured signal sounds or looks. There is no indication that the portion of a system which receives should be considered separately from that which displays.

The factors listed in the legislative history do speak of the size of the area where the transmission will be played and "the extent to which the receiving apparatus is altered . . . for the purpose of improving the aural or visual quality of the performance," id. And it is true, as defendants argue, that most of the cases involving the Section 110(5) exemption deal with the enhancement factor, see, e.g., Rogers v. Eighty-Four Lumber Co., 617 F. Supp. 1021, 1022-1023 (W.D. Pa. 1985); Sailor Music v. The Gap Stores, Inc., 516 F. Supp. 923, 924-925 (S.D.N.Y.), aff'd, 668 F.2d 84 (2d Cir. 1981), cert. denied, 456 U.S. 945, 72 L. Ed. 2d 468, 102 S. Ct. 2012 (1982). The reason, however, is that these cases have to do not with interception of blacked-out television programming, where the difficulty is in intercepting a signal, but with the playing of music for which no royalties have been paid. In this sort of case, the question as a practical matter is whether the defendant establishment is of the size and kind that Congress would expect to obtain a license through a subscription music service. . . . In the present case, however, the NFL and Cardinals are not saying the bar owners can display their programs if a license fee is paid; these plaintiffs intend that their work not be performed at all outside their aegis, making the fact of reception rather than just its quality the primary consideration. The question in this instance, therefore, is how likely the average patron who watches a blacked-out Cardinals game at one of the defendant restaurants is to have the ability to watch the same game at home? If it is likely—that is, if such systems are the "kind commonly used in private homes"—then the Section 110(5) exemption applies.

However, as the District Court in this case stated:

> There are less than 1,000,000 dish systems in use, and many of these are confined to commercial establishments. The dishes do have residential use when the home is so situated that access to television station broadcasting by standard television antennae is poor. Television sets can be purchased for $100.00 or more [while] dish systems cost no less than $1,500.00 and for desired reception, $3,000.00 to $6,000.00 or more.

Given these facts, the Court's finding that satellite dishes are not "commonly found in private homes" is not clearly erroneous. There was testimony that the number of such receivers has been growing rapidly, Tr., Preliminary Hearing (November 29, 1984), Vol. II at 104-105, and while some day these antennae may be commonplace, they are not now.

C

The Copyright Act protects "original works of authorship fixed in any tangible medium," 17 U.S.C. § 102(a), including "motion pictures and other audiovisual works," 17 U.S.C. § 102(a)(6). As for live broadcasts, such as the football games at issue here, the Act states that "[a] work consisting of sounds, images, or both, that are being transmitted, is 'fixed' . . . if a fixation of the work is being made simultaneously with its transmission," 17 U.S.C. § 101; "to 'transmit'" is defined as "to communicate . . . by any device or process whereby images or sounds are received beyond the place from which they are sent." Id. The defendants claim that no infringement took place because they intercepted the clean feed, and it was the dirty feed which was fixed under the Act and for which the plaintiffs sought copyright protection. In making the argument that the clean and dirty feeds represent separate works, defendants depend on the quoted definitions, as well as a third provision of Section 101 which states that each draft version of a work "prepared over a period of time," id., constitutes a separate work.

The District Court rejected this theory on two grounds. Not only could the argument rule out any protection for live broadcasting by satellite transmission but, the Court said, it also ignored the fact that the game, and not the inserted commercials and station breaks, constituted the work of authorship.

We agree. . . . Congress surely was aware that the images and sounds from a live broadcast do not go directly from camera or microphone to a home television or radio. To hold that this transmission process nevertheless represents the performance of separate works would gut the plain purpose of the "fixation" definition, as well as distort the concept of a "work prepared over a period of time."

• • •

Accordingly, permanent injunctive relief was appropriate as to the defendants McBee & Bruno's, Inc., Michael Badalamenti, and Talayna's of South St. Louis, Inc. Their violation of the Copyright Act fully supports the grant of such relief. As to these defendants, there is no need to discuss the District Court's holding that the Communications Act was also violated. All of the violations proved against them on this record were violations of the Copyright Act, at least, and we do not believe that either side in this case is concerned about anything these defendants might do in the future that would violate the Communications Act without also violating the Copyright Act.

■ ■ ■ ■

Fundamental Concepts

Copyright Protection

The purpose of copyright is specifically to protect those who have put much time and energy into some creative project. These creators deserve to reap the financial benefits of their work. The law is economically motivated, designed to protect the rights of those who provide the many creative endeavors we hear and see daily.

A copyright gives the owner of the work the exclusive right to copy, reproduce, distribute, publish, perform or display the work. There are two fundamental criteria for copyright protection: 1) the work must be original, and 2) it must be in some tangible form which can be reproduced (Copyright Act, 1994). Registration of a copyright is not required for protection. The protection exists as soon as the work is fixed in some tangible form, such as on paper, a video tape, a cassette tape, on canvas, and so forth, and lasts for the life of the creator plus 50 years (except in the case of works "made for hire," where the copyright lasts for the life of the creator plus 75 years). The federal government grants registration of a copyright, which does not create the copyright, but does provide some procedural advantages in enforcing rights under law.

There are now eight broad categories of copyright protection, including: 1) literary works; 2) musical works; 3) dramatic works; 4) pantomime and choreographic works; 5) pictorial, graphic, and sculptural works; 6) motion pictures and other audio visual works; 7) sound recordings; and, 8) architectural works (Copyright Act, 1994).

To appreciate what can be copyrighted, it is instructive to consider what cannot be. "In no case does copyright protection for an original work of authorship extend to any idea, procedure, process, system, method of operation, concept, principle, or discovery, regardless of the form in which it is described, explained, illustrated, or embodies in such work" (Copyright Act, 1976). Government documents and works in the public domain do not have copyright protection either. Works in the public domain include those with expired copyrights and works where copyright has not been requested (Talab, 1986).

The most interesting area not given protection is "ideas." An idea cannot be copyrighted, however, the description of the idea can be. For example, it would be difficult to copyright a play in basketball. It is an idea. The description of a play and how it works can be copyrighted, yet the idea or concept cannot. Once the play is seen, and others determine how it is performed, they can use it without violating copyright laws. Similarly, an aerobics instructor's ideas for hand movements to instruct classes for the deaf, may not be the subject of a copyright. The pictures or descriptions of the movements may be copyrighted, however, the movements themselves cannot. There is no way to copyright hand motions. Specific copyright protection is provided for choreography for a dance that will be done the same way with the same music every time, however, hand motions that represent words, used differently with different music, cannot hold a copyright. Once someone sees them, they can be used.

Works that do not hold originality cannot be considered for copyright (Copyright Act, 1994). This would include standard works such as calendars, height and weight charts, tape measures, and lists of tables (Talab, 1986). This allows freedom to make use of these articles. The outline of a calendar cannot be copyrighted, but the format and the pictures that go with the calendar can be. This allows intramural programs, for example, to use a common calendar and add their own dimensions including pictures, special events, and any additional information specific to their programs. Similarly, no copyright can be held for blank forms which are used to obtain information (Copyright Act, 1976). Therefore, agencies can use anyone's accident report form or registration form. They are designed to gather information and not to convey it.

Works where authorship is small cannot hold a copyright (Copyright Act, 1994). This includes slogans, titles, names, variations, typographic ornamentation, lettering, or coloring. If slogans, titles, names, etc., were copyrighted, there would be a loss of freedom to speak. Such words like "uh huh" would then belong to certain companies like Pepsi, and with those words, Pepsi's right to control how they are used. These short sayings are protected by the trademark laws (see Chapter 5.31).

Government works or works paid for by tax dollars cannot hold copyrights. Works found in the government document section of the library are for public use (Copyright Act, 1976).

Facts also cannot be copyrighted. Information in newspaper articles can be used by others if they are published facts. One cannot use the article verbatim, but they can use the facts. Research data cannot be copyrighted for the same reason. They are facts. Any raw data collected can be used by anyone. In *Feist v. Rural Telephone Service Co.* (1991), Feist Publication published a telephone book. They had done all the research to put it together. Rural Telephone Service used the Feist book and reorganized it using addresses as the listing. The court found that Feist had published facts. Rural Telephone used the facts, just in a different way. It was not infringement.

Rights of the Copyright Owner

A copyright gives its owner certain rights to the works, including: 1) the right to reproduction; 2) the right to preparation of derivative works including translation from language to language and from one form to another (i.e., from book to movie, from movie to play); 3) the right to public distribution; 4) the public performing rights which include live renditions that are face to face, on recordings, broadcasts, and retransmissions by cable; and 5) the right to the public display, specifically written or art work (Copyright Act, 1994). This section has been strengthened with the Visual Artist Rights Act of 1990 which has become section 106A of the Copyright Act (Copyright Act, 1994). Among the rights afforded artists by this law is the right to prevent any intentional distortion, mutilation, or other modification of that work. This allows the artist to control the visual art work until his or her death. If a wall mural was painted at a sport club, that wall mural could not be changed or removed without the artist's permission until the artist dies. The rationale behind the law is to preserve the work for posterity as an artifact of our present culture (Gorman, 1991). The only way it could be removed if painted after the 1990 law is if permission were granted from the artist in writing.

Who is the owner of the copyright? It vests initially in the author or creator of the work. However, in the case of a "work made for hire," it is the employer or person for whom the work was prepared that is the owner of the copyright. Section 201(b) of the Copyright Act provides that "the employer or other person for whom the work was prepared is considered the author for the purpose of this title, and, unless the parties have expressly agreed otherwise in a written instrument signed by them, owns all of the rights comprised in the copyright." In *Baltimore Orioles v. Major League Baseball Players* (1986), the players claimed part ownership of the copyright to televised games since they were the ones being filmed and retained ownership in their own likenesses. The Seventh Circuit, however, found for the Orioles, based on the fact that the players were working for the club at the time of the game and the filming, and, therefore, the Orioles owned the copyright, not the players. This was likened to actors and actresses who do not own the copyright of the films in which they appear unless specifically stated in the contract. Even if the contract gives an actor a percentage of the film's profit, it does not mean that he or she owns a percentage of the copyright unless specifically stated.

Fair Use

An important section of the law for those who are not creators, but are users of copyrighted works, is the fair use section (§107). The section was passed to strike a balance between the copyright monopoly and the greater interest of society (Hohensee, 1988). There are four tests to ascertain fair use: a) the purpose and the character of use, whether it is for commercial or for nonprofit educational purposes; b) the nature of the copyrighted work; c) the amount and substantiality of the material used in comparison with the whole; and d) the effect of the use on the potential market or value of the work (Copyright Act, 1994). Fair use allows for "criticism, comment, news reporting, teaching, scholarship or research" (Copyright Act, 1994).

A primary motivator for the passage of the fair use section, was the use of copyrighted works for educational purposes. The educational fair use test is based on three rules: a) brevity (using small parts of the whole); b) spontaneity (if there is time to request permission, it should be requested); and, c) cumulative effect (how will it affect the creator?). In *Basic Books, Inc. v. Kinkos Graphics* (1991) the court considered whether the production of professors' course packets, that were a compilation of articles directly relating to one course, were a violation of copyright or educational fair use. The court found that Kinkos had violated the copyright laws in creating the packets. Kinkos' motivation was not educational, but to make a profit from the works of others, and, therefore, the educational fair use exemption did not apply. Kinkos advertised and did its best to get the business of professors. According to Martin (1990), the case was not decided using the fair use test. If that was the case, in his opinion, there should have been joint infringement against the professors as well, since the professors provided the material to be copied to be used for their courses. No professors were named in the case. Instead, the court looked at the profit motive and the amount of commercialism used by a national corporation selling copyrighted works.

A case involving circumstances similar to *Kinkos*, yet yielding an opposite finding was decided by the Sixth Circuit in *Princeton University Press v. Michigan Document Services* (1996). In concluding that the production of professors' course packets was not a copyright infringement, the Sixth Circuit examined the four tests for fair use. First, the court found that the production of packets by Michigan Document Services was for educational, not commercial, purposes. Secondly, the nature of the works in question were of the type that are protected by "fair use" or education/non-fiction. Thirdly, the amount of material reproduced was considered non-substantial. In the *Kinkos* case the copying was 5.2 percent to 25.1 percent of the original work and in the Michigan Document Services it ranged from 5 percent to 33 percent, yet the court found it to be non-substantial. Finally, the use through reproduction in professors' packets would not significantly affect the potential market for or value of the original work. The professors maintained that they would not require the material if they could not use it in a professor packet and over 100 authors indicated that their reason for writing the material was not for economic gain but for the spread of their ideas and critique of their work.

Music and Performance

Musical scores that are performed by band and chorus should be purchased. However, there are guidelines in §110 of the Copyright Act, similar to the educational fair use guidelines, to allow for music and dramatic performances by non-profit agencies, religious institutions, or for educational uses. Performance of music is legal without paying royalties if it is for non-profit and all money goes to charity. Music and dramatic works can be performed in classrooms, for religious assembly, and for transmission to the public, without any purpose of direct or indirect commercial advantage and without payment of any fee or other compensation for the performance to its performers, promoters, or organizers. There can be no direct or indirect admission charged unless the proceeds, after deducting the reasonable costs of producing the performance, are used exclusively for educational, religious, or charitable purposes and not for private financial gain (Copyright Act, 1994). This would not include colleges and universities playing their pep music at games. Licenses must be secured from performance rights agencies. This exemption also does not include music played at conferences even though one may define that as an educational setting (Dickson, 1990). For conferences, conventions or workshops, special licenses must be purchased to allow the playing of background music, music at socials, or live performances. This license is purchased by the convention center or the conference directors and is negotiated based on the size of the conference, the use or the music, and number of conferees.

Public Performance Restrictions

According to the Copyright Act, a performance or display is public if it is open to the public or at any place where a substantial number of persons outside of a normal circle of a family and its social acquaintances is gathered. This includes any place where people are not specifically invited and there is use of music or video displays. For public performances, a license must be obtained. This even includes dormitory public areas. Both in 1987 and in 1990 there was an attempt to seek an exemption for nursing homes and long term care medical facilities so that these facilities could show movies without a license. According to the Congressional Record (1990), the lobbying by the motion picture industry was so strong that this exemption did not pass. Nursing homes, who often use videos as a leisure activity for their residents, must obtain a license to show them in their public areas even though they do not charge a fee for viewing and the people who would be watching live in the facility. Thus the same would be true for college dormitories. In order to show a video in a public setting, one must have a license.

Music is also affected by public performance restrictions. Playing cassette tapes, for example, in a public place is prohibited without a license. If a manager of a fitness center, for example, wants to play background music in the center and people paid to be members, the manager must obtain a license. If that same center has aerobic instructors who play tapes during exercises, the center must have a license, especially if there is profit (Bath, 1992). It is not the responsibility of the aerobics instructor to get the license, it is the responsibility of the center in which the class is being given. It is not particularly expensive and the amount is decided by the size of the facility, the amount of use, and the number of participants in the program. Cases involving copyright infringement for public performances of music include: *Tallyrand v. Stenko* (1990), involving background music played in a skating rink; *Broadway Music, Inc. v. Melody Faire* (1990), involving a club where musical compositions were performed by live artists, *Tallyrand Music Inc. v. Charlie Club*

Inc. (1990), where the health club's license covered music played in their restaurant and bar, but not for aerobics classes; and, *Broadway Music Inc. v. Blueberry Hill Family Restaurants, Inc.* (1995), where a restaurant chain operated jukeboxes that patrons played for free.

Television and Radio Broadcasting

The Copyright Act protects any original works of authorship fixed in any tangible medium, including motion pictures and other audiovisual works. The broadcast, by radio or television, of a live sporting event is eligible for protection. The Act has become a significant source of protection for the major professional sports leagues to combat the unauthorized interception of commercial-free feeds of broadcast signals. The issue has focused on sports bars where sports fans gather to watch satellite transmission of games that could only be seen through the use of satellite dish antenna systems (Sutphen, 1992). The professional sports leagues contend that the piracy of distant network satellite signals of games both devalues advertising revenues when patrons at sports bars watch contests commercial free, and affects local ticket sales when a blacked-out game is broadcast in a local sports bar.

In 1976, Congress enacted §110(5), the "home-use" exemption, to limit the exclusive rights granted copyright owners under §106(4) to perform and publicly display their copyrighted work. Section 110(5) bars a finding of infringement when the transmission is received by equipment similar to the type "commonly used in private homes." Thus, the clause exempts commercial businesses that use standard radio or television equipment in their establishments to provide entertainment as long as they are not transmitting cable or some other pay-per-view transmission. Sports bars have attempted to use the "home-use" exemption to exempt their interception of satellite feeds by contending that satellite dish equipment is commonly used in private homes. Such arguments have, at least to date, been unsuccessful. Thus, sports bars or other public establishments desiring to transmit cable or pay-per-view broadcasts must have a license. (*National Football League v. Play by Play Sports Bar*, et al., 1995; *National Football League v. McBee & Bruno's, Inc.*, 1986; and, *Cablevision Systems Corp. v. Midland Enterprises*, 1994).

This "home-use" exemption clause does not include rebroadcasting. It is a copyright infringement to tape a copyrighted program and exhibit it at another time in a public setting without explicit permission from the producers. The broadcasting rights of time and place are reserved for the broadcasters. On the other hand, it is legal to tape a show for later viewing if it is done in the confines of a home with friends and family. This is considered time shifting and has been held legal in non-public settings (*Sony v. Universal Studios,* 1984). In *Sony*, Universal Studios attempted to enjoin the production of home-use videotape recorders, under the theory that the machines could be used for the unauthorized copying of movies owned by Universal Studios, to be viewed at a later time. In finding for Sony, the court found that in-home time shifting would not cause any actual harm to Universal Studios. The result in *Sony*, however, did not affect the right to time shift in public places, which remains a copyright violation. A sports bar, for example, cannot tape a game for later viewing in their establishment without infringing on copyright.

Recent Developments

The most recent issues in copyright involve the internet. The information on the internet is open to anyone with access to the net, yet retain copyright protection and cannot be copied, used or sold without permission from the author. Those on the internet are also artists in their own right and should receive the same protection as those who work in other mediums.

Computer software and games have also been the subject of copyright litigation. Several computer game companies are using copyright protection to safeguard their games. At issue in these disputes is the fine line between the idea of the game and the game itself.

References

A. Cases

Baltimore Orioles v. Major League Baseball Players, 805 F.2d 663 (7th Cir. 1986).
Basic Books, Inc. v. Kinkos Graphics Corp., 758 F.Supp. 1522 (S.D.N.Y. 1991).
Broadcast Music, Inc. v. Blueberry Hill Family Restaurants, Inc., 899 F.Supp. 474 (N.D.Nev).
Broadcast Music, Inc. v. Melody Fair Enterprises, Inc., 1990 WL 283743 (W.D.N.Y. 1990).
Cablevision Systems Corp. v. 45 Midland Enterprises, Inc., 858 F.Supp. 42 (S.D.N.Y. 1994).
Feist Publications v. Rural Telephone Service Co., 111 S.Ct. 1282 (1991).
Harrison/Erickson, Inc. v. Chicago Bulls Limited Partnership, 1991 WL 51118 (S.D.N.Y.).
National Football League v. McBee & Bruno's, Inc., 792 F.2d 726 (8th Cir. 1986).
National Football League v. Play by Play Sports Bar, et al., 1995 WL 753840 (S.D. Tex. 1995).
Princeton University Press v. Michigan Document Services, 1996 WL 54741 (6th Cir.).
SONY Corp. v. Universal Studios, 464 S.Ct. 774 (1984).
Tallyrand Music Inc. v. Charlie Club Inc., 17 USPZ 2d 1395 (N.D. Ill. 1990).
Tallyrand Music Inc. v. Frank Stenko, 1990 WL 169163 (M.D. Pa. 1990).

B. Publications

Bath, M. (February, 1992). Permission to Use Music: It's the Law. *Aquatics International*, 6.
Dickson, J.F. (March, 1990). Copyright Laws Change Meeting Tunes. *Successful Meetings*, 31-33.
Gorman, R.A. (1990). Visual Artists Rights Act of 1990. *Journal of the Copyright Society of the U.S.A.*, 38, 233-241.
Hohenese, J.M. (1988). The Fair Use Doctrine in Copyright: A Growing Concern for Judge Advocates. 19 *Military Law Review* 155-197.
Martin, S.M. (1992). Duplication of Error. *Journal of Copyright Society of the U.S.A.*, 429, 429-525.
Sutphen, Lynne S. (1992). Sports Bars' Interception of the National Football League's Satellite Signals: Controversy or Compromise. 2 *Seton Hall Journal of Sport Law* 203-231.
Talab, R.S. (1986). *Common Sense Copyright: A Guide to New Technologies*.

C. Legislation

Copyright Remedy Clarification Act, 104 U.S.C. 2749 (1990).
USCS Title 17
Visual Artists Rights Act of 1990, 104 U.S.C. 5128 (1990).

5.51

Tax Law

Professional Sport Issues

James T. Gray
National Sports Law Institute
Marquette University Law School

It is often said that in life that there are only two guarantees: death and taxes. A similar adage is also appropriate for professional athletes: retirement and taxes. Over the last twenty years player free agency, television exposure and endorsements have provided many individual and team athletes with salaries ranging from the hundreds of thousands to the tens of millions of dollars.

While player employment salaries and endorsement income has received significant public attention, the importance of tax issues and concerns has sometimes been ignored or misunderstood by professional athletes and their advisors. City, state and federal tax laws are often viewed as complex, intricate and, at times, puzzling. Tax laws often change, especially when a new political party takes charge of either the Presidency, Congress, Governor's Office, State Legislature or City Hall. As a result, there are those within the professional sports industry, such as tax lawyers and accountants, who spend their entire professional lives interpreting tax statutes, case law and Internal Revenue Service rulings.

■ ■ ■ ■

Representative Case

SARGENT v. COMMISSIONER OF INTERNAL REVENUE
United States Court of Appeals for the Eighth Circuit
929 F.2d 1252 (1991)

OPINION:

This case, on appeal from the United States Tax Court, is one of first impression for this Court. Initially, the Commissioner of Internal Revenue issued Notices of Deficiency with respect to the federal income taxes of Gary A. Sargent for the years 1978 through 1981; and for Steven M. Christoff for the years 1980 through 1982.

Sargent and Christoff (hereinafter "Appellants") were hockey players with the Minnesota North Stars Hockey Club (hereinafter the "Club"). Appellants' personal service corporations (PSC), created to represent the business associations of each Appellant, contracted with the Club to provide each Appellant's services to the Club as a hockey player and, in the case of Sargent, also as a con-

sultant. The North Stars paid each PSC for the use of each Appellant's services; each PSC, in turn, paid each Appellant a salary and contributed the remainder to each PSC's qualified pension plan. The Commissioner proposed to disallow these pension deductions and elected to tax Appellants on the entire amount paid by the Club to the PSC.

Appellant Sargent filed a Petition with the Tax Court on March 11, 1986, contesting the deficiencies. Appellant Christoff did likewise on May 17, 1988, and May 18, 1988. The case was tried in the United States Tax Court, New York, New York, on November 16, 1988; and on November 13, 1988, Judge Tannenwald, Jr., writing for the majority, issued an opinion upholding the deficiencies proposed by the Commissioner. We reverse the decision of the Tax Court and hold that Appellants were employees of their respective personal service corporations; and, therefore, Appellants should not be taxed on the pension deductions of their PSCs.

•••

Background

The facts are set forth in detail in the Tax Court's opinion, and we shall state only the essentials: Appellants were both professional hockey players with the Minnesota North Stars Hockey Club. Prior to signing with the North Stars, Appellant Sargent sought out the assistance of Attorney Arthur Kaminsky concerning the benefits of incorporation. Kaminsky advised Sargent that incorporation provided two primary benefits: increased bargaining power and the possibility of placing money into a pension plan.

Based upon his consultations with Kaminsky, Sargent incorporated Chiefy-Cat, Inc. (Chiefy-Cat) on July 20, 1978. Sargent was the sole shareholder, president, and sole director of this personal service corporation. On July 20, 1978, Sargent entered into an Employment Contract with Chiefy-Cat wherein he agreed to provide his services as a professional hockey player and consultant exclusively for Chiefy-Cat for the period July 1, 1978, to June 30, 1984. At the same time, Chiefy-Cat agreed to furnish the services of Sargent as both a hockey player and consultant to the Club. In exchange, the Club agreed to pay Chiefy-Cat a set salary during each respective playing season. Further, Sargent's employment agreement with Chiefy-Cat provided that Chiefy-Cat agreed to pay Sargent a set salary during each respective season.

Chiefy-Cat withheld and paid the applicable federal and state income taxes and timely filed Employers Quarterly Federal Tax Returns and Forms W-2 and W-3. On March 5, 1980, the Commissioner of the Internal Revenue Service issued a letter whereby the pension plan established by Chiefy-Cat and covering Sargent was determined to be a qualified pension plan. That favorable determination is still in effect and is not an issue before this Court.

Christoff followed substantially the same route toward incorporation. He employed the services of Attorney Kaminsky, and sought the same benefits as those sought by Sargent. Thus, on August 11, 1980, Christoff incorporated RIF Enterprises, Inc. (RIF), and entered into an employment agreement with RIF identical—for the most part—to that between Sargent and Chiefy-Cat. Likewise, RIF contracted with the North Stars and agreed to provide Christoff's services as a hockey player to the Club. In exchange, the Club agreed to pay RIF a salary during each respective hockey season. From this salary, RIF directed contributions to the PSC's qualified pension plan.

During the years at issue, neither Sargent nor Christoff were considered employees of the Club for purposes of the National Hockey League Players' Pension Plan. In each case, the Club paid Chiefy-Cat and RIF, respectively, the amounts that it would otherwise have contributed to the Players' Pension Plan on their behalf. The sole issue before this Court is whether Sargent and Christoff should be taxed now on those amounts contributed by their respective PSC's to each PSC's qualified pension plan.

The Tax Court takes the position that because Sargent and Christoff were members of a hockey "team," the requisite control over them—for purposes of taxation—was lodged in the hockey Club, and not in their respective PSCs, with which they had a contractual employment relationship. We reject this contention.

With respect to the "control" factor, which is heavily relied upon by the Tax Court, the Regulations state:

> In this connection, it is not necessary that the employer actually direct or control the manner in which the services are performed; it is sufficient if he has the right to do so.

It seems to this Court that legal analysis is forgotten if we simply measure the control element of an employment relationship by whether the employee is or is not a member of a superficially defined "team." Eventually, the issue becomes mired in a game of definitions: If the organizational structure is itself mislabeled a "team," a personal service corporation, as a matter of law, is a forbidden tax deferment tool for each and every person providing his or her services to that organization. On the other hand, if the organization to which the services are provided is not defined as a "team," then those same service-providers are free to create a PSC and subject that PSC's legitimacy to traditional common law and tax code analysis, regardless of the level of control exerted over those persons by the organization. Such an arbitrary approach is specious at best.

Accordingly, within Regulation § 31.3121(d)-(1)(c)(2), two necessary elements must be met before the corporation, rather than the service-recipient, in this case the North Stars Hockey Club, may be considered the true controller of the service-provider. First, the service-provider must be just that—an employee of the corporation whom the corporation has the right to direct or control in some meaningful sense. See Vnuk v. Commissioner, 621 F.2d 1318, 1320-21 (8th Cir. 1980); Johnson v. Commissioner, 78 T.C. 882 (1982). Second, there must exist between the corporation and the person or entity (Club) using the services a contract or similar indicium recognizing the corporation's controlling position. See Pacella v. Commissioner, 78 T.C. 604 (1982); Keller v. Commissioner, 77 T.C. 1014 (1981), aff'd 723 F.2d 58 (10th Cir. 1983); Johnson, supra.

These two elements were applied in a case strikingly similar to the one before us. In Johnson, supra, Charles Johnson, a professional basketball player with the San Francisco Warriors, created a PSC and the IRS sought to tax Johnson for the entire amount paid to his PSC by the Warriors. Without ever addressing whether Johnson was or was not a member of a "team," the Tax Court ultimately held the contracts to be dispositive of the issue of control:

> In the case before us, we accept arguendo that the [PSC-Johnson] agreement was a valid contract which required the payments with respect to [Johnson's] performance as a basketball player ultimately to be made to the [PSC]. We also accept arguendo that the [PSC-Johnson] agreement gave [the PSC] a right of control over [Johnson's] services, . . . Thus, the first element [of control] is satisfied.

Ultimately, Johnson was required to pay individual income tax on the entire amount paid to his PSC, but only because his PSC had no contractual arrangement with the Warriors basketball team. Said the Tax Court regarding the second prong of the "control" test: "crucial is the fact that there was no contract or agreement between the Warriors and [the PSC]." Id. at 884. We are not faced with such a dilemma in this case. Not only did Appellants have a contractual arrangement with their respective PSCs, thereby passing the first prong of the analysis, each PSC also had a contractual relationship with the North Stars Hockey Club. Consistent with its analysis in the past, the Tax Court in Johnson concluded that the existence of bona fide contracts between the parties satisfied the requisite elements of control. Indeed, the Tax Court at no time concerned itself with whether Johnson was or was not a member of a "team."

The Tax Court's "team" analysis further breaks down when one looks at a decision handed down by the Tax Court just one day after the case before us. In Pflug v. Commissioner, 1989 Tax Ct. Memo LEXIS 615, 58 T.C.M. (CCH) 685, 1989 T.C. Memo 615 (1989), an actress entered into an exclusive employment contract with her husband's corporation, Charwool Production, Inc. ("Charwool"), of which she was an officer. Subsequently, Charwool entered into a contract with 20th Century Fox Studios, agreeing to provide the services of Ms. Pflug for a new TV series. Although the ultimate issue was whether Ms. Pflug was subject to self-employment taxes on income received from Charwool, the Court was first required to decide whether Ms. Pflug was an employee of Charwool. In holding that Ms. Pflug was an employee of Charwool, and not an employee of 20th Century Fox Studios, the Tax Court held the contracts between the respective parties to be dispositive and stated:

> The fundamental question is whether Charwool had the right to exercise dominion and control over the activities of [Pflug], not only as to results but also as to the means and methods used to accomplish the result. We find, by virtue of the contract [Pflug] entered with Charwool, Charwool had the requisite right to control [Pflug].

This Court is perplexed to find that those same contractual arrangements which were dispositive of the issue of "control" in Pflug were summarily discarded in the case before us. By the same token, those same "team" factors which were dispositive of the issue of control in the case before us were not even discussed in Pflug.

Was not Joanne Pflug a part of a team every bit as "controlled" as Sargent and Christoff? Like a hockey team in which different players assume different roles to insure success, the members of Pflug's team included the cast, writers, directors, and producers all working toward the common goal of producing a successful TV series. More importantly, just as a hockey player has a generalized set of plays tailored to fit his talents and the talents of his teammates, so, too, Ms. Pflug's "plays" included movements carefully choreographed to mesh with other cast members, a script prepared for her to follow, cue cards to insure that little or no deviation from the designed "play" occurred, and numerous retakes to guarantee that ultimate control vested in the hands of the studio, not Ms. Pflug's PSC. Nevertheless, the Tax Court concluded that Ms. Pflug was an employee of her PSC.

There can be little question that Ms. Pflug was part of a team under more stringent production controls than those placed on either Sargent or Christoff by the Club. But, as the Tax Court concluded, ". . . by virtue of the contract [Pflug] entered with Charwool, Charwool had the requisite right to control [Pflug]." Id. Appellants' contractual arrangements, which were every bit as bona fide as those entered into by Ms. Pflug, should and do provide the requisite control for Appellants to be considered employees of their respective PSCs.

Once the "team" analysis of control is disregarded, this Court is able to fall back on ample Tax Court precedent which upholds the sanctity of contractual relations between taxpayers and their respective personal service corporations. In Haag v. Commissioner, 88 T.C. 604 (1987), the contractual arrangements between a doctor and his PSC again dictated the Courts' disposition of the case. The Tax Court stated:

> We find that the employment agreement effectively gave the [PSC] the right to control petitioner's medical practice.

Although the Commissioner argues that in each of these cases the employer-employee relationship was never addressed, this Court thinks otherwise. Each time the legitimacy of the employee's relationship with the corporation was raised, the Tax Court pointed to the existence of a contractual relationship between the corporation and the employee/service-provider as the rationale for upholding the legal significance of the PSC. In Keller, supra, for example, the Tax Court respected the contractual arrangements entered into by the taxpayer and the PSC, and held them out as the basis for distinguishing its decision in Roubik v. Commissioner, 53 T.C. 365 (1969), stating:

> The corporation (in Roubik) did not enter into any arrangements to provide the services of its purported employees; personal contractual obligations between the taxpayers and the parties for whom they provided services persisted.

• • •

Quite simply, we agree with the position taken by the Tax Court in Keller, supra, when it stated: "we find that an employment relationship was created in this case by the employment agreement and that it was maintained by the parties to the agreement after execution." 77 T.C. at 1032. Appellants in this case entered into bona fide arms lengths agreements with their respective PSCs. For this reason, each is considered to be an employee of that PSC, and not an employee of the North Stars Hockey Club.

II

By rejecting the Tax Court's "team" test, and embracing the viability of the contractual relations between Appellants and their personal service corporations, we have effectively decided the only issue presented for our deliberation: By whom were Appellants employed? Thus, because Appellants were employees of their respective PSCs, they were improperly taxed on the entire amount paid by the North Stars Hockey Club to the PSCs.

• • •

Unfortunately, taxpayers will often go to great lengths to evade unlawfully the payment of income taxes. Whether it simply be lying on their tax forms, assigning income to those who have not earned it, or sheltering income in nonexistent or improper tax-avoidance investments, each is destructive to the often painful revenue-production responsibility of the IRS. In this case, however, we are presented with taxpayers who have fulfilled each and every task required of them in order to become properly incorporated. More importantly, for purposes of this case, Appellants took steps to insure that each was a contractually-bound employee of his respective PSC. That these contracts of employment were recognized and respected by the North Stars Hockey Club, the National Hockey League and the Minnesota Office of Administrative Hearings lends substantial credibility to the fact that Appellants were employees of their respective PSCs—and not the North Stars Hockey Club.

• • •

In conclusion, this Court finds that Appellants were, at all times relevant to this case, employees of their respective personal service corporations. Furthermore, the PSCs established by Appellants are legitimate corporate entities, created to conduct Appellants' business. Appellants, therefore, are obligated to pay income tax only on those amounts paid to them as salary by their respective PSC. For all of the reasons articulated above, the decision of the United States Tax Court is

Reversed.

■ ■ ■ ■

Fundamental Concepts

Federal Taxation of Player Salaries

The most important issue for professional athlete income is the tax consequences of large sums of money earned over a short period of time. For instance, an average taxpayer usually has a median annual income from $30,000 to $50,000 over a working career from 30 to 35 years. However, many professional athletes have a career from four to six years while earning income ranging from $100,000 to $10 million dollars a year and being taxed at the highest rates. The issue for most athletes is the timing of payment of taxes and the availability of tax shelters.

Deferred Compensation. Deferred compensation allows highly compensated professional athletes to reduce their current income and receive it at a later date at a lower tax rate. In order to defer their income until after retirement, athletes have utilized pension plans, individual retirement accounts, employment contracts which spread compensation over a five to ten year period after retirement and establishing personal service corporations (see *Sargent v. Commissioner*, 1991).

A personal service corporation (PSC) is an entity formed by a professional athlete who becomes the sole or majority stock holder. The athlete then contracts with the PSC to perform personal services. In turn, the PSC will contract with a team or an athletic organization who wishes to acquire the services of the athlete. Once a PSC and a team enter into a contract for a player's services, employment compensation is paid to the PSC. The PSC withholds and pays applicable federal and state income taxes. The remaining revenue can be used to establish a pension plan with payments made to athletes when they are retired and at a lower tax rate.

Bonuses. In professional sports, bonuses such as signing, roster, statistical performance and volume of play are included in the athlete's gross income. However, not all bonuses are considered "wages" for withholding purposes. The issue of tax withholding is not whether a tax is paid, but rather the timing of that payment.

Signing bonuses which pay an athlete for his signature on a contract are not contingent on future play and, therefore, are not subject to federal withholding. For example, New York Jets quarterback Neil O'Donnell received a five year deal worth $25 million and included a $7 million signing bonus. By avoiding income withholding, athletes such as O'Donnell defer the payment of their income tax. The money that would normally be withheld as tax can instead be invested until the tax is due the following year.

On the other hand, a roster bonus paid for making the team's active roster is considered wages. Withholding must be paid because the athlete upon making the team is committed to future play. Similarly performance bonuses based upon individual or team statistics are considered wages and are subject to federal withholding.

In addition to the time when professional athletes receive their compensation, tax shelters were formerly available to minimize their income tax bill. For example, the 1986 Tax Reform Act (Act) removed many of the tax shelters which highly compensated professional athletes could use to protect their large incomes from federal taxation.

Tax Shelters—Passive Losses. Prior to the time the Act became law, the use of passive losses to reduce an athlete's final tax bill was popular. A passive gain or loss is created through the conduct of a trade or business in which the athlete does not materially participate. (See Treasury Regulation 1.469-5T(a)(1) on page 11 for materially participate definition.)

For example, assume an athlete with a salary of one million dollars invested in two limited partnerships in which he did not materially participate. One partnership generated $600,000 worth of loss for the athlete and the other generated $200,000 in income. The $600,000 passive loss would first be used to offset the $200,000 passive gain. The remaining $400,000 passive loss would then be used to offset the athlete's one million dollar salary reducing his gross income to $600,000 ($1 million - $400,000 = $600,000). However, under current tax law, passive losses cannot be used to offset wages, active business income or investment income derived from interest, dividends and royalties.

Tax Shelters—Limited Partnerships. Another tax shelter which was eliminated under the Act pertained to limited partnership investments. Prior to the passage of the Act athletes were able to invest in limited partnerships which were attractive because many were created to generate paper losses. In addition, limited partnerships were viewed as good investments because athletes were only liable for the amounts they contributed to the venture. As a result, athletes could use limited partnership losses to offset their active income as well as enjoy limited personal liability as it pertained to the investment. However, the Act stated that limited partners do not materially participate in the partnership, regardless of their level of participation. Therefore, all loss generated by a limited partnership are considered passive losses.

Federal Tax Rates.   In exchange for the elimination of these tax shelters, along with many others, the Act reduced tax rates from a maximum rate of 50 percent to a maximum rate of 28 percent for individual taxpayers. The Revenue Recognition Act of 1990 increased the top marginal tax rate to 31 percent. In 1993, President Clinton passed the Deficit Reduction Bill. Under this law, the top income tax rate increased from 31 percent to 36 percent for taxable incomes in excess of $140,000 for joint returns and $115,000 for individual returns. The law imposed an additional 10 percent surtax for those people with taxable incomes over $250,000 which results in a 39.6 percent tax rate for those who earn at high income levels.

Travel Expenses.   When athletes travel in pursuit of their trade or business, reasonable and necessary travel expenses are deductible. Expenses which are often deducted by an athlete on the road include transportation, meals and lodging, which are not extravagant, baggage charges, laundry, and other expenses incurred in pursuit of business.

The issue of travel expenses is a significant one for individual sport athletes such as golfers, tennis players and jockeys. The tax home for individual athletes is his residence provided that the residence is a regular place of abode in real and substantial sense. If an athlete simply travels from one event to the next and never establishes a tax home, there is no "duplication" of expenses and, therefore, travel expenses will not be deductible.

State and City Tax Implications on Player Salaries

Interstate and intercity taxation is one of the most recent financial planning concerns which many professional athletes are encountering. While commenting on the professional athlete state tax issue, Gabe DiCerbo, Finance Director of Taxpayer Services of the New York State Department of Taxation said "what triggered our interest in athletes is their salaries are getting bigger and bigger. We suddenly found there was now enough dollars to make it worth our while."

Presently there are an increasing number of states and cities which host leagues, tours and teams that require tax payments from athletes for not only their current employment in their jurisdictions but for back taxes as well. Professional athletes are easy targets for tax collection because the government can determine when the player was in the state and how much he earned for the appearance by virtue of published league and tour game schedules as well as player salaries and tournament earnings.

A primary concern for a professional athlete is a determination of their state of residency. The term "resident" is consistently defined by most state taxing authorities. In general, a resident includes a person present in the state for other than a temporary or transitory purpose. Although no one factor is determinative, a court may review such factors as an athlete's domicile at birth, family location, state licenses, payment of taxes as well as locations of business and investment interests.

Acquiring residency in Alaska, Florida, Nevada, South Dakota, Texas, Washington or Wyoming means no imposition of a state tax on athlete's personal income. On the other hand, California imposes a tax at 11 percent of personal income and New York City, which combines state and city taxes, has established a personal income tax rate of 12.355 percent.

When states require athletes to pay taxes based upon their personal income, two formulas are used. The first formula is the Games Played Method where the taxing authority determines how many games were played within its state compared to how many games were played overall. This fraction is then applied to the players compensation for performance:

$$\frac{(\text{Number of Games in State A})}{(\text{Total Number of Games})} \quad \text{X Total Compensation for Services}$$

This fraction of the player's income is subsequently taxed by the state.

The second formula is the Duty Days Method. The taxing authority compares the number of days an athlete worked in the state to the total number of days, including official pre-season activity, regular season and post-season participation, that the athlete actually worked or had to be available for work.

$$\frac{(\text{Number of Days Athlete Worked})}{(\text{Total Number of Days Actually Worked or Had to be Available for Work})} \quad \text{X Total Compensation for Services}$$

In addition to state tax laws, professional athletes are taxed by cities on income earned within their borders. Cities which tax an athlete's personal income include Philadelphia, New York, Detroit and Cleveland. In Philadelphia, the city government expected to generate at least $8 million a year from professional athletes, with additional revenues for collecting back taxes from 1986. For example, an NFL football player earns an annual salary of $1.4 million, which is about $90,000 per game. The city of Philadelphia has a city tax rate of 4.3125 percent. The NFL player has to pay a $3,800 tax bill for working in Philadelphia for one game.

Recent Developments

Attorney Disciplined for Failure to File Complete Athlete Tax Returns. In *In re Jackson* (1994) an agent for NBA player Gerald Wilkins was suspended for six months from practicing law for violating the attorney code of professional responsibility. The agent was both an attorney and certified public accountant and assisted Wilkins in the preparation of his federal tax returns.

The Internal Revenue Service disallowed significant business deductions paid to an unincorporated business, Gerald B. Wilkins Enterprises; claims for personal exemptions for a dependent for failure to meet the support test; duplicate deductions of travel expenses; gifts to Gerald Wilkins' mother that were claimed as "agent's fees"; and deductions or losses claimed for expense and depreciation on automobiles used entirely for personal purposes.

The Court concluded that the lawyer claimed substantial amounts of business deductions for Wilkins with full knowledge that there was no documentation to justify these deductions and these actions constituted "dishonesty." As a result, the lawyer was found to have committed malpractice and had his law license suspended for six months. In addition, the lawyer had to pay Wilkins $63,447.97 together with attorneys fees and costs.

Travel Expenses. In *Henderson v. Commissioner* (1995), a lightning technician employed by Walt Disney's World On Ice, stayed in hotel rooms while working and stayed in his parents' home while not on tour. He paid no rent to his parents and had no ownership interest in their house. In disallowing his federal travel expense deductions, the court noted that the concept of a tax home requires that a traveling taxpayer incur substantial, continuous and duplicative living expenses back home.

Payment of Taxes. Each year on April 15th, the federal government and many state governments require payment on personal taxable income. Under the federal Internal Revenue Code section 61, income is taxable from any source derived. Taxable income is gross income less allowable deductions. For example, a professional athlete's gross income usually includes employment compensation, endorsements, bonuses, prize money, personal appearance fees, licensing income and movie or book royalties.

However, some notable professional athletes have not reported their taxable income as it pertains to sports autograph shows. In 1995, former baseball player Darryl Strawberry was sentenced to six months of home confinement for evading up to $120,000 in taxes between 1986 and 1990. That same year, former Brooklyn Dodger Edwin "Duke" Snider and former San Francisco Giant Willie McCovey pleaded guilty to tax evasion relating to an Atlantic City, New Jersey card show. Snider was sentenced to two years probation and paid the Internal Revenue Service about $27,000 in fines. McCovey paid approximately $21,000 in fines and was scheduled to be sentenced sometime in 1996. In 1990, baseball great Pete Rose pleaded guilty to tax evasion. He served five months in prison and paid a $50,000 fine for failing to report $354,968 in personal income from 1986 to 1989.

References

A. Cases

In re Jackson, 650 A.2d 675, (1994).

Henderson v. Commissioner, T.C. Memo. 1995-559, Nov. 27, 1995.

Sargent v. Commissioner of Internal Revenue, 929 F.2d 1252 (8th Cir. 1991).

B. Publications

Baker, William H. (1990). The Tax Significance of Place of Residence for Professional Athletes. 1 *Marquette Sports Law Journal* 1-39.

Baker, William H. "Allocation of Non-Resident Football Player's Income to the State of New York" and "Athlete Travel Expense Deductions." *For the Record: The Official Newsletter of the National Sports Law Institute*, Vol. 6, No. 5, 6-8.

Greenberg, Martin J. (1993). *Sports Law Practice*, Vol. 1 and Vol. 2.

Meisel, Chris. State Taxation Issues Affecting Professional Athletes. *For the Record: The Official Newsletter of the National Sports Law Institute*, Vol. 5, No. 2, 5-8.

Meisel, Chris. State and City Taxation Issues Affecting Professional Athletes. *For the Record: The Official Newsletter of the National Sports Law Institute*, Vol. 5, No. 3, 6-8.

C. Legislation

Tax Reform Act of 1986

Internal Revenue Code section 469

Treasury Regulation 1.469-5T(a)(1) (1991); I.R.C. § 469(h)(1) provides that a taxpayer shall be treated as materially participating in an activity if the tax payer is involved in the activity on a basis which is (a) regular, (b) continuous and (c) substantial.

Revenue Ruling 58-145, 1958-1 Cumulative Bulletin 360 (1958)

Revenue Ruling 75-472, 1975 Cumulative Bulletin 60 (1975)

Treasury Regulation § 1.162-2(a) (1990)

5.52

Tax Law

Amateur Sport Issues

Dr. Carolyn Lehr
University of Georgia

With the increased solicitation of income to support amateur athletic programs an understanding of tax laws, codes and regulations has become more and more important for the amateur sport administrator. Tax policy is complex and sweeping. On the federal level tax laws are determined by legislative, administrative and judicial sources. The Internal Revenue Code (IRC) is a collection of statutes. The Internal Revenue Service (IRS) enforces these laws and exercises this power through general tax policies and inspection. Lastly, federal courts adjudicate disputes and thus court opinions influence tax law.

This chapter will address the various tax codes, IRS regulations, and court decisions that can influence business strategies and decisions in amateur sport, and more specifically intercollegiate athletics.

■ ■ ■ ■

Representative Case

NATIONAL COLLEGIATE ATHLETIC ASSOCIATION v. COMMISSIONER OF INTERNAL REVENUE
United States Court of Appeals for the Tenth Circuit
914 F.2d 1417 (1990)

OPINION:

The National Collegiate Athletic Association (NCAA), the petitioner in this case, appeals from the decision of the tax court, which determined a deficiency of $10,395.14 in unrelated business income tax due for the 1981-1982 fiscal year. On appeal, the NCAA challenges the court's conclusion that revenue received from program advertising constituted unrelated business taxable income under I.R.C. § 512, not excludable from tax as a royalty under section 512(b)(2), I.R.C. § 512(b)(2). We reverse.

I

The NCAA is an unincorporated association of more than 880 colleges, universities, athletic conferences and associations, and other educational organizations and groups related to intercollegiate athletics, for which it has been the major governing organization since 1906. The NCAA is also an "exempt organization" under section 501(c)(3) of the Code, I.R.C. § 501(c)(3), and hence is exempt from federal income taxes. One of the purposes of the NCAA, as described in the organization's constitution, is "to supervise the conduct of . . . regional and national athletic events under the auspices of this Association." Pursuant to this purpose, the NCAA sponsors some seventy-six collegiate championship events in twenty-one different sports for women and men on an annual basis.

The most prominent of these tournaments, and the NCAA's biggest revenue generator, is the Men's Division I Basketball Championship. The tournament is held at different sites each year. In 1982, regional rounds took place at a variety of sites, and the Louisiana Superdome in New Orleans was the host for the "Final Four," the tournament's semifinal and final rounds. In that year, the Championship consisted of forty-eight teams playing forty-seven games on eight days over a period of almost three weeks. The teams played in a single-game elimination format, with each of the four regional winners moving into the Final Four.

The NCAA contracted with Lexington Productions, a division of Jim Host and Associates, Inc. ("Host" or "Publisher"), in 1981 to print and publish the program for the 1982 Final Four games. The purpose of such programs, according to the NCAA's then-director of public relations, is:

> to enhance the experience primarily for the fans attending the game. . . . [It also] gives the NCAA an opportunity to develop information about some of its other purposes that revolve around promoting sports [as a] part of higher education and demonstrating that athletes can be good students as well as good participants.

Prior to the middle of the 1970s, the host institution produced the Final Four program. The NCAA took over production until the late 1970s, when it began contracting with Host for the Final Four program. In 1982, Host began producing the programs for all rounds of the Championship. The motive for contracting the program production to Host was, according to the NCAA, to achieve consistency and quality at each round's game sites; making a profit was not the primary incentive.

The "Official Souvenir Program" for the 1982 Final Four round of the tournament was some 129 pages long, and it featured pictures of NCAA athletes such as Michael Jordan and articles on the NCAA itself, on New Orleans, on individual athletes, on championships from prior years, and on the Final Four teams: Georgetown, Houston, Louisville, and North Carolina. Advertisements made up a substantial portion of the program, some of which were placed by national companies. Among the products and services so displayed were Buick automobiles, Miller beer, Texaco motor oil, Fuji film, Maxwell House coffee, Nike sneakers, McDonald's fast food, Coca-Cola soda, Xerox photocopiers, ESPN cable network, and Popeyes Famous Fried Chicken. Other advertisers were local New Orleans merchants.

• • •

The NCAA's total revenue from the 1982 Men's Division I Basketball Championship was $18,671,874. The NCAA reported none of this amount as unrelated business taxable income on its federal income tax return for the fiscal year ending August 31, 1982. The Commissioner mailed the NCAA a notice of deficiency in which he determined that the NCAA was liable for $10,395.14 in taxes on $55,926.71 of unrelated business taxable income from the program advertising revenue. The NCAA petitioned the tax court for a redetermination of the deficiency set forth by the Commissioner. The tax court determined that this revenue was unrelated business taxable income, and that it was not excludable from the tax as a royalty.

• • •

Section 511 of the Code imposes a tax on the unrelated business taxable income of exempt organizations. Section 512(a)(1) of the Code defines the term "unrelated business taxable income" as "the gross income derived by any organization from any unrelated trade or business . . . regularly carried on by it. . . ." The term "unrelated trade or business" means "any trade or business the conduct of which is not substantially related . . . to the exercise or performance by such organization" of its exempt function. I.R.C. § 513(a). Under the heading "Advertising, etc., activities," section 513(c) provides that "the term 'trade or business' includes any activity which is carried on for the production of income from the sale of goods or the performance of services. . . . An activity does not lose identity as a trade or business merely because it is carried on . . . within a larger complex of other endeavors which may, or may not, be related to the exempt purposes of the organization." I.R.C. § 513(c).

The NCAA's advertising revenue therefore must be considered unrelated business taxable income if: "(1) It is income from trade or business; (2) such trade or business is regularly carried on by the organization; and (3) the conduct of such trade or business is not substantially related (other than through the production of funds) to the organization's performance of its exempt functions." . . . If a taxpayer shows that it does not meet any one of these three requirements, the taxpayer is not liable for the unrelated business income tax.

The NCAA concedes that its program advertising was a "trade or business" not "substantially related" to its exempt purpose. The only question remaining, therefore, is whether the trade or business was "regularly carried on" by the organization. The meaning of the term "regularly carried on" is not defined by the language of the statute.

Accordingly, we turn to the Treasury Regulations for assistance.

Section 1.513-1(c) of the Treasury Regulations provides a discussion of the phrase "regularly carried on." The general principles set out there direct us to consider "the frequency and continuity with which the activities productive of the income are conducted and the manner in which they are pursued." Treas. Reg. § 1.513-1(c)(1). As a cautionary note, the regulations emphasize that whether a trade or business is regularly carried on must be assessed "in light of the purpose of the unrelated business income tax to place exempt organization business activities upon the same tax basis as the nonexempt business endeavors with which they compete."

The regulations then move beyond the general principles and set out a process for applying the principles to specific cases. The first step is to consider the normal time span of the particular activity, and then determine whether the length of time alone suggests that the activity is regularly carried on, or only intermittently carried on. See id. § 1.513-1(c)(2)(i). If the activity is "of a kind normally conducted by nonexempt commercial organizations on a year-round basis, the conduct of such [activity] by an exempt organization over a period of only a few weeks does not constitute the regular carrying on of trade or business." As an example of a business not regularly carried on, the regulations describe a hospital auxiliary's operation of a sandwich stand for only two weeks at a state fair. In contrast, the regulations deem the operation of a commercial parking lot every Saturday as a regularly-carried-on activity.

If the activity is "of a kind normally undertaken by nonexempt commercial organizations only on a seasonal basis, the conduct of such activities by an exempt organization during a significant portion of the season ordinarily constitutes the regular conduct of trade or business." The operation of a horse racing track several weeks a year is an example of a regularly-conducted seasonal business, because such tracks generally are open only during a particular season.

A primary point of contention in this case is whether the NCAA's advertising business is normally a seasonal or year-round one, and whether it is intermittent or not. The tax court noted that the Commissioner looked at the short time span of the tournament, concluded that it was as much a "seasonal" event as the operation of a horse racing track, and then argued that the time involved in the tournament program advertising made it a regularly carried on business. The court observed that the NCAA, which did not agree with the Commissioner's "season" conclusion, also focused on the tournament itself in contending that the event's short time span made the activity in question intermittent. The tax court rejected these arguments as "placing undue emphasis on the tournament itself as the measure for determining whether petitioner regularly carried on the business at issue. . . . Although sponsorship of a college basketball tournament and attendant circulation of tournament programs are seasonal events, the 'trade or business' of selling advertisements is not."

We agree that to determine the normal time span of the activity in this case, we should consider the business of selling advertising space, since that is the business the Commissioner contends is generating unrelated business taxable income. There is no dispute that the tournament itself is substantially related to the NCAA's exempt purpose and so, unlike the horse racing track, it should not be the business activity in question. See American College of Physicians, 475 U.S. at 839 ("Congress has declared unambiguously that the publication of paid advertising is a trade or business activity distinct from the publication of accompanying . . . articles"). Since the publication of advertising is generally conducted on a year-round basis, we conclude that if the NCAA's sale of program advertising was conducted for only a few weeks, that time period could not, standing alone, convert the NCAA's business into one regularly carried on.

In regard to the question of how long the NCAA conducted its advertising business, the tax court stated that "it is inappropriate to decide whether the trade or business at issue is regularly carried on solely by reference to the time span of the tournament itself." Rec., vol. I, doc. 13, at 15-16. The tax court, observing that the agency relationship between the NCAA and Host allowed the court to attribute Host's activities to the NCAA, noted that the NCAA had "not produced any evidence . . . regarding the extent or manner of Host's conduct in connection with the solicitation, sale, and publication of advertising for the tournament programs." Id. at 18. The court went on to conclude that "without such evidence [the NCAA] has not proven that neither it nor Host carried on the activity of selling program advertising regularly. [The tax court] will not assume Host's conduct in this regard was infrequent or conducted without the competitive and promotional efforts typical of other commercial endeavors." We believe the tax court focused its analysis in the wrong direction.

The tax court held, and the Commissioner argues, that the amount of preliminary time spent to solicit advertisements and prepare them for publication is relevant to the regularly-carried-on determination, and that the length of the tournament is not relevant. This position is contrary to the regulations and to existing case law. The language of the regulations alone suggests that preparatory time should not be considered. The sandwich stand example in the regulations, for instance, included a reference only to the two weeks it was operated at the state fair. See Treas. Reg. § 1.513-1(c)(a)(i). The regulations do not mention time spent in planning the activity, building the stand, or purchasing the alfalfa sprouts for the sandwiches.

The case closest to the one here also does not evaluate preparatory time. In that case, Suffolk County Patrolmen's Benevolent Ass'n v. Commissioner, 77 T.C. 1314 (1981), an exempt organization staged a professional vaudeville show every year as a fundraising event, using a company with which it had contracted. The organization derived the vast majority of its receipts from the sale of advertising in a program guide distributed to show patrons and to anyone who requested it. The shows generally consisted of three or four performances stretching over two weekends. The tax court found that preparation for the shows and the program, including the solicitation of advertisements, lasted eight to sixteen weeks, but it then emphasized that:

> nowhere in the regulations or the legislative history of the tax on unrelated business income is there any mention of time apart from the duration of the event itself. . . . The fact that an organization seeks to insure the success of its fundraising venture by beginning to plan and prepare for it earlier should not adversely affect the tax treatment of the income derived from the venture.

As in Suffolk County, the advertising here was solicited for publication in a program for an event lasting a few weeks. The NCAA did put on evidence as to the duration of that event. While the length of the tournament is irrelevant for purposes of assessing the normal time span of the business of selling advertising space, we hold that, contrary to the tax court's conclusion, the tournament must be considered the actual time span of the business activity sought to be taxed here. The length of the tournament is the relevant time period because what the NCAA was selling, and the activity from which it derived the relevant income, was the publication of advertisements in programs distributed over a period of less than three weeks, and largely to spectators. Obviously, the tournament is the relevant time frame for those who chose to pay for advertisements in the program. This case is unlike American College of Physicians, 475 U.S. at 836, where advertisements were sold for each issue of a monthly medical journal. Accordingly, we conclude that the NCAA's involvement in the sale of advertising space was not suf-

ficiently long-lasting to make it a regularly-carried-on business solely by reason of its duration.

The next step of the regulation's analysis is to determine whether activities which are intermittently conducted are nevertheless regularly carried on by virtue of the manner in which they are pursued. In general, according to the regulations, "exempt organization business activities which are engaged in only discontinuously or periodically will not be considered regularly carried on if they are conducted without the competitive and promotional efforts typical of commercial endeavors." Treas. Reg. § 1.513-1(c)(2)(ii). . . . On appeal, the Commissioner initially agreed with the tax court that the record was devoid of evidence with which the NCAA could show that Host's efforts were not of a sufficiently competitive and promotional nature. But the Commissioner then went on to focus on the Final Four program, a part of the record. He characterized the program's advertisements as "typical print media advertisements," and distinguished them from the advertisements in the vaudeville show programs, which "'more closely resembled complimentary contributions than commercial selling agents.'" Appellee's Brief at 27 (quoting Suffolk County, 77 T.C. at 1322). The sentence referring to sports events in the regulations was, according to the Commissioner, directed more at advertising in high school sports programs than at the type of advertising in the program here.

• • •

We conclude that the advertising here is an infrequent activity. The programs containing the advertisements were distributed over less than a three-week span at an event that occurs only once a year. We consider this to be sufficiently infrequent to preclude a determination that the NCAA's advertising business was regularly carried on.

Our conclusion is buttressed by the regulation's admonition that we apply the regularly-carried-on test in light of the purpose of the tax to place exempt organizations doing business on the same tax basis as the comparable nonexempt business endeavors with which they compete. See Treas. Reg. § 1.513-1(c)(1). The legislative history of the unrelated business income tax also convinces us that we must consider the impact an exempt organization's trade or business might have on its competition. The tax was a response to the situation prevailing before 1950, when an exempt organization could engage in any commercial business venture, secure in the knowledge that the profits generated would not be taxed as long as the destination of the funds was the exempt organization. The source of those funds did not affect their tax status. . . . As more and more exempt organizations began acquiring and operating commercial enterprises, there were rumblings in

Congress to do away with the perceived advantage enjoyed by these organizations.

• • •

Although we have observed that the purpose of the unrelated business income tax was to prevent unfair competition between companies whose earnings are taxed and those whose are not, it is not necessary to prove or disprove the existence of actual competition. . . . Viewed in this context, we conclude that the NCAA program, which is published only once a year, should not be considered an unfair competitor for the publishers of advertising. Application of the unrelated business tax here therefore would not further the statutory purpose. We hold that the NCAA's advertising business was not regularly carried on within the meaning of the Code.

The decision of the tax court is REVERSED.

■ ■ ■ ■

Fundamental Concepts

The 16th Amendment reaffirmed the federal government's power to levy tax on personal income. Subsequently, the Internal Revenue Code (IRC) included tax exempt (non-profit) organizations. IRC 501 defines and describes the qualifications for tax exempt organizations, while IRC 501 (c) (3) designates the organizations or a section of the organizations which qualify under religious, charitable, literary or educational purposes. Within the athletic arena, colleges and universities are not the only organizations who qualify as tax exempt. According to Gaul and Gorowski (1993) part of the NFL, NHL, PGA and USTA are among tax-exempt sports groups. The distinction in these organizations are their purposes, educational or charitable.

Prior to 1950 the Internal Revenue Code classified organizations as totally taxable or totally tax exempt. In 1950 the unrelated business income tax (UBIT) was introduced following the decision made in *Mueller, C.F. v. Commissioner*, (3rd Cir. 1951). Subsequently, sections of the IRC 501, 501 (c) (3), 512 and 513 were included in the Code to deal with UBIT. These sections clarified the tax exempt status of the monies generated by an organization. Specifically, exempt status applies to income generated from those activities that are **substantially** related to the organization's purpose. Consequently, those activities that generate income that is unrelated to the organization's purpose may be taxed or the organization may even lose it's tax exempt status. (Craig and Weisman, 1994).

Income generated by non-profit organizations is thus designated as related or unrelated. If income is related to a tax-exempt organization's tax-exempt purpose, then the income remains tax-exempt. If deemed unrelated, however, the gross income, less allowable expenses, is taxed using the regular corporate income tax rate, approximately 34 percent. (Craig and Weisman, 1994) There are restrictions regarding the extent of unrelated income permitted. Organizations could lose their tax exempt status if unrelated income becomes a considerable portion of their business operations. (IRC 501 (c) (3)).

A simplified definition of unrelated business income is **business** or **trade** generated by a tax exempt organization which is **regularly** carried on and **not substantially** related to the purpose of the organization (Lehr, 1993). These three factors, business or trade, regular basis, and unrelated to the purpose of the organization are the essential elements for unrelated income tax to be levied. IRC 513 identifies or clarifies these three factors. First, is the income generated by business or trade? This would involve the sale of goods or services with a profit motive or an activity that created unfair competition. Second, is the trade or business performed on a regular basis? "Regular" activities are determined by frequency and duration. The business or trade in question is also compared with similar activities conducted by for profit entities. Lastly, is the business or trade substantially related to the purpose of the organization? This is ambiguous since non-profit organizations would claim that all activities are related to their purpose. The IRS may think differently, and has the discretionary power to make a determination on a case by case basis.

Taxation issues are present when athletic programs conduct various activities which generate income. Clearly, some of these activities are related to the institution's educational purpose while others do perplex the UBIT issue (Craig and Weisman, 1994).

Under the current interpretations of the IRS the following revenue sources **do not** to have UBIT inferences:

Ticket Sales.   Athletic events are considered educational experiences and contribute to the mission of the institution.

Program Sales and Concessions.   Program sales and refreshments are usually provided at athletic events, thus these are related to the institution's purpose. The sale of merchandise and advertisement is another topic that will be discussed in a later section.

Television and Radio Rights.   When an institution contracts for these rights, the income is considered related to the exempt organization's purpose: promotion of the university/college.

Licensing Fees and Interest.   Licensing fees are considered royalty income. The sale of names and logos are thus exempt from UBIT as long as the organization is not actively involved in the solicitation of the revenues (Craig and Weisman, 1994). Likewise, dividends, interest and endowment income are considered "passive" activities and are not subject to UBIT.

Revenue from Bowls/Tournaments.   These revenues elevate the programs of institutions and thus revenues are not subject to UBIT.

Craig and Weisman (1994) and Fry (1991) identified income generating activities that are subject to UBIT. Although challenges have been made, skillful management may limit tax liability.

Advertisement Revenue.   Advertisement comes in many forms: game programs and television/radio. Are these forms of advertisements subject to UBIT? The answer is yes, no, sometimes.

Program Advertisement.   If the organization solicited the advertisement and the programs contain a substantial amount of advertisement, UBIT would be applicable. Some deviation from this criteria may alter the tax status. (*United States v. American College of Physicians*, 1986). The decision in this case differentiated the content of the advertisement. If the content of the advertisements was educational, associated with sport, or connected to the local tourism industry, it may be related to the purpose of the organization and thus may not be subject to UBIT.

The cases that seem most relevant to taxation of revenue generated from sporting event program advertisement were the decisions rendered in *National Collegiate Athletic Association v. Commissioner* (1990) and *Suffolk County Patrolmen's Benevolent Association, Inc. v. Commissioner of Internal Revenue* (1981). At issue in the *NCAA* case was the parties' interpretation of what constituted "regularly carried on." The IRS contended that the length of the Men's Division I Basketball Championship was not the issue. Rather, what seemed relevant was the amount of time spent to solicit advertisement and the preparation of the publication. The IRS contended this time period would constitute "regularly carried on." The Tax Court (92 T.C. 456, 1989) agreed. On appeal, however, the Tenth Circuit Court (*NCAA v. Commissioner*, 1990) reversed the Tax Court finding and held that the NCAA's involvement in the sale of advertising space was not a regularly carried on business and therefore revenue generated was not subject to UBIT. The court also examined the contractual agreement between the NCAA and the program printer and publisher. In addition to printing the program, the publisher was contracted to secure program advertisement. With regard to this contractual agreement the court referred to *Suffolk County Patrolmen's Benevolent Association, Inc. v. Commissioner of Internal Revenue* (1981) which stated:

Additionally, respondent (Commissioner) would have us find that petitioner's (Suffolk) activities was regularly carried on because an independent professional organization was under contract to produce and promote shows (including the program guide). . . . It is entirely reasonable for an exempt organization to hire professionals in an effort to insure the success of a fundraiser, and there are no indications in the regulations or legislation history of sections 511 through 513 that the use of such professionals would cause an otherwise infrequent intermittent activity to be considered regularly carried on. (77 T.C. 1323)

Thus, the *NCAA* and *Suffolk* decisions present an important aspect to program advertisement and lend credence to new strategies to limit UBIT.

Television/Radio Advertisement.   When universities maintain an in-house network, advertising revenue is taxable. Again, if the television or radio rights are sold to a third party, the revenue generated by the contractual agreement may not be taxable.

Merchandise Sales.   Because selling of merchandise has a profit motive and might create unfair competition this endeavor is subject to UBIT.

Debt-Financed Property.   Debt-financed property is usually exhibited in the form of property held to provide income (sky-box suites) and thus will be taxed (IRC 514).

Rental Income.   The renting of athletic facilities may seem another source of income to help finance athletic programs. Athletic administrators need to review their lease agreements to determine if rental fees would be exempt income or subject to UBIT. The problem lies in the interpretation of the IRS and if the rented property was "real" or "personal." Generally, rental income from "real" property is exempt from tax provided that 50 percent of the total rental was received from "real" property as opposed to "personal" property (IRC 512). "Real" property will be the building, field, and stadium. Interpretations from the IRS define "personal" property as utilities, maintenance and security (Craig and Weisman, 1994).

Another issue involves a facility built for both related activities: classes, student clubs, and student recreation, and commercial uses: ice shows and public skating. *Rensselaer Polytechnic Institute v. Commissioner* (1983) illustrates the need for accurate record keeping in a multi-use facility, and emphasizes the difference in direct deductible expenses, variable expenses and fixed expenses.

Corporate Sponsorship of Events and Signage.   Many organizations rely on corporate sponsors to stage contests and events or to increase revenues. The "bowl" controversy began a series of IRS interpretations, proposed audit guidelines and possible legislation.

In 1991, the IRS took the position that sponsorship fees paid to tax-exempt organizations such as the Cotton Bowl were subject to UBIT (Crawford 1993) (Tech. Adv. Mem. 91-47-007, Aug. 16, 1991). Prior to that decision non-profits avoided taxation by characterizing these fees as "royalties." The IRS thus took the position that these fees were not charitable contributions, but rather commercial advertising. (John Hancock stated that they received $5 million worth of publicity in return for its $1 sponsorship fee, Crawford, 1993)

In 1992, guidelines were published that clarified the IRS's position. (Proposal Examination Guidelines Regarding Treatment of Exempt Organization Corporate Sponsorship Income, *Internal Revenue Bulletin No. 1992-5*, Feb. 3, 1992). Public comment did not support the hard line drawn by the IRS. As a result the IRS issued proposed regulations (Proposed Treas. Reg. 1.51 3-4, 58 Fed. Reg. 5690, 1993) which softened its position on sponsorship as advertising. These proposed regulations recognize that revenue generated by sponsorships that reflect mere recognition and acknowledgments would not be subject to UBIT. Logos and slogans could be used on banners, signage, scoreboard, naming of the event, and on uniforms. On the other hand, the sponsorship would be considered advertising if the fee was contingent on factors such as attendance or broadcast ratings, or if there was a presence of selling activities such as an inducement to buy, sell, rent or lease the sponsor's product or service (Crawford, 1993). Although these proposed regulations are a departure from the previous position of the IRS, they are still confusing, and leave interpretation open to the IRS; what is meant by logo, slogan, " regularly carried on?" Currently these proposed regulations are the enforcement tool used by the IRS.

Other Tax Issues

Taxation and the Student Athlete. There are two taxation issues that concern the student athlete. First, the perspective athlete is responsible to include as income the value of the official visits in the recruiting process (transportation, lodging, meals, and entertainment). The second, involves the portion of the athletic scholarship which is regarded as income. Currently an athlete should include as income the room and board portion of the athletic scholarship. Institutions are required to notify the athlete of these requirements (Mingelgreen and Caratzola, 1987), (IRC 117).

Employee Compensation. Some colleges and universities make available to faculty and staff discounts on the purchase of tickets to athletic events. The IRC (Section 1.6-21 (5)) provides that discounts to employees that exceed 20 percent for goods and/or services must be included in the employee's compensation as reported on the W-2 Form for income tax purposes.

Preferred Seating. Colleges and universities have instituted preferred seating policies which afford individuals who contribute to a scholarship fund the right to purchase preferred seating at athletic events. The IRS has ruled that these contributions qualify for deductions to the extent that they exceed the fair market value of benefits received. Most institutions have placed the fair market value of preferred seating at 20 percent, thus the contributor can deduct 80 percent of the contribution as a charitable contribution.

Nonresident Alien (NRA) Student. There are specific rules that apply to scholarship payments made to, or on behalf of NRA students. The institution must generally withhold and remit to the IRS 14 percent of the amount of any taxable portion of the scholarship. This withholding requirement creates a problem for the student as well as the institution.

Recent Developments

Currently Congress is considering legislation, similar to that introduced in 1992 and 1993, that would exempt organizations such as the NCAA from UBIT on "qualified sponsorship payments" received in connection with "qualified public events" (Hoffman and Van der Bellon, 1995). According to Hoffman and Van der Bellon (1995) the legislation indicates that the sponsor could not receive a substantial return benefit other than the use of a name or trade logo which acknowledges the sponsor's product or service. Furnishing the sponsor privileges such as facilities and services which are connected with the event would also be acceptable. A "qualified public event" would be either: an event substantially related to the purpose of the exempt organization, for example a football game sponsored by a conference, **or** an event conducted infrequently: an annual event or a tournament of no more than a month in duration. This bill addresses the "bowl controversy," tournaments, and a singular regular contest, but does not address season long sponsorship or scoreboard signage. According to Haffman and Van der Bellon (1995) these forms of sponsorship would not be "qualified public events," and thus revenue generated would be subject to UBIT. In this case the athletic administrator must decide on single contest sponsorship, or that sponsorship fees be placed in a scholarship fund that may not be subject to UBIT.

This Senate bill provision is part of the controversial Reconciliation Act of 1995. At this time the Senate, House and President are negotiating. Athletic administrators need to monitor this legislation closely.

References

A. Cases

Mueller, C.F. v. Commissioner, 14 T.C. 922 (1950), rev'd, 190 F. 2d 120 (3rd Cir. 1951).

National Collegiate Athletic Association v. Commissioner of Internal Revenue, 92 T.C. 456 (1989), rev'd, 914 F.2d 1417 (10th Cir. 1990).

Rensselaer Polytechnic Institute v. Commissioner, 732 F. 2nd 1058 (1983).

Suffolk County Patrolmen's Benevolent Association, Inc. v. Commissioner of Internal Revenue, 77 T.C. 1314.

United States v. American College of Physicians, 475 U.S. 834 (1986).

B. Publications

Ciccolella, M. (1991). A Taxing Question. *Collegiate Athletic Management, 3* (1), 24, 26.

Comacho, D. and Dunn, J. (1992). NCAA v. Commissioner of I.R.S.: When Will the Internal Revenue Service Consider an Activity Regularly Carried On? *Journal of College and University Law, 19*, 39-47.

Craig, C. and Weisman, K. (1994). Collegiate Athletics and the Unrelated Business Income Tax. *Journal of Sport Management, 8*, 36-48.

Crawford, C. (1993). IRS Softens its Position on Sponsorships as Advertising. *The Journal of Taxation, 79*, 214-216.

Crawford, C. (1992). IRS Attacks Exempt Organization Income from Corporate Sponsorship Fees. *The Journal of Taxation, 76*, 230-235.

Fry, K. (1991). Taxing Examples; Certain Revenue Producing Activities in Your Department May Be Subject to the UBIT. *Collegiate Athletic Management, 3* (1), 25.

Gaul, G. and Borowski, N. (May 3, 1993). Tax-exempt Status Shortchanges U.S. of Billions, *Atlanta Journal Constitution.*

Haimes, D. (1992). Corporate Sponsorship of Charity Events and the Unrelated Business Income Tax: Will Congress or the Courts Block the IRS Rush to Sack the College Football Bowl Games? *Notre Dame Law Review, 67* (4), 1079-1120.

Hoffman, J. and VanderBellen, A. (August 16, 1995). IRS, Taxes and Corporate Sponsorship. *The NCAA News*, 4-5.

I.R.C. 1.6-21 (5), 117, 501, 512, 513, 514, and 517.

Koeberle, B. (1992). The Legal Implications of Taxation on Non-profit Athletic Events. *The Sports, Parks, & Recreation Law Reporter, 5* (4), 51, 53-54.

Lehr, C. (1993). The IRS and Intercollegiate Athletics. Paper Presented at the Sixth Annual Sport, Physical Education, and Law Conference, Jekyll, GA.

Mingelgreen, M. and Caratzola, F. (October, 1987). Tangled Up in Tax Reform, *Athletic Business*, 36-39.

Mott, R. (November 13, 1995). Senate Tax Legislation Would Clarify Treatment of Sponsorship Revenue. *The NCAA News*, 5, 9.

Proposed Examination Guidelines Regarding Treatment of Exempt Organization Corporate Sponsorship Income. (1992). *Internal Revenue Bulletin No. 1992-5.*

Proposed Treas, Reg. 1.51 3-4, *58 Fed. Reg. 5690*, 1993.

Schnee, E. and Brock, E. (1991). Opportunities Exist to Reduce Unrelated Business Income from Advertising Revenue. *The Journal of Taxation, 74*, 240-245.

Tech. Adv. Mem. 91-47-007, Aug. 16, 1991.

Wirtschafer, N. (1994). Fourth Quarter Choke: How the IRS Blew the Corporate Sponsorship Game. *Loyola of Los Angeles Law Review, 27* (4), 1465-1511.

5.60

Sport Agent Regulation

T. Jesse Wilde
Huckvale & Company Law Offices

As recent as twenty years ago most professional athletes negotiated their own player contracts. They had little reason to do otherwise. Being inseparably bound to a team through a reserve system, with no competing professional leagues to look to for employment, professional athletes were left with few alternatives. Contract negotiation in these circumstances for most players was more a matter of taking what was offered or refusing to play.

During the 1970s and 1980s, however, other options became available to players, giving them the bargaining leverage they had previously lacked. Through litigation, arbitration, collective bargaining, and, in some instances, the emergence of competing professional leagues, players gained greater freedom to market themselves to the highest bidder. As a result, the price for a relatively scarce supply of talent began to rise (Rypma, 1990). Expanded media coverage and escalating rights fees paid by networks to leagues made professional sports even more popular and profitable than in years past. The increased revenues enjoyed by franchise owners allowed them to meet, albeit grudgingly, the increasing player salary demands (Dow, 1990). As professional sports evolved into a multi-billion dollar industry the need for professional representation became more and more essential for many athletes seeking to maximize their individual worth. Likewise, many would-be agents seized the opportunity to provide their services to professional athletes, to reap the economic benefits of an association with, and service to, a high-priced talent pool (Wilde, 1992).

While few would argue that the services of a competent agent can be extremely valuable for a professional athlete, the emergence of the sport agent in professional sports has not, however, been without problems. First, the intense competition for a limited supply of quality athletes has encouraged corruption (Shropshire, 1989). Until recently, corrupt or unscrupulous agents had everything to gain and nothing to lose by bending or breaking the rules in the competitive pursuit for talented clients. Through offers of money, gifts or other inducements, many agents persuade college players to sign representation contracts before the expiration of their collegiate eligibility, and thereby violate collegiate eligibility rules (Shropshire, 1989). While no one is certain how deep the problems run, NCAA insiders estimate that close to 100 percent of projected first and second round National Football League draft prospects and the top 50 college basketball players declaring annually for the National Basketball Association draft are in contact with, and have received benefits from, sports agents prior to the expiration of their college eligibility (Hagwell, 1995). Second, while agents perform professional services for their athlete clients, there are no professional requirements or standards to which they must rise (Dow, 1990). The industry has evolved beyond contract negotiation, with many agents now providing additional services, including: soliciting, negotiating and securing additional income opportunities, providing financial advice and income management services, and furnishing general guidance on legal and tax matters (Narayanan, 1990). Few agents have expertise in all areas, yet many attempt to compete with those who profess such knowledge.

Whether through corruption or incompetence, the abuses of the agent-player relationship, committed by a relative minority of agents, have taken their toll on the profession's reputation and have prompted measures from a variety of sources to regulate sport agents (Dunn, 1988).

■ ■ ■ ■

Representative Case

U.S. v. WALTERS
United States Court of Appeals for the Seventh Circuit
997 F.2d 1219 (1993)

OPINION: EASTERBROOK, Circuit Judge.

Norby Walters, who represents entertainers, tried to move into the sports business. He signed 58 college football players to contracts while they were still playing. Walters offered cars and money to those who would agree to use him as their representative in dealing with professional teams. Sports agents receive a percentage of the players' income, so Walters would profit only to the extent he could negotiate contracts for his clients. The athletes' pro prospects depended on successful completion of their collegiate careers. To the NCAA, however, a student who signs a contract with an agent is a professional, ineligible to play on collegiate teams. To avoid jeopardizing his clients' careers, Walters dated the contracts after the end of their eligibility and locked them in a safe. He promised to lie to the universities in response to any inquiries. Walters inquired of sports lawyers at Shea & Gould whether this plan of operation would be lawful. The firm rendered an opinion that it would violate the NCAA's rules but not any statute.

Having recruited players willing to fool their universities and the NCAA, Walters discovered that they were equally willing to play false with him. Only 2 of the 58 players fulfilled their end of the bargain; the other 56 kept the cars and money, then signed with other agents. They relied on the fact that the contracts were locked away and dated in the future, and that Walters' business depended on continued secrecy, so he could not very well sue to enforce their promises. When the 56 would neither accept him as their representative nor return the payments, Walters resorted to threats. One player, Maurice Douglass, was told that his legs would be broken before the pro draft unless he repaid Walters' firm. A 75-page indictment charged Walters and his partner Lloyd Bloom with conspiracy, RICO violations (the predicate felony was extortion), and mail fraud. The fraud: causing the universities

to pay scholarship funds to athletes who had become ineligible as a result of the agency contracts. The mail: each university required its athletes to verify their eligibility to play, then sent copies by mail to conferences such as the Big Ten.

After a month-long trial and a week of deliberations, the jury convicted Walters and Bloom. We reversed, holding that the district judge had erred in declining to instruct the jury that reliance on Shea & Gould's advice could prevent the formation of intent to defraud the universities. 913 F.2d 388, 391-92 (1990). Any dispute about the adequacy of Walters' disclosure to his lawyers and the bona fides of his reliance was for the jury, we concluded. Because Bloom declined to waive his own attorney-client privilege, we held that the defendants must be retried separately. Id. at 392-93. On remand, Walters asked the district court to dismiss the indictment, arguing that the evidence presented at trial is insufficient to support the convictions. After the judge denied this motion, 775 F. Supp. 1173 (N.D. Ill. 1991), Walters agreed to enter a conditional Alford plea: he would plead guilty to mail fraud, conceding that the record of the first trial supplies a factual basis for a conviction while reserving his right to contest the sufficiency of that evidence. In return, the prosecutor agreed to dismiss the RICO and conspiracy charges and to return to Walters all property that had been forfeited as a result of his RICO conviction. Thus a case that began with a focus on extortion has become a straight mail fraud prosecution and may undergo yet another transformation. The prosecutor believes that Walters hampered the investigation preceding his indictment. See In re Feldberg, 862 F.2d 622 (7th Cir. 1988) (describing some of the investigation). The plea agreement reserves the prosecutor's right to charge Walters with perjury and obstruction of justice if we should reverse the conviction for mail fraud.

"Whoever, having devised . . . any scheme or artifice to defraud, or for obtaining money or property by means of false or fraudulent pretenses, representations, or promises . . . places in any post office or authorized depository for mail matter, any matter or thing whatever to be sent or delivered by the Postal Service . . . or knowingly causes [such matter or thing] to be delivered by mail" commits the crime of mail fraud. 18 U.S.C. § 1341. Norby Walters did not mail anything or cause anyone else to do so (the universities were going to collect and mail the forms no matter what Walters did), but the Supreme Court has expanded the statute beyond its literal terms, holding that a mailing by a third party suffices if it is "incident to an essential part of the scheme," Pereira v. United States, 347 U.S. 1, 8, 98 L. Ed. 435, 74 S. Ct. 358 (1954). While stating that such mailings can turn ordinary fraud into mail fraud, the Court has cautioned that the statute "does not purport to reach all frauds, but only those limited instances in which the use of the mails is a part of the execution of the fraud." Kann v. United States, 323 U.S. 88, 95, 89 L. Ed. 88, 65 S. Ct. 148 (1944). Everything thus turns on matters of degree. Did the schemers foresee that the mails would be used? Did the mailing advance the success of the scheme? Which parts of a scheme are "essential?" Such questions lack obviously right answers, so it is no surprise that each side to this case can cite several of our decisions in support. Compare United States v. McClain, 934 F.2d 822, 835 (7th Cir. 1991), and United States v. Kwiat, 817 F.2d 440, 443-44 (7th Cir. 1987), among cases reversing convictions because use of the mails was too remote or unforeseeable, with Messinger v. United States, 872 F.2d 217 (7th Cir. 1989), among many cases holding that particular uses of the mails were vital to the scheme and foreseeable.

"The relevant question . . . is whether the mailing is part of the execution of the scheme as conceived by the perpetrator at the time." Schmuck v. United States, 489 U.S. 705, 715, 103 L. Ed. 2d 734, 109 S. Ct. 1443 (1989). Did the evidence establish that Walters conceived a scheme in which mailings played a role? We think not— indeed, that no reasonable juror could give an affirmative answer to this question. Walters hatched a scheme to make money by taking a percentage of athletes' pro contracts. To get clients he signed students while college eligibility remained, thus avoiding competition from ethical agents. To obtain big pro contracts for these clients he needed to keep the deals secret, so the athletes could finish their collegiate careers. Thus deceit was an ingredient of the plan. We may assume that Walters knew that the universities would ask athletes to verify that they were eligible to compete as amateurs. But what role do the mails play? The plan succeeds so long as the athletes conceal their con-

tracts from their schools (and remain loyal to Walters). Forms verifying eligibility do not help the plan succeed; instead they create a risk that it will be discovered if a student should tell the truth. Cf. United States v. Maze, 414 U.S. 395, 38 L. Ed. 2d 603, 94 S. Ct. 645 (1974). And it is the forms, not their mailing to the Big Ten, that pose the risk. For all Walters cared, the forms could sit forever in cartons. Movement to someplace else was irrelevant. In Schmuck, where the fraud was selling cars with rolled-back odometers, the mailing was essential to obtain a new and apparently "clean" certificate of title; no certificates of title, no marketable cars, no hope for success. Even so, the Court divided five to four on the question whether the mailing was sufficiently integral to the scheme. A college's mailing to its conference has less to do with the plot's success than the mailings that transferred title in Schmuck.

To this the United States responds that the mailings were essential because, if a college had neglected to send the athletes' forms to the conference, the NCAA would have barred that college's team from competing. Lack of competition would spoil the athletes' pro prospects. Thus the use of the mails was integral to the profits Walters hoped to reap, even though Walters would have been delighted had the colleges neither asked any questions of the athletes nor put the answers in the mail. Let us take this as sufficient under Schmuck (although we have our doubts). The question remains whether Walters caused the universities to use the mails. A person "knowingly causes" the use of the mails when he "acts with the knowledge that the use of the mails will follow in the ordinary course of business, or where such use can reasonably be foreseen." United States v. Kuzniar, 881 F.2d 466, 472 (7th Cir. 1989), quoting Pereira, 347 U.S. at 8-9. The paradigm is insurance fraud. Perkins tells his auto insurer that his car has been stolen, when in fact it has been sold. The local employee mails the claim to the home office, which mails a check to Perkins. Such mailings in the ordinary course of business are foreseeable. e.g., United States v. Richman, 944 F.2d 323 (7th Cir. 1991). Similarly, a judge who takes a bribe derived from the litigant's bail money causes the use of the mails when the ordinary course is to refund the bond by mail. e.g., United States v. Murphy, 768 F.2d 1518, 1529-30 (7th Cir. 1985). The prosecutor contends that the same approach covers Walters.

No evidence demonstrates that Walters actually knew that the colleges would mail the athletes' forms. The record is barely sufficient to establish that Walters knew of the forms' existence; it is silent about Walters' knowledge of the forms' disposition. . . . In the end, the prosecutor insists that the large size and interstate nature of the NCAA demonstrate that something would be dropped into the mails. To put this only slightly differently, the prosecutor submits that all frauds involving big organizations necessarily are mail frauds, because big organizations habitually mail things. No evidence put before the jury supports such a claim, and it is hardly appropriate for judicial notice in a criminal case.

• • •

There is a deeper problem with the theory of this prosecution. The United States tells us that the universities lost their scholarship money. Money is property; this aspect of the prosecution does not encounter a problem under McNally v. United States, 483 U.S. 350, 97 L. Ed. 2d 292, 107 S. Ct. 2875 (1987). Walters emphasizes that the universities put his 58 athletes on scholarship long before he met them and did not pay a penny more than they planned to do. But a jury could conclude that had Walters' clients told the truth, the colleges would have stopped their scholarships, thus saving money. So we must assume that the universities lost property by reason of Walters' deeds. Still, they were not out of pocket to Walters; he planned to profit by taking a percentage of the players' professional incomes, not of their scholarships. Section 1341 condemns "any scheme or artifice to defraud, or for obtaining money or property" (emphasis added). If the universities were the victims, how did he "obtain" their property?, Walters asks.

According to the United States, neither an actual nor a potential transfer of property from the victim to the defendant is essential. It is enough that the victim lose; what (if anything) the schemer hopes to gain plays no role in the definition of the offense. We asked the prosecutor at oral argument whether on this rationale practical jokes violate § 1341. A mails B an invitation to a surprise party for their mutual friend C. B drives his car to the place named in the invitation. But there is no party; the address is a vacant lot; B is the butt of a joke. The invitation came by post; the cost of gasoline means that B is out of pocket. The prosecutor said that this indeed violates § 1341, but that his office pledges to use prosecutorial discretion wisely. Many people will find this position unnerving (what if the prosecutor's policy changes, or A is politically unpopular and the prosecutor is looking for a way to nail him?). Others, who obey the law out of a sense of civic obligation rather than the fear of sanctions, will alter their conduct no matter what policy the prosecutor follows. Either way, the idea that practical jokes are federal felonies would make a joke of the Supreme Court's assurance that § 1341 does not cover the waterfront of deceit.

Practical jokes rarely come to the attention of federal prosecutors, but large organizations are more successful in gaining the attention of public officials. In this case the mail fraud statute has been invoked to shore up the rules of an influential private association. . . . The NCAA depresses athletes' income—restricting payments to the value of tuition, room, and board, while receiving services of substantially greater worth. The NCAA treats this as desirable preservation of amateur sports; a more jaundiced eye would see it as the use of monopsony power to obtain athletes' services for less than the competitive market price. Walters then is cast in the role of a cheater, increasing the payments to the student athletes. Like other cheaters, Walters found it convenient to hide his activities. If, as the prosecutor believes, his repertory included extortion, he has used methods that the law denies to persons fighting cartels, but for the moment we are concerned only with the deceit that caused the universities to pay stipends to "professional" athletes. For current purposes it matters not whether the NCAA actually monopsonizes the market for players; the point of this discussion is that the prosecutor's theory makes criminals of those who consciously cheat on the rules of a private organization, even if that organization is a cartel. We pursue this point because any theory that makes criminals of cheaters raises a red flag.

Cheaters are not self-conscious champions of the public weal. They are in it for profit, as rapacious and mendacious as those who hope to collect monopoly rents. Maybe more; often members of cartels believe that monopoly serves the public interest, and they take their stand on the platform of business ethics, e.g., National Society of Professional Engineers v. United States, 435 U.S. 679, 55 L. Ed. 2d 637, 98 S. Ct. 1355 (1978), while cheaters' glasses have been washed with cynical acid. Only Adam Smith's invisible hand turns their self-seeking activities to public benefit. It is cause for regret if prosecutors, assuming that persons with low regard for honesty must be villains, use the criminal laws to suppress the competitive process that undermines cartels. Of course federal laws have been used to enforce cartels before; the Federal Maritime Commission is a cartel-enforcement device. Inconsistent federal laws also occur; the United States both subsidizes tobacco growers and discourages people from smoking. So if the United States simultaneously forbids cartels and forbids undermining cartels by cheating, we shall shrug our shoulders and enforce both laws, condemning practical jokes along the way. But what is it about § 1341 that labels as a crime all deceit that inflicts any loss on anyone? Firms often try to fool their competitors, surprising them with new products that enrich their treasuries at their rivals' expense. Is this mail fraud because large organizations inevitably use the mail? "Any scheme or artifice to defraud, or for obtaining money or property by means of false or fraudulent pretenses, representations, or promises" reads like a description of schemes to get money or property by fraud rather than methods of doing business that incidentally cause losses.

None of the Supreme Court's mail fraud cases deals with a scheme in which the defendant neither obtained nor tried to obtain the victim's property. . . . We have been unable to find any appellate cases squarely resolving the question whether the victim's loss must be an objective of the scheme rather than a byproduct of it, perhaps because prosecutions of the kind this case represents are so rare. According to the prosecutor, however, there have been such cases, and in this circuit. The United States contends that we have already held that a scheme producing an incidental loss violates § 1341. A representative sample of the cases the prosecutor cites shows that we have held no such thing.

• • •

Many of our cases ask whether a particular scheme deprived a victim of property. E.g., Lombardo v. United States, 865 F.2d 155, 159-60 (7th Cir. 1989). They do so not with an emphasis on "deprive" but with an emphasis on "property"—which, until the enactment of 18 U.S.C. § 1346 after Walters' conduct, was essential to avoid the "intangible rights" doctrine that McNally jettisoned. No one doubted that the schemes were designed to enrich the perpetrators at the victims' expense; the only difficulty was the proper characterization of the deprivation. Not until today have we dealt with a scheme in which the defendants' profits were to come from legitimate transactions in the market, rather than at the expense of the victims. Both the "scheme or artifice to defraud" clause and

the "obtaining money or property" clause of § 1343 contemplate a transfer of some kind. Accordingly, following both the language of § 1341 and the implication of Tanner, we hold that only a scheme to obtain money or other property from the victim by fraud violates § 1341. A deprivation is a necessary but not a sufficient condition of mail fraud. Losses that occur as byproducts of a deceitful scheme do not satisfy the statutory requirement.

Anticipating that we might come to this conclusion, the prosecutor contends that Walters is nonetheless guilty as an aider and abettor. If Walters did not defraud the universities, the argument goes, then the athletes did. Walters put them up to it and so is guilty under 18 U.S.C. § 2, the argument concludes. But the indictment charged a scheme by Walters to defraud; it did not depict Walters as an aide de camp in the students' scheme. The jury received a boilerplate § 2 instruction; this theory was not argued to the jury, or for that matter to the district court either before or after the remand. Independent problems dog this recasting of the scheme—not least the difficulty of believing that the students hatched a plot to employ fraud to receive scholarships that the universities had awarded them long before Walters arrived on the scene, and the lack of evidence that the students knew about or could foresee any mailings. Walters is by all accounts a nasty and untrustworthy fellow, but the prosecutor did not prove that his efforts to circumvent the NCAA's rules amounted to mail fraud.

REVERSED

■ ■ ■ ■

Fundamental Concepts

The saga of Norby Walters and Lloyd Bloom is well-documented. In 1989, Walters was sentenced to five years in prison, but in 1990 his conviction was overturned and remanded for a new trial by the Seventh Circuit (913 F.2d 388). Walters subsequently pleaded guilty to federal mail fraud charges to avoid more serious racketeering and conspiracy charges, however, in 1993, his conviction pursuant to his guilty pleas was also overturned by the Seventh Circuit (997 F.2d 1219). Ultimately, Walters was forced out of the sport agent business. Bloom, whose conviction on racketeering charges was also overturned, was found shot to death in his home in August 1993 (Mott, 1995). While their unscrupulous conduct went unpunished by the courts, no case has been as responsible for focusing public awareness on the problems associated with the unscrupulous conduct of some sport agents, and prompting the development of agent-specific legislation designed to prevent recurrences of unethical, unscrupulous and illegal conduct by sport agents. As a result of Walters, for example, several states rushed to enact sport agent legislation to protect the innocent college athlete and prevent colleges from encountering difficulties with their various sanctioning athletic associations (Powers, 1994).

Sport Agent Legislation

The old adage, that simply having a client is the lone prerequisite for calling oneself a sport agent, is no longer entirely accurate. Now, in addition, such a title often requires registration and payment of fees under some state legislative scheme (Rodgers, 1988-89). The list of states with some form of sport agent legislation has grown from California, which was the first to pass such legislation in 1981, to include 24 states across the country, including: Alabama, Arkansas, California, Florida, Georgia, Illinois, Indiana, Iowa, Kentucky, Louisiana, Maryland, Michigan, Minnesota, Mississippi, Nevada, North Carolina, Ohio, Oklahoma, Pennsylvania, South Carolina, Tennessee, Texas, Virginia, and Washington. (Powers, 1994).

The boom period for state legislation occurred during the mid to late-1980s in response to the outrage spawned by the well-publicized misdealings of such notorious sport agents as Norby Walters and Lloyd Bloom. During 1988 alone, for example, 12 states passed athlete agent legislation (Rodgers, 1990).

State legislative schemes, through the incorporation of civil and criminal penalty provisions, attempt to ensure that all agents in all sports abide by the rules (Dunn, 1988). An obvious disadvantage with state-by-state agent legislation is the confusion resulting from conflicting laws between various states, there being no federal agent legislation at present. In addition, current state legislation does not create any objective standards for competency. An attempt is made to control the corruption, but not the incompetence.

State sport agent legislation varies immensely in form and content. A division, however, can be made in general terms between early legislation (early to mid-1980s), which concentrated on regulating the agent, and the current legislative trend (mid-1980s to present), which focuses on the economic havoc an unscrupulous agent can cause a college or university (Rodgers, 1988-89).

Early Legislation. Although the specific statutes vary substantially in form and content, state sport agent legislation enacted during the early to mid 1980s, in general terms, typically includes provisions for agent registration, payment of fees, posting of surety bonds, contract approval, and criminal penalties for agent misconduct. The California legislation, passed in 1981 and amended in 1985, for example, focuses on protecting the athlete through an extensive licensing, registration and regulation program (Cosgrove, 1990). The legislation does not prohibit contact with a student-athlete prior to the expiration of his collegiate eligibility, but it does impose a limit on fees chargeable by the agent and requires the posting of a $25,000 surety bond (California Athlete Agencies Act of 1981).

In 1987, Texas became the fourth state to enact sport agent legislation. Although tailored after its California predecessor, the Texas statute has a number of important distinctions. Most notably, the statute prohibits any contact with a student-athlete prior to the expiration of the athlete's eligibility, except in state sponsored sport agent interviews to be conducted at each institution during the athlete's final year of eligibility. In addition, the Texas legislation requires that copies of the signed representation contract be filed with the university athletic director and the Secretary of State's office within five days of signing. The student-athlete is given 16 days thereafter to cancel the contract (Texas Athlete Agent Act of 1987).

The Current Trend. From the late 1980s to the present, the focus of state sport agent statutes shifted away from protecting the athlete, to addressing the economic damage an unscrupulous agent could cause for a college or university. This current legislative trend is characterized by provisions requiring notice to school and state before and/or after the signing of a representation contract, waiting periods for valid contracts, the creation of causes of action in favor of colleges and universities for agent misconduct resulting in damages, and an abandonment or modification of the onerous registration requirements common in earlier legislative schemes (Rodgers, 1989-90).

The statement of legislative intent in the first section of the Florida statute illustrates the focus of this current legislative trend:

The Legislature finds that dishonest or unscrupulous practices by agents who solicit representation of student athletes can cause significant harm to student athletes and the academic institutions for which they play. It is the intent of the Legislature to protect the interests of student athletes and academic institutions by regulating the activities of athlete agents which involve student athletes at colleges or universities in the state. (Florida Athlete Agents Act of 1988).

The Florida statute is arguably the most stringent in the country, as the state targets both the agent and the athlete for civil and criminal penalties for statutory violations (Rodgers, 1988-89). Indicative of the current legislative trend, the Florida statute does not, for example, prohibit contact between an athlete and an agent prior to the expiration of the athlete's collegiate eligibility. It does, however, prohibit offering inducements to sign, and requires both the athlete and the agent to give notification of the signing of a representation contract prior to participating in any athletic event or within 72 hours of the signing, which ever first occurs. The athlete is given 10 days after this notification to rescind the contract. Failure to notify renders the contract void and also constitutes a criminal offense for both the athlete and the agent (Florida Athlete Agents Act of 1988). Only Florida, Iowa and South Carolina have such a provision imposing criminal sanctions on athletes for failing to give notice of signing (Rodgers, 1988-89). Florida's statute also holds the student or agent liable in damages that result to the college from an athlete's subsequent ineligibility if the student or agent fails to notify the athletic director that the student has entered into a contract (Florida Athlete Agents Act of 1988).

Other legislative schemes incorporate a variety of novel provisions which deserve some mention. The Indiana statute provides another example of notice provisions. However, in Indiana, the notice by the agent to the athletic director of the university or college is required 10 days prior to the execution of the representation contract (Indiana Failure to Disclose Recruitment Act of 1988). Only Georgia, Ohio and Minnesota have similar provisions requiring this prior notice (Rodgers, 1988-89).

Minnesota is one of only a few states that specifically include non-collegiate athletes within the scope of its legislation. The Minnesota statutory definition of "student athlete" includes not only a current college athlete but "any individual who may be eligible to engage in collegiate sports in the future" (Minnesota Athlete Agents Act of 1988). High school athletes, such as baseball or hockey players who are commonly drafted out of high school, are protected under the Minnesota statute, but would not receive the same protection under most other state regulatory schemes. Only Louisiana, Maryland, Mississippi, Oklahoma, and Kentucky have similar provisions (Rodgers, 1988-89).

Kentucky employs a seemingly much simpler solution to address agent misconduct by prohibiting any contact whatsoever with an athlete until the expiration of his collegiate eligibility. The Kentucky legislation imposes a criminal prohibition on recruiting or soliciting, directly or indirectly, a student athlete to enter into an agent contract, professional sports services contract, or other sports related contract before the student athlete's eligibility for collegiate athletics has expired (Kentucky Athlete Agents Act of 1988). The statute does not prohibit activity by agents once an athlete's eligibility has expired, and, like many of the more recent statutes, has no agent registration requirement (Cosgrove, 1990).

Nevada has also followed this current trend of choosing not to impose licensing and registration requirements on sport agents. Rather, its regulatory scheme emphasizes the potential damage which can flow from an agent whose activities have caused a student-athlete or institution to violate rules of the NCAA of which the institution is a member. Nevada became one of the first states to statutorily list the specific revenue items that may be considered in calculating a damage claim against an unscrupulous agent, including loss of television revenue, a decline in ticket sales, loss of post-season revenue, and other opportunities through which the institution would have realized revenue if the NCAA rules had not been violated (Nevada Athlete Agents Act of 1989). Tennessee has enacted similar provisions (Tennessee Athlete Agents Act of 1988).

Agent-specific legislation has not been the panacea many anticipated. States have appeared less than enthusiastic in devoting their limited resources to policing legislative requirements. Not surprisingly, agents prone to abuse have ignored these statutory provisions and continued to conduct business as usual. In addition, differing state requirements have created an administrative nightmare for many honest agents doing business in several states. This, coupled with a perceived lack of enforcement, often encourages the breach of these provisions. State legislation is also criticized as being primarily designed to keep student athletes eligible and playing for state universities, rather than protecting the athletes and their future professional careers, since many classes of athletes are left unprotected by most legislative schemes. State regulatory efforts also, for the most part, create no objective standards for competency to which an agent must rise for entry into the profession. As evidenced throughout this discussion, the failure to require special training of sport agents is one of the major difficulties with the industry as a whole.

The regulation of sport agents under state legislation may also fail constitutional muster. Sport agent activity clearly involves interstate activities within federal power under the Commerce Clause of the Constitution (Dow, 1990). The industry is truly national in scope. Federal sport agent legislation would address jurisdictional ambiguities and substantive inconsistencies of existing state regulation, erase multiple application and fee requirements, and eliminate forum shopping by agents who attempt to avoid states that have legislation (Goodman, 1990).

Although never formally introduced to Congress, federal sport agent legislation was proposed by the National Sports Lawyers Association in its draft Professional Sports Agency Act of 1985. The proposed statute addressed many recurring concerns relevant to the sport agent industry, including standards for training, experience and competence, but failed to gain legislative support (Dow, 1990). One could reasonably surmise that if such a measure failed to gain the requisite support in the wake of sport agent scandals in the late-1980s, then the imminent passage of a federal sport agent statute seems unlikely when other, perhaps more pressing issues, are attracting the attention of federal legislators.

A compromise proposal between state-by-state legislative schemes and federal legislation is the development of a Model Sports Agency Act. Much like the Uniform Securities Act, such a model statute would promote uniformity among the states, while allowing each state the latitude to adopt certain provisions deemed necessary. Reciprocal agreements could exist between states to overcome the burden of agents having to register in more than one jurisdiction (Dow, 1990). Under this alternative, legislators could also begin to focus on screening prospective agents, by regulating the standards for entrance into the profession. The regulation of professional occupations, such as doctors and lawyers, has traditionally been a matter of state concern (Rypma, 1990). The model statute could establish objective criteria for entrance into the profession, including, for example, the successful completion of a comprehensive examination to evaluate the candidate's knowledge of concepts fundamental to competent athlete representation. Such concepts would include collective bargaining agreements, basic player contract issues, free agency restrictions, arbitration procedures, and relevant tax law (Rypma, 1990).

Other Regulatory Efforts

Agent-specific legislation is not the only legal means used to regulate the conduct of athlete agents. Other common law or statutory remedies, while not specifically directed at agents, have been used to attempt to control their abusive conduct. For example, the common law civil remedies of breach of contract, misrepresentation, fraud, deceit, and negligence have been applied in cases of agent misconduct (Shropshire, 1989). In addition, various federal and state criminal statutes have been used, albeit unsuccessfully, to attempt to criminally sanction agent misconduct. Sport agent Jim Abernethy, for example, who had signed and provided illegal payments to an athlete before his eligibility had expired, was indicted and convicted at trial on a charge of tampering with a sports contest in the state of Alabama. Abernethy's conviction was overturned on appeal when the Alabama Court of Criminal Appeals construed the Alabama tampering statute in a manner favorable to Abernethy and sport agents in general (Narayanan, 1990). Sport agents Norby Walters and Lloyd Bloom, as described above, were federally indicted for conspiracy to commit extortion, and other multiple charges involving violations of the Federal Mail Fraud Statute (Goodman, 1990), and the Federal Racketeer Influenced and Corrupt Organizations Act (Narayanan, 1990).

In addition to the foregoing, organizations directly or indirectly interested in monitoring the conduct of the athlete or agent or both, include the National Collegiate Athletic Association, professional team sports players' associations, the Association of Representatives of Professional Athletes, and the American Bar Association, have also become involved in regulating this relationship.

The National Collegiate Athletic Association (NCAA). By the mid-1970s, repeated instances of agent abuse prompted the NCAA, an unincorporated association of almost 1000 members and the primary regulator of intercollegiate athletics, to promulgate regulations in an attempt to limit the likelihood of an unscrupulous agent preying on a talented, young and financially naive athlete (Wilde, 1992). NCAA rules provide that an individual will lose eligibility for intercollegiate competition if the student-athlete contracts orally or in writing to be represented by an sport agent, or if the student-athlete receives any type of payment or promise of payment (*NCAA Manual*, 1995-96, art. 12.3.1).

In a further attempt to prevent agents from "preying" on student-athletes, the NCAA established a voluntary player-agent registration program in 1984 (Rypma, 1990). The program required disclosure of an agent's education and background, and imposed notification requirements upon the agent prior to contact with a student-athlete (Rypma, 1990). The program's primary flaw, however, was its voluntariness. The NCAA could assume no jurisdiction over an sport agent. Agents prone to abuse would simply not register, and the NCAA was powerless to monitor, regulate or sanction their activities. Further, as with most regulatory efforts aimed at sport agents, the program also failed to require agents to meet any particular competency qualifications prior to registration. Citing these limitations, the NCAA discontinued its program in 1989 (Rypma, 1990).

The NCAA has not, however, ceased all efforts to control the unscrupulous activities of agents. The Association has drafted prototype legislation for use by states considering the adoption of sport agent legislation (Cosgrove, 1990). In addition, in 1988 the NCAA began requiring student-athletes, participating in the Division I men's basketball tournament and in sanctioned college football bowl games, to sign an affidavit certifying that the athlete has not signed with an agent. This practice continues to date (Cosgrove, 1990). Further, the NCAA authorizes and encourages its member institutions to establish professional sports counseling panels for student-athletes. Under NCAA rules (*NCAA Manual*, 1995-96, art. 12.3.4) these panels are given authority to assist student-athletes with career choices and in securing competent agent representation. Such panels may review a professional sports contract, assist an athlete in deciding whether to stay in college or to seek a professional career by ascertaining the athlete's professional market value, and provide advice and guidance in the selection of a reputable agent.

Professional Team Sport Players' Associations. In 1983, the National Football League Players' Association (NFLPA) became the first professional team sport players' union to initiate an player-agent certification program (Rypma, 1990). The 1982 collective bargaining agreement between the NFL and NFLPA had reserved the exclusive right for the NFLPA or "its agent" to negotiate individual NFL player contracts. The 1983 program was established to certify agents as "NFLPA Contract Advisors," who, under the program, are required to use a standard representation agreement, to comply with certain limits on compensation for contractual negotiations, and attend periodic training seminars (Ring, 1987). Fines, suspensions, and/or revocations of licenses are among the penalties imposed for noncompliance.

Despite the program's intent to protect athletes from agent incompetence and corruption, several problems persisted. First, the program, in its original form, did not address the corruption occurring in intercollegiate athletics. Until recently, the NFLPA certification program did not apply to regulate agents negotiating a player's first contract with the league (Dunn, 1988). Only agents representing current NFL players were covered. Alerted to the potential for agent abuse of athletes who had yet to sign their first NFL contract, the program was amended in 1989 to include agents negotiating on behalf of these prospective players (Shropshire, 1989). Second, the plan is limited in scope. The plan regulates only "contract advisors" of NFL players, and its rules prohibit the charging of excessive fees for only contract negotiation and money-handling services. Agents providing other services can charge excessive fees, and effectively evade the plan's restrictions (Dunn, 1988). Third, the plan is devoid of any specific criteria for granting or denying agent certification. The NFLPA's program, not unlike the plans implemented by other players' unions, expects applicants to disclose their educational, professional, and employment background, yet does not require any minimum levels of training, education, skill, or knowledge as a condition for representing professional athletes (Rypma, 1990). The only criteria, in fact, to deny certification concern misconduct such as fraud, embezzlement, and theft (Shropshire, 1989).

In 1986, the National Basketball Players' Association (NBPA) adopted regulations governing player agents. These regulations loosely parallel the NFLPA program. Certified agents are required to use a standard representation agreement and to comply with certain limits on compensation for contractual negotiations (Rypma, 1990). Like the NFLPA plan, fines, suspensions, and/or revocations of licenses are among the disciplinary measures imposed for noncompliance. One key distinction between the NBPA and NFLPA schemes, until recently, was the inclusion within the NBPA program of agents negotiating a contract for a player who has yet to sign with an NBA team (Dunn, 1988).

The Major League Baseball Players' Association (MLBPA) adopted its agent certification plan in its 1985 labor agreement, but delayed implementation of the plan until 1988 (Rypma, 1990). Not surprisingly, the plan is similar to its football and basketball counterparts. One major distinction, however, is that the MLBPA plan does not restrict the fees chargeable by an agent for service rendered. The agent, however, is required to provide an itemized statement of fees to the MLBPA (Dunn, 1988).

At the time of this writing, the National Hockey League Players' Association had no agent certification program, but was developing plans to implement a program in the near future.

The Association of Representatives of Professional Athletes (ARPA). The ARPA was founded in 1978 to provide competent and honest representation to professional athletes. It remains the only self-regulating organization within the sport-agent profession. The ARPA's Code of Ethics attempts to ensure integrity, competence, dignity, management responsibility, and confidentiality from agents in the representation of their clients (Dunn, 1988). Yet, notwithstanding its laudable intentions, the ARPA has done little to address the problems of agent incompetence and corruption. Since the ARPA cannot compel agents to join the organization, it is unlikely that agents prone to abuse or corruption will be interested in associating themselves with the ARPA. In addition, even for members of the ARPA, there is no enforcement mechanism for violators of its Code of Ethics (Dunn, 1988).

The American Bar Association (ABA). The ABA's Code of Professional Responsibility has some relevance here. The ABA Code proposes standards of integrity and conduct for all attorneys, and has been adopted in some form or another by many state bar associations. The obvious deficiency here is that while many sport agents are attorneys, the Code has no effect on agents who are not lawyers (Shropshire, 1989).

Recent Developments

Florida Sport Agent Prosecution. The state of Florida is becoming more and more vigilant in enforcing its athlete agent regulations—witness the 1995 prosecution of Joel Segal who received a $3500 fine and probation for violating the Florida statute's prohibition against offering student athletes inducements to sign representation contracts prior to the expiration of their collegiate eligibility (Mott, 1995).

In addition, Florida has amended its athlete agent legislation to require, effective October 1, 1995, all agents registering under the statute to pass an examination on Florida law and NCAA bylaws regulating agents. The sport agent competency exam is the first of its kind to be implemented under a state legislative scheme. The amended legislation also requires agents to complete 20 hours of continuing education within every two year period, mandates the posting of a $15,000 surety bond, enhances the state's enforcement rights, increases the registration fees, and escalates the penalties for noncompliance with legislative requirements (Curtis, 1995).

Sports Agent Settles Civil Suit with USC.   In October 1995, sports agent Robert Caron settled a civil suit, brought against him by the University of Southern California, by agreeing to pay the university $50,000 in damages and to abide by a permanent injunction forbidding him to induce USC athletes to enter into representation contracts with him prior to the expiration of their college eligibility. The suit, believed to be one of the first of its kind, alleged that Caron had intentionally interfered with the contractual relationship between the university and three of its football players, by inducing the athletes to breach their scholarship contracts and lose their collegiate eligibility by accepting gifts and enticements provided by Caron in his effort to secure their future representation (*NCAA News*, October 30, 1995).

Special NCAA Committee Announced.   During his state-of-the-association address at the opening of the NCAA's 1996 Annual Convention, executive director Cedric Dempsey announced that the NCAA is preparing to strike out at unscrupulous agents. Dempsey outlined the creation of a special committee formed to study the issue and present legislative proposals for the January 1997 Convention. The committee's membership will include representatives from the NCAA's enforcement staff, professional leagues, professional players' associations, high schools and state legislatures (Wieberg, 1996). Possible legislative proposals already being discussed to curb unscrupulous sport agent activity include more stringent sanctions against a student-athlete for violating NCAA rules by accepting inducements or signing a representation contract prior to the expiration of collegiate eligibility. Inserting "pay-back" clauses into a student-athlete's financial aid agreement, for example, could require the player to pay back the value of his scholarship if he is found to have lost his eligibility through signing with an agent (Wieberg, 1995).

References

A. Cases
U.S. v. Walters and Bloom, 711 F. Supp. 1435 (N.D. Ill. 1989), reversed and remanded, 913 F.2d 388 (7th Cir. 1990).
U.S. v. Walters, 997 F.2d 1219 (7th Cir. 1993).

B. Publications
Cosgrove, David B. (1990). A Survey of State Sport Agent Legislation: Origins And Effects. 16 *Journal of College and University Law* 433-448.
Curtis, Ted. (1995). The Sunshine State's Tough New Law: Florida Enacts the Nation's Strictest Athlete Agent Regulation. 1 *The Sports Lawyer* 1, 7-8.
Dow, T. Andrew. (1990). Out of Bounds: Time to Revamp Texas Sports Agent Legislation. 43 *Southwestern Law Journal* 1091-1118.
Dunn, David Lawrence. (1988). Regulation of Sports Agents: Since at First It Hasn't Succeeded, Try Federal Legislation. 39 *The Hastings Law Journal* 1031-1078.
Goodman, Mark C. (1990). The Federal Mail Fraud Statute: The Government's Colt 45 Renders Norby Walters and Lloyd Bloom Agents of Misfortune. 10 *Loyola Entertainment Law Journal* 315-333.

Hagwell, Stephen R. & Mott, Ronald D. (1995). Agents Confirm Problems Run Deep. *NCAA News.* September 25, 1995, 1, 13.

Mott, Ronald D. & Hagwell, Stephen R. (1995). Concern Mounts Over Sports Agents' Influence. *NCAA News.* September 18, 1995, 1, 14.

Narayanan, Ash. (1990). Criminal Liability of Sports Agents: It Is Time to Reline the Playing Field. 24 *Loyola of Los Angeles Law Review* 273-316.

Powers, Alec. (1994). The Need to Regulate Sports Agents. 4 *Seton Hall Journal of Sport Law* 253-276.

Ring, Bart Ivan. (1987). An Analysis of Athlete Agent Certification and Regulation: New Incentives with Old Problems. 7 *Loyola Entertainment Law Journal* 321-335.

Rodgers, J. Mark. (1988-89). States Revamp Defense Against Agents. 6 *The Sports Lawyer* 1-7.

———. (1990). Update: 19 States Target Sports Agents. 8 *The Sports Lawyer* 1-5.

Rypma, Curtis D. (1990). Sports Agents Representing Athletes: The Need for Comprehensive State Legislation. 24 *Valparaiso University Law Review* 481-519.

Shropshire, Kenneth L. (1989). Athlete Agent Regulation: Proposed Legislative Revisions and the Need for Reforms Beyond Legislation. 8 *Cardozo Arts & Entertainment Law Journal* 85-112.

Wieberg, Steve. (1995). Misconduct by Agents Under Growing Scrutiny. *USA Today.* October 5, 1995, 10C.

———. (1996). NCAA Will Push To Regulate Agents. *USA Today.* January 8, 1996, 11C.

Wilde, T. Jesse. (1992). The Regulation of Sport Agents. 2 *Journal of Legal Aspects of Sport*, 18-29.

———. (1995). Sports Agent Settles Lawsuit with Southern California. *NCAA News.* October 30, 1995, 24.

C. Legislation and Regulations

California Athlete Agencies Act of 1981. Cal. Lab. Code §§ 1500-1547 (1981).

Florida Athlete Agents Act of 1988. Fla. Stat. Ann. §§ 468.451-468.457 (1988).

Indiana Failure to Disclose Recruitment Act of 1988. Ind. Cod. Ann. § 35-46-4 (1988).

Kentucky Athlete Agents Act of 1988. Ky. Rev. Stat. Ann. § 518.010 (1988).

Minnesota Athlete Agents Act of 1988. 1988 Minn. Laws 701 §§ 1-2 (1988).

NCAA Manual, 1995-96, art. 12.3.1 and 12.3.4.

Nevada Athlete Agents Act of 1989. 1989 Nev. Legis. Serv. 382 §§ 1-11.

Tennessee Athlete Agents Act of 1988. 1988 Tenn. Pub. Acts 853 §§ 1-12.

Texas Athlete Agent Act of 1987. Tex. Rev. Civ. Stat. Ann. art. 8871 §§ 1-11. (Vernon Supp. 1990).

U.S. Constitution art. I, § 8, cl. 3.

5.70

Workmen's Compensation Legislation

John T. Wolohan
Iowa State University

Under common law, when an employee was injured on the job, there was a good chance the injuries would go uncompensated due to the doctrines of assumption of risk, contributory negligence and the fellow servant rule (Larson, 1992). Those injured workers who could overcome the above defenses, usually faced a series of other problems before they received any compensation for their injuries. First, the injured workers, faced with little or no income, were under enormous financial pressure to settle their claim. The injured worker therefore usually received much less then the true value of their claim in order to support themselves and their families. Second, even if the injured employee was able to withstand the financial pressure and could afford to litigate the claim, the employer was often able to use the court system to his or her advantage and delay paying the employee any compensation. Finally, if the injured worker was lucky enough to recover his or her damages, the award was usually reduced by hefty attorney fees (Prosser & Keeton, 1984).

In an effort to protect injured workers and do away with the injustice of the common law system, states began to enact workmen's compensation legislation modeled after the German and English systems (Larson, 1992). The first state to enact workmen's compensation was New York in 1910 (Larson, 1992). By 1949, every state in the country had enacted some form of workmen's compensation law. The workmen's compensation legislation, which is different in every state, provide benefits, including lost wages, usually around one-half to two-thirds of the employee's weekly wages, and medical care, to an employee who is injured or killed in the course of employment, regardless of fault (Larson, 1992). "The right to compensation benefits depends on one simple test: Was there a work connected injury?" (Larson, 1992). In exchange for this protection, the injured worker agrees to forego any tort claim he or she might have against the employer (Larson, 1992).

Workmen's compensation is therefore a form of strict liability. It does not matter whether the injury was caused by the employee's negligence or pure accident, *all the employee has to show is that he or she was injured in the course of employment* (Larson, 1992). As a result, the injured worker receives quick financial assistance with minimal interruption in his or her life.

■ ■ ■ ■

Representative Case

RENSING v. INDIANA STATE UNIVERSITY BOARD OF TRUSTEES

Supreme Court of Indiana

444 N.E.2d 1170 (1983)

OPINION:

This case is before this Court upon the petition to transfer of defendant-appellee, Indiana State University Board of Trustees (Trustees). The plaintiff-appellant, Fred W. Rensing, was a varsity football player at Indiana State University who suffered an injury on April 24, 1976, during the team's spring football practice which left him a quadriplegic. Rensing filed a claim with the Industrial Board of Indiana (Industrial Board) seeking recovery under workmen's compensation for permanent total disability as well as medical and hospital expenses incurred due to the injury. The Industrial Board rejected his claim finding that an employer-employee relationship did not exist between Rensing and the Trustees and, therefore, he was not entitled to benefits under the Workmen's Compensation Act, Ind. Code § 22-3-1-1 et seq. (Burns 1974). The Court of Appeals, Fourth District, reversed the decision of the Industrial Board on the basis that Rensing was an "employee" for pay within the meaning of the statute and his employment by the Trustees was also within the coverage of the statute.

We now grant transfer and reverse. The opinion and decision of the Court of Appeals are hereby vacated, and plaintiff's petition to transfer is granted. The decision of the Full Industrial Board is reinstated.

The facts established before the Industrial Board were summarized by the Court of Appeals:

The undisputed testimony reveals the Trustees, through their agent Thomas Harp (the University's Head Football Coach), on February 4, 1974 offered Rensing a scholarship or "educational grant" to play football at the University. In essence, the financial aid agreement, which was renewable each year for a total of four years provided that in return for Rensing's active participation in football competition he would receive free tuition, room, board, laboratory fees, a book allowance, tutoring and a limited number of football tickets per game for family and friends. The "agreement" provided, inter alia, the aid would continue even if Rensing suf-

fered an injury during supervised play which would make it inadvisable, in the opinion of the doctor-director of the student health service, "to continue to participate," although in that event the University would require other assistance to the extent of his ability.

The Trustees extended this scholarship to Rensing for the 1974-75 academic year in the form of a 'Tender of Financial Assistance.' Rensing accepted the Trustees' first tender and signed it (as did his parents) on April 29, 1974. At the end of Rensing's first academic year the Trustees extended a second "Tender of Financial Assistance" for the 1975-76 academic year, which tender was substantially the same as the first and provided the same financial assistance to Rensing for his continued participation in the University's football program. Rensing and his father signed this second tender on June 24, 1975. It is not contested the monetary value of this assistance to Rensing for the 1975-76 academic year was $2,374, and that the "scholarship" was in effect when Rensing's injuries occurred.

• • •

Rensing testified he suffered a knee injury during his first year (1974-75) of competition which prevented him from actively participating in the football program, during which time he continued to receive his scholarship as well as free treatment for his knee injury. The only requirement imposed by the Trustees (through Coach Harp) upon Rensing was attendance at his classes and reporting daily to the football stadium for free whirlpool and ultrasonic treatments for his injured knee.

• • •

As noted above, the financial aid agreement provided that in the event of an injury of such severity that it prevented continued athletic participation, "Indiana State University will ask you to assist in the conduct of the athletic program within the limits of your physical capabilities" in order to continue receiving aid. The sole assistance actually asked of Rensing was to entertain prospective football recruits when they visited the University's Terre Haute campus.

During the 1975 football season, Rensing participated on the University's football team. In the spring of 1976 he partook in the team's annual three week spring practice when, on April 24, he was injured while he tackled a teammate during a punting drill.

• • •

The specific injury suffered by Rensing was a fractured dislocation of the cervical spine at the level of 4-5 vertebrae. Rensing's initial treatment consisted of traction and eventually a spinal fusion. During this period he developed pneumonia for which he had to have a tracheostomy. Eventually, Rensing was transferred to the Rehabilitation Department of the Barnes Hospital complex in St. Louis. According to Rensing's doctor at Barnes Hospital, one Franz U. Steinberg, Rensing's paralysis was caused by the April 24, 1976 football injury leaving him 95-100 percent disabled. (Rensing v. Indiana State University Board of Trustees, supra, at pp. 80-82 (footnotes omitted))

Rensing's appeal to the Industrial Board was originally heard by a Hearing Member who found that Rensing had "failed to sustain his burden in establishing the necessary relationship of employer and employee within the meaning of the Indiana Workmen's Compensation Act," and rejected his claim. Id. at p. 83. The Full Industrial Board adopted the Hearing Member's findings and decision; then this decision was reversed by the Court of Appeals.

In this petition to transfer, the Trustees argue that there was no contract of hire in this case and that a student who accepts an athletic "grant-in-aid" from the University does not become an "employee" of the University within the definition of "employee" under the Workmen's Compensation Act, Ind. Code § 22-3-6-1(b), (Burns Supp. 1982). On the other hand, Rensing maintains that his agreement to play football in return for financial assistance did amount to a contract of employment.

• • •

Here, the facts concerning the injury are undisputed. The contested issue is whether the requisite employer-employee relationship existed between Rensing and the Trustees so as to bring him under the coverage of our Workmen's Compensation Act. Both the Industrial Board and the Court of Appeals correctly noted that the work-

men's compensation laws are to be liberally construed. Prater v. Indiana Briquetting Corp., (1969) 253 Ind. 83, 251 N.E. 2d 810. With this proposition as a starting point, the specific facts of this case must be analyzed to determine whether Rensing and the Trustees come within the definitions of "employee" and "employer" found in the statute, and specifically whether there did exist a contract of employment. Ind. Code § 22-3-6-1, supra, defines the terms "employee" and "employer" as follows:

(a) "Employer" includes the state and any political subdivision, any municipal corporation within the state, any individual, firm, association or corporation or the receiver or trustee of the same, or the legal representatives of a deceased person, using the services of another for pay.

(b) The term "employee" means every person, including a minor, in the service of another, under any contract of hire or apprenticeship, written or implied, except one whose employment is both casual and not in the usual course of the trade, business, occupation or profession of the employer.

The Court of Appeals found that there was enough evidence in the instant case to support a finding that a contract of employment did exist here. We disagree.

It is clear that while a determination of the existence of an employee-employer relationship is a complex matter involving many factors, the primary consideration is that there was an intent that a contract of employment, either express or implied, did exist. In other words, there must be a mutual belief that an employer-employee relationship did exist. . . . It is evident from the documents which formed the agreement in this case that there was no intent to enter into an employee-employer relationship at the time the parties entered into the agreement.

In this case, the National Collegiate Athletic Association's (NCAA) constitution and bylaws were incorporated by reference into the agreements. A fundamental policy of the NCAA, which is stated in its constitution, is that intercollegiate sports are viewed as part of the educational system and are clearly distinguished from the professional sports business. The NCAA has strict rules against "taking pay" for sports or sporting activities. Any student who does accept pay is ineligible for further play at an NCAA member school in the sport for which he takes pay. Furthermore, an institution cannot, in any way, condition financial aid on a student's ability as an athlete. NCAA Constitution, Sec. 3-1-(a)-(1); Sec. 3-1-(g)-(2). The fundamental concerns behind the policies of the NCAA are that intercollegiate athletics must be maintained as a part of the educational program and student-athletes are integral parts of the institution's student body. An athlete receiving financial aid is still first and foremost a student. All of these NCAA requirements designed to prohibit student-athletes from receiving pay for participation in their sport were incorporated into the financial aid agreements Rensing and his parents signed.

Furthermore, there is evidence that the financial aid which Rensing received was not considered by the parties involved to be pay or income. Rensing was given free tuition, room, board, laboratory fees and a book allowance. These benefits were not considered to be "pay" by the University or by the NCAA since they did not affect Rensing's or the University's eligibility status under NCAA rules. Rensing did not consider the benefits as income as he did not report them for income tax purposes. The Internal Revenue Service has ruled that scholarship recipients are not taxed on their scholarship proceeds and there is no distinction made between athletic and academic scholarships. Rev. Rul. 77-263, 1977-31 I.R.B. 8.

As far as scholarships are concerned, we find that our Indiana General Assembly clearly has recognized a distinction between the power to award financial aid to students and the power to hire employees since the former power was specifically granted to the Boards of Trustees of state educational institutions with the specific limitation that the award be reasonably related to the educational purposes and objectives of the institution and in the best interests of the institution and the state. Ind. Code § 20-12-1-2(h) (Burns 1975).

Furthermore, we find that Ind. Code § 22-4-6-2 (Burns 1974) is not applicable to scholarship benefits. In that statute, which deals with contributions by employers to unemployment insurance, employers are directed to include "all individuals attending an established school . . . who, in lieu of remuneration for such services, receive either meals, lodging, books, tuition or other education facilities." Here, Rensing was not working at a regular job for the University. The scholarship benefits he received were not given him in lieu of pay for remuneration for his services in playing football any more than academic scholarship benefits were given to other students for their high scores on tests or class assignments. Rather, in both cases, the students received benefits based upon their past demonstrated ability in various areas to enable them to pursue opportunities for higher education as well as to further progress in their own fields of endeavor.

Scholarships are given to students in a wide range of artistic, academic and athletic areas. None of these recipients is covered under Ind. Code § 22-4-6-2, supra, unless the student holds a regular job for the institution in addition to the scholarship. The statute would apply to students who work for the University and perform services not integrally connected with the institution's educational program and for which, if the student were not available, the University would have to hire outsiders, e.g., workers in the laundry, bookstore, etc. Scholarship recipients are considered to be students seeking advanced educational opportunities and are not considered to be professional athletes, musicians or artists employed by the University for their skills in their respective areas.

In addition to finding that the University, the NCAA, the IRS and Rensing, himself, did not consider the scholarship benefits to be income, we also agree with Judge Young's conclusion that Rensing was not "in the service of" the University. As Judge Young stated:

> Furthermore, I do not believe that Rensing was "in the service of" the Trustees. Rensing's participation in football may well have benefited the university in a very general way. That does not mean that Rensing was in the service of the Trustees. If a student wins a Rhodes scholarship or if the debate team wins a national award that undoubtedly benefits the school, but does not mean that the student and the team are in the service of the school. Rensing performed no duties that would place him in the service of the university. (Rensing v. Indiana State University, supra, at 90)

• • •

Courts in other jurisdictions have generally found that such individuals as student athletes, student leaders in student government associations and student resident-hall assistants are not "employees" for purposes of workmen's compensation laws unless they are also employed in a university job in addition to receiving scholarship benefits.

• • •

All of the above facts show that in this case, Rensing did not receive "pay" for playing football at the University within the meaning of the Workmen's Compensation Act; therefore, an essential element of the employer-employee relationship was missing in addition to the lack of intent. Furthermore, under the applicable rules of the NCAA, Rensing's benefits could not be reduced or withdrawn because of his athletic ability or his contribution to the team's success. Thus, the ordinary employer's right to discharge on the basis of performance was also missing. While there was an agreement between Rensing and the Trustees which established certain obligations for both parties, the agreement was not a contract of employment. Since at least three important factors indicative of an employee-employer relationship are absent in this case, we find it is not necessary to consider other factors which may or may not be present.

We find that the evidence here shows that Rensing enrolled at Indiana State University as a full-time student seeking advanced educational opportunities. He was not considered to be a professional athlete who was being paid for his athletic ability. In fact, the benefits Rensing received were subject to strict regulations by the NCAA which were designed to protect his amateur status. Rensing held no other job with the University and therefore cannot be considered an "employee" of the University within the meaning of the Workmen's Compensation Act.

It is our conclusion of law, under the facts here, including all rules and regulations of the University and the NCAA governing student athletes, that the appellant shall be considered only as a student athlete and not as an employee within the meaning of the Workmen's Compensation Act. Accordingly, we find that there is substantial evidence to support the finding of the Industrial Board that there was no employee-employer relationship between Rensing and the Trustees, and their finding must be upheld.

For all of the foregoing reasons, transfer is granted; the opinion of the Court of Appeals is vacated and the Industrial Board is in all things affirmed.

The judgment and determination of the Industrial Board are affirmed.

■ ■ ■ ■

Fundamental Concepts

The basic policy behind the workmen's compensation system is that "the cost of the product should bear the blood of the worker" (Prosser & Keeton, 1984). In other words, since the employer is required by the state to compensate the employee through private insurance, state funded insurance or self-insurance any damages suffered by an employee. The employer should treat the cost of the injuries and workmen's compensation insurance as part of the cost of production. These extra costs are then added to the cost of production and passed on to the consumer.

While every state has its own workmen's compensation laws, there are two elements that every injured employee must satisfy before he or she can recover workmen's compensation benefits. The first element the person must show is that he or she was an employee of the organization. An employee is defined as any person in the service of another under any contract of hire. In reviewing the relationship between an individual and sports organization to determine if he or she was in fact an employee, the Courts have used an "economic reality test" (*Coleman v. Western Michigan Univ.*, 1983). Under the economic reality test, the court examined the following factors to determine whether there existed an expressed or implied contract for hire:

1. Does the employer have the right to control or dictate the activities of the proposed employee;
2. Does the employer have the right to discipline or fire the proposed employee;
3. The payment of "wages" and, particularly, the extent to which the proposed employee is dependent upon the payment of wages or other benefits for his daily living expenses;
4. Whether the task performed by the proposed employee was "an integral part" of the proposed employer's business (*Coleman v. Western Michigan Univ.* at 225).

In *Coleman v. Western Michigan Univ.* (1983), the Court of Appeals of Michigan citing the Rensing decision also concluded that scholarship athletes are not employees within the meaning of the workmen's compensation statute (at 228). In particular, the Court found that Coleman could only satisfy the third factor of the "economic reality test," that his scholarship did constitute wages. As far as the other factors, the court found that the university's right to control and discipline Coleman required by the first two factors was substantially limited (at 226). In considering the fourth factor, the court held "that the primary function of the defendant university was to provide academic education rather than conduct a football program" (at 226). The term "integral," the court held, suggests that the task performed by the employee is essential for the employer to conduct his business. The "integral part" of the university is not football, the court said, but education and research (at 227).

The second element every employee must establish before he or she can collect workmen's compensation is that the injury suffered by the employee must have occurred in the course of his or her employment.

Sport managers must be conscious of workmen's compensation in the following areas: staff employees, volunteers and scholarship athletes. With staff employees, it is clear that the sport manager should follow the local laws governing workmen's compensation insurance. How volunteers and scholarship athletes are classified is much more difficult. For example, there are a number of states, including California, Oregon, Minnesota and Tennessee, which allow "volunteers" to be covered under the employer's workmen's compensation plan (Wolohan & Wong, 1996).

Although covering "volunteers" under your workmen's compensation plan may seem like a less attractive option, considering the up front expense for the school of paying for workmen's compensation insurance, there are a number of important benefits from this option. First, by covering "volunteers" under your workmen's compensation plan, if a volunteer is ever injuried, you can save you organization both time and money by avoiding a negligence lawsuit. Second, by covering "volunteers" under your workmen's compensation plan, you save your school from any bad publicity that a lawsuit would generate. Finally, you also protect your volunteers from financial hardship by providing them benefits under workmen's compensation (Wolohan & Wong, 1996).

As illustrated by *Rensing v. Indiana State University Board of Trustees* the difficult workmen's compensation cases involve scholarship athletes. For example, in most states, workmen's compensation insurance rates are determined by actuarial tables that take into account the number of accidents and claims for that particular group of employees. If athletes were suddenly added into the group of school employees, the number of injuries and claims of the group would rise substantially. This would make it difficult, if not impossible, for colleges and universities to find an insurance company willing to insure them. Even if the school could find an insurance company, the increased exposure would require the insurance company to raise rates. Faced with higher insurance rates and/or the potential liability of self insuring, many schools will be forced to reevaluate whether the increased cost and exposure is worth having an athletic program.

Other possible consequences of considering scholarship athletes as paid employees include:

Additional Workmen's Compensation Claims. If scholarship athletes were considered employees of their school, there could be an increase in the number of workmen's compensation claims filed and benefits paid (Wolohan, 1994).

Tax Effect on School. If scholarship athletes are considered employees of their school, there are be some interesting tax questions for not only colleges or universities but for scholarship athletes as well. Does the scholarship athlete now have to pay taxes on the value of his or her scholarship? Also, will schools now be required to pay FICA and Medicare tax on the student's income? If so, how are the taxes to be paid? (Wolohan, 1994).

Employee Benefits. If scholarship athletes are considered employees of their school, are scholarship athletes eligible for employee benefits? Besides tuition, room, board and books, are scholarship athletes now going to be eligible for life, medical, and dental insurance? How about the school's employee retirement plan—would scholarship athletes be eligible? (Wolohan, 1994).

Non-Scholarship Athletes. Even if scholarship athletes are considered employees of their school, athletes who do not receive an athletic scholarship will still not be covered by workmen's compensation. Since these athletes receive no compensation, they have no contractual relationship with the university to compete in athletics. Therefore, the athlete can never be deemed employees. (Wolohan, 1994)

Recent Developments

Kent Waldrep v. Texas Christian University

In March 1993, in a ruling that could change college athletics, the Texas Workmen's Compensation Commission ruled that former Texas Christian University (TCU) football player Kent Waldrep was an employee of TCU when he was paralyzed during a football game in 1974 (*NCAA News*, March 31, 1993).

At the time of his injury, Kent Waldrep was in his third year at TCU. However, due to his injury Waldrep was no longer able to satisfy his athletic commitment to the University, and was forced to leave the university after TCU withdrew his scholarship for the next school year (Wolohan, 1993). In May 1991, having incurred an estimated $500,000 in medical expenses, Waldrep filed a workmen's compensation claim with the Texas Workmen's Compensation Commission. In his claim Waldrep argued that since his scholarship to TCU was directly related to his performance on the athletic field he should be considered an employee of TCU. As an employee, Waldrep argued that he is entitled to workmen's compensation benefits for any injuries he received in the course of his employment.

The Texas Workmen's Compensation Commission agreed with Waldrep and held that he was an employee of TCU and that his injury occurred in the course of that employment. The Commission ruled Waldrep was entitled to workmen's compensation benefits covering his past and future medical expenses plus a weekly salary, retroactive to 1974, for the rest of his life. On March 25, 1993, the same day the Commission made its ruling, attorneys for the Texas Employers' Insurance Association filed a notice of appeal with the Travis County District Court in Austin, Texas (Flint v. Waldrep, cause # 93-03451, Travis County District Court, filed March 1993).

State Legislation Covering College and Professional Athletes

In *Graczyk v. Workers' Compensation Appeals Board*, the California Court of Appeals denied workmen's compensation benefits to Ricky Graczyk after he sustained head, neck and spine injuries while playing football for California State University, Fullerton.

The Appellate Court, overturning the decision of the California Workers' Compensation Appeals Board, ruled that it was the intent of the state legislature to exclude Graczyk, and all scholarship athletes, from receiving workmen's compensation benefits for injuries received on the playing field (*Graczyk* at 499). The court points out that the California State Legislature specifically amended the state's workmen's compensation statute to exclude "any person, other than a regular employee, participating in sports or athletics who receives no compensation for such participation other than the use of athletic equipment, uniforms, transportation, travel, meals, lodging, or other expenses incidental thereto" from the definition of employee (at 499). The California State Legislature amended the statute further in 1981 when it specifically excluded "[a]ny student participating as an athlete in amateur sporting events sponsored by any public agency, public or private nonprofit college, university or school, who receives no remuneration for such participation other than the use of athletic equipment, uniforms, transportation, travel, meals, lodging, scholarships, grants in aid, and other expenses" from the definition of employee (at 499, fn. 3.) (West's Ann.Cal.Labor Code §3353 (k)). Hawaii, New York and other states have followed California's example of expressly excluding scholarship athletes from workmen's compensation benefits.

Another area where states have amended their workmen's compensation statutes is to exclude professional athletes. In *Tookes v. Florida State University*, Claim No. 266-39-0855, a basketball player at Florida State University suffered a knee injury during the 1981-82 season which required him to sit out most of the season. As a result of his injury, Tookes filed a workmen's compensation claim for lost wages and medical expenses. Tookes argued that he was an employee of the University, due to his athletic scholarship, and therefore entitled to workmen's compensation benefits (Wong, 1988). The Florida Department of Labor and Employment Security and Industrial Claims Judge, however, disagreed. The judge determined that there was no employer-employee relationship between Tookes and the University. Even if there was an employer-employee relationship between Tookes and the University, the judge held that Tookes would still be ineligible for benefits. If Tookes was employed by the University to play basketball, under Florida law he would be considered a professional athlete and therefore a member of a class specifically excluded under the Florida Workers Compensation Statute (Wong, 1988). Besides Florida, there are at least five other states that restrict workmen's compensation benefits to professional athletes or have considered amending their state workmen's compensation statutes to exclude professional athletes (Wolohan, 1994).

NCAA Catastrophic Insurance Policy

One of the reasons scholarship athletes have sought workmen's compensation benefits in the past is to recover out of pocket medical expenses. Although, most schools will pay the medical expenses of injured athletes, there usually is a limit to their generosity. In fact, it is not uncommon for a school to stop paying an injured athlete's medical and other bills. This is especially true when the injury is permanently disabling and the injured athlete requires prolonged medical care.

In an effort to alleviate such hardships, and perhaps to prevent future court challenges on the status of scholarship athletes, the NCAA in August 1991 implemented a Catastrophic Insurance Plan covering every student who participates in college athletics. The NCAA's Catastrophic Insurance Plan, which covers not only student athletes, but also student coaches, student managers, student trainers and cheerleaders. The NCAA's Catastrophic Insurance Plan automatically insures every college athlete who participates in NCAA sports against catastrophic injuries. The NCAA's plan is similar to workmen's compensation in that it provides medical, dental and rehabilitation expenses, plus lifetime disability payments to students who are catastrophically injured, regardless of fault. The plan also includes $10,000 for burial expenses in the case an athlete was to die during practice or a game.

The NCAA plan is more attractive than workmen's compensation in a number of ways. First, scholarship athletes can collect benefits without litigating the issue of whether or not the athlete is an employee of the college or university. Second, the NCAA's plan provides the athlete with benefits immediately, without time delays, litigation costs and the uncertainties involved in litigation. Finally, another benefit of the NCAA's plan is that it guarantees that catastrophically injured athletes will receive $60,000 toward the cost of completing their undergraduate degree. The money that is above and beyond any other benefits he or she receives is paid right to the school.

References

A. Cases
Coleman v. Western Michigan Univ., 125 Mich. App. 35, 336 N.W. 2d 224 (1983).
Graczyk v. Workers' Compensation Appeals Board, 153 Cal. App. 3d 997, 229 Cal. Rptr. 494 (1986).
Rensing v. Indiana State University Board of Trustees, 437 N.E. 2d 78 (1982).
Rensing v. Indiana State University Board of Trustees, 444 N.E. 2d 1170 (1983).
State Compensation Fund v. Industrial Commission, 135 Colo. 570, 314 P. 2d 288 (1957).
University of Denver v. Nemeth, 257 P.2d 423 (1953).
Van Horn v. Industrial Accident Commission, 219 Cal. App. 2d 457, 33 Cal. Rptr. 169 (1963).

B. Publications
Larson, A. (1992). *The Law of Workers Compensation.*
NCAA Catastrophic Injury Insurance Policy
Prosser, W.L., Keeton, W.P. (1984). *The Law of Torts*, (5th ed.).

Wolohan, J.T., edited by Wong, G.M. (June 1993). Ruling May Have Texas-Size Impact. *Athletic Business*, 17, 22-23.

Wolohan, J.T. (1994). Scholarship Athletes: Are they Employees or Students of the University? The Debate Continues. 4 *Journal of Legal Aspects of Sport* 46-58.

Wolohan, J.T., & Wong, G.M. (March 1996). Pitching In. Schools have Alternatives in Determining Volunteers' Legal Status. *Athletic Business*, 20, 10-14.

Wong, G. M. (1988). *Essentials of Amateur Sports Law*.

————. *NCAA News*, March 31, 1993, 1.

C. Selected Readings

Atkinson, M. (1983-84). Workers' Compensation and College Athletics: Should Universities be Responsible for Athletes Who Incur Serious Injuries? 10 *Journal of College & University Law* 197-208.

Rafferty, R.C. (1983). Rensing v. Indiana State University Board of Trustees: The Status of the College Scholarship Athlete—Employee or Student? 13 *Capital University Law Review* 87-103.

Whitmore, M. R. (1991). Denying Scholarship Athletes Worker's Compensation: Do Courts Punt Away A Statutory Right? 76 *Iowa Law Review* 763- 804.

5.81

Title VII of the Civil Rights Act of 1964

Lisa Pike Masteralexis
University of Massachusetts-Amherst

The Civil Rights Act of 1964 is a comprehensive federal law prohibiting discrimination in numerous settings, including elections, housing, federally funded programs, education, employment, and public facilities and accommodations. Title VII of the Civil Rights Act addresses employment discrimination and is the centerpiece of the act (Zimmer, Sullivan, and Richards, 1988). When it was enacted it represented the first comprehensive federal law prohibiting employment discrimination. Id. While an employer may distinguish between applicants or employees, Title VII places limits on an employer's criteria for making such distinctions. As a general rule, when the distinction is made on the basis of an employee's characteristics, such as race, gender, religion, or national origin, it will be considered discriminatory.

■ ■ ■ ■

Representative Case

MORRIS v. BIANCHINI

United States District Court, Eastern District of Virginia
1987 U.S. Dist. LEXIS 13888

OPINION: MEMORANDUM OPINION

Plaintiff, Linda Peden Morris ("Morris"), instituted this suit pursuant to Title VII of The Civil Rights Act of 1964, 42 U.S.C. § 2000e, et. seq., alleging that The Sporting Club ("Club") and its owners and directors refused to promote Morris to the position of athletic director of the Club on the basis of sex. The defendants answered the suit denying plaintiff's allegations and further alleging that the male selected to be athletic director was better qualified and the Club had a legitimate nondiscriminatory reason for the failure to promote Morris. For the reasons set forth below, judgment is entered in favor of the plaintiff on her complaint for sex discrimination.

• • •

I. Findings of Fact

After reviewing the pleadings, evidence, authorities, and argument of counsel, the court makes the following findings of fact:

Plaintiff, Linda Peden Morris, is a white female with a Bachelor of Science Degree in Recreation Administration from Radford University issued in May, 1983. She had received an Associate Degree in Recreation Management and Physical Activities in May, 1980, from Marymount College. She was employed by The Sporting Club located in McLean, Virginia, from March, 1983, until she resigned in January, 1985, when she learned that David

Tashiro was promoted to the position of athletic director of the Club.

The defendants, Richard Bianchini (the Club director), Jack Naiman (an owner), David Johnson (an owner), and Richard Erdenburger (director of the Cherry Creek Colorado Club), all participated in the employment decision to promote Mr. Tashiro over plaintiff.

The Sporting Club is a health fitness facility offering health services for members. Aerobics, running, biking, swimming, water aerobics, weight training and racquetball are services provided for members. The Club itself is divided into four major operating departments: maintenance, sales, the restaurant, and athletics.

Plaintiff commenced her employment with the Club in March, 1983, and was initially hired as an intern. The internship was required by Radford University in order to complete a Degree in Recreation Management. Plaintiff interned at all four departments of the Club. The internship lasted from March, 1983, to May, 1983. Plaintiff was a receptionist, aerobics instructor, and worked in weight training and water aerobics. She subsequently became a full-time employee at the Club in June, 1983. She received pay on an hourly basis without a formal title or job description. She worked in the nautilus area, taught aerobics and water aerobics classes, worked at the front desk, and also acted as a life guard.

In December 1983, plaintiff was hired as a weight training specialist at the Club, a supervisory position. She programmed club members, supervised a part-time volunteer staff of approximately twenty persons, conducted staff meetings, and was responsible for overseeing the maintenance of the nautilus equipment.

Between December, 1983, and May, 1984, plaintiff also served as water aerobics coordinator. She supervised the water aerobics program and pool area, recruited, trained and evaluated staff, and conducted three to five water aerobics classes a week.

In June, 1984, plaintiff was promoted to the position of fitness coordinator and received a salary increase of $5,000. The promotion was approved by the acting club director, Mitch Mayday, who worked in the Denver headquarters. In her new position, plaintiff organized and coordinated the aerobics program in addition to the water aerobics program.

Between June, 1984, and January, 1985, plaintiff also performed the duties of assistant athletic director. During this time, she acted for the athletic director in his absence.

When plaintiff was employed with the Club, Bruce Morris was the athletic director. She and Morris started dating in August, 1983, and the relationship became serious in July, 1984. Plaintiff and Bruce Morris married on April 5, 1986. It was well known at the Club that Bruce Morris and plaintiff were dating.

The personal relationship between plaintiff and Bruce Morris caused no problems with their working relationship. If anything, Morris was tougher on his wife-to-be than other employees in order to avoid any appearance of impropriety.

Plaintiff received a number of favorable evaluations from Bruce Morris which also had to be signed off by the Club director, Mayday. Plaintiff was believed to be a good instructor and performed her job very well.

On October 9, 1984, David Tashiro became employed by the Club as weight training specialist. Tashiro had previously been employed from 1983 to 1984 at the Nautilus Life Fitness Center in Herndon, Virginia. The defendants hired Tashiro in October, 1984, with the intention of promoting him to athletic director. He was paid a substantially higher salary than plaintiff had received as weight training specialist.

The Club was not happy with Bruce Morris's performance as athletic director. (Testimony of Bianchini, plaintiff, and Kenny). The feeling was that Bruce Morris lacked the leadership necessary for the position, and the members complained about his performance. He also lacked the motivation to be a good athletic director. Morris was subsequently fired on January 3, 1985. At that time, plaintiff sought to replace him as athletic director.

On December 1, 1984, defendant Richard Bianchini became the new Club director, replacing John F. Kenny. Bianchini had no prior experience in the recreation health field. Bianchini started his activities with the Club in November, 1984, and worked with the former director, Mr. Kenny, during a transitional period. In early December, 1984, Bianchini sent Tashiro to Denver to be interviewed for the position of athletic director. Based on Tashiro's Denver interview, Erdenburger recommended Tashiro for athletic director. (Plaintiff's Exhibit 29). On January 3, 1985, Bianchini fired Bruce Morris and then selected Tashiro to replace Morris as athletic director. In selecting Tashiro, Bianchini did not feel bound by the job description qualification requirements.

Previously, on September 14, 1983, the Club's board of directors met in Denver. It was determined that all new employees with supervisory positions should have a Bachelor's Degree in a health related field and that internships should be considered when making hiring decisions.

Tashiro worked as athletic director for less than five months and was fired in May, 1985. He did not live up to defendants' expectations. . . . Tashiro had no college degree nor did he possess a degree in a health related field. . . . Prior to being hired as athletic director, Tashiro's experience was limited primarily to the weight training field with nautilus machines. He had no experience in aerobics, water aerobics, or run, bike, and swim programs.

Prior to her resignation, plaintiff asked Bianchini why she had not been promoted to athletic director. He refused to respond to her inquiry.... Plaintiff resigned after learning that she had been passed over for promotion in favor of a less experienced male.

• • •

The defendants had a policy of not promoting women. Kaye Campbell-Forsman, assistant athletic director, was not promoted to the position of athletic director, although she was as well qualified as the man (Dan Cohen) who was ultimately hired. Kaye Campbell-Forsman was hired by the Club director, Greg Demko, in August, 1980. Her performance was outstanding.... In April, 1981, Demko was fired. Campbell-Forsman performed the duties of acting athletic director after Demko left. The Club refused to promote Campbell-Forsman from assistant athletic director to the position of athletic director. Forsman had applied twice to be athletic director and was passed over.

Instead of Campbell-Forsman, the defendants hired Dan Cohen, who lasted ten days in the position. Subsequently they hired Bruce Ponder as athletic director, again passing over Campbell-Forsman.... Campbell-Forsman asked why she was not selected as athletic director. She was told by Ed Martinez, an athletic director of the Denver Club, that the Club had a policy not to hire women for the McClean Club for the athletic director position.... [Yet, it] was defendants' stated policy to hire people from within the Club whenever possible.

On January 28, 1985, the plaintiff filed a timely charge with the Fairfax County Human Rights Commission. The parties have stipulated that the plaintiff has exhausted her administrative remedies.

On June 19, 1986, the plaintiff received Notice of Right to Sue from the Equal Opportunity Commission. She has timely filed this suit. (Plaintiff's Exhibit 28).

Plaintiff's lost wages total $12,444.84.

The defendants intentionally discriminated against the plaintiff on the basis of her sex and have engaged in a pattern of discrimination.

II

In McDonnell Douglas Corp. v. Green, 411 U.S. 792, 93 S. Ct. 1817, 36 L.Ed.2d 668, (1972), the Supreme Court set forth the allocation of proof in a disparate treatment Title VII case. Initially, the plaintiff bears the burden of establishing a prima facie case of discrimination by a preponderance of the evidence. The plaintiff may meet this burden by showing:

(i) that he belongs to a [protected] minority; (ii) that he applied and was qualified for a job for which the employer was seeking applicants; (iii) that, despite his qualification, he was rejected; and (iv) that, after his rejection, the post remained open and the employer continued to seek applicants from persons of complainant's qualifications.

By establishing a prima facie case, the plaintiff creates a rebuttable presumption of unlawful discrimination.... After the plaintiff has established a prima facie case, the burden of production shifts to the defendant "to articulate some legitimate, nondiscriminatory reason for the employee's rejection." McDonnell Douglas Corp. v. Green, 93 S. Ct. at 1824. The defendant need only produce evidence sufficient to raise a genuine issue of fact with respect to the alleged discrimination; the defendant need not produce evidence which persuades the trier of fact that the employment action was lawful. Burdine, 101 S. Ct. at 1094. The ultimate burden of persuading the trier of fact that the defendant intentionally discriminated against the plaintiff remains at all times with the plaintiff. Burdine, 101 S. Ct. at 1094-95. The plaintiff may carry this burden by persuading the trier of fact by the preponderance of the evidence that the articulated reasons for the employment decision are pretextual. Burdine, 101 S. Ct. at 1095.

In a pattern or practice case, "the initial burden is to demonstrate that unlawful discrimination has been a regular procedure or policy followed by the employer." International Brotherhood of Teamsters v. United States, 431 U.S. 324, 97 S. Ct. 1843, 1867, 52 L.Ed.2d 396 (1977). As stated in Teamsters, a plaintiff must:

[P]rove more than the mere occurrence of isolated or "accidental" or sporadic discriminatory acts. It [has] to establish by a preponderance of the evidence that ... discrimination was the [defendant's] standard operating procedure—the regular rather than the unusual practice.

This creates an inference "that individual hiring decisions were made in pursuit of the discriminatory policy and ... require[s] the employer to come forth with evidence to dispel that inference." In a disparate treatment pattern or practice case, the alleged pattern or practice which is the "'regular or standard operating procedure' ... [must] so demonstrably treat women in relatively unfavorable ways that it justifies a rebuttable inference that it proceeds from an intention to treat them differently simply because of their sex." Stastny v. Southern Bell Tel. & Tel. Co., 628 F.2d 267, 273 (4th Cir. 1980) [emphasis added]. Such a pattern or practice may be shown "by a cumulation of evidence, including statistics, patterns, practices, general policies, or specific instances of discrimination.

In the instant case, plaintiff has established a prima case of disparate treatment. She belongs to a protected minority, and has proved by the preponderance of the evidence that she sought the job of athletic director and was qualified for the position, but David Tashiro was promoted instead.

Defendants have met their burden of articulating a legitimate nondiscriminatory reason for not promoting plaintiff—namely, their claim that David Tashiro was better qualified. Superior qualifications are a legitimate nondiscriminatory reason for taking an employment action. Young v. Lehman, 748 F.2d 194, 198 (4th Cir. 1984). In the face of such a justification plaintiff must show she was better qualified:

> The rule in this circuit is that where relative qualifications are advanced as the nondiscriminatory reason for an employment decision, the plaintiff has the burden of establishing that she was better qualified than the successful applicant. Once the Navy's evidence showed that its reason for promoting Iekel was based on relative qualifications, Young had the burden of proving the reason pretextual, i.e., that she was better qualified.

Here, the court feels that plaintiff has met her burden of establishing that she was better qualified than David Tashiro. First, plaintiff had a college degree in Recreation Administration, while Mr. Tashiro did not. The Club's board of directors had previously determined that for all supervisory positions applicants would be preferred (i.e., considered better qualified) if they possessed a Bachelor's Degree in a health related field. In addition, plaintiff had a wider range of experience in the health fitness field than Tashiro. While Tashiro had worked almost exclusively in the weight training area, plaintiff had experience in water aerobics, aerobics, and weight training.

In addition, plaintiff had more experience with the operation of this particular health club, including experience in supervisory positions. She had worked in all of the Club's operations during her internship with the Club from March, 1983, to May, 1983. According to the Club's own policy, internships were to be considered a plus in making employment decisions. Before he became athletic director, Tashiro had only worked as weight training specialist at the club, a job plaintiff had already held. In addition, when Tashiro was hired as weight training specialist, the plan was to eventually promote him to athletic director. At this time, he had no experience in the Club. Plaintiff, on the other hand, had a wide range of experience at the Club in weight training, in water aerobics, as fitness director, and as an intern. In terms of familiarity with the Club and

the various aspects of the Club's services, plaintiff was far better qualified than Mr. Tashiro.

• • •

Moreover, there is ample direct evidence in this case that defendants had a policy of not promoting women to the position of athletic director. This is one of those rare Title VII cases where there is credible direct evidence of intent to discriminate.

• • •

The court also finds that plaintiff has met the burden of establishing a pattern or practice of discrimination. Again, this is one of those rare Title VII cases where there is credible direct evidence of a policy to discriminate. As detailed above, the McLean Club had a policy not to hire women as athletic director. While the Club apparently did so to cater to their customer's preference for a male macho image, such a customer preference cannot excuse discrimination. To allow businesses to follow such customer preferences would only serve to entrench the sexual stereotypes Congress sought to address in passing Title VII. Under Title VII, customer preference "may be taken into account only when it is based on the company's inability to perform the primary function or service it offers" or where the customer preference is related to abilities to perform the job. Here, there is no evidence that the Club would be unable to provide fitness services without a male macho image or that females are in any way less able to be athletic directors. To the contrary, there is evidence the clubs in Denver and San Diego provide fitness services with female athletic directors and without a male macho image.

In addition to direct evidence of a policy to discriminate, specific incidents provide evidence of a pattern and practice of discrimination. . . . Defendants might argue that a small number of incidents of discrimination is insufficient to show a pattern. The court first notes that even though the number of incidents is small, when compared with the number of times the position of athletic director was open, the number is significant.

• • •

III

Remedies

The primary remedial provision of Title VII, 42 U.S.C. § 2000e-5(g), provides:

> If the court finds that the [defendant] has intentionally engaged in or is intentionally engaging in an unlawful employment practice . . . the court may enjoin the [defendant] from engaging in such unlawful employment practice, and order such affirmative action as may be appropriate, which may include, but is not limited to, reinstatement or

hiring of employees, with or without back pay . . . or any other equitable relief as the court deems appropriate.

When the court determines that a plaintiff has been discriminated against in violation of Title VII, the court retains broad powers to grant injunctive relief under the remedial provision of Title VII. Patterson v. Greenwood School Dist., 696 F.2d 293, 295 (4th Cir. 1982). Moreover, the court is "under a duty to render a decree which will both eliminate past discrimination and bar discrimination in the future." United States v. County of Fairfax, 629 F.2d 932, 941 (4th Cir. 1980), cert. denied, 449 U.S. 1078, 101 S. Ct. 858, 66 L.Ed.2d 801 (1981). In addition, "[a]n injunction warranted by a finding of unlawful discrimina-

tion is not prohibited merely because it confers benefits upon individuals who were not plaintiffs or members of a formally certified class." Evans v. Harnett County Bd.of Education, 684 F.2d 304, 306 (4th Cir. 1982). The injunction, however, must not be too broadly stated. See Davis v. Richmond, F.& P. R. Co., 803 F.2d 1322, 1328 (4th Cir. 1986). Here, plaintiff is entitled to an injunction prohibiting sex discrimination in choosing athletic directors for the McLean Club.

As to reinstatment, plaintiff testified that she does not wish to be reinstated to her former position. Plaintiff is entitled to her back wages in the stipulated amount of $12,444.84. She is also entitled to counsel fees and costs.

■ ■ ■ ■

Fundamental Concepts

Scope.   Title VII broadly prohibits discrimination in employment. Section 703 (a) states,

It shall be an unlawful employment practice for an employer—
(1) to fail or refuse to hire or to discharge any individual, or otherwise discriminate against any individual with respect to his compensation, terms, conditions, or privileges of employment, because of such individual's race, color, religion, sex, or national origin; or
(2) to limit, segregate, or classify his employees or applicants for employment in any way which would deprive or tend to deprive any individual of employment opportunities or otherwise adversely affect his status as an employee, because of such individual's race, color, religion, sex, or national origin. 42 U.S.C. §§ 2000e-2(a).

Title VII applies to **employers** with 15 or more employees working at least twenty calendar weeks and whose organizations impact interstate commerce. Title VII, however, excludes the United States and some departments of the District of Columbia, Native American tribes and bona fide membership clubs, such as country clubs from its definition of employer. To be considered a bona fide membership club under Title VII, the club must qualify for tax-exempt status under the charitable exemption provision of the Internal Revenue Code and must be established for defined social or recreational purposes or for a common literary, scientific, or political objective.

Graves v. Women's Professional Rodeo Association, Inc. (8th Cir. 1990) makes clear that professional associations which sanction events will not be considered employers unless they clearly fit the definition of employer. In *Graves*, a male rodeo barrel racer charged that the defendant non-profit association which organized female rodeo contestants and sanctioned events had discriminated against him on the basis of gender when it denied him membership. The court found that the WPRA was not an "employer" under Title VII as its members were not employees. The court relied on the two key factors in determining the WPRA was not an employer. First, the WPRA did not pay wages, withhold taxes, or pay insurance for members. Second, while the WPRA did exercise a degree control over members through its rules, those rules only permitted an opportunity for members to compete for prize money raised by sponsors, not by WPRA.

Administration of Title VII.   The Equal Employment Opportunity Commission (EEOC) is a five member, presidentially appointed administrative agency charged with the administration of Title VII (*EEOC*

v. National Broadcasting Co., Inc., 1990). As a governmental agency the EEOC carries out a number of functions. First, the EEOC investigates charges of employment discrimination and attempts to conciliate alleged violations (Player, 1988). Where the EEOC does not find reasonable cause to go forward with conciliation or where conciliation is not fruitful, the complaining party may proceed with a private Title VII lawsuit.

Second, the EEOC may file suit in federal district court to enforce Title VII. For example in *EEOC v. National Broadcasting Co., Inc.* (S.D.N.Y. 1990), the EEOC brought suit on behalf of a female applicant for the position of television sports director alleging sex discrimination in violation of Title VII. In addition, the EEOC may intervene in any private employment discrimination lawsuit.

Third, the EEOC creates guidelines and regulations for the interpretation of Title VII. While the guidelines and regulations do not possess the full force and effect of law, they are subject to great judicial deference. For example, in *Meritor Savings Bank, FSB v. Vinson* (1986), the U.S. Supreme Court relied on EEOC guidelines to define hostile environment sexual harassment.

Classes Protected Under Title VII

Title VII specifically prohibits employment discrimination against individuals on the basis of race, color, religion, gender, or national origin. In general, any employment decision, practice, or policy which classifies individuals and treats them differently on those bases will violate Title VII.

Race. While much of the United States' Civil Rights Movement focused on the treatment of African-Americans, Title VII's definition of race is much more broad. It is not limited to ethnological races, but protects all classes of people from dissimilar treatment, including, but not limited to Hispanics, Native Americans, Asian-Americans. As Player (1988) elaborates, "ethnologists may not classify Hispanics as a 'race,' yet discrimination against American Hispanics is said to be 'racial' because of their mixed race heritage" (p. 299). The same can be said of those from the Middle East where discrimination against Semitic people would be racial (*Id.*). For instance, Zimmer, Sullivan, and Richards (1988) raise as an example the discrimination of the Holocaust in which no distinction was made between religious and non-religious Jews or Jews from various national origins, but rather the discrimination was made upon racial lines. These two examples are also indicative of discrimination on the basis of national origin.

Racial discrimination cases involving coaches and athletic directors have arisen from decisions made in the course of public school desegregation. For example in *Cross v. Board of Education of Dollarway, Arkansas School District* (E.D. Ark. 1975), the plaintiff, a black high school football coach in an all-black elementary and high school in a segregated school district was demoted to assistant coach when his school became the junior high and the black high school students were moved into the white high school. Twice Cross was passed over for the position and white coaches with fewer qualifications were hired. On the second instance the school superintendent suggested that the defendant school board deviate from its policy to promote within to search outside the district for a white coach. The superintendent was of the opinion that the white players would not play for a black coach and that the community was not ready for a black head coach and athletic director. The school board then, never even considered Cross' application for the position. The court found the school board's refusal to even consider Cross' application was clear evidence of individual disparate treatment on the basis of Cross' race. As a result Cross was entitled to back pay in the amount equal to difference in the amount he would have received and that which he did receive as assistant coach. In addition, the defendant was ordered to promote Cross to head football coach and athletic director or to compensate him at a salary comparable to the positions.

Color. An employer's distinction on the basis of skin pigment or the physical characteristics of an applicant or employee's race would be deemed discrimination. For instance, if an employer favors light-skinned African-Americans over dark-skinned African-Americans, it is treating African-Americans differently as a race on the basis of color. Thus, color-based discrimination will often intersect with race-based discrimination.

National Origin.   With regard to national origin, the court focuses on one's ancestry. This does not include regions of the United States such as Puerto Rico. Title VII does not prohibit employment discrimination solely on the basis of citizenship. For example, in *Dowling v. United States* (D. Mass. 1979), the plaintiff argued that the National Hockey League and the World Hockey Association only hired Canadian referees, and thus discriminated against him on under Title VII on the basis of his national origin. The court dismissed the claim as it stated that Title VII does not bar employment discrimination on the basis of alienage or citizenship. However, the lack of United States citizenship may not be used as a method of disguising discrimination which is actually based on race or national origin. In other words, an employer may follow a policy of employing only United States citizens, but may not give unequal treatment to different non-citizens based on their country of origin. Rules which require communication in "English-only" are allowed *only* where the employer can prove that such a rule is a business necessity.

Sex.   Title VII has primarily been relied upon by women, but it also applies to men. The gender of the employee discriminated against, not the gender of the athletes the employee coaches is the basis for the Title VII discrimination "on the basis of sex" claim. The plaintiffs in *Jackson v. Armstrong School District* (W.D. Penn. 1977) lost their Title VII claim due to the fact that they were paid less money because they were coaching girls basketball, rather than due to the fact that they were women as the defendant established that the men coaching girls basketball were paid the same amount as the women.

Title VII's protection against gender-based discrimination includes **sexual harassment**, but does *not* include discrimination on the basis of sexual orientation. In 1978 Congress amended Title VII's language "on the basis of sex" to include protection against discrimination on the basis of pregnancy, childbirth, or other related medical condition (including abortion). In other words, an employer cannot refuse to hire or cannot fire a qualified woman because she is pregnant, has had a child, or has had an abortion. Likewise, an employer cannot leave coverage for pregnancy or childbirth related conditions out of an insurance or disability plan offered to all employees. An employer may, however, refuse to include coverage for abortion, except where the life of the mother is endangered.

Religion.   All well-recognized faiths and those considered unorthodox beliefs, provided the court is convinced that the purported belief is sincere and genuinely held, and not simply adopted for an ulterior motive, are protected under Title VII. An employer must make a **reasonable accommodation** to an employee's religious practices and observances, unless it would place an **undue hardship** on the employer. An employer's obligation is simply to make a reasonable accommodation to an employee. For example, in *Simmons v. Sports Training Institute* (1990), the plaintiff a Seventh Day Adventist whose religion prohibited him from working on the Sabbath, from sundown Friday until sundown Saturday, sued his employer for religious discrimination. After his conversion to the religion, the plaintiff only informed the employer that he could not work on Saturdays, so the employer accommodated his religious practices by changing his schedule to Monday through Friday 6:00 am-2:00 pm. Thereafter the defendant hired the plaintiff's brother to work the graveyard shift, as well as the Saturday shift, which had previously been covered by his brother prior to his conversion to the Seventh Day Adventist religion. This required the brother to work a double shift. Eventually, the brother fell asleep on the job and in an effort to keep his brother employed, the plaintiff swapped shifts with his brother. The plaintiff, however, against his employer's wishes, had his brother work double shifts for three weeks in a row. The plaintiff had requested the time off and was granted two of the three weeks. The plaintiff took the third week against his employer's wishes and was fired for insubordination. The plaintiff charged discrimination on the basis of his religious needs. The court refused to find religious discrimination had anything to do with the firing as the employer had reasonably accommodated the employee and the employee was fired for an unauthorized vacation.

Theories of Liability

Courts applying Title VII have established four theories of liability: individual disparate treatment, systemic disparate treatment, disparate impact, and retaliation.

Disparate Treatment. Disparate treatment of an employee occurs when the employer *intentionally discriminates* against a worker and thus, acts with an illegal motive. Disparate treatment may occur in one of two forms: individual, where an employer treats one person with discriminatory animus or systemic, where an employer acts in furtherance of a pattern or practice of discrimination.

Individual Disparate Treatment. There are two ways in which a plaintiff or the EEOC can prove intentional discrimination. The first is where **direct evidence of intent** exists through statements made by the defendant. An example is in *Morris v. Bianchini* (1987), above, where the plaintiff and another women were passed over for promotion to athletic director of the health and fitness club in favor of less qualified males, the reason they were given was that the club sought "a macho, male image" for its athletic director. This statement was used as evidence of an intent by the club's management to discriminate on these two qualified women in favor of a less qualified candidate simply on the basis of his gender.

A second example is in *Biver v. Saginaw Township Community Schools, et al.* (6th Cir. 1986), the plaintiff female alleged discrimination in failing to hire her for a boys or girls basketball team coaching position. The court accepted as evidence of the school superintendent's discriminatory intent his statement that "hell would freeze over before he would hire a woman for a boys' coaching position[.]" (*Id.*) The superintendent claimed that it was not discriminatory as his policy was to hire men to coach boys and women to coach girls. The plaintiff, however, attacked the credibility of the superintendent's explanation by showing many instances in which men were hired to coach girls.

A second method by which one can prove discrimination is through the use of an **inference**. A plaintiff can establish an inference for the court by comparing how an employer treats similarly situated employees of different protected classes. The model for reliance on an inference to prove discriminatory animus was established by *McDonnell Douglas Corp. v. Green* (1973). According to *Texas Department of Community Affairs v. Burdine* (1981), the McDonnell Douglas model is as follows: "[f]irst, the plaintiff has the burden of proving by the preponderance of the evidence a prima facie case of discrimination. Second, if the plaintiff succeeds in proving the prima facie case the burden shifts to the defendant 'to articulate some legitimate nondiscriminatory reason for the employee's rejection.' Third, should the defendant carry this burden, the plaintiff must then have an opportunity to prove by a preponderance of the evidence that the legitimate reasons offered by the defendant were not its true reasons, but were a pretext for discrimination."

"The ultimate burden of persuading the trier of fact that the defendant intentionally discriminated against the plaintiff remains at all times with the plaintiff" (*Burdine*, 1981). Under this widely relied upon standard a plaintiff can establish a **prima facie case** by proving:

(if applicant)
1. Applicant is a member of a protected class
2. Applicant applied for job for which employer was seeking applicants
3. Applicant was qualified to perform job
4. Applicant was not hired
5. Employer filled position with non-minority or continued to search

(if employee)   1.   Employee is within protected class
                   2.   Employee was performing task satisfactorily
                   3.   Employee was discharged or adversely affected by change in working conditions
                   4.   Employee's work was assigned to one in non-minority category

The burden that shifts to the defendant is to rebut the plaintiff's presumption by producing evidence that the plaintiff was rejected and someone else preferred for a **legitimate, nondiscriminatory reason** (*Burdine*, 1981). The defendant's burden is one of production, not persuasion. For the reason to be legitimate it must be lawful, clear, and reasonably specific. Id. In other words, when comparing the chosen applicant or employee with the plaintiff, the defendant should elaborate on the criteria necessary for hiring or promotion, the basis for the comparison of the candidates, and that the person hired or promoted, rather than the plaintiff possessed the qualities the defendant was seeking (*Herman v. National Broadcasting Co., Inc.*, 1984). The defendant need not prove that the chosen employee was a superior candidate, but simply that there were legitimate, nondiscriminatory reasons to justify the employer's decision. In addition, it is more difficult for a defendant to raise this defense without clear qualification criteria for hiring. For instance, in *Jackson v. World League of American Football* (S.D.N.Y. 1994), the court refused to grant summary judgment in a racial discrimination case where the World League of American Football had not set clear qualifications for the position of head football coach.

Once the employer provides a legitimate, nondiscriminatory reason for the alleged discrimination, the burden then shifts back to the employee to prove that the legitimate reason is in fact a **pretext** for intentional discrimination. There are a number of ways a plaintiff may establish evidence of pretext. According to Player (1988), these include providing direct evidence of prejudice toward the plaintiff or members of the protected class; presenting statistical evidence of an unbalanced work force; presenting evidence of the rejection of a high number of protected class members; and proving that the articulated reason for rejection has not been consistently applied to members of the majority as it has to protected class members. An example of this last point occurred in *Davis v. McCormick* (N.D. Ind. 1995), where the plaintiff female coach was subject to a more stringent disciplinary policy and that her discipline was arguably more severe than any male coach's discipline. The court found that this raised a reasonable inference that the plaintiff's discipline was a pretext for intentional discrimination. A plaintiff may also present the fact that the proffered legitimate, nondiscriminatory reason was not given to the plaintiff at the time the employment decision was made as evidence that it was an afterthought and thus, pretextual (Player, 1988). For example, in *Baylor v. Jefferson County Board of Education* (11th Cir. 1984), a black teacher and coach argued that the defendant school board's transfer of him to a teaching (only) position was racially motivated. Baylor successfully proved that the defendant's legitimate, nondiscriminatory reason for the job transfer was developed after his hearing and decision to transfer him out of coaching were made. Finally, failing to comply with the usual hiring procedures may indicate that discriminatory actions were involved. For instance, in *Cross v. Board of Education of Dollarway, Arkansas School District* (E.D. Ark. 1975), the school superintendent suggested that the school board deviate from its policy of promoting from within to search outside the district for a white coach. As a result, the school board never even considered Cross' application for the position and hired a white coach from outside of the school district with similar experience.

Harassment.   The EEOC has long viewed harassment on the basis of race, color, religion, sex, or national origin as violative of Title VII. The Supreme Court in *Meritor Savings Bank, FSB v. Vinson* (1986) stated that, "[t]he Commission has held and continues to hold that an employer has a duty to maintain a working environment free of harassment based on race, color, religion, sex, [or] national origin . . . and that the duty requires positive action where necessary to eliminate such practices or remedy their effects." Courts have applied this theory to harassment on the basis of race (*Firefighters Institute for Racial Equality v. St. Louis*, 1977), religion (*Compston v. Borden, Inc.*, 1976), national origin (*Cariddi v. Kansas City Chiefs Football Club*, 1977), and gender (*Meritor Savings Bank, FSB v. Vinson*, 1986). By far, the application of the harassment theory is most developed for discrimination on the basis of sex. This chapter will limit the discussion to sexual harassment, but the hostile environment theory of liability can be applied to all forms of harassment on the basis of one's membership in a protected class.

Sexual Harassment.   Sexual harassment is a type of disparate treatment employment discrimination. A discussion of sexual harassment is worthy as it is a form of disparate treatment discrimination, establishing sexual harassment varies a bit from the standard *McDonnell Douglas* model. Sexual harassment occurs when one in power or authority relegates an employee to a vulnerable, inferior work place position through sexual coercion and/or unwelcome sexual advances and innuendoes. Sexual harassment is rarely founded upon a romantic or physical attraction. Rather it is used to build and sustain power by treating members of the opposite sex as sexual objects.

Types of Sexual Harassment.   Early courts, wary of getting involved in work place disputes between men and women, recognized sexual harassment only in narrowly defined situations involving the granting or denial of a woman's employment opportunities on the basis of her entering into a sexual relationship with a superior (*Barnes v. Costle*, 1977; *Miller v. Bank of America*, 1979). This type of sexual harassment, called *quid pro quo* (this for that) occurs when a subordinate's employment opportunities are conditioned upon entering into a sexual relationship with a superior.

The law now prohibits a second type, called **hostile environment** sexual harassment. In *Meritor Savings Bank, FSB v. Vinson* (1986), the U.S. Supreme Court quoted EEOC guidelines to state that hostile environment sexual harassment occurs when the work place is permeated with ". . . conduct [of a sexual nature which] has the purpose or effect of unreasonably interfering with an individual's work performance or creating an intimidating, hostile, or offensive working environment" (*Meritor*, at 65 quoting 29 C.F.R. §1604.11(a)(3)). In *Meritor,* the Supreme Court neither established the standard of review to determine whether a work place is hostile, nor defined the behavior necessary to constitute a hostile environment. The Supreme Court did, however, state that to be actionable, the sexual harassment must be so severe or pervasive that it alters employment conditions and creates an abusive working environment.

Determining whether an environment is hostile or abusive can only be accomplished by reviewing all of the circumstances (*Harris v. Forklift Systems, Inc.*, 1993). The Court found that these may include, but are not limited to "the frequency of the discriminatory conduct; its severity; whether it is physically threatening or humiliating, or a mere offensive utterance; and whether it unreasonably interferes with an employee's work performance." While defining which actions create this abusive work environment is also best considered on a case-by-case basis, a combination of the following actions, when sufficiently severe, may create a hostile work environment: jokes, suggestions, abuse, or harassment of a sexual nature; unnecessary patting, pinching, squeezing, brushing against one's body, or putting one's hands or arms on another; constant leering or ogling; remarks about one's clothing or body which carry a sexual tone; pressure for sexual favors; and/or the posting or distributing of pornographic material.

Two-pronged Test for Sexual Harassment.   In *Harris*, the Supreme Court reaffirmed its *Meritor* decision and rejected the reasonable woman standard in favor of a **reasonable person standard of review** and established a two-pronged test for sexual harassment which includes both objective and subjective elements. The Court further stated that the plaintiff need not prove psychological injury to establish that she was sexually harassed. The Court reasoned that "Title VII comes into play before the harassing conduct leads to a nervous breakdown."

The first prong requires the plaintiff to show that the conduct is severe or pervasive enough to create an objectively hostile environment that a reasonable person would find hostile or abusive. The second prong requires the plaintiff subjectively perceived the environment to be hostile and abusive, thereby altering the employment climate.

Employer Liability for Sexual Harassment. The Supreme Court has *not* addressed the issue of employer liability, other than to recognize that Congress defined "employer" to include any agent of the employer, thereby evincing some intent to rely upon agency theories (*Meritor* at 72). The Court noted, however, some inconsistency in the EEOC's standards of employer liability as stated in the agency's brief submitted in *Meritor* as amicus curiae (Id.). While the *EEOC's Guidelines on Discrimination Because of Sex* state that the employer shall be held strictly liable for the actions of its agents and supervisory employees (*EEOC Guidelines* at §1604.11(c), 1990), the brief stated that this standard would only be imposed for quid pro quo harassment (*Meritor* at 72). Liability for the harassment is imputed to the employer because it has delegated to the supervisor authority to hire, fire, manage, and promote the employee. If a supervisor is acting within the scope of his employment and sexually harasses an employee, the employer will often automatically be held liable for the supervisor's actions regardless of whether the employer was put on notice of the sexual harassment. However, where hostile environment sexual harassment is alleged, provided a sexual harassment policy is in place, the EEOC requires actual notice. Finally, the Court noted that the Guidelines require facts to be examined on a-case by-case basis.

With respect to harassment between employees, *EEOC Guidelines* state that an employer is responsible where the employer (or its agents or supervisors) knows of or should have known of the conduct (*EEOC Guidelines* at §1604.11(d), 1990). The employer is not liable, however, if it can show that it responded to the sexual harassment with immediate and appropriate corrective measures.

Finally, employers may also be liable for sexual harassment committed by non-employees, such as independent contractors or service people. In sport, many times team physicians or athletic trainers may be considered independent contractors. The employer will be held liable if the employer knows of or should have known of the conduct, fails to take immediate and appropriate corrective actions, and exercises a sufficient degree of control over the non-employee.

Systemic Disparate Treatment. Under the theory of systemic disparate treatment plaintiffs are challenging broad sweeping employment policies which are discriminatory, for instance, an employer's policy not to hire women or to segregate employees by race or national origin would raise systemic concerns.

A plaintiff's initial burden is to "establish by preponderance of the evidence that discrimination is an employer's standard operating procedure—the regular, rather than the unusual practice" (*Hazelwood School District v. United States*, 1977, quoting *Teamsters v. United States*, 1977). This will create an inference that individual hiring or promotion practices were made in furtherance of this discriminatory policy.

When challenging system-wide patterns or practices, plaintiffs will often rely upon the use of statistical evidence bolstered with evidence of individual discriminatory treatment. The statistics will compare the racial, ethnic, or gender balance of the qualified labor population with the population of a work force which draws employees from that population. In *Teamsters* (1977), the court stated that statistics showing an imbalance are probative because such imbalance is often a telltale sign of purposeful discrimination. Absent discrimination it is assumed that over time nondiscriminatory work place practices will result in a work force which is representative of a region's general population.

Once a plaintiff establishes a presumption of a discriminatory pattern or practice, the burden then shifts to the employer to demonstrate why an inference of discriminatory animus could not be drawn from the plaintiff's evidence. Here the defendant has two options. First, the defendant can attack the plaintiff's statistical evidence as inaccurate or insignificant. Second, the employer may seek to provide a non-discriminatory explanation for the apparently discriminatory result. As with individual disparate treatment, once a defendant produces this explanation, the burden will shift to the plaintiff to persuade the court that the defendant's stated explanation is in fact a pretext for discrimination. This chapter's significant case, *Morris v. Bianchini*, was a great example of direct evidence of systemic disparate treatment as the plaintiff established that the health club had engaged in a practice of not promoting women to the athletic director position in order to maintain a "male macho" image.

Disparate Impact. Disparate impact discrimination exists where a plaintiff is challenging a neutral employment practice, regardless of intent, which has a discriminatory effect upon a protected group. According to the court in *Wynn v. Columbus Municipal Separate School District* (N.D. Miss. 1988), the disparate impact model is often misunderstood and misapplied. This model only applies where the employer has instituted a specific procedure, usually a criterion for employment which the plaintiff can show has a causal connection between a protected class' imbalance in the work force (*Pouncy v. Prudential Insurance Co. of America,* 1982).

The prima facie case requires that the employee or the EEOC prove that the employment practice or policy has an adverse impact on the protected group of which the employee is a member. This is usually established through statistical evidence documenting the impact of the practice on the protected class. The use of statistical evidence is difficult and the plaintiff's methodology may be attacked as being flawed. For instance, in *Wynn v. Columbus Municipal Separate School District* (N.D. Miss. 1988), the plaintiff female coach used the disparate impact model to challenge her employer's practice of having the head football coach also serve as the athletic director. She argued that such a practice had a disparate impact on females, because it was extremely rare that a female would be qualified to be a head football coach. The plaintiff presented as evidence an examination of her state, Mississippi. Of the 192 high school athletic directors in the state only 62 were not head football coaches, no women were head football coaches, and just two athletic directors were women. The court found her theory flawed on two grounds. First, the fact that very few women in Mississippi were selected to serve as athletic director had very little relationship to the issue of whether the defendant Columbus School District discriminates against women as athletic director. Second, the plaintiff's statistical evidence is drawn from a pool which includes not only females from the protected class, but a number of non-members of that class, namely males who are not qualified as football coach and thus, are denied the athletic director position as well. The court stated the better approach would be to consider the discriminatory treatment of qualified female coaches in the Columbus Schools who had been denied the position of athletic director. Thus, the plaintiff lost on her disparate impact claim, but was successful under her disparate treatment theory.

The employer may then rebut the plaintiff's argument by attacking the statistical analysis or producing evidence that the practice is job-related. This requires proof that the challenged employment practice is necessary to achieve some legitimate business objective, the practice actually achieves that objective, and there is no reasonable method of accomplishing the objective without a discriminatory impact on the protected class.

Once the employer shows the barrier is job-related, the burden shifts back to the plaintiff to prove that the barrier is a pretext for discrimination, by showing that there are other adequate devices which do not discriminate against a protected class.

Retaliation. Title VII also provides a cause of action for retaliation in response to a plaintiff's filing of a claim of employment discrimination. Section 704 (a) of Title VII provides that:

> it shall be an unlawful employment practice for an employer to discriminate against any of his employees [because that employee] has opposed an practice made an unlawful employment practice by this subchapter, or because he has made any charge, testified, assisted or is participating in any manner in an investigation proceeding, or hearing under this chapter. 42 U.S.C. §2000e-3(a).

The plaintiff's burden of proof in retaliation claims mirrors that in other Title VII suits. The plaintiff bears the initial burden of establishing a prima facie case of retaliation. To establish the prima facie retaliation case, the plaintiff must show by a preponderance of the evidence that 1) the plaintiff engaged in a statutorily protected activity; 2) adverse action was taken against the plaintiff by the employer subsequent to and contemporaneously with such activity; and 3) a causal link exists between the protected activity and the adverse action (*Jalil v. Advel Corp.*, 1989). Once the plaintiff has established a prima facie case, the defendant may introduce evidence providing legitimate, nonretaliatory reasons for its conduct. If the defendant properly introduces such evidence, then the burden shifts back to the plaintiff to show that the defendant's justification is merely pretext for covering up unlawful retaliation.

A good example of a retaliation case is *Burkey v. Marshall County Board of Education* (N.D.W. Va. 1981), in which the plaintiff filed an EEOC complaint and was transferred from junior high school to an elementary school. The defendant school district argued that the reason for the transfer was to save money. The plaintiff was able to rebut this reason by showing that Burkey's transfer saved the district no money.

Additional Defenses

Bona Fide Occupational Qualification.   It is not illegal to discriminate on the basis of religion, gender, or national origin, where an employer can show the classification is a bona fide occupational qualification. Race and color are never bona fide occupational qualifications. The bona fide occupational qualification defense requires the employer to prove that members of the excluded class could not safely and effectively perform essential job duties and the employer must have a factual basis for believing that persons in the excluded class could not perform the job. The bona fide occupational qualification must also be reasonably necessary to the normal operation of the business. Finally, customer preference cannot be the basis for a bona fide occupational qualification. For example in *Morris v. Bianchini*, the court refused to accept a health club's stated customer preference for a director who possessed a macho male image as a defense to a practice of not hiring qualified women for the position.

Business Necessity.   Business necessity serves as a defense to a disparate impact discrimination claim, where the employer may seek to prove that a particular practice is job-related.

Affirmative Action.   Affirmative action involves giving preference to those under-represented in the work place. These policies often possess goals/timetables for increasing the percentage of the under-represented to rectify past discrimination. The affirmative action policy may be voluntary or court-ordered as a result of a Title VII or IX lawsuit. Affirmative action policies often result in discrimination against the over-represented classes, termed reverse discrimination. It is legal provided:

a.   The discrimination results from a formal, systematic program.
b.   The program is temporary, operating only until its goals are reached.
c.   The program does not completely bar the hiring/promotion of non-minorities.
d.   The program does not result in the firing of non-minority workers.
e.   The program does not force the employer to hire/promote unqualified workers.
f.   Where the program is court-ordered, it must be based upon actual evidence of discrimination.
g.   Where the program is voluntary, it must be based either on actual evidence of discrimination or evidence that those in under-represented groups had been under-utilized in the past.

Remedies.   Section 706(g) provides the following power to remedy employment discrimination under Title VII:

> If the court finds that the respondent has intentionally engaged in or is intentionally engaging in an unlawful employment practice . . . the court may enjoin the respondent from engaging in such unlawful employment practice, and order such affirmative action as may be appropriate, which may include, but is not limited to, reinstatement or hiring of employees with or without back pay . . . or any other equitable relief as the court deems appropriate. . . .

A successful plaintiff most often is awarded back pay. A back pay order requires the defendant to pay all lost wages and benefits which would have been earned were it not for the illegal discrimination. The trial court may grant interest on these wages.

Recent Developments

1. The Civil Rights Act of 1991 was introduced into Congress with the stated goal of negating five United States Supreme Court decisions which severely limited important protections granted by employment discrimination laws. Cathcart and Snyderman (1992) state that when the law was enacted it appeared to reach beyond a simple restoration of prior laws and put into effect the following changes to Title VII:

   - Jury trials and compensatory and punitive damages for all claims of intentional discrimination under Title VII (this had been only available for racial and ethnic discrimination).

   - In disparate impact cases the employer must demonstrate that the challenged practice is job related for the position in question and is consistent with a business necessity.

   - Defendants will be liable for declaratory or injunctive relief and attorney's fees where a plaintiff proves that race, color, religion, national origin, or sex was a motivating factor for any employment practice, even if other factors also motivated the employment decision (called mixed motive cases). A plaintiff is not, however entitled to backpay, reinstatement, or compensatory or punitive damages.

   - It eliminates challenges to affirmative action consent decrees from individuals who had notice and an opportunity to object when the decree was entered or whose interests were adequately represented by another.

   - It prohibits the practice of "race norming" which is a practice whereby test scores are adjusted on the basis of race or other Title VII classification.

2. Since the *Meritor Savings Bank, FSB v. Vinson* (1986) Supreme Court sexual harassment decision, federal courts of appeal have varied in their application of agency theories to supervisors' conduct in sexual harassment cases. While there is no clear trend, recent decisions in several courts of appeal, evidence a possible expansion of employer liability in hostile environment cases, regardless of notice, and particularly where supervisory employees are accused. The following appellate cases have held employers to a strict liability standard when supervisory personnel sexually harass employees: *Sparks v. Pilot Freight Carriers*, 1987 (strict liability for managers in quid pro quo and environment cases); *Karibian v. Columbia University*, 1994 (strict liability standard for high-level supervisors where no reasonable means of complaint or no action taken by employer when notified of harassment); and *Kelly-Zurian v. Wohl Shoe Co.*, 1994 (strict liability standard in hostile environment claims when harasser is agent or supervisor). It is unlikely, though, that the issue will be resolved in the near future as the Supreme Court recently declined to review *Karibian v. Columbia University* (1994), which expanded the scope of employer liability and raised important issues regarding employer responses to sexual harassment complaints.

3. Although it has not been addressed on the federal level, a handful of progressive states have added protection against discrimination on the basis of sexual orientation in their employment

discrimination laws. At the same time, and possibly in response to this movement, a number of regions have sought to prohibit homosexuality in their state and/or local governments.

4. The majority of published cases in sport are in educational institutions. Although no documented evidence exists as to why this is the case, a few assumptions may by made. First, as positions in sport go, those in education may feel more secure as employees. Although athletic positions do not have tenure or are members of a union, those who are also teachers may perceive that this protection also covers them in their coaching positions. Second, employees in educational settings may be more familiar with their rights due to their work environment. Third, cases in other areas of sport may settle prior to trial and thus, no public record exists. Fourth, employment discrimination cases are often complex and litigation can be costly. Unless one is a player or at the top levels of upper management, the salaries are often low and victims may not have the resources to pursue such litigation.

References

A. Cases

Barnes v. Costle, 561 F.2d 983 (D.C. 1977)

Baylor v. Jefferson County Board of Education, 733 F.2d 1527 (11th Cir. 1984)

Biver v. Saginaw Township Community Schools, et al., 805 F.2d 1033 (6th Cir. 1986)

Burkey v. Marshall County Board of Education, 513 F. Supp. 1084 (N.D.W. Va. 1981)

Cariddi v. Kansas City Chiefs Football Club, 568 F.Supp. 87 (8th Cir. 1977)

Compston v. Borden, Inc., 424 F. Supp. 157 (S.D. Ohio 1976)

Cross v. Board of Education of Dollarway, Arkansas School District, 395 F. Supp. 531 (E.D. Ark. 1975)

Davis v. McCormick, 898 F. Supp. 1275 (C.D. Ill. 1995)

Dowling v. United States, 476 F. Supp. 1018 (D. Mass. 1979)

EEOC v. National Broadcasting Co., Inc., 753 F. Supp. 452 (S.D. N.Y. 1990)

Firefighters Institute for Racial Equality v. St. Louis, 549 F.2d 506 (8th Cir. 1977)

Franklin v. Gwinnett County Public Schools, 112 S.Ct. 1028 (1991)

Graves v. Women's Professional Rodeo Association, 907 F. 2d 71 (8th Cir. 1990)

Harris v. Forklift Systems, Inc., 114 S.Ct. 367 (1993)

Hazelwood School District v. United States, 433 U.S. 299 (1977)

Herman v. National Broadcasting Co., Inc., 774 F.2d 604 (7th Cir. 1984)

Jackson v. Armstrong School District, 430 F. Supp. 1050 (W.D. Penn. 1977)

Jackson v. World League of American Football, 65 Fair Emp. Prac. Cas. 358 (S.D.N.Y. 1994)

Jalil v. Advel Corp., 873 F. 2d 701 (3d Cir. 1989)

Karibian v. Columbia University, 812 F.Supp. 413 (S.D.N.Y. 1993), rev'd 14 F.3d 773 (2d. Cir. 1994), *cert.* denied 1994 Lexis 4577 (1994)

Kelly-Zurian v. Wohl Shoe Co., 22 Cal. App. 4th 397 (Cal. Ct. App. 1994)

McDonnell Douglas Corp. v. Green, 411 U.S. 792 (1973)

Meritor Savings Bank, FSB v. Vinson, 477 U.S. 57 (1986)

Miller v. Bank of America, 600 F.2d 211 (9th Cir. 1979)

Morris v. Bianchini, et al., 43 Fair Emp. Prac. Cases 647 (E.D. Va. 1987)

Pouncy v. Prudential Insurance Co. of America, 668 F.2d 795 (5th Cir. 1982)

Sparks v. Pilot Freight Carriers, 830 F. 2d 1554 (11th Cir. 1987)

Simmons v. Sports Training Institute, 52 Fair Emp. Prac. Cas. 1322 (S.D.N.Y. 1990)

Teamsters v. United States, 431 U.S. 324 (1977)

Texas Department of Community Affairs v. Burdine, 450 U.S. 248 (1981)

Wynn v. Columbus Municipal Separate School District, 692 F. Supp. 672 (N.D. Miss. 1988)

B. Publications

Cathcart, D.A. and Snyderman, M. (1992). "The Civil Rights Act of 1991," 8 *The Labor Lawyer* 849-922

Player, M.A. (1988). *Employment Discrimination Law*, St. Paul, Minn: West Publishing Co.

Zimmer, M.J., Sullivan C.A., and Richards, R.F. (1988). *Cases and Materials on Employment Discrimination*, Boston: Little, Brown, and Co.

C. Legislation

Title VII of the Civil Rights Act of 1964, 42 U.S.C.A. §2000e et seq. (1990)

5.82

The Age Discrimination in Employment Act (ADEA)

Lisa Pike Masteralexis
University of Massachusetts-Amherst

The Age Discrimination in Employment Act (ADEA) prohibits employment discrimination on the basis of age. ADEA has become particularly important as our society's people are living longer, more productive lives and as a result our work force is becoming older. In addition, downsizing is the modus operandi of the business world and often downsizing involves early retirement packages or the elimination of positions for older workers as younger workers are viewed as a more cost efficient work force. Therefore a familiarity with ADEA is important for any sport manager.

■ ■ ■ ■

Representative Case

AUSTIN v. CORNELL UNIVERSITY

891 Federal Supplement
United States District Court,
N.D. New York.
July 20, 1995.

In this age discrimination lawsuit, defendants Cornell University, Richard Costello and William Szabo (collectively, "Cornell") moved for summary judgment against plaintiffs Edward W. Austin and Henry L. McPeak, who previously held seasonal positions at Cornell's golf course. In the alternative, Cornell sought summary judgment dismissing the complaint against the individual defendants, Costello and Szabo.

• • •

Cornell owns, operates, and maintains the Robert Trent Jones Golf Course in Ithaca. At all times relevant to this lawsuit, defendant Costello was the Head Golf Professional at the Ithaca course, and defendant Szabo was Cornell's Associate Director of Athletics for Operations and Facilities in charge of overseeing the course. Plaintiffs Austin and McPeak each worked at the golf course over several summer seasons. McPeak, who formerly worked full time at Cornell, worked as a volunteer ranger from 1988 until 1990 and as a paid ranger in 1991 and 1992. Austin worked primarily in the golf course's pro shop from 1988 until 1991 and as a ranger in 1992. The duties of a golf course ranger include monitoring play on the course to ensure that members are complying with golf etiquette and playing fast enough to prevent bottlenecks and gaps in play on the course.

Before the start of the 1993 golf season, Cornell decided not to rehire Austin and McPeak. Costello, Szabo, and Richard Deibert, the golf course superintendent, jointly made the decision. At the time of this action, McPeak was 67 years old and Austin was 73 years old. Costello told Austin and McPeak during separate telephone conversations that the golf course was undergoing a reorganization in which Cornell would not need their services and that plaintiffs should not take the decision personally. Costello did not tell plaintiffs that their prior service had been deficient in any way. Costello also did not ask plaintiffs whether they would have been willing to work increased hours.

According to the deposition testimony of Costello, Szabo and Deibert, the reorganization stemmed from Cornell's decision to lower golf course fees and thus increase membership. To accommodate the anticipated increased use of the course, Cornell instituted a "double wave" system of play in which parties would tee off simultaneously on the first and tenth holes, play their nine holes, and then cross over to finish the remaining nine holes on the course. The double wave system required course rangers to work harder in monitoring the pace of play and in coordinating cross-overs. The golf course reorganization also included the consolidation of approximately 20 seasonal positions into about 16 or 17 jobs. Fewer people worked more hours to perform the same work. Szabo testified that he wanted to reduce the number of people on the Cornell payroll.

Costello, Szabo and Deibert concluded in March 1993 that McPeak and Austin were not qualified for the ranger duties. Defendants claims that during the 1992 season, they received numerous complaints from members regarding the slow rate of play on the golf course. Deibert and Costello also claim to have observed problems on the course such as bottlenecks, and Deibert claims to have seen plaintiffs socializing or looking for lost golf balls instead of monitoring play on the course.

• • •

Both Austin and McPeak testified during their depositions that Cornell never criticized their performance as rangers. Rather, they claimed that their work was praised. Because plaintiffs were seasonal workers, Cornell did not conduct formal evaluations of their performance. In his deposition, Costello, who served as plaintiffs' immediate supervisor, testified that he tried to manage his employees using positive reinforcement rather than criticism.

• • •

After deciding not to rehire plaintiffs, Cornell placed an advertisement in a local newspaper for the ranger positions. Cornell eventually hired four people to work as rangers during the 1993 golf season, although no more than three rangers were employed simultaneously during the season. All four of these employees were younger than plaintiffs. Three individuals were in their 20s, and one employee was in his 50s.

On October 14, 1993, plaintiffs filed complaints with the Equal Employment Opportunity Commission and the New York State Division of Human Right, alleging that Cornell discriminated against them because of their age.

• • •

Defendants contend that they are entitled to summary judgment because Austin and McPeak failed to raise genuine issues of material fact with respect to their age discrimination claims. Specifically, Cornell argues that it did not rehire plaintiffs because they were not qualified to work as rangers at the reorganized golf course. Plaintiffs respond that they have sufficient evidence of defendants' discriminatory intent.

Plaintiff's claims under the ADEA are governed by the familiar burden-shifting analysis of McDonnell Douglas-Burdine. EEOC v. Ethan Allen, Inc. 44 F.3d 116, 119 (2d Cir.1994) (citations omitted). Plaintiffs first must create an inference of discrimination by establishing a prima facie case by a preponderance of the evidence. Id. Defendants then have a burden of production to offer a legitimate, nondiscriminatory reason for the employment decision. Id. In order to prevail, plaintiffs finally must demonstrate that defendants' articulated reason was merely a pretext for discrimination. Id. The ultimate burden of proving age discrimination always remains with plaintiffs. Gallo v. Prudential Residential Servs., 22 F.3d 1219, 1224 (2d Cir.1994).

A. Unlawful Termination Claim

In their complaint, plaintiffs claim that Cornell discriminated against them "by dismissing them and/or denying them employment on the basis of their age." Compl. ¶ 30. Defendants argue first that plaintiffs presented no prima facie case of unlawful termination because Austin and McPeak were seasonal employees whose limited term of employment ended at the completion of the 1992 golf season. Unlawful termination cannot occur where a party is not an employee at the time of the alleged discrimination. See Hyland v. New Haven Radiology Assocs., 794 F.2d 793, 796 (2d Cir.1986).

Plaintiffs have not responded to this argument. Indeed, during his deposition, McPeak admitted that he was not claiming Cornell dismissed him but rather that Cornell failed to rehire him for the 1993 gold season. Def.Aff.Ex. E, at 135. Similarly, Austin stated during his deposition that Cornell never hired him to work during the 1993 golf season. Id. Ex. D., at 93-94. thus, there is no dispute that Austin and McPeak were seasonal employees. Any claim of unlawful termination therefore is dismissed for plaintiffs' failure to establish a prima facie case.

B. Unlawful Refusal to Hire

Defendants next contend that plaintiffs failed to establish a prima facie case of unlawful refusal to hire because Austin and McPeak were not qualified for the 1993 ranger positions. Plaintiffs respond that they raised genuine issues of fact with respect to their ability to work as rangers. Moreover, plaintiffs contend they produced sufficient evidence that Cornell's explanation for its action is merely a pretext for discrimination.

1. Prima Facie Case

In order to make a prima facie case of unlawful refusal to hire, plaintiffs must show that (1) they belong to the protected age group; (2) they applied for an were qualified for the ranger position; (3) they were not hired despite their qualifications; and (4) the ranger positions ultimately were filled by younger people. Taggart v. Time Inc., 924 F.2d 43, 46 (2d Cir.1991). The relevant inquiry is whether the plaintiffs were rejected "because of circumstances which give rise to an inference of unlawful discrimination." Id. Direct evidence, statistical evidence, or circumstantial evidence will support the inference of discrimination. Id. There is no dispute that Austin and McPeak are both older than 40 and thus within the age group protected by the ADEA. See 29 U.S.C. § 631(a). Similarly, there is no dispute that Cornell did not hire plaintiffs and that people younger than plaintiffs filled the ranger positions in 1993. However, Cornell contends that plaintiffs failed to show that they applied and were qualified for the ranger positions.

• • •

To establish a prima facie claim, plaintiffs need only make "a minimal showing of qualification" and demonstrate that they possess the basic skills necessary to perform the job. Owens v. New York City Hous. Auth., 934 F.2d 405, 409 (2d Cir.), cert. denied, 502 U.S. 964, 112 S.Ct. 431, 116 L.Ed.2d 451 (1991) (citation omitted). See also Chambers v. TRM Copy Ctrs. Corp., 43 F.3d 29, 37 (2d Cir.1994) (holding that plaintiff in employment discrimination case has a de minimis burden at prima facie stage). Because Austin and McPeak worked as rangers in 1992 and received no criticism from their supervisors, they raised an issue of fact as to whether they were qualified to work as rangers in 1993. Defendant Szabo testified that plaintiffs could understand the new double wave system of play, although he also stated his belief that plaintiffs could not implement it successfully. Def.Reply Aff.Ex. C, at 121-22. Moreover, it is undisputed that defendants only assumed that plaintiffs would not work longer hours. Drawing all reasonable inferences in favor of the nonmoving plaintiffs, a trier of fact could conclude that Austin and McPeak possessed the basic skills required to work as rangers and thus were qualified for the 1993 seasonal positions.

2. Nondiscriminatory Rationale

Because plaintiffs established a prima facie case, the burden of production shifts to defendants to offer a legitimate, nondiscriminatory reason for their decision. Defendants claim that plaintiffs were not rehired because they could not perform satisfactorily in the reorganized ranger position, which demanded working increased hours and closer monitoring of play. Cornell based its assessment of plaintiffs' performance on the complaints it received from golfers, the defendants' own observations, and the survey responses it collected. On its face, the golf course reorganization is an age-neutral reason for defendants' decision.

3. Pretext for Discrimination

The burden shifts again to plaintiffs to show that Cornell's justification is a pretext for age discrimination. Plaintiffs must produce "sufficient evidence to support a rational finding that the legitimate, nondiscriminatory reasons proffered by the employer were false, and that more likely than not the employees['] age was the real reason for the [employment action]." Woroski v. Nashua Corp., 31 F.3d 105, 110 (2d Cir.1994)(citation omitted); see also Gallo, 22 F.3d at 1224-25. Austin and McPeak claim that the following facts constitute evidence of Cornell's discrimination: (1) Deibert stated during his deposition that he thought Cornell should "try some fresh help for the ranger positions"; (2) Szabo testified during his deposition that he though Austin was too timid to be a good ranger and that neither plaintiff could handle the stress of the job, Pl.Decl.Ex. F, at 95, 109; (3) A golf course survey returned by former Head Golf Professional Jim Fenner stated that "you can't run a pro shop with part-time senior citizens," id, Ex. H; (4) Cornell encouraged students to apply for the ranger positions and hired four inexperienced people younger than plaintiffs for the jobs; (5) Cornell never criticized plaintiffs' performance, never disciplined them, and never gave them an opportunity to improve; and (6) Cornell initially did not tell plaintiffs that their poor performance was a factor in Cornell's decision. Drawing all reasonable inferences in favor of the nonmoving plaintiffs, at least some of these facts support the conclusion that age discrimination was the reason for Cornell's action.

• • •

Consequently, with respect to their refusal to hire claim, Austin and McPeak established a prima facie case of age discrimination, which Cornell effectively rebutted by articulating the golf course reorganization as the legitimate basis for its decision. However, plaintiffs raised genuine issues with respect to whether Cornell's explanation was pretextual. A rational trier of fact, drawing all reasonable inferences in favor of plaintiffs, could conclude that age more likely than not was the basis of Cornell's decision. Defendants' motion for summary judgment regarding this claim therefore is denied. However, because plaintiffs conceded that they were seasonal workers, they failed to establish a claim of unlawful termination. Defendants' motion for summary judgment regarding this claim is granted.

III. Individual Liability

Cornell contends in the alternative that individual defendants Costello and Szabo cannot be held liable for discrimination under the ADEA. Defendants argue that these individuals are not "employers" as defined by 29 U.S.C. § 630(b), which establishes the scope of ADEA liability. Plaintiffs respond that individual agents of an employer may be held liable for age discrimination if they exercised supervisory control over the dispute employment decision.

The provisions of the ADEA apply to an "employer." 29 U.S.C. § 623(a). The ADEA defines employer as "a person engaged in an industry affecting commerce who has twenty or more employees for each working day in each of twenty or more calendar weeks in the current or preceding calendar year ... [and] [t]he term also means ... any agent of such a person. . . ." Id.

• • •

Although courts are divided on the imposition of individual liability under the ADEA, I will adopt the reasoning of prior decisions in the Northern District of New York. Thus, Costello and Szabo may be individually liable for discriminatory acts they performed while exercising supervisory control over plaintiffs' employment. In this case, it is clear that defendants, Szabo and Costello controlled plaintiffs' employment with Cornell. There is not dispute that they, along with Deibert, jointly decided not to rehire plaintiffs. Moreover, Costello was plaintiffs' direct supervisor. Thus, the individual defendants participated in the process that plaintiffs claim was discriminatory, and I will not dismiss the complaint against them. Defendants' motion accordingly is denied.

■ ■ ■ ■

Fundamental Concepts

Scope.   Enacted in 1967, ADEA draws its substantive provisions directly from Title VII and uses virtually identical language. Section 623 (§4) states,

> (a) It shall be an unlawful employment practice for an employer—
> (1) to fail or refuse to hire or to discharge any individual, or otherwise discriminate against any individual with respect to his compensation, terms, conditions, or privileges of employment, because of such individual's age; or
> (2) to limit, segregate, or classify his employees or applicants for employment in any way which would deprive or tend to deprive any individual of employment opportunities or otherwise adversely affect his status as an employee, because of such individual's age; or
> (3) reduce the wage rate of any employee to comply with this chapter.
> 29 U.S.C. § 623 (§4).

ADEA applies to workers over the age or 40, but exempts several classes of workers, in particular public safety personnel (such as police officers, pilots, train engineers), certain top-level managers, and until 1994, tenured college professors over 70. Currently there is no maximum age limit to protection.

ADEA applies to **employers** with 20 or more employees working at least twenty calendar weeks and whose organizations impact interstate commerce and which operate within or outside of the United States. Title VII, however, excludes the United States and some departments of the District of Columbia. Unlike Title VII Native American tribes, religious organizations and bona fide membership clubs, such as country clubs are not excluded from its definition of employer.

Theories of Liability

An individual challenging an employment decision under the Act bears the ultimate burden of demonstrating by a preponderance of the evidence that age was a determining factor in the employer's decision, and that "but for" the employer's age-based animus the challenged employment decision would not have been made (*Shreve v. Cornell University*, 1988, citing *Pena v. Brattleboro Retreat*, 1983). Since ADEA's language mirrors Title VII, courts applying ADEA have adopted Title VII's four theories of liability: individual disparate treatment, systemic disparate treatment, disparate impact, and retaliation. This chapter will not go through the same degree of detail on these for theories as is available in Chapter 5.81 Title VII, so please refer to that chapter for greater detail on these theories.

Disparate Treatment. Disparate treatment of an employee occurs when the employer *intentionally discriminates* against a worker and thus, acts with an illegal motive. Disparate treatment may occur in one of two forms: individual, where an employer treats one person with discriminatory animus or systemic, where an employer acts in furtherance of a pattern or practice of discrimination.

Individual Disparate Treatment. There are two ways in which a plaintiff or the EEOC can prove intentional discrimination. The first is where **direct evidence of intent** exists through statements made by the defendant.

A second method used when one is relying on circumstantial evidence is through the use of an **inference**. A plaintiff can establish an inference for the court by comparing how an employer treats similarly situated employees of different protected classes. In *McDonnell Douglas Corp. v. Green* (1973) and *Texas Department of Community Affairs v. Burdine* (1981), the United States Supreme Court developed the following framework for evaluating these claims: "[f]irst, the plaintiff has the burden of proving by the preponderance of the evidence a prima facie case of discrimination. Second, if the plaintiff succeeds in proving the prima facie case the burden shifts to the defendant 'to articulate some legitimate nondiscriminatory reason for the employee's rejection.' Third, should the defendant carry this burden, the plaintiff must then have an opportunity to prove by a preponderance of the evidence that the legitimate reasons offered by the defendant were not its true reasons, but were a pretext for discrimination" (*Burdine*, 1981).

"The ultimate burden of persuading the trier of fact that the defendant intentionally discriminated against the plaintiff remains at all times with the plaintiff" (*Burdine*, 1981). Under this widely relied upon standard a plaintiff can establish a **prima facie age discrimination case** by proving:

(if applicant)
1. Applicant is a member of the protected class (over 40)
2. Applicant applied for job for which employer was seeking applicants
3. Applicant was qualified to perform job
4. Applicant was not hired
5. Employer filled position with non-minority or continued to search

(if employee)
1. Employee is within protected class (over 40)
2. Employee was performing task satisfactorily
3. Employee was discharged or adversely affected by change in working conditions
4. Employee's work was assigned to one in non-minority category

The burden that shifts to the defendant is to rebut the plaintiff's presumption by producing evidence that the plaintiff was rejected and someone else preferred for a **legitimate, nondiscriminatory reason** (*Burdine*, 1981).

Once the employer provides a legitimate, nondiscriminatory reason for the alleged discrimination, the burden then shifts back to the employee to prove that the legitimate reason is in fact a **pretext** for intentional discrimination. There are a number of ways a plaintiff may establish evidence of pretext. According to Player (1988), these include providing direct evidence of prejudice toward the plaintiff or members of the protected class; presenting statistical evidence of an unbalanced work force; presenting evidence of the rejection of a high number of protected class members; and proving that the articulated reason for rejection has not been consistently applied to members of the majority as it has to protected class members. A plaintiff may also present the fact that the proffered legitimate, nondiscriminatory reason was not given to the plaintiff at the time the employment decision was made as evidence that it was an afterthought and thus, pretextual. (Player, 1988).

Age Harassment. The EEOC has long viewed harassment on the basis of race, color, religion, sex, or national origin as violative of Title VII. The Supreme Court in *Meritor Savings Bank, FSB v. Vinson* (1986) stated that, "[t]he Commission has held and continues to hold that an employer has a duty to maintain a working environment free of harassment based on race, color, religion, sex, national origin, **age**, or disability, and that the duty requires positive action where necessary to eliminate such practices or remedy their effects."

In *Eggleston v. South Bend Community School Corporation* (N.D.Ind. 1994), a coach and teacher who filed a claim under ADEA and had entered into a conciliation agreement with the school in accordance with EEOC procedures, brought an action for, among other things, retaliation and harassment based on age which he was subjected to as a result of enforcing his rights under ADEA. The defendant school corporation argued that the plaintiff failed to establish a prima facie case of age discrimination because "[a]t best the allegations of harassment . . . collectively amount to nothing more than a personality dispute or a mere inconvenience . . . and thus fail to achieve the level of an adverse action by the employer necessary to make out a prima facie case." The court, relying on EEOC Guidelines and the Supreme Court precedent in *Meritor* which addressed hostile environment sexual harassment, found that an ADEA action based on hostile environment harassment was feasible.

Criteria and Standards for Age Harassment. The EEOC has outlined criteria for determining whether an action creates harassing, and therefore unlawful, behavior. The **criteria** are the same as those in Title VII harassment cases. They are that "the conduct: (i) has the purpose of effect of creating an intimidating hostile or offensive work environment; (ii) has the purpose or effect of unreasonably interfering with an individual's work performance; or (iii) otherwise adversely affects an individual's employment opportunities." The **reasonable person standard** is used for determining whether the harassment is actionable. Under this standard the court will determine whether the conduct is sufficiently severe or pervasive to alter the conditions of employment and to create an intimidating, hostile work environment.

Systemic Disparate Treatment. Under the theory of systemic disparate treatment plaintiffs are challenging broad sweeping employment policies which are discriminatory. According to Zimmer, Sullivan, and Richards (1987), aside from the practice, now generally illegal, of mandatory retirement at a certain age, there may be few facially discriminatory policies in place which adversely affect older workers. The cases will more likely emerge from a *Teamsters v. United States* (1977) type analysis, where patterns of discrimination against older workers will emerge from statistical evidence.

When challenging system-wide patterns or practices, plaintiffs will often rely upon the use of statistical evidence bolstered with evidence of individual discriminatory treatment. The statistics will compare the racial, ethnic, or gender balance of the qualified labor population with the population of a work force which draws employees from that population. In *Teamsters* (1977), the court stated that statistics showing an imbalance are probative because such imbalance is often a telltale sign of purposeful discrimination. Absent discrimination it is assumed that over time nondiscriminatory work place practices will result in a work force which is representative of a region's general population.

Once a plaintiff establishes a presumption of a discriminatory pattern or practice, the burden then shifts to the employer to demonstrate why an inference of discriminatory animus could not be drawn from the plaintiff's evidence. Here the defendant has two options. First, the defendant can attack the plaintiff's statistical evidence as inaccurate or insignificant. Second, the employer may seek to provide a nondiscriminatory explanation for the apparently discriminatory result. As with individual disparate treatment, once a defendant produces this explanation, the burden will shift to the plaintiff to persuade the court that the defendant's stated explanation is in fact a pretext for discrimination.

Disparate Impact. Disparate impact discrimination exists where a plaintiff is challenging a neutral employment practice, regardless of intent, which has a discriminatory effect upon a protected group. Neutral selection devices such as educational achievement, physical requirements, or scores on a test for the very purpose of excluding persons on the basis of age may constitute an ADEA violation (Player, 1988).

The prima facie case requires that the employee or the EEOC prove that the employment practice or policy has an adverse impact on the basis of age. This is usually established through statistical evidence documenting the impact of the practice on older workers. The use of statistical evidence is difficult and the plaintiff's methodology may be attacked as being flawed.

The employer may then rebut the plaintiff's argument by attacking the statistical analysis or producing evidence that the practice is job-related. This requires proof that the challenged employment practice is necessary to achieve some legitimate business objective, the practice actually achieves that objective, and there is no reasonable method of accomplishing the objective without a discriminatory impact on the protected class.

Once the employer shows the barrier is job-related, the burden shifts back to the plaintiff to prove that the barrier is a pretext for discrimination, by showing that there are other adequate devices which do not discriminate against a protected class.

Retaliation. ADEA also provides a cause of action for retaliation in response to a plaintiff's filing of a claim of age discrimination. Section 4 (d) of ADEA provides that:

> It shall be unlawful for an employer to discriminate against any of his employees or applicants for employment . . . because such individual . . . has opposed a practice made an unlawful employment practice by this subchapter, or because such individual has made any charge, testified, assisted or participated in any manner in an investigation proceeding, or litigation under this chapter. 29 U.S.C. §623.

The plaintiff's burden of proof in ADEA retaliation claims mirrors that of Title VII retaliation suits. The plaintiff bears the initial burden of establishing a prima facie case of retaliation. To establish the prima facie retaliation case, the plaintiff must show by a preponderance of the evidence that 1) the plaintiff engaged in a statutorily protected activity; 2) adverse action was taken against the plaintiff by the employer subsequent to and contemporaneously with such activity; and 3) a causal link exists between the protected activity and the adverse action (*Jalil v. Advel Corp.*, 1989). The causal link may be established by showing a proximity in time between the filing of a charge and the alleged negative action (*Eggleston v. South Bend Community School Corporation,* 1994). Once the plaintiff has established a prima facie case, the defendant may introduce evidence providing legitimate, nonretaliatory reasons for its conduct. If the defendant properly introduces such evidence, then the burden shifts back to the plaintiff to show that the defendant's justification is merely pretext for covering up unlawful retaliation.

A good example of a retaliation case is *Eggleston v. South Bend Community School Corporation* (N.D.Ind. 1994), in which the plaintiff filed an EEOC ADEA complaint and the following negative actions occurred. First a school board member stated that "[i]t will be a cold day in hell before Gene Eggleston coaches in this system." Second, the plaintiff's evaluation system changed so that the Head Football Coach, a named defendant in the ADEA action evaluated his work as coach. Third, the supervisory coaching staff's 'micro-management' of the plaintiff's responsibilities as coach led to a dispute and the removal of an assistant coach who served the plaintiff. The defendants raised as legitimate, nondiscriminatory reasons for the actions 1) a different interpretation of the school board member's statement, 2) the change in evaluation was system-wide and not done with discriminatory animus toward the plaintiff, 3) the school denied dispute was related to the plaintiff's age discrimination claim. The court refused to dismiss the retaliation claim as it found that there were genuine issues of fact in dispute over the defendants' stated legitimate nondiscriminatory reasons for the alleged retaliatory actions.

Additional Defenses

Bona Fide Occupational Qualification.   It is not illegal to discriminate on the basis of age, where an employer can show the classification is a bona fide occupational qualification reasonably necessary to the normal operation of the employer's business. The language is so similar to Title VII that the United States Supreme Court has construed the two virtually the same (Player, 1988, citing *Western Airlines v. Criswell,* 1985). Thus, an age-based bona fide occupational qualification defense requires the employer to prove that older workers could not safely and effectively perform essential job duties and the employer must have a factual basis for believing that older workers could not perform the job. The bona fide occupational qualification must also be reasonably necessary to the normal operation of the business. Finally, customer preference cannot be the basis for a bona fide occupational qualification.

Seniority Systems.   A seniority system may be exempt from ADEA where the seniority system does not require or permit involuntary retirement and can serve as a defense so long as the system is not rooted in age discrimination (Zimmer, Sullivan and Richards, 1987). In fact a valid seniority system should favor older workers since increased seniority will be positively correlated with age.

Bona Fide Employee Benefit Plans.   In ADEA Congress allowed for employers to make actuarial distinctions according to age provided that the terms of a bona fide employee benefit plan (retirement, pension, insurance) were not a subterfuge to evade compliance with ADEA [29 U.S.C. §623 (§4 (f)(2))]. This section stems from a congressional recognition that costs tend to increase for older workers who as a group are more subject to illness, long-term disability, and death (Zimmer, Sullivan and Richards, 1987). From a fairness perspective, employers should not have these additional costs imposed upon them. The defense only applies to benefit plans and does not allow employers to make wage distinctions or reduce benefits such as paid vacations or sick leave based on an employee's age (Player, 1988). The benefit plans must be valid ones and the reduction in benefits must be based on demonstrable actuarial distinctions reflecting the actual variation in costs for older workers. For instance, an employer's failure to provide layoff income or severance pay for older workers because they have pensions is discriminatory as the employer's system is not a valid plan and is not based in actuarial distinctions. Health care benefits cannot be eliminated at a certain age for an employee or a spouse and the benefits provided must be the same as benefits provided to younger employees and their spouses.

"Reasonable Factors Other Than Age."   Under ADEA, an affirmative defense exists which is very similar to the Equal Pay Act approach outlined in chapter 5.85. The defense allows a defendant make a differentiation between employees based on reasonable factors other than age. This exceeds the simple burden of production on the employer to establish a legitimate, nondiscriminatory defense to a prima facie case. With this defense, once the prima facie case or age discrimination is established by a plaintiff and the burden shifts to the employer, the employer can try to persuade the court that the employer's decision was based on age neutral factors.

Remedies. Section 7 of ADEA provides the following power to remedy age discrimination:

> Liquidated damages shall be payable only in cases of willful violation of [ADEA]. In any action brought to enforce [ADEA] the court shall have jurisdiction to grant such legal or equitable relief as may be appropriate to effectuate the purposes of [ADEA], including without limitation judgments compelling employment, reinstatement, or promotion, or enforcing the liability for amounts deemed to be unpaid minimum wages or unpaid overtime compensation under this section. 29 U.S.C. §626.

ADEA incorporates the remedy provisions of the Fair Labor Standards Act and thus, the collection of back pay is determined by that act. Once liability is established under ADEA, the fact finder will determine the appropriate amount of back pay. If the conduct was willful, liquidated damages in the amount of the back pay will be also awarded. In addition. courts are granted the power to use equitable relief to put the plaintiff back in the position he/she would have been in had their not been illegal age discrimination.

References

A. Cases

Austin v. Cornell University, 891 F. Supp. 740 (N.D.N.Y. 1995)

Eggleston v. South Bend Community School Corp., 858 F. Supp. 841 (N.D. Ind. 1994)

Pena v. Brattleboro Retreat, 702 F.2d 322 (2d Cir. 1983)

Shreve v. Cornell University, 1988 U.S. Dist. LEXIS 3109 (N.D.N.Y. 1988)

Teamsters v. United States, 431 U.S. 324 (1977)

Western Airlines v. Criswell, 472 U.S. 400 (1985)

B. Publications

Player, M.A. (1988). *Employment Discrimination Law*, St. Paul, Minn: West Publishing Co.

Zimmer, M.J., Sullivan C.A., and Richards, R.F. (1988). *Cases and Materials on Employment Discrimination*, Boston: Little, Brown, and Co.

C. Legislation

Age Discrimination in Employment Act, 29 U.S.C.A. §§ 621-634 (1990)

—— 5.83 ——

Title I of the Americans with Disabilities Act

Mary A. Hums
University of Massachusetts-Amherst

What do the following athletes have in common: Jim Eisenreich (baseball), Magic Johnson (basketball), Ann Cody (track and field), and Trisha Zorn (swimming)? Each has some type of disability. Eisenreich has Tourette's Syndrome. Johnson is HIV-positive. Cody is confined to a wheelchair as a result of a spinal cord injury. Zorn is visually impaired. Yet, each has had successful athletic careers. Athletes with disabilities are becoming more and more visible every day, but what about other people with disabilities who wish to work as sport managers in some segment of the sport industry? What barriers do they face and what kind of legal protections do they have against employment discrimination? In addition to addressing facility issues, the Americans With Disabilities Act (ADA) provides guidelines for employers when dealing with employees with disabilities. These guidelines help ensure equal opportunity for people with disabilities by opening up the definition of who is a "qualified individual" to people of all abilities.

■ ■ ■ ■

Representative Case

MADDOX v. UNIVERSITY OF TENNESSEE
United States Court of Appeals for the Sixth Circuit
62 F.3d 843 (1995)

OPINION: BAILEY BROWN, Circuit Judge.

The plaintiff-appellant, Robert Maddox, a former assistant football coach at the University of Tennessee, brought suit against the school, its Board of Trustees, and its athletic director, Doug Dickey (collectively "UT"), under § 504 of the Rehabilitation Act of 1973, as amended, 29 U.S.C. § 701, et seq., and the Americans with Disabilities Act of 1990 ("ADA"), 42 U.S.C. § 12101, et seq., alleging discriminatory discharge on the basis of his disability, alcoholism. The district court granted UT's motion for summary judgment, concluding that Maddox was not terminated solely by reason of, or because of, his handicap, but rather, because of a well-publicized incident

in which Maddox was arrested for driving under the influence of alcohol. Maddox appealed. We AFFIRM.

I. Facts

On February 17, 1992, Doug Dickey, acting as UT's athletic director, extended to Maddox an offer of employment as an assistant football coach. The position did not carry tenure and was terminable at will in accordance with the policies of the Personnel Manual. As part of the hiring process, Maddox completed an application. On the line after "Describe any health problems or physical limitations, which . . . would limit your ability to perform the duties of the position for which you are applying,"

517

Maddox wrote "None." In response to the question "have you ever been arrested for a criminal offense of any kind?" Maddox replied "No." These responses were not accurate. According to what Maddox alleges in this lawsuit, he suffers from the disability of alcoholism. Also, Maddox was arrested three times before 1992, once for possession of a controlled substance, and twice for driving a motor vehicle under the influence of alcohol. As to the first answer, Maddox claims that it is in fact correct because "it has never affected my coaching ability . . . I never drank on the job." As to the second question, Maddox claims that another university employee, Bill Higdon, advised him not to include the information concerning his prior arrests on the application.

On May 26, 1992, after Maddox began working at UT, a Knoxville police officer arrested Maddox and charged him with driving under the influence of alcohol and public intoxication. According to newspaper reports, the accuracy of which is not contested, Maddox backed his car across a major public road at a high rate of speed, almost striking another vehicle. When stopped by the officer, Maddox was combative, his pants were unzipped, and he refused to take a breathalyzer. He also lied to the arresting officer, stating that he was unemployed. This incident was highly publicized, and UT was obviously embarrassed by the public exposure surrounding the event.

Maddox entered an alcohol rehabilitation program at a UT hospital after his arrest. UT first placed Maddox on paid administrative leave. In June 1992, however, Dickey and then Head Coach Johnny Majors determined that the allegations were accurate and jointly issued a letter notifying Maddox that his employment was being terminated. They testified that termination was necessary because of: 1) the criminal acts and misconduct of Maddox; 2) the bad publicity surrounding the arrest; and 3) the fact that Maddox was no longer qualified, in their minds, for the responsibilities associated with being an assistant coach. Both Dickey and Majors deny that they were aware that Maddox was an alcoholic or that Maddox's alcoholism played any part in the decision to discharge him. Nevertheless, Maddox brought this action alleging that the termination was discriminatory on the basis of his alcoholism in violation of his rights under the Rehabilitation Act and the ADA. UT responded by filing a motion for summary judgment which the district court granted. The court recognized that, under both statutes, a plaintiff must show that he was fired by reason of his disability. In the court's view, summary judgment was appropriate because Maddox could not establish the existence of a genuine issue of material fact with respect to whether he had been fired by reason of his status as an alcoholic rather than by reason of his criminal misconduct. Maddox now appeals.

II. Analysis

1. Standard of Review

Review of a grant of summary judgment is de novo, utilizing the same test used by the district court to determine whether summary judgment is appropriate. A court shall render summary judgment when there is no genuine issue as to any material fact, the moving party is entitled to judgment as a matter of law, and reasonable minds could come to but one conclusion, and that conclusion is adverse to the party against whom the motion is made.

2. Maddox Was Not Terminated Because of His Disability

Maddox raises a number of issues on appeal which he contends show that the district court erred in granting summary judgment to the defendants. Maddox first alleges that the district court erred in analyzing his claim under the Rehabilitation Act. Section 504 of the Act provides, "no otherwise qualified individual with a disability . . . shall, solely by reason of her or his disability, be excluded from the participation in, be denied the benefits of, or be subject to discrimination under any program or activity receiving Federal financial assistance." 29 U.S.C. § 794(a). Thus, in order to establish a violation of the Rehabilitation Act, a plaintiff must show:

> (1) The plaintiff is a "handicapped person" under the Act; (2) The plaintiff is "otherwise qualified" for participation in the program; (3) The plaintiff is being excluded from participation in, being denied the benefits of, or being subjected to discrimination under the program solely by reason of his handicap; and (4) The relevant program or activity is receiving Federal financial assistance.

It is not disputed in this case that UT constitutes a program receiving Federal financial assistance under the Act. Likewise, we assume, without deciding, that alcoholics may be "individuals with a disability" for purposes of the Act. . . . Thus, our analysis focuses on whether Maddox is "otherwise qualified" under the Act and whether he was discharged "solely by reason of" his disability. The burden of making these showings rests with Maddox.

In support of its motion for summary judgment, UT contended that both factors weighed in its favor. First, Dickey and Majors contended that they did not even know that Maddox was considered an alcoholic in making both the decision to hire and fire him. Moreover, they contended that Maddox was discharged, not because he was an alcoholic, but because of his criminal conduct and behavior and the significant amount of bad publicity surrounding him and the school. UT alternatively contended that Maddox is nevertheless not "otherwise qualified" to continue in the position of assistant football coach.

The district court granted UT's motion for summary judgment, specifically holding that UT did not discharge Maddox solely by reason of his disability. The court found it beyond dispute that Maddox's discharge resulted from his misconduct rather than his disability of alcoholism. The court noted,

> It cannot be denied in this case, Mr. Maddox was charged with . . . [driving while under the influence and public intoxication] which would not be considered socially acceptable by any objective standard. The affidavit testimony of Mr. Dickey and Mr. Majors is clear on the point that it was this specific conduct, not any condition to which it might be related, which provoked the termination of Mr. Maddox's employment.

As a result, the court found it unnecessary to decide the alternative ground of whether Maddox was "otherwise qualified."

Maddox contends that the district court erred in distinguishing between discharge for misconduct and discharge solely by reason of his disability of alcoholism. Maddox claims that he has difficulty operating a motor vehicle while under the influence of alcohol and therefore he characterizes drunk driving as a causally connected manifestation of the disability of alcoholism. Thus, Maddox contends that because alcoholism caused the incident upon which UT claims to have based its decision to discharge him, UT in essence discharged him because of his disability of alcoholism. In support, Maddox relies on Teahan v. Metro-North Commuter R.R. Co., 951 F.2d 511, 516-17 (2d Cir. 1991), cert. denied, 121 L. Ed. 2d 24, 113 S. Ct. 54 (1992), in which the Second Circuit held that a Rehabilitation Act plaintiff can show that he was fired "solely by reason of" his disability, or at least create a genuine issue of material fact, if he can show that he was fired for conduct that is "causally related" to his disability. In Teahan, the defendant company discharged the plaintiff because of his excessive absenteeism. The plaintiff responded by claiming that his absenteeism was caused by his alcoholism and therefore protected under the Rehabilitation Act. The district court disagreed and granted summary judgment for the employer because, the court found, Teahan was fired for his absenteeism and not because of his alcoholism. The Second Circuit reversed the district court's grant of summary judgment on appeal, however, rejecting the court's distinction between misconduct (absenteeism), and the disabling condition of alcoholism. The court presumed that Teahan's absenteeism resulted from his alcoholism and held that one's disability should

not be distinguished from its consequences in determining whether he was fired "solely by reason" of his disability. Id. Thus, Maddox argues that, in the instant case, when UT acted on the basis of the conduct allegedly caused by the alcoholism, it was the same as if UT acted on the basis of alcoholism itself.

We disagree and hold that the district court correctly focused on the distinction between discharging someone for unacceptable misconduct and discharging someone because of the disability. As the district court noted, to hold otherwise, an employer would be forced to accommodate all behavior of an alcoholic which could in any way be related to the alcoholic's use of intoxicating beverages; behavior that would be intolerable if engaged in by a sober employee or, for that matter, an intoxicated but nonalcoholic employee.

Despite Teahan, a number of cases have considered the issue of misconduct as distinct from the status of the disability. In Taub v. Frank, 957 F.2d 8 (1st Cir. 1992), the plaintiff Taub, a heroin addict, brought suit against his former employer, the United States Postal Service, alleging discriminatory discharge under the Rehabilitation Act. The Post Office discharged Taub after he was arrested for possession of heroin for distribution. The district court granted the Post Office's motion for summary judgment and Taub appealed. The First Circuit affirmed and held that Taub could not prevail on his Rehabilitation Act claim because his discharge resulted from his misconduct, possession of heroin for distribution, rather than his disability of heroin addiction. The court reasoned that addiction-related criminal conduct is simply too attenuated to extend the Act's protection to Taub.

The conduct/disability distinction was also recognized by the Fourth Circuit in Little v. F.B.I., 1 F.3d 255 (4th Cir. 1993). In Little, the F.B.I. discharged the plaintiff, known by his supervisors to be an alcoholic, after an incident in which he was intoxicated on duty. The district court granted summary judgment in favor of the F.B.I. on the basis that the plaintiff was no longer "otherwise qualified" to serve as an F.B.I. agent. The Fourth Circuit affirmed, noting as an additional basis that the plaintiff's employment was not terminated because of his handicap. The court noted, "based on no less authority than common sense, it is clear that an employer subject to the . . . [Rehabilitation] Act must be permitted to terminate its employees on account of egregious misconduct, irrespective of whether the employee is handicapped." Id.; see also Landefeld v. Marion Gen. Hosp., Inc., 994 F.2d 1178, 1183 (6th Cir. 1993) (Nelson, J., concurring) ("The plaintiff was clearly suspended because of his intolerable conduct, and not solely because of his mental condition.")

Moreover, language within the respective statutes makes clear that such a distinction is warranted. Section 706(8)(c) of the Rehabilitation Act states:

"Individuals with a disability" does not include any individual who is an alcoholic whose current use of alcohol prevents such individual from performing the duties of the job in question or whose employment, by reason of such current alcohol abuse, would constitute a direct threat to property or the safety of others.

Likewise, the ADA specifically provides that an employer may hold an alcoholic employee to the same performance and behavior standards to which the employer holds other employees "even if any unsatisfactory performance is related to the alcoholism of such employee." 42 U.S.C. § 12114(c)(4). These provisions clearly contemplate distinguishing the issue of misconduct from one's status as an alcoholic.

At bottom, we conclude that the analysis of the district court is more in keeping with the purposes and limitations of the respective Acts, and therefore, we decline to adopt the Second Circuit's reasoning in Teahan. Employers subject to the Rehabilitation Act and ADA must be permitted to take appropriate action with respect to an employee on account of egregious or criminal conduct, regardless of whether the employee is disabled. In the instant case, for example, while alcoholism might compel Maddox to drink, it did not compel him to operate a motor vehicle or engage in the other inappropriate conduct reported. Likewise, suppose an alcoholic becomes intoxicated and sexually assaults a coworker? We believe that it strains logic to conclude that such action could be protected under the Rehabilitation Act or the ADA merely because the actor has been diagnosed as an alcoholic and claims that such action was caused by his disability.

3. Pretext

Maddox alternatively contends that even if UT has successfully disclaimed reliance on his disability in making the employment decision, the district court nevertheless erred in determining that Maddox had produced no evidence that the reasons articulated by UT were a pretext for discrimination. A Rehabilitation Act plaintiff may demonstrate pretext by showing that the asserted reasons had no basis in fact, the reasons did not in fact motivate the discharge, or, if they were factors in the decision, they were jointly insufficient to motivate the discharge

Maddox first alleges that Dickey and Majors knew that Maddox was an alcoholic. Setting aside for a moment the legal significance of this statement, it is not supported factually in the record.

• • •

Maddox also claims that he knew of other coaches in the football program who drank alcohol in public and who were arrested for DUI but who were not discharged. This point is also irrelevant. Whether Maddox had such knowledge is immaterial. There is no evidence in the record establishing that Majors or Dickey had knowledge of the public intoxication of any other coach, or failed to reprimand or terminate any coach who they knew to have engaged in such behavior.

Maddox finally contends that UT's conclusion that he is no longer qualified to be an assistant coach at UT is without merit. Maddox claims that his misconduct did not affect his "coaching" responsibilities because an assistant coach's duties are limited to the practice and playing fields, and do not comprise of serving as a counselor or mentor to the players or serving as a representative of the school. Maddox relies on the fact that none of these functions were explained to him in his formal job description.

We first note that this allegation seems more appropriate for determining whether he was "otherwise qualified" rather than whether he was discharged because of his disability. Nevertheless, Maddox's position is simply unrealistic. It is obvious that as a member of the football coaching staff, Maddox would be representing not only the team but also the university. As in the instant case, UT received full media coverage because of this "embarrassing" incident. The school falls out of favor with the public, and the reputation of the football program suffers. Likewise, to argue that football coaches today, with all the emphasis on the misuse of drugs and alcohol by athletes, are not "role models" and "mentors" simply ignores reality.

The district court's grant of summary judgment in favor of the defendants is AFFIRMED.

■ ■ ■ ■

Fundamental Concepts

The Americans with Disabilities Act of 1990 (ADA) is not limited to facility accessibility issues, but also addresses employment issues as well. It is important to remember that the ADA covers the entire scope of the employment process. According to Miller, Fielding and Pitts (1993), sport managers must be aware of

ADA requirements as they relate to selection criteria, application accessibility, job application and interview inquiries, medical exams and inquiries, reasonable accommodations, and essential job functions. This chapter focuses primarily on the question of reasonable accommodation. Before examining the ADA's application to sport organizations, some basic definitions must be established.

Employer.   According to Title I, §12111 [sec. 101] (5)(a) of the ADA, the term "employer" means ". . . a person engaged in an industry affecting commerce who has 15 or more employees for each working day in each of 20 or more calendar weeks in the current or preceding calendar year, and any agent of such person." In *Jones v. Southeast Alabama Baseball Umpires Association* (1994), an umpire who wore a prosthetic leg had his request to work an increased number of varsity high school baseball games denied and proceeded to file an ADA claim. The Umpires' Association filed for summary judgment, claiming it did not fall under ADA coverage because it did not employ umpires for more than 20 weeks. Jones was able to show that since the Association assigned umpires during both the school year and for summer youth games, it actually employed umpires for approximately six months, and therefore the Association's request for summary judgment was denied.

Disability.   According to the Preface and Part I. Employment, §12103 [Sec. 3] (2), the term "disability" means: a) a physical or mental impairment that substantially limits one or more of the major life activities of such individual; b) a record of such impairment; or c) being regarded as having such an impairment. The ADA does not specifically define "major life activities." These are usually considered basic functions such as walking, talking, seeing, hearing, caring for oneself, breathing, sitting, standing, lifting, reaching, learning, working, reasoning and remembering (Allen, 1993).

Qualified Individual with a Disability.   According to Title I, §12111 [Sec. 101] (8) of the ADA, a "qualified individual with a disability" means: ". . . an individual who, with or without reasonable accommodation, can perform the essential functions of the employment position that such an individual holds or desires." In order to be qualified, a person must still meet certain prerequisites for the position. For example, a teacher who could not pass the required national teachers' examination could be considered not qualified for a teaching position (*Pandazides v. Virginia Board of Education*, 1992). In *Sawhill v. Medical College of Pennsylvania* (1996), the plaintiff, a licensed clinical pathologist, was told his termination was because he did not fit into his department's future plans, but he later discovered his termination was related to his disability (clinical depression). The plaintiff alleged termination based on his disability in violation of the ADA. The defendant's motion to dismiss was denied. The term "qualified individual with a disability" does "not include any employee or applicant who is currently engaging in illegal use of drugs, when the covered entity acts on the basis of such use" (42 U.S.C. 12112(a)). In *Collings v. Longview Fibre Company* (1995), Collings and seven other employees alleged Longview Fibre wrongfully terminated them for their drug addiction disability in violation of the Americans with Disabilities Act. The employees were discharged because of their drug related misconduct at work and not because of their alleged substance abuse disability. The regulations accompanying the ADA indicate that employers may discharge or deny employment to people illegally using drugs, and the courts have recognized a distinction between termination of employment because of misconduct and termination because of a disability.

Reasonable Accommodation/Undue Hardship.   In order to comply with the ADA, employers must make reasonable accommodations for their workers with disabilities. However, employers only need to do so if providing the reasonable accommodation does not result in undue hardship. According to Title I, §12111 [sec. 101] (9) of the ADA, a **"reasonable accommodation"** may include:

(a) making existing facilities used by employees reasonably accessible to and usable by individuals with disabilities; and

(b) job restructuring, part-time or modified work schedules, reassignment to a vacant position, acquisition or modification of equipment or devices, appropriate adjustment or modifications of examinations, training materials or policies, the provision of qualified readers or interpreters, and other similar accommodations for individuals with disabilities.

According to Title I, §12111 [sec. 101] (10)(a) of the ADA, an **undue hardship** is ". . . an action requiring significant difficulty or expense, when considered in light of the factors set forth in subparagraph (b)":

(b) In determining whether an accommodation would impose an undue hardship on a covered entity, factors to be considered include:

(i) the nature and cost of the accommodation needed under this Act;

(ii) the overall financial resources of the facility or facilities involved in the provision of reasonable accommodation; the number of persons employed at such a facility; the effect on expenses and resources, or the impact otherwise of such accommodation upon the operation of the facility;

(iii) the overall financial resources of the covered entity; the overall size of the business of the covered entity with respect to the number of its employees; the number, type and location of its facilities; and

(iv) the type of operation or operations of the covered entity, including the composition, structure, and functions of the workforce of such entity; the geographic separateness, administrative, or fiscal relationship of the facility or facilities in question to the covered entity.

The courts have interpreted the meaning of reasonable accommodation and undue hardship differently in different cases (Churchill, 1995). Some reasonable accommodations include: working at home for an employee who experiences pain while commuting (*Sargent v. Litton Systems*, 1994); taking a leave of absence for alcoholism treatment (*Schmidt v. Safeway*, 1994); eliminating heavy lifting and strenuous work (*Henchey v. Town of North Greenbush*, 1993); allowing a police officer to carry food, glucose and an insulin injection kit (*Bombrys v. City of Toledo*, 1993); and, transferring an employee to a city where better medical care was available (*Buckingham v. United States*, 1993). There are instances, however, when the courts have indicated that the requested accommodations were unreasonable or would have resulted in undue hardship. Reasonable accommodation did not require allowing an employee who has unpredictable violent outbursts to remain in the workplace (*Mazzarella v. U.S. Postal Service*, 1993), accommodating frequent or unpredictable absences (*Jackson v. Veteran's Administration*, 1994), or assigning limited tasks that substantially reduce an employee's contribution to the company (*Russell v. Southeastern Pennsylvania Transportation Authority*, 1993).

According to the President's Commission on Employment of People with Disabilities Job Accommodation Network, of workplace accommodations made between October 1992 and September 1994, 18 percent were cost-free, 50 percent cost $500 or less, 10 percent cost between $501-$1000, 8 percent cost between $1001-$2000, 9 percent cost between $2001-$5000 and 5 percent cost greater than $5000 (Epstein, 1995). Providing reasonable accommodations for employees need not be excessively expensive or complicated.

Some examples of reasonable accommodations are provided by Vernon-Oehmke (1994). A sales associate with quadriplegia had his desk raised so his wheelchair could fit, a special handling device added to his telephone and was allowed flexible work hours in order to take advantage of transportation and personal care requirements. A groundskeeper with limited use of one arm was provided a detachable extension arm for a rake so he could hold the rake with his impaired arm while controlling the rake with his healthy arm. A data entry operator with visual impairment used a modified desk layout, shifting from the right to the left side of the desk. Persons with psychiatric disabilities have been allowed the use of sick leave for emotional as well as physical illness. An entry level worker who loses concentration and accuracy amid distractions was reserved an enclosed office space.

Recent Developments

HIV. A question facing sport managers, particularly in professional sports, is the issue of HIV-positive athletes and their ability to participate in sport as employees who are covered by the ADA. If an HIV-positive professional athlete retains the physical skills to compete at his or her professional level, then he or she is a "qualified individual with a disability" within his or her specific sport organization. The next, and more difficult, issue is whether or not the athlete poses a significant threat to other athletes, such that accommodating the participation of such an athlete creates an undue hardship on an employer. Currently, there have been no confirmed cases of HIV transmission involving contact between professional sports participants. Boxing commissions, however, are now beginning to consider and implement policies barring HIV-positive boxers from fighting. Boxers and other individual sport athletes, however, may not fall under ADA coverage as employees, whereas team sport athletes would. Sport managers must keep current with medical findings regarding HIV transmission, and must also keep in mind that any HIV-positive athletes they employ may be protected by the ADA, as well as the Rehabilitation Act and any applicable state laws.

Obesity as a Disability?   Another recent discussion has focused on whether or not being excessively overweight constitutes a disability. This becomes a timely issue in light of the tragic death of Major League Baseball umpire John McSherry, who was overweight at the time of his death. Shortly afterwards, two other umpires who were overweight voluntarily took time off from umpiring with concerns about their health.

References

A. Cases

Bombrys v. City of Toledo, 849 F.Supp. 1210 (N.D. Ohio 1993)

Buckingham v. United States, 998 F.2d 735 (9th Cir. 1993)

Collings v. Longview Fibre Company, 63 F.3d 828 (1995)

Henchey v. Town of North Greenbush, 831 F.Supp. 960 (N.D.N.Y. 1993)

Jackson v. Veteran's Administration, 22 F.3d 277 (11th Cir. 1994)

Jones v. Southeast Alabama Baseball Umpires Association, 864 F.Supp. 1135 (M.D. Ala. 1994)

Mazzarella v. U.S. Postal Service, 849 F.Supp. 89 (D. Mass. 1993)

Pandazides v. Virginia Board of Education, 804 F.Supp. 794 1992).

Russell v. Southeastern Pennsylvania Transportation Authority, 2 A.D. Cas. [BNA] 1419 (E.D. Pa. 1993)

Sargent v. Litton Systems, 841 F.Supp. 956 (N.D. Cal. 1994)

Sawhill v. Medical College of Pennsylvania, 1996 U.S. Dist. LEXIS 4097

Schmidt v. Safeway, 864 F.Supp. 991 (D. Ore. 1994)

B. Publications

Allen, J.G. (1993). *Complying with the ADA: A Small Business Guide to Hiring and Employing the Disabled.* New York: John Wiley & Sons.

Churchill, S.S. (1995). Reasonable Accommodations in the Workplace: A Shared Responsibility. *Massachusetts Law Review*, June, 73-83.

Epstein, S.B. (1995). In Search of a Bright Line: Determining When an Employer's Financial Hardship Becomes "Undue" Under the Americans with Disabilities Act. *Vanderbilt Law Review*, 48, 391-478.

Miller, L.K., Fielding, L.W., & Pitts, B.G. (1993). Hiring Concerns Impacting the Sport Practitioner. *Journal of Legal Aspects of Sport*, 3, 3-15.

Vernon-Oehmke, A. (1994). *Effective Hiring and ADA Compliance*. New York: American Management Association.

C. Legislation

Americans with Disabilities Act of 1990, 42 U.S.C.A. §12101 et seq. (West, 1993)

Title IX of the Educational Amendments of 1972

Mary A. Hums • Lisa Pike Masteralexis
University of Massachusetts-Amherst

The annual athletic department budget at Marion Heights College has a line item for coaches' salaries. When the monies are divided up, the coaches for the men's sports end up with two-thirds of the money while the coaches of the women's sports get the other one-third. Because of this, the only coaches who will work for these salaries to coach the women's sports lack experience and knowledge of their sports, and so the play on the field suffers, the women's teams have losing records and morale is low among the female athletes. Knowing that Title IX includes a component involving coaches, rumors begin to fly among the women athletes on the Marion Heights College campus about the possibility of initiating a Title IX investigation of the program.

■ ■ ■ ■

Representative Case

HARKER v. UTICA COLLEGE OF SYRACUSE UNIVERSITY

United States District Court, Northern District of New York
885 F. Supp. 378 (1995)

OPINION:

Introduction

This case is before the court on defendants' motion for summary judgment. Plaintiff, a former women's basketball coach at Utica College (the "College"), brought this action pursuant to Title VII, Title IX, and the Equal Pay Act, alleging that she was discriminated against based on her gender and that her employment contract was not renewed by defendants after she complained about the inequities between her job and that of the male basketball coach. Defendants, Utica College, James Spartano, College Athletic Director and Michael Simpson, College President, deny these allegations, and move for summary judgment on the grounds that: (1) plaintiff's claims under Title IX regarding the College's athletic program generally are not justiciable; (2) plaintiff cannot state a prima facie case of discriminatory termination, and can produce

no evidence that she was discharged because of her gender; and (3) plaintiff's salary disparity claim fails because she cannot show she was paid less than similarly situated male employees.

Background

Plaintiff was hired to coach the women's basketball team at Utica College for the 1990-91 academic year. At the time of her hiring in 1990, plaintiff had a bachelor's degree and nine years of college basketball coaching experience at the Division III and junior college levels. After accepting the position, plaintiff agreed to the terms of her contract with defendant James Spartano, the Athletic Director at the College. Under the terms of her original contract, plaintiff was employed for ten months, and received compensation of $25,000 for coaching basketball and performing teaching duties, with an additional $3,000 for coaching women's softball. These terms were consistent with the original offer submitted by Mr. Spartano to the plaintiff, she did not attempt to negotiate any changes in the compensation or benefits provided.

Since 1987, the head coach of the men's basketball team at the College has been Edwin Jones. Mr. Jones was hired as men's head coach in 1987 after the College dropped from a Division I school to a Division III school. At the time of his appointment as head coach, Mr. Jones had a master's degree, and a total of fourteen years of college coaching experience, the last six coming as an assistant at the College when it was in Division I. In 1987, Mr. Jones was given a multi-year contract with a starting salary of $23,000. By 1990, when plaintiff was hired, Mr. Jones had seventeen years coaching experience, including nine years at the College, and was making $32,500. In addition to this compensation, as part of his contract, Mr. Jones negotiated an arrangement whereby the College would pay for half of his auto insurance and provide him with a monthly auto allowance. This was a continuation of an arrangement that was in place while Mr. Jones had served as an assistant coach at the College, the purpose of which was to reimburse him for expenses incurred in connection with recruiting trips.

Plaintiff's contract was renewed in 1991, when her salary was increased to $25,765, and again in 1992, when her salary was increased to $29,916. In early March 1993, however, defendant Spartano approached defendant Simpson regarding plaintiff's performance of her coaching duties. At that time, defendant Spartano expressed concern about whether the College was going to be able to field a women's basketball team for the 1993-94 season. This concern was based upon defendant Spartano's realization that only one member of the 1992-93 team would be returning to the team for the next season if plaintiff remained as coach. In addition to the dwindling number of returning players to the 1993-94 women's basketball team, the defendants were concerned with the fact that plaintiff had not been successful in recruiting new players for the team.

As early as January 1993, defendant Spartano met with plaintiff in regard to her recruiting efforts for the 1993-94 team. Another meeting was held in February, at which point defendant Spartano asked plaintiff to provide him with a list of players that she was recruiting for the 1993-94 team. Plaintiff ultimately provided him with a list of names of recruits and defendant Spartano proceeded to investigate the recruits on the list. As a result of his investigation, defendant Spartano found that the names on the list were primarily students who had expressed an interest in basketball on their Admissions materials rather than players who had been actively recruited by plaintiff, and that no high quality players had committed to play for the College.

In addition to this perceived failure to adequately recruit, defendant Spartano also informed defendant Simpson of his concern over complaints that members of the 1992-93 team had regarding plaintiff's coaching.

• • •

As a result of her poor recruiting and bad rapport with her players, on April 5, 1993, defendant Spartano notified plaintiff that he had recommended that her contract not be renewed for the 1993-94 year by defendant Simpson. That same day, plaintiff met with defendant Simpson to discuss defendant Spartano's recommendation. Plaintiff claims that, during this meeting, she complained about the inequities that existed between the terms of her employment and those of Mr. Jones. Soon after this meeting, defendant Simpson had a meeting with defendant Spartano in which Simpson approved the recommendation that plaintiff's contract not be renewed. Defendant Spartano then met with plaintiff and notified her of defendant Simpson's decision. Thereafter, plaintiff submitted her letter of resignation.

Discussion

Plaintiff's Claims

Title VII Retaliation

Section 704 of Title VII of the Civil Rights Act of 1964 prohibits retaliatory actions against employees who oppose alleged discriminatory practices. Cosgrove v. Sears, Roebuck & Co., 9 F.3d 1033, 1038 (2d Cir. 1993). Section 704(a) of the statute provides:

> It shall be an unlawful employment practice for an employer to discriminate against any of his employees or applicants for employment . . . because she has opposed any practice made an unlawful employment practice by this subchapter.

42 U.S.C. § 20003-3(a). In order to establish a prima facie case of retaliation under Title VII plaintiff must show: (1) she was engaged in protected activity which was known to the defendant, (2) she suffered an adverse employment action, and (3) there was a causal connection between the protected activity and the adverse employment action. Johnson v. Palma, 931 F.2d 203, 207 (2d Cir. 1991).

• • •

Examining the record in the light most favorable to plaintiff and drawing all possible inferences in her favor causes the court to find that she has established a prima facie case of retaliation under Title VII. Therefore, as stated above, the burden shifts to the remaining defendants, Simpson and the College, to show that they had legitimate, nondiscriminatory reasons for not renewing her contract.

In regard to the decision not to renew plaintiff's contract, defendant Simpson stated that he made the final decision after individual meetings with defendant Spartano and the plaintiff. His decision was based primarily upon two factors, (1) plaintiff's failure to properly perform her duties, particularly her failure to recruit new players and (2) student complaints regarding plaintiff's coaching. In addressing this phase of the burden-shifting analysis, the Supreme Court has stated that "the determination that a defendant has met its burden of production (and has thus rebutted any legal presumption of intentional discrimination) can involve no credibility assessment." Therefore, the court, without weighing the credibility of the reasons set forth, finds that defendants have met their burden by producing legitimate, nondiscriminatory reasons for the non-renewal of plaintiff's contract.

In light of the legitimate reasons offered by the defendants for the non-renewal, the burden shifts back to plaintiff to rebut the reasons given for her non-renewal. The burden is shifted back to the plaintiff because, "the plaintiff at all times retains the ultimate burden of persuasion."

In her attempt to prove that the reasons set forth by defendants for their decision not to renew her contract were pretextual, the plaintiff has failed to cite to anything in the record which would serve to rebut those reasons. . . . Therefore, defendants Simpson and Utica College are entitled to summary judgment on plaintiff's Title VII retaliation claim.

Title VII Discrimination

In order to establish a prima facie case of discriminatory discharge, plaintiff must show that she (1) was a member of a protected class; (2) was qualified for the position; (3) was discharged from that position; and (4) the discharge occurred in circumstances which give rise to an inference of gender discrimination. Rosen v. Thornburgh, 928 F.2d 528, 532 (2d Cir. 1991). As with a Title VII retaliation claim, once the plaintiff has established a prima facie case, the burden of production shifts to the defendants to articulate a legitimate, nondiscriminatory reason for the discharge. Id. (citation omitted). Once the defendants have satisfied this prong of the test, the plaintiff must establish by a preponderance of the evidence that the reasons set forth by defendants are merely pretextual. Id.

In the case at bar, plaintiff has satisfied the first element of the prima facie case, as she is a member of a protected class. There is some question as to whether she was qualified for the position, as her contract was not renewed due to her poor performance of her duties. There is also a question of whether plaintiff's non-renewal was under circum-

stances which give rise to an inference of gender discrimination. . . . The record clearly indicates that the College had legitimate reasons for hiring defendant Spartano to be interim coach of the women's basketball team after plaintiff's contract was not renewed. The record also clearly illustrates that defendants initially attempted to replace plaintiff with a woman coach, but were unsuccessful in doing so. Finally, it is uncontroverted that the College hired a woman, Susan Betler, as plaintiff's permanent replacement. Accordingly, the circumstances surrounding plaintiff's non-renewal are not sufficient to raise an inference of gender discrimination, and plaintiff has failed to establish a prima facie case of discriminatory discharge. . . . Therefore, defendants are entitled to summary judgment on this claim.

Equal Pay Act Claim

Plaintiff asserts a claim under the Equal Pay Act ("EPA"), 29 U.S.C. § 206(d)(1), based on the fact that her salary was less than that of Ed Jones, the male coach of the men's basketball team. The EPA states, in pertinent part,

> No employer . . . shall discriminate . . . between employees on the basis of sex by paying wages to employees . . . at a rate less than the rate at which he pays wages to employees of the opposite sex in such establishment for equal work on jobs the performance of which requires equal skill, effort, and responsibility, and which are performed under similar working conditions, except where such payment is made pursuant to (i) a seniority system; (ii) a merit system; . . . or (iv) a differential based on any other factor other than sex.

29 U.S.C. § 206(d)(1). Therefore, in order to state a prima facie case of wage discrimination under the EPA, plaintiff must establish that: (1) the College pays different wages to her male counterpart; (2) plaintiff and her male counterpart perform equal work on jobs requiring equal skill, effort and responsibility; and (3) the jobs are performed under similar working conditions. Corning Glass Works v. Brennan, 417 U.S. 188, 94 S. Ct. 2223, 2228 (1974). Once plaintiff has established a prima facie case, the burden of production shifts to the defendants to show that the difference in wages was a result of one of the exceptions outlined in the EPA. . . . If defendants satisfy their burden of proving legitimate business reasons for the disparity in salaries, the plaintiff can rebut defendants' explanation by showing that the proffered reasons are merely pretextual.

It is undisputed that throughout her three year tenure at the College, plaintiff's salary, for coaching basketball, went from $25,000 in 1990-1991, to $25,765 in 1991-92 and, finally, to $29,916 in 1992-93. The men's basketball coach, Mr. Jones, earned $32,500, $33,475 and $34,814 over that same period of time. Similarly, it is also undisputed that the position of head women's basketball coach required equal skill, effort and responsibility and was performed under similar conditions to that of the job of men's head basketball coach. Accordingly, plaintiff has established a prima facie case under the EPA.

The defendants have set forth several reasons for the disparity in salary between plaintiff and Mr. Jones. These reasons include differences in education, experience and length of service with the College. Defendants argue that these are legitimate, non-gender based, reasons for the differences in salary and, therefore, they are entitled to summary judgment.

• • •

Defendants contend that as a result of these stated reasons, they have satisfied their burden of showing legitimate, non-gender based, reasons for the disparity in salaries between the male coach of the men's basketball team and plaintiff. In addressing an Equal Pay Act claim, the Supreme Court has stated that the Act "contemplates that a male employee with 20 years' seniority can receive a higher wage than a woman with two years' seniority." Corning Glass, 94 S. Ct. at 2232. Similarly, the Seventh Circuit has stated that "employers may prefer and reward experience, believing it makes a more valuable employee, for whatever reason. And it is not [the court's] province to second-guess employers' business judgment." Fallon v. State of Ill., 882 F.2d 1206, 1212 (7th Cir. 1989). In the case at bar, the record clearly shows that the male coach had nine years seniority over plaintiff at the time that she was hired, therefore, the court finds that the defendants have established a legitimate reason for the wage differences between them.

Plaintiff has failed to set forth any arguments which could serve to rebut the reasons established by defendants for the differences in pay. . . . Defendants' motion for summary judgment is, therefore, granted.

Title IX

Plaintiff has also alleged that the defendants violated Title IX by discriminating against her in the terms and conditions of her employment. Title IX provides, in relevant part, that

> No person . . . shall, on the basis of sex, be excluded from participation in, be denied the benefits of, or be subjected to discrimination under any education program or activity receiving Federal financial assistance.

20 U.S.C. § 1681(a). The Supreme Court has held that an implied private right of action exists under Title IX. Cannon v. University of Chicago, 441 U.S. 677, 99 S. Ct.

1946, 60 L. Ed. 2d 560 (1979). In addressing such actions, "courts have interpreted Title IX by looking . . . at the caselaw interpreting Title VII." Yusuf v. Vassar College, 35 F.3d 709, 714 (2d Cir. 1994). Therefore, the court must employ a Title VII discrimination analysis in order to determine whether a cause of action exists under Title IX.

In her claim, plaintiff asserts that she suffered discrimination because: (1) she had to raise money to pay for warm-up clothing for her team; (2) the men's baseball team played on campus while the women's softball team had to use off-campus city facilities; (3) the male coaches got to run summer camps while she was not permitted to do so; (4) the women's teams had to share locker rooms while the men's teams did not; and (5) her teams never received any financial support from the booster club.

These allegations are sufficient to create an inference of discrimination such that the burden of production would shift to the defendants to articulate nondiscriminatory reasons for the allegedly discriminatory terms and conditions. The court will address those proffered reasons seriatim.

Fundraising

Defendants argue that plaintiff has offered no support for the allegation that she suffered discriminatory terms and conditions of employment because she was forced to raise money to purchase warm-up suits for her players while the College paid for the warm-ups for the male teams. The court agrees, and the record supports that the College purchased warm-ups for the men's basketball team and the women's basketball and soccer teams. Furthermore, in her deposition testimony, plaintiff repeatedly stated that she did not know whether the warm-ups used by other teams were purchased by the College or through independent fund-raising by the teams.

Athletic Fields

Defendants have provided legitimate reasons for the fact that plaintiff's softball team had to play on a city-owned, off-campus field while the men's baseball team got to play on-campus. The defendants do not contest the fact that the softball field was owned by the City of Utica and located off-campus, they do, however, point out that the field was adjacent to the College and only 200 yards from the College Athletic Center. Additionally, the record clearly indicates that the softball field, while owned by the City, was maintained by the College and was in superior condition to the on-campus baseball field.

Summer Camps

Plaintiff also alleges that she received inequitable treatment because she was forced to run a girls' basketball camp in conjunction with Mr. Jones, the coach of the men's team. She argues that she was discriminated against because she was not permitted to run her own girls' camp, and she was not allowed to be present at the boys' camp. This argument is weakened, however, by the fact that plaintiff admitted at her deposition that she had never been told that she could not work at the boys' camp, but only that she had never been invited to do so. Additionally, plaintiff asserts that she was told that if she wanted to run a girls' basketball camp, she would have to run it with Mr. Jones. Defendants deny that plaintiff was ever told that she could not run her own camp, and plaintiff failed to identify who it was who told her so. Drawing all possible inferences in her favor, the court assumes that plaintiff was told that she had to run the girls' camp in conjunction with Mr. Jones. Nevertheless, such an allegation, standing alone, does not constitute an act of discrimination sufficient to defeat defendants' motion for summary judgment.

Locker Rooms

Defendants have set forth legitimate reasons to rebut the allegations of discriminatory terms and conditions of employment resulting from the shared locker rooms. Defendants state that the only reason that the women's teams had to share the two locker rooms was because all four teams wanted to use them, while only two of the men's teams wanted to use the two men's locker rooms.

Booster Club Funds

The record belies plaintiff's allegation that she was discriminated against by the fact that her teams never received any booster club money. In fact, the record contains copies of at least ten vouchers denoting disbursement of over $7,000 to the plaintiff from the booster club. These disbursements covered everything from clothing for the women's basketball and softball teams to spring training softball trips to Myrtle Beach, South Carolina.

As stated above, defendants have satisfied their burden of production by articulating legitimate reasons for all of the terms and conditions of employment which plaintiff has claimed to be discriminatory. Plaintiff has failed to direct the court to anything in the record which would serve to rebut these reasons, or create a question of material fact as to any of them. Accordingly, defendants are entitled to summary judgment on plaintiff's Title IX claim.

Conclusion

In light of the above, the court finds that defendants have produced evidence sufficient to show that the non-renewal of plaintiff's contract was the result of legitimate, nondiscriminatory reasons. Additionally, the court finds that plaintiff has failed to create any question as to the credence of the stated nondiscriminatory reasons. Therefore, defendants are entitled to summary judgment on all plaintiff's claims.

■ ■ ■ ■

Fundamental Concepts

Scope. According to Title IX of the Educational Amendments of 1972, §1681. [§901]:

(a) No person in the United States shall, on the basis of sex, be excluded from participation in, be denied the benefits of, or be subjected to discrimination under any education program or activity receiving Federal financial assistance . . .

In *Broussard v. Board of Trustees for State Colleges and Universities* (E.D. La. 1993), a female concessions and ticket sales manager in the athletic department at Southeastern Louisiana University filed suit under Title IX for employment discrimination when her position was eliminated, she was transferred out of the athletic department, and a new title was created for a male who basically took over her responsibilities. The defendant argued that Title IX did not apply to employment discrimination. Relying on *North Haven Board of Education v. Bell* (1982), the court held that Title IX does apply to employment discrimination by educational institutions.

The U.S. Supreme Court has also recognized a private cause of action for individual plaintiffs against educational institutions (*Cannon v. University of Chicago*, 1979 and *Franklin v. Gwinnett County Public Schools*, 1992). However, as was the case in *Bowers v. Baylor University* (W. D. Tex. 1994) and *Clay v. Board of Trustees of Neosho County Community College* (D.Kan. 1995), courts will not extend Title IX to employment discrimination claims against individual defendants. The same is true for other employment discrimination statutes, however, most discrimination statutes do hold employers liable for the actions of their agents.

Application. The application of Title IX to employment discrimination cases is far from clearly defined. The U.S. Supreme Court in *North Haven Board of Education v. Bell* (1982) held that "Title IX proscribes employment discrimination in federally funded education programs." It would appear that applying Title IX to employment discrimination cases would duplicate Title VII, yet because the language in the statute does not directly address employment discrimination, it may not provide the procedural and substantive limitations of Title VII. Courts have applied Title VII standards to Title IX employment discrimination by individuals in educational institutions. For instance, in *Bartges v. University of North Carolina at Charlotte* (W.D.N.C. 1995), the court initially focused on Bartges' Title VII claims of individual disparate treatment and retaliation. On the basis of Bartges' failure to establish a prima facie case of discrimination under Title VII, the court entitled the defendant to summary judgment on the plaintiff's Title IX claim. Had Bartges been successful under Title VII, the court would have then applied those same standards to Title IX.

Rather than redefine the standards and models prohibiting gender-based discrimination under Title VII please refer to the gender discrimination section, including sexual harassment in Chapter 5.81—Title VII. To be successful under Title IX then, a plaintiff will have the burden of establishing a prima facie case of individual or systemic disparate treatment, sexual harassment, disparate impact, or retaliation in accordance with Title VII. A defendant will have the burden of producing a legitimate nondiscriminatory reason for the action or can rely on the other defense of a bona fide occupational qualification or a business necessity. In *Harker v. Utica College of Syracuse University* (N.D.N.Y. 1995), the plaintiff establishes an inference of discrimination under Title IX, just as she would under Title VII and the defendant university produces a legitimate, nondiscriminatory reason for each aspect of discrimination she claimed she suffered.

Remedies. Actions brought under Title IX will enable a successful plaintiff to receive the same remedies available under Title VII, with one limitation. Where there is duplication in the employment discrimination claims, a successful plaintiff will not be granted duplicate remedies for each cause of that legal action. For example, in *Tyler v. Howard University* (D.D.C. 1993), the court stated that while the U.S. Supreme Court recognizes "a variety of remedies, at times overlapping, to eradicate employment discrimination," the court concluded that a lost wages award for sex discrimination under three causes of action, for sex discrimination arising from the same wrong would cause the three separate damage awards to merge into one award. Thus, the court reduced that portion of Tyler's damage award from $1.8 million to $600,000.

Recent Developments

The majority of cases in employment discrimination in athletics under Title IX have been brought in the past decade. Most have been brought by coaches and have dealt with disparities in pay between male and female coaches or disparities in pay for coaches coaching female versus those coaching male teams or for actions taken by employers in retaliation for exercising their rights to enforce Title IX. There are a number of possible reasons why these cases are developing. First, until the Civil Rights Restoration Act of 1987, the holding of *Grove City College v. Bell* (1984) limited Title IX's application to only those educational programs which were direct recipients of federal funding. Where athletic departments are not direct recipients, Title IX was not an available remedy to challenge gender discrimination in athletics. Second, in 1992 the United States Supreme Court in *Franklin v. Gwinnett County Public Schools* held that an individual could bring suit under Title IX for intentional discrimination and that there was no evidence that Congress intended to restrict a victim of intentional discrimination from collecting compensatory damages and attorney's fees. Thus, *Franklin* has given victims of intentional discrimination (and their attorneys) a financial incentive in bringing suit under Title IX. Third, as a result of the two aforementioned actions and Title IX's twentieth anniversary, groups such as the Women's Sports Foundation and the Trial Lawyers for Public Justice have begun to mobilize women in sport to enforce their rights. In reflecting upon twenty years of Title IX, women's athletics had moved significantly forward, yet their were still obstacles to reaching equality, namely in terms of participation and employment.

Title IX has been relied upon to challenge discrimination in coaches' compensation. One reason is that the Equal Pay Act is narrow and Title IX will take into account a wider range of discriminatory actions because it relies on Title VII theories of liability. For instance, *Stanley v. University of Southern California* (9th Cir. 1994), provides an example of the difficulty a female coach may have in proving an Equal Pay Act claim. Stanley lost due to the court's finding that the male coach possessed more experience, and faced a greater degree of pressure and responsibility in coaching the men's basketball team due to the large fan following and the media attention the team received. In Equal Pay Act claims there is simply a comparison of salaries and job duties and responsibilities, whereas with Title IX such factors as a school's discriminatory patterns and policies may be considered (disparate impact). In addition, a school's discriminatory animus which may be evidenced by a lower salary being paid to a coach can be challenged. For instance, assume an athletic department had a pattern or practice of only hiring women for part-time or assistant coaching positions and hired only men, including less qualified candidates for all head coaching positions. Under the Equal Pay Act the women coaches bringing suit would be compared to other assistant or part-time coaches and there may either be no pay disparity or it may be justified by differences in the positions. Yet to attack the hiring practices, the plaintiff would present a prima facie case for systemic disparate treatment and seek monetary damages and an injunction to prohibit the athletic program from continuing to engage in such a pattern or practice.

Another consideration courts have made in examining salary disparities under Title IX employment discrimination has been to require that there must ultimately be a negative impact on the *athletes* themselves in order for there to be a cause of action involving coaches' compensation. If paying women's coaches less, for example, results in athletes on a given team always having less skilled coaches, or always having only part-time coaches, so that the athletes themselves suffer, that is not an acceptable situation. If on the other hand, comparable men's and women's teams are coached by nationally respected coaches, and the women's coach is paid less (based on nondiscriminatory factors), there may not be grounds for an employment discrimination case involving Title IX, since both teams are receiving high caliber coaching and the athletes are not adversely affected. A Title IX violation only occurs when the compensation policies deny female athletes coaching that is equivalent to their male counterpart. It is difficult to ascertain whether or not the lower pay for female coaches actually results in a negative impact on the female athletes (Wong & Barr, 1994). For example, in *Deli v. University of Minnesota* (1994), Ccach Deli brought a Title IX action claiming the university paid her at a lower level than coaches of certain men's sports. Although she filed her claim after the statute of limitations had expired, the court considered her claim in arguendo. Given the success of her teams, the court found that Deli did not offer sufficient evidence to prove that the athletes she supervised received lesser quality coaching as a result of the difference between her salary and the male coaches' salaries, and so she did not establish a prima facie claim for a Title IX violation. Such a standard does not appear to reward the coach who works hard and is successful despite a low salary and implies a correlation between low pay and poor quality which may not in fact exist. The court's reliance on such a standard likely arises from the Office of Civil Rights (OCR) Policy Interpretations which apply to athletics and are codified at 34 C.F.R. §106 et seq. Section 106.41(c) prohibits discrimination between males and females in athletic programs on the basis of 13 major program components. Section 106.41(c)(5) addresses the opportunity to receive coaching. Under this program component female athletes may argue that a salary disparity has a negative impact on the *athletes* themselves. Keep in mind that in these policies are in place to allow athletes to seek equality in their athletic programs through increased athletic department expenditures on their coaching staff.

There have also been a handful of cases involving coaches who were retaliated against for supporting Title IX complaints at their institutions. After a jury decided Cal-State Fullerton fired its volleyball coach for his support of a Title IX suit, the coach was awarded $1.35 million in damages (Herwig, 1994). Two former coaches at the State University of New York-Oswego received a $135,000 settlement as a result of retaliatory actions by the university for the coaches having filed a Title IX compliant ("Title IX Settlement," 1995).

In *Clay v. Board of Trustees of Neosho County Community College* (D.Kan. 1995), John Clay, a former women's basketball coach brought an action against the college and its athletic director on a number of points, including retaliatory discharge prohibited by Title IX. The court held that the coach had a private cause of action for retaliation under Title IX, the college board's decision not to renew coach's contract would have been substantially motivated by impermissible purposes if the athletic director's negative recommendation was the result of the coach's Title IX complaints, and the athletic director was not subject to individual liability under Title IX. In denying the defendant's motion for summary judgment, the *Clay* court noted that the question of whether Title IX provided a private cause of action for damages for retaliation against a whistle blower had not yet been addressed in the Tenth Circuit. The trial court was instructed to rely on Title VII's protection against retaliation for guidance.

References

A. Cases

Bartges v. University of North Carolina at Charlotte, 908 F. Supp. 1312 (W.D.N.C. 1995)

Broussard v. Board of Trustees for State Colleges and Universities, 61 Fair Emp. Prac. Cas. 710 (E.D. La. 1993)

Cannon v. University of Chicago, 441 U.S. 66 (1979)

Clay v. Board of Trustees of Neosho County Community College, 905 F.Supp. 1488 (D. Kan. 1995)

Deli v. University of Minnesota, 863 F.Supp 963 (D. Minn. 1994)

Franklin v. Gwinnett County Public Schools, 112 S.Ct. 1028 (1992)

Grove City College v. Bell, 465 U.S. 565 (1984)

North Haven Board of Education v. Bell, 456 U.S. 512 (1982)

Stanley v. University of Southern California, 13 F.3d 1313 (9th Cir. 1994)

Tyler v. Howard University, Civ. No. 91-CA11239 (D.D.C. 1993)

B. Publications

Bonnette, V., & Daniel, L. (1990) *Title IX Athletics Investigator's Manual, 1990*. Washington: Office for Civil Rights, Department of Education.

Herwig, C. (1994, February 10). Fired Cal State-Fullerton Coach Wins $1.35M in Gender Lawsuit. *USA Today*, p. 6C.

Title IX settlement. (1995, October 18). *USA Today*, p. 1C.

Wong, G.M., & Barr, C.A. (October 1994). Pay Attention: Athletic Administrators Need to Understand Equal Pay Issues. *Athletic Business*, 10, 14.

C. Legislation

Educational Amendments of 1972, 20 U.S.C. §§ 1681-1688

—— 5.85 ——

Equal Pay Act

Mary A. Hums
University of Massachusetts-Amherst

Big State University, a Division I basketball school, pays its head men's basketball coach a salary of $115,000, while the head women's basketball coach is paid $55,000. Can the wage disparity be justified? Is coaching men's basketball sufficiently different from coaching women's basketball? Does the head women's basketball coach have a cause of action under the Equal Pay Act?

■ ■ ■ ■

Representative Case

STANLEY v. UNIVERSITY OF SOUTHERN CALIFORNIA
United States Court of Appeals for the Ninth Circuit
13 F.3d 1313 (1994)

OPINION:

Marianne Stanley, former head coach of the women's basketball team at the University of Southern California (USC), appeals from an order denying her motion for a preliminary injunction against USC and Michael Garrett, the athletic director for USC (collectively USC).

Coach Stanley contends that the district court abused its discretion in denying a preliminary injunction on the ground that she failed to present sufficient evidence of sex discrimination or retaliation to carry her burden of establishing a clear likelihood of success on the merits. Coach Stanley also claims that the court misapprehended the nature of the preliminary injunction relief she sought. In addition, she argues that the district court clearly erred in finding that USC would suffer significant hardship if the preliminary injunction issued. Coach Stanley further asserts that she was denied a full and fair opportunity to present testimonial evidence at the preliminary injunction hearing and to demonstrate that USC's purported justification for paying a higher salary to George Raveling, head coach of the men's basketball team at USC, was a pretext

for sex discrimination and retaliation. We affirm because we conclude that the district court did not abuse its discretion in denying the motion for a preliminary injunction. We also hold that the district court did not deny Coach Stanley a full and fair opportunity to present evidence of sex discrimination, retaliation, and pretext.

I. Pertinent Facts

Coach Stanley signed a four-year contract with USC on July 30, 1989, to serve as the head coach of the women's basketball team. The expiration date of Coach Stanley's employment contract was June 30, 1993. Coach Stanley's employment contract provided for an annual base salary of $60,000 with a $6,000 housing allowance.

Sometime in April of 1993, Coach Stanley and Michael Garrett began negotiations on a new contract. The evidence is in dispute as to the statements made by the parties. Coach Stanley alleges in her declarations that she told Garrett that she "was entitled to be paid equally with the Head Men's Basketball Coach, George Raveling[,] and that [she] was seeking a contract equal to the one that USC had paid the Head Men's Basketball Coach" based on her outstanding record and the success of the women's basketball program at USC. She also requested a higher salary for the assistant coaches of the women's basketball team. According to Coach Stanley, Garrett verbally agreed that she should be paid what Coach Raveling was earning, but he asserted that USC did not have the money at that time. He indicated that "he would get back [to her] with an offer of a multi-year contract . . . that would be satisfactory." Garrett alleges in his affidavit, filed in opposition to the issuance of the preliminary injunction, that Coach Stanley told him that "she wanted a contract that was identical to that between USC and Coach Raveling."

On April 27, 1993, Garrett sent a memorandum which set forth an offer of a three-year contract with the following terms:

1993-94 Raising your salary to $80,000 with a $6,000 housing allowance.

1994-95 Salary of $90,000 with a $6,000 housing allowance.

1995-96 Salary of $100,000 with a $6,000 housing allowance.

Presently, Barbara Thaxton's base salary is $37,000 which I intend to increase to $50,000. It is not my policy to pay associate or assistant coaches housing allowances. Therefore that consideration is not addressed in this offer.

The memorandum concluded with the following words: "I believe this offer is fair, and I need you to respond within the next couple of days so we can conclude this matter. Thank you." According to Garrett, Coach Stanley said the offer was "an insult."

Coach Stanley alleged that, after receiving this offer, she informed Garrett that she "wanted a multi-year contract but his salary figures were too low." Coach Stanley also alleged that she told Garrett she "was to make the same salary as was paid to the Head Men's Basketball Coach at USC." Garrett asserted that Coach Stanley demanded a "three-year contract which would pay her a total compensation at the annual rate of $96,000 for the first 18 months and then increase her total compensation to the same level as Raveling for the last 18 months." He rejected her counter offer.

• • •

Garrett sent a memorandum to Coach Stanley on July 15, 1993, in which he stated, inter alia:

My job as athletic director is to look out for the best interests of our women's basketball program as a whole, and that is what I have been trying to do all along. The best interests of the program are not served by indefinitely extending the discussions between you and the University, which have already dragged on for weeks. That is why I told you on Tuesday that I needed a final answer that day.

Since I did not hear from you, as it now stands the University has no offers on the table. If you want to make any proposals, I am willing to listen. Meanwhile, for the protection of the program, I must, and am, actively looking at other candidates. I am sorry that you feel distressed by this situation. As I have said, I have to do what is best for our women's basketball program.

Finally, I was not aware that you were in Phoenix on official University business. Your contract with the University expired at the end of June, and I must ask you not to perform any services for the University unless and until we enter into a new contract. I will arrange for you to be compensated on a daily basis for the time you have expended thus far in July on University business.

Coach Stanley did not reply to Garrett's July 15, 1993 memorandum. Instead, on August 3, 1993, her present attorney, Robert L. Bell, sent a letter via facsimile to USC's Acting General Counsel in which he indicated that he had been retained to represent Coach Stanley. Bell stated he desired "to discuss an amicable resolution of the legal dispute between [his] client and the University of Southern California." Bell stated that if he did not receive a reply by August 4, 1993, he would "seek recourse in court." On August 4, 1993, USC's Acting General Counsel sent a letter to Bell via facsimile in which he stated that "we are not adverse to considering carefully a proposal from you for an 'informal resolution.'"

II. Procedural Background

On August 5, 1993, Coach Stanley filed this action in the Superior Court for the County of Los Angeles. She also applied ex parte for a temporary restraining order (TRO) to require USC to install her as head coach of the women's basketball team.

The complaint sets forth various federal and state sex discrimination claims, including violations of the Equal Pay Act (EPA), 29 U.S.C. 206(d)(1) (1988), Title IX, 20 U.S.C. § 1681(a) (1988), the California Fair Employment and Housing Act (FEHA), Cal. Gov't Code § 12921 (West Supp. 1993), and the California Constitution, Cal. Const. art. 1, § 8 (West 1983). The complaint also alleges common law causes of action including wrongful discharge in violation of California's public policy, breach of an

implied-in-fact employment contract, intentional infliction of emotional distress, and conspiracy. As relief for
this alleged conduct, Coach Stanley seeks a declaratory
judgment that USC's conduct constituted sex discrimination, a permanent injunction restraining the defendants
from discrimination and retaliation, an order "requiring
immediate installation of plaintiff to the position of Head
Coach of Women's Basketball at the USC," three million
dollars in compensatory damages, and five million dollars
in punitive damages.

On August 6, 1993, the Los Angeles Superior Court
issued an oral order granting Coach Stanley's ex parte
application for a TRO, pending a hearing on her motion
for a preliminary injunction. . . . On the same day that the
TRO was issued, USC removed the action to the District
Court for the Central District of California. On August 11,
1993, the district court ordered that the hearing on Coach
Stanley's motion for a preliminary injunction be held on
August 26, 1993, and that the TRO issued by the state
court be extended and remain in effect until that date.

• • •

Pursuant to Coach Stanley's request, the district court
reviewed Coach Raveling's employment contract in camera. Later that day, the district court denied the motion for
a preliminary injunction.

III. Discussion

The gravamen of Coach Stanley's multiple claims
against USC is her contention that she is entitled to pay
equal to that provided to Coach Raveling for his services
as head coach of the men's basketball team because the
position of head coach of the women's team "requires
equal skill, effort, and responsibility, and [is performed]
under similar working conditions." She asserts that USC
discriminated against her because of her sex by rejecting
her request. She also maintains that USC retaliated against
her because of her request for equal pay for herself and her
assistant coaches. According to Coach Stanley, USC retaliated by withdrawing the offer of a three-year contract and
instead presenting her with a new offer of a one-year contract at less pay than that received by Coach Raveling.

We begin our analysis mindful of the fact that we are
reviewing the denial of a preliminary injunction. There
has been no trial in this matter. Because the hearing on the
preliminary injunction occurred 21 days after the action
was filed in state court, discovery had not been completed.
Our prediction of the probability of success on the merits
is based on the limited offer of proof that was possible
under the circumstances. We obviously cannot now evaluate the persuasive impact of the evidence that the parties
may bring forth at trial.

A. Standard of Review

We review the denial of a motion for preliminary injunction for abuse of discretion. . . . An order is reversible
for legal error if the court did not apply the correct preliminary injunction standard, or if the court misapprehended the law with respect to the underlying issues in
litigation. An abuse of discretion may also occur if the district court rests its conclusions on clearly erroneous findings of fact.

• • •

B. There Has Been No Clear Showing of a Probability of Success on the Merits of Coach Stanley's Claim for Injunctive Relief

1. Merits of Coach Stanley's Claim of Denial of Equal Pay for Equal Work.

The district court concluded that Coach Stanley had
failed to demonstrate that there is a likelihood that she
would prevail on the merits of her claim of a denial of
equal pay for equal work because she failed to present
facts clearly showing that USC was guilty of sex discrimination in its negotiations for a new employment contract.
The thrust of Coach Stanley's argument in this appeal is
that she is entitled, as a matter of law, "to make the same
salary as was paid to the Head Men's Basketball Coach at
USC." Appellant's Opening Brief at 9. None of the authorities she has cited supports this theory.

In her reply brief, Coach Stanley asserts that she has
"never said or argued in any of her submissions that the
compensation of the men's and women's basketball
coaches at USC or elsewhere must be identical." Appellant's Reply Brief at 2. Coach Stanley accuses USC of
mischaracterizing her position. This argument ignores her
insistence to Garrett that she was entitled to the "same salary" received by Coach Raveling. The denotation of the
word "same" is "identical." Webster's Third New International Dictionary 2007.

In her reply brief, Coach Stanley asserts that she
merely seeks equal pay for equal work. In Hein v. Oregon
College of Education, 718 F.2d 910 (9th Cir. 1983), we
stated that to recover under the Equal Pay Act of 1963, 29
U.S.C. § 206(d)(1) (1988), "a plaintiff must prove that an
employer is paying different wages to employees of the
opposite sex for equal work." Hein, 718 F.2d at 913. We
concluded that the jobs need not be identical, but they
must be "substantially equal." Id. (internal quotation and
citation omitted).

The EPA prohibits discrimination in wages "between
employees on the basis of sex . . . for equal work, on jobs
the performance of which requires equal skill, effort, and

responsibility, and which are performed under similar working conditions." 29 U.S.C. § 206(d)(1) (1988). Each of these components must be substantially equal to state a claim. Forsberg v. Pacific Northwest Bell Tel., 840 F.2d 1409, 1414 (9th Cir. 1988).

Coach Stanley has not offered proof to contradict the evidence proffered by USC that demonstrates the differences in the responsibilities of the persons who serve as head coaches of the women's and men's basketball teams. Coach Raveling's responsibilities as head coach of the men's basketball team require substantial public relations and promotional activities to generate revenue for USC. These efforts resulted in revenue that is 90 times greater than the revenue generated by the women's basketball team. Coach Raveling was required to conduct twelve outside speaking engagements per year, to be accessible to the media for interviews, and to participate in certain activities designed to produce donations and endorsements for the USC Athletic Department in general. Coach Stanley's position as head coach did not require her to engage in the same intense level of promotional and revenue-raising activities. This quantitative dissimilarity in responsibilities justifies a different level of pay for the head coach of the women's basketball team.

• • •

The evidence presented by USC also showed that Coach Raveling had substantially different qualifications and experience related to his public relations and revenue-generation skills than Coach Stanley. Coach Raveling received educational training in marketing, and worked in that field for nine years. Coach Raveling has been employed by USC three years longer than Coach Stanley. He has been a college basketball coach for 31 years, while Coach Stanley has had 17 years experience as a basketball coach. Coach Raveling had served as a member of the NCAA Subcommittee on Recruiting. Coach Raveling also is the respected author of two bestselling novels. He has performed as an actor in a feature movie, and has appeared on national television to discuss recruiting of student athletes. Coach Stanley does not have the same degree of experience in these varied activities. Employers may reward professional experience and education without violating the EPA. Soto v. Adams Elevator Equip. Co., 941 F.2d 543, 548 & n.7 (7th Cir. 1991).

Coach Raveling's national television appearances and motion picture presence, as well as his reputation as an author, make him a desirable public relations representative for USC. An employer may consider the marketplace value of the skills of a particular individual when determining his or her salary. Horner, 613 F.2d at 714. Unequal wages that reflect market conditions of supply and demand are not prohibited by the EPA. EEOC v. Madison Community Unit Sch. Dist. No. 12, 818 F.2d 577, 580 (7th Cir. 1987).

The record also demonstrates that the USC men's basketball team generated greater attendance, more media interest, larger donations, and produced substantially more revenue than the women's basketball team. As a result, USC placed greater pressure on Coach Raveling to promote his team and to win. The responsibility to produce a large amount of revenue is evidence of a substantial difference in responsibility. See Jacobs v. College of William and Mary, 517 F. Supp. 791, 797 (E.D. Va. 1980) (duty to produce revenue demonstrates that coaching jobs are not substantially equal), aff'd without opinion, 661 F.2d 922 (4th Cir.), cert. denied, 454 U.S. 1033 (1981).

Coach Stanley did not offer evidence to rebut USC's justification for paying Coach Raveling a higher salary. Instead, she alleged that the women's team generates revenue, and that she is under a great deal of pressure to win. Coach Stanley argues that Jacobs is distinguishable because, in that matter, the head basketball coach of the women's team was not required to produce any revenue. Jacobs, 517 F. Supp. at 798. Coach Stanley appears to suggest that a difference in the amount of revenue generated by the men's and women's teams should be ignored by the court in comparing the respective coaching positions. We disagree.

• • •

At this preliminary stage of these proceedings, the record does not support a finding that gender was the reason that USC paid a higher salary to Coach Raveling as head coach of the men's basketball team than it offered Coach Stanley as head coach of the women's basketball team. Garrett's affidavit supports the district court's conclusion that the head coach position of the men's team was not substantially equal to the head coach position of the women's team. The record shows that there were significant differences between Coach Stanley's and Coach Raveling's public relations skills, credentials, experience, and qualifications; there also were substantial differences between their responsibilities and working conditions. The district court's finding that the head coach positions were not substantially equal is not a "clear error of judgment."

• • •

IV. Conclusion

The district court did not abuse its discretion in denying a mandatory preliminary injunction. Coach Stanley did not meet her burden of demonstrating the irreducible minimum for obtaining a preliminary injunction: "that there is a fair chance of success on the merits." Martin v. International Olympic Comm., 740 F.2d at 675. Because mandatory preliminary injunctions are disfavored in this circuit, we are compelled to review the record to determine whether the facts and the law clearly favor Coach Stanley. Anderson, 612 F.2d at 1114. The evidence offered at the hearing on the motion for a preliminary injunction demonstrated that Coach Stanley sought pay from USC equal to Coach Raveling's income from that university, notwithstanding significant differences in job pressure, the level of responsibility, and in marketing and revenue-producing qualifications and performance. A difference in pay that takes such factors into consideration does not prove gender bias or violate the Equal Pay Act. The unfortunate impasse that occurred during the negotiations for the renewal of the employment contract of an outstanding basketball coach followed the offer of a very substantial increase in salary—not sex discrimination or retaliation. Because Coach Stanley failed to demonstrate that the law and the facts clearly favor her position, the judgment is AFFIRMED.

■ ■ ■ ■

Fundamental Concepts

According to §206 (d)(1)[§3] of the Equal Pay Act of 1963:

> No employer having employees subject to any provisions of this section shall discriminate, within any establishment in which such employees are employed, between employees on the basis of sex by paying wages to employees in such an establishment at a rate less than the rate which he pays wages to employees of the opposite sex in such establishment for equal work on jobs the performance of which requires equal skill, effort and responsibility, and which are performed under similar working conditions, except where such payment is made pursuant to (i) a seniority system; (ii) a merit system; (iii) a system which measures earnings by quantity or quality of production; or (iv) a differential based on any factor other than sex . . .

The scope of the Equal Pay Act is narrow, focusing on wage rate differentials between the sexes. Before examining the Equal Pay Act's application to sport organizations, some basic concepts will be reviewed.

Historically, women have been paid less than men, and the purpose of the Equal Pay Act is to address this inequity. There may, however, be circumstances where men's wage rates are less than women's wage rates and the difference is based on sex. In such instances, men may also utilize the Equal Pay Act.

To maintain a claim under the Equal Pay Act, the plaintiff must first establish the position with which she is comparing herself. That position is called the comparator. For a collegiate women's basketball coach, for example, her comparator may be the men's collegiate basketball coach at the same institution. The plaintiff must then demonstrate her wage rate was different even though her position was substantially equal to that of the comparator's position with respect to skill, effort, responsibility and similar working conditions.

Equal Work. Four criteria determine whether or not jobs are considered equal (Gold, 1993). The first of these is **skill**, meaning the ability needed to perform the job duties. Second is **effort**, which is the physical and mental exertion needed to perform the job duties. Third is **responsibility**, or the extent to which a worker supervises others, makes decisions, or is held accountable for business operations. Finally, **working conditions**, or the surroundings or hazards in the worker's job environment must be considered.

Courts have interpreted equal work for coaches in different ways. In *EEOC v. Madison Community School District #12* (1987), the court ruled that high school coaching positions, regardless of the sport or gender of the coach, were sufficiently alike as to constitute equal work. However, in *Stanley v. University of Southern California* (1994) and *Deli v. University of Minnesota* (1994), the courts ruled that differences in spectator appeal, squad size and media and public relations responsibilities made coaching positions held by men and women, even when coaching the same sport, not substantially equal. In *Tyler v. Howard University* (1993), Tyler, the women's basketball coach, claimed she received lower salary and benefits than the men's basketball and football coaches, and that she performed the same duties with better results. Tyler was awarded $138,000 in damages under the Equal Pay Act (Wong & Barr, 1993). The differences in responsibilities between a female high school basketball coach and her male counterpart were found to be insubstantial in *Burkey v. Marshall County Board of Education* (1981). In *Burkey*, the court acknowledged differences did exist, but found the differences were solely based on a district policy which did not allow the girls' teams to play as many games as the boys' teams.

Pay Differentials Between Men And Women. In some situations, pay differentials are acceptable between men and women, however, the employer must prove the pay differential is based upon one of three objective, gender-neutral factors (Gold, 1993). The first of these factors is a **seniority system**. If seniority is used as a basis of different wage rates, the employer must show that a legitimate, consistent system exists, and that the system is not intentionally used to perpetuate wage differentials between the sexes. In *Harker v. Utica College of Syracuse University* (1995), the court ruled that a male head basketball coach possessing nine years seniority over a female head basketball coach established a legitimate reason for a wage differential. Secondly, pay differentials may result from wage scales based on **merit systems/piece rates**. Employees can be legally rewarded for productivity based on the quantity of what they produce. For example, if both men and women are paid $8 for each widget they produce, and a man produces 10 widgets an hour while a woman produces 8 widgets an hour, their wage rates are the same, but the more productive employee may be paid more. Employers must take care, however, to be sure pay differentials are as objective and measurable as possible and not subjective in nature. Finally, **factors other than sex** may also influence pay differentials. These factors must, however, be gender-neutral. According to Player (1988), these factors must be those that reasonably would be utilized in establishing salary rates, and must be rationally related to bona fide employer concerns. Examples of these factors include shift differentials, training programs, and temporary and part-time assignments. Courts have held that the sex of a team does *not* constitute a factor other than sex. In *EEOC v. Madison Community School District #12* (1987), the court held the reference to 'factors other than sex' refers to the sex of the employee, not the sex of the employer's customers, clients or suppliers.

Suggestions for Employers. Sovereign (1989) offers the following three suggestions for managers. First, managers should have rational reasons for employees' compensation levels. Next, employers must explain to employees how their wages are determined. Third, as much as possible, employers should correct wage differentials between the sexes rather than trying to justify them. In addition to this advice, Sharp & Fitzgerald (1996) suggest managers construct accurate job analyses and write specific job descriptions as a means of justifying wage differentials.

Recent Developments

It appears the courts have made distinctions between high school and college coaches in cases involving the Equal Pay Act. It may be that this distinction between high school and college coaches is due to the level of competition involved, or it may be a result of the plaintiff's choice of which other coach or coaches to be compared with. In *Stanley*, the plaintiff specifically sought a salary equal to her male counterpart, the men's basketball coach George Raveling. On appeal, the court affirmed the lower court's rejection of the injunction sought by Stanley. In a trial on the merits the court granted USC's motion for summary judgment since it found the men's and women's head basketball coaching jobs were not substantially equal, and therefore, do not require equal pay (*Stanley v. the University of Southern California* (C.D. Cal. 1995)).

Given the narrow scope of the Equal Pay Act, coaches may have a better chance of winning an employment discrimination suit using Title IX, because in a Title IX action, the coach can bring in factors such as the sex of the athletes. For example, in *Pitts v. State of Oklahoma*, No. CIV-93-1341-A (W.D. Okla., 1994), the coach of a women's intercollegiate golf team brought both Equal Pay Act and Title IX actions when she claimed female coaches were being paid less than their male counterparts. The jury agreed there was discrimination based on gender in violation of Title IX, yet found the University had not violated the Equal Pay Act. As discussed above, in *Tyler* the plaintiff coach was successful on both her Equal Pay Act and Title IX claims.

As yet, any sport related cases raising an Equal Pay Act claim have involved amateur athletics on either the college or high school levels. It will be interesting to see if this trend continues, or if any cases will surface involving professional sport, the health and fitness industry or the recreational sport industry.

References

A. Cases
Burkey v. Marshall County Board of Education, 513 F. Supp. 1084 (1981)
Deli v. University of Minnesota, 863 F.Supp. 958 (D.Minn. 1994)
EEOC v. Madison Community School District #12, 818 F.2d 577 (7th Cir. 1987)
Harker v. Utica College of Syracuse University, 885 F.Supp. 378 (N.D.N.Y. 1995)
Pitts v. State of Oklahoma, No. CIV-93-1341-A (W.D. OK, 1994)
Stanley v. The University of Southern California, 1995 U.S. Dist. LEXIS 5026 (C.D. Cal 1995), *aff'd*, 13 F.3d 1313 (9th Cir. 1994)
Tyler v. Howard University, Civ. No. 91-11239 (D.D.C. 1993)

B. Publications
Sharp, L., & M. Fitzgerald (1996). *Job Descriptions and Performance Appraisals: Keys to a Successful Pay Equity Defense*. Presented at the Annual Conference of the Society for the Study of Legal Aspects of Sport and Physical Activity, Albuquerque, N.M.
Gold, M.E. (1993). *An Introduction to the Law of Employment Discrimination*. Ithaca, N.Y.: ILR Press.
Player, M.A. (1988). *Employment Discrimination Law*. St. Paul, Minn.: West Publishing Company.
Sovereign, K.L. (1989). *Personnel Law*. (2d Ed.). Englewood Cliffs, N.J.: Prentice Hall.
Wong, G.M., & Barr, C.A. (1993). Equal Payback: Women's Coach Wins Landmark Title IX/Equal Pay Act Case. *Athletic Business*, Sept., 13-14.

C. Legislation
Equal Pay Act of 1963, 29 U.S.C.A. §201 et seq. (West, 1993)

5.90

Health and Fitness Club Issues

Jay M. Ablondi
International Health, Racquet & Sportsclub Association

There are several legal issues that impact how health and fitness club managers operate their facilities. The purpose of this section is to give sport managers a basic understanding of how many legal issues impact the operation of a health and fitness facility. Most of these topics or issues are covered in more depth in other chapters and are discussed here only as they relate to health clubs. Now more than ever, managers need to know the laws affecting their clubs or risk finding themselves on the losing end of a costly lawsuit.

Fundamental Concepts

Health Club Membership Agreements

Many club managers don't realize this, but the membership contracts they have with the members of their fitness facility might be illegal. Thirty-seven states plus the District of Columbia have specific laws that stipulate what can and cannot be in a health club service agreement. If a membership contract violates a statute in this area it may be deemed null and void.

In an attempt to offer health club consumers some sort of financial protection, many state legislatures passed laws regulating the health club industry. For example, many states stipulate that health club contracts cannot be longer than three years in duration while others specifically outlaw lifetime contracts. A common provision in state health club statutes concerns membership cancellation. Most states allow for a "cooling-off " period of usually three business days immediately after a person enters into a health club contract. During this period a consumer can cancel his or her contract for any reason and is entitled to a full refund of money paid.

After the "cooling-off" period has expired, most states allow consumers to cancel their health club agreements for specific reasons, such as death or disability, or if the member moves or if the club moves its location or substantially changes the services offered. If a consumer meets the requirements under this provision, he or she is entitled to a pro rata refund equal to the unused portion of the membership agreement. In addition, many states stipulate that the consumer's right to cancellation must be included and specify the exact language and print size of the notification in the membership contract. States have also placed restrictions on how early a club operator can "pre-sell" memberships in a facility which has not yet opened for business. Some states require health clubs to maintain a surety bond so that if the club goes out of business money will be available for consumer refunds. Club managers should ensure that their membership contracts comply with the applicable state laws. An overview of health club consumer protection laws is summarized in an informative table prepared by the International Health, Racquet & Sportsclub Association (IHRSA). See Chapter 3.10 for more information regarding contracts.

The Legal Implications of Couples Memberships

As the health and fitness club industry has matured, club owners have recognized that they can no longer cater only to the "single" class that traditionally made up the vast majority of their membership. In order to attract a wider segment of the population, many club operators developed special discount rates for families and married couples.

Inevitably, the question arises, "If a club offers a couples membership, what are its legal obligations regarding unmarried, gay, or lesbian couples?" In 1993, A gay couple filed suit against a fitness center in New York City charging that the club discriminated against them by refusing to sell them a discounted family membership. Two gay club members tried to enroll their partners at a half-priced fee that was offered to members' families but were told by officials at the club that they did not qualify. The New York City Human Rights Commission ruled that the club's policy violates a city ordinance which states that businesses may not discriminate on the basis of sexual orientation or family status. The club was forced to change its policy and pay a fine.

In 1992, a complaint was brought against a Philadelphia club which permitted unmarried heterosexual couples to obtain a couples membership but denied gay and lesbian couples the same benefit. The Philadelphia Human Rights Commission ruled that this policy violated the Philadelphia Fair Practices Ordinance. In response, the club discontinued all discount memberships for unmarried couples. The club's new policy, which is in compliance with the law, extends benefits to legally married couples only. Some cities and counties provide legal recognition for heterosexual and homosexual couples who live together in the form of a domestic partnership registry. Club managers should find out if they are operating in a jurisdiction with a domestic partnership registry before they determine their couples policy. (See Table 1)

Table 1
Areas that Prohibit Discrimination Based on Sexual Orientation[a]

States	Counties		Cities
Connecticut	Alameda County, CA	Berkeley, CA	Cambridge, MA
Hawaii	San Mateo County, CA	Laguna Beach, CA	Ann Arbor, MI
Massachusetts	Santa Cruz County, CA	Los Angeles, CA	East Lansing, MI
New Jersey		Oakland, CA	Minneapolis, MN
Vermont		San Francisco, CA	Ithaca, NY
Wisconsin		Santa Cruz, CA	New York, NY
		West Hollywood, CA	Philadelphia, PA
		Washington, DC	Seattle, WA
		West Palm Beach, FL	Madison, WI
		Takoma Park, MD	

[a]National Gay & Lesbian Task Force Policy Institute

This issue extends beyond "couple" memberships. In 1996, a gay couple filed a complaint against a fitness facility in Chicago after the gym's management ejected the couple for kissing at the club. The two men said that the owner and a former manager told them to leave because their public displays of "affection" broke the club's rules. The complaint alleges that the club violated Chicago's Human Rights Ordinance and accuses the club of using a double standard. "If a husband and wife kiss hello there, no one bats an eye," said one of the complainants. "We just want equal treatment." The club owner is disputing the complaint because he says it is without merit. He told a local newspaper reporter that "this is a gym, not a motel." To avoid charges of illegal discrimination, all members of a club should be held to the same standards of behavior. See Chapter 4.14 for more information regarding the rights of groups.

Sexual Harassment

Due to the "social" atmosphere at health and fitness clubs and the predominance of casual or revealing workout attire at most clubs, club managers need to be aware of the possibility that sexual harassment could occur at the facility. The Equal Employment Opportunity Commission (EEOC)—the federal agency charged with enforcement of federal anti-discrimination law—defines sexual harassment as unwelcome sexual advances, requests for sexual favors and other verbal or physical conduct of a sexual nature when 1) submission to such is a condition of employment—known as "quid pro quo" harassment, or 2) such conduct interferes with an individual's work performance or creates an "intimidating, hostile or offensive work environment."

Sexual harassment can occur between club employees, club members, or both. It is the club manager's responsibility to establish and enforce policies aimed at preventing sexual harassment. Club managers should have a written sexual harassment policy which has been reviewed by an attorney. Employees should understand the policy and it should be part of the club's member conduct policies. If a club manager observes conduct that could be considered harassment, or if a harassment complaint is brought to the manager's attention, the manager should follow the club's harassment procedures accordingly. Managers need to be diligent in making sure that they are providing an environment that is free of harassment for both employees and members. See Chapter 5.81 for more on sexual harassment.

Women Only Health Clubs

Is the exclusion of men from "women only" health clubs a violation of anti-discrimination laws? This question raises a complicated legal issue which the court system has just recently begun to address. The courts and state legislatures have recognized certain situations in which gender-based discrimination in public places is acceptable because there is a compelling and overriding privacy issue involved (e.g., rest rooms and showers).

Some courts have spoken on this issue. In *LivingWell (North), Inc. v. Pennsylvania Human Relations Commission* (1992), the state alleged that LivingWell violated the Pennsylvania Human Relations Act by refusing to admit men. LivingWell successfully argued that its customers had a privacy interest which permitted them to discriminate on the basis of sex. The club contended that their members had a legitimate privacy interest because of the special circumstances involved in exercising (e.g., compromising body positions, self-consciousness about her own body). The court ruled that excluding men from a women only club does not violate the state's anti-discrimination law. The court found that: 1) LivingWell established that a legitimate privacy interest existed; 2) including men as members would undermine the club's business operations; and, 3) there is no other way to protect the member's privacy interest other than excluding men. The court recognized that there are certain situations which "warrant the exclusion of the opposite sex for privacy reasons"

Another related issue involves Title VII of the Civil Rights Act, the federal law which prohibits employers from discriminating against potential employees on the basis of gender. In *U.S. EEOC v. Audrey Sedita* (1990), at issue was the hiring policy of the Women's Workout World health club chain in Illinois. In this case, the Equal Employment Opportunity Commission (EEOC) claimed that the club's policy of hiring only women for the positions of manager, assistant manager and instructor was discriminatory. The EEOC argued that the club was in violation of Title VII because in this case gender is not a bona fide occupational qualification (i.e., a qualification that an employee must possess in order to perform the essential duties of a job).

Women's Workout World argued that their customers prefer female personnel in those particular positions because such employees would be exposed to nudity, club members in awkward positions while exercising, and the employees in question would have to perform body measurements involving intimate touching. To prove that their policy was based on customer preference, the club submitted a petition signed by 10,000 members declaring that they would no longer patronize Women's Workout World if men were employed in the three positions. This was important because the livelihood of a business is one factor in determining a bona fide occupational qualification. It is important to note that customer preference doesn't usually justify discrimination, however, the stakes are different when an individual's privacy rights are at issue. This case never went to trial because an out-of-court settlement was reached.

Illinois, New Jersey, and Tennessee recognize the privacy issue involved in health clubs. Each of these states has specifically exempted health clubs and gyms from their human rights laws which otherwise prohibit sex discrimination in public accommodations.

The Americans with Disabilities Act

Health club managers must make sure that they are in compliance with two areas of the ADA: Employment (Title I) and Public Accommodation (Title III). Health clubs are not allowed to discriminate against qualified individuals with disabilities in regard to job application procedures, hiring, advancement, termination, compensation, and training. A qualified individual is any person who can perform the essential duties of the job. Employers are required to reasonably accommodate people with disabilities unless they can demonstrate that the accommodation would impose an "undue hardship" on the business.

Regarding public accommodation in health clubs, the ADA indicates that an exercise class cannot exclude a person who uses a wheelchair because he or she cannot do all of the exercises and derive the same results from the class as persons without a disability. The facility must be accessible to the disabled and must be able to provide people with disabilities a means by which they can achieve their exercise goals. Title III of the ADA guarantees people with disabilities the chance to partake "fully and equally" in programs and services offered at health clubs and other public accommodations. Club managers who ignore the requirements of the ADA may be sued by either an individual with a disability or the U.S. Department of Justice. For more information regarding the rights of persons with disabilities, see Chapter 4.27.

Eating Disorders. Eating disorders, such as anorexia and bulimia, can be dangerous and even life threatening if proper care is not taken. Many anorexics and bulimics exercise excessively so these disorders may be recognized more readily in a health club setting. Club managers should be familiar with the symptoms associated with an eating disorder. While club managers do not have any specific obligation to inform members about anorexia and bulimia, doing so might prove to be prudent. Managers should require all members to read a disclaimer which informs them about the problems, symptoms and medical risks of anorexia and bulimia. According to the U.S. Department of Justice, anorexic and bulimic people are a protected class under the Americans with Disabilities Act, because they are perceived to have a disability. Since the ADA prohibits clubs and other public accommodations from discriminating against a person with a disability, a club manager cannot prevent an anorexic or bulimic person from using the facility.

AIDS. AIDS can be a difficult subject for club managers to deal with because of the stigma surrounding this disease. Many people are ignorant as to how AIDS is contracted and this ignorance can lead to fear and discrimination. A club that terminates a membership or refuses to sell a membership to a prospect with AIDS runs the risk of being sued for violating the laws against discrimination. Club members and prospective members are protected by the anti-discrimination law.

Employees with AIDS are also protected against discrimination. Courts have not been sympathetic to the argument that fear of the disease by co-workers—and presumably members—is a justification for discrimination. For example, a manager faced with employees who refuse to work with a co-worker with AIDS cannot fire the employee with AIDS. Rather, the manager would be required to discipline the other employees for their refusal to work.

Under the Americans with Disabilities Act, the only time a health club or other place of public accommodation can exclude an individual with a disability like AIDS from the club is if that individual's participation would result in a direct threat to the health or safety of others. This determination must be based on reasonable judgment that relies on current medical evidence. Current medical evidence has determined that AIDS is contracted through the exchange of bodily fluids, therefore, a person cannot get AIDS through casual contact with an infected person. Health club activity, including the use of pools, whirlpools and saunas, is considered to be "casual contact." Club managers need to follow federal guidelines to ensure that club employees and members are not needlessly exposed to another person's blood. The Occupational Safety and Health Administration (OSHA) under the U.S. Department of Labor provides guidelines in this area.

If it is brought to a club manager's attention that someone has AIDS, the manager should ensure that only those with an absolute need to know are told. If a club manager or an employee discusses a person's health status indiscreetly, the club could be sued for violation of privacy. The best approach may be to implement an AIDS education program for all club employees. The American Red Cross has a well-respected program dealing with this issue.

Music Copyright Fees

The United States Copyright Act of 1976 grants copyright owners, in this case composers and/or publishers of popular music, the exclusive right to publicly perform or authorize the public performance of their copyrighted works. This law makes it a copyright infringement to perform a copyrighted musical work in a public place without the consent of the copyright owner. The use of records, tapes, or radio music in aerobic classes or as background music may be considered a public performance, thus clubs are required to obtain a music license. A similar law, called the Canadian Copyright Act, grants artists copyright protection in Canada.

Broadcast Music Inc. (BMI), the American Society of Composers, Authors and Publishers (ASCAP) and the Society of European Stage Authors and Composers (SESAC) are the three major music licensing organizations which provide blanket licenses for virtually all copyrighted music in the United States. Composers and publishers grant ASCAP, BMI or SESAC the right to license, in bulk, the public performance of their copyrighted music works. BMI, ASCAP and more recently SESAC have heightened their efforts to license fitness industry businesses which play popular music over public address systems or use recorded music in aerobic dance classes.

The general rule is that, if the club uses radio music, a licensing fee must be paid to ASCAP, BMI, and SESAC. The playing of radio music in public areas is a public performance of copyrighted music, except when played through a "homestyle" radio receiver with minimum amplification. Music played in aerobic classes, even if the club or instructor has purchased 'taped' music, is also subject to a copyright fee. It is virtually impossible to play only music copyrighted by BMI and not ASCAP or vice versa. BMI, ASCAP, and SESAC enforce the copyright law. Each asks health club managers to enter into a licensing agreement. If the manager refuses, the licensing organization will send in an agent to log the use of any songs it has the right to license. Armed with evidence of a violation, the licensing organization may sue in federal court for copyright infringement. Statutory damages range from $500 to $100,000 per infringement depending upon the nature and severity of the violation.

In 1991, the Supreme Court ruled in favor of two retail store chains who refused to pay copyright fees to BMI and ASCAP (*Edison Brothers Stores Inc. v. Broadcast Music Inc.*, 1991). The court based its decision on the "homestyle" exemption language in the Copyright Act, which focuses on the type of equipment used to deliver music. The "homestyle" exemption states that a single receiver apparatus of the kind commonly found in private homes must be used. Additionally, the transmission must be provided free of charge and cannot be "further transmitted" to the public. The court also found that the physical size, not the financial size, of the establishment is relevant to whether or not this exemption applies. Generally, a single receiver should be in close proximity to two, or possibly as many as four, speakers. An argument could be made that it is possible that a club, if it meets the "homestyle" criteria, may be exempt from paying a fee for the use of background music. However, the "homestyle" exemption would not apply to aerobic classes. To date, there has not been a case involving a health club and the "homestyle" exemption.

In general, the music used in health clubs is considered a "public performance" and requires the business owner to pay a royalty. See Chapter 5.40 for more information regarding copyright law.

Independent Contractor vs. Employee

In the health and fitness industry, club managers must decide upon which basis to employ a person—as an employee or as an independent contractor. In general, a worker is an employee under the common law rules if the person for whom he or she works has the right to direct and control the work, both in the final results and in the details of when, where, and how the work is to be done. On the other hand, an independent contractor is a person who sells his or her services to perform a specific task. The independent contractor ordinarily uses his or her own methods and receives no training from those who purchase the services. While the business owner is required to pay taxes (e. g. social security, workman's compensation) for each employee, an independent contractor is responsible for paying his or her own taxes.

Club managers may be tempted to classify aerobic instructors, tennis pros or personal trainers as independent contractors in order to save payroll costs, however, the U.S. Internal Revenue Service (IRS) will scrutinize each worker to determine if he or she has been properly classified. The financial implications of misclassifying employees can be significant. If a misclassification is identified, employers can be responsible for back taxes, fines and other employee benefits such as medical insurance and retirement accounts. Traditionally, the IRS will consider all workers to be employees unless the employer proves that the worker meets the IRS requirements for independent contractor status. In general, the IRS views aerobic instructors as employees, not independent contractors. Because of these facts, many club managers have determined that it is safer to treat all of their instructors as employees and not risk a costly IRS audit. See Chapter 2.12 for more information regarding independent contractors.

Unfair Competition in the Health and Fitness Industry

Many commercial health club managers are faced with what they consider unfair competition. Unfair competition may occur when a taxpaying business has to compete for customers with entities that are either tax-exempt or worse—operated by the government. A study conducted by the International Health, Racquet and Sportsclub Association (IHRSA) found that tax-exempt health clubs can operate their facilities for as much as 33 percent less than their taxpaying counterparts. This advantage is due to the fact that tax-exempt organizations do not pay federal or state income taxes or property taxes and are eligible for reduced postal rates. Many tax-exempt fitness clubs receive free advertisements in the form of public service announcements. Such competition may come from a YMCA, Jewish Community Center, municipal park and recreation department, or nonprofit hospital.

Recent Developments

A student who suffered brain damage at a University of Arizona fitness facility was awarded $5 million because the court found that the university's emergency response was inadequate (*Spiegler v. State of Arizona*, 1995). Illinois and Pennsylvania require health clubs to have at least one cardiopulmonary resuscitation (CPR) trained person on premises at all times. This requirement is under consideration by several other state legislatures, most notably in New York. Club managers should ensure that their own emergency policies and procedures are in accordance with the prevailing standards of care.

In response to complaints by business owners, several state legislatures have passed laws regulating the collection practices of music licensing groups: BMI, ASCAP, and SESAC. Colorado, Idaho, Illinois, Indiana, Maryland, Minnesota, Missouri, New York, Oklahoma, Texas, Virginia, West Virginia, and Wyoming have passed laws in this area. Generally, these laws regulate only the collection practices of music licensing groups because any change in the copyright law itself must occur at the federal level. In the 104th Congress (1995-96), "The Fairness in Music Licensing Act" was introduced. This legislation would exempt truly small businesses, including certain health clubs, from having to pay licensing fees for incidental use of the radio or television, provide access to the song titles represented by the societies and provide for a local arbitration system for grievances to be resolved. The 104th Congress also introduced the Independent Contractor Simplification Act (HR 1972) in an effort to clarify for businesses the criteria used by the IRS to determine a worker's proper tax status.

References

Cases

Commonwealth of Mass. v. U.S. Health, Inc., Mass. Suffolk Superior Court Civil Action No. 89-0282-B, (1995)

Edison Brothers Stores Inc. v. Broadcast Music Inc., No. 90-328C(1) (E.D.Mo. 1991)

Sioux Valley Hospital Association v. South Dakota Board of Equalization, 513 N.W. 2d 562 (1994)

Spiegler v. State of Arizona, Cause No. CV 92-13608 (AZ Maricopa County Superior Court, 1995).

U.S. EEOC v. Audrey Sedita, No. 87 C 2790 (N.D. Ill. 1991)

LivingWell (North), Inc. v. Pennsylvania Human Relations Commission, No. 2676 C.D. (Commonwealth Ct. of Penn. 1992)

Index of Selected Cases

Cases and page numbers in bold type indicate *Representative Cases*. Notes indicated with "n."

Subject Index

property interest 258
substantive due process 258
duty 26, 28
advising of participatory risk 109–110
for providing safe premises 107–111
of care 116–117
of emergency care 79–80, 82
of inspection 108
of maintenance and repair 108–109
origin of 28–29
to keep safe 110–111
to provide supervision 119–120
to provide transportation 116
to warn of concealed dangers 109

E

emergency care 77
duty of 82
planning for 80–82
emergency medical situations 110
emergency, medical 188
employment process 128–131
employment tort 122–132
Equal Pay Act 322, 533–539
equal protection 68
eligibility standards 270
gender equity 309–315, 316–326
intermediate scrutiny 268–269
rational basis 269
strict scrutiny 267–268
exculpatory agreement 63–69
exculpatory clause 75
expert witness 8

F

facility, facilities 99
leasing 38
maintaining 188
fair comment 161–162
first aid 188
emergency, medical 188
foreseeability 89–90

G

gambling 388–389
game rules, violation of 98–99
gender discrimination 131–132
See also sex discrimination
Good Samaritan statutes 60, 82
governmental claim 7
governmental function 57

H

handicapped athletes 339–347
health and fitness issues
Americans with Disabilities Act 543–544
AIDS 543–544
club membership agreements 540
couples memberships 541–542
discrimination 362
eating disorders 543
music copyright fees 544–545
sexual harassment 542
women-only clubs 542–543
high school athletic associations
academic standards 294–295
conduct issues 301–308
disabled students 288, 298, 339–347
drug testing 328–337
eligibility issues 290–300
"home schooling" 300
judicial review 287
longevity 295
pre-game invocations 354
redshirting 295
state action 248–249, 251
transfer rules 295

I

immunity
governmental 57–60
recreational use 59–60
sovereign 57–60
statutory 40, 59–60
volunteer 60
in loco parentis 61
independent contractor 38, 117, 119
injunctions 238, 241–242
instruction 97–98
proper 99–100
insurance 190–196
cash value 194
coinsurance 194
conditions 191
contractual agreements 191
coverage 191–192
declarations 191
deductible 194
endorsements 191
exclusions 191
NCAA Catastrophic Insurance Plan 490
policy 190–191
replacement cost 194
insurance coverage 192–196
advertising liability 194
automobile 195